CW00648722

PENGUIN REFERENCE
The Penguin Book of Word Histories

Fred McDonald studied English Language and Literature as a mature student at Goldsmiths' College, London, and followed this by an MA in Old and Middle English at King's College. She then joined Oxford University Press as assistant editor on the *New Shorter Oxford English Dictionary*, and also answered queries for the Oxford Word and Language Service (OWLS). Since leaving to become a freelance she has contributed, as lexicographer, etymologies editor, and occasionally managing editor, to more than twenty English dictionaries and language reference books, including the *New Penguin English Dictionary*, and has broadcast on place names and other aspects of the English language. She is co-author of *Questions of English*, based on enquiries to OWLS, and of *The Guinness Book of British Place Names*.

The Penguin Book of
WORD HISTORIES

Fred McDonald

PENGUIN BOOKS

PENGUIN BOOKS

Published by the Penguin Group
Penguin Books Ltd, 80 Strand, London WC2R 0RL, England
Penguin Group (USA) Inc., 375 Hudson Street, New York, New York 10014, USA
Penguin Group (Canada), 90 Eglinton Avenue East, Suite 700, Toronto, Ontario, Canada M4P 2Y3
(a division of Pearson Penguin Canada Inc.)
Penguin Ireland, 25 St Stephen's Green, Dublin 2, Ireland (a division of Penguin Books Ltd)
Penguin Group (Australia), 250 Camberwell Road,
Camberwell, Victoria 3124, Australia (a division of Pearson Australia Group Pty Ltd)
Penguin Books India Pvt Ltd, 11 Community Centre,
Panchsheel Park, New Delhi – 110 017, India
Penguin Group (NZ), 67 Apollo Drive, Rosedale, North Shore 0632, New Zealand
(a division of Pearson New Zealand Ltd)
Penguin Books (South Africa) (Pty) Ltd, 24 Sturdee Avenue,
Rosebank, Johannesburg 2196, South Africa

Penguin Books Ltd, Registered Offices: 80 Strand, London W2CR 0RL, England

www.penguin.com

First published 2010
1

Copyright © Fred McDonald, 2010

The moral right of the author has been asserted

Set in 7.5/10 Stone Serif
Typeset by Macmillan Publishing Solutions
Printed in England by Clays Ltd, St Ives plc

ISBN: 978–0–140–28298–6

www.greenpenguin.co.uk

Mixed Sources
Product group from well-managed
forests and other controlled sources
www.fsc.org Cert no. SA-COC-1592
© 1996 Forest Stewardship Council
FSC

Penguin Books is committed to a sustainable future
for our business, our readers and our planet.
The book in your hands is made from paper
certified by the Forest Stewardship Council.

Contents

Acknowledgements   vi

Introduction   vii

The Penguin Book of Word Histories   1

Acknowledgements

Grateful thanks to the lexicographers, past and present, who made this book possible, to Frances Kelly for her efforts on my behalf, to the good folk at Penguin for their exemplary patience, to Trish Stableford for her professional expertise but above all for her friendship, and to my husband Tony for all the reasons he knows and some he probably doesn't.

INTRODUCTION

The English language

If, as is thought, all humankind stems from common African ancestors, it stands to reason that, as the Bible says, 'the whole earth was of one language, and of one speech' (Genesis 11:1). But as humankind began to scatter, driven by economic forces, enmities or simple curiosity, it evolved into races and tribes with much in common, but physically and culturally distinct. So did the language.

The most widespread language race was Indo-European, which originated in Eastern Europe about 5,000 years ago and spread to India in the east, the Atlantic in the west, Russia and Scandinavia in the north, and the Mediterranean in the south. Its descendants include most European languages, Sanskrit, whence the major languages of the Indian subcontinent, and some Middle Eastern tongues. English belongs to the Germanic branch of the Indo-European family: its closest relatives are Frisian, German, Dutch, and the Scandinavian languages.

Old English

There are no written records of Indo-European or Germanic; what we know of them has been extrapolated from their descendants. For us the story of English begins with the coming of the Anglo-Saxons. Legend says that when the Romans left in the fifth century AD, the British King Vortigern offered land to the Saxon brothers Hengest and Horsa if they would protect his vulnerable kingdom from other Germanic raiders, but the gamekeepers quickly turned poacher and overran the land with fire and the sword, pushing the unfortunate Britons ever north- and westwards.

However, we now know that there was not one single invasion. The 'Anglo-Saxons', as the Germanic settlers came to be called, were a mixture of Angles,

Saxons, Jutes, and Frisians. Archaeological evidence shows that Germanic settlements were established in Roman times, that the invasions which ousted many Britons followed a period of peaceful immigration, and that the newcomers co-existed with the remaining Britons, gradually assimilating them.

Whether or not the Britons were evicted physically, they were certainly displaced linguistically and culturally. They spoke a Celtic language (also from Indo-European), which later separated into Welsh, Cornish, and Breton, and few traces of this remain in English. The main survival is in the names of major topographic features, such as rivers, hill ranges, and forests, and in a few English place names where a Celtic element is combined with an Anglo-Saxon one, usually revealing that the Anglo-Saxons did not understand the Celts: **Bredon**, for example, is a combination of a Celtic word for 'hill' with Anglo-Saxon *don* 'hill', now with 'on-the-hill' added for good measure.

By about the 8th century the various dialects spoken by the Anglo-Saxons had shaken down into what we now call Old English (although there were still local variations), the West Saxon form becoming dominant. Old English is incomprehensible to the modern reader, but many of its words survive in some form. Among these are the place-name elements (settlement names, especially in southern England, are overwhelmingly of Anglo-Saxon origin), everyday words such as *sun, moon, day, night, man, woman, book, house, horse, cow, now, then*, and the often disregarded little words that enable us to make sentences, express relationships, and ask questions: *a, the, and, but, this, that, on, in, up, down, how, what*, etc. Onto this sturdy root-stock were grafted elements from other languages.

Latin

This is the first and by far the most important of these languages, spoken throughout the Roman Empire by its rulers and those who had direct dealings with them. Before Germanic settlers came to England, Germanic tribes had traded with the Romans and served in their armies. The Anglo-Saxons in England adopted Latin words in their names for existing settlements, notably *castra* 'a camp', appearing as **caster** or **-chester**, and *wicus* 'a dwelling, farm, or settlement', appearing as **Wick**, **-wich**, or **-wick**. Latin was the language of the Church, and some of the earliest borrowings (e.g. *candle, font, bishop*) reflect this. Latin also fathered French, Spanish, Italian, and Portuguese, which have all contributed to English – more of those later.

Perhaps Latin's most important role was as an international language: historical, scientific, and philosophical works were written in Latin, and anyone with any learning spoke it. It remained so for many years, and until the last century educated people throughout Europe could pick a Latin word 'off the shelf' and use it for their own ends, knowing that their peers would understand it.

Compared to modern English, Latin had a fairly small vocabulary, but it worked its words very hard, adding prefixes and suffixes to extend or change their meanings, so that a single Latin verb, for example, may have many English descendants: Latin *vertere* (see VERSE) is a good example.

Old Norse

The Anglo-Saxon Chronicle records the first Viking raid in 787. In the following years Scandinavian pirates raided settlements, especially monasteries, around the coast of England. In 850 a Viking army over-wintered in England, and from then on they sought land as well as plunder, at first as bases for a season's raiding, later as permanent homes. Although the Chronicles tend to lump them together as 'Danes' or 'heathens' (a foreigner is a foreigner, after all), there were two main groups, the Danes and the Norwegians. They spoke related dialects of a language we now call Old Norse, which was similar to Old English, having some words in common and others almost the same, and could probably make themselves understood fairly well.

The Norwegians mainly settled in the Shetlands, north and north-west Scotland, Ireland, Wales, and north-west England, the Danes generally settling in the east and north-east of England. The Danes might have overrun the whole of England, which was then divided into separate kingdoms, often at odds with each other. But in the 9th century King Alfred of Wessex united the kingdoms, held the Danes to a draw, and divided the country with the Danish leader Guthrum. The Danes ruled the north and east (thereafter called the Danelaw), the Saxons keeping the south and west. The Scandinavians added about 10,000 new words to English, including *call, fellow, hit, loose, low, sky, window*, and *wrong*. Some replaced English words, others co-existed: *shirt* and *skirt*, *breach* and *break* are basically Old English and Old Norse versions of the same word (the Scandinavians generally used a *k* sound where the Anglo-Saxons used *ch*). Other borrowings, especially place-name elements such as *-by* and *-thwaite*, were confined to areas of Scandinavian settlement: although the boundaries have changed over the years, the north-south linguistic divide persists to this day.

By the end of the 10th century Old English was an established language (albeit with regional variations). Parts of the Bible and other important works had been translated into it, and it had a thriving literature of its own. That was about to change.

French

As every schoolboy knows, in 1066 William Duke of Normandy defeated Harold at the Battle of Hastings and became King of England. French became the language of power, the feudal system was introduced, and the whole fabric of English society was changed forever. As usual, it's not as simple as that. For one thing, Normandy was founded by the Vikings, who, after over a century of raiding and forcible annexation, were granted land by the French king, much as Alfred had ceded land to the Danes, and the new language was Norman, rather than Parisian, French. For another, there had been comings and goings between the English, Norman, and French courts for many years (Edward the Confessor, the last Saxon king, had French as his first language), and the beginnings of the feudal system (originally French, adopted by the Normans) were already established. Old English had already borrowed some words from Parisian French.

There was one big, important difference between the Scandinavians and the English. The Scandinavians travelled widely (to Russia, Istanbul, Sicily, and North America), and wherever they went, they assimilated those parts of the local culture they found useful, and learned the local language. The English tended to stay at home and speak English: you can't help thinking that they spoke loudly and slowly while waving their arms about, and that their descendants are even now demanding fish and chips in tourist resorts around the world. Despite Norman dominance, English survived.

Middle English (11th–14th centuries)

English did change, though. Old English was grammatically very complex: its verbs, adjectives, and pronouns changed according to their function in the sentence, usually by adding a suffix (an inflection). Nouns were regarded as masculine, feminine, or neuter, with no obvious logic (*wheat* was masculine, *oats* were feminine, *corn* was neuter), and the adjectives describing them and the articles (*the, a*) would have different forms accordingly as in modern French and German. Old Norse grammar was similar but different, Latin and French different again.

Such complexities are baffling to foreigners. In a foreign country you may well know the right word but not the correct form – enough to make yourself understood, but not to speak correctly – and where languages interact with each other, as Old Norse and French did with Old English, the nuances of correct usage are lost. This process had begun before the Norman Conquest, but accelerated after it.

Only a few of the Old English inflections now survive, for example in the personal pronouns (*I, me, mine*), the *s* of the plural and possessive, and the *-ed* of the past tense of verbs. Grammatical gender and case endings all but disappeared in Middle English, and with them most of the numerous possible forms: a noun is now marked only as singular or plural, and its adjective does not change.

In this period England was an us-and-them society, with the ruling classes speaking Anglo-Norman French and the lower orders speaking English. England did not have a king with English as his mother tongue until the accession of Henry IV in 1399. It follows that many of the French words adopted into English concerned the court, chivalry, the law, and good living (*justice, felony, duke, baron, chivalry, forest,* as well as hunting and hawking terms). English words survived for the more mundane aspects of life.

However, the Normans needed to communicate with their new subjects, if only to tell them what to do. While the aristocracy could carry on speaking French, those lower down the social scale, the NCOs of society, had to learn some English. Norman clergymen were drafted in to parishes and had to speak to parishioners, however inexpertly: a 12th-century book of 'English' sermons, written in a kind of phonetics, shows how difficult some of the newcomers found this.

Gradually England and English absorbed the newcomers and their language, aided by a love of words that is found in Old English poetry and persists to this day. By the end of the 14th century English was developing as a literary language, and was becoming recognizable to us: with modernized spelling, good footnotes, and some concentration older schoolchildren can tackle Chaucer. There were still large regional variations (there is a story of a northerner in London being unable to buy *eyren*, though the locals were quite willing to sell him *egges*), but the dialect spoken in the area which included London and the university cities of Oxford and Cambridge was becoming the standard.

English also borrowed words from Parisian French (some of which had, in turn, been borrowed from continental Germanic tribes), sometimes alongside the Norman French forms (see CATTLE, WALLOP).

Modern English (post-1500)

The standardization of English was helped enormously by the introduction of printing in the 1470s by William Caxton. Books, which had previously been laboriously copied by scribes, could now be printed in thousands, each one exactly like the others. (Despite this, spellings varied enormously: one correct spelling per word is largely an 18th-century idea.) And instead of being ruinously expensive, owned only by the Church and the aristocracy, books now became affordable to the rising middle classes. Education spread, more and more people could read, and although Latin was still the language of the Church and scholarship, the newly literate man in the street read English.

The Renaissance brought about a new enthusiasm for learning, initially about the classics, increasingly about the important scientific discoveries that were taking place. Once again, Latin words were adapted for new uses, and foreign words flooded into English, notably from Greek, the language of philosophy and science since Roman times, and from Arabic, the language of alchemy and mathematics.

English has continued to welcome words from many sources: South American words such as *tomato* and *puma* (usually via Spanish or Portuguese), Indian words such as *bungalow* and *gymkhana*, musical terms from Italy (*piccolo, pianissimo*), terms in psychology from Germany (*Gestalt*), cookery terms from France (*bain marie, omelette*), and food and drink from almost anywhere (*spaghetti, oloroso, balti*). The fact that a Welsh pub could offer 'traditional balti' in the 1990s shows how quickly and thoroughly these words are assimilated.

English as a world language

In the early 17th century Britain began to establish colonies abroad, first in North America and India, later in the West Indies, Australia and New Zealand, Africa, and Hong Kong. To each place the settlers took the English of their own time, and in each place it changed, little by little, adapting to local circumstances as it always has. Increasingly British English is taking words from these offspring, partly as a result of people from the (former) colonies coming to settle in Britain, partly because of the spread of mass communications. A film or television programme made in one country can be shown in many others: some American terms have come into British English via the Australian soaps so popular with young teenagers. In this way British English continues to import and export words.

The English are famous for their resistance to learning other languages, apparently convinced that everyone should speak English – and they are getting their way. English is now the major world language, the chief language of North America, Australia, New Zealand, and a number of other countries, and spoken in some form almost everywhere. Although Chinese has more native speakers, English is more widespread and more people use it as a second language. It is the official language used by air traffic control and in shipping, and the main language of international business, science, engineering, and computing. Scientists and inventors no longer reach for a Latin word for a new object or concept.

English has emerged from its long history as a rich, flexible language, with reasonably simple grammar and a huge vocabulary, expanding by thousands of new words every year. It is one of the easiest languages to get by in, and one of the hardest to speak like a native: its word-hoard produces many near-synonyms that are not quite interchangeable. Long may it thrive.

About this book

Words are like people. Some stay close to their ancestors in meaning and form, like a child that goes into the family business and lives its life in the town where it was born. There is little to say about these, and they are not included. Others change their appearance, take on new roles, influence, or are influenced by, other words, go up or down in the world, and end up quite different from their parents and other family members. This book aims to trace their family trees and their stories, and to reveal the processes, attitudes, and individual writers that have influenced the language.

Up to a point the book follows normal dictionary conventions: an alphabetical sequence of entries, each with a headword (in **bold** type), followed by the date the word was first recorded in English and its origin, then an account of its life story, with the dates of significant developments. Some senses have a label, e.g. (Australia), indicating that this sense is only used there; if the label is in italics the sense originated there but is now more widespread.

Many entries then have a further paragraph or paragraphs giving additional information, which may include brief details of related words (in **bold** type, in **_bold italics_** if the word has been borrowed from another language and is still used virtually in its original form, or in SMALL CAPITALS* if the word has an entry of its own (the asterisk tells you that this entry also deals with more than one word)).

A few things worth noting:

Dates

It is seldom possible to give a strictly accurate date of a word's first appearance in English. Dictionaries that give dates base them on the first written record, but words are usually spoken long before they are written down (especially so with slang), and the further back you go the less written evidence there is. The *Oxford English Dictionary* gives the first recorded example for each word and sense, but if you look at the examples you will realize that, very often, the writer of it feels no need to explain the word, suggesting that it was already in use. Because of this, I have avoided giving firm dates. 'Middle English' (ME) covers the period from the 11th to the 14th centuries, thereafter the century is given until the twentieth century, when it is usually possible to get closer. If an exact date is known, I give it.

Word origins

The account of the word's origin, in square brackets, is less detailed than you will find in a larger dicionary, leaving more space to tell the word's story. Forms from 'parent' languages are often omitted if they are not essential to an understanding of the word's pedigree. Hence, for example:

[French, from ...] indicates that the word was virtually the same in French as it is in English.

[Via French from ...] indicates that the French word was similar to the English one, but not the same.

[(Via French from) Latin ...] indicates that the English word was borrowed from French, and also independently from Latin.

Names

Name studies is a distinct branch of linguistics which dictionaries do not venture into. However, names begin as brief descriptions, although the form may have fossilized so that it is no longer recognizable as an ordinary word, and they are included if they are related to the headword and fit naturally into the story. Place names usually consist of two elements, one saying what the place is (a town, hill, etc.), the other saying what is special about it, e.g. what is found or grown there, or who it belongs to. Surnames could be based on someone's physical appearance, their occupation, or where they came from. It follows that many place names became surnames, and in such cases I do not differentiate, just referring to 'the name'.

The hope is that you will browse, picking up bits of information as you go, finding words in unexpected places, and ending up with some insight into the richness of the English language.

A

aback [Old English *on baec*, from *baec* **back**: related to *bacon'* (at BEEF). Written as two words until the 15c] At or to the back; surviving in **taken aback**, originally referring to a ship whose sails were blown back against the mast so that it stopped or was blown backwards (18c), hence disconcerted (19c).

abacus [ME. Latin, from Greek *abakos* 'slab, drawing-board spread with sand or dust', probably from Hebrew *'ābāq* 'dust'] Originally a board spread with sand on which to write, draw or tot up figures (the earliest sense in English). Later, a tally was kept by placing counters in columns marked on the board, and in Roman times the counters were strung on wires. The sense 'counting frame' is first recorded in the 17c, though various forms of it were used during the Middle Ages. The Greek sense 'slab' survives in architecture, where an *abacus* is a slab on the capital of a column (16c).

abandon [ME. Old French *abandoner*, from *bandon* 'control' (in the phrase *mettre a bandon* 'to put under someone else's control'), of Germanic origin: related to BAN*] To bring under control; to put in someone else's control, hence **1 abandoned** having surrendered to something (good or bad); given up to your natural instincts (17c), whence **abandon** wildness, lack of restraint (19c) **2** to give up or desert (15c).

abash [ME. Old French *esbair*, *esbaisse-* 'to astound', from *bair* 'to gape': see BAY*] To make someone embarrassed or ashamed; shortened to *bash* to make or become daunted or disconcerted (–17c), whence **bashful** daunted (15–18c); diffident, shy (16c).

abate [ME. Old French *abatre* 'to fell', from *batre* 'to beat': see BATTER*] To put an end to, hence **1** to (cause to) diminish or die down (the shortened form **bate** survives mainly in **with bated breath** hardly breathing) **2** to make or become legally null and void (15c).
  Old French *abatre* produced **abattoir** and REBATE*.

abdicate [16c. Latin *abdicare* 'to reject or disown', from *ab-* 'away' + *dicare* 'to declare'] **1** to disown or disinherit a child (–19c) **2** to resign or be deprived of a right or responsibility; to renounce the throne (17c).
  Latin *dicare* is the ancestor of **condition**, **dedicate**, INDEX*, and PREDICAMENT*. Related to DICTATE*.

aberration [16c. Latin *aberrare* 'to wander or deviate', from *errare* (see ERR*)] A deviation from a path, hence from the accepted way of doing things, now a (usually unwelcome) departure from the norm (19c).

abet [ME. Old French *abeter* 'to urge on', from *beter* 'to hunt with dogs, to hound', of Germanic origin: related to BITE*] To urge someone to do something (good or bad), hence to encourage or help them to commit a crime (15c).

abject [15c. Latin *abjectus*, literally 'thrown away', ultimately from *jacere* 'to throw' (ancestor of JET*)] Rejected; wretched, degraded; humiliated or humiliating: phrases such as *abject poverty* probably led to the modern sense 'extreme, total' (*abject failure*).

able [ME. Old French, from Latin *habilis* 'suitable, fit, handy', from *habere* 'to hold'] Easy to handle or use, also fit, suitable (both –18c), hence **1** physically fit; surviving mainly in **able-bodied** and in **disabled** (17c) **2** having the knowledge or power to do something, hence to empower or make capable (replaced by 15c **enable**) **3** skilful, clever (16c) **4 disable** to make unfit for use (17c).

Latin *habilis* produced medieval Latin *habilitare* 'to make able', whence **habilitate** and **rehabilitate**; *habere* is the ancestor of HABIT*.

ablution [ME. (Via Old French from) Latin *abluere* 'to wash clean or wash away', from *lavare* 'to wash' (ancestor of LAVATORY*)] In alchemy: purification using liquids, hence ritual washing of the body or of sacred vessels (16c); washing yourself (18c); **the ablutions** a place with washing facilities (1950s).

abominable [ME. Old French, from Latin *abominabilis*, from *abominari* 'to shun as a bad omen', from *ominis* 'omen'. Once widely believed to be from Latin *ab-* 'away' + *homine* 'human being', and to mean literally 'inhuman', hence often spelt *abhominable*] Morally or physically disgusting, detestable; watered down to 'very bad' (19c).

Latin *ominis* produced **omen** and **ominous** serving as an (originally either good or bad) omen.

Aborigines [16c. Latin *ab origine* 'from the beginning', from *origo, origin-* 'beginning, source'; from *oriri* 'to rise or be born'] The original inhabitants of Italy and Greece; the indigenous peoples 'discovered' by Europeans (17c), now almost exclusively those in Australia. The noun **Aboriginal** (18c), now the preferred term, was also used in the 19c for an early White settler or a White person born in Australia, as opposed to a later immigrant.

Latin *origo* produced **origin, original** (earliest in **original sin** an innate tendency to sin caused by Adam and Eve's disobedience to God: see the Bible, Genesis 3), and **originate**. *Oriri* produced ABORT* and ORIENT*.

abort [16c. Latin *aboriri*, from *oriri*: see ABORIGINES*] To miscarry (still the technical term), also to end a pregnancy, or something else, prematurely, now applied to a flight or mission (1960s, *US*).

Latin *aboriri* produced **abortive** a stillborn child or animal (ME–18c), hence premature, stillborn; fruitless, unsuccessful.

abound [ME. Latin *abundare*, ultimately from *unda* 'a wave'] To overflow, hence to be plentiful; to teem with.

Abundant [from *abundare*] also developed from 'overflowing' to 'plentiful': both were once believed to come from Latin *habere* 'to have', and were often spelt *habound, habundant*. Latin *unda* is the ancestor of SOUND³*.

abracadabra [17c. Latin from Greek, perhaps based on **Abraxas**, the name of the supreme deity of a 2c Gnostic sect] First mentioned as a mystical word worn on an amulet to ward off the plague 'in former times', later used as a conjuror's magic word, hence an impressive-sounding but nonsensical word; jargon or gibberish (19c).

abroad [ME. From BROAD*] **1** widely scattered, widespread **2** out and about, not at home; out of your own country (15c); (jokingly) other countries (*abroad is full of foreigners*, 19c).

abscond [16c. Latin *abscondere* 'to put out of sight', from *condere* 'to put away, to preserve', from *dare* 'to put'] To hide or cover, specifically to hide from the law, hence to flee from justice or custody.
  Latin *abscondere* produced **sconce** a screen to protect a candle flame, later a candle or lamp bracket; *condere* fathered **condiment** [Latin *condimentum* 'a preservative'] and **recondite** [Latin *recondere* 'to put away, to hide']. *Dare* is the ancestor of DATA*.

absolute [ME. Latin *absolvere*: see ABSOLVE*] Freed from an obligation (–17c) or from limitations, hence **1** complete, total (*absolute zero, decree absolute*), hence **absolutely** in an absolute way; very, extremely (16c); used to reinforce a negative (*absolutely not!*, 18c) and as an emphatic 'yes' (19c) **2** unrestricted, independent (*absolute monarch*, 15c).

absolve [ME. Latin *absolvere, absolut-* 'to set free', from *solvere* 'to loosen'] **1** to free from an obligation or liability, hence **(a)** to pronounce free from blame or guilt (16c) **(b)** to give formal remission from sin (16c, ME in **absolution** such remission), largely replacing **assoil** [ME, via French from Latin *absolvere*] **2** to clear up, to find an answer to (15–17c, outlived by RESOLVE and SOLVE).
  Latin *absolvere* produced ABSOLUTE; *solvere* is the ancestor of SOLVE*.

abstain [ME. Via Old French from Latin *abstinere* 'to hold back', from *tenere* 'to hold'] To avoid or refrain from, hence to fast; to refrain from sex or alcohol (with the noun **abstinence**), or from using your vote (19c, with the noun **abstention**).
  Abstemious looks like a relative, but comes from Latin *ab* 'away' + *temetum* 'strong drink'. Latin *tenere* is the ancestor of TENOR*.

abstract [ME. (Via Old French from) Latin *abstrahere, abstract-* 'to draw away', from *trahere* 'to pull' (ancestor of TRACT*)] To extract or separate, hence **1** a summary (the essentials extracted) **2** separated from the material world (15c), hence **(a)** withdrawn, preoccupied (16c, now usually as **abstracted**) **(b) abstract art** which does not portray material objects (1950s).

absurd [15c. (Via French from) Latin *absurdus* 'out of tune', from *surdus* 'hard of hearing, hard on the ear'] **Absurdity** is recorded once meaning 'lack of harmony', and *absurd* once meaning 'out of tune', but the usual sense has always been ridiculous or silly, 'out of tune' with reason.

abuse [ME. Via French from Latin *abuti, abus-*, from *uti* USE*] To misuse, hence **1** to ill-treat: **(a)** to violate or defile; defilement (16c) (surviving, just, in **self-abuse** masturbation) **(b)** to injure or harm by (repeated) ill-treatment; such treatment (16c) **(c)** corrupt practice (16c); improper use, now especially of a drug, alcohol, etc. **(d)** coarse or insulting language (16c); to hurl this at someone (17c) **2** to misrepresent (–18c); to deceive (15–19c); deception, delusion (16–17c): surviving in **disabuse** (17c).

abyss [ME. Via late Latin from Greek *abussos* 'bottomless', from *bussos* 'depth'] The bottomless pit once believed to be under the world, later identified with hell, hence any deep chasm (16c).

Abyss largely replaced **abysm** [Old French *abisme*, ultimately from Greek *abussos*] in both senses, whence **abysmal** like an abyss, later extremely bad.

academy [ME. Via French from Latin *academia*, from Greek *akadēmeia* 'to do with Akadēmos', a legendary Greek hero] The name of a garden where Plato (5c Greek philosopher) taught, on land formerly sacred to Akadēmos, hence (both formerly also as **academe**) **1** Plato's school of philosophy (16c) **2** an educational establishment: **(a)** for higher learning and the arts, hence **academic** to do with, or (someone) engaged in, higher learning, especially as opposed to technical or practical knowledge (16c), hence purely theoretical (*an academic question*, 19c) **(b)** for skills (*military/riding academy*, 16c) **(c)** in the UK, a publicly funded secondary school with some private sponsorship and a degree of independence (2000).

Academe came to mean the academic world, now largely replaced by its source, Latin *academia*. Plato's name is found in **Platonic love** spiritual, non-sexual love (a 16c concept, from the idea that the highest form of human love is ultimately based on the soul's love for God, felt to be compatible with Plato's idea of archetypes).

accent [ME. (Via French from) Latin *accentus* 'intonation', from *cantus* 'song', from *canere* 'to sing' (ancestor of CANT*)] The tone of something said, hence **1** prominence given to a syllable by stress or pitch (15c); stress in poetry or, later, music (16c), hence a particular emphasis (17c); to give one (largely replaced by **accentuate**); something that does so, a contrasting detail **2** a characteristic pronunciation (*a French/upper-class accent*, 16c) **3** a mark indicating stress, intonation, or pronunciation (16c).

access [ME. (Via French from) Latin *accessus* 'approach, entrance', from *accedere* 'to approach, to go to, to join or be added', from *cedere* 'to go'] **1** the onset of illness; an attack or fit, later an emotional attack (18c, from modern French) **2** the means of approaching or entering a building etc., hence **accessible** possible to reach or enter **3** the right or opportunity to use or contact something/someone, hence **(a)** *accessible* available (16c); easy to understand (1960s) **(b)** to gain access to (1960s).

Latin *accedere* produced **accede** and **accessory**, literally 'someone/something joined or added'; *cedere* is the ancestor of CEDE*.

accolade [17c. French, from Provençal *acolada* 'an embrace around the neck', ultimately from Latin *collum* 'neck' (ancestor of **col** and **collar**)] The ceremonial embrace or kiss (now a touch with a sword) by which a monarch bestows knighthood, hence a public expression of esteem (19c).

accommodate [16c. Latin *accommodare* 'to make suitable', from *commodus* 'fitting, convenient': see COMMODIOUS*] To adapt one thing or person to another, hence

1 to supply someone's needs, especially for space or lodgings; **accommodation**, **accommodations** US lodgings or premises (17c) **2** to reconcile people or settle differences, hence *accommodation* a compromise (17c).

accord [OE. Old French *acord* (noun), *acorder* (verb), ultimately from Latin *cors*, *cord-* 'heart'] To reconcile one person with another (–18c); to come to an agreement (ME), hence **1** reconciliation, consensus; a formal agreement **2** to agree or consent to (ME–19c); consent (surviving mainly in *of your own accord*) **3** to be consistent or harmonious (ME); conformity, harmony.

    Accord produced CHORD; Old French *acord* produced **accordion** [via German *Akkordion*, from *Akkord* 'accord, harmony']. Latin *cors* is the ancestor of CORDIAL*.

ace [ME. French, from Latin *as* 'unity, a unit'] A single spot etc. on a dice, domino or playing card; a card etc. marked with one, hence **1** a tiny amount, a hair's breadth (16c) **2** in tennis: a serve that beats the opponent (19c); in golf: a hole in one (early 20c): these senses, plus the ace often being the most valuable card, led to the association with excellence: a successful fighter pilot (World War I); someone who excels (*US*); *ace!* excellent! (1970s).

ache [Old English *aece* (noun), *acan* (verb)] In Middle English the verb was spelt and pronounced *ake*; the noun spelt *atche* and pronounced *aitch*; this persisted until the 19c, although from *c.*1700 the verb's pronunciation was gradually adopted for the noun. The modern spelling is largely due to Samuel Johnson (18c critic, poet, and lexicographer), who mistakenly derived *ache* from Greek *akhos* 'pain'.

acid [17c. (Via French from) Latin *acidus*, from *acere* 'to be sour', from *acer* 'sour'] Sour, tart, hence **1** a sour substance, specifically one which turns litmus red and dissolves many metals, hence the **acid test** for gold using nitric acid, the only one that dissolves gold (19c); any conclusive test **2** sarcastic, bitter (18c) **3** describing an intense 'biting' colour (early 20c) **4** the hallucinogenic drug LSD, derived from lysergic acid (1960s, *US*), hence **acid rock** music associated with hallucinogens.

    Latin *acer* is the ancestor of **acrid**, **acrimonious**, EAGER, and *vinegar* (at VINTAGE). Related to Latin *acerbus* 'bitter, sharp', whence **acerbic** and **exacerbate**.

acme [16c. Greek *akmē*, literally 'highest point', also 'pimple'. Often written in Greek letters until the 19c] The peak of perfection or achievement. A popular name for small companies (partly because it puts them near the top of listings), and adopted by the American animator Chuck Jones as the trade name of fiendish devices in cartoons.

    Acne comes from a misreading of Greek *akmē*.

acquit [ME. Old French, from medieval Latin *acquitare* 'to pay a debt', from *quitare* 'to set free: see QUIT*] To settle your own or, later, someone else's debt; to release someone from a liability or obligation, hence **1 acquit yourself** to free yourself from an obligation by doing your part **2** to declare that someone has no responsibility for a crime.

acre [Old English *aecer*] **1** an arable field; surviving in **God's acre** a graveyard (translating German *Gottesacker*), in place names (*Benacre*, *Long Acre*), and the surnames **Acre(s)**, **Acker(s)**, someone who lived by a field, and **Ackerman** a ploughman **2** as much land as a team of oxen could plough in a day, later formalized as 220 yards × 22 yards (approximately 201 × 20 metres), hence **(a)** 4,840 square yards (0.405 hectares) **(b)** a linear measure of 220 or, less commonly, 22 yards: replaced by *furlong* (at STADIUM), surviving in road names (*Twelve Acre Lane*) **3 acres** a large expanse (*acres of sail,* 19c); **the acres** your estate.

act [ME. Latin *agere, act-* 'to carry out, perform, or do': see AGENT*] **1** something done, a deed (*Act of God, caught in the act*), an action **2** to do something: **(a)** to decide a legal case (15c only) or to pass proposed legislation into law (survived by **enact**), hence (a written record of) a decree or decision; a statute **(b)** to have an effect on something (18c) **3** to perform (in) a play (16c), hence **(a)** to behave as if playing a role (17c); such a pretence (1920s) **(b)** to do someone's job temporarily (*acting sergeant,* 18c) **4** a section of a play (16c), hence a short performance, a turn (19c).

Descendants of Latin *actus* include **action**, originally (the taking of) legal proceedings, **active**, **actor** originally an agent or administrator, **actual** originally active, practical, hence real, **actuary** originally a registrar, **counteract**, **react**, **redact** to draw up a document, statement, etc., now to edit, especially to omit confidential information, and TRANSACT*.

acute [ME. Latin *acutus*, literally 'sharp, sharpened', from *acuere* 'to sharpen', from *acus* 'needle'. All major English senses existed in Latin and the dates of their adoption are not significant] **1** brief and severe (*acute illness/the problem is acute*) **2** pointed (16c), hence **acute angle** a pointy angle, less than 90° **3** sharp, shrill, high (16c), hence **acute accent**, originally showing pitch in music or stress in speech **4** quick-witted, shrewd (16c), shortened to **cute** (18c), which came to mean ingenious, quaintly or endearingly attractive (19c, cf. CUNNING*) **5** intense (*acute pain,* 17c) **6** sensitive (*acute hearing,* 18c). Cf. OBTUSE.

Latin *acuere* produced **acumen**, literally 'sharpness'; *acus* produced **acupuncture** the treatment of disorders by inserting needles at specific points (whence **acupressure** using pressure instead), and **aglet** the tag on the end of a lace.

adamant [OE. Latin *adama(n)s*, from Greek *adamas* 'invincible' (from *daman* 'to subdue'), used for the hardest metal, later for the hardest stone, then known: Latin *adama(n)s* was later used for the even harder diamond. Early writers took Latin *adama(n)s* to be from *adamare* 'to be attracted to', and translated *lapidem adamantem* 'hard stone' as 'lodestone, magnet'] A legendary stone with various contradictory qualities: it could act as a magnet or stop one working; it was sometimes said to be a diamond, although a diamond could counteract its power. The modern sense arose in phrases such as *an adamant heart* (16c).

Latin *adama(n)s* produced medieval Latin *diamas, diamant-*, whence French *diamanté* [literally 'set with diamonds'] and **diamond**.

add [ME. Latin *addere*, literally 'to give to', from *dare* 'to give'] To join one thing to another, hence **1** to make an additional remark **2** to join one number to another; to add numbers together (15c). To **add up** figures dates from the 18c, hence to make a (correct) total (19c), to make sense (1940s).

Latin *addere* produced **addendum**, literally 'something added to'; *dare* is the ancestor of DATA*.

addict [16c. Latin *addictus* 'bound, pledged', past participle of *addicere*, from *dicere* 'to say, swear' (ancestor of DICTATE*)] **1** formally bound or sentenced to (16c only) **2** devoted to (–19c), whence **addicted**, which gradually replaced it, and then produced the verb *addict* to devote yourself, originally to a person or cause (16–17c), hence *addicted* 'devoted' to strong drink (17c) or a drug (early 20c); *addict* someone hooked on drugs etc.

address [ME. French *adresser*, ultimately from Latin *directus* (see DIRECT*)] To set up, to prepare or put to rights, hence **1** to apply yourself to something; to face a target, problem, etc. (19c) **2** to direct or send something; the name of the person and place something is sent to (18c), hence **(a)** to write this on the thing to be sent (19c) **(b)** a residence or location (19c); a place in a computer's memory where data is to be stored (1950s) **3** to approach and speak to someone (15c); a polite or formal approach (16c); a formal speech (17c), hence to speak to a particular audience, in a particular way, or using specific words (18c); **form of address** a way of speaking to someone (19c).

adherent [ME. (Via French from) Latin *adhaerere* 'to stick to', from *haerere* 'to stick' (ancestor of **cohere**, **hesitate** and **inherent**)] Following, a follower. The oldest of a family (followed by **adherence** and **adhesion**, 15c), most of whom originally referred to attachment to a party or cause, next to physically sticking to something, followed by sticking to a rule or principle. **Adhesive** (17c) is the odd man out: it has never meant 'following a cause' and the earliest sense is 'sticking to a principle': 'sticky' dates from the 18c and 'a sticky substance' from the 19c.

adjourn [ME. Ultimately from Old French *a jorn nome* 'to the day named', from *jo(u)r, jornee* 'day': see JOURNEY*] To order someone to appear on the day named, hence to defer proceedings to a particular day or indefinitely (15c); to interrupt a meeting intending to resume it later or elsewhere.

adjust [17c. Obsolete French *adjuster*, ultimately from Latin *ad-* 'to' + *juxta* 'near' (ancestor of JOUST*)] To arrange or harmonize, hence **1** to move, rearrange, adapt, or alter slightly (17c); to adapt yourself to circumstances (1920s) **2** to settle conflicting interests (17c), specifically to assess an insurance claim.

adlib [18c. Abbreviation of Latin **ad libitum** 'according to pleasure'] Written on musical scores to mean 'interpret or improvise freely', hence improvised, unrehearsed, spontaneous (1920s, *US*); to play or speak without rehearsal; a spontaneous remark.

admiral [ME. Old French, from Arabic *amīr* 'commander', from *amara* 'to command'. The Arabs in Spain and Sicily created the title *amīr-al-mā* or *amīr-al-bahr* 'commander of the sea'; Christian writers assumed *amīr-al* 'commander of the' to be one word, and added the *d* by association with Latin *admirabilis* 'admirable': French and English had spellings with and without *d* until the 16c] A Saracen commander (–15c), hence **a(d)miral of the sea** or **navy** the chief officer in the English navy, shortened to *a(d)miral* after the original sense became obsolete.

Admiral used to be a variant of *admirable* (at ADMIRE), whence, probably, the **red** and **white admiral** butterflies.

Arabic *amīr* produced **emir**, originally adopted for a male descendant of Muhammad, later a title for various Muslim rulers.

admire [ME. Via French from Latin *admirari* 'to wonder at', from *mirari* 'to wonder', from *mirus* 'wonderful'] To marvel (at), to feel or express surprise or astonishment (16c, but implied in Middle English **admirable** and **admiration**); to regard with surprise and approval (15c); to approve of or respect, hence **1** admirer someone who admires (16c); a suitor (18c) **2** to like or wish to do something (17c, now dialect and US) **3** to express approval or esteem (19c).

Latin *mirari* is the ancestor of **marvel**, **miracle**, **mirage**, **mirror**, and the names **Mirabelle** and **Miranda**.

admit [ME. Latin *admittere* 'to send to, to let in', from *mittere* 'to send' (ancestor of MISSION*)] To allow into a place, hence to let something into your mind, to acknowledge its truth (15c); to acknowledge a fault or crime (1930s).

adore [ME. Old French, from Latin *adorare*, from *orare* 'to speak or pray' (ancestor of ORACLE*)] To worship as a god (surviving mainly in hymns); to revere and love; loosely, to like very much (19c). Hence **adorable**, originally 'worthy of worship' (17c), now often means merely 'charming, cute' (*c.*1900).

adult [16c. Latin *adultus*, past participle of *adolescere* 'to come to maturity', from *alescere* 'to be nourished, to grow or grow up', from *alere* 'to nourish'] Grown up, mature; an adult person (17c); suitable or intended for adults (1920s), hence **1** sexually explicit (1950s) **2** suitable or intended for the elderly (1960s, US).

Latin *adolescere* produced **adolescent**, literally 'coming to maturity': first used as a noun (15c) but rare until the 18c, when the adjective appeared. *Alere* is the ancestor of **alimentary**, **alimony** nourishment, means of living, hence maintenance paid to a divorced spouse, Latin *alumnus* [literally 'nursling'] adopted for a former student, and **coalesce** [Latin *coalescere*, literally 'to grow up together'].

adultery [ME. Old French *avouterie* from, ultimately, Latin *adulterare* 'to corrupt', from *alterare* 'to change', from *alter* 'other'. Originally spelt *avoutrie*: the spelling began to change in the 15c to conform to the Latin] Sexual intercourse with someone other than your spouse. Hence [all ME, from Old French] **adulterer**, **adulteress** and the unaccountably rare **adulter** to commit adultery, also to spoil by mixing with something inferior (–18c), a meaning gradually replaced by **adulterate** [16c, directly from Latin *adulterare*], which also meant to commit adultery (17–19c).

Latin *alter* is the ancestor of **alter** [via French from late Latin *alterare*, literally 'to make other'], **altercate**, **alternate**, **altruism** [via French from Italian *altrui* 'another person'], and **subaltern**, originally (someone) of inferior rank.

advance [ME. Via Old French from late Latin *abante* 'in front', from Latin *ante* 'before' (ancestor of ANTE*)] The underlying sense is 'to move, or move something, forward', hence **1** to help progress; to promote someone (surviving mainly in **advancement** promotion, preferment), specifically to help a child get on by spending money it stood to inherit, hence to pay money early, the money paid (16c) **2** progress, a step forward; to make progress (17c), hence **advanced** having progressed, ahead of its time **3** to bring forward (15c); to put forward for consideration (16c); a personal approach (now usually plural and amorous, 17c)

4 to increase (16c); to increase, or an increase, in price (17c), surviving in the auctioneer's *any advance on £500?*

advantage [ME. Old French, from *avant* 'in front', from late Latin *abante* (see ADVANCE*)] Literally 'being in front', hence a superior position; something that helps you get ahead; **advantaged** having advantages or privileges (16c); **take advantage (of)** to make use of circumstances or opportunities, especially to make unfair use of someone's good nature or innocence.

Old French *avantage* was shortened to **vantage**, surviving mainly in **vantage point**. French *avant* is found in **avant-garde** [with *garde* 'guard': see WARD*] the front of an advancing army (shortened to **vanguard** and then to **van**), hence the innovative writers and artists of a period; progressive, ultra-modern.

adventure [ME. Via Old French from Latin *adventurus* 'about to happen', from *advenire* 'to arrive', from *venire* 'to come'] Chance, luck; a chance event; a risky or exciting incident, hence to risk; to dare to do something dangerous or uncertain, largely replaced by the shortened form **venture**, which came to mean a risky undertaking, especially a business enterprise (16c).

Latin *advenire* produced **advent**, **adventitious**, and AVENUE*. Latin *venire* is the ancestor of VENUE*.

advertise [ME. Via Old French from Latin *advertere*, from *vertere* 'to turn'] To turn towards, hence to turn your own or someone else's attention to something (15–19c); to bring something to people's attention in order to sell it (18c). The idea of turning your mind to something is also found in medieval Latin *inadvertentia* 'inattention, carelessness' [from *inadvertere*, from *in-* 'not' + *vertere*], whence **inadvertent**.

Latin *adversus* [literally 'turned towards', from *advertere*] could also mean 'turned to face', hence 'opposite, against', whence **adversary** an opponent or enemy (see also DEVIL), **adverse** hostile, harmful, and **adversity** misfortune, hardship, things going against you. *Vertere* is the ancestor of VERSE*.

advice/advise [ME. Old French *avis* (noun), *aviser* (verb), ultimately from Latin *ad-* 'to' + *videre* 'to see' (ancestor of VISION*). Originally beginning *av-*; the *d* probably introduced by William Caxton (15c English printer). Noun and verb have had both spellings during their history; the current situation dates from the 17c: cf. DEVICE/DEVISE, LICENCE/LICENSE, PRACTISE] To look at or consider (–17c); a viewpoint, hence an opinion asked for or given; to give one; to caution or warn (15c), hence (to give) a formal notification (16c).

advocate [ME. Via Old French from Latin *advocatus* 'counsel', from *advocare* 'to call as a witness', from *vocare* 'to call'] Someone who speaks on another's behalf, specifically one who pleads their client's case in court (surviving in Scots, and in the US in the general sense 'lawyer'), hence to speak in favour of (16c); someone who does so (18c).

Latin *advocatus* fathered Dutch **advocaat** [shortened from *advocatenborrel* 'advocate's drink', because it was thought to clear the throat], Spanish **avocado** [replacing *aguacate* from Nahuatl *ahuacatl* 'testicle' (adopted for the vegetable because of its shape), whence also **guacamole** (with Nahuatl *molli* 'sauce')], and French **avocet**, adopted for a bird with black and white plumage, resembling an advocate's robes. Latin *advocare* produced *avow* (see VOW*); *vocare* is the ancestor of VOUCH*.

aerial [16c. Latin, from Greek *aerios*, from *aēr*: see AIR*] Thin as air, ethereal, imaginary; light as air (17c); produced, being, or flying in the air, hence **1** to do with or using aircraft (19c) **2 aerial wire** a wire or rod for transmitting or receiving radio waves (*c*.1900, quickly shortened to *aerial*).

affect [15c. Latin *affectare* 'to aim at, seek, or desire', from *afficere, affect-*, literally 'to do to', from *facere* 'to do'] To like or love; to like to do or have (16c), to do so ostentatiously; to feign a liking or opinion, hence **1 affectation** feigned or ostentatious liking or behaviour, intended to impress (16c) **2 disaffect** to (cause to) dislike (17c); to alienate.

Latin *affectare* produced **affection** an emotion or feeling, later a kindly or loving one, which probably influenced the early meaning of *affect*. Latin *afficere* produced **affect** to attack or afflict, hence to influence or move, and Spanish *aficionado* a devotee, originally of bullfighting. *Facere* is the ancestor of FACT*.

affinity [ME. Via Old French from Latin *affinis* 'related by marriage', literally 'bordering on', from *finis* 'end, border'] Relationship by marriage, later the close relationship between a child's parents and godparents (cf. GODFATHER), hence **1** kinship generally; likenesses suggesting a common origin (16c) **2** voluntary association or companionship (–17c), hence a liking or attraction (17c); the tendency of chemicals to combine (18c) **3 affinity group** of people with common interests (1970s, *US*), hence **affinity card** a discount card issued to group members, now usually a credit card paying a percentage to a charity.

Latin *affinis* produced **paraffin** [German, with Latin *parum* 'barely': from its low affinity]; *finis* is the ancestor of FINE*.

affirm [ME. Via Old French from Latin *affirmare*, from *firmus* FIRM*] To make firm, to strengthen, later **1** to confirm a statement (–17c), contract, or law; to assert something, hence in law: to make a solemn assertion in lieu of an oath (15c) **2 affirmative** positive, assertive (15c); used to express confirmation or agreement (19c, *US military*).

affix [ME. Latin *affigere, affix-*, from *figere* FIX*] To fix or fasten to; an appendage or addition (16c), hence an element added to a word (17c): a **prefix** [17c, via Latin *praefigere* 'to fix in front'] or a **suffix** [18c, via Latin *suffigere* 'to fix behind or under, whence also **soffit**].

affluence [ME. French, from Latin *affluere* 'to flow towards', from *fluere* to flow] A plentiful flow, hence abundance, wealth (16c), hence **affluent** in the sense 'wealthy' (18c), whence **affluential** (someone) rich and powerful, and **affluenza** guilt and lack of motivation arising from wealth (both 1980s, US). The earliest sense of *affluent* was 'flowing towards' (15–18c), whence *affluence* a movement of things or people towards a place (16c).

The opposite of Latin *affluere* was *effluere* 'to flow out or away', ancestor of **effluence** (whence **effluent** a stream of liquid, especially industrial waste or sewage), **effluvium**, and **efflux**, all basically meaning 'an outflow'. Latin *fluere* is the ancestor of FLUENT*.

afford [Old English *geforthian*, from *forthian* 'to further', from FORTH*] To do or accomplish, later to manage or have the means to do or give (15c), hence **1** to offer or provide (*the trees afford shelter*, 16c) **2** to have enough money for (19c).

affray [ME. Anglo-Norman French *affrayer* 'to frighten', occasionally 'to attack', ultimately of Germanic origin] **1** to disturb, alarm, or scare away (surviving in the past participle, now spelt **afraid**); fright, terror (–16c) **2** an attack or assault (–16c); a brawl or skirmish (15c), now only in the legal sense 'a breach of the peace caused by fighting or rioting'. Shortened to **fray**: the sense 'a fight, fighting' survives mainly in literary phrases (*ready for the fray*); the sense 'fright' survives in Scots.

aftermath [15c. From Old English **after** + **math** 'mowing'] A second growth after mowing or harvest (15c), hence the result of, literally something that grows up after, an event (19c).

Math is related to the surname **Mather(s)** [Old English *maethere* 'mower'], and to **mead**, **meadow**, and **mow**, whence the surname **Mower**.

again [Old English *ong(a)ean*, from a Germanic word meaning 'opposite'] In the opposite direction, back to the beginning, surviving in the old-fashioned **turn again** 'turn back', whence **Turnagain** in the names of cul-de-sacs. Hence **1** back to a former state (*drunk again!*, ME) **2** once more, repeatedly (ME). The meaning 'opposite' survives in **against** [ME, from *again*].

agenda [17c. Latin, plural of *agendum* 'something to be done', from *agere* 'to do': see AGENT*. Until the 18c the singular was *agend* (plural *agends* or *agenda*); **agendum** has sometimes been used as the singular since the 19c, but *agenda* (plural *agendas*) is generally accepted] **1** matters of ecclesiastical practice, things to be done as opposed to things to be believed **2** (a list of) the items to be dealt with at a meeting (19c); things to be done or achieved (*a busy/her own agenda*, 1960s).

agent [15c. Latin *agere*, *agent-* 'to lead or drive', later 'to carry on, to do'] Someone/something that produces an effect, hence **1** someone who acts on another's behalf (16c); a steward or representative; a computer program that can do routine tasks automatically (1980s) **2** the means by which something is achieved (16c).

Latin *agere*'s descendants include ACT*, AGENDA, **agile**, AGITATE*, *ambiguous* (at AMBIT), ASSAY*, EXACT*, **-gate** (*fumigate*, NAVIGATE), PRODIGAL, and SQUAT*.

aggravate [15c. Latin *aggravare* 'to make heavy', from *gravis* 'heavy' (ancestor of GRIEVE*)] To weigh down, hence **1** to oppress (–18c) **2** to add weight to (16c), hence to strengthen or increase, now only to increase the seriousness of something, to make it worse **3** to annoy (16c), hence *aggravation* annoyance, trouble (19c), annoying or aggressive behaviour, shortened to **aggro** (1960s).

aggregate [ME. Latin *aggregare* 'to herd together', from *gregis* 'a flock'] The underlying sense is 'collected into one', hence **1** the sum total; to win/lose **on aggregate** by the total score in all games **2** (something) made up of many parts (17c); specifically a rock consisting of fragments loosely held together (18c); a building material made of sand or gravel mixed with cement (19c).

Latin *gregis* is the ancestor of **congregate**, **egregious** [Latin *egregius*, literally 'outside the flock'], originally meaning remarkably good, **gregarious**, and **segregate**.

agitate [15c. Latin *agitare* 'to set in motion', from *agere*: see AGENT*] To drive away, later **1** to disturb or excite (16c), hence **agitation** nervousness, anxiety (17c) **2** to shake something (16c) **3** to discuss or debate (17c), hence **agitator**, literally someone who will not let a matter rest (18c); *agitate* to campaign actively (19c).

Latin *agitare* produced **cogitate** [Latin *coagitare* 'to shake together', hence 'to turn over in your mind'].

agnail [Old English *angnaegl*, from *ang* 'tight, painful' + *naeg(e)l* 'nail'] A corn on the toe (–19c); a painful swelling around a nail (16c); later, influenced by **hangnail** [17c, from HANG], a strip of torn skin beside the nail (19c).

Old English *naeg(e)l* produced the **nail** on fingers and toes, also a small spike for fastening, whence **Naylor** a nail-maker.

agony [ME. Via Old French or late Latin from Greek *agōnia* 'struggle for victory in the games', later 'mental struggle, anguish', from *agōn* 'contest', from *agein* 'to lead or drive'] Mental suffering, specifically Christ's anguish at Gethsemane (see the Bible, Matthew 26:36–42), hence **1** the mental and physical anguish of dying (15c); intense mental or physical pain (17c) **2** (influenced by *agonize*) **agony column** the personal column of a newspaper or magazine (19c), now the advice column; **agony aunt/uncle** who writes it (1970s).

Greek *agōn* produced **agonize** to cause or suffer agony, also to struggle, especially mentally, and PROTAGONIST*. *Agein*'s descendants include -**agogue** (PEDAGOGUE, *synagogue* at SYNTHESIS), and **stratagem** [Greek *stratēgēma* 'to lead an army', with *stratos* 'army'].

agree [ME. Old French *agreer* from Latin *gratus* 'pleasing' (ancestor of GRACE*)] To please or be pleased with, hence **1** to approve of or consent to (15c); to reach a consensus (16c) **2** to be or become harmonious (15c); to have the same opinion; to be consistent; to be suited by something (originally as in *I agree with this*, 16c; later *this agrees with me*, 17c); to get on well together (17c).

aid [15c. French *aide* (noun), *aider* (verb), from Latin *adjuvare* 'to give help to', from *juvare* 'to help or please'] (To give) help, hence **1** someone/something that helps **2** material or financial assistance, specifically that given by one country to another (1940s).

French *aide* was adopted in **aide-de-camp** an officer's assistant (shortened to **aide**, which came to mean an assistant or ancillary worker, *US*), and **aide mémoire** a help to the memory: *aider* produced the international radio distress signal **mayday** [from *venez m'aider* 'come and help me']. Latin *adjuvare* produced **adjutant** [Latin *adjutare*, literally 'to help continuously'] and **adjuvant** (an) auxiliary, hence something that augments a drug etc.; *juvare* produced **jocund** [Latin *jucundus* 'pleasant': influenced by Latin *jocus*: see JOKE] and probably **jury** makeshift (*jury rig*).

aim [ME. Via Old French from Latin *aestimare* 'to assess' (ancestor of ESTEEM*)] To calculate or evaluate (–15c), to guess or estimate (–19c), hence to work out a course, hence **1** **(a)** to point a weapon or direct a missile; the aiming of something (*to take/a good aim* **1**5c); **aim high** so that the missile will go further, hence to be ambitious **(b)** to direct something at a particular audience (19c) **2** to try to do something; an objective or ambition (17c).

air Three words intertwined: I [ME. Via Old French *aire* and Latin *aer* from Greek *aēr*] The gas we breathe; the space containing it that surrounds the earth, hence **1** fresh or open air; to expose to the air (16c), hence to make public (17c) **2** the air as a medium for radio waves (1920s), hence **on (the) air** broadcasting or being broadcast, hence **off (the) air** (1940s); *air* to broadcast or be broadcast (1950s) **3** as a place where aeroplanes etc. fly, earliest in **aircraft** originally balloons or airships (19c), now only aeroplanes II [16c. French, probably from Old French *aire* 'nature, quality', literally 'place of origin', from Latin *ager* 'field'] Outward appearance; manner or style; a stylish or confident manner, hence **give yourself airs** III [16c. Italian *aria* from Latin *aer* (see I)] A melody or song.

Greek *aēr* produced AERIAL, **aero-** (*aerobatics, aeroplane* at PLANE, and **aerobic** needing oxygen, whence **aerobics** exercise aimed at improving the body's utilization of oxygen). Latin *ager* is the ancestor of **agrarian**, *agriculture* (at CULTURE), and PILGRIM*. Italian *aria* was adopted for a long solo song, and produced *malaria* bad air arising from marshes, hence the disease it was once thought to cause.

aisle [ME. Old French *ele* 'wing' (the original spelling in English), from Latin *ala*. The spelling changed in the 17c by association with *isle* and with modern French *aile* 'wing' (whence **aileron**, literally 'little wing')] Part of a church parallel with the nave, later (by confusion with ALLEY) a passage between rows of seats in the nave (18c), hence in a theatre or other building, later one between seats in a vehicle (19c) or shelves in a supermarket (1950s).

alarm [ME. Via French from Italian *allarme*, from *all'arme!* 'to arms!'] A call (*alarm!*) to take up arms, hence **1** a sense of impending danger; to make someone feel this (17c); **alarmed** frightened or apprehensive; **alarmist** (someone) spreading alarm or panic (18c) **2** a warning of approaching danger (16c); (a device for making) a sound that acts as a warning or wakes someone up, hence *alarmed* fitted with an alarm (1960s).

albatross [17c. Alteration, influenced by Latin *albus* 'white', of 16c *alcatras*, applied to various seabirds, from Spanish *alcatraz* 'pelican' and Portuguese *alcatraz* 'frigate-bird', both from Arabic *al-ghaṭṭās* 'the diver'. The American prison island of **Alcatraz** was named from the pelicans seen around it] Applied to several species of large seabirds, especially the wandering albatross, which often follows ships and was believed to bring good luck. Hence a burden or disadvantage (1930s), from Samuel Taylor Coleridge's *The Rime of the Ancient Mariner* (1798), in which the mariner shoots an albatross, the ship is becalmed, and his companions die of thirst, their curses hanging on him like a dead albatross.

album [17c. Latin, 'a blank tablet', from *albus* 'white'] A blank book for autographs [from the German use of Latin *album amicorum*, literally 'tablet of friends'], hence one in which to put stamps, photographs, etc. (19c); a holder for a set of recordings (1950s), hence a compilation of recordings.

Descendants of Latin *albus* include the name **Alban**, **albino**, **Albion** a poetic name for Great Britain (from the white cliffs of Dover), **albumen**, AUBURN, and **daub** [via French from Latin *dealbare* 'to whiten, whitewash, or plaster'].

alchemy [ME. Via Old French from medieval Latin *alchimia*, from Arabic *al-kīmiyya* 'the chemistry', from Greek *khēm(e)ia* 'the art of transmuting metals']

The medieval study of the transformation of substances, whose chief aims were turning base metal into gold and discovering a universal panacea and the elixir of life, hence **1** an alloy, mainly brass, resembling gold **2** a seemingly magical power of transmuting (17c).

The alchemist was also called a **chemist** [via French from medieval Latin *alchimista*, from *alchimia*]: the current sense arose as the modern science of **chemistry** grew out of alchemy. *Alchimia* also produced **chemical**, originally to do with alchemy or chemistry.

alcohol [16c. Via French or medieval Latin from Arabic *al-kuhl* 'the kohl'] A powder, specifically kohl, obtained by heating a substance until it vaporized, the powder being deposited as the vapour cooled, hence a distilled liquid or 'spirit' (17c), regarded by alchemists as very powerful, specifically **spirit of wine**, the part that makes you drunk. Hence **1** **alcoholic** caused by or containing alcohol (18c); (a person) addicted to alcohol (19c), hence *chocoholic*, *workaholic*, etc. **2** **alcopop** a traditionally soft drink containing alcohol (1990s).

alert [16c. Via French from Italian *all' erta* '(be) on the lookout', literally 'to the watchtower!'] Watchful, vigilant (*military*), hence **1** wide awake, lively (18c) **2** a warning of an attack (18c); to put someone on their guard (19c); a state or period of readiness (World War II).

algebra [ME. Ultimately from Arabic *al-jabr* 'the reunion of broken parts', from *jabara* 'to reunite or restore'] Bone-setting (–17c, probably from Spanish, in which it survives). The mathematical sense (16c) comes via Italian from the title of a widely translated 9c mathematical treatise *ilm al-jabr wa'l-muqābala* 'the science of restoring what is missing and equating like with like'.

Algorism, the Arabic or decimal system of writing numbers, comes via Old French and medieval Latin from Arabic *al-Khwārizmī*, literally 'the man from Khiva', referring to Abū J'afar Muḥammad ibn Mūsā, author of this treatise; **algorithm** is a variant, influenced by Greek *arithmos* 'number' (whence **arithmetic**).

alias [15c. Latin, 'at another time, otherwise', from *alius* 'other' (ancestor of ALIEN*)] Adopted meaning 'also called' before an alternative name, hence **1** such a name, especially a criminal's false one (17c) **2** **aliasing** the distortion of recorded sound or, later, a visual image, when transferred from an analogue to a digital system (1950s), hence **antialiasing** the reduction of this (1990s).

alibi [17c. Latin, from *alius* 'other' (see ALIEN*) + *ubi* 'where' (whence **ubiquitous**)] Elsewhere (–18c), hence **1** a plea that someone accused of a crime was elsewhere when it was committed (18c); to provide evidence supporting this (*c.*1910, *US*); a person or evidence that does so (1940s) **2** an excuse of any kind (1920s, *US*).

alien [ME. Old French, from Latin *alienus* 'belonging to another', from *alius* 'other'] Belonging to another person, family, place, or context, hence **1** foreign; a person, later a plant or animal (19c), from another country; a creature from another planet (1940s) **2** different; distasteful, repugnant (18c). The association of foreignness with oddness and undesirable traits is also found in BARBARIAN, **outlandish**, originally 'foreign' (ME), and STRANGE.

Latin *alienus* produced ALIENATE; *alius* is the ancestor of ALIAS and ALIBI.

alienate [ME. Latin *alienare*, literally 'to make other', from *alienus*: see ALIEN*] **1** to estrange, hence **alienation** isolation, estrangement; mental estrangement, insanity (15c); **alienist** an expert in mental illness (19c, US) **2** to transfer property (15c). The two senses come together in the American legal term **alienation of affections**, the transference of your spouse's affections to a lover who is held responsible for your loss (19c).

allay¹ [Old English *alecgan*, from *lecgan* LAY*] To put down or aside (–12c); to abandon a principle, to annul or abolish a law (–17c), hence to quash (–17c); to quell a disturbance or strong emotion (*allayed our fears*, ME); to diminish, mitigate, or alleviate.

This development was influenced by ALLAY² and by obsolete *allege* to (cause to) diminish [ultimately from Latin *alleviare* 'to lighten' (whence **alleviate**), from *levare* 'to raise': see LEVER].

allay² [ME. Old French *al(e)ier* 'to combine': see RALLY*] To moderate or modify, to mix a precious metal with a baser one; such a mixture: almost entirely replaced by **alloy** [French *aloier*, a later form of *al(e)ier*].

allege [ME. Anglo-Norman French *alegier* 'to declare in court', ultimately from Latin *lis* 'law suit' (ancestor of **litigate**)] To declare on oath (–18c); to make a statement or accusation which must then be proved.

Allegation (the making of) an accusation in court, later a statement yet to be proved, comes from Latin *allegare* 'to cite', literally 'to send to or for' (from *legare* 'to send', ancestor of LEGATE*), confused in meaning with *alegier*.

allegiance [ME. Anglo-Norman variant of Old French *ligeance*, from *li(e)ge* 'entitled to feudal service', from medieval Latin *litus*, *laetus* 'serf', probably of Germanic origin and related to LET*] Loyalty and service owed to your feudal superior (surviving in the **oath of allegiance** to the Sovereign taken by Members of Parliament and other public servants), hence loyalty or commitment to a person or cause (18c).

Old French *liege* was adopted for a lord, his vassal, or their feudal relationship: it survives mainly in the historical terms **my liege**, **liege lord**, and **liege man** 'vassal'.

alley [ME. Old French *alee* 'walking, passage', from *aler* 'to go', from Latin *ambulare* 'to walk' (ancestor of AMBLE*)] A corridor or covered walkway (surviving in *skittle/bowling alley*); a pathway in a garden or maze (15c); the aisle in a church (now N English dialect); a narrow pathway between buildings, hence **alley cat** a feral town cat (*c*.1900); a disreputable person, a prostitute (1940s, US).

allot [15c. Old French *aloter*, from *loter* 'to divide into lots', from *lot* 'portion', of Germanic origin: related to LOT*] To share out arbitrarily, originally by drawing lots, later to assign something to someone or for a specific purpose (16c), hence **allotment** something allotted (16c), now specifically a small urban plot of land rented for cultivation (19c).

allow [ME. Old French *alouer*, partly from Latin *allaudare* 'to praise' (from *laus* 'praise'), partly from medieval Latin *allocare*, literally 'to put in place', from *locare* 'to place': see COUCH*] **1** to approve of or accept; to accept as true, to concede

2 to give something to someone as a right, a fair share, or to meet their need, hence to let someone have or do something; **allowance** a ration or sum of money allowed (15c) **3** (also **make allowances**) to make concessions in special circumstances (17c).

Latin *laus* produced **laud** (to) praise; *allocare* produced **allocate** to authorize, especially payment, hence to authorize a share of something for a particular person or purpose.

along [Old English *andlang*, from *lang* LONG*] **1** from end to end of, through or parallel to the length of **2** onward, further on in space or time (ME). Hence **along with**, **alongside** onward or together with (16c); **all along** throughout, all the time (17c); **alongshore** along or by the shore (18c), shortened to **longshore** (19c), whence **longshoreman** a docker (*US*).

Old English *andlang* produced **endlong**; *lang* produced *gelang*, whence **along** to do with, because of, together with, shortened to **long** (now dialect), whence **belong**.

alphabet [16c. Via late Latin from Greek *alphabēton*, from *alpha* and *bēta* the first letters of the Greek alphabet] The Greek alphabet, extended to others in the 17c, a move initially deplored by scholars but generally accepted by the 18c. Hence **1** the rudiments of a subject (16c) **2** an agreed set of characters or symbols (19c).

Alsatian [17c. Medieval Latin *Alsatia* 'Alsace'] Literally 'from or to do with Alsace', a sense not recorded until the 19c. Originally used to describe the Carmelite monastery in Fleet Street, London, which retained the medieval right of providing sanctuary from arrest (as fugitives could take refuge in Alsace, a long-disputed territory between France and the German states). Hostility to all things German during World War I led to the British adopting the name **Alsatian (wolf)dog** for the German Shepherd Dog, which is neither from Alsace nor directly descended from the wolf.

aluminium [From 18c *alumina* aluminium oxide, ultimately from Latin *alumen* **alum**] The British chemist Sir Humphrey Davy (b.1778), who tried to isolate the metal in the early 19c, suggested the name *alumium*, but later changed it to **aluminum** (still the US form). In the UK this was felt to have 'a less classical sound' and the name was quickly changed to match the names of metals such as *titanium* and *uranium*. Davy also named other metals after the substances from which he tried, sometimes sucessfully, to extract them: **calcium** [Latin *calx*, *calc-* 'lime'], **magnesium** [medieval Latin *magnesia*, ultimately from Magnēsia, an ancient city in Asia Minor], *potassium* (at POT), and **sodium** [from **soda**, originally obtained from the ashes of saltwort: probably ultimately from Arabic *suwwād* 'saltwort'].

amalgam [15c. French *amalgame* or medieval Latin *amalgama*, ultimately from Greek *malagma* 'soft mass'] A softened mass made by combining gold or silver with mercury; any alloy with mercury, hence any blend of substances (17c), whence **amalgamate** to make an amalgam; to unite organizations etc. (19c).

amateur [18c. Via French and Italian from Latin *amator* 'lover', from *amare* 'to love', from *amor* 'love'] Someone who is fond of something, specifically one who does something for the love of it rather than for money, hence done by an amateur (19c); (also as **amateurish**) as if done by an amateur; not very good.

Hamfatter meaning an inexpert jazz musician (19c, US slang) may have come about because jazz trombonists greased their slides with ham fat, but is probably a pun on *amateur*. *Amateur* was altered to **ham** an amateur telegraph or radio operator: either *amateur* or *hamfatter* is the source of *ham* a bad actor or acting.

Latin *amor*'s descendants include the names **Amabel** (shortened to **Mabel**), **Amanda** (shortened to **Mandy**), and French **Aimée** (Anglicized to **Amy**), whence the surname **Amey**, Spanish *amoroso* a lover (17–19c), also a sweet sherry, **amorous**, French *amour* (surviving mainly in *amour propre*, literally 'self-love'), whence **enamour** and **paramour** your (secret or adulterous) lover [French *par amour* 'for love']. Related to AMIABLE*.

amaze [Old English *amasian*] To stupefy, bewilder, or confuse (–18c); stupefaction, bewilderment (ME–18c); to fill with wonder, to astonish (16c); wonder, astonishment (replaced by 17c **amazement**). Shortened to **maze** to stupefy (surviving in the southern US), hence **1 the maze** stupefaction, delirium, delusion; *maze* a state of bewilderment **2** a delusion or deception, hence a labyrinth; any confusing network, tangle, or muddle (16c).

Amazon [ME. Latin from Greek, of unknown origin: said by the Greeks to be from *a* 'without' + *mazos* 'breast', in the belief that the Amazons cut off their right breasts to facilitate wielding weapons] One of a legendary race of female warriors said to have lived in Scythia, hence any female warrior (16c); an athletic or formidable woman (17c).

The name of the **River Amazon** comes from a Tupi or Guarani word meaning 'wave', which Spanish explorers mistakenly associated with the legendary Amazons, partly because the local tribesmen were beardless.

ambassador [ME. Via French and Italian from medieval Latin *ambactia*, from Latin *ambactus* 'servant, vassal', from Gaulish *ambactos*. The word also began with *em-* or *im-* until at least the 16c, *embassador* surviving in the US until the 19c] An official messenger, specifically one sent by one monarch or state to another, later a diplomat living in a foreign country to represent their own (16c), hence a worthy representative (*a great ambassador for the sport*, 1980s).

Latin *ambactus* produced **embassy**, which was originally also spelt *ambassy*: Johnson (see ACHE) considered this spelling 'quite obsolete', but again, it survived well into the 19c.

ambit [ME. Latin *ambitus* 'circuit', from *ambire* 'to go around', from *ambi-* 'both ways, around' + *ire* 'to go'] The surroundings or precincts of a building, town, etc., hence a circumference or boundary (16c); the extent or scope of something (17c).

Latin *ambire* later meant 'to go around canvassing for votes', and its noun, *ambitio*, came to mean 'desire for office or popularity', whence **ambition** an inordinate desire for power, later the aspiration to be or do something; a goal or aim. Descendants of *ambi-* include *ambidextrous* at RIGHT, **ambient**, and **ambiguous** [Latin *ambiguus* 'doubtful, shifting, from *ambigere* 'to go around', from *agere* 'to lead': see AGENT*]. Latin *ire* is the ancestor of EXIT*.

amble [ME. Via Old French from Latin *ambulare* 'to walk'] Of a horse etc.: to move both legs on one side at the same time (replaced by PACE); this gait, hence, because it is comfortable for the rider, to ride at an easy pace; to walk in a leisurely way (16c); a leisurely pace or stroll (17c).

Latin *ambulare* is the ancestor of ALLEY, **ambulance** [French, from *hôpital ambulant* 'mobile hospital'], originally a vehicle in which wounded soldiers were treated in the field, PERAMBULATE*, and **preamble.**

amenable [16c. Via Old French from late Latin *minare* 'to drive animals', from Latin *minari* 'to threaten': see MENACE*] Subject to law or to some authority, hence obeying authority; willing to cooperate (19c).

amend [ME. Anglo-Norman French *amender*, ultimately from Latin *emendare*, literally 'to remove a fault', from *menda* 'fault'] **1 (a)** to correct or reform another person (–18c) or yourself **(b)** restitution or reparations (surviving in *make amends*) **2 (a)** to rectify; to remove errors from a text or legal document (15c), largely replaced by **emend** [also from *emendare*] **(b)** to improve a document etc. by a minor change or addition **3** to repair something broken (replaced by *mend* below) **4** to recover from (–17c) or cure (–19c) a disease; recovery (16–17c).

Quickly shortened to **mend**, now usually meaning 'to repair', sense 4 surviving in *on the mend*. Latin *menda* is the ancestor of **mendacious** and **mendicant**.

amiable [ME. French, from late Latin *amicabilis* 'amicable', from Latin *amicus* 'friend'] Friendly, kind, also lovely, lovable, hence (combining the two) pleasant, likeable. **Amicable** [also from *amicabilis*] was originally applied to things, meaning 'pleasant or benign'; the current sense 'in a friendly spirit', was influenced by *amiable*.

Latin *amicus* produced the surnames **Amis** and **Bellamy**, and *inimicus* 'unfriendly', whence **enemy, enmity,** and **inimical.** Related to AMATEUR*.

ampersand [19c. From the phrase *and per se and* '& in or by itself is *and*'] The ampersand (&), originally standing for Latin *et* 'and', was used by medieval scribes, and later appeared at the end of the alphabet in children's primers. Pupils reciting their ABC would end '*x, y, z, and per se and*' [Latin ***per se*** 'by, in, or of itself'] without knowing what it meant, slurring it to *ampersand*, which became the name of the symbol.

amputate [16c. Latin *amputare*, from *putare*, literally 'to clean', hence 'to prune, to clear up or settle' (ancestor of COUNT*)] To lop off or prune, hence to 'prune' a diseased part of the body (17c).

anathema [16c. Ecclesiastical Latin from Greek, 'something devoted', later 'something devoted to evil', from *anatithenai* 'to dedicate', literally 'to put up', from *tithenai* 'to put' (ancestor of THESIS*)] Someone/something damned or cursed; a formal pronouncement of damnation or excommunication, hence an object of loathing; (the object of) a general curse.

angel [Old English *engel*, via a prehistoric Germanic word from Latin *angelus*, from Greek *aggelos* 'messenger', from *aggelein* 'to announce' (ancestor of *evangelist* at GOSPEL)] A superhuman, spiritual being acting as God's messenger or attendant; **(guardian) angel** a spirit who watches over someone (ME), hence **1** the pub name **The Angel**, often originally a pilgrims' hostel run by a religious house **2** an innocent or extremely kind person (16c), hence **(a)** a financial backer, especially in the theatre (19c) **(b)** a nurse (1970s).

Angels were formerly considered the lowest of nine ranks of a celestial hierarchy: the only others to have survived in popular culture are the **archangels**, next above the angels [ultimately from Greek *arkhaggelo*, from *arkhi-* 'chief' (see ARCHIVE*)], the **cherubim** [ultimately from Hebrew *kĕrūb*] the second rank, whose wings formed God's throne; now often portrayed as small, plump, winged boys (partly because infants who died were thought to become angels, partly from a mistaken association of Hebrew *kĕrūb* with Aramaic *kĕ-raḇyā* 'child-like'), hence **cherub** an attractively innocent child, and the **seraphim** [via late Latin from Hebrew *śĕrāpim*] the highest rank, who surrounded God's throne and sang his praises, hence **seraphic** like a seraph, blissful, serene.

Latin *angelus* was adopted for a devotional exercise commemorating Christ's Incarnation [from the opening words *Angelus domini* 'the angel of the Lord']; its descendants include the name **Angela** and the plant **angelica** [Latin *herba angelica* 'angelic herb', from its taste and fragrance].

anger [ME. Old Norse *angr* 'grief', *angra* 'to grieve'] (To cause) grief or distress, hence **1** to enrage; rage **2** inflammation, to irritate or inflame, surviving in dialect and in **angry** meaning 'inflamed' (15c).

angle¹ [ME. (Via French from) Latin *angulus* 'corner'] A corner, the space between two diverging lines or planes, hence **1** the degree of divergence (16c) **2** to direct something into a corner (16c) or obliquely (19c); the (oblique) direction from which you see or approach something, hence to present information from a particular viewpoint (1930s) **3** also **Nangle**: the surname of someone who lived in an odd corner of land.

angle² [Old English *angul*] A fishing hook; fishing tackle, hence to fish with a hook and line (ME); to try to get something by artful means (16c).

Related to *Angul* (now **Angeln**), a district in Schleswig-Holstein (so called because of its hook-like shape), from which the **Angles** [Latin *Anglus*, of Germanic origin, whence **Anglo-**] came to settle in England in the 5c, giving their name to the country [Old English *Englaland* 'Angles' Land'] and to **East Anglia**: see also *Anglo-Saxon* at SAXON. Place names such as **Englefield** pinpoint Angles in areas belonging to other folk.

animate [ME. Latin *animare* 'to give life to', from *anima* 'life, breath, soul, mind'] **1** alive, living **2** to bring to life (15c), to make lively; to inspire to action (16c); to make cartoon characters appear to move (19c). Hence **animated** (16c), *animate* (19c) full of life and energy.

Animate produced **animation** liveliness, later the technique of moving cartoons, whence **animatronics** [with *electronic*] the use of computer technology to animate models or puppets, pioneered by the Disney Corporation, **anime** Japanese animated films [representing Japanese pronunciation of a shortened form of *animation*], which replaced **Japanimation**, and **claymation** animation using (clay) models (1990s). Latin *anima*'s descendants include **animadvert**, *animal* (at BEAST), **animism**, **animosity** spiritedness, courage, later a spirit of hostility, **equanimity** literally 'even-mindedness', **magnanimity** literally 'greatness of spirit', **pusillanimous** literally 'having a small, weak spirit' [with Latin *pullus*: see POOL*], and **unanimous** literally 'of one mind'.

announce [15c. Via French from Latin *annuntiare* from *nuntiare* 'to make known', ultimately from *nuntius* 'messenger'] To make something known; to proclaim the arrival of someone/something (18c), hence **announcement** the announcing of something, a notice or proclamation.

Announce has largely replaced **annunciate** [also from *annuntiare*], except in **The Annunciation** the announcement to the Virgin Mary that she was to bear God's son (see the Bible, Luke 1:28–39). Latin *nuntiare* produced **denounce**, **enunciate**, PRONOUNCE, and **renounce**; *nuntius* fathered Italian *nuncio* a (papal) messenger, before being adopted itself in this sense.

annoy [ME. Old French *anui* (noun), *anuier* (verb), ultimately from Latin *in odio* (from *odium* 'hatred') in *mihi in odio est* 'it is hateful to me'] To be offensive to (ME only); (to cause) discomfort or distress (–16c); to bother, irritate, or anger; something that does so (–19c, outlived by **annoyance**).

Shortened to **noy** (now dialect), whence **noisome** noxious, unpleasant, smelly. Old French *anui* evolved into *ennui* boredom; Latin *odium* was adopted meaning 'repugnance, contempt', having fathered **odious**.

ante [19c. Latin *ante* 'before'] A stake put up by a card player before the cards are dealt (*US*), hence to put up an ante; to give or pay up; an advance payment; **to raise/up the ante** to increase the amount required, to try to get more out of a situation.

Latin *ante*'s descendants include ADVANCE, ADVANTAGE*, **ancient**, **ante-** (*antenatal*, *antechamber*), ANTICIPATION, ANTIQUE*, and VAMP.

antelope [ME. Via Old French or medieval Latin from late Greek *antholops*] A fierce mythical creature that lived by the Euphrates, using its long serrated horns to cut down trees and evade capture. The current sense dates from the 17c.

anthem [Old English *antefn*, ultimately from Greek *antiphōnos* 'responding', from *anti* 'opposite, in exchange' + *phōnē* 'sound'] An antiphon (a song or hymn in which groups of singers take alternate parts), later prose set to music to be sung in church (ME), hence a song of praise or celebration (15c), or one with particular significance (*national anthem*, 19c).

Greek *anti* produced **anti-** 'opposite, against, preventing' (*anticlockwise*, *anti-Semitism*, *antifreeze*); *phōnē* was added to many Greek words, and produced **-phone** (*earphone*, *telephone* at TELEGRAPH) and **phon(o)-** (*phonetics*, *phonograph*).

anthrax [ME. Latin, from Greek *anthrax* '(hot) coal, carbuncle'] A carbuncle; a (fatal) disease whose symptoms include skin ulcers (19c).

Greek *anthrax* produced **anthracite** a reddish gem described by the Roman scholar Pliny (16–18c); Davy (see ALUMINIUM) reborrowed it for a kind of hard coal.

anticipation [16c. Latin *anticipare*, from *ante* (see ANTE*) and *capere* 'to take' (ancestor of CATCH*)] Action taken before the proper time, hence **anticipate** to mention, think about, or do something ahead of time (16c); to take action to prevent or prepare for; to expect or look forward to (18c).

antipodes [ME. Via French or late Latin from Greek, from *anti* 'against, opposite' and *pous*, *podos* 'foot' (ancestor of PODIUM*)] Those who live on the opposite side of the earth (Ethiopia, according to one early writer) and have their feet towards you, hence where they live (16c), later specifically Australia and New Zealand, as being opposite Europe (19c).

antique [15c. (Via French from) Latin *antiquus, anticus* 'former, ancient', from *ante*: see ANTE*] Ancient, hence belonging to a bygone age (16c), specifically to ancient Greece or Rome, hence **1** a relic of a former time, valued for its age; to make something look like one (1920s) **2** old-fashioned or out of date (17c).

Latin *antiquus* fathered Italian *antico* 'antique', whence **antic** grotesque; a grotesque or absurd action.

apocryphal [16c. From *Apocrypha* (see below), from Christian Latin *apocrypha scripta* 'hidden writings', because they were not generally published] Literally, to do with or from the Apocrypha, the fourteen books added to the Septuagint and Vulgate versions of the Old Testament but not accepted as authentic by the Jews or included in the Protestant Bible (17c), but recorded earlier in the current sense 'probably not true'.

apology [16c. Via French or late Latin from Greek *apologia* 'a speech in your own defence', ultimately from *logos* 'word, speech, debate, reason, ratio'] A formal defence of an action or belief, largely replacing **apologetic** in this sense (ME), both superseded by *apologia* (18c). Hence an explanation or excuse; an expression of regret for a fault or wrongdoing; **an apology for** a poor substitute (18c), from the idea of apologizing for the absence of the real thing.

Descendants of Greek *logos* include **logarithm** [with Greek *arithmos* 'number'], **logic, logo** a symbol or character representing a word, attitude, or idea, later an organization's symbol or badge [shortened from **logogram** or **logotype**], **-logue** (*analogue* at DIGIT, *dialogue*), **-logy** (*geology, tautology*), whence **-logist** (*psychologist*), and **syllogism**. Related to Greek *legein*, whence ECLECTIC*.

apostrophe [16c. Strictly speaking, two words, both from Greek *apostrophein* 'to turn away', from *strephein* 'to turn' (ancestor of CATASTROPHE*)] **I** [via Latin] a passage in a speech or piece of writing in which the author 'turns aside' to address an (absent or imaginary) person or thing **II** [via French or late Latin from Greek *apostrophos*, literally 'turned away'] the omission of one or more letters from a word (–17c); the punctuation mark (') that shows this, hence used for the possessive form of a noun (e.g. *boy's* in *the boy's shoes*: 17c, originally replacing *e* in words whose possessive form ended in *-es*, a remnant of Old and Middle English inflections). The placing of the apostrophe when there is more than one owner (*the boys' shoes*, 18c) was originally disputed because no letter had been omitted. The apostrophe was also used with the plural of foreign words ending in a noun (e.g. *avocado's*), where the plural of a similar English word would have ended in *-es*, and sometimes before the *s* of other plurals (more or less obsolete by the 19c). Nowadays fewer and fewer people understand how to use the apostrophe: some publishers do not use it at all and it is making a comeback in plurals, the so-called greengrocers' apostrophe (*apple's*). It may die out.

apothecary [ME. Via Old French from late Latin *apothecarius* 'storekeeper', from *apotheca* 'storehouse', from Greek *apothēkē*, from *apotithenai* 'to put away', from *tithenai* 'to put'] A shopkeeper selling non-perishable commodities such as preserves, spices, and drugs, gradually restricted to one who prepared and sold medicines (the Apothecaries' Company of London separated from the Grocers' in 1617). Now largely replaced by *chemist* (at ALCHEMY), **pharmacist** [ultimately from

Greek *pharmakon* 'drug, medicine'], or N American **druggist** [ME **drug**, from Old French *drogue*, of unknown origin].

Latin *apotheca* fathered Spanish ***bodega*** a wine warehouse; in Spanish-speaking areas of the US, a small grocery store that may sell alcohol, and French ***boutique*** a small shop, hence describing a small and distinctive hotel etc. Greek *tithenai* is the ancestor of THESIS*.

appal [ME. Old French *appallir*, from *pale* 'pale', from Latin *pallidus*, from *pallere* 'to be pale'] To make or become pale, dim, or feeble (–19c), hence **1** to dismay (15c); to horrify or scandalize **2** to lose flavour, to become flat or stale (15c), shortened to **pall** (18c).

Pale was adopted from Old French. Latin *pallidus* gave rise to **pallid**, and *pallere* to **pallor**.

apparatus [17c. Latin, from *apparare* 'to make ready for', from *parare* 'to make ready' (ancestor of PARADE*)] The underlying sense is 'preparation for doing something', hence the equipment needed, specifically that in a laboratory or a gymnasium; **(critical) apparatus** the background material needed to study a text (18c).

apparel [ME. Old French *apareillier*, perhaps from Latin *parare* 'to make ready (ancestor of PARADE*), or from Latin *ap-* 'to, towards' + *par* 'equal', PAR*] (What is needed) to prepare; furnishings or equipment; that for personal use, now only clothing; to equip, arm, or dress.

apparent [ME. Via Old French from Latin *apparere*: see APPEAR*] Plainly visible; evident or obvious (15c), hence **1 heir apparent** the unquestioned successor **2** likely, probable (16–18c); **apparently** evidently, seemingly (16c).

appeal [ME. Old French *appeler* 'to call (upon), to accuse, from Latin *appellare* 'to accost, address, or approach', literally 'to drive towards', from *pellere* 'to drive'] The underlying meaning is '(to make) an approach', hence **1** (to make) an approach to a higher court or authority, hoping to change the decision of a lower one; a judicial review of a case **2** to approach someone for help (16c); a plea for help, especially for donations (19c) **3** to be attractive to a particular person or group (18c); attractiveness (early 20c).

Shortened to **peal**, originally the ringing of a bell as a summons to prayer etc. Latin *appellare* produced Old French *rapeler* 'to call back', whence **repeal**. *Pellere* is the ancestor of PULSE*.

appear [ME. Via Old French from Latin *apparere*, from *parere* 'to be or become visible'] To come into view, hence **1** to present yourself in public, specifically in court, later as an actor or performer (18c); to be published or become available **2** to be visible (–18c), hence to be plain or obvious; to seem to be (15c).

Latin *apparere* produced APPARENT and **apparition** an (unexpected) appearance; what appears, hence something strange or unexpected, specifically a ghost. Latin *parere* is the ancestor of **transparent** [via *transparere* 'to shine through'].

appease [ME. Old French *apaisier*, from *pais* **peace**, from Latin *pax* (ancestor of PAY*)] To settle strife, to bring peace, hence to pacify someone, later specifically by giving in to their demands (15c), now often (especially as **appeasement**) alluding to the UK's concessions to Nazi Germany in an attempt to avoid World War II.

append [15c. Latin *appendere* 'to hang on', from *pendere* 'to hang' (ancestor of PENDANT*)] **1** to hang something on like a pendant, hence **appendix** a small part growing from the surface of an organ (17c), specifically the **vermiform** (worm-shaped) **appendix** in the intestine **2** to attach (16c), hence *appendix* a subsidiary section added to a book or document (16c); *append/appendix*: to add as an appendix (19c).

Latin *appendere* fathered Old French *apentis* 'an appendage', whence **pentice** a lean-to, arcade, or porch (ME–19c), altered to **penthouse** by association with French *pente* 'slope' and HOUSE.

apple [Old English *aeppel*] The fruit; something resembling it: (*custard/oak apple*), **love apple** an early name for the tomato (16c), once believed to be an aphrodisiac and identified with the forbidden fruit in the Garden of Eden (see the Bible, Genesis 3), which was popularly called an apple (whence **Adam's apple**, supposed to be a bit of the fruit that stuck in Adam's throat). The **apple of your eye** (OE) was originally the pupil, thought to be a solid sphere, hence someone/something equally precious; the **Big Apple** as a name for New York is said to have been introduced by the sports writer John FitzGerald in 1921, referring to the New York racetracks: he heard it from Black stable hands in New Orleans, for whom the big-money New York tracks were as tempting as a big shiny apple.

apply [ME. Old French *aplier* from Latin *applicare* 'to fold towards', from *plicare* 'to fold'] **1** to put something on or touching something else, specifically to put a dressing on a wound, hence **(a)** to administer any remedy **(b)** to bring a thing, your mind, or your energy to bear on something **(c)** to use a word, principle, or law in particular circumstances, hence to refer or be relevant to (15c, rare before the 18c) **2** to go to a place; to approach a person, specifically with a formal request (17c) **3** (shortened to, and surviving as, **ply**) to work at assiduously (15c), hence **(a)** to wield a tool etc. vigorously (16c) **(b)** to offer insistently (*plied us with food*, 16c) **(c)** (only as *ply*) to go or wait somewhere regularly, especially in hope of work (*ply for hire*, 18c), hence to travel regularly between certain places (19c).

Latin *applicare* fathered French *appliquer*, whence *appliqué* a piece of material sewn onto another to decorate it; (to decorate using) this technique. Latin *plicare* is the ancestor of PLY*.

appoint [ME. Old French *apointer*, from *a point* 'to a point': see POINT*] The underlying sense is 'to bring to a certain point or condition', hence **1** to arrange or settle something definitely, specifically **(a)** to settle on someone for a post or responsibility (hence **disappoint** to deprive someone of a post etc., hence to frustrate or let down, 15c) **(b)** to fix a time or place for something (16c, ME in **appointment** a pre-arranged meeting) **2** to fit something out, surviving mainly in **well-appointed**.

appreciate [16c. Late Latin *appretiare* 'to set a price on', from *pretium* PRICE*] To set the right price on, hence to value; to be grateful for; to be aware of or sensitive to; to raise or rise in price (18c, *US*: probably influenced by Middle English **depreciate** to underrate or undervalue; to make or become less valuable, 17c).

apprehend [ME. (Old French *aprendre* from) Latin *apprehendere* 'to learn', from *prehendere* 'to get hold of': cf. CLEVER*] To grasp, physically or mentally (–19c), hence **1** to arrest someone (16c) **2** to become aware (17c), specifically of danger, to anticipate nervously (now usually **be apprehensive**).

Old French *aprendre* is the source of **apprentice** (whence the surname **Prentice**), and Latin *prehendere* of PRISE*.

appropriate [ME. Latin *appropriare* 'to make your own', from *proprius* 'own' (ancestor of PROPER*)] To take possession of something, hence **1** to take something for your own use or for a particular purpose, later without the owner's permission (16c), hence **misappropriate** to appropriate money etc. for an illegal or improper use **2** attached or belonging to (16c), hence characteristic of; suitable (for).

approve [ME. Via Old French from Latin *approbare*, from *probare* 'to test': see PRO-BABLE*] To prove or demonstrate (–17c, hence **disapprove** to disprove, 15c); to confirm or sanction, hence to have or express a favourable opinion of, hence *disapprove* to view unfavourably (17c).

Latin *approbare* produced **approbate** to approve formally (now N American), and **approbation** confirmation, proof (ME–18c); formal endorsement or approval.

apron [ME. Old French *naperon*, from *na(p)pe* 'tablecloth', from Latin *mappa* 'napkin'. Originally spelt *napron*; the current spelling (16c) comes from the wrong division of *a napron*: cf. EKE*] A protective garment worn over the front of your clothes, hence something similar in shape or function, for example a cover for your legs in an open carriage (18c), the part of a stage in front of the curtain, which originally jutted out into the auditorium (19c); a paved area for parking aircraft (1920s).

Old French *na(p)pe* produced **napery**, **napkin**, and the surname **Napier**, **Napper** someone who sold, or the servant in charge of, napery. Latin *mappa* is the ancestor of **map** [from medieval Latin *mappa mundi*, literally 'sheet of the world'], and perhaps of **mop**.

apt [ME. Latin *aptus* 'fitted, suitable', from *apere* 'to fasten'] Fit or ready for, hence **1** likely or prone to (16c, implied in 15c **aptitude** natural tendency or inclination); having a talent for, quick to learn, hence *aptitude* natural ability **2** appropriate or relevant (16c).

Latin *aptus* produced **inept** [Latin *ineptus* 'unsuitable'] and **lariat** [via Spanish *reatar* 'to retie' from Latin *aptare* 'to adjust']. *Apere* is the ancestor of ATTITUDE. Related to Latin *copula* a link or connection, whence **copulate** and **couple**.

aquaplane [*c*.1910. Latin *aqua* 'water' + PLANE*] A board like a water-ski towed behind a speedboat (*US*); to ride on one, hence of a vehicle: to skid on a wet surface, the wheels 'riding' on a film of water (1960s).

Latin *aqua* is used in pharmacy etc. for water or a watery fluid, and as an abbreviation for **aquamarine**. It appears in words such as *aquarium* and *aqueduct*, and produced *aqua vitae* etc. (at VITAL), **ewer** [via Old French], French **gouache** [via Italian *guazzo* from Latin *aquatio* 'watering'], and **sewer** [Norman French *se(u) wiere* 'sluice from a fishpond', ultimately from Latin *ex-* 'out of' + *aqua*] a channel built to drain marshy land, later one for waste water and excrement.

arc [ME. Old French, from Latin *arcus* 'a bow or curve'] The apparent path of a celestial body, especially the sun, from horizon to horizon, hence part of a circle's circumference (16c); a curve or arched shape; later specifically the arch-shaped luminous discharge of electricity between electrodes (19c).

Latin *arcus* is the ancestor of ARCADE, **arch**, and **archer**, literally a 'bow-er', one who shoots with a bow.

arcade   [17c. French, via Italian or Portuguese from Latin *arcus*: see ARC*] A covered walkway formed by a series of arches (17c), later any covered walk or avenue, specifically one containing shops or stalls (19c), hence (**amusement**) **arcade** a covered space containing coin-operated games (*c*.1900).

archipelago   [16c. Italian, from Greek *arkhi-* 'chief, greatest', from *arkhein*: see ARCHIVE*) + *pelagos* 'sea, lake, lagoon'] Former name of the Aegean sea, hence any stretch of water which, like the Aegean, has many islands, hence a group of islands.

Greek *arkhi-* is found in *archetype* (at TYPE), and **architect** [Greek *arkhitekton*, literally 'chief builder'], and produced **arch-** (*archangel* at ANGEL, *arch-enemy*); its use with words such as *rogue* or *wag* led to **arch** being used alone to mean 'self-consciously mischievous or playful'.

archive   [17c. Via French from Latin *archiva*, *archia*, from Greek *arkheia* 'public buildings or records', from *arkhē* 'government, rule', from *arkhein* 'to rule'] (A repository for) public records, hence a collection of historical documents or information; to place records in one (19c); to transfer computerized data to a less frequently used file or medium (1970s).

Greek *arkhē* produced **-arch** (*matriarch, monarch*) and **-archy** (HIERARCHY, *oligarchy*). Greek *arkhein* is the ancestor of ARCHIPELAGO*.

Arctic   [ME. Via Old French and Latin from Greek *arktikos* 'of the north' from *arktos* 'bear', hence the constellation known as the Great Bear or by its Latin name, **Ursa Major**] (To do with) the north pole or the polar region, hence bitterly cold (17c). The **Arctic Circle** originally referred to an imaginary circle in the heavens that, for any given latitude, contained all the stars visible throughout the year (apparently so named because it was originally defined as the latitude where the Great Bear skimmed the horizon but never disappeared below it).

Antarctic [Greek *antarktikos* 'opposite the north'] appeared in Middle English in the general sense 'southern, opposite to the Arctic': though long postulated in Europe and mentioned in Maori legend as early as the 7c, the existence of the Antarctic region was not proved until Captain Cook's explorations (1772–75). The star **Arcturus** [Greek *Arktouros*, literally 'bear-guard', with *ouros* 'guard'] is so named from its position at the Great Bear's tail. Latin *ursa* 'bear' produced **ursine** to do with or like a bear, and the names **Orson** and **Ursula**.

ardent   [ME. Old French from Latin *ardens* 'burning', from *ardere* 'to burn' (ancestor of **ardour** and **arson**)] Flammable (surviving in **ardent spirits** alcohol, now usually referring to a fiery taste); burning, fiery (15c), hence 'burning' with lust or enthusiasm.

area   [16c. Latin, 'level piece of open ground'] **1** an (empty) piece of land, or of space in a building (16c), hence **(a)** a courtyard (17c); a sunken one outside a basement (18c) **(b)** a field of knowledge or activity (17c) **(c)** a region or neighbourhood (18c);

a vicinity **(d)** land or space used for a specific purpose (*dining/parking area*, 19c); a distinct part of any surface **2** the size of a surface (16c).

Latin *area* came to mean 'bird of prey's nest' (whence **eyrie**), and produced French *are*, whence **hectare** [with Greek *hekaton* 'hundred'].

arena [17c. Latin *(h)arena* 'sand'] The floor of an amphitheatre, which in Roman times was spread with sand to soak up the blood; the whole amphitheatre; a stadium; any scene of action or conflict (18c).

aristocracy [15c. Via Old French from Greek *aristokratia*, from *aristos* 'best' + -*kratia* 'power, rule'] Government of a state by its best citizens, later by the rich and well-born (16c), as opposed to **democracy** rule by the people [Greek *dēmos* 'people, land'], hence the nobility, regardless of who rules (17c). **Aristocrat** is from French *aristocrate*, coined during the Revolution of 1790 for a member of the aristocracy, or someone who thought aristocrats should rule.

Greek *dēmos* is the ancestor of **demagogue**, -**demic** (*endemic*, *epidemic*), and **demography**.

ark [Old English *aerc*, from Latin *arca* 'chest'] A container with a lid, specifically **1** a food bin (surviving in N England) **2 Ark (of the Covenant)** the chest containing the tablets of Jewish law **3** a covered ship, specifically Noah's Ark (see the Bible, Genesis 6–8), hence **(a)** any ship (15c); a large flat-bottomed river-boat (19c, US) **(b)** a place of refuge (17c).

Ark produced the surname **Arkwright**, someone who made chests. Latin *arca* is the ancestor of EXERCISE*.

arm [ME. Via French from Latin *armare* 'to equip for fighting', from *arma* 'arms, armour'] **1 arms: (a)** armour, hence a knight's emblem, often worn on a tabard, literally a **coat of arms**, over his armour; this later became his family symbol, hence the *(coat of) arms* of a family, country, or organization **(b)** weapons (singular in words such as *firearm*, *sidearm*) **2** to equip with armour or weapons, hence with something that strengthens or protects, hence **(a) armed** having a weapon or weapons (*armed guard*); prepared or equipped (*armed with the facts*, 16c) **(b) disarm** to deprive of a weapon etc.; to remove someone's wish to harm, to win them over (17c) **(c)** to prepare or activate a weapon (early 20c) **3** a branch of the armed forces (18c), hence a division of an organization (1950s), sometimes seen as belonging to **arm** an upper limb [Old English *(e)arm*].

Latin *armare* produced Spanish *armadillo*, literally 'little armed man', ARMATURE, and ARMY*.

armature [ME. Latin *armatura* (whence **armour**), from *armare*: see ARM*] Arms or armour, hence something that protects or supports, hence **1** a plant or animal's protective outer covering (18c) **2** the keeper of a magnet (18c), hence the core and windings of an electromagnetic machine (19c); part of an electric machine that moves in response to magnetic or electromotive force (19c) **3** an internal supporting framework for a sculpture or model (*c*.1900).

army [ME. Old French *armee*, ultimately from Latin *armata* 'armed', from *armare*: see ARM*] An armed expedition or force, originally on land or sea, the latter gradually superseded by *navy* (see NAVIGATE), hence **1** a large military force (15c); a country's entire land forces (17c) **2** a large number of people or things (16c); a number of people united for a cause.

Latin *armata* fathered Spanish **armada** a fleet of warships, hence a large army; a large fleet of any craft.

aroma [ME. Old French *aromat*, ultimately from Greek *arōma* 'spice'] A fragrant herb or spice (–18c); the fragrance of one, hence any pleasant smell (19c).

array [ME. Old French *arei* (noun), *areer* (verb), ultimately of Germanic origin] To prepare, hence **1** to put in order, originally for battle, hence **(a)** (an) orderly arrangement, especially in lines or ranks; an imposing or well-ordered series of people or things (19c); a set of numbers and/or symbols in a particular order; a particular arrangement of computerized data (1950s) **(b)** (the mustering of) a militia (15c) **2** attire, dress; to dress, adorn, or embellish, hence **arrayment** outfit, dress (15c), shortened to **raiment**.

Related to **curry** to groom a horse: **curry favour** is an alteration of *curry Favel*, a horse in a medieval fable whose name became a byword for deceit.

arrear [ME. Old French *ar(i)ere* 'behind' from medieval Latin *adretro*, from Latin *retro* 'backwards'] In or to the back (–19c), behind, overdue (–19c), hence an outstanding duty or debt; **in arrears** behind with payments.

Old French *ar(i)ere* produced *reredorter* (at DORMITORY) and *reredos* (at ENDORSE). Latin *retro* produced **rear** (situated) at the back, back, last, and appears in *retroactive*, *retrofit*, etc., and RETROGRADE*.

arrive [ME. Old French *ariver*, ultimately from Latin *ripa* 'bank, shore' (whence *riparian* and *river*)] To reach the end of a voyage; to reach a place by any means; to reach a conclusion or decision or, later, a certain stage of development (16c), hence to be professionally or socially successful (19c).

arsenal [16c. Via French and Italian from Venetian Italian *arzana* 'workshop', applied specifically to the naval dockyard in Venice, from Arabic *dār-aṣ-ṣ inā'a*, literally 'house of manufacture'] A shipyard (–19c), later a government establishment for making or storing weapons, hence a store of literal or figurative weapons (17c).

Arsenal football team began life at Woolwich Arsenal in SE London: when it moved to N London it gave its name to the nearest underground station. It has since moved again.

art and **science** both originally meant acquired, as opposed to natural, wisdom or skill. Hence **the (liberal) arts** or **sciences** the medieval quadrivium (music, geometry, arithmetic, and astronomy) and trivium (grammar, rhetoric, and logic): *art* or *the arts* later came to mean (the skill of creating) literature, music, painting, and sculpture (the **fine arts**), also history, philosophy, and languages, while *science* or *the sciences* refers to the study of natural phenomena. *Art* went on to mean **1** craft, technique (17c) **2** cleverness, cunning (17c), hence **artful (a)** learned, skilful, wise; cunning, crafty **(b)** skilfully planned or done (18c).

Both words were adopted into Middle English from Old French, *art* from Latin *ars, artis* 'skill', whence **artisan**, ARTIFICE*, and **inert** [Latin *iners, inert-* 'unskilled, inactive'], *science* from Latin *scire* 'to know', whence CONSCIENCE*, NICE*, **omniscient**, *plebiscite* (at PLEBEIAN), and **prescient**.

artery [ME. Via Latin from Greek *artēria*, probably from *aeirein* 'to raise'] **1** the windpipe (–17c: the Greeks thought the arteries were air ducts because they are empty after death) **2** a blood vessel taking blood around the body from the heart, hence an important channel of communication or transport (19c).

Related to **aorta** the main artery [Greek *aortē*, used by Hippocrates (Greek physician, born *c*.450 BC) for branches of the windpipe, and by Aristotle (Greek philosopher, 4c BC) in its current sense].

artichoke [16c. Northern Italian *articiocco* from Spanish *alcarchofa*, from Arabic *al-kharšūfa*. The word has had many spellings, including *hortichoke*, from the idea that the plant 'choked' the garden, and *h(e)artichoke*, because the globe artichoke was said to have a *choke* (its inedible centre, literally something that choked you) at its heart] An edible thistle, the globe artichoke. Hence, from their similar flavours, the **Chinese** or **Japanese artichoke**, and the **Jerusalem artichoke** [*Jerusalem* here is a corruption of Italian *girasole* 'sunflower', the family to which it belongs, ultimately from Greek *guros* 'a ring': see VEER].

article [ME. French, from Latin *articulus* 'small joint or part', from *artus* 'joint'] A distinct part of a document, a clause, paragraph, or point, hence **1 articles** a formal agreement, specifically for an apprenticeship; **articled clerk** one 'apprenticed' to a solicitor **2** a particular piece of business, a matter or subject (15c), hence an item for sale, an object of a particular kind (18c) **3** a short factual piece in a magazine (18c).

Latin *articulus* produced ARTICULATE; *artus* produced **arthritis**.

articulate [15c. Latin *articulare* 'to divide into segments', from Latin *articulus*: see ARTICLE*] (Also **articulated**) made up of segments divided by joints, hence **1** of sounds: made up of clearly distinguishable parts (16c), hence *articulate* of speech: fluent and clear; of a person: able to express themselves, an emotion etc., clearly; to do so (17c) **2 articulated lorry** with tractor and trailer connected by a flexible joint (1930s), shortened to **artic** (1950s).

artifice [ME. Old French from Latin *artificium*, from *ars*, *art-* + *-ficium* 'making' from *facere* 'to make'] Technical skill, craftsmanship (–18c), hence **1** cleverness, cunning (17c), an ingenious device, trick or plan **2** (a product of) human skill as opposed to nature (19c, influenced by *artificial*).

Latin *artificium* produced **artificer** a craftsman; a military or naval technician (popularly shortened to **tiffy**), and **artificial** made by human skill, not natural, imitation, feigned. Latin *ars* produced ART* and **artefact** [also with *facere* (ancestor of FACT*)].

asparagus [OE. Medieval Latin *sparagus* from Latin *asparagus*, from Greek *asparagos*] First recorded as *sparagi*; in the 16–17c usually called by the French name *sperage*. Latin *asparagus*, used by herbalists, became more widely known in the 17c, and was often shortened to *sparagus*. By 1650 this had become **sparrow-grass**, the usual name until the 19c when the Latin form came back into fashion.

aspect [ME. Ultimately Latin *aspicere*, *aspect-* 'to look at', from *specere* 'to look' (ancestor of SPICE*)] **1** gaze, contemplation, regard (–19c), hence the way someone/something looks to the eye or mind (15c); a part or facet that presents itself (17c); a point of view **2** the relative positions of celestial bodies; of a planet: to look on and influence another (15c) **3** to look at or face (16–17c); the position, or the side, of a building etc. facing in a certain way (17c).

aspersion [15c. Latin *aspergere, aspers-* 'to sprinkle on', from *spargere* 'to sprinkle' (ancestor of **disperse, intersperse,** and **sparse**)] The sprinkling of someone with liquid, specifically in baptism; later a slander or false insinuation, regarded as spattering or staining (16c, chiefly in **cast aspersions**); defamation, slander (17c).

asphodel [15c. Latin *asphodilus* from Greek *asphodelos*] Applied to various, originally Mediterranean, plants of the lily family, some of which have white or yellow flowers, later to an immortal flower said to cover the Elysian fields (17c).

The medieval Latin variant *affodilus* produced **affodil,** originally applied to the asphodel but later erroneously to the narcissus. The variant **daffodil** was used for both kinds of flower until the 17c, when *(d)affodil* became restricted to the narcissus, and then to the wild yellow variety. *Affodil* survives in poetry and dialect, along with the variants **daffidowndilly, daffodilly,** and **daffydilly.**

assassin [16c. Via French or medieval Latin from Arabic *ḥašīšī* 'hashish-eater', from *ḥašīš* 'dry herb, **hashish**'] A member of a medieval Ismaili Shi'ite Muslim sect who were said to murder religious and political rivals, using hashish to give them visions of Paradise before facing capture and death, hence someone who murders a public figure for religious or political ends (17c).

assay [ME. Old French *assaier, essayer* 'to try', ultimately from Latin *exigere, exact-*, literally 'to drive out': see EXACT*] **1** (to carry out) a test of quality or fitness, now especially of the purity of metal (15c) **2** (to make) an attempt to do something (15c); to try to overcome something/someone. The variant **essay** (16c) came to mean a short piece of non-fictional prose, literally an attempt to deal with a subject.

assess [15c. Latin *assidere, assess-*: see ASSIZE*] To decide the amount of a fine or tax (15c), hence to value something for taxation (19c, 16c in **assessment**); to judge or evaluate (1930s).

asset [16c. From the Anglo-Norman French legal phrase *aver asetz* 'to have enough', from Old French *asez* 'enough', ultimately from Latin *satis* (ancestor of SATISFY*)] **Assets** sufficient means to pay a deceased person's debts and legacies; property owned by a person or firm, whether or not it meets their liabilities, hence *asset* an item of such property; someone/something regarded as valuable or beneficial (17c).

assize [ME. Old French *assise*, from *asseoir* 'to sit or settle', from Latin *assidere* 'to sit by', later 'to sit beside and assist a judge', also 'to attend to', from *sedere* 'to sit'] A sitting of a consultative or legislative body, hence **1 assizes** periodic court sessions formerly held in England and Wales; *assize* a judicial inquest; its verdict (16c) **2** an edict made by an assize; one setting standards for weights and measures or, shortened to **size,** the amount of a payment or tax (–18c: cf. ASSESS); a standard set. Hence *size* how big something is or how much it measures; a standard or proper measurement (16c); to make or adjust to a certain size (17c); to measure or estimate its size (19c).

Old French *assise* may be the source of **size** a mixture for sealing porous surfaces. Latin *assidere* produced ASSESS and **assiduous;** *sedere* is the ancestor of SESSION*.

associate [ME. Latin *associare*, from *socius* 'companion, friend'] To join or ally with another or others; joined, allied; **association** the act of joining or uniting (16c). Hence **1** to put things together (16c), now especially in your mind; a thing placed or found with another (17c) **2** a partner, ally, or companion (16c), hence **(a)** *association* a society (16c); **Association Football** played according to the rules of the Football Association (19c, often shortened to **soccer**) **(b)** *association* social interaction, now specifically in prison (17c) **(c)** (describing) someone who is a member of a society or who shares a responsibility, but has lower status (19c).

Latin *socius* is the ancestor of **dissociate** to separate physically or mentally [via *sociare* 'to unite'] and SOCIAL*.

assume [ME. Latin *assumere*, literally 'to take up', from *sumere* 'to take'] **1** to take a living person up into heaven (mainly in the **Assumption** of the Virgin Mary) **2** to take on or take up with someone **3** to claim, appropriate, or start using something; to pretend to have something (*an assumed name*, 17c) **4** to take something as being true for the sake of argument (15c) **5** to take on an office, duty, role, or responsibility (16c).

Presume [Latin *praesumere*, literally 'to take up beforehand, to anticipate', from *sumere*] shares the senses 'to take on something' and 'to take as being true' (also formerly 'to appropriate'), but without authority or grounds for doing so. Latin *sumere* is the ancestor of SUMPTUOUS*.

astonish [16c, from Middle English *astone* 'to stun or stupefy' (–18c), from Old French *estoner*, ultimately from Latin *tonare* 'to thunder'] To stun, bewilder, or dismay (–18c), hence to amaze (17c).

Astoned stunned, insensible, astonished [past participle of *astone*], developed into **astound**, replaced by **astounded**, whence the verb *astound*. Old French *estoner* produced **stun**. Latin *tonare* is the ancestor of **detonate** and **tornado** [alteration (influenced by Spanish *tornar* from Latin *tornare*: see TURN) of Spanish *tronada* 'thunderstorm', from *tronar* 'to thunder'].

astronomy [ME. Via French and Latin from Greek *astronomia* 'arrangement of the stars', from *astron* 'star'] The study of stars and planets, originally including **astrology** [Greek *astrologia* 'study of the stars'], which was adopted for the practical uses of astronomy, e.g. measuring time, predicting tides and eclipses, and ascertaining the planets' influence on human affairs: the current division of senses dates from about the 17c. **Astronomical** in the sense 'enormous' (19c) comes from the almost unbelievable distances encountered in astronomy.

Greek *astron* produced **astro-** (*astronaut*, *astrophysicist*), **disaster** [via French from Italian *disastro*, literally 'ill-starred'], and perhaps **stroll** [probably from German dialect *strollen*, *strolchen*, from *Strolch* 'vagabond, fortune-teller', from Italian *astrologo* 'astrologer']. Greek *aster* was adopted for a genus of plants with star-shaped flowers, and is the ancestor of **asterisk** and **asteroid**.

asylum [ME. Latin, from Greek *asulon* 'refuge', from *asulos* 'inviolable', from *a-* 'not, no' + *sulon* 'right of seizure'] A place of refuge, originally for criminals, later for the insane or destitute (18c), hence sanctuary or protection (*political asylum*).

atlas [16c. Latin, named after Atlas, a Titan said to hold up the pillars of the universe] A person who bears a great burden, hence **1** the **atlas vertebra** the top bone of the spinal column that supports the skull **2** a book of maps (17c: coined by Mercator: see CHEAP: early atlases often had a frontispiece depicting Atlas).

The **Atlas** mountains in NW Africa were named after the Titan because the heavens were supposed to rest on them (Perseus, son of the Greek god Zeus, showed Atlas the head of the gorgon Medusa, the sight of which turned men to stone and poor Atlas into a mountain). **Atlantic** [Greek *Atlantikos* 'to do with Atlas'] originally referred to these mountains, hence to the sea near the W African coast, subsequently to the whole ocean.

atom [ME. Via Old French and Latin from Greek *atomos* 'indivisible', also 'a moment', from *a-* 'not' + *temnein* 'to cut' (ancestor of TOME*)] The smallest medieval unit of time, less than a sixth of a second, later a hypothetical particle of matter so small that it could not be divided (15c), hence a very small bit of something (17c); the smallest particle of a chemical element (19c).

atone [ME. From *at one*] To become reconciled (–17c), extremely rare before the 16c, when it was re-formed from **atonement** reconciliation, specifically between God and man, hence to reconcile people; to appease an offended person (17–19c); to make amends for an offence.

atrium [16c. Latin, perhaps originally the place where smoke escaped through a hole in the roof, from or related to *ater* 'black'] A central court in a Roman house; a covered court or portico, hence **1** a central hall or glassed-in court in a house (19c) or through several storeys of a building (1960s, *US*) **2** a chamber in the body, specifically one of the upper chambers of the heart (19c).

Latin *ater* produced *atrox, atroc-* 'black-looking, frightful, cruel', whence **atrocious** and **atrocity**.

attach [ME. Old French *atachier, estachier*, ultimately of Germanic origin] To fasten one thing to another, hence **1** to seize with legal authority **2** to join an organization (17c); **be attached** to join a military unit etc. for special duties (19c), hence modern French *attaché* someone attached to an embassy staff (19c), hence **attaché case** for documents such as attachés carried **3** to become devoted to someone (18c) **4** to attribute to or associate with someone/something (19c).

Old French *estachier* produced **detach** [via Old French *destachier*] and Italian *staccato* [Italian *(di)staccare*, from *destachier*]. Related to STAKE*.

attack [17c. French *attaquer* from Italian *attacare* 'to attach' (in the phrase *attacare battaglia* 'to join battle'), ultimately of Germanic origin and related to STAKE*] To assault physically; to try to kill or destroy; a physical assault, hence **1** to assault verbally (17c), a verbal assault (18c) **2** of a disease: to afflict; a bout of illness, emotion, etc. (*an attack of conscience*, 19c) **3** to begin to corrode, dissolve, or damage something (18c) **4** to go on the offensive in a sport or contest (18c); the players who do so; an attacking move **5** to tackle something vigorously or confidently (19c); a vigorous beginning, especially in music; [influenced by Italian *attaca*] verve, brilliance, decisive style.

attend [ME. Via Old French from Latin *attendere* 'to stretch towards', from *tendere* 'to stretch'] To pay attention to or be present at, hence **1** to deal with or take care of; to serve or wait on; to accompany or escort **2** to go to regularly (*attend school/church*);

to visit a sick person regularly or professionally (16c) **3** to occur with or as a result of something (*success attended their efforts*, 17c).

Shortened to **tend** 'to mind', whence **tender 1** a minder (surviving mainly in *bartender*) **2** a boat that ferries things to and from a ship; a truck carrying a locomotive's fuel and water; a firefighter's vehicle. Latin *tendere* is the ancestor of TEMPT*.

attic [16c. Via Latin from Greek *Attikos*] **Attic** to do with Athens or Attica, hence **attic (order)** a small column (in the Attic style), and the horizontal part it supported, above the main facade of a building (17c); **attic (storey)** a small storey at the top of a building (18c), hence *attic* a room in the attic storey (19c).

attire [ME. Old French *atir(i)er*, from *a tire* 'in order', from *tire* 'order, rank', from *tirer* 'to draw out, to endure', probably from *martirer* 'to torture' (from the idea of stretching on the rack), ultimately from Greek *martur* 'witness'] To prepare or equip, originally for war, hence **1** a set of armour and weapons (–15c); shortened to **tire** the metal protecting a wheel's rim (15c); the variant **tyre** (–17c) was revived in the UK for the rubber equivalent (19c), the Americans keeping *tire* **2** to dress or adorn; clothing.

Old French *atir(i)er* produced **artillery**, literally 'equipment for war', *tire* produced **tier**, and *tirer* produced **retire** [via *retirer* 'to withdraw'] and **tirade** [literally 'a volley'], adopted for long angry speech. Greek *martur* produced **martyr** someone, originally a Christian, who died for their faith (see WITNESS).

attitude [17c. French, from Italian *attitudine* 'fitness, posture', from late Latin *aptitudo* 'aptitude', from Latin *aptus* 'fit' (see APT*)] The placing or posture of a figure in art, hence **1** the posture accompanying an action or feeling (18c); (behaviour that shows) a settled opinion or way of thinking (19c), hence [probably from phrases such as *I don't like your attitude*] an assertive or arrogant manner (1960s, *US*) **2** the angle of an aircraft in relation to the direction of travel or to the horizontal (early 20c).

attract [15c. Latin *attrahere*, *attract-* 'to pull towards', from *trahere*, *tract-* 'to draw' (ancestor of TRACT*)] To pull towards yourself or itself, especially by invisible means, originally by inhaling or suction, later by magnetism or charm, hence **attractive** appealing, pleasing, alluring (16c), whence *attract* to draw attention, to appeal to (17c), whence **attraction** something that attracts, especially tourists or customers (19c).

attrition [ME. Late Latin *attritio*, from *atterere* 'to rub away', from *terere*, *trit-* 'to rub'] **1** regret for sin from fear of damnation, falling short of **contrition** sincere remorse [ME, via French from Latin *contritio*, from *contrere* 'to rub together, to bruise', here referring to the 'bruising' of the soul] **2** abrasion of skin or tissue (15c); rubbing, grinding, or wearing away (17c), hence the gradual wearing down of an army by constant harassment (World War I); gradual loss of staff etc.

Latin *terere* is the ancestor of **detriment** and **detritus** [both via Latin *deterere* 'to wear away'], and **trite** [Latin *tritus*, literally 'well worn'].

auburn [15c. Old French *auborne*, *alborne*, from Latin *alburnus* 'off-white', from *albus* 'white' (ancestor of ALBUM*)] Very pale blonde; later also spelt *abrun(e)* or *aburn* and thus associated with *brown* and *burn*, hence the current sense 'reddish brown' (16c).

audience [ME. Old French, from Latin *audientia*, from *audire* 'to hear'] Hearing or listening, hence **1** a formal hearing or interview with an important person **2** people listening (15c), hence those who attend a performance or read a book (18c), or watch or listen to a broadcast (1920s).

Latin *audire* is the ancestor of **audible**, **audio-** (*audiotape*), whence **audio** (electronic reproduction of) sound, **audit** an examination of accounts (originally read out), **audition** the action or power of hearing, hence the 'hearing' of an actor etc. seeking work, to test or be tested in this way, **obeisance** and **obey** [both via Latin *oboedire* 'to listen to'], and of **oyez** [Old French, literally 'hear, listen!', from *oïr* 'to hear'].

augur [ME. Latin] **1** a Roman official who interpreted omens from natural phenomena, including birds' behaviour (cf. AUSPICE); a prophet or soothsayer **2** to begin something with rites that included the observation of omens (16c: cf. *inaugurate* below) **3** to make predictions from omens (16c) **4** to be an omen, to promise well or ill (18c).

Latin *augur* produced *augurare* 'to take omens from natural phenomena, to consecrate or instal ceremonially when these are favourable', whence **inaugurate**.

aunt [ME. Via Anglo-Norman French *aunte* from Latin *amita* 'father's sister'] The sister of one of your parents, loosely, an older female relative or, to a child, a family friend, hence **1** a wise and kindly older woman (19c); a conservative or timid one **2** a female animal that helps care for another's offspring (19c). **Uncle** [ME, via Old French from Latin *avunculus* 'mother's brother', whence **avuncular**] has a similar but more disreputable history: **1** an older male relative or family friend; your mother's lover (1960s) **2** an older man who helps you (16c); a pawnbroker (18c).

Aunt, auntie, and *uncle* were used as informal forms of address to older people, in the US especially elderly Black people, hence **Uncle Tom** a slave in Harriet Beecher Stowe's novel *Uncle Tom's Cabin* (1852): portrayed as the victim of a cruel system, Tom's good nature led to *Uncle Tom* becoming a contemptuous term for an obsequious Black man.

aura [ME. Latin from Greek] A gentle breeze (–18c); a subtle emanation (18c), hence **1** a warning sensation before an epileptic fit or migraine **2** a force said to emanate from and envelop a person or thing, discernible by psychics etc. (19c).

Latin *aura* produced French *essorer* 'to fly up', whence **soar**.

aurora [ME. Latin *aurora* 'dawn', *Aurora* 'goddess of the dawn'] Dawn, the first light of day, hence, because in their simplest form they resemble an approaching sunrise, 18c **aurora borealis** the northern lights [Latin *borealis* 'northern', from Greek *Boreas* 'god of the north wind'] and **aurora australis** the southern lights [Latin *australis* 'southern', from Auster 'god of the south wind', whence also **Australia**], whence *aurora* one of these (19c); a similar phenomenon.

auspice [16c. (Via French from) Latin *auspicium*, from *auspex* 'observer of birds', from *avis* 'bird' (ancestor of AVIATOR*) + *specere* 'to look at' (ancestor of SPICE*)] The observation of birds' behaviour for predicting the future; a (favourable) omen, originally one derived from birds (cf. AUGUR), hence **1** **auspicious** favourable, suggesting future success **2** a helpful influence, patronage (17c, surviving mainly in *under the auspices of*).

authentic [ME. Via Old French and Latin from Greek *authentēs* 'author, perpetrator', from *autos* 'self, same' (see AUTOMATON*) + *hentēs* 'doer'] (As if) from the author, authoritative, hence **1** legally valid **2** real, genuine (15c).

author [ME. Old French *autor*, from Latin *auctor*, from *augere* 'to increase, promote, or originate'] Someone who originates, invents, or causes something, specifically someone who writes books.

Old French *autor* evolved into *auteur* , adopted for a film director who exercises strong creative control. Latin *augere* is the ancestor of **auction**, **augment**, and **authority**, which has the underlying sense 'the power of a creator'.

autograph [17c. Via French or late Latin from Greek *autographos* 'written yourself', from *autos* (see AUTOMATON*) + *graphos* 'writing', from *graphein* 'to write' (ancestor of GRAPHIC*)] **1** someone's signature, hence one written for a friend or fan (18c): said by Johnson (see ACHE) to have long been collected 'by foreigners'; to put your autograph on something (19c) **2** a document in the author's handwriting, hence written or painted by the author or artist's own hand (19c); your own handwriting (19c).

automaton [17c. Latin, from Greek *automatos* 'acting by itself', from *autos* 'self'] Something able to move by itself, hence a 'living machine', a robot or a person acting mechanically without thought. Hence **automatic 1** done like an automaton without conscious thought (18c) **2** self-acting or self-regulating (18c), whence **(a) automation** the use or introduction of automatic devices (1940s), whence **automate** (1950s) **(b) auto-** (*autocue*, *autopilot*).

Greek *automatos* produced German *automat* an automaton, hence a cafeteria supplying food from vending machines (US), whence **Laundromat**, a trade name for an automatic washing machine (*US*), later (also as **laundermat**) a launderette. Greek *autos* produced AUTHENTIC, **auto-** (AUTOGRAPH, *automobile* at MOBILE), and **tautology** [ultimately from Greek *to auto* 'the same'].

avail [ME. From obsolete *vail* 'to be useful', from Old French *valoir* 'to be worth', from Latin *valere* 'to be strong' (ancestor of VALID*)] To be effectual, useful, or advantageous, hence **1** advantage, benefit, profit (15c); **to no avail** useless, ineffectual **2 avail yourself** to make use of (15c), hence **available** useful, valid (15c, surviving as a legal term); able to be used; accessible or obtainable (19c).

avatar [18c. Sanskrit *avatāra* 'descent', from *ava* 'away' + *tar-* 'to cross over'] The appearance of a Hindu god, especially Vishnu, as a person or animal, hence **1** someone/something that embodies a quality, concept, etc. (19c); an archetype **2** a temporary manifestation (19c) **3** a computer-generated image of a person (1990s), now especially in role-playing games.

avenue [17c. French, from *avenir* 'to arrive or approach', from Latin *advenire*: see ADVENTURE*] A way of reaching a place (*military*), hence **1** the drive of a country house, often bordered by trees, hence **(a)** a broad or tree-lined road or path; an urban street, originally tree-lined (18c), now frequently used, without much meaning, in street names **(b)** parallel lines of trees, statues, etc. bordering a path **2** a way of achieving something (1920s).

French *avenir* fathered *misavenire* 'to turn out badly', whence **misadventure** bad luck, (a) misfortune; an accidental cause of death not involving crime or negligence.

average [15c. French *avarie* 'damage to a ship or cargo', via Italian from Arabic *'awārīyah* 'damaged goods', from *'awār* 'damage at sea, loss'. Originally spelt *averay* or *averie*; changed in the 16c by association with *damage*] Money apart from normal freight charges paid by the owner of goods in transit, later the financial loss to the owners of a damaged cargo and/or vessel (16c); the equitable sharing of the loss by all parties, hence the division of a total by the number of items added up (18c); the amount arrived at by doing so, hence an ordinary or middling amount or level; a mean.

aviator [19c. French, from Latin *avis* 'bird'] A heavier-than-air flying machine (obsolete before World War I); the pilot of one, originally as distinct from an **aeronaut** a balloonist [18c, via French from Greek *aer* (see AIR*) + *nautēs* 'sailor', from *naus*: see NOISE].

Aeronautics, originally defined as 'the pretended art of sailing in a vessel thro' the air or atmosphere', was well established as 'the science of flight' by the 1820s; **aviation** referring to powered flight (19c).

Latin *avis* is the ancestor of AUSPICE, **aviary**, *bustard* (at TARDY), and Italian *ocarina* [literally 'little goose', because its mouthpiece resembles a goose's beak], and is one parent of **ostrich** [the other being Greek *strouthos* 'sparrow', later 'ostrich', shortened from *megas strouthos*, literally 'big sparrow', or *strouthokamelos* 'camel sparrow', because of its long neck].

award [ME. Anglo-Norman French *awarder* 'to consider or ordain', ultimately from Norman French *warder* 'to judge or guard': see WARD*] (To come to) a serious or judicial decision, hence (to hand down) a fine or penalty (16c), later an honour or prize (19c).

away [Old English *onweg, aweg*, literally 'on the way', from *weg* WAY*] To or at another place or state; absent, uninvolved, whence **awayward** (turned) in a different direction (ME, whence **wayward** contrary, perverse, wilful), and **way** to or at a great distance (19c); to a great extent (1940s); very, extremely (1990s).

awe [Old English *ege*, replaced in Middle English by forms from related Old Norse *agi*] Terror, dread, later dread mixed with reverence and wonder. **Awful** originally meant 'inspiring awe' (OE), hence impressive, majestic, remarkable (16c, largely replaced by **awesome**), later remarkably bad, dreadful (19c).

Awfully took its early senses from *awful*, but is now a neutral 'very, extremely'. A similar progression is found in *frightfully, terribly*, and *terrific(ally)* (at TERROR), and TREMENDOUS.

awkward [ME. From obsolete *awk* 'left-handed, perverse' (cf. RIGHT), from Old Norse *afugr* 'back to front'] Upside down, back to front; perverse, cantankerous (16c); clumsy or ungainly; embarrassing or embarrassed (18c); difficult to manage or deal with (19c).

B

bachelor [ME. Old French *bacheler*, sometimes said to be from *bas chevalier* 'low knight' (i.e. of the lowest order of knighthood); but perhaps related to medieval Latin *baccalarias* 'tenant farmer, student'] A young knight; a junior member of a guild; someone with a first academic degree (these senses surviving as a surname, also spelt **Batchelor**). Hence an unmarried man (perhaps too young to establish his own household) or, occasionally, woman (17c); a young male animal with no mate (19c).

The usual word for an unmarried woman was *spinster* (see SPIN): this came to suggest one sadly 'left on the shelf', so **bachelor girl** and **bachelorette** (*Canadian*) were coined for an independent single woman. The former died out as these became common: the latter survives in N America, particularly referring to a bride's **bachelorette party** or 'hen night'.

Medieval Latin *baccalarias* changed to *baccalaurius* by association with *bacca lauri* 'laurel berry' (from the laurels awarded to scholars), whence **baccalaureate** a first degree; a set of examinations paving the way to higher education.

badge [ME. Origin unknown] An emblem identifying a knight and his followers, hence one worn as a sign of rank or office, by a licensed trader, or to show membership of an organization, now often simply as a souvenir or to carry a slogan; a distinguishing sign or token of any kind (16c).

Badger may come from *badge* meaning 'knight's emblem', because of its distinctive head markings, or from French *bêcheur* 'digger'; the verb probably comes from badger-baiting. *Badger* replaced **brock** [Old English *brocc*, of Celtic origin], which survives as the traditional name of badgers in stories, as a surname, and in place names (*Brocklebank, Brockham*).

baffle [16c. Origin unknown] To fool or cheat; also to ridicule or disgrace, although this may be a different word, hence **1** to confuse or perplex (17c), hence **bafflegab** confusing or pretentious jargon (1950s, US) **2** to frustrate or impede (17c), hence a device that controls the flow of a fluid or the emission of sound or light (19c).

bag [ME. Perhaps from Old Norse *baggi* and related to BAGGAGE] A flexible container, hence **1** something resembling this, e.g. an udder; **bags** loose-fitting trousers (16c); puffiness under the eyes (19c) **2** a bagful; this used as a measure, hence the amount of game killed (19c); to catch or kill game, hence to get or take (*bagged all the hot water*); to claim (mainly in children's slang **bags I**, *c.*1910) **3** to bulge like a bag (15c), hence **baggy** (18c).

baggage   [15c. French *bagage* (from *baguer* 'to tie up'), or *bagues* 'bundles', both probably of Germanic origin and related to BAG] The things you take when you travel (the usual term in American English, largely replaced in British English by *luggage*: see LUG), but creeping back. Hence **1** portable military equipment (16c); **bag and baggage** a soldier's bag of personal belongings plus the army's equipment: **to march out with bag and baggage** was to retreat honourably without surrendering either **2** rubbish, nonsense, trash (16c, now only dialect), hence riff-raff; a disreputable woman or (until the 17c) man; a flirtatious young woman, a minx (17c) **3** burdens (17c), now particularly mental or emotional ones.

bail¹   [ME. Old French *bail(le)*, from *baillier* 'to take charge of' (ancestor of **bailiff**), from Latin *bajulare* 'to bear a burden', from *bajulus* 'carrier', later 'administrator'] Custody, jurisdiction (–16c), hence custody of a prisoner by someone giving sureties that they would return when required (–19c); the release of, or to release, the accused against such sureties (15c); what is pledged; to provide it (16c), hence **bail someone out** to get them out of trouble.

Probably influenced by **bail/bale (out)** to scoop water out of a boat [Middle English *bail* 'bucket', also ultimately from Latin *bajulus*]; later to jump out of an aircraft (in British English usually *bale*, perhaps from the idea of dropping a bale of goods through a trapdoor; *bail* is the usual North American spelling).

bail²   [ME. Old French *bail(le)* 'palisade, enclosure', perhaps from Latin *baculum* 'rod, staff'] The outer wall of a castle, hence **1** a wall between courtyards; a courtyard (16c, cf. *bailey* below) **2 bails** a palisade (16c), hence *bail* a crossbar; the crosspiece of a wicket (18c); the bar holding the paper against the platen of a typewriter (1930s).

Old French *bail(le)* produced **bailey** the outer wall, later the outer court, of a castle, surviving mainly in the **Old Bailey**, Central Criminal Court in London, named from the road on which it stands which ran alongside a rampart known as the *bailey* outside the city wall, and in **motte and bailey castle** a fort on a mound surrounded by a bailey: French *motte* largely replaced Old French *mote* in the sense (fortified) mound or hill: *mote* survives meaning a tumulus or barrow, and in the variant **moat** a surrounding ditch. Latin *baculum* is the ancestor of DEBACLE*.

bain-Marie   [French, literally 'bath of Mary', a translation of medieval Latin *balneum Mariae*, a mistranslation of medieval Greek *kaminos Marias* 'furnace of Mary or Maria', an Egyptian alchemist of the 2c BC (sometimes identified with Miriam, sister of Moses: see the Bible, Exodus), who was credited with inventing heating and distillation apparatus] *(St) Mary's bath*, Latin *balneum Mariae*, or the semi-Anglicized *balneo of Mary* were used from the 15c for various means of heating used in alchemy and later in cookery; the current form was adopted in the 18c.

bait   Two Middle English words intertwined: **I** [Old Norse *beit* 'pasture', *beita* 'food', from *bita* 'to bite', of Germanic origin and related to BITE*] **1** food used to attract an animal, hence **(a)** to put food on a hook or in a trap **(b)** an enticement or temptation **2** to feed an animal, especially on a journey; the food given (15c); a snack between meals (now dialect) **II** [Old Norse *beita* 'to hunt with dogs or hawks', also from *bita*] to torment a captive animal with dogs, hence to tease or harass someone; (also as **bate**) a fit of temper, as the person harassed might have (19c) **III** (combining the two) to tempt or chivvy someone into doing something (16c).

bake [Old English *bacan*] To cook, later to harden, using dry heat; to be cooked or hardened in this way, hence **1** to become uncomfortably hot (ME) **2** a baked dish (16c); a social gathering where baked food is served (19c, *US*).

Bake produced the surnames **Backhouse** someone who lived or worked in a bakehouse, **Baker**, and *Baxter* (see BREW*). Old English *bacan* is probably the ancestor of **batch**, originally the quantity of bread baked at one time.

balance [ME. French, ultimately from Latin *(libra) bilanx* '(scales with) two pans', from *bi-* 'two' + *lanx* 'plate, pan'] A pivoted beam supporting two scale pans for weighing things, hence **1** the scales of justice, reason, or fate (now chiefly in **hang in the balance** to be undecided) **2** to weigh one thing against another, to decide their relative importance (16c); to compare credits and debits in a set of accounts, hence the difference between the two (18c), an amount left over **3** to equal in weight or importance (16c); to equal or cancel out; (to bring or keep in) a state of equilibrium (17c); **well-balanced** sane, sensible (19c).

bald [ME. Perhaps from Celtic *bal* 'white mark', or related to Old English *bael* 'fire'] **1** hairless, hence **(a)** without fur or feathers; of a tyre: having no tread (1930s) **(b)** unadorned, plain, stark **2** having white marks, surviving mainly in **bald eagle** which has a white head, **piebald** [from PIE*], and **skewbald** [either from Latin *scutum* 'shield' (ancestor of SQUIRE*), or related to Old Norse *sky* 'cloud' (the original sense of its descendant, **sky**)].

ballad [15c. French *ballade* from Provençal *balada*, from Latin *ballare* 'to dance', from Greek *ballizein*] A simple song, originally one to dance to; a sentimental or romantic song, later often distributed as broadsheets, hence **1** a popular satirical song, similarly published (16c) **2** a popular narrative poem, originally sung (18c) **3** a slow, romantic pop song (1930s).

Greek *ballizein* is the ancestor of **ball** a dance, and French *ballet* [via Italian *balleto* 'little dance'].

ballistic [18c. Latin *ballista* a device for hurling large missiles (16c), from Greek *ballein* 'to throw'] To do with missiles, hence **ballistics** the science of missiles, now especially firearms; **ballistic missile** one that is propelled towards its target rather than being guided to it (1940s), the explosive warheads in such weapons leading to **go ballistic** to become extremely angry (1980s).

Descendants of Greek *ballein* include the surname **Ballaster** someone who made crossbows, DEVIL, EMBOLISM*, *hyperbole* (at HYPE), **metabolism** [Greek *metabolē* 'change', from *metaballein*, literally 'to throw differently'], PARABLE*, PARLIAMENT*, PARLOUR, PAROLE, **problem** [via French and Latin from Greek *problēma*, literally 'something thrown in the way'], and SYMBOL.

ballot [16c. Italian *ballotta* 'small ball', from *balla* 'ball', ultimately of Germanic origin] A coloured ball placed in a container to register a vote, hence a secret vote; (to vote by) a system of secret voting; to ask those entitled to vote to do so (19c).

To **blackball** comes from the system of voting against someone by putting a black ball in a container, a positive vote being shown by a white ball. Italian *balla* is related to **ball**, **balloon**, and **bollock**: the variant *palla* is one parent of *pall-mall* (at MAUL).

bank

balsa [17c. Spanish *balsa* 'raft'] A raft or fishing boat from the Pacific coast of S America, hence (the wood from) a tropical American tree, used for making rafts (19c).

baluster [17c. French *balustre* from Italian *balaustro*, from *balaust(r)a* 'wild pomegranate flower' (because the shape of early balusters resembled the flower), ultimately from Greek *balaustion*] A short pillar shaped like a narrow vase, later one supporting a handrail. **Banister** is an early alteration, which was quickly accepted despite initially being condemned as 'vulgar'.

French *balustre* produced **balustrade** a row of balusters supporting a rail or parapet.

ban [Old English *bannan*: the noun partly via related Old French *ban*] To summon or call to arms (–ME), hence **1** an announcement or summons (ME, surviving as **banns** announcements of a forthcoming marriage) **2** to curse or damn (ME); to prohibit or exclude; a formal prohibition (17c).

Old French *ban* produced **banal** to do with compulsory feudal service; the current meaning 'commonplace, trite' is from a later French sense 'applying to all'. Related to ABANDON, **bandit**, **banish** and **contraband** [via Spanish from Italian *contrabando*, literally 'against the proclamation'].

band Strictly speaking, three words intertwined: dictionaries vary as to how they divide them. I [ME. Old Norse *band*, related to BIND*. Replaced by BOND in senses 1 and 2] **1** a restraint, shackle, or leash, hence **bandog** a chained guard dog (ME), now a ferocious type of cross-breed (1970s) **2** an obligation or binding agreement (replaced by *bond*) **3** a string used to bind something II [15c. French *bande*, probably of Germanic origin and related to BANNER] an organized group of soldiers or, later, outlaws; a group of people with a common purpose; a group of musicians, or of people or animals travelling together (17c), hence a herd or flock (19c, N *American*) III [15c. Old French *bande*, *bende* (whence **bandage**), of Germanic origin and related to BIND*] **1** a circle of metal or a strip of flexible material to go around something (*wedding band, waistband*); an endless belt on a machine (18c), **2** a distinct or contrasting stripe, hence a narrow stratum (19c), a range of values, radio frequencies, etc. within set limits, a discrete section of a recording (20c). IV [15c. French *bander*, from *bande* (see III above)] **1** to bind (–19c, influenced by I above) **2** to put a band around something (16c) **3** to unite in a group (16c, influenced by II above) **4** to mark with a band or stripe (18c); **5** to divide into a band or range, specifically to separate pupils by ability (1960s).

French *bander* also meant 'to take sides', specifically in tennis, whence **bandy** to throw or hit a ball to and fro, hence to exchange blows or insults, to pass gossip or someone's name around casually. *Bander* may also be the source of **bandy** a kind of tennis, later of hockey; a curved stick used in the latter, hence bow-legged.

bank¹ [ME. Old Norse *bakki*. Related to BANK², ³ and BENCH] A (sloping) shelf of land, originally beside a river (whence the surnames **Bankhead** and **Banks** for someone who lived on one); a raised margin round a pond etc., hence **1** a heap of earth, snow, etc. with a sloping side; a dense mass of cloud or fog (17c) **2** to confine within a bank or banks, later also **embank** (16c), whence **embankment**

an artificial bank (19c) **3** to pile earth etc. up into a bank (16c, hence **bank up the fire** to pile fuel or ashes onto it so that it burns slowly); (to make) a slope on the inside of a bend (early 20c); to tilt when turning, as though on a banked curve.

bank² [15c. (Via French from) Italian *banca* 'bank, bench, table', from medieval Latin *banca, bancus*, of Germanic origin] **1** a moneylender's table or shop, hence **(a) banker** a money lender (16c) **(b) bankrupt** insolvent, an insolvent person [16c, from Italian *banca rotta* 'broken table', influenced by Latin *ruptus* 'broken' (see ROUTE), because an insolvent banker had to publicly smash his table] **(c)** (to own) a business offering financial services (17c); to have an account with, or deposit money in, such a business (19c); a money-box (*piggy bank*, 1940s) **2** a fund of money (16–18c), hence **(a)** the cash or chips controlled by one player, against which the others bet (18c) **(b)** a store of something (*blood bank*, 1930s, *US*); a place where this is kept or collected **3** to stake your money or hopes on something (19c), to rely on something happening, hence **bankable** sure to bring success (1950s).

Italian *banca* produced French ***banquette*** a ledge along a rampart or trench from which soldiers fire; an upholstered bench along a wall, and MOUNTEBANK. Related to BANK¹*.

bank³ [ME. French *banc*, ultimately of Germanic origin] A bench or platform; a rowers' bench in a galley (16c), hence a tier of oars; a number of similar objects arranged in rows or tiers (19c).

French *banc* produced **banquet**. Related to BANK¹*.

banner [ME. Old French *ban(i)ere*, ultimately from medieval Latin *bandum*, of Germanic origin and probably related to BAND II] A flag acting as a standard, hence **1** the surname **Bannerman**, a standard-bearer **2** one displaying an emblem or, later, slogan, carried in procession, often stretched between two poles, hence **banner (headline)** a newspaper headline stretching across the page (*c.*1910, *US*), whence *banner* an advertisement etc. across the top of a web page (1990s) **3** a flag awarded as a distinction (19c, *US*).

banyan [16c. Portuguese, from Hindi *baniyā* 'merchant', from Sanskrit] A Hindu trader or merchant, hence (because traders built a pagoda under one of these trees) a kind of Indian fig tree (17c).

bar [ME. French *barre* (noun), *barrer* (verb): probably related to BARRICADE, **barrier**, **embargo**, and EMBARRASS*] A rod, pole, or beam, hence **1** one fastening a door; to fasten a door with one; to shut in or out, hence **barring** (16c), *bar* (18c) except, excluding **2** a barrier: **(a)** at the entrance to a city (surviving in place names, e.g. *Potters Bar, Perry Bar*) **(b)** at which a prisoner stands in court; one separating the bench from the rest of the court: advanced students were invited to stand at the bar and join in the proceedings, hence **be called to the bar** to become a barrister; **be called within the bar** to become a King's/Queen's Counsel; **the Bar** barristers or (*US*) lawyers collectively (16c) **(c)** a sandbank at the mouth of a river or harbour (16c) **(d)** a line on a musical score dividing one metrical unit from another (17c), such a unit **3** to stop a court case by a legal objection (15c), hence to stop someone having or doing something; to prohibit or prevent an action (16c); a prohibition or obstacle **4** a counter or, later, room where liquor is served (15c);

one offering a commodity or service (*juice*/*heel bar,* 1950s), hence **bar(r)ista** someone who makes and serves drinks in a coffee bar (*c.*2000) **5** a line or stripe (15c), hence **barcode** (1980s) **6** an oblong block of metal, soap, chocolate, etc. (16c); a block of metal used as currency (18c), hence a pound sterling (slang, early 20c, usually in **half a bar**) **7** a rail at which dancers practise (19c), later also French **barre** (early 20c).

barb [ME. French *barbe* from Latin *barba*] A beard (–17c), hence **1** a point facing away (like a beard hanging down) from the main point of a spear, fishhook, etc. to stop it coming out, hence a pointed or hurtful remark (18c) **2** a growth like a beard or whisker on an animal's head (15c); a barbel, hence applied to several kinds of fish having barbels (19c).

Latin *barba* produced **barbel** and **barber** (also as a surname with the variant **Barbour**), and **rebarbative** [French *rébarbatif*, from Old French *(se) rebarber* 'to confront', literally 'to face beard to beard'].

barbarian [ME. (Via Old French from) Latin *barbarianus*, from *barbarus* 'foreign', from Greek *barbaros* 'foreign, especially in speech, ignorant'] Having different speech or customs, specifically not belonging to the Greek, Roman, or Christian civilizations, hence **1** a foreigner (15–19c) **2** a coarse or violent person (15c); uncivilized, savage (16c, now largely replaced by **barbarous**). Cf. ALIEN*.

Greek *barbaros* produced the name **Barbara**, perhaps originally given to a foreign slave, BRAVE*, and **rhubarb** [via Old French from, ultimately, Latin *rha barbarum*, from Greek *Rha* the river Volga, beside which rhubarb was grown].

barge [ME. French, or Latin *barca* 'boat', both probably from Greek *baris* 'Egyptian boat'] A small sailing ship, hence **1** a ceremonial boat (15c); a ship's boat for senior officers and VIPs (16c) **2** a flat-bottomed cargo boat used on estuaries and canals (15c), hence to move clumsily like a barge (19c); to push or bump into heavily (early 20c).

Latin *barca* produced **embark** to board a boat, hence to set out on a voyage or enterprise, and probably **bark**, also originally a small sailing ship, later (also **barque**) a larger, ocean-going vessel.

barn [Old English *ber(e)n*, from *baer, bere* 'barley' + *(a)ern* 'house'] A building for storing grain, hay, etc., hence **1** one for housing livestock and farm vehicles (18c, N American) **2** a tiny unit (10^{-24} sq.m) used in measuring the cross-section of nuclei (1940s, said to be an ironic use of *as big as a barn door*).

Old English *ber(e)n* produced the name **Barnes**. *Baer, bere* is the ancestor of **barley** and of **Bar-** or **Ber-** in names (e.g. *Barlow, Berwick*).

barricade [16c. French, from *barrique* 'barrel', from Spanish *barrica*: related to **barrel**, and probably to BAR*. Originally spelt *barricado* (words believed to be of Spanish, Portuguese, or Italian origin were sometimes given the ending *-ado*)] A makeshift barrier across a street etc., originally referring to those the Parisians built using barrels of rubble in 1588, hence to block or protect with a barricade; to shut in or out with one (17c).

barrow¹ [Old English *bearwe*: related to BEAR¹*] A stretcher; a bier; a handcart, wheelbarrow, or wheeled stall in a market (ME), hence **barrow boy** a market trader (1930s); a brash or unorthodox businessman.

barrow²　[Old English *beorg*: related to BOROUGH*] **1** a mountain, gradually shrinking to a hill or mound; obsolete by the 18c except in the names of individual hills in the west and north of England and as an element in other place names (usually as **Bar-**, sometimes as **-borough** or **-burgh**: cf. BOROUGH) **2** a burial mound, long obsolete except in W England dialect, but revived by modern archaeologists.

base¹　[ME. (Via French from) Latin *basis* 'stepping, step, pedestal', ultimately from Greek *banein* 'to stand, walk, or go'] The part of a column between the shaft and the pedestal or pavement, hence the lowest part; a foundation or starting point (these senses largely shared by Latin *basis*, 16c); to build on or develop something from a base (19c). Hence **1** the most important part; the main ingredient (15c) **2** a (military) headquarters from which operations are launched or coordinated (19c), hence **(a)** in baseball and rounders: one of the places where players may stop **(b)** to station someone at a particular place (early 20c).

　Base produced **basic**. Greek *banein* is the ancestor of **acrobat** [literally 'one that walks on tiptoe', with Greek *akros* 'tip, peak'] and **diabetes** [Greek *diabētēs* 'a siphon' (from the copious amount of urine which is a symptom), from Greek *diabanein* 'to go through'].

base²　[French *bas* from medieval Latin *bassus*] **1** low, short **2** of inferior quality (*base metal*) **3** low in the social scale (15c), hence **(a)** menial, degrading **(b)** lacking morals or principles, despicable (16c) **(c) baseborn** of humble origin (16c), illegitimate (17c).

　French *bas* produced *bascule* (at RECOIL), **bass** 'low' in various musical senses [influenced by related Italian *basso*, which is also used in music and produced **bassoon**], the surnames **Bass(e)** and **Basset(t)** a short person, and **basset (hound)**, from its short legs.

basilica　[16c. Latin, literally 'royal palace', from Greek *basilikē*, from *basileus*: see BASILISK*] A large hall with a semicircular apse, used for public assemblies or law courts in the ancient world. Roman emperors granted some basilicas to the early Christians as places of worship, hence **1** a church built on this plan **2** a Roman Catholic or Greek Orthodox church granted special privileges because of its antiquity or importance.

basilisk　[ME. Latin, from Greek *basiliskos*, literally 'little king', from *basileus* 'king'] A legendary reptile (said to have a crown-shaped mark on its head), whose bite, breath, or mere glance was fatal to all living things, hence **1** a heraldic figure of a wyvern with a cock's head **2** a malicious person (15c) **3** a brass cannon (16c, other firearms of the period were also named after serpents) **4** a New World lizard with a prominent crest (19c).

　The mythical reptile was also called a **cockatrice** [via Old French from medieval Latin *calcatrix* 'tracker' (translating Greek *ikhneumon*), from Latin *calcare* 'to tread or track', from *calx* 'heel']: the resemblance to COCK led to the belief that it was hatched from a cock's egg, or that it would die if it heard a cock crow. Travellers to basilisk country took cocks with them for protection, also mirrors, as the creature's reflection would frighten it to death.

　Greek *basileus* is the ancestor of the names **Bas(e)ley** or **Baz(e)ley** and **Basil**, of **basil** the 'king' of herbs, prized for its culinary and medicinal uses (it even cured basilisk bites), and of BASILICA. Latin *calx* produced *inculcare* 'to stamp in with the heel', whence **inculcate**. Greek *ikhneumon* was applied to a creature said to eat crocodile eggs or to dart into crocodiles' mouths and chew its way out through their stomachs, whence **ichneumon: 1** the Egyptian mongoose, which eats crocodile eggs **2** a fly that lays eggs in the larvae or pupae of other insects, the hatchlings eating their way out.

bastard [ME. Via Old French from medieval Latin *bastardus*, probably from *bastum* 'pack saddle', implying that the father was a packhorse drover who left in the morning] Illegitimate; an illegitimate child, first recorded in personal names (*William the Bastard*), hence **1** of mixed or inferior breeding **2** of inferior quality (15c, hence **bastardize** in the sense 'cheapen or degrade', 16c); in plant and animal names: resembling the named species (*bastard mahogany/trout*, 16c) **3** irregular, unauthorized (16c) **4** a nasty person (19c), now informally someone of the kind described (*poor/lucky bastard!*); something unpleasant or annoying (1930s).

Old French *ba(s)t* 'pack saddle' [from Latin *bastum*] produced *bat* in **bat-horse** a packhorse carrying officers' baggage, hence **batman** a soldier in charge of it; an officer's servant.

batter [ME. Old French *batre* 'to beat', ultimately from Latin *battuere*] To hit repeatedly, hence **1** to damage by beating or wear (16c) **2** to attack with a battering ram (16c) or, later, with artillery; to attack a person, their opinions, etc. strongly and persistently.

Old French *batre* produced ABATE*, **batten**, pancake **batter** [via Anglo-Norman French *batture* 'beating'], and BATTERY. Latin *battuere* produced *bat* in **not bat an eyelid** [a survival of Middle English *bate* 'to beat or flutter'], **battalion**, **battle**, and **combat**, and perhaps the **bat** for hitting a ball [via Old English *batt* 'thick stick, club'], and *battledore* (at SHUTTLE).

battery [ME. Old French *baterie*, from *batre*: see BATTER*] Metal articles shaped by hammering (–19c), hence **1** a number of pieces of artillery used together, hence **(a)** an artillery emplacement (16c) **(b)** a connected set of Leyden jars (an early device for producing electricity, 18–19c), hence a modern battery (19c) **(c)** a group of things to be used together, specifically a series of psychological tests (1920s) or poultry cages (1930s) **2** battering, beating (16c), now mainly in *assault and battery*.

baulk [Old English *balc* from Old Norse *bálkr* 'partition'] A ridge or mound, specifically a ridge of land left unploughed, hence **1** to leave an unploughed ridge (ME), hence to omit intentionally; to refuse to do or tackle something (16c) **2** a large squared piece of timber (ME), specifically the tie beam of a house **3** an obstacle or stumbling block (15c), hence to hinder or thwart (16c); a setback (17c).

Old English *balc* appears in a few names as **Balk-**. Old Norse *bálkr* is the ancestor of *bulk* in **bulkhead**.

bay¹ [ME. Old French *(a)bai* (noun), *(a)baiier* (verb): imitating the sound] The cry of a large dog or pack of hounds; to bark or howl, hence **1** **at bay** cornered and forced to face baying hounds; **hold/keep at bay** to keep (originally hounds) at a distance (16c) **2** to shout or bawl, especially to demand something (16c).

bay² [ME. French *baie* from Latin *baca* 'berry'] A (laurel) berry, hence a kind of laurel whose leaves are used in cooking (16c), hence **1** bay(s) its leaves used to garland a hero or poet (16c), hence fame, glory **2** bayberry the fruit of the bay tree (16c), later (the fruit of) an unrelated Caribbean tree (18c), whose leaves and fruit are used to make **bay rum** (19c).

bay³ [ME. French *baie*, from *bayer* 'to gape' (Old French *bair*), from medieval Latin *batare*] **1** a section of a wall between two pillars or buttresses **2** bay (window) a window that sticks out from a wall (15c) **3** a recess or compartment (*bomb/sick/loading bay*, 16c).

Despite appearances **bay** 'indent in a coastline' is probably not related; it comes via a different Old French word *baie* from Spanish *bahia*, of unknown origin.

beach [Perhaps from or related to Old English *b(a)ece* 'stream, brook'] Pebbles washed by the waves (16c dialect, surviving at least until the 19c in SE England); the seashore. Hence to deliberately run a ship onto the beach, for example to repair it (19c); **beached** stranded out of the water.

Old English *b(a)ece* survives as -**bach, Bec-**, or -**bech** in place names. Related to **beck** a brook [Old Norse *bekkr*].

beacon [Old English *bēcan*: related to BECKON and BUOY] A sign or omen (–ME); an ensign or standard (–15c), later a signal fire (ME), hence **1** a signal station or watch tower; a hill suitable for one (16c, now mainly in their names) **2** a light used as a signal, warning, or guide, hence a source of inspiration or guidance **3** a radio transmitter whose signal indicates the position of a ship, aircraft, etc. (*c.*1920).

bead [Old English *gebed*: related to BID] Prayer; **beads** prayers said using a rosary, hence a small ball strung on a rosary, necklace, etc. (ME), hence **1** a tiny drop of liquid (16c, whence **beady eyes** small, round, glittering ones, 19c); a small knob forming the front sight of a gun (19c, hence **draw a bead on** to take aim at) **2** (also as **beading**) an ornamental moulding resembling a string of beads (18c); a narrow semicircular moulding (19c); the thickened inner edge of a pneumatic tyre (early 20c).

beam [Old English *bēam*] **1** a tree (now only in the names of species, e.g. **hornbeam**), hence **(a)** a horizontal, load-bearing timber etc. in a building **(b)** (the bar of) a balance (15c) **(c)** a transverse timber in a ship (17c, hence **on your beam ends** destitute, because a ship with its beam ends touching the water may well founder); either side of a ship; a ship's width **(d)** a pivoted (originally timber) shaft in an engine (18c) **2** a ray of light, hence **(a)** a bright smile (like a sunbeam, 16c); to smile broadly (19c) **(b)** to shine brightly (17c) **(c)** a parallel flow of any kind of radiation or particles (19c); a directional radio signal (1920s), to direct radio signals to a specific area. Cf. RAY.

Old English *bēam* occasionally appears in place- and surnames as **Bam-** or **Bem-**, when it usually means a plank bridge. Related to BOOM².

bear¹ [Old English *beran*] **1** to hold or carry (*bear a grudge/title/scar/signature*), hence to hold or conduct yourself in a certain way (ME, hence **bearing** demeanour) **2** to be able to carry or cope with; to endure or tolerate (16c), hence **(a)** to be fit for (*doesn't bear thinking about*, 16c) **(b)** *bearing* that takes the friction of a moving part (18c) **3** to give birth to (hence **born**, from *boren*, past participle of *beran*); to produce **4** to move something (ME), later to (try to) move in a certain direction (*bear left*), hence **(a)** to be aimed at a target (17c); to affect or be relevant to **(b)** *bearing* location or direction of movement; **get/lose your bearings** to find out/forget where you are.

Old English *beran* produced BERTH. Related to BARROW[1], **bier**, and BIRTH.

bear² [Old English *bera*] The large carnivore, later applied to similar animals (*ant/koala bear*), hence **1** a rough or bad-tempered person, later a large, lovable one (1950s) **2** originally **bearskin seller**: someone who contracts to sell stocks at a certain price on a future date, hoping to buy them more cheaply in the meantime (18c, probably from the idea of selling a bear's skin before catching the bear), hence a **bear market** in which share prices are falling: cf. BULL **3** the police, a policeman [1970s, US; also as **Smokey (Bear)**, short for *Smokey the Bear* a character used in fire-prevention campaigns and often seen on posters etc. 'watching' the roadside].

Bear produced the surname **Bearman**, someone who kept a dancing bear or bears for baiting. Related to the names **Barnard(o)** and **Bernard**.

beast [ME. Old French *beste*, ultimately from Latin *bestia*] Any member of the animal kingdom, later specifically a (large) mammal, hence **1** a crude, lustful, or cruel person (cf. BRUTE), hence **beastly**, now often merely unpleasant or annoying and also applied to things, and **bestial 2** a mythical or heraldic creature **3 beastie** (18c, mainly Scots and US), **minibeast** an insect or other small creature (1990s) **4** the surname **Best**, given to an animal-keeper or a violent person.

Beast replaced **deer** [Old English *deor*], originally meaning any (wild) mammal, and has been largely replaced in a general sense by **animal** [Latin, from *animale* 'living being', from *animalis* 'living', from *anima* 'life, breath, soul' (ancestor of ANIMATE*)].

beat [Old English *bēatan*] To strike repeatedly, hence **1** to make a path by trampling, hence the route patrolled by a policeman etc. (18c); the area in which someone regularly works, hunts, etc. (19c) **2** to beat a drum (ME), hence **(a) beat a retreat** to beat the signal for retreat (18c), hence to retreat **(b)** a stressed note in music (19c); the rhythm of music, especially the strong rhythm of rock or jazz (early 20c) **3** to produce or shape by beating (ME); to stir vigorously **4** to pulsate or throb (ME); a stroke or pulse (18c) **5** to defeat (ME, cf. THRASH, TROUNCE); to tire out; to baffle **6** to sail to windward (15c, perhaps from sense 1: cf. *thrash*), hence **beat your way** to travel, especially with difficulty (19c).

The terms **beat generation** and **beatnik** may be from **beaten** meaning 'exhausted, defeated' or from **deadbeat** a lazy, disreputable person, although the founder member Jack Kerouac connected them with **beatitude** blessedness [ultimately from Latin *beatus* 'blessed'].

beckon [Old English *bēcnan*: related to BEACON*] To gesture to someone, originally for any purpose, later to bring them to you (16c). Shortened to **beck** (ME) which came to mean a signal or gesture; **be at someone's beck and call** to be subject to their unspoken and spoken commands.

bedlam [15c. Contraction of Bethlehem, the town in Israel where Christ was born] The Hospital of St Mary of Bethlehem, founded in London in 1297 and later used as hospital for the insane, hence **1** a madman, specifically one discharged from Bedlam with a licence to beg (16c, surviving in the names of fields where beggars congregated) **2** a lunatic asylum (17c); a place or situation of uproar or confusion.

beef [ME. Old French *boef* from Latin *bos, bovis* 'ox, cow, beef' (ancestor of **bovine** and BUGLE)] **1** the meat of an ox, bull, or cow; (the carcass of) an ox raised for meat **2** muscle, strength, power (19c), hence **beefy** muscular (19c); **beef up** to make more powerful (1940s); **beefcake** (pictures of) muscular men (1940s, modelled on **cheesecake** pictures of attractive women, 1930s); **beef** or (*US*) **beefsteak tomato** a large, firm variety **3** to protest or complain (19c, *US*, from the idea of resisting like a stubborn ox); a protest or grievance.

Beef is one of several instances where the word for the animal comes from Old English while that for the meat is from Old French, leading to speculation that the Saxons tended the beasts but their Norman masters ate them, others being **calf/veal**, **sheep/mutton**, and **pig**/PORK or **bacon**, although *bacon*, originally the back and sides of a pig's carcass, is ultimately of Germanic origin and related to ABACK.

beer [Old English *bēor*, ultimately from Latin *biber* 'drink', from *bibere* 'to drink'] Uncommon until the 16c when hops were introduced; *beer* was then used for the new-fangled drink flavoured with them, as opposed to traditional **ale** [Old English *(e)alu*], which came to refer to lighter, paler beers and which survives in brand names, as an old name for a celebration at which ale was served (cf. *bride ale* at BRIDE), and in **Real Ale** beer produced and served by traditional methods (1960s). Both *ale* and *beer* have long been used for brewed or fizzy drinks made from other ingredients (*ginger ale, root beer*). In modern use *beer* is the overall term and includes ale, **lager** [19c, from German *Lager-Bier* 'beer brewed for storing', from *Lager* 'storehouse'], *porter* (see PORT[3]), and STOUT.

Latin *bibere* is the ancestor of **beverage**, the surnames **Beveridge** and some instances of **Bevin**, **bibulous**, **imbibe**, and probably of **bib** to tipple (surviving mainly in *wine bibber*), whence, probably, the bib tied under a child's chin, hence the part of a pinafore or dungarees covering the chest. *Lager* is related to LAY*.

beige [19c. French, of unknown origin] A fine woollen fabric, usually sold undyed and unbleached, hence the colour of unbleached wool.

belfry [ME. Old French *berfrei* (later *belfrei*), perhaps ultimately from a Frankish word meaning 'to protect peace'. Originally spelt *berfrey*: the spelling altered in the 15c (as in French), partly by association with *bell*] A movable tower used in attacking fortifications, later a watchtower or bell tower (15c), hence the place in a church where the bells are hung or where bell-ringers stand (16c); an ornamental frame holding a ship's bell (18c).

belly [Old English *belig*] A bag, purse, or pod (–ME); the human, later an animal's, abdomen (ME), hence the bulge of a pot, sail, etc. (16c); the underside of a plane's fuselage (World War I).

Old English *belig* appeared in (*blǣst*)*belig*, literally 'blowing-bag', probably the ancestor of **bellows**. Related to **billow** and probably to **bolster** a long narrow pillow; to support (as if) with one.

Bible

bench [Old English *benc*: related to BANK[1]*] **1** a long seat; one reserved for certain people, hence such people, e.g. judges, bishops (ME), Members of Parliament (*Front/Back/Treasury bench*, 19c), officials and reserves at a game (early 20c) **2** a merchant's or banker's counter (ME), later a workman's table **3** a shelf of land (ME), hence **(a)** the surname **Binch**, **Binks** who lived on one **(b)** **benchmark** a surveyor's mark left on a point which has been surveyed (19c), hence a point of reference, a standard; to measure the performance of a computer system by running a specially designed program (1970s); the result of such a test (1980s).

bend [Old English *bendan*, later associated with BAND III] To bind (OE only); a band, a fetter (–15c), hence **1** to bring a bow into tension by pulling the string; to (make something) bow or curve (ME), hence **(a)** to (make someone) stoop or bow **(b)** to turn your steps etc. (15c), later your attention, efforts, eyes, or ears towards something, hence **bent** determined, resolved; a natural inclination or talent (cf. INCLINE*) **(c)** to pervert (*bend the rules*, 16c, rare before the 19c), hence *bent* dishonest; stolen (*c*.1910, *US*: cf. *crooked* at CROOK); homosexual (1920s) **2** a diagonal band of colour on a heraldic shield (ME).

bereave [Old English *berēafian*, from *rēafian* 'to pillage, rob, or steal': related to ROBE* and perhaps to RIP] To plunder or rob (ME, also as **reave**), hence to take a precious possession or much-loved person; to leave widowed or orphaned. The Old English past participle was *berēafode*: by the 17c this had separated into **bereft** lacking or deprived of something; feeling a sense of loss, and **bereaved** having lost a loved one.

berserk [19c, apparently introduced by Scott (see DOFF). Old Norse *berserkr*, probably from *bjorn* 'bear' + *serkr* 'coat, shirt', but perhaps based on *berr* 'bare'] (Also as **berserker**) a warrior in Norse history and legend (depicted in medieval tapestries fighting naked or clad in bearskins), famed for reckless courage and savagery, hence madly aggressive or angry, now usually in **go beserk**.

The late arrival of the word into English reflects a late 18c interest in Old Norse language and literature, resulting in a number of English translations that appealed to the Romantics.

berth [17c. From BEAR[1] sense 4] **1** sufficient room for a ship to manoeuvre or swing at anchor (17c), hence **give someone/something a wide berth** to steer clear of them **2** to moor a ship in a suitable place (originally with room to swing); such a place (18c), hence **(a)** living space for a ship's crew (18c), hence a job, originally on a ship **(b)** someone's place in a barracks, vehicle, etc.; a bed on board a ship or vehicle (19c) **(c)** a parking space or loading bay (1930s).

Bible [ME. Old French, from Christian Latin *biblia* 'books' (later regarded as singular), from Greek *biblion* 'book', from *biblos* 'papyrus, scroll', of Semitic origin] (A copy or edition of) the Christian or Hebrew Scriptures, hence the sacred writings of any religion; an indispensable manual (19c).

Bible replaced **bibliotheca** [Latin, from Greek *bibliothēkē* 'library', from *biblion* + *thēkē* 'repository', from *tithenai* 'to put' (ancestor of THESIS*)], used in the Old English period for the Christian Scriptures, and re-borrowed for a collection of books (19c), partly replacing its descendant, French *bibliothèque*, formerly naturalized but now treated as French.

bid [Strictly speaking, two words: one from Old English *biddan* 'to ask', the other from Old English *bēodan* 'to proclaim, to offer, to issue a challenge'. Both developed the sense 'to demand or command' and were regarded as the same word by the end of the Middle English period] The senses 'to invite' (ME), and 'to express or wish' (*bid him farewell*) are from *biddan* and have the past tense **bad**, **bade**, or **bid**. *Bēodan* produced the senses **1** to offer, now usually (to offer) the price you are prepared to pay (ME); **bid fair** to offer a good chance of success **2** to try to do (17c); an attempt (19c) **3** to claim to be able to win a certain number of tricks in a card game (18c). The usual past tense is *bid*, although *bade* survived at least until the 18c.

Old English *biddan* is related to BEAD. *Bēodan* produced *forbēodan*, literally 'to command not to', whence **forbid**, and is related to **beadle** originally a town crier or court usher (–17c), later a ceremonial usher or a parish officer who kept order in church (also as a surname, with variants including **Biddle** and **Buddle**).

bide, abide [Both from Old English *bidan*] *Abide* is generally later than *bide* in all senses. **1** to wait expectantly (surviving in Scots and in **bide your time** await your opportunity) **2** to stay in a certain condition or place, hence **(a)** to stand firm; to endure or put up with (now mainly in *can't abide*) **(b)** to reside (ME. *bide* in this sense survives in Scots).

Abide produced **abode** waiting, delay (ME–17c), hence a temporary stay (–18c); the place where you stay; a home.

bidet [17c. French, from *bider* 'to trot', of unknown origin] A small horse (–19c). The current sense developed in French (because you sit astride it) and was adopted in the 18c, both word and object being regarded as French and therefore mildly improper until well into the 20c.

bill¹ [Old English *bile*] A bird's beak, hence **1** something resembling it: **(a)** the human nose or mouth, an animal's muzzle or snout (now only of the duck-billed platypus, 19c) **(b)** a strip of land sticking out into the sea (ME, mainly in place names, e.g. *Selsey Bill*) **(c)** the point of an anchor fluke (18c) **2** to peck (ME); of doves: to stroke each other's bills (16c), hence **bill and coo** to exchange caresses and endearments.

bill² [ME. Anglo-Norman French *bille* or Anglo-Latin *billa*, from Latin *bulla*, literally 'bubble', later 'seal, a sealed document'] **1** a written list, catalogue, or inventory (*bill of fare/lading*), hence **(a)** a list of goods and charges; to send one (19c) **(b) bill of health** an official statement of the health of a ship's company (17c), hence **clean bill of health** with no infectious diseases listed, hence a good report **(c)** (a list of items on) a theatre programme (19c, *US*) **(d) fill/fit the bill** to fulfil a list of requirements (19c) **2** an official (originally sealed) document, hence **(a)** a petition (–18c); one to the monarch, later to Parliament, asking for changes in the law (16c), hence draft legislation presented to Parliament **(b)** a papal edict (15c only: outlived by Middle English **bull**, also from Latin *bulla*) **(c) bill of exchange** a written instruction to pay someone a sum of money (16c), hence *bill* a banknote (17c, *US*) **3** a printed advertising poster, placard, or leaflet (15c), hence **(a)** to advertise something (17c) **(b) billboard** a notice board or hoarding (19c, *US*) **(c) top billing** the most prominent position on a poster etc. (1960s); stardom.

Latin *bulla* is the ancestor of BILLETT, BOWL[2]*, BULL, **bulletin**, BULLION*, and **ebullient** [via Latin *ebullire* 'to bubble up'] boiling vigorously, hence bubbling over with excitement or enthusiasm.

billet [15c. Anglo-Norman French *billette* or Anglo-Latin *billetta*, literally 'small bill', from *billa*: see BILL[2]] A short written document; an official order requisitioning accommodation (17c, the verb 'to assign accommodation or quarter troops' is recorded slightly earlier); a place where someone is billeted (19c).

bind [Old English *bindan*] To tie or fasten, hence **1** to tie together, hence **(a)** to make into or form a solid mass, e.g. to fasten the pages or parts of a book together (ME); to form a chemical bond (early 20c) **(b)** to marry; to join by ties of affection or loyalty (16c) **2** to wrap with a ribbon, cord, etc., e.g. to bandage a wound (ME); to reinforce or decorate with bands of material **3** to restrain, confine, or obstruct, hence **(a)** to put someone under a legal or moral obligation (ME); to contract someone as an apprentice (15c) **(b)** a position in which you cannot act freely (19c); **double bind** an unresolvable dilemma (1950s) **(c)** to bore or tire (1920s), hence a boring duty, a nuisance (1930s).

Related to BAND II, BEND, BOND, BUNDLE, and **riband** (with the variant **ribbon**).

bird [Old English *brid, bird*, of unknown origin] A chick or fledgling (surviving in N English dialect), hence **1 (a)** a small, later any, bird (ME); a game bird (16c); an aircraft (1930s) **(b) get the bird** (formerly *the goose*) to be hissed by an audience (19c), hence **give someone the bird** to dismiss them scornfully; to raise your middle finger at them as an obscene gesture of contempt (1960s, US) **(c)** a prison sentence, prison (1920s, short for rhyming slang *birdlime* 'time') **2** a child or young man (ME–16c); a girl or young woman (ME, old-fashioned by the 19c but revived in 20c slang); a person of a particular kind (*a cunning old bird*, 19c); an excellent person, animal, or thing (19c, US).

Bird replaced **fowl** [Old English *fugol*: related to FLEET*] as the everyday word, except in a few compounds (*wild/waterfowl*), in place names (*Foulness, Fowlmere*), and names such as **Fowler, Fullerton** referring to bird-catchers: *fowl* now usually refers to poultry.

birth [ME. Old Norse *byrth*: related to BEAR[1]*] The emergence of a baby or young animal from the mother's body, hence **1** parentage, descent, lineage; **birthright** rights, privileges, or property that your parentage entitles you to (16c), later a natural or moral right that you are entitled to from birth (17c) **2** origin or beginning (17c).

biscuit [ME. Old French *bescoit, besquit*, ultimately from Latin *bis* 'twice' + *coctus* 'cooked', from *coquere, coct-* 'to COOK*'. Originally spelt *besquite*: the usual spelling from the 16–18c was *bisket*, reflecting the pronunciation: the current form is from modern French] A flat, crisp cake, originally baked and then dried in a cool oven so that it would keep for use as emergency rations (modern biscuits are baked only once, although baking twice lasted until at least the 18c). Hence **1** pottery between its first and second firings (18c) **2** a small round cake eaten with meat and gravy (19c, US) **3** one of the three square sections of a soldier's mattress (World War I).

The idea of cooking twice is also found in Italian **ricotta**, traditionally produced from whey left over from making pecorino cheese [Latin *recocta*, from *coquere*], and in German **Zwieback** [literally 'twice bake'], which is baked as a loaf, then sliced and dried.

bit¹ [Old English *bita*: related to BITE*] A bite, a mouthful (–17c), hence **1** a scrap of food (ME); a small piece or amount of anything (16c); a small sum of money (17c), specifically an obsolete silver coin of the southern US and the Caribbean, worth a varying fraction of the Spanish dollar; in the US, one-eighth of an American dollar, hence **two bits** 25 cents **2** (also as **bit of fluff, skirt**, etc.) a dismissive term for a young woman (19c) **3** everything to do with a particular role in life (*the whole marriage, mortgage, kids bit*, 1950s, *US*).

bit² [1940s. Blend of *binary* and DIGIT, probably influenced by BIT¹] A unit of information expressed as either 0 or 1 in binary notation, hence **byte** a group of eight bits, used as a unit in measuring a computer's memory [1960s, probably an arbitrary formation based on *bit* and BITE, but perhaps suggested by *binary digit eight*].

Nibble [from or related to Low German *nibblen* 'to gnaw'] to take small bites of something, hence a small amount of food, was adopted for half a byte, but as computer memory is now measured in gigabytes it is seldom used.

bitch [Old English *bicce*] A female dog; a man (ME), at first not necessarily derogatory, a promiscuous (ME) or spiteful (18c) woman, hence **1** an awkward or unpleasant thing (19c) **2** any woman (19c); a strong, feisty one; your girlfriend (1990s) **3** **bitchy** spiteful (1920s, *US*), *bitch* to speak or behave spitefully (1930s) **4** to complain continually (1940s, *US*).

Cf. DOG* and **minx** a pet dog, later a prostitute or a cheeky, flirtatious girl [origin unknown].

bite [Old English *bītan*] To pierce, grip, cut, or sever with the teeth, hence **1 (a)** to wound or damage with the teeth or a sharp implement; such a wound (17c); **(b)** to cause sharp physical or mental pain (ME, hence **biting** stinging, sharp, sarcastic); to have the intended (bad) effect (1970s) **2** to nibble (ME–17c), hence a piece bitten off, a mouthful (16c); a snack (19c); **sound bite** a brief extract from an interview or statement designed to be broadcast (1980s) **3** to grasp (16c); to take the bait (17c), hence to accept a suggestion or respond to provocation (18c) **4** to deceive or swindle (18c), hence **put the bite on** to extort money from (1930s, *US*) **5** the way your teeth come together when you bite (19c).

Related to ABET, BAIT, BIT¹, ², the **bit** of a horse's bridle, also the cutting part of a tool or drill, and probably to *bitts* (at BITTER).

bitter [Old English *biter*] **1** sour, sharp, pungent, hence a bitter-tasting medicine (18c, hence **bitters** a bitter drink used as a digestive, now an alcoholic one used in cocktails); beer made bitter with hops (19c) **2** painful, difficult; painful to think about or accept (19c) **3** full of anger or animosity; of words: cutting, harsh (ME), expressing grief or regret; resentful (15c) **4** of weather: harsh (*bitter wind/cold*, ME).

To the bitter end comes from **bitts** [probably of Low German origin and related to BITE*] a pair of posts on a ship's deck around which ropes are fastened or belayed, the **bitter end** being the first coil around the bitts and therefore the last to be paid out: the current meaning may have been influenced by the biblical phrase *her end is bitter as wormwood* (Proverbs 5:4).

bivouac [18c. French, probably from Swiss German *Biwacht*, literally 'extra watch', a citizens' patrol which helped the town watch in emergencies: related to WAKE*] A night watch by the whole army, hence to remain in the open without tents (19c); a temporary, makeshift encampment, hence (to camp in) a makeshift tent or camp; **bivvy** a makeshift shelter or small tent (World War I).

blame [ME. Old French *bla(s)mer*, ultimately via ecclesiastical Latin *blasphemare* 'to revile or reproach', from Greek *blasphēmein*, from *blasphēmos* 'evil speaking' (whence **blasphemy**)] To find fault with someone for something they have done, hence **1** (to fix) the responsibility for an offence, mistake, etc. **2 blamed** a euphemism for 'damned' (19c, US).

blanch [ME. Old French *blanchir*, from *blanc* 'white', of Germanic origin] To whiten or bleach, hence **1** to peel almonds (exposing the white kernel) by scalding them, hence to cook quickly and lightly in boiling water (18c) **2** to make or turn pale with fear etc. (17c).

Old French *blanc* produced the names **Blanchard**, **Blanche**, and **Blanchflower**, BLANCMANGE, BLANK, BLANKET, and probably **plonk** cheap wine [*Australian*, a corruption of *vin blanc* 'white wine']. Related to BLEAK*.

blancmange [ME. Old French *blanc mangier* 'white food', from *blanc* (see BLANCH*) + *mang(i)er* 'to eat', ultimately from Latin *mandere* 'to chew'. Originally as *blancmanger*, the final -*r* began to disappear in the 18c, when the word was often Anglicized as *blomange* or *blamange*; the current spelling partly restores the French form, but the 18c pronunciation has survived] A dish of white meat or fish, and sometimes rice, in a cream sauce (–15c); a milk jelly (16c), now usually a dessert made with coloured, flavoured cornflour.

Old French *mang(i)er* produced **mange** a skin disease caused by mites (whence **mangy** suffering from mange; poor and dirty-looking), **manger**, and modern French *mangetout*, literally 'eat all'; Latin *mandere* produced **mandible** the (lower) jaw, later a bird's beak, and **manducation** eating, especially as part of the Eucharist.

blank [ME. Old French *blanc*: see BLANCH*] White, pale, colourless (–19c); of paper: left white, not written on (15c), hence **1** a document with spaces to be filled in (16c); such a space; a dash or space in place of an omitted word (18c), hence **(blankety-)blank** in place of a swear word (19c) **2** the disc of a coin before the design is stamped (16c); a piece of metal from which a finished article will be made (19c), hence empty, without what is expected (*blank cartridge/cheque/verse/wall*), hence 'empty': **(a)** without result or success (16c); a losing lottery ticket, now usually in **draw a blank** to be unsuccessful, to search in vain (from the idea of drawing a covert) **(b)** having or showing no interest or knowledge (*a blank expression*, 16c); a period you know or remember nothing about (17c); **blank something out** to suppress the memory of it (18c); **blank someone** to ignore or pretend not to know them (1980s) **3** the white spot in the centre of a target (16c), hence **point blank** aimed directly at the blank without allowance for the missile dropping; the distance from which the missile will hit the target in this case.

blanket [ME. Old Norman French, or Old French *blanchet*, from *blanc*: see BLANCH*] Undyed woollen cloth; a large piece of cloth, originally woollen, used as a covering, rug, or garment, hence a thick covering (*blanket of snow*, 17c); to cover everything or cover completely; inclusive, indiscriminate (*blanket ban/bombing*, 19c).

blatant [1590s. Perhaps an alteration of Scots *blaitand* 'bleating', or from Latin *blatire* 'to babble'] Earliest in the **Blatant Beast**, a many-tongued monster symbolizing slander in Edmund Spenser's allegory *The Faerie Queene*, hence offensively noisy (17c); obvious, shameless, bare-faced (19c).

bleak [Old English *blāc*, later also from related Old Norse *bleikr*] Shining, white (–15c); pale, pallid, colourless (now only dialect), hence colourless from lack of vegetation, bare, exposed (16c); cold, dull, inhospitable, cheerless (18c); hopeless, dire.

Old English *blāc* produced the surnames **Blacker** someone who bleached cloth, and **Blake** (which can also come from *black*). Related to BLANCH* and **bleach**.

bless [Old English *blētsian*, *blœdsian,* literally 'to mark with blood', ultimately from *blōd* BLOOD*] To consecrate by a religious rite, perhaps originally involving blood or sacrifice, or with the sign of the cross, hence **1 not have a penny to bless yourself with** from the cross on an old silver penny, or from the practice of crossing someone's palm with a coin **2** to praise or thank God [translating Latin *benedicare* 'to praise']; to ask God to favour or protect, hence **bless you!** said when someone sneezes (an early symptom of the plague); to devoutly wish well, hence **give your blessing** to give your consent and good wishes **3** to give happiness or good fortune (by association with *bliss*), hence **be blessed with** to feel fortunate because you have something (17c).

Old English *blētsian* produced the surnames **Blessed**, **Blest**, and **Blisset**.

bloat [ME. Probably from or related to Old Norse *blautr* 'soft'] **1** soft and wet: recorded only once, but probably surviving in dialect **2** to soak a herring in brine before smoking it (16c), whence **bloat herring** one cured in this way, replaced by **bloater** (19c).

Possibly the same word as, or related to, **blout** soft and flabby (ME only), reappearing when Shakespeare used it: 'Let the blowte king tempt you again to bed' (*Hamlet* III iv 182). In later editions this was printed as **bloat**, perhaps by association with *bloat herring,* and taken to mean 'swollen with self-indulgence or pride' (bloaters being softer and plumper than kippers). Hence **1** to blow out, inflate; to swell (usually as **bloated**); a disease of cattle in which the stomach swells **2** a conceited or obnoxious person (US).

blood [Old English *blōd,* ancestor of BLESS and related to **bleed**] The bodily fluid, hence **1 (a)** bloodshed, murder **(b)** blood shed in sacrifice, especially Christ's blood as a symbol of atonement **2** blood as one of the cardinal humours (ME, see HUMOUR), or the source of emotions or desire, hence **hot-blooded** impulsive, passionate (16c); **cold-blooded, in cold blood** callous(ly), without emotion (cf. *sang froid* at SANGUINE) **3** blood as the means of passing on hereditary characteristics (ME); (good) parentage, lineage, race, stock, hence **(a)** a (frequently rowdy) young aristocrat (16c); *bloody drunk* as drunk as one, whence **bloody** very, extremely; confounded, damned (17c), later thought to refer to Christ's blood or to be short for *by Our Lady* and producing euphemisms including *bally, bleeding, blessed, blooming,* and *ruddy*. As late as 1964 *bloody* in the film *My Fair Lady* caused much comment: it now seems rather tame **(b) blood horse** a thoroughbred (18c) **(c)** *blue blood* see SANGUINE.

blouse [19c. French, of unknown origin] A long, loose shirt or smock, usually belted at the waist, worn by French peasants and workmen, later a battledress jacket gathered into a waistband; a woman's shirt, originally tucked in at the waist.

French *blouse* produced ***blouson*** [literally 'small blouse'], adopted for a short jacket like a battledress top.

bludgeon [18c. Origin unknown] A stout stick or club; to beat with one (19c), hence **bludgeoner** someone who uses one, shortened to **bludger** a pimp, specifically one who robbed the prostitute's clients (British slang), hence someone who lives off others (1900s, Australia and New Zealand), whence **bludge** to avoid work; to cadge or scrounge (1940s); an undemanding job; a spell of (paid) idleness.

bluestocking A contemptuous term for a man wearing blue worsted stockings instead of formal black silk (17c), hence informally dressed; later applied to the literary gatherings held by three 18c London society ladies, where informal dress was accepted. The women who attended became known as *blue-stocking ladies* or *blue-stockingers*, hence *bluestocking* an educated woman (19c).

bluff¹ [17c. Dutch *bluffen* 'to brag' or *bluf* 'bragging'] To blindfold or hoodwink, hence to try to deceive your opponents at poker as to the value of your hand (19c, *US*); to pretend to be strong, confident, or prepared to do something in order to intimidate; such a pretence; **call someone's bluff** to defy someone who is bluffing, originally by demanding to see a card player's hand.

bluff² [17c. Origin unknown] Having a broad, flat front (*nautical*); of a ship's bows: with little or no rake; of a coastline: almost perpendicular. Hence **1** a steep, rugged cliff or headland **2** abrupt, rough, or surly (18c); blunt but good-natured (19c).

board [Old English *bord*, combining two Germanic words, one meaning 'board, plank', the other meaning 'border, edge, ship's side': influenced in Middle English by related Old French *bort* 'edge, ship's side' and Old Norse *borth* 'board, table'] **1** a plank, hence a thin, rigid piece of material (ME); such material (*cardboard, chipboard*) **2** a table: **(a)** one used for food (ME, whence **sideboard**, originally a side table in a dining hall); the provision of meals (*board and lodging*); to provide or receive board and lodging (16c) **(b)** one used for meetings (ME); those attending; a body of governors, directors, etc. (16c) **(c) above board** without deception, literally with your hands in full view on the table (17c) **3** an edge or border (–16c), surviving in **seaboard** the coastline or shore (18c) **4** the side of a ship, surviving in **outboard**, **overboard**, etc., *starboard* (at PORT¹), and **go by the board**, literally to be swept overboard (17c). Hence *board* to come alongside a ship to attack or capture it (15c); to get into a ship or vehicle (16c); to let people do so (1970s).

Old English *bord* produced the names **Borden** and perhaps **Bordley** where boards were made, and **Bor(e)land** and **Bor(th)wick** the home farm (supplying the lord's table).

bob¹ [ME. Origin unknown: possibly two different words] **1** to hit, to buffet (–17c); to rap, tap, or bounce against something (17c) **2** (to make) a quick down-and-up movement (17c); (to make) a quick curtsy (19c).

bob² [ME. Origin unknown] A bunch or cluster, a posy (surviving in Scots); a rounded mass, a knob (16c), hence **1** the weight on a pendulum or plumb-line (17c); a pendant (17c) **2** a knot or bunch of hair or ribbon (17c), whence **bobble** (1920s).

Hence **bobtail** to dock a horse's tail (16c, presumably from the resulting knob-like shape), hence **1** a horse or dog with a docked tail (17c) **2 bobtail discharge** a dishonourable discharge that cuts short a serviceman's career (19c, *US*). *Bobtail* was shortened to **bob**, whence **1 bobcat** a short-tailed American lynx **2 bob(sled)**, **bob(sleigh)** originally (one of) a pair of short sleds used to carry logs, hence a sporting sled with two pairs of short runners **3** to cut a woman's hair short; such a haircut; **bobby pin** used in short hair **4 bobby** small, short, found in **bobby socks/sox** ankle socks, and perhaps also in **bobby calf** a young male calf destined for imminent slaughter, although the earlier term **staggering bob** suggests that it may be from *Robert* (at HOBBY).

bogey [19c. Perhaps of Celtic origin] **1** a name for the Devil, hence **(a) bogey(man)** an (imaginary) source of terror, a goblin or bugbear; in underworld slang: a police-man (1920s); an unidentified enemy aircraft (World War II) **(b)** in golf: the number of strokes a good player was thought to need for a hole or course (19c, said to be because a player claimed that this standard, regarded as an imaginary opponent, was 'a regular bogeyman'); a score of one more than this (1940s, when new materi-als for golf balls made it easier to equal the bogey: British players lowered the stan-dard, usually by one stroke per hole, while American players used PAR for the new target score, keeping *bogey* for the old one) **2** a piece of nasal mucus (1930s).

The youngest of a group of related words meaning 'someone/something strange and terrible', often invoked to intimidate children: the earliest is **bug** (whence **bugaboo** and **bugbear** an imaginary bear-like creature, later a niggling problem or annoyance), later **bogle** and probably **boggle** to start or shy (presum-ably at a bogey), hence to hesitate; to be baffled or overwhelmed; to make a mistake. BOGUS may be related.

bogus [18c. Probably related to BOGEY*] A machine for making counterfeit coins (–19c, the story goes that when one was found in Ohio no one knew what it was, and it was dubbed a *bogus*, probably meaning simply a strange object), hence a counterfeit coin; false, fake (19c).

Bohemian **1** a native or inhabitant of Bohemia, now part of the Czech Republic (15c) **2** [via French] a gypsy (from the belief that gypsies came from Bohemia), hence an unconventional, free-and-easy person (introduced from French by the 19c novelist William Thackeray).

Gypsy is an alteration of *Egyptian*, as some people believed gypsies came from Egypt (they actually originated in India). Once considered offensive, the term has been re-adopted by gypsies themselves to distinguish them from New Age and other travellers. Non-gypsies often use **didicoi** [perhaps an alteration of Romany *dik akei* 'look here'] to distinguish travellers, seen as dirty and dishonest, from the respectable **Romany** gypsy [from Romany *rom* 'man'].

boisterous [ME. Probably from Old French *boistous* 'rough, clumsy', from Latin *buxus* 'made of box wood', ultimately from Greek *puxos* 'boxwood' (ancestor of BOX[1]*)] Rough, coarse, tough (–18c); of wind or weather: stormy, wild (16c); of a person or animal: rough, violent; good-naturedly rough, noisy, and energetic (17c).

bolt [Old English, of unknown origin. The underlying sense is apparently 'cylinder'] **1** an arrow, specifically a short, broad one as used in a crossbow, later a flash of lightning accompanied by thunder (16c, 15c in **thunderbolt**: from the idea of a god hurling a missile to earth with a clap of thunder). Hence to move quickly: **(a)** to spring up or back (ME–19c), whence **bolt upright (b)** to shoot or eject like a bolt (15c); to drive an animal from its lair (16c); to escape (originally of an animal from its lair, hence **bolt hole** the hole by which it escapes, now one in which to take refuge); to flee or rush off; of a horse: to run out of control (19c); of a plant: to run to seed **(c)** to gulp food rapidly without chewing (18c) **2 (a)** a bar or pin for fastening a door, gate, etc. (ME); to fasten with one (16c) **(b)** a bar with a screw thread (ME); to fix together with a nut and bolt (18c) **(c)** a sliding rod or plate in a rifle that ejects the cartridge and closes the breech (17c) **3** a roll of cloth (15c).

bomb [16c. French *bombe* from Italian *bomba*, probably via Latin *bombus* from Greek *bombos* 'booming'] **Bomb of fire** a fireball used as a weapon (16c only, translating Spanish *bomba de fuego*), hence *bomb* an explosive mortar shell (17c), now a container filled with explosives, gas, etc. with a detonator, hence **1** to attack with bombs, hence **(a) (to go like a) bomb** to travel quickly (1950s); to be a success (1960s) **(b)** to fail, to flop (1960s, *US*) **2 lava/volcanic bomb** a rounded mass of lava thrown out of a volcano (18c).

French *bombe* was adopted for a dome-shaped dessert. Greek *bombos* is the ultimate ancestor of BOUND[3], and probably of **bombard**.

bombast [16c. Old French *bombace*, from medieval Latin *bombax*, alteration of *bombux* 'silk, silkworm', from Greek] Raw cotton or cotton fibre, often used as padding, hence inflated language, empty rhetoric. **Fustian** [via French *fustaigne* from medieval Latin *fustaneum* '(cloth) from Fostat' (a suburb of Cairo)], originally a mixture of linen or cotton and wool (ME), later a coarse twilled cotton, also came to mean 'pompous language' at this time.

Latin *bombyx* produced **bombax**, a genus of tropical trees with seeds surrounded by silky fibre, and **bombazine** raw cotton, later a twilled cotton or silk fabric.

bonanza [19c. Spanish, 'fair weather, prosperity', from medieval Latin *bonacia* 'calm seas', an alteration, influenced by Latin *bonus* 'good', of *malacia* in the same sense] A rich deposit of ore (originally used by miners in Nevada, where veins of silver were found), hence a source of sudden wealth or success.

bond [ME. Variant of BAND I] A shackle or fetter, now usually plural (influencing BONDAGE), hence **1** a constraint; a promise or agreement, hence **(a)** a legal document which binds one person to pay or recompense another (16c, hence **bond paper** good-quality paper used for such documents); to pledge by a bond **(b)** surety, bail (17c, now chiefly US) **(c)** secure storage of goods by customs authorities pending payment of duty (19c) **2** something that fastens or sticks things together (ME); to hold together or adhere (19c), hence (to form or be held by) an emotional tie (1960s).

bondage [ME. Anglo-Latin *bondagium* from Middle English *bond* 'householder', later 'peasant, serf' from Old Norse *bóndi* 'tiller of the soil', ultimately from *búa* 'to dwell': influenced by BOND] Serfdom, slavery, feudal tenure, hence the condition of being constrained, controlled, or tied up; sexual activity involving physical restraints (1960s).

Middle English *bond* survives, just, in **bondman/woman** serf, slave, villein. Old Norse *bóndi* produced *-band* in HUSBAND: *búa* is the ancestor of BOOTH*.

bonfire [ME. Originally *bone-fire* or, in Scotland and N England, *banefire*: these spellings survived until the 19c, although *bonfire* appeared in the 16c. The later spelling and the burning of heretics probably misled Johnson (see ACHE) into deriving it from French *bon* 'good'] An open-air fire on which bones were burnt (–17c), hence **1** a funeral pyre (16–17c) **2** a fire for burning heretics or proscribed literature (16c), hence one for burning rubbish (18c) **3** a large open-air fire as part of a celebration (16c).

booby [17c. Probably from Spanish *bobo*, from Latin *balbus* 'stammering'] **1** a stupid or childish person, hence **booby prize** awarded to the person who comes last (19c); **booby trap** a trap set as a practical joke (19c), later a hidden or disguised explosive device (World War I); to set such a trap (World War II). Shortened to **boob** (early 20c, *US*), hence (to make) a stupid mistake (1930s); **boo-boo** a prank (early 20c); a stupid mistake (1950s) **2** a tropical seabird which had no fear of man and was easily caught (17c): the **dodo** [Portuguese *doudo* 'simpleton'] and the **dotterel** [from DOTE] were similarly named from their misplaced confidence.

boogie [Early 20c. Perhaps via W African English *bogi-bogi* 'to dance' from Hausa *buga* 'to beat drums'] A party, especially one where the guests contributed to their host's rent (US), hence **boogie-woogie** a kind of blues played at such parties (1920s), shortened to *boogie* (1940s), hence to dance to this or, later, to rock music (1950s); to have sex (1970s). Cf. JAZZ.

book [Old English *bōc* (noun), *bōcian* (verb)] **1** a document, charter, or deed; to grant land by a charter (surviving in the place names **Boughton** and **Buckland**, given to land granted by charter) **2** a collection of pages bound together, hence **(a)** a text long enough to fill one or more of these; specifically the Bible (ME); a script or libretto (16c); a magazine (19c) **(b)** one of the major divisions of a long text (ME) **(c)** a set of things (e.g. stamps, matches) bound together like a book (15c) **3** an account or record (–17c); to keep or enter in one (ME), hence **(a)** a ledger (15c), hence **bookkeeper** someone who keeps **the books** the accounts (16c) **(b)** a list of bets (19c), hence **make a book** to take bets, whence **bookmaker (c)** to make or record a reservation (19c) **(d)** to record an offender's details (19c); the total of accusations made against them (1920s), **throw the book at** to bring all possible charges, **get/do the book** to get/serve the maximum sentence (US).

Probably related to **beech** [Old English *bēce*], on which runes were carved, and to **buckwheat** [from early Dutch or Low German] whose grains resemble beechmast.

boom¹ [15c. Ultimately imitative: perhaps from Dutch *bommen*] **1** to hum or buzz; (to make) a loud, deep, resonant sound **2** to rush along (16c, originally said of a ship and perhaps influenced by BOOM², a boom being used to set a sail at the optimum angle to the wind), hence of trade or profits: to increase suddenly (19c, *US*); a sudden increase in activity or amount.

boom² [16c. Dutch: related to BEAM] A beam or pole, specifically one marking a channel (–18c), hence **1** a floating barrier, often made of timbers or spars (17c) **2** a spar securing the base of a ship's sail (17c); a connecting spar in an aircraft (early 20c); a movable arm supporting a camera, microphone, etc. (1930s).

boot [ME. (Via Old Norse) from Old French *bote*] **1** a shoe reaching above the ankle, hence **(a)** a protective cover (16c) **(b)** to kick someone/something hard (19c) **(c) bootleg** describing smuggled or illicitly sold liquor (19c, from the practice of hiding things in long boots) or pirated recordings (1920s) **(d) bootstrap** a strap inside a boot for pulling it on (19c), hence **pull yourself up by your own bootstraps** (1920s), to get on by your own efforts, hence **bootstrap loader/routine** a simple program enabling a computer to start up and load its own operating system (1960s), whence **boot (up)** to start up a computer (1980s) **2** a step on a coach (16–19c), hence a space near it where attendants sat (17c); a separate compartment in a coach; a luggage compartment in a coach (18c) or car (1930s).

Old French *bote* is one parent of ***sabot*** a wooden shoe [with ***savate*** 'shoe' (adopted for a kind of boxing in which kicking is allowed)], whence **sabotage** [French *saboter* 'to walk noisily, to bungle, to damage or destroy']. Probably related to BUTT³*.

booth [ME. Old Norse *buth*, from *búa* 'to live', also 'to prepare'] A temporary dwelling or shelter; a tent or covered stall at a fair or market; a lightweight structure at which something is sold or business transacted (*tollbooth, ticket booth*); such a structure within a building (*polling booth*, 19c), hence a small area in a restaurant etc. with a table flanked by benches (1950s).

The surname **Booth, Boothman** was given to someone who lived in a small hut. Old Norse *búa* appears as **Booth-** in place names, and is the ancestor of BONDAGE, BOUND², and possibly of **bustle**.

borough [Old English *burg, burh*] A fortress, a fortified town or manor house (–15c, surviving in place names, mainly for a community larger than a village: largely replaced by TOWN); one having a charter or a municipal authority, or which returned a member to Parliament; an administrative district of London or of New York City (19c).

The Scots variant **burgh** 'town with a charter' is one parent of **burgher** an inhabitant of a burgh, borough, or (now usually continental) town [the other being related Dutch and German *burger* 'someone/something from a (fortified) town']. Old English *burg* produced **burrow** and names including **B(o)urke** and **Brough(am)**, and appears in others as **Berry(-)**, **-berry**, **-borough**, **Bur-**, **-burgh**, and **-bury**. Related to BARROW², **borrow**, BOURGEOIS*, BURIAL, BURY, and HARBOUR.

bound¹ [ME. Old French *bodne, bonde*, from medieval Latin *bodina*, of unknown origin] A boundary mark or line, hence **1** to set bounds, to limit or restrict; to form the boundary of (16c), whence **bounder**, literally something that forms the bounds or border (16–19c), altered to **boundary** (17c) **2 (a) beat the bounds** to symbolically trace the boundaries of a parish, beating landmarks along the route (16c) **(b) out of bounds** where you must not go (17c).

bound² [ME. Old Norse *búinn*, past participle of *búa*: see BOOTH*. Originally *boun*; the *-d* was added as if to form a past participle, probably influenced by the past participle of *bind*] Ready, prepared, dressed (–19c); ready to leave for, or on the way to, a place (ME); about to do something (19c), now often with the sense 'be certain to', influenced by the past participle of *bind* in the sense 'oblige'.

bound³ [16c. French *bondir* 'to resound', later 'to rebound', from Latin *bombilar* 'to buzz', from *bombus*: see BOMB*] To bounce or recoil (–17c, outlived by **rebound** [Old French *rebondir*]; (to) leap or spring (16c).

bounty [ME. Old French *bonte* 'goodness', from Latin *bonitas*, from *bonus* 'good'] Goodness, virtue (–17c), hence kindness, graciousness, generosity; a generous act; a gift or gratuity, hence a sum paid to recruits on enlistment (18c), to merchants to encourage particular forms of trade, for the killing or capture of outlaws or the scalp of a Native American (19c, *US*), or for killing vermin.

Bounty produced **bounteous** and **bountiful** generous, later ample, abundant. Latin *bonus* influenced BONANZA, and fathered French *bon* 'good', whose descendants include *bonbon*, **bonhomie** [French *bonhomme* 'good fellow', later 'peasant farmer', whence the name **Bonham**], **boon** in *boon companion*, **Budgen** [from *bon Jean* 'good John'], **debonair** [from *de bon aire* 'of good disposition', whence the surname **Bonar**], and probably **bonny**. *Bonus* was adopted (probably by members of the London Stock Exchange), meaning something to the good, something (especially money) over and above what is due or expected, whence, probably, **bunce** money, commission, profit.

bourgeois [French, 'citizen or freeman of a city or burgh' (as distinct from a peasant or gentleman), from Old French *burgeis*, ultimately from Latin *burgus* 'castle, fort', later 'fortified town', of Germanic origin and related to BOROUGH*] Adopted meaning 'to do with or typical of the French bourgeois class' (16c), hence middle-class (18c); conventional, unimaginative, selfishly materialistic; in communist terminology: capitalistic, reactionary (19c); a capitalist.

Old French *burgeis* produced **burgess** a citizen or freeman of a borough (surviving as a surname); a member of its governing body (now only US).

bout [16c. From 15c *bought* 'bend, loop, coil of rope', of Low German origin and related to BOW¹*] A bend or curve, now only the curve of a violin's side, hence a 'turn' of work, a spell of exercise (hence a boxing or wrestling match), drinking (17c), or illness (19c).

bow¹ [Old English *boga*] A bend, a curved line, something curved (often in compounds, of which **elbow** [Old English *elnboga* 'arm bend'], **oxbow**, **rainbow**, and **saddle-bow** survive), hence **1** a weapon for shooting arrows; a violin bow, originally curved (16c) **2** an arched bridge (surviving in place names) **3** a knot with a double loop (16c); a ribbon tied in one **4** a curved part of a wall (18c), hence **bow window** a curved bay window.

Old English *boga* produced the names **Boland**, **Bowes**, **Bowman**, and **Bowyer**. Related to BOUT, BOW²*, and probably to **akimbo** [originally as *in kenebowe*: probably from Old Norse], which until recently has always referred to the arms with hands on hips, but now sometimes refers to legs with knees apart.

bow² [Old English *būgan*] To bend or stoop, hence **1** to bend or kneel in respect or submission, hence to submit, to accept something unwillingly; to bend your head or body in acknowledgement or agreement (17c); **bow out** to withdraw formally or gracefully (19c) **2** to bend something over or downwards (ME); to force downwards or crush (17c).

Old English *būgan* produced BUXOM. Related to BOW¹*.

bower [Old English *būr*] A dwelling, especially an ideal one, hence **1** an inner room; a lady's bedroom or boudoir **2** an arbour or summerhouse (15c).

Old English *būr* is probably the ancestor of **burly** stately, imposing; strong, sturdy, heavily built. Related to **build**.

bowl¹ [Old English *bolle, bolla*] A (usually round) open container; this as part of a pipe, spoon, etc. (ME); a natural basin (19c); a stadium (early 20c), especially in the names of American football stadiums, hence an important contest held in one (1930s).

Related to Afrikaans *biltong* [Dutch *bil* 'buttock' + *tong* 'tongue', referring to the strips of meat], **bole**, **boll**, **boulder**, BULK, and BULWARK.

bowl² [15c. Old French *boule*, from Latin *bulla* 'bubble': see BILL²*] A sphere or ball, now a ball rolled at a jack or pins in various games; to play such a game; to roll a ball etc. along the ground (16c), hence **1** to roll along, to move quickly and smoothly (17c) **2** in cricket: to send a ball to a batsman (18c, the ball being originally rolled or thrown underarm).

Old French *boule* produced *boulet* 'a small ball', whence **bullet**, originally a ball shot from a small cannon.

box¹ [Old English, probably via late Latin *buxis* from Latin *pyxis* 'box made of boxwood', from Greek *puxos* 'the box tree'] A case or (lidded) container; one with its contents (ME), hence **1** to enclose (as if) in a box **2 Christmas box** in which apprentices collected tips (16c); a tip given to tradesmen etc., traditionally on **Boxing Day**, formerly the first working day after Christmas **3** (a box underneath) the coachman's seat in a carriage (17c) **4** a compartment (*witness/loose box*, 17c), hence **(a) box office** where boxes, and later other seats, in a theatre could be booked (18c) **(b) horse box** a stall in a railway truck or ship (19c); a vehicle for transporting horses **5** a protective case (*cricket box*, 15c); a simple shelter (*sentry/ signal/phone box*, 18c); a small country house used while hunting, shooting, etc. **6** an area marked out by lines in some sports (19c).

Greek *puxos* is the ancestor of BOISTEROUS, of the **box tree** (the usual meaning of **Box-** in place names), and of **pyx** the container for consecrated bread at the Eucharist.

box² [15c. Origin unknown] A blow, obsolete except as a slap on the ear or side of the head; to strike or slap (16c); to fight with your fists (17c), to take part in **boxing** organized fighting using padded gloves (18c). Hence **boxer** a pugilist (17c), hence **1 Boxer** a member of a 19c Chinese secret society (*c.*1900, the Chinese name was *yi hé quán*, literally 'righteous harmonious fists') **2** a breed of dog with a flattened nose like a pugilist's, originating and named in Germany (1930s).

boy [ME. Origin uncertain; probably Germanic] **1** a male servant or assistant, surviving mainly in **potboy, best boy** the chief electrician's assistant in a film crew (1930s, *US*) **2** a male child or youth; a son of any age; a man regarded as immature **3** a member of a group of men (15c), now especially in **the boys** a man's friends, colleagues, or team-mates; a man of a particular kind (*backroom/barrow boy*) or from a particular area (1940s) **4 yob** [*boy* spelt backwards] a youth (19c); a lout (1920s).

In sense 1 *boy* replaced **knave** [Old English *cnafa*], which survives meaning a rogue, and as the jack in cards (see JACK-IN-THE-BOX). **Lad** [perhaps of Scandinavian origin] has a similar history: the sense 'male servant' survives in **stable lad** who may be of any age or either sex: the sense 'a lively, irresponsible man' (*bit of a lad*) spawned **laddism** such behaviour, and the female **ladette**. Cf. GROOM, KNIGHT, PAGE.

Girl [origin unknown] originally meant a child of either sex; confined to female children it followed the history of *boy*, the 'female servant' sense surviving as 'female employee', especially a secretary, clerk, or shop assistant. **Lass** [*N English*, probably of Scandinavian origin] has always been feminine.

brace [ME. Old French *bracier*, from *brace* 'the two arms', from Latin *bracchia*, plural of *bra(c)chium* 'arm', from Greek *brakhiōn*] **1** to embrace (–16c); to surround or encircle, hence the mark {, or loosely [, used to unite lines of text or, in pairs, to enclose a section (17c) **2** to hold or fasten; a clasp, buckle, or clamp (15c), hence **(a)** a pair, originally of hounds (15c, probably from the leash holding them together), later of pistols, game birds, etc. **(b)** a tool holding a drill bit (16c) **(c)** a device for straightening teeth (1950s) **3** something that strengthens or supports, hence **(a) braces** for holding trousers up (18c) **(b)** to make firm or rigid (18c) **4** to make tight or tense (15c); to tone up (hence **bracing** invigorating, 18c); **brace yourself** to prepare yourself for something difficult or unpleasant.

Latin *bra(c)chium* is the probable ancestor of German **pretzel** [*US*: a monk is said to have devised the pretzel's shape to represent arms folded in prayer]. Greek *brakhiōn* is the ancestor of **brachiosaurus** a dinosaur with forelegs longer than its hindlegs, and of **embrace**.

bracket [16c. (Via French from) Spanish *bragueta* 'codpiece', also (perhaps because of the shape) 'bracket, corbel', from French *brague* 'mortise', in plural 'breeches', via Provençal from Latin *bracae* 'breeches', of Gaulish origin and probably related to BREECH] **1** an L-shaped support; a shelf or support fixed to a wall (17c), hence a support made of two pieces joined at an angle (like the legs of a pair of breeches) **2** (perhaps likened to a pair of legs, or perhaps by association with BRACE) one of the marks used in pairs to enclose a piece of text, hence to enclose or link with brackets (19c); something that falls within defined limits (*tax/price bracket*), hence to group or class things or people together.

braid [Old English *bregdan*] (To make) a sudden, especially side-to-side, movement (–17c), hence **1** to draw a sword or brandish a spear etc. (–17c); a blow, attack, or outburst (ME–17c) **2** to twist in and out, to interweave, to plait; something woven, a plait (16c), hence **(a)** a ribbon etc. plaited into or tying up the hair; to tie up or plait the hair with one (18c) **(b)** a woven band or plait of silk, gold, etc. (16c); to trim with this (19c).

Old English *bregdan* is probably one ancestor of **embroider** [the other being Old French *(em)broder*, of Germanic origin]. Related to **upbraid** [Old English *upbrēdan*] to bring something up as grounds for reproach (–18c), hence to censure or scold.

braise [18c. French *braiser*, from *braise* 'live coals, cinders'] To cook in a tightly closed pan, originally by burying it in live coals, hence (the makings of) a braised dish.

French *braise* is the ancestor of **brazier** a container for live coals or, later, a fire, and of *breeze* in **breeze block**, made of cinders mixed with sand and cement.

brand [Old English] Burning (–14c); a piece of charred or burning wood, hence **1** (the blade of) a weapon (surviving in poetry, perhaps from the image of it flashing in the light); **brand new** as if still glowing from the forge (16c) **2** to mark by burning (ME); the permanent mark produced (16c), hence **(a)** a stigma (as criminals were often branded), to stigmatize (17c) **(b)** a mark of ownership (17c); a trademark (19c); goods bearing a trademark or trade name; to mark or label with a trade name.

Relatives include **brandish**, **brandy** [shortened from *brandy-wine*, from Dutch *brandewijn* 'distilled wine'], *brim* (in BRIMSTONE), **brindled**, and **burn**.

brass [Old English *braes*, of unknown origin] An alloy of copper and tin (superseded by *bronze* below), now of copper and zinc, hence **1** objects made of brass, e.g. musical instruments (ME); an inscribed (brass) plate (16c); a brass ornament, especially on a horse's harness (early 20c); **brass hat** an officer (Boer War, from the gold braid on his cap); **big/top brass** officers collectively (19c, *US*) **2** copper (ME); copper or bronze coins; money, cash (16c) **3** hardness, toughness (ME); effrontery (16c); **as bold as brass**, **brazen** shameless **4** a prostitute (1930s, from rhyming slang *brass nail* 'tail').

Bronze [via French from Italian *bronzo*, probably from Persian *birinj* 'brass'] is first recorded meaning to coat with bronze, later to make or become bronze-coloured, to suntan; the noun also formerly meant 'hardness, effrontery'. See also GOLD sense 3.

brave [15c. French, from Italian *bravo* 'bold, excellent' or Spanish *bravo* 'courageous, untamed, savage', ultimately from Latin *barbarus*: see BARBARIAN*] **1** courageous, intrepid, daring, hence **(a)** bravado (16–19c) **(b)** a hired thug (16–19c) **(c)** courageous people collectively (17c); a (Native American) warrior (18c) **(d)** to face something courageously **2** excellent, admirable (16c) **3** splendid, spectacular, showy (16–18c, revived by 19c Romantics). Senses 2 and 3 are also found in the Scots form **braw**.

Spanish *bravo* produced **bravado** ostentatious but perhaps false courage, later a hired thug. Italian *bravo* was adopted for a hired thug and as a cry meaning 'well done' (the feminine form *brava*, addressed to women, and the superlative *bravissimo* are still generally regarded as Italian), and produced *bravura* a difficult piece of music to perform, hence brilliant, ambitious, daring, such a performance.

breach [ME. Old French *breche*, ultimately of Germanic origin] Breaking physically, fracture (–17c), hence **1** a break, a gap; a gap in defences made by an attack (16c), hence **step into the breach** to defend it; to replace someone unexpectedly absent **2** the breaking of a contract or obligation (*breach of confidence/contract*); a violation (*breach of the peace*, 16c); a break in continuity; a breakdown of friendly relations **3** to break through; to go above a figure or beyond a limit (16c); of a whale: to leap out of the water (19c).

Related to Old English *br(a)ec* 'newly cultivated land', which appears in names such as **Bircham, Bratton, Breckland,** and **Bretton,** and to **break**.

bread [Old English: related to BREW*, BROIL*, and **broth**] A staple food made of baked dough, hence essential food (ME); your livelihood (18c), hence **1 (a) bread and butter** your livelihood; routine work providing a steady income **(b) bread-winner** the person whose earnings support a household (19c) **2** money (1930s: *dough* in this sense dates from the 19c; both *US*).

breech [Old English *brēc*, plural of *brōc*] A garment covering the loins and thighs (–17c), hence **1 breeches** short trousers (ME, often pronounced and spelt **britches**) **2** the buttocks (16c, surviving mainly in *breech birth*); an animal's hindquarters (implied in **breeching** a strap around a draught horse's hindquarters); the back part of anything, specifically the rear part of a rifle or shotgun barrel.

Old English *brēc* produced the name **Bracegirdle**, someone who made belts to hold up your breeches. Perhaps related to BRACKET.

breed [Old English *brēdan*: related to BROOD] To carry a child from conception to birth; to hatch young from the egg, hence **1** to produce offspring, to reproduce (ME); to produce or be produced; to rear animals or plants and develop strains or characteristics; to mate one animal with another (19c) **2** birth, lineage, extraction (15c); a strain or race (16c) **3** to bring up, educate, or train a child (15c), hence **breeding** the rearing and education of children (16c); the result of birth, lineage, and upbringing; **ill/well-bred** having bad/good manners.

breeze [16c. Probably from Old Spanish and Portuguese *briza*] A north or north-east wind, specifically the north-east trade wind of the tropics (–18c); the north-east wind of the Atlantic coast of tropical America (17c), hence **sea breeze** a cool, usually light, onshore wind, whence **1 land breeze** the corresponding offshore wind that blows at night **2 breeze** a light wind, hence to move in an easy, carefree way (early 20c, *US*); something easy (1920s, *US*).

brew [Old English *brēowan*: related to BREAD*] To make beer etc. by infusion and fermentation, hence **1** to be fermented or infused (ME); to make by mixing or infusion without fermentation (17c), specifically **brew (up)** to make tea (19c) **2** to concoct or foment (ME); to develop ominously (16c); a mixture of things or people likely to do so (1990s) **3** the amount or quality of beer etc. made at one time (16c).

Outside the monasteries, beer was often brewed by women: **brewster** originally meant a female brewer, as **baxter** meant a female baker and **dexter** a female dyer; these terms were later also used for men and subsequently became surnames.

bribe [ME. Old French *bri(m)ber* 'to beg', of unknown origin] To steal, rob, or extort (–17c), hence theft, extortion, stolen goods (–16c); money demanded or offered for favours (15c); to give a bribe.

bride [Old English *brȳd*] A woman recently, or about to be, married, hence to do with a bride or wedding, surviving mainly in **bridegroom** [Old English *brȳguma* 'bride's man', altered by association with GROOM], otherwise replaced by **bridal** [15c, shortened from **bride ale** a wedding feast; later associated with adjectives ending in -*al*].

brief [ME. Via Old French from late Latin *breve* 'a (brief) note or dispatch', from Latin *brevis*] **1** short (hence **briefs** short knickers or trunks, 1930s); concise **2** an official letter or document, specifically one from the Pope, shorter and less formal than a bull **3** an abstract or summary (16c); a summary of a case for the instruction of counsel (17c); to instruct counsel (19c), hence **(a)** (to give) information and instructions about a task; **briefing** such information (*c*.1910); a meeting at which this is given; **debrief** to get or give information about an event etc. afterwards (World War II) **(b)** your legal representative (20c slang).

Brief produced *breve* (see LARGE sense 3b). Latin *brevis* is the ancestor of **abbreviate**, **abridge** **breviary** originally an abridged version of the psalms, and **brevity**.

brigand [ME. Via Old French from Italian *brigante* 'foot-soldier, skirmisher' (literally 'brawling'), from *brigare* 'to fight, brawl', from *briga* 'strife'] A lightly armed irregular foot-soldier (–18c), hence one who lives by robbery and pillage, a bandit (15c).

Italian *briga* is the ancestor of **brigade** and **brigantine** originally a small vessel used mainly for spying or piracy.

brimstone [Old English *brynstān*, literally 'burning stone'] The popular name for sulphur until at least the 17c. Sulphur's flammable nature and foul smell led to its association with the fires of hell; allusions to *fire and brimstone* are frequent in the Bible, and the word is now seldom used alone except in the names of sulphur-coloured plants and insects (*brimstone butterfly*, 19c).

brisk [16c. French *brusque* 'lively, fierce' (later borrowed meaning 'curt, offhand, abrupt'), from Italian *brusco* 'sour', ultimately from Latin *bruscum* 'coarse, rough'] **1** active, vigorous, efficient; stimulating, invigorating, hence **(a)** acting quickly and without fuss (17c) **(b)** of business: busy **(c)** hurried, hasty (17c); peremptory **2** pleasantly tart (16c); of wine: not stale or flat.

broach [ME. French *brochier* 'to prick, to stitch', *broche* 'a spit', ultimately from Latin *brocc(h)us* 'projecting'] **1** to prick (–16c) or pierce; to tap a cask (15c), hence to start on something, to raise a subject (16c) **2** a pointed rod; a lance, needle, skewer, or spit, surviving chiefly as **brooch** an ornamental pin.

French *brochier* produced **brochure** [literally 'something stitched'], adopted for a (stitched) pamphlet. French *broche* produced **brochette** a small skewer or pin, specifically one on which chunks of meat are cooked, or one to fasten a medal etc. to clothing. Latin *brocc(h)us* fathered Italian **broccoli** [literally 'little shoots'].

broad [Old English *brād*] Wide; also spacious; wide open, hence **1** fully expanded or developed (*broad daylight*); **The Broads** (in East Anglia) lakes formed where rivers widen out (17c) **2** obvious, easily understood (*a broad hint*, ME); of a regional accent: strong, distinct (16c) **3** plainly, bluntly (ME); blunt, outspoken (15c); bawdy, ribald (16c) **4** unrestrained (17c), hence tolerant, liberal (19c), hence **broadminded**, **Broad Church** Anglicans favouring a liberal interpretation of doctrine (*c*.1850, modelled on *Low* and *High Church*), an organization tolerating a range of opinions among its members **5** widespread, far-ranging, general (19c); not detailed (*a broad outline*).

Broad produced ABROAD. Old English *brād* produced **breadth** (earlier as *bread*, the *-th* added on the pattern of *length* and *strength*), and appears in place names meaning 'wide, spacious' (*Bradford, Bradley*), along with related Scandinavian *breithr* (*Braithwaite, Brayton*): in surnames it sometimes means 'fat'.

broil [ME. Old French *bröollier*, ultimately of Germanic origin and related to BREAD*] To mix in a confused way (−17c); (to engage in) a noisy or violent quarrel (15c); to involve in such confusion or quarrelling (16c). Largely replaced by **embroil** [also from Old French *bröollier*, which is probably the ancestor of Italian *imbroglio*].

brood [Old English *brōd*: related to BREED] Offspring, young, specifically chicks hatched and reared together, hence **1** a family's children (ME); a group with a similar origin or characteristics (15c) **2** the nurturing of young in the egg or womb (ME, now mainly in **brood bitch/mare** etc. kept for breeding, 16c); to sit on or hatch eggs (15c); of a hen: to protect chicks under her wings, hence **(a)** to nurse an idea or grudge **(b) brooding** hanging over, looming (17c) **(c) broody** of a hen: ready to brood eggs (16c); of a woman: longing for a baby (19c).

broom [Old English *brōm*] A yellow-flowered shrub; a long-handled brush (15c), originally one made of broom or heather twigs, now called a **besom** [Old English *bes(e)ma*], which originally meant a bundle of rods or twigs used to flog miscreants (−ME), replaced by **birch** [Old English *birce*], birch twigs being most commonly used. In Scotland and N England *besom* is also used as a mildly derogatory word for a woman or girl.

Old English *brōm* appears in names as **Bram-** or **Brom-**, less commonly as **Bran-** or **Bren-**, and is related to **bramble** [Old English *brem(b)el*, which appears as **Bram-** or **Brem-**]. Old English *birce* appears as **Birch-** or **Birk-**, some of the latter being from related Scandinavian *birki*.

brothel [ME. Ultimately from Old English *brēothan* 'to degenerate, deteriorate', of unknown origin] A worthless man or woman (−16c); a prostitute (15−17c), hence **brothel (house)** (16c).

Brothel outlived **bordel (house)** [ME−19c, from Old French *bordel*, literally 'cabin' (of Germanic origin), whence Italian *bordello*].

brother [Old English *brōthor*. The plural has had many forms; in early Middle English **brethren** became the standard and remained so until the 17c] The son of one or, usually, both of your parents, hence **1** a close male friend: the alteration **buddy** (19c, *US*) also means someone who befriends and supports a person with AIDS (1980s) **2** a man recognized as your equal; a fellow-citizen or countryman; a (fellow) member of a religious community, later of a guild or trade union (ME), hence a friendly form of address to any man (early 20c). *Brethren* was used for members of the early church and was later adopted by various Christian associations (*Plymouth Brethren*): **brethren** or **bred(ren)** has become (Black) slang for a friend. In names, *Brother-* usually means a younger brother, and sometimes comes from related Old Norse *brother*: **Brether-** (from *brethren*) usually refers to a religious community.

Sister [Old English *sweoster*] developed similarly: the '(fellow) member' senses tend to be later, because *brethren/brothers* 'the members collectively' included women, because many organizations did not originally admit women, or because women's organizations were founded later. *Sister* became the title for a (senior) nurse; it is also used for a (fellow) prostitute, a (fellow) Black woman (*US*), a fellow gay man, or a (fellow) feminist. Shortened to **sis** and to **sissy**, which came to mean an effeminate person or a coward and is one parent of **prissy** (*US*), the other being *prim* (at PRIME).

browse [15c. Old French *broster*, from *bro(u)st* 'young shoot', probably of Germanic origin] To feed on the leaves and shoots of bushes, hence, because the animals move frequently from bush to bush, to look through a book casually (19c, *US*); to look at goods or objects in a similar way (1970s); to read or search out data files on a computer network (1980s), now specifically on the internet (1990s: cf. SURF), hence **browser** a program that facilitates this.

brush [ME. French *brosse*, probably ultimately from Latin *bruscum* 'knot on a maple': the verb partly from related French *brosser*] **1** an implement with hairs or bristles attached to a handle, hence **(a)** to clean or clear away (as if) with one (15c); to apply something with one (19c) **(b)** something resembling a brush, e.g. a fox's tail (16c); an electrical conductor with metallic strips (19c); a drumstick ending in wire bristles (1920s) **2 (a)** a brief (unpleasant) encounter **(b)** to touch in passing (17c); to injure by doing so; a graze (18c).

Latin *bruscum* is the ancestor of **brush 1** cut or broken twigs or branches (perhaps used to make brushes: cf. BROOM) **2** (land covered with) bushes or undergrowth.

brute [15c. Via French from Latin *brutus* 'heavy, dull, stupid'] Of an animal: incapable of reasoning or understanding, hence **1** unthinking, senseless, cruel (16c, largely replaced by **brutal**); such a person (cf. BEAST) **2** a (large, powerful) animal (17c).

buccaneer [17c. French *boucanier*, from *boucan* 'a barbecue or smoking rack', from Tupi *mukem*] A French settler who lived by hunting wild oxen in Spanish America, drying and smoking the meat on a *boucan*, some of whom turned to plunder and piracy when the Spanish authorities banned their hunting. Hence a Caribbean, later any, pirate (19c), a flamboyant, unscrupulous adventurer or businessman.

buck [Partly from Old English *buc* 'male deer', partly from Old Norse *bokki* 'male goat'] A male goat (–16c); a male roe or fallow deer, later applied to the male of other animals and, contemptuously, to a Native American, Black, or Aboriginal man (19c, *US*). Hence **1** a man (ME), rare until the 18c, when it came to refer to an impetuous young dandy, hence **buck up** to dress up (19c); to make or become more lively or cheerful **2** of a male rabbit: to copulate (16–19c); of a horse: to jump with its back arched like a copulating rabbit (19c).

Buck a dollar may refer to a buck's skin, more valuable than a doe's, while **pass the buck** comes from the game of poker, a *buck* being an object (often, it is said, a knife with a buckhorn handle) put in front of the player whose turn it was to deal or bid: these explanations are tenuous. **Buck** a sawhorse, later a short vaulting horse, comes from related Dutch *bok* (as in Afrikaans *springbok*) or German *bock* 'goat'.

buckle [ME. Old French *bocle* from Latin *buccula* 'cheek-strap', from *bucca* 'cheek']
1 a fastener with a hinged pin; to fasten with one, hence (from the idea of buckling on armour) to prepare yourself for battle or a task (16c), surviving in **buckle down/to 2** [via French *boucler* 'to curve or bulge' (like a cheek)] to give way or crumple (16c).

Old French *bocle* also meant 'shield boss', hence *escu bocler* 'shield with a boss', whence **buckler**. *Bouclé* [past participle of *boucler*] was adopted for a fabric or yarn with a crinkly or knobbly effect.

budget [15c. Old French *bougette*, literally 'small leather bag', from Latin *bulga* 'bag, knapsack' (whence BULGE), of Gaulish origin] A pouch, wallet, or bag (surviving in dialect at least until the 19c), hence **open the budget** of the Chancellor of the Exchequer: to make a statement to the House of Commons of revenues and expenditure expected in the coming year and the financial measures proposed (18c, from the idea of showing the contents of a bag), later a plan for the resources of any organization, family, or individual (19c); to draw one up; the money needed or available for something, hence **on a budget** having limited money; *budget* suitable for someone on a budget, cheap (1950s).

buff [16c. Via French and Italian from late Latin *bufalus*, ultimately from Greek *boubalos* 'antelope, wild ox' (whence **buffalo**)] A buffalo (–18c), hence leather made from buffalo hide; dressed ox-leather resembling this, hence **1** military dress, often made of buff leather **2** (of) the yellowish colour of buff leather, hence, from the buff uniforms formerly worn by volunteer firemen in New York, someone who avidly attends fires (*c.*1900), hence a knowledgeable enthusiast (*wine buff*, 1930s) **3** the bare skin, usually as **in the buff** nude (17c) **4** a polishing wheel or pad covered with buff leather (19c), hence to polish.

buffer [19c. Probably from 16c *buff* 'to sound like hitting something soft', ultimately imitative] Something that reduces the shock or impact of one thing on another, hence to do so; (to be) a protective intermediary.

Probably related to Old French *bufe*, whence **buff** a blow (surviving in **blind man's buff**) and **buffet** to knock about, and perhaps to **buff** to stutter or splutter, surviving in **buffer** an old-fashioned, incompetent, or indecisive man.

buffet [15c. Old French *buf(f)et*, of unknown origin] A low stool or footstool (now only Scots and N English). In French, *buffet* came to mean a sideboard (adopted in the 18c), hence a place where food is laid out on a sideboard or counter for people to help themselves; (describing) a meal served in this way (19c).

bug [17c. Perhaps ultimately from Old English *-budda* as in *scearnbudda* 'dung beetle': *shorn bug*, presumably from *scearnbudda*, survived in dialect as late as the 18c: cf. *sharn* at SHARD] **1** an insect that bites and sucks; a bedbug or louse; loosely, any beetle or grub **2** (a person with) an obsession (19c, *US*, perhaps because lice are difficult to detach) **3** a fault in a machine, system, or computer program (19c: it is often said that an insect was squashed between the contacts of a relay in an early electromechanical computer, causing the machine to fail; however, early examples predate the computer) **4** (an illness caused by) a virus or germ (*c.*1910) **5** (to equip with) an alarm system or listening device (1920s) **6** to pester or annoy (1940s). Hence **debug** to remove faults or programming errors (1940s), listening devices (1960s), or lice.

bugger [ME. (Via early Dutch) from Old French *bougre* 'heretic', from medieval Latin *Bulgarus* 'Bulgarian', particularly one belonging to the Orthodox Church and therefore regarded as a heretic by the Roman Church] A heretic, specifically an Albigensian, hence, from a common association of heresy with forbidden sexual practices, someone who has anal sex or sex with an animal (16c); to do so; a nasty or awkward person or thing (18c), now often simply a person of the kind described (*poor/lucky bugger*, 19c); to ruin or spoil (early 20c, hence **buggered** ruined, exhausted); **bugger about/around** to mess about or potter around (1940s). Also used as a swear word, stronger than *damn*, since the 18c (see also FUCK).

Sod a man who has anal sex [short for **Sodomite**, literally a citizen of Sodom (see the Bible, Genesis 18–19)] developed similarly, but also produced **Sod's law** the 'natural law' that states that if something can go wrong, it will; probably a stronger version of **Murphy's law**, *Murphy* being a character who invariably made mistakes in US Navy training cartoons.

bugle [ME. Old French, from Latin *buculus* 'bullock', diminutive of *bos* 'ox' (ancestor of BEEF*)] A buffalo or wild ox, hence **bugle horn** a hunting horn made of an ox's horn, soon shortened to *bugle*; later applied to a brass or copper hunting horn and hence, after Hanoverian light infantry battalions began to use hunting horns to send signals, to a small military trumpet (18c, cf. CORNET, HORN).

bulge [ME. Old French *bou(l)ge* from Latin *bulga*: see BUDGET] A (leather) bag, hence (probably from its shape) **1** (now only as the variant **bilge**) **(a)** the lowest part of a ship's hull (15c); **bilge (water)** the dirty water that collects there (17c), hence rubbish, nonsense (19c) **(b)** the widest part of a barrel or cask (16c) **2** to swell or protrude (17c); a swelling or protrusion (18c), hence a temporary increase in volume, numbers, etc. (19c).

bulk Strictly speaking, two words: I [ME. Old Norse *bálki* 'heap, cargo'] a ship's (entire) cargo; the total amount of a commodity, hence **1** a pile or large quantity (15c); to heap up (17c) **2 to sell in bulk** to sell a whole cargo (17c), later to sell in large quantities; *bulk* to combine consignments (19c) II [15c. Probably ultimately from Old English *būc* 'belly, pitcher', later 'body'] the belly, later the whole trunk, now specifically a large physical frame, hence the (large) volume, weight, or size of something; a large mass or shape (16c), hence **1** to be or seem large, thick, or weighty, hence to make something (seem) thicker and heavier (1930s); something that adds weight or volume, specifically roughage in the diet (1940s) **2** the mass of something (17c); the greater part or number (18c).

Old Norse *bálki* is related to BOWL[1]*. Old English *būc* is probably the ancestor of **bucket**.

bull [Old English *bula* from Old Norse *boli*] **1** an uncastrated bovine animal; a male seal, elephant, rhinoceros, or whale (ME) **2** stock bought up in order to raise the price (18c); a speculator who buys stock for this reason (cf. BEAR[2]); **bull market** in which prices are rising.

Bull meaning 'idle talk, nonsense' and 'unnecessary spit and polish or red tape', may be from **bullshit** or may be from Old French *bo(u)ler* 'to deceive or cheat', hence a ridiculous or contradictory statement.

Bull produced BULLDOZE. Old English *bula* appears in names as **Bol-** or **Bul-**, and produced **bullock**, which appears in a few names as **Bulk-** and has replaced **rother** [Old English *hryther*], which survives in names (also as **Ruther-**).

bulldoze [19c. From BULL + *doze*, an alteration of **dose** (via French and Latin from, ultimately, Greek *didonai* 'to give')] A severe punishment (from the idea of 'a dose fit for a bull'), hence to intimidate or coerce; **bulldozer** a person who does so; a large earth-moving machine (1930s), whence *bulldoze* to move or demolish with a bulldozer (1940s); to act or deal with forcefully.

Descendants of Greek *didonai* include **anecdote**, originally a secret or hitherto unpublished detail [via French and Latin from Greek *anekdotos* 'unpublished', ultimately from *ekdidonai* 'to give out'] and **antidote**.

bullion [ME. Old French *bouillon*, from *bo(u)illir* 'to boil', from Latin *bullire* 'to bubble', from *bulla* 'bubble': see BILL²*] A mint (–18c, from the idea of 'boiling' or melting metal), hence metal in a lump to be made into coins (15c); gold or silver as bars or ingots (16c); a lot of money.

French *bouillon* was adopted meaning 'stock, broth'; *bouillir* produced **boil** and French *bouilli* [literally 'boiled'] adopted for boiled meat (17–19c), whence *bully* in **bully beef**. Latin *bullire* produced **parboil** [via Old French from late Latin *perbullire* 'to boil thoroughly', the original English sense; the current sense arose by confusion with *part*].

bully [16c. Probably from early Dutch *boele* 'lover'] Sweetheart, darling, of either sex, later used when speaking to a male friend, hence **1** a good chap, a fine fellow, later a braggart, hence someone who intimidates weaker people (17c); to do so (18c); **bully (boy)** a hired thug **2** (usually in forms of address) gallant, hearty (–19c), hence very good, first rate (19c, *US*); **bully for you** well done!

bulwark [15c. Early Dutch or Low German *bolwerk* 'rampart made of tree trunks', from *bol* 'tree trunk' + *werk* 'work'] A rampart, a protecting wall or embankment, hence something/someone that gives protection or support.

Low German *bolwerk* produced French **boulevard** '(a promenade on the site of) a rampart', borrowed for a broad avenue, later a wide urban street (*US*). *Bol* is related to BOWL¹*, and *werk* to WORK*.

bum Two words intertwined: I [ME. Origin unknown] **1** the buttocks, hence a bailiff (17c, originally **bum bailiff**, because he sneaks up from behind); **bum fodder** toilet paper, hence **bumf**, **bumph** boring printed material, especially official forms (19c) **2** an idler, a tramp (now usually associated with II) II [19c. Ultimately from German *bummeln* 'to stroll or loaf about'] **1** a tramp; to wander round like one; to cadge or scrounge **2** of poor quality, worthless, hence **bummer** a bad experience (1960s, originally one due to hallucinatory drugs); a disappointment or failure.

bundle [ME. Early Dutch *bundel*: related to BIND*] A collection of things tied or wrapped up together, hence **1** to tie in a bundle (16c), hence **(a)** to pack things hurriedly (18c); to put or move unceremoniously (*bundled her into a taxi*, 19c) **(b)** to package things to be sold together (1960s); such a package, hence **unbundle** to charge separately for such items **2** a collection of parallel tissues etc. in an animal or plant (18c) **3** to wrap up warmly (16c); **bundle up (with)** to share a bed, fully clothed, with someone of the opposite sex (formerly allowed during courtship in some parts of England and Wales, 18c) **4** a large amount of money (*c*.1900, *US*: cf. PACKET, PARCEL), hence **go a bundle on** to bet a large sum on; to like very much.

bunker [16c. Origin unknown] A seat, bench, or chest (Scots), hence **1** (probably) **bunk** a narrow bed (18c) **2** a bank in a field (19c); a sandpit, usually backed by a bank, on a golf course (19c); a military dugout (World War II), a reinforced underground shelter **3** a large fuel container (19c).

buoy [ME. Probably from early Dutch *bo(e)ye*] A fixed floating object used to mark a hazard or channel, hence **1** to provide or mark with a buoy or buoys (16c) **2 (life)buoy** a device for keeping you afloat (19c).

Related to BEACON* and to Spanish *boya*, whence **buoy 1** to rise to or float on the surface (16–17c); **buoyant** able to do so; resilient, lighthearted **2 buoy (up)** to keep someone/something afloat; to keep up someone's spirits; to encourage.

bureau [17c. French, from Old French *burel* 'baize' (originally usually brown), from *buire* 'dark brown', from Latin *burrus* 'reddish brown', from Greek *purros* 'red', from *pur* 'hearth, fire'] A writing desk with drawers and, often, a baize writing surface (17c), hence **1** an office; an office or business with a specific function (*information/marriage bureau*, 1920s) **2** a chest of drawers (19c, US).

Baize was brought to England by French and Dutch refugees; the word comes via Dutch from French *baies*, plural of *bai* '(reddish) brown', from Latin *badius*.

Descendants of Greek *pur* include **empyrean** the highest part of heaven, once believed to be a realm of pure fire and light, **pyre**, **pyrethrum** [Latin, from Greek *purethron* 'feverfew' (used to treat fever), from *puretos* 'fever'], **pyrites** originally a mineral used for striking fire, and **pyro-** (*pyroclastic, pyromania*). French *bai* produced **bay** (describing) a brown or chestnut horse with a black mane, tail, and legs, also as a surname given to redheads, and **Bayard** the name of a magnificent chestnut horse in medieval romances, which became a byword for reckless courage.

burial [Old English *byrgels*: related to BOROUGH*. Spelt *buriels* in Middle English: the ending changed by association with nouns ending in -*al*, and because the *s* was mistaken for a plural ending] **1** a grave or tomb (–17c, recently revived as a technical term in archaeology) **2** an interment or funeral (ME).

bury [Old English *byrgan*: related to BOROUGH*] To put a corpse in a grave, tomb, or the sea, hence to put or hide anything in the ground (ME); to cover with earth or other material; to put out of sight or out of mind (15c); to engross yourself in something (*buried himself in his work*).

bush [ME. Partly from Old French *bos(c)*, *bois* 'wood', partly from related Old Norse *buski*] A shrub with many woody stems; a clump of shrubs, hence **1** a thicket (16–17c); reintroduced [probably from related Dutch *bosch*] for wooded, uncultivated, and sparsely populated country in former British colonies (17c) **2** a bunch of ivy, formerly used as a wine-seller's sign **3** to grow thick like a bush (15c); a thick mass of hair (16c); pubic hair (1920s).

Bush produced the variant **bosk**, whence **bosky**. French *bois* produced **bouquet**, literally 'little bush', and **hautboy** [French *hautbois*, with *haut* 'high'], the former name, and the source of, **oboe**, and is related to **ambush** [Old French *embuschier*] originally to hide troops (as if) in the bushes. Old Norse *buski* produced the name **Busby**.

busk [17c. Obsolete French *busquer* 'to seek', from Italian *buscare* or Spanish *buscar*, ultimately of Germanic origin] To cruise about, to tack; to go around the streets, pubs, etc. selling goods or entertaining (19c), hence **busker** a street entertainer; *busk* to improvise a song etc. (1960s).

bust [17c. Via French and Italian from Latin *bustum* 'tomb, sepulchral monument'] The torso or upper part of a large sculpture (17c only), hence **1** a sculpture representing someone's head and shoulders **2** a woman's breasts (18c) or chest measurement (19c).

but [Old English *butan*, from *bi* **by** + *ūt* **out**] Outside, hence **1** without, lacking; except (*everyone but me*), hence used to join clauses with opposite meanings **2** the part of a house into which the outer door opened, surviving in Scots **but and ben** a two-roomed cottage, the *ben* being the inner room [Old English *binnan*, from *bi* + **in** (related to INN*)].

Old English *butan* is found in **about** [Old English *onbutan* 'on the outside']; *by* produced *because* (at CAUSE), and *ūt* is found in **utmost** and UTTER.

butler [ME. French *bouteillier* from *bouteille*, from medieval Latin *butticula* 'small cask', from Latin *buttis* 'cask'] The servant who served wine or had charge of the wine-cellar; now the head (male) servant in a household.

French *bouteille* produced **bottle**. Latin *buttis* is the ancestor of **butt** a cask, and of **buttery** originally a place where liquor was stored.

butt¹ [ME. Old French *bo(u)ter*, of Germanic origin] To hit or thrust; to hit or shove with the head or horns; to thrust or jut out, hence **1** (probably) a promontory or headland (16c, now only in a few place names such as *The Butt of Lewis*) **2 butt in** to intervene or interfere (*c.*1900, *US*), hence **butt out** to stop interfering (1970s).

Old French *bo(u)ter* produced **buttress** [from *ars bouterez* 'thrusting arch'] and REBUT. Related to **button** [French *bouton* 'stud, knob'].

butt² [ME. Old French *but* 'target, goal', of unknown origin, probably influenced by French *butte* 'mound, target'] A mound with a target for archery or shooting practice; **butts** a practice ground for archers, usually with a butt at each end (surviving in place names), hence **1** an end or boundary mark (now US), hence [partly from **abut** in the sense 'to end at or border on', ultimately from Old French *but*] to lie, place, or join end to end **2** a target; an aim or goal (16c); the 'target' of teasing, ridicule, or bullying (17c).

Old French *but* produced French *débuter* 'to make the first stroke in a game', whence *début* (to make) a first public appearance. French *butte* was adopted for a hill with steep sides and a flat top (N American), and is probably the ancestor of British dialect **butt** a mound or hillock.

butt³ [15c. Of Germanic origin] The thicker end of something; the handle of a gun, fishing rod, etc., hence the buttocks (now mainly N American); the trunk of a tree just above the ground (17c); the stub of a cigar or cigarette (19c).

Butt belongs to a family of words of Germanic origin with the basic meaning 'something thick', including **butt** a ridge of ploughed land, also the earliest sense of **buttock** [Old English *buttuc*], **butt** a flatfish, whence **halibut** [literally 'holy butt'] eaten on holy days when meat was forbidden; **turbot** [via Old French from

Old Swedish *tornbut*, literally 'thorn butt', from the spines on its back], and probably BOOT.

buxom   [ME. Ultimately from Old English *būgan*: see BOW²] Obedient, obliging, kindly (–19c); good-tempered and lively (16c), hence (from the traditional association of plumpness with an easy-going nature) plump, cheerful, vigorous and attractive.

C

cabal [16c. French *cabale*, ultimately from Hebrew *qabbālāh* 'tradition', from *qibbēl* 'to receive or accept'] The Kabbalah, a body of mystic Jewish teachings (–18c), hence a secret (17–18c); a conspiracy; a political clique or faction, influenced by the initials of Charles II's ministers (Clifford, Ashley, Buckingham, Arlington, and Lauderdale).

The Kabbalah has been adopted for a system of beliefs founded in the US in 1965, based on interpretations of the Jewish Kabbalah.

cabin [ME. French *cabane* via Provençal from late Latin *capanna, cavanna*] A shelter (–19c), hence **1** a small room on a ship **2** a small, simple dwelling (15c), whence **cabinet** in the same sense (16–17c), which came to mean **(a)** a small or private room; one where the sovereign's advisers met (17c); a government's chief ministers **(b)** [influenced by French *cabinet* 'closet', from Italian *gabinetto* 'closet, chest of drawers', also from late Latin *capanna*] a jewel case (16c); a piece of furniture for storing or displaying objects, hence one containing a radio or television (1940s).

cabriolet [18c. French *cabriole*, later form of *capriole* 'a leap', ultimately via Italian *capriolo* 'roebuck', from Latin *capreolus* 'small goat, kid', from *caper* 'goat'] A sprung two-wheeled carriage with a hood (because of its bouncy motion), hence a soft-topped car (*c.*1910). Shortened to **cab** (19c): **1** a hackney carriage (with a hood); a taxi **2** the driver's compartment of a lorry, train, etc. (thought to resemble the carriage's hood).

French ***capriole*** was adopted for a leap, skip, or prance, originally in dancing, later by a trained horse, and was shortened to **caper**, which came to mean a playful act, a prank, later a risky activity or a scam. Latin *caper* produced **Capricorn** the constellation and sign of the zodiac [Latin *capricornus* 'goat-horned', with *cornu* 'horn': see CORNET*] and French ***chevron*** an inverted V-shape in heraldry (probably from the image of kids leaping and butting each other), hence a V-shaped badge or stripe. Related to the surname **Cheever** a goatherd or a stubborn person.

cachet [17c. French, from *cacher* 'to hide', also 'to press down', ultimately from Latin *cogere* 'to drive together': see SQUAT*] **1** a seal for a document, hence a distinguishing mark (19c); a quality giving distinction or prestige **2** a medicinal capsule (19c).

French *cacher* produced **cache** a place to hide things; (to place in) a hidden store, hence **cache (memory)** an auxiliary computer memory enabling rapid access to data.

cadet [17c. French, from Gascon dialect *capdet*, literally 'little chief', ultimately from Latin *caput* 'head' (ancestor of CAPITAL*)] A younger son, hence a gentleman, often a younger son, who joined the army without a commission, intending to work his way up (shortened in Scotland to **caddie**), hence a military or police trainee (18c); a member of a youth organization offering military-style training (19c). *Caddie* later meant an odd-job man or errand-boy (18c, cf. *cad* below), now a golfer's assistant. **Cad** (shortened from *cadet* or *caddie*) originally meant a passenger picked up by a coachman for his own profit, later a bus or coach conductor or an odd-job man; in Eton and Oxford University: a lad who ran errands for students, or a contemptuous term for any townsman (cf. SNOB), hence someone who does not behave like a gentleman.

cadre   [19c. French, from Italian *quadro*, ultimately from Latin *quadrum* SQUARE*] A frame, framework, or plan, hence the 'framework' or skeleton force of trained soldiers, supplemented by recruits when needed; (a member of) a core of political activists (1930s); in Communist China: a holder of a Party, governmental, or military office (1960s).

Italian *quadro*, or its Spanish equivalent, *cuadro*, produced French **quadrille** each of four groups of riders taking part in a tournament or display, hence **1** a riding display **2** a square dance performed by four couples.

cake   [ME. Old Norse *kaka*] A small, flat, round loaf of bread, hence **1** a loaf of sweetened bread (15c); a baked mixture of flour, fat, sugar, and egg **2** a flat, rounded mass of some other food (*fishcake, pancake,* 15c); a small block (*cake of soap,* 16c); to form into one (17c); to encrust (*caked with mud,* 1920s). **To take the cake** (later **the biscuit**) comes from the **cakewalk**, an informal competition of elegant walking with a cake as the prize, popular among African-Americans in the 19c, hence a dance based on this (early 20c).

Related to **cookie** [Dutch *koekje* 'little cake'] and to French **quiche** [ultimately from German *Kuchen* 'cake'].

calibre   [16c. Via French or Italian from Arabic *qālib* 'mould', ultimately from Greek *kalapous* 'shoemaker's last'] The diameter of a bullet, cannonball, etc., hence **1** social standing (–18c, probably from a figurative use in French), hence someone's character or worth (17c) **2** the internal diameter of a gun barrel, later of any cylinder (18c), whence **calibrate** to measure this (19c); to check the tube of a measuring instrument etc. for irregularities before marking a scale on it; to mark the scale; to check a measuring instrument against a standard (*c.*1900).

The variant **calliper** first appears in **calliper compasses** for measuring bullets, later shortened to **callipers**, hence a leg brace having two metal rods like the legs of a pair of compasses.

callow   [Old English *calu*, ultimately from Latin *calvus* 'bald'] Bald (–15c); without feathers, unfledged (15c), hence young and inexperienced (16c).

Old English *calu* appears as **Cal-** in place names, usually of bare hills. Latin *calvus* produced *calvaria* 'skull', whence **Calvary**, the site of Christ's crucifixion.

cameo   [15c. Old French *came(h)u*] A precious stone having layers of different colours, hence (something resembling) one carved to give a raised design in one colour against a background of another; a medallion with a profile carved in this way, hence a written sketch or portrait (19c); **cameo (part)** a small character part in a play, film, etc. (1950s).

camp [16c. French *c(h)amp* via Italian from Latin *campus* 'field, level ground', applied to the Campus Martius at Rome, used for sports and military drill] An army's quarters, hence **1** (the site for) a collection of huts, tents, caravans, etc. where people stay temporarily; to set one up; to live outdoors or in temporary accommodation; to stay somewhere (*reporters camped on her doorstep*) **2** a body of troops, later nomads, travellers, etc., moving and camping together; a group with similar aims (19c); **a foot in both camps** a connection or sympathy with two opposing factions.

Latin *campus* was adopted for university grounds (originally at Princeton University), and is the ancestor of Old English *camp* '(enclosed) field' (appearing as **Camp-** or **Comp-** in place names), CAMPAIGN*, CHAMPION*, and probably SCAMP*.

campaign [17c. Old French *c(h)ampagne* (whence **champagne** and *champignon*), via Italian from Latin *campania*, from *campus*: see CAMP*] Open country, hence time the army spends 'in the field' away from its barracks; the manoeuvres practised, hence a series of military operations; a series of actions with a specific aim (18c); to organize or take part in one.

can¹ [Old English *cunnan*] To know (–19c); to know how to (ME), hence **1** to have the ability, power, or opportunity to (ME); to be likely to; to be allowed to (19c, now often replacing *may*: see MAIN) **2** to learn or study (ME, surviving in the variant **con**).

The original sense survives in Scots **canny** clever, prudent (whence **uncanny** strange, eerie), and COUTH. Related to CUNNING, KEEN, **ken** to make known (OE–17c); to know (now Scots), your range of knowledge (*beyond our ken*), **kith** knowledge (OE–15c), hence the country and the people you know, surviving in **kith and kin** your country, later your friends and family, now usually just your family, and to **know**.

can² [Old English *canne*, perhaps ultimately from Latin *canna*: see CANE*] A container for liquids, now specifically a metal one, hence **1** one for preserving food or drink (19c, *US*), hence **(a)** to preserve food etc. in one, hence **canned** prerecorded (*canned laughter*, *c*.1900) **(b)** prison (early 20c, *US*) **(c)** a protective jacket for the fuel element in a nuclear reactor (1940s) **2** a bin (*trash can*, 19c, US).

Can is replacing **tin** in sense 1 as aluminium replaces tin or tin plate, especially for drinks cans; the Australians still use **tinny** for a can of beer.

cancel [15c. Old French, from Latin *cancellare*, from *cancelli* 'lattice, barrier' (whence CHANCELLOR*)] To cross out, originally by crossed lines, hence **1** to invalidate a document, now especially a ticket, by marking, tearing, etc.; to annul a contract; to reverse an instruction (16c); to call off an action or event **2** to cross out a common factor from each side of an equation (16c), hence **cancel out** to neutralize an effect (17c).

cancer [OE. Latin, translating Greek *karkinos* 'crab, creeping ulcer'] **1 Cancer** a constellation said to represent a crab that Hercules crushed; the sign of the zodiac originally corresponding to this; someone born under it (19c) **2** a malignant tumour (from the crablike pattern of distended veins around it), hence an evil that spreads like one (17c, cf. *canker* below).

Latin *cancer* produced French *chancre* adopted for a syphilitic ulcer, having produced **canker** a tumour (ME–17c), later applied to various kinds of ulcer and disease or to an evil or corrupting influence.

candid [17c. (Via French from) Latin *candidus*, from *candere* 'to be white, to glisten'] White (–19c); pure, clear, innocent; fair, unbiased; sincere, frank; of a photograph: unposed, informal (1920s), hence **candid camera** for taking informal photographs, often secretly (1930s), later the name of a US television show where hidden cameras filmed people's reactions to artificial situations.

Latin *candidus* produced **candidate** [via *candidatus* 'white-robed', because those seeking office wore white] and **candour**. Descendants of *candere* include **candida** a yeastlike white fungus, **candle**, **chandelier**, **chandler** originally a candle-maker or seller, **incandescent**, and INCENDIARY*.

candy [16c. Short for Middle English **sugar candy**, via Old French from Arabic *sukkar* (see SUGAR*) + *qandī*, ultimately from Sanskrit *khanda* 'fragment'] (To produce) crystallized sugar; to coat, preserve, or sweeten with it, hence a sweet or sweets collectively (19c); now often someone/something decorative (*eye/arm candy*). **Candy stripe** (19c, *US*) came from a popular kind of striped candy.

cane [ME. Old French, from Latin *canna*, from Greek *kanna*, *kannē*, of Semitic origin] The hollow stem of certain plants; the solid stem of others, hence **1** a length of cane for inflicting punishment (16c), to punish (as if) with one (17c) **2** a walking stick, originally one made of Malacca cane (17c) **3** to weave canes into baskets etc. (17c).

Cane produced the surname **Cain(e)**, **Ka(y)ne** a tall, thin person or someone who gathered canes. Latin *canna* produced Spanish *canasta* adopted for a game played with two packs (a 'basketful') of cards [via Latin *canistrum* 'basket', whence also **canister** originally a wicker container], Italian *cannelloni*, **cannon**, **canyon**, and CHANNEL* (all with the underlying sense 'tube'), **caramel** [via French and Spanish from Provençal *canamel* 'sugar cane'], and probably CAN².

cannibal [16c. Spanish *Canibales* (plural), a variant of *Caribes*, from Arawak *carib*] A member of the Carib, who inhabited the Antilles and neighbouring S American coastal regions at the time of the Spanish conquest and were said to eat humans, hence a person who eats another; an animal that eats its own species (18c); **cannibalize** to use one thing as a source of parts for another (1940s).

Carib produced **Caribbean** and perhaps **Caliban**, the name of Shakespeare's subhuman character in *The Tempest*, who may be based on fanciful travellers' tales of the Carib.

cant [16c. Latin *cantus* 'song' and *cantare* 'to sing', both from *canere* 'to sing, play, or chant'] Singing (–18c); to sing or chant (–19c), hence (perhaps from the singing of religious mendicants) **1** to whine or beg (–19c); a whining way of speaking (17c) **2** (to use) words repeated mechanically, like a religious chant or a beggar's plea; (to use) beggars', later any, slang or jargon; (to use) hypocritically pious language (17c). Cf *patter* (at PATERNOSTER).

Latin *canere*'s descendants include ACCENT, **accentor** a genus of songbirds, **cantata**, **canticle**, **canto**, **cantor**, **chant** [via French *chanter* 'to sing', whence also **shanty** a sailors' song], **descant**, **enchant** [via French from Latin *incantare*, whence also **incantation**], **incentive** [Latin *incentivus* 'setting the tune'], and **recant** [Latin *recantare*, literally 'to sing or call back'].

canteen [18c. French *cantine* from Italian *cantina* 'cellar', probably from *canto* 'corner, nook', from Latin *cant(h)us* 'rim, iron tyre', probably of Celtic origin]

A military shop for provisions, hence **1** a set of cooking or eating utensils, or a flask, originally for soldiers (19c) **2** a cafeteria in a factory, school, etc. (19c), hence **canteen culture** reactionary attitudes passed informally from experienced personnel (originally in the police force) to new recruits (1980s).

Latin *cant(h)us* is the ancestor of **cant** to bevel, slope, or tilt, of French *canton* a corner, hence a 'corner' of land, a district, whence **cantonment** a military encamptment, of **chamfer** [via French *chant* 'edge' (from *cant(h)us*) + *fraindre* 'to break' (from Latin *frangere*: see FRACTION*)], and probably of **decant**.

canvass [16c. Variant of Middle English **canvas** 'coarse hemp cloth', from Old Norman French *canevas*, ultimately from Latin *cannabis* 'hemp', from Greek *kannabis*] To toss someone in a canvas sheet (–17c), later to discuss (perhaps from the notion of tossing ideas about); to discuss doing something; to seek support for it; to seek votes or custom; to ask someone's opinions or voting intentions (17c).

Latin *cannabis* was adopted for Indian hemp, or the drug prepared from it.

capable [16c. French, from Latin *capabilis*, from *capere* 'to take or hold' (ancestor of CATCH*)] Able to take in, capacious; able to take in mentally (–17c); able to do something, hence **1** good, bad, or cheeky enough to do something **2** competent, efficient, able (17c).

capital [ME. French, from Latin *capitalis*, from *caput* 'head'] (To do with) the head, top, or beginning (–17c), hence **1** principal, chief (*capital city*) **2** at the head of a page etc., hence **capital letter** beginning a name or sentence (17c) **3** involving the loss of your head, hence your life (*capital punishment/offence*, 15c) **4** stock, money, etc. to start a business (16c, cf. PRINCIPAL); accumulated or invested wealth, hence **capitalism** the system of using private capital (18c); **capitalize** to convert income or assets into capital; to turn something to your advantage **5** top class, excellent (18c).

Latin *capitalis* is the ancestor of CATTLE*. *Caput*'s descendants include **biceps**, **triceps**, and **quadriceps**, muscles with two, three, and four 'heads' or points of attachment, **cabbage** a brassica that forms a head, CADET*, **cape** a headland, **capital** the top of a column [via Old French from Latin *capitellum*, literally 'little head'], **Capitol**, CAPITULATE*, **caprice**, CAPTAIN*, **decapitate**, PRECIPITATE*, and perhaps CHAPEL* and CHAPTER: see also CORPORAL.

capitulate [16c. Medieval Latin *capitulare*, from Latin *capitulum* 'heading, chapter', from *caput* 'head'] To draw up under headings; to draw up articles of agreement (–19c) or terms of surrender (17c); to surrender.

Medieval Latin *capitulare* produced **recapitulate** to repeat the main points, to summarize, shortened to **recap**. Latin *caput* is the ancestor of CAPITAL*.

captain [ME. Old French *capitain* from Latin *capitaneus*, from *caput* 'head'] A leader, hence **1** an officer in the armed services, police, etc.; a naval officer commanding a ship (16c), hence the master of any ship (17c); a foreman or supervisor; the leader of a sports team (19c); the chief pilot of a civil aircraft (1920s) **2** to be captain, to lead (16c).

Old French *capitain* replaced *chevetaine* [also from Latin *capitaneus*], whence **chieftain**, its spelling influenced by **chief** [Old French *ch(i)ef* 'head, leader', also ultimately from Latin *caput*]. Old French *ch(i)ef* produced *chef* (at COOK) and MIS-CHIEF*; Latin *caput* is the ancestor of CAPITAL*.

caption [ME. Latin *captio*, from *capere* 'to take, seize' (ancestor of CATCH*)] Seizing, capture; legal seizure or arrest (15c); a warrant for this; a statement at the head of it saying where, when, and by whose authority it was issued (17c), hence a heading of a chapter, article, etc. (18c, *US*); a title or short explanation of an illustration (19c, *US*); a film or television subtitle (1920s).

car [ME. Norman French *carre* from Latin *carrus*, from Gaulish *carros* 'cart, wagon'] Any wheeled vehicle (–18c), later specifically a ceremonial or passenger vehicle, hence **1** the passenger compartment of a balloon, airship, or lift (18c) **2 (motor) car** an automobile (19c).

　　Latin *carrus* is the ancestor of CAREER, **carry** [via Old Norman French *charier*, whence also **carriage** the act, means, or way of carrying], CHARGE*, and CHARIOT*. Related to **carpenter** [via French from late Latin *carpentarius (artifex)* 'carriage (maker)', from *carpentum* 'carriage'].

caravan [15c. Via French or Italian from Persian *kārvān*] A group of travellers and pack-animals in desert or hostile regions; a group of vehicles travelling together (17c); a covered wagon or carriage (shortened to **van**, 19c); a mobile home used by Gypsies, showmen, or, later, holidaymakers (19c).

　　Van came to mean **1** a closed railway truck **2** a vehicle for prisoners **3** a vehicle for carrying light goods or making service calls.

card [ME. French *carte* from Latin *c(h)arta*: see CARTEL*] A playing card, hence **1** a (printed) piece of stiff paper (*birthday/business/cigarette/index card*, 16c), hence **(a)** the list of races at a meeting, formerly printed on a card (19c) **(b)** a small piece of plastic with information embossed or encoded on it (*credit/phone card*, 1960s); a printed circuit board resembling one (*SIM card*, 1980s) **2 discard** to reject a card from a hand (16c), hence to get rid of **3 card(board)** the material itself (19c) **4** a person of a certain kind (*knowing old card*, 19c, perhaps from phrases such as *good/ doubtful card* referring to playing cards likely/unlikely to win), hence an amusing or eccentric one.

cardinal [Old English, ultimately from Latin *cardinalis* 'acting as a hinge', hence 'chief, principal', from *cardo* 'hinge'] **1** one of the chief dignitaries of the Roman Catholic church, who wear scarlet robes, hence applied to various red flowers, birds, insects, etc. (16c) and to the colour (19c) **2** chief, principal (15c): **cardinal numbers** one, two, etc., as opposed to the ordinal numbers first, second, etc. (16c); **cardinal points** of the compass, north, south, east, and west (16c).

career [16c. French *carrière* from Italian *carriera*, ultimately from Latin *carrus*: see CAR*] A racecourse, a tilting ground (–18c), hence **1** a short gallop, a charge (–17c); to rush wildly (17c) **2** a course, path, or road (17c); your course through life (19c); (your progress in) a profession; dedicated to this (*career diplomat*, 1920s).

carouse [16c. From German *gar aus trinken* 'to drink up'] **To drink/quaff carouse** to drink the whole glass (–17c), hence *carouse* to drink a glass at one go; (to take part in) a noisy drinking party (17c).

carousel [17c. Via French from Italian *carosello* 'tilting match', of unknown origin] A tournament where knights took part in mounted games; a merry-go-round with galloping horses, hence a circular conveyor belt for luggage at an airport (1960s); a rotating holder for photographic slides; **carousel fraud** in which goods are repeatedly imported and exported, the perpetrator claiming, but not paying, VAT each time (*c.*2000).

carpet [ME. Via Old French or medieval Latin from obsolete Italian *carpita* 'woollen counterpane', ultimately from Latin *carpere* 'to pluck, to pull to pieces', also 'to slander'] A fabric used for bedspreads or tablecloths; a thicker (patterned) one used as a floor covering (15c); something thought to resemble this (*carpet of snow/flowers*, 16c). Hence **1** to reprimand (19c, because servants were summoned to the carpeted parlour for the purpose), whence, probably, **on the carpet** and the military **on the mat** (both *c.*1900) **2 carpet-bagger** a profiteer or political opportunist (originally a northerner in the southern states after the American Civil War, carrying his belongings in a **carpet bag** made of thick patterned material).

Latin *carpere* produced **excerpt** and **scarce** [both via Latin *excerpere* 'to pluck out'], and influenced the development of **carp** [Old Norse *karpa* 'to brag'] to speak, say, or tell (ME–16c); to whinge or find fault.

carrion [ME. Old Norman French *caroi(g)ne*, ultimately from Latin *caro* 'flesh'] A corpse or carcass (–18c); rotting flesh, refuse.

Old Norman French *caroi(g)ne* also meant 'a cantankerous woman', and produced **crone** [via early Dutch *caroonje*, *croonje* 'carcass, old ewe']. Latin *caro's* descendants include **carnage, carnal, carnation** (at CLOVE), **carnival** (at SHRIVE), **carnivore** [with Latin *vorare* 'to swallow', whence **devour** and **voracious**], **charnel house**, and **incarnate** [Latin *incanari* 'to be made flesh'].

cart [ME. Old Norse *kartr*] A chariot or carriage (–17c); a farm or goods vehicle, originally distinguished from a wagon by having two wheels instead of four, later by being smaller; a light carriage or van (19c). Hence **1** to carry in a cart; to move or carry roughly, unceremoniously, or with difficulty (19c) **2 in the cart** in trouble (19c, because condemned prisoners were taken to the gallows in a cart).

Cart produced the surnames **Carter** who carried goods in a cart, and **Cartwright** who made carts.

cartel [16c. Via French from Italian *cartello* 'placard', from *carta* 'paper, letter', from Latin *c(h)arta*, from Greek *khartēs* 'papyrus leaf'] **1 cartel of defiance** a written challenge **2** (a written agreement for) the exchange or ransom of prisoners (17c) **3** [via German *Kartell*] **(a)** a political agreement or coalition, originally that between the Conservatives and National Liberal parties in Germany (1887) **(b)** an agreement between suppliers to control the market (*c.*1900).

Italian *carta* produced **carton**, CARTOON, and CARTOUCHE*. Greek *khartēs* produced CARD, **cartography, cartulary, chart**, and CHARTER.

cartoon [16c. Italian *cartone*, literally 'large paper', from *carta*: see CARTEL*] A full-size drawing made as a design for a painting etc.; a drawing, originally full-page, in a newspaper (19c); a humorous or satirical drawing; a sequence of these in a strip; a film made by animating a sequence of drawings (early 20c).

cartouche [16c. Via French from Italian *cartoccio* 'paper case', from *carta*: see CARTEL*] **1** a paper or parchment case containing powder and shot, outlived by its variant **cartridge**, which came to mean a metal case containing powder and a bullet, hence a case and its contents for slotting into a machine (*ink cartridge*, *c.*1915) **2** a decorative panel or corbel representing an unrolled scroll (17c); an ornate scroll-shaped frame (18c); a frame containing a name in Egyptian hieroglyphics (19c).

case¹ Strictly speaking, two words, both Middle English and from Latin *casus* 'a fall', from *cadere* 'to fall'] **I** [Directly from Latin *casus,* translating Greek *ptōsis*, applied by Aristotle (see ARTERY) to any derived, inflected, or extended form of a word] any form of a noun, adjective, or pronoun that shows its relationship to other words in the sentence; this relationship **II** [Via Old French *cas* 'an occurrence'] an event or incident (–16c, surviving in *in that/any case*, **in case** in the event); an incident with relevant facts and circumstances; an instance or example, hence **1** an instance of disease or injury; a person being treated by a doctor, social worker, etc.; a person of a specified kind (*a hard case*, 19c); an unusual person, a 'character' (*US*) **2** a lawsuit (16c); the arguments presented by one side; any set of arguments.

Latin *cadere*'s descendants include *accident* (at FORTUNE), **cadaver**, **cadence**, **cascade**, CASUAL*, **chance**, CHEAT*, CHUTE*, **coincide**, **decadent**, **decay**, **deciduous**, INCIDENT, OCCASION*, and **recidivist** [Latin *recidere* 'to fall again'].

case² [ME. Old French *c(h)asse*: see CASH*] **1** a container (*bookcase, display case, suitcase*); one of a pair for printer's type (16c), the top one holding the capitals, the lower one small letters, hence **upper/lower case** capital/small letters respectively **2** a protective covering (*seed/pillow case*); an animal's skin (16–18c), hence to skin an animal (16c, now chiefly N American), hence, probably, to examine closely (early 20c); to study premises before robbing them **3** the frame of a door, window, etc. (16c), hence **staircase** the walls, banisters, etc. supporting a flight of stairs (17c), the stairs with their banisters and landings; the rooms reached by a staircase (18c).

cash [16c. Old French *c(h)asse* or Italian *cassa* 'box', both from Latin *capsa*, from *capere* 'to hold' (ancestor of CATCH*)] A cash box (–18c); its contents, coins and banknotes; to exchange a cheque, token, etc. for cash (19c); **cash your chips** to exchange gambling chips for cash when leaving the casino, hence to die.

Descendants of Old French *c(h)asse* include CASE²*, **casket**, **cassette**, **chase** a frame for setting type, and **enchase** [via French *enchasser* 'to encase, to set jewels'] to ornament, engrave, or emboss, whence **chase** in the same senses. Latin *capsa* is the ancestor of **caisson**, **capsule**, **casement**, **cashier** someone who handles cash, CHASSIS*, and probably **capsicum**.

cashier [16c. Flemish *kasseren* from Old French *casser* 'to annul', ultimately from Latin *cassus* 'null' (see QUASH*)] To disband or dismiss troops (–18c); to dismiss someone from a position of authority, later specifically to dismiss a military or naval officer with disgrace (18c).

casino [18c. Italian, literally 'small house', from *casa* 'house', from Latin *casa* 'hut, cottage'] Italian *casino* came to mean a country house, hence, from the house parties held in them, a meeting-hall for dancing, music, and, later predominantly, gambling.

Italian *casa* was altered by British troops in World War II to **karzy** a lavatory. Latin *casa* is the ancestor of **chalet**, **chasuble** a clerical vestment [via Latin *casubla* 'hooded cloak', literally 'little cottage'], and French *chez*.

cask [16c. French *casque* or Spanish *casco* 'helmet', perhaps ultimately from Latin *quasssare* 'to shake to pieces': see QUASH*] **1** the helmet of a suit of armour, surviving in the 17c spelling **casque**, which came to mean a horny, helmet-like growth on a bird, insect, or reptile (18c) **2** a (wooden) barrel.

cassock [16c. French *casaque* 'long coat', from Italian *casacca* 'riding coat', probably from Turkic *kazak* 'vagabond, nomad' (ancestor of **Cossack** and **Kazakh**)] A soldier's long coat or cloak; a long coat or gown worn by both sexes, later especially by scholars, hence a priest's or chorister's robe (17c).

cast [ME. Old Norse *kasta*] Largely replaced by THROW, except in: **1** to throw away; what is thrown: (*outcast, castaway, worm cast*) **2** to place (*cast your vote/cast doubt on*), hence to calculate (from the idea of placing counters); to prepare a horoscope, hence (to make) a conjecture, surviving mainly in **forecast** (ME) **3** to shape using a mould or form (15c); (describing) what is made (*cast iron, plaster cast*) **4** to turn or twist (15c, cf. WARP*), hence **(a)** a squint **(b)** to turn a scale (16c, surviving in *casting vote*) **(c)** to make a loop or knot (16c), hence **cast on/off** in knitting (19c) **(d) castor** a swivelling wheel (18c) **5** to scatter (16c), hence **(a)** the distribution of dramatic roles; the actors given parts; to assign parts (18c) **(b) caster/castor** a perforated container for sprinkling sugar or spices (17c), hence **caster/castor sugar** (19c) **(c) broadcast** of seed: scattered rather than sown in rows (18c); to sow in this way (19c); to spread news etc. widely, especially by radio or television (1920s); (to take part in) a transmission, hence **narrowcasting** to a specified audience (1930s), *webcast* (at WEB), etc.

caste [16c. Spanish and Portuguese *casta* 'lineage, race, breed', feminine of *casto* 'pure, unmixed', from Latin *castus* 'pure, chaste'] **1** a race of people (–18c), hence **half-caste** (someone) of mixed race (18c, now considered offensive) **2** one of the hereditary classes in Hindu society (17c), hence a system of rigid social divisions (19c); a social class that keeps to itself; the status conferred by caste or class, hence **outcaste** someone outside the caste system; someone rejected by their peers (also as *outcast*, from CAST).

Latin *castus* is the ancestor of **castigate** [Latin *castigare*, literally 'to make chaste', whence also **chasten** and **chastise**], of **chaste**, and of **incest** [via Latin *incestum* 'unchastity'].

casual [ME. (Via Old French from) Latin *casualis*, from *casus* 'a fall': see CASE[1]*] Accidental, fortuitous, hence **1** unpredictable, irregular, occasional (15c); **casual labourer/worker/staff** taken on when needed (19c) **2** unplanned, random (17c); superficial, perfunctory (19c); nonchalant, unconcerned (early 20c); informal (1930s), hence **casuals** for informal wear (1940s).

Latin *casualis* produced **casualty** chance (15–19c), hence a chance event, an accident or disaster; the loss of a soldier by death, wounds, or desertion, hence someone killed or injured; something lost or destroyed (*a casualty of spending cuts*).

cataract [ME. Latin *cataracta* 'waterfall, floodgate, portcullis', from Greek *kataraktēs* 'down-rushing', from *katarassein* 'to rush or plunge down', from *arassein* 'to strike or smash'] **1** a portcullis or window grating (–19c, rare until the 17c); an opaque film over the lens of the eye (15c) **2** a waterfall, a torrent (16c).

catastrophe [16c. Via Latin from Greek *katastrophē* 'overturning, a sudden turn', from *strophē* 'turning' from *strephein* 'to turn'] The dénouement of a play, particularly a tragedy, hence **1** a disastrous outcome; a terrible accident (18c), hence **catastrophize** to perceive a situation as a disaster (1980s) **2** an event that overturns the accepted order of things (17c); a sudden or violent change in the earth's structure (19c).

Greek *strophe* was adopted for (the lines chanted during) a movement from right to left by a Greek chorus, followed by an opposite movement, the **antistrophe**: the two words came to mean the first and second forms respectively in a poem with two alternating metres. *Strephein*'s descendants include APOSTROPHE, **strepto-** twisted, having a twisted chain of molecules etc. (*streptococcus, streptomycin*), and perhaps STROP*.

catch [ME. Old French *chacier*, ultimately from Latin *captare* 'to try to catch', from *capere* 'to take'. The original past tense was *catched*: **caught** appeared in Middle English (becoming standard in the 19c), influenced by Old English *lachen* (past tense *laughte*) 'to seize or capture' (which *catch* replaced), surviving mainly in **latch** a fastening (ME) and **latch on to** to attach yourself to a person or idea (early 20c): its current past tense **latched** appeared in the 15c] To chase (–16c); to capture, trap, or entangle; to get involuntarily (*catch cold/fire*); what is caught. Hence **1** something that catches, a fastening; a snag **2 catch on** to grasp with your mind (16c, cf. CLEVER*); **catchy** of a tune: easy to remember (19c) **3** to reach or overtake (17c), to be in time for **4** to surprise someone doing something (17c) **5 catchment area** from which rainfall is collected (19c), or the users of a school, hospital, etc. are drawn (1950s).

Catch produced *Catchpole* (at POOL), and probably **ketch** a sailing boat. Latin *capere*'s descendants include **accept**, ANTICIPATION, CAPABLE, **capacious**, **capacity**, **capstan**, CAPTION, **capture**, CASE[2]*, CASH*, CATER*, CHASE*, CONCEIVE, COP*, **deceive**, **except**, **inception**, **incipient**, **intercept**, **municipal** [Latin *municipium* 'town', from *municeps* 'citizen', from *munus* 'public duty'], OCCUPY*, *participate* (at PART), **perceive** [Latin *percipere* 'to obtain, to grasp'], **precept**, PRINCIPAL*, RECEIVE*, **recover** [via French from Latin *recuperare* 'to take back', whence also **recuperate**], and **susceptible** [via Latin *suscipere* 'to take up'].

cater [ME. Shortening of **achatour** (–18c), from Old French *ac(h)ater* 'to buy', ultimately from Latin *captare*, from *capere* 'to take' (ancestor of CATCH*)] Someone who buys provisions, especially for a large household (–17c, superseded by **caterer**), hence to buy or supply provisions (16c), to supply and prepare food and drink for a large number of people or for a special occasion; to supply whatever someone wants (*cater for all tastes*, 17c).

catholic [ME. (Via Old French from) Latin *catholicus*, from Greek *katholikos* 'universal', from *holos* 'whole'] **1** [from Greek *katholikē ekklēsia* 'universal church', hence all Christians, later confined to 'true' believers (not heretics)] **(a)** (describing) the early church, and churches regarding themselves as its continuation: the Western church after the Eastern churches broke away, calling themselves **Orthodox** [ME, ultimately from Greek *orthos* 'straight, right' + *doxa* 'opinion, repute, glory', from *dokein* 'to think'], the Roman Catholic church after the Reformation, the Anglican church as opposed to Nonconformists **(b)** the community of Roman Catholic, Orthodox, and Protestant churches; all Christians **2** useful or interesting to a wide range of people (16c); interested in a wide range of things; eclectic, broadminded.

Greek *holos* is one parent of HOLOCAUST; *ekklēsia* produced **Eccles(-)** in place names [via a Celtic word adopted by the early, pagan Anglo-Saxons to name Romano-British settlements that had a Christian church], the Old Testament book **Ecclesiastes**, and **ecclesiastic**; *orthos* produced **ortho-** (*orthodontic, orthopaedic* at PEDAGOGUE); *doxa* produced **doxology**, **heterodox**, and **paradox**; *dokein* produced **dogma**, and is related to DOCTOR*.

cattle [ME. Old Norman French *catel*, variant of Old French *chatel*, ultimately from Latin *capitalis*: see CAPITAL*] Personal property, wealth, goods (–15c), hence **1** livestock, formerly including all farm animals, including poultry and bees, since the 17c increasingly restricted to bovine animals, hence a contemptuous term for people (16c) **2** an item of property (15–18c), outlived by **chattel** [ME, from Old French *chatel*], which also briefly meant 'property' and 'livestock'.

The identification of personal wealth with livestock is also found in Latin *pecu*: see PECULIAR.

caudle [ME. Old French *chaudel*, ultimately from Latin *calidus* 'warm', from *calere* 'to be warm'] A drink for invalids of warm gruel containing sugar, wine, and spice; to give one (17c), hence the dialect variant **coddle** to treat as an invalid, to treat indulgently or over-protectively (19c), also as **mollycoddle** [from *Molly* (a pet form of Mary) a milksop].

Coddle is recorded earlier meaning 'to simmer', but this may be a different word. Latin *calidus* produced **cauldron**, **chowder,** and **scald**; *calere* is the ancestor of CHAFE*.

cause [ME. Via Old French from Latin *causa* 'cause, lawsuit'] What makes something happen or exist; (to be) the reason or justification for something, especially an action (*have/show cause*), specifically for going to law; one party's case; the side of a question someone takes, a principle that you support.

Cause produced **because** [shortened from *by cause that* 'for the reason that']. Latin *causa* is the ancestor of **accuse** [via French from Latin *accusare*, from *ad cause* 'to the (legal) case'], **excuse** [via Latin *excusare*, literally 'to remove from accusation'], and RUSE*.

caution [ME. French, from Latin *cautio*, from *cavere, caut-* 'to take heed'] **1** security, bail, a guarantee (surviving in the US, as a Scottish legal term, and in **caution money** deposited as security for good behaviour, 19c) **2 (a)** a warning (16c), now especially an official warning of the consequences of future bad behaviour; to give somebody one (17c) **(b)** carefulness, prudence (17c); prudent foresight (largely replacing **precaution** [16c, from Latin *praecavere*, from *cavere*]); a prudent action, especially to avoid danger (17–19c, outlived by *precaution*).

A form of Latin *cavere* appears in schoolboy slang *cave!* 'look out!' and **keep cave** to act as lookout: another form, *caveat* [literally 'let him/her beware'], was adopted for a warning or proviso.

cavalcade   [16c. French, from Italian *cavalcata*, from *cavalcare* 'to ride', ultimately from Latin *caballus* 'horse' (ancestor of CHIVALRY*)] A ride on horseback; a mounted raid, hence a company of riders (17c); a procession of riders, later including vehicles (whence **motorcade** a procession of motor vehicles, *c*.1910); a dramatic series of things or events.

cede   [16c. Latin *cedere, cess-* 'to go, to retreat'] To give way or yield to (–18c), hence to give up, especially territory (18c).

Descendants of Latin *cedere* include **abscess**, ACCESS*, **antecedent** [via French from Latin *antecedere* 'to go before', whence **ancestor**], **cease**, **concede**, **decease** [Latin *decedere* 'to go away', hence 'to die or retire', whence also **predecessor**], **exceed**, **intercede**, **precede**, PROCEED*, RECEDE*, **secede**, **succeed** [Latin *succedere* 'to go after', later 'to get close to, to do well'].

ceiling   [ME. From **ceil** 'to line with wood or plaster' (–17c), perhaps ultimately from Latin *caelum* 'heaven' (whence **celestial**) or *celare* 'to hide' (whence OCCULT*)] The action of plastering or panelling a room; the materials used to line a room or a ship's hull (15c) or to hide roof-beams (16c), hence a room's upper surface; an upper limit, originally the maximum altitude at which an aircraft can fly (early 20c); the altitude of the lowest cloud layer (1930s).

cell   [ME. (Via Old French from) Latin *cella* 'storeroom, chamber'] A religious house dependent on a larger one; a hermit's dwelling; a room, originally for one, in a monastery or prison, hence **1** a compartment or cavity (15c); one of the basic structural units of a living being (17c, first described as tiny bladders in plant tissue: their significance was realized in the 19c); a compartment containing electrodes for generating electricity, usually one of several in a battery (19c) **2** a space marked out by lines (19c); a box for information in a table or spreadsheet (1950s), hence a unit of data storage in a computer **3** a small group forming part of a larger (political) organization (1920s) **4** the area covered by one short-wave radio transmitter in a network (1970s), hence **cellular telephone** a mobile radio-telephone using such a network, shortened to **cellphone**.

Latin *cella* is the ancestor of **cellar** a storehouse (ME–19c); an underground storeroom, hence a wine store or someone's stock of wines, and of some instances of the surnames **Kellner** and **Seller** the steward of a wine cellar.

census   [17c. Latin, from *censere* 'to assess or judge'] A tax, especially a poll tax (–19c, replacing Middle English *cense*, also from Latin *census*), hence the registration of citizens and property, usually for taxation, in ancient Rome; an official count of a population (18c); any systematic count or survey.

Latin *census* is the probable source [via early Dutch] of **excise** a tax, specifically one on goods for the domestic market, hence the government department that collects it. Latin *censere* produced **censor** originally a Roman magistrate who carried out censuses and acted as a guardian of public morals, and **censure**.

centre   [ME. (French, from) Latin *centrum*, from Greek *kentron* 'ox goad, sharp point, point of a pair of compasses', from *kentein* 'to prick'] The mark made by the stationary point of a pair of compasses (–16c), hence **1** the middle **2** a point around which something revolves (15c), around which things gather or are grouped (17c), or from which something goes out (18c); a place where facilities are concentrated (*shopping/training centre*, 19c, *US*) **3** someone/something in the centre (16c), e.g. the filling of a chocolate etc., a player or position in midfield **4** to place in the centre (16c); to focus on, be concentrated in, or revolve round the centre (17c); to pass a ball towards the middle (19c).

Greek *kentron* is the ancestor of **concentrate**, **concentric**, ECCENTRIC, and **epicentre** [with Greek *epi* 'on, near, above'].

century [ME. Latin *centuria* 'a group of one hundred', from *centum* 'a hundred'] **1** a company in the Roman army, originally of a hundred men (earlier in **centurion**, its leader) **2** a group of a hundred things (16c), hence **(a)** originally as *a century of years*, a period of a hundred years (17c) **(b)** one hundred dollars or pounds (19c) **(c)** a score of a hundred in a game (19c).

Latin *centum* is the ancestor of **cent** a hundred (surviving in **per cent**), later a hundredth, hence (a coin worth) a hundredth of an American dollar or of the principal unit of some other currencies, of **centenary**, **centennial**, and **centi-** a hundred or hundredth (*centipede*, *centimetre*).

cesspool [17c. Probably an alteration, influenced by *pool*, of ME *suspiral* 'vent, water pipe, settling tank', from Old French *souspirail* 'air-hole', from Latin *suspirare* 'to breathe deeply', from *spirare* 'to breathe'] A trap under a drain to catch solids, later an underground tank for liquid waste and sewage.

Cess in *cesspool* produced **cesspit** a pit for sewage; a dirty or immoral place. Latin *spirare* is the ancestor of SPIRIT*.

chafe [ME. French *chauffer* 'to heat', ultimately from Latin *calefacere*, from *calere* 'to be warm'] To make or become warm (surviving in **chafing dish**), hence **1** to inflame someone's feelings (–18c); to make or become annoyed (15c) **2** to rub something to warm it (15c); to wear, damage, or injure by rubbing (16c); to rub against something (17c).

French *chauffer* produced **chauffeur** 'fireman, stoker', adopted for a motorist (some early cars being steam-powered). Latin *calere* is the ancestor of **calorie**, CAUDLE*, and **nonchalant** [from Old French *non* 'not' + *chalant* 'being concerned'].

chair [ME. Old French *chaiere* from Latin *cathedra* 'seat, bishop's throne', from Greek *kathedra*] A seat for one person, hence **1** one for someone important: **(a)** the seat from which a professor delivers lectures, hence a professorship (19c) **(b)** a bishop's throne (15c), hence the office or authority of a bishop (17c): cf. *see* and *cathedral* below **(c)** (the seat of) someone presiding at a meeting etc. (17c); to preside (1920s). Hence **chairman**, **chairwoman** (both 17c), *chairwoman* being rare until the 19c: both changed by 1970s feminists to **chairperson**, or shortened to *chair* **(d)** a bard's seat at an Eisteddfod (19c) **2** something resembling a chair, e.g. a socket on a railway sleeper to hold a rail (19c).

See [Anglo-Norman French *se(d)*, ultimately from Latin *sedes* 'seat', from *sedere* 'to sit': see SESSION*] followed a similar path: a seat (ME–16c); a bishop's throne (–19c), hence (the area under) his jurisdiction or authority. Latin *cathedra* is the ancestor of **cathedral** to do with a bishop's throne or see, hence **cathedral**

(church) housing the bishop's throne, and of French *chaise*, adopted for a light carriage and in *chaise longue* [literally 'long chair'].

chalk [Old English *cealc*, ultimately from Latin *calx* 'lime, limestone', probably from Greek *khalix* 'pebble'] Lime (–16c, rare in Middle English); a soft form of limestone; a piece of it for writing, marking, rubbing on a billiard cue, etc. (15c); to do so; a chalk mark, especially to record a score (16c), hence **by a long chalk** by a wide margin.

Old English *cealc* appears in place names as **Chal-**. Latin *calx* is the ancestor of *calcium* (at ALUMINIUM), **calculate** [via Latin *calculus* 'pebble (on an abacus)', itself adopted for a method of calculating], and **causey** [via Old Norman French *cauciée* 'road paved with limestone'] a mound, embankment, or dam (ME–18c); a road on top of one (perhaps the original sense); a raised path, also as *causey-way*, shortened to **causeway**.

challenge [ME. Old French *chalengier* from Latin *calumniari*, from *calumnia* **calumny**] (To bring) an accusation or charge (–17c); to call to account, hence **1** a sentry's call for a password etc.; to give it (18c) **2** (to issue) an invitation to take part in a duel, contest, etc.; a test of your abilities and character (1950s), hence **challenged** lacking a physical or mental attribute (*visually challenged*, 1990s, *US*) **3** to dispute, deny, or object to; such an objection, especially to a juror.

chamber [ME. French *chambre* from Latin *camera* 'vault, arched chamber', from Greek *kamara* 'object with an arched cover'] A room, hence **1** a bedroom or private room; a judge's private office (17c); **chambers** a suite of lawyers' offices **2 (a)** a reception room or hall in an official residence **(b)** (the meeting-hall of) a (legislative) assembly (cf. *camera* below) **(c)** the treasury of a government or corporation (cf. *chamberlain* below) **3** a compartment or cavity (15c); one for ammunition in a gun (16c).

Chamber may be the source of *chum* (at COMRADE). Latin *camera* was adopted for a legislative chamber in Italy or Spain; the treasury of the papal curia, or (a building with) an arched or vaulted roof; it is also found in **bicameral** having two legislative chambers, in *camera obscura* [literally 'dark chamber'] a darkened box or room into which an image of its surroundings is projected through a lens, shortened to *camera* and applied to any apparatus for taking pictures, and in **in camera** in a judge's chamber. It is the ancestor of French *cabaret* a French inn, re-borrowed for a nightclub with entertainment, hence the entertainment, **chamberlain** a personal servant, literally a servant of the bedchamber (whence the surname **Chambers** and Scottish **Chalmers**), later an officer managing a royal or noble household, and COMRADE*.

champion [ME. Old French *c(h)ampion* from medieval Latin *campio* 'fighter', from Latin *campus*: see CAMP*] A brave, skilful fighter, hence **1** one who fights on someone else's behalf; to do so (19c) **2** the overall winner of a contest or competition (18c), hence excellent, splendid (19c, *N English*).

Old French **Campion** and **Champion** survive as surnames: **Kemp**, also from Latin *campus*, has the same meaning. **Campion**, the flower, may be related, as some species are said to have been used for victors' garlands in the ancient world.

chancellor [ME. Via Old French from late Latin *cancellarius* a court usher who stood at the barrier separating the public from the judges, later a secretary, from Latin *cancelli* 'lattice, barrier'] The monarch's secretary, later applied to various high-ranking officials. Hence **chancellery** the position of chancellor (ME), his department or staff (17c); shortened to **chancery**, which was also applied to the Court of the Lord Chancellor, now a division of the High Court of Justice.

Latin *cancelli* produced CANCEL and **chancel** the (railed-off) part of a church near the altar.

channel [ME. Old French *chanel* from Latin *canalis* 'pipe, groove, channel', from *canna*: see CANE*] The course of a waterway; (to make) a groove or tube for liquid to flow along, hence **1** a navigable course through hazards (16c), hence **(a)** a route for information etc. (*the proper channels*, 16c); a path for an electrical current or signal (19c), a frequency band for telecommunications or broadcasting (1920s); a radio or television station (1950s) **(b)** to direct something along a route (17c) **2** a strip of water between two pieces of land or larger bodies of water (16c) **3** a groove or furrow, e.g. in architecture (17c).

Latin *canalis* fathered **canal** a pipe or tube for liquid; an artificial watercourse.

chaos [15c. French or Latin, from Greek *khaos* 'void, abyss'] A chasm or abyss, a vast empty space (–17c); the infinite space and formless matter supposed to have existed before the ordered universe (16c), hence a state of confusion or disorder; the behaviour of a system which, although obeying certain rules, appears random because of its extreme sensitivity to conditions (1970s).

The Flemish chemist J. B. van Helmont (1577–1644) adopted Greek *khaos* for an occult principle thought to exist in all matter. As the sound of Greek *kh* is similar to Dutch and Flemish *g*, the word came into English as **gas**: the current sense produced **gasoline**, originally a kind of lighting and heating oil, now the N American word for petrol and often shortened to *gas*.

chapel [ME. Old French *chapele* from medieval Latin *cappella* 'small cloak', from Latin *cappa* 'hood, hooded cloak', probably from *caput* 'head'. The first *chapele* housed half of St Martin's cloak: see *Martin* (at MARTIAL)] A place for Christian worship other than a parish church or cathedral, hence **1** one in an institution or private household **2** a place for private worship, especially in a large church or cathedral **3** a non-Anglican place of worship, originally a Roman Catholic church, now usually a Nonconformist one (17c).

Medieval Latin *cappella* produced *cappellani*, the custodians of St Martin's cloak, whence **chaplain** originally the clergyman of a chapel, and the surname **Chaplin** a chaplain or his servant. Latin *cappa* is the ancestor of Italian *a capella* [literally 'in chapel style'] adopted describing unaccompanied singing, **cap**, **cape** a cloak, **Capuchin** a member of an order of Franciscan friars who wore pointed hoods [via Italian *cappuccino* 'someone wearing a *cappucio*, a hood or cowl': **cappuccino** was later applied to espresso coffee with milk, the colour of a Capuchin's habit], CHAPERONE, COPE[2], and ESCAPE*.

chaperone [ME. French *chaperon*, literally 'small hood', from *chape* 'hood', from Latin *cappa*: see CHAPEL] A hood or cap (–19c), hence someone who accompanies a young unmarried woman (later some other vulnerable person), sheltering their charge as a hood shelters the face (18c).

charisma

chapter [ME. French *chapitre* from Latin *capitulum*, literally 'small head', from *caput* 'head' (ancestor of CAPITAL*)] A main division of a book, specifically one of the books of the Bible, hence **1** a scriptural passage or lesson read at certain Roman Catholic services; part of a monastic rule read to the assembled monks or canons, hence an assembly or the body of canons, monks, or members of an order of knighthood; a local branch of a society (19c, *US*) **2** part of a history, a period or sequence of events (17c).

char [Old English *cerr* (noun), *cierran* (verb)] To turn (–17c); a turn (–18c, surviving in **ajar**, literally 'on the turn', 17c); a spell or piece of work (–17c: cf. TURN*); an odd job (ME, now largely replaced by its variant **chore**, 18c); to do chores (16–19c), whence **char(lady/woman)** who does so; *char* to be one.

character [ME. Via French and Latin from Greek *kharaktēr* 'marking tool', from *kharassein* 'to cut or engrave' (probably the ancestor of **gash**)] A distinctive mark, hence **1** a letter or symbol (15c) **2** a distinctive feature or quality (16c, largely replaced by 17c **characteristic**); those that make something what it is (17c); the effect they produce (*full of character*); a person with particular characteristics (*a flamboyant/shady character*), hence a fictional (17c) or unusual (18c) person **3** to engrave, inscribe, or write (16–18c); to portray or describe, a description (17c), hence (combined with sense 2); a written summary of someone's qualities; (good) reputation; moral strength (18c).

charge [ME. French, from late Latin *car(ri)care* 'to load', from Latin *carrus* CAR*] To burden, a burden (–18c), hence **1** to load or fill ready for use; what is needed to do so (17c) **2** (to burden with) a duty or responsibility; the responsibility of minding someone/something; the person or thing minded (16c), hence **in someone's charge** in their care, **in charge** taking care of, in control (19c) **3** (to burden with) a financial liability: **(a)** to demand a price for something (18c); the price (19c) **(b)** to put something on an account (19c), hence **charge account/card 4** to lay blame on, to accuse; an accusation (15c) **5** to attack by rushing at; such an attack (16c); to rush carelessly (19c).

Latin *carricare* produced Spanish **cargo**, **caricature** [via Italian *caricare* 'to load', also 'to exaggerate'], and **discharge** [via Old French from late Latin *discar(ri)care*] to unload or release (*discharge a cargo/gun/bankrupt, discharge from a job/hospital*); to fulfil an obligation (thus relieving yourself of it); the act of discharging or being discharged; what is released, a flow.

chariot [ME. French, from *char* 'cart', ultimately from Latin *carrus* CAR*] Any wheeled vehicle, specifically a ceremonial carriage; later [by confusion with Old French *charet* 'small *char*'] a two-wheeled vehicle used in warfare and racing.

Old French *char* produced French *char à bancs*, literally 'cart with benches' (see BANK³), whence **charabanc**.

charisma [17c. Christian Latin, from Greek *kharisma*, from *kharis* 'favour, grace'] A gift from God, especially a talent (surviving in the **charismatic** churches, featuring gifts such as speaking in tongues), hence the 'talent' of leadership [1930s, via German]; a magnetic personality (1960s).

Greek *kharis* produced **Eucharist** [via Old French and Latin from Greek *eukharistos* 'grateful, thankful', from *kharizesthai* 'to show favour'].

charity [OE. Via French from Latin *caritas*, from *carus* 'dear'] Christian love towards others; kindness, natural goodness (ME), hence **1** generosity to the needy; money or help given to them; an organization set up to help them (16c) **2** a benevolent or tolerant attitude towards others (15c).

Latin *carus* produced **caress** and French *cher* 'dear', whence **cherish** literally 'to treat as dear'.

charm [ME. Via French from Latin *carmen* 'song, verse, incantation'] (The reciting of) a spell, hence **1** to use a spell; to put one on someone/something; to enthral, captivate, or delight (15c); an indefinable power of doing so (16c); **charms** (sexually) attractive features **2** an object having magical powers, a talisman or amulet (16c); a trinket worn on a bracelet (19c).

charter [ME. Via French from Latin *chartula*, from *c(h)arta*: see CARTEL*] **1** a document from the monarch or legislature, hence **(a)** to grant or establish by a charter **(b)** a right or privilege granted by one or, later, publicly acknowledged (16c); (to give) permission or licence to do something **(c) chartered** being a member of a professional body having a Royal charter (*chartered accountant*, 19c) **2** a written contract between individuals, hence **charter-party** [via French from medieval Latin *charta partita* 'divided charter'] an agreement written in duplicate on one sheet of paper which is then divided so that the two parts can be fitted together to prove authenticity (15c, cf. COUNTERPART, *deed poll* at POLL, *indenture* at INDENT), shortened to *charter* and confined to an agreement to hire a ship (16c), later also a vehicle or aircraft, hence to hire one (19c); to do with such a hiring (*charter flight*, 1920s); the conveyance hired (1950s).

chase [ME. Old French *chacier*, ultimately from Latin *capere* 'to take' (ancestor of CATCH*)] **1** to drive away **2** to pursue or hunt; pursuit, hence **(a) the chase** hunting with hounds **(b)** a tract of land reserved for hunting (15c, surviving in place names) **(c) steeplechase** a horse race over fences, originally between fox-hunters riding across country between church steeples (18c, often shortened to *chase*); a foot race over obstacles (19c) **(d) wild goose chase** a mounted game in which competitors follow the leader at intervals, like wild geese in flight (16c), hence an erratic course, later, the origin having been forgotten, a hopeless pursuit (like hunting wild geese on horseback); a hopeless search (17c).

Old French *chacier* produced **chassé** a gliding dance step in which one foot displaces the other (whence **sashay** to perform a chassé, to walk with attitude, and probably **shey-shey** a shuffling Jamaican dance), and PURCHASE.

chassis [17c. French, ultimately from Latin *capsa* 'box': see CASH*] A (sliding) window frame (–18c, its variant, **sash**, survives); the sliding frame of a mounted gun (19c); the main frame of a vehicle (*c.*1900), hence the body of a person or animal (1930s); a mounting for the parts of an electronic device.

cheap [Old English *cēap*, ultimately from Latin *caupo* 'small trader, innkeeper'] Trade, buying and selling (–ME), hence **1** a market place (surviving in place names, e.g. *Cheapside*, *Chepstow*) **2** a bargain, especially a good one (–16c), hence **(a)** inexpensive (15c); charging low prices (16c); costing less than usual (18c) **(b)** of poor quality (16c); achieved without much effort; contemptible, hence **cheapskate** a mean person [19c, US, from *skate* a worn-out horse, of unknown origin], whence *cheap* mean, stingy (1930s, US).

Old English *cēap* produced **chapman** a trader (surviving as a surname), later a customer, shortened to **chap**, now meaning a man or boy, and perhaps **chop** in *chop and change*. Related to the names **Chippendale** and **Chipperfield**, to **Chipping** in place names, to **Copeland** and **Copeman** [both from Old Norse *kaup*], and to **Kremer** 'shopkeeper', the original name of a distinguished 15c Flemish cartographer who much preferred the Latinized form **Mercator** [from *mercari*: see MARKET].

cheat [ME. From **escheat** 'land reverting to the feudal lord if a tenant has no eligible successor', from Old French, from Latin *excidere* 'to fall away', from *cadere* 'to fall' (ancestor of CASE[1*])] Land forfeited to or confiscated by the feudal lord; to claim land, especially unfairly, hence to deceive or swindle (16c); to break rules for your own advantage; someone who does (17c); to be unfaithful to your partner (1930s, *US*).

check [ME. Old French *eschec* via medieval Latin and Arabic from Persian *šāh* 'king'] Said in a chess game when a king is threatened; (to put the king in) this position (**checkmate** follows the same path from Persian *šāh māt* 'the king is dead'). Hence (because you must protect the king before doing anything else) to stop, obstruct, or restrain (15c); to stop and inspect something (17c), hence to verify; a means of doing so, hence **1** (**cheque** in British English) a counterfoil (18–19c); a form (with a counterfoil) instructing a bank to transfer funds (18c) **2** a receipt for something deposited; to deposit something (19c, US) **3 check in/out** to record entering or leaving (*c.*1920, *US*); **checkout** a payment desk in a supermarket (1960s).

Old French *eschec* produced **chess** and **exchequer** or **chequer** a chessboard (ME–19c), hence, because accounts were kept using counters on a squared cloth, a department dealing with royal or government revenues: a pub called **The Chequers** may once have been used to collect local taxes or distribute dole. Hence *chequer*, later also **check**, a squared pattern. Persian *māt* 'dead' produced Spanish *matador*, **matt** lustreless, dull, and *mate* in **stalemate** when a chess player cannot move except into check, hence a deadlock [with Anglo-Norman French *estale* 'fixed position', from Old French *estal*: see INSTALMENT].

cheek [Old English *cēoce*] The jaw or jawbone (–ME), hence **1** the side of the face, hence **cheeks (a)** side pieces (ME) **(b)** the buttocks (17c) **2 (to give) cheek** to speak insolently (19c), hence *cheek* insolence; impudence, effrontery; **cheeky** impertinent, (playfully) disrespectful; amusing but mildly improper. Cf. JOWL.

Old English *cēoce* produced *acēocian* **choke** to suffocate or be suffocated by blocking or squeezing the throat, hence to smother; to obstruct or be obstructed.

cheer [ME. Via Old French and Latin from Greek *kara* 'head'] The face (–16c); the expression (–19c); the state of mind it shows (hence **wotcher**, an alteration of *what cheer?* 'how are you?'), especially a good mood, hence **1 cheerful** happy, optimistic; bright and pleasant; **cheery** in good spirits, genial (15c), considered 'a ludicrous word' by Johnson (see ACHE); **cheerless** gloomy, dispiriting (16c) **2 cheer (up)** to make or become more cheerful **3** (to give) a shout of approval or encouragement (17c).

cherry [ME. Anglo-Norman French *cherise*, from medieval Latin *ceresia*, ultimately from Greek *kerasos*] The fruit, hence **1** its tree; a related or similar tree; the wood of any of them (18c) **2** a young girl (19c); the hymen, virginity (perhaps from the idea of something small and sweet).

The form *cherry* came about because *cherise* was mistaken for a plural: something similar happened to **pease**, an earlier form (surviving in **pease pudding**) of **pea** [Old English *pise*, plural *pisan*, ultimately from Greek *pison*]. *Cherise* evolved into French **cerise** adopted meaning 'cherry red'. Greek *kerasos* is the ultimate ancestor of German **Kirsch** [short for *Kirschwasser* 'cherry water'].

chest [Old English *cest*, *cyst*, ultimately from Latin *cista*, from Greek *kistē* 'box' (ancestor of **cistern**)] A large, heavy box, hence **1** the strongbox or treasury of an institution (ME); its funds (16c) **2** the 'box' containing the heart and lungs (ME).

chestnut [16c. Old English *cisten*, via Old French from Latin *castanea*, from Greek *kastanea*. *Cisten* evolved into *chesten(-nut)*, shortened to *chesnut* or *chestnut*: the latter prevailed after being adopted by Johnson (see ACHE)] (The reddish-brown nut of) the sweet chestnut tree, hence **1 pull someone's chestnuts out of the fire** and **cat's paw**, from the fable of the monkey who, rather than burn himself, persuaded a cat to get roast chestnuts for him **2** (a horse of) a similar colour **3** the unrelated horse chestnut (because the nuts look similar); *horse* may come from the horseshoe-shaped scar left when a leaf falls, or because the Turks used the nuts to treat sick horses, but may simply mean 'large, coarse', as in *horse ant/mussel* etc. **4** a hard brown lump, about the size of the nut, on a horse's leg (18c) **5** an old, stale joke or story (19c, *US*), said to come from a play in which one character tells a story involving a cork tree, interrupted by another who claims to have heard him tell it twenty-seven times before, always with a chestnut.

Greek *kastanea* produced **castanet** [via Spanish *castañeta*, literally 'little chestnut'].

child [Old English *cild*. The original plural was also *cild*; the form *c(h)ildra* arose by association with Old English words with similar plurals, and evolved into *childre* or *childer* (surviving in N English dialect), which acquired the then common plural ending *-n* or *-en*] A (female) fetus or new-born baby (surviving in *with child*, *childbirth*); a boy or girl between babyhood and puberty, hence **1** (the title of) a young nobleman or gentleman (surviving in poetry as **childe**, and the usual sense of **Chil-** in place names); any youth **2** an immature or naive person **3** your son or daughter (replacing **bairn** [Old English *bearn*], which survives in Scotland and N England); a member of a tribe, clan, or country; a person from or influenced by something (*child of the devil/the sixties*).

chiropodist [18c. Ultimately from Greek *kheir* 'hand' + *pous, pod-* 'foot'] Someone who treats the feet and, formerly, the hands. Originally regarded as pretentious and usually translated as 'corn-cutter', it gained respectability in the late 19c and **chiropody** was then coined from it. Gradually being replaced by **podiatrist**, **podiatry** [early 20c, *US*, also from Greek *pous*].

Greek *kheir* is the ancestor of SURGERY*, and *pous* of PODIUM*.

chisel [ME. Old Norman French, ultimately from Latin *caedere*, *caes-*, *cidere*, *cis-* 'to cut'] **1** a cutting tool; to cut or shape with one (16c) **2** to swindle (19c, surviving mainly in **chiseller**): perhaps a different word, the original spelling being *chizzle*; however, *gouge* also had this meaning in the 19c.

Latin *caedere*'s descendants include **cement** [via Latin *caementum* 'rough-hewn stone'], **-cide** killing (*homicide*), something that kills (*pesticide*), **circumcise**, **concise**, **decide**, **excise** to cut out, **precise** [French *précis*, itself adopted meaning a summary], and **scissors**.

chivalry [ME. Old French *chevalerie* from medieval Latin *caballarius* 'horseman', from Latin *caballus* 'horse'] Knights or mounted soldiers collectively (replaced by 16c **cavalry**, also from Latin *caballus*); the rank of knight (15c); the medieval system of knighthood, including its moral codes (18c); knightly virtues; honourable and courteous behaviour, especially towards women. As in **chivalrous** brave (ME, archaic by the 16c, but re-emerging in the late 18c with the added senses 'honourable, courteous'), the later senses marking renewed interest in the medieval period by historians and Romantics.

Latin *caballus* is the ancestor of CAVALCADE and of **cavalier**, which gives a different picture of a mounted soldier: originally a horseman, especially a cavalryman or a gentleman with military training, hence a vigorous or flamboyant military man; a fashionable gentleman, especially one escorting a lady, hence jaunty, free and easy, shading into offhand, careless, arrogant. Applied derogatorily by Parliamentarians to the more swashbuckling and belligerent supporters of Charles I, hence a Royalist in the Civil War.

chivvy [18c. From *Chevy Chase*, a former hunting ground and the scene of a skirmish celebrated in a popular 15c ballad] **1** a hunting cry; a hunt or pursuit (19c), hence to harass **2** the face (19c rhyming slang).

chord [ME. Originally *cord* (shortened from ACCORD), altered in the 17c by association with *chord* 'string of a musical instrument': see CORD] Agreement, reconciliation (–15c); musical harmony (15–18c), hence two or more notes played together (18c).

chorus [16c. Latin, from Greek *khoros* 'dance, band of dancers'] A group of singers and dancers in ancient Greek drama: in Attic tragedy they commented on moral and religious matters between the acts, hence **1** an actor who speaks the prologue and epilogue and comments on events **2** a song sung by the chorus; the refrain of a song, in which the audience often joins; anything uttered by many at once (*a chorus of birdsong/protest,* 17c); a composition for many voices **3** a choir (17c); those who sing an opera's choral parts; the supporting performers in a musical (19c).

Greek *khoros* is the ancestor of **chorea** (a disease causing) jerky, involuntary movements, **choreography**, and *Terpsichore* (at MUSE[1]).

Christ [Old English *Crīst* from Latin *Christus*, from Greek *Khristos* 'anointed one' (from *khreien* 'to anoint'), translating Hebrew *māšīāḥ* 'messiah'] The Messiah expected by the Jews, given as a title to Jesus of Nazareth by those who believe that he fulfilled Jewish prophecy.

Jesus, *Christ*, and *Jesus Christ* have long been used as oaths or exclamations and, being blasphemous, have many euphemisms, including **crikey, criminy, cripes, crumbs, gee (whiz), Gemini** (whence **jiminy cricket** and possibly JINGO and Scots **jings**), **jeepers (creepers), jeez, Judas Priest,** and perhaps *cats* in **suffering cats**. Cf. DEVIL, GOD. Latin *Christus* produced CHRISTEN*; Greek *khreien* is the ultimate ancestor of **cream**.

christen [Old English *crīsten*, from Latin *Christianus*, from *Christus* CHRIST] (A) Christian (replaced by **Christian** from Latin *Christianus*, ME), hence to make Christian (–19c); to baptize someone into the Christian church (ME), hence **1** to name or rename someone at their baptism (15c); to give a name or nickname (17c) **2** to adulterate or splash with water **3** to use for the first time (early 20c).

Latin *Christianus* produced **cretin** [via (Swiss) French], applied to someone physically deformed and mentally retarded by a congenital deficiency of thyroid hormone (as a reminder that they were nevertheless Christian souls), and loosely and offensively to a fool.

chronic [15c. Via French and Latin from Greek *khronikos* 'to do with time', from *khronos* 'time'] Of a disease: long-lasting, constantly present or recurring, hence **1** having chronic illness (*a chronic invalid*, 19c) **2** constant, continual, persistent (usually of something bad, 19c); habitual, inveterate; **something chronic** severely, badly (*c*.1910).

Greek *khronos* is the ancestor of **chronicle**, of **chrono-** (*chronology, chronometer*), of *crony* (at COMRADE), and of **synchronize**.

church [Old English *cir(i)ce*, ultimately from Greek *kuriakon doma* 'house of the Lord', from *kurios* 'lord'] **1** a building for public Christian worship; a temple or mosque (–17c); to take someone (especially a woman after childbirth) to church for a special service or rite (ME); to conduct such a service **2** Christians collectively (hence **the Church invisible** all Christians, past and present, **the Church visible** those still on earth, both 16c); a Christian denomination or congregation **3** the clergy; religious authority **4** a non-Christian religious organization (ME).

Old English *cir(i)ce* produced Old Norse *kirkja*, whence **kirk**, the Scots and N English equivalent of *church*, now specifically the Church of Scotland. *Church* and *kirk* appear in place- and surnames (*Churchill, Kir(k)by*), sometimes distinguishing a village having a church (*Church Stretton, Kirklevington*), *kirk* sometimes with the name of the saint to which the village church was dedicated, notably in **Kirkoswald**, which combines Old Norse *kirk* with an Anglo-Saxon saint, using Celtic word order.

churl [Old English *ceorl*] A man (–ME); the lowest-ranking Anglo-Saxon freeman; after the Norman Conquest, a serf, hence a peasant; a rough, ignorant, surly man, surviving mainly in **churlish**.

Scorn for country folk is also found in **boor** [Low German *bör* or Dutch *boer* 'farmer'], **bumpkin** [possibly from early Dutch *bommekijn* 'little barrel', hence 'squat person'], CLOWN, *corny* (at CORN), RUSTIC, VILLAIN, and **yokel** [originally a dialect word for the green woodpecker, from its cry, resembling a maniacal laugh], possibly in HOYDEN and JERK, and sometimes implied in *peasant* (at PAGAN). For a different perspective, see *bonhomie* (at BOUNTY), and cf. COCKNEY.

Old English *ceorl* appears as **Carl-**, **Charl-**, and **Chorl-** in place- and surnames. *Boor* is related to *bour* in **neighbour** [Old English *nēahgebūr*, with *ne(a)h* NIGH]; Dutch *boer* produced Afrikaans **Boer**.

chute [19c. French, 'a fall', ultimately from Old French *cheoir* 'to fall', from Latin *cadere*: influenced by, and influencing, SHOOT] A cataract or cascade of water (*N America*); a sloping channel or slide, to send down one. Hence **1** a narrow passage for cattle: cf. *shoot* sense 3 **2** a slide or roller coaster, especially with water at the bottom (early 20c, later also as **shute**).

French *chute* produced **parachute** [with French *para-* 'protector of, protection against': see PARADE*], whence **para-** in **parascending** and *paratrooper* (at TROOP).

cipher [ME. Via Old French and medieval Latin from, ultimately, Arabic *ṣifr*, from *ṣafira* 'to be empty'] A nought (superseded by *zero* below), hence **1** an (Arabic) numeral (15c); a symbol or hieroglyph (16–19c); secret writing, originally with made-up characters (16c); (text written in) a code, hence **decipher** to convert a cipher to ordinary writing; to interpret something written in code or hard to understand (17c) **2** someone/something that fills a space but is not important (16c).

Zero a nought [also ultimately from Arabic *sifr*] shares sense 2 of *cipher*, and came to mean the point on a scale (marked by a nought) from which values are reckoned, hence **1** describing a starting point (*zero hour*, **ground zero** originally the epicentre of a nuclear explosion) **2** a gunsight setting that allows for wind and elevation, hence **zero in** to aim a gun or missile; to focus on; to close in on.

circus [ME. Latin, from Greek *krikos*, *kirkos* 'circle, ring'] A round or oval arena in ancient Rome for chariot races, gladiatorial contests, etc., hence **1** an open space where several streets meet (18c), hence **the Circus** the British Secret Service (1960s, from its headquarters in Cambridge Circus, London, but with overtones of sense 2) **2** a (travelling) show in which clowns, acrobats, etc. perform in a ring (18c), hence (a scene of) lively, confused, and often trivial activity (*media circus*, 19c, *US*).

Latin *circus* produced *circa* around, approximately, **circle** (whence **circlet**), **circuit**, **circular**, **circulate**, **circum-** around (*circumnavigate*, *circumstance* at STATION), and **search** [via Old French *cherchier* and late Latin *circare* 'to go round']. Old French *cherchier* produced **research** [via obsolete French *rechercher*, literally 'to search closely', whence *recherché* rare, exotic, obscure].

cite [15c. French *citer* from Latin *citare* 'to move, excite, or summon', from *ci(e)re* 'to set going, to call'] To summon before a court (earlier in **citation** a summons); to call up, arouse, or excite (16c), hence to 'call up' or quote an author, book, or passage, especially in support of an argument; to mention as an example or proof (17c); to mention in an official despatch (World War I, *US*).

Latin *citare* produced **recite** [Latin *recitare*, literally 'to call up again'] and **resuscitate** [Latin *resuscitare*, from *suscitare* 'to raise']; *ciere* is the ancestor of EXCITE* and SOLICIT*.

city [ME. French *cité* from Latin *civitas* 'citizenship, citizens, the community or State' (later applied to the independent states of Gaul, and then to their principal town), from *civis* 'citizen'] A town; a large or important one, specifically one given the title of *city* by Royal charter and having a degree of autonomy. Hence **the City** within the ancient London boundaries, governed by the Lord Mayor and Corporation (16c) and containing the Bank of England and the Stock Exchange, hence the business and financial community (17c).

A city does not necessarily have a cathedral, though many do. In Gaul the principal towns became centres of episcopal authority and the Normans followed this pattern in England, moving some episcopal sees from smaller towns. At the

Reformation Henry VIII granted city charters to towns in which his new bishoprics were established.

Latin *civitas* produced **citadel** a fortress defending a city and providing refuge for its inhabitants, hence a Salvation Army meeting hall. Latin *civis* is the ancestor of CIVIL*.

civil [ME. French, from Latin *civilis*, from *civis* 'citizen'] To do with citizens or society, hence **1** to do with citizens' rights and duties; **civil law** dealing with agreements between citizens; **civil war** between citizens rather than states **2** not ecclesiastical, military, or naval, hence **civil engineer** who designs and builds public utilities (17c, originally as distinct from an engineer who built fortifications and armaments); **civilian** a non-military employee of the East India Company (18c), later someone not in the armed forces or police; **civil service** the non-military parts of the East India Company (18c), now the non-military branches of public administration.

French *civil* produced **civilize**, whence **civilization**. Latin *civilis* produced **civility** citizenship, hence good citizenship, orderly behaviour (surviving in N Ireland); politeness, courtesy, whence *civil* polite. *Civis* is the ancestor of CITY* and **civic**.

claim [ME. Via Old French from Latin *clamare* 'to call, cry, or appeal'] To assert your right to, hence **1** (the right to make) such a demand; the thing claimed, hence **stake a claim**, originally to claim a piece of land by marking it out with stakes (19c, *US*) **2** to demand, deserve, or require (*claimed our attention*, 17c); such a demand **3** (to make) an assertion that something exists or is true (19c).

Latin *clamare* is the ancestor of **acclaim** [via *acclamare* 'to shout for'], **clamour**, **proclaim**, and RECLAIM.

class [16c. Latin *classis* 'the Roman people or army', later a section of either] Any of the six divisions of the Roman people, based on wealth, instituted in the 6c BC, hence a category of people or things, originally a set of students taught together, hence **1** a period of teaching **2** a rank in society (18c); high social rank, hence high quality, elegance (19c); **classy** elegant, stylish **3** see TAXONOMY.

Classical and **classic** [from Latin *classicus* 'of the highest *classis*'] both originally meant 'first class, excellent', and were then applied to the works of ancient Greek and Roman authors, partly because these were studied by students in class and partly because they were considered superior to vernacular works, hence **1** describing art, architecture, etc. of ancient Greece and Rome, or modelled on it; **classics** (the study of) Greek and Roman literature **2** describing something that reaches or sets a standard; excellent of its kind; of lasting value.

clear [ME. Via Old French from Latin *clarus*] Bright, brightly shining; of the sky, weather, etc.: sunny, cloudless, hence **1** easily seen or understood (cf. SEE*); easily seen through, transparent, translucent **2** of the complexion: glowing, healthy, unblemished **3** free from obstructions, encumbrances, debt, guilt, etc.; apart, out of reach (15c) **4** to make or become clear; to pass by or over without touching.

Clear produced *clerestory* (at HISTORY). Descendants of Latin *clarus* include *chiaroscuro* [Italian, from *chiaro* 'clear, bright' + *oscuro* 'dark' (from Latin *obscurus*, whence **obscure**)], **claret**, **clarify**, **clarinet**, **clarion**, **clarity**, **declare**, French *éclair* [literally 'lightning'], and names including **Cla(i)re**, **Clara**, **Clarence**, **Clarice**, and **Claridge**.

cleave [Old English *cleofan*. The original past tense was *clove* (surviving in **clove hitch** a knot in which the rope emerges in two parallel lines, 18c): *cleaved* appeared in Middle English, perhaps borrowed from **cleave** to stick or cling to [Old English *cleofian*], and evolved into **cleft** (15c)] To split something, hence **1** to split or come apart (ME) **2** to penetrate (16c); to cut a path through (19c).

Probably related to **cleft** a crevice, originally spelt **clift**, which survives as a surname: the modern spelling is by association with *cleft* above, and to **clove** of garlic [Old English *clufu*]. **Cleave** 'to stick to' is related to **clammy**, **clay**, **climb** (whence **clamber**), and perhaps to CLEVER.

clench [Old English *clencan*] To secure with a nail etc., especially by beating the end over after it has gone through, hence **1** the beaten end (ME); something that fastens or grips firmly **2** to grasp firmly (ME); the variant **clinch** came to mean to cling to your opponent in a fight (19c); such a move or hold, hence to embrace (*US*), an embrace (*c*.1900) **3** to close your teeth or fist tightly **4** to settle something decisively (16–19c), surviving as *clinch*.

The Scots and N English variant **clink** survives mainly in **clinker built**, describing a boat made of overlapping planks fastened with clenched nails. Related to **cling**.

clerk [OE. Christian Latin *clericus*, from Greek *klērikos* 'to do with the Christian clergy', from *klēros* 'lot, heritage' (from the Bible, Deuteronomy 18:2 '…the Lord is their inheritance', referring to the Levites, the priestly tribe of the Israelites). Formerly also spelt **clark**, whence the surname] A member of the clergy, hence, because the clergy were literate, a scholar; a person who draws up or copies documents or keeps records (16c), originally a senior official, now also a junior employee; an assistant in a shop or hotel (18c, US).

Latin *clericus* is the ancestor of the surnames **Clarges** a clergyman's servant, and **Cleary** a clerk, of **clergy**, originally meaning 'learning, scholarship', and of **clerical** originally 'learned'.

clever [ME. Perhaps of Low German origin and related to CLEAVE* 'to stick to'] Recorded once in Middle English meaning quick to catch hold, resurfacing meaning deft, dextrous (16c); later nimble, agile, hence mentally agile, quick to catch on (18c); showing intelligence, ingenious.

The ideas of catching hold and learning are linked in many English words, including APPREHEND, CATCH, COMPASS, COMPRISE, CONCEIVE, **forget** [Old English *forgietan*, ultimately from a Germanic word meaning 'to lose your hold'], *gather* and *recollect* (both at COLLECT), **get**, **grasp**, HINT, NIMBLE, *perceive* (at CATCH), and **take in/on board**. Cf. SEE.

clew [Old English *cliwen*. The variant **clue** appeared in the 15c: both forms were found in most senses until the 19c] A rounded mass (–18c); a ball of string, hence **1** the thread used by Theseus in Greek mythology to find his way out of the Labyrinth (ME), hence *clue* something that gives guidance in a difficult situation (16c) or that helps solve a puzzle, crime, or crossword **2** *clew*: **(a)** the thread of life spun by the Fates (17c) **(b)** the corner of a sail where the sheets are attached **(c)** the cords of a hammock (18c).

client [ME. Latin *cliens*, variant of *cluens* 'heeding', from *cluere* 'to hear or obey'] A person under someone's protection and patronage, a dependant (surviving in client state), hence someone 'protected' by a legal adviser (15c) or using any professional services (17c); a customer; a person being helped by a social worker, counsellor, etc. (1920s, *US*), ironically introduced to lessen the idea of dependency.

climate [ME. Via (French and) Latin from Greek *klima* 'a slope, a zone', from *kli-nein* 'to lean' (ancestor of **cline**)] A zone between two lines of latitude (–18c); any region of the earth (15–18c); one considered in relation to its atmospheric or weather conditions (17c): largely replaced in these senses by **clime** [15c, also from Latin *clima*]. Hence a region's normal weather pattern (17c); prevailing conditions (*economic/moral climate*).

clock [ME. Early Dutch and Low German *klocke*, ultimately from medieval Latin *clocca* 'bell': probably introduced by Flemish clockmakers brought to England by Edward I] A bell; an instrument (with a bell) for recording time. Hence **1 of the clock** specifying the time according to the newfangled clock, rather than shown by the sun's movement (shortened to **o'clock**, 18c) **2** to time something (19c), hence **(a)** to attain a certain speed or time **(b)** to watch or notice (1940s) **3** someone's face, likened to a clock face (1920s); to hit them in it (1940s) **4** a measuring instrument, originally with a dial (1930s); a speedometer or mileometer, hence to turn a vehicle's mileometer back (1970s).

Medieval Latin *clocca* fathered French *cloche* 'bell' (whence **cloak**, from its shape, also in French), adopted for a bell-jar to protect a plant, and again for a bell-shaped hat.

clog [ME. Origin unknown] A lump of wood; one tied to a person or animal to stop them running away, hence **1** to restrict with one; to hinder by sticking, like clay or mud (16c); to block or become blocked **2** a wooden or wooden-soled shoe (15c).

close [ME. Old French *clore*, *clos-* (verb), *clos* (noun and adjective), from Latin *claudere* 'to shut or shut in'. The 'hissing' *s* of the noun and adjective was inherited from *clos*; the pronunciation of the verb was probably by association with Old English *clysan*, also ultimately from Latin *claudere*, which it replaced] **1** to enclose; an enclosed space (*cathedral close*); a narrow passage or entry; a cul-de-sac (18c, mainly in place names) **2** shut (up); to shut, hence **(a)** hidden, secret, secretive (15c) **(b)** stifling, stuffy (16c) **(c)** restricted (*close season*, 19c) **3** to bring or come together (from the idea of closing a gap), hence **(a)** near; intimate (*close friend/relative*); stingy (17c, cf. NIGH) **(b)** tight, tightly (*close fitting*) **4** (to bring or come to) an end (15c); to settle a matter (17c).

Latin *claudere*'s descendants include **clause**, **claustrophobia**, **cloister**, CLOSET, **conclude**, **disclose**, literally 'to open up' (ME–18c), hence to reveal, ENCLOSE*, EXCLUDE*, FORECLOSE, **occlude**, **preclude** to bar the way (15–18c), hence to make something impossible, **recluse**, and **seclude**.

closet [ME. Old French, from *clos*: see CLOSE*] A private room, hence **1** a lavatory (15c, short for *closet of ease* and surviving in 19c **WC**, short for *water closet*: cf. LAVATORY, TOILET) **2** a cabinet (17c); a cupboard or storage space (now N American). Hence private, secret (17c), virtually obsolete but recreated in the 1960s from **come out (of the closet)** to stop hiding your homosexuality.

clot   [Old English *clot(t)*] A lump: **1** a hard lump of earth (ME, largely replaced by the variant **clod**), hence a clumsy, awkward or stupid person (16c) **2** a lump of coagulated liquid (*blood clot*, ME); to coagulate; *clod* in these senses survived until the 18c.

Old English *clot(t)* fathered dialect *clodder* a clotted mass, and *clotter* to cover with clods; these produced **clutter** (to form) a clot (15–17c), hence to crowd or heap together; (to fill with) an untidy collection of things. Related to **cleat** a wedge, later a projection to stop your foot or a rope from slipping, CLOUT, and **cluster**, probably to CLOUD, and perhaps to CLOWN.

cloth   [Old English *clāth*] (A piece of) woven fabric; a garment (–ME); clothing (ME–17c); the uniform of a household or profession (surviving in **man of the cloth** a clergyman); your profession as shown by this (17c).

The plural of Old English *clāth* was *clāthas*, whence **clothes**. The verb **clothe** comes from *clāth* via two Old English verbs: *clathian*, past tense *geclathod*, whence **clothed** (now the usual past tense), and *claethan*, past tense *claethde*, whence **clad**, surviving as an old-fashioned past participle and in **cladding** a protective covering, whence *clad* to cover with cladding.

cloud   [Old English *clūd*: probably related to CLOT*] A mass of earth or rock; a hill (surviving in place names); a mass of water vapour in the sky (ME, replacing Old English *w(e)olcen*, which also meant 'sky' and survives in poetic **welkin**), hence a mass of dust, smoke, insects, etc. **On Cloud Nine** comes from a classification of cloud systems used by the American Weather Bureau, cumulo-nimbus being the ninth and highest.

clout   [Old English *clūt*: related to CLOT*] **1** a metal plate; a patch; a cloth or rag (ME), hence a garment; an archery target, originally a piece of canvas, laid on the ground (16c) **2** perhaps a different word: (to give) a heavy blow (ME), hence power or influence (1950s, *US*).

clove   [ME. Old French *clou de gilofre*, literally 'nail of the clove' (from its shape), *clou* from Latin *clavus*, *gilofre* ultimately from Greek *karuophullon*, from *karuon* 'nut' + *phullon* 'leaf'] A dried flower bud used as a spice (replacing *girofle* or *gilofre*). Old French *clou de gilofre* produced English *clowe (of) gilofre*, shortened to *clowe* or *clove*: the longer form survived into the 16c and was also applied to a clove-scented species of pink. Eventually *clove* became confined to the spice and (*clove*) *gilofre* to the **(clove) pink**. *Gilofre* was altered to **gillyflower** (17c, by association with *flower*), used to name various unrelated scented flowers.

The clove pink is the ancestor of the modern **carnation** [perhaps from Greek *karuophullon*, or via French and Italian from Latin *carnatio* 'fleshiness', from *caro* 'flesh']. **Pink** may be from *pink eye* a small or half-shut eye [probably from early Dutch *pinck* 'small']; the flower gave its name to the colour.

Latin *clavus* produced CLOY; Greek *karuophullon* produced **chervil**; Latin *caro* produced **carnation** 'flesh-coloured' and CARRION*; Dutch *pinck* produced *pinkje* 'the little finger', whence **pinkie**.

clown   [Probably of Low German origin; perhaps related to CLOT*] A peasant (16c), an uncouth or stupid person, such a character in a play (17c), hence a comic performer (18c). Cf. CHURL*.

cloy [15c. Obsolete *accloy* 'to drive a nail into', via Old French from medieval Latin *inclavare*, from Latin *clavus* 'a nail' (whence CLOVE)] To fasten or pierce with a nail (–18c); to stop up with a nail or peg (–17c), hence to choke (16c); to satiate.

club [ME. Old Norse *clubba*, variant of *klumbal*: related to **clump**] A heavy stick with a thickened end, hence **1** a stick used in ball games (*golf club*, 15c) **2 clubs** the suit of playing cards marked with a trefoil (16c: the symbol was taken from French cards, where the name of the suit is *trefle*, and the name from Spanish *basto* or Italian *bastone* 'club, baton', the symbol on Spanish or Italian cards) **3** to gather into a club-shaped mass (17c); **club (together)** to come together for a common purpose or to share expenses, hence *club* an association for pursuing a common interest, or later, for social purposes; its premises, hence an establishment providing facilities or entertainment for members (19c); **nightclub** where members could drink, dance, etc. after normal licensing hours, now shortened to *club* and open to all (19c), whence **(night)clubbing** going to (night)clubs (1930s).

coach [16c. French *coche*, from Hungarian *kocsi* (*szeker*) '(wagon) from Kocs', a town in Hungary] A large carriage; one for public use (17c), hence **1** to convey or travel in a coach (17c); to teach or train privately or intensively (18c, apparently from the idea of speeding the student's progress, like a coach); a private tutor or trainer (19c) **2** a railway carriage (19c); a single-decker bus (1920s).

coal [Old English *col*] A glowing ember (*hot/live coals*); a charred piece of wood; charcoal (ME); a solid black fossil fuel.
   Coal produced **charcoal** [with an unknown first element], whence **char** to make into charcoal, to blacken by burning, **cole/coal tit** (from its black head), **collier** originally a charcoal-burner or seller, whence the surname **Colyer**, and probably **collie** an (originally black) sheepdog, either directly or via **colley dog**, from **colley** a kind of sheep with black legs and face.

coast [OE. Via Old French *coste* from Latin *costa*] The rib or side (–19c), hence **1** the 'side' or borderland of a country or district (ME–17c); the sea shore (originally *sea coast/coast of the sea*); to sail within sight of the shore or from port to port along it (15c), hence **coaster** a person or ship that does so (16c); a small tray for a decanter (which 'coasts' around the table, stopping at each diner, 19c), hence a mat for a bottle etc. **2** to slide downhill on a toboggan (18c, *N American*, from a later French sense 'hillside'); to move using momentum (19c); to progress without effort (1930s).
   Old French *coste* produced **costard** a large, ribbed apple (whence the surname **Coster** and **costermonger**, who sold them), and modern French *côte*, whence **cutlet** [via French *côtelette* 'small rib']. Latin *costa* produced **accost** to lie or go alongside [16–17c, via Italian], now to approach someone boldly or aggressively.

coax [16c. From *cokes* 'a fool', of unknown origin] **1** to fondle, hence to persuade, originally by caresses or flattery (17c), now usually by gentle persistence **2** to make a fool of (17c, probably the underlying sense despite appearing later).

cock [Old English *cocc*, probably from medieval Latin *coccus*; later from French *coq*] A male bird, hence **1** a male chicken, hence the leader of a flock, the best (16c), surviving in **cock of the walk** (*walk* here being where fighting cocks were kept) **2** in the names of bird species (*woodcock, peacock*), hence **cocker (spaniel)**

bred for flushing woodcock (19c) **3** perhaps from the shape, resembling a cock's head: **(a)** (a spout with) a tap (15c), hence, perhaps, **cock-a-hoop** (from the effect of laying the tap in the 'hoop' or rim and drinking the barrel dry) **(b)** (to raise) the hammer of a gun (16c), hence **half-cock(ed)**; **go off at half-cock** to fire, later to act or speak, prematurely **(c)** to turn up or at an angle, hence **cock-eyed** having a squint (19c), topsy-turvy, nonsensical, drunk (1920s, *US*) **4** the penis (17c), earlier in *pillicock* [*pill* being a N English dialect word for penis, probably of Scandinavian origin], whence **pillock 5** nonsense (19c), said to be from **cock and bull story** [of uncertain origin] or suggested by **poppycock** [*US*, from Dutch *pappekak*, literally 'soft dung'].

The perceived character of the domestic cock produced **cockade** [from French *bonnet à la coquarde*, from *coquard* 'saucy', from *coq*], **coquetry** and **coquette** [from French *coquet* 'wanton', literally 'young cock'], and **cocky** lecherous, over-confident, cheeky, but not *cocksure* (see GOD). *Cock* produced **cockerel** a young domestic cock, COCKNEY, COCKPIT, and COCKTAIL, and is the first element, expressing size and vigour, of **cockchafer**. It also influenced the spelling of **cockatoo** [via Dutch *kaketoe* from Malay *kakatua*], **cockatiel** [from Dutch *kaketielje* 'small *kaketoe*'], *cockatrice* (at BASILISK), and **cockroach** [earlier *cacaroch*, from Spanish *cucuracha*].

cockney   [ME. From COCK + obsolete *ey* **egg** (Old English *ǣg*)] A small misshapen egg, said to have been laid by a cock (–17c); a pampered child or effeminate man (–18c); a town-dweller, regarded as affected or puny by country folk (16–19c), hence one born in London, properly within the sound of the bells of St Mary-le-Bow (17c).

cockpit   A pit for cockfights (16c), hence **1** a place of conflict **2** the ground floor of a theatre's auditorium (traditionally a rowdy area), shortened to *pit* (17c), hence **(orchestra) pit** a place at the front of this for the orchestra (19c) **3** an area in the aft lower deck of a warship where the wounded were taken (18c); the well in a yacht's stern where the helm is (19c), hence the place from which an aircraft (*c.*1910) or racing car (1930s) is controlled.

cocktail   (Having) a tail like a cock (17c); (a horse) having a tail with the muscles nicked to make it stand up, hence (because mainly working horses were nicked), a racehorse that is not a thoroughbred (19c), hence, probably, a mixed alcoholic drink (*US*, the spirit being adulterated); a dish of mixed food (*fruit/prawn cocktail*, 1920s); a mixture of drugs etc. (1970s).

code   [ME. French, from Latin *codex* 'a block of wood', later one split into writing tablets, hence a book] A collection of Roman statutes, hence **1** any set of laws (18c) or regulations (19c); a society's or individual's mores **2** a system of characters, symbols, etc. used to send secret messages (19c) or containing information (*bar code, postcode*), hence **(a)** to put something into code; **decode** to decipher or interpret **(b)** a system by which genetic information is stored (1950s); to provide genetic information (1960s).

Latin *codex* produced *cockboat* (at SWAIN) and **codicil** an amendment to a will [via Latin *codicillus*, literally 'small codex'], and was adopted for a set of statutes or rules (16–18c), later a book of manuscript texts or an official list of drugs.

cohort   [15c. (Via Old French from) Latin *cohors* 'an enclosed space', later 'people gathered in one, a group of soldiers or attendants': see COURT*] One-tenth of a legion in the Roman army; a division of any army (16c); a band of warriors, hence a group of people with a common aim (18c), born in the same year (1940s), or having something else in common. The plural *cohorts*, meaning troops, forces, or supporters, produced a singular sense 'an assistant or colleague' (1950s, *US*).

coin [ME. French *coin* 'wedge, cornerstone', later 'die', from Latin *cuneus* 'wedge'. In the 17–18c the variant **quoin** was found in all senses; it is now the only spelling of senses 1 and 2] **1** the outer angle of a wall; a cornerstone **2** a wedge **3** a die for stamping metal money; to do so, hence **(a)** (a piece of) money produced; cash **(b)** to make money, to show a profit (16c); **coin money** to make it without effort (19c) **(c)** to invent a word or phrase (16c).

Coin produced the surnames **Coyne**, **Conyer(s)** who made coins or were misers; Latin *cuneus* produced **cuneiform** wedge-shaped, hence (describing) an early form of writing using wedge-shaped impressions on clay tablets.

cole [Old English *cāwel*, *caul*, ultimately from Latin *caulis* 'hollow stem, cabbage'] Cabbage, any brassica. Hence **1** colewort [ME, with *wort* 'a plant': see ROOT*], shortened to **collard** (18c, *US*), now one that does not form a heart **2** kale, kail [ME, Scots and N English variants, influenced by related Old Norse *kál*] **3** colcannon [18c, Irish], **kailkenny** [19c, Scots] (the second elements may mean 'whiteheaded') a dish of cabbage and mashed potato.

Latin *caulis* produced **cauliflower** [literally 'flowered cabbage', with Latin *flos, flor-* FLOWER*], **choux (pastry)** originally applied to round filled pastries [plural of French *chou* 'cabbage'], **coleslaw** [US, from Dutch *koolsla*, from *kool* + *sla* from French *salade* SALAD*] originally as *cold-slaw*, suggesting that *cole* was no longer a familiar word, whence **hot slaw** cabbage cooked with vinegar and sugar and served warm, **kohlrabi** first mentioned as being 'cultivated as food for cattle in England, and as a vegetable in India and Germany' [German alteration, influenced by *Kohl* 'cabbage', of Italian *cavolo rapa* (with Latin *rapa*: see TURNIP)].

collateral [ME. Medieval Latin *collateralis* 'side by side with', from Latin *lateralis* 'sideways, on the side', from *latus* 'side' (ancestor of LATITUDE*)] Side by side, parallel, hence **1** from a common ancestor by a different line; a collateral relative (17c) **2** accompanying, additional, hence **collateral (security)** something pledged in addition to the main obligation of a contract (16c); property as security for a loan (19c, *US*); **collateral damage** besides that intended (1980s).

collect [ME. Via Old French or medieval Latin from Latin *colligere*, *collect-*, from *legere* 'to choose, collect', also 'to read'] Replaced by **gather** [Old English *gaderian*] in sense 1, replacing it in sense 2. To bring together, hence **1** to put two and two together, to infer **2** collect yourself to control your feelings (17c): cf. *compose yourself, pull yourself together, self-possession* **3** to take from various sources (17c) **4** to get and keep related objects (18c, ME in *collection*) **5** to come together, to assemble or accumulate (18c) **6** to pick up or call for (19c).

Latin *colligere* produced **coil**, **collect** a short prayer [via Latin *collecta* 'a gathering'; perhaps originally said by those gathering for Mass, or a prayer summing up thoughts for that day], CULL, and **recollect** [Latin *recolligere* 'to gather again, to recall']. *Legere* is the ancestor of LEGEND*. *Gather* is related to GAD and **together**.

college [ME. (Via French from) Latin *collegium* 'partnership, association', from *collega* 'partner, **colleague**', from *com* 'together' + *legare* 'to depute' (ancestor of

LEGATE*)] An association of people sharing duties and privileges, surviving mainly in their names (*College of Arms*) and in **electoral college**. Hence a community of clergy living together (ME); a body of teachers, scholars, and students, especially in higher or specialized education; its premises (cf. *university* at UNIVERSE*).

colony [ME. Latin *colonia* 'farm, settlement', from *colonus* 'farmer, settler', from *colere* 'to cultivate, to inhabit' (ancestor of CULTURE*)] A settlement, mainly of retired soldiers, acting as a garrison in newly conquered territory in the Roman Empire; an independent city founded by immigrants (16c); a community in a new country owing allegiance to the mother country, hence **1** a country ruled by another (17c) **2** animals, insects, etc. of one kind living as a community (17c) (a place occupied by) a distinct group of people (*nudist colony*, 18c); an expatriate community (19c).

comb [Old English *camb*] An implement for tidying hair, hence **1** something resembling it: a chicken's serrated crest; a honeycomb (because the plates of cells hang parallel to each other like a comb's teeth, ME); a tool or machine for dressing wool, flax, etc. **2** to use a comb (ME); to search thoroughly (*c*.1900, 19c in **beachcomber**: perhaps suggested by *to go over/through with a fine-tooth(ed) comb*).

    The verb *comb* replaced **kemb** [Old English *cemban*], which survives in **kempt** combed, neat, now usually a humorous back-formation from **unkempt**: cf. **dishevelled** [Old French *descheveler*, from *chevel* 'hair', from Latin *capillus*] having the hair loose, hence uncombed, untidy, with the back-formation **dishevel**. Old English *camb* produced the surname **Camber**, **Kember**, or **Kempster** a comb-maker or seller, or a flax-comber (cf. *brewster* etc. at BREW), and **oakum** [Old English *acumbe*, literally 'off-combings']. Latin *capillus* produced **capillary**. Related to **cam** [Dutch *kamrad* 'toothed wheel', from *kam* 'comb'].

comfort [ME. Via Old French from late Latin *confortare*, from Latin *fortis* 'strong' (ancestor of FORCE*)] To strengthen, encourage, or invigorate (–18c); encouragement, support (surviving in the legal phrase *aid and comfort*), hence **1** support or relief for someone in distress; to support, console, or soothe; someone/something that does so **2** to cheer, (to give) pleasure or enjoyment (–17c); **comforts** the things that make life easy and pleasant (17c); *comfort* physical and material well-being (19c).

commend [ME. Latin *commendare*, literally 'to entrust completely', from *mandare* 'to entrust', later 'to order': see MANDATE*] **1** to entrust, now only to God's protection **2** to praise formally; to mention or suggest as desirable or suitable **3** to convey someone's regards (*commend me to your mother*).

    Latin *commendare* produced *recommendare*, whence **recommend**, which has shared the senses of *commend*. Latin *mandare* produced *commandare*, which was used more or less interchangeably with *commendare* in medieval Latin and fathered Old French *comander*, whence **command**, **commandant**, **commandeer** [via Afrikaans and Dutch], Portuguese *commando* originally a militia of white settlers in S Africa, and **commodore** [via Dutch].

commission [ME. French, from Latin *committere*, *commiss*-: see COMMIT*] Delegated authority, hence **1** a warrant giving authority, especially to a military officer or a ship's captain, hence **(a)** to give one (17c) **(b)** to prepare a ship and bring it into service; to bring equipment into use; **out of commission** not in service or working order **2** a group of people given authority (15c) **3** a task entrusted to someone else (16c); an order for a piece of work; to give one (18c) **4** authority to act for someone in business (17c); payment according to the results.

Latin *committere* produced several words with the underlying sense 'someone given authority': French **commis** a deputy or clerk (16–19c), re-adopted for a junior chef or waiter, Russian *commissar* the head of a government department in the USSR, **commissary** specifically an officer entrusted with supplying troops with provisions, hence a store of provisions for troops or employees, a restaurant in a film studio (*US*), French **commissionaire** a person entrusted with small tasks or errands; a member of an association of ex-soldiers employed as messengers, porters, etc., hence a uniformed usher, and **commissioner** someone entrusted with, or appointed by, a commission.

commit [ME. Latin *committere* 'to entrust, to engage in', from *com* 'together' + *mittere* 'to put or send' (ancestor of MISSION*)] **1** to place for safe keeping or to be dealt with (*commit to memory/his body to the ground*), hence **(a)** to send to prison or a psychiatric hospital **(b)** to refer a parliamentary bill to a committee (16c) **2** to entrust someone with a duty (–16c); to promise that you or someone else will do something (18c); to dedicate yourself, resources, etc. to a cause **3** to do wrong (*commit a felony/adultery*, 15c).

Commit produced **committee** a person, or one of a group, entrusted with a task etc. (15–17c); the whole group.

commodious [15c. Via French or medieval Latin from Latin *commodus* 'suitable, convenient', literally 'with the proper measure', from *modus* 'a measure'] Beneficial, useful (–18c); convenient, serviceable (16–19c), hence providing convenient accommodation; roomy, spacious.

Latin *commodus* is the ancestor of ACCOMMODATE, French **commode** originally adopted for a tall headdress for women, later applied to such conveniences as a brothel-keeper, a chest of drawers, a privy, or a seat containing a chamber pot, and **commodity** something useful or valued, especially something to be traded. *Modus* is the ancestor of MODE*.

common [ME. Via Old French from Latin *communis*, literally 'sharing duties', from *munus* 'duty, service, gift'] The community, the people (–17c); the ordinary people as opposed to the aristocracy (–18c), surviving in **commoner** and **House of Commons**. Hence **1** (a piece of land) belonging to the community; shared by a community (*common room, Common Market*), by many people (*common knowledge*), or by people or things (*common factor*) **2** known to many (*common criminal*); familiar, widespread, not unusual **3** to do with or typical of ordinary people; vulgar (19c). See also *commonplace* (at TOPIC).

Latin *communis* is the ancestor of **commune, communicate, communion, communism, community,** and **incommunicado**. Descendants of *munus* include **immune** [via Latin *immunis* 'exempt from a liability'], *municipal* (at CATCH), **munificent**, and **remuneration**.

commute [ME. Latin *commutare* 'to change completely, to exchange' from *mutare* 'to change' (ancestor of MEW*)] To exchange one thing for another, hence to change one kind of obligation, punishment, or payment for another (17c), whence **commutation ticket** a season ticket (individual fares being commuted to a single payment, 19c, *US*); **commuter** someone using a commutation ticket or who does the same journey regularly, hence *commute* to do so, a commuter's journey (1960s).

companion [ME Old French *compaignon*, literally 'one who eats bread with another', ultimately from Latin *panis* 'bread'] A friend or comrade, hence **1** a member of an order of knighthood (16c) **2** a handbook (seen as a helpmeet, 18c); a piece of equipment containing several useful items (*smoker's companion*, 18c) **3** something that matches or goes with another (18c).

Companion in *companionway* is an alteration of obsolete Dutch *kompanje* 'quarterdeck' [via Old French from Italian (*camera della*) *compagna* '(storeroom for) provisions', also from Latin *panis*]. The *compagna* was a structure built on the main deck, and the meaning 'something above the deck' carried into Dutch and English, where *companion* originally meant a raised window on the quarterdeck letting light into the officers' cabins below, hence **companion ladder** leading to the officers' quarters; **companionway** a staircase between decks.

Latin *panis* is the ancestor of **accompany**, **company**, Spanish *panada* a thickening for soups etc., originally made from bread [from Italian *panata*] and *panatela* [used in American Spanish for a long thin biscuit, later for the cigar, from Italian *panatello* 'small loaf, from *panata*], Italian *panet(t)one* and *panforte* [literally 'strong bread'], **pannier** a large basket for provisions, later one of a pair slung across a horse's back [via French from Latin *panarium* 'bread basket'], **pantry** originally a bread cupboard, and **pastille** [Latin *pastillus* 'small loaf or roll', later 'aromatic lozenge'].

compass [ME. French *compas* 'scope, circle', also 'artifice, subtlety', and *compasser* 'to measure', ultimately from Latin *passus*: see PACE*. All main senses appeared in English at about the same time and appear in other European languages: their development is uncertain] **1** a circle (–17c); a circumference, hence **(a)** a circumscribed area; limits, range, scope (16c) **(b)** to surround, confine, or include (largely replaced by **encompass**); to grasp (16c), hence to understand or achieve (cf. CLEVER*) **(c)** (to go round) a circuit **(d)** (to make) circular or curved (16c) **2** a device: **(a)** (pair of) **compasses** for drawing circles and measuring distances **(b)** for finding direction (15c) **3** ingenuity, cunning, a crafty scheme (–16c); to contrive, especially by underhand means (largely replaced by *encompass*).

competent [ME (Via French from) Latin *competere* 'to coincide, to be appropriate', from *com* 'together' + *petere* 'to seek'] Suitable, appropriate (–18c), hence **1** befitting your status **2** sufficient or adequate for your needs, hence **competence**, **competency** an adequate supply (15–18c), an adequate income (16c) **3** having sufficient qualifications or authority (15c); having adequate skill, capable (17c).

A later sense of Latin *competere*, 'to strive with', produced **compete**; *petere* is the ancestor of PETULANT*.

complain [ME. Old French *complaindre*, ultimately from Latin *plangere* 'to lament, to beat your breast, to strike noisily'] To lament, to express sorrow or dissatisfaction, hence **1** to state a grievance formally; to bring a charge **2** to make a mournful sound (17c). Hence **complaint** an expression or cause of sorrow, dissatisfaction, or a grievance, hence **(a)** an accusation or charge **(b)** an ailment.

Complain and *complaint* largely replaced **plain** [Old French *plaindre* from Latin *plangere*]. *Plaindre* produced **plaintiff** and **plaintive**; *plangere* produced **plangent**.

complex [17c. (Via French from) Latin *complectere, complex-*, literally 'to plait together', from *plectere* 'to plait'] Made up of (many) parts, hence **1** intricate, hard to analyse or disentangle (18c): cf. **complicated** [17c, from Latin *complicare*, from *plicare* 'to fold': see PLY] **2** something complex: **(a)** a connected group of repressed ideas (*inferiority complex, c.*1906); an exaggerated feeling, an obsession (*c.*1920) **(b)** a set of buildings etc. (*sports complex*, 1930s).

Latin *complectere* produced COMPLEXION. Latin *plectere* produced **pleach**, *plexus* (at SOLAR), and **perplex** [via Latin *perplectere* 'to plait thoroughly'].

complexion [ME. French, from Latin *complectere*: see COMPLEX*] The combination of bodily humours thought to determine your constitution and temperament (cf. TEMPER), hence **1** the appearance of your skin, originally as showing these (16c) **2** the nature or appearance of something (16c).

comply [16c. Ultimately from Latin *complere* 'to fill up, finish, fulfil', from *plere* 'to fill', from *plenus* 'full'] To accomplish or fulfil (–17c); to fulfil the demands of courtesy (17c), hence to be agreeable; to oblige or obey.

Latin *complere* produced **accomplish**, **complete**, **complement** [literally 'completion, something that completes'], and **compliment** [via Italian *complimento* 'fulfilment (of the demands of courtesy)']. Latin *plere* produced **deplete**, EXPLETIVE, IMPLEMENT, **replete**, and SUPPLY*; *plenus* produced **plenary**, *plenipotentiary* (at POSSE), **plenty**, and **replenish**.

compost [ME. Old French, from Latin *componere*: see COMPOUND*] A combination or compound, hence **1** a dish of fruit cooked in syrup (15–18c, replaced by modern French *compote*, 17c) **2** an organic mixture used as manure (15c).

compound [ME. French *compondre* from Latin *componere, composit-* 'to put together', from *ponere* 'to put': see POSE*] **1** to combine or mix; to make something by doing so, hence **(a)** made in this way; a mixture (17c) **(b)** to add interest to a sum borrowed and charge interest on the total (16c) **(c)** to add to, increase, or complicate (1960s) **2** to settle a matter, specifically by paying or accepting money (15c); to condone an offence for money or for private reasons (17c): **compound a felony/offence** is now often taken to mean 'to add to it, to make it worse', by association with 1c above.

Compound 'an enclosure' comes via Portuguese or Dutch from Malay *kampong*, later adopted for an enclosure or village in Malaysia.

Latin *componere* produced **component**, **compose**, **composit**, and COMPOST.

comprise [ME. French *compris(e)*, past participle of *comprendre*, from Latin *comprehendere* 'to grasp fully', from *prehendere* 'to grasp'] To seize (–17c), hence **1** to grasp mentally (–17c), outlived by **comprehend** [also from *comprehendere*] **2** to include, contain, or consist of (15c); to constitute (18c).

Comprehend shares the sense 'to include, contain, or consist of', now most commonly in **comprehensive** inclusive, all-embracing. Latin *prehendere* is the ancestor of PRISE*.

compromise [Via French from Latin *compromittere* 'to make mutual promises', from *promittere* 'to **promise**', from *mittere* 'to send' (ancestor of MISSION*)]

(To reach) an agreement, to go to arbitration (–17c), hence **1** to reach agreement by making mutual concessions (15c); such an agreement (16c); (the finding of) a middle way (18c) **2** to expose yourself to criticism, suspicion, or danger (17c); **compromised** damaged or disgraced (19c).

comrade [16c. French *camarade*, from Spanish *camarada* 'room-mate', from Latin *camera*: see CHAMBER*] Someone who shares your quarters, hence a fellow soldier, a friend or companion. Adopted by communists and socialists as an egalitarian alternative to *Mr, Mrs*, etc. (19c), hence a (fellow) communist or socialist.

 Chum [*Oxford University slang*: probably short for *chamber-fellow*] also originally meant a room-mate; the Cambridge equivalent was **crony** [from Greek *khronios* 'long-lasting', perhaps used to mean 'contemporary', from *khronos* 'time'].

 French *camarade* produced **camaraderie**. Greek *khronos* is the ancestor of CHRONIC*.

conceive [ME. French *concevoir* from Latin *concipere*, *concept-*, literally 'to take in', from *capere* 'to take' (ancestor of CATCH*)] To take in physically or mentally (cf. CLEVER*), hence **1** to become pregnant; **be conceived** to be created in the womb **2** to understand; to form an idea; to devise or originate, whence **conceit** (ME, modelled on *deceit*) and **concept** (16c), both meaning 'an idea formed in the mind'; *conceit* went on to mean **(a)** a fancy or whimsical object (15c); a fanciful or witty expression (16c); a fanciful notion, a whim **(b)** a personal opinion (15c); a favourable one (16c), now of yourself, pride, vanity (17c).

concern [ME. (Via French from) Latin *concernere*, literally 'to sift together', from *cernere* 'to sift, discern' (ancestor of CRIME*)] To be relevant to; to affect or involve (15c), hence **1** to be important to you (16c); something you are involved in; a business (chiefly in *going concern*); **concerns** business or affairs **2** (to cause) anxiety (17c); something you care or worry about.

concert [16c. French *concerter* from Italian *concertare* 'to harmonize', perhaps ultimately from Latin *concernere*: see CONCERN. At first often confused with, and hence spelt, CONSORT] To unite, to bring into agreement or harmony, hence **1** a group of musicians (16c, surviving as *consort*); a (harmonious) combination of sounds (17c); a public musical performance, originally by a consort **2** to agree to act together (*concerted action/effort*, 17c); **in concert** together (18c).

 An Italian-sounding ending was added to *concert* to give **concertina**. French *concerter* produced *desconcerter*, literally 'to throw out of harmony', whence **disconcert** to upset someone's progress or plans, to spoil their self-possession. Italian *concertare* produced *concerto*.

concoct [16c. Latin *concoquere*, *concoct-* 'to cook together', from *coquere* COOK*] To refine metals or cook food (–19c); to prepare a dish from numerous ingredients (17c), hence to make up an elaborate story or scheme (18c).

concur [ME. Latin *concurrere*, literally 'to run together', from *currere* 'to run'] **1** to act together; to agree or express agreement **2** to happen together, to coincide (15c).

 Latin *concurrere* produced **concourse** a gathering, a throng, hence an open area where people may gather in a public building etc. (*US*). *Currere* is the ancestor of CURRENT*.

conduct [ME. (Old French *conduit* from) Latin *conducere* 'to bring or lead to', from *ducere* 'to lead'] **1** provision for guidance or safe passage, such as an escort or pass (surviving in **safe conduct**) **2** to lead, guide, or escort **3** to direct or command; direction, management, hence **(a)** self-management, behaviour (16c) **(b)** to manage a business or meeting (17c), an orchestra (18c), or a bus (19c, back-formation from **conductor**) **4** to be a channel for; a channel or pipe (surviving as **conduit**); to convey energy or electricity (18c).

Latin *conducere* produced **cond** to direct or guide, shortened to **con**, whence a submarine's **conning tower**, **conduce** to lead or bring to (ME–17c); to promote or encourage, surviving mainly in **conducive**, **conduit**, and the surname **Condy, Cundy** someone who lived by one. *Ducere* is the ancestor of DEDUCE*.

confection [ME. French, from Latin *conficere*, *confect-* 'to put together', from *facere* 'to make'] A mixture, especially a medicine; one mixed with a preservative or sweetener, hence a preserve or sweet, whence **confectioner** someone who makes or sells these (16c); **confectionery** sweets and cakes (18c).

Latin *conficere* produced **comfit** a sugared nut, seed, etc., Italian *confetti* 'comfits', referring to real or imitation sweets thrown during Italian carnivals, hence the paper shapes thrown at weddings, and **discomfit** literally 'to undo', originally to defeat in battle. *Facere* is the ancestor of FACT*.

confer [ME. Latin *conferre*, *collat-*, from *ferre* 'to bring or carry, to bear'] To bring together (–17c), hence **1** to talk seriously (coming together to do so, 15c); to discuss, hence **conference** [16c, from French] serious conversation, discussion; a formal meeting; a meeting of an association, hence an association, originally of businesses, now also of sports teams or clubs (19c) **2 collations** an extract from John Cassian's *Collationes Patrum in Scetica Eremo Commorantium* 'Conferences of, or with, the Egyptian Hermits' (*c.*415) read in Benedictine monasteries before a small meal at the end of the day, hence *collation* a light meal, especially at an unusual time (16c) **3** to contribute, to give (16c, earlier in **collation**) **4** *collation* the comparing, later the gathering and ordering, of pages, hence the verb **collate** (16c): the idea is also found in **cf.** [short for Latin *confer* 'compare!'].

Descendants of Latin *ferre* include **circumference**, DEFER*, **-fer** 'bearing' (*aquifer*, *conifer*), **fertile**, INFER, **interfere**, PERIPHERY*, **prefer**, **prelate**, REFER*, **suffer**, *superlative* (at SUPERANNUATED), TRANSLATE*, and **vociferate**.

confident [16c. Latin *confidere*, from *fidere* 'to trust', from *fides* 'trust'] Certain, convinced, self-assured; (someone) entrusted with secrets (17–19c), altered to **confidant(e)**, imitating French pronunciation.

Latin *confidere* produced **confide** to trust or have faith in, hence to trust someone with your private thoughts, **confidence** faith in, trust, hence faith in yourself (the opposite is **diffidence** [Latin *diffidere* 'to mistrust']), **confidential** confident (17c only); suggesting closeness or intimacy; private or secret; entrusted with private matters (*confidential secretary*). *Fidere* produced **affiance** and **affidavit** [both via Latin *affidare* 'to declare on oath'], French *fiancé(e)*, **fiduciary**, and the dog's name **Fido**. *Fides* is the ancestor of FAITH*.

confound [ME Via Old French from Latin *confundere*, *confus-* 'to pour or mix together', from *fundere* 'to pour' (ancestor of FUSE*)] To disorder, to mix up physically

(ME) or mentally (16c), hence **1** to embarrass, bewilder, or perplex **2** to overthrow, defeat, or ruin, hence used as an oath, a milder version of *damn*.

Confound had two past participles: **confounded** and **confused**: the latter produced **confuse**, which replaced *confound* in senses 2 and 3.

conjure [ME Via French from Latin *conjurare* 'to swear an oath together', from *jurare* 'to swear', from *jus* 'right, law'] To oblige someone to do something by making them swear to, or by appealing to them in the name of someone/something sacred or precious (–18c), hence to summon a spirit or demon using such a name (hence **a name to conjure with** one powerful enough to use) or by means of a spell; to use spells; to practise magic; to do 'magic' tricks (16c); **conjure up** to produce something (as if) by magic.

Latin *jurare* produced **abjure**, **jury**, and **perjure**: *jus* is the ancestor of JUST*.

conker [19c. Probably ultimately from Greek *kogkhē* 'mussel, cockle', but associated with, and formerly often spelt, **conquer** (ultimately from Latin *conquirere* 'to seek for', from *quaerere* 'to seek')] A snail-shell, used in the game of *conkers* or *conquerors* in which two shells were pressed or smashed together, the undamaged one being the 'conqueror'; a horse chestnut used in a similar game.

Conquer originally meant to acquire, later to take by force, hence to subdue. Greek *kogkhē* produced Old French *cockille*, whence **cockle** whence the surname **Cockell** a cockle-seller or a pilgrim wearing a shell as a badge (cf. SCALLOP), **conch**, originally a mussel or oyster, and modern French *coquille*. Latin *quaerere* is the ancestor of QUEST*.

conscience [ME. Via French from Latin *conscientia,* from *conscire* 'to share in the knowledge of, to know in your heart', from *scire* 'to know'] **1** your innermost thoughts or convictions (–17c) **2** the sense of right and wrong, originally as a quality, like *prudence*, which everyone had more or less of, later an individual's moral sense. Hence **conscientious** governed by conscience or a sense of duty (17c).

Because of the final *-s* sound *conscience* was mistaken for a plural, with the singular *conscion*, whence **conscionable** having a conscience, conscientious (surviving in **unconscionable**). Latin *conscire* produced **conscious**, originally being aware of your own wrongdoing. *Scire* is the ancestor of *science* (at ART*).

conscription [ME. Latin *conscriptio* 'levying of troops', from *conscribere* 'to write down together, to enrol', from *scribere* 'to write' (ancestor of SCRIPT*)] Putting in writing (–17c); enrolment or enlistment of soldiers (16–17c). Re-borrowed (*c*.1800) from French meaning 'compulsory enlistment', along with *conscript* a conscripted soldier; **conscript** 'to enlist compulsorily' is a back-formation from *conscription* (19c, US).

conservative [ME. Latin *conservare*: see CONSERVE*] Tending to conserve. Used in 1830 to describe the British political party that aimed to preserve existing political institutions and the established Church, and eventually adopted as the Party name, hence opposed to radical change; cautious, moderate; of an estimate: deliberately low (*c*.1900, US).

conservatory [16c. Latin *conservatorium,* from *conservare*: see CONSERVE*] Something that preserves (–17c); a place where things are preserved, now a greenhouse or room for delicate plants (17c),

Latin *conservatorium* produced Italian **conservatorio**, an orphanage or school where the children were taught music, which was adopted for a musical academy, whence French **conservatoire** and *conservatory* in the same sense.

conserve [ME. Via French from Latin *conservare*, from *servare* 'to keep'] To keep carefully; to save for later use, hence **1** a preparation of fruit, flowers, herbs, etc. preserved in sugar (15c), originally for medicinal purposes, now specifically a kind of jam **2 conservation** preservation, specifically of the environment, wildlife, and natural resources (early 20c).

Latin *conservare* produced CONSERVATIVE and CONSERVATORY*. *Servare* is the ancestor of OBSERVE, PRESERVE, and RESERVE*.

consign [ME. (Via French from) Latin *consignare* 'to mark with a sign', from *signum* 'a mark or sign' (ancestor of SIGN*)] To mark with the sign of the cross (–18c), especially at baptism or confirmation; to commit or dedicate someone to God (16–18c), hence to entrust someone/something to someone's care (16c); to hand over formally; to send to a particular place or fate (17c); to send or deliver goods, hence **consignment** a quantity of goods sent (18c).

consist [ME. Latin *consistere* 'to stand firm, to exist', from *sistere* 'to stop, place', from *stare* 'to stand'] **1** to exist or be inherent in (–19c); to be made up of (16c); to be based on **2** to stand firm, to stay the same (16–17c), hence **consistency** permanence of form; the firmness or density of a substance (17c) **3** to exist together, to be compatible, to agree (16–19c), hence (combining senses 2 and 3) **consistent** constant, dependable, coherent, without contradiction, true to type (17c).

Latin *sistere*'s descendants include **assist**, **desist**, **exist**, **insist**, **persist**, **resist**, **-stice** stopping (*armistice*, *solstice* at SOLAR), and **subsist** [Latin *subsistere* 'to stand still'] to exist; to (just) provide for yourself (*subsistence farming*); *stare* is the ancestor of STATION*.

consort [15c. Via French from Latin *consors* 'sharing, partner, partnership', from *com* 'together' + *sors* 'lot, destiny'] A partner or companion; a ruler's spouse (16c), hence to associate with habitually; to play or sing together regularly; a group of musicians (cf. CONCERT).

Latin *consors* produced **consortium**; *sors* is the ancestor of **assort**, **sorcerer** [Latin *sortes* 'responses made by oracles', plural of *sors*], and **sort**.

contain [ME. French *contenir* from Latin *continere* 'to hold or keep together', from *tenere* 'to hold'] **1** to have inside; to include or consist of; to (be able to) hold a certain amount **2** to keep inside, to restrain, control, or repress; to control your emotions (17c).

French *contenir* produced COUNTENANCE; Latin *continere* is the ancestor of CONTENT, CONTINENT, and **continue**, and *tenere* of TENOR*.

contemporary [17c. Medieval Latin *contemporarius*, ultimately from Latin *com* 'together' + *tempus* 'time' (ancestor of TEMPER*)] Belonging to, existing, or occurring at the same time, hence **1** (a person) of a similar age **2** belonging to the present time (19c); ultra-modern (1920s, the predominant sense during the mid 20c, now becoming old-fashioned).

content [ME. (Via French from) Latin *contentus* 'contained', also 'satisfied' (from the idea of your desires being contained), from *continere*, *content-* CONTAIN*] **1** (now usually plural) what is in a container or, later, a book (16c), hence **(a)** the ideas expressed in a work of art (19c) **(b)** the amount of a substance in a mixture (*sugar content, c.*1900) **2** reasonably happy, satisfied, willing to accept, hence **(a)** pleased (surviving in *well content*): used, now only in the House of Lords, to express consent (15c) **(b)** to satisfy or be satisfied (15c); to accept or make do with, hence **content(ment)** quiet happiness; **contented** satisfied, quietly happy (16c).

contest [16c. Latin *contestari* 'to call on to witness', from *testari* 'to witness': see TESTAMENT*] To witness or swear to a fact or statement (–17c); to swear against it, to dispute or challenge (17c); to argue; to fight or compete for something; a competition.

context [ME. Latin *contexere, context-* 'to weave together', from *texere* 'to weave' (ancestor of TEXT*)] The 'weaving together' of words and sentences (–17c); the text produced (16–17c), hence the text surrounding a word or passage and affecting its significance; the conditions or circumstances in which something exists or happens (19c).

continent [ME. Latin *continens, continent-* 'holding together', hence 'restrained', also 'continuous, uninterrupted', from *continere*: see CONTAIN*] **1** exercising self-restraint, hence chaste, celibate; able to control your bladder and bowels (1940s, 18c in **incontinence**) **2** [from Latin *terra continens* 'continuous land'] an uninterrupted tract of land (16–17c), hence **(a)** the mainland; **the Continent** mainland Europe (17c); **Continental** typical of this (18c) **(b)** any of the great land masses of the earth (17c).

contingent [ME. Latin *contingere* 'to be in contact with, to come to, to befall', from *tangere* 'to touch'] **1** possible but not certain, as likely to happen or be true as not, hence (something) happening by chance (16c); conditional, depending on circumstances (17c); something that may happen in certain circumstances (largely replaced by **contingency**, also from Latin *contingere*) **2** a share or quota received (18c); a quota of troops supplied by a region or power; the troops concerned, hence a distinct group forming part of a larger gathering.

Latin *contingere* produced **contiguous**; *tangere* is the ancestor of TACT*.

contract [ME. Via Old French from Latin *contrahere, contract-* 'to draw or bring together', hence 'to limit', from *trahere* 'to draw' (ancestor of TRACT*)] **1** (to enter into) a binding agreement, originally to marry; the document recording it (16c), hence to become involved in or acquire something, now usually something bad (*contracted pneumonia/debts*) **2** to bring together; to concentrate (–18c); to limit or confine (16c); to make or become smaller or shorter.

contretemps [17c. French, originally '(motion) out of time', from *contre* 'against' (from Latin *contra*) + *temps* 'time', from Latin *tempus* (ancestor of TEMPER*)] In fencing: a thrust at an inopportune moment or at the same time as your opponent's (now a feint intended to produce a counter-thrust), hence **1** an embarrassing mishap or mistake (18c) **2** a dispute or disagreement (1960s).

control [ME. Anglo-Norman French *contreroller* 'to keep a copy of a roll of accounts', ultimately from medieval Latin *contrarotulus* 'copy of a roll', from *rotula* 'small wheel': see ROLL*] To check accounts against a duplicate record (–18c), hence **1** to check by comparison (16c); a standard to compare with, especially in a scientific experiment (19c) **2** to regulate or restrain (16c); restraint, restriction; **controls** by which a machine is guided or managed (*c*.1900) **3** someone who guides or directs (18c); a being that guides or channels messages to a Spiritualist medium (19c); someone who controls a spy (1960s) **4** a place where something is controlled (*c*.1900, originally part of a motor rally where speed is restricted); a checkpoint.

convene [ME. Latin *convenire* 'to come together', hence 'to unite, to agree', from *venire* 'to come'] **1** to meet for a common purpose; to call a meeting (16c) **2** to agree, harmonize, or suit (15c, rare since the 17c).

Latin *convenire* produced CONVENIENT, CONVENT*, CONVENTION, and **covenant**. *Venire* is the ancestor of VENUE*.

convenient [ME. Latin *convenire*: see CONVENE*] Appropriate, suitable (–18c), hence **1** at a suitable time or place (15c) **2** easily used or available (15c); handy, nearby (19c).

convent [ME. Old French *co(n)vent* from Latin *conventus*, from *convenire*: see CONVENE*. Spelt *covent* until the 17c, surviving in **Covent Garden**, London, formerly owned by Westminster Abbey] An assembly (–17c); a group of people (–16c), specifically the twelve apostles, hence a group of twelve religious people plus a superior; (the premises of) a religious community, now usually of nuns. Cf. **coven** [ME, also via Old French from Latin *convenire*] an assembly (–17c), now a group of (originally 13) witches).

convention [15c. French, from Latin *convenire*: see CONVENE*] A formal meeting or agreement; general agreement (18c); an accepted rule or way of behaving (19c). Hence **conventional** to do with a convention (15c); conforming to accepted ways (19c); of weapons: other than the newfangled nuclear (1950s).

converse [ME. French *converser* from Latin *conversari* 'to move among, to occupy yourself with', from *versare* 'to occupy yourself', literally 'to turn yourself round', from *vertere* 'to turn'] To live among or spend time with (–18c); to trade or to have sexual relations with (–19c, surviving in the legal term **criminal conversation** adultery); to exchange ideas with (16c), surviving in **conversation** the exchange of ideas and information by talking; informal talk, a chat (17c), whence *converse* to have a conversation.

French *converser* produced **conversant** living or associating with (ME–19c), hence familiar with, knowledgeable about. Latin *conversari* produced Italian **conversazione** a social gathering for discussing art or literature; *vertere* is the ancestor of VERSE*.

convert [ME. French *convertir*, ultimately from Latin *convertere* 'to turn around', from *vertere* 'to turn' (ancestor of VERSE*)] **1** to cause to change direction (–18c); to reverse or transpose (surviving mainly in **converse** opposite, the reverse, 16c) **2** to (cause to) change from a sinful life, later to a different religion, party, or opinion, hence someone who does so (16c, replacing *converse*) **3** to turn to a different purpose (surviving in the legal term **convert to one's own use** to appropriate illegally); to change something's character, form, or function; to undergo such change (16c); to be designed to do so (*sofa converts to a bed*, 1930s) **4** to exchange for an equivalent (*convert pounds to dollars*, 16c).

convey   [ME. Via Old French from medieval Latin *conviare*, from Latin *via* 'way, road' (ancestor of TRIVIAL)] To accompany or escort someone (–18c); to take from one place to another, hence **1** to communicate or express (*convey our sympathy*) **2** to transfer property by legal process (15c), hence **conveyance** (a document effecting) such transference, **conveyancing** preparing such documents (18c) **3** *conveyance* a vehicle (16c).

The Scots variant **convoy** came to mean a protective escort (15c), hence people, vehicles, or, especially, ships travelling with one (16c) or as a group (17c, short-lived but revived via **in convoy** in such a group, World War I). Latin *via* is the ancestor of TRIVIAL*.

convict   [ME. Latin *convincere, convict-* 'to overcome', later 'to prove beyond doubt', from *vincere* 'to conquer'] **1** **(a)** to find someone guilty **(b)** convicted, found guilty (–19c); a convicted criminal (15c), now one serving a prison sentence (18c) **2** to satisfy someone that something is true (–17c, replaced by **convince**, also from Latin *convincere*), hence **conviction** a firm belief **3** to conquer or overcome (15–17c, the original sense of *convince*, 16–17c) **4** (combining senses 1 and 2) to make someone aware of their sins (16c).

Latin *vincere* is the ancestor of EVICT*, **invincible**, PROVINCE, **vanquish**, **victory**, and the names **Victor**, **Victoria**, and **Vincent**.

convivial   [17c. Latin *convivialis*, from *convivium* 'a feast', from *com* 'together' + *vivere* 'to live' (ancestor of VICTUAL*)] Fit for a feast; involving good food and pleasant company, hence fond of these, sociable (18c).

cook   [Old English *cōc*, ultimately from Latin *coquus*, from *coquere* 'to cook'] A man employed to prepare food, hence **1** to prepare food by heating (ME), hence **(a)** **cook up** to make up, to invent (17c, cf. CONCOCT) **(b)** **cook the books** to invent figures in the accounts (17c) **(c)** to be cooked (19c); to swelter **2** a woman employed to cook (16c, replacing **cookess**): as cooking came to be regarded as a female occupation, male cooks adopted the French title *chef* (short for *chef de cuisine* 'head of the kitchen': see CAPTAIN*).

Latin *coquere* is the ancestor of BISCUIT*, CONCOCT, **cuisine** [French, from Latin *coquina* 'kitchen', whence Old English *cycene* **kitchen**], **culinary** [Latin *culina* 'kitchen, stove', whence Old English **kiln**], **decoct**, PRECOCIOUS*, and Italian **terra-cotta**, literally 'baked earth' [with Latin *terra*: see TERRACE*].

coordinate   [17c. From **co-** 'together' (from Latin *com-*) + Latin *ordinare* 'to put in order': see ORDAIN*: probably modelled on SUBORDINATE] (To make) equal in rank, hence **1** **(a)** a partner, equal, or equivalent (19c) **(b)** each of a set of numbers that together pinpoint a position, e.g. on a map **(c)** **coordinates** clothes that match or go together (1950s) **2** to (make things or people) work together (19c), hence **coordination** the balanced and effective action of interrelated parts (*hand and eye coordination*).

Latin *com-* 'with, together, completely' was added to many Latin words, also appearing as **col-**, **con-**, and **cor-**.

cop [18c. From obsolete *cap* 'to arrest', via Old French from Latin *capere* 'to seize' (ancestor of CATCH*)] To catch, get, or steal, hence **1** an arrest (*a fair cop*, 19c); **copper** a policeman (19c) **2 cop it** to get into trouble, to be punished (19c); to be killed **3** something acquired (19c); its value (usually negative, *not much cop*) **4 cop out** to avoid getting, especially to evade a responsibility or decision (1940s, *US*); **cop-out** an evasion, a pretext or excuse.

cope[1] [ME. Old French *co(l)per*, from *co(l)p* 'a blow', from medieval Latin *colpus*, from Latin *colaphus* 'blow with the fist', from Greek *kolaphos*] To come to blows with or meet in battle (surviving in dialect), hence to prove yourself a match for (16c); to deal with successfully.

Old French *co(l)per* produced COUPON*. Medieval Latin *colpus* is the ancestor of **coppice** a small wood where the trees are regularly cut back (shortened to **copse**), hence to cultivate trees in this way, and of COUP.

cope[2] [ME. Medieval Latin *capa* from Latin *cappa* 'hood, hooded cloak': see CHAPEL*] A long outdoor cloak (–18c); a ceremonial cape worn by some Christian priests, hence **1** to dress someone in a cope; to 'cloak' the top of a wall with masonry or tiling (16c); **coping** the topping **2** the surname **Cope** someone who made or sold capes, or who wore a distinctive one.

copy [ME. Via French from Latin *copia* 'abundance, wealth, power, the right or means to do something', in medieval Latin 'transcript', from phrases meaning 'the right to transcribe'] **1** abundance, plenty (–17c) **2** a transcript of a document, hence **(a)** to transcribe or reproduce a document; in computing: to reproduce data at another location (1950s); to send a copy of a letter or email to a third party (1980s) **(b)** a single specimen of a printed or published work (16c) **(c)** (to make) a reproduction or imitation of any object (17c); to imitate someone's work, actions, ideas, etc. **3** an original to be copied (15c); text prepared for printing; material for an item in a newspaper etc. (19c); the text of an advertisement (*c.*1900).

Latin *copia* appears in *cornucopia* (at CORNET) and produced **copious**.

cord [ME. French *corde* from Latin *chorda*, from Greek *khordē* 'gut, string of musical instrument' (made of gut); the spelling **chord** arose in the 16c, reflecting its Latin ancestor, and has replaced *cord* in some senses] (A piece of) thin rope, hence **1** the string of a musical instrument (–19c, surviving as *chord*, mainly in **strike a chord** to produce a memory or response, probably from the idea of plucking the heart-strings but associated with CHORD) **2** a cord-like structure in the body (18c) **3** a straight line joining two points on a curve (16c, quickly replaced by *chord*) **4** a measure of cut wood, probably measured with a length of cord (17c) **5** rib on a fabric (18c); a ribbed fabric, especially **corduroy** [18c, with **duroy** a kind of worsted, of unknown origin], hence **cords** corduroy trousers (19c) **6** electric flex (19c, N American except in **cordless**).

Cord produced **cordite** (from its stringy appearance), and surnames including **Coard** and **Cordell** for a cord-maker. Latin *chorda* produced CORDON.

cordial [ME. Medieval Latin *cordialis*, from Latin *cor* 'heart'] To do with the heart (–17c), hence **1** a medicine, food, or drink that stimulates the heart or circulation; one that comforts or cheers; a drink of sweetened or flavoured spirits (16c);

a concentrated fruit or herbal drink (18c) **2** heartfelt, sincere (15c); warm, friendly, and polite (18c).

Latin *cor* is the ancestor of ACCORD*, **concord**, COURAGE*, **discord**, MISERICORD, QUARRY, and RECORD, and perhaps of CORE.

cordon [15c. Italian *cordone*, literally 'a large cord', and French *cordon*, literally 'a small cord', both from Latin *chorda*: see CORD] **1** an ornamental cord or braid; a ribbon or sash forming part of the insignia of an order of knighthood (18c), hence French **cordon bleu** [literally 'blue cord'] a member of a distinguished chivalric order, specifically the French Order of the Holy Ghost (who wore blue sashes), hence superior (French) cuisine (from the excellent food served at their meetings); (the holder of) a first-class distinction; a first-class cook. The English equivalent is **blue ribbon/riband** the highest honour, the first prize (19c) **2** a line of troops or police to keep people in or out of an area (18c); to surround with one (19c); (usually as French **cordon sanitaire**) one round an infected area to prevent the spread of disease; a series of buffer states protecting a country from infiltration or attack.

core [ME. Perhaps from or related to Latin *cor*: see CORDIAL*] The central part of an apple etc., hence **1** (describing) the central or most important part of anything (*core curriculum*, 15c: cf. *heart* at COURAGE) **2** to remove the core (15c) **3** **hard core** **(a)** hard material used for foundations (19c) **(b)** an irreducible nucleus (1930s); an intransigent minority (1950s), hence committed, fanatical, blatant, whence **hard-core (pornography)** depicting sexual acts explicitly, whence **soft (core)** titillating, mildly erotic (1960s).

corn [Old English] A small hard particle, such as a grain of salt or sand (surviving in dialect and in **corned beef**, originally preserved with salt 'corns'), hence a small hard seed, especially of a cereal plant; cereal plants or their seeds collectively. **Corny** was originally used to describe beer with a strong malty taste (ME); the sense 'rustic, unsophisticated', hence 'sentimental, hackneyed, trite' dates from the 1930s: cf. CHURL*.

Old English *corn* appears in place- and surnames, and produced *cyrnel*, literally 'little corn', whence **kernel**.

cornet [ME. French, ultimately from Latin *cornu* 'horn, tip'] **1** a wind instrument made of, or resembling, an animal's horn; a woodwind, now a brass, instrument (cf. BUGLE, HORN) **2** something shaped like a horn: a cone of paper for carrying sweets etc. (16c); a cone-shaped ice cream wafer (1920s).

Latin *cornu* is the ancestor of *cor* in French **cor anglaise** [literally 'English horn'], of the **corn** on your toe, of -**corn** (*Capricorn* at CABRIOLET, *unicorn*), **corner**, **cornet** a women's headdress, originally one with two 'horns' worn by the Sisters of Charity, later one with strips of lace hanging down from it, hence a (cavalry troop's) pennon or standard, a mounted standard-bearer, and of late Latin **cornucopia** [literally 'horn of plenty': see COPY].

corporal [OE. Via Old French from, ultimately, Latin CORPUS*] **1** [via medieval Latin *pallium corporale*, literally 'cloth for the body'] a vestment used at the Eucharist (–17c); a cloth on which the bread and wine are placed (ME) **2** to do with or belonging to the human body (*corporal punishment*, ME).

Corporal a non-commissioned officer comes from French *caporal* or Italian *caporale*, ultimately from Latin *caput* 'head' (ancestor of CAPITAL*).

corporate [ME. Latin *corporare*, from Latin CORPUS*] **1** forming or being a **corporation** a body of people having its own legal existence, now a civic authority or large industrial company; to do with or belonging to one **2** to form into a corporation; to unite or combine into one body; both largely survived by **incorporate**.

corpus [ME. Latin *corpus* 'body'] The body of a human or animal (rare after the 17c), first found in oaths such as *God's corpus*. Hence **1** the 'body' or main part: **(a)** of an organ (*corpus of the uterus*, 17c) **(b)** a principal sum, as opposed to interest or income from it (19c) **2** a body of writings or data (18c).

Latin *corpus* is found in in **Corpus Christi** [literally 'the body of Christ'] a festival in honour of the Eucharist, in legal terms such as **corpus delicti** [literally 'the body of the crime'] the evidence that a crime has been committed, sometimes erroneously used for a corpse as evidence that someone has been killed, and **habeas corpus** [literally 'you may have the body'], and in the names of some masses of specialized tissue, e.g. the **corpus luteum** (yellow body) in the uterus. Its descendants include CORPORAL, CORPORATE*, **corporeal**, **corpulent**, **corpuscle** literally a tiny body, and CORSE*.

correct [ME. (Via French from) Latin *corrigere*, *correct-* 'to make straight', literally 'to rule completely', from *regere* 'to guide or rule' (ancestor of REGIMENT*)] **1** to put someone/something right; to point out or eradicate errors or bad behaviour, hence without errors, right, accurate (15c); acceptable, proper, polite (17c) **2** to rectify or compensate for a defect (16c) or for different conditions (18c).

Latin *corrigere* is the ancestor of **corrigible** able to be corrected, capable of improvement or reformation (earlier and more common in **incorrigible**), and of **escort** originally a body of armed guards for a traveller [via Italian *scorta*, past participle of *scorgere* 'to guide or conduct'].

corridor [16c. French, from Italian *corridore*, alteration (by association with *corridore* 'runner') of *corridoio* 'place for running', from *correre* 'to run', from Latin *currere* (ancestor of CURRENT*)] A strip of land protected by a parapet (–18c); a passage or covered way (17–19c), hence **1** a passage inside a building or a railway train (19c) **2** a strip of land allowing access through another country's territory (*c.*1920); (**air**) **corridor** a route that aircraft must follow, especially through foreign airspace (1920s), hence *corridor* the path a spacecraft must follow to re-enter the atmosphere safely (1970s) **3** the land along a major route and influenced by it (1960s).

corrode [ME. Latin *corrodere* 'to gnaw away', from *rodere* 'to gnaw'] Both *corrode* and **erode** [17c, from Latin *erodere*, literally 'to gnaw out'] mean 'to destroy gradually', by chemical action, disease, wear, or the effects of weather or water. Since the 19c *corrode* has been used for chemical action, *erode* for wear, weather, and water: both are used meaning 'to (cause to) deteriorate or diminish'.

Latin *rodere* is the ancestor of **rodent**, literally 'gnawing', and **rostrum** [Latin, literally 'beak, snout, muzzle'] originally a platform in the Forum in Rome decorated with the beak-heads of captured warships: a **beak-head** [from **beak** a bird's bill, via from Latin *beccus*, of Celtic origin] was a projection on the bows, some-times in the shape of an animal's or bird's head, used to pierce enemy ships.

corsage [ME. French, from *cors*: see CORSE*] (The size and shape of) the body (–17c). Re-adopted for the 'body' of a woman's dress, the bodice (19c), hence a posy worn on it (early 20c).

corsair [16c. Via French and Old Provençal from Italian *corsaro*, from Latin *cursarius*, from *cursus* (see COURSE) in the sense 'plunder'] A Muslim privateer preying on Christian shipping on the Barbary coast, hence any pirate; a pirate ship (17c).

Italian *corsaro* produced Hungarian *huszar* 'pirate, raider, light horseman', whence **hussar** one of a body of light horsemen in the Hungarian army, hence applied to British regiments modelled on them.

corse [ME. Old French *cors* from Latin CORPUS*] The living body of a human or animal (–16c); a dead human body (surviving in poetry), altered to **corps(e)** by association with its Latin ancestor (the final *e* was rare until the 19c).

Old French *cors* produced CORSAGE, **cors(e)let** a piece of armour, later a tight-fitting garment, covering the trunk (whence **corselette** a woman's foundation garment), and **corset** a close-fitting or laced bodice, later one worn as a foundation garment or for support. The alteration **corps** was adopted for a military force with particular skills or duties, hence an organized group (*corps de ballet, diplomatic corps*).

cosmetic [17c. Via French from Greek *kosmētikos*, from *kosmein* 'to arrange or adorn', from *kosmos*: see COSMOS*] The art of adorning or beautifying the body, hence **1** (a substance) used for this purpose; **cosmetic surgery** to improve your appearance (1920s) **2** designed merely to improve appearances, superficial (1950s).

cosmos [ME. Greek *kosmos* 'order, ornament', later 'the world or the universe', so called by Pythagoras who regarded the physical world as a perfectly ordered system] The universe as a whole (rare until the 19c); an ordered system (19c); order, harmony. Hence **cosmic: 1** of this world, worldly (recorded once in the 17c) **2** to do with the universe (19c); universal, infinite, immense; to do with the universe other than the earth; to do with travel beyond the earth [1950s, suggested by Russian *kosmischeskii*, from Greek *kosmos*], hence **cosmonaut** a (Russian) spaceman [1950s, partly from Russian *kosmonavt*, from Greek *kosmos* + *nautēs* 'sailor', on the pattern of English *astronaut*].

Greek *kosmos* is the ancestor of COSMETIC, **cosmology**, **cosmopolite** [via Greek *kosmopolitēs*, literally 'citizen of the world'], whence **cosmopolitan**, and of *-cosm* in MICROCOSM*.

costume [18c. French, from Italian *custume* 'custom, fashion, habit', from Latin *consuetudo*: see CUSTOM*] In art or literature: the appropriate customs, fashions, etc. of the time and place in which the work is set (–19c, surviving in **costume drama/piece**); the style of clothing, hair, etc. of a particular time, place, or type of person (19c), hence **1** clothing for a particular occasion, season, or activity (19c) **2** the clothes worn for a fancy-dress party, play, or film (19c); **costume**

jewellery artificial jewellery (1930s, *US*) **3** a complete set of outer garments, specifically a woman's dress (19c), now a woman's matching jacket and skirt.

cottage [ME. Anglo-Norman French *cotag* and Anglo-Latin *cotagium*, from Old English **cot** or related **cote**, both meaning 'small dwelling, shelter'] A small, humble rural house, hence **1** a small urban house for factory workers etc. (18c), later any small house; a holiday home (19c, *US*) **2** a public lavatory where homosexual men meet (1940s).

Cottage may originally have referred to the tenure of a cot. Cottage-dwellers were known by terms such as *coterell, cotman, cotsǣta, cotset(la), cottar* or *cott(i)er*: most of these died out with the feudal system but some survive as surnames and others were revived by 19c historians to describe holders of particular kinds of tenancy.

Cot and *cote* appear as **Cot-, -cot(t)** in place names, and survive in **dovecot(e)**, in dialect and poetry, and in the surname **Coates**. *Cotset* is probably the source of **cosset** a lamb brought up on the bottle, hence a spoiled, pampered child; to fondle or pet; to pamper or over-protect. Related to **coterie** a small exclusive group [French, 'group of joint tenants', ultimately from Low German *kote* 'cottage'].

couch [ME. Via Old French from Latin *collocare*, literally 'to place together', from *locare* 'to place', from *locus* 'a place'] To put or lay in place, hence **1** to lay flat or in layers (–18c); to decorate with thread laid on the cloth and stitched down **2** to put together; to put words together, to phrase in a certain way (16c) **3** to lie or crouch down, now chiefly of an animal in its lair, hence a place to lie: **(a)** a lair, now only an otter's **(b)** a piece of furniture to lie or sit on, especially a long seat, originally with a low back and one arm, now often simply a sofa; **couch potato** someone who spends hours on the couch watching television (1970s, *US*), possibly with a pun on *tuber* and a television tube, but probably just from the idea of vegetating **4** to bring down or lower, especially to lower a lance into position to attack (15c).

Latin *collocare* produced **collocate**; *locare* produced ALLOW*, **locate**, and **location** (**dislocation** is earlier); *locus* is the ancestor of LOCAL*.

count [ME. Via Old French *co(u)nter* from Latin *computare* 'to reckon up, to settle an account', from *putare* 'to clean', hence 'to prune, to clear up or settle'] **1** to add up or check items to determine the total number; (the result of) such a reckoning, the total (15c); to say numbers in order (*count to 10*, 16c), hence **count on** to make the basis of your calculations or plans, to rely on (17c) **2** to include or be included in a total or reckoning, hence to be important or significant (19c) **3** to tell or recount (–18c); an account or story (15–16c); a declaration, plea, or indictment (16c); an item in it (*two counts of manslaughter*) **4** to consider to be (*count yourself lucky*).

Old French *co(u)nter* had the senses 'to enumerate' and 'to narrate', which it passed on to **account** (ME–17c), hence a statement of an event, of someone's conduct, or of money, goods, etc. expended or owed. Both senses were also found in **reckon** [Old English *gerecenian*], originally to relate, later to mention a number of things in order, hence to count up or calculate, to estimate or regard as. **Tell** [Old English *tellan*] developed similarly: 'to enumerate' survives mainly in **teller** a voting officer or bank clerk, and **tell off** to enumerate your sins, to scold.

Old French *co(u)nter* also produced COUNTER, **discount**, modern French *raconteur*, and **recount**. Latin *computare* produced **compute** to calculate, hence **computer** a person, later a machine, that does so; *putare* is the ancestor of AMPUTATE, **depute** [via Old French from Latin *deputare* 'to consider to be', in late Latin 'to destine or assign'], **dispute**, **impute**, **putative**, and **repute**. *Tell* is related to **tale** and **talk**.

countenance [ME. Old French *contenance* 'bearing, behaviour', literally 'contents', from *contenir*: see CONTAIN*] Bearing, demeanour, hence **1** calmness, composure **2** facial expression, hence the face **3** your manner towards someone, showing approval or disapproval, hence to show regard for; to favour (16c); to approve or allow.

counter [ME. Via Old French from Latin *computarium*, from *computare*: see COUNT*] **1** something used in counting, especially a small disc, hence one used in a game to keep score or show a player's position (16c) **2** a table where money is counted (–17c); a desk etc. in a shop where goods and money are exchanged (17c), a service desk in a bank, library, etc. (19c); the place where food is displayed in a cafeteria; a work surface in a kitchen (mid 20c).

counterpart [15c. From **counter-** 'corresponding, matching' (via French from Latin *contra* 'against') + PART*] Each of the two parts of an indenture (see *indenture* at INDENT), hence **1** a copy of a legal document **2** each of two parts that fit together and complete each other (17c); in music: a part written to accompany another (18c) **3** a person or thing that naturally goes with or complements another (17c); a person or thing that is similar to another, or has a similar function, in a different context.

Counter-, meaning 'corresponding' etc., appears also in *counterfeit*, *counterfoil*, etc. In **counter** to oppose, *counteract*, *countermand*, etc., and **encounter** originally to meet as an enemy, the meaning is 'against'. **Contra-** (*contradict*, *contrary*, CONTRETEMPS, etc.) always means 'against'.

coup [ME. French, from medieval Latin *colpus* 'a blow': see COPE¹*] **1** a blow given or received in combat (–16c) **2** [re-borrowed from modern French] an unexpected and successful stroke or action (18c).

French *coup* is also found in *coup de grâce* a fatal blow, especially to end suffering, hence the final act that ends something, and *coup d'état* [literally 'blow of State'], the overthrow of a government, shortened to *coup*.

coupon [19c. French, literally 'piece cut off', from *couper* 'to cut', from Old French *co(l)per*: see COPE¹*] A detachable piece of a stock certificate to be given up in return for payment of interest (19c), hence **1** a voucher to be cut from a book, originally for railway tickets and hotel accommodation (19c, introduced by Thomas Cook), later for rationed goods (World War I), hence any voucher **2** a part of an advertisement etc. to be cut out and sent to the advertiser for goods or further information (*c*.1900); an entry form for a competition, especially a football pool.

French *couper* produced *coupé* [shortened from *carrosse coupé* 'cut carriage'] a closed carriage for two passengers, modelled on a larger four-seater, hence a two-door car with a hard top (unusual for the time) and, originally, two seats, *découpage* the art of decorating with paper cut-outs, and **recoup** originally to cut short.

courage [ME. Old French *corage* from Latin *cor* 'heart' (ancestor of CORDIAL*)] The heart as the basis of thoughts and feelings (–17c), hence anger, arrogance, lust, pride (–17c), also spirit, confidence; boldness, bravery, fortitude. Hence **discourage** to dishearten (ME); to dissuade or deter; to try to prevent (17c); **encourage** to hearten (ME); to urge or recommend (15c); to foster or promote (17c).

The **heart** [Old English *heorte*] was also seen as the source of kindness and good feelings (hence **hearty**, **heartless**: cf. CORDIAL), and especially of love. *Heart* also means the central or innermost part of something (cf. CORE).

courier Strictly speaking, two words, both ultimately from Latin *currere* 'to run' (ancestor of CURRENT*)] I [ME, via Old French] a fast, literally a running, messenger, hence **1** a messenger for a clandestine organization (1920s) **2** a person or company that delivers packages quickly (1970s); to send something by courier II [16c, via French and Italian] a mounted soldier used as a skirmisher or scout (–17c); a messenger sent ahead of travellers to arrange accommodation or fresh horses (17c); someone employed to help tourists during their trip (19c).

course [ME. French *cours*, from Latin *cursus*, from *currere* 'to run'] A run or gallop (–17c); movement along a path, hence **1** the path (*watercourse/racecourse/golf course*, etc.); the route of a ship, aircraft, etc. (16c) **2** the ability or opportunity to run or flow; to do so quickly or freely (15c) **3** the chasing of hares, now usually as **coursing 4** the progress of time or events, hence **(a)** the normal progression of events; the normal procedure; a way of proceeding (*the wisest course*, 16c); a planned series (*course of antibiotics/lectures*); a curriculum **(b)** a step in a series: a part of a meal; a row or layer (*damp course*, 15c).

Coarse (15c, spelt *course* until the 17c) may be the same word. Originally meaning 'common, ordinary' (perhaps in the normal course of things), hence of poor quality; the sense 'rough, harsh' (16c) may be from coarse (*ordinary*) cloth for everyday wear; the senses 'unrefined, uncivilized, rude, obscene' date from the 17c.

Latin *cursus* produced CORSAIR; *currere* is the ancestor of CURRENT*.

court [ME. Old French *cort* '(a building with) a courtyard', later 'a monarch's residence', also 'a legal or administrative assembly', by association with Latin *curia* '(the meeting place of) one of the main divisions of the Roman people', ultimately from Latin *cohors* 'an enclosed space', from *hortus* 'garden'] **1** a ruler's residence, household, and associates, hence (to give or seek) the flattering attention typical of courtiers (16c); to woo, hence to risk attracting something (*courting disaster*, 1930s) **2** a formal assembly of the sovereign, ministers, and officials; (a meeting of) a legislative body; its meeting place **3** **court(yard)** an open space surrounded by buildings or walls, hence *court*: **(a)** a large building with a courtyard, surviving in the names of former manors (*Tottenham Court*) and apartment or office blocks (with or without courtyards) **(b)** a space marked out for a game (16c) **(c)** a yard opening off a street; a courtyard surrounded by houses (17c) **(d)** a large space within a building (*Palm Court, food court*), originally in the building housing the Great Exhibition of 1851.

Latin *cohors* produced COHORT, French **cortège** a retinue of court attendants, later of mourners, **courtesan** literally a female courtier, **courtesy** literally manners fit for court, later (a gesture of) politeness or respect (whence **curtsy**), and **courtier**.

Latin *hortus* produced the name **Hortense, horticulture, orchard** [Old English *ortgeard*, with YARD²] originally a garden growing herbs and fruit trees, and **ortolan** a small garden bird [French from Provençal, literally 'gardener'].

cousin   [ME. Via Old French from Latin *consobrinus* 'mother's sister's child', ultimately from **soror** 'sister' (ancestor of **sorority**)] **1** a child of your parent's sibling, since the 17c often called a **first cousin** (largely replacing *cousin-german*: see GERM), hence **second cousin** a child of your parent's first cousin, and so on **2** any close relative other than a sibling or parent (–18c), hence someone/something having much in common with another; a form of address used by a monarch to another monarch or nobleman (15c); **kissing cousin** a relative or friend sufficiently close to be greeted with a kiss (1950s, US).

couth   [Old English *cuth*, past participle of *cunnan* CAN¹] Famous, known, familiar (–16c), hence **1 uncouth** unfamiliar, strange (–17c); ignorant (ME–17c); awkward, vulgar, rude (17c, cf. *ignorant* at IGNORE, RUDE), whence *couth* cultured, polite (19c) **2** Scots **couthie** kindly, affable (18c); pleasant, cosy.
     Old English *cuth* appears in the name **Cuthbert**, and probably produced **cuddle**.

cove   [Old English *cofa*] **1** a small chamber or closet **2** a cave; a small sheltered valley (ME), bay, or inlet (16c); a narrow recess in a mountain or cliff (19c) **3** an arch or vault (16c), a concave moulding like the shoulder of an arch (17c), also called **coving** (18c).
     Old English *cofa* appears as **Cof-** or **Cov-** in place names. Related to *cubby* in **cubby hole.**

coy   [ME. Old French *coi, quei*, from Latin *quietus:* see QUIET*] Quiet, unassuming (first recorded as a surname); modest, bashful, shy, especially of a girl, hence provocatively pretending to be so (16c); annoyingly reticent, evasive (1960s).

craft   [Old English *craeft*] Strength, power (–16c); ability, skill, ingenuity (*handicraft, roadcraft*), hence **1 (a)** a skilled trade; those who practise one (ME), hence **craftsman** (originally *craft's man*) a skilled tradesman; one who does anything with skill and care (19c) **(b)** to make something skilfully (ME, extremely rare before the 1960s, when it was probably re-created from *craftsman*) **2** an ingenious device or stratagem (–17c); a magic spell, also occult art or skill (ME–16c), guile, cunning, hence **crafty** [Old English *craeftig* 'strong'] meaning 'cunning, wily' (ME): cf. *artful* (at ART), *cunning* (at CAN¹) **3 small craft** small boats collectively (15c, perhaps requiring 'small craft' (less skill), to handle than larger vessels), hence *craft* boats collectively (18c); a single vessel; later an aeroplane (19c) or spaceship (1960s).
     Related to Swedish *kraft* 'strength', whence **kraft paper.**

crane   [Old English *cran*] A wading bird with long legs, neck, and bill; a similar bird, hence **1** a tall lifting device with a long jib (resembling the bird, ME); a movable support with a long arm; a moving platform for a camera (1930s) **2 cranesbill** applied to several wild geraniums whose fruits have a long spur like a crane's beak (16c) **3 crane your neck** to stretch to get a better view (18c).
     Geranium comes via Latin from Greek *geranion*, from *geranos* 'crane'; the garden geranium is a related species, the **pelargonium** [via Latin from Greek *pelargos*

'stork']. Old English *cran* appears in place names (*Cranford/Cranbrook*). Related to **cranberry** [German *Kranbeere* 'crane berry'].

crank [Old English: related to **cringe** and **crinkle**] A sharply bent axle, shaft, or handle, hence **1** to bend sharply (18c); bent, distorted (18c, Scots), hence **(a)** awkward, difficult to do (18c, now only Scots) **(b)** (earlier as **cranky**) sick or infirm (18c: cf. CROOK), hence *cranky* peevish, difficult to please (19c); odd, eccentric; *crank* an eccentric idea or person (cf. CROTCHET) **2** to operate with a crank (19c); to turn over or start a car engine with one (*c.*1910); **crank up** to increase inexorably, as if wound up with a crank (1930s); to inject heroin etc. (1970s).

crate [ME. Latin *cratis* 'hurdle, wickerwork' (ancestor of GRIDDLE*)] A hurdle (–16c); a basket or slatted wooden box, hence an (old) aeroplane (1920s, early aircraft being made with wooden struts).

craven [ME. Probably from Old French *cravanter* 'to crush or overwhelm', from Latin *crepare* 'to rattle, crack, or burst'] Defeated, overcome, hence admitting defeat, abject, cowardly; a coward (16c); a cock that will not fight.
Latin *crepare* produced **crevice** [via Old French *crevace* (from *crever* 'to split'), whence modern French *crevasse*], **decrepit** old, feeble, later dilapidated, and **discrepance** [via *discrepare* 'to be discordant'], largely replaced by **discrepancy**.

craze [ME. Perhaps from Old Norse] To (cause to) shatter (–19c), hence **1** especially of pottery: to crack (15c); to produce, later to develop, small cracks in the glaze, hence *crazed* (15c), *crazy* (16c) full of cracks; **crazy paving/quilt** made of irregular pieces, resembling crazed pottery (19c) **2 (a)** to break someone's physical or mental health (15c), hence *crazed*, *crazy* sick or infirm (16–19c), mad, absurd; wildly enthusiastic (19c) **(b)** a mad idea, a mania (19c); a fad.

creature [ME. French, from Latin *creatura*, from *creare* 'to create'] Something created, hence **1** any member of the animal kingdom; a person of a certain kind (*creature of habit*); a despicable person, especially someone's puppet (17c) **2** something good (17c, from the biblical phrase 'every creature (*creation*) of God is good', I Timothy 4:4); a material comfort, especially food, hence **the creature** alcoholic drink, especially whisky.
Latin *creare* fathered *recreare*, literally 'to re-create, to restore', whence **recreation** refreshment, originally food, later (an activity providing) mental and emotional refreshment.

credence [ME. French, from medieval Latin *credentia*, from *credere* 'to believe, trust, or entrust'] **1** belief, acceptance as true **2** trustworthiness, hence **letter of credence** a letter of introduction or recommendation, largely replaced by **credential letter(s)** or **credentials** (17c), now meaning proofs of your identity, status, etc. **3** safekeeping (15–16c), hence, perhaps, a cupboard or sideboard (16–19c, surviving in the Italian form *credenza*, 19c); a small table, shelf, etc. for things used in the Eucharist (19c).
Latin *credere*'s descendants include **credible**, CREDIT, **credulous**, **creed**, and **grant** [via Old French *creanter, greanter* 'to assure, guarantee, or promise', whence also **miscreant** (via Old French *mescreant* 'unbelieving'), originally (describing) a heretic].

credit [16c. French *crédit*, ultimately from Latin *creditum*, from *credere*: see CREDENCE*] Belief, trust; to believe or trust, hence **1** trust in someone's intention and ability to pay (15c in **creditor**), hence **(a)** an arrangement to defer payment **(b)** a reputation for honesty and solvency; money available to support this (17c) **(c)** (to make) a record of money paid or paid into a bank (18c) **2** trustworthiness (–19c); good reputation; causing this (*does you credit/a credit to you*), hence **(a) discredit** (to cause) loss of reputation or confidence (16c) **(b)** acknowledgement of merit or achievement (17c), now, that a student has completed a course or course unit (*c.*1900); **credits** acknowledgements of people's contributions to a film etc. (early 20c) **(c)** to attribute a good quality or achievement to someone (19c).

French *crédit* produced **accredit** to authorize or vouch for; to provide with credentials; to recognize officially.

creep [Old English *creopan*] To crawl or drag yourself along the ground; to move or approach slowly, timidly, or stealthily (ME); slow or stealthy movement (15c), hence **1** to insinuate yourself (ME); an obsequious or unpleasant person (19c, *US*) **2** to advance or develop gradually (ME); to change shape gradually under pressure (19c); such change (cf. *mission creep* at MISSION) **3** to feel as if covered with crawling insects (ME), hence **the creeps** a feeling of disgust or fear (19c); **creepy** producing it **4** of a plant: to grow over a surface or up a support (15c); **creeper** such a plant (17c) **5** (an enclosure with) a low entrance (19c), especially allowing only young animals to enter and feed **6** **(brothel-)creepers** soft-soled (suede) shoes (19c).

Senses 1 and 2 are partly shared by **crawl** [probably of Scandinavian origin]: the two words come together in **creepy-crawly**.

crescendo [18c. Italian, literally 'growing, ultimately from Latin *crescere*: see CRESCENT*] A direction to play a piece of music with a gradual increase in volume (18c); such an increase or piece, hence a build-up to a climax; a climax (1920s, *US*).

crescent [ME. Old French *creissant* 'growing', ultimately from Latin *crescere* 'to grow'] The moon between new and full; the shape of the moon in its first and, later, last quarter (15c), hence **1** this shape as an ornament or symbol, adopted by the Turkish sultans (16c) and later by Muslims in general **2** something crescent-shaped (17c), specifically a street or row of houses (18c).

Old French *creissant* evolved into *croissant* (called a *crescent* in N America). Latin *crescere* is the ancestor of **accrue**, **concrete** [Latin *concrescere* 'to grow together'], CRESCENDO, CREW, **decrease**, **excrescence**, **increase**, **increment**, and RECRUIT.

crest [ME. Old French *creste* from Latin *crista* 'tuft, plume'] A plume on a helmet that identifies the wearer, hence **1** **elevate your crest** to show readiness for battle, **crestfallen** dejected, disheartened (16c) **2** the heraldic symbol of a family etc. **3** a tuft of feathers or hairs on top of a bird's or animal's head **4** the top of a helmet; a summit or culmination; a ridge (whence, probably, **crease** a fold or wrinkle, 16c); to reach a summit or ridge (19c).

crew [15c. Old French *creüe* 'increase', from *croistre* 'to grow', from Latin *crescere*: see CRESCENT*] A band of soldiers serving as reinforcements (–16c), hence any organized armed band (16c); a group of people, animals, or things; a squad of workers or, later, sailors (17c), hence **1** the sailors manning a ship (technically, everyone but the captain, but sometimes excluding the officers); to man a ship

(1930s) **2** the people manning an aircraft (early 20c) or spaceship (1960s) **3** the technicians working on a film (1950s).

crib [Old English] A manger or hayrack, hence **1** the manger in which the Christ-child was laid; a baby's bed (17c); a model of the Nativity scene (19c) **2** an animal's stall; a confined space (16c, hence to confine or hamper, 17c); a room; a (small) house; a public house or brothel (19c) **3** a basket (ME–19c); a (slatted) storage bin (17c); a framework of bars or slats **4** to steal or pilfer (18c, perhaps originally from a bin), hence to plagiarize a passage or translation; a plagiarized passage (19c); a translation used by students.

Related to French *crèche* 'manger, hayrack', adopted for a Nativity model, hence a day-care centre for children.

crime [ME. Via French from Latin *crimen* 'judgement, indictment, offence', ultimately from *cernere, cret-* 'to judge, separate, or sift'] Sinfulness (rare since the 17c); a sinful, later an illegal, act, hence **1** illegal activity, law-breaking (15c) **2** something deplorable or shameful (16c).

Latin *crimen* produced **incriminate** and **recriminate** [via *criminare* 'to accuse'], Latin *cernere*'s descendants include **ascertain**, **certain**, CONCERN, CONCERT*, **decree**, DISCRETION*, **excrete**, and SECRET*.

crisis [ME. Latin, from Greek *krisis* 'decision', from *krinein* 'to decide'] The turning point of a disease, later of a situation (17c); an uncertain or dangerous time; a time or situation calling for decisive action.

Greek *krinein* produced *kritēs* 'a judge', whence **criterion**, **critic** someone who passes judgement, later specifically on artistic works, **critical** which has senses related to both *crisis* and *critic* (*a critical moment/critical report*), and **critique**.

crook [ME. Old Norse *krókr*] A hook, hence **1** something hook-shaped, specifically a shepherd's staff with a hooked end, hence a bishop's crozier; a sharply curved part of anything; a curve or bend (15c) **2** to make or become bent, hence **crooked** deformed, bent with age (ME), whence perhaps *crook* 'sick, infirm' (Australian: cf. CRANK), and the surname **Crook** for someone with bent limbs or back **3** deceit, trickery, a trick (–17c, hence *crooked* dishonest, corrupt, probably influenced by Old Norse *krókóttr* 'cunning, deceitful', but cf. RIGHT); a criminal or swindler (19c, *US*).

Old Norse *krókr* is the ancestor of CROTCHET*, the names **Croxford** and **Cruikshank**, ENCROACH, and perhaps of **crotch** and **crouch**. Related to *crozier* (at CRUSADE), **crutch**, and **lacrosse** [Canadian French *(jeu de) la crosse* '(game of) the hooked stick'].

crop [Old English *cropp*: ultimately from a prehistoric Germanic word meaning 'rounded mass'; the sense 'top' developed in English] **1** a pouch in a bird's gullet **2** a plant top, especially picked for use (ME, now dialect), hence **(a)** to cut off the top; to graze; to pick flowers or fruit **(b)** the produce of cultivated plants; such plants; a season's produce (16c); to harvest or yield a crop (17c); to raise crops, to farm (19c, *US*) **(c)** to cut short (16c); a short haircut (18c); to cut off or mask part of a photograph (19c) **(d) crop out/up** of rock: to stick through the earth like a growing crop (17c, hence **outcrop**, 19c); **crop up** to appear or happen unexpectedly **3** the stock of a whip (15c); a short whip (*riding crop*, 19c).

Crop produced the surname **Cropper, Crapper** someone who harvested produce or polled cattle. Related to **croup** an animal's hindquarters, French *croupier* 'pillion rider', hence an advisor standing behind a card player, usually sharing the stake and winnings (cf. GALLERY sense 2a), later someone who takes in and pays out bets in a casino, **crupper** a strap over a horse's croup, and **group**, literally a knot or cluster.

cross [ME. Old Norse *kross* from Old Irish *cros* (replacing Old English *cruc*), ultimately from Latin CRUX*] **1** (a monument representing) the structure on which Christ was executed (earliest in place names, e.g. *Crossfield, Crosby*); a cross as a symbol of Christ, his crucifixion, or Christianity, hence **(a)** its shape; to trace it as a blessing or act of devotion, or to seal a vow (*cross your heart*) **(b)** a burden or trial (borne for Christ's sake as Christ carried his cross to his execution) **2** a mark or figure with two intersecting lines: **(a)** as a heraldic symbol; a cross-shaped medal (*George Cross*, 17c) **(b) cross out** to cancel by marking with a cross or, later, by drawing a line through; *cross* to cross someone's name out to debar them (16–18c); to thwart or oppose, hence opposite, contrary (*cross purposes*); perverse, argumentative (–19c); irritable, angry (17c) **3** to (cause to) intersect, hence **(a)** to go over; to pass a boundary (15c); to breed an animal or plant with one of a different kind (18c); a hybrid **(b)** an intersection (16c), hence **crossroad(s)** a road junction (18c); a moment of decision (19c, cf. *crucial* at CRUX) **4** to go or extend from side to side, end to end, or corner to corner (16c); such a movement or stroke (19c) **5** involving interchange or reciprocal action (16c); to pass in opposite directions (*the letters crossed in the post*, 18c).

Crisscross 'Christ's cross', alteration of **cross of Christ** or **croscrist**, the figure of the cross preceding the alphabet in a child's primer, was taken for a doubling of *cross*, and came to mean to go across and back repeatedly, also a network of intersecting lines. Old English *cruc* produced the surname **Crouch(er)**, who lived by a cross, and **crutched** describing orders of friars who wore or carried a conspicuous cross. The usual Old English word for Christ's cross was **rood**, surviving in **rood screen** a screen topped with a cross separating the choir or chancel of a church from the nave.

crotchet [ME. French *crochet*, from *croc* 'hook', from Old Norse *krókr*] A small hook, especially **1** an ornamental hook or pin **2** a decorative leaf-shape on a spire or gable (largely replaced by 17c **crocket**, also from French *crochet*) **3** a musical note; originally formed by adding a 'hook' to the stem of a minim, then written as a solid note: when the minim became a hollow note in the 15c the hook was transferred to the quaver (see also LARGE sense 3b) **4** a whim, a perverse idea (16c), hence **crotchety** peevish, 19c: cf. CRANK); a fanciful device (17c).

French *crochet* was adopted for a kind of knitting using a small hook; the N French variant *croquet* 'bishop's crook', later 'hockey stick', was adopted for a ball game played with a mallet, and fathered **roquet** to strike, or the striking of, an opponent's ball in this game. Old Norse *krókr* is the ancestor of CROOK*.

crowd [Old English *crūdan*] To press or push (–ME), hence **1** to press on, to hurry, originally of a ship (rare between ME and 17c, now only US: later uses perhaps from **crowd on sails** to cram the masts with sails for speed) **2** to push in a barrow (ME, now US and dialect) **3** to push your way into a confined space or through a mass of people (15c) **4** to gather or press together in a mass (15c), hence a mass of people (16c) or of things (17c) crammed together; a group of people with something in common (*the in-crowd*, 19c) **5** to cram people or things into a small space (16c); to fill a place to overflowing (17c) **6** to come close to someone in an intimidating way (17c); to pressurize.

crown [ME. Via Old French from Latin *corona* 'wreathe, chaplet, crown', from Greek *korōnē* 'something curved', from *korōnis* 'curved'] A circlet worn by a monarch as a symbol of their authority (ME), hence **1** (to confer) the title and authority of a monarch, hence **the Crown** the monarch as Head of State (16c) **2** (to award) a crown, garland, etc. as a symbol of honour, achievement, or victory; an award or distinction; a culmination or highest achievement (15c) **3** the top: **(a)** of the head (hence to hit on the head, 18c); of a hat (15c); of a hill (16c); of a tooth (19c), hence (to fit) an artificial one **(b)** the centre of a (cambered) road (17c); **crown bowls** played on a cambered green (19c) **4** something resembling or marked with a crown, e.g. a coin (15c); a size of paper (38 x 51 cm), originally having a crown as a watermark (18c).

Latin *corona* is recorded once in Old English referring to Christ's crown of thorns; it was reborrowed for things resembling a crown, e.g. the top of a cornice; a 'halo' round the sun, moon, etc., or round an electrode, and for a Havana cigar (originally a trade name). Latin *corona* produced **coronary** literally 'like a crown', applied to nerves, blood vessels, etc. encircling a body part, particularly the heart, hence **coronary (thrombosis)** a clot in the coronary artery; loosely, a heart attack (US). Other descendants include *corolla* [literally 'little crown'] adopted for the whorl of petals forming a flower head, **corollary** [Latin *corollarium* 'money for a garland', hence 'a tip, something extra', from *corolla*], **coronation**, **coroner**, originally an officer responsible for the monarch's private property, and **coronet**.

crucial [18c. French, from Latin CRUX*] Like or to do with a cross: **1** in anatomy: crossing, cross-shaped (18c, largely replaced by 19c **cruciate**, also from Latin *crux*) **2** that decides between hypotheses [19c, from *experimentum crucis* 'experiment at the cross(road)', from the 16c British philosopher Francis Bacon's phrase *instantia crucis* 'instance of the cross', which he explained as a metaphor from a signpost at a crossroad], hence decisive, very important.

crude [ME. Latin *crudus* 'raw, rough'] Not processed or refined, hence **1** not properly thought out or finished (17c); unskilfully planned or made; approximate, not corrected, adjusted, or explained (19c) **2** rough, rude, blunt (17c); coarse, obscene. Cf. RUDE.

Latin *crudus* fathered French *crudités*. Related to **cruel**.

cruise [17c. Probably from Dutch *kruisen* 'to cross', from *kruis* 'cross', from Latin CRUX*] To sail to and fro across the sea seeking for ships to plunder or, later, to protect shipping (whence **cruiser** a privateer, later a fast warship), hence **1** to wander about seeking something, now especially sexual partners **2** (to go on) a pleasure voyage (19c), hence **(a)** *cruiser* a boat designed for this **(b)** to travel at a comfortable, steady speed (early 20c).

crumb [Old English *cruma*. The final *b* was added in the 16c, perhaps from related **crumble**, but also by association with words such as *climb* and *dumb*] A small particle, especially of bread, cake, or biscuit, hence **1** the soft inner part of a loaf (ME) **2** a tiny amount (*a crumb of comfort*, 16c) **3** a body louse, resembling a crumb (19c, US), hence **crumby**, **crummy** lousy, filthy, shoddy, worthless (19c); *crumb* a lousy, filthy, or insignificant person (early 20c).

crusade [ME. Old French *croise* 'cross', from Latin CRUX*. Originally *croiserie*: the current spelling evolved under the influence of Spanish *cruzado* and medieval Latin *cruciata*, both meaning 'marked with a cross', crusaders being blessed with the sign of the cross before setting out] A war or expedition sanctioned by the Christian church for religious ends (15c), specifically one of the medieval campaigns to wrest the Holy Land and Spain from the Muslims, hence (to carry on) a vigorous campaign with a religious or moral purpose (18c).

Old French *croise* is one parent of **crozier** [the other being Old French *croce* 'crook' (related to CROOK*)] someone who carried a cross or a bishop's crook in procession (surviving as a surname), hence an archbishop's processional cross.

crux [17c. Latin *crux* 'cross' (for crucifixion), hence 'torment, misery'] **1** a cross, chiefly in **crux ansata** [literally 'cross with a handle'] an ankh **2** something difficult to explain, a puzzle [18c, probably from medieval Latin *crux interpretum* 'interpreter's cross', something that mentally 'crucified' an interpreter], hence the chief problem or essential point (19c, perhaps influenced by *crucial*).

Descendants of Latin *crux* include CROSS*, CRUCIAL*, **crucible** [via Latin *crucibulum* 'night light', probably in front of a crucifix], **crucify**, CRUISE, CRUSADE*, and **excruciating** [via Latin *excruciare* 'to torture'].

cubicle [ME. Latin *cubiculum*, from *cubare* 'to lie down'] A bedroom (–17c); reintroduced for a small partitioned space in a dormitory (19c), hence any small compartment (1920s).

Latin *cubare* is the ancestor of **concubine**, **covey**, INCUMBENT*, and of *incubus* and *succubus* (at NIGHTMARE).

cuckold [OE. Old French *cucuault*, from *cucu* **cuckoo**, imitating its call] A man whose wife is unfaithful (who may have someone else's chicks in his nest); to make a cuckold of (16c). Hence **cuckquean** [from *cuckold* + *quean* 'woman': see KING] a woman whose husband is unfaithful (16c, inexplicably rare since the 17c).

Until the 16c *cuckoo* existed side by side with Scots and N English **gowk** [Old Norse *gaukr*]: both developed the sense 'fool', and *cuckoo* the sense 'foolish, crazy', whence, probably, **kook** a crazy or eccentric person. **Cuckoo pint**, the wild arum, owes its name to its column of red berries (*pint* being short for **pintle** 'penis' [Old English *pintel*]), the red and knobbly appearance perhaps suggesting disease.

cull [ME. Old French *coillier*, *cuieller*, ultimately from Latin *colligere*: see COLLECT*] To select from a large number; selecting, a selection (17c), originally for good qualities (hence to pick flowers etc., surviving in the surname **Culpepper** a spicer), later in order to reject unsuitable or surplus items or animals.

culpable [ME. Anglo-Norman variant of Old French *coupable* (the usual English spelling until the 15c), from Latin *culpabilis*, from *culpare* 'to blame', from *culpa* 'fault, blame'] Guilty of a crime or sin, deserving punishment, or, later, blame or censure.

Anglo-Norman French *culpable* appeared in the clerk's response to a plea of 'not guilty': *Culpable: prest d'averrer notre bille* '(You are) guilty: (we are) ready to prove our indictment', entered in the court records as the abbreviation *cul.prist*. As French died out in English courts this was apparently misinterpreted, the Clerk addressing the accused as *culpri(s)t*, hence **culprit** the accused or guilty person.

cult [17c. (Via French from) Latin *cultus*, from *colere*: see CULTURE*] Worship (17c only); a system of worship, with its rituals, symbols, etc. (*the cult of the Virgin*); the idolization of a person or thing (18c), hence **1** a religious sect, now especially one regarded as fanatical or misguided (19c) **2** (describing) someone/something 'idolized' by an in-group (*c*.1900).

culture [ME. (Via French from) Latin *cultura* 'care, cultivation', from *colere*, *cult-* 'to inhabit, till, protect, or worship'] A piece of cultivated land (–18c); cultivation of the land (cf. *agriculture* below), hence **1** to cultivate land, crops, or animals (16c, now rare); to cultivate, or the cultivation of, bacteria, tissue, etc. (19c); the growth obtained **2** cultivation of the mind, education (16c); refinement, sophistication; artistic and intellectual pursuits (19c); the arts, language, customs, and beliefs of a time, place, or people; a society or group defined by this; the attitudes and behaviour of a particular group (*drug culture*).

Latin *cultura* combined with *ager* 'field' to produce *agricultura*, whence **agriculture** originally tilling the soil but later including all farming activities, whence **-culture** (*apiculture*, *horticulture*). Latin *colere* is the ancestor of COLONY, CULT, and **cultivate**.

cunning [Old English *cunnan* (whence CAN[1]*) or related Old Norse *kunna* 'to know'] Knowledge, learning (–16c), hence **1** knowledgeable, learned (–17c); clever, shrewd (17c) **2** knowledge of the occult (ME–16c), hence craftiness, guile (15c); devious, wily (16c) **3** skilful (ME), skilfully planned or done, ingenious (15c), hence quaint, charming (19c, *US*). Cf. *artful* (at ART), *crafty* (at CRAFT), *cute* (at ACUTE).

cupidity [15c. (Via French from) Latin *cupiditas*, ultimately from *cupere* 'to desire'] **1** greed for (someone else's) money or possessions **2** strong desire, lust (16c).

Latin *cupiditas* produced **covet** to desire greedily or, formerly, sexually; *cupere* is the ancestor of **concupiscence** excessive desire, lust, and of **Cupid** the Roman god of love, usually depicted as a winged, naked boy carrying arrows and a bow with a double curve, hence **Cupid's arrow/dart** the overwhelming power of love, **Cupid's bow** a double curve, especially of the top lip, **kewpie doll** (the trade name of) a chubby doll with a curl or topknot (*US*).

curate [ME. Medieval Latin *curatus*, from Latin *cura*: see CURE*] **1** someone responsible for the spiritual welfare of laymen; a vicar's or parish priest's assistant (16c); **curate's egg** something only partly good (19c, from a cartoon showing a curate being served a bad egg at the bishop's table: desperate for patronage, he insists that 'parts of it are excellent') **2** a supervisor or steward (15–17c): cf. *curator* below **3** in Ireland: a liquor-seller's assistant (*c*.1900), perhaps thought to affect the parish's spiritual state.

Latin *cura* produced **curator**, originally a spiritual pastor, later a legal guardian (surviving in Scots law), and re-borrowed for an overseer or steward (replacing *curate*), hence the custodian of a museum, library, etc., whence **curate** to act as curator.

curb [15c. French *courber*, from Latin *curvare* from *curvus* 'curved, bent' (ancestor of **curve**)] To bend or bow (–19c), hence **1** (a bit with) a chain that goes under the horse's jaw, used to make the horse bend its neck or to check a headstrong animal, hence (to use) a check or restraint (17c) **2** an (originally curved) edging or frame (16c); a raised margin or edging (18c, spelt **kerb** in British English since the 19c).

curd [15c. Variant of Middle English **crud**, which it replaced except in dialect: origin unknown] The solid part of sour milk, hence **1** a similar substance (*lemon/ bean curd*); the edible head of cauliflower or broccoli (18c) **2** to congeal or coagulate, whence **curdle** (16c), which has replaced it.

Crud produced Scots **crowdie** a soft cheese, and resurfaced meaning 'filth, slime, excrement' (1940s, US).

cure [ME. French, from Latin *curare* 'to take care of', from *cura* 'care'] Care, concern, responsibility, also to take care of or responsibility for (–17c), hence **1 the cure of souls** the spiritual care of a parish **2** (to give) medical care (–18c); (to give) successful treatment, hence **(a)** a remedy (15c); a method or course of treatment (19c); a stay at a health resort for treatment **(b)** to put something right (15c) **3 (a)** to preserve by salting or pickling (17c); the method or substance used (18c) **(b)** to improve by a chemical process (19c); the process used or quality obtained (*c.*1900); to undergo such treatment (1920s).

Latin *cura* is the ancestor of **accurate**, CURATE*, French *curette* a surgical instrument for cleaning out a cavity, CURIOUS, **manicure**, **pedicure**, PROCURE*, SCOUR, **sinecure** [from Latin *(beneficium) sine cura*] originally an ecclesiastical benefice without the cure of souls, and SURE*.

curfew [ME. Old French *cuevrefeu*, from *cuvrir* 'to cover' + *feu* 'fire'] A regulation, common in medieval towns, requiring fires to be extinguished at night to avoid accidents, hence **1** (the bell rung as) a signal for this; the regular ringing of any bell **2** an order for people to stay indoors at night or at other specified times (19c).

curious [ME. Via French from Latin *curiosus*, from *cura*: see CURE*] Careful, diligent (–18c), hence **1** assiduous, eager to learn, inquisitive, nosy **2** needing careful study, obscure, occult (–18c); interesting, remarkable (–19c), hence **curiosity** (17c), **curio** an interesting object (19c) **3** carefully, elaborately or skilfully made (–19c, surviving, just, in **curiously**) **4** [from French] odd, strange (18c).

current [ME. Old French *corant*, from *courre* 'to run', from Latin *currere*] Running or flowing (–19c), hence **1** something that does: **(a)** a stream of water or air **(b)** a general trend or tendency (16c, more common in **undercurrent**) **(c)** (the rate of) a flow of electricity (18c) **2** in circulation (15c): **(a)** of money (15c), hence **currency** legal tender, anything used as money (18c) **(b)** of facts, theories, etc.: generally known or accepted (16c) **3** in the present, happening now (17c); **current account** a bank account for present needs (19c).

Latin *currere* is the ancestor of of CONCUR*, CORRIDOR, CORSAIR, COURIER, COURSE*, and CURSOR, **discourse**, EXCURSION*, **incur** and **incursion** [both from Latin *incurare* 'to run in'], **intercourse**, **occur**, **precursor**, RECOURSE*, **succour** [Latin *sucurrere*, literally 'to run after'], Latin *curriculum* 'running, course', adopted for (the content of) a course of study, and in *curriculum vitae*, literally 'course of life', and producing **curricle** a light two-wheeled carriage.

cursor [ME. Latin, from *currere*: see CURRENT*] A runner; a running messenger, hence a movable marker on a slide rule or other instrument (16c), or on a computer screen (1960s).

Latin *cursor* produced *cursorius* 'to do with or like a runner', whence **cursory** passing rapidly over, hasty, superficial.

curt [15c. Latin *curtus* 'cut short, abridged'] Short, shortened, hence concise, brief (17c); terse, abrupt (19c).

Latin *curtus* is the ultimate ancestor of **curtal** to cut short, later especially to dock a horse's tail [French *courtault* 'something shortened', from *court* 'short'], altered to **curtail** by association with *tail* or French *tailler* 'to cut'.

custard [ME. Anglo-Norman French *crustarde* (the original English spelling), ultimately from Latin *crusta* 'rind, shell, crust'] An open pie, usually containing meat or fruit in a sauce thickened with eggs, hence the sauce, later a sweetened, cooked sauce of eggs and milk (16c); a similar sauce of milk thickened with cornflour or a proprietary mix (19c).

Latin *crusta* is the ancestor of **crust**, **crustacean**, and of several words adopted in the 19c and 20c with meanings closer to the original sense of *custard*: Italian *crostini* fried or toasted bread with a savoury topping, French *croustard* a case of fried bread, pastry, or potato with savoury or sweet filling, and French *croûte* fried bread or pastry on which game or savouries are served, whence *croûton* a piece of fried bread served with soup, *en croûte* on or in pastry.

custom [ME. Old French *c(o)ustume*, ultimately from Latin *consuetudo*, from *consuescere* 'to accustom', from *suescere* 'to become accustomed' (ancestor of **accustom**, COSTUME, and **desuetude**)] A traditional or habitual practice, hence **1** a traditional service or payment to your lord; a duty levied on goods going to market, hence **Customs** duty levied on imports; the place where imports are examined to ascertain duty (1920s) **2** to do something habitually (–17c), hence **(a) customer** someone who habitually buys from a trader (15c), later any purchaser; someone you deal with frequently (15–17c), hence someone you have to deal with (*a tough customer*, 16c) **(b)** the regular buying of goods from a particular trader (16c); (regular) business or customers **(c)** made or modified for a particular customer (*custom car*, 19c), hence **customize**.

cybernetics [1948, coined by Norbert Wiener, an American mathematician, from Greek *kubernētēs*, 'steersman', from *kubernan* 'to steer or control'] The science or study of control systems, hence **cyber-** in terms relating to electronic communications, especially via computers, e.g. **cyberspace** the notional space in which electronic information exists (1980s), **cybercafé** an internet café (*c*.2000); a virtual meeting place.

Greek *kubernan* produced Latin *gubernare*, whence **govern** [via French] and **gubernatorial**.

cycle [ME. Via French or late Latin from Greek *kuklos* 'circle'] **1** a period of time
between regularly-repeated events; a sequence of such events (17c) or operations
(19c), hence **(a)** to (cause to) go through a cycle **(b)** a series of songs, poems, etc.
on a theme (17c) **2 bicycle** a two-wheeled vehicle powered by its rider [19c, with
Latin **bi-** 'having two'], soon shortened to *cycle* or **bike**: all three forms came to
mean to ride a bicycle; a **biker** now rides a motorcycle.

 Bicycle produced **BMX** [short for *bicycle motocross*]. Greek *kuklos* is the ancestor
of **cyclone**, **encyclical** [via Latin from Greek *enkuklios* 'circular, general'], whence
also **encyclopaedia** [with Greek *paideia* 'general education'].

cynic [16c. Latin *cynicus* from Greek *kunikos*, probably from *Kunosarges*, the name
of a gymnasium where the philosopher Antisthenes (born *c.*444 BC) taught, but
popularly taken to mean 'doglike, churlish' (cf. DOG*), *kunōn* 'dog' becoming a
nickname for a Cynic] A member of a school of philosophers founded by Antisthenes, who rejected pleasure and family ties in favour of self-control and self-
knowledge, and were outspoken critics of society, hence someone who distrusts
or sarcastically criticizes other people's motives.

 Greek *kunōn* produced Greek *kunosoura* 'dog's tail, Ursa Minor', whence **cyno-
sure**, also used for the constellation and for the pole star in it, long used to guide
travellers, hence **1** something that serves as a guide **2** the centre of attention.

D

dab [ME. Imitative] **1** (to give) a tap, pat, or peck; to pat or press with something soft (16c): **(a)** to apply something in this way; to daub or plaster; this act (18c); a blob of something dabbed on **(b)** squarely, exactly (17c, surviving in N American **slap/smack dab**) **(c)** (probably) **dab (hand)** an expert (17c), perhaps originally someone with a light, deft touch **(d) dabs** fingerprints (1920s) **2** to drop something (18c, now dialect); the variant **dob** survives in Australia, meaning **(a)** to inform on or incriminate someone (1950s, presumably from the idea of dropping them in it) **(b)** to put money in a collection (1950s) **(c)** to impose a responsibility on someone (1960s) **(d)** to kick a goal (1960s).

Dab is the probable source of **dabble** to sprinkle or splash; to splash around in shallow water, hence to be involved in something casually. Related to **dap** to fish by bobbing the bait on the water, later to skip across water like a stone, and (via the variant **dib**), to **dibber**, or **dibble** a tool for planting bulbs etc. (from the idea of pecking the ground).

daft [Old English *gedaefte*: probably related to **daffy**] The underlying sense is probably 'fit, suitable', hence 'behaving properly', 'showing fitness or aptitude' (cf. APT). **1** meek, humble, gentle (–ME); simple, stupid (ME); reckless; crazy (15c): cf. SILLY **2** (as **deft**) skilful, dexterous (15c).

dainty [ME. Old French *daintie, deintie*, earlier *deintiet*, from Latin *dignitas* 'worthiness, beauty', from *dignus* 'worthy'] High quality (–15c), hence **1** (something) choice or delicious; a delicacy **2** excellent, handsome (–19c); delightful, delicately pretty **3** having delicate tastes, fastidious (16c).

Old French *deintiet* produced **daintith** something choice, surviving in Scots and as a surname. Latin *dignitas* produced **dignity**, whence **dignitary**; *dignus* produced **condign**, **deign** to see fit or condescend to [via Latin *dignare* 'to consider worthy'], **dignify**, **disdain** [Old French *desdeignier* from Latin *dedignari* 'to treat as unworthy'], and **indignation** disdain, contempt (–16c); anger caused by contemptuous treatment [Latin *indignari* 'to consider unworthy'].

dais [ME. Old French *deis* from Latin *discus* 'disc, dish, tray', later 'table', from Greek *diskos* DISC*] A raised table for dignitaries in a hall; the platform for it or for seat(s) of honour. Obsolete by 1600 in England (surviving in Scots meaning 'a seat'); revived in the late 18c.

Latin *discus* was adopted for the disc thrown by athletes, and produced **dish** and Italian *desco*, whence **desk** a table with a writing surface, hence the section of a newspaper etc. that deals with a particular subject (*news/city desk*); a service counter (*information desk*).

dally [ME. Old French *dalier*, of unknown origin] To chat idly (–15c), hence to amuse yourself: **(a)** by flirting or teasing (15c, earlier in **dalliance**) **(b)** by dabbling in something (16c), hence to waste time, to dawdle.

damn [ME. Via Old French from Latin *dam(p)nare* 'to inflict loss on', later 'to sentence', from *damnum* 'loss, damage'] To convict and sentence (–19c, replaced by **condemn** [via Old French from Latin *condemnare*, from *damnare*]), hence **1** to condemn as bad or worthless **2** of God: to condemn someone to hell, hence **(a)** used in oaths or to express annoyance (with the US variants **dang**, **darn**) **(b)** **damned** condemned to hell; deserving damnation or condemnation, hence **do your damnedest** to do your worst, later your utmost (19c) **3** to cause damnation, condemnation, or failure (*damning evidence*).

Latin *damnum* is the ancestor of **damage** (to cause) loss or harm, now usually physical harm, hence **damages** compensation for loss or harm, and **indemnity** [via French from Latin *indemnitas* 'freedom from loss or harm'].

damp [ME. Early Low German, 'vapour, steam'] Bad air; poisonous gas (now usually in a mine), hence **1** to stifle, suppress, or extinguish (15c): **(a)** to extinguish or slow a fire (15c), hence the **damper** in a chimney that controls the draught (18c) **(b)** to suppress a sound or vibration (16c) **(c)** to depress, disappoint, or discourage (16c) **(d)** *damper* something that suppresses your appetite (18c); a flour-and-water cake baked in hot ashes (19c, Australia and New Zealand) **2** a visible vapour, a mist (17–19c); to moisten (largely replaced by **dampen**, 19c); slight wetness or high humidity (18c); moist, humid.

danger [ME. Old French *dangier*, ultimately from Latin *dominus* 'lord, master' (ancestor of DOMINATE*)] The jurisdiction or power of a lord (–19c), hence **in someone's danger** at their mercy; **in danger (of)** at risk (from), hence *danger* risk, peril (15c); something that may cause harm, a risk.

dash [ME. Imitating the sound] **1** to crash into, or throw something down, violently, to break by doing so, hence to ruin or frustrate (*dashed our hopes*, 16c); to daunt **2** (to make) a quick or violent stroke; a hurried pen stroke (16c), hence **(a)** **dash off** to write or sketch rapidly **(b)** a short pen stroke used in punctuation, music, or the Morse code **3** to move quickly hence **(a)** liveliness, vigour (18c); **dashing** spirited, lively, flamboyant; **cut a dash** to behave or dress strikingly **(b)** a sudden rapid movement (19c); a short race, a sprint **4** to splash with water or mud, hence **(a)** a splash of liquid (16c); a small quantity added to a mixture **(b)** **dash(board)** in front of a carriage to keep out road dirt (19c); an instrument panel at the front of a vehicle or aircraft (*c*.1900).

data [17c. Latin, plural of *datum* 'something given', from *dare* 'to give', also 'to play'] Facts or figures forming the basis of reasoning or calculation, hence information gathered and kept for future reference (19c); text, images, and sounds stored by a computer (1940s). Strictly speaking, *data* is plural, although often taken to mean 'information' and treated as singular. The singular form **datum**, not found in English until the mid 18c, is comparatively rare.

Latin *datum* produced **date** [from the Latin formula used on letters, *data (epistola)* '(letter) given or delivered', followed by the time or place], and DIE*. Latin *dare* is the ancestor of ABSCOND*, ADD*, **dative** the grammatical case that expresses the indirect object or recipient, **edition** [literally 'what is published', ultimately from Latin *edere* 'to give out'], MANDATE*, **perdition**, RENDER*, TRADITION, and *vend* (at VENAL).

daze [ME. Old Norse *dasathr* 'weary, numb with cold'] **1** to stun or stupefy; to bewilder; bewilderment (19c) **2** to make or become blind or confused by bright light (whence 15c **dazzle**, which has largely replaced it).

   Dazed produced **dastard** a dazed or stupid person; a treacherous coward, surviving mainly in **dastardly**. *Dazzle* came to mean glitter, a bright confusing light; stretched to **razzle-dazzle** (something) deceptively showy; glamorous excitement (**razzmatazz** may be an alteration), a spree, shortened to **razzle** (*on the razzle*).

deal [Old English *dǣl* (noun), *dǣlan* (verb): related to DOLE and ORDEAL] **1** a part or portion (–18c); a share; a quantity (*a good/great deal*) **2** to divide into portions or shares (–ME); to share out (–16c); to distribute (ME), later specifically playing cards (16c) **3** to fight, quarrel, or compete with (–18c); to associate or be concerned with (ME), hence **(a)** to do business; to trade in a commodity (16c); a business transaction; a bargain or arrangement (19c) **(b)** to treat someone, later also to behave, in a certain way **(c)** to cope with (15c); to take effective action against (*I'll deal with you later!*, 16c).

dean [ME. Old French *deien*, from Latin *decanus* 'commander of ten men', from *decem* 'ten' (ancestor of DECIMATION*)] **1** the head of ten monks, or of a cathedral chapter; **(rural) dean** a clergyman supervising a group of parishes **2** an officer in a medieval guild **3** a senior member: **(a)** the senior or most influential member of a group (15c, largely replaced by **doyen(ne)**, also from Old French *deien*) **(b)** a senior member of a university's academic staff (16c).

dear [Old English *dēore*] Glorious, noble, honourable (–17c); respected, loved, precious, hence **1 (a)** (used when speaking to) someone you love (ME), hence beginning a letter, originally affectionate or polite (15c), later simply conventional (17c) **(b)** lovable, sweet (*a dear little kitten/cottage*, 18c); a lovable person **2** important, valuable (–17c); expensive; at great cost **3 Oh dear!**, **dear dear!**, probably originally short for *dear God* (17c), certainly so in **the dear knows!** (19c).

   Old English *dēore* produced *dēorling*, literally 'little dear', whence **darling**. *Dear* produced **dearth** famine, scarcity (making food expensive).

debacle [French *débâcle*, from *débâcler* 'to unbar', from *bâcler* 'to bar', from Latin *baculum* 'staff, rod'; the French spelling survived well into the 20c] The breaking up of ice in a river (19c), hence a sudden flood or rush of water; a rout; a complete or ludicrous failure.

   Latin *baculum* is the ancestor of **bacillus**, French *baguette*, **imbecile** physically weak; (someone who is) mentally feeble [via Latin *imbecillus*, literally 'without support'], and perhaps of BAIL²*.

decent [16c. (Via French from) Latin *decere* 'to be fitting'] Suitable, appropriate, hence **1** appropriate to your rank (–17c), later to your financial circumstances (18c); reasonable, good enough **2** conforming to accepted standards of propriety; respectable; wearing enough to receive visitors (*are you decent?*, 18c) **3** kind, considerate (*c*.1900).

decimation [15c. Latin *decimare* 'to take one tenth', from *decimus* 'tenth', from *decem* 'ten'] **1** (the levying of) a tax of one tenth **2** the Roman punishment of executing one man in ten of a mutinous legion (16c), hence *decimate* to kill or destroy a tenth (17c), now often to kill or destroy a large proportion (partly from a misunderstanding of *decimate* as 'to kill nine in ten', partly by confusion with *devastate*).

Latin *decimus* produced **deci-** (*decibel*, *decilitre*), **decimal**, and **dime** [Old French *di(s)me*, from Latin *decima (pars)* 'tenth (part)'], originally a tenth, hence an American coin worth one-tenth of a dollar; *decem* is the ancestor of DEAN*, Latin *December* the tenth month of the Roman calendar, becoming the twelfth when January and February were added *c.*700 BC (similarly *September* [Latin *septem* 'seven'], *October* [Latin *octo* 'eight'], and *November* [Latin *novem* 'nine']), DENIER*, **dicker** a set of ten, especially of hides, hence to barter (US, from bartering for hides with Native Americans), to exchange or haggle, and of *dozen* and *duodenum* (at DOUBLE).

deck [15c. Early Dutch *dekken* 'to cover', and *dec* 'roof, cloak': related to THATCH*] **1** to cover or clothe (–17c); to adorn (16c) **2** (the material used for) a covering (*nautical*); a structure covering a space in a ship, hence the floor of the space above; a storey in a bus etc. (19c); any kind of floor or platform: **(a)** the ground (1920s, *airmen's slang*), hence to knock someone down (1950) **(b)** the flat surface of a record player etc. (1950s), now including the works **3** a pack of cards (stacked like a ship's decks, 16c); a similar-sized pack of illicit drugs (1920s).

decline [ME. French *decliner* from Latin *declinare*, literally 'to bend aside', from *clinare* 'to bend'] To turn aside, hence **1** to deviate: **(a)** to deviate from the equator or, formerly, the ecliptic (hence **declination** the angular distance of a heavenly body from the celestial equator); of a compass needle: to deviate from the north-south line (17c, 15c in *declination*) **(b)** of a noun, adjective, or pronoun: to vary in form according to number, gender, etc. (15c); to state these variations; **declension** a group of words with similar forms (cf. INFLECT) **2** to turn or go down: **(a)** to decay or diminish; deterioration; a fall or slump (19c) **(b)** to bow or droop **(c)** to slope downwards (15c); a downward slope (16c): cf. INCLINE **(d)** to 'turn down' something suggested (17c).

Latin *clinare* is the ancestor of INCLINE and of **recline** to lie down; to (cause to) tilt backwards; to lie back.

deduce [15c. Latin *deducere*, *deduct-* 'to lead out', from *ducere* 'to lead'] To convey, hence **1 (a)** to infer from something already known **(b)** to trace or show something's origin **2** to subtract (–19c), survived by **deduct** [15c, also from Latin *deducere*], which had all the meanings of *deduce*. The relationship survives in **deduction** (15c), which means both 'subtraction, something subtracted' and 'the process or result of deducing'.

Latin *ducere* produced *dux* 'leader', adopted in some parts of the world for a school's top pupil, and which in turn produced **ducat** originally a silver coin issued by the Duke of Apulia, **duchess**, **duchy**, and **duke**. Other descendants include **abduct**, **aqueduct**, CONDUCT*, **doge**, **douche** [French, from Italian *doccia* 'conduit pipe'], **duct**, **educate**, **educe**, ENDUE, INDUCE*, **introduce**, PRODUCE*, REDUCE*, SEDUCE*, **subduction**, and **subdue** [both from Latin *subducere* 'to lead or bring under'], **traduce**, and *viaduct* (at TRIVIAL).

deed [Old English *dēd, dǣd*: related to DOOM*] An intentional act, hence **1** a brave or skilful one; action, as opposed to speech; **indeed** in reality, certainly (ME, two words until the 17c) **2** a legal document which transfers property or creates a contract (ME); to transfer by deed (19c, *US*).

default [ME. Old French *defaute* (the original English spelling) from *defaillir* 'to fail', ultimately from Latin *fallere* 'to deceive or disappoint' (ancestor of FAIL*). The *l* was added to conform to Latin *fallere* (15c), becoming standard in the 17c but not usually pronounced until the 18c. **Fault**, also via Old French from Latin *fallere*, and also originally meaning 'absence or scarcity', has a similar spelling history] **1** absence or scarcity, hence **in default of** in the absence of; *default* a preset option that a computer adopts unless the user chooses an alternative (1960s) **2** failure to act, to meet an obligation, appear in court, etc., hence **(a) by default** because someone does not appear, something is not done, or something does not happen **(b)** culpable neglect, usually with bad consequences, largely replaced by *fault* (*at fault, your fault*) **3 (a)** a moral or material imperfection **(b)** an error (both largely replaced by *fault*).

defeat [ME. Old French *de(s)fait*, past participle of *de(s)faire* 'to undo', from medieval Latin *disfacere*, from Latin *facere* 'to do' (ancestor of FACT*)] To undo or do away with (–17c); to annul, hence to make someone/something fail (15c); to outdo or overcome (16c), hence victory (*our defeat of the Armada*) or ruin (*our defeat by the barbarians*).

defend [ME. Via French from Latin *defendere*, literally 'to strike against', from *fendere* 'to strike'] **1** to prevent (–19c); to ward off an attack (both shortened to **fend**) **2** to support or protect against attack, harm, criticism, or an accusation; to resist an opponent's attack in a game (18c, 17c in **defence**).

Fend came to mean to protect or provide for (usually yourself), and produced **fender** and **forfend**. *Defence* was shortened to FENCE. Latin *fendere* (found only in compounds) produced OFFEND. Related to MANIFEST.

defer [ME. Via French from Latin *differre, dilat-*, literally 'to carry apart', from *ferre* 'to bring or carry'. Essentially the same word as **differ**, the two being synonymous until about the 17c. After they parted company the stress in *defer* shifted to the first syllable by association with *prefer* and *refer*] **1** (now only *defer*) to put on one side (–15c); to put off **2** (now only *differ*) to be dissimilar, hence **(a)** to make dissimilar or distinct (largely replaced by 19c **differentiate**) **(b)** to hold dissimilar views (16c, ME in **difference** a disagreement or quarrel).

Different, now usually used with *from*, was formerly seen with *against, with*, and *than* (which died out in British English but is creeping back from N America); *different to*, always regarded as incorrect, has proved remarkably hardy. Latin *differe* produced **dilatory** causing delay, later slow, tardy, and **indifferent** making no distinction, having no interest; neither good nor bad, not very good, poor. *Ferre* is the ancestor of CONFER* and of **defer** to give way to [via Latin *deferre* 'to carry away'].

defy [ME. Old French *de(s)fier*, ultimately from Latin *fidus* 'faithful', from *fides* FAITH*] To renounce your allegiance to, to turn against (–17c), hence **1** to resist or refuse to obey **2** to challenge to fight; such a challenge (16c, now US); to challenge someone to do something apparently impossible (17c).

degree [ME. French *degré*, ultimately from Latin *gradus* 'step'] A step in a flight, a rung of a ladder (surviving in heraldry), hence **1** a step in descent from a common ancestor, hence the closeness of descendants, **prohibited/forbidden degrees** those too close to marry **2** a step on the social ladder, rank or station **3** a step in a process, hence **(a)** a level of proficiency; an academic qualification **(b) by degrees** little by little (16c) **4** a step on a scale, hence a unit of measurement **(a)** for angles and circles, later of latitude and longitude (17c) **(b)** of temperature (18c) **5** the relative extent, amount, intensity, or level of something; the relative severity of a crime (17c) or burn (19c); a limited amount (*a degree of freedom*, 17c); **to a degree** to some extent (18c).

Descendants of Latin *gradus* include **degrade**, **centigrade**, GRADE*, **gradual**, **graduate**, RETROGRADE*, and Latin *gradi*, *gress-* 'to proceed or step', whence **aggression**, **congress**, **digress**, **egress**, **ingredient**, **ingress**, PROGRESS, and **transgress** [Latin *transgradi*, literally 'to step across', hence 'to go beyond a limit or prohibition': cf. TRESPASS].

deity [ME. Via Old French from ecclesiastical Latin *deitas*, coined by St Augustine from *deus* 'god'] The divine nature of God; (the status of) a divine being, hence **1** an object of worship (16c) **2 the Deity** God (16c).

Latin *deus* appears in *deus ex machina* (at MACHINE), and fathered French *adieu* [literally 'to God', committing you to God's care], its Spanish equivalent *adios*, and **joss** a Chinese figure of a god [via Javanese *dejos* and Portuguese *deus*], whence **joss stick** an incense stick, and Australian **josser** a clergyman.

delicate [ME. French *délicat* or Latin *delicatus* 'pleasing', perhaps from or related to *deliciae*: see DELICIOUS*] Delightful, pleasant, charming (–18c), hence **1** fond of pleasure; lazy, self-indulgent; weak and effeminate (–17c), hence **(a)** frail, sickly **(b)** fastidious (16c); squeamish (17c) **(c)** sensitive, perceptive (16c); calling for sensitivity (*delicate negotiations*, 18c) **2** of food: dainty and delicious, whence **delicacy** a choice food **3** exquisite, dainty (15c), hence **(a)** fragile (16c) **(b)** skilful, deft (*a delicate touch*, 16c) **(c)** slight, subtle (17c); subtly pleasing (*a delicate shade of green*, 19c).

French *délicat* produced *délicatesse* 'delicacy', whence Dutch *delicatessen* 'delicacies', adopted meaning a place that sells them (*US*), now shortened to **deli**.

delicious [ME. Old French, from late Latin *deliciosus*, from Latin *deliciae* 'delight, pleasure', from *delicere* 'to allure', from *lacere* 'to entice'] Delightful, giving great pleasure or amusement, hence pleasing to the senses, especially of taste or smell.

The source of such coinings as *bootylicious*, *doggylicious*, and probably of **luscious**. Latin *delicere* produced **delectable**, **delight**, and Italian *dilettante* [literally 'delighting'] adopted for an amateur artist or art-lover, hence someone who dabbles.

deliver [ME. French *delivrer*, ultimately from Latin *liberare* 'to free' (whence **liberate** and LIVERY): see LIBERAL*] To save or set free; to free from, hence **1** to help a woman in childbirth (unburdening the woman and releasing the child); to give birth **2** to unburden your mind, to speak your thoughts; to give a lecture or speech **3** to give up or hand over, hence to take a parcel, goods, etc. to an address or recipient; **deliver (the goods)** to provide what is expected or promised (1940s, *US*) **4** to land a blow or throw a missile (16c).

delta [ME. Latin from Greek, from Phoenician *daleth*] The fourth letter (Δ, δ) of the Greek alphabet, hence **1** the triangular deposit of sand and soil at the mouth of a river (originally the Nile, 16c); anything triangular (*delta wing*, 17c), hence [via Latin *deltoides*] **deltoid** triangular (18c); the large triangular shoulder muscle **2** the fourth in a series (17c); a fourth-class mark in an exam (*c.*1910).

deluge [ME. French, ultimately from Latin *diluvium*, from *diluere* 'to wash away, to dissolve', ultimately from *lavare* 'to wash'] A flood, especially Noah's (see the Bible, Genesis 6–8), hence a heavy downpour (16c); a vast or overwhelming amount; to flood or overwhelm.

Latin *diluvium* produced **antediluvian** before Noah's flood; ancient, antiquated, extremely old-fashioned. *Diluere* produced **dilute**; *lavare* is the ancestor of LAVATORY*.

demarcation [17c. Spanish *demarcación*, Portuguese *demarcação*, ultimately of Germanic origin and related to MARK*] A boundary, originally in **line of demarcation** that laid down by the Pope in 1493 to divide the New World between the Spanish and Portuguese. Hence *demarcation* the setting of a boundary (19c); clear division (whence **demarcate** to set limits; to separate or distinguish, 19c); **demarcation dispute** about the division of workers' duties (1930s).

demeanour [15c. From Middle English *demean* 'to control or manage', hence 'to manage yourself, to behave in a certain way', from Old French *demener* (whence, probably, **mien**), ultimately from late Latin *minare* 'to drive animals, to drive with threats', from *minari* 'to threaten': see MENACE*] Conduct, behaviour, hence **1** manner, bearing, or appearance **2** **misdemeanour** bad behaviour; a bad deed; an indictable offence, formerly, and still in the US, one less serious than a felony.

demon [Strictly speaking, two words, both Middle English, from Greek *daimōn* 'divinity, genius': the spelling **daemon**, common until the 19c, survives in sense 1] **I** [via Latin *daemon*] **1** a guiding spirit **2** a minor deity or demi-god (16c); a person with 'superhuman' energy or skill (19c) **II** [via Latin *daemonium* or Greek *daemonion*, literally 'lesser god', used in translations of the Bible for heathen deities] an evil spirit; a hideous or malignant creature (17c); a personification of something evil or harmful (*demon drink*, 18c).

The poet John Milton coined **Pandemonium** [Greek *pan* 'all' (see PANOPLY) + *daimōn*] for the capital of hell in *Paradise Lost* (1667), hence a hellish or chaotic place; uproar.

demonstration [ME: **demonstrate** appears in the 16c. (Via Old French from) Latin *demonstratio*, from *demonstrare* 'to point out' from *monstrare* 'to show', from *monstrum* 'warning, portent': see MONSTER*] The action of pointing out, making known, or exhibiting; something that does so, a sign or indication (–17c), hence **1** proving, a proof **2** an expression of feeling (16c); a public display of feelings about an issue or cause (19c, shortened to **demo**, 1930s) **3** a show of military force (19c) **4** a practical display of how something is done or how something works (19c, 17c in *demonstrate*).

Latin *monstrare* produced **monstrance** demonstration, proof, hence the container in which the consecrated Host is shown to the congregation in the Roman Catholic Mass, MUSTER, and **remonstrate** to show or make plain (16–18c), hence to make plain your reasons for opposing something.

demur [ME. Old French *demeure, dem(o)urer* (verb), *demeure* (noun), ultimately from Latin *morari* 'to delay', from *mora* 'delay'] To linger, procrastinate, or delay (–17c); procrastination, delay (–18c); in law: to enter a **demurrer**, an objection to the validity of an opponent's point although it may be factually correct, thus delaying the action pending a ruling (17c), hence (to make) any objection.

Old French *demourer* produced DEMURE* and **demurrage** procrastination, delay, now only in loading or unloading a chartered ship, railway truck, or lorry. Latin *mora* is the ancestor of **moratorium**.

demure [ME. Old French *demo(u)re*, past participle of *demo(u)rer* (see DEMUR), influenced by Old French *mur, meür* 'grave', from Latin *maturus* 'ripe, timely' (ancestor of MATURE*)] Calm, settled, still (–15c); grave, serious, composed (15c); (affectedly or falsely) modest, coy (17c).

denier [15c. French, from Latin *denarius*, a silver coin worth ten copper ones, from *deni* 'containing ten', from *decem* 'ten'] A French coin of low value (15c); the weight of one (16–18c), hence a unit of weight for silk (19c), later one for measuring the fineness of yarn, equal to the weight in grams of 9,000 metres of it.

Latin *denarius* produced the *d* in *£.s.d.* (at POUND[1]), the surname **Denyer** for a poor person, Arabic and Persian *dinar*, Spanish *dinero* adopted as a slang term for money, and **groat** [from medieval Latin *denarius grossus* 'thick penny']. Latin *decem* is the ancestor of DECIMATION*.

denigrate [15c. Latin *denigrare*, from *niger* 'black' (ancestor of NEGRO*)] To blacken or darken (–19c), hence to blacken someone's character (16c, virtually obsolete by the 18c, revived in the 19c).

depart [ME. French *départir*, ultimately from Latin *dispertire*, from *partire* 'to part': see PART*] To divide or separate (–18c), hence **1** to deviate; to abandon or change a practice **2** to set out on a journey (15c); to die (16c), hence **the (dear) departed** the deceased (18c).

French *départir* produced **department** division, distribution, separation (ME–17c), hence a specialized part of an organization or shop (whence **department store**, *US*); a branch of public administration; an area of expertise or responsibility.

depend [ME. Via French from Latin *dependere*, from *pendere* 'to hang' (ancestor of PENDANT*)] To hang down or from something, hence **1** to be in suspense, to be awaiting an outcome (–18c); to be determined or influenced by it (15c) **2** to rely on for support (15c); to rely on confidently, to count on.

deplore [16c. Via French or Italian from Latin *deplorare*, from *plorare* 'to weep or cry out' (ancestor of **explore** and **implore**)] To weep or grieve for, to regret deeply, hence **deplorable** very sad, regrettable (17c), later very bad, contemptible (18c), hence *deplore* to disapprove of strongly (19c).

depose [ME. French *déposer* from Latin *deponere*, *deposit-* 'to put down or away', later 'to testify' (whence DEPOSIT and DEPOT), from *ponere* 'to place': see POSE*] **1** to put down or put away, especially for safe keeping (–18c, replaced by DEPOSIT) **2** to remove from office, to dethrone **3** to testify, especially on oath (also as **depone**), hence **deposition** (the giving of) testimony, especially a sworn, written statement (15c).

deposit [16c. Latin *depositum*, from *deponere*: see DEPOSE*] **1 on/in deposit** put aside or away, especially for safe keeping (16c) **2** to give money as security (17c); a pledge or part payment **3** an accumulated layer of dust, sediment, etc. (18c) **4** a storehouse (18c, *US*), elsewhere called a **depository** [Latin *depositorium* 'storehouse'] or **depositary** [Latin *depositarius* 'trustee']: both date from the 17c and, probably because of the similarity of spelling, have both meanings. Cf. DEPOT.

depot [18c. French *dépôt*, from Latin *depositum*, from *deponere*: see DEPOSE*] A military base where stores (and formerly prisoners of war) are deposited, or troops assembled, hence a storehouse for goods; a place where vehicles are kept and maintained (19c); a bus or railway station (*US*).

deprave [ME. (Via French from) Latin *depravare*, from *pravus* 'crooked, perverse'] To disparage; to misrepresent, to corrupt a word or text (15c), hence to corrupt morally, usually as **depraved**.

Depravity is an alteration, suggested by *deprave*, of **pravity**, also ultimately from Latin *pravus*.

deprecate [17c. Latin *deprecari*, from *precari* 'to pray'] To try to avert by prayer (15c in **deprecation**); to plead or protest against, hence (by association with *depreciate* at APPRECIATE) to belittle or underrate (19c, still widely regarded as incorrect, although **self-deprecation** is well established).

Latin *precari* produced **imprecate**, **pray**, and **prayer** [via Old French from Latin *precarius* 'obtained by pleading or prayer', whence also **precarious** at someone else's pleasure, hence unstable, uncertain, risky].

derelict [16c. Latin *derelinquere*, *derelict-* 'to abandon completely', from *relinquere* 'to leave behind', from *linquere* 'to leave'] Abandoned by the owner or occupier; left to decay; a neglected or abandoned ship or building; a person neglected by society, a down-and-out (18c). Hence **dereliction 1** deliberate neglect of a duty or obligation (19c), whence *derelict* a negligent person (N American) **2** land gained when water 'abandons', i.e. recedes from, it (18c).

Latin *relinquere* produced **relict** and **relinquish**; *linquere* is the ancestor of **delinquent** someone who fails in a duty, later an offender, **relic**, and **reliquary**.

derive [ME. (Via French from) Latin *derivare*, from *rivus* 'brook, stream'] To draw off a fluid (–19c), hence to get or come from a source (15c); to be formed from; to trace or show the origin of something. Hence **derivative** (something) derived (15c); not original (16c); (describing) a financial product whose value depends on that of an underlying asset (1960s).

Latin *rivus* produced **rival** [Latin *rivalis* 'using (hence competing for) the same stream'], and perhaps *rivulet* (at RIVIERA).

derogate [15c. Latin *derogare*, from *rogare* 'to ask or question' (ancestor of PROROGUE*] To repeal part of a law, hence **1** to lessen the force or authority of (–17c);

to detract from or disparage (16c, whence **derogatory**) **2** to deviate from a norm or standard of behaviour (17c).

derrick [17c. Surname of a rapist who was sentenced to death but reprieved by the Earl of Essex on condition he become the public hangman; he later executed Essex for treason] A hangman (–18c); the gallows, hence a lifting tackle resembling it on a ship (18c); a crane (19c); a framework over an oil well supporting the drilling apparatus.

derring-do [Alteration of Middle English *dorryng* or *duryng do* 'daring to do'] Used by Chaucer in *Troilus and Crysede* (*c.*1370) describing Troilus as 'in no degree second, / In duryng do that longeth to (i.e. what is proper for) a knight'; the poet John Lydgate, following Chaucer, describes Troilus as equal to any man 'In dorryng do...For to fulfil that longeth to a knight' (1430). Spenser (see BLATANT) misinterpreted this (printed *derrynge do* in 16c editions) as meaning 'manhood, chivalry'; Scott (see DOFF) subsequently used it to mean 'daring action, desperate courage' (19c).

describe [15c. Latin *describere*, *descript-* 'to copy, write down, or delineate', from *scribere* 'to write' (ancestor of SCRIPT*)] **1** to portray in words; to define something and list its characteristics, hence **descript** described (17c), surviving mainly in **nondescript**, originally applied to a species, disease, etc. not previously identified or described, later meaning hard to describe or classify (19c); with no distinctive features **2** to trace an outline (15c); to move as though doing so (16c).

desert [Two words, both Middle English and ultimately from Latin *deserere*, *desert-* 'to leave or forsake', from *serere* 'to join or entwine'] **I** [via French from Latin *desertare*] to give up or abandon, hence **1** forsaken, abandoned (later also **deserted**, 17c) **2** to abandon someone/something you have a duty to (17c); to fail someone in time of need (*her courage deserted her*) **II** [via late Latin *desertum* 'an abandoned place'] an area supporting little life, now usually a hot, dry region but formerly including other uncultivated land, hence uninhabited, lonely; barren.
   Latin *serere* is the ancestor of **assert**, **dissertation**, **exert**, **insert**, and **series**, whence **serial** (something) belonging to or forming one. Late Latin *desertum* produced Gaelic *diseart* 'hermit's cell, church', whence the place- and surname **Dysart**.

deserve [ME. Via Old French from Latin *deservire*, *desert-* 'to serve well', from *servire* SERVE*] To earn by serving well (–18c), hence to be worthy of or entitled to; to be worthy of good or bad treatment, reward or punishment; earlier in **desert** deserving; what is deserved (*just deserts*).

design [ME. (Via French or Italian from) Latin *designare*, literally 'to mark out', from *signare* 'to mark', from *signum* 'a mark' (ancestor of SIGN*)] **1** to signify (–17c); to call by a name, to identify or describe (–19c); to nominate for, or appoint to, an office (16–18c). Replaced in these senses by **designate** (18c, ME in **designation**) **2** to plan, hence **(a)** to make a plan for a work of art, building, etc.; the plan (17c); the way something is planned or made with regard to its function and appearance, hence **designer** someone who designs, especially clothes (17c), hence describing fashion items carrying a famous designer's label (1960s) **(b)** to devote to, to intend or create for, a specific purpose (16c, also as *designate*, 18c);

a purpose or intention; a goal, an end in view (17c) **(c)** (to hatch) a plot (16c, hence **have designs on** to be plotting to get, 17c); hypocritical scheming (18c) **(d)** a decorative pattern (17c).

desperate [ME. Latin *desperare*, *desperat-* 'to lose hope' (ancestor of **despair**), from *sperare* 'to hope'] Despairing, hence **1** made reckless by despair or need (15c), hence **(a)** a reckless or violent criminal (17–18c), altered to pseudo-Spanish **desperado (b)** extremely anxious to have or do something (1950s) **2** extremely grave (*a desperate shortage of food*, 15c); undertaken as a last resort (*desperate remedies*, 16c).

despite [ME. Old French *despit*, from Latin *despicere* 'to look down on' (whence **despise**), from *specere* 'to look at' (ancestor of SPICE*)] Contempt, scorn, hence (also shortened to **spite**) **1** contemptuous treatment or behaviour; to show contempt **2** contempt for or defiance of opposition (–18c), hence **in despite of** notwithstanding, in defiance of (now as **in spite of** or *despite*) **3** (now only *spite*) malice, desire for revenge; to harm or humiliate someone maliciously.

dessert [16c. French, from *desservir* 'to clear the table', from *servir* 'to serve', from Latin *servire* SERVE*] Nuts, fruit, sweets, etc. to nibble after a meal when the table has been cleared, hence the last course of a meal, the pudding (18c, *US*).

destine [ME. Via French from Latin *destinare* 'to make firm, to establish', from *stare* 'to stand'] To predetermine or decree; to devote to, or intend for, a purpose (16c), hence **be destined** to be fated or intended to; to be bound for a place (18c). Hence **destination** the fact of being destined for a purpose (ME) or a place (18c), the place itself (19c); **destiny** fate (ME).

Latin *destinare* produced **predestinate** of God: to destine, to preordain, specifically to preselect for heaven or hell; *stare* is the ancestor of STATION*.

destroy [ME. Old French *destruire*, ultimately from Latin *destruere*, from *struere* 'to build'] To tear down, to smash, hence **1** to ruin; to ruin financially or professionally (18c) **2** to rescind or abolish; to put an end to; to kill; to euthanase an animal (19c). Hence **destruction** demolition, devastation, ruin, slaughter (ME), whence (probably from *self-destruction*) **destruct** to deliberately destroy your own missile etc. (1950s, *US*).

Latin *struere* is the ancestor of **construct** [Latin *construere* 'to build up', later 'to put together or analyse a sentence', whence also **construe**], **instruct** [Latin *instruere* 'to set up, to provide with'], **obstruct** [Latin *obstruere* 'to build against'], and **structure**.

desultory [16c. Latin *desultorius* 'like or to do with a *desultor*', a circus rider who vaulted from horse to horse, ultimately from *salire* 'to leap' (ancestor of SALIENT*)] Jumping, skipping, or flitting about, hence passing aimlessly from one thing to another; fitful, unmethodical; disconnected, random (18c).

detail [17c. French *détailler*, from Old French *taill(i)er* 'to cut': see TAIL*] To describe minutely, to treat item by item; such a description or treatment; small matters or items collectively, hence **1** a particular, a small or minor part (18c); in art: the treatment of a small part in isolation (19c) **2** in military use: (the distribution of) the orders of the day, assigning personnel to specific duties (18c); to assign, or those assigned, to a specific task.

detect [ME. Latin *detegere, detect-*, from *tegere* 'to cover'] To uncover, expose, or display (–18c), hence **1** to expose the real nature of (16c), hence **detective** to do with such investigations (19c), whence **detective (policeman)** who investigates crime, whence *detect* to do so, to be one (1920s) **2** to notice or discover the existence of (18c).

Latin *tegere* produced **integument**, **protect**, **tile**, **tuil(l)e** a curved piece of armour for the thigh, now a thin curved biscuit, and the **Tuilleries** gardens in Paris, on the site of a tile works. Related to TOG*.

determine [ME. Via French from Latin *determinare* 'to limit or fix', from *terminare* 'to end', from *terminus* 'end, boundary' (ancestor of TERM*)] To bring or come to an end (surviving mainly as a legal term); to limit, to settle or decide, hence **1** to decide, later to make you decide, to do something, hence **determined** firm, resolute (17c); **determination** resolve, firmness, tenacity (19c) **2** to ascertain precisely (17c).

develop [17c. French *développer*, ultimately from Latin *dis-* 'reverse, undo', with a second element of unknown origin, also found in ENVELOP] To unfold, unroll, or unfurl (surviving mainly in heraldry and as a mathematical term meaning to flatten a curved surface), hence **1** to reveal or find out (18c); to reveal or be revealed in stages; to make visible (19c); to reveal the image on a photographic film **2** to arise and increase (18c); to evolve (19c).

device/devise [ME. Via Old French (where much of the sense development took place), from Latin *dividere* 'to force apart', from *videre* 'to separate'. In modern use *device* is used for the noun, *devise* for the verb. Cf. ADVICE/ADVISE*] To distinguish or distribute (–15c), also to order or decide (–19c), later **1** to plan, contrive, or invent; a mechanical contrivance or artistic design **2** to bequeath, now only property; this action; a clause in a will bequeathing property **3** intent, inclination (surviving in *leave to your own devices*).

Latin *dividere* produced **divide**, **dividend**, and INDIVIDUAL.

devil [Old English *dēofol*, ultimately via Latin from Greek *diabolos* 'accuser, slanderer' (from *diaballein* 'to slander', from *dia* 'across' + *ballein* 'to throw'), used to translate Hebrew *śāṭān* **Satan**, literally 'the adversary', who originally reported wrongdoers to God and was sometimes allowed to tempt the good (see the Bible, Job 1, 2), but was later regarded as God's enemy] The arch-enemy of God and mankind in Jewish, Christian, and Islamic theology; the leader of the rebellious angels who were thrown out of heaven, hence **1** an evil spirit: **(a)** one of the devil's minions who tempt and torment mankind; **bedevil** to harass or tease (16c) **(b)** one that possesses someone (17c), hence **blue devils** depression (18c), hence **the blues** music originating in African-American songs about misery and hardship (*c.*1900) **2** a vicious person or animal (17c); a troublesome, mischievous, or high-spirited one (hence **the devil**, **devilment** high spirits, mischief, 18c); a person of the kind described (*poor/lucky devil!*) **3** a subordinate, e.g. a printer's errand boy, a junior barrister (17c) **4** a highly spiced dish (hot as hellfire, 18c); (to cook with) a peppery sauce or seasoning **5** applied to various fearsome or unpleasant things, animals, or plants, and to topographical features, earthworks, etc. that could surely have been made only by the Devil.

The devil is also known as **Beelzebub** [Latin, translating Hebrew *ba'al zebūb* 'Lord of the Flies' (another of his epithets); see the Bible, 2 Kings 1:2], **Belial** [Hebrew *bĕliyya'al* 'worthlessness'], LEVIATHAN, *Lucifer* (at LUCID), **Mephistopheles** [popularly derived from Greek *mē* 'not', *phos* 'light', and *philos* 'loving'], and **Prince of Darkness**. He also has many nicknames, used to avoid mentioning him (he may well appear if you do!), the earliest being Old English *se ealdra* 'the Old One', and FIEND: others include **the Beast**, BOGEY, **the deuce** [Low German *duus*, probably ultimately from Latin *duos* 'two', (the worst throw with two dice)], **Dickens** [a pet form of Richard], the DRAGON or *the serpent* (at WORM), **the (old) Enemy** or **Adversary**, the euphemistic **Goodman**, MISCHIEF, and **Old Nick** or **Old Harry**.

Greek *diabolos* produced **diabolical**; *ballein* is the ancestor of BALLISTIC*.

dial [ME. Medieval Latin *diale* 'clock-face', probably originally in a phrase such as *rota dialis*, literally 'daily circle or wheel', ultimately from Latin *dies* 'day' (ancestor of JOURNEY*)] **1** a mariner's compass (–17c) **2** a sundial (15c); any timepiece (–17c); the face of one, later of any measuring instrument, hence **(a)** any device with a pointer showing a value (18c); one that shows which frequency a radio is tuned to (1920s) **(b)** a disc with numbered holes on an old-fashioned telephone (19c); to turn the dial or, later, press the keys of a telephone to call up the number required (1920s); **dial up** to access a computer via a telephone line (1970s) **(c)** someone's face (19c).

diaper [ME. Old French *dia(s)pre* from medieval Latin *diasprum*, a white silky fabric, from medieval Greek *diaspros* 'pure white', from *aspros* 'a silver coin', from Latin *asper* 'rough' (ancestor of **asperity** and **exasperate**), sometimes applied to bas-relief on carvings and coins] A kind of ornamental silk, later a cotton fabric woven with a small pattern (15c), hence a towel or napkin made of this (16c), specifically a baby's nappy (19c, N American).

dictate [16c. Latin *dictare* 'to say firmly or repeatedly', from *dicere* 'to say'] **1** to say words to be written down **2 (a)** [from Latin *dictatum* 'something dictated'] an authoritative instruction (*dictates of conscience*) **(b)** to prescribe, lay down, or decide (17c); to give orders.

Latin *dictare* produced **dictator** a Roman magistrate who ruled with absolute power during an emergency, hence an absolute ruler, a tyrant, **ditty**, **indict**, and **indite**. Latin *dicere* is the ancestor of ADDICT, **benediction**, **diction**, **dictionary**, **dictum**, **ditto** [via Italian *detto* 'said'], **edict**, JUDGE*, *jurisdiction* (at JUST), **predict**, *valediction* (at VALID), and *verdict* (at VERY). Related to ABDICATE*.

die [ME. French *dé* (plural *dés*), from Latin *datum*: see DATA*] **1** (plural **dice**) a small cube with numbered faces (surviving mainly in **the die is cast**), used in the game of **dice** played with two of them, hence **(a)** *dice* one of these cubes; a small cube of food; to cut into dice **(b) dicey** risky (1950s) **2** (plural **dies**): **(a)** the plain part of a pedestal between the base and the cornice (17c), also called a *dado* [17c, Italian, from Latin *datum*], which later referred to the lower part of a wall when decorated differently from the upper (18c), or a wooden trim separating the two **(b)** an engraved stamp for making coins, embossed paper, etc. (17c), hence applied to various devices for shaping materials (19c).

diet [Strictly speaking, two words, both ultimately from Latin *diaeta* '(prescribed) way of living', from Greek *diaita* 'course of life'] I [ME, via Old French] what you habitually eat (*staple diet*); the kind of food eaten (*vegetarian diet*); to feed on particular kinds of food; to restrict the kind or amount of food eaten, originally as a punishment, hence **1** (to follow) a prescribed eating regime **2** suitable for particular nutritional needs (17c), now usually low in calories (1960s, *US*) **II** [15c, via medieval Latin *dieta* 'a day's allowance, work, etc.', also 'a day set for a meeting', influenced by Latin *dies* 'day' (ancestor of JOURNEY*)] a conference or congress; (the regular meeting of) a legislative assembly (16c).

dig [ME. Perhaps from Old English *dīc* DITCH*] To break up or remove earth with the hands, paws, a spade, etc.; to make a hole etc. by doing so. Hence **1 dig out/ up** to extract, hence to find out by research (19c); *dig* to study closely; to understand, appreciate, or enjoy (1930s, *US*) **2** to thrust or force into (16c); (to give) a sharp poke or nudge; a sharp remark (19c) **3 dig in** to dig a trench etc. to shelter in (19c), hence **digger** an ordinary soldier, a mate (World War I, Australian) and probably **diggings** or **digs** lodgings (19c, the place where you are 'dug in') **4** an archaeological excavation (19c); to make one (early 20c).

digest [ME. Latin *digerere*, literally 'to carry away', hence 'to divide, distribute', from *gerere* 'to carry' (ancestor of GESTURE*). The main senses developed in Latin] To break down and absorb food in the body, hence **1** to break down a substance using heat, chemicals, etc. (15c) **2** to break down and organize methodically, hence **the Digest** [Latin *digesta* 'matters digested'] the collected and abridged writings of Roman jurists, hence a systematic compilation of laws or legal opinions (16c); a collection or summary of information; a magazine, book, or broadcast containing abridgements of items originally published elsewhere (1920s) **3** to absorb mentally (16c).

digit [ME. Latin *digitus* 'finger, toe'] **1** each of the Arabic numerals 0–9 (as originally counted on your fingers), hence **digital** to do with or using digits (15c); expressing data in digits (*digital computer/watch*, 1930s); representing sound or light waves by means of pulses expressed as digits (*digital radio*, 1960s) **2** a finger or toe (17c); the equivalent part of an animal (19c).

When digital devices appeared a label was needed for the existing non-digital ones: **analogue** a parallel word or thing [Greek *analogon* 'in due proportion', from *logos*: see APOLOGY*] was used to mean representation by physical means, e.g. mechanical rotation, voltage, etc.

Latin *digitus* produced **digitalis** the genus name of the foxglove [suggested by German *Fingerhut* 'thimble, foxglove', from the flower's shape], hence the drug made from it.

din [Old English *dyne*] A loud, cacophonous, or persistent noise; to subject someone to it (17c), hence to fix something in someone's mind by repeating it over and over (18c).

dint [Old English *dynt*, later also from related Old Norse *dyntr*] A blow, especially with a weapon (–19c), hence **1** its force (ME); **by dint of sword** by force of arms (–18c), hence **by dint of** by means of (16c) **2** (largely replaced by the variant **dent**: see also INDENT) to make a shallow depression in a surface (ME), hence **(a)** such a depression (16c) **(b)** to damage or weaken (1930s).

diploma [17c. Latin, from Greek *diplōma* 'folded paper', from *diploun* 'to fold', from *diplous* 'double'] An official document, especially the original manuscript:

1 one conferring an honour, privilege, or licence; a university or college certificate **2** a State paper, hence [via French] **diplomatic** to do with official or historical documents (18c), hence to do with the management of international relations (probably due to the publication of the original texts of important public documents, many of which dealt with international affairs), hence skilled in negotiating, prudent, tactful (19c).

direct [ME. Latin *dirigere*, *direct*- 'to arrange in lines', also 'to send in a straight line', from *regere* 'to put straight'] **1** straight, going or leading straight from one thing or place to another, hence **(a)** straight to the point, frank (16c) **(b)** without intermediary, intervention, or delay (16c) **(c)** of an electric current: flowing in one direction only (19c) **2** to send, later to address, a letter etc.; to address a remark; to send or guide in a particular direction; to guide or advise; to instruct, order, or supervise (15c); to conduct a musical performance (19c); to supervise a film or play (*c*.1910).

Latin *dirigere* produced **dirge** the Roman Catholic Office of the Dead [from Latin *Dirige, Domine, Deus meus, in conspectu tuo viam meam* 'Direct, O Lord, my God, my way in your sight', the beginning of a hymn formerly part of this service], hence a song of mourning; a slow, mournful, or tedious piece of music. Other descendants include ADDRESS, **dirigible** able to be directed, hence a balloon or airship you can steer, and DRESS*. Latin *regere* is the ancestor of REGIMENT*.

disc [17c. Via French or Latin from Greek *diskos* 'quoit, dish, disc' (ancestor of DAIS*), from *dikein* 'to throw'. Originally spelt *disk*, surviving in American English, whence its re-adoption in sense 4] The apparent shape of the sun, hence a flat, round object: **1** a quoit or discus (18–19c) **2** a disc-shaped part of an animal or plant (18c); a layer of cartilage between vertebrae (19c) **3** a gramophone record (19c), hence French **discothèque** [from Italian *discoteca* 'record library', modelled on *biblioteca* 'library': see BIBLE] a place where records are played for dancing (1950s), shortened to **disco** (1960s, *US*), which also describes the music played (1970s) **4 (a) disk** a thin round plate that stores information for use in a computer (1950s) **(b) compact disc (CD)** on which data is optically recorded (1970s); **DVD** [short for *digital video*, or *versatile*, *disc*] a high-quality, large capacity CD (1990s).

discipline [ME. Latin *disciplina* 'instruction of pupils', from *discipulus* 'learner, disciple', from *discere* 'to learn'] **1** (to carry out) chastisement, correction, or self-mortification to promote spiritual growth **2** instruction or education (–17c), hence **(a)** a branch of learning **(b)** (military) training; order and obedience in the army, a school, etc. (17c) **3** the rules and punishments by which religious practices are maintained (15c, seen as concerning the Church's disciples or followers, as opposed to doctrine, the domain of the 'teacher'); to formally rebuke or punish a member of an organization, originally a Church (19c).

discretion [ME. Latin *discernere*, *discret*- 'to distinguish or set apart', from *cernere* 'to sift or separate', later 'to judge or decide'] Discernment, judgement (–17c), hence **1 (a) indiscretion** lack of judgement; an imprudent action (17c); a sexual misdemeanour (19c) **(b)** the ability or freedom to rely on your own judgement (15c) **2** tact, reticence.

Latin *discernere* produced **discern** and DISCRIMINATE, and also **discreet** showing discernment or judgement, prudent, tactful, and **discrete** separate (*discrete* being the usual spelling for both until the 16c); *cernere* is the ancestor of CRIME*.

discriminate [16c. Latin *discriminare*, from *discrimen* 'distinction', from *discernere*: see DISCRETION*] Distinct, clearly distinguished (earlier and mainly in **indiscriminate**); to be, make, or perceive a difference or distinction, hence to judge or treat people differently because of their race, age, sex, etc. (19c).

discuss [ME. Latin *discutere*, *discuss*- 'to break up, disperse', later 'to investigate', from *quatere* 'to shake' (ancestor of QUASH*)] **1** to drive away, disperse, dispel (–19c) **2** to investigate or try a matter judicially (–17c), hence to examine something by debating or talking about it (15c).

disease [ME. Old French *disaise*, from *aise* 'comfort, convenience': see EASE*] Discomfort, inconvenience, anxiety (ME–18c), re-created in the early 20c from *ease*); something causing this: an annoyance or grievance (–18c); illness (15c); an ailment (16c).

dismal [ME. Via Anglo-Norman French from medieval Latin *dies mali* 'evil days'] Any one of the two days in each month marked as unlucky in the medieval calendar (–15c), hence unlucky (–17c); causing misfortune, disaster or dismay (16c); dreary, depressing; miserable (17c).

dismiss [ME. Old French *de(s)metre* 'to send away', ultimately from Latin *dimittere*, from *mittere* 'to send'] **1** to set free **2** to remove someone from a job etc. for incompetence or bad behaviour (15c) **3** to send away or allow to leave (16c): **(a)** to disperse an assembly or disband an army **(b)** to put something out of your mind, to reject or refuse to consider it; to reject an appeal to a higher court (17c).

Old French *de(s)metre* produced Anglo-Norman French **demise** 'sent away', adopted for a transfer of property, hence a death causing this; any death; an end. Latin *mittere* is the ancestor of MISSION*.

disparage [ME. Old French *desparagier*, from *parage* 'equality of rank', ultimately from Latin *par* 'equal', PAR*] To marry someone of lower rank or to be disgraced by doing so (–18c), hence to discredit; to treat or speak of contemptuously (16c).

dispense [ME. Via Old French from Latin *dispensare* 'to disburse or distribute', later 'to deal with', from *dispendere* 'to weigh or pay out', from *pendere* 'to weigh, to pay'] **1** to give out, hence **(a)** to administer justice or a sacrament **(b)** to supply prescribed medicine (16c) **2 dispense with** (to have the power) to grant a **dispensation**, a relaxation of a law or obligation in a particular case; to release someone from a vow or obligation (16c), hence to do away with a requirement; to manage without something thought of as necessary (17c), hence **indispensable** in the sense 'essential, necessary'.

Latin *dispendere* fathered Old French *dispencier* 'dispenser', whence **spencer** a butler or steward, surviving as a surname (with the variants **Despencer**, **Spence**, and **Spens(er)**; the synonymous **Spender** is also ultimately from *dispendere*. The 2nd Earl Spencer gave his name to a short double-breasted tail coat; later applied to a short, tight jacket or bodice for women and children, and thus to a similar woollen undergarment. Latin *pendere* is the ancestor of PENDANT*.

display [ME. Old French *despleier* from Latin *displicare* 'to scatter, disperse' (in medieval Latin 'to unfold'), from *plicare* 'to fold' (ancestor of PLY*)] To unfold, unfurl, or spread out, hence **1** to make visible or evident; to show prominently or ostentatiously (17c), hence **(a)** an exhibition or show; showiness, ostentation (19c) **(b)** of a bird: (to adopt) stylized behaviour as a means of communication (*c*.1900) **2** to lie or place with the limbs spread (surviving in heraldry); to spread out troops (16–19c, cf. *deploy* below).

Shortened to **splay**, which came to mean 'to spread or be spread out awkwardly'. Old French *despleier* evolved into *deployer*, whence **deploy**, used by Caxton (see ADVICE) to mean 'display', and reborrowed meaning 'to spread out troops in an extended line', hence to position troops for action; to organize resources.

disport [ME. Old French *desporter*, literally 'to carry away', from *porter* 'to carry', from Latin *portare*: see PORT³*] Amusement, entertainment, diversion (that carries you away from sadness or boredom); a pastime or game, hence to amuse yourself; to behave playfully, especially in a way that attracts attention (19c). Shortened to **sport**, which came to mean **1** play, fun, joking (15c), hence to play with or treat lightly (17c); a laughing stock or plaything, hence **sport (of nature)** a plant or animal different from the normal type (regarded as nature's prank, 17c); *sport* to produce or undergo mutation (18c) **2** a (competitive) game or pastime involving physical effort and skill (16c); such activities collectively, hence (combining 1 and 2) **(good) sport** someone who is fair-minded, easy-going, a good loser, and can take a joke (19c) **3** to show or wear ostentatiously (18c).

Old French *porter* produced *deporter* 'to behave', literally 'to bear yourself', whence **deport**, surviving mainly in **deportment**: a similar sense is found in **port** '(dignified) bearing' [also from *porter*], whence **portly** stately, dignified, imposing; stout. Latin *portare* also produced **deport** 'to banish' [French *déporter* from Latin *deportare* 'to send or carry off'].

dispose [ME. French *disposer*, from Latin *disponere*, *disposit-*, from *ponere* 'to put': see POSE*] To place or arrange things; to arrange matters, hence **1** to deal out, distribute (–19c); to formally assign or hand over (–16c); **dispose of** to give away or get rid of (17c); **disposal** the power to dispose of or use, usually in *at your disposal* (17c) **2** to make fit or ready; to put someone in the right frame of mind, hence **disposed** prepared, fit, in good health (–17c, surviving in **indisposed**); ready or inclined to do something; **well-disposed** inclined to approve, friendly, sympathetic (15c); **disposition** temperament (15c).

distemper [ME. Late Latin *distemperare*, from Latin *temperare* 'to mix in proper proportions': see TEMPER*] **1** to mix in the wrong proportions (ME only); to upset or derange, especially the balance of humours, hence to trouble physically or mentally; a disturbance of humours (16c), the resulting ill temper or ill health; an illness, now specifically a viral disease affecting animals; a disturbed state (17c) **2** [via Old French] to mix with a liquid, to soak or dilute, hence a method of painting with powder colours mixed with water, size, etc. (17c); (to paint with) this mixture (19c).

Italian *pingere a tempera* 'to paint with distemper' produced **tempera**, a paint-ing technique using an emulsion, usually of pigment and egg white.

distil [ME. (Via French from) Latin *distillare*, ultimately from *stillare* 'to drip', from *stilla* 'a drop'] To give or come out in tiny drops or in a vapour; to boil something and condense the vapour; to purify, separate, concentrate, or to obtain an essence or spirit, especially whisky, in this way. The variant **still** survives for an apparatus or place for distilling (16c).

Latin *stillare* produced *instillare*, whence **instil** to add liquid drop by drop, hence to introduce an idea, feeling, principle, etc. gradually or covertly.

distract [ME. Latin *distrahere*, *distract*-, from *trahere* 'to draw or drag' (ancestor of TRACT*). The original past participle, *distract*, changed to **distraught** under the influence of *straught*, former past participle of STRETCH; the modern form **distracted** appeared in the 16c] To pull in different directions (–17c), hence **1** to divert someone or their attention **2** to confuse, perplex, or drive mad by conflict-ing emotions or demands, mainly in *distracted* and *distraught*, and in *distrait* [ME–16c, past participle of French *destraire*, from Latin *distrahere*; re-adopted in the18c].

distress [ME. Via Old French from, ultimately, Latin *distringere* 'to pull apart', also 'to detain', from *stringere* 'to pull tight'] **1** (to cause) hardship, poverty, physical or mental anguish; (to subject to) severe pressure or stress, hence **(a)** danger requiring urgent assistance (*a ship in distress*, 17c) **(b)** physical exhaustion, col-lapse (19c) **(c)** to damage an object to make it look antique (1940s, *US*) **2** the seizure of property to make the owner fulfil an obligation or to punish them for not doing so, surviving as a legal term and in **distress sale**; it is now usually called **distraint** (18c), from **distrain** to subject to a distress [ME, via Old French *destrein-dre* from Latin *distringere*].

Stress [partly short for *distress*, partly via Old French *estrece* from Latin *stringere*] originally meant to compel or constrain: the sense '(to place) emphasis' comes from the idea of putting on pressure. Latin *distringere* also produced DISTRICT; *stringere* is the ancestor of STRICT*.

district [Medieval Latin *districtus* '(territory of) jurisdiction', from Latin *distring-ere*, *distric-*: see DISTRESS*] The territory under the jurisdiction of a feudal lord (17c), hence an administrative area; an area surrounding a particular place or having its own identity (*red light district*, 18c).

ditch [Old English *dīc*] A trench; one for drainage (ME), hence **1** a small stream; the sea (1920s, naval slang); to make an emergency landing in water **2** an embankment (ME), replaced by related **dyke** [Old Norse *dik(i)*] a trench, also the heaped-up material dug out to make it **3** to dig a ditch (ME) **4** to throw some-thing into a ditch (19c); to discard, abandon, or jilt (*c*.1910, *US*).

Old English *dīc* produced the place- and surnames **Deighton**, **Digby**, **Diss**, and **Ditton**, and probably DIG.

divers [ME. French, 'different, odd, wicked' from *diversus* 'contrary, different, separate', from Latin *divertere* 'to separate', literally 'to turn aside', from *vertere* 'to turn'] **1** different (–18c, outlived by the variant **diverse**); various, sundry **2** only as *diverse*: varied, changeable (16c).

Latin *divertere* produced *diversare* 'to turn continually', whence **diverse 1** to vary, to be or make different, replaced by **diversify 2** to turn aside, replaced by **divert**. **Divorce** is from Latin *divortere*, a variant of *divertere*. Latin *vertere* is the ancestor of VERSE*.

divine [ME. Via Old French from Latin *divinus*, from *divus* 'godlike'] **1** the study of the nature of God (outlived by **divinity** and by **theology**, ultimately from Greek *theos* 'god', whence ENTHUSIASM*); a theologian **2** to do with, coming from, or sacred to, a deity, hence having 'superhuman' beauty, talent, etc.; excellent, delightful **3** the seeking of knowledge by supernatural means (outlived by **divination**); to predict or discover by such means.

Related to DEITY* and to Italian *diva* [literally 'goddess'], adopted for a distinguished woman (opera) singer.

dock [ME. Probably ultimately of Germanic origin] The solid part of an animal's tail, hence to cut this short; to shorten or reduce, now especially to withhold part of someone's pay.

Probably the ancestor of **docket** a summary or abstract; a list of cases to be tried, matters to be discussed, or contents.

doctor [ME. Via Old French from Latin, from *docere* 'to teach'] A teacher; a learned person; someone holding a **doctorate**, the highest university degree; an authority on a subject, now especially medicine, hence **1** to treat a sick person (18c) **2** to alter, disguise, or adulterate **3** to repair or improve (19c) **4** to neuter an animal (*c*.1900).

Latin *docere* is the ancestor of **docent** a private teacher in a university, a (voluntary) guide in a museum etc. (both US) **docile** originally meaning 'easy to teach', **doctrine** literally 'what is taught', hence a set of beliefs or principles, DOCUMENT, and **indoctrinate** to teach, hence to teach a doctrine or ideology in a way that discourages critical thought. Related to *orthodox* (at CATHOLIC).

document [ME. French, from Latin *documentum* 'lesson, proof' (in medieval Latin 'written instruction'), from *docere*: see DOCTOR*] **1** teaching (–19c); to teach (17–19c) **2** evidence, proof (–19c), hence written evidence (15c); a written record; an official paper; to prove or support by written evidence (18c); to record in writing (19c). Hence **documentary** to do with or consisting of documents (19c); to do with evidence or teaching, hence factual (1920s); a factual film etc. (1930s), whence **docudrama** a dramatization of real events (1960s); **docutainment** based on real events but designed to entertain (1970s), and **docugame** a computer game based on real events (*c*.2000).

doff [ME. Contraction of *do off*, from **do** (Old English *dōn*): related to DOOM*] To take off a garment; to put aside or get rid of (16c). *Doff* and its opposite **don** [ME, from *do on*] virtually disappeared in the 17c: Johnson (see ACHE) described *doff* as 'scarcely used except by rustics'. Both were revived as archaisms (18c), and popularized by Sir Walter Scott (influential Scottish poet and novelist, b.1771).

dog [Old English *docga*, of unknown origin] The domestic canine; a male dog, fox, or wolf (ME); a related or similar animal (18c). Hence **1** a contemptible man (ME); a rake, often a term of envious reproof (*lucky/sly old dog,* 17c); something poor or disappointing (1930s, *US*); an ugly woman; a slow or difficult horse (1940s, *military slang*) **2** (from a dog following its master or prey): **(a)** to follow closely (16c); to chase or harass (cf. *hound* below); to trouble persistently (17c) **(b) dog star** [translating Greek *kuon* or Latin *canicula* 'small dog'] said to follow at Orion's heels: it rises with the sun in midsummer and seemed to make it hotter, hence the star's modern name **Sirius** [Greek *Seirios* (*aster*) 'scorching (star)'] and **dog days** [translating Latin *dies canicularis*] the hottest time of the year, regarded as enervating, unhealthy, and, later, unlucky **(c) dogged** tenacious, persistent (18c) **3** in terms for food, e.g. **(a) dogsbody** dried peas boiled in a cloth (19c, nautical slang); ship's biscuits soaked and mashed with sugar: later applied to a junior officer, hence someone who does all the menial jobs (1920s) **(b) dogs** sausages (19c); **hot dog** a hot sausage in a roll (*c.*1900) **4 dogging** having sex in a public place with a stranger (1990s).

Contempt for dogs is also shown in **a dog's life** a miserable one, **dog Latin** a spurious or incorrect form (whence **doggerel**), in the names of inedible or 'inferior' plants (*dog daisy/fennel*: the **dog rose**, however, was used to treat rabies). The surnames **Dockett**, **Dogget**, and some instances of **Dodgson** and **Doig**, were also probably derogatory. Cf. BITCH, **cur** a (bad-tempered) dog, a contemptible man [probably from Old Norse *kurr* 'grumbling'], CYNIC, FEISTY, and TYKE.

Dog replaced **hound** [Old English *hund*] as the usual term for the domestic animal in early Middle English; this now usually refers to a hunting dog, hence to pursue or harass (cf. sense 2 above).

dole [Old English *dāl*: related to DEAL*] **1** a portion (–16c); a share (ME); your share, your fate **2** the distribution of charitable gifts; to distribute them, hence **(a)** the goods or money distributed (17c); unemployment benefit (post-World War I) **(b)** to give out (sparingly) (18c).

doll, **dolly** [16c. Pet forms of *Dorothy* (see ENTHUSIASM*)] A girlfriend or mistress (–17c), hence **1** a model person as a child's toy (17c); a puppet (19c); a ventriloquist's dummy (early 20c); **corn dolly** originally a human figure made of the last cornstalks cut [1950s alteration of *kirn baby/dolly*, from **kirn** a harvest-home feast (16c), the last corn harvested (18c), of unknown origin] **2** an attractive or pleasant (perhaps not very bright) person (18c), not always female; **doll up** to dress smartly or elaborately (*c.*1900) **3** *dolly* a device with 'legs' at the bottom and handles or 'arms' at the top, for agitating washing in a tub (18c), sometimes applied to the tub, and later to various useful devices, now especially a wheeled platform for a film or television camera (1920s).

dollar [16c. Flemish or Low German *daler* from German *Taler*, short for *Joachimstaler*, literally 'from Joachimstal' (now Jáchymov), in the Czech Republic, applied to a coin made of the silver mined there] A German silver coin, later called a **thaler** (18c): both terms were also applied to various European coins, and *dollar* to a Spanish coin used in Spanish and British colonies in the New World which became the monetary unit of the newly fledged United States of America in 1785; the name was kept when the US began minting its own coins, and was later adopted by other former colonies introducing their own currencies. The Spanish coin was worth eight *reals* and was marked with a figure 8 (hence **pieces of eight**); the dollar sign ($) is probably based on this.

dollop [16c. Perhaps of Scandinavian origin] A clump of grass or weeds in a field (surviving in eastern English dialect); a shapeless or soft lump (18c), now usually a helping of (soft) food (19c); to serve out or cover in dollops.

dolphin [ME. Old French *dau(l)phin* via Provençal *dalfin* from Latin *delphinus*, from Greek *delphis*] A small toothed whale; a similar species, also a mythical fish of the Nile, hence **1** one as a symbol of love, diligence, speed, also salvation and resurrection (from the belief that dolphins rescued drowning sailors, and that it was a dolphin that swallowed Jonah: see the Bible, Jonah 1, 2) **2** applied to various devices thought to resemble a dolphin, including a mooring buoy (18c).

In 1349 the future King Charles V of France bought the Viennois in SE France, taking **Dauphin**, the family name of the previous owners (whose crest was a dolphin), as a title; this became the hereditary title of the king's eldest son after Charles gave the province to his. Greek *delphis* produced **delphinium** [via *delphinion* 'larkspur': the flower shape is thought to resemble the curve of a dolphin's back or a lark's hind claw] and **Delphi** in ancient Greece where the god Apollo established an oracle (he is said to have turned himself into a dolphin, swum to a ship, and forcibly recruited the crew to guard it). Delphi had formerly been called *Pytho*, and the previous oracle had been guarded by a serpent or monster, **Python**, which Apollo killed; its name was given to the snake in the 19c.

domain [ME. French *domaine*, alteration of *demeine*, ultimately from Latin *dominus*: see DOMINATE*] The possession and use of land (–17c), outlived by *demesne* below); (the ownership of) heritable property, especially land, hence **1** a ruler's territory (18c) **2** your sphere of influence; an area or subject in which you predominate **3** the scope of a subject, law, etc., hence **in the public domain** not protected by patent or copyright (19c, *US*); not or no longer secret **4** a 'place' in a computer network used in a network address (1980s).

Old French *demeine* produced **demesne**, applied specifically to land occupied and worked by its owner, especially the home farm or park of an estate. *Domain* is not recorded in this sense, but produced Scots **mains** home farm (surviving in place names and as a surname), and the land around the Government House in Sydney was called **The Domain**: *domain* came to mean a public park in Australia and New Zealand after The Domain became one.

dome Strictly speaking, two words, both from Latin *domus* 'house': I [16c, directly from *domus*] a house, a home; a grand house or other building. II [via French from Italian *duomo* 'house (of God), cathedral', hence 'cupola' (which many had)] a roof (17c) or building (1950s) shaped like an upturned bowl; something resembling this, e.g. the roof of a cavern (18c); a rounded hilltop (19c); the head.

Latin *domus* is the ancestor of **domestic**, **domicile**, and of **major-domo** the chief male servant in a large household [via Spanish and Italian from medieval Latin *major domus* 'chief of the house'].

dominate [17c. Latin *dominari*, from *dominus* 'lord, master of a household'] To control or have authority over (17c, but implied in **domination**, ME); to influence strongly; to be the most important, conspicuous, or influential thing or person (19c); to occupy a commanding or superior position. **Dominator** (15c) and the female equivalent **dominatrix** (16c) also pre-date *dominate*: the latter was extremely rare until about the 1970s, when it re-emerged meaning a dominant woman in a sado-masochistic relationship.

Latin *dominari* produced **domineer**. *Dominus* appears in **anno domini** 'in the year of the Lord', usually shortened to AD, and is the ancestor of *dame* and *damsel* (at LORD*), DANGER, DOMAIN*, the name **Dominic**, DOMINION*, DON*, DUNGEON*, **predominate**, and probably DOMINO. Related to **daunt**, originally to tame or subdue [Old French *donter*, from Latin *domitare* 'to subdue' (whence **indomitable**)].

dominion [ME. Old French, ultimately from Latin *dominium*, from *dominus*: see DOMINATE*] **1** the power or right to govern **2** territory ruled, later applied to territory outside England, later Great Britain, owing allegiance to the Crown (17c).

Latin *dominium* was adopted as a legal term meaning 'ownership, control', whence **condominium**, literally 'joint dominium', originally joint control of a state's affairs by other states, later (a unit in) an apartment block jointly owned by the owners of the individual units (shortened to **condo**), which produced **dockominium** a privately owned mooring in a marina, or a waterside condominium with its own moorings.

domino [17c. French, probably ultimately from Latin *dominus*: see DOMINATE*] The development is largely a matter of conjecture: in French it meant a priest's winter cloak, perhaps from the ritual formula *benedicamus Domino* 'let us bless the Lord' (for providing a warm cloak?); in Spanish and English it meant a cloak with a mask worn at masquerades. The word may have been applied to the tiles used in the game of dominoes (*c.*1800) because the spots looked like eyes peeping through a mask: however, it may be that the winner's cry of *domino!* on playing the last tile also goes back to *benedicamus Domino*, 'bless the Lord, (I've won!)'. In 1954 the US President Dwight D. Eisenhower used 'falling domino principle' to suggest that a political event in one country would lead to its occurrence in others, as a falling domino will fell a whole line, whence **domino effect/ theory**.

don [16c. Latin *dominus*: see DOMINATE*] **1** [via Spanish] a respectful title or form of address for a Spanish man; a Spanish noble or gentleman (17c) **2** a distinguished man; a university teacher, especially at Oxford or Cambridge (17c) **3** [via Italian] a high-ranking Mafia member (1950s, *US*).

Latin *dominus* produced French *dan*, adopted as a title or respectful form of address and sometimes added to the names of poets after Spenser (SEE BLATANT) applied it to Chaucer, **Dom** the title of some Roman Catholic dignitaries, and Latin **Domine** [the form of *dominus* used when speaking to a lord], adopted as a polite form of address to a clergyman or other professional, hence a schoolmaster (surviving in Scots **dominie**); a pastor of the Dutch Reformed Church (now mainly in the Dutch and Afrikaans form **dominee**).

donkey [18c. Originally pronounced *dunky*: perhaps from the colour **dun** (Old English, probably related to **dusk**), or from the name **Duncan** (from Gaelic **Donagh** 'brown warrior', often taken to mean 'brown head')] A small, strong beast of burden with long ears, proverbially regarded as obstinate and stupid, hence **1 donkey engine** a small or auxiliary engine (19c); **donkey jacket** a workman's jacket (*c.*1920); **donkey work** hard or unglamorous work **2** a fool (19c) **3 donkey's years** (early 20c) may be a pun on *donkey's ears*, or refer to the animal's longevity: it's been said that a good donkey will last you a lifetime, but so will a bad one.

Donkey replaced **ass** [Old English *assa*, ultimately from Latin *asinus*] as the usual word for the domestic animal: *ass* now usually means a fool or one of the donkey's wild cousins. Latin *asinus* is one parent of **Fortnum**, a name meaning literally 'strong little donkey' [with Old French *fort* 'strong', from Latin *fortis*: see FORCE*].

doom [Old English *dōm*] A law or decree (–17c); a legal judgement or sentence, hence **1** (a depiction of) the Last Judgement, when God will judge the world (ME), hence **doomsday (a)** the day of the Last Judgement; the end of the world **(b) Doomsday/Domesday Book** William the Conqueror's comprehensive survey of England (originally a popular name reflecting its thoroughness) **2** your destiny or (dreadful) fate (ME); impending ruin or disaster (16c); to destine or condemn to such a fate (17c).

Related to DEED, **deem** [Old English *dēman*] to judge (–17c); to consider to be, whence the surname **Dempster** someone who judged minor disputes, and to DOFF*.

dope [19c, *US* in most senses. Dutch *doop* 'sauce', from *doopen* 'to dip or mix'] A thick liquid, hence **1** a mixture, ointment, syrup, etc., specifically **(a)** the thick, treacly preparation of opium used for smoking, hence any narcotic; (to give) a drug to improve or impede sporting performance (*c*.1900), hence, perhaps, true or misleading information (an advantage or hindrance) **(b)** Coca-Cola (early 20c), perhaps because it was supplied to retailers as a concentrated syrup, or because it originally contained cocaine (hence its name) **(c)** varnish applied to the cloth surfaces of early aircraft to keep them taut and airtight (*c*.1910) **2** to smear, daub, or adulterate with dope.

Dope 'a fool' is first recorded in English dialect, and may be a different word.

dormitory [15c. Latin *dormitorium*, from *dormire* 'to sleep'] A bedroom; a communal one in an institution (16c), hence **1** a resting place (17c) **2** a hostel or hall of residence (19c, US) **3** (describing) a community whose inhabitants commute to work elsewhere (1920s).

Latin *dormire* produced **reredorter** a lavatory at the back of a monastic dormitory [with French *arere* 'back, backwards': see ARREAR*], and Old French *dormir*, whence **dormant, dormer** originally a bedroom or dormitory window, and probably **dormouse** [via Anglo-Norman French *dormeus* 'sleepy': the spelling changed by association with *mouse*].

dote [ME. Probably related to early Dutch *doten* 'to be silly or childish'] To act or talk foolishly (–19c); to be or become foolish in old age (hence **dotage**), hence to be excessively and indulgently fond of someone (15c).

Dote is the source of *dotterel* (at BOOBY) and perhaps **dotty** 'stupid, crazy'.

double [ME. Via Old French from Latin *duplus*, from *duo* 'two'] Consisting of two, two-fold, repeated; to make double, to multiply by two; to increase twofold. Hence **1** twice as much or many; (something) of twice the usual size, strength, volume, etc.; for or involving two people instead of one (*double bed, doubles match*): often opposed to **single** [Old French, from Latin *singulus*: related to SIMPLE]

2 dual, ambiguous; deceitful **3** (to produce) a copy or duplicate (–19c), hence **(a)** someone/something very like another (18c); a stand-in (19c) **(b)** **dub** to copy previously recorded sound (1920s); to add sounds to a soundtrack (1930s); to mix recorded sounds (1950s), hence a form of (originally Jamaican) popular music made by remixing recorded music and adding sound effects (1970s); a kind of poetry originally accompanied by this (1980s) **4** to line a garment, hence **doublet** a lined jacket (whence **singlet**, originally an unlined one, 18c).

Latin *duo*'s descendants include *deuce* (at DEVIL), **doubloon** a Spanish gold coin double the value of a pistole, **dual**, **duet**, **duo-** (*duologue*, *duopoly*), Italian *duo* a duet; a couple, especially of performers, **duplicate**, **duplicity**, and also Latin *duo-decim* 'twelve' [with Latin *decem* 'ten' (ancestor of DECIMATE*), whence **dozen** [via French] and **duodenum** part of the small intestine, so called because of its length, about twelve fingers' width. Related to DOUBT*.

doubt [ME. Old French *douter* from Latin *dubitare* 'to waver or hesitate', from *dubius* 'wavering, uncertain'] **1** to be uncertain; this feeling; a reservation **2** (to feel) fear (–18c); to be afraid of.

Old French *douter* produced **redoubtable** [via *redouter* 'to fear']. Latin *dubitare* produced **indubitable**; *dubius* is the ancestor of **dubious**. Related to DOUBLE*.

down [Old English *dūn*, perhaps ultimately of Celtic origin] A hill (surviving as **-don** in place names), hence open high ground, especially **the Downs** the chalk uplands of S England (ME), whence *Down* (a sheep of) a breed raised there (19c, 18c in **Southdown**).

Related to **down** in or to a lower place [shortened from *adown*, from Old English *of dūne* 'off the hill'], **dune** [French, from early Dutch *dūne*], and TOWN*.

dowry, dower [ME. Both from Old French *douaire*, from medieval Latin *dotarium*, from Latin *dotare* 'to endow', from *dos, dot-* 'dowry'] In Middle English both meant: **1** a natural gift or talent **2** (now *dower*) the share of a man's estate which his widow inherits, hence **dower house** a house on an estate for the owner's widow **3** (now *dowry*) money or property a woman brings to her marriage (or gives to a religious house on entering it); that given by a man to his bride or her family.

Latin *dotare* is the ancestor of **dowager** a widow who has inherited a title or property from her husband, hence a dignified elderly woman, and of **endow** to provide with a dowry, property, or a permanent income.

drag [ME. Old Norse *draga* or related Old English *dragan*; the noun partly from early Low German *dragge* 'grapnel'] **1** to pull forcefully or with difficulty **2** something dragged, e.g. a dragnet (hence to search a river etc. with a dragnet or grappling hook, 16c), a sledge (16c, the original sense of related **dray**); a cart; a private coach (18c) **3** to trail along the ground (15c), hence **(a)** a hunted animal's scent trail (18c); a smelly lure for hounds (19c) **(b)** women's clothing worn by men (19c, *theatrical slang*, perhaps from a long dress trailing on the ground) **4** to progress slowly or against resistance (18c), hence **(a)** something that impedes progress (18c); the force that resists motion through a fluid, especially of an aircraft through the air (early 20c) **(b)** a nuisance, a boring person or event (19c) **5** a street (19c, perhaps from the idea of carts etc. being dragged along it), hence **drag race**, originally held illegally on public roads (1950s).

Drag produced **draggle** and perhaps DROGUE. Probably related to DRAW, to the place names **Draycot(t)** and **Drayton** (where something is dragged), and to **dredge** something for dragging or scooping up stuff from a riverbed etc., to clear out or search a river with one.

dragon [ME. French, from Latin *draco*, from Greek *drakōn* 'serpent', perhaps from *derkesthai* 'to look' and meaning literally 'one with a (deadly) glance': cf. BASILISK] **1** a huge serpent (–18c); the Devil (the serpent in the Garden of Eden); a cruel, later a strict or formidable, person (18c) **2** a mythical winged, fire-breathing reptile (gradually replacing **drake** [Old English *draca*, ultimately from Greek *drakōn*], hence **(a)** applied to species of lizard, especially the Komodo dragon (1920s) **(b) to chase the dragon** to smoke heroin by heating it and inhaling the fumes; as the powder melts the fumes appear to writhe like a dragon's tail (1960s).

French *dragon* produced **dragonet** a small or baby dragon, later a brightly-coloured fish, and DRAGOON. Latin *draco* produced Romanian *dracul*, a title, indicating membership of the chivalric Order of the Dragon, of Vlad the Impaler (the prototype of Prince Dracula in a 15c story and of Bram Stoker's *Dracula,* 1897), and RANKLE. Greek *drakōn* is the ancestor of **draceana** a tropical shrub with brightly coloured leaves and irritant sap (a related species, the **dragon tree**, yields a red resin known as **dragon's blood**, used to colour varnishes etc.), **Draco**, the name given to an Athenian lawmaker known for his severe sentences (whence **draconian**), **dragons** [via Old French *dragonce*] the earliest name of the **dragon arum** or **green dragon**, believed to cure snake bite, and probably of its relative, **tarragon**.

dragoon [17c. French *dragon*: see DRAGON*] A kind of gun, said to breathe fire, hence a mounted infantryman, originally equipped with one. In 17c France dragoons were billeted on Huguenots to 'persuade' them to renounce their heresy, hence to force or harass someone into doing something.

drama [16c. French *drame* (the original English spelling) and late Latin *drama* from Greek, from *dran* 'to do, act, or perform'] A serious play; plays as a genre (17c), hence an exciting or emotional real-life situation (18c); an exciting or gripping quality (1930s).

French *drame* produced **melodrama** [with Greek *melos* 'song, music' (whence *melody* at ODE)] a play with music, often sensational and over-emotional, hence such a play without music, a similar real-life situation. Greek *dran* produced *drastikos*, whence **drastic** active, effective, originally applied to medicine, especially one with a dramatic effect, hence extreme, severe.

drape [ME. French *drap* 'cloth', from Latin *drappus*, perhaps of Celtic origin] To weave (–17c), hence **1 draper** someone who weaves or, later, sells cloth; **drapery** cloth, fabrics; curtains, linens, etc. (17c) **2** *drape* [from *drapery* or directly from French *drap*] a cloth (17c); a hanging or curtain (19c, US); to cover or hang with fabrics; to arrange cloth or clothing in graceful folds, hence **(a)** of fabric or clothing: to hang well (1940s); the way it hangs **(b)** to recline limply (1940s).

Old French *drap* is probably the ancestor of **drab** originally a kind of undyed cloth, hence of a similar shade; dull, uninteresting, and of **trap** an ornamental or protective cloth spread over a horse and its harness (ME–18c), whence **trappings** (a cover for) an ornamental harness; the outward signs of status, whence, probably, **traps** belongings, baggage.

draw   [Old English *dragan*] The basic sense is 'to move or pull along'; *draw a picture* etc. comes from the idea of moving a pencil across paper. The verb has, in effect, five nouns: its own *draw,* **drawer**, and **drawing** (all ME), and and **draught** [ME, from related Old Norse *drattr*] and its variant **draft** (16c, now the only N American spelling), basically meaning 'drawing, something drawn'.
   Draw produced WITHDRAW and is related to DRAG*.

dreary   [Old English *drēorig*, from *drēmor* 'gore': related to **drowsy**, and probably to **drizzle**] **1** gory, bloody (–16c); dire, dreadful (17c) **2** sorrowful, grieving (–19c). Hence (combining 1 and 2) dismal, depressing, dull (17c, shortened to **drear** in poetry).

dredge   [ME. Old French *dragie*, probably ultimately from Greek *tragemata* 'spices, confectionery'] **1** a comfit (–17c, replaced by modern French *dragée*, which also means a small sugar-ball used on cakes **2** a mixture of spices; to sprinkle with spices, sugar, or flour (16c); **dredger** a perforated container for dredging (17c).

drench   [Old English *drenc* (noun), *drencan* (verb): related to **drink** and **drown**] A (medicinal) drink (–ME), now only one for animals, hence to force one down a person or animal, hence to drown or be drowned (ME); to be submerged; to soak (16c).

dress   [ME. Old French *dresser* 'to prepare', ultimately from Latin *directus*: see DIRECT*] **1** to direct or guide (–16c), hence **(a)** to train a horse (–18c, cf. *dressage* below) **(b)** to punish or reprimand (surviving in *dress down*) **2** to put in place or in order (–17c); to come, or bring troops, into formation for a parade (18c) **3** to prepare (–18c), hence **(a)** to prepare or season food (**mutton dressed as lamb** is a pun on this sense); **dressing** seasoning or sauce for food (16c); *dress* to add dressing (18c) **(b)** to prepare yourself by putting on (appropriate) clothes, hence the clothes worn (16c); a woman or girl's frock (18c) **(c)** to prepare stone, hides, etc. for use (15c) **(d)** to treat soil with fertilizer (16c) **4** to equip or adorn: **(a)** to provide a play with costumes and props (18c) **(b)** to adorn a ship with flags (18c) or a shop window with goods (19c) **5** to treat a wounded person (15c) or a wound (17c) with a protective covering **6** to arrange the hair (16c, surviving mainly in **hairdresser**).
   Old French *dresser* produced *dressage* advanced training for horses, **dresser** originally a side table for preparing food, and **redress** [via *redresser* 'to rearrange or repair'].

dribble   [16c. From **drib** 'to drip, to progress little by little' (16c, rare since the 17c), alteration of **drip** from Old English *dryppan*] **1** to (allow to) trickle or drip; to let saliva trickle from your mouth (17c); a trickle of liquid or saliva **2** to move a ball by a series of small taps or kicks (19c).
   Drib came to mean a small or insignificant quantity, surviving mainly in *dribs and drabs*. Related to **droop** [Old Norse *drúpa*], **drop** [Old English *dropa*], and EAVESDROP.

drivel   [Old English *dreflian*, of uncertain origin] **1** to dribble or slobber; saliva dribbling from the mouth (ME); largely replaced by the 19c alteration **drool**, which came to mean 'to feel or show excessive desire or emotion' from the idea of salivating at the sight of food (1950s) **2** to babble or talk childishly; childish talk, nonsense (19c).

drogue [18c. Perhaps from DRAG*] A board, tub, etc. tied to a harpoon line to slow the whale down; a canvas cone towed behind a boat to steady it (19c); one serving as a brake on an aircraft (*c.*1920), hence **1** a windsock (1930s); a similarly shaped target towed behind an aircraft; an unmanned aircraft, originally used as a target (1950s) **2** an auxiliary parachute (1940s) **3** the funnel-shaped connecter on the end of a tanker aircraft's refuelling line (1940s).

dub [ME. Anglo-Norman French *(a)duber* or Old French *adober* 'to equip with armour, to repair', of unknown origin] **1** to confer knighthood by a ceremonial touch with a sword, hence to give someone a title, name, or nickname **2** to equip, clothe, adorn, or trim (–18c), hence to dress a fishing fly, later leather or cloth (17c); to smear (now usually leather) with grease, hence **dubbing** grease for treating leather (18c), shortened to **dubbin** (19c).

dud [ME. Origin unknown] A garment (surviving as **duds** clothes, later things, belongings); coarse or ragged clothes (16c), hence **dudman** a person wearing them, a scarecrow (17c), whence *dud* an ineffective person or thing (19c); a counterfeit coin; counterfeit, useless (early 20c).

due [ME. Old French *deu,* past participle of *deveir* 'to owe', from Latin *debere*] Owing or payable, hence **1** that ought to be, or be done, fitting, proper, right, hence **(a)** merited, deserved; your rights or deserts; **give someone their due** to treat or speak of them fairly (16c) **(b)** directly and exactly (*due west,* 16c) **(c) in due course** after a proper interval (19c) **2** a debt (–19c); **dues** a fee, toll, or charge; your debts or obligations (18c); **pay your dues** to meet your obligations, later to undergo hardships, especially to gain experience (1940s, US slang) **3 due to** caused by, attributable to (17c); because of (19c, regarded as incorrect but now well ensconced): cf. *owing to* (at OWE) **4** payable on a certain date (19c); expected at a certain time.

Old French *deu* produced **duty**, literally 'something owed', which has largely replaced **devoir** [also from *deveir*]. The phrase *put yourself in devoir* 'to put yourself under an obligation' produced **endeavour** to exert yourself (ME–17c); exertion, effort, hence (to make) a strenuous effort or attempt to do something.

duel [15c. French, from Italian *duello* or Latin *duellum* (an older form of *bellum* 'war'), which survived in poetry and was revived in medieval Latin to denote single combat, probably influenced by Latin *dualis* 'of two'] Armed combat between two people to settle a legal case, hence any contest between two people or parties (16c); a formalized fight to settle a quarrel (17c); to fight one.

Latin *bellum* is the ancestor of **bellicose**, **belligerent**, and **rebel** [Latin *rebellare,* literally 'to make war again', whence also **revel** (via Old French *se reveler* 'to rebel or carouse')].

dull [Old English *dol,* later also from early Dutch or Low German *dul*] **1** slow-witted, stupid; sluggish, listless (ME) **2** of a blade etc.: blunt (ME); of pain: not intense or acute **3** uninteresting, boring (ME) **4** of a colour: not vivid (ME); of weather: overcast (16c).

Probably the source of **doldrum** a sluggish or stupid person (–19c), hence **the doldrums** a period of listlessness and despondency; an area of the ocean near the equator with little wind, hence a period of stagnation and lack of progress.

dumb [Old English] **1** unable to speak, hence **(a)** speechless from fear or shock (ME), whence **dumbstruck** (16c), **dumbfound** [17c, from CONFOUND] **(b)** deliberately not speaking (ME) **(c)** done without speech (*dumb show*, 16c) **(d)** **dummy** a dumb person (16c); an imaginary fourth player in whist (18c); a model of a human body (*ventriloquist's/tailor's dummy*, 19c), hence an imitation or substitute; an imitation teat to soothe a baby (early 20c); (to make) a feigned pass or kick to mislead your opponent; **dummy run** a practice or tryout (World War I, *naval slang*) **2** producing no sound, hence without something you would expect (16c): **dumbell**, (originally **dumb-bell**) an exercise machine similar to the device for swinging a church bell (18c); **dumb barge** with no means of propulsion (19c) **3** stupid, ignorant [ME, probably influenced by related Dutch *dom*, German *dumm* 'stupid']; of a computer terminal: unable to process data (1970s); **dumb down** to make (1930s) or become (1990s) less intellectually demanding.

dump [ME. Probably of Scandinavian origin] To fall or drop suddenly (–15c); to thump (16c, Scots); then not recorded until it reappeared in the US meaning 'to put or throw down carelessly; to throw out or discard' (18c), hence **1** a place where things are left or discarded: **(a)** a dirty, dreary or unpleasant place (19c) **(b)** a store for provisions, ammunition, etc. (World War I) **2** to flood a market with cheap goods (19c) **3** to abandon permanently or temporarily (*dump the kids on grandma*, early 20c); to discard a friend or lover **4** to defecate (early 20c, *US*); this act (1940s); **dump on** to criticize, abuse, or defeat (1960s) **5** to copy or list stored data without processing it (1950s); a printout or listing of it.

    Dump in **down in the dumps** is a different word [probably from early Dutch *domp* 'vapour, haze', related to DAMP] originally meaning a reverie (16–17c), hence **dumps** vagueness, perplexity, depression.

dunce [16c] A follower of the 13c theologian John Duns Scotus, ridiculed by later humanists and reformers as enemies of learning, hence **1** a pedant (–18c) **2** a slow learner.

dungeon [ME. French *donjon*, probably from medieval Latin *dangio* 'lord's tower', ultimately from Latin *dominus*: see DOMINATE*] **1** a prison cell in or under a castle **2** the castle keep. Until the 17c *dungeon* and *donjon* were used in both senses; *donjon* then died out but was revived by Scott (see DOFF) in sense 2, for which it is now the usual spelling.

duress [ME. Via Old French from Latin *duritia* 'hardness', from *durus* 'hard, tough'] Oppression, violence, cruelty (–17c); forcible restraint or confinement (15c), hence coercion by (real or threatened) imprisonment or violence, especially illegal coercion of someone held in custody before their trial.

    Latin *durare* 'to harden or endure' [from *durus*] produced **durable**, **duration**, **during**, the surname **Dur(r)ant**, **endure**, and **obdurate**. *Durus* is the ancestor of **durum** a kind of wheat with hard seeds, and perhaps of **dour**.

dwarf [Old English *dweorg*] A very small person, hence **1** a member of a race of small people in Scandinavian folklore, skilled in mining and metalwork **2** small (16c), hence **(a)** (describing) a small animal or plant variety **(b)** (describing) a small, dense star (*c*.1910) **3** to stunt (17c); to become small or undersized (19c); to make look small by comparison **4** a small person with a large head, small limbs, and other abnormalities (19c), as opposed to a **midget** [19c, from **midge** a small fly, from Old English *mycg(e)*] who is normal in everything except size.

dwell [Old English *dwellan*] To mislead, hinder, or delay (–ME); to linger, hesitate, or pause (ME); to stay where or as you are, hence **1** to live somewhere permanently; **dwelling** the house etc. where you live **2 dwell on** to think, speak, or write about at length.

dynamic [18c. Via French from Greek *dunamikos*, from *dunamis* 'force, power', from *dunasthai* 'to be able'] **Dynamics** the study of motion or the forces producing it; (the study of) forces causing change (19c), hence *dynamic* to do with such forces; characterized by action or sudden change; active, energetic.

Greek *dunamis* produced **dynamite** the explosive [translating Swedish *dynamit*, the name given by its inventor, 19c chemist Albert Nobel], hence someone/something that is (potentially) very harmful or exciting, and **dynamo** [short for **dynamo-electric machine**] a machine that converts mechanical to electrical energy. *Dunasthai* is the ancestor of **dynasty**.

E

eager [ME. Old French *aigre* 'keen', ultimately from Latin *acer* 'sharp, pungent' (ancestor of ACID*)] **1** pungent, sour, tart (–18c) **2** of a medicine: acting quickly and violently, hence impetuous, angry (surviving in dialect); keen.

ease [ME. Old French *aise* 'opportunity, elbow room, convenience', ultimately from Latin *adjacere* 'to lie close, from *jacere* 'to lie', also 'to throw'] Comfort, convenience, hence **1** (to bring about) freedom or relief from pain, annoyance, anxiety, or effort **2** freedom or relief from constraint (15c); to loosen or relax; **at ease** relaxed, in a relaxed way (19c) **3** to relax your efforts, to slow down (16c); to move or manoeuvre slowly and gently (17c) **4** absence of awkwardness or embarrassment (17c, 15c in **easy**).

Old French *aise* produced DISEASE and **malaise** [from *mal* 'bad', from Latin]. Latin *adjacere* is the ancestor of **adjacent**, and *jacere* of JET*.

eavesdrop [ME. Probably from Old Norse *upsardropi*, from *ups* 'eaves' + *dropi* 'a drop'] The dripping of water from the eaves; the land on which it falls, hence **eavesdropper** someone standing there to listen to conversations inside the house (15c), whence *eavesdrop* to listen to a private conversation (17c).

Old Norse *ups* is related to **eaves** [Old English *efes*] and **over** [Old English *ofer*], and *dropi* to DRIBBLE*.

eccentric [ME. Latin *eccentricus* from Greek *ekkentros*, literally 'out of centre', from *kentron*: see CENTRE*] In early astronomy: a circle or orbit of which the earth is not the precise centre, hence **1** of circles: not concentric, having different centres (16c) **2** having the axis or support off-centre (17c), hence **(a)** of an orbit: elliptical (17c) **(b)** an eccentric wheel used to convert circular to fore-and-aft motion (19c). Hence (combining 1 and 2) irregular, anomalous (17c); (describing) an unconventional, harmlessly odd person (19c).

eclectic [Greek *eklektikos*, from *eklegein* 'to pick out', from *legein* 'to gather, also 'to speak'] To do with or belonging to those philosophers in ancient Greece and Rome who adopted doctrines from various schools of thought (17c), hence choosing, borrowing, or derived from a variety of sources (19c).

Greek *legein*'s descendants include **dialect**, **dyslexia**, and **lexicon**: related to *logos* (see APOLOGY*).

economic [ME. (Via Old French from) Latin *oeconomicus*, from Greek *oikonomikos*, from *oikonomia*, from *oikos* 'house' + *nemein* 'to manage, to distribute fairly': this and other descendants of *oikos* often began *oe-* until the early 20c] Household management (–17c), hence (to do with) the management of resources, originally of a household (16–18c), later of a community (19c). The idea of thrift and reducing expenditure arose in the 17c, producing **economical** sparing, thrifty; using resources efficiently (18c), **economize** to make savings, and **economy** cheaper or better value (*economy class/size*, 1950s, *US*).

Descendants of Greek *oikos* include **diocese**, **ecology** whence **eco-** (*ecosystem*, *eco-friendly*), **ecumenical** [Greek *oikoumenikos* 'to do with the whole (inhabited) world', from *oikein* 'to inhabit'], and **parish** [via Old French from ecclesiastical Latin *parochia* 'diocese', from, ultimately, Greek *paroikos* 'neighbour, neighbouring', from *para* 'near']. Greek *nemein* produced **Nemesis**, the name of the Greek goddess of retribution, hence **1** an avenger; an invincible or implacable enemy (*US*) **2** deserved punishment.

edify [ME. Via French from Latin *aedificare*, from *aedis* 'dwelling' + *facere* 'to make'] To build (rare since the 18c); to establish, build up, or strengthen, hence to strengthen spiritually or morally; to improve someone's morals or intellect (15c).

Latin *aedificare* produced **edifice**; *facere* is the ancestor of FACT*.

eerie [ME. Probably from Old English *earg* 'cowardly'. *Scots and N English*, spreading south in the 19c] Fearful, apprehensive; superstitiously afraid, hence causing such fear, strange, weird (18c).

effect [ME. (Via Old French from) Latin *effectus*, from *efficere* 'to accomplish', from *facere* 'to make'] A result of an action, hence **1** accomplishment, fulfilment (surviving in *bring into effect*); reality, fact, surviving in *in effect* **2** the intended result (–17c); the meaning or intent (*to this effect*, 16c) **3** to bring something about (16c) **4** something acquired as the result of an action (17c), hence **effects** belongings, movable property (18c) **5** the 'result' of a work of art, the impression it produces (18c), hence **effects** (the means of producing) lighting, sounds, etc. used to enhance a film or broadcast (19c) **6** a scientific phenomenon (*Doppler effect*, 19c).

The variant *effeck* was shortened to *feck* in Scotland and N England, surviving in **feckless** useless, ineffectual, irresponsible. Latin *efficere* produced **efficacious** and **efficient**; *facere* is the ancestor of FACT*.

effete [17c. Latin *effetus* 'having borne fruit or young', later 'worn out from doing so', from *f(o)etus* 'bearing young, pregnant, pregnancy, young offspring'] No longer fertile, past breeding; no longer vigorous, hence decadent, degenerate (18c); weak, self-indulgent, effeminate (*c*.1900).

Latin *f(o)etus* was adopted meaning 'unborn young', and is the ancestor of **fawn** a young deer; the colour of one, light brown.

eke [Old English *ēaca* (noun), *ēcan* (verb)] An addition, increase, or extension; to increase, lengthen, or add to (both now chiefly Scots), hence **1 eke-name** an additional name (ME), whence, by wrong division of *an eke-name*, **nickname** (15c) **2 eke out** to 'stretch' a supply (16c); **eke out a living** to get by with difficulty (19c).

Wrong division also produced **adder** [Old English *a naeddre*], *ammunition* (at MUNITION), APRON, **newt** [*an evet*, a variant of **eft**, from Old English *efeta*], **umpire**

[Old French *nonper* 'not equal', from Latin PAR*], and surnames such as **Nash** and **Noak(es)**, **Noke(s)**, whose owners lived by an ash and an oak respectively.

elaborate [16c. Latin *elaborare*, from *labor* 'work' (ancestor of LABOUR*)] To produce by work or effort (–19c); to develop, to work out in detail (17c), hence **1** detailed, intricate; richly or extravagantly decorated **2** careful, painstaking (17c) **3** to enlarge on or explain in detail (1930s).

elder [Old English *(i)eldra*, comparative of *(e)ald* old] Older than someone else; the older of two people, hence **1** a parent or ancestor (–18c); someone given respect or authority, especially because of their age and experience (ME, but cf. *alderman* below): **(a)** an official in the early Christian church [translating Greek *presbuteros*, from *presbus* 'old man': cf. *presbyter* below], later in some Protestant churches (17c) **(b) elder statesman** a member of a body of retired statesmen who advised the Japanese emperor (1920s); an experienced person who is consulted unofficially (1930s) **2 elderly** approaching old age (17c), whence *elder* to do with or for the elderly (*eldercare/Elderhostels*, 1970s, N American) **3** a nickname for the elder of two people with the same name, surviving as a surname.

Old English *(e)ald* produced **alderman** originally an Anglo-Saxon chief or nobleman, and appears as **Al(d)-** in place- and surnames. Greek *presbuteros* produced **priest** [via Old English *prēost*, which appears as **Pres-** in names] and Latin **presbyter** adopted for an early church elder, hence a senior clergyman in some churches, in others, a member of the **presbytery** a ruling council of elders [from medieval Latin *presbyterium*, whence also **Presbyterian** to do with, or a member of, a church ruled by a presbytery].

elect [ME. Latin *eligere*, *elect-* 'to select', from *legere* 'to choose'] **1** to choose someone for an office etc., especially by voting; elected but not yet in office (*president elect*, 15c) **2** chosen, selected (15c); (someone) chosen by God for salvation (–17c), surviving in **the elect** those chosen (16c), hence any specially selected group (17c) **3** to choose to do one thing rather than another (16c).

Latin *eligere* is the ancestor of **elegant**, **eligible,** and **elite**, and *legere* of LEGEND*.

element [ME. Via French from Latin *elementum* 'principle, rudiment', used to translate Greek *stoikheion* 'step, component part'] One of the constituents of the material world, originally earth, air, fire, or water, hence **1 (a) the elements** the weather **(b)** earth, air, or water as a creature's natural habitat (16c); **in your element** in your natural surroundings, doing something you like and are good at **2** a substance forming part of a more complex one, hence **(a)** a substance that cannot be broken down chemically (17c) **(b)** a small part (19c); a component; a factor **3 the elements** the letters of the alphabet, hence the rudiments of a subject.

elf [Old English] A small being with magical powers, originally believed to cause diseases and nightmares and to steal children, substituting their own offspring, later more or less synonymous with *fairy* (at FATE), but sometimes distinguished by being male or more mischievous, hence a mischievous creature or child (16c). Hence **elfin** to do with or like an elf (16c); small and strangely attractive (18c).

Elf produced the name **Alfred**, and appears as **Elph-** in a few surnames. Related to Norman French **Aubrey** (**Oberon**, the king of the fairies, is a variant of the pet form **Auberon**), and to **oaf** [Old Norse *álfr*] an elf's child, a changeling, hence a deformed or idiot child, a stupid or clumsy person, a lout.

elixir [ME. Medieval Latin from Arabic *al-'iksīr*, from *al* 'the' + *'iksīr* from Greek *xērion* 'powder for drying wounds', from *xĕros* 'dry'] A miraculous substance believed by alchemists to turn base metal into gold or to prolong life indefinitely (15c), hence **1** the quintessence of something (17c) **2** a powerful remedy or panacea (17c, later in the names of quack remedies); a sweet mixture used to disguise the taste of medicine.

Greek *xĕros* produced **xero-** dryness (in medical words), and in **xerography** a dry photocopying process, whence the tradename **Xerox**.

elocution [ME. Latin *eloqui*, *elocut-* 'to speak out', from *loqui* 'to speak'] Oratorical or literary style (–19c); oratory, eloquence (16–18c), hence the art of speaking (17c), especially of voice production and correct pronunciation.

Latin *eloqui* produced **eloquent**; *loqui*'s descendants include **circumlocution**, **colloquy**, **grandiloquence**, **interlocution**, **loquacious**, **magniloquent**, **obloquy** [late Latin *obloquium*, literally 'speaking against'], *soliloquy* (at SULLEN), and **ventriloquy** [Latin *ventriloquus* 'speaking from the belly', from *venter* 'belly'].

elope [16c. Anglo-Norman French *aloper*, probably from early Dutch *ontlopen* 'to run away', from *lopen* 'to run': related to LEAP*] To run away or abscond, hence in law, to run away from your husband with a lover (17c), in popular use, to run away to get married (19c).

elude [16c. Latin *eludere*, literally 'to finish play', later, of a gladiator, 'to dodge or parry a blow', hence 'to mislead or baffle an opponent', from *ludere* 'to play', from *ludus* 'game, play' (ancestor of LUDICROUS*)] To delude or baffle (–17c); to evade or escape from (17c); to escape your memory or understanding (18c).

embarrass [17c. Via French and Spanish from Italian *imbarazzare*, from *imbarazzo* 'obstacle, obstruction', from *imbarrare* 'to block or bar': related to BAR*] **1** to encumber, hence **embarrassed** encumbered by debts, short of money (19c) **2** to perplex, hence to make someone feel awkward, self-conscious, or ashamed (19c).

embolism [ME. Via late Latin from Greek *embolismus*, from *emballein* 'to throw in', from *ballein* 'to throw'] **1** the insertion of days or a month into a calendar to bring it into line with the solar year **2** a prayer inserted into the Mass (18c) **3** the blocking of a blood vessel by something, usually a clot, carried by the bloodstream (19c); the object causing it (*c.*1900), partly replacing **embolus** [19c, from Greek *embolos* 'stopper', from *emballein*].

Greek *emballein* produced **emblem** [via Latin *emblema* 'inlaid or raised design']; *ballein* is the ancestor of BALLISTIC*.

eminence [ME. Latin *eminere* 'to project, to stand out', from *minere* 'to stand'] A height or high position, hence **1** a high social position, superiority; a title given to an important person, now only a cardinal (17c); a distinguished person (1930s) **2** a protuberance (chiefly in anatomy); a high place, a hill (17c).

French *éminence grise* [literally 'grey eminence'], a person who has power but no official position, was originally the nickname of Père Joseph, the grey-clad confidential secretary to Cardinal Richelieu (the *éminence rouge* 'red eminence', from his scarlet robes). Latin *minere* produced *imminere* 'to hang over', whence **imminent**, and *prominere* 'to jut out', whence **prominent** and perhaps **promontory**. Related to MENACE*.

emotion   [16c. French, from *émouvoir* 'to excite', from Latin *emovere*, literally 'to move out', from *movere* MOVE] **1** a public disturbance (–18c, outlived by **commotion** (ME), also ultimately from Latin *movere*] **2** physical (17–19c) or mental agitation **(a)** strong feeling causing it (19c). Hence **emote** to make an exaggerated show of emotion (*c*.1915, *US*); *emoticon* (at ICON).

empire   [ME. French, from Latin *imperium*: see IMPERIAL] **1** an extensive territory, or a number of territories or states, ruled by a single authority; a large, widespread commercial organization (1950s); the part of an organization an individual controls **2** an emperor's position or (period of) rule (17c), hence describing styles of furniture, clothing, etc. from the time of Napoleon I, emperor of the French (1804–15).

empty   [Old English *ǣm(e)tig*, from *ǣm(e)tta* 'leisure', perhaps from *ā* 'no, not' + *mōt* 'meeting, MOOT*'] At leisure, unoccupied (–ME), hence unoccupied in the sense 'containing nothing'; to make or become so (16c), replacing **empt** [Old English *ǣmtian* 'to be unoccupied', from *ǣm(e)tta*)].

   Idle [Old English *īdel*] swapped meanings with *empty*: originally vacant, void, unoccupied (–ME), hence indolent (ME); to pass time indolently (17c); of an engine: to (be made to) run with no load (early 20c).

enclose   [ME. Old French *enclore*, ultimately from Latin *includere*, from *claudere* 'to shut'] To shut in or imprison (now mainly in **enclosed order** a religious order whose members are secluded from the outside world), hence **1** to surround or contain; to surround with walls, hedges, etc. (15c), specifically to fence in common land to bring it into cultivation (16c) **2** to put something in a container, specifically to put a document in an envelope with a letter (18c).

   Latin *includere* is the ancestor of **include**, which also originally meant to shut in; *claudere* is the ancestor of CLOSE*.

encroach   [ME. Old French *encrochier* 'to seize or latch on to', from *crochier* 'to hook', from *croc* 'hook', from Old Norse *krókr* (ancestor of CROOK*)] To obtain unlawfully or by force (–17c), hence to make inroads into someone's property or rights (16c); to go beyond proper limits.

encumber   [ME. French *encombrer* 'to block up', from *combre* 'barrier, river barrage', of Gaulish origin] **1** to trouble or harass (–17c) **2** to hamper, obstruct, or block up, hence to fill with useless matter or things (15c); to burden with debts or responsibilities.

   Probably the source of **cumber** to overwhelm, destroy, harass, or distress, later to bother or inconvenience; an inconvenience or encumbrance, surviving mainly in **cumbersome** and **cumbrous**, both originally meaning 'causing obstruction, difficult to get through', hence troublesome, inconvenient, unwieldy, needlessly complicated.

endorse   [15c. Medieval Latin *indorsare*, from Latin *dorsum* 'the back': superseding *endoss* (ME–17c), from Old French *endosser*, from *dos* 'back', from Latin *dorsum*. The spelling **indorse** survives in legal use and in the US] To write on the back of a document, especially to sign a bill of exchange on the back to accept responsibility for paying it, hence **1** to confirm, vouch for, or recommend (17c) **2** to sign the back of a cheque to make it payable to someone else (19c) **3** to record an offence on a driving licence etc. (19c).

Latin *dorsum* produced **dorsal** to do with or on the back (*dorsal fin*); French *dos* produced *dos-a-dos* 'back to back', whence **do-se-do** a square-dancing movement in which people pass back to back, *dossier* a bundle of papers labelled on the back, adopted for a collection of documents on a subject, and **reredos** an ornamental screen or hanging behind an altar [with *arere* 'behind': see ARREAR*].

endue [ME. French *enduire*, from Latin *inducere* 'to lead in', from *ducere* 'to lead'] **1** to assume a different form, later (influenced by Latin *induere* 'to put on clothes') to put on a garment; to clothe **2** (by association with *endow* at DOWRY) to endow, now only with a quality or ability.

Latin *inducere* produced INDUCE*; *ducere* is the ancestor of DEDUCE*.

engage [ME. French *engager*, from *gage* 'someone/something pledged': see WAGE*] To pawn or pledge something; to pledge yourself to do something (16c), hence **1 (a)** to enter into a contract (16c), specifically with an employee or employer; **be engaged** to have promised to marry (18c), to have an appointment (19c) **(b)** to reserve something (18c); **engaged** occupied or in use (19c) **2** to involve yourself or someone else in an activity or undertaking (17c): **(a)** to begin fighting an enemy **(b)** to attract and hold someone's attention (18c); to charm or fascinate (now chiefly in **engaging**); to draw into conversation (early 20c) **(c)** of parts of a mechanism: to come together ready to start working (19c).

engine [ME. French *engin*, from Latin *ingenium* 'intellect, talent', from *gignere* 'to beget'] **1** natural talent, ingenuity, cunning (surviving in Scots as **ingine**); the product of ingenuity, a plot, tool, or weapon, e.g. a trap or snare (15c), a large mechanical weapon such as a catapult, a machine (*steam engine*, 17c), a powered vehicle (*traction/railway engine*, 19c) **2** an agent or driving force (*engine of change*, 16c). The shortened form **gin** (ME) survives as a kind of trap, a windlass, a hoist, and a machine for separating cotton fibres from seeds, and produced the surname **Ginn** a trapper or a cunning person.

Latin *ingenium* is the ancestor of **engineer** originally a designer of fortifications and weapons, later of machines and other devices, hence to (secretly) make something happen, of the surnames **Gane, Gaine(s), Jenner**, and some instances of **Ingham** (all engineers), and of *ingenious* (at INGENUOUS). *Gignere* is the ancestor of GINGERLY*.

enhance [ME. Anglo-Norman French *enhauncer*, ultimately from late Latin *inaltare*, from Latin *altus* 'high'] To raise, to make higher (–16c), hence **1** to exaggerate, to make something appear greater **2** to raise the price or value of something; to make more important, beautiful, or useful (16c).

Descendants of Latin *altus* include **altar**, **altitude**, Italian *alto*, **exalt**, **haughty**, and **hawser**, originally a rope for hauling a boat upstream.

enigma [16c. Via Latin from Greek *ainigma*, from *ainissesthai* 'to speak allusively or obscurely', from *ainos* 'fable'] A riddle or parable (–19c), hence something (17c) or someone (early 20c) hard to understand.

enjoy [ME. Old French *enjoier* 'to give joy to' (from *joie* 'joy'), or *enjoïr* 'to rejoice', both from Latin *gaudere* 'to rejoice'] To be joyful (–16c), hence **1** to be happy because you have something; to take pleasure in; to have the use or benefit of (*enjoyed good health*) **2** to make someone happy (15–17c), hence **enjoy yourself**, literally to make yourself happy, to have a good time (17c) **3** (combining 1 and 2) **enjoy!** enjoy yourself or what you have (1960s, *US*, modelled on Yiddish).

Old French *joie* produced **joy** and **rejoice**. Latin *gaudere* is the ancestor of **gaud** a showy ornament or trinket, whence **gaudy** tastelessly showy, and of **gaudy** (a) celebration (16–19c), hence a feast, especially an annual dinner held by a college for former members.

enormity [ME. Via French from Latin *enormitas*, from *enormis* 'irregular, abnormal', from *norma* 'standard' (ancestor of NORMAL*)] Deviation from a moral or legal standard; a crime or transgression, gradually becoming exaggerated into wickedness, a monstrous act, probably by association with **enormous** [16c, also from *enormis*], which until the 19c meant 'shocking, outrageous, wicked' as well as 'huge'. *Enormity* went on to mean enormous size (18c, still regarded as incorrect).

ensconce [16c. From 15c **sconce** 'small fortification or earthwork', from Dutch *schans* 'brushwood, brushwood screen for soldiers', from Middle High German *schanze*] To fortify (–19c); to hide behind a fortification (–18c), hence to hide or settle yourself in a safe or comfortable place (rare before the 19c, when popularized by Scott: see DOFF).

ensemble [15c. French, ultimately from Latin *simul* 'at the same time' (ancestor of **assemble** and **simultaneous**)] Together, simultaneously. French *(tout) ensemble* [literally '(all) together'] was adopted for (the effect of) something taken as a whole (18c), hence *ensemble* **1** (the effect of) a group of performers working together (19c) **2** something, specifically a woman's outfit, made up of various items (1920s).

ensign [ME. French *enseigne*, from Latin *insignia*, plural of *insigne* 'mark, sign, badge of office', ultimately from *signum* SIGN*] **1** a signal or rallying cry (Scots, rare since the 16c) **2** a characteristic sign (15c); a symbol, emblem, or badge of office; a military or naval standard, hence a standard-bearer (16c), later applied to various junior military or naval officers.

Latin *insignia* was adopted for badges or emblems collectively, later a single item, with the plural **insignias** (still widely deplored).

ensure [ME. Anglo-Norman French *enseürer* from Old French *aseürer*, ultimately from Latin *securus* 'untroubled': see SURE*] **1** to make someone sure or confident, to convince (rare since the 16c); to promise that something will happen or is true (–17c, outlived by **assure** from Old French *aseürer*) **2** to make safe or certain, to secure, hence **(a)** to secure a sum of money if something untoward happens (17–18c), replaced by the variant **insure**, or by *assure* if the event is inevitable (*life assurance*) **(b)** to make sure that something will happen (18c).

enterprise [ME. Old French, past participle of *entreprendre* 'to undertake', literally 'to take between', from *entre* (from Latin *inter*: see INTERIM*) + *prendre* 'to take', from Latin *prehendere*] A (new or risky) undertaking, hence **1** to undertake or attempt such a venture or a difficult task (15c); the initiative or willingness to do so, hence **enterprising** showing initiative (17c) **2** organized activity intended to make a profit (*private enterprise*, 18c); a business or firm (19c).

Old French *entreprenour* [from *entreprendre*], literally 'someone who undertakes', hence a manager, was borrowed in the 15c but did not survive; its descendant, *entrepreneur* was adopted for a producer of musical entertainments (outlived by Italian *impresario* [from *impresa* 'an undertaking', ultimately from Latin *prehendere*]): the current sense produced **intrapreneur** someone who uses their entrepreneurial skills for the benefit of their employer (*US*). Latin *prehendere* is the ancestor of PRISE*.

entertain [ME. French *entretenir*, ultimately from Latin *inter* 'among' (see INTERIM) + *tenere* 'to hold' (ancestor of TENOR*)] To keep up, maintain, or carry on (–19c), hence **1** to maintain in a certain condition or treat in a certain way (15–17c); to treat a guest hospitably (15c) **2** to accept and keep in your mind (16c); to occupy your mind; to do so agreeably, to amuse (17c).

enthusiasm [17c. Via French or Latin from Greek *enthousiasmos*, from *enthous*, *entheos* 'possessed by a god, inspired', from *theos* 'god'] Possession or inspiration by a god (–18c); a mistaken sense of this, hence extravagant religious emotion; passionate interest in, or eagerness to do, something (18c); a craze (early 20c). **Enthuse** (19c, *US*) is a back-formation.

Greek *theos* is the ancestor of **apotheosis**, **pantheon**, **-theism** (*pantheism*), **-theist** (*atheist*), **theo-** (*theology* at DIVINE*, *Theophany* at EPIPHANY*), and of the names **Dorothy** (whence DOLL*), **Theodore**, and **Timothy**.

entire [ME. French *entier*, ultimately from Latin *integrum*, neuter of *integer* 'untouched, whole', from *tangere* 'to touch'] **1** whole, complete, hence **(a)** absolute, in every way (15c) **(b)** in one piece, undivided (15c); not broken or impaired (16c); not castrated (18c) **2** having integrity, blameless, incorruptible, honest, sincere (–18c).

Latin *integer* was adopted meaning a whole number, and produced **integral**, **integrate**, and **integrity**, which maintains the sense of moral as well as physical wholeness. Latin *tangere* produced **intact**, literally 'untouched', and TACT*.

envelop [ME. Old French *envoluper*, from *en-* 'in' + an element of unknown origin also found in DEVELOP: the noun via modern French *enveloppe*] To wrap up; to be the covering, to surround or contain (16c), hence **envelope** something that does so: **1** a folded paper cover for a letter (18c) **2** in maths: a curve or surface that forms a tangent to a number of others (19c); a line that joins the peaks of a graph (1920s), hence **push the envelope** to approach or try to raise the limits of what is possible (1980s, *aviation slang*, referring to graphs of aircraft performance).

envoy [17c. Old French *envoyer* 'to send', from *en voie* 'on the way', from Latin *via* 'way'] A representative sent by one monarch or government to another, a diplomat, hence any representative; an agent or messenger.

Old French *envoy* 'sending, dispatch' [from *envoyer*] was adopted for the concluding part of a literary work (now in the modern French spelling *envoi*), and produced *invoy* a list of goods sent and the charges for them, which survives in its plural, **invoice**. Latin *via* is the ancestor of TRIVIAL*.

epicure   ME. A follower of the Greek philosopher Epicurus (born *c*.341 BC), who taught that the greatest good was pleasure, defined as the freedom from physical or emotional pain achieved by living a simple, virtuous life and cultivating friendships (–18c, outlived by **Epicurean**), later a person whose 'greatest good' is sensual pleasure, especially food and drink (16c), originally a glutton, now usually a person with refined tastes.

epiphany   [ME. Greek *epiphainein* 'to manifest', from *phanein* 'to show' (ancestor of PHANTOM*)] A Christian festival held on 6 January, in the Western church celebrating the showing of Jesus to the Magi, the first Gentiles to see him, hence the manifestation of any divine or superhuman being (17c); any important revelation or realization (19c).

Greek *phanein* produced **theophany** [Greek *theophaneia*, with *theos* 'god'], occasionally used for the festival; the Greek name **Theophania** (with variants in other European languages) was formerly given to girls born then. The name survived as the French surname **Tiffany**, which became popular as a girls' name as a result of the film *Breakfast at Tiffany's* (Tiffany & Co. being a high-class jewellers in New York). Greek *theophaneia* produced **tiffany** a kind of thin silk or, later, muslin, traditionally worn on the feast of Epiphany.

episode   [17c. Via French from Greek *epeisodion* 'addition', from *epeisodios* 'coming in besides', from *eisodios* 'coming in', from *hodos* 'way, journey'] A passage of dialogue between songs in Greek tragedy, hence a story forming part of a longer one: **1** an incident or period in history or in life (18c) **2** an instalment of a serial (early 20c).

Greek *hodos* is the ancestor of **anode** literally 'a way up' and **cathode** literally 'a way down', of **exodus** literally 'a way out', the name of the second book of the Bible which tells of the Israelites' escape from Egypt, hence the departure of a large number of people, of **method**, **odometer**, PERIOD, and **synod** [Greek *sunodos* 'assembly', literally 'a way or journey together'].

epitome   [16c. Latin, from Greek, from *epitemnein* 'to cut into or cut short', from *temnein* 'to cut' (ancestor of TOME*)] A summary or abstract, hence a representation of something on a small scale; a typical example.

equal   [ME. Latin *aequalis*, from *aequus* 'level, even, equal'] Identical or equivalent in size, amount, number, value, etc.; of a surface: level, even, hence **1** on the same level (16c); (someone) of the same rank or having the same qualities, abilities, rights, etc. **2** fair, just, impartial (16–18c); acting or affecting impartially or uniformly (17c) **3** to make, be, or become equal (16c); to produce something equal (17c) **4** evenly balanced between opposing forces or sides (17c) **5** sufficient for the demands made (*equal to the task*, 17c), a sense also found in **adequate** [17c, also from Latin *aequus*].

Latin *aequalis* fathered French *égal*, whence **egalitarian**. *Aequus* produced **equanimity** literally 'evenness of mind' [with Latin *animus* 'mind'], **equi-** (*equidistant*, *equivalent* at VALID), EQUITY, **iniquity** literally 'unfairness', and Latin *aequare* 'to make equal', whence **equable**, **equate**, **equation**, and **equator** [from medieval

Latin *circulus aequator diei et noctis* 'circle equalizing day or night'] originally referring to the celestial equator or equinoctial.

equity [ME. French *équité* from Latin *aequitas*, from *aequus*: see EQUAL*] Fairness, impartiality; a fair or reasonable decision or action, hence the recourse to natural justice and fairness to mitigate or supplement law (16c); a system of laws, administered by special courts, based on equitable precedents; a right recognized by such a court (17c), hence **equity of redemption** the right of a mortgagor to redeem the property by paying the money owed, even if this is overdue; *equity* **1** the value of such property when all charges on it have been paid (19c); **negative equity** when the property is worth less than what is owed (1950s, *US*) **2** the value of a company after all its liabilities are met (*c.*1900, *US*), hence **equities** the ordinary shares of a company, giving the right to a share in the company's equity and profits after holders of debentures and preferred shares have been paid (1930s).

err [ME. Old French *errer* from Latin *errare*] To wander (–17c); to go astray, hence to behave badly; to make a mistake.

French had another verb *errer* 'to travel' [from late Latin *iterare*, from Latin *iter* 'a journey' (ancestor of ITINERARY*)]: both had the present participle *errant* and the two words became confused, coming into Middle English with the senses 'travelling, wandering' and 'straying, erratic'. *Errant* survives mainly in **knight errant** one travelling in search of adventure, and in the variant **arrant**, which originally meant 'wandering' (ME–17c), frequently applied to vagabonds, highwaymen, and other roving criminals and coming to mean 'notorious, blatant' (15c). Latin *errare* is the ancestor of ABERRATION, **erratic**, **erroneous**, and **error**.

escape [ME. Old French *eschaper*, ultimately from medieval Latin *ex-* 'off, away, out' + *cappa* 'hooded cloak': see CHAPEL*. The underlying sense is of taking off your cloak, hence of throwing off restraint] To free yourself from captivity; this action, hence **1** to avoid capture, danger, or something unpleasant; a way of doing so (*fire escape*, 15c); a distraction from the realities of life (19c), hence **escapism** (the seeking of) distraction (1930s) **2** to avoid being seen or found; to elude someone's memory (*her name escapes me*, 17c) **3** to be uttered unintentionally **4** to break or leak out of a container (15c); a leakage (19c); **escape velocity** sufficient velocity to break out of a planet's gravitational field (1940s).

The shortened form **scape** survives in poetry and in **scapegoat** a goat allowed to escape sacrifice and go into the wilderness, symbolically bearing the community's sins (see the Bible, Leviticus 16:20–22), hence someone who takes the blame, and **scapegrace** a lazy or mischievous person (from the idea of 'escaping' God's grace). Related to **escapade** an escape from confinement or restraint (17–19c); an adventurous or irresponsible action (19c), and to **scarper** [from Italian *scappare* 'to escape', influenced by rhyming slang *Scapa Flow* 'to go'].

espy [ME. Old French *espier* (verb), *espie* (noun), ultimately of Germanic origin] To look out (for); to watch secretly, hence **1** someone who does so **2** to find out by doing so; to see or find out by chance (15c).

Espy shares most senses with **spy** [also from *espier*], which came to mean to watch an enemy secretly (originally only in wartime); someone who does so, originally by entering the enemy camp in disguise. Old French *espie* evolved into *espion*, whence **espionage**.

essence [ME. French, from Latin *essentia*, from *esse* 'to be'] **1** what makes something what it is; its most important or indispensable property, characteristic, or element (16c), hence **(a)** a (fragrant) concentrated extract of a plant etc.; a perfume **(b)** an underlying principle or spirit **2** **fifth essence** [translating medieval Latin *quinta essentia*, itself a translation of Greek *pemptē ousiā* 'fifth being'], the fifth element (after earth, air, fire, and water), once believed to make up the heavenly bodies and to be latent in all things, the isolation of which was one of the aims of alchemy: more commonly called the **quintessence** (15c), which came to mean the purest extract of a substance (16c); the purest or most perfect example **3** an entity (16c), now only an immaterial or spiritual being.

Latin *essentia* produced **essential** purest, most perfect; to do with the essence of something, hence (something) basic, fundamental, or necessary. *Esse*'s descendants include **entity**, INTEREST, POSSE*, PRESENT*, and PROUD*.

esteem [ME. Via French from Latin *aestimare* 'to estimate'] Value, worth, reputation (–18c); to value or appraise; to estimate a number, quantity, etc. (15–18c), hence to judge (16–18c); (to have) an opinion, now usually (to have) a high opinion of, (to) respect.

Latin *aestimare* is the ancestor of AIM and of **estimate**, which briefly meant 'intellectual ability', but acquired the senses of *esteem*; the two later diverged, *esteem* referring mainly to a judgement of character, *estimate* to a judgement of numbers, but retaining the earlier sense in **estimable** originally able to be estimated or appraised, and **estimation**.

ether [ME. (Via Old French from) Latin *aether*, from Greek *aithēr* 'the upper air'] A substance once believed to fill the space beyond the moon's sphere and to make up the stars and planets; this region, the heavens, hence **1** the space or substance above the clouds (16c) **2** a rarefied substance existing throughout the universe, once believed to carry electromagnetic waves (17c), hence radio as a medium or art form (19c) **3** a colourless liquid used as a solvent or anaesthetic (18c, because its lightness and volatility were thought to be like the ether). The early senses survive in **ethereal** to do with the heavens (16c); resembling the ether; light, insubstantial, delicate (17c).

ethnic [ME. Christian Latin *ethnicus*, from Greek *ethnikos* 'heathen', from *ethnos* 'nation, people, culture', used to translate Hebrew *goy* '(foreign) nation'] **1** someone who is not Christian or Jewish, a heathen or pagan (–18c); to do with heathen or pagan nations (15c, now rare) **2** to do with or belonging to a race or nation (19c), hence to do with or typical of people sharing a particular racial, national, or cultural heritage (1940s, *US*); (a person) belonging to such a group; foreign, exotic (chiefly US).

Greek *ethnos* produce **ethno-** (*ethnology*). Greek *ethnikos* was translated in the Bible by late Latin *gentiles* [from Latin *gentilis*: see GENTLE*], whence **gentile**. Hebrew *goy* passed into Yiddish, and thence into English, as a Jewish term for a Gentile.

euphuism [16c. From *Euphues*, a character in John Lyly's romances, from Greek *euphues* 'shapely', from *eus* 'good, well, easy' + *phuein* 'to grow'] A style imitating

Euphues, marked by much alliteration, antitheses, and similes, hence affected or pompous language (19c, probably from that of Sir Percie Shafton, described as a Euphuist, in Walter Scott's novel *The Monastery*).

Greek *eus* also appears in words such as **euphemism**, **euphonium** [Greek *euphōnos* 'well-sounding'], *euphoria* (at PERIPHERY), **euthanasia**, and *evangelist* (at GOSPEL). Greek *phuein* is the ancestor of PHYSIC*.

evade [15c. Via French from Latin *evadere*, literally 'to go away', from *vadere* 'to go'] To get away, to escape, hence **1** to escape doing something, especially by cunning or trickery; to (cunningly) avoid a duty, question, etc. (17c); to avoid paying taxes by misrepresenting your financial affairs, or to defeat the intention of a law while obeying the letter of it **2** to elude or baffle (18c).

Latin *vadere* is the ancestor of **invade**, **pervade**, and **vamoose** [*US*, via Spanish *vamos* 'let's go']. A form of it appears in *vade mecum* [literally 'go with me'], adopted for a handbook or other handy article.

evening [Old English *æfnung*, from *æfnian* 'to approach evening', from *æfen* (see *even* below)] The time or process of night falling (–16c); the time between sunset and bedtime (ME), hence **1** the last part of someone's life or a period of time (17c) **2** an evening's activities (*a musical evening*, 18c).

Old English *æfen* evolved into **even** the latter part of the day, surviving in dialect, poetry, and in **Evensong** and **eventide** (whence **eventide home** an old people's home, originally one run by the Salvation Army); the evening, later the day, before a church festival or any special occasion, shortened to **eve** or to **e'en**, which survives in poetry and in **Halloween** [shortened from *All-Hallow-Even*] the eve of the feast of All Saints (SEE HOLY).

ever [Old English *aefre*] Always, at all times (*evergreen*, *forever*), hence **1** on all occasions; at any time (*did you ever meet her?*/*whenever*) **2** in any way, at all (*however*) **3** increasingly (*ever harder*, ME); to a great extent (*ever so much*); also used for emphasis (*she was ever so late*/*why ever did you marry him?*).

Ever produced **whatever**. Old English *aefre* produced **every** and **never**. Related to **aye** always [Old Norse *ei*], **nay** [Old Norse *nei*, from *ei*], and WIGHT*.

evict [ME. Latin *evincere*, *evict-*, literally 'to defeat utterly', from *vincere* 'to conquer' (ancestor of CONVICT*)] **1** to defeat a country or enemy (–17c); to defeat someone by argument or litigation (–18c); to prove or disprove something (–18c); these senses were shared from the 16–19c by **evince** [also from Latin *evincere*], which came to mean to be evidence for something (17c); to indicate or reveal something's presence (19c) **2** to recover (the title to) property by legal process, hence to make a tenant etc. leave by legal process (16c); to throw someone out.

exact [ME. Latin *exigere*, *exact-*, literally 'to drive out', later 'to demand', 'to weigh, test or examine', and 'to complete or perfect', from *agere* 'to lead or drive'] **1** to demand; to force to give or pay **2** completed, perfect (16–18c); accurate, precise, strict, punctilious (16c).

Latin *exigere* produced ASSAY*, **examine**, **exigency**, literally 'what is demanded', and **exiguous** scanty, small (literally 'weighed precisely'); *agere* is the ancestor of AGENT*.

exaggerate [16c. Latin *exaggerare*, from *aggerare* 'to make a pile', from *agger* 'a heap', from *aggerere* 'to bring to', from *gerere* 'to bring' (ancestor of GESTURE*)]

To pile up or accumulate (–17c), hence to 'heap up' praise or blame, to emphasize a virtue or fault (–18c); to make something seem greater than it is.

example [ME. Old French, alteration of *essample*, from Latin *exemplum*, from *eximere*, *exempt-* 'to take out, deliver, or free', from *emere* 'to buy, get or take'] **1** an instance that bears out or illustrates a statement or principle; a problem or exercise designed to illustrate a principle or technique (17c) **2** (someone showing) behaviour worthy of imitation **3** (someone given) a punishment intended as a deterrent.

Anglo-Norman French *assample*, a variant of *essample*, produced **sample**, which formerly shared the senses 'typical instance' and 'model of behaviour', and came to mean a small part or amount by which the whole may be judged. Latin *exemplum* produced **exemplar** and **exemplify** before being adopted for a moralizing or illustrative story. *Eximere* produced **exempt**; *emere* is the ancestor of PEREMPTORY, **pre-emption** the buying of something before others have a chance to, whence **pre-empt** to do so (*US*); to prevent something by acting first, PREMIUM, PROMPT*, REDEEM*, and VINTAGE*.

excite [ME. (Via French from) Latin *excitare*, literally 'to summon repeatedly', from *exciere* 'to summon', from *ciere* 'to move or call' (ancestor of CITE*)] To move, stir up, or instigate; to produce or provoke an action or reaction (largely replaced by **incite**, also from Latin *ciere*), hence to rouse something latent or dormant: **1** to make something more active; to magnetize or electrify (17c) **2** to arouse emotions, to make interested or eager (19c).

exclude [ME. Latin *excludere*, *exclus-*, from *claudere* 'to shut'] To keep or shut out, hence **1** to omit (15c) **2** to debar from membership or deny a privilege (15c), hence **exclusive** available only to certain people (18c) or from a certain source (19c); of a news item, etc.: appearing in only one publication; such an item (*c.*1900).

Latin *excludere* produced **sluice** a device to control a flow of water; an overflow channel; to (let water) flow through one; to rinse or flush with water. Latin *claudere* is the ancestor of CLOSE*.

excursion [16c. Latin *excurrere*, *excurs-* 'to run out', from *currere* 'to run' (ancestor of CURRENT*)] An escape from confinement, hence **1** a sortie or raid (surviving in **alar(u)ms and excursions** loud, confused noise or activity, originally a stage direction) **2** a digression in speech or writing (–18c, replaced in literary use by **excursus**, also from Latin *excurrere*, 19c); a deviation from a path (17c, surviving in astronomy); a short journey (17c) or pleasure trip (18c); a sudden surge in a nuclear reactor's output (1950s) **3** (the distance covered by) an alternating or oscillating motion (18c).

execrable [ME. French, from Latin *execrabilis*, from *exsecrari* 'to curse', literally 'to make profane', from *sacrare* 'to devote or consecrate', from *sacer* 'holy'] Expressing or involving a curse, hence accursed, dreadful (–17c); detestable (15c); of very poor quality, indescribably bad (18c).

Latin *exsecrari* produced **execrate** to curse, hence to feel or express loathing for. *Sacrare* produced **desecrate**, **sacrament**, and **sacre** to dedicate to religious use, to sanctify, outlived by **consecrate** [also from *sacrare*], but surviving in **sacred**. *Sacer* is the ancestor of SACRIFICE*.

execute [ME. Via French from medieval Latin *executare*, from Latin *exsequi*, *exsecut-* 'to follow up or carry out', from *sequi* 'to follow' (ancestor of SEQUEL*)] To do, to carry out, hence **1** to perform a skilled action or movement **2** to implement a legal decision (especially a death sentence), later the provisions of a will etc. **3** to produce a work of art from a design (18c); to perform a piece of music.

A person who executes may be an **executant** who performs music, an **executioner** who carries out a death sentence, an *executive* (see below) or an **executor** who deals with a will. **Executive** originally meant to do with executing, hence the enactment of laws; the branch of government that does so; the head of a government or state, hence any group or person that manages an organization; a senior manager, hence suitable for executives or their busy, expensive lifestyles (*executive jet*).

exercise [ME. Via French from Latin *exercere* 'to keep busy, to practise', literally 'to drive on or out', from *arcere* 'to keep in' (whence **arcane** and **coerce**), from *arca* 'chest, ARK'] **1** the use or practice of power, a right, a skill, etc.; to use or practise them **2** practice or practising in order to improve; to train by practising (15c); a task performed to improve or test (16c) **3** military training (–19c); a parade or drill (16c); **exercises** training manoeuvres under simulated combat conditions **4** physical exertion to improve or maintain health; to take this; to make an animal etc. do so **5** to tax your powers (16c); to worry or vex.

exhibit [ME. Latin *exhibere* 'to hold out', hence 'to offer or present', from *habere* 'to hold' (ancestor of HABIT*)] **1 (a)** to put forward for consideration; to present a document as evidence in court; a document, later an object, presented (17c) **(b)** to display an object or objects (16c); an object displayed (19c), hence **exhibition** a public display of objects or demonstration of skill (18c), hence a sight or spectacle, surviving mainly in *make an exhibition of yourself* and in **exhibitionism** compulsive displaying of the genitals (19c); attention-getting behaviour (early 20c) **(c)** to show signs of something (*exhibited symptoms of stress*, 18c) **2** to (offer to) pay expenses (15–17c); maintenance, support (–18c); to provide a student with this (16–19c), hence *exhibition* a grant awarded to a student (16c).

exit [15c. Latin *exire*, *exit-* 'to go out', from *ire* 'to go'] **1** [from Latin *exit* 'he/she/it goes out'] a stage direction indicating that someone leaves the stage (earlier as the plural, **exeunt**): these outlasted **exeat/exeant** 'let him/them go out' (–16c); *exeat* survives in the sense 'permission to leave (temporarily)' (18c) **2** an actor's departure from the stage (16c); a departure from any place or situation (17c); to make your exit, hence **(a)** a way out (17c); a slip road leading off a main road (1950s) **(b)** to go out (1970s).

Latin *exire* produced ISSUE; *ire*'s descendants include AMBIT*, COUNT*, INITIATE*, **obituary**, PERISH, *sedition* (at SEDUCE), **sudden** [via Anglo-Norman French from late Latin *subitanus*, ultimately from Latin *subire* 'to go secretly', hence 'to take by surprise'], and TRANCE*.

expedition [ME. Latin, from *expedire* 'to extricate', literally 'to free the feet', later 'to put in order', from *pes*, *ped-* 'foot': cf. *impede* (at IMPEACH)] The act of dealing with or doing something quickly and efficiently, hence **1** the act of dispatching troops or setting off on a military mission (15c), hence a journey by a group for a specific purpose (16c); the people travelling (17c) **2** promptness, speed, efficiency (16c).

Expedition is the noun belonging to **expedite**, which however is later in most senses. Latin *expedire* produced **expedient** appropriate or advisable; such an action, later (one that is) practical but not necessarily right. Latin *pes* is the ancestor of PIONEER*.

experience [ME. French, from Latin *experientia*, from *experiri* 'to try out'] **1** testing, trying out (–17c); a test to try or prove something (–18c); proof by practical demonstration (–18c); to test, try, or prove by this means (16–18c): outlasted in these senses by **experiment** [ME, also from Latin *experiri*] **2** observation of, or contact with, something as a source of knowledge; something you are involved with that affects you or adds to your knowledge (*a frightening experience/work experience*); to be affected or involved in one (16c); the sum of your experiences; the knowledge or skill gained (17c).

Latin *experiri* produced **expert**, literally 'experienced'. Related to **peril** [from Latin *periculum* 'experiment, risk'] (a cause of) danger, whence **perilous**, altered to **parlous**.

expletive [ME. Latin *expletivus*, from *explere* 'to fill out', from *plere* 'to fill': see COMPLY*] Added merely to make up the numbers or fill a space, hence a word or phrase added to fill out a sentence or line of verse (17c); a meaningless exclamation (19c), now usually a swear word.

explode [16c. Latin *explaudere* 'to drive out by clapping', from *plaudere* 'to clap'] To reject scornfully (–19c); to clap, boo, or hiss a play off the stage (17–19c), hence to force out violently or noisily (17–19c); to (make something) expand, burst, or shatter, to blow up (18c), hence **1** to give vent to an emotion (19c) **2** to increase dramatically (early 20c) **3** to show something on a diagram with its parts in the right relative positions but separated from each other, as though blown apart (1950s).

Explode produced **implode** to (make something) collapse inwards. Latin *plaudere* is the ancestor of PLAUSIBLE*.

exploit [ME. Old French *esploit* (noun), *espleiter* (verb), ultimately from Latin *explicare* 'to unfold', later 'to explain', from *plicare* 'to fold'] Progress, speed, success (–16c); to accomplish or achieve (–18c); to get on or prosper (–17c), hence **1** an attempt to overcome or capture (15–18c); a military endeavour; a daring action (16c) **2** [from modern French] to make use of a resource (19c); to take advantage of something/someone selfishly.

Latin *explicare* (the opposite of *implicare* at IMPLY) produced **explicate** to unfold, spread out, or display, to unravel or disentangle (16–18c), hence to explain; to develop a theory, and **explicit** fully explained, also outspoken, hence describing or showing clearly, leaving nothing to the imagination. Latin *plicare* is the ancestor of PLY*.

exponent [16c. Latin, literally 'showing, explaining', from *exponere* 'to publish, exhibit, or explain', literally 'to put out', from *ponere* 'to put': see POSE*] **1** a figure or symbol accompanying a number that states how many times the number is multiplied by itself, hence **exponential** to do with an exponent (18c); increasing or growing rapidly **2** someone/something that explains, interprets, or provides an example of (19c); an advocate or supporter.

Latin *exponere* is also the ancestor of **expose**, **exposition** the action of interpreting or showing; something that does so, now specifically a large exhibition, shortened to **Expo** (originally applied to the 1967 World Fair at Montreal), and of **expound**.

express [Strictly speaking, two words, both ME and ultimately from Latin *exprimere*, *expres-* literally 'to press out', from *premere* PRESS*] **I** [via Old French *expresser* and medieval Latin *expressare* 'to keep pressing out'] **1** to press or squeeze out; to give out in response to pressure or a stimulus (17c) **2** to represent or depict in a sculpture or picture, later in music or, especially, in language (hence **expression** a word, phrase, or figure of speech, 17c); to communicate an emotion, idea, etc. in any of these media (hence **expressionist** an artist, writer, etc. whose work aims to represent inner experience rather than the physical world, 19c), or by actions or signs (hence the *expression* on your face, 18c); in maths: to represent a value etc. by a figure, symbol, or formula **3** to state explicitly (16c, cf. 11) **II** [via Old French from Latin *expressus* 'pressed out', later 'distinctly shown'] **1** stated definitely and explicitly (–17c, surviving in **expressly**) **2** intended or designed explicitly for a purpose, hence **(a)** a special messenger (16c, surviving in the names of newspapers); to send by one (18c, *US*); a private organization carrying mail or goods quickly (*Pony Express*, 19c); **express delivery** quick delivery by special messenger (19c) **(b)** express (train) a special train (19c); one making few or no stops, hence *express* fast, designed for high-speed operation (19c); **expressway, express route** for high-speed traffic (1940s).

Latin *expressus* fathered Italian *(caffè) espresso*, literally 'pressed out (coffee)', made by forcing steam through the ground beans, Anglicized into **expresso**.

exquisite [ME. Latin *exquisitus* 'carefully sought out, choice, excellent', from *exquirere* 'to seek out', from *quaerere* 'to seek' (ancestor of QUEST*)] Accurate, precise, careful (–18c), hence **1** of language: carefully chosen, apt, also unusual or affected (15–17c); of food: choice, dainty, delicious (16c); of objects: delicate, intricate, and beautifully made; excellent, beautiful **2** intense (*exquisite pleasure/pain*, 17c) **3** discriminating and sensitive (17c).

extenuate [15c. Latin *extenuare*, literally 'to thin out', from *tenuis* 'thin' (ancestor of **attentuate** and **tenuous**] to make thin, to emaciate, hence to diminish, underrate, or make light of (16c); to treat a crime as less serious; to find an excuse or mitigating circumstance (18c).

extinct [15c. Latin *exstinguere*, *exstinct-* 'to quench completely', from *stinguere* 'to quench', apparently also 'to prick' (perhaps by confusion with related *stigare* 'to prick', also 'to incite')] **1** to put out a fire; of a fire, light, candle etc.: no longer burning, later applied to disease, hope, vices, etc. compared to fire; of a volcano: no longer active (19c) **2** to abolish, (to make) null and void **3** to kill, to wipe out (–17c); no longer alive or in existence (–17c); having died out (17c).

The verb *extinct* was replaced by **extinguish** [also from *exstinguere*]; the verb **distinct** [Latin *distinguere* 'to separate', literally 'to mark out by pricking', from *stinguere*] was replaced by **distinguish** at the same time. Latin *stinguere* produced

instinct instigation, impulse (ME–18c); later an innate natural impulse; *stigare* produced **instigate**.

extol [ME. Latin *extollere*, from *tollere* 'to raise'] To lift up or out (–17c); to raise in rank (–18c), hence to raise in esteem, to praise enthusiastically (15c).

extravagant [ME. Latin *extravagari*, *extravagant-*, from Latin *extra* (see *extraordinary* at ORDINARY) + *vagari* 'to wander': see VAGARY*] Diverging, discrepant, irrelevant (–17c), also irregular, abnormal, improper, unsuitable (–18c), hence unreasonable, unrestrained (16c); unreasonably or absurdly elaborate or abundant; unreasonably expensive (18c); spending too heavily, wasteful.

Latin *extravagari* fathered **astray** [via Anglo-Norman French *astrey*, shortened to *strey*, whence **stray**] and **extravaganza** [Italian *estravaganza* '(an) extravagance'].

F

fable [ME. Old French, from Latin *fabula* 'story', from *fari, fant-* 'to speak'] A story, hence **1** a myth; myths in general; an unlikely tale; something existing only in the popular imagination (16c); **fabled** mythical, imaginary (17c) **2** a story designed to deceive **3** a short story with a moral.

Fable probably produced **fib** (to tell) a lie. Latin *fabula* produced **confabulation** (a) conversation [via *confabulari* 'to converse'], shortened to **confab** (later altered to **conflab**), and **fabulous** belonging to or typical of fable; amazing, astonishing; wonderful, excellent. Latin *fari* is the ancestor of **affable**, FATE*, FAY*, **ineffable**, **infant**, literally '(one) without speech', **infantry** [via Italian *infante* 'youth, foot-soldier'], and **preface**.

fabric [15c. Via French from Latin *fabrica* 'something made', from *faber* 'artisan'] **1** a building (–19c); the basic structural units of one (17c), specifically a church **2** any manufactured material (18c, now specifically a textile); the material of which something is made (19c).

Latin *fabrica* produced **fabricate** to make or manufacture, later to make up something false (hence **fabrication** a lie or forgery), and French *forger*, whence **forge** to make, hence **1** to shape by heating and hammering; a furnace or workshop for this **2** to make an illegal copy.

face [ME. French, utimately from Latin *facies* 'form, appearance', later 'face'] The front of the head, the visage, hence **1** this expressing feelings, hence **(a)** a grimace (*make a face*) **(b)** command of facial expression, coolness, effrontery (16c) **2** the visible part or surface, especially the front; to turn or be positioned so that this points a certain way (*it faces east/face the front*, 16c); **face (up to)** to confront bravely; to consider or accept (18c) **3** outward appearance (15c); disguise, (a) pretence **4** to provide with **facing** a (decorative) outer layer (16c); **facings** visible (contrasting) cuffs, collar, or lapels **5** reputation, image (19c, earliest and chiefly in **lose/save face**, modelled on Chinese).

French *face* produced **deface**, **efface** originally to 'wipe out' an offence [from French *effacer*, literally 'to remove the face'], **façade** a face or front, a (deceptive) appearance, **facet** [French *facette*, literally 'small face'], and **surface**. Latin *facies* is the ancestor of **superficial**.

facsimile [16c. From Latin *facere* 'to make' + *simile* 'a likeness', from *similis* 'like'. Spelt *fac simile* until the 19c] The making of an exact copy, especially of writing (–17c); such a copy (17c), hence describing a system for transmitting a copy of a document electronically (*facsimile telegraph/transmission*, 19c); shortened to **fax** (1940s), hence (to transmit) such a copy (1970s); a machine for doing so.

Latin *simile* was adopted for a figure of speech that likens one thing to another; *similis* is the ancestor of SIMULATE*, and *facere* of FACT*.

fact   [15c. Latin *factum* 'something done', from *facere*, *fact-* 'to make or do'] **1** an action or deed, originally a good one, later a crime (16c, surviving in *before/after the fact*) **2** truth, reality (16c); something known to have happened or be true (17c), hence **faction** a blend of fact and fiction (1980s), **factoid** a questionable 'fact' [1973, coined by American author Norman Mailer].

Latin *facere*'s descendants include AFFECT*, ARTIFICE*, **beneficent**, **benefit**, CHAFE*, CONFECTION*, **counterfeit**, DEFEAT, **defect**, **deficient**, **deficit**, EFFECT*, **-facient** that brings about (*abortifacient*), FACSIMILE*, FACTOR*, FACTOTUM, FACULTY*, FASHION*, **feasible**, FEAT, FEATURE, FETISH, **-fic** (*scientific*), **-fice** (*edifice*, *precipice*), **-ficial** (*beneficial*), **-ficient** (*efficient*, *sufficient*), FORFEIT, **-fy** (*glorify, putrefy*), Spanish *hacienda* [from Latin *facienda* 'things to be done'], **infect**, MAGNIFY*, **malfeasance**, *manufacture* (at MANAGE), OFFICE*, **perfect** [Latin *perficere*, literally 'to do thoroughly'], PONTIFF*, **prefect** [Latin *praeficere* 'to set first or over'], PROFIT*, **refectory** [Latin *reficere* 'to refresh', literally 'to remake'], SACRIFICE*, *specific* (at SPICE*), *spinifex* (at SPINE), **suffice** [Latin *sufficere* 'to make up to, to be enough'], and **surfeit** [via Old French *surfaire* 'to overdo'].

factor   [ME. (Via French from) Latin *factor*, from *facere*: see FACT*] **1** someone who does or makes something (–19c); someone who does so for someone else, an agent (now mainly Scots); to act as one (17c) **2** any of the numbers multiplied together to produce a specific result (17c); something that influences or contributes to a result or process (19c), hence **factor in/out** to include/exclude from an assessment or calculation (1970s).

Latin *factor* appears in **benefactor** and **malefactor** good- or evil-doer, and is the ancestor of **factory**, strictly speaking three words: **1** [via English *factor*] the work or position of a factor (Scots) **2** [via Portuguese *feitoria*] a trading station for factors in a foreign country **3** [via late Latin *factorium* 'oil press'] a place where goods are manufactured.

factotum   [16c. Medieval Latin, from Latin *fac* 'do!' (from *facere*: see FACT*) + *totum* 'everything' (whence **total**). Originally as *dominus* or *magister factotum* 'Master Do-Everything', or *Johannes factotum* 'John Do-Everything'; often spelt *fac-totum* until the 19c] A jack of all trades, hence a servant with many duties, or who manages all his master's affairs.

faculty   [ME. Via French from Latin *facultas*, from *facilis* 'easy', from *facere*: see FACT*] The power or ability to do something, hence **1** a particular aptitude, hence **(a)** a branch of learning; now (the students and staff of) a university or college department (in N America, all a university's teaching staff); all the members of a profession, especially medicine (16c) **(b)** a physical or, later, mental ability (*still has all his faculties*, 15c) **2** means, resources, property, surviving mainly in **faculty theory** the theory that everyone should be taxed according to their means **3** the freedom or right to do something (16c); an authorization or dispensation.

The opposite of Latin *facultas* was *difficultas*, ancestor of **difficulty**, whence **difficult**. Latin *facilis* is the ancestor of **facile**, **facilitate**, and **facility**.

fag¹ [15c. Origin unknown] A flap (15c only); a remnant of cloth etc. (16c), hence **fag end** what is left over when the best has been used (17c), specifically a cigarette end (19c), hence *fag* a (cheap) cigarette.

fag² [16c. Origin unknown: perhaps related to FLAG] To tire or flag; to tire yourself out with work (18c), hence **1** a tiring or tedious task, drudgery (18c); a public schoolboy who does such tasks for an older boy; to be or to use a fag (19c) **2 fagged (out)** weary (19c).

faggot [ME. French *fagot* from Italian *fagotto*, ultimately from Greek *phakelos* 'bundle'] A bundle of firewood, hence **1** a bunch of herbs (15c); a bundle of reeds, metal rods, etc. (16c), hence **(a)** a miscellaneous collection of things (17c); a meatball made of offal, suet, and breadcrumbs (19c) **(b) faggoting** a kind of drawn-thread work in which the remaining threads are tied together like faggots (19c); a stitch resembling this **2** a term of abuse, especially for an old woman (19c), hence an effeminate gay man (early 20c, *US*), shortened to **fag** (1920s).

fail [ME. Old French *faille* (noun), *faillir* (verb), ultimately from Latin *fallere* 'to deceive or disappoint': the noun largely replaced by 17c **failure**] **1** to be or become inadequate; to weaken or fade **2** to prove inefficient or unreliable; to neglect or omit to do something; such an omission (surviving in *without fail*) **3** to fall short of a standard; to be unsuccessful in doing or achieving something; a lack of success (15c), now mainly in an exam.
   Latin *fallere* is the ancestor of DEFAULT*, FALLACY, **false**, Italian *falsetto*, and *faucet* (at TAP).

fair¹ [Old English *faeger*] Pleasing, hence **1** beautifully; beautiful (now usually of a woman); of hair or skin: light **2** gracious(ly), courteous(ly), hence initially attractive, specious, plausible (ME) **3** promisingly, auspiciously, surviving in **bid fair** to appear likely to succeed (ME) **4** smooth, even (ME); to smooth a surface (19c); **fairing** a structure added to streamline a vehicle **5** physically or, later, morally clean, blameless (ME), hence honest, just, impartial, equitable (18c) **6** clear, unobstructed (ME), surviving in dialect, in place names (*Fairford, Fairmile*), and in **fairway** a navigable channel between rocks etc. (17c); the closely mown area on a golf course between the tee and the green (*c.*1900) **7 (a)** of an amount or fortune: large, considerable (ME); reasonable, adequate (19c) **(b)** considerably, completely, quite (ME, surviving in British dialect and in former colonies); moderately (15c), replaced by **fairly** (19c) **8** of weather: bright, sunny (ME); of wind: favourable (15c) **9** in neat handwriting (16c); **fair copy** material transcribed after final corrections (19c).

fair² [ME. Via Old French from late Latin *feria*, singular of Latin *feriae* 'holy days' (when fairs were often held). The spelling **fayre** died out *c.*1800 but has recently been revived in sense 1a and 1c as an affectation] **1** a large (livestock) market, with amusements and sideshows which often outlived it, hence (all 19c) **(a)** a commercial exhibition **(b)** a sale of goods to raise money for charity **(c) (fun)fair** a (travelling) collection of rides, sideshows, etc. **2 fairs** in Scotland: a period when a town's factories traditionally close for holidays (18c). Cf. FEAST, WAKE.

faith [ME. Old French *feid, feit*, from Latin *fides* 'trust, confidence, something inspiring this, trustworthiness'] **1** complete confidence or belief in someone (originally God) or something, especially without proof; a set of religious beliefs or principles; belief in religious doctrines **2** a vow, promise or trust (–17c); the obligation to fulfil it; **keep (your) faith** to do so, to be loyal, hence *faith* allegiance, loyalty **3** (both ME) **(a) bad faith** [Latin *mala fides*] insincerity, intent to deceive **(b) good faith** [Latin *bona fides*] honesty, honest intentions. These Latin phrases were later adopted as legal terms: *bona fide* [literally 'with good faith'], being used to mean 'genuine(ly), sincere(ly)' (16c); *bona fides* was then taken as its plural and used to mean 'proofs of sincerity, credentials' (1940s).

Latin *fides* is the ancestor of CONFIDENT*, DEFY, **fealty**, FIDELITY*, and **perfidy**.

fallacy [15c. Latin *fallacia*, from *fallax* 'deceiving', from *fallere* 'to deceive' (ancestor of FAIL*)] Deception, guile, a trick or a lie (–18c, replacing ME *fallace*, also from Latin *fallacia*), hence **1** a plausible but flawed argument (16c); a belief based on one, a delusion **2** deceptiveness (18c).

fame [ME. Old French, from Latin *fama* 'report'] **1** reputation, especially good reputation gained by achievements **2** what people say, report, or rumour (–19c); to tell or report **3** (combining 1 and 2) the condition of being much talked about or very well known; **famed, famous** well known or celebrated.

Latin *fama* produced **defame** [via *diffamare* 'to give a bad report about'] and **infamous** [via *infamis*, literally 'without fame'].

familiar [ME. (Via French from) Latin *familiaris*, from *familia*: see FAMILY] Belonging to, or like one of, the household, hence **1** a household member, a servant, now only in a pope's or bishop's household; **familiar (spirit)** one expected to come when called (15c) **2** friendly, informal, or intimate; unduly so, impertinent **3** well known, often encountered, easily recognized (15c); well acquainted with (16c).

family [ME. Latin *familia* (whence FAMILIAR), from *famulus* 'servant'] **1** household servants or a nobleman's retinue **2** the descendants of a common ancestor, hence a group with common ties or interests (16c) or significant common features (17c) **3** (combining 1 and 2) a household, including parents and their children, servants, and lodgers (16c); a couple and their children (17c, now often **nuclear family**, as opposed to **extended family** including grandparents, uncles, aunts, cousins, etc.); a couple's children. Hence to do with the family, intended or suitable for families (*family car/viewing*, 19c) **4** see TAXONOMY.

fanatic [16c. (Via French from) Latin *fanaticus* 'of a temple, inspired by a god', from *fanum* 'temple' (whence PROFANE)] Of behaviour or speech: suggesting possession by a god or demon; (someone who is) excessively enthusiastic, especially about religion. Shortened to **fan** a keen supporter, a devotee (19c, *US*), whence **fanzine** a magazine for fans (1940s, *US*).

fang [OE. Old Norse *fang* 'to capture or grasp'] **1** something seized, booty, spoils (now only Scots) **2** a firm grip (ME–17c); something with one: **(a)** a rope to hold a fore-and-aft sail (16c, now as the variant **vang**) **(b)** a trap (16c, now only Scots) **(c)** a large pointed tooth; a snake's venom tooth (19c).

Related to *fangled* in **newfangled** fond of (easily gripped by) new things, hence novel, disconcertingly new and different.

fantasy [ME. Via Old French and Latin from Greek *phantasia* 'appearance, imagination', from *phantazein* 'to make visible': see PHANTOM*. Formerly also spelt *phantasie*

(17–19c)] The idea formed in the mind of something perceived by the senses (–16c) or of something imagined; imagination, hence **1** an ingenious invention or design (15c); a musical work in an impromptu style (16c, largely replaced by Italian *fantasia,* also from Greek *phantasia,* 18c) **2** an unfounded idea or supposition; caprice, a whim, hence an arbitrary preference or desire (15–17c), replaced by **fancy: (a)** in **take a fancy to, fancy free** not in love; **fancy man** a woman's lover or pimp (19c); **fancy woman** a mistress or prostitute; **fancy yourself** to be conceited **(b)** to select as a likely winner (19c) **3** to imagine (15c); to indulge in unrealistic ideas or dreams (16c, now usually *fancy* or **fantasize**, 1920s); something imagined, a day dream (19c); (an example of) a type of fiction featuring imaginary worlds and supernatural events (1940s).

Fancy also came to mean: **1** creative imagination; the ability to produce decorative designs or articles, hence elaborate or decorative, not plain; such an article **2** **the Fancy** those with the same hobby or interest, especially boxing **3** to breed, or the art of breeding, animals or plants for (exaggerated) characteristics.

farce [ME. Old French *farce* 'stuffing', *farsir* 'to stuff', from Latin *farcire*] To cram or stuff (–17c); to stuff with forcemeat (**force** being an alteration of *farce*: –18c).

In France, *farce* came to mean an impromptu comic episode 'stuffed into' a religious drama, later a comic interlude between acts of a secular play, hence a short comic play, later a full-length one, often with ludicrous events and misunderstandings; an absurd situation or event.

fare [Old English: related to *ferry, ford,* and GABERDINE] To go, to travel (–19c); travelling, a journey (–18c, surviving in dialect *eel-fare* the passage of young eels up a river, whence **elver** a young eel, 17c). Hence **1** to travel or get on well or badly, hence **(a)** to have good or bad luck or treatment; to be entertained or fed well or badly (ME), hence the food or drink provided **(b) farewell**, literally 'may you get on well' (ME) **(c) welfare** good progress or fortune (ME), well-being, hence (the official provision of) support for those in need (early 20c) **2** a journey that you pay for (ME); the price paid; a paying passenger (16c).

farm [ME. Via French from medieval Latin *firma* 'a fixed payment', from Latin *firmare* 'to fix or settle': see FIRM*] A fixed annual rent or tax, hence **1** to rent (–18c) or let (16c) land; **farmer** someone who works on someone else's land (–16c), or cultivates rented or, later, their own land; *farm* a piece of (originally rented) land where crops or animals are reared (16c); a place where something is produced, processed, or stored (*fish/wind/tank farm,* 19c). See also *farmstead* (at STEAD) **2** a fixed amount accepted in lieu of actual moneys collected; (to allow someone) to collect rents, taxes, etc. in return for a fixed sum (16c); to take, or (often as **farm out**) to get someone else to take, a responsibility in return for a fee.

fascia [16c. Latin, 'band, door frame'] A horizontal band of wood, stone, brick, etc. on a building, hence (usually as **facia**) the nameplate over a shop (19c); a car's dashboard (1920s).

Latin *fascia* is the ancestor of **fess**, a heraldic term meaning a horizontal stripe. Related to Latin *fascis* 'bundle', the plural of which, **fasces**, was used for a bundle of rods bound round an axe, used as a symbol of authority in ancient Rome and adopted by the Italian *partito nazionale fascista,* a right-wing political party that ruled Italy from 1922 to 1943, whence **fascist** (originally with the Italian plural *fascisti*); quickly applied to other right-wing, authoritarian organizations, ideas, or individuals.

fashion   [ME. Old French *façon*, from Latin *factio* 'making, doing', from *facere*: see FACT*] Shape, form, or appearance, hence **1** a particular shape or style; an accepted style of clothing, decoration, entertainment, etc. (15c); that adopted by the social elite (*a lady of fashion*, 16c); that currently popular (17c) **2** a manner or way or behaving (surviving mainly in *in my fashion, after a fashion*); a prevailing custom (15c) **3** to form; to make or adapt in a particular way (16c).

Latin *factio* came to mean 'a group of people acting together', whence **faction** a dissenting group within a larger one; dissension or intrigue within a group.

fast   [Old English *fæst*), *faeste* (adverb)] Firmly fixed, stable, immovably (*fast asleep/colour, stuck fast*), hence **1** constant, standing firm (*fast friend*), largely replaced by **steadfast** [ME, literally 'firmly in place', from STEAD] **2** of a fortress: secure, unassailable (–17c, surviving in -**fast** in a few place names and **fastness** stronghold, fortress) **3** firmly tied or fastened (ME); **fast and loose** a fairground trick in which the punter tried to secure the loop of a folded belt with a stick, the trickster ensuring failure **4** close, immediate (surviving, just, in *fast by*: cf. HARD); immediately, at once; rapid(ly); **live fast** to use up your energy too quickly (17c), hence *fast* dissipated, immoral, promiscuous.

Related to **avast!** stop! [Dutch *hou'vast, houd vast* 'hold fast!'], **fast** to go without food, **fast** a period of fasting [Old Norse *fasta*], whence **breakfast** the meal that breaks the night-time fast, and to **fasten**.

fastidious   [ME. Latin *fastidiosus*, from *fastidium* 'loathing, disgust'] Disagreeable, distasteful (–18c), hence finding things distasteful or disgusting (16–17c); squeamish, particular, fussy about cleanliness or propriety (17c).

fate   [ME. (Via Italian from) Latin *fatum* 'that which is spoken', from *fari* 'to speak'] The power popularly supposed to predetermine everything that happens, destiny, hence **1** the result of this, your destiny; a bad result, death or destruction; the final outcome (18c) **2** a goddess of destiny (16c), especially one of the three Greek, Roman, or Scandinavian ones known as **the Fates**. Cf. *destiny* (at DESTINE), see also FAY*.

Latin *fatum* produced **fatal** decreed by fate (ME–18c, surviving in **fatalism**), decisive; deadly, disastrous, and FAY*. *Fari* is the ancestor of FABLE*.

father   [Old English *faeder*] The male parent, hence **1** God, especially as distinct from Christ and the Holy Spirit **2** a paternalistic ruler or superior, originally a feudal lord; a spiritual teacher or leader (ME); (the title of) a priest, abbot, etc.; **Holy Father** the Pope (15c: cf. *pope* below); **father(s)** the elder(s) or leader(s) of a community **3** a forefather, a patriarch **4** a founder or inventor (ME), hence **(a)** to originate or encourage (16c); someone/something that does so **(b)** the first, largest, or most extreme example (17c), later also **the father and mother** or the *daddy* **5** to beget a child (15c); to be or act as the father; to foster; someone who does so (16c); **fatherland** your native country (17c): **mother country/land** is earlier (16c) and also applied to a country in relation to its colonies **6** a respectful title for an old man (16c).

The major senses of **mother** [Old English *mōdor*] are similar: it has also come to mean: **1** inherited or learned from your mother (*mother tongue/wit*, 17c) **2** a pet's woman owner (1920s), now usually *Mum*: *father* is not used in this way, though *dad* is **3** a despicable person (1950s, US, short for *motherfucker*: see FUCK).

Dad(dy), **Pa(pa)**, **Ma(ma)**, **Mum(my)**, etc. reflect a baby's first attempts at speech. Similar words exist in most languages, notably Latin *mamma* 'mother, breast' (whence **mammal** and **mammary**) and Greek *pap(p)as* 'father, bishop, patriarch', whence **pope** and **poplin** originally made at Avignon, which was papal property until 1791.

fathom [Old English *faethm*] Something that embraces, hence **fathoms** the outstretched arms (OE only); *fathom* a unit of measurement based on the span of the outstretched arms, later standardized at six feet (1.83 metres) and used to measure the depth of water, hence to measure depth (16c); to get to the bottom of something, to investigate or understand it.

fatigue [17c. Via French from Latin *fatigare* 'to drive to breaking point', from *ad fatim*, *affatim* 'abundantly, to bursting point'] To tire out, hence **1** an action or task that does so; non-military tasks done by soldiers (18c); **fatigues** clothes worn for these (19c) **2** weariness caused by exertion or, later, by (repeated) stress (*metal fatigue*, 18c), hence inability to respond or perform adequately following prolonged or repeated exposure (*battle/compassion fatigue*, 19c).

Latin *fatigare* produced **fatigable** apt to tire, and **indefatigable** untiring, tireless. **Defatigable** 'easily tired' was formed from *fatigable* (17–18c), and was reinvented as a back-formation from *indefatigable* (1940s).

favour [ME. Old French, from Latin *favor*, from *favere* 'to show kindness to'] **1** exceptional kindness and goodwill, hence **(a)** to treat kindly, to indulge or oblige; to treat gently, to avoid hurting or straining (*favours his left leg*, 16c) **(b)** a kind act (*do me a favour*, 16c) **2** (to have or show) liking, approval; partiality or preference, hence **(a)** something that attracts these, charm, beauty (–17c); appearance (15c, surviving mainly in **ill-favoured** unattractive, ugly), hence to look like or take after someone **(b)** **in/out of favour** liked/not liked (16c) **(c)** something given or worn as a sign of favour (16c). Hence [via Italian] **favourite** (someone/ something) preferred (16c); a ruler's chosen, intimate companion; the competitor most fancied to win; **favouritism** unfair preferential treatment of one person (18c) **3** aid, support; to help, support, or facilitate; to prove advantageous to; **in your favour** to your advantage.

fay [ME. Old French *faie*, from Latin *fata* 'the Fates', plural of *fatum*: see FATE*] A being in human form with magical powers; a small, delicate, winged and usually benevolent one, a fairy.

The original sense survives in Italian *fata morgana* an illusion or mirage [literally 'Fairy Morgan', King Arthur's sister, believed to cause a mirage frequently seen in the Strait of Messina]. *Fay* influenced the development of FEY. Old French *faie* produced *faierie*, whence **fairy** the world of fairies (largely replaced by **faerie**, a deliberate archaism introduced by Spenser: see BLATANT); a single fairy; a small graceful woman or child; a gay man.

faze [Old English *fēsian*, of unknown origin] Originally as **feeze**: to drive or frighten away; to frighten (ME). Virtually obsolete in British English since the 17c but apparently surviving in the US, where the variant *faze* appeared meaning to disconcert or disturb (19c).

fear [Old English *fǣr* (noun), whence *fǣran* (verb)] **1** danger, a sudden calamity (OE only); (to produce) the feeling that danger is near; great anxiety or apprehension (ME); to be afraid of (15c) **2** to revere (surviving in **godfearing**); reverence, awe (ME).

feast [ME. Old French *feste* from Latin *festum*: see FESTIVAL*] A periodic religious celebration such as Christmas or a saint's day (partly replaced by FESTIVAL), hence **1** (to take part in or lay on) a celebratory meal or banquet; an ample or elaborate meal; to eat heartily and with enjoyment; to entertain or honour someone, originally with a banquet (–16c, replaced by *fête* below) **2** an annual village festival, originally on the feast day of the saint to which the church was dedicated (16c), sometimes evolving into, or being revived as, the village fête.

Old French *feste* evolved into *fête*, adopted for a festival or entertainment, hence to hold one in someone's honour (cf. *feast* above), and again for an open-air bazaar: cf. FAIR².

feat [ME. French *fait* from Latin *factum* 'something done': see FACT*] A deed, a course of action (–18c); a noble or brave one (15c); a remarkable action or achievement, especially one showing strength, skill, or courage.

feature [ME. Old French *feture*, *faiture* 'form', from Latin *factura* 'manufacture, formation', from *facere* 'to make or do' (ancestor of FACT*)] Form, shape, or proportion, especially of the body (–18c, but used as an archaism by 19c poets); a part of the body (ME–18c) or face (15c), hence a distinctive, characteristic, or prominent part (17c), hence **1** a prominent item in a newspaper, magazine, etc. (19c); **feature (film)**, **main feature** the main film in a cinema programme (*c*.1910) **2** to give prominence to; to present as (19c, *US*) or to be (1940s) a special or important element.

fee [ME. Anglo-Norman French, variant of Old French *f(i)eu*, *fie(f)*, from medieval Latin *feudum*, ultimately of Germanic origin] (Tenure of) a piece of land in return for service to your feudal superior, hence (tenure of) a heritable estate: earliest in **fee tail** restricted to a designated heir or heirs (see TAIL); **fee simple** without restriction; the heritable right to a paid position (–19c); the money due to the holder, later to a professional person for their services (16c); a sum paid for a right or service (*admission/membership/tuition fee*).

Old French *f(i)eu*, *fie(f)* produced **enfeoff** to put someone in possession of a feudal tenancy, **fief(dom)** the land held, later something that you control, and Scots **feu** a feudal tenure in return for money rather than service, now a perpetual lease for a fixed sum. Latin *feudum* is the ancestor of **feudal**, coined by 17c historians to describe the system. Related to FELLOW.

feign [ME. French *feindre*, *feign-* (also *faindre*), from Latin *fingere* 'to shape, form, or contrive'] To make something (rare after Middle English); to do so in order to deceive, to forge a document, invent a story, excuse, etc., hence to lie or dissemble (–16c); to avoid a duty by false pretences (–16c); to pretend (*feigned sickness/innocence*).

Old French *feindre*, *faindre* produced FEINT/FAINT; Latin *fingere* is the ancestor of **effigy** and **fiction**. Related to **figment**, originally an invented statement or story, and to FIGURE*.

feint/faint [ME. Old French *feindre, faindre*: see FEIGN*] Feigned, simulated, false, hence **1** (nearly always *feint*) to deceive; (–17c); a simulated blow or attack to mislead your opponent (17c); to make one (19c) **2** (nearly always *faint*) shirking, lazy, cowardly, weak (surviving in *faint heart*), hence **(a)** (to become) weak or dizzy from fear, exhaustion, hunger, etc.; to swoon; a swoon (*a dead faint*, 19c) **(b)** barely perceptible, dim, indistinct, pale, hence (describing) the faint lines on paper to guide handwriting (19c, usually as **ruled feint**).

feisty [16c. Ultimately from Old English *fist* 'to fart'] **Fisting hound, dog**, or **cur** a contemptuous term for a lapdog, traditionally bad-tempered and with poor digestion from indulgent feeding, hence **f(e)ist** a small (snappy) dog (18c, US), whence *feisty* excitable, touchy, aggressive (19c), now usually determined, assertive, self-reliant (1960s). Cf. DOG*.

Distantly related to **petard** a small bomb [French, from *peter* 'to fart', whence the surname **Petters**: see also HOIST] and perhaps to **fizzle** originally to fart quietly, but not to **fart** itself [Old English], which is related to **partridge** [via French from Latin *perdix*], whose wings make a sharp whirring sound when it takes off.

fellow [Old English *fēolaga*, literally 'one who lays out money', from Old Norse *félagi*, from *fé* 'cattle, property, money' (related to FEE*) + *lag* 'laying down' (related to LAY*)] A business partner, colleague, or ally (rare since the 17c); a companion or associate (ME), hence **1** a counterpart or match; an equal **2** a member (now often a privileged one) of a society with common interests, or of a university or its governing body, now specifically a graduate student supported by a university to teach or do research (19c) **3** a man or boy; a servant or lower-class man; your boyfriend (19c) **4** belonging to the same group, occupation, etc. (*fellow citizen*, 16c).

felon [ME. French, from *fel* 'wicked, cruel' (whence **fell** in the same sense), from medieval Latin *fel(l)o*, of unknown origin] Wicked, murderous, cruel (–16c), hence **1** a wicked or cruel person **2** a painful abscess or whitlow. Hence **felony** wickedness, anger, deceit, treachery (–16c); grave or violent crime, such a crime, formerly, and still in the US, distinguished from a *misdemeanour* (see DEMEANOUR); *felon* someone guilty of a felony.

fence [ME. Short for *defence*: see DEFEND*] Defending, defence (–16c); a means of defending (–18c), hence **1** (to enclose with) a railing or barrier; a similar structure for horses to jump (19c) **2** **fencing** the art or sport of fighting with swords (16c); *fence* to practise this; to parry or evade questions (17c), to engage in repartee **3** a person who handles stolen goods (17c, perhaps 'protecting' the thief from the law); to do so.

feral [17c. Latin *fera* 'wild animal', from *ferus* 'wild'] To do with or like a wild animal, hence **1** savage, fierce **2** untamed, uncultivated **3** wild, but formerly domesticated or having domesticated ancestors (19c).

Latin *ferus* produced **fierce** and perhaps **zebra** [Italian, Spanish, and Portuguese, meaning 'wild ass', perhaps ultimately from Latin *equiferus* 'wild horse', with *equus* 'horse' (whence **equestrian** and **equine**)]. Related to **ferocious**.

ferment [ME. Via French from Latin *fermentum*, from *fervere* 'to boil'] To undergo or to subject to a process such as that of yeast on sugar, which breaks down the substance fermented and produces heat and bubbling, hence to make or become excited (17c); to stir up emotion or trouble; agitation, excitement.

Latin *fervere* is the ancestor of **effervescent** boiling, hence bubbling, fizzy, exuberant, **fervent**, **fervid**, and **fervour**, all having the ideas of heat and strong emotion. **Foment** to put a hot (medicated) dressing on, later to stir up strong feeling, trouble, etc., which looks similar, is from Latin *fovere* 'to cherish', also 'to warm'.

ferret   [ME. Via Old French from, ultimately, Latin *fur* 'thief'] A domesticated kind of polecat, used for hunting rabbits and rats in their burrows; to hunt or to drive out (as if) with one, hence to rummage through or search out (16c); someone who does so, a detective (17c).

Latin *fur* is the ancestor of **furtive** and **furuncle** a boil [via Latin *furunculus*, literally 'little thief', used for a growth on a vine thought to be 'stealing' the sap].

festival   [ME. Old French, from medieval Latin *festivalis*, from *festum* 'feast day', from *festus* 'joyous'] To do with or suitable for a feast or feast day (partly replaced by **festive**, 17c), hence a feast day (16c); an occasion for feasting or celebration; a (regular) series of special events or performances (*beer/film festival*, 19c).

Latin *festum* is the ancestor of FEAST*, German *Fest* 'celebration', adopted for a special gathering (*songfest*, *gabfest*, US) and in *Festschrift* a collection of writings in honour of a scholar, **festal**, **festoon** [via Italian *feston* 'festal ornament'], and Spanish *fiesta*.

fetish   [17c. Via French from Portuguese *fetiço* 'charm, sorcery', literally 'artificial', from Latin *facticius*, from *facere* 'to make or do'] An object used by W African peoples as an amulet or charm, later one believed to contain a spirit, hence **1** an obsession (*makes a fetish of punctuality*, 19c) **2** an object or non-sexual part of the body that arouses sexual excitement in some people.

Latin *facticius* produced **factitious** made by human beings, hence artificial, false. *Facere* is the ancestor of FACT*.

feud   [ME. Old French *fe(i)de*, from early Dutch and Low German *vēde*] Hostility, enmity, ill-will; a bitter, prolonged, and often violent quarrel between families or other groups (15c), hence any prolonged quarrel (16c); to take part in one (17c).

Related to **foe** [Old English *fāh*] involved in feud, hostile, hence a hostile person, your enemy.

fey   [Old English *faege*] Doomed to die, at the point of death, hence **1** distracted, preoccupied (as you well might be, 18c); dreamy, other-wordly, now often in an affected way **2** (influenced by FAY) having, or associated with, magical powers.

fiddle   [Old English *fithele*, ultimately from Latin *vitulari* 'to celebrate a festival, to be joyful'] A violin or similar instrument; to play one (ME), hence to make aimless movements, to mess about; to tinker (16c), hence **1** to cheat or swindle (17c); a swindle (19c) **2** a fuss or inconvenience (19c); **fiddly** small and awkward (1920s).

Violin [Italian *violino* 'small viola', ultimately from Latin *vitulari*] gradually became the standard term, *fiddle* becoming informal or disparaging. It was lengthened to **fiddlededee** nonsense, and to **fiddle-faddle** idle talk; trifling, petty;

to fuss about trifles, whence **fidfad** someone who does so, whence, probably, **fad** a personal preference, a whim, a craze, and **faddy** fussy, particularly about food. **Fiddlestick** 'a violin bow' came to mean 'something trivial', whence **fiddlesticks** nonsense.

fidelity [ME. (Via French from) Latin *fidelitas*, from *fidelis* 'faithful', from *fides* 'trust'] Loyalty, faithfulness; veracity or accuracy (16c), hence **high fidelity** accuracy of recorded sound to the original (1930s), shortened to **hi-fi** (1950s).

Latin *fidelis* produced **infidel**, literally an unbeliever. *Fides* is the ancestor of FAITH*.

field [Old English *feld*] A tract of open, treeless land (surviving in place names as **Fel-** or **-feld**); a piece of (usually enclosed) land put to a particular, originally agricultural, use, hence **1** the scene of **(a)** a battle (ME); military manoeuvres (17c); **field artillery/hospital/telegraph** etc. for use while on campaign **(b)** a sport (*hunting/playing field*, 18c), hence **(i)** those who take part, especially the runners in a race other than the favourite or leader (18c); to select a competitor or team (1920s) **(ii)** in cricket: the side not batting, deployed around the field (18c); to stop and return the ball (19c); to answer questions as they arise (*c.*1900) **2 (a)** the country (ME), surviving in **field sports** (17c) **(b)** the natural environment (*field trip/guide*,18c) **(c)** a sphere of action, influence, or expertise (18c) **3** a background for a design or picture (ME); a large surface or expanse (16c).

fiend [Old English *fēond*] An enemy (–ME), hence the Devil; a demon or evil spirit; an extremely wicked or cruel person (ME); a mischievous or annoying one (17c); an addict or enthusiast (*dope/cricket fiend*).

figure [ME. Via French from Latin *figurare* 'to form or fashion', from *figura* 'a form or shape'] The distinctive form of a person or thing (–17c): **1** a picture, statue, etc. of a human form, hence **(a)** a person as they appear to others (*a figure of fun/a respected figure*) **(b)** the shape of the body **(c) figurine** a small statue (19c) **2** a two-dimensional shape; to decorate with such shapes or a pattern (*figured silk*); such a pattern (16c); a 'pattern' or sequence of movements made by a dancer or skater (19c) **3** a symbol representing a number; a number or amount (19c); to calculate or understand (*N American*); to be understandable, to make sense (*that figures*, 1950s, US) **4** to form or shape (–18c), surviving in **configure**, **disfigure**, and **transfigure** [all ME, ultimately from Latin *figurare*] **5** to foretell or herald (–16c), surviving in **prefigure** (15c) **6** a diagram or illustrative drawing **7** a rhetorical expression, usually in **figure of speech**; a metaphor, hence **figurative** metaphorical **8** to feature, to be significant (17c).

Senses 6 and 7 come from the use of Latin *figura* to translate Greek *skhēma*: see SCHEME. Related to FEIGN*.

file [ME. French *filer* 'to spin, to string on a thread', ultimately from Latin *filum* 'a thread'] To string documents on a thread to keep them in order; such a string (16c); (to put a document in) a folder etc., hence **1** to put a document officially on record; to make a formal application (*file for divorce*); to send in a news report (1950s) **2** [via French *file* 'a thread'] a line of people one behind the other (16c, hence *rank and file* at RANK[1]); to move in a line (17c) **3** a collection of instructions or data treated as a single entity by a computer (1950s).

French *file* produced **defile** originally a place where troops can march only in single file. Latin *filum* is the ancestor of **filament**, **filigree**, FILLET, and PROFILE.

filibuster [16c. Ultimately from Dutch *vrijbuiter*, literally 'one who plunders freely', from *vrij* 'free' and *buit* 'plunder'] **1** a pirate (recorded once) **2** [via French *flibustier*] a pirate preying on Spanish colonies in the West Indies (18c) **3** [Spanish *filibustero*, from French *flibustier*] a member of a band of American adventurers who stirred up revolution in several Latin American states (19c), hence someone taking part in unauthorized military action; someone who obstructs the passing of legislation, usually by a long or irrelevant speech; (to use) such a tactic.

Dutch *vrijbuiter* produced **freebooter**; *vrij* is related to FREE*, and *buit* to **booty**.

fillet [ME. French *filet*, ultimately from Latin *filum*: see FILE*] A band of material, later of nerve or muscle fibre, hence **fillets** the loins (15c); *fillet* a piece of meat from this area; a boneless piece of meat or fish; to bone meat or fish (19c).

filter [ME. Via Old French from medieval Latin *filtrum*, of West Germanic origin] (A piece of) felt (–15c); this or other material used to strain something (16c), later anything that stops particles, rays, etc. passing through, hence **1** to put or go through a filter (16c); to move or trickle slowly (18c) **2** to obtain or remove something by filtering (18c).

Modern Latin *filtrare* [from *filtrum*] produced **filtrate** to put or go through a filter; filtered liquid, whence **infiltrate** to make a liquid permeate a substance gradually; to get someone into enemy lines, an organization, etc. surreptitiously, whence **exfiltrate** to withdraw troops, an agent, etc. surreptitiously. Related to Old English **felt**.

finance [ME. French, from *finer* 'to bring to an end, to settle a debt', from *fin* 'end, payment', from Latin *finis*: see FINE*] Payment of a debt, ransom, or compensation (–16c); a tax, taxation, revenue (15–17c), hence **finances** the monetary resources of a country, organization, or individual (18c); *finance* the management of these; to manage money (19c); (to provide) necessary funds.

French *fin* produced **fine** termination, conclusion (surviving in **in fine** finally, to sum up); (money paid on) the conclusion of a law suit, hence a penalty of any kind, now a monetary one; to impose one.

fine [ME. Via French from Latin *finire* 'to finish', from *finis* 'end, limit'] The underlying sense is 'finished, perfected', hence 'very good of its kind'. Hence to make clear or pure (whence 16c **refine**); to make less coarse (16c); to make or become slimmer (19c).

Fine produced **finery**, **fingering** (at GROGRAM), and probably **finical** and **finicking** fastidious, too particular, too elaborate or detailed; altered to **finicky**. Latin *finire* produced **define**, **definite**, **finish**, and FINITE*; descendants of *finis* include AFFINITY, **confine**, **final**, FINANCE*, FINESSE, and **finish**.

finesse [ME. French, ultimately from Latin *finis*: see FINE*] Purity, clarity; delicacy; dexterity (16c); subtlety, tact; artfulness, cunning, a subtle strategy; in cards: to try to win a trick with a card of low value (18c); such an attempt (19c); to use, or to achieve something by, tact or cunning.

finite [ME. Latin *finitus*, from *finire*: see FINE*] Having an end or limits, hence **1** able to be counted or measured (16c) **2** of a verb: having a specific number, tense, or person (18c), as opposed to the earlier **infinitive** [ME, from Latin *infinitus*], hence the infinitive form of a verb, in English usually preceded by *to* (16c).

Latin *infinitus* produced **infinite**, **infinitesimal** immeasurably small, and **infinity** boundlessness; an unbounded space, time, amount, etc.; (a point at) an immeasurably great distance.

fire [Old English *fyr*] The light, heat, and flames produced by burning; the process of burning, hence **1** a pile of burning material; a domestic heater (*electric fire*, early 20c) **2** destructive burning, a conflagration (ME) **3** to set light to (ME); to set light to gunpowder etc. (16c), hence **(a)** to shoot a gun; shooting (*heavy/friendly fire*); **fire away!** start shooting (guns, questions, etc., 18c: cf. SHOOT sense 1b) **(b)** to discharge a bullet or other missile; to launch something forcibly; to throw someone out (19c, US), hence to dismiss someone from a job **4** a burning passion or emotion (ME); to make or become excited **5** to treat using fire or heat (17c); to bake pottery **6** to use a fuel (*gas-fired central heating*, 18c).

firm [ME. Via French from Latin *firmus* 'stable, strong, immovable'; the verb via Latin *firmare*] Securely fixed, steady, stable, hence **1** settled, established; to establish, settle, or ratify (–19c), replaced by **confirm** [ME, also from *firmare*], re-emerging as **firm up** (1980s) **2** (to make or become) hard, solid, or compact **3** steadfast, resolute, determined **4** [from a later sense of *firmare* 'to confirm by signing'] a signature (16–18c), hence a group of people who set up a business (and sign the necessary documents, 18c), hence **(a)** the business **(b)** a group acting together.

Latin *firmare* produced FARM and **firmament** [Latin *firmamentum*, literally 'a support', used to translate Hebrew *rāqîʿa* 'the sky', then seen as a vault supporting the clouds and stars]. Latin *firmus* is the ancestor of AFFIRM, **furl** [via French *fer(m)lier* 'to bind firmly'], **infirm**, **infirmary**, and **infirmity**.

fish [Old English *fisc* (noun), *fiscian* (verb)] Any animal living entirely in water (surviving in *shellfish, jellyfish*, etc.); a cold-blooded vertebrate with gills and fins; to (try to) catch fish, hence **1** to try to get something by indirect means (*fishing for compliments*, 16c), hence **phishing** dishonestly trying to obtain someone's personal details via the internet (1990s) **2** to feel, dredge, or dive for something under water (17c); to search for or pull out (*fished around in her bag/fished out some money*); to (try to) remove an obstruction from the borehole of a well (*c*.1910); such an obstruction (1930s).

fistula [ME. Latin, 'tube, pipe, flute'] **1** an ancient Roman wind intrument **2** a long, pipelike ulcer (15c); an abnormal or artificial passage in the body.

Latin *fistula* produced **fester** an ulcer or (suppurating) sore [via Old French *festre*]; to ulcerate or suppurate, hence to rot; to rankle or become more bitter.

fit¹ [ME. Origin unknown] (To be) suitable or proper, hence **1** of the right size (–18c); to be or to make something the right size and shape (16c) **2** (to make) sufficiently good or worthy (16c) **3** (to make something) ready, hence **(a)** to equip (16c); to instal equipment (17c) **(b)** ready or liable to do something (*fit to drop*, 16c) **(c)** ready for physical activity, in good health (18c); sexually attractive (1990s) **4** to (cause to) conform or agree with (*fits in well/fits the facts,*16c); **fit up** to gather enough (false) evidence to convict someone (19c, *Australian*) **5** the surname **Fitt** a polite or pleasant person.

fit² [Old English *fitt*] Conflict, struggle (OE only); a painful, frightening, or exciting episode or experience (ME–17c), hence **1 (a)** an episode of a recurrent illness (16c) **(b)** a convulsion; to have one (1960s) **(c)** a sudden uncontrollable outbreak or outburst (*a coughing fit/fits of laughter*); a sudden strong emotional reaction (*don't tell Mum, she'll have a fit*, 19c, US) **2** a sudden, short spell of activity (16c); **in fits and starts** spasmodically; **fitful** irregular, spasmodic (19c).

fix [ME. Ultimately from Latin *figere, fix-* 'to fasten'] **1** to fasten securely, to make firm or stable, hence a position from which it is hard to escape, a predicament (19c) **2** to make hard or rigid (15c) **3** to establish, settle, or ascertain (16c), hence a calculation of position (1920s); an understanding or identification of something **4** to make permanent and unalterable (17c) **5** to make ready for use; to mend, correct, or alter (18c), hence an illegal dose of a narcotic drug (regarded as 'mending' the recipient, 1930s) **6** to organize something or make it happen (18c); to do so stealthily or fraudulently; an illicit arrangement, a swindle (1920s) **7** to deal with or punish someone (19c).

Latin *figere* is the ancestor of AFFIX*, Latin **fibula** 'brooch, clasp', adopted for the outer bone of the lower leg (because of the shape it makes with the tibia), French *fiche* 'a peg', later 'an index card (that 'pegs' a piece of information) or a slip of paper', whence **microfiche** (shortened to **fiche**), and **transfix**, and probably of **fish(plate)** a plate used to strengthen a rail etc.

flag [16c. Origin unknown: perhaps related to FAG²] Hanging down, drooping (–18c), hence **1** to hang; to flop about; to become limp; to droop or fade (17c); to become weak, especially through fatigue; to wane or decline **2** a (hanging) piece of cloth used as an emblem or signal, hence **(a)** to communicate by means of a flag or flags (19c); **flag (down)** to stop a vehicle or its driver by waving or signalling **(b)** something resembling a flag; a tag or badge (*c*.1910); to mark with one (1930s).

flagrant [15c. (Via French) from Latin *flagrare* 'to blaze' (ancestor of **conflagration**)] Blazing, burning, glowing, hence of an offence: glaring, scandalous, blatant (18c).

flail [Old English, ultimately from Latin *flagellum* 'whip', from *flagrum* 'scourge'] A wooden handle attached to a free-swinging bar, used for threshing; a weapon resembling this (15c); a whip or scourge, hence **1** to beat (as if) with a flail (15c) **2** to thrash about or swing something wildly (19c).

Latin **flagellum** produced **flagellate** and, probably, **flog**, and was adopted for a whiplike projection from a cell.

flame [ME. Via Old French from Latin *flamma*] A glowing body of burning gas; **the flames** (death or destruction by) fire; **flaming** fiery, burning hot (17c). Hence **1** a 'burning' emotion; to kindle (15–17c) or feel (16c) one (cf. *inflame* below), hence **(a)** to flare up with anger (16c); (to send) an abusive or threatening email (1980s) **(b)** **(old) flame** a (former) lover (17c) **2** to shine or glow like a flame; a bright beam of light; brilliance, brilliant colouring; the reddish-orange colour of a flame (18c).

Latin *flamma* fathered French **flambé** [literally 'singed'], adopted for a kind of porcelain or glaze fired in a particular way, later for food doused with spirit which is then set alight, *flambeau* a flaming torch, *flamboyant* 'blazing', adopted meaning brightly-coloured, showy, dashing, **flammable** liable to catch fire, and **inflame** to catch fire (hence **inflammable** likely to do so: largely replaced in official use by **flammable** because the *in* of *inflammable* could be taken to mean 'not'); to arouse a strong feeling (hence **inflammatory**); to make (especially a part of the body) hot (hence **inflammation**).

flap [ME. Probably imitative] **1** to slap; a slap (–18c) **2 (a)** to toss (now dialect), hence **flapjack** a pancake (17c); a flat cake made with oats and syrup (1930s) **(b)** to throw or fall down (17c) **3** to make something swing, or move up and down, vigorously; to do so (16c); something hinged or joined at one edge so that it can, hence **(a) flappy** able or apt to flap, loose, flaccid (16c), altered to **flabby** soft, sagging, weak (17c); having flabby flesh, overweight (18c), whence **flab** excess body fat (1950s) **(b)** a young girl (17c, said to be one who still wore her hair 'flapping', i.e. loose or in a pigtail: now only N English dialect), whence **flapper** a prostitute (19c); a frivolous young woman (*c*.1900, but associated with the 1920s) **(c)** the movement or sound of flapping (18c); to fuss, worry, or panic (19c); a panic or fuss; a military alert (*c*.1910).

The variant **flop** generally describes a softer or clumsier movement: it has come to mean to fail dismally, a failure, and has produced **flipflop** something that flaps or flops, now especially a kind of soft rubber sandal.

flare [16c. Origin unknown] To spread out and display, originally your hair, hence **1** to widen gradually (17c); a gradual widening out, the part that does so (*c*.1900); **flares** flared trousers (1960s, *US*) **2** to burn with spreading but unsteady flame (17c); a similar light (19c); a sudden burst of light or flame, hence **(a)** a device that produces one **(b)** a sudden outburst of emotion; **flare up** to suddenly become angry; to suddenly recur or intensify **(c)** to burn off waste gases in the open air; this flame.

flash [ME. Probably imitating the sound] To splash water about (–17c); of waves: to move quickly, to rise and break, hence, from the ideas of sudden, quick movement and light sparkling on water: **1** to move swiftly (15c); **flash dry/freeze** to do so rapidly (1940s) **2** to suddenly burst into flame (15c); (to make) a sudden, brief burst of fire or light (16c), hence **(a)** an instant (*in a flash*, 17c) **(b)** a coloured patch (*shoulder flash*, 19c); any bright patch or streak of colour (1970s) **3** to (make something) appear suddenly and briefly (16c); to expose the genitals deliberately in public **4 flashy** sparkling, brilliant (17c), hence (also *flash*) ostentatious, gaudy; ostentatiously clever or attractive; *flash* to display ostentatiously (18c) **5** a sudden rush of water; **flash flood** a sudden, brief, destructive flood (1940s).

flask [Old English *flasce*, *flaxe*, from medieval Latin *flasco*, of unknown origin] **1** a container for liquids (–ME) **2** a powder horn [16c, probably via French] **3** a narrow-necked glass or, later, metal container for liquids [17c, via Italian *fiasco* below].

Medieval Latin *flasco* produced Italian **fiasco** an utter failure [from *fare fiasco* 'to make a bottle', also 'to make a mistake, to fail' (said to be from anglers hooking straw-covered wine bottles instead of fish)] and **flagon** [via Old French *flacon*].

flat [ME. Old Norse *flatr*] Horizontal, level, even and smooth; without much depth, hence **1** a piece of flat land (*salt flats*); a flat part **2** featureless, dull (16c); without energy, 'fizz', or variation.

Flat 'an apartment' is an alteration of related Old English **flet** the floor or ground, also a dwelling (–15c); in Scots, a storey. **Flatter** [from Old French] may be ultimately from a related Germanic word meaning 'to smooth, stroke, or pat'.

flaunt [16c. Origin unknown] To show off; to display possessions or abilities provocatively or defiantly (19c). The idea of defiance probably led to *flaunt* being used since the 1920s in place of **flout** to treat (now usually a law) with contempt [16c, perhaps related to **flute**: the German phrase *pfeifen auf*, literally 'to pipe at', also meant 'to disdain']; this use is considered incorrect but is beginning to appear in dictionaries.

flavour [ME. Old French *flaor*, probably ultimately from a mixture of Latin *flatus* 'blowing, breath' (from *flare* 'to blow') and *foetor* 'stench' (from *fetere* 'to stink'). Cf. SAVOUR, which probably influenced the spelling] Fragrance, smell; to smell; to give scent or taste to (16c), hence the element in taste that partly depends on smell (17c); something's distinctive taste, hence **1** (a touch of) a unique characteristic (17c) **2** a substance added to food to give it a distinctive taste (19c).

Latin *flatus* produced **flatulent**; *flare* produced **conflate** originally to fuse metals [via Latin *conflare*, literally 'to blow together'], INFLATE*, and French *soufflé* [literally 'puffed up']; *fetere* produced **fetid**.

flaw [ME. Perhaps from Old Norse *flaga* 'slab'] The underlying sense is 'a detached piece': **1** a snowflake **2** a tongue of flame **3** a fragment or splinter; a crack (15c, perhaps earlier in **whitlow**, an alteration of *whiteflaw*); a defect; a failure or shortcoming (18c) **4** turf, a turf (18c); a season's harvest of peat (19c).

Old Norse *flaga* is the ancestor of **flag** a paving stone, also a turf (surviving in E Anglian dialect). Probably related to **flake**, which also formerly meant a spark or tongue of flame, a defect or blemish, or a sheet of ice (largely replaced by **floe**, also probably related).

fleet [Old English *flēotan*] To float (now dialect); to float or drift past or away (ME); to move (away) quickly (largely replaced by related FLIT, surviving mainly in 16c **fleeting**].

Old English *flēotan* produced *flēot* **fleet** a group of naval ships, later a number of people, birds, etc. moving together (ME–17c), surviving in dialect and revived for vehicles, boats, or aircraft travelling together or with the same owner (19c). Related to **flee**, **fleet** a creek, inlet, or stream, surviving in place names, **flight**, FLOAT*, **flood**, **flow**, **flutter**, FLY, *fowl* (at BIRD), and perhaps **fluster** to make slightly drunk, hence to confuse or agitate.

flexible [ME. (Via French from) Latin *flexibilis*, from *flectere, flex-* 'to bend'] Pliable; adaptable, variable, hence **1** **flex** flexible insulated cable (*c.*1900) **2** **flexitime** variable working hours (1970s).

Latin *flectere* is the ancestor of **deflect**, **flex** to (make something) bend, to (be able to) bend or contract, *genuflect* (at GENUINE), INFLECT, and REFLECT*.

flip [16c, probably a contraction of Middle English **fillip** to flick your fingertip against your thumb, this movement: imitating the sound] **1** a hot drink of beer and spirits (probably from the idea of whipping something up), now one of spirits or wine beaten with egg and sugar **2** (to make) a sudden movement (19c);

a somersault **3** (to take) a short flight in an aircraft (*c*.1915) **4 flip (your lid)** to become very excited or angry (1950s, *US*).

Flip produced **flippant** nimble, also talkative, fluent, hence playful, not serious, treating serious matters lightly: *flip* later followed the same path.

flirt [16c. Probably suggested by the action: words beginning with *fl* often refer to something quick or sudden] **1** (to give someone) a smart tap or blow; to move something quickly; to spread a fan etc. quickly **2** (to make) a sharp 'dig' or jest; a young girl likely to do so, hence someone who behaves in a playfully amorous way; to do so (17c); to toy briefly with an idea etc. (19c).

flit [ME. Old Norse *flytja*] To move or take away (now Scots or dialect); to move quickly or lightly, hence **1** flitter (to make) restless, fluttering movements; to move restlessly from place to place, shortened to *flit* (16c) **2** to move house, especially to avoid creditors (16c); such a move (19c).

Related to **fleet** swift [Old Norse *fljótr*] and, more distantly, to FLEET*.

float [Old English *flotian*, later also from related Old French *floter*: the noun partly from Old English and Old Norse *flot* 'a floating state', partly from Old Enigsh *flota*, Old Norse *floti* 'ship, fleet'] **(On) float** the state of moving or resting on the surface of liquid (–18c, replaced by **afloat**); to do so, hence **1** to move or drift along on the surface (ME) or through the air (17c); to move unsteadily like a floating object (16c); to waver or fluctuate (*floating voter*); to move casually from place to place (*c*.1900, *US slang*); of a currency: to find its own level according to market forces (1960s) **2** something that floats: **(a)** a buoyant object used to stop something (ME) or someone (19c) sinking **(b)** a raft or flat-bottomed boat (ME); a flat-bodied vehicle (*milk float*, 19c); a decorated one in a carnival procession **(c)** a device that floats on the surface of a liquid and regulates its level (18c) **(d)** a soft drink with ice cream floating in it (*c*.1915) **3** to make something float (18c); to 'launch' a company, shares on the stock market, etc. (19c), hence **(a)** to put forward an idea **(b)** a supply of change at the start of business (*c*.1900).

Old French *floter* produced **flotsam** wreckage and cargo found floating. Old Norse *floti* produced Spanish **flotilla**, literally 'a small fleet'. Related to FLEET*.

flora [16c. Latin *flos, flor-*: see FLOWER*] The name of an ancient Italian goddess of fertility and flowers, hence nature's power to produce flowers, the plants of a particular time, region, or habitat (18c). Hence **floral** [Latin *Floralis*] to do with the goddess Flora (17c), with flowers (18c), or with a region's flora (19c).

Another Italian goddess, **Fauna**, later gave her name to the animals of a particular time etc.; her brother Faunus, often identified with the Greek god Pan, gave his name to **faun**, a similar Roman god.

floss [18c. French *soie floche* 'floss silk', from Old French *flosche* 'down, nap of velvet', perhaps from Latin *floccus*] The silk surrounding a silkworm's cocoon, hence **1 floss (silk)** rough silk broken off when winding a cocoon, later untwisted silk embroidery thread, hence **(dental) floss** (*c*.1910), *floss* to use it (1970s) **2** the silky fibres around some seeds **3** a downy or fluffy surface; fluff, a fluffy mass; **candy floss** a mass of spun sugar (1950s); something attractive but frivolous or worthless. Hence **flossy** made of or like floss (19c); fancy, showy, flashy, also cheeky, saucy (*N American*), whence perhaps **floozie** a flashy, disreputable woman (*c*.1900, *US*).

Latin *floccus* produced **flock** a tuft or particle of wool or cotton (*flock mattress/ wallpaper*).

flourish [ME. Latin *florere* 'to flower', from *flos*: see FLOWER*] To grow, thrive, flower, or succeed, hence **1** to adorn (originally with flowers), embellish, or decorate (–17c); (an) embellishment (16c); a fanfare; an ostentatious gesture (17c) **2** to be at the peak of your powers at a particular time (16c, cf. FLOWER).

Florence in Italy takes its name from Latin *Colonia Florentia* 'flowering' or 'flourishing colony': Florence Nightingale (so named because she was born there) made *Florence* a popular name for girls.

flower [ME. Old French *flo(u)r* from Latin *flos, flor-*. The original spelling, *flour*, had died out by the 17c except in sense 2] The (colourful) part of a plant containing the reproductive organs; a plant grown for its flowers; to blossom; **flowered** or **flowery** decorated with (a pattern of) flowers. Hence **1** a precious possession (originally a woman's virginity) **2** the finest example or part, hence the finest quality of meal, surviving as **flour** finely ground (wheat) grain **3 flowers** fine words or phrases, hence *flowery* full of ornate or elaborate expressions **4** to grow or thrive; to be at or attain the height of excellence (cf. FLOURISH).

Descendants of Latin *flos* include French **fleur** 'flower', which became popular as a girl's name after being used in John Galsworthy's *Forsyte Saga*, FLORA, *floret*, **florid**, **Florida** the American state [from Spanish *florida* 'flowering', probably in *Pascua florida*, literally 'flowering Easter', the Spanish term for Palm Sunday, the day on which the peninsula was discovered in 1513], **florist**, and FLOURISH*.

fluent [16c. Latin *fluere* 'to flow'] **1** flowing freely, smoothly, or abundantly (now only of speech or language; otherwise replaced by *fluid*); of movement: easy, graceful (19c) **2** able to speak with ease, especially in a foreign language.

Latin *fluere* is the ancestor of AFFLUENCE*, **confluence**, **fluctuate**, **flue**, **fluid**, **flume**, FLUOR*, **flush** a run of cards of one suit, **fluvial**, **flux**, INFLUENCE*, *mellifluent* and *mellifluous* (at TREACLE), **reflux**, and **superfluous** [Latin *superfluere* 'to overflow'].

fluor [17c. Latin, from *fluere*: see FLUENT] A flow, stream, or discharge (17c only); a fluid state or mass (–18c); any mineral more fusible and softer than a gem (17c); one used as a flux or containing fluorine (18c).

Latin or English *fluor* produced **fluorine** and its compound **fluoride** (whence **fluoridate**), and **fluorspar** calcium fluoride, whence **fluorescence** light or other radiation emitted by some substances, including fluorspar.

flush [ME. Probably suggested by the action (cf. FLIRT)] To move quickly, hence **1** to spring or fly up suddenly; to make a game bird etc. do so (15c); to drive or bring out into the open (1950s) **2** to (cause to) rush or spurt out (16c), hence **(a)** of blood: to rush to the face (16c, perhaps influenced by *blush*); to blush; to (cause to) glow with colour, light, or emotion (*flushed with success*, 17c); such a glow **(b)** a sudden rush of water (16c); to clean or dispose of something with one (18c); a device for doing so (19c) **3** (probably from sense 2, with the idea of a stream level with its banks): **(a)** having plenty, especially of money (16c); full to overflowing (17c) **(b)** even, level, in the same plane; not sticking out or indented.

fly [Old English *flēogan*: related to **fly** a winged insect (Old English *flēoge*)*] To move through the air using wings, an engine, etc.; to make something fly (16c);

to pilot or travel in an aircraft (early 20c). Hence **1** to move or travel quickly, hence **(a)** (by confusion with *flee*) to run away; to leave hurriedly (ME), hence, perhaps, surreptitious (*fly tipping/posting*, *c*.1900) **(b)** a stagecoach (18c); a light carriage (19c) **2** of a hawk: to attack (ME); to rush at violently (16c) **3** a speed-regulating device (16c), hence **flywheel** (18c) **4** of a flag etc.: to wave or flutter (17c); to raise or display a flag; something attached at one side like a flag, e.g. the flap covering a fastening or at the entrance of a tent **5** to go or leap over (18c), hence **(a)** the roof of a tent (19c); **flysheet** a protective covering over a tent **(b) flies** the space above the front of a stage (19c).

focus [17c. Latin 'domestic hearth'] The underlying sense is 'place where things come together', like a family round the hearth: **1** the place where rays of light etc. converge after reflection or refraction (17c); to make them converge (18c); to adjust a lens to do so (19c) **2** the primary site in the body of a disease or infection (17c) **3** the centre of attention or activity (18c) **4** to concentrate or be concentrated on (19c) **5 focus group** of people thought to be representative of (a section of) society, brought together to give their opinions (1980s).

Latin *focus* produced French *foyer* 'hearth, home, focus', adopted for a centre of activity or attention, later a place in a theatre where the audience gathers, hence the entrance hall of any public building, and French *fusil* a flint in a tinderbox, later a kind of flintlock musket, whence *fusilier* a soldier armed with one, and *fusillade* (to shoot down with) a concentrated or sustained burst of gunfire.

foible [16c. French, from Old French *f(i)eble* (whence **feeble**), from Latin *flebilis* 'lamentable', from *flere* 'to weep'] Physically or, later, mentally weak (–18c), hence a slight weakness of character, a quirk (17c).

foil[1] [ME. Old French *fouler* 'to trample', ultimately from Latin *fullo* 'fuller'] To trample, hence **1** to tread ground to destroy a trail or scent, hence (to bring about) a setback or defeat (15c) **2** (influenced by *foul*) to soil or pollute; to violate someone's chastity (replaced by *defoul, defile* below).

Old French *fouler* produced **defoul** to oppress (ME–17c), later to debauch, corrupt, desecrate, or pollute, altered to **defile** by association with obsolete **befile** 'to soil' [Old English *fȳlan*: related to **filth** and **foul**]. Latin *fullo* produced **fuller** someone who cleans and thickens cloth (also as a surname), originally by treading or beating it in water (cf. *Walker* at WALK), whence **full** to do so.

foil[2] [ME. Via Old French from Latin *folium* 'leaf'] **1** the leaf of a plant (–16c), surviving in plant names (*cinquefoil, trefoil*), and architectural ornaments based on them **2** metal as a thin flexible sheet; the metal coating of a mirror; a leaf of metal put under a gemstone to increase its brilliance (16c); something/someone that sets off another **3** part of a document detached and kept as a record (15c, replaced by its descendant, **counterfoil**, 18c) **4** see *aerofoil, hydrofoil* (at PLANE).

Latin *folium* is the ancestor of **defoliate, exfoliate, foliage** originally a design or decoration based on leaves, **folic acid** (found in leafy green vegetables), and FOLIO*.

foist [16c. Dutch dialect *vuisten* 'to take in the hand', from *vuist* 'fist': related to **finger, fist**, and **five**] To palm a dice to produce it at the 'right' moment (16c only), hence to introduce something surreptitiously; to palm off something worthless; to impose someone or something unwanted.

folio [ME. Latin, from *folium* 'leaf', in medieval Latin used in references to mean 'on leaf so-and-so'] **1** a numbered sheet of paper etc., either loose or in a bound volume; the page number in a printed book (17c) **2 in folio** [via Italian *in foglio*] in the form of a full-size sheet folded once (16c), whence *folio* the largest size of book, in which each page is half a standard sheet.

Latin *folio* produced FOIL²* and **portfolio** [Italian *portafogli*, from *portare* 'to carry' (from Latin: see see PORT³*) + *fogli* 'sheets of paper'] a case for loose papers; (one containing) samples of someone's creative work or the official documents of a State department, hence a minister's responsibilities; the range or a list of some-one's investments.

folly [ME. French *folie* 'madness', from *fol* 'mad, foolish', from Latin *follis* 'bel-lows, windbag, empty-headed person'] Foolishness; a foolish act or idea; an expensive, ornate but useless building (16c, from the idea of a foolish undertak-ing, but probably influenced by a later sense of French *folie* 'delight, a favourite dwelling'; until the 19c *folly* was occasionally used to name a pleasant place). The idea of something delightful and frivolous probably lies behind **The Follies**, a show featuring glamorous girls (*c*.1900, US).

Old French *fol* produced **fool** a halfwit; a clown; probably also the dessert, originally a kind of trifle made with clotted cream. Latin *follis* produced *folliculus* 'little bag', whence **follicle**.

force [ME. French, ultimately from Latin *fortis* 'strong', of music: 'loud'] Physical strength or energy, hence **1** this exerted to achieve a result; compulsion, coer-cion, to compel by physical or other means **2** a country's military strength, hence its troops, ships, etc. (*Armed Forces*); an organized body of workers (*workforce*, 19c); the police **3** power other than physical (*the force of law*) **4** in physics: an agency or influence that produces (a change of) motion (17c); its strength or intensity.

Descendants of Latin *fortis* include COMFORT, **effort**, **enforce**, **fort**, French *forte* someone's strong point, Italian *forte* and *fortissimo* directions to play music (very) loud (see also *panforte* at COMPANION, *pianoforte* at PLAIN), **fortify**, **fortitude**, *Fortnum* (at DONKEY), **fortress**, **reinforce**, and probably **forge (ahead)**.

foreclose [ME. French *forclore*, from *for-* 'out' (from Latin *foris*: see FOREST*) + *clore* (see CLOSE*)] **1** to stop someone escaping or leaving (ME only); to prevent some-one doing something; to take away their right to redeem a mortgage (18c) **2** to exclude or debar.

forest [ME. Via Old French from Latin *forestis silva*, literally 'woodland outside', from *foris* 'outside', from *fores* 'door'] A large tract of woodland and scrub reserved for hunting, usually owned by the monarch, and with its own officers and laws; a similar tract of land, sometimes mixed with pasture, now usually a large, dense wood or the trees in it (17c); a dense mass or large number of upright objects.

Latin *fores* is the ancestor of **foreign** and FORFEIT, the surname **Forrest(er)** and some instances of **Forster** and **Foster**. Related to FORUM*.

forfeit [ME. Old French *forfet*, *forfait*, from *forfaire* 'to transgress', from *for-* 'out' (from Latin *foris*: see FOREST*) + *faire* 'to do' (from Latin *facere*: ancestor of FACT*)] (To commit) a crime or offence (–19c); to lose the right to something as a penalty;

to surrender something, or the thing surrendered, as a penalty, now usually in a game.

forlorn [Old English, from *forleosan* 'to lose completely', from *leosan* 'to lose'] **1** morally 'lost', depraved (–17c) **2** deprived of something/someone (ME); abandoned, desolate, lonely and miserable (16c).

Old English *leosan* produced **lorn** lost, ruined, doomed; abandoned, bereft, surviving mainly in **lovelorn**. Related to, and influencing, **forlorn hope** [an alteration of Dutch *verloren hoop*, literally 'lost troop'] a band of soldiers picked to launch an attack and not expected to survive, hence a desperate or futile hope or attempt, and to LOSE*.

form [ME. French *forme* from, ultimately, Latin *forma*: the verb via Latin *formare*] The shape or configuration of something, hence **1** to make or shape: **(a)** a mould, block, etc. used to do so **(b)** to shape someone's character etc. **(c)** to create and develop an idea, alliance, etc. (18c) **2** to make up, to be part of **3** the way in which something is made (–17c); a particular shape or mode (*in liquid form, a form of carbon*) **4** a prescribed way of doing things, hence **(a)** behaviour according to set rules; (mere) ritual; **good/bad form** good/bad behaviour or manners **(b)** a set order of words (partly replaced by FORMULA); a document with blanks to be filled in (19c) **(c)** to arrange in a set order; to get into order (*form fours*, 18c), hence **formation** an arrangement of troops, ships, etc. (18c), whence **formate** to get into or move in formation (1920s) **(d)** a long, backless seat (probably from the idea of sitting in a set row) **(e)** a rank or degree (15–18c), hence a class of schoolchildren of similar age or ability (16c) **5** the physical condition of a racehorse, athlete, etc. (18c, hence **in (good) form** in good shape, performing well); *form* a record of past performances, hence a criminal's record (1950s) **6** shape or structure, as opposed to content, in art (19c).

French *forme* produced *platform* (at PLATE*). Latin *formare* produced **conform**, FORMAT, INFORM*, **reform** re-establish, rebuild, or repair (ME–17c), hence to remake in a better form, and **transform**. Latin *forma* is the ancestor of **formal** [via Latin *formalis* 'according to form'], FORMULA*, and **uniform** [with Latin *unus* 'one' (whence UNIT*)] having or keeping the same form, appearance, or character, hence identical clothing worn by the armed forces, schoolchildren, etc.

format [19c. Via French and German from Latin *formatus liber*, literally 'shaped book', from *formare* (see FORM*) + *liber* 'book' (ancestor of LIBEL*)] The physical characteristics, such as shape and size, of a book or other object; the way something is arranged or done (1950s), specifically the handling of data in a computer; to put into a format (1960s).

formula [17c. Latin, literally 'little form', from *forma*: see FORM*] A prescribed or customary way of saying, writing, or doing something, hence **1** a prescription or recipe (18c); baby food made according to one **2** a general rule or principle (18c), or the ingredients of a chemical (19c), expressed in symbols; these symbols **3** a category of racing car, usually expressed in terms of engine size or technical specifications (*Formula One*, 1920s).

Formula produced **formulaic** expressed (as if) in a formula, unoriginal, and **formulate** to express in a formula or in carefully chosen words, hence to draw up something in detail. Latin *formula* produced medieval Latin *formularius liber* 'book of formulae', whence **formulary** a collection of set forms of ritual or, later, of the details of drugs.

forsake [Old English *forsacan*, from *sacan* 'to quarrel, to accuse': related to SAKE*] To decline or refuse (–17c); to give up something valued; to deny or renounce allegiance to God, your lord, etc. (ME), hence to abandon, withdraw from, or desert.

forth [Old English] **1** forward, onwards, surviving in **back and forth 2** forward, into view, now only with certain verbs (*bring/come/put/show forth*), formerly with a wider selection where *out* has largely replaced it (*lay/set/stand/stretch forth*) **3** away or out from a place **4** onwards from a point in time (*from this day forth*).

Forth produced AFFORD and **forward**, and is found in **forthcoming**, **forthright**, and **forthwith**, originally 'along with, at the same time'. Related to **before**, **first**, **fore-** (*forehand, foresee*), **former**, and **further**.

fortune [ME. French, from Latin *Fortuna*, a goddess personifying luck or chance, from *fors* 'chance, luck'] (The personification of) luck or chance as it affects your life, hence **1** your luck or fate (*tell your fortune*) **2** good luck, prosperity (16c, earlier in **fortunate** and **unfortunate**); a large amount of money.

Latin *fors* produced **fortuitous** (happening) by chance, accidental, now often used to mean 'lucky', probably by association with *fortunate*. **Luck** [probably from early Dutch *geluc* 'happiness, good fortune'] usually means good fortune, though it can mean simply chance. An **accident** [Old French, from Latin *accidere* 'to happen', from *cadere* 'to fall' (ancestor of CASE[1]*)] was originally just an event, now only an unplanned, usually unfortunate one, the neutral sense surviving in **by accident**.

forum [ME. Latin, literally 'what is out of doors'] The marketplace or public square in a Roman city, where business was conducted and the law courts were situated, hence a court or tribunal (17c); a meeting for discussion (18c, now also on the internet); a periodical etc. in which people may express opinions.

Forensic [from Latin *forensis* 'to do with the forum'] literally means 'to do with or used in a court of law', hence **forensic science** used in the detection of crime; **forensic evidence** scientific evidence of crime; **forensics** the gathering of forensic evidence; a department that does so. Related to FOREST*.

fossil [16c. French *fossile*, from Latin *fossilis* 'dug up', from *foder* 'to dig'] **1** a fossilized fish found, hence believed to have lived, underground (16c only) **2** found buried in the earth (17c); a rock, mineral, etc. dug out of the earth (17–19c), hence (combining 1 and 2) a trace of a life form preserved in the earth's strata (18c); (someone/something) belonging to the past and incapable of further development (19c); **fossil fuel** formed in the earth from prehistoric plant life.

Latin *foder* produced *fossa* 'a ditch', which produced **fosse** a canal, ditch, or moat (earliest in **Fosse Way**, a Roman road between Axminster and Lincoln, having a ditch on one, or sometimes each, side), and was later adopted as a medical term for a shallow depression or cavity in the body.

foster [Old English: related to **feed**, **fodder**, and **food**, and [via Old French] to **forage** and **foray**] Food (–17c); to feed or nourish, hence **foster father/mother/child** etc., regarded as family because they feed others, or are fed, in the household, sometimes by nursing or being nursed (until about the 17c *foster mother* also meant a wet nurse, her husband being the child's foster father and other children she nursed being foster brothers and sisters). Hence to nurse or bring up a child (ME, now only someone else's on a temporary basis); to cherish, protect, or encourage the development of something.

found [ME. Via French from Latin *fundare*, from *fundus* 'bottom, base', also 'a piece of land'] To lay the base of a building; to create or establish something new; to base something on firm grounds (*founded on fact*). Hence **foundation** the founding or the basis of something: **1** an endowment for maintaining an institution (cf. *fund* below); such an institution (*foundation school*, 16c); an organization funding the arts, research, etc. (*c*.1900, *US*) **2 foundations** the part of a building below ground level that supports the rest (15c); **foundation stone** one forming part of the foundations (17c), now a commemorative one laid above ground **3** (describing) a base layer (*foundation garment*, 19c).

Latin *fundus* produced **founder** [via Old French *(es)fondrer* 'to sink, submerge, or collapse', literally 'to go to the bottom'], **fund** a foundation or basis (17–18c), hence to finance something; the money to do so, FUNDAMENT, **profound**, and **profundity**.

fountain [ME. Via French from Latin *fontanus* 'of a spring', from *fons* 'a spring'] **1** a natural spring, hence the principal source of a stream, information, etc. (15c, since the 16c also as **fountainhead** and **fount**, probably a back-formation) **2** an artificial water feature with a jet or jets of water (16c), hence **drinking fountain** (19c); **soda fountain** originally a container for soda water with a pipe for drawing it off (19c, US) **3** a small reservoir for liquid (18c); **fountain pen** containing one.

Latin *fons* produced ecclesiastical Latin *fontes baptismi* 'baptismal waters', whence **font**. Related to Old English *funta* 'spring', which appears as **Font-** or **-font** in place names.

fraction [ME. French, from ecclesiastical Latin *fractio* 'breaking (bread)', from Latin *frangere, fract-* 'to break'] **1** the breaking of bread in the Eucharist; the action of breaking or disrupting (16c) **2** the state of being broken; a fracture or fissure (–18c); disruption of harmony or peace (16–18c, whence **fractious** peevish, quarrelsome, 17c) **3** a number that is not a whole number; a small proportion or piece.

Latin *frangere* is the ancestor of *chamfer* (at CANTEEN), **defray** [French *defrayer*, from *frais* 'expenses, damages caused by breakage', from Latin *fractum* 'breakage'], **diffract**, **fracture**, FRAGILE*, FRAGMENT*, **frangible**, **infraction**, **infringe**, REFRACTION*, and **saxifrage** [Latin *saxifraga* 'rock-breaking', because it often grows in cracks]. Related to SUFFRAGE.

fragile [ME. (Via French from) Latin *fragilis*, from *frangere*: see FRACTION*] **1** morally weak, apt to sin (–17c) **2** easily broken or damaged (16c) **3** physically weak, delicate (19c).

Latin *fragilis* fathered French *fraile*, whence **frail**, which shares all three senses.

fragment [ME. (Via French from) Latin *fragmentum*, from *frangere*: see FRACTION*] A broken-off or detached piece; a small portion; a piece left when the whole is lost or destroyed (16c); part of something not completed. Hence **1** to break into fragments (19c), whence **defrag** to consolidate computer files to optimise storage space (1970s) **2 fragmentation bomb/grenade** one designed to break into small fragments on impact (World War I), whence **frag** to kill with one (1970s, US slang).

fragrance   [17c. (Via French from) Latin *fragrantia*, from *fragrare* 'to smell sweet'] Sweetness of smell (17c, earlier in **fragrant**); a pleasant smell, hence **1** a perfume or cologne (19c) **2** to give something a pleasant smell (19c, rare until *c.*1990, when it was adopted by advertisers).

Latin *fragrare* is the ultimate ancestor of French *flair* 'the sense of smell', also 'intuition' (from the idea of sniffing something out), adopted meaning 'natural discernment or perception of quality', hence a natural sense of style; a natural talent.

frame   [Old English *framian*, from *fram* 'forward' (whence **from**): related to FUR-NISH*] To be useful (–ME); to prepare something, later specifically timber, for use (ME–15c); to make and fit the wooden parts of a building, hence **1** the wooden skeleton of a building (hence **framework**, 16c); a supporting structure (16c); something that encloses, supports, or shows off (*window/picture frame*); to do so (*hair framing her face*, 18c); to set in a frame **2** any structure made of parts fitted together (ME–18c); structure or constitution (*her slight frame*, 16c); **frame of mind** your mental or emotional state **3** to make, devise, or invent (ME); a contrivance or plan (16c); a conspiracy or plot, especially to incriminate someone (*c.*1900, also as **frame-up**, *US slang*); to do so (1920s) **4** to shape something (15–18c), hence **(a)** to 'shape' or set your mind etc. to do something (16c) **(b)** to express something in a particular way (17c).

franchise   [ME. French, from *franc(he)*: see FRANK*] Freedom (–17c), to set free (largely replaced by 15c **enfranchise**), hence **1** freedom from prosecution **2** a right or privilege, hence **(a)** citizenship (15c); the right to vote (18c) **(b)** powers granted to a company set up for the public interest (19c, *US*); authorization to sell a company's products or services (1950s); to grant this (1960s).

frank   [ME. Old French *franc(he)*, from medieval Latin *francus* 'free', *Francus* 'a Frank' (because only Franks in Gaul had full political freedom), of Germanic origin] Free, not enslaved or captive (–17c); free from obligation or restriction, hence **1** liberal, generous; producing abundant or good quality flowers or fruit (15–17c), hence of high-quality, surviving in **frankincense** [Old French *franc encens* 'high-quality incense'] **2** sincere, candid, outspoken (16c); open, undisguised (18c) **3** (to put) a signature on a letter showing that it is to be sent free of charge (18c); (to put) a mark on a letter recording prepayment of postage (1920s); (to put) a mark on a postage stamp to show that it has been used (1930s).

Old French *franc(he)* produced FRANCHISE* and the surname **Francombe** [Anglo-Norman French *franchomme* 'free man']. Latin *francus* is the ancestor of the (former) French, Belgian, and Swiss unit of currency, the *franc*, originally a gold coin used in medieval France bearing the legend *Francorum rex* 'king of the Franks', and of the names **Francis** and **Franklin** a freeman or freeholder. Related to **France, Frankfurt**, literally 'ford of the Franks', and **French**.

fraught [ME. Early Dutch *vracht*] **1** to hire, or the hiring of, a ship or, later, a vehicle for carrying cargo; the cargo; to load or carry it (15c): replaced in these senses by **freight** [15c, from *vrecht*, a variant of *vracht*] **2** to supply or equip, hence provided or equipped with; full of, likely or designed to produce (*fraught with danger*, 16c); causing distress (1960s); distressed, tense, anxious.

fray [ME. French *frayer*, ultimately from Latin *fricare* 'to rub'] **1** of a deer: to rub the velvet off its antlers **2** to wear or be worn ragged by rubbing, hence **(a)** to unravel the edge of something to make a fringe (19c) **(b)** to wear the nerves (early 20c); to become strained (*tempers started to fray*).

Fray is probably one parent of FRAZZLE. Latin *fricare* is the ancestor of **dentifrice** and **friction**.

frazzle [19c. Probably partly from FRAY*: *East Anglian dialect*, re-imported into British English from the US] To fray or wear something out, later to burn or char, hence a worn out or burnt state or thing (*worn/burnt to a frazzle*).

freak [16c. Origin unknown] An impulse or whim; a prank (18c), hence **freak (of nature)** one of nature's pranks, (describing) something/someone abnormal (*freak weather conditions*, 19c), hence **1** an unconventional person; a hippy (1960s); a drug addict; someone obsessed (*fitness/control freak*) **2 freak (out)** to have or cause intense emotions, hallucinations, etc. (1970s).

free [Old English *frēo*] Not a captive, slave, or serf, not ruled by another, hence **1** to liberate, to release **2** able to move or act without restriction, hence **(a)** not attached or combined **(b)** spontaneous, open, plain-spoken (17c) **3** exempt from a rule, penalty, or payment, hence (given) without payment or obligation (ME) **4 free of/from** to rid of something undesirable, hence without it (*free from care/carefree*, ME).

Free produced the surnames **Freebody**, **Freeman**, and some instances of **Fry**, also **Freedman** a former slave. Old English *frēo* produced **freedom**. Related to **friend** [Old English *frēond*] someone not bound by social obligation or sexual love, only by affection.

frenzy [ME. Via French from medieval Latin *phrenesia*, from Latin *phrenesis*, from Greek *phrēn* 'the mind'. The alternative spelling *phrensy* died out in the 20c] (Temporary) insanity; uncontrollable rage; a state of wild excitement, enthusiasm, or agitation (16c); a sudden burst of activity.

Greek *phrēn* is the ultimate ancestor of **frantic** and **frenetic**, both originally meaning insane [via French and Latin from Greek *phrenitis* 'delirium': both formerly spelt *phr-*], and is one parent of **schizophrenia** [with Greek *skhizein* 'to split', whence **schism**, **schist** an easily split rock consisting of layers of different materials, and **schistosome** (with Greek *sōma* 'body') the blood fluke, whose segmented body is easily broken].

fresh [Old English *fersc*] Not salt, fit for drinking; of food: not salted, preserved, or processed, hence [partly from related Old French *freis, fresche* 'new'] **1** new, as new: **(a)** not stale, worn out, or spoiled by time (*fresh in your memory*) **(b)** recently made or done (*fresh bread/freshly baked pies*) **(c)** new and different or additional (*a fresh start, fresh evidence*) **(d)** newly arrived (*fresh from Paris*), hence **freshman** a newcomer or novice (16c); a first-year student (now usually **fresher**) **(e)** of the wind: rising again after dying down (16–18c); brisk, strong **2** to make fresh, to renew or strengthen (ME), largely replaced by 15c **refresh** and 17c **freshen 3** a pool or stream of fresh water, or a rush of water, a flash flood (16c, largely replaced by **freshet** [probably from Old French *freschette*, from *fresche*] **4** [perhaps influenced by German *frech* 'impudent'] cheeky, overfamiliar (19c, *US*); **get fresh** to make (unwanted) sexual advances (1920s).

Probably related to Italian *fresco* 'cool, fresh', adopted for a (method of) painting on wet plaster, originally as *in fresco* 'in the fresh (plaster)', a translation of Italian *al fresco,* itself adopted as one word to mean 'in the fresh air', and to FRISK.

fret   [Old English *fretan*: related to **eat** and **etch**. Cf. CORRODE*] To devour (–16c); to gnaw away (ME); to destroy gradually by corrosion, disease, friction, etc.; to (cause to) chafe or rub; to irritate, annoy, or worry; to distress yourself, to worry or brood (16c).

fringe   [ME. Old French, ultimately from Latin *fimbria* 'fibre, thread, fringe'] An ornamental edging of loose threads or tassels, hence **1** something resembling this: an edging of hairs or fibres on an animal or plant (17c); hair worn hanging over the forehead (19c) **2** an edge or margin (16c); on the side, not mainstream or conventional (*fringe benefit/theatre/medicine*); a peripheral or unconventional group (*lunatic fringe, c.*1910).

frippery   [16c. French *friperie* from Old French *freperi*, from *frepe* 'rag', of unknown origin] (A shop selling) second-hand clothes (–19c), hence cheap finery (17c); (something) of little value or importance; ostentation, mere show (18c).

frisk   [ME. Old French *frisque*: probably related to FRESH*] Lively, spirited, playful (–19c); (to give) a playful leap (16c); to skip or dance, hence to move briskly (17c); to search someone by running your hands quickly over them (18c, *slang*).

fritter   [18c. From US *flitter* 'fragment, rag' (17–19c), ultimately from Middle English *fitter* 'to break into pieces'] To spend or get rid of a little at a time; to waste time, money, or energy on unimportant matters.

frock   [ME. French *froc*, of Germanic origin] **1** a monk's or priest's long gown; the status of a priest, hence to invest as a clergyman (16c); **defrock** (16c) or **unfrock** (17c) to strip one of his office **2** a man's long coat or tunic; **frock coat** a man's long-skirted coat (19c) **3** a garment with a skirt worn by children of both sexes (16c), now by a woman or girl, a dress; a theatrical costume **4** see *smock* (at SHIFT).

front   [ME. French, from Latin *frons, front-*] **1** the forehead; the face; this expressing emotion, hence demeanour, especially confidence; impudence (17c, co-existing with **effrontery**, also from Latin *frons*) **2** the foremost part, originally of an army etc.; the part of a battleground nearest the enemy or where fighting is taking place, hence **(a)** an area of activity thought to resemble this (*home/economic front,* World War I); a political group (*National Front*) **(b)** an interface between air masses of different temperatures etc. (*c.*1920) **3** the face of a building; the part of a book, etc. that you naturally reach first, hence **(a)** land facing a road, river, etc. (18c, earlier as **frontage**); a seaside promenade **(b)** a person or organization serving as a cover for illict activities (*c.*1900); to act as one (1930s, *US*) **4** to face boldly (16c, co-existing with **confront**, also ultimately from Latin *frons*) **5** a forward or leading position (*to/at the front*, 17c).

Descendants of Latin *frons* include **affront** [via Old French from Latin *ad frontem* 'to the face'], **frontier**, and **frontispiece** [Latin *frontispicium* 'facade' (the earliest English sense)].

fruition [ME. French, from Latin *frui*, *fruct-* 'to enjoy, to have the use of'] **1** the pleasure of possessing something (–19c) **2** (by association with *fruit* below) the bearing of fruit (19c); a successful outcome.

Latin *frui* produced **fructify** to bear fruit, **fructose** a fruit sugar, and **fruit** originally produce in general. Related to Latin *fruges* 'produce, fruit', whence **frugal** and **frugivorous** fruit-eating.

fuck [16c, but probably much older: a Middle English poem contains the pseudo-Latin *fuccant* 'they fuck'. Always offensive, and omitted from dictionaries until well into the 20c. Origin unknown] To have sex (with); the sexual act (17c); a woman considered in sexual terms (19c).

By the 20c (perhaps much earlier) *fuck* was being used as a stronger substitute for *damn*, and **fucking** for *bloody*. It has many euphemisms, including **(sweet) Fanny Adams** (for **fuck all** nothing at all), poor Fanny being a murder victim whose name had become sailors' slang for tinned meat, and possibly **muck about**. *Fuck* is still offensive but now ubiquitous and virtually meaningless, leading to a 'need' for stronger words, whence **motherfucker** and **motherfucking** (both *US*), with euphemistic **mother-loving**.

fudge [17c. Probably an alteration of 16c **fadge** 'to fit, to be consistent', of unknown origin] To fit in, to turn out as expected, also to mix up, to merge, hence **1** to fit things together clumsily; to cobble facts etc. together so as to be superficially convincing; a made-up story (18c); to gloss over discrepancies or inconvenient facts (1980s); a makeshift or dishonest solution **2** a sweet made of milk, sugar, and butter beaten together and boiled (19c).

fume [ME. Via French from Latin *fumare* 'to smoke', from *fumus* 'smoke'] Smoke, hence **1** fragrant or odorous smoke; a smell **2** a (harmful or irritant) vapour or gas, hence **in a fume** irritable, angry; *fume* to be so (16c) **3** to expose something to fumes; to perfume or fumigate **4** to emit fumes (16c).

Latin *fumare* fathered Italian *parfumare* 'to fill with (the smell of) smoke', whence **perfume**. Latin *fumus* produced **fumigate** to perfume; to rid of pests or germs using fumes, and **fumitory** a grey-leafed plant [medieval Latin *fumus terrae* 'smoke of the earth'].

fun [17c. Variant of **fon** 'a fool, (to be) foolish, to make a fool of' (ME–16c), of unknown origin] To trick or cheat (17c); a hoax or practical joke; amusement, merriment; playful joking or mockery: denounced as 'a low cant word' by Johnson (see ACHE), and still regarded as informal in the 19c; (something/someone) amusing or entertaining (19c). Hence **funny** comical, amusing, humorous (18c, **funny bone** is a 19c pun on **humerus**, the bone's Latin name); odd, strange, suspicious (19c).

Fon produced **fond** foolish, infatuated; (over-affectionate, doting; foolishly optimistic (*fond hope*), whence **fondling** a fool; a much-loved or pampered person, a pet, whence **fondle**, originally to pamper.

function [16c. French, from Latin *fungi, funct-* 'to perform or carry out'] An action, use, or role for which someone/something is suitable or designed, hence **1** an official duty; a religious rite; an official ceremony or social occasion (19c) **2** the performance of a function (*liver function*); to perform a duty or role (19c) **3** in maths: a variable quantity regarded in relation to other variables on which its value depends (18c); something dependent on another factor or factors. Hence **functional** to do with use rather than structure or form (17c); practical, utilitarian, designed for use (1920s).

Latin *fungi* produced *defungi* 'to finish', whence **defunct** dead, no longer used, and *perfungi* 'to get through, to be done with', whence **perfunctory** done or acting merely out of routine or duty; hasty, superficial.

fundament [ME. (Via French from) Latin *fundamentum*, from *fundare* FOUND*] Foundation, founding, basis (–17c), hence **1** the buttocks or anus **2 fundamental** to do with basic principles or structure; **fundamentals** such principles (17c); **fundamentalism** strict adherence to religious tenets seen as fundamentals of the faith (1920s).

furbish [ME. Old French *fourbir*, of Germanic origin] To remove rust from; to burnish or polish; to clean up (16c), hence (also, and now usually, as **refurbish**, 17c); to renovate, restore, or redecorate.

Old French *fourbir* produced the surname **Frobisher**, someone who polished metal.

furnish [ME. Old French *f(o)urnir* 'to accomplish, complete, or supply', ultimately of W Germanic origin] To provide with what is necessary or useful; to prepare or equip, now to equip with **furniture** movable, functional items (tables, chairs, etc., 16c), or with equipment, fittings, or accessories (*door/street furniture*).

Old French *furnir* produced PERFORM and **veneer** (to apply) a thin, decorative surface layer, hence a misleading outward appearance (*veneer of civilization*). Related to FRAME.

fuse [16c. Latin *fundere, fus-* 'to pour or melt'] To melt or be melted because of intense heat, hence **1** to (cause to) combine, originally by melting together (17c), hence **fusion** such a union, specifically **(a)** the combining of nuclei, with a resulting release of energy (1940s) **(b)** (describing) music, food, etc. combining elements from different styles or cultures (1980s) **2** a part of an electrical circuit that melts and breaks the circuit if too much current is passed through it (19c); to provide with a fuse (1920s); to (cause to) stop working because the fuse melts (1930s); **blow a fuse** to make a fuse melt (*c.*1900); to fly into a rage (1920s).

The **fuse** that detonates a bomb, originally a tube filled with combustible material, comes from Italian *fuso* 'spindle', from Latin *fusus*, whence also French **fuselage**. Latin *fundere* is the ancestor of CONFOUND*, **diffuse**, **effuse**, **fondant** [via French *fondre*, whence also **fondue**, **font** a typeface (originally cast in metal), and **found** to melt and mould metal, whence **foundry**], **funnel**, **infuse** originally meaning to pour a liquid ingredient into a mixture, **perfuse**, **profuse**, REFUND, **suffuse**, **transfuse**, and probably of **futile** [Latin *futilis* 'that pours out easily', later 'leaky', hence 'worthless'].

G

gaberdine [16c. Old French *gauvardine*, earlier *gallevardine*, perhaps from early High German *wallvart* 'pilgrimage', from *wallen* 'to go' (related to WALK*) + *vart* 'journey' (related to FARE*)] A long, loose coat or smock of coarse material worn by pilgrims, hence (usually **gabardine**) a kind of twilled material used to make coats (*c.*1900).

gad [ME. Back-formation from **gadling** 'companion', later 'wanderer, tramp', from Old English *gædeling*, from *gæd* 'fellowship': related to *gather* (at COLLECT*)] **1 gad (about)** to wander idly, restlessly, or in search of pleasure, hence **gadabout** someone who does so (19c) **2** of cattle: to rush about wildly (16c), surviving mainly in **gadfly** a biting fly that drives them wild, hence someone who torments another (17c).

gag [ME. Perhaps from the sound of choking] **1** to strangle or suffocate (–15c) **2** something put into (or later, over) the mouth to keep it open for surgery or to prevent speech (16c); to use one; to silence someone (as if with a gag) (17c); the (premature) ending of debate in a legislative assembly (19c, *US*) **3** to (cause to) retch (18c) **4** (perhaps from the idea of being thrust in like a gag) an ad lib or piece of business introduced into an act (19c); a joke, a hoax or prank; to make jokes.

gaggle [ME. Imitating a goose's cackle] Of geese: to cackle, hence **1** of a person: to cackle or chatter **2** a flock of geese (15c); a noisy or disorderly group of people; an untidy group of things, especially aircraft (World War II).

This is one of many Middle English collective nouns obsolete by the end of the 17c but revived by antiquarians. Some (e.g. *pride of lions, charm of finches*) survive: others (*kindle of kittens, rag of colts*) are found mainly in lists of collective nouns.

gallant [ME. French *galant*, from *galer* 'to have fun, to make a show', from *gale* 'pleasure, rejoicing', of Germanic origin] **1** splendidly dressed, stylish, showy **2** brave and chivalrous **3** (combining 1 and 2): **(a)** fine, excellent; majestic, noble **(b)** a fashionable young man (or, formerly, woman); a ladies' man; a woman's suitor or lover **(c)** polite and attentive to women (17c) **(d)** (to be) flirtatious or amorous (whence, perhaps, 19c **gallivant**).

Old French *galer* produced **regale** to entertain lavishly; *gale* produced French or Italian *gala* showy dress, finery, hence a festive occasion; a special sports event (*swimming gala*). Related to WALK*.

gallery [ME. Via Old French from Italian *galleria* 'portico', formerly also 'church porch', from medieval Latin *galeria*, perhaps an alteration of *galilea* 'Galilee': a porch or chapel furthest from the altar was called a *galilee* (15–19c), as Galilee was the province furthest from Jerusalem] A covered walkway with one or both sides open; a long narrow balcony: hence **1 (a)** a long narrow room or corridor (16c), e.g. one used to display works of art (hence a place where art is exhibited and/or sold); **shooting gallery** one with targets for shooting practice (19c); a place where drug addicts can 'shoot up' (1950s, *US*) **(b)** a horizontal underground passage (17c) **2** a balcony inside a building (16c): **(a)** the highest one in a theatre, with the cheapest seats; those seated there (17c, hence **play to the gallery** to try to appeal to the unsophisticated), hence the spectators at a card game who bet on the players and offer advice (19c, cf. *croupier* at CROP); the spectators at a golf match **(b)** a glass-fronted control room of a television studio (1950s).

In Italy, *galleria* came to mean an arcade of shops, hence a shopping mall or department store elsewhere, originally one in tiers around a central space.

galley [ME. Old French *galie* from medieval Latin *galea* or medieval Greek *galaia*, perhaps from Greek *galeos* 'shark'] A (Greek or Roman) ship with sails and oars, usually rowed by slaves or convicts, hence **1** a large rowing boat (16c) **2** (perhaps from the use of *galley slave* to mean 'drudge') a ship's or aircraft's kitchen (18c); (describing) a kitchen with two parallel work surfaces (1990s) **3** [via modern French *galée*] an oblong tray for holding set type (17c), hence **galley (proof)** a proof, originally taken from a galley, in the form of a long strip, not divided into pages (19c).

Old French *galie* produced French *galion*, literally 'large galley', whence **galleon** [via early Dutch or Spanish].

galvanize [19c. French *galvaniser*, from Luigi Galvani (1737–98), Italian physiologist, who discovered that muscles moved by means of electricity produced by chemical reactions in the body] **1** to stimulate a muscle or nerve by means of (especially chemically produced) electricity; to stimulate or shock someone into acting **2** to coat with metal, originally by electrolysis, now often to coat iron with zinc, although no electricity is used in the process.

In the early 20c a galvanized iron vessel used in the US army was called a **G.I. can**: later *G.I.* was taken to stand for *government issue*, and was applied to various items provided for soldiers, and eventually to an enlisted man.

gambol [16c. Alteration of French *gambade*, from Italian *gambata*, from *gamba* 'leg', from late Latin *gamba* 'horse's leg, hock', from Greek *kampē* 'bend'] A horse's leap or bound (16c only); a playful leap or skip; to caper or frolic.

French **gambade** was adopted in the same senses (16c only) and revived by Scott (see DOFF), who probably introduced the Spanish form **gambado**: both survive mainly in dictionaries. Italian *gamba* produced **gambado** a rider's protective legging, and **gambit** [via *gambetto*, literally 'a tripping up'].

Greek *kampē* is the ultimate ancestor of Norman French *gambe* 'leg' (whence **gammon**), a variant of Old French *jambe*, whence **jamb** the 'leg' of a doorway.

game [Old English *gamen* (noun), *gamenian* (verb)] Fun, pleasure; to jest or amuse yourself (both now dialect), hence an amusement or pastime (ME): **1** sport derived from hunting, shooting, etc.; (describing) the creature(s) hunted, hence an object of pursuit; an end in view; **fair game** that can legitimately be pursued (19c) **2** a competitive pastime with rules, hence **(a)** an episode of play, a match

(b) an activity, scheme, lovemaking, etc. regarded as a game; **(on) the game** (engaged in) burglary (18c) or prostitution (19c); an industry or business (*the advertising game*, 1950s) **(c)** performance, strategy, or tactics in a game or scheme; a ruse or trick (17c) **(d) Games** an (international) event with many sporting contests (originally in ancient Greece, which also included dramatic and musical contests); **games** sports and athletics in schools (19c) **(e)** to play card games etc. for money (16c) **(f) gamecock** a fighting cock (17c), hence *game* the courage and spirit of one (18c); spirited, plucky; ready and willing (19c) **(g)** a bit of fun, a lark (19c).

Old English *gamen* produced **gamble** and probably *gammon* in **backgammon**.

gamut [ME. Medieval Latin *gamma ut*, from *gamma* the third letter of the Greek alphabet (transliterated as *G*) + *ut* (see below)] **1** the lowest note in the medieval musical scale, G an octave and a half below middle C **2** a scale based on seven hexachords containing all the notes used in medieval music (15c), hence the full range of notes a singer or instrument can produce (17c); the whole range or scope of anything.

Ut is the first word of a Latin hymn for St John the Baptist's day in which each phrase begins on the next note on the scale, the initial syllables being adopted for the notes: *Ut queant laxis resonare fibris Mira gestorum famuli tuorum, Solve polluti labii reatum, Sancte Iohannes*. Another note *si* [from the initials of *Sancte Iohannes*] was added in the 18c, and *ut* was replaced by Italian *do*. In the 19c *si* was changed to *te* to avoid having two notes beginning with the same letter, and arbitrary spelling changes produced the modern scale: **doh**, **ray**, **me**, **fah**, **soh**, **lah**, **te**.

gang [Old English *gang* (noun), *gangen* (verb), from Old Norse *gangre* 'journey, group'] **1 (a)** travelling; a journey; to walk or go (surviving in Scots) **(b)** a way, road, or passage, surviving in **gangway** and **gangplank 2** a group of people that go together (ME): **(a)** of labourers (17c), hence **ganger** their foreman (19c) **(b)** of slaves, prisoners, or criminals (18c), hence **gangster** a member of a criminal gang (19c), altered to *gangsta* in **gangsta rap** rap music with violent lyrics (1990s) **(c)** to form or join a gang (*gang up with/against*, 19c).

Probably the source of **gangling** or **gangly** straggling, lanky. Related to *go* (at WEND).

gantry [ME. French *gantier*, from Latin *cantherius* 'nag', also 'rafter' (probably because of the horse's prominent backbone), from Greek *kanthēlios* 'pack ass', from *kanthēlia* 'panniers'] A wooden frame for a barrel or barrels, later a large frame for mounting a crane, railway signals, power cables, etc.

French *gantier* came to mean 'timberyard', and produced Canadian French *chantier* 'a lumberjacks' camp or cabin', whence **shanty** a rough dwelling.

gape [ME. Old Norse *gapa*: related to **gap**] To open your mouth wide, hence **1** to stare open-mouthed (whence, probably, **gawp**, 17c); such a stare (17c) **2** to be or become wide open; a split or opening (17c) **3** to yawn; a yawn (16c) **4** the width of an open mouth or beak (18c).

garb [16c. Via French from Italian *garbo*, of Germanic origin and related to GEAR] Grace, elegance, style; a prevailing style or fashion (both –17c), hence outward appearance (17c); clothing; to clothe (19c).

garble [ME. Via Anglo-Latin and Italian *garbellare* from Arabic *garbala* 'to sift', perhaps ultimately from Latin *cribrum* 'sieve'] To rid of unwanted matter or rubbish (–19c); to pick out the best (15c); to pick out the facts that suit you (17c); to (intentionally) distort or jumble the meaning of something.

garnish [ME. Old French *g(u)arnir*, of Germanic origin] **1** to equip or arm (–19c); to fit out or embellish (15c); to decorate a dish of food (17c); such decoration **2** in law: to warn; to serve notice on a third party for the purpose of legally seizing money belonging to a debtor or defendant, hence **garnishee** this third party (17c); to recover money by a **garnishee order** requiring them to surrender it (19c).

   Old French *g(u)arnir* produced *garnement* 'equipment', whence **garment**. Related to WARRANT*.

garret [ME. Old French *garite*, from *g(u)arir* 'to equip or defend', of Germanic origin] A watchtower (–16c), hence a room at the top of a house.

   Old French *g(u)arir* produced **garrison** (a means of) defence or protection (ME–17c), hence troops stationed in a fortress or town. Related to WARRANT*.

gasket [17c. Probably from French *garcette* 'little girl', later 'thin rope' (perhaps from a little girl's pigtail), from *garce*, feminine of *gars* 'boy'] A plaited cord for securing a furled sail; a strip of plaited hemp or tow for caulking a joint (19c), hence a seal around a joint or between machine parts (*c*.1900).

gate¹ [Old English *gaet*, *geat*. The original pronunciation would have been *yat* or *yet*, which survives in N English dialect, in a few place names, and the surname **Yates**, **Yeat(e)s**: the current pronunciation has been standard since the 16c] An opening in a wall that can be closed by a movable barrier, hence **1** (something resembling) such a barrier (*floodgate*, *tailgate*) **(b)** a frame for holding saws (19c); a device in a movie camera or projector for holding a frame of film (early 20c) **2** an entrance or exit (ME): **(a)** a gap in a cliff, a pass (earliest in place names, e.g. *Margate*, *Yatton*) **(b)** the number of people coming through the gates to attend a sporting event (19c); the total admission fees **3** to provide or control access (as if) with a gate (*gated community*, 17c); **gated** confined to school grounds (19c); **gate-crasher** who comes uninvited (1920s), whence **gatecrash** (1930s).

   In 1972 Republican operatives broke into the Democrats' headquarters in Washington DC, hoping to find material that would help in the re-election of President Richard Nixon; the ensuing scandal, dubbed **Watergate** after the complex housing the Democrats' offices, led to Nixon's resignation: -**gate** has since been applied to many scandals (*Irangate*).

gate² [ME. Old Norse *gata*] A way, hence **1** a road, path, or street, surviving in place names (e.g. *Harrogate*) and in street names in Scotland, N England, and the Midlands **2** a way of behaving or doing something, surviving in the Scots variant **gait** your way of walking.

   Gate produced *runagate* (at RENEGADE). Related to **gauntlet** in **run the gauntlet** [alteration of *gantlope*, from Swedish *gatlopp*, from *gata* 'lane' + *lopp* 'course, running']: the spelling changed by association with unrelated **gauntlet** glove [Old French *gantelet* 'small glove', from *gant* 'glove', of Germanic origin].

gay [ME. French *gai*, of unknown origin] **1** happy, light-hearted; pleasure-loving, hedonistic, dissolute; leading such a life (19c); engaged in prostitution

2 bright, colourful, showy; something bright, an ornament (surviving in dialect and in **nosegay**) **3** of an animal: lively, alert (19c); of a dog's tail: carried erect (1950s) **4** homosexual; a (male) homosexual (probably 19c: well established, though little known outside gay circles, by the 1930s, and adopted by homosexual men in the 1960s). This sense has eclipsed the earlier senses, (although **gaiety** and **gaily** survive), and has led to the teenage slang sense 'without a girl- or boyfriend, unattractive, unpopular' (*c*.2000), later 'no good, broken'. *Gaiety* replaced **gayness** (–17c), which was revived meaning 'homosexuality' in the 1970s.

gazette [17c. (Via French from) Italian *gazzetta*, originally Venetian *gazeta de la novità* 'a *gazeta*'s worth of news, a *gazeta* being a Venetian coin of low value] A newsletter; a newspaper; (the title of) an organization's official newspaper, specifically an official journal giving notice of government appointments, bankruptcies, etc., hence **be gazetted** to be the subject of a notice in it.

Italian *gazzetta* produced *gazzettiere* 'journalist', whence **gazetteer**: the sense 'a geographical index' comes from the title of a 17c publication, *The Gazetteer's or Newsman's Interpreter: Being A Geographical Index.*

gear [ME. Old Norse *gervi*: related to GARB] The underlying sense is 'equipment, apparatus'. **1** clothing; arms, armour; tackle, harness (hence **gear (up)** to harness an animal, 17c; to get ready); tools; rigging (16c) **2** household goods; movable property, 'stuff' **3** a mechanism (*steering/landing/winding gear*, 16c); the mechanism that connects a motor with its work (19c, hence **in gear** connected), especially that used to change the relationship between the speed of the motor and that of the wheels, hence **gearing** the arrangement or ratio of gears; the ratio of a company's debts to the value of its shares (1930s).

gender [ME. Old French *gendre*, ultimately from Latin GENUS*] A sort or class (–18c), hence a grammatical category of nouns in some languages, sometimes arbitrary but often based on sex (masculine, feminine, and neuter), hence the state of being masculine, feminine, or neuter; the male or female sex; sex expressed by cultural, rather than biological, distinctions (1960s).

Old French *gendre* evolved into modern *genre*, adopted for a type of painting, literature, etc.

general [ME. French, from Latin *generalis* 'of the whole class', from Latin GENUS*] To do with or including all or most members of a group, or parts of a whole, hence **1** controlling (a substantial part of) an institution, hence **captain general** [translating French *capitaine général*] a commander-in-chief (16c), shortened to *general* and also applied to commanders of divisions **2** not restricted or specialized; applying or happening in most cases; usual, prevalent.

General produced **gen** [from the official phrase 'for the general information of all ranks'], whence **genned up** well-informed.

generation [ME. French, from Latin *generare* 'to beget or produce', from Latin GENUS*] **1** offspring, progeny, hence **(a)** offspring considered as a step in descent from an ancestor, hence a stage in development **(b)** those born at about the same time considered as a group; the time it takes to produce a new generation (19c), usually reckoned as thirty years **2** the act of reproducing or process of being reproduced **3** the process of producing, now specifically electricity.

Latin *generare* produced **engender** [via French from Latin *ingenerare*] and, later, **generate**, which has partly replaced it.

generous [15c. Via French from Latin *generosus*, from Latin GENUS*] Of noble birth; noble, courageous, magnanimous, not mean or petty, hence (both 17c) **1** open-handed **2** ample, abundant.

The association of high rank and benevolence is also found in **benign** [ultimately from Latin *bene* 'well' + *-genus* 'born'], GENTLE, KIND, and LIBERAL. Cf. **mean** [Old English *(ge)mǽne*] humble, poor; unkind, unpleasant; niggardly, whence **demean** to lower in status, to debase.

genesis [OE. Latin from Greek, 'generation, creation, birth'] **1 Genesis** the name of the first book of the Bible, which tells of the world's creation **2** the way something comes into being, its origin (17c), whence **-genesis** production, origin (*biogenesis, parthenogenesis*).

Genesis produced **genetic** (whence **genetics** the study of natural development, later of heredity and inherited characteristics), which became the adjective connected with **gene** [German *Gen*, from *Pangen* **pangene** a supposed ultimate unit of living matter or heredity, from Greek *pan* 'all' + *genos* 'kind, race, offspring'], and is related to **Eugene, Eugenia**, meaning 'well-born', to **eugenics** the study of improving the human race by selective breeding, and to GENUS*. Greek *pan* produced PANOPLY*; *genos* is the ancestor of **-gen** 'producing' (*allergen, pathogen*), **genealogy, genocide** [coined to describe the systematic extermination of Jews and gypsies by the Nazis], and **hetero-** and **homogeneous**.

genial [16c. Latin *genialis*, from GENIUS] **1** to do with marriage or procreation, hence encouraging growth (17c); of weather: mild and pleasant **2** to do with your natural disposition (17c, hence **congenial** having the same temperament). Hence (combining 1 and 2) pleasant, good-natured, cheerful (18c).

genius [ME. Latin, ultimately from *gignere* 'to beget'] In Roman mythology, a person's guardian spirit, assigned at their birth, also that of a place or institution, hence **1** a demon or spirit (16c, cf. *genie* below) **2** a quality that characterizes a place, period, or people (17c) **3** an innate ability or inclination (17c); (a person having) extraordinary creative or intellectual abilities.

These senses were shared by **genie** [French *génie*, from Latin *genius*]: French *génie* was used to translate Arabic *jinni*, a spirit that could take human or animal form and influence human affairs, hence the *genie* in Aladdin's lamp.

Latin *genius* produced GENIAL; *gignere* is the ancestor of GINGERLY*.

gentle [ME. French *gentil*, from Latin *gentilis* 'of the same clan or nation, from a good family', from *gens, gent-* 'family, race'] Noble, well-born, entitled to a coat of arms (surviving in *gentleman* etc. below) hence **1** courteous, chivalrous; kindly, benevolent (16c, cf. GENEROUS*); of an animal: quiet, docile (16c); to make one so (18c) **2 gentleman** a man of a noble, later of a good, family, hence **(a)** an honourable, courteous man of any rank (cf. GENEROUS*); a polite way of addressing or, later, referring to a man (16c: **gent** was a standard abbreviation until the 19c; the feminine **gentlewoman** has been largely replaced by *lady* at LORD) **(b)** a man of good family in a nobleman's household; a superior manservant (*gentleman's gentleman*) **(c)** a man of independent means (18c), hence a smuggler; **gentleman of**

the road a highwayman, gypsy, or tramp **3** suitable for a gentleman (15c); **the gentle craft** shoemaking (see SNOB) **4** moderate, mild (*a gentle breeze*, 16c) **5** soft, pliant (16–18c), hence an anglers' maggot, whence (with a pun on sense 3) **the gentle art/craft** angling.

Old French *gentil* produced **genteel** and **jaunty**, which both originally meant 'fashionable, stylish', also 'well-bred', and GENTRY.

gentry [ME. Old French *genterise*, variant of *gentelise* 'nobility', from *gentil*: see GENTLE*] Social superiority, good breeding, courtesy; the upper classes below the aristocracy (16c), whence **gentrify** to make an area middle-class, to alter or renovate property in accordance with middle-class tastes (1970s).

genuine [16c. Latin *genuinus*, from *genu* 'knee', referring to the Roman custom of a man taking a child on his knee to acknowledge paternity; later associated with GENUS] Natural, native, not foreign or acquired (–18c), hence **1** real, true, not artificial or feigned (17c); authentic; sincere (19c); of a horse or greyhound: that does its honest best (1930s) **2** purebred (18c).

Latin *genu* produced **genuflect** [with Latin *flectere* 'to bend' (ancestor of FLEXIBLE*)].

genus [16c. Latin *genus*, *gener-* 'class, race, kind'] **1** a class containing a number of subordinate classes **2** see TAXONOMY. Hence **generic** belonging to a genus (17c); applicable to a large class, hence general, non-specific; (describing) a product, especially a drug, without a brand name or trademark (19c).

Latin *genus* is the ancestor of **congener**, **degenerate**, GENDER*, GENERAL*, GENERATION*, GENEROUS*, and **miscegenation** [with Latin *miscere* 'to mix' (ancestor of MEDDLE*)]. Related to *gene* (at GENESIS).

germ [ME. Via French from Latin *germen* 'bud, seed, sprout, offshoot'] A part of an organism which can develop into a similar one, hence **1** a rudiment from which something may develop (16c) **2** a plant seed (19c); the embryonic centre of one, especially of a cereal **3** the 'seed' or cause of a disease (19c); a (pathogenic) micro-organism.

Latin *germen* produced **germane** relevant, a variant of **german** having the same parents (surviving in the technical term **cousin-german** first cousin, and perhaps in *German measles* at MEASLES), and **germinate**.

gesture [15c. Medieval Latin *gestura*, from Latin *gerere*, *gest-* 'to bear, perform, or behave'] Posture, bearing, deportment (–19c); the use of posture and movement for effect in oratory; (to make) a movement expressing a thought or feeling (16c); something done (merely) as a courtesy or formality, or to express an attitude (*c.*1910).

Latin *gerere* is the ancestor of **congest**, DIGEST, **gestation**, **gesticulate**, **ingest**, JEST*, REGISTER, and **suggest**.

geyser [19c. Icelandic *Geysir*, the name of a particular spring in Iceland: related to **gust** and perhaps to **gush**] A spring that spouts hot water and steam intermittently, hence a gas-fired domestic water heater.

ghastly [ME. Ultimately from Old English *gǣstan* 'to terrify' (whence **aghast**). The *gh-* spelling was apparently introduced by Spenser (see BLATANT)] **1** terrifying, gradually fading to shocking, nasty **2** (influenced by related GHOST) like a ghost or corpse (16c); deathly pale.

ghost [Old English *gāst*. The *gh-* spelling was introduced by Caxton (see ADVICE) probably influenced by related Flemish *gheest*] The soul or spirit (–19c); the spirit or essence of God (surviving in **Holy Ghost**); the spirit as the source of life (surviving in *give up the ghost*); a dead person's spirit in the next world (–17c); one that makes itself known to the living (ME), hence **1** (from a ghost's pale, nebulous appearance) a faint mark or trace (17c); a false image on a photograph or screen (19c) **2** a person who does creative work for which someone else takes the credit (*ghostwriter*, 19c) **3 ghost town** a formerly busy place now (almost) deserted (1931); **ghost site** a website that is no longer updated (1990s).

Related to GHASTLY and to German *Geist* in **poltergeist** literally 'noisy ghost', and **Zeitgeist** literally 'spirit of the time'.

ghoul [Arabic *gūl*] In Arabic mythology: a spirit believed to rob graves and devour corpses (18c), hence someone with a morbid interest in death, disaster, or repulsive things (19c).

giddy [Old English *gidig*: related to GOD] Literally, possessed by a god, hence mad, foolish, stupid (–ME), hence **1** feeling unsteady, dizzy (ME); causing this feeling (16c); whirling around (19c) **2** excitable, impulsive, frivolous (16c, earlier in **giddiness**).

The meaning of **dizzy** [Old English *dysig*: related to **doze**] has followed the same path, although the madness was not attributed to divine possession.

gift [ME. Old Norse *gipt*: related to **give**] **1** giving; the ability to give; **in someone's gift** within their right to give **2** something given, a present or donation: **(a)** a virtue or ability thought to be miraculously bestowed (*gift of tongues*); a natural talent or ability, hence **gifted** exceptionally clever or talented **(b)** a bribe (–17c), inadvertently revived in **free gift**, given as an inducement to buy something (19c) **(c)** an unexpected advantage or benefit (19c); something unexpectedly easy. **3** to give someone a present (16c); to give as a present, to give away (17c).

gin [18c. Ultimately from Latin *juniperus* **juniper**] A spirit flavoured with juniper berries, introduced from the Netherlands and also called by its Dutch name **genever**, **geneva** [alteration of *genever* by association with the Swiss city of Geneva], or **Hollands**. Originally a cheap imitation of Dutch genever and sometimes flavoured with less desirable substances, *gin* now means both the Dutch drink and the generally drier, but equally wholesome, English variety.

Gin in **gin rummy** is apparently a pun on **rummy**, as if it were based on the drink **rum**: the origins of both are unknown.

ginger [Old English *gingifer(e)*, *gingiber*, later combined with Old French *gingimbre*, both from medieval Latin *gingiber*, *zingiber*, from Greek *ziggiberis*, from Pali *siṅgivera*, probably ultimately from Sanskrit *śṛṅga* 'horn' + *vera* 'body' (from the antler-like shape of the root)] A spicy root, hence **1** (of) the reddish-yellow colour of dried or preserved ginger (19c); a nickname for someone with red hair **2 ginger up** to put ginger into a horse's anus to make it appear lively (19c); to enliven or stimulate; **ginger group** a small group of people that tries to stir up the majority (1950s).

Latin *gingiber* produced **gingerbread** [via Old French from medieval Latin *gingibratum* '(something) made of ginger'] originally as **gingebrar** (preserved) ginger, later a cake flavoured with ginger (hence the current spelling, by association with *bread*); a ginger biscuit made into fancy shapes and formerly often gilded, hence **1** elaborate carving or showy decoration **2 take the gilt off the gingerbread** to make something less attractive.

gingerly [16c. Probably from Old French *gensor* 'delicate', from *gent* 'graceful', from Latin *genitus* '(well-)born', from *gignere* 'to beget'] Elegantly, daintily, also effeminately, mincingly (–17c), hence tentatively, cautiously.

Latin *gignere* is the ancestor of **congenital**, ENGINE*, **genital**, GENIUS*, **indigenous**, INGENUOUS*, **primogeniture**, **progenitor**, and **progeny**.

gird [Old English *gyrdan*: related to GIRDLE and GIRTH] To encircle your own or someone else's waist; to put on a belt etc., hence **1** to fasten a sword around your waist; to prepare or brace yourself; **girder** a bracing beam (17c) **2** to surround, encircle, or enclose (ME); **girt** surrounded.

girdle [Old English *gyrdel*: related to GIRD*] **1** a belt or band, hence to surround (as if) with one (16c); to ring-bark a tree (17c) **2** a ring of bone (*pelvic girdle*, 17c) **3** a corset (1920s, *US*).

girth [ME. Old Norse *gjord*: related to GIRD*] **1** a belt to secure a saddle etc., hence to put a girth around, to encircle; to put a measuring-line round; the measurement around (17c) **2** a girder (17c, US: cf. *gird*).

gist [18c. Old French, from *gesir*, *gis-* 'to lie', from Latin *jacere*: see JET*] When French was the language of the law courts the phrase *cest action gist* 'this action lies' was used when the grounds for proceeding were stated, hence **gist** the essential grounds of an action; the main point or meaning of something (19c).

Related to Old French *giste* 'resting place', whence modern French *gîte* an inn, now a holiday home.

glad [Old English *glaed*] Bright, shining (–17c), hence bright, cheerful, happy, pleased, hence **1** to be, become, or make glad (–17c), replaced by **gladden** (ME, but extremely rare before the 16c) **2** in surnames for cheerful people (*Gladman*, *Gladwyn*).

Related to GLAZE*, and probably to **glade** a clearing (a bright space) in a wood; an area of wetland with tall grasses (US), whence **everglade** originally in **the Everglades**, a large wetland in Florida: *ever* here may mean 'endless'.

glance [ME. An alteration (probably influenced by *glent* below), of obsolete **glace**, from Old French *glacier* 'to slip, to ice, to give a gloss to', ultimately from Latin *glacies*] **1** to move or strike something obliquely; of a weapon, tool, etc.: to slide off **2** to shine or flash. Hence (combining 1 and 2) to look away as if dazzled (16c); (to give) a sideways or hurried look.

Glent [probably of Scandinavian origin] had a similar range of meanings: the alteration **glint** survives meaning (to make) a brief flash. Old French *glacier* produced *glacé*, **glacier**, and **glacis** a sloping bank, especially as part of a fortification, now a buffer zone. Latin *glacies* produced **glacial** and **glaciate**.

glaze [Middle English *glasen*, from Old English *glaes* **glass**: related to GLAD*] **1** to fit a window with glass **2** to make something shine like glass; (to cover with) a smooth, glassy coating, hence **(a)** to cover the eyes with a film (16c); to make them appear dull, fixed, or glassy; of the eyes: to be or become glazed (18c) **(b)** to cover with a protective or decorative coating (16c); such a coating (18c): hence **deglaze** to remove it (19c); to take the 'coating' of meat residues from a pan to make gravy etc. [1970s, via French].

glee [Old English *glīo, glēo*] Entertainment, fun, also mockery (–17c), hence **1** musical entertainment; an (unaccompanied) part song (17c) **2** joy, delight (ME), now often a rather smug jubilant feeling.

glib [16c. Perhaps from or related to Dutch *glibberig* or Low German *glibberich*] Slippery, smooth; moving easily; easy, offhand; of a speaker: fluent, slick, superficial, and not necessarily sincere.

glimpse [ME. Of Germanic origin] **1** to shine faintly or intermittently (largely replaced by *glimmer* below) **2** to glance briefly. Hence (combining 1 and 2) a faint or fleeting appearance (16c); a momentary or imperfect view; to get one (18c).
  Glimpse and related **glimmer** may have influenced each other, or may have developed independently: *glimmer* originally meant to shine brightly; **glimmering** also meant an indistinct view, a faint notion, shortened to *glimmer*. **Gleam** [Old English *glaem*] a bright light, later a subdued, fleeting, or reflected one, is also related.

glitch [1960s. Origin unknown] Astronauts' slang for a sudden surge of current, often causing a malfunction (*US*), hence a malfunction, a minor problem; to malfunction (1980s).

glitter [ME. Old Norse *glitra*] To sparkle or shimmer; to be splendid or showy; splendour, showiness, glamour (17c); tiny pieces of sparkling material used as decoration or (often **glitter dust**) as a cosmetic (1960s).
  Glitter produced **glitterati** the rich and fashionable [*US*, suggested by *literati*], and **glitzy** glamorous, showy, gaudy [*N American*, suggested by **ritzy** 'superior, glamorous' from **The Ritz**, a name given to luxury hotels founded by the Swiss hotelier César Ritz]: **glitz** is a back-formation.

gloat [16c. Perhaps of Scandinavian origin] To look with a furtive or sideways glance (–18c); to cast amorous or admiring glances (17–18c); to look at lustfully or greedily; to look at or think about with smug or malicious pleasure (18c); such a look or feeling (19c).

globe [ME. (Old French, from) Latin *globus*] **1** a spherical object **2** a planet or star (16c), specifically the earth, hence **global** to do with or involving the whole world (19c, hence **globalization**, 1950s); to do with or applied to a whole system or group, comprehensive **3** (combining 1 and 2) a spherical map of the earth (**terrestrial globe**) or the constellations (**celestial globe**) (16c).

gloom [ME. Origin unknown] **1** to look sullen or depressed, to frown or scowl; such a look (16c, Scots) **2** of the weather: to be or become dull **3** to make dark or sombre (16c), hence **gloomy** dark, shadowy; *gloom* murky darkness (17c) **4** to make dismal or despondent (18c); despondency; *gloomy* dismal, disheartening.

The dialect variant *glum* 'to frown' is probably the source of **glum** meaning 'morose, dejected'.

glory [ME. Via Old French from Latin *gloria*] Exaltation, praise, or honour, hence **1** something that brings or shows this; a special distinction or ornament; a halo (17c, earlier as *gloria*, later as **gloriole**) **2** praise and thanks offered to God, hence the pious phrase **glory be to God**, whence the exclamation **glory be!** (19c) **3** the splendour and bliss of heaven, hence **(a)** outstanding beauty or magnificence; pomp, majesty **(b)** a state of exaltation (17c), hence **in his glory** at the height of his happiness, prosperity, or triumph **4** to rejoice in or pride yourself on; pride, boastfulness (–18c, surviving in **vainglory**).

Latin *gloria* was adopted for various hymns of praise beginning with it, for a kind of fabric, and as a first name (in George Bernard Shaw's play *You Never Can Tell*, 1898). Its descendants include **Gloriana**, the name of a character in Spenser's *The Faerie Queene* (see BLATANT), often used as an epithet of Elizabeth I, whom she resembled.

glue [ME. Via French from late Latin *glus*, *glut-*, from Latin *gluten*] An adhesive substance obtained by boiling hides and bones, hence (to stick with) any adhesive, hence **1** to fix firmly or keep close (*kids glued to the television*) **2 glue sniffing** inhaling the fumes of plastic cement or a similar substance (1960s).

Latin *gluten* is the ancestor of **glutinous**, and was adopted as the original name of fibrin, a substance involved in blood clotting, and later for a substance found in (wheat) flour that gives dough its elastic texture.

glut [ME. Probably via Old French from Latin *gluttire* 'to swallow': related to **glutton**] To overeat, over-indulge, or overfeed; to sicken by doing so, hence a surfeit or excess (16c); a supply that exceeds demand; to overstock a market with goods (17c).

gnostic [16c. Via ecclesiastical Latin from Greek *gnōstikos*, from *gnōsis* 'knowledge', from *gignōskein* 'to know, think, or judge'] **1 Gnostic** a member of a pre-Christian and early Christian sect who believed that esoteric knowledge of spiritual matters (**gnosis**) could free humanity from the material world **2** to do with (spiritual) knowledge (17c).

The 19c biologist Thomas Huxley regarded as 'Gnostics' those who eagerly accepted doctrines claiming to explain God and the world, and coined the term **agnostic** [with Greek *a-* 'not, without'] to describe himself and his view that you can truly know only material phenomena. Greek *gignōskein* produced **diagnosis**, **gnomic**, **gnomon** the pin of a sundial [Greek *gnōmōn* 'judge, inspector, indicator', whence also *physiognomy* (at PHYSIC)], and **prognosis**.

goal [ME. Origin unknown] Recorded once meaning a boundary or limit, and re-emerging in the modern sense (16c), having presumably survived in some rural sport (ignored by the literate) in which a ball had to cross a line in order to score. Hence the finishing point of a race or journey; something you want to achieve (17c).

gob [ME. Old French *gobe* 'mouthful, lump', from *gober* 'to swallow', perhaps of Celtic origin] A mass or lump (now mainly US and dialect): **1** a lump or mouthful of food, especially meat or gristle (16c) **2** a lump of any slimy or viscous material;

to cough up or spit a lump of phlegm or saliva (19c) **3** a lump of glass from which a single vessel is made (1920s).

Probably the source of **gobble** to eat quickly, whence **gobbledegook**, introduced to polite society in the 1940s and assumed to be from a turkey's **gobble** [imitative], but previously slang for a prostitute offering fellatio [from *gobble the goo*], and perhaps of JOB[1]. Old French *gobe* produced **gobbet** literally a small gob. Possibly related to **gob** mouth [perhaps from Scottish or Irish Gaelic], whence **gab** (idle) talk, and **gobsmacked**.

goblin [ME. Probably via Anglo-Norman French from medieval Latin *gobelinus*, a mischievous spirit that haunted Évreux in N France in the 12c, perhaps ultimately from Greek *kobálos* 'rogue'] A mischievous and sometimes evil spirit in the shape of a small, grotesque man.

Probably related to German *Kobold, Kobalt* a (mischievous) household spirit or a goblin found in mines, hence an apparently worthless ore believed to harm the silver with which it was found, adopted as **cobalt**. Cf. **nickel** [German *Kupfernickel*, the miners' term for the copper-coloured ore from which it was obtained (from *Kupfer* 'copper' + *Nickel* 'rascal, demon'): so called because despite its appearance it yielded no copper].

god [Old English] A superhuman being believed to have power over nature and human affairs, hence **1** the Supreme Being, creator and ruler of the universe **2** an idol; someone/something worshipped or idolized.

Euphemisms appear in: **begad, begorra(h)**, and **by gum** [*by God*], **cocksure** [*God sure*], **(cor/gor) blimey** [(*God*) *blind me*], **doggone** [*God damn*], **drat** [*od rat (it)* for *God rot (it)*], **egad** [*oh God*], **Gawd** (whence **Gawd-help-us** a stupid or exasperating person, **Gawd-forbid** rhyming slang for *kid* meaning 'child'), **golly, gosh**, and **strewth** [*God's truth*]. God in the person of Christ appeared in **gadzooks** [*God's hooks*] and **Od's bod(i)kins**, both referring to the nails fastening Christ to the cross, and **zounds** [*God's wounds*]. See also DEAR; cf. CHRIST.

God appears in GODFATHER*, **goodbye** [from *God be with you*, influenced by *good* in *good morning* etc.], and GOSSIP. Related to GIDDY.

godfather A man who sponsors an adult at baptism, or who formally takes responsibility for a child's Christian upbringing (OE), hence a man who sponsors, supports, or cares for someone/something (16c: cf. GOSSIP*); the head of a criminal organization, especially of the American Mafia (1960s, from or popularized by Mario Puzo's novel *The Godfather* or the film made from it).

Probably the source of **gaffer** (a respectful title or form of address for) an elderly man, hence the leader of a group of workmen; the chief electrician of a film crew. The female equivalents, **godmother** and **gammer**, did not develop further senses, except in **fairy godmother** a female benefactor.

goggle [ME. Perhaps related to JOG*] To look sideways, to squint, to roll your eyes; to look with wide-open or bulging eyes, hence **goggles** spectacles, originally to correct a squint, now worn to protect the eyes (16c).

gold [Old English] The precious metal, hence **1** (gold) coins, money, wealth (BRASS and **silver** [Old English *siolfor*] also have this sense) **2** made of gold, gold-coloured (ME), later also **golden**, which replaced related *gilden* [Old English *gylden*]; this colour **3** (the adjective also *golden*): (something) valuable or precious; (something) excellent, the best, *silver* being second best, hence the gold and silver medals in sport, *bronze* (at BRASS) being adopted for third place (19c): see also *golden jubilee* (at JUBILEE). **Platinum** [19c, alteration of 18c *platina* (cf. ALUMINIUM), from Spanish *plata* 'silver', ultimately from Greek *platus* 'broad, flat' (ancestor of PLATE*)], now often more valuable than gold, has been adopted for something even better (*platinum disc/credit card*) **4** *golden*: in the names of financial incentives (*golden handshake*, 1960s) **5** also **Gould**: a surname for a goldsmith or someone with yellow hair: *Gold* in Jewish surnames (e.g. *Goldfarb*), is from related German or Yiddish *Gold*.

Related to *gall* (at HUMOUR), **gild** to coat with gold or gold leaf [Old English *gyldan*], whence **gilt**, and to **yellow** [Old English *geolu*, whence also **yolk**].

goon [19c. Perhaps from dialect *gooney* 'simpleton', of unknown origin, but influenced by a subhuman character, Alice the Goon, in Popeye cartoons: see JEEP] A simple, affectionate person (19c only); a dull or stupid one (1920s, *N American*); a hired thug (1930s, *N American*); a German prison camp guard (World War II).

Alice gave her name to *The Goon Show*, a British radio series (1951–60), noted for its absurd and surreal humour; its cast was known as *The Goons*, and *goon* came to mean someone who has a similar sense of humour or who acts bizarrely.

goose [Old English *gōs*] **1** a large, long-necked water bird; the female bird (ME); its flesh as food (16c) **2** a simpleton (ME) **3** a tailor's iron with a handle like a goose's neck (17c) **4** a sound like a goose's hiss; one expressing disapproval of a performance (19c, cf. *to get the bird* at BIRD) **5** to poke someone between the buttocks [19c, perhaps from a supposed resemblance of the outstretched arm and hand to a goose's neck and beak, or from **gooseberry bush** as a slang term for the female pudendum (under which babies were found)].

The association of geese with foolishness is also found in **gunsel** a naive or homosexual youth [*US*, from Yiddish *gendzel* from German *Gänslein* 'gosling'], later, influenced by *gun*, an informer or (armed) criminal, and probably in **gonzo** eccentric, far-fetched, also a fool [*US*, probably from Spanish *ganso* 'goose, fool'], and **gull** a fool, a dupe; to fool or deceive [probably from obsolete **gull** yellow, also a gosling, from Old Norse *gulr*], whence **gullible**.

Goose probably produced **goosander** and **gooseberry** [although this may be an alteration of French *groseille* 'redcurrant' (a former sense of *gooseberry*). Old English *gōs* appears in place names (*Gosport, Gosford*) and produced **goshawk** [Old English *gōshafoc* 'goose hawk', probably from its size and barred plumage, resembling a greylag goose], the surname **Gossart**, **Gozzard** a goose herd, and **gossamer** [literally 'goose summer', because it is plentiful during St Martin's summer, a spell of fine weather around the saint's day (11 November)]. Geese have long been associated with St Martin and also with St Michael, probably because fattened geese were taken to market in the autumn; **goose fairs** were held in many towns at Michaelmas (29 September), and geese were traditionally eaten to celebrate both saints' days (**cook someone's goose** may refer to the premature cooking of the bird intended for the holiday). Related to **gander** and **gannet**.

gopher [18c. Perhaps from Canadian French *gaufre* 'honeycomb': see WAFER*] Applied to various creatures whose burrows 'honeycombed' the land, originally the **gopher tortoise**, now usually a North American rodent (19c). Hence a system for searching out information on the internet (1990s), partly from the idea of 'burrowing' in the system, partly because the rodent is the mascot of the University of Minnesota, where it was developed, and partly from **gofer** someone who runs errands [1960s, from *go for*].

gore¹ [Old English *gor*] Dirt, filth, slime (–17c); thick or clotted blood (16c); blood shed violently (15c in **gory** bloody, bloodstained, hence involving bloodshed, horrific, 16c).

gore² [Old English *gāra*] A triangular piece of land (surviving in names such as **Garwood** and **Kensington Gore**), hence **1** a triangular piece used to shape a skirt or sail (ME); one as part of the surface of a globe, balloon, umbrella, etc. (18c) **2** a strip of land between two towns etc. (17c, US).

Related to Old English *gār* 'spear', which appears in names as **Gar-** and **Gor-**, and which produced **garfish** [from its long body and pointed jaw], **garlic** [Old English *gārlēac*, literally 'spear leak', from its spear-shaped leaves], the names **Gerald**, **Gerard**, **Gervase**, and **Jarvis**, and perhaps **gore** to stab.

gorge [ME. Old French *gorge* (noun), *gorger* (verb), ultimately from Latin *gurges* 'whirlpool'] The throat, hence **1** (the contents of) a hawk's crop or, later, stomach (hence **my gorge rises at** it makes me sick); of a bird of prey: to fill its gorge, hence **(a)** to fill up, to overfill, to choke **(b)** to eat greedily; to gobble up (17c) **2** something resembling a throat: the neck of a bastion (17c); a concave moulding (18c); a deep narrow valley.

Old French *gorge* produced **gorget** a piece of armour for the throat, later a (decorative) collar, hence a coloured patch on an animal's breast or throat; *gorger* is the ancestor of **disgorge** to bring up food from the stomach (partly replaced by **regurgitate**, ultimately from Latin *gurges*), hence to pour or empty something out, and of **engorge** to feed greedily, whence **engorged** crammed, congested, or swollen. **Gargle**, **gargoyle**, and **gurgle** are probably related.

gospel [Old English *god spel* 'good news' (from *god* **good** + *spel* SPELL²), translating Latin *evangelium*, itself translating Greek *euaggelion*, from *eus* 'good' + *aggelein* 'to announce'] The message of salvation through Christ; the Christian religion; (one of) the records of Christ's life written by the four Evangelists, hence something regarded as undeniably true (ME); a principle or doctrine thought to offer social or political 'salvation'.

Greek *euaggelion* produced **evangelist** one of the authors of the Gospels; a Christian missionary; someone eager to share their beliefs or enthusiasm. Greek *eus* produced EUPHUISM*.

gossip [ME. Literally 'brother or sister in God', from GOD + Old English *sib* '(someone) related by birth'] Your baptismal sponsor or your child's godparent, hence a close friend; one with whom you share idle talk and rumours, hence someone who indulges in such talk (16c); to do so (17c); such talk (19c). Cf. GODFATHER.

The importance of the godparent's relationship with the godchild and its parents also appears in AFFINITY, Scots **cummer** [French *commère*, literally 'co-mother'] your child's godmother, later a close female friend, and French **compère** 'godfather', briefly adopted for a male friend or sugar-daddy. (*Commère* and *compère* were re-adopted meaning 'mistress or master of ceremonies').

Sib produced **sibling** a relative (OE–15c), revived for a brother or sister (*c*.1900).

Gothic [16c. French *gothique* or late Latin *gothicus*, from *Gothi* 'the Goths', a Germanic tribe that invaded the Roman Empire from the 3–5c, ultimately from the Goths' name for themselves] To do with the Goths or their language, hence **1** to do with the Germanic tribes (17–19c) **2 (a)** to do with the Dark Ages (17c), hence gloomy, horrific; **(b)** to do with the Middle Ages, medieval, romantic. Hence describing a novel or, later, film full of gloom, horror, and supernatural happenings in a medieval setting (18c), whence **goth**, **gothic** (describing) a style of rock music with mystical lyrics whose fans wear black clothes and whitened faces with heavy black make-up, resembling characters in gothic films (1980s) **3** (describing) medieval styles of handwriting or architecture regarded as barbarous by Renaissance scholars (17c); barbarous, uncouth, crude (18c).

grace [ME. Via Old French from Latin *gratia*, from *gratus* 'pleasing, grateful'] **1** attractiveness, charm; elegance, hence **(a) The Graces** the three sister-goddesses in classical mythology believed to bestow beauty, charm, and happiness (16c) **(b)** an attractive quality or feature; an embellishment (16–18c), surviving in **grace (note)** in music; **(c) grace (with)** to add beauty, elegance, or charm to (16c); *grace* a way of behaving thought to do so (17c, surviving in *airs and graces*) **(d)** an amenable attitude (*have the grace to, with (a) bad/good grace*, 16c) **2** favour, surviving in *in someone's good graces*; benevolence and courtesy to your inferiors, hence **(a)** someone able to show grace, a royal or noble person; **Your Grace** used to address a duke, duchess, or archbishop (16c) **(b)** the unearned love and mercy God gives to humanity, hence **a state of grace** freedom from sin (through atonement); **fall from grace** to, or a lapse from, this state; to lose a favoured or privileged position; **year of grace** reckoned from the birth of Christ **3** a favour: **(a)** a pardon; **Act of Grace** a formal pardon granted by Act of Parliament (17c) **(b)** an (originally God-given) talent or virtue **(c)** a privilege or dispensation; the granting of a delay or period of immunity (18c); **days of grace** extra time allowed to pay a debt **4** gratitude, thanks (–16c); a short prayer of thanks at a meal.

Latin *gratia* produced *coup de grâce* (at COUP), **disgrace** [via French from Italian *dizgrazia*, literally 'disfavour'], *gratis* [via Latin *gratiis* 'from kindness or favour'], and **ingratiate**. Descendants of *gratus* include AGREE, **congratulate**, **grateful** [from obsolete *grate* 'pleasing, agreeable, thankful'], **gratify**, **gratitude**, GRATUITY, and **ingrate** unfriendly, ungrateful; such a person.

grade [16c. French, from Latin *gradus* 'step' (ancestor of DEGREE*)] **1** a unit for measuring angles, a degree (16c only) **2** to award a university degree to (16c only) **3** to rank according to quality, size, etc. (17c), hence **(a) upgrade** to raise in rank, to improve (originally to improve stock by breeding with better animals, 19c), whence **downgrade** (1930s) **(b)** a rank or standard (19c); a mark awarded to a student's work; a class or form in school (N American) **4** (the degree of) a slope (whence, probably, **gradient**); to produce or alter one.

graffiti [19c. Plural of Italian *graffito*, from *graffio* 'a scratch', perhaps ultimately from Latin *graphium*: see GRAFT] Drawing or writing scratched on an ancient wall, e.g. at Rome or Pompeii, hence drawing or writing unofficially scratched, painted, or sprayed in a public place; to produce this (1980s). Strictly speaking, a single drawing or piece of writing should be a **graffito**, although *a piece of graffiti* is the usual term.

Italian **graffito** and its earlier form *sgraffito* are used for a form of decoration produced by scratching through a surface layer to reveal a different colour underneath.

graft [ME. Old Norse *groftr* 'digging': related to GRAVE*] **1** a ditch or moat **2** the earth moved by a spade in one go (16c), whence, probably, *graft* meaning 'hard work, to work hard' (19c), and perhaps in the sense 'money obtained by corruption, to make money corruptly' (19c: **grift** is probably an alteration, *c*.1915).

grail [ME. Old French *graal* from Latin *gradalis* 'dish'] **(Holy) Grail** the dish or cup Christ used at the Last Supper, the object of knightly quests, hence something elusive but eagerly sought.

Sometimes called **sangrail** or **sangreal** [Old French *saint* ('holy') *graal*]: the mistaken belief that this comes from French *sang real* '(Christ's) real, or royal, blood' encouraged the persistent rumour that the real Holy Grail is Christ's blood, preserved in the descendants of his children with Mary Magdalene (see MAUDLIN).

grain [ME. French, from Latin *granum*] A plant seed, a fruit pip (–19c); a fruit or berry (–17c), hence **1** the seed or seeds of a cereal plant; cereal plants, hence a small unit of weight (based on a grain of wheat); a tiny amount (*a grain of truth*) **2** a small, hard roundish particle of sand, salt, etc. **3** (the dye made from) kermes, an insect found on certain trees and once thought to be a berry; any fast dye, hence **ingrain** to dye with kermes or other fast dye (–17c), **ingrained, dyed in the grain** (influenced by sense 4) dyed with kermes etc.; deeply rooted, inveterate, inherent (16c) **4** a granular appearance or texture, hence **(a)** (the pattern formed by) the arrangement of fibres in wood, paper, etc. (16c), hence **against the grain** against your inclination (17c, because it is harder to cut wood across the grain), **cross-grained** having an irregular grain, difficult to cut (17c), bad-tempered, difficult **(b)** a rough or wrinkled appearance of leather (16c).

French *grain* produced GROGRAM*: a later sense 'spice, ingredient' produced **gravy** [French *gravé*, a misreading of *grané* 'stew, sauce']. Latin *granum* is the ancestor of **gram** applied to kinds of pulse [via Portuguese *grão*], GRANGE*, **granite** [via Italian *grano*, whence **granita** a coarse-grained water ice], **granule** [Latin *granulum* 'little grain'], and GRENADE*.

grammar [ME. Old French *gramaire* from Latin *grammatica*, from Greek *grammatikē tekhnē* 'art of letters', from *gramma* 'something written, letter of the alphabet', also 'a small weight', from *graphein* 'to write'] **1** (the study of) the rules by which words are put together; a book setting out the rules (16c), hence (a book on) the basic principles of any subject (17c) **2** Latin (16c), hence **grammar school** set up to teach it, later a secondary school with a wider curriculum: in the UK, one for the academically bright (1944); in the US, a school between primary and high school (19c), later an elementary school.

In the Middle Ages Latin *grammatica* and **gramarye** [from Old French *gramaire*] both meant 'scholarship, learning', especially about astrology and the occult: obsolete by the 16c, but revived by Scott (see DOFF) and surviving in popular literature. *Grammar* didn't have this sense (grammar schools were never Hogwarts), but its Scottish variant **glamour** emerged in *to cast the glamour over* to enchant, hence magic, enchantment; bewitching beauty or charm; romantic, exciting but often illusory attractiveness; sexual attractiveness, especially aided by clothes and make-up (*US*).

Modern French *grammaire* produced **grimoire** a manual of black magic. Greek *gramma* produced **-gram** (*cardiogram, parallelogram*) and **gram(me)** a unit of mass in the metric system; *graphein* is the ancestor of GRAPHIC*.

grange [ME. French, from medieval Latin *granica villa* 'grain house', from Latin *granum* GRAIN*] A granary, later a farmstead, especially one belonging to a monastery or feudal lord and used to store produce and tithes, whence the surname **Gra(i)nger** given to its steward.

Granary comes from Latin *granarium* [from *granum*], whence also **garner** [via Old French *gernier*] a storehouse, hence **1** to store in one; to gather or harvest and store **2** a surname given to the storekeeper or someone who lived nearby.

graphic [17c. Via Latin from Greek *graphikos*, from *graphē* 'writing, drawing', from *graphein* 'to write'] Drawn with a pencil or pen (17c only), hence **1** described clearly and vividly **2** to do with or producing pictures (18c) **3** to do with handwriting (18c). Hence (combining 2 and 3) **graphic arts** those based on line rather than colour (e.g. drawing, calligraphy, etching); **graphic design** the art of integrating text, typography, and illustrations (1950s); **graphics** the result of this (1960s); **graphic novel** a full-length story told as a cartoon strip (1970s) **4** to do with or involving diagrams or figures (19c), hence **(a) graphic formula** a chemical formula in which the relationship of the elements is shown by lines, shortened to **graph** a diagram showing the relationship between varying quantities **(b) graphic equalizer** a device that allows the strength of different sounds or frequencies to be varied, the strength of each being displayed electronically as a graph (1960s) **5 (computer) graphics** the use of computers to produce visual images; these images (1960s).

Greek *graphein* is the ancestor of the surname **Graff** a scribe, GRAFFITI, **graft** originally a shoot with a tapered end (like a stylus) inserted into a slit in another plant so that it will grow there, GRAMMAR*, **-gram** something written (*telegram*), **-graph** something written or drawn (AUTOGRAPH, *photograph*), something that writes down or records (*seismograph*, TELEGRAPH), **-grapher** someone who writes, draws, or records (*biographer, cartographer*), or who studies a certain subject (*geographer*), **graphite** the 'lead' in pencils, **-graphy** writing in a certain way (*calligraphy*) or on a certain subject (*biography*), hence a subject studied or written about (*oceanography*), and of PROGRAMME.

grapple [ME. Old French *grapil* 'small hook', from *grap(p)e* 'hook', of Germanic origin] A device with hooks used for dragging or grasping (later called a **grappling iron** or **hook**), hence to grab or hold with a grapple or with your hands (16c); to grip firmly, especially in wrestling or a hand-to-hand fight, hence to fight hand-to-hand; to wrestle with a problem.

Old French *grapil* produced **grapnel** a grappling iron; *grap(p)e* is the ancestor of **grape** [via Old French *graper* 'to gather (grapes)', using a hook], whence **grapefruit** [which grow in clusters like grapes]. **Cramp**, **crimp**, and Italian *grappa* are related.

gratuity [15c. Old French *gratuité* or medieval Latin *gratuitas* 'gift', probably from Latin *gratuitus* 'voluntary, spontaneous', from *gratus*: see GRACE*] Favour, a favour or kindness (–17c); a gift, usually of money, decided by the giver (16c); one given for good service, a tip; a sum of money given on retirement or to a serviceman or woman on discharge (19c).

Latin *gratuitus* produced **gratuitous** free, not earned or paid for, hence unwarranted, uncalled-for, without reason or justification.

grave [Old English *grafan*] **1** to dig or excavate (surviving in dialect); to bury (ME–19c) **2** to carve or sculpt (surviving in poetry and in **graven image** an idol: see the Bible, Exodus 20:4); to cut into a hard surface (ME–17c); to carve lettering or a design on a surface (largely replaced by its descendant, 15c **engrave**).

Related to **grave** a burial place [Old English *graef* 'grave, pit, trench', whence some instances of **Grave-** or **-grave** in place names (more commonly from Old English *graf(e)*, *graefe* 'brushwood, thicket, **grove**')], more distantly to GRAFT and GROOVE, and probably to Swedish *grav* 'trench' in *gravlax* (originally made by burying the salmon with salt, herbs, etc.), and to GRUB.

gravity [15c. (Via French from) Latin *gravitas*, from *gravis* 'heavy, serious'] **1** seriousness: the opposite of **levity** [16c, from Latin *levitas*, from *levis* 'light' (in weight)] **2** heaviness, weight (17c); the tendency to go downwards; the force that draws things towards the centre of the earth, or towards each other.

Latin *gravitas* was adopted meaning a solemn demeanour, having previously produced **gravitate** to be moved by gravity, hence to go towards a certain point. *Gravis* is the ancestor of AGGRAVATE, **grave** meaning serious, and GRIEVE*. Latin *levis* is the ancestor of LEVER* and of **levitate**, originally to rise because of lightness.

graze [Old English *grasian*, from *graes* **grass**] To feed on growing grass, hence **1** to put an animal out to graze (16c: cf. *grazier* below); **grazing** pasture **2** of a person: to eat small amounts at frequent intervals (1970s, *US*); to take and eat food in the supermarket without paying; to keep switching television channels without watching much of any (cf. BROWSE).

Perhaps the source of **graze** to touch in passing (from the idea of cropping grass); to cause or suffer a slight abrasion by doing so; such an abrasion. *Grass* is the ancestor of **grazier** someone who grazes or fattens cattle. Related to **green**, **grow**, and perhaps to GROOM*.

grease [ME. Old French *graisse*, ultimately from Latin *crassus* 'solid, fat, thick, dense'] The fat part of an animal's body (–17c); melted animal fat; this or something similar used as a lubricant; to anoint, smear, or lubricate with it, hence **grease the wheels** to make things run smoothly, to meet expenses (15c); **grease someone's palm** to bribe them (16c), hence *grease* a bribe (18c); protection money.

Latin *crassus* produced **crass** coarse, thick, dense; stupid, insensitive. A similar connection is found in **dense**, **fathead**, and THICK.

greet [Old English *grētan*] To begin on; to approach (OE only), hence **1** to accost or attack (–15c) **2** to speak to someone when you meet them, now in a polite or friendly way; to express or send good wishes, surviving mainly in the **greeting** (*Dear Sir*) beginning a letter, and in **greetings card/telegram** (19c) **3** of a sight or sound: to meet the eye or ear (17c) **4** to receive or respond in a certain way (*the suggestion was greeted with derision*, 19c).

Old English *grētan* is one ancestor of **greet** to weep or complain (surviving in Scots and N English dialect), the other being related Old English *grēotan* 'to cry', whence probably **regret** originally a lament.

grenade [16c. French, from Old French *(pome) grenate* '**pomegranate**' (ME, influenced by Spanish *granada* 'pomegranate'), from *pome* 'apple' (from Latin *pomum* 'fruit, apple') + Latin *granatum*, literally 'having many seeds', from *granum* 'seed, GRAIN*'] A pomegranate (–17c); a small, similarly shaped explosive shell, hence a glass 'bomb' that releases chemicals for clearing drains, extinguishing fires, etc. (19c).

French *grenade* fathered **grenadier** a soldier who threw grenades, hence a tall, strong soldier (having the necessary reach and strength), surviving in **Grenadier Guards**, and **grenadine** a cordial made from pomegranates. Old French *pome* was adopted for an apple or similar fruit, hence a (metal) ball or orb, and produced **pomander** [from *pome d'embre*, literally 'apple of ambergris'] and the name **Pomeroy** someone who lived near an apple orchard. Spanish *granada* became the name of an Andalucian city and province, perhaps because the city occupies four hills, like the four sections of a pomegranate, or because the fruit was grown nearby (**Grenada** in the Caribbean is named after it), and produced **granadilla** a passion fruit. Latin *pomum* produced POMMEL*; *granatum* produced **garnet** [via Dutch and Old French, because the stone is the colour of pomegranate seeds], and some instances of the surname **Garnett** a grower or seller of pomegranates.

griddle [ME. Old French *gredil, gridil,* ultimately from Latin *cratis* 'hurdle, wickerwork'] A metal framework for cooking over a fire, replaced by **gridiron** [ME, alteration of *griddle* by association with *iron*] and by *grill* below. Hence **1** (also *gridiron*) a large griddle for torturing people **2** a metal plate heated and used for cooking (15c, also as **girdle**); to cook on one **3** a miners' sieve (18c).

Gridiron was applied to various frameworks of parallel or intersecting bars or lines: the shortened form **grid** shares most of its senses, and was also applied to a distribution network for power, water, etc.

Latin *cratis* is the ancestor of CRATE, of **grate** a framework of metal bars (surviving in N America, otherwise replaced by **grating** or by *grille* below), hence a fire basket; a hearth, and of **grill** [via Old French *gr(a)il*, whence also **grille**, applied to various metal frameworks] a griddle, now a burner that sends heat downwards, hence **1** a dish of grilled food; a restaurant that serves grills **2** to interrogate.

grieve [ME. Old French *grever* 'to burden, encumber, or harm', from Latin *gravare*, from *gravis* 'heavy, serious'] To harass, oppress, or trouble (–19c); to hurt or damage (–16c); to hurt mentally, to make someone very sad or, formerly, angry or resentful (surviving in **aggrieved** and **grievance**); to feel or show sorrow or regret (16c).

Old French *grever* produced **grief** hardship, suffering (surviving in *come to grief*); mental distress; deep sorrow. Latin *gravare* produced **grievous**; *gravis* is the ancestor of GRAVITY*.

grim [Old English: ultimately from a Germanic word meaning 'mask'] Savage, cruel; stern, unrelenting; frightening, unnerving; extremely unpleasant and depressing; of a smile or laugh: without mirth (17c). In place names, especially of ancient earthworks, *grim* is sometimes the nickname, meaning 'the masked one', of the Norse god Woden, said to go around in disguise.

Related to **grimace** [French, from Spanish *grimazo* 'caricature', from *grima* 'fright'], to surnames such as **Grimble** and **Grime(s)** and probably to **grime**.

grin [Old English *grennian*: related to **groan**] To show your teeth in pain or, formerly, anger; to smile broadly, usually showing your teeth (15c); such a smile (17c). The Scots and N English variant **girn** went on to mean to pull a grotesque face (now usually **gurn**); to complain.

gringo [19c. Spanish, originally 'gibberish', later 'foreigner', perhaps an alteration of *griego* 'Greek', from Latin *Graecus*: the saying 'it's all Greek to me' also exists in Spanish] In Spain, a foreigner; in Latin America, a White North American or Briton (usually derogatory).

gripe [Old English *grīpan*: related to **grip** and **grope**] To seize, to grasp or pinch, hence **1** this act (ME); a grip or hold (16c); a painful pinch, hence (to cause) colic (as if squeezing the bowels, 17c) **2** a penny-pincher (16c); to keep short of money (17c) **3** to complain (1930s, *US*); a complaint or grievance.

grogram [16c. French *gros grain* 'coarse grain' (see GROSS*, GRAIN*)] A coarse, stiff fabric of silk or wool and mohair; (a garment) made of this.

In 1740 Admiral Edward Vernon, nicknamed Old Grog from his grogram cloak, ordered the rum served to sailors to be diluted, the name **grog** being given to this and similar diluted spirits (later to alcoholic drink in general, *Australia* and *New Zealand*), hence **groggy** drunk; dazed, weak, or dizzy.

French *grosgrain* was adopted for various ribbed fabrics. Its opposite, *fin grain*, is the probable source of **fingram** a fine woollen cloth (17–18c), later changed to **fingering** and applied to a fine knitting wool.

groom [ME. Origin unknown: possibly related to GRAZE*] A boy or man; a male attendant or servant (cf. BOY*): **1** one who looks after horses (now someone of either sex, cf. *lad* at BOY) **(a)** applied to various officials in a royal household (*Groom of the Chamber*, 15c): cf. MARSHAL* **(b)** the surname **Groom(e) (c)** to clean and brush a horse (19c); of an animal: to clean itself or another, hence to make yourself neat and smart (*well-groomed*); to prepare someone for a role, originally as a politician (*US*); to seduce a child (1990s) **2** short for *bridegroom* (at BRIDE, 17c), hence **groomsman** a bridegroom's attendant, the best man.

groove [ME. Obsolete Dutch *groeve* 'furrow': related to GRAVE*] A mine shaft or pit; to sink one (15c); an (artificial) channel (17c), hence **1** a fixed routine, a rut (19c) **2** a track cut in a phonograph cylinder or gramophone record (*c*.1900), hence, perhaps, **in the groove** playing jazz, later doing anything, enthusiastically and well (1930s); *groove* to do so; a good style or feeling; **groovy** good, excellent.

gross [ME. Old French *gros(se)* 'large', from Latin *grossus* 'bulky, coarse', probably of Germanic origin] Thick, bulky, massive (–18c), hence **1** of letters: large, hence **gross up** to write in a large, clear hand (15–16c); to make a fair copy of; to prepare the final form of a document: outlived by **engross** [via Anglo-Norman French *engrosser* or medieval Latin *ingrossare*] **2** coarse (–18c); of a person or behaviour: lacking culture or decency (16c), hence repulsive, disgusting (1950s, *N American*)

3 obvious (15–18c); flagrant (*gross misconduct*, 16c) **4 gross up** to buy up, to corner the market (15–16c), also as **engross** [via Old French *en gross*, medieval Latin *in grossa* 'in bulk, wholesale'], which later meant to need or use all of (17c), hence to absorb all your attention (18c) **5** twelve dozen [15c, from French *grosse douzaine* 'large dozen'] **6** entire, whole, without deductions (16c), hence to make a certain amount of profit before tax etc. (*grossed £15m*, 19c).

Old French *gros* produced GROGRAM* and **grosbeak** a finch with a thick bill. Latin *grossus* is the ancestor of **grocer**, originally a wholesaler.

grotesque [16c. Via French from Italian *pittura grottesca* 'cave paintings', from Italian *grotta* 'cave', from Latin *crypta* '(underground) chamber', ultimately from Greek *kruptein* 'to hide'] An artistic style in which fantastic animal or human forms are interwoven with foliage and flowers (first found in excavated Roman buildings), hence **1** (someone/something) comically or disturbingly distorted (17c); wildly incongruous, fantastically absurd (18c) **2 grotty** ugly, nasty, dirty (1960s, altered to **grody**, US), whence **grot** dirt.

Italian *grotta* produced **grot** or **grotto** a picturesque (artificial) cave. Latin *crypta* produced **crypt**, originally a grotto. Greek *kruptein* is the ancestor of **cryptic**, **crypto-** secret, hidden, invisible, **cryptogram** a coded message (whence **decrypt**, **encrypt**), and **krypton** a rare, colourless, odourless gas, also the name of Superman's home planet, whence **kryptonite** a mysterious substance to which he is vulnerable.

ground [Old English *grund*] **1** the bottom of the sea, a well, a container, etc., hence **(a) grounds** lees, dregs **(b) aground** of a boat etc.: touching the bottom (15c); *ground* to (cause to) run aground (15c) or sink (17c) **2** a building's foundations (–18c); to lay them (ME–17c), hence **(a)** *ground(s)* the basis of a system, belief, etc.; the reason for an action (hence **groundless**, 17c); to establish or base on **(b)** a foundation for work, e.g. cloth to be embroidered (ME); a preparatory coat of paint, hence **background** the part behind the chief objects in a picture etc. (17c), hence **foreground (c)** to instruct someone in the elements of a subject (ME), hence **grounding** this instruction, the knowledge gained (17c) **3** (the surface of) the earth, hence **(a)** a region or country (–17c); land you occupy (ME); land, an opinion, etc. you defend (*stand your ground*); a piece of land with a specific use (*football ground*); **grounds** land belonging to a building (15c) **(b)** to bring to or put on the ground, to knock down (ME); to come to the ground, to land (18c); to prevent an aircraft from flying (1930s), hence to keep a child at home as a punishment (1980s).

grout [Old English *grūt*] Coarse meal, hence **1 grouts** (porridge made from) crushed or husked grain, especially oats: replaced by **grits** [plural of **grit** bran, chaff, from Old English *grytte*] coarse oatmeal (16c); (porridge made from) any coarse grain (US), or **groats** [Old English *grotan*] (both related) **2** sediment, dregs (ME); mud, slime; plaster or mortar (17c); to apply these (19c).

Related to **grit** [Old English *grēot* 'sand, gravel'] and GRUEL.

grub [ME. Probably of Germanic origin and related to GRAVE*] To dig; to break the soil, hence **1 (a) grub up** to dig up, to uproot **(b)** to clear the ground of roots etc., hence to work laboriously; **grub(ber)** a labourer or drudge, hence **money-grub(ber)** someone intent only on making money (18c) **2** a maggot or caterpillar (found in the soil, 15c), hence **(a) Grub Street** (street infested with grubs, now Milton Street) in London, where many struggling or hack writers lived; such writers or their work (17c, influenced by sense 1) **(b) grubby** infested with grubs (18c); dirty (19c) **3** of an animal: to root about for food (17c), hence **(a)** food, whence *grubstake* (at STAKE) **(b)** to rummage (19c).

grudge   [15c. Old French *grouchier* 'to murmur', probably of Germanic origin] To grumble; grumbling, discontent, reluctance, hence **1** to be unwilling to give or allow; (also **begrudge**) to resent someone having something **2** (deep-seated and lasting) resentment or animosity, hence **grudge fight/match** in which there is personal animosity between contestants (17c).

   Hence the variant **grouch** a fit of temper or sulks; a grumbler. **Grouse** to grumble; (a reason for) a complaint, and GRUNT* are probably related.

gruel   [ME. Old French, ultimately of Germanic origin and related to GROUT*] Flour, meal; (oat) meal cooked in water or milk, especially as food for invalids or convicts, hence **get/have your gruel** to be defeated, punished, or killed (18c); **gruelling** arduous, exhausting (19c).

grunt   [Old English *grunnettan*, probably related to GRUDGE*] To make a deep, guttural sound, like a pig, hence **1** this sound (16c) **2** (also **grunter**) applied to various fish who make a similar noise when caught (17c): the **gurnard** also does so [ME, ultimately from Latin *grunnire* 'to grunt'] **3** an unskilled assistant, a menial (1920s, US slang); an American infantryman, especially in Vietnam, hence **grunt work** menial work (1970s).

   Grunt produced **gruntle** to make quiet little grunts; to grumble, whence **disgruntle**, literally 'to grumble a lot', whence **disgruntled** discontented, fed up, whence the humorous back-formation **gruntled** pleased, satisfied.

guide   [ME. French *guider*, earlier *guier*, of Germanic origin] To show the way; someone who does, hence **1** to direct, influence, or advise; someone/something that does; a manual (17c); **guide(book)** containing information for tourists (18c) **2** to control the movement of a vehicle, tool, etc. (15c); something that does so (17c); something that marks a position or guides the eye (19c) **3** a military scout (16c), hence **(Girl) Guide** a member of an international girls' organization founded in 1909 (cf. SCOUT sense 3).

   Old French *guier* is one parent of **guy(rope)** a rope that holds or steadies something, originally on a ship [the other being Low German and Dutch *gei*]. Related to WIT*.

guile   [ME. Old French, probably of Old Norse origin] Deceit, cunning, treachery; to deceive or defraud (–17c), surviving in dialect and in **beguile** (ME), which came to mean to charm or amuse (16c, hence **beguiling** charming, fascinating); to divert your attention, hence to pass time pleasantly.

   The source of the surname **Guyler** a deceitful person. Probably related to **wile** trickery, deceit, hence **1** to entice; to get by cunning; **wiles** enticing or persuasive behaviour **2 wile (away)** to pass time pleasantly (influenced by *beguile* and WHILE).

guise   [ME. French, ultimately of Germanic origin] Manner, style, custom, habit (–18c); a way of dressing, hence external or assumed appearance **(a)** disguise or pretence; (to wear) a disguise, mask, or fancy dress (15c), hence **guiser** a mummer; an odd-looking person (18c, Scots, whence, perhaps, **geezer** a bloke, 19c); one of a group of children in disguise, especially at Halloween, offering entertainment in return for sweets.

French *guise* produced **disguise** to change your usual style of dress, originally with no sense of deceit (ME). Related to **wise** way [Old English *wīse*], surviving mainly in **otherwise** [Old English *on ōthre wisan* 'in another way'], and to WIT*.

gulf [ME. Via French from Italian *golfo*, ultimately from Greek *kolphos* 'bosom', later 'trough between waves, abyss'] **1** a large inlet **2** a chasm; a wide gap, a huge difference of opinion etc. (see the Bible, Luke 16:26) **3** a whirlpool (15c), hence **engulf** to swallow up (16c); to overwhelm.

gullet [ME. French *goulet* 'bottleneck', from Old French *go(u)le* 'throat', from Latin *gula*] The passage for food in the throat, hence a narrow passage, a gorge or ravine (17c, now mainly dialect).

Gully [also from Old French *goulet*] followed the same path, replacing *gullet* in the sense 'ravine'. Old French *go(u)les*, plural of *go(u)le*, was used for pieces of red-dyed fur worn at the neck, whence **gules** the heraldic term for red.

gum [ME. Old French *gomme*, ultimately via Latin and Greek from Egyptian *kemai*] The sticky juice of some plants; a similar synthetic substance; something resembling either. Hence **1** such a substance used as glue, as a fabric stiffener, in food products, etc. (15c), hence **(a)** to treat with gum (16c) **(b)** something made with gum, e.g. **gum boot/shoe** made of rubber (19c), hence *gumshoe* to move stealthily, as if in soft shoes (*c.*1900), hence a detective **(c)** (a sweet made with) a similar gelatinous mixture (19c) **(d) (chewing) gum**, originally from sapodilla or spruce gum (19c), whence **bubble gum** (1930s) **2 gum (tree)** that produces gum, especially the eucalyptus (17c) **3 gum up** to make or become clogged with a thick or sticky substance (19c).

gun [ME. Perhaps from the Scandinavian female name *Gunnhildr*, from *gunnr* + *hildr*, both meaning 'war'] Any large war machine for hurling rocks, bolts, etc. (–16c); a cannon (hence the firing of one as a salute or signal, 17c); a portable firearm (15c). Hence **1** to provide with a gun or guns (17c, hence **outgunned** having less firepower) **2** to shoot (*gun down*, 17c); **gun for** to intend to harm (19c) **3** a member of a shooting party (19c); someone armed with a gun (*hired gun*, 1930s, *US*) **4** a device that ejects a substance (*grease gun*, 19c), hence a car's accelerator, which injects fuel into the engine (early 20c), hence **give it the gun** (*c.*1915), *gun* (1930s) to open the throttle; to accelerate sharply.

As *gun* became applied to smaller firearms, a cannon became known as a **great gun**, hence **1 blow great guns** to blow a gale (sounding as loud as cannon); **go great guns** to do something rapidly or successfully **2** an important person, surviving mainly as **big gun**.

gut [Old English *guttas* (plural)] **Guts** the bowels, the entrails; the alimentary canal, hence **1** to cut these out (ME); **gutted** extremely disappointed or upset (feeling empty inside, 1970s) **2** the stomach, a (large) one (*beer gut*, ME), hence **(a) guts** a greedy person (16c); *gut(s)* to eat greedily (17c) **(b)** courage, determination (formerly believed to come from the stomach, 19c: the idea also survives in *not have the stomach for*) **(c)** of a feeling, reaction, etc.: instinctive (1950s) **3** intestinal tissue (ME), hence **(a) (cat)gut** thread or cord made from the intestines of various animals (probably not cats, 16c) **(b)** a fibre from silkworms used for fishing lines (19c) **4** the internal parts of something (17c), hence **(a)** to remove or destroy them **(b)** the substance, the essentials; to extract these (18c).

gutter [ME. Old French *gotiere*, ultimately from Latin *gutta* 'a drop'] A watercourse, hence **1** a trough to carry off rainwater from a roof or street, hence a filthy channel (19c); a degraded existence (cf. *guttersnipe* at SNIPE) **2** (to make) a groove or channel, hence **(a) gutter (stick)** a device that separates two pages set for printing (17c), hence *gutter* the space between facing pages of an open book or between stamps on a sheet (19c) **(b)** of a candle: to burn away quickly because the molten wax has made a channel on one side (18c).

Latin *gutta* produced **gout 1** a disease once thought to be caused by drops of infected fluid in the blood **2** a drop, later a large blob, of blood etc.

guy [19c. Named after Guy Fawkes, conspirator in the Gunpowder Plot to blow up Parliament in 1605] A home-made effigy of Guy Fawkes burned on a bonfire on **Guy Fawkes** or **bonfire night**, 5 November, the anniversary of the Gunpowder Plot, hence **1** to parade a guy around the streets in the days before Guy Fawkes night, hence to mock or ridicule **2** a strange, oddly dressed person, hence any man (*US*); **guys** people of either sex.

gymnasium [16c. Latin, 'place for training, school', from Greek *gumnasion*, from *gumnazein* 'to exercise', from *gumnos* 'naked' (Greek athletes usually trained naked)] **1** a place equipped for physical exercises (now usually having exercise machines and shortened to **gym**) **2** a high school or college in Continental Europe (17c).

Gymnasium influenced the spelling of **gymkhana** [Urdu *gendḵānah* 'racket court', from Hindi *gēd* 'ball' + Persian *ḵānah* 'house'] a public sports facility in India, later an athletics display, now a meeting for mounted games.

H

habit [ME. Via Old French from Latin *habitus* 'having, holding, consisting of', later 'constitution or condition; the way you live, behave, or appear', from *habere* 'to have or consist of'] **1** clothing; that worn by a particular profession or rank, or for a particular activity (*nun's/riding habit*) **2** demeanour or posture (–17c), hence a characteristic way of growing (*a trailing habit*, 17c) **3** nature, disposition; usual or customary behaviour; a regular, repetitive, sometimes unconscious action or way of behaving; an addiction (*drug habit*, 19c).

A similar development from 'hold or possess' to 'act in a certain way' is found in **behave** [ME, from **have** (Old English *habban*, whence HOBNOB)].

Latin *habitus* produced the legal term **habit and repute** [medieval Latin *habit et reputatus* 'held and reputed (to be so)'], **habitual** originally meaning 'in your nature', **habituate**, French *habitué*, and **malady** [Latin *male habitus* 'in bad condition']. Latin *habere*'s descendants include ABLE, EXHIBIT, INHABIT*, **inhibit**, **prebend** (the property providing) an allowance made to a cathedral clergyman [via French from Latin *praebenda* 'things to be supplied' (whence **provender**), from *praebere* 'to supply', from *prae* 'before' + *habere*], and **prohibit** [Latin *prohibere*, literally 'to hold back'].

hack [Old English *haccian* 'to cut in pieces'] To cut or chop with repeated heavy blows; (to make) a rough, irregular cut, gash, or wound **2** (to give) a short, hard, dry cough (19c) **3** a hacking blow (19c); a try or attempt (N American); **hack (it)** to cope with (*US*, perhaps from the idea of hacking your way through difficulties: cf. HAGGLE) **4 hacker** someone who uses or programs computers as a hobby (1970s, *US*, said to be from a Yiddish expression for an inept carpenter, hence someone with no manual skills, but perhaps related to sense 3), hence *hack* to be a hacker; **hack into** to access a computer system illicitly, originally as a challenge (1980s) **6 hack and slash** describing violent films or computer games (1980s).

hackle [ME. Alteration of **hatchel**, ultimately of West Germanic origin and related to **hook**] **1** a comb, originally for flax (as the northern variant **heckle**); to comb with one **2** a long feather or feathers which the domestic cock raises when angry (probably because the raised feathers resembled a comb's teeth, but influenced by **hackle** a bird's plumage [ME, from Old English *hacele* 'a cloak']), hence **(a) hackles** the hairs on a dog's neck and back which it raises when angry or afraid **(b)** *heckle* to harangue (16c, *Scots*); to interrupt a public speaker or performer with aggressive remarks (17c).

hackney [ME. Anglo-Norman French *hakeney* or Anglo-Latin *hakeneius*, probably from Hackney in E London, where horses were pastured] **1** a horse kept for hire (later also **hack**), hence **(a)** to drive hard or overwork (often the fate of a hired horse, 16c); **hackneyed** made trite or commonplace by overuse **(b)** now only *hack*: someone, especially a writer, hired to do menial work (16c); an active, uncritically loyal member of a political party **(c)** a vehicle kept for hire (17c), surviving in **hackney carriage** the official name of a taxi in the UK, and as *hack* (18c, N American) **2** (now *hack*) an ordinary riding horse, hence to ride for pleasure (16c); (a horse for) such a ride **3** only as *hackney*: a high-stepping harness horse (19c).

haggard [16c. French *hagard*, perhaps of Germanic origin and related to HEDGE*] Of a hawk: caught as an adult, hence wild, unmanageable; of a person: wild-eyed, unkempt, gaunt (17c).

haggle [16c. Old Norse *höggva*] **1** to chop clumsily, to hack or mangle **2** to get on with difficulty (cf. HACK); to argue or wrangle (17c), now especially in order to agree on a price.

    Hassle, also originally 'to hack', may be a blend of *haggle* and *tussle* (at TOUSE): the current senses emerged in the US. Old Norse *höggva* produced **haggis**, and is related to **hay**, **hew**, and **hoe**.

halcyon [ME. Latin *(h)alcyon*, from Greek *halkuōn*, alteration (influenced by *hals* 'salt, sea' and *kuōn* 'conceiving'), of *alkuōn* 'kingfisher'] A mythical bird, identified with the kingfisher, that nested on the sea around the winter solstice, charming the wind and waves to stay calm, hence **1 halcyon days** fourteen days of calm weather at this time (16c); a happy or prosperous period; *halcyon* calm, peaceful, idyllic **2** the kingfisher, now specifically a tropical genus.

half [Old English *h(e)alf*] **1** one side of an object, or of an argument or transaction, surviving in **on behalf of**, **on someone's behalf** [ME, from Old English *be healfe* 'by the side'] **2** (forming) either of two equal or corresponding parts; something equal to this, e.g. a half-pint of beer, each of two equal periods of play in a game, a child's reduced fare (1930s) **3** partially, to some extent (*half-starved*); partial, incomplete, imperfect (*a half smile, half-brother*, ME), hence **not half (a)** not sufficiently or at all **(b)** completely, certainly (16c) **4 half-back** a player between the forwards and backs (19c), shortened to *half* (*left/scrum half*).

hall [Old English *h(e)all*] Any large roofed space, now only as specified (*market/ town hall*), hence **1** a large house; the main one on an estate, now chiefly in names (*Toad of Toad Hall*), also as a surname for someone who lived close to or worked at one; a public room in one (ME), hence **(a)** a large room or building for public gatherings (*banqueting/music/village hall*) **(b)** an entrance-room (17c); a vestibule or lobby; a corridor (N American) **2** a guild's or fraternity's building (ME), whence **hallmark** (18c, from Goldsmiths' Hall in London, where articles are assayed and stamped) **3** a building where students lived or were taught (ME, surviving in **hall of residence** and in the names of some colleges); (a meal taken in) a college or university dining room (16c).

    Related to **Valhalla** the hall where Odin received the souls of heroes [Old Norse *Valhöll*, from *valr* 'those slain in battle' + *höll* 'hall'], and to **HOLE***].

halt [16c. (Via French, Italian, or Spanish) from German *halten* 'to stop or hold'] (To make) a temporary stop on a journey; to stop (17c, often as a military command), hence **1** to make something stop (18c) **2** a stopping-place, especially a small unmanned railway station (early 20c).

Related to HOLE*. **Halting** 'stopping and starting' is not related: it comes from **halt** [Old English *healtian*] to limp, later to hesitate.

ham [Old English *ham, hom*] The back of the knee, later of the thigh; the thigh and buttock (15c); an animal's hock, hence **1** an animal's thigh as food, now specifically a cured pig's ham (17c); **ham-fisted/handed** clumsy (literally 'having fists/hands like hams': early 20c, *aviators' slang*). Cf. HOUGH: see also AMATEUR **2 hamstring** a tendon behind the knee or hock (16c); to cripple by cutting it (17c); to thwart or hinder.

hamburger [17c. German] **1** Hamburger (describing) someone/something from Hamburg in N Germany **2 Hamburg(er) steak** a flat cake of seasoned minced beef (19c, *US*); *hamburger* this served in a bun (early 20c), shortened to **burger** (1930s), hence **cheeseburger** etc. with added ingredients (1960s). HAM was then taken to mean cured pork, hence **beefburger, veggieburger**, etc.

The names of other foreign foods were similarly altered: **Bologna sausage** became **polony** (UK) and **baloney** (*US*, coming to mean 'nonsense' because sometimes made from donkey meat); German *Frankfurter wurst* 'sausage from Frankfurt(-am-Main)' became **frankfurter**, and *Wienerwurst* 'Viennese sausage' became **wiener** or **weenie**.

hand [Old English] The end of the arm, beyond the wrist, hence **1** something resembling this (*hand of a clock/of bananas*); a measurement (4 inches, 10.2 cm) based on a hand's width (16c) **2** side, position (*left/right hand, beforehand*); **at hand** nearby, partly replaced by **handy 3** possession, care, control (*in your hands, out of hand*); an owner (ME, surviving in *change hands, first/second hand*) **4** help (*give/lend a hand*), hence **(a)** a share in an action (16c) **(b)** a manual worker (17c); one of a (ship's) crew **5** to touch, grasp, or manipulate (ME, outlived by **handle** [Old English *handlian*], which came to mean the part you hold to do so), hence *handy* dextrous, skilful **6 (**something) operated or done with the hands (*hand brake, hand-picked, handwriting*); a pledge, now of marriage (sealed by holding or shaking hands, ME); a style of writing; a round of applause (16c) **7** (describing) something held in the hand (*handkerchief, hand of cards*, 16c) **8** hand **(on/over/round)** to pass (as if) with your hand(s) (17c).

Hand produced HANDICAP and HANDSOME; Old English *hand* produced **handcraft**, changed to **handicraft** under the influence of **handiwork** [Old English *handgeweorc*].

handicap [17c. From 'hand in cap'] A game in which one person offered to exchange a possession for something belonging to another, an umpire deciding the difference in value. All three deposited forfeit money in a cap and the umpire announced his valuation; the opponents showed their acceptance or rejection by withdrawing their hands either full or empty. Hence a horse race in which an umpire decided the weight each horse must carry, the owners originally showing acceptance or dissent in a similar way (18c), hence **1** any contest in which an inferior competitor is given an advantage; (to give) this advantage **2** the extra weight given to the superior horse (19c), hence (to give) a disadvantage.

handsome [15c. From **hand** + *-some* as in *cumbersome*] Easy to use or deal with (–16c); handy, convenient, suitable (16c); apt, appropriate, clever (now US); fitting, proper; generous, magnanimous, ample; impressive, fine; good-looking.

hang [Partly from Old English *hangian* 'to dangle', partly from Old Norse *hanga* 'to suspend'. The earlier past tense **hanged** survives in sense 1; in other senses the past tense is **hung**] To suspend or be suspended, hence **1** to kill or be killed by hanging (originally by crucifixion) **2** to (cause or allow to) droop or bend; of a horse: to (try to) veer to one side (1950s), hence, perhaps, **to hang a left/right** (1960s, *US*) **3** to depend on **4** to attach or be attached (*hang a door/picture/wallpaper*, ME); **5** to be or remain in suspense (ME), hence to pause or hesitate (*hang fire, a hung jury*, 17c); **hang about/around** to stay; **hang on/in** to endure **6** the way something hangs, is poised, or handles (18c), hence **get the hang of** to come to understand or manage, to get the knack (19c, *US*).

The practice of forming the past tense by changing the verb died out during the Old English period: *hung* probably arose by association with changes such as *sang, sung*. A similar story is found in **shit**: the past tense **shitted** is now regarded as correct, but **shat** (perhaps by association with *sit, sat*) is common and may become dominant.

Related to **hanker** originally to linger or wait around, to *henge* in **Stonehenge**, and to **hinge** on which something hangs or relies.

hap [ME. Old Norse *happ*] **1** (to have) good or bad fortune; to come across something by chance (outlived by its descendant, **happen**) **2** something that comes about by chance; to do so (whence 15c **mayhap**, short for 'it may hap'): outlived by *happen* **3** good fortune, success, prosperity (–17c), surviving in **hapless** and in **happy** originally 'fortunate' **4** chance seen as controlling events, whence **perhaps**, literally 'through chances' (15c), and **haphazard** (16c, literally 'hazard of chance').

harbinger [ME. Old French *herbergier*, from *herbergere* 'to provide lodging for', from *herberge* 'lodging', from Old Saxon *heriberga* 'shelter for an army', from *heri* 'army': related to HARBOUR*] Someone who provided lodging (–16c) or who went ahead to find lodgings, hence a herald or forerunner (16c); a sign of something to come.

harbour [Old English *herebeorg* (noun), *hereborgian* (verb), from *here* 'army' + *beorge* 'shelter'] (A) shelter, hence **1** a sheltered anchorage (ME); to shelter in one (16c); (to stay in) an overnight stop for troops or tanks (1930s) **2** to give lodgings to (ME–17c), hence **(a)** to shelter a criminal, vermin, etc. **(b)** to keep an idea, suspicion, or grudge in your mind **3 coldharbour** a crude roadside shelter for drovers or travellers (ME, surviving in place names).

Old English *here* appears as **Har-** or **Her-** in place names (*Harmsworth, Hereford*), and is related to HARBINGER, **harness**, HARRY*, HERALD, and perhaps **harangue**; *beorg* is related to BOROUGH*.

hard [Old English *h(e)ard*] **1** firm, difficult to penetrate, cut, or fragment: **(a)** of money: in gold or coin (18c); **hard cash** coins and notes (not cheques or credit); **hard currency** backed by assets (19c) **(b)** a firm beach or foreshore, a roadway or jetty across a foreshore (19c) **(c)** of the penis: erect (19c); **hard (on)** an erection. See also *hard core* (at CORE), *hardware* (at WARE²) **2** courageous, bold, later tough: cf. *hardy* below **3** callous, harsh, severe; without concession or compromise (*hard bargain, the hard left*, 17c) **4** difficult to endure, hence **hardship** adversity (ME)

5 strenuous, laborious; strenuously, vigorously (cf. FAST), hence **(a)** difficult to do, understand, or to control (ME); of liquor: strongly alcoholic (18c); of a drug: addictive (1960s) **(b)** having difficulty (surviving in **hard of hearing**) **(c)** with difficulty, scarcely (16c, largely replaced by **hardly**) **6** extremely, intensely (now mainly US); to the fullest extent (*hard over*, 16c, *nautical*) **7** close, close by (ME, surviving in **hard by**, **hard on the heels**) **8** of water: containing minerals making it difficult for soap to lather (17c) **9** of a fact: unable to be explained away (19c); of news: factual, objective, real (1920s).

Often opposed to **soft** [Old English *softe* 'meek, mild, gentle'] whose equivalent senses are generally later; this is also true for most of the *hard/soft* phrases (e.g. *hard/soft drug/sell*). **Hard-** appears in place- and surnames, and is related to **-ard**, **-art** (*dastard* at DAZE, *braggart*), and to **hardy** [Old French *hardi*, of Germanic origin] bold, daring (whence **foolhardy**), later tough, robust.

hark [ME. Probably from Old English *heorcian*, whence **hearken**] To listen attentively (later called to get hounds' attention before a command), hence **hark back!** go back! (to find a lost scent), hence to return to a subject; to resemble something in the past.

harlequin [Obsolete French, or Italian *Arlechinno*, from *Herlequin*, the name of the leader of a legendary troop of demon horsemen, perhaps ultimately from Old English *Herla cyning* 'King Herla', a mythical figure identified with Woden] A character in French comedy based on Arlechinno in the Italian *commedia dell'arte* (16c); a character in English pantomime, dressed in a multicoloured costume, hence **1** gaily coloured (18c); variegated **2** a buffoon (19c) **3 harlequinade** a pantomime or play featuring Harlequin (18c); clowning, buffoonery (19c).

The *commedia dell'arte* also produced PANTALOON*, PUNCH, and **zany** [from **Zanni** a comic servant, short for Italian *Gianni* or *Giovanni* 'John', a stock name of such characters]. See also SKIRMISH.

harlot [ME. Old French, 'young man, knave'] **1** a male servant (–16c); a beggar, tramp, or rascal (–17c); an itinerant juggler or clown (–15c), these senses producing the surname **Arlot(t) 2** a lecher (15c), later a promiscuous woman, a prostitute.

harry [Old English *her(g)ian*] To raid; to plunder (ME); to attack repeatedly; to worry, goad, or torment (15c). The variant **harrow** survives, just, in the **harrowing of hell**, when, between his death and resurrection, Christ raided hell to rescue the souls of the good; it produced **harrower**, a kind of hawk (16c), changed to **harrier** by association with **harrier** a hound for hunting hares [ME, from **hare** (Old English *hara*)].

Harry produced **hurry**, lengthened to **hurry-scurry**, whence **scurry**. *Harry* and *hare* are probably the parents of **hare** to harass, worry, or frighten (16–17c), whence **harum-scarum** [with **scare** (Old Norse *skirra*)]. Related to HARBOUR*.

harvest [Old English *haerfest*] Autumn (–18c), hence (the season for) reaping and gathering grain or, later, other crops (ME), hence **1** to do so; to gather up (19c); to remove tissue for experiments or transplantation (1940s); to cull wild animals **2** the crops gathered; (to receive) the product of any activity or effort.

hash [16c. French *hacher*, from *hache* 'axe', ultimately of Germanic origin] To cut, especially meat, into small pieces; to hack or mangle, hence **1** a dish of chopped (cooked) meat with potatoes (17c), hence **(a)** to make into or serve as hash; to mull over or discuss exhaustively (1950s, whence **rehash**, 1960s) **(b)** later also *rehash*: something presented in a new guise (17c); *rehash* to do so (19c) **(c)** a jumbled mixture, a mess (18c) **(d) hashery**, **hash house** a cheap restaurant or boarding house; **hasher**, **hash slinger** a waiter (all 19c, *US*) **2 hash browns** chopped cooked potatoes, fried until brown [*c*.1900, *US*, contraction of *hashed brown(ed) potatoes*] **3 hash (mark/sign)** the character # [1980s, perhaps an alteration of *hatch* below].

French *hacher* produced **hatch** to inlay a surface with metal strips or mark it with lines; **hatching** (the drawing of) parallel lines to represent shading. *Hache* produced *hachette* 'a small axe', whence **hatchet**; **bury the hatchet** comes from the Native American custom of burying their weapons when making peace.

haul [15c. Variant of Middle English *hale*, via French from Old Norse *hala*] **1** to pull, drag, or tug, hence **(a)** a pull (17c); the pulling out of a fishing net; the fish caught (18c); an amount seized, stolen, etc. **(b)** to transport goods, especially by road (18c), hence **haulage** the business or cost of transportation (19c); **haulier** a person or company that transports goods by road (early 20c) **(c)** the distance hauled, a journey (*long/short haul*, 19c) **2** to trim a ship's sails to sail closer to the wind (16c); to change course; of the wind: to change direction relative to the boat (18c).

Hale produced **halier** a rope and tackle for raising or lowering sails, altered to **halyard** by association with YARD[1].

haunt [ME. French *hanter*, of Germanic origin and related to HOME*] To do or use habitually (–16c); to visit frequently, hence **1** of a thought or feeling: to occur to or trouble frequently; of a ghost or spirit: to visit repeatedly (16c) **2** a place frequented.

havoc [ME. Anglo-Norman French *havok*, alteration of Old French *havo(t)* 'plundering, devastation', perhaps of Germanic origin] **1 cry havoc** to give an army the order *havoc!* 'plunder!' **2** devastation, destruction, chaos (15c).

hazard [ME. Via French and Spanish from Arabic *az-zahr* 'chance, luck', from Persian *zār* or Turkish *zar* 'dice'] A dice game in which the chances are complicated by arbitrary rules; to play this (15c); to stake something in a game (16c); to take a chance or risk; a risk of loss or harm; (a source of) danger.

The source of the surname **Has(s)ard**, **Hassett**, or **Hazzard** a gambler or risk-taker.

head [Old English *heafod*] The part of a human or animal beyond the neck, hence **1** the top (often opposed to **foot** [Old English *fōt*]): the top of a page or section (hence **heading**, **headline**, 19c), of a boil or pimple (ME, hence *come to a head*); the 'business end' of a tool etc.; the froth on beer; the end of the bed where your head lies; the end of the table where important people sit; the source of a river, hence a body of water etc. to provide power (*good head of steam*); the pressure it exerts **2** the front (ME), hence **(a)** a boat's bows (15c); **heads** a boat's toilet (formerly in the bows, 18c) **(b) head(land)** a promontory (16c) **(c)** to go in or to the front (18c); **head (off)** to overtake and turn aside **3** (describing) a ruler or leader; to be one, to lead (ME) **4** the mind (ME); (a person with) a certain kind of mind (*a wise head, an airhead*); mental aptitude (*a head for figures*) **5** a person, cow, etc. as a unit (*the trip cost £12 a head/400 head of sheep*, 16c) **6** to face or move in a certain direction (17c); *heading* the direction followed.

hearse [ME. Old French *herce* 'harrow', from Latin *hirpex*, from Samnite *(h)irpus* 'wolf' (from its teeth)] **1** a latticework placed over a distinguished person's coffin (probably from the resemblance of the latticework to a harrow); a framework over the bier to support the pall (16c), hence the bier itself (17c); a vehicle that takes a coffin to the funeral **2** a harrow (15–18c).

Old French *herce* produced **rehearse** [via Old French *rehercier*, literally 'to harrow again', from *hercier* 'to harrow'] to repeat something aloud, hence to practise a performance.

heaven [Old English *heofon*] **1** the vault containing the sun, moon, and stars, hence **heavenly bodies** stars, planets, comets, etc. (ME) **2** (often **the heavens**) the sky; the regions beyond it (mainly in **heaven and earth** the universe); the home of God and the angels, hence **(a)** in Judaism: each of seven celestial regions; in Islam: each of seven stages of blessed life after death, hence **seventh heaven** the highest of these, the most blissful state (19c) **(b)** God, Providence (*Heaven help us!*) **(c)** a beautiful or blissful state or place (ME) **(d) heavenly** divine, holy; wonderfully good or beautiful (ME); delightful (19c). Cf. PARADISE.

hectic [ME. Via Old French and Latin from Greek *hektikos* 'habitual', later 'to do with or suffering from tuberculosis' (a chronic disease), from *hexis* 'habit, state of mind or body', from *ekhein* 'to stay in a certain condition, to hold or keep'] To do with or characteristic of tuberculosis or similar diseases, hence feverish, flushed (19c); full of feverish excitement or activity (*c*.1900).

Greek *ekhein* produced **eunuch** [via Latin from Greek *eunoukhos*, literally 'keeper of the bedroom', with *eunē* 'bed'] and HECTOR.

hector [ME. Greek *hektōr* 'holding fast' (the name of a Trojan hero in Homer's *Iliad*), from *ekhein*: see HECTIC] A brave warrior; a swaggering bully (17c, specifically one of a gang of London youths), hence to bluster; to browbeat or intimidate.

hedge [Old English *hecg*] A line of bushes forming a boundary or barrier; to make, repair, or surround something with one (ME); to confine or restrict (16c), hence **1** to hem in with conditions (16c); to prevaricate **2** to enclose in something else, specifically to safeguard a debt by including it in one with better security (17–18c); to reduce the risk of a bet or speculation by making an opposing one; a means of doing so; **hedge fund** an investment vehicle designed to make money despite a falling market (1940s).

Old English *hecg* appears in names such as **Heacham**, **Heckfield**, **Hedge(s)**, and **Heigham**. Probably related to HAGGARD and **hawthorn** (often used for hedges).

heel [Old English *hēla*, *haela*: related to HOUGH] The foot immediately below the ankle; the corresponding part on an animal. Hence **1** the part of a sock, shoe, etc. at the heel (ME) **2** something resembling a heel; the end part or remains, e.g. of a loaf or cheese (15c); the lower or handle end (17c); the thickest part (18c) **3** to provide with a heel (17c); to give a gamecock spurs or a person a weapon (18c), hence **heeled** equipped, armed (19c, *US*); **well-heeled** wealthy **4** to kick, urge on, or push in with the heel (19c) **5** a command to a dog to follow closely (19c), hence **heeler** a (disreputable) follower, especially of a politician (US), whence perhaps *heel* a despicable person (early 20c).

hell [Old English: related to HALL*] The underworld, the place where souls go after death; this as a place of punishment inhabited by demons and the damned, hence **1** the inhabitants or powers of hell (ME), hence **(a) hell cat** a spiteful or furious woman or, occasionally, man (17c) **(b) from hell** particularly bad (1980s, *US*) **2** a place of confinement, punishment, misery, or chaos (ME); a gambling den (18c).

Euphemisms include **Hades** [Greek *haidēs*, originally a name of Pluto, the god of the dead; used to translate Hebrew *šĕ'ōl*, the home of departed spirits, identified with hell or a place for souls awaiting judgement], **Halifax** an industrial city in N England, and **heck** (*N English dialect*).

henchman [ME. Old English *hengest* 'stallion' (see STUD) + MAN] A nobleman's page or squire; a Highland chief's closest attendant (18c); a loyal follower, now often of a politician or criminal (19c). Cf. MARSHAL*.

Hengest survives in place names (e.g. *Henstridge*, *Hinksey*), and was the name of one of the reputed leaders of the first Anglo-Saxon settlers, the other being his brother **Horsa**, whose name also means 'stallion' [Old English *hors* **horse**].

herald [ME. Old French *herau(l)t* (noun), *herauder* (verb), of Germanic origin and related to HARBOUR* and to WIELD*] An official who issued a ruler's proclamations, carried messages between Heads of State, organized tournaments and State ceremonies, and ruled on etiquette, precedence, and the use of armorial bearings, hence **1** a messenger or envoy; to go before or announce the approach of someone/something; someone who does so (16c) **2 heraldry (a)** the profession or study of devising, granting, or blazoning arms, of associated protocol, and of tracing genealogies (16c); armorial bearings, insignia, or devices **(b)** the pomp and ceremony connected with a herald's work (17c).

hermetic [17c. From Hermes Trismestigus (Hermes Thrice-greatest), the name the Greeks gave to the Egyptian god Thoth, whom they associated with Hermes (their god of science: see MERCURY) and regarded as a teacher of the occult] **1** to do with alchemy and the occult; obscure, esoteric **2 hermetic seal** an airtight seal or closure (from a magical seal accredited to Hermes Trismestigus), hence *hermetic* airtight, isolated, free from outside influences (18c).

Related to **hermaphrodite** [from Hermaphroditus, the son of Greek Hermes and the goddess Aphrodite, whose body became merged with that of a nymph] and the name **Hermione**, meaning 'dedicated to Hermes'.

hero [15c. Latin *heros*, from Greek *hērōs*] A man, often the offspring of a god and a mortal, with superhuman strength, courage, or skill; an outstandingly brave man or, later, woman (largely replacing the feminine form **heroine**, which survives in sense 2), hence **1 heroic** typical of or fit for a hero (16c); as brave as one; **heroics** recklessly bold behaviour (18c) **2** such a man as the subject of an epic (17c), hence **(a)** the chief male character in a story, play, etc. **(b) heroic verse**

a form used in epic poetry; *heroic* of language: extravagant, exaggerated; of a statue: larger than life-size (18c); unusually large or great **3** someone you look up to (17c).

Latin *heros* produced German **heroin**, which inflates the user's self-esteem.

herring [Old English *hǣring*] A small edible fish. Hence **1 herringbone** **(a)** (a bone from) a herring's skeleton (16c) **(b)** (having) a zigzag pattern or weave, like the two sets of a herring's ribs joining the spine (17c) **(c)** (to sew with) an asymmetrical cross stitch (18c); in skiing: to climb a slope by walking with the skis pointed outwards (*c.*1900): both producing a herringbone pattern **2 red herring** a herring smoked to a reddish-brown colour (15c), hence (from the practice of dragging one across a trail to teach hounds not to be distracted from the real scent) something irrelevant or misleading (19c).

hide [Old English *hȳd*] An animal's skin, hence **1 hidebound** having skin stretched tightly over the bones (16c); of a tree: unable to grow because its bark is too inflexible, hence conservative, inflexible, narrow-minded (17c) **2** to flay (18c); to flog (19c), surviving mainly in **hiding** a beating (cf. TAN).

hierarchy [ME. Via Old French and medieval Latin from Greek *hierarkhia* 'rule of a high priest', from *hierarkhēs* 'high priest', from *hieros* 'sacred' + *-arkhē* 'rule, government': see ARCHIVE] **1** in Christian theology: each of three divisions of angelic beings, hence **(a)** an element of any threefold system **(b)** angels collectively (16c) **(c)** a body of clergy organized into ranks (17c); (the formal grading of) a body of people, animals, or things ranked one above the other **2** rule in sacred matters; (a system of) rule by priests.

Greek *hieros* appears in **hieroglyphic** [Greek *hierogluphikos*, with *gluphe* 'carving'] the ancient Egyptian writing system (**hieroglyph** is a back-formation), hence (describing) a picture, figure, or symbol with a hidden meaning.

hijack [1920s. Origin unknown] To steal (originally contraband) goods in transit (*US*); to take control of a vehicle by force and steal its load, take its passengers hostage, or divert it to another destination; such an attack (1950s); to take over an idea, course of action, etc. (1970s). Hence **carjack** (1990s, *US*) and **skyjack** (1960s).

hike [19c. Origin unknown] To walk vigorously (*W England dialect*), hence **1** to do so for pleasure; such a walk **2** to march or trek; such a march, hence to force to move; to shove, pull, or hoist (**hoick** is probably a variant); a sudden increase (*price hike,* 1930s, *N American*).

hilarity [ME. Via French from Latin *hilaritas*, from *hilaris* 'cheerful', from Greek *hilaros* 'joyful, propitious'] Cheerfulness, contentment, calm joy; great amusement or mirth (19c).

Latin *hilaris* produced **exhilarate**, literally 'to make cheerful', and the name **Hilary**.

hinder [Old English *hindrian*] To injure or damage (–18c); to delay, obstruct, or prevent (ME); to be an obstacle to.

hint [17c. Obsolete *hent* 'to grasp, get hold of', from Old English *hentan*: related to **hunt**. The underlying idea is 'something that may be grasped': cf. CLEVER*] **1** an opportunity (–19c) **2** a subtle suggestion or clue that an alert person may understand, hence **(a)** to give information indirectly; a tip-off (18c) **(b)** a trace (*a hint of pink*, 19c).

hinterland [19c. German, literally 'land behind'] The (deserted or uncharted) land behind a coastline or river, hence **1** the land around, and trading through, a port (*c*.1900); the fringes of a town or city (1930s) **2** the subconscious mind (*c*.1900); the private interests or cultural background of a public figure (1990s).

Related to **behind** [Old English *behindan*], whence, probably, **hind** (*hind leg/ hindsight*).

hip [1900s. Perhaps from Wolof *hepi* 'to see' or *hipi* 'to open your eyes'] Wise to, clued up, aware of the latest trends (*African-American*, also as **hep**), hence **hip-** or, more commonly, **hepcat** (1930s), **hipster** (1940s) someone who is so; **hippy** a would-be hepcat (1940s), adopted by Whites for a young person who advocated universal peace and love, dressed unconventionally, and often lived communally and used hallucinogenic drugs (1950s), regarded by themselves as wise and by others as, at best, naive.

Probably the source of **hip-hop**, an originally African-American culture that includes rap music, graffiti, and break-dancing.

hippodrome [16c. (Via French from) Latin, from Greek *hippodromos*, from *hippos* 'horse' + *dromos* 'race, course'] A course for chariot or horse races in ancient Greece and Rome, hence **1** a modern circus or, later, variety theatre (19c, surviving in theatre names) **2** a race or contest in which the result is fixed (19c, *US*); to fix a result.

Greek *hippos* appears in **hippocampus** [with Greek *kampos* 'sea monster'] a mythical creature, half horse and half dolphin, later a seahorse, hence one of the two seahorse-shaped ridges in the brain associated with memory, **hippogriff** [with Latin *gryphus* 'griffin'] a mythical creature with a horse's body and an eagle's head and wings, **hippopotamus** [ultimately from Greek *hippos ho potamios* 'horse of the river'], and *Phil(l)ip* (at PHILANDER). Greek *dromos* produced **-drome** (*aerodrome*, *velodrome*), **palindrome** [with Greek *palin* 'back, again'], and **syndrome** [with Greek *sun* 'together']. Related to **dromedary**, a camel often used for racing.

history [ME. Latin *historia* 'finding out, narrative', ultimately from Greek *histōr* 'a wise or learned man'] An account of real or imagined events or people; the study or a systematic account of actual events (15c) or phenomena (*natural history*, 16c); the course of events or of human affairs (17c).

History produced **herstory** history from a woman's angle, or emphasizing women's roles: the word may not survive but, like other linguistic changes advocated by feminists in the 1960s and '70s (e.g. *person* instead of *man*, the abandoning of female terms such as *authoress*, *heroine*), it made its point. Latin *historia* produced **historiated** describing initial letters decorated with figures of people and animals [(via French from) medieval Latin *historiare* 'to decorate with (historical) scenes'], **storey** the floor of a building (perhaps originally a tier of windows depicting Bible stories, whence **clerestory** a row of clear windows), and **story** originally an account believed to be true, especially of a biblical event or saint's life.

hit [Old English *hittan* from Old Norse *hitta*] To meet with, to find (by chance), hence **1** (to give) a blow, shot, etc. that meets its target (ME); a successful attempt

(19c); a successful record, film, etc. **2** (to strike) a blow (ME); to strike someone/something; to affect or occur to someone suddenly and forcefully (19c).

hitch [ME. Origin unknown] To move or lift with a jerk; to move jerkily, hence **1** to limp (16c); a limp, a fault in a horse's gait (17c) **2** to catch on something (16c); to catch or fasten temporarily, hence **(a)** a means of doing so (*clove hitch*, 18c) **(b)** a temporary obstacle or problem **(c) hitch (up)** to harness a horse etc. (19c, hence **get hitched** to get married); to join two things so that one powers the other; *hitch* a means of doing so, hence to get a lift in a vehicle (joining something that will move you); also **hitchhike** (cf. HIKE) to travel by doing so (1920s); such a journey.

hobby [ME. Alteration of **Robbie**, pet form of **Robert**, once a traditional name for a horse (surviving in **Dobbin**, an alteration of **Robin**, another pet form)] A small horse or pony, whence **hobby horse 1** a figure of a horse in a mummer's play etc. (16c) **2** a child's toy horse (16c), hence **(a)** a favourite leisure activity (17c, shortened to *hobby*, 19c); a subject that you go on about **(b)** a velocipede (19c) **3** a horse on a fairground ride (18c).

    Robert produced a number of surnames beginning **Dob-**, **Hob-**, or **Rob-** (the pet form **Bob** may be the source of *staggering bob* at BOB[2]), and was also a name for the **robin**, a garden bird considered by some to bring bad luck, probably regarded as akin to a **dobby** or **hob**(goblin), a mischievous or spiteful household sprite (often called **Robin Goodfellow** to placate him): **play hob** 'to play the devil' survives in the US.

hobnob [19c. From *hob and nob*, *hob or nob*, probably meaning 'give and/or take', said by two people drinking to each other, from *hab nab* 'to have/not have', from Old English *habban* **have**] To drink together or to each other, hence to socialize or be on familiar terms, especially with your social superiors.

    Have is the source of *behave* (at HABIT), and is related to **haft**, *heavy* (at LIGHT[1]), and to **heave** [Old English *hebban*], whence, probably (on the pattern of *cleave/cleft*, *weave/weft*), **heft 1** weight, heaviness (surviving mainly in **hefty**) **2** to lift something, later specifically in order to test its weight or balance.

hocus-pocus [17c. From pseudo-Latin *hax pax max Deus adimax*, perhaps based on Latin *hoc est enimis corpus meum* 'this is truly my body', used in the Mass] A 'magic' phrase used by conjurors, hence conjuring, sleight of hand, trickery; to play tricks, to deceive. Also shortened to **hocus**, which later meant to drug a person or animal, or to spike a drink with a drug (19c).

    Altered to **hokey-pokey** deception, trickery (**hanky-panky** is probably a further alteration), also the American name of the dance called the **hokey-cokey** in the UK. It probably influenced **hokey-pokey** ice cream sold in the streets [said to come from the Italian vendors' *ecco un poco* 'here's a little', offering a tempting sample]. *Hocus* is probably the source of **hoax**, and perhaps of **hokum** melodramatic, sentimental, or humorous business designed to captivate an audience (US, *theatrical slang*), hence nonsense, whence **hokey** overacted, overdone, false (US).

hoist [15c. Alteration of **hoise** (–18c), probably from Dutch or Low German] To raise or lift up, especially using a mechanical device, hence **1** this act, a lift-up (17c) **2** to rob or steal (18c); (to go) shoplifting, whence the American variant

heist to rob or steal (19c); a robbery or hold-up (1930s) **3** something hoisted; a group of flags hoisted as a signal (19c) **4** a lifting device, a winch, lift, etc. (19c).

The past participle of *hoise* survives in **hoist by his own petard**, literally 'lifted by his own bomb' (see also *petard* at FEISTY).

hold [Old English *haldan*] To watch (surviving in **behold**), hence to watch over; to keep; to grasp, other senses developing from this in Middle English. *Behold* produced **beholden** obliged, indebted (ME), although not recorded itself in equivalent senses.

hole [Old English *hol*] **1** a hollow place, a cavity, hence **(a)** a hiding place (ME), surviving in *priest's hole* and in **hole up** to take refuge, to hide yourself **(b)** the inside of a ship or aircraft where cargo is carried (15c, earlier as *holl*, altered to **hold** by association with HOLD) **(c)** a prison cell (16c); an unpleasant place (17c); an awkward situation (18c) **(d)** a cavity that you have to get a ball into in golf etc. (16c); a pocket on a billiard or pool table; to get a ball into one (17c) **2** an opening; a perforation; to make one, specifically in a ship.

Old English *hol* may be the source of a ship's **hull**, which however may be the same word as **hull** the outer covering of a fruit or seed [related Old English *hulu*, from *helan* 'to cover']. Also related to HALL*, HALT, to Old English *h(e)alh* 'corner, cave, recess', surviving as **Hal-** and **-hall** in place names, HELL, **helmet**, and **hollow** [Old English *holh*, which appears in names as **Hol-** or **-hall**].

holocaust [ME. Via French and Latin from Greek *holokauston*, from *holos* 'whole' + *kaustos* 'burnt', from *kaiein* 'to burn'] A sacrificial offering completely consumed by fire; large-scale sacrifice, slaughter, or destruction (17c); **the Holocaust** the (period of) genocide of the Jews by the Nazis during World War II, often used to include other ethnic and social groups exterminated at the same time, and generally the persecution of Jews under the Nazi regime.

Greek *holos* produced CATHOLIC, **holism** the tendency in nature to produce 'wholes' (bodies or organisms) from the ordered grouping of units [coined by the S African statesman Jan Smuts], whence **holistic** comprising or to do with all parts or aspects of a whole, and **holograph** a document entirely handwritten by its author, later (also as **hologram**) a three-dimensional photographic image. Greek *kaiein* produced **calm** [via late Latin *cauma* '(a resting place for) the heat of the day', from *kauma* 'burning heat'], **caustic** burning, corrosive, hence sarcastic, biting, **cauterize**, and **ink** [via French and Latin from Greek *egkauston* 'purple ink used for Roman emperors' signatures', from *enkaiein* 'to burn in' (whence also **encaustic**)].

holy [Old English *hālig*] **1** dedicated to religious use, sacred, consecrated **2** belonging to a deity, divine **3** free from evil, morally and spiritually perfect, hence pious, devout, also sanctimonious, especially in **holier than thou** [early 20c, based on the Bible, Isaiah 65:5].

Holy is found in *halibut* (at BUTT[3]), **holiday** originally a religious festival (holy day) on which no work was done (whence the surname **Halliday**, **Hol(l)iday**, someone born on such a day), **hollyhock** originally the marsh mallow, which has medicinal uses [with Old English *hoc* 'mallow'], and **holystone** a piece of soft sandstone for scouring a ship's decks (probably because sailors worked on their knees, and the name **Halliwell**, **Holywell** (someone who lived by a sacred spring).

Old English *hālig* produced *halga* 'someone/something holy', whence **hallow** a saint, and *halgian* 'to make or treat as holy', whence the verb **hallow**. Related to WHOLE*.

homage [ME. French, ultimately from Latin *homo, hominis* 'man'] A formal, public acknowledgement of feudal allegiance, the vassal declaring himself to be his lord's 'man', hence reverence, respect, deference; a work reverently imitating another artist's style (1990s, usually with modern French pronunciation).

Latin *homo* was adopted for the genus to which humans belong, and produced Spanish *hombre* a man, adopted for one of Spanish descent (US), **homicide, hominid** a member of the family of primates of which humans are the only living species, and **homunculus** a tiny person; a fetus considered as a fully formed human. Related to HUMAN* and HUMBLE*.

home [Old English *hām*] A settlement, a village or town (surviving in place names ending in -hampstead and some ending in -ham and -hampton), hence **1** see *homestead* (at STEAD) **2** (to do with) the place where you live, come from, or, later, (feel) you belong (ME), hence **(a)** to go home (*homing pigeon*, 18c) **(b) homely** like home, informal, comfortable, unpretentious (ME); of a person: plain, not beautiful **(c)** an institution for those who cannot live independently (19c) **(d)** domestic (*home help/movie*); the domestic unit (*broken home*) **(e)** to give, now usually a pet, a home **(f)** (at) a team's own ground **(g) homeboy, homey** someone from your home town, later from your peer group (1960s, *African-American*) **3** as opposed to foreign (*Home Office, home rule*, 16c) **4** (to) a point aimed at (*hit home*, 16c); **home in** to be directed to a target or destination (1920s); **home in on** to focus on (1950s) **5** a place where something originated or flourishes (18c); **home page** the introductory page of a website (1990s) **6** a place of safety in a game (19c).

Related to **hamlet, hangar**, HAUNT, and to *hunky* in **hunky-dory** [*US*, from Dutch *honk* 'home, base (in a game)' + *dory* of unknown origin].

hone [Old English *hān*] A stone (–ME), surviving as a surname for someone who lived by a (boundary) stone; a whetstone (ME); to sharpen on one (19c); to polish or perfect a skill etc.

honest [ME. Via Old French from Latin *honestus*, from *honos, honor* **honour**] Held in, or deserving, honour or respect (–17c); worthy, decent, virtuous, hence **1** chaste, surviving in **make an honest woman of** to marry an unchaste woman, restoring her respectability **2** sincere, truthful, not deceitful or fraudulent; of a thing: genuine, unadulterated (16c); of money etc.: gained fairly (17c).

hoop [Old English *hōp*] **1** a measure for dry goods (–11c) **2** a metal band binding a barrel's staves (ME); one of the equally spaced bands on a quart pot, hence **(a)** the amount of liquor contained between them (16–17c, a similar arrangement may be the source of sense 1) **(b)** something resembling this, e.g. a child's toy (17c); a ring through which an acrobat or performing animal jumps (18c, hence **go/(be) put/jump through hoops** to (have to) go to great lengths to please someone or achieve something); a horizontal band of colour on a garment (19c).

horde [16c. Polish *horda*, from Turkish *ordu* 'camp, army'] A tribe or troop of Tartar or other nomads, hence **1** a large (unwelcome) crowd (17c) **2** in anthropology: a loose social group of about five families (19c); to form or live in one.

Turkish *ordu* produced **Urdu** [via Persian and Urdu *zabān i urdū*, literally 'language of the camp'].

horn [Old English: related to German *Horn*, whence **alpenhorn, flugelhorn**, etc.] A bony growth on an animal's head, the material it is made of (ME), hence **1** something (originally) made of, shaped like, or sticking out like one (*shoe/cream horn*); a promontory (now mainly in place names); a snail's antenna; an erect penis (19c, hence **horny** sexually aroused) **2** (an animal horn used as) a wind instrument ; a (brass) one with a flared end (*hunting/French horn*: cf. BUGLE, CORNET): **(a) hornpipe** a small pipe (ME); a (sailors') dance to it (15c); the music for this (18c) **(b)** a device for sounding a warning (*fog/klaxon horn*, 19c) **3** a horned animal (ME, surviving in **shorthorn, longhorn**, both 19c) **4** to butt or gore (16c), hence **horn in** to butt in, to interfere (*c*.1910, US).

horrid [16c. Latin *horridus* 'bristling', later 'rough, rude, wild, savage', from *horrere* 'to bristle, later 'to shudder'] **1** rough, shaggy (now rare) **2** dreadful, frightful (17c); unpleasant, nasty.

Latin *horridus* produced **ordure** [French, from *ord* 'filthy']; *horrere* is the ancestor of **abhore, horrible, horrific, horrify**, and **horror**.

hose [Old English *hosa*: related to German *Hosen* 'trousers', whence **Lederhosen**] A covering for the leg and sometimes the foot, hence **1** as a plural: stockings (ME); tight-fitting trousers (*doublet and hose*, 15c). Hence **hosier** a maker or seller of hose (ME, as a surname); **hosiery** their business or goods (18c) **2** a flexible tube or pipe (ME); to spray with water from one (19c).

hospital [ME. Old French, from medieval Latin *hospitale* 'hospitable place', from Latin *hospitalis* 'hospitable', from *hospis* 'host, guest', probably from *hostis*: see HOST[1]] **1** a guest house or shelter for pilgrims, travellers, or strangers (–18c) **2** (also **spittle, spital**) a charitable institution that cares for the needy, the aged, or the infirm (surviving in names, e.g. **Christ's Hospital** originally a school for poor children, **Greenwich Hospital** originally for aged sailors, and **Spitalfields** next to the former St Mary's Hospital which cared for the sick and poor); an establishment where the sick are treated (16c); **hospitalize** to admit someone to hospital (recorded once in the 17c, re-emerging *c*.1900) **3** a lodging house for university students (16–18c).

Hospice [19c, from Latin *hospitium*, from *hospis*] shared senses 1 and 2: it now means a nursing home for the dying. **Hostel** [ME. Old French *(h)ostel* from medieval Latin *hospitale*] replaced *hospital* in senses 1 and 3: it now provides basic accommodation for workers, the homeless, and (young) travellers.

Latin *hospis* produced **hospitable, hospitality**, and HOST[2]. Old French *(h)ostel* produced *hostelier* **hosteler** someone who looks after guests and strangers, especially in a religious house; a hostel- or innkeeper (whence **hostelry**); a stableman at an inn (usually as **ostler**); the form **hostler** survives for someone in charge of an engine shed (US). **Hotel** and **hotelier** are from the modern French equivalents.

host¹ [ME. Via Old French from Latin *hostis* 'stranger, enemy', in medieval Latin 'army'] An army; a large number of people or things, hence **the heavenly host, hosts of heaven 1** the multitude of angels **2** the sun, moon, and stars. Hence **Lord (God) of Hosts** God as the Lord of heaven, the universe, or the Israelite armies.

Latin *hostis* produced **hostile** and, probably, Latin *hospis* 'host, guest', whence HOSPITAL*.

host² [ME. Via Old French from Latin *hospis*: see HOSPITAL] *Host,* **hostess** someone who entertains a guest (ME), now the presenter of a radio or television show with a live audience (1940s). Hence *host*: **1** to act as host (15c) **2** an animal or plant on which a parasite lives (19c) **3** the recipient of a tissue transplant (*c.*1900) **4** *hostess* a woman who entertains guests in a nightclub (1930s, sometimes a euphemism for prostitute) or attends to airline passengers, replaced by *stewardess* or, later, *attendant*, but surviving in **hostie** (Australian and New Zealand slang).

hough [Old English *hōh*: related to HEEL] A human heel, hence **1** a projecting ridge of land; a rise or cliff, surviving in names such as **Hooton**, **Ho(u)ghton**, **Huff**, and **Hutton**, and as **-hoe** or **-how 2** the hollow behind the knee; the back of this end of the thigh (cf. HAM), hence (now usually as the variant **hock**) the joint on an animal's hind leg corresponding to the human ankle (ME); a joint of meat extending upwards from it; a knuckle of pork etc.

house [Old English *hūs*: related to HUSBAND*] **1** a dwelling, especially with two or more storeys, hence **(a)** its inhabitants, replaced by **household** (ME) except in the sense 'family line, dynasty' **(b) house(hold)** to do with a house or household (*house arrest, housekeeper, household appliances*), **household troops** who guard the royal family (18c) **2** a building where something happens, is sold, kept, or produced (*slaughter/coffee/hen house, warehouse, playhouse, hothouse*). Hence **(a)** (the premises of) a religious community, a legislative assembly (*Houses of Parliament*, 16c), or a business (*publishing house*, 16c) **(b)** (a performance at) a theatre or cinema (*first/second house*, 17c) **(c)** (the pupils living in) a school boarding house (19c), hence (the members of) a division of a school not based on age **3** to provide with a house; to keep or store in a building **4** a division of the zodiac (ME).

housewife [ME. From HOUSE + *wife* (at MAN): the early spelling *hus(e)wif*, which persisted until the 19c, affected that of later senses] **1** a woman whose main occupation is managing her household **2** a shameless (young) woman (16c, later altered to **hussy**) **3** a small sewing kit (18c, often spelt and pronounced **hussive**).

hoyden [16c. Dutch *heiden* 'heathen': the underlying sense is probably 'country dweller': cf. CHURL*] A rude, ignorant man (–18c); a noisy, rude, or boisterous woman or girl (17c).

Related to **heath** and **heathen**, and probably to **hoit** to behave boisterously (16–17c), whence **hoity-toity** boisterous, playful, later arrogant, haughty.

hub [16c. Origin unknown: the underlying sense may be 'rounded mass'] **1** a lump of clay at the back of the hearth; the back and sides of a grate; a shelf beside the grate where pans can be warmed, surviving as **hob**, which now means a surface with hotplates or burners (1960s) **2** *hob*: a (rounded) pin used in games (16c), whence **hobnail** a broad-headed nail **3** the central part of a wheel (17c), hence a centre of activity or interest (19c).

huckster [ME. Probably of Low German origin] A pedlar or small shopkeeper, hence **1** a derogatory term for a broker or middleman; a person who sells unscrupulously or aggressively; an advertising agent or copywriter, especially for radio or television (1960s) **2** to bargain or haggle (16c); to be a huckster (17c).

Probably related to **hawker** someone who travels around selling goods, technically one with a cart or van, as opposed to a **pedlar/peddler** who walks [alteration of **pedder** (surviving in Scots and dialect, and as a surname), perhaps ultimately from Latin *pes* 'foot': see PIONEER]. **Hawk** and **peddle** are both back-formations.

huddle [16c. Perhaps of Low German origin] **1** to hide or hush up (–19c) **2** to heap, mix up, or crowd together, hence **(a)** a (confused) mass of people or things; **go into a huddle** to crowd together, especially to talk privately (1920s); *huddle* a brief gathering of players during a game to receive instructions (1930s); a pause while a bridge-player considers their next move **(b)** confusion, disorderly haste (17c); to do something carelessly or hastily **3** to hunch or crouch down in fear or for shelter (18c); to crowd together in this way.

Probably related to **hide** to conceal [Old English *hydan*], and to **hugger-mugger 1** secrecy, concealment; secret; secretly **2** disorder, confusion; disorderly, confused. One of a number of similar formations, including *hucker-mucker*, *huddermudder*: the second element may be from **mucker** 'to hoard money' [perhaps from **muck** in an obsolete sense 'money'].

huff [16c. From the sound of blowing] To blow (surviving in **huff and puff**), hence **1** to 'puff up' with pride, arrogance, or anger; to take offence, hence **in a huff** in a fit of pique; **huffy** touchy, easily offended (17c) **2** in draughts: to take an opponent's piece (originally also blowing on it) if they fail to take yours (17c).

hulk [Old English *hulc*, perhaps ultimately from Greek *holkas* 'cargo ship', from *helkein* 'to pull'] A large cargo ship; any large unwieldy craft, hence **1** a large clumsy person or thing (ME); **hulking** massive, clumsy, unwieldy (17c) **2** a derelict ship (17c); one used for storage, lodgings, or as a prison.

human [ME. Via French from Latin *humanus*: originally also **humane**] To do with or characteristic of mankind: **1** as distinct from God or the gods, imperfect (16c) **2** as distinct from the lower animals (18c), hence having the (better) qualities attributed to man, kind, compassionate (19c): earlier in **inhuman** (ME), *humane* (15c), and **humanity** kindness, benevolence (ME) **3** a human being, a person (16c).

Humanity came to mean **1** human nature, the human race **2** learning concerned with human society, hence **(the) humanities (a)** the fine arts, history, and philosophy, formerly also grammar and rhetoric (cf. *the (liberal) arts* at ART) **(b)** the classics. Related to HOMAGE*.

humble [ME. Via Old French, from Latin *humilis* 'low, lowly', from *humus* 'ground, soil'] **1** unassertive, deferential **2** lowly, modest, unpretentious, hence **3** to reduce someone's rank, importance, or pride.

Latin *humilis* produced **humiliate** and **humility**: *humus* is the ancestor of **exhume**, **inhume**, and **transhumance** the seasonal moving of livestock to new grazing, and was adopted for the part of the soil made up of decayed plant material. Related to HOMAGE*.

Humble in **eat humble pie** is a pun based on **umbles** 'offal', regarded as inferior food [alteration of Old French *numbles* 'loin' (of meat), ultimately from Latin *lumbulus*, literally 'small loin', from *lumbus* loin]. Latin *lumbus* also produced **lumbago**, **lumbar**, and **sirloin** the upper, choicest part of a loin of beef [via Old French *surlonge*, literally 'above the loin']: there is no truth in the oft-repeated tale that an English king knighted a particularly fine sirloin, although this probably influenced the current spelling.

humour [ME. Via Old French from Latin *(h)umor* 'moisture', from *humere* 'to be moist'] Moisture, damp, vapour (–17c); a bodily fluid (surviving in **aqueous** and **vitreous humour**, the fluids in the eyeball), specifically the **cardinal humours** below, the relative proportions of which were thought in ancient and medieval times to decide a person's physical and mental qualities, hence **1** a person's mental disposition (15c, cf. COMPLEXION, TEMPER); a characteristic mood (16c, surviving in **good-humoured**); a whim or fancy (popular in the 16–17c despite being ridiculed by Shakespeare among others), hence to indulge someone's mood or whim **2** what makes something amusing (16c); the ability to appreciate or express this.

The cardinal humours were BLOOD, believed to cause a ruddy complexion and a courageous, passionate, optimistic disposition, **phlegm**, believed to produce a calm, sluggish, apathetic nature [via Old French and Latin from Greek *phlegma* 'inflammation, heat' (hence enervation resulting from it), from *phlegein* 'to burn'], **choler** secreted by the liver, believed to cause bad temper and bitterness [via Old French from Latin *cholera*, from Greek *kholera* 'bilious disorder', from *kholē* 'bile'], earlier called **gall** [Old English *gealla*: related to GOLD*], later called (yellow) **bile** [French, from Latin *bilis*], and **melancholy** an imaginary fluid thought to be produced by the spleen and to cause a sullen, gloomy nature, sadness, and depression [via Old French from Latin *melancholia*, from Greek *melankholia*, literally 'black bile', the humour's later name].

Blood's supposed influence survives in SANGUINE. *Choler* came to mean (an illness causing) nausea and diarrhoea (–18c), replaced by Latin **cholera**, now confined to a specific disease. *Gall* survives mainly in **gall bladder**, where bile is stored, and in **gall stones**, which form there. *Melancholy* came to mean clinical depression (outlived by Latin **melancholia**). The **spleen** [via French and Latin from Greek *splēn*] came to be regarded as the source of depression, anger, and spite (surviving in **splenetic** and **vent your spleen**), and the area around it, the **hypochondria** [literally 'under the breastbone', from Greek *khondros* 'cartilage (of the breastbone)'] came to mean depression, now unfounded anxiety about your health.

Latin *humere* produced **humid**. Greek *kholē* produced **cholesterol**, first found in gall stones, whence **sterol** applied to the class of substances including cholesterol, whence **steroid** a class of compounds including the sterols.

hump [17c. Probably of Low German or Dutch origin] To hunch your back, hence **1** **humpback** (someone with) a hunched back; *hump* such a shape (18c), hence

(a) to have sex with a woman (18c, from the curve of the man's back)
(b) to shoulder a burden (19c); to move something with difficulty **(c)** a rounded
mass (19c); a mound; a mountain barrier (*c.*1910, *US*), hence **over the hump** over
the worst **2** a complaint, slight, or snub (from the idea of hunching your shoulders in annoyance); **the hump** annoyance, resentment (18c).

hunch [15c. Origin unknown] **1** to push or shove (now mainly US and Scots),
hence **(a)** a push (17c, now mainly Scots) **(b)** to push up your shoulders (17c,
probably influenced by 16c **hunchbacked** humpbacked, of unknown origin); to
sit in a hunched position (1930s) **(c)** to nudge someone to draw their attention
to something (19c, US), hence a hint; an intuitive feeling **2** [perhaps a different
word, related to 19c **hunk**, probably of Dutch origin] a large lump or slice (18c).

hurl [ME. Origin unknown] **1** to move suddenly or violently; to drive or throw
forcefully, whence **hurling** an Irish game similar to hockey (later called **hurley**); a
Cornish game in which two sides tried to drive or carry a ball to a distant goal
(17c); *hurl* to play either of these (16c) **2** strife, commotion (–17c, surviving in
hurly-burly) **3** (to go for) a 'spin' in a vehicle (16c, Scots and N English: also found
in *hurlpool, hurlwind,* so perhaps confused with WHIRL, but cf. WARP*).

hurt [ME. Old French *hurter,* perhaps ultimately of Germanic origin] To strike, to
knock against, to collide (–17c, the original sense of Middle English **hurtle,** from
hurt); a knock or blow, especially one causing pain or injury (–19c), hence (to
cause) physical injury; to injure or harm in any way; (to suffer) mental or emotional distress; to suffer or be a source of pain (*my leg hurts,* 16c).

husband [ME. Old Norse *húsbóndi,* from *hús* 'house' + *bóndi* 'occupier and tiller of
the soil', from *búa* 'to dwell'] The male head of a household (ME only), hence
1 the manager of a household, a steward (surviving in 18c **ship's husband** an
agent appointed by a ship's owners to look after it in port), whence **husbandry**
household management (–17c); thrift, economy; *husband* to manage resources
thriftily (15c) **2** a (tenant) farmer (–18c, later also **husbandman**), hence *husbandry*
agriculture, farming **3** a man in relation to his wife.
    Old Norse *hús* is related to HOUSE, HUSK, and HUSTINGS. *Bóndi* is the ancestor of
bondage (at BOND), and *búa* of BOOTH*.

husk [ME. Probably from Low German *hũske* 'sheath', literally 'little house':
related to HUSBAND*] The dry outer covering of grain etc., hence **1** a (worthless)
outer part (16c); to remove it; to undress (1940s, African-American) **2 husky
(a)** dry as a husk (16c); having a dry throat (18c); of the voice: low and slightly
rough **(b)** tough, strong (19c, *N American*), perhaps influenced by **husky** a large,
strong sled dog, originally called an **Eskimo dog** [19c, abbreviation of obsolete
Ehuskemay or Newfoundland dialect *Huskemaw* 'Eskimo'], hence Eskimos and
their language (now considered offensive).
    Eskimo [from an Algonquian word probably meaning 'people who speak a dif-
ferent language'] also came to be regarded as offensive (perhaps from a mistaken
belief that it came from Abnaki *askimo* 'raw-flesh-eater'), and those from Canada
and Greenland prefer to be called **Inuit** [plural of Inuit *inuk* 'person']; however, it
is the only word for the people as a whole and is still used by archaeologists and
anthropologists. It also survives in **Eskimo pie** a kind of choc-ice (US trademark),

Eskimo roll a complete roll-over in a kayak, and **Esky** a coolbox (Australian trademark).

hustings [ME. Old Norse *hústhing* 'house of assembly', from *hús* 'house' (here specifically a royal household) + *thing* 'an assembly or parliament'] **Husting** an assembly or council; one summoned by the monarch, later applied to the highest court of the City of London, hence *hustings* the part of the Guildhall where this was held, or the platform where the Lord Mayor and Aldermen sat (18c); a temporary platform from which parliamentary candidates were nominated and addressed the electors, hence electoral proceedings.

Old Norse *hús* is related to HUSBAND*. Old Norse *thing* was adopted for an assembly in areas of Scandinavian settlement in Britain, and survives in the place names **Dingwall** and **Tynwald Hill** [both from Old Norse *thingvölr* 'assembly field']: related to Old English **thing** an assembly, hence a matter for discussion; any matter; an entity; an inanimate object.

hustle [17c. Dutch *hutselen*] To shake about (–19c); to jostle (18c); to push or hurry someone into a place or action, hence **1** rough pushing or jostling (19c); lively, noisy activity **2** to move hurriedly, to bustle (19c) **3** to sell goods aggressively (19c, N American); to push someone into buying, hence **(a)** to steal or swindle; to live by petty crime **(b) hustler** an aggressive salesman, petty criminal, prostitute, or swindler **(c)** a swindle, a scam (1960s, US).

hyacinth [16c. Via French from Latin *hyacinthus*, from Greek *huakinthos*] **1** a blue gem, perhaps a sapphire, later a reddish variety of zircon **2** a flower with dark markings interpreted as Greek *aiai* 'alas', said to have sprung from the blood of **Hyacinthus**, a youth loved and accidentally killed by the god Apollo; a plant of the lily family with a spike of (originally blue) flowers, hence applied to various plants with (usually) blue flowers, and adopted by the 18c Swedish biologist Linnaeus for the bluebell (18c) **3** a blue-black variety of domestic pigeon (19c).

Latin *hyacinthus* evolved into medieval Latin *jacinthus*, whence **jacinth**, an earlier name for the gem, and occasionally used for the flower and the pigeon. Both *hyacinth* and *jacinth* have been used as first names, originally for boys.

hydra [ME. (Via Old French and) Latin from Greek, meaning 'water snake', from *hudōr* 'water'] A mythical aquatic monster with many heads that grew back as fast as they were cut off, hence **1** a difficult or multifaceted problem (15c) **2** any terrible reptile (16c) **3** a kind of polyp, named by Linnaeus (see HYACINTH) because, if it is cut up, each piece can grow into a whole animal.

Greek *hudōr*'s descendants include **hydrangea** [literally 'water vessel' (with Greek *aggeion* 'vessel'), because of its cup-shaped seed capsule], **hydrant**, **hydraulic**, **hydro-** (*hydroelectric*), **hydrogen**, and **hydropsy** retention of fluid in the tissues, popularly shortened to **dropsy**.

hype [1920s. Perhaps short for **hyperbole** rhetorical exaggeration (ME, from Greek *huperbolē* 'excess, exaggeration', from *huper* 'over, beyond, too much' + *ballein* 'to throw'), and influenced by **hyped up** stimulated, worked up (1930s, US), as though from an injection of a drug, from **hypodermic (needle/syringe)** [19c, from Greek *hupo* 'under' + *derma* 'skin'] To cheat or short-change (US); someone who does so; cheating, deception, lies (1940s), especially deceptively inflated advertising or publicity (1960s).

Greek *huper* produced **hyper-** in *hypermarket*, *hypertension*, and in **hyperactive**, whence **hyper** excitable, highly strung; Greek *hupo* produced *huphen* 'together' (whence **hyphen**), and **hypo-** (*hypochondria* at HUMOUR, *hypothermia*). *Ballein* is the ancestor of BALLISTIC*, and *derma* of **dermatitis**, **epidermis**, **pachyderm**, and *taxidermy* (at TAXONOMY).

hysteric/hysterical [Both 17c, via Latin from Greek *husterikos* 'to do with the womb', from *hustera* 'womb'] To do with, caused by, or suffering from *hysterical passion* (later called **hysteria**), a syndrome characterized by convulsions, paralysis, or absence of sensation with no physical cause, and extreme emotional outbursts, once thought to be commoner in women and to be associated with the womb. Hence **1** *hysteria* wild excitement; uncontrollable laughter or crying **2 hysterics** hysterical convulsions or outbursts (18c); an uncontrollable fit of sorrow, anger, or mirth; *hysterical* hilarious (1960s).

I

icon [16c. Latin, from Greek *eikōn* 'likeness, image'] A picture, especially a portrait (–18c): see also *Veronica* (at VERY) a statue; **iconic** describing ancient Greek statues, often of athletes, in conventional poses (17c), hence conventional, typical. Hence *icon* a representative symbol: **1** a religious image, especially in the Orthodox church (19c), but implied in **iconoclast** someone who hates or destroys them (17c) or who challenges accepted beliefs (19c) **2** a symbol resembling what it represents (*c.*1910); a small symbolic picture on a computer screen (1980s), whence **emoticon** a symbolic picture made from standard characters, used in emails to convey emotions, e.g. :-) 'happy', :-O 'shocked' (1990s).

idea [ME. Latin, from Greek *idea* 'appearance, form', later 'mental image', from *idein* 'to see'] **1** in Platonic philosophy: an archetype, hence the conception of something at its most perfect or of a standard to be aimed at (16c, cf. IDEAL); a design; a plan of action **2** a mental image, something imagined (16c); a thought or way of thinking (17c); a notion, belief, or opinion (18c).

Latin *idea* produced IDEAL, **ideology** the study of the nature of ideas, now the ideas, beliefs, or doctrines of a person, group, or society, often forming the basis of a political or economic theory.

ideal [ME. Late Latin *idealis*, from *idea*: see IDEA*] To do with or existing as an archetype (ME), hence **1** a perfect example (15c); perfect, excellent (17c) **2** a standard or principle to be aimed at (15c) **3** existing only in the imagination (17c); visionary, unrealistic, impractical.

identify [17c. Latin *identificare*, literally 'to make the same', from *idem, ident-* 'same'] **1** to regard and treat as identical (17c); **identify with** to associate strongly or feel a strong affinity with (18c) **2** to establish who or what something is (18c). Hence **identification** identifying or being identified (17c); something that does so (1940s, *US*), shortened to **ID** (1950s) and to **ident** a short broadcast that identifies a television channel (*c.*2000).

Latin *idem* is used to mean 'in the same (previously mentioned) work', and produced **identical** and **identity** sameness; your essential, unchanging self; (the characteristics that make up) your unique personality; what distinguishes you, especially your name.

idiom [16c. Via (French and) Latin from Greek *idiōma* 'private property, peculiar phraseology', ultimately from *idios*: see IDIOSYNCRASY*] The language of a people or country, later of an area or group; a natural or characteristic way of using language, hence **1** an expression whose meaning cannot be deduced from the individual words (*take French leave, kick the bucket*) **2** a characteristic artistic, musical, or literary style (1920s).

idiosyncrasy [17c. Greek *idiosugkrasia*, from *idios* 'own, private' + *krasis* 'mixture'] Your unique physical constitution (surviving as a medical term for someone's abnormal reaction to a food or drug); your unique mental constitution, a unique way of thinking or behaving; a quirk or eccentricity.

Greek *idios* produced **idio-** unique, personal (*idiolect, idiopathic*), IDIOM, and **idiot** [via Greek *idiōtēs* 'private person, layman, ignorant person']: *krasis* is related to Greek *kratēr* 'mixing bowl', whence **crater.**

idyll [16c. Latin *idyllium* from Greek *eidullion*, literally 'small picture', from *eidos* 'form, picture'] A short (verse) description of idealized rural life, hence **1** a piece of music with a pastoral theme (19c) **2** a scene, time, or experience fit for an idyll (19c), one of (often temporary) happiness and peace.

Greek *eidos* is the ancestor of **idol**, and appears in **kaleidoscope** [Greek *kalos* 'beautiful' + *eidos* + SCOPE] a toy producing a constantly changing pattern of coloured shapes, hence a complex, colourful, and constantly changing scene.

ignore [15c. (Via French from) Latin *ignorare* 'to not know'] **1** to not know about (rare since the 17c, surviving mainly in **ignorance** and *ignorant* below) **2** to refuse to recognize, to disregard (19c); to reject an indictment because of insufficient evidence, replacing **find/return/bring in an ignoramus,** *ignoramus* being the endorsement put on the document [16c, Latin, literally 'we do not know', from *ignorare*]: *ignoramus* an ignorant person is probably from George Ruggle's satire *Ignoramus* (1615), depicting an incompetent lawyer.

Latin *ignorare* produced **ignorant** knowing nothing, hence knowing nothing about good manners (informal or dialect: cf. *uncouth* at CAN[1], RUDE). Related to NOTICE*.

ilk [Old English *ilca*: related to LIKE[2]*] Same, the same; the same person or thing; the same name or place (all surviving in Scots); the current sense 'a family, class, or sort' (18c) comes from a misunderstanding of the phrase **of that ilk** used when a laird and his estate have the same name (*Moncrieff of that ilk* 'Moncrieff, laird of Moncrieff').

ill [ME. Old Norse *illr* 'evil, difficult'] **1** evil(ly); wicked(ness) **2** unlucky, disastrous(ly) (*an ill wind*); bad luck, trouble **3** unsatisfactory, inferior; in an unsatisfactory way **4** (causing) pain or injury, harmful; a disease; of health: poor (15c); of a person: in poor health; sick, nauseous (1920s).

illuminate [ME. Latin *illuminare*, from *lumen* 'light, a light or opening'] Cf. ILLUSTRATE. To light up, to shine light on, to decorate with lights, hence **1** to enlighten spiritually or, later, intellectually (15c, earlier in **illumine**); to shed light on a subject **2** to decorate a manuscript with gold, silver, or colours (15c); to add lustre to, to make splendid (17c) **3** to direct a beam of microwaves or other radiation at (1960s).

Latin **lumen** was adopted for a tube or cavity in an organism or cell, and as the unit for measuring luminous flux, and is the ancestor of **luminary** a source of light, hence of enlightenment, an influential person, and of **luminescence** and **luminous.**

illusion [ME. French, from Latin *illudere*, *illus-* 'to mock', from *ludere* 'to play', from *ludus* 'play' (ancestor of LUDICROUS*)] Deceiving, a deception (–17c); a false impression or appearance, hence **1** its ability to deceive or the mind's ability to be deceived by it (17c) **2** a misapprehension of something seen (18c); an erroneous belief.

Although used loosely in both senses, an *illusion* differs from a **delusion** a false belief not based on appearance [also ultimately from *ludere*], and a **hallucination** a perception of something that is not really there [Latin *alucinari* 'to dream, to be distracted or deceived', from Greek *alussein* 'to be troubled or distraught'].

illustrate [16c. Latin *illustrare*, from *lustrare* 'to brighten' (whence **lustre**), from *lustrum* 'purification'] Cf. ILLUMINATE. **1** to light up or enlighten (–19c, ME in **illustration**), hence to explain, especially by giving examples; to clarify or decorate a text with diagrams or pictures (17c) **2** to add lustre to, surviving mainly in **illustrious** [16c, from Latin *illustris* 'bright, evident, distinguished, famous', from *illustrare*], literally 'having the lustre conferred by rank or fame'.

image [ME. French, from Latin *imago* 'a likeness', later 'natural form or shape'] A painted or sculpted likeness or portrait; to make one (19c). Hence **1** a likeness reflected in a mirror or produced by a lens, now also by infra-red radiation, X-rays, etc.; to produce one (18c) **2** appearance or form (now often alluding to the Bible, Genesis 1:27: *God created man in his own image*); a counterpart or copy (16c: see also *spitting image* at SPIT[1]); an embodiment or typical example **3** (to form) a mental picture, hence the public's perception of someone/something (*c*.1900, rare until re-created by the advertising industry in the 1950s) **4** a (vivid) description (16c); a simile, metaphor, or other figure of speech, hence **imagery** the use of these.

Latin *imago* is the ancestor of **imagine**, and was adopted for the final form of an insect when metamorphosis is complete.

immaculate [ME. Latin *immaculatus*, literally 'spotless', from *macula* 'spot, mesh, blemish'] **1** free from moral stain, hence **immaculate conception** the conception of the Virgin Mary, also of Christ, believed to be free from Original Sin (17c) **2** spotlessly clean, neat and tidy (16c) **3** in perfect condition (19c); without fault, error, or blemish.

Latin *macula* was adopted as the medical term for a spot, and is the ultimate ancestor of **mail** (one of the rings or plates making up) flexible armour, French **maquette** a preliminary model or sketch, French **maquis** brushwood, scrub (the bushes being likened to spots): adopted referring to thick Mediterranean scrub where outlaws often hid, hence (a member of) the French Resistance in World War II, and **trammel** [via late Latin *tremaculum*] a fishing or fowling net; a hobble or fetter; an impediment, hence **untrammelled** unimpeded, unrestrained.

imp [Old English *impa*, *impe*, ultimately from Greek *emphutos* 'implanted, grafted', from *emphuein* 'to implant', from *phuein* 'to plant, to make grow' (ancestor of PHYSIC*)] A sapling (surviving in Scots and in the name **Impey**); a scion of a noble family; (someone regarded as) a child of the Devil, hence a little devil; a mischievous child (17c). Cf. SCION*.

impact [17c. Latin *impingere*, *impact-* 'to drive something into or at', from *pangere* 'to drive or fix in'] **1** to pack in tightly (surviving mainly in **impacted**) **2** the striking of one thing against another, a collision (18c), hence **(a)** the effect of one; the effect or influence of one thing, person, action, etc. on another (19c); **impact (on)** to have a strong effect on (1930s) **(b)** to strike or collide with (early 20c); to make something do so (1940s).

Latin *impingere* p.oduced **impinge** to strike, thrust at, or fix on forcibly, hence to encroach on, interfere with, or affect. Latin *pangere* is the ancestor of **compact** to pack together, hence tightly packed, condensed, concise, **page** of a book, and perhaps of PAGEANT.

impart   [ME. Via Old French from Latin *impartire*, from *pars, part-* PART] To give part of, to share, hence (both 16c) **1** to give something a particular quality **2** to share a story or information, to tell.

impeach   [ME. Old French *empe(s)cher*, from Latin *impedicare* 'to shackle the feet', from *pedica* 'a shackle', from *pes, ped-* 'foot'] To impede, to damage or impair (–17c), later to accuse (15c), specifically of treason or serious crime, hence to remove someone from office because of serious misconduct.

The Anglo-Norman form of *empe(s)cher* produced **appeach** with the same range of meanings (ME–18c); shortened to **peach**, which survives as an old-fashioned slang term meaning to inform on someone. Latin *impedere* [also literally 'to shackle the feet', from *pes*] produced **impede** and **impediment** an obstruction or hindrance, hence **1** a physical impairment (*speech impediment*) **2** baggage (now usually as the Latin plural *impedimenta*): cf. EXPEDITION. *Pes* is the ancestor of PIONEER*.

impel   [ME.Latin *impellere, impuls-*, literally 'to drive towards', from *pellere* 'to drive'] To make something move, to drive or propel, hence to drive, force, urge, or incite someone to act (15c).

Latin *impellere* produced **impulse** a physical or mental driving force, hence a sudden urge or whim: *pellere* is the ancestor of PULSE*.

imperial   [ME. French, from Latin *imperialis*, from *imperium* 'command, authority, empire', from *imperare* 'to command', from *parare* 'to prepare'] To do with an empire or emperor, hence **1** majestic, august; domineering, dictatorial [16c, largely replaced by **imperious**, also from Latin *imperium*] **2** applied to the parliament and institutions of Great Britain (as being above those of the constituent countries, 18c), hence describing weights and measures formerly used throughout Great Britain and the British Empire (19c).

Latin *imperium* produced EMPIRE; *imperare* produced **emperor** [Old French *emperere*, from Latin *imperator* 'commander'] and **imperative**. *Parare* is the ancestor of PARADE*.

impetus   [17c. Latin, from *impetere* 'to rush at, to attack', from *petere* 'to go towards'] The force or energy with which something moves; the force that makes something happen, an impulse or stimulus.

Latin *impetere* produced **impetigo**, applied to various (rapidly spreading) skin diseases, and **impetuous**; *petere* is the ancestor of PETULANT*.

implement   [ME. Latin *implere* 'to fill up or fulfil', later 'to employ', from Latin *plere* 'to fill': see COMPLY] **1** [via medieval Latin *implementa*, literally 'things employed'] a piece of equipment, an article of furniture, dress, etc.; a tool, instrument, utensil, or weapon (16c) **2** [via late Latin *implementum* 'filling up, fulfilment'] fulfilment of a contract etc. (17c); to fulfil a contract or undertaking (18c); to put a plan or decision into effect.

imply [ME. Old French *emplier* from Latin *implicare*, from *plicare* 'to fold, to involve'] To entwine or entangle (–19c), hence to involve as a logical necessity, to entail (16c); to require the existence of something not expressly stated, hence to express indirectly, to hint at or insinuate. In the 16–17c used interchangeably with **employ** [15, from Latin *implicari* 'to be involved in', from *implicare*], both meaning 'to involve or imply' and 'to use'.

Latin *implicare* produced **implicate** to entangle, to imply, especially involvement in a crime, and **implicit** implied or understood; of faith: coming from the Church, not arrived at independently, hence depending on authority, unquestioning, with no doubts or reservations. *Employ* may be the source of **ploy** an activity, later a game, escapade, or trick, hence a deceptive tactic. Latin *plicare* is the ancestor of PLY*.

import [ME. Latin *importare* 'to bring in', in medieval Latin 'to imply or mean, to matter', from *portare* 'to carry': see PORT[3]] **1** to signify or imply; significance, meaning, implication (16c). Hence **important** significant, having significant consequences (ME); of a person: having authority or influence (18c) **2** to matter (15c) **3** to bring in (16c), specifically goods from another country; something brought in (17c); to transfer data into a computer or application from another (1970s): the opposite of **export** [15c, from Latin *exportare*, from *portare*].

importune [ME, via French from Latin *importunus* 'inconvenient, unseasonable', from *im-* 'not' + **Portunus**, the god who protected harbours, from *portus* 'harbour, PORT[1]*'] Untimely (–18c, replaced by 16c **inopportune**); inconvenient, troublesome (–19c); persistently demanding (replaced by **importunate**, 16c); to be importunate (16c); to accost someone to offer sexual services (19c).

impose [15c. French *imposer*, based on Latin *imponere*, *imposit-*, 'to put in or on', from *ponere* 'to put': see POSE] **1** to lay blame (–17c) **2** to levy a tax, duty, etc. (16c); to lay down a law or punishment, hence **imposition** a piece of work a schoolchild must do as a punishment (18c) **3** to force on someone (17c): **(a)** to make demands on them (earlier in *imposition* an unfair or inconvenient demand) **(b)** to pass something off on them (earlier in **impostor** a deceiver, especially one who passes themselves off as someone else) **4** to influence someone by an impressive appearance or manner (17c), hence **imposing** large, impressive, daunting (18c).

impress [ME. Old French *empresser* 'to press in', from *presser* 'to press', from Latin *premere* PRESS*. Influenced by Latin *imprimere*: see IMPRINT] **1** to apply with pressure; to press one thing on another so as to leave a mark, hence **impression** such a mark; a cast or copy: **(a)** a print taken from type etc. (16c); (the printing of) a number of copies at one time; a reprint, as opposed to new edition, of a book (1920s) **(b)** a representation of someone/something by an artist or performer (1950s); an impersonation of a well-known person **2** to fix something in someone's mind, hence *impression* the effect, opinion, or mental image of something; a (vague or mistaken) idea or belief (17c) **3** to affect or influence deeply (18c); to make a good impression on (19c).

imprint [ME. Via French from Latin *imprimere* 'to press in', from *premere* PRESS*. Cf. IMPRESS] **1** (to make) an impression, physically or in the mind (ME); the lasting mark of an experience or influence (17c); **imprinting** the rapid development of a young animal's identification with its own species or a surrogate (1930s) **2** a publisher's name, date of publication, etc. printed in a book (18c); a division of a publishing house with its own book list (1970s).

Latin *imprimere* produced **imprimatur** [literally 'let it be printed'] an official authorization by the Roman Catholic church to print a religious work, hence official permission or approval.

improvement [ME. Anglo-Norman French *emprowement*, ultimately from Old French *prou*: see PROUD*] Profitable management (–16c); the cultivation or development of land (15c); **improve** to use something profitably (16c), hence to increase the price or value, originally of land (17c); to make or become better.

impudent [ME. Latin *impudens, impudent-*, from *pudens* 'ashamed, modest', from *pudere* 'to feel or make ashamed'] Shameless, immodest (–18c); disrespectful, cheeky (16c).

Latin **pudendum** [singular of *pudenda* 'the shameful (parts)', from *pudere*] was adopted for the human, especially female, external genitalia.

impugn [ME. Latin *impugnare* 'to assail', from *pugnare* 'to fight', from *pugnus* 'fist' (ancestor of **pugilist, pugnacious**, and **repugnant**)] To assault, to attack physically (–17c), hence to argue against (15c); to question someone's actions, honesty, etc.

incendiary [ME. Latin *incendiarius*, from *incendium* 'conflagration', from *incendere* 'to set fire to', from *candere* 'to glow'] (Easily) combustible, causing fire, hence **1 (a)** an arsonist (15c); to do with arson (17c) **(b)** designed to catch fire on impact (19c); an incendiary bomb (World War II) **2** a person (16c) or thing (17–18c) that arouses strong feelings or strife.

Latin *incendere* produced **incense** a substance burnt for its fragrance [via Christian Latin *incensum* 'something burnt'], and **incense** [via Old French *incenser* 'to inflame'] to excite or arouse (ME–17c), later to enrage or exasperate. *Candere* is the ancestor of CANDID*.

incident [ME. (Via French from) Latin *incidere* 'to fall upon, to happen to', from *cadere* 'to fall' (ancestor of CASE¹*)] Related to, or occurring as a consequence of, hence **1** an event that is part of a larger action or scene; a distinct piece of action in a literary work (17c) or a war (1920s); an event with potentially serious consequences (*an international incident*, *c*.1910); a fracas or public disturbance (1930s) **2** of an expense: incurred in addition to the main sum (–18c), superseded by **incidental** (18c), hence **incidentals** such expenses **3** apt or liable to happen (15c), hence **incidence** the rate or manner of occurrence (19c).

incline [ME. Via Old French from Latin *inclinare* 'to lean towards', from *clinare* 'to bend' (ancestor of DECLINE*)] To bend or bow towards, forward, or inward, hence **1** to bend your mind towards something, to favour; to make or be willing to do; to tend to be or do (16c): cf. *bent* (at BEND), LEAN¹, French **penchant**, literally 'a leaning', and **propensity**, literally 'a hanging towards' [both ultimately from Latin *pendere* 'to hang' (ancestor of PENDANT*)], and **proclivity** [Latin *proclivitas* 'a leaning toward', from *clivus* 'a slope'] **2** to tilt or slope (15c); a slope (16c); **inclination** (the amount of) a deviation of one line or plane from another (17c).

incumbent [ME. Anglo-Latin *incumbens*, from Latin *incumbere* 'to lie or lean on', from *cumbere* 'to lie'] **1** someone holding an ecclesiastical benefice, later some other post (17c); occupying a benefice etc. **2** falling to someone as a duty or obligation (16c) **3** hanging, leaning, or lying over (17c); in botany and zoology: lying flat.

Latin *cumbere* is also found in **recumbent** [Latin *recumbere* 'to lie back'] and **succumb** [Latin *succumbere* 'to lie under'] to overwhelm, later to be overwhelmed, to give in to. Related to CUBICLE*.

indent [ME. Medieval Latin *indentare*, from Latin *dens* 'tooth'] To make a notch in; to give a jagged edge or outline; to divide a document leaving jagged edges, hence **indenture** an agreement written in duplicate on a sheet which was then divided in this way (its authenticity could be proved by fitting the edges together: cf. *charter party* at CHARTER, COUNTERPART, *deed poll* at POLL), hence *indent* (to write) an order for goods with a duplicate or counterfoil (18c) **2** to leave a blank space at the beginning of a line of writing (17c); such a space (19c).

Indent influenced **indent** [from *dent*: see DINT] to inlay or emboss (ME–18c), later to make a dent in: the two converge in **indentation** (the action of making) a notch, recess, or dent. Descendants of Latin *dens* include **dandelion** [via French *dent-de-lion* 'lion's tooth', from its jagged leaves], **dentist**, and **trident**.

index [ME. Latin *index*, *indic-* 'forefinger', from or related to *indicare* 'to point towards', from *dicare* 'to proclaim'] **Index finger** the forefinger, the one you point with, hence *index* a pointer or indicator (16c); something that 'points' to a conclusion or fact: **1** a list or catalogue (16c); an alphabetical list of topics in a book; **The Index** [Latin *Index Librorum Prohibitorum* 'List of Forbidden Books'] an official list of works proscribed by the Roman Catholic church (17c), hence to provide a book with an index (18c); to add something to an index or *The Index* **2** in maths: a small symbol above or below the line indicating a value or function (17c); a number or formula expressing a relationship or ratio (19c); (a number on) a scale that relates variables to each other or to a base number (*retail price index*, 19c), hence **indexed**, **index-linked** linked to, usually, the cost of living index (1970s) **3** a symbol of a hand with a pointing finger used to call attention to a paragraph etc. (18c) **4** in engineering: to move from one predetermined position to another (*c*.1900); one such movement (1960s).

Latin *indicare* produced **indicate**; *dicare* is the ancestor of ABDICATE*.

Indian [ME. Latin *India*, from *Indus,* from Greek *Indos* 'the River Indus', from Persian *hind* (the name later extended by the Greeks and Persians to the area around the river, and subsequently to all the country east of it), from Sanskrit *sindhu* 'river, the Indus'] To do with or originating in India; a native or inhabitant of the Indian subcontinent or, since 1948, the Republic of India, hence **1** a member of one of the indigenous peoples of the Americas (16c, because European explorers thought they had reached some part of India), now usually regarded as offensive and largely replaced by Native American **2** an indigenous inhabitant of the

Philippines, especially one who has become a Christian (17c), or of Australia or New Zealand (18–19c).

Indy, an obsolete variant of India, survives in the plural **Indies**, originally India and the adjacent regions of SE Asia, later called the **East Indies** to distinguish them from the **West Indies** of the New World. *East Indies* is now restricted to the Malay archipelago, *West Indies* to the islands separating the Caribbean Sea from the Atlantic.

Greek *Indikos* [from *Indos*] produced **Indic** the name of a large group of languages spoken in the subcontinent, and **indigo** [via Portuguese] a blue dye originally obtained from India. Persian *hind* is the ancestor of **Hindi** and **Hindu**, and Sanskrit *sindhu* of **Sind** a province in the Indus valley. The American state of **Indiana** was named because of the large numbers of Native Americans who lived there.

individual   [ME. Medieval Latin *individualis*, from Latin *individuus*, from *dividuus* 'divisible', from *dividere* 'to force apart': see DEVICE*] Indivisible (–17c); existing as an indivisible entity (17c), hence **1** (to do with) a single person or thing, or a single member of a group; intended to serve one person (19c) **2** distinctive, (a person or thing) having characteristics that distinguish them from others of a similar kind **3** a human being, a person (18c).

indolence   [17c. Latin *indolens*, from *dolere* 'to suffer or give pain'] **1** insensitivity or indifference to pain, also freedom from pain, a state of ease without pain or pleasure (–18c) **2** love of ease, laziness (18c).

Latin *dolere* produced **condole** [Latin *condolere*, literally 'to suffer with]', **dole** grief, sorrow (surviving mainly in **doleful**), and Latin *dolor* 'pain, grief', whence the (originally Spanish) name **Dolores** (pet forms **Lola**, **Lolita**) given to girls born on 15 September, the feast of the Seven Sorrows of Mary, and **dolour** pain or distress (now only mental).

induce   [ME. Latin *inducere*, literally 'to lead in', from *ducere* 'to lead'] **1** to bring about: **(a)** to persuade or influence someone to do something; **inducement** an incentive (16c) **(b)** to initiate labour artificially (16c) **2** to infer, deduce (16c, earlier and more common in **induction**).

Latin *inducere* produced ENDUE and **induct** to introduce someone formally into a benefice, later into a post or military service; *ducere* is the ancestor of DEDUCE*.

indulgence   [ME. French, from Latin *indulgentia*, from *indulgere* 'to be kind, to yield, to allow': **indulge** is apparently a back-formation (17c)] **1** the gratification of someone's whims; the yielding to their or, later, your own inclinations (17c), hence **(a)** something allowed as a favour or luxury **(b)** (undue) leniency or toleration **(c)** extra time granted to settle a debt (19c) **2** in Roman Catholicism: the partial remission of a punishment for sin (the sale of indulgences was one of the factors leading to the Reformation) **3** a grant of religous liberty to Nonconformists (17c); a licence allowing Scottish Presbyterians to hold services.

industry   [ME. (Via French from) Latin *industria*] Diligence, hard work; regular employment in useful work, later especially in manufacturing, hence trade and manufacture collectively (*heavy industry*, 16c); a particular branch of this (*the* *steel/tourist industry*); a profitable activity compared to an industry (*the heritage/ boy band industry* (1960s).

infer [15c. Latin *inferre* 'to bring in', from *ferre* 'to bring' (ancestor of CONFER*)] **1** to bring in or bring about (–18c) **2** (from medieval Latin) to deduce, to draw a conclusion (16c) **3** to imply (widely regarded as incorrect, but used by many otherwise reputable writers).

infernal [ME. French, from Christian Latin *infernalis*, from Latin *infernus* 'below, underground', in Christian use 'hell'] To do with hell or the underworld; diabolical, fiendish; extremely unpleasant or annoying (18c).

Latin *infernus* fathered Italian **inferno**, adopted with reference to Dante's epic *Divine Comedy* (14c), hence a place resembling hell, a large, out-of-control fire. Related to Latin *inferus* 'low', whence **inferior** 'lower'.

infest [ME. (Via French from) Latin *infestare* 'to assail', from *infestus* 'hostile'] To torment or harass (rare since the 17c); to overrun or take over (16c), now chiefly of parasites or vermin.

inflate [ME. Latin *inflare*, literally 'to blow into', from *flare* 'to blow'] To distend or be distended with air or gas, hence **1** to 'puff up' with pride, satisfaction, etc. (16c), hence **inflated** of literary style: overblown, bombastic (17c) **2** to increase greatly or beyond reasonable limits (19c), hence **inflation** an (undue) increase in the money supply in relation to the goods available, leading to rising prices; *inflate* to bring about (19c) or undergo (1960s) inflation.

Inflate produced its opposite, **deflate**, and **stagflation** [with *stagnation*] an economic state of stagnant demand and high prices. Latin *flare* is the ancestor of FLAVOUR*.

inflect [ME. Latin *inflectere*, from *flectere* 'to bend' (ancestor of FLEXIBLE*)] To bend (inwards), hence **1** to modify the form of a word according to its function, tense, number, etc. (16c: cf. DECLINE); **inflection** an inflected form; a prefix or suffix used to form one **2** *inflection* change of intonation in singing or speaking (16c); a change of tone or pitch; *inflect* to do so (19c).

influence [ME. (French, or) medieval Latin *influentia*, from Latin *influere* 'to flow in', from *fluere* 'to flow'] An influx (–18c); a flow of ethereal fluid or, later, occult force from the stars believed to affect human destiny or character, hence the indirect or imperceptible effect one person or thing has on another (16c); the power of producing this (17c); to exercise this power (18c); someone/something that does so. Shortened informally to **fluence** a mysterious, magical, or hypnotic power (*c*.1900).

Medieval Latin *influentia* fathered Italian **influenza** [literally 'influence', also '(an outbreak of) an epidemic' (probably caused by the stars' influence), specifically an 18c epidemic in Italy, hence adopted as the name of the disease, usually shortened to **flu**]. Latin *influere* is the ancestor of **influx**, and *fluere* of FLUENT*.

inform [ME. Via Old French from Latin *informare*, from *formare*: see FORM*] To form or shape; to mould the character; to teach; to impart knowledge of a particular fact (15c); to tell the authorities about someone's wrongdoing, especially for a reward (16c). Hence **information** facts collected or communicated (ME, shortened informally to **info**, *c*.1910), whence **1 disinformation** (the dissemination of) deliberately false information, especially by a government (1950s, translating Russian *dezinformatsiya*) **2 infomercial** [with *commercial*] an advertising broadcast resembling a documentary; **infotainment** [with *entertainment*] a broadcast that gives information in an entertaining way (both 1980s).

ingenuous [16c. Latin *ingenuus*, literally 'native, inborn', later 'freeborn', ultimately from *gignere* 'to beget'] Noble, generous, high-minded (–18c); honest, frank, candid (17c); innocent, unworldly.

From the 16c to the 18c *ingenuous* was confused with **ingenious** [ultimately from Latin *ingenium* 'intellect, talent': see ENGINE*] intelligent, discerning, talented; inventive; clever and original; and both words shared all their senses. This survives in **ingenuity** [from *ingenuus*] originally 'nobility, honesty, candour': current senses come from *ingenious*.

Latin *ingenuus* produced the French feminine form *ingénue*, adopted for (an actress playing) a naive young woman; *gignere* is the ancestor of GINGERLY*.

inhabit [ME. (Via French from) Latin *inhabitare*, from *habitare* 'to have possession of', from *habere* 'to have'] To dwell or reside; to live in permanently. Co-existing with, and now largely replacing, synonymous **habit** [Latin *habitare*], hence the pairs **habitable** and **uninhabitable**; **habitant** and **inhabitant**.

Latin *habitare* produced **binnacle** the 'home' of the ship's compass [originally spelt *bittacle*: via Spanish *bitácula* or Portuguese *bitacola* from Latin *habitaculum* 'a dwelling place'], **cohabit**, and **habitat**. Latin *habere* is the ancestor of HABIT*.

inherit [ME. Via Old French from Latin *inhereditare* 'to appoint as heir', from Latin *heres* 'heir' (ancestor of **heir**, **hereditary**, and **heritage**)] **1** to receive as a right (*the meek shall inherit the earth*); to receive property, a title, etc. when the previous holder dies; to receive a quality or characteristic from an ancestor (16c); to take something over from a previous owner or occupier (*inherited his office when he left*, 19c) **2** to make someone your heir (–16c, surviving in **disinherit**); to be, or to succeed as, an heir.

initiate [16c. Latin *initiare* 'to begin', from *initium* 'beginning', from *inire* 'to go in', from *ire* 'to go'] **1** to introduce someone with rites or ceremonies into a group, organization, or religion, or to some (esoteric or occult) knowledge; someone who has (just) been initiated (19c) **2** to introduce, to begin or set going (17c), hence **initiative** this action (18c), the first step in a process, hence **(a)** the right, power, ability, or willingness to take it; drive, resourcefulness, self-motivation (early 20c) **(b)** a plan put forward to tackle a particular problem (1940s).

Latin *initiare* produced **commence** [via Old French from Latin *com* 'together' + *initiare*]; *initium* produced **initial**; *ire* is the ancestor of EXIT*.

inn [Old English] A dwelling; a temporary one (ME), hence **1** a public house, originally one providing food and accommodation for travellers **2** [translating Latin *hospitium* (see *hospice* at HOSPITAL*)] a hall of residence for students, preserved in the names of some buildings formerly used for this purpose, notably **Gray's Inn** and **Lincoln's Inn** (housing law students), which became two of the four **Inns of Court**, which admit people to the bar.

Inn produced the surname **Inman** an innkeeper, and probably **inmate** [with MATE] a housemate, lodger, or subtenant, now usually someone living in an institution. Related to *ben* (at BUT) and to **in**.

innuendo [16c. Latin, literally 'by giving a nod to', from *innuere* 'to nod to, to signify', from *nuere* 'to nod'] Namely, that is to say (used in legal documents to introduce a clarification of the previous passage); such a clarification; in an action for libel or slander: the alleged implication of an expression which is not in itself actionable (17c), hence a remark with a (suggestive) double meaning; the use of such remarks.

inoculate [ME. Latin *inoculare* 'to graft, to implant', from *oculus* 'eye, bud'] To graft a bud or shoot into a plant of a different type (–19c); to introduce infected matter into the body, especially to produce immunity (18c); to introduce micro-organisms into a culture medium (19c).

The earliest form of inoculation against disease was carried out in 1796 by Dr Edward Jenner, using matter from a cowpox sore, because he noticed that people with cowpox escaped smallpox. He called cowpox **vaccine disease** [Latin *vaccinus* 'of a cow', from *vacca* 'cow'], and **vaccine** came to be used for a preparation of cowpox, or later of any disease-causing organism, used for inoculation (hence **vaccinate** to inoculate), and later for a program that protects a computer from a virus.

Descendants of Latin *oculus* include **eyelet** [Old French *oillet*, literally 'little eye'], INVEIGLE, **monocle**, **ocular** to do with the eye; an eyepiece, whence **binocular(s)**, French *trompe l'oeil* literally 'deceives the eye', and ULLAGE.

inquire/enquire [ME. Old French *enquerre*, ultimately from Latin *inquirere* 'to inquire into', from *quaerere* 'to ask'. Originally spelt *enquere*, later also *inquere* to conform to the Latin verb: the current spellings (from Latin) arose in the 16c. In modern British English *enquire* is generally used when asking a question, *inquire* being used for investigating formally or officially; the same is true for **enquiry/inquiry**. No such distinction is made in American English] **1** to examine or investigate (–18c); to hold an investigation **2** to ask a question; **enquire after** to ask after (17c) **3** to search for, to try to find (–18c); to ask for or ask to see.

Latin *inquirere* produced **inquest**, **inquisition**, and **inquisitive**; *quaerere* is the ancestor of QUEST*.

insect [17c. Latin *(animal) insectum* 'cut up (animal)', from *insecare, insect-* 'to cut up or cut into', from *secare* 'to cut'] Any small cold-blooded creature with a segmented body, now only an invertebrate with three segments, six legs, and (usually) wings.

Latin *(animal) insectum* was used to translate Greek *(zōion) entomon* [from *entomos* 'cut up', from *temnein* 'to cut'], whence **entomology** the study of insects. Latin *secare* is the ancestor of SECTION*, and Greek *temnein* of TOME*.

inspire [ME. Via French from Latin *inspirare*, from *spirare* 'to breathe'] **1** to breathe or blow into; to breathe life or a soul into; of a supernatural being: to impart a truth or idea to someone, as if by breathing it into them, hence to fill someone with noble thoughts or with the desire to do something; to arouse or provoke a feeling (16c); to suggest or prompt an action (19c) **2** to breathe in, to inhale: the opposite of **expire** [ME, via Old French from Latin *ex(s)pirare* 'to breathe out'] to give out your last breath, to die, hence to die out, to become invalid with time.

instalment [18c. Alteration of obsolete *estalment* (16–18c), from Old French *estaler* 'to place or settle', from *estal* 'a place', of Germanic origin] An arrangement to pay by regular fixed sums (18c only); one of these payments; one of the parts of a story etc. published at different times (19c).

Old French *estaler* probably produced **stale** to urinate (said of horses and cattle, who take up a distinctive position to do so); *estal* produced **stale** describing wine or beer whose sediment had settled with long standing, hence of food, air, etc.: not fresh, *stalemate* (at CHECK), and **stall** a decoy (15–16c); (to act as) an accomplice, later (to use) an evasive trick or delaying tactic, and is one parent of STALL*. Probably related to STAND*.

instance   [ME. French, from Latin *instantia* 'presence, persistence, urgency' (used in medieval Latin to translate Greek *enstasis* 'objection'), from *instare* 'to be present, to press upon', from *stare* 'to stand'] **1** urgency in speech, urgent pleading, surviving in **at the instance of** at the suggestion or urging of **2** a particular case cited to disprove a general assertion (16–17c); an example illustrating a general truth; to cite a case or example (17c).

Latin *instare* produced INSTANT; *stare* is the ancestor of STATION*.

instant   [ME. Via French from Latin *instare*: see INSTANCE] **1** pressing, urgent **2** present now or at the time, current, hence **(a)** in the current month (shortened to **inst.**, probably obsolete) **(b)** a moment; the present or a particular moment (16c), hence **instantly** at this instant, at once **3** occurring immediately (16c); quickly and easily prepared (*c.*1910); instant coffee (1950s); **instantized** made in an instant form (1960s).

institute   [ME. Latin *instituere* 'to establish, arrange, or teach', from *statuere* 'to set up': see STATUS*] **1** to establish someone in an office or position **2** to set up or initiate, hence something instituted (15c): **(a)** an established law or custom (largely replaced by **institution**) **(b)** also as *institution*: (the building housing) an organization set up to promote a cause, education, or (usually *institution*) for the care of the sick or disabled (18c), hence **institutionalized** dependent on the care and routine of an institution (*c.*1900) **(c)** *institution* a long-established person or thing (19c) **3** a principle of instruction (16c); **institutes** a digest of the elements of a subject, especially a legal abstract.

instrument   [ME. (French, from) Latin *instrumentum*, from *instruere, instruct-* 'to set up', also 'to teach', from *struere* 'to build'] Something used to produce or achieve something, hence **1** a device for producing music; to arrange music for instruments (19c) **2** a person used as a means to an end, a dupe **3** a formal legal document; to draw one up (18c); to petition someone by means of one **4** an implement or tool (15c); a measuring device; to equip with such devices (1940s).

Latin *instruere* produced **instruct**; *struere* is the ancestor of DESTROY*.

insular   [16c. Latin *insularis*, from *insula* 'island'] **1** an islander; to do with, or characteristic of, islanders (18c); ignorant of, and indifferent to, other cultures or ideas **2** to do with islands, living or situated on an island (17c): **(a)** of climate: temperate because of the sea's influence (19c) **(b)** a kind of Latin script used in the British Isles in the early Middle Ages (*c.*1900) **3** like or forming an island (17c); detached, separate (19c).

Latin *insula* is the ancestor of the surname **Eyles**, **Il(l)es**, **Isles**, or **Lisle** [via Anglo-Norman French *isle* 'island'], **isle** and **islet** [via Old French *ile*], **isolated** (whence isolate), **insulate** to make into an island; to detach or isolate, especially to surround with materials that do not conduct electricity, heat, or sound, **insulin** a hormone produced in the **islets of Langerhans**, clusters of cells in the pancreas [named after Paul Langerhans, 19c German pathologist, who first described them], and **peninsula** [with Latin *paene* 'almost'].

Island is from unrelated Old English *ēgland*, from *ēg* 'an area (partly) surrounded by water or marsh' (whence some instances of **-ey** in place names, others being from Old English *ea* 'river') + LAND.

insult [16c. Strictly speaking, two words, although each has influenced the other: both ultimately from Latin *salire* 'to leap' (ancestor of SALIENT*)] **1** [via Latin *insultare*, literally 'to keep jumping on'] to exult or boast, hence to exult over, to treat scornfully (17c); an offensive remark or action; something so contemptible or worthless as to be offensive **2** [via French or ecclesiastical Latin from Latin *saltus* 'a jump'] a (sudden) attack or assault (17c), hence **(a)** to make one **(b)** an attack of a disease; (something that causes) physical injury (*c*.1900).

intelligence [ME. Via French from Latin *intelligentia*, from *intelligere*, *intellect-* 'to understand', literally 'to choose among', from *legere* 'to gather or pick out', also 'to read'] The ability to learn and understand, hence **1** a spirit or other being with this **2** comprehension, knowledge (15c); information, especially about a (potential) enemy (16c); (those involved in) the collection or communication of it (17c) **3 intelligence quotient (IQ)** a measure of someone's intelligence, the average being 100 [1920s, from German] **4 artificial intelligence (AI)** the use of computers etc. to perform functions normally requiring human thought (1950s).

Latin *intelligentia* is the source [via Russian and Polish] of **intelligentsia**. *Intelligere* produced **intellect** and **intellectual** [via Latin *intellectus* 'understanding'], **intelligible** able to understand (ME–18c), later to be understood, and **intelligent** having intelligence; of a device or system: able to respond to different situations and to make deductions from information. *Legere* is the ancestor of LEGEND*.

intend [ME. French *entendre* 'to turn your mind to, to hear, to understand', from Latin *intendere*, *intent-* (literally 'to stretch towards'), from *tendere* 'to stretch'] To turn your mind to (–17c), hence **1** to pay attention to or look after (–18c); to direct, oversee, or supervise (18–19c): cf. *superintend* (at SUPERINTENDENT) **2** to plan to do or contemplate doing something (15c) **3** to design or destine something for a person or purpose (16c) **4** to mean by saying (16c).

French *entendre* produced **entente** 'an understanding', adopted for (the parties to) an amicable understanding between states, specifically in the **entente cordiale** between Britain and France. Latin *intendere* produced **intense** [via Latin *intensus* 'tightly stretched, strained'], **intent** concentrating, engrossed [from the past participle], **intent** and **intention** [via Latin *intentus* 'purpose'], and SUPERINTENDENT. *Tendere* is the ancestor of TEMPT*.

interest [ME. Old French from Latin, from *interesse* 'to be between, to take part in', from *esse* 'to be'] (A right to) a share, later specifically a financial share. Hence **1** a benefit or advantage; **in the interests of** to the benefit of **2** a personal or commercial involvement, especially affecting your impartiality (16c), hence **(a)** a business, principle, etc. that is important to a number of people (17c); these people: cf. *vested interests* (at VEST) **(b)** to involve someone in something (17c); **be**

interested to wish to be involved, to feel curiosity or concern; *interest* (to arouse) such feelings (18c); something that does so (19c); a hobby or pursuit **3** [from a medieval Latin sense of *interesse*, 'compensation for non-payment of a debt'] money charged for credit or a loan (16c).

Interest produced **disinterested** and **uninterested**. Strictly speaking, the former now means 'impartial', the latter 'not curious or concerned'; however, both words have had both meanings, and the distinction is often disregarded. Latin *esse* is the ancestor of ESSENCE*.

interim [16c. Latin, from *inter* 'between, among'] **1** a provisional or temporary arrangement, originally between the German Protestants and the Roman Catholic church; provisional, temporary (17c) **2** in the meantime, meanwhile; an intervening period (17c).

Latin *inter* is the ancestor of ENTERPRISE*, **entrails**, **inter-** (*interloper* at LOAFER, *international*), **interior**, **intern**, and **internal**.

interlude [ME. Medieval Latin *interludium*, from *ludus* 'play' (ancestor of LUDICROUS*)] A light dramatic item performed between acts of a morality play, hence **1** (something performed or done during) an interval between acts of a play or between broadcast items (17c) **2** an interval during which something happens that contrasts with what goes before or after (18c).

internecine [17c. Latin *internecinus*, from *internecare* 'to slaughter, to destroy utterly', from *necare* 'to kill', from *nex* 'death, destruction'] War to the death (translating Latin *internecinus bellum*), hence deadly, involving great slaughter. Johnson (see ACHE) interpreted *inter-* (here meaning 'completely') as 'between' (as in INTERIM) and defined *internecine* as 'endeavouring mutual destruction', hence the current sense, to do with internal conflict (19c).

Latin *nex* produced **pernicious** deadly, destructive (surviving in **pernicious anaemia**, formerly always fatal); wicked, malicious; harmful. Related to Greek *nekros* 'corpse', whence **necro-** (*necrophilia*, *necropolis* at POLICY).

interpolate [17c. Latin *interpolare* 'to polish up', from *polire* POLISH*] **1** to refurbish (–18c); to insert new material; to falsify a text by doing so **2** to estimate or calculate the value of a function that lies between known values (18c), whence to **extrapolate** to estimate or calculate values outside a series from those within it (19c); to predict or infer from previous events or known facts **3** to throw a remark into a conversation (19c).

intimate [17c. Latin *intimare* 'to announce, to make familiar', from Latin *intimus* 'inmost', also 'a close friend'] Inmost, deep-seated, hence **1** essential, intrinsic **2** deeply personal or private **3** of a relationship: very close, hence **(a)** a close friend or associate **(b) be intimate (with)** to have sex (19c, 17c in **intimacy**); involving the sexual organs or bodily orifices (*intimate search*, 1920s) **(c)** having or trying to create a close, friendly atmosphere (*c*.1915) **4** of knowledge: resulting from close familiarity, thorough, deep.

Latin *intimare* also produced **intimate** to announce formally, later to indicate or imply, to mention in passing.

intrigue [17c. Via French and Italian from Latin *intricare* 'to entangle or perplex', from *tricare* 'to play tricks', from *tricae* 'tricks, perplexities', from *tricari* 'to make difficulties'] **1** to deceive or cheat; (to carry on) an underhand plot or an illicit love affair **2** to puzzle or perplex; to fascinate or make curious (19c) **3** complexity, something complicated; to entangle or complicate.

Latin *intricare* produced **intricate**; *tricare* is probably the source of TRICK*; *tricae* produced **extricate**, originally to unravel or clear of difficulties.

introvert [17c. Modern Latin *introvertere*, literally 'to turn in', from *vertere* 'to turn'] **1** to turn your thoughts inwards, hence in Jung's psychology, someone more concerned with their own thoughts and feelings than the world outside (*c*.1915) **2** to turn or bend inwards physically (18c).

The opposite of *introvert* was **extravert** to turn outwards or inside out; the variant **extrovert** was rare until the early 20c, when it was influenced by *introvert* and became the more common form. Latin *vertere* is the ancestor of VERSE*.

intrude [ME. Latin *intrudere*, literally 'to thrust in', from *trudere* 'to thrust'] **Intrusion** the taking over of an office, right, or vacant estate without a legitimate claim (surviving as a legal term), hence *intrude* to do so (16c); to enter forcibly; to go or butt in where you are not wanted; to introduce something unwelcome.

Latin *trudere* is the ancestor of **abstruse** [via French from Latin *abstrudere*, literally 'to thrust away'] hidden (16–18c), hence obscure, hard to understand, and of **extrude**, **obtrude**, and **protrude**.

inveigle [15c. Old French *aveugler* 'to blind', from *aveugle* 'blind', ultimately from Latin *ab-* 'away from' + *oculus* 'eye' (ancestor of INOCULATE*)] To deceive (–18c); to win over by coaxing or flattery, to entice or seduce (16c).

invent [15c. Latin *invenire*, literally 'to come upon', from *venire* 'to come'] **1** to discover (originally and surviving in **Invention of the Cross** a festival commemorating the supposed discovery of Christ's cross) **2** to plan or plot (16–17c), hence to produce by ingenuity, to devise or originate.

Latin *invenire* produced *inventarium* 'a list of things found', whence **inventory**. Latin *venire* is the ancestor of VENUE*.

inveterate [ME. Latin *inveterare* 'to make old', from *vetus*, *veter-* 'old' (ancestor of VETERAN*] Originally of a disease: chronic; firmly established, persistent (16c); obstinately persisting in a (bad) habit.

invidious [17c. Latin *invidiosus*, from *invidia* 'ill will', from *invidere* 'to regard with malice', from *videre* 'to see'] Giving or likely to give offence or arouse ill-feeling, hence **1** likely to arouse envy **2** of a comparison: unfair (18c).

Latin *invidia* produced **envy** [via French], originally simply hostility or spite; *videre* is the ancestor of VISION*.

invoke [ME. Via French from Latin *invocare* 'to call upon', from *vocare* 'to call'] To call upon a deity in prayer or as a witness; to call upon or summon a spirit (17c, ME in **invocation**), hence **1** to give rise to a feeling or idea (17c) **2** to call for some thing or action (17c); in law: to call for papers or evidence from another case (19c), hence to appeal to for support or confirmation; to cite as an authority **3** to call for something to be observed or put into effect (19c); to do so.

Latin *vocare* is the ancestor of **evoke** [Latin *evocare*, literally 'to call out'] to summon a spirit, hence to 'call up' a memory, feeling, or response, and of VOUCH*.

iota [ME. Greek *iōta*, of Phoenician origin] The ninth and smallest letter (ι) of the Greek alphabet, hence the smallest or a very small quantity (17c).

Greek *iōta* is the ancestor of **jot** the smallest letter or part (see also *not one jot or tittle* at TITLE), hence to write down briefly or hastily.

iris [ME. Latin *iris, irid-*, from Greek *iris, Iris* the goddess of the rainbow. The main senses existed in Greek and their English dates are not significant] **1** a mineral (now a variety of quartz) that produces iridescent reflections **2** the plant, which has varieties in many colours **3** a rainbow (15c); a combination of brilliant colours **4** a coloured halo (15c); the coloured part of the eye that controls the amount of light admitted (16c); a diaphragm that does the same for a lens (19c).

Latin *iris* is the ancestor of **iridescent** and **iridium** a metal that produces brightly coloured compounds.

issue [ME. French, ultimately from Latin *exire* 'to go out': see EXIT*] To go or come out; this action, hence **1** an exit or outlet; the mouth of a river; (the cause of) a discharge of blood, pus, etc. **2** to come from a source: **(a)** (as) proceeds or revenue (surviving as a legal term) **(b)** as a descendant; offspring, progeny **(c)** an outcome or consequence; to derive, turn out, or result (16c) **3** the end of an action or legal proceeding; a point still in question at the end of a legal case; a matter of contention, hence **(a) join issue** to submit an issue jointly for a decision; to accept the other side's contention as the issue to be settled; to engage in the argument (16c); to take the opposing view (17c, replaced by **take issue**, 19c) **(b) at issue** under discussion, contentious (18c); **make an issue of** to make a fuss about (1920s) **(c)** a subject of concern (17c); a dilemma (19c) **4** to let or give out (15c); to give or be given out publicly or officially (17c); what is issued (19c): **(a)** (the number of) shares, coins, copies of a newspaper, etc., issued at one time **(b)** a thing or amount distributed, especially in the armed forces **(c)** in a library: the number of books lent (1950s); a system for recording the loans.

item [ME. Latin, from *ita* 'thus, so'] Likewise, also, used to draw attention to or introduce a new statement or an entry in a list, hence **1** an entry in a list of accounts (16c); an individual member of a set; a piece of information or news (19c); in computing: any quantity of data treated as a unit (1950s), hence a couple in a relationship (1970s, *US*) **2** to list the members of a set (17c, replaced by 19c **itemize**).

iterate [ME. Latin *iterare* 'to repeat', from *iterum* 'again'] **1 iteration** the repetition of an action, hence *iterate* to repeat one; in maths: to repeat the use of a formula, each time substituting the result of the previous calculation (*c*.1900) **2** to state again or repeatedly (largely replaced by 15c **reiterate** [from Latin *reiterare*]).

itinerary [ME. Latin *itinerarium*, neuter of *intinerarius* 'to do with a journey or roads', from *iter, itiner-* 'journey, road'] A route, a course of travel, hence **1** an account of a journey (15c) **2** a guide book for travellers (16c); a travel plan (19c).

Latin *itiner-* produced *itinerari* 'to travel', whence **itinerant** going from place to place, especially in the course of your work (originally of a circuit judge); someone who does so.

J

jabot [19c. French *jabot* 'a bird's crop', later the frill on a shirt-front, sticking out like a bird's crop] A frill on the front or at the neck of a shirt, later a cascade of frills on a blouse.

jackanapes First recorded in 16c satires as *Jack Napes* (probably based on *Jack an ape*, and perhaps already used as a name for a pet monkey), the nickname of the unpopular William de la Pole who dominated the government of the weak King Henry VI and whose symbol was an ape with a ball and chain. Hence someone who behaves like de la Pole or like a cheeky monkey: an impertinent upstart, a mischievous child.

The present form comes from 18c *Jack-a-Napes*, probably intended to mean 'Jack of Naples': at this time tame apes were being imported from Italy as fashion accessories. See also JOCKEY*.

jacket [ME. French *jacquet* 'a short *jacque*', i.e. a sleeveless leather tunic, sometimes reinforced for protection in battle, perhaps from *Jacques* used as a general name for a peasant, from Latin *Jacobus*, ultimately from Hebrew *Ya'aqob*] A short coat, later extended to various coverings: an animal's skin (17c); the insulation of a boiler (19c), a book's dust wrapper, a potato skin.

French *jacque* is the probable source of **jackboot** a long boot worn by cavalry soldiers, hence military oppression (revived by the boot's association with Nazi soldiers). Latin *Jacobus* produced **Jacob** and [via the variant *Jacomus*] **James**, hence **Jacobean** to do with St James the Apostle, King James I and VI or his time, or, occasionally, Henry James the novelist, and **Jacobite** (describing) a supporter of James II and his heirs.

jack-in-the-box [16c. The name *Jack*: see JOCKEY*] A cheat, especially one who gave tradesmen an empty box instead of one containing money (–18c), hence the child's toy, which also gives you a surprise when you open it (18c).

Jack is used here to mean 'a man' (also found in **Jack Frost**, **Jack-o'-lantern** originally a nightwatchman with a lantern, and *Jack Tar* at TAR), later specifically a workman (*lumberjack/steeplejack/jack of all trades*), a youth, hence the knave in cards (adopted when the card's value came to be shown in its corner, to avoid confusion with K for king, whence *jackpot* at POT), or the male of some animals, whence **jackass** (see also *jackrabbit* at RABBIT). See also JACKKNIFE.

jackknife [18c. The name *Jack*: see JOCKEY*] A large folding knife; to double up like one (19c), hence **1** (to perform) a dive in which you double up in the air with straight legs (1920s) **2** of an articulated lorry: to fold against itself (1940s).

Jack was applied to various tools and labour-saving devices (e.g. *bootjack, jack hammer*), as though Jack was there to help, originally one that turned a spit, now a lifting device, hence **jack up** to raise with one.

jade [ME. Origin unknown] **1** a worthless or worn-out horse, hence to make or become tired or worn out (17c) **2** a headstrong or disreputable woman (16c) **3** (combining 1 and 2) **jaded** tired or bored from overindulgence (17c).

jag [ME. The *j* perhaps suggesting a sudden forceful movement, the *-ag* sharpness and unevenness (as in *rag*)] **1** to stab or pierce (surviving in Scots, N England and US dialect), hence **(a)** a sharp point or projection **(b)** a prick (17c); an injection (19c, Scots: cf. *jab* at JOB²) **2** to cut or pink a garment for decoration; an ornamental point on a garment (cf. TAG*), hence **jagged** cut in this way; having a sharp, ragged edge (15c).

jail [ME. Old French *jaiole*, ultimately from Latin *cavea* 'cage'. **Gaol**, from the Old Norman French form of *jaiole*, is now the standard spelling in British official use; otherwise both spellings occur. Only *jail* is used in the US] A prison for convicted criminals; imprisonment (15c); to imprison (17c).
    Latin *cavea* is the ancestor of **cage** and perhaps **decoy** originally an enclosed place into which wildfowl are led and captured [perhaps from Dutch *de kooi* 'the cage', ultimately from *cavea*].

jam [18c. The *j* as in *jag*; the *-am* as in *cram*] **1** to press or squeeze in; to push or ram forcibly (*jammed on the brakes*, 19c); to bruise or crush **2** to become fixed or wedged; to wedge or obstruct, hence **(a)** people or things crowded together so that none can move (*traffic/log jam*, 19c); an awkward situation (1920s, *US*) **(b)** to obstruct a radio signal (World War I).
    Jam fruit spread (hence something easy, good, or pleasant; **jammy** easy, lucky) may be related to sense 1, or may be a separate word of unknown origin. *Jam* (to play) improvised music (*African-American*) may be from the sense 'something pleasant', but is probably from an African language, perhaps Wolof *djam* 'inspiration' or Swahili *jaame* 'something good'.

jamboree [19c. Origin unknown] A noisy celebration, a spree (*US slang*), hence the name given to the 1920 International Rally of Scouts in London, and subsequently applied to any large Scout rally.

jangle [ME. Old French *jangler*, possibly of Germanic origin] To talk excessively or noisily, the sound of this; to grumble or squabble; squabbling, bickering, hence **1** to make a harsh, unmusical noise (15c) **2** to irritate or upset (17c).

jape [ME. Apparently combining the form of Old French *japer* 'to yap' with the sense of Old French *gaber* 'to mock'] A trick: **1** a deception or fraud (–19c); to deceive; to mock or insult (–19c); to seduce or have sex with (15c, probably causing *jape* to disappear in all its senses by about 1600; it was revived by 19c writers, including Scott: see DOFF) **2** a jest or joke; to joke or jeer.

jar [15c. The *j* as in JAG, the *r* suggesting discordant sound] **1** a harsh or discordant sound (hence **nightjar** a nocturnal bird with a churring call, 17c), hence **(a)** to (cause to) make one (16c) **(b)** to grate on the ear or nerves (16c) **2** disagreement, a petty squabble; to bicker (16c) **3** to jolt (16c); (to shake or vibrate from) a jolt or shock (18c); to affect or injure by means of one (19c) **4** to clash, to be or seem inappropriate or out of place (17c).

Jar a container [via French from Arabic] first appeared in 16c travellers' tales, referring to a large earthenware pot found in the East.

jargon [ME. Old French *jargoun, gergon*, of unknown origin] (To make) a twittering or chattering noise (–15c, revived by 19c writers), hence **1** nonsense, gibberish; to talk unintelligibly (16c) **2** a cipher or code (16–18c) **3** a hybrid or debased form of language (17c), often used contemptuously of speech the listener did not understand **4** (combining 1–3) the language of a particular profession or group (17c), often unintelligible to others.

jaunt [16c. Origin unknown] To tire a horse out by riding it up and down; to traipse about; a tiring or troublesome journey; any journey (17c); (to take) a pleasure trip.

jazz [Early 20c. Origin unknown: probably of African origin but sometimes said to be named after Jasper (Jas), a slave known for his enthusiastic dancing, or Jasbo Brown, an itinerant musician in Mississippi. The dates given show when senses came to the notice of White society so the development of *jazz* and *jive* is a matter of conjecture] **1** a kind of (originally) African-American music characterized by syncopation and improvisation; to play or dance to this (by 1920) **2** energy, excitement, liveliness (*jasm* in this sense, probably of African origin, was recorded in 1860, but may not be related); **jazz up** to liven or brighten up; **jazzy** lively, bright, gaudy **3** meaningless talk, nonsense, rubbish (*c.*1918: cf. *jive* below), hence **(a)** to lie or exaggerate **(b)** something unpleasant (1930s) **(c)** miscellaneous, unspecified things (*all that jazz*, 1950s) **4** (to have) sexual intercourse (cf. BOOGIE).

Jive [probably of W African origin] has a similar history: **1** a kind of jazz, hence **(a)** to play it or dance to it; the dance **(b) jive (talk)** a kind of Black English associated with jazz musicians **2** idle, foolish, or insincere talk (*African-American*); to mislead or flatter; to taunt or sneer at; to talk or act foolishly; something worthless or unpleasant.

jean [15c. Old French *Janne*, from medieval Latin *Janua* 'Genoa', an Italian city] From Genoa, Genoese (–17c), hence **jean (fustian)** a heavy twilled cotton fabric from Genoa (16c); made of this or a similar fabric, now usually denim (18c); **jeans** hardwearing (denim) trousers (19c).

Denim was originally a kind of serge [from French *serge de Nîmes*, a city in S France], while **serge** [via French from Latin *serica lana* 'silken wool', from *sericus* 'silk'] was originally a woollen fabric used for curtains and bedhangings: see also *fustian* (at BOMBAST). **Genoa** also gave its name to a kind of velvet, a fruit cake, and a large jib used on a racing yacht (now often shortened to **genny** or **jenny**).

jeep [1930s. Partly from *Eugene the Jeep*, a character of great strength and resourcefulness who appeared in the Popeye series of cartoons by E. C. Segar, partly from *GP*, standing for *General Purpose* (vehicle)] Briefly applied to a commercial vehicle (1937, probably from Eugene); later to a small, tough, four-wheel-drive vehicle used in the US Army (1941): in this sense sometimes said to be short for *jeepers creepers*, an officer's remark after riding in the prototype.

Other characters from the Popeye cartoons include Alice the Goon (see GOON) and the burger-loving J. Wellington Wimpy, whose name was adopted by a chain of hamburger bars.

Jehovah [16c. The consonants *JHVH or YHWH* representing the Hebrew name of God, too holy to be spoken, with the vowels of Hebrew *'aḏōnāy* 'my Lord' inserted] The name of the Jewish, and subsequently Christian, God, especially in the Old Testament. **Yahweh** (19c) is now considered the correct form, though *Jehovah* is still more common. **Adonai** [ME, from Hebrew *'aḏōnāy*] is used in Judaism and in the Old Testament.

jejune [17c. Latin *jejunus*] **1** fasting, hungry (–18c) **2** not nourishing; meagre or barren, hence intellectually unsatisfying, boring, simplistic; childish, naive (19c, perhaps from a mistaken belief that the word comes from French *jeune* or Latin *juvenis* 'young').

Latin *jejunus* produced **jejunum** the second part of the small intestine, usually empty after death, and **dine** to eat **dinner** [via Old French *disner* 'to eat dinner', from *desj(e)uner* 'to break a fast'] the main meal of the day (but cf. TEA*): *dine* produced **diner** someone who dines; a railway dining-car (*US*), hence a café (originally built to resemble a dining-car).

jelly [ME. French *gelée* 'frost, jelly', from Latin *gelata* 'frozen', from *gelare* 'to freeze', from *gelu* 'frost'] Meat or fish stock, later fruit juice, set with gelatine (16c), hence **1** **jellied** covered, set in, or cooked with jelly (15c) **2** to (make something) set like jelly (17c), partly replaced by the back-formation **jell** (18c), which came to mean 'to take shape, to cohere' (*c.*1900, cf. *gel* below) **3** something with a jelly-like consistency (*petroleum/royal jelly*, 17c) **4** a clear fruit preserve (18c); in the US: jam **5** (a dessert made from) a proprietary mix of flavoured gelatine (19c, in the US usually known by the proprietary name **Jello**, 1930s), hence **jelly shoes/ sandals**, **jellies** made of a moulded plastic that looks like jelly.

Latin *gelata* produced **gelatine** (whence **gel** (to form) a soft jelly-like colloid; to take shape) and **gelignite** [with Latin *ignis* 'fire']. *Gelare* produced **congeal**, originally 'to freeze' [Latin *congelare*, literally 'to freeze together'].

jeopardy [ME. Old French *jeu parti* 'a divided (i.e. even) game', from *jeu* 'game' (from Latin *jocus* JOKE*) + *partir* 'to divide', from Latin *partire*: see PART*] A problem in chess etc. (–15c); a position in which the chances of winning or losing are even (–16c), hence a dangerous situation; risk, danger. Hence **jeopard** to put at risk (ME–17c, revived by Scott: see DOFF); **jeopardize** (17c) is more common.

jerk [16c. Origin unknown] **1** (to give someone) a lash with a whip (–18c); (to 'lash' with) satire or ridicule; a sarcastic remark **2** to wrench or yank; to jump or twitch, hence **(a)** (to suffer) an involuntary muscular spasm (19c) **(b)** to serve soda (19c, US, probably from the action of working the soda fountain); **soda jerk(er)** someone who does so **(c)** in weightlifting: a lift in which the barbell is thrust upwards quickly from shoulder level (*c.*1910); to perform this (1930s) **(d) physical jerks** physical or gymnastic exercises (*c.*1920). *Jerk* unpleasant person, fool (1930s, *US*) may be from **jerk off** to masturbate (1930s, *US*), or may be from **jerkwater** describing a train running on a small branch line (19c, *US*, from the need to 'jerk' water from streams with a bucket on a rope), hence small, insignificant, inferior.

Jerry [World War I. Probably an alteration of *German*, influenced by the name *Jerry*] (A) German; a German soldier or aircraft; Germans or German soldiers collectively. Hence **jerry can**, **jerrican** a five-gallon metal container, originally one captured from the Germans (World War II).

jersey [16c] (Something) from Jersey, the largest of the Channel Islands: **1** a fine woollen worsted, later any plain machine-knitted fabric **2** a knitted pullover or sweater (19c); a football, rugby, or cycling shirt **3** a breed of dairy cattle (19c).

The neighbouring island of **Guernsey** gave its name to a similar breed of cattle and to a kind of sweater (sometimes altered to **gansey**), hence the 'jersey' worn by Australian Rules players.

jest [ME. Old French *geste*, *jeste*, from Latin *gesta* 'actions, exploits', from *gerere* 'to carry, wield, or perform' (ancestor of GESTURE*)] A heroic deed; a story of such deeds, originally in verse (surviving as **gest**, used mainly by students of medieval literature); an idle tale, a lampoon (–17c), hence (to make) a mocking or jeering speech (16c); (to make) a joke; fun, joking, merriment. Hence **jester 1** a professional reciter of gests (ME) **2** someone who jests (16c); a professional clown in a medieval court.

jet [16c. French *jeter* 'to throw', ultimately from Latin *jactare*, literally 'to throw repeatedly', from *jacere* 'to throw', also 'to lie down'] **1** to (make something) stick out or project (–18c, surviving as **jut**); something that does so, specifically a jetty (17–18c) **2** to throw out (17c, surviving in E English dialect); a stream of liquid, gas, etc. forced out through a narrow opening (17c), hence **(a)** to spurt out (17c) **(b)** a spout or nozzle for producing a jet (19c) **(c) jet (engine)** an engine powered by a jet of combustion gases (1940s); **jet (aircraft/fighter/plane**, etc.) one with jet engines, hence *jet* to travel or convey in one, *jet lag* (at LAG[1]), **jet set** wealthy people who regularly jet (1950s).

French *jeter* produced **jetty**; Latin *jactare* produced JETTISON; *jacere*'s descendants include ABJECT, **conjecture**, **deject** to bring down, to conquer or humble, hence to dishearten, EASE*, **ejaculate**, **eject**, GIST, **inject**, **interject**, **joist**, OBJECT, PROJECT, **reject**, SUBJECT, and **trajectory**.

jettison [ME. Old French *getaison* from Latin *jactatio*, from *jactare*: see JET] The action of throwing goods overboard to lighten a ship; to do so (19c); to abandon or get rid of; to discard something from an air- or spacecraft (1940s). Shortened to **jetsam** jettisoned goods washed up on shore (16c).

jig [16c. Perhaps from or related to French *giguer* 'to dance', from *gigue* 'a fiddle', of Germanic origin] (Music for) a lively folkdance; to play or, later, dance a jig; to dance in a lively or jerky way (17c); to (make something) move jerkily (later also as **jiggle**). Hence **1** a device that moves up and down or from side to side (18c), now especially one that guides cutting or drilling tools and holds the work in place, hence **(a)** to use a jig (18c) **(b) jigsaw** a saw for cutting curves (19c), **jigsaw (puzzle)** made by cutting up a picture with a jigsaw (*c.*1910), a complex whole **(c)** to provide a workshop with jigs (*c.*1900), hence **rejig** to re-equip a workshop (1940s), to reorganize or rearrange (1960s) **2 jig-jig**, **jig-a-jig** (to have) sexual intercourse (19c, pidgin).

Jigger has some senses connected with *jig*: someone who dances a jig or who works a mechanical jig; a lure jigged up and down to attract fish; various kinds of light vehicle; of a fish: to tug repeatedly at a line. Others are unexplained and may represent different words: these include **1** an illicit still; (a measure for) a drink of spirits **2 jiggered** damned; tired out, broken, ruined [perhaps an alteration of *buggered*] **3** to manipulate facts or figures in order to mislead (*US*).

jingo [17c. Origin uncertain, possibly an alteration of **Jesus**: see CHRIST] **1** hey/ high jingo! a conjuror's call to make something appear (–18c, the opposite of **(hey) presto!** [16c, from Italian *presto* 'quick, quickly'] to make something disappear); an exclamation when something does so **2 by jingo** used in a popular song adopted by those who advocated sending a British fleet against Russia in 1878: the chorus ran *We don't want to fight, yet by Jingo! if we do, We've got the ships, we've got the men, and got the money too'*, hence *jingo* such a supporter, a zealous patriot; **jingoism** bellicose patriotism.

job¹ [16c. Perhaps from 15c *job* 'a piece', possibly an alteration of GOB] **1** originally **job of work**: a piece of work, hence **(a)** a (difficult) task (17c); a task or transaction carried out for money; a crime (18c) **(b)** to do piecework or odd tasks (*jobbing gardener*, 17c) **2** your paid employment (17c); your role in it; **jobsworth** a (deliberately obstructive) petty official who follows regulations to the letter (1970s, from *it's more than my job's worth*) **3** personal profit or interest (17–18c); a public service or office turned to private advantage; to gain money or advantage from one (18c); **jobbery** the making of such gains (19c) **4** to buy and sell as a middleman (17c); to deal in stocks and shares on your own account (18c); **jobber** someone who does either **5** something turning out well or badly (*good job you noticed, make the best of a bad job*, 17c); **the job** what's needed (*do/just the job*, 17c) **6 job (lot)** a collection of articles sold together (19c) **7** an example of its kind (*the bird was a little brown job*, 1920s).

job² [ME. The sound apparently expressing a brief, forcible action] To peck, stab, poke, or prod; this action (16c). Largely replaced by the variant **jab** (19c, *Scots*), which came to mean (to throw) a short, straight punch, and (to give) an injection (1920s, *US*): cf. JAG.

jockey [16c. Pet form of **Jock**, Scots form of **Jack**, pet form of **John**] A lad or servant; one who manages horses, hence **1** a horse-dealer (17c), hence a fraud or cheat; to trick or outwit (18c) **2** a postillion or mounted courier (17–19c); a (professional) rider in a horse race, hence **(a)** to ride as a jockey (18c); to manoeuvre to gain an advantage, like a jockey in a race (19c) **(b)** someone who operates a machine (*c.*1912, *N American*), hence **disc jockey** someone who plays records in a club, on radio, etc. (1940s), shortened to **DJ** or **deejay (c) jockey wheel** a small wheel that 'rides' on another (19c); one on a trailer that is lifted and 'rides' when the trailer is hitched (1950s).

Jack is found in JACKANAPES, JACK-IN-THE-BOX*, and JACKKNIFE.

jog [16c. Probably from Middle English *shog*, of Germanic origin] To shake, push, or jolt, hence **1** to move as if shaken or jolted; to walk or run with a heavy, jolting pace or, later, with a gentle, steady one; to do so for exercise (1940s); such a run **2** (to give) a gentle push or nudge (*jogged his memory*, 17c).

Jog produced **joggle**. *Shog* may be related to GOGGLE, and **shag** to shake or toss about (surviving in dialect); to have sex with; this act.

joint [ME. Old French, from *joindre* 'to join', from Latin *jungere, junct-*] **1** joined, combined, united; sharing a job or role (15c); done, owned, made, etc. by two or more people or parties **2** a place where things or parts join; a place or structure where parts are connected but usually able to move in relation to each other. Hence **(a)** a part around a joint (15c); this part of an animal used for food; to divide a carcass into joints **(b)** to connect with a joint (16c) **(c)** a place where people meet (19c, *US*), especially for drinking or dancing, later for taking drugs (hence, probably, equipment for doing so, 1930s, a marijuana cigarette, 1960s), hence any house or building; a tent or stall at a fair or circus (1920s); **the joint** prison (1950s, US).

Old French *joindre* produced **join** and **rejoinder** a defendant's response to the plaintiff's reply to the defendant's plea [from Old French *rejoindre* 'to reply (again)']. English has borrowed several verbs from Old French descendants of Latin *jungere*, taking nouns from the Latin: these include **adjoin/adjunct**, **conjoin/conjunction**, **enjoin/injunction**, and **subjoin/subjunctive**: other descendants include **jointure** originally the joint holding of property by a husband or wife, **junction**, **juncture** a joint or joining; a critical situation or moment, a 'crossroads', and JUNTA.

joke [17c. Latin *jocus* 'jest, wordplay'] Something said or done to make people laugh (*slang*), hence **1** a ridiculous person, thing, or situation; a laughing stock (18c); someone/something you cannot take seriously **2** to make a joke; **joker** someone who does so (18c); a (usually unpleasant) man (19c); a playing card with the figure of a jester, often used as a trump or wild card, hence a minor clause in a document that changes its effect in a way that is not obvious (*c*.1900, *US*); a drawback, a snag.

Latin *jocus* is the ancestor of JEOPARDY, **jocose**, **jocular** (but not *jocund*: see AID), JUGGLER*, and probably **jewel**.

journal [ME. Old French *jurnal* from Latin *diurnalis*, from *diurnus*: see JOURNEY*] **1** a book containing the services and prayers for the day (–16c), now called a **diurnal 2** a book for travellers describing the daily stages of the route (–17c: cf. JOURNEY); a record of travel (17–18c); a ship's log(book) **3** a record of commercial transactions entered as they occur (15c) **4** an official daily record of proceedings (16c) **5** a personal diary (17c) **6** a daily newspaper (17c, now mainly in names: hence **journalist**, **journalism**, **journalese** a hackneyed style of writing associated with newspapers); a periodical dealing with matters of current interest to a particular group.

journey [ME. Old French *jornee*, ultimately from Latin *diurnum* 'daily portion', later 'day', from *diurnus* 'of the day, daily', from *dies* 'day'] A day, hence **1** a day's travel, estimated at 32 km or 20 miles (–16c: cf. JOURNAL sense 2); the distance actually travelled (15c); an expedition from one place to another; a progression from one state to another (*a spiritual journey*); to make one **2** a day's work, hence **journeyman** a tradesman who has finished his apprenticeship, no longer bound by indentures but paid by the day (15c).

Old French *jornee* produced ADJOURN and JOURNAL, Latin *diurnum* produced
sojourn to stay temporarily (literally for a day), a temporary stay; *dies* is the ancestor of DIAL, **diary**, DISMAL, MERIDIAN, and **quotidian** [via Old French from, ultimately, Latin *quotidie* 'each day']: see also DIET.

joust [ME. Old French *j(o)uster* 'to bring together', ultimately from Latin *juxta*
'near'] To join battle, to fight, especially on horseback (–17c); single combat; this
as a sport or exercise; a series of such encounters, a tournament; to take part in
one.

Joust produced **jostle**, originally to have sex with. Latin *juxta* is the ancestor of
ADJUST and **juxtapose**.

jovial [16c. Latin *jovialis*, from *Jovis* 'Jove', the chief god of ancient Rome, also
known as Jupiter (from Latin *Juppiter*, from *Jovis Pater*, literally 'Jove Father')]
1 under the influence of the planet Jupiter (–19c), hence cheerful, good-
humoured, convivial, as those born under Jupiter's influence were thought to be
2 to do with the planet (17c, largely replaced by **Jovian**).

jowl [Old English *ceafl*: the three words *jowl* all originally began with *c* or *ch*: no
one knows why they changed. The current spelling first appeared in *jowl* meaning 'head'] The jawbone, the (lower) jaw, hence **1** (idle or malicious) talk
(ME–16c); to talk idly, to chatter (ME only, in the form *chavel*: probably the source
of **shiver** to tremble with cold, with chattering teeth) **2** the side of the face (17c,
surviving mainly in **cheek by jowl**), probably influenced by **jowl** [Old English
ceole] the throat; a dewlap, which in turn may have been influenced by **jowl** head
[15c, origin unknown], now only the head and shoulders of certain fish as food.
Cf. CHEEK.

jubilee [ME. Via French from Latin *jubilaeus (annus)* '(year) of jubilee', an alteration (influenced by Latin *jubilare* 'to rejoice', whence **jubilant** and **jubilation**) of
Greek *iōbēlaios*, ultimately from Hebrew *yōḇēl*, originally 'ram, ram's-horn trumpet', with which the jubilee year was proclaimed] The **year of Jubilee**, observed
by the Israelites every fifty years, during which slaves were freed, alienated property returned to its owners, and land left untilled, hence **1** in Roman Catholicism: a year during which sins are forgiven in return for acts of piety or repentance
(15c) **2** the fiftieth anniversary, or a celebration of fifty years (rare before the
19c), now usually called the **golden jubilee** by analogy with a golden wedding,
hence **silver jubilee** celebrating twenty-five years; **diamond jubilee** celebrating
sixty years, originally of Queen Victoria's reign **3** a time of celebration (15c);
general or public rejoicing (16c); the sound of this; a joyful African-American folk-
song (19c).

judge [ME. Via French from Latin *judex, judicis*, from *jus* 'law' + -*dicus* 'speaking'
from *dicere* 'to say'] **1** (someone authorized) to try a case in a law court, hence
(a) to decide a question; to give a ruling; to form or give an opinion; to appraise
(b) (to act as) an adjudicator or umpire **2** a person given temporary authority to
govern, specifically among the ancient Israelites (surviving in the biblical *Book of
Judges*).

Descendants of Latin *judex* include **adjudge**, **adjudicate**, **hoosegow** a prison
[Latin-American Spanish *juzgao*, from Spanish *juzgado* 'tribunal', from Latin

judicatum, literally 'thing judged'], **judicial**, **judiciary**, **judicious**, and **prejudice**, literally 'prejudgement'. Latin *jus* is the ancestor of JUST*, and *dicere* of DICTATE*.

juggernaut [17c. Via Hindi from Sanskrit *Jagannātha*, literally 'lord of the world', one of Krishna's titles, from *jagat* 'world' + *nātha* 'lord, protector'] An image of the Hindu god Krishna carried in procession on a huge cart, hence **1** something to which people blindly devote themselves or are sacrificed (19c, because devotees are said to have thrown themselves under the cart's wheels); a destructive and implacable force **2** a large lorry (19c).

juggler [Old English, via Old French *j(o)uglere*, from Latin *joculator*, from *joculari* 'to jest', ultimately from *jocus*: see JOKE*] A sorcerer; a conjuror or jester, later a deceiver or trickster. **Juggle** is a back-formation, originally meaning 'to entertain with jesting or tricks' (ME): the current sense dates from the 19c.

Old French *j(o)uglere* produced modern *jongleur* a wandering entertainer in medieval England and France.

jumper [19c. Probably from **jump** 'short coat' (17c, now dialect), from Middle English **jupe** 'loose jacket or tunic' (now only Scots), from Old French *juppe, jubbe* (whence **jupon** a tunic worn with armour), from Arabic *jubba*] A sailor's loose jacket or overshirt; a knitted jersey (early 20c); **jumper (dress)** a pinafore dress (1930s, US), perhaps influenced by French *guimpe* [from Old French *guimple*, of Germanic origin and related to **wimple**] a blouse or yoke worn under a low-necked dress.

junk [ME. Origin unknown] **(Old) junk** an old or inferior rope or cable (–18c); old rope for recycling (17c), hence **1 (salt) junk** a sailors' word for salt meat, compared to old rope (18c) **2** a piece or lump of something (18c) **3** discarded material or goods, originally still of some use (19c); rubbish, hence describing things of low or doubtful value (*junk bond/food/jewellery/mail*, 1930s) **4** narcotics, especially heroin (1920s), hence **junky** a drug addict.

junket [ME. French *jonquette*, from *jonc* 'rush', from Latin *juncus*] A rush basket; a cream cheese or pudding, originally made in a rush basket or served on a rush mat, now a dish of sweetened, flavoured curds; any sweet delicacy (16c); a feast; a picnic, outing, or party; (to go on) a trip taken at someone else's (especially at public) expense (19c, *N American*).

Latin *juncus* is the ancestor of **jonquil** a kind of narcissus thought to resemble a rush, and of **junco** a reed bunting, now applied to various buntings of Central and N America.

junta [17c. Spanish and Portuguese, literally 'conference', ultimately from Latin *jungere* 'to join' (ancestor of JOINT*)] A Spanish or Italian council or committee (17c); a cabal (18c), now a political or military clique that seizes power after a coup.

just [ME. Via French from Latin *justus*, from *jus, juris* 'law, right'] **1** righteous, morally upright **2** legally or morally right; correct, appropriate; impartial, fair-minded; fair, equitable, well deserved **3** of a measurement: accurate, precise (–19c), hence exactly, precisely, accurately (15c): **(a)** (almost) exactly at the moment in question; very recently, very soon (17c) **(b)** no more than, only (17c);

neither more nor less than (19c) **(c)** actually, really; **just so** exactly in that way (18c); exactly as it should be.

Descendants of Latin *jus* include CONJURE*, **injury**, JUDGE*, **jurisdiction** [with Latin *dicere* 'to say' (ancestor of DICTATE*)], **jurisprudence** [with Latin *prudentia* (see PROVIDENCE) meaning 'knowledge, skill'], **jury** [via Latin *jurare* 'to swear'], **justice**, JUSTIFY, and the name **Justin**, feminine **Justine**.

justify [ME. Via French from Latin *justificare*, from *justus*: see JUST*] **1** to treat justly (–17c); to prove or maintain rightness or innocence; to free from sinfulness through faith or God's grace **2** to make something exact (16c); to adjust the spaces between words in a text so that all the lines are the same length.

K

Kaffir [16c. Arabic *kāfir*, from *kafara* 'to doubt or deny'] **1** a derogatory term for a non-Muslim, becoming rare in the 20c but re-emerging (also as **Kuffar**) among Muslims in western countries (*c*.2000) **2** a member of a Bantu people, especially the Xhosa, in South Africa, hence **(a)** their language (19c) **(b)** any Black African (19c), hence **(White) Kaffir, Kaffirboetie** [Afrikaans *boetie* 'little brother'] a White person thought to favour Black Africans (1920s) **(c) Kaffirs** South African mining shares (19c).

Applied to Black Africans *Kaffir*, always derogatory, is now considered extremely offensive and is legally actionable in South Africa. The terms **kaffir beer** and **kaffir corn**, traditionally brewed and grown by Black Africans, are going out of favour. So far, *kaffir* survives respectably in the names of various southern African plants and animals.

kamikaze [19c. Japanese, literally 'divine wind', from *kami* 'divinity' + *kaze* 'wind'] In Japanese tradition: a gale that destroyed the Mongol invasion fleet in 1281, hence a Japanese suicide pilot or his plane that attacked enemy ships (World War II), hence (a person or deed that is) reckless or self-destructive (1960s); in surfing: a deliberate fall or crash.

keel [ME. Old Norse *kjölr*] The main structural element of a ship, running the length of the hull, hence **1 (a) on an even keel** with the keel level (16c), hence balanced, stable (19c) **(b) keel over to capsize** (19c); to fall over or collapse **2** a ship (16c); a yacht with a keel (19c) **3** something resembling a ship's keel: **(a)** a ridge-shaped part of an organism (16c) **(b)** the main structural part of an aircraft's fuselage (19c).

Keel a flat-bottomed boat (originally one used in E England, later, as **keelboat**, a N American riverboat) is from related Dutch *kiel* 'ship', whence also **keelhaul**.

keen [Old English *cēne*] **1** wise, clever (–15c) **2** brave, daring (–17c); powerful, strong (–16c); fierce, savage, cruel (–17c) **3** of an edge or point: sharp (ME), hence acute, intense (*keen wind/sense of smell*) **4** of a person: eager, enthusiastic (ME), hence **keen on** very interested in (17c), attracted to (1930s).

Senses 1 and 2 survive in some instances of the surname **Keen**, given to those with such qualities. **Keen as mustard** is said to come from an advertisement for Keen's mustard showing a smiling family with the slogan 'Keen as Keen's mustard', with a pun on sense 4 and the mustard's sharp taste. Related to CAN[1]*.

keep [Old English *cēpan*, of unknown origin] To (try to) seize (–15c), hence **1** to lie in wait for (–15c); to watch (for) (–17c); to pay attention to (ME–16c), hence to observe a religious festival; to abide by a law, custom, promise, etc.; to continue or maintain (*keep a diary/the peace, house/bookkeeper*, 16c) **2** to maintain possession of (ME), hence **(a)** to safeguard (*keep a secret*); to protect or defend, hence the strongest tower of a castle (16c) **(b)** to maintain financially; sustenance, maintenance (*earn your keep*, 19c) **(c)** to provide with continuously (*the hens keep us in eggs*). Hence **3** to (cause to) stay in a place, position, or condition (*kept to her bed/keep your chin up/how are you keeping?*, ME); to be able to be stored without spoiling, or to be postponed **4** to restrain or refrain from doing something (ME).

kermes [16c. Via French from Arabic *qirmiz*, the insect] **1** kermes (oak) a small evergreen Mediterranean tree **2** (the dried bodies of) a kind of scale insect that forms hard berry-like galls on the kermes oak, used to make a red dye (17c); this dye.

Arabic *qirmiz* produced **carmine** (the colour of) a crimson pigment obtained from **cochineal** [via French or Spanish from Latin *coccinus* 'scarlet', from Greek *kokkos* 'berry, seed, grain'] a similar scale insect in Central America, originally mistaken for grains or berries, and **crimson**.

key [Old English *cǣg*, of unknown origin] An instrument that operates a lock, winds a clock, etc., hence a means of access, control, or understanding (*key to success/a map*), hence **1** something that 'locks': a surface prepared so that plaster etc. will stick (15c, hence to prepare one, 19c); **key(stone)** the wedge-shaped central block that locks an arch together **2** a lever or button on a musical instrument (15c), a telephone, calculator, computer terminal etc. (19c), hence **keyboard (a)** these keys (19c); also **key (in):** to enter data using a keyboard (1960s) **(b)** (describing) a musical instrument with keys (19c) **3** later **keynote**: the note on which a musical scale is based (15c, probably a translation of Latin *clavis* 'key'), used in medieval music for a note or tone, particularly this one, hence *key* **(a)** the scale (*minor key/key of C*) **(b)** the pitch of a voice etc. (16c); a characteristic tone or level of intensity; **keyed up** raised in pitch etc. (18c), tense, excited **(c)** *keynote* (expressing) the most important points (*keynote speech*, 18c) **3** the winged seed of an ash tree (growing in bunches like keys, 16c).

Latin *clavis* appears in the names of early keyboard instruments (e.g. *clavichord, clavier*), and produced **clavicle** the collarbone [Latin *clavicula* 'small key', from its shape], French *clef*, that shows the pitch of a stave, **conclave**, originally a locked or private room, and French *enclave* [from Old French *enclaver* 'to enclose'].

kid [ME. Old Norse *kith*] A young goat, hence **1** soft leather made from a kid or lamb (15c), hence **with kid gloves** very gently or delicately **2** a young roe-deer (15c) or, later, antelope **3** a child (16c); a young criminal (*Billy the Kid*, 19c); **kid brother/ sister** your younger sibling (19c, US) **4** an indentured servant (16c) **5** to deceive, joke with, or tease (19c, probably from the idea of making a child or goat of).

Kid produced the surnames **Kidd(e), Kidman, Kyd(d)** a frisky person or a goatherd, and **kidnap** to abduct a child or other person, originally to work on the American plantations [*nap* perhaps a variant of **nab** to arrest or seize, of unknown origin].

kilt [ME. Of Scandinavian origin] To gather and tuck up a long skirt, hence a knee-length pleated 'skirt' forming part of a Scotsman's national dress (18c), derived from an earlier garment consisting of a long piece of woollen cloth, one end of which was pleated and fastened round the waist, the other end, now separate and called the **plaid** [16c, from Scottish Gaelic *plaide*] being draped round the upper body.

Tartan the fabric from which the kilt and plaid were made [perhaps from Old French *tertaine, tiretaine*, ultimately from Latin *Tyrius* '(cloth) from Tyre', a town in Lebanon] now often refers to its distinctive chequered patterns; *plaid* also came to mean the fabric and pattern. Both now describe anything with such a pattern; *kilt* is also used for a woman's pleated skirt.

kin [Old English *cynn*] A group of people descended from a common ancestor, hence **1** a class of people, animals, plants, etc. (replaced by KIND) **2** your race or family; your relative(s) (ME), hence **next of kin** (being) your closest relative (15c) **3** relationship by birth (ME), largely replaced by **kinship**, which also means relationship by marriage or similarity (19c) **4** (also **akin**) related or similar to (16c).

Kin fathered **kindred** kinship, resemblance, affinity, also a family, tribe or clan. Related to KIND, German *Kind* 'child', adopted in *kindergarten* [literally 'children's garden'], and KING.

kind [Old English *gecynde*] Natural, proper, appropriate; your natural position in society (–17c); well-born or well-bred (ME), hence **1** having, showing, or arising from, a gentle and benevolent nature (ME, cf. GENEROUS) **2** agreeable, pleasant (ME–18c), surviving in **take kindly (to)** to find pleasant, to accept willingly **3** grateful (15c, surviving in dialect and in *thank you kindly*).

Related to KIN and to **kind** nature or a natural characteristic, hence a group of animals etc. with shared ancestry and/or characteristics; a class or sort (replacing KIN): hence **mankind** [replacing Old English *mancynn* 'man kin, the race of men'].

king [Old English *cyn(in)g*] A male (hereditary) ruler, hence **1** God or Christ as the supreme ruler (*King of Kings/Heaven*) **2** a man pre-eminent in his sphere (ME); the best (or biggest) animal, plant, etc. of its kind **3** something of great, or the greatest, importance, e.g.: **(a) king bee** (–18c), changed to **queen bee** when her gender was recognized **(b)** the chess piece which must be defended (15c) **(c)** the playing card, originally the most valuable (16c) **4 king-size(d)** larger than usual (19c).

Queen [Old English *cwēn*] a king's wife or consort, later also a female monarch, is earlier in sense 2, though often referring to beauty rather than size or strength, and in senses 3 and 4 to something slightly smaller or less important. It also means a mature female cat or an effeminate gay man: **quean** 'a gay man' is ultimately from related Old English *cwene* 'woman', surviving in Scotland for a young girl, a sweetheart, or a hussy.

King appears in the names of places (formerly) belonging to the monarch; *Queen* is less common, later, and usually refers to a specific queen; **Quen-** in names sometimes means 'queen', sometimes 'woman' [from *quean*]. Old English *cyn(in)g* appears as **Ken-** in a few names, and produced **kingdom** originally a monarch's authority, later the community or territory ruled, hence a 'realm' of nature (*the animal kingdom*: see also TAXONOMY), and is related to KIN*.

kiosk [17c. Via French from Turkish *köşk* 'pavilion' from Persian *kušk*] An open-sided summerhouse in some Middle Eastern countries, hence **1** a similar structure used as a shelter or bandstand elsewhere (19c) **2** a booth (19c) **3** a thick post on which advertisements are posted (19c).

kit [ME. Early Dutch *kitte*, of unknown origin] A wooden tub or pail; a basket or box, hence a set of things (originally a soldier's uniform, equipment, and personal necessities, 18c), especially in a container, hence **1 kit(bag)** a strong bag for a serviceman's kit (19c) **2** the clothing and/or equipment needed for any activity; **kit out/up** to provide someone with this (*c.*1915); **get your kit off** to strip (1980s) **3** a set of parts from which something may be assembled (19c).

kite [Old English *cȳta*, of unknown origin] A hawk with a soaring flight, hence a toy or similar device that soars on the end of a string (17c), hence **1 fly a kite** to suggest something to see how people react **2 (flying) kites** the highest sails on a ship **3** (alluding to a paper kite) a bill used to raise money on credit; a (bad) cheque (1920s), hence **to (fly a) kite** to pass one, to raise money fraudulently **4** an aeroplane (*c.*1905) **5** the surnames **Keate(s)**, **Keating**, **Kite**, given to a rapacious person.

knack [ME. Origin uncertain] **1** a trick or deception (15c); a particular, usually intuitive, skill (16c); a quick and easy way of doing something; an ingenious device; a small decorative object, whence **(a) knick-knack** (17c), which has replaced it **(b) knacker** a harness-maker or saddler (16c, probably from the small fittings on a harness) **2** (perhaps a different word) a worn out horse (18c); someone who buys such horses for slaughter, or derelict houses, ships, etc. for scrap (19c).

Perhaps the same word as **knack** a sharp blow or sound; to make such a sound, hence **knacker** someone/something that does so; **knackers** castanets, later testicles [ultimately an imitation of the sound, but perhaps immediately from Low German or Dutch *knak*: related to German *knackwurst* a sausage whose thick skin cracks open when bitten]. The two words come together in *knacker* to kill or castrate; to exhaust or ruin.

knar [ME. From or related to early Dutch or Low German *knorre* 'knot, knob'] **1** a rugged rock or stone (surviving in dialect) **2** a knot in wood; a large bark-covered protuberance on a tree.

Knar produced **knur** a hard swelling in the body or on a tree trunk, whence **knurl** a knot or knob; a small beading or ridge, **knurled** knotty, knobbly, or ridged, whence **gnarled** knotted, twisted, or misshapen, and **gnarl** a knar on a tree.

knickerbocker [19c. Named after Diedrich Knickerbocker, pretended author of Washington Irving's *History of New York* (1809)] **1 Knickerbocker** a descendant of one of the original Dutch settlers of the New Netherlands (later divided into New York and New Jersey), hence any New Yorker **2 knickerbockers (a)** men's or women's short trousers gathered at the knee (resembling Dutchmen's breeches pictured in Irving's book, 19c), hence **(b)** women's underpants, originally reaching to the knee: shortened to **knickers** in both senses, short-lived in (a) but now the only form for (b) **(c) knickerbocker glory** a layered sundae (1930s, said to be named from the hooped stockings women wore with knickerbockers).

knight [Old English *cniht*] A boy, a youth (OE only); an attendant or servant; a servant (–ME, cf. BOY*); a military servant to a man of high rank; a feudal tenant holding land in return for military service (ME); a man given privileged military status by the monarch after having served as a page and squire; to confer this, hence **1 (a)** such a man as a lady's attendant or champion; a man devoted to a lady or cause; a noble or chivalrous man; **knight in shining armour** a protector or rescuer (19c); **white knight** a company that rescues another from a hostile take-over bid (1980s) **(b)** a member of an order of knighthood (*Knight of the Garter*, 15c) or of some secret, religious, or political societies (19c) **(c)** a man granted a (formerly hereditary) title next below a baronet because of his achievements or public service (16c) **2** a chess piece, usually shaped like a horse's head (15c).

knit [Old English *cnyttan*: related to KNOT*] To tie in or with a knot, hence **1** to knot string to make a net (ME); to make (a garment etc. with) rows of interlocking loops; a knitted fabric or garment **2** to combine or unite closely (ME); to join or grow together (*the bone is starting to knit, close-knit community*, 15c); **knit your brows** to draw them together, to frown (16c).

knob [ME. Early Low German *knobbe* 'knot, knob, bud'] A rounded lump, hence **1 (a)** a swelling, a wart or pimple **(b)** a rounded handle or control button **(c)** an ornamental boss (18c) **2** a rounded hill or mound (17c) **3** a small piece of butter, coal, etc. (17c) **4** the head (18c, cf. *nob* below) **5** the penis (1950s).

Knob fathered **knobble** a small knob (whence **knobbly**), and perhaps **nob** the head. A variant of Low German *knobbe* produced the later forms **(k)nub**, **(k)nubble**, and **(k)nubbly**: *nub* developed the sense 'main point or gist', and produced **nubby**. Probably related to KNOT*.

knot [Old English *cnotta*: the underlying sense is 'knob'] **1** a length of string inter-twined (with another) as a fastening; a way of tying one, hence **(a)** a tangle **(b)** a tie, a bond; **tie the knot** to get married (ME) **(c)** an intricately shaped flower bed (15c, surviving mainly in **knot garden** with such beds) **(d)** to tie (in) a knot (16c, replacing KNIT) **(e)** one of the divisions (marked by knots) in a log line to measure speed (by counting the knots let out while a sandglass ran, 17c), hence a unit of measurement equal to one nautical mile per hour **2** a knob (ME): **(a)** an orna-mental boss, stud, or fastening **(b)** a hillock (mainly in place names) **(c)** (to form) a hard lump; a whorl in timber where a branch grew; a node **(d)** a small cluster **(e)** **knotgrass/weed** with jointed stems (16c) **(f)** the surname **Knott** a thickset person or one who lived by a hillock.

Related to KNIT, **knout** [via French and Russian from Old Norse *knútr*], and probably to KNOB*.

kowtow [19c. Chinese *kĕtóu*, from *kĕ* 'to knock' + *tóu* 'head'] The former Chinese custom of kneeling and touching the ground with your forehead to show respect or submission; to do so, hence to act obsequiously; a submissive or servile act.

L

label [ME. Old French, literally 'ribbon', probably of Germanic origin and related to LAP¹*] A narrow strip of cloth; a piece of cloth, paper, cardboard, metal, etc. on or with something and bearing information about it (17c), hence **1** to attach, or mark with, a label **2** (to describe or categorize with) a descriptive word or phrase (19c) **3** a trade name (often appearing on labels, c.1900); the company trading under it **4** (to mark with) a dye etc. used to identify a substance so that it can be observed during a chemical reaction (1930s) **5** a number or word that identifies part of a computer program (1950s).

labour [ME. Old French, from Latin *labor*] (To) work or toil, hence **1** to work hard or despite difficulties, hence **(a)** of a woman: to give birth (15–18c, revived in the 20c); childbirth (16c) **(b)** to move or travel with difficulty (15c); of a ship: to roll or pitch heavily (17c) **2** a task (*labours of Hercules/labour of love*); the work or workers needed for it (18c); the supply of workers for a particular job, industry, or employer; their contribution to production, hence (manual) workers collectively, especially as a social class or political force (19c), hence **Labour Party** a British political party formed in 1906 to represent them, later applied to similar parties elsewhere **3** to suffer from a disadvantage or defect (*labour under a misapprehension*, 15c) **4** to work by beating or rubbing (15–17c); to beat or thrash (16–17c, surviving in dialect and in **belabour**) **5** to talk about at great length or in excessive detail (15c).

Latin *labor* is the ancestor of ELABORATE, **laboratory** [via medieval Latin *laboratorium* 'work place'], and **laborious**.

labyrinth [ME. Via French and Latin from Greek *laburinthos*] In Greek mythology: the maze constructed to contain the Minotaur, a monster with a man's body and a bull's head, hence **1** any maze; a complex or confusing structure or situation (16c) **2** a complex anatomical cavity, especially the inner ear (17c).

lac [15c. (Via medieval Latin from) Portuguese *lac(c)a*, from Hindi *lākh* or Persian *lāk*] A resinous substance secreted by an insect and used to make shellac and dye, hence **1** a varnish (originally) made from lac (16–18c, largely replaced by *lacquer* below) **2** goods coated with lac or lacquer (17c) **3** a pigment prepared from lac (17c), surviving in the variant **lake**, which came to mean a pigment produced by combining an organic substance with a metallic oxide.

Lac produced *shellac* (at SHELL). Portuguese *lac(c)a* produced **lacquer** lac (16–18c), later a varnish made from shellac; a resinous wood varnish that could take a hard polish; a hard coating made of a polymer in a volatile solvent, hence **1** to coat with lacquer; lacquered goods **2 (hair) lacquer** a fixative for a hairstyle.

lace [ME. Old French *laz, las* (noun), *lacier* (verb), from, ultimately, Latin *laqueus* 'noose'] **1** a noose, snare, or net (–17c); a delicate openwork fabric (16c) **2** a cord, hence **(a)** one used to draw edges together, hence **lace (up)** to fasten or, later, be fastened with one; *lace* to thread with one (15c); to thread one through holes or round hooks (17c); to thread a film etc. through a machine (1940s) **(b)** ornamental braid, surviving in **gold/silver lace (c) necklace** an ornamental string of beads, jewels, etc. (16c) **3** to trim with lace or a lace (16c); to enhance with streaks of colour (17c); to enhance a drink with a dash of spirits; to enhance or adulterate any food or drink.

Old French *laz* produced **latchet** a strip, loop, or thong; *lacier* produced **interlace**, and perhaps **lash** to tie, originally to lace up a garment. Latin *laqueus* fathered Spanish *lazo*, whence **lasso** (*US*).

lack [ME. Probably from an Old English word related to **leak**] **1** to be absent or missing; an absence or shortage; to be without or in need of (16c); need, poverty (16c); famine, starvation **2** a (moral) defect, an offence (–16c); (one bringing) disgrace or shame, hence **alack** an exclamation expressing reproach or regret (15c), hence **alack the day**, **alack-a-day** literally 'shame on the day' (16c), shortened to **lackaday** (17c), altered to **lackadaisy** (18c), whence **lackadaisical** sentimental, dreamy, listless (like someone given to crying *lackaday!*).

lade [Old English *hladan*] **1** to load: **(a)** to load cargo on a ship; of a ship: to take on cargo (ME); **bill of lading** a receipt for the cargo given by the ship's master (16c) **(b) laden** heavily loaded (15c); weighed down, oppressed (16c) **2** to take a fluid from a river, container, etc. with a ladle or scoop; to bale (16c).

Old English *hladan* produced **ladle** (whence the surname **La(i)dler** a ladle-maker), and perhaps *larboard* (at PORT[1]). Related to **lathe**.

lag[1] [15c. Perhaps from a distortion of **last** 'hindmost, latest' (*fog, seg, lag* meaning 'first, second, last' survive in some English dialects), from Old English *latost*: related to **late**, **latter**, and LET*] **1** hindmost, last, belated; the last person (16c) **2** to fall behind (16c), hence **(a) laggard** falling behind, hanging back (16c); someone who does so (18c) **(b)** the time elapsing between related events (19c); **jet lag** the delayed physiological effects of flight across time zones (1960s).

lag[2] [17c. Probably of Scandinavian origin and related to LAY*] A barrel stave (surviving in dialect); one used to make a covering for a boiler etc. (19c), hence **lagging** insulation material; *lag* to cover a boiler, pipe, etc. with it.

lair [Old English *leger*: related to LAY*] A place to lie: **1** a grave or burial plot (now Scots) **2** a bed or couch **3** an enclosure for domestic animals, especially on the way to market (ME), hence **lairage** the lodging of animals in one (19c) **4** a wild animal's den (ME); a private retreat (19c).

lake [ME. Partly via Old French from Latin *lacus* 'basin, pool, lake', partly from Old English *lacu* 'small stream'] A pond or pool (now chiefly US); a large area of water surrounded by land, hence a large ornamental pond in a park (19c).

Latin *lacus* produced **lacuna** 'a hollow, gap, or defect', adopted meaning 'hiatus, gap, omission', **lacustrine**, and **lagoon** [via Spanish or Italian]. Old English *lacu* survives as -**lake** or -**lock** in place names, and is related to *Leach* (at LEECH), and to **leach** to water (OE–16c), later to percolate water through something, hence removing soluble material, hence to extract or be extracted in this way.

lam [16c. Probably of Scandinavian origin and related to **lame** (Old English *lama*)] To beat or thrash; to hit out (19c); to run away, to 'beat it' (*US*), hence **on the lam** on the run.

Lam produced **lambaste** [with **baste** 'to beat', probably of Scandinavian origin] to beat; to scold or criticize severely.

lance [ME. French *lance* (noun), *lancier* (verb), from Latin *lancea*] A horseman's spear, hence **1** to throw like one; to push out (16c only, outlived by **launch** [ME, from French *lancier*]) **2** to pierce with one; to pierce with a sharp instrument to let out pus etc. (15c) **3** a soldier with a lance (largely replaced by 16c **lancer**), hence **free lance** a mercenary (19c); (later one word) a politician with no permanent allegiance; a self-employed person working for a number of clients (now also **freelancer**) **4** something resembling a lance: a small, sharp surgical knife (15c, replaced by **lancet** [French *lancette*, literally 'small lance']); a fishing spear or harpoon (18c); **thermic lance** a tool using heat to cut hard materials (1920s).

Latin *lancea* is the ancestor of **lancepesade** [via French from Italian *lancia spezzata*, literally 'broken lance', hence a soldier on a hopeless mission, a devoted follower] an old or experienced soldier, hence a low-ranking non-commissioned officer, whence (by analogy) *lance* in **lance corporal** etc.

land [Old English] The earth's surface not covered by water, hence **1** a distinct part of it (*native land/marshland*, **landed** owning or consisting of land): in place names -**land** may mean a district, estate, or part of a village **2** ground, soil **3** to come or bring to land (ME): **(a)** to bring a fish ashore (17c), hence to get something you want (*land a job*, 19c) **(b)** to come or bring to a specific place (*land up in*, *land a blow*, 17c); to come to a stopping place on a journey (hence **landing** a resting place in a flight of stairs, 18c) **(c)** to fall on or encumber with (19c).

Old English *land* appears in *island* (at INSULAR), as **Lam-** or **Lan(d)-** in surnames, in **landmark** (an object marking) a boundary; a conspicuous object used as a guide; something marking an important development, and in *outlandish* (at ALIEN). Related to *land* in HINTERLAND, in German *Landlaufer* (see LOAFER), in the **landrace** pig [Danish, literally 'national breed'], and in LANDSCAPE, and to *laund* (at LEA).

landscape [16c. Dutch *landschap*, from *land* 'land' + *scap* 'state, condition'] A picture of natural scenery (whence *seascape*, *cityscape*, etc.), hence **1** (a view of) such scenery (17c) **2** to lay out a garden or park, especially imitating natural scenery (19c); to incorporate roads, buildings, etc. attractively **3** of a picture etc.: horizontal, wider than it is tall (1930s, cf. *portrait* at PORTRAY).

Related to LAND*, **shape** [Old English *sceap*], and -**ship** (*citizenship, hardship, craftsmanship*) [Old English -*scipe*].

lantern [ME. Via French and Latin from Greek *lamptēr* 'torch, lamp', from *lampein* 'to shine' (whence **lamp**)] A transparent or translucent case containing a light, hence **1** a structure with windows on all sides on top of a building **2** the room at the top of a lighthouse, containing the light (15c).

lap[1] [Old English *laeppa*] A fold or flap, especially on a garment, hence **1** a lobe of the ear, liver, etc. (–18c); a fold of flesh or skin (ME) **2** a fold of a toga etc. used as a pouch (ME–17c); a skirt front held up to catch or carry something; a seated person's thighs, where a child etc. may be held, hence a sheltered place or situation (*the lap of luxury*, 17c) **3** to coil or fold material around (ME); a sheet of material wound on a roller (19c); the amount of rope etc. needed to encircle a reel; one circuit of a racetrack or field; to lead a competitor by a circuit; to travel one (*lapped at 70 m.p.h.*, 1920s) **4** to lay one thing partly over another (17c); to extend beyond: replaced by 18c **overlap**.

Lap produced **lapel**, and **lappet**, which has largely replaced it in sense 1. Probably related to LABEL.

lap² [Old English *lapian*] To scoop up liquid with your tongue, hence **1** to splash gently (making a similar sound, 19c) **2** to take or consume eagerly (19c).

Old English *lapian* produced Old French *la(m)per* 'to gulp down', whence *lampons* 'let us drink' (used as a refrain), the probable source of **lampoon**.

lapse [ME. Latin *labi*, *laps-* 'to glide, slip, or fall'] **1** of time: to pass (largely replaced by **elapse** [16c, Latin *elabi* 'to slip away', from *labi*]); the passing of time **2** the termination of a right or contract because it is not used; to allow this (17c); to become void in this way (18c) **3** a slip of the tongue etc., a slight error (15c); a moral slip; (to make) a fall from a standard or (back) into an inferior state (16c: cf. *relapse* below).

Latin *labi* produced **collapse**, **prolapse**, and **relapse** originally to slip back into sin or heresy.

lard [French, from Latin *lar(i)dum* 'bacon'] (Fat) bacon or pork (–18c); rendered pork fat, hence **1** to insert strips of fat into lean meat before cooking; to embellish speech or writing with unnecessary words (16c, also as **interlard**) **2** to smear with fat or grease **3** similar fat from another animal (15c).

Latin *lar(i)dum* produced **larder** [via *lardarium* 'a store of, or for, meat'], the surname **Larder**, **Lard(i)ner** the person in charge of the larder, and French *lardon* a strip of fat used for larding, whence **lardons** diced bacon.

large [ME. French, from Latin *largus* 'abundant'] **1** generous, open-handed, prodigal, lavish (–17c, surviving as a surname) **2** copious, abundant (–17c, hence **largely** to a great extent, on the whole) **3** spacious, roomy (–17c); broad, wide (–18c); big (15c), hence **(a)** of writing: lengthy (now rare), hence at length, fully (16c), surviving mainly in **writ large** written in full, exaggerated **(b)** the longest note in early music, twice or three times the duration of a *long*, which in turn was twice or three times the duration of a **breve** [a variant of BRIEF], originally a short note which became longer as shorter notes were introduced: the **semibreve**, the **minim** half the length of a semibreve [Latin *minimus* 'least, smallest', from *parvus* 'small': see MAXIMUM], the CROTCHET, half the length of a minim, and the *quaver* (at QUAKE) **4** unrestrained (–17c), hence **at large** not confined **5** of the wind: favourable (16c); **by and large** close to, but just off, the wind (17c); on the whole (18c).

French *large* produced **enlarge** and *largesse* liberality, generosity (ME–17c); generous giving; what is given. Latin *largus* fathered Italian *largo* 'broad', adopted as a musical direction meaning 'slowly and with dignity'; a piece of music played in this way, whence *larghetto* [literally 'little largo'] (a piece in) a fairly slow time.

larva [17c. Latin] **1** a disembodied spirit, a spectre (–19c) **2** a mask or disguise, hence used by Linnaeus (see HYACINTH) for an immature insect, amphibian, etc. that is nothing like the adult.

lash [ME. Probably imitative] To move quickly or suddenly, hence **1** a sudden, violent blow (–17c): **(a)** (to give) one with a whip, hence the flexible part of a whip; to whip to and fro; (**eye)lash**, one of a row of hairs on the eyelid (18c) **(b) lash (out)** to launch a sudden physical or verbal attack **2** to throw; to apply liberally; of rain or, formerly, tears: to pour, hence **lash out** to spend lavishly, to squander (16c); **lashings** lots (19c, *Anglo-Irish*).

last [Old English *lǽstan]* To follow a leader or a course of action (–15c); to go on, hence to continue to exist or happen; to be sufficient or available for a period of time.

Related to the shoemaker's **last** [Old English *lǽste*], which originally meant a footprint or track, and to LEARN*.

latitude [ME. Latin *latitudo* from *latus* 'broad'] Breadth, width, hence **1** the angular distance north or south of the earth's equator or the ecliptic of a celestial body (from early rectangular maps, the 'breadth' being north-south, the 'length' [**longitude**, from Latin *longus* 'long', whence LOUNGE*] being east-west), hence **latitudes** a region of the earth defined by this (*temperate latitudes*, 17c) **2** the range within which something may vary (–18c); extent, range, scope (17c), hence scope for some freedom of action or belief.

Latin *latus* is the ancestor of COLLATERAL, **dilate**, and **lateral** to do with a side, at or to the side, whence **bilateral**, **equilateral**, and **quadrilateral**.

launder [ME. Contraction of **lavender** (–16c, surviving as a surname), from Old French *lavandier(e)*, ultimately from Latin *lavanda* 'things to be washed', from *lavare* 'to wash'] A person who washes clothes or linen (–17c, replaced by 15c **launderer**, 16c **laundress**), hence **1** to do so (16c, hence to be washable, *c*.1900); to alter something to make it acceptable (1960s); to pass illegally acquired money through a legitimate business or bank account to disguise its 'dirty' origins (1970s) **2** a water trough or channel, specifically one for washing ore in a mine (17c).

Launder produced **laund(e)rette** and *Laundromat* (at AUTOMATON). Old French *lavandiere* produced *lavanderie*, whence **lavendry** (ME–16c), shortened to **laundry** laundering; a place where this is done; items (to be) washed. Latin *lavare* is the ancestor of LAVATORY*, and may have influenced **lavender** the plant, which was used in soap and to perfume laundry [via Anglo-Norman French from medieval Latin *lavendula*, perhaps from Latin *lividus* 'bluish': see LIVID].

laurel [ME. Via Old French and Provençal from Latin *laurus*] A tree or shrub of the genus *Laurus,* especially the bay tree; its foliage used to garland a hero or poet (Apollo, the Greek god of poetry, having vowed to wear laurel leaves after the nymph Daphne escaped his advances by being changed into a laurel: cf. BAY[2]), hence **(poet) laureate** a title given to a distinguished poet, since the 17c the official court poet. See also *baccalaureate* (at BACHELOR).

Daphne [Greek *daphnē* 'laurel'] gave her name to a genus of flowering shrubs which includes the spurge laurel. Latin *laurus* produced the names **Laura** (variants include **Lauren, Lori, Lowri**) and **Laurence** or **Lawrence** [Latin *Laurentius* 'a man from Laurentium', an ancient Italian city named from its laurel trees]; pet forms include **Larry** (perhaps the source of Australian **larrikin** a (young) hooligan), **Laurie,** and **Law**, surviving as a surname and in **Lawson**.

lavatory [ME. Late Latin *lavatorium* from Latin *lavare* 'to wash'] A basin or bath for washing, hence **1** a (medicinal) wash (15–17c, outlived by Middle English **lotion**, also from Latin *lavare*) **2** the washing of the celebrant's hands at the offertory or after washing the communion vessels (16c), largely replaced by 18c **lavabo** [Latin, 'I will wash' (from *lavare*), from Psalm 26:6: *Lavabo inter innocentes manus meas* 'I will wash my hands in innocence', the psalm accompanying the action in Roman Catholicism], which also means the towel and basin used (18c), and is occasionally used for a washroom or toilet (1930s) **3** a washroom (17c); one with a toilet (19c, cf. CLOSET, TOILET); the toilet itself (1930s).

Latin *lavare* is the ancestor of ABLUTION, DELUGE*, **dilute**, **latrine** [French, from Latin *latrina*, shortened from *lavatrina*], LAUNDER*, **lava** [Italian, meaning 'stream caused by a sudden downpour', later 'stream of molten rock', originally from Vesuvius], and **lave** to wash or bathe [via Old English *lafian* and French *laver*, whence also **lavage** and **lavish**], hence the surname **Laver** a launderer.

lay [Old English *lecgan*] **1** to make something/someone lie down, hence to have sex (with) (1930s, *US*, now often as **to get laid**); a woman considered as a sexual partner (*a good/easy lay*) **2** to deposit (*lay an egg/a bet*) **(b) lay aside/away/by/off/up** to put away or aside (ME); to place or set (*lay a cable/table, lay hands/eyes on*); to spread out on a surface (*lay a carpet*), hence **layer** a stratum (17c) **3** lay (down) to establish (*lay the foundations/lay down the keel*); **lay down the law** to state the law on a certain point, hence to be dogmatic (19c) **4** to put forward (*lay a claim*); to allege (*lay blame/a charge*, ME) **5** to lie (ME, usually regarded as incorrect), hence **(a) lie/lay back** to recline; **laid back** relaxed, easy going (1970s, *US*) **(b)** the way something lies (*lay of the land*, 19c) **(c) layabout** an idler (1930s) **6 lay out** to spend money (15c), hence **outlay** expenditure (17c, *Scots and N English dialect*).

Lay produced **inlay** to set something into a surface; what is set. Old English *lecgan* produced ALLAY[1], and probably **ledge** and **ledger** originally a large bible or breviary (laid on a lectern or shelf). Related to **belay** originally to surround, **beleaguer** [Dutch *belegeren*, literally 'to camp around'], FELLOW, *lager* (at BEER), LAIR, **law** [Old English *lagu* from Old Norse *lag* 'something laid down'], **lie** [Old English *licgan*: the dialect form **lig** developed the senses 'to laze about' and 'to freeload, to go to or gatecrash parties'], **low** [Old Norse *lágr*], whence **below**, and probably to LAG[2].

lea [Old English *lēa(h)*] An open space in woodland (surviving as the names **Leigh** and **Lee**, and as the elements **-leigh** or **-ley**), hence open land, pasture, a meadow. The variant **ley** (pronounced 'lay') came to be used for the supposed straight line linking important sites (1920s, now usually as **ley line**).

Laund [Old French *launde* 'heathland': related to LAND*] also developed from 'clearing' to 'pasture': the later spelling, **lawn**, now means an area of mown grass, keeping the sense 'clearing' in the New Forest, and is also a surname for someone who lived in one.

lead [Old English *lēad*, perhaps of Celtic origin] The metal, hence **1** (something) made of this (ME), e.g. the plummet of a plumb, or sounding, line; **heave the lead** to take soundings; **swing the lead** to shirk or malinger (World War I, *Forces slang*, perhaps an alteration of 19c **swing the leg** to feign injury or sickness) **2** black **lead** graphite (once thought to be a form of lead, 16c); a stick of this used in a pencil (17c, shortened to *lead* in the 19c); (to use) a preparation of graphite for polishing cast iron (19c) **3** the surname **Le(a)dbetter, -bitter**, literally a 'lead-beater'.

league [ME. (Via French from) Italian *lega*, from *legare* 'to bind', from Latin *ligare*] A military, political, or commercial pact; an association of individuals, societies, etc. (19c), later of sports clubs that compete with each other, hence (those show-ing) a certain level of ability (1950s); **league table** a list of the members of a sport-ing league in ranking order (*c*.1910), a comparison of performance in any area (1950s); **out of/not in my league** markedly better or worse than me.

Italian *legare* produced **legato** 'bound', adopted as a direction to play music smoothly with no breaks between notes. Latin *ligare* is the ancestor of LIAISON*, **lien, ligament, ligature, oblige** and **obligate** [Latin *obligare* 'to bind to'], RALLY*, **religion** [Old French, from Latin *religio* 'obligation, bond', later 'monastic life' (bound by vows), the original sense in English], and RELY.

lean¹ [Old English *hleonian*: related to **ladder** and **lid**, and probably to LEAN²] **1** to lie down and rest (now only Scots); to rest or recline against something (ME), hence **lean on (a)** to rely on for support **(b)** to put pressure on, to intimidate (1960s) **2** to bend or incline (*lean forward/back/over*); to incline or tend towards something (ME); to be partial or favourable to (16c): cf. INCLINE*.

lean² [Old English *hlaene*: probably related to LEAN¹] Thin, hence meagre, poor in quality or quantity (ME); low in essential or valuable elements; without rich or unnecessary ones, hence **1** (meat) containing little or no fat (15c) **2** efficient, economical (1980s): cf. SLIM*.

leap [Old English *hlyp* (noun), *hleapan* (verb)] To jump or spring; a jump, hence **1** a sudden transition or advance; to make one (ME); to go quickly past or over something without stopping, hence **leap year** in which the dates following 29 February apparently 'leap' from the expected day of the week to the next **2** a place over or from which to leap (*Lover's Leap*), also as **-lip** in place names.

Related to *lap* in **lapwing**, LOAFER*, **lope** [variant of Scots *loup*, from Old Norse *hlaupa*] a leap; to leap or bound; to run away; (to run with) a long, bounding stride; to canter, and WALLOP*, and probably to ELOPE.

learn [Old English *leornian*] **1** to acquire knowledge or a skill; to hear or find out a fact **2** (replacing obsolete *lere*, from related Old English *lǣran*) to teach (ME), surviving in colloquial use, in the surname **Larner** a teacher, and in **learned** instructed, taught, later educated, erudite, knowledgeable, specifically about the law (15c, surviving in *my learned friend*); scholarly (16c).

Related to LAST* and **lore** instruction, education, what is learned or taught (now dialect), hence collective or traditional knowledge or beliefs.

leave [Old English *lēaf*] Permission, hence **1** permission to depart (ME), hence **take your leave** to get permission to go, to say goodbye to **2 leave (of absence)** permission to be absent from your normal place or duties (18c); (a period of) authorized absence (19c). Hence (with elements of 1 and 2) **take French leave** to leave without saying goodbye to your host (18c, a custom then current in France); to be absent without permission.

Related to **furlough** [Dutch *verlof*, from *ver* 'for' + *lof* 'permission'], **lief**, and **love**, but not to *leave* to bequeath (at LIVE).

lecture [ME. Via Old French or medieval Latin from Latin *legere*: see LEGEND] Reading, a reading; a text to be read, hence **1** a (moral) lesson (16c); a lengthy reprimand; to reprimand at length (18c) **2** (to give) a formal speech on a particular subject (16c); **lecturer** someone who gives lectures in a university (17c), now one with an academic teaching post below the rank of professor, whence *lecture* to hold such a post.

lee [Old English *hlēo*: related to *luke* in **lukewarm**] Protection, shelter (surviving mainly in *in/under the lee of*); a sheltered condition or place (ME–17c); the sheltered side of an object (15c); the side away from the wind. Hence **leeward** (the side) away from the wind (16c); **leeway** the sideways movement of a ship blown (slightly) off course (17c), hence freedom within set limits (19c); permissible variation.

leech [Old English *lǣce*] A physician; now usually humorously and by association with **leech** a kind of blood-sucking worm [Old English *lǣce, lyce*], especially the kind used in medicine to let blood, hence someone who clings to or preys on another (16c); to drain of energy, money, etc. (1920s); to latch on to like a parasite, to exploit (1960s).

The surname **Leach** may have belonged to a physician, a bloodthirsty person, or to someone who lived by a boggy stream [Old English *laecc, laece*: related to LAKE*].

leer [16c. Perhaps from obsolete **leer** 'face, cheek', from Old English *hlēor*] To look sideways or askance; to look or stare with a sly or lascivious expression, hence such a look; looking in this way (17–19c), whence probably **leery** sharp, knowing, streetwise, wary (18c), altered to **lairy** flashily dressed, showy (*c*.1900, *Australia and New Zealand*), whence **lair** to act or dress flashily (1920s); someone who does so.

leg [ME. Old Norse *leggr*] A limb of a quadruped or insect; a biped's lower limb; this from the knee downwards, hence **1** (part of) a bird's or animal's leg as food **2** something resembling a leg: **(a)** a support or prop (15c); the stem of a glass etc. (15c only, replaced by *shank* below) **(b)** the part of a garment covering the leg (15c); **leggings** a garment, or protective coverings, for the legs (18c) **3** a side of a triangle (regarded as standing on its base: 17c, replacing *shank*); a branch of a forked or jointed object, hence, in nautical use, a run made on a single tack (19c); a stage in a journey, race, or competition (1920s) **4 leg it** to walk quickly or run (17c); **leg work** preliminary work involving running errands, gathering information, etc. (19c) **5 leggy** having long (attractive) legs (18c); of a plant: long-stemmed, spindly (19c).

Shank [Old English *sceanca*] originally meant the shinbone, later the whole leg (hence **Shanks' mare/pony** your own legs as transport), hence a shaft, stem, or straight part.

legate [ME. Via French from Latin *legare, legat-* 'to depute, to send as an envoy', also 'to bequeath'] **1** a papal ambassador, now a cardinal on a special mission; a representative, envoy, or messenger, hence **legation (a)** a legate's mission, purpose, position (17c), or official residence (19c) **(b)** a group of legates (17c); (the entourage of) a diplomat below the rank of ambassador **2** to bequeath (15c), hence **legacy** what is bequeathed; a long-lasting effect (16c).

The closest in meaning of Latin *legare*'s children is **delegate** (to authorize someone to be) a deputy or representative; to entrust authority or a duty to them, hence **delegation** a group of delegates. Other descendants are *allegation* (at ALLEGE), COLLEGE*, and RELEGATE*. Related to LOYAL*.

legend [ME. Via French from medieval Latin *legenda* 'what is to be read', from Latin *legere* 'to read', also 'to choose or gather'] **1** an account of a saint's life or historical event; a traditional, popular tale which may not be true (17c); such stories collectively (19c); the subject of such a tale (*a legend in her own lifetime*, *c.*1915) **2** a list or record (–17c); a compilation of extracts from sacred books to be read at religious services (15c, largely replaced by **lectionary** [18c, also from Latin *legere*] **3** something written: an inscription or motto (15c); a caption for an illustration (*c.*1900); an explanation of symbols on a map (1960s).

Latin *legere*'s descendants include COLLECT*, CULL, ELECT*, INTELLIGENCE*, **lectern**, LECTURE, **legible**, LEGION, **legume** [so called because it is easily gathered], **lesson** originally something to be read or listened to [via French *leçon*], NEGLIGENCE*, and **select**.

legion [ME. Old French, from Latin *legere*: see LEGEND*] A body of Roman infantry; a large body of soldiers, hence **1** a large number of people or things; innumerable, widespread (17c), often with reference to the Bible, Mark 5:9: *my name is Legion: for we are many* **2** applied to distinct parts of modern armies (16c) and to associations of ex-service personnel (post World War I), hence **legionnaire's disease** a form of pneumonia, so called from an outbreak in 1976 among people attending a convention of the American Legion.

lens [17c. Latin *lens*, *lent-* 'lentil' (from the similarity of shape)] A piece of glass etc. with one or two surfaces curved to bend light, hence **1 (a)** the structure in the eye that focuses light on the retina (18c); a facet of a compound eye (19c) **(b)** a device for changing the direction of sound, electrons, etc. (1920s), hence **lensing** the bending of radiation by a strong gravitational field **2** a lens-shaped piece of rock, ice, etc. (19c); to become lens-shaped (1920s).

Latin *lens* produced **lentigo** 'lentil-shaped spot', adopted as the technical term for a freckle or pigmented patch on the skin, and **lentil** [via Latin *lenticula*, literally 'small lentil'].

Lenten [Old English *lencten*: related to LONG*] **1** springtime (–ME, probably with reference to the lengthening days) **2** the penitential period before Easter (–17c). Shortened to **Lent** in both senses, *Lenten* now being understood as an adjective 'to do with Lent'.

less [Old English *lǽssa* (adjective), *lǽs* (adverb)] Used as the comparative of **little** [Old English *lytel*]: **1** smaller in number, fewer (now regarded as incorrect, but still common); not so big or so much (ME) **2** a smaller amount, quantity, or number (*less said the better, less than no time*) **3** to a smaller extent, degree, or amount, hence **nevertheless**, **nonetheless** (literally 'not less') despite that, however **4** of lower status or importance, largely replaced by **lesser** (ME); the smaller, younger, or less important of two people or things (*St James the Less*): obsolete after a noun, replaced before one by **lesser** (17c) **5** minus, with this subtracted (*less 10% discount*) **6** to make or become less (ME, largely replaced by **lessen**) **7** let alone, even less likely or acceptable (17c, now only as **much** or **still less**).

Less produced **in** or **on less** 'on a lesser condition, except', which became one word and then changed, by association with **un-** 'not', to **unless**, sometimes shortened to *less*, especially in the US. Old English *læs* produced the phrase *thy læs the*, literally 'by which less that', later *the laeste*, whence **lest**. Related to **least**.

let [Old English *lætan*] **1** to leave, to refrain from taking, using, or doing, to leave a job, bequest, etc. to someone else (–17c) **2** to allow, hence **(a)** to allow someone to use land, property, or, formerly, money for rent or interest; the period that something is let (17c); to be let (18c) **(b)** to allow or, later, to make someone/something escape or go (*let blood/loose, let in/out/down*), hence **inlet** letting in, admission (ME); a small arm of the sea (16c); an entrance (17c); **outlet** a place where something comes out or is made available (*retail outlet*, ME); a means of expressing emotion, energy, etc. (17c) **(c)** used to introduce a command or suggestion (*let me go/drive, let's eat*, ME) **3** to cause, surviving in *let someone know*. Related to ALLEGIANCE*, LAG[1]*, and **let** [Old English *lettan*] to prevent or obstruct (surviving in **let and hinder**), hence an obstruction (surviving mainly in **without let or hindrance**); in tennis etc.: obstruction of the ball so that it must be played again; a replay.

lethal [16c. Latin *let(h)alis*, from *letum* 'death'] **1** causing spiritual death or damnation **2** (capable of) causing physical death (17c); extremely destructive (19c).

The *h* in *lethalis* came about by association with *Lethe*, the Latin name of a river in Hades, whose water made the newly dead forget their past [from Greek *lēthē* 'forgetfulness, oblivion', whence **lethargy**].

letter [ME. French *lettre* from Latin *lit(t)era* 'letter of alphabet', (plural) 'epistle, literature'] **1** a symbol representing a sound in an alphabet, a character, hence **(a)** a typeface or font (16c) **(b)** **letters** a qualification shown by its initial letters (19c, now chiefly in *to have letters after your name*); *letter* a school or college award for sporting achievement, similarly shown by the initials or an abbreviation of the establishment's name (*c.*1910, US) **2** something written, an inscription, document, or text (–18c), hence **(a)** a written communication **(b)** *letter(s)* a formal legal document (*letter of credit/intent/introduction, letters of administration, letters patent*) **3** literal or precise meaning (*letter of the law*) **4** letters (knowledge of) writing or literature, surviving in **man of letters** a scholar.

Latin *lit(t)era* is the ancestor of **alliteration** the repetition of one letter to begin words in a line of verse, LITERAL, **literary** to do with letters of the alphabet (17–18c), later with good writing, LITERATE*, **obliterate** [via Latin *oblitterare*, literally 'to remove letters'], and **transliterate** to represent words or sounds written in one alphabet with the letters of another.

level [ME. Old French *livel*, ultimately from Latin *libra* 'scales, balance'] An instrument for indicating a horizontal line, hence **1** horizontal; (to make) horizontal, even, or flat (15c); lying or moving horizontally (17c) **2** to bring a weapon to the right angle for use, to aim (15c); to aim a look, accusation, etc. (16c) **3** a real or imaginary horizontal line from which height is measured (16c), hence **(a)** to determine the height from it **(b)** a position in relation to it (19c); a relative height, amount, or value **4** on the same horizontal plane (16c); equal to, consistent with, hence **(a)** balanced, steady (16–17c), re-emerging in **level-headed** (19c, *US*) **(b) on the level** honest(ly), straightforward(ly) (19c); **level with** behave or speak honestly to someone (1920s, *US*) **(c)** level with the brim (*a level teaspoonful*, *c*.1900) **5** to place on the same horizontal plane (16c): **(a)** to knock down, to flatten (17c) **(b)** to remove inequalities; **level up/down** to standardize (18c) **6** something horizontal: **(a)** a passage in a mine (16c); a level tract of land (*Somerset Levels*, 17c); a storey in a building (1960s); a stratum in the earth **(b)** a social or intellectual stratum or standard (17c); a layer of meaning (*the film works on many levels*, 1960s).

Latin *libra* is found in *libra pondo* (see POUND¹*), and produced **deliberate** [via *deliberare* 'to weigh carefully', from *librare* 'to weigh'] and **equilibrium** [from *aequilibrium* 'equal balance'].

lever [ME. Old French *levier*, *leveor*, from *lever* 'to raise or rise', from Latin *levare*, from *levis* 'light in weight'] A bar used with a pivot to move something heavy, hence **1** an arm that operates a machine (19c) **2** to use a lever (19c, earlier in **leverage** the action or a way of levering); to move or raise with difficulty **3** a means of exerting (moral) force (19c); *leverage* increased power to get things done; the ratio of a company's debt to its equity, used to maximize returns (1930s, *US*); to speculate using borrowed capital (1970s).

Old French *lever* produced **Levant** the former name of the eastern Mediterranean region [French, literally 'rising', hence the point where the sun rises], **levee** [from *levé* 'rising'] a monarch's reception for visitors shortly after getting up, later a British monarch's afternoon assembly; a reception or assembly at any time (now chiefly N American), **levee** an embankment beside a river [*US*, from *levée*, feminine past participle of *lever*], and **levy** the raising of, or to raise, a tax or a (conscript) army; what is raised. Descendants of Latin *levis* include *allege* (at ALLAY¹), *carnival* (at SHRIVE), **elevate**, **leaven**, **legerdemain** [ME, from French *leger de main*, literally 'light of hand'], **levitate** and **levity** (at GRAVITY), and RELIEVE*: see also ALLAY¹.

leviathan [ME. Late Latin, from Hebrew *liwyāṯān*] A huge real or imaginary sea creature: **1** in the Bible, a serpent killed by God (Psalms:74:14, Isaiah 27:1, hence a name for the Devil); a symbol of God's creative power (Job 41) **2** used by the political thinker Thomas Hobbes (b.1588) for an all-powerful Commonwealth governing for the people's benefit but not answerable to them, hence any totalitarian regime **3** an extremely powerful or wealthy man (17c) **4** any huge thing, especially a ship (19c).

lewd [Old English *lǣwede*, of unknown origin] Not in holy orders, lay (–19c), hence uneducated, ignorant (ME); crude, vulgar; good-for-nothing, wicked, vile; lascivious, indecent, obscene.

liaison [17c. French, from *lier* 'to bind', from Latin *ligare*] **1** a binding or thickening agent **2** an intimate relationship, especially an adulterous one (19c) **3** communication and cooperation, originally between military units (19c), hence **liaise** (1920s, *military slang*).

French *lier* is probably the source of **liable** bound or obliged to do or pay, hence susceptible to, apt or likely to do, and of **liana**. Latin *ligare* is the ancestor of LEAGUE*.

libel [ME. Old French, from Latin *libellus*, literally 'little book', from *liber* 'book'] **1** a formal document, a written statement; one setting out the plaintiff's case in a lawsuit, a written indictment **2** a little book (surviving in Scots). Hence (combining 1 and 2) a leaflet etc. making a public accusation or defaming someone's character (16–18c); (to make) a false or defamatory statement (17c); (to publish) a libellous document, film, etc. Cf. *slander* (at SCANDAL).

Latin *liber* is the ancestor of **library** and of Italian *libretto* 'little book', adopted for the text of an opera.

liberal [ME. French, from Latin *liberalis*, from *liber* 'free, a free man'] Worthy of, or suitable for, a free man, later for a gentleman or educated person, hence **1** generous, open-handed; given generously **2** free, unrestrained, lax (–18c); of an interpretation or translation: not rigorous or literal **3** of education: developing the mind and providing cultural knowledge rather than professional or vocational skills; *liberal arts* see ART **4** broad-minded, tolerant (18c); progressive, especially in political and religious matters; someone with such views (19c).

Latin *liber* produced DELIVER*, LIBERTINE, and **liberty**.

libertine [ME. Latin *libertinus*, from *libertus* 'freed man', from *liber*: see LIBERAL] **1** a freed slave **2** a member of one of the 16c sects who believed that the gospel freed Christians from obedience to civil or moral law, hence a freethinker; someone not restricted by convention or morality, especially in sexual matters.

licence/license [ME. Via Old French from Latin *licentia*, from *licere* 'to be lawful or permitted'. Noun and verb used both spellings until well into the 19c: in British English *licence* is now the noun, *license* the verb, in American English both are usually spelt *license*. Cf. ADVICE/ADVISE*] Freedom of action, hence **1** (official) permission to do or, later, own something; an official permit, hence **(a)** to grant (a) licence **(b)** a certificate of competence from certain colleges and universities (15c); **licentiate** the holder of one, now usually in a profession **2** excessive freedom or lack of restraint; an artist's or writer's freedom to distort facts or artistic rules for effect (16c).

Latin *licere* is the ancestor of **leisure**, and of **licit** lawful, permissible, and its more common opposite, **illicit**.

lickerish [15c. Alteration of **lickerous** (ME–17c), Anglo-Norman variant of Old French *lecheros*, from *lechier* 'to lick, to be debauched or gluttonous', of Germanic origin] **1** gluttonous; lustful (17c) **2** tasty, sweet, tempting (16c). The variant **liquorish** [16c, by association with *liquor* (at LIQUID)] probably influenced the spelling of **liquorish** the sweet [ME, Anglo-Norman French *lycorys*, via late Latin from Greek *glukurrhiza*, from *glukus* 'sweet' + *rhiza* 'root': the earlier spelling **licorice** survives in N America].

Old French *lechier* produced **lecher** a lewd or promiscuous man, whence **lech** to feel or behave lecherously, to lust after, and is related to **lick** [Old English *liccian*]. Greek *glukus* is related to **glucose**; *rhiza* produced **rhizome**.

light¹ [Old English *lēocht*, *līht* (adjective), *līhten* (verb)] Weighing little, or less than normal (opposite of **heavy** [Old English *hefig*]), hence **1** with little force or pressure (cf. *heavy* intense, oppressive); delicate (*a light touch*, cf. **heavy handed**) **2** to make light or lighter; to unload (ME, whence **lighter** a boat used for unloading ships, 15c), replaced by **lighten 3** to descend from or onto (largely replaced by **alight**, originally to jump down lightly), hence **light on** to find by chance **4** not dense, thick, or rich (*light diet/soil/traffic*); **lite** low in alcohol, calories, etc. (1960s, *US*) **5 lights** the lungs (ME, because of their lightness) **6** to lift or move along (19c, nautical), hence **light out** to set off (*US slang*).

Light is related to **lung** [Old English *lungen*], and *heavy* to *have* (at HOBNOB).

light² [Old English *lēoht, līht* (noun and adjective), *līhtan* (verb)] The radiation that enables us to see, hence **1** not dark: **(a)** full of light; to provide with light (ME) **(b)** pale (ME); **lighten** to make paler **2** a source of light (*put the light on*) (a pane of) a window (ME) **3** (to be) bright, shining, luminous, or burning (–18c, replaced by **alight**, ME); to set burning, to ignite (ME); a flame, match, etc. for doing so (17c) **4** spiritual or mental knowledge or insight (surviving mainly in *shed light on*); to bring this (ME, outlived by *lighten* and **enlighten**: cf. SEE*); mental capacity or knowledge (16c, surviving in *according to his lights*) **5** brightness: **(a)** vivacity, animation (16c); **light up** to produce this (18c) **(b) (high)light** a bright part of a picture (17c); (to put) a light tint in the hair (1940s); *highlight* an outstanding feature (19c); to draw attention to (1930s) **6 bring/come to light** to discover or be discovered.

like¹ [Old English *līcian*: related to LIKE²] To be pleasing to, to suit (surviving in dialect); **like yourself** to take pleasure in (ME–16c), hence *like* to find agreeable or pleasant, hence **1** to think well of; to prefer, hence what you like (18c, chiefly in **likes and dislikes**) **2** to want to do, later to be or have (19c).

like² [ME. Old Norse *(g)likre*] Similar; a similar thing; in a similar way, hence **1** to compare (outlived by **liken**) **2** -like similar to, suitable, appropriate (*ladylike*) **3 likely** apparently true, probable; apparently suitable; able, vigorous, or good-looking (15c, now US and dialect).

Related to **each**, ILK, **likeness**, **-ly** as in *beastly*, *manly* [Old English *-lic*] and as in *greatly*, *secondly* [Old English *-lice*], and **lychgate** a covered gateway to a church-yard, where the coffin rested before going into the church [Old English *lic* 'form, body'].

lilt [ME. Origin unknown] To sound an alarm (–16c); to raise your voice (15–17c), hence to strike up a song (17c); a (merry) song or tune; to sing, play, or speak merrily or with a jaunty rhythm (18c); a way of speaking in which the voice's pitch varies pleasantly.

limber [ME. Perhaps ultimately from Latin *limon* 'shaft'] The shaft of a cart, hence **1** the detachable shaft and front wheels of a gun carriage (15c) **2** (probably from the easy movement of a shaft) flexible, supple (16c); lithe, nimble, hence **limber (up)** to make or become limber (18c).

Limber produced **limbo**, a West Indian dance in which incredibly limber danc-ers squeeze under a low bar.

lime [Old English *līm*: related to **loam** , which originally meant clay or mud] Any sticky substance, specifically **1 (bird)lime** used to catch birds; to smear with bird-lime etc. (ME); to catch in this way; to trap or ensnare **2** mortar or cement (sur-viving in Scots), hence calcium oxide, the chief constituent of mortar, obtained by heating **limestone** and also called *quicklime* (see QUICK), hence **(a) (slaked) lime**

a mixture of this and water **(b)** (to treat with) various calcium compounds (17c) **(c) limelight** intense white light produced by heating lime (19c), formerly used in the theatre, hence the focus of (public) attention **(d) limescale** a deposit caused by calcium etc. in hard water.

limousine [*c.*1900. French, originally a hooded cloak worn in the former French province of Limousin] A car with a covered outside seat for the driver, later a luxury car, originally with a separate chauffeur's compartment (1920s, colloquially shortened to **limo**, 1960s); a passenger vehicle on a fixed route to and from an airport (1960s, US).

linden [Old English *lind* 'lime tree'] Made of lime wood (–ME); **linden (tree)** a lime tree (16c).

Old English *lind* appears in names such as **Lindsell** and **Lindop**; the variant **line** survives as a surname, and was altered to **lime**, now the usual name of the tree and its wood. Related to LITHE*.

The small green citrus fruit is from an unrelated tree [via French and Spanish from Arabic *līma* 'citrus fruit', whence also **lemon**]. **Limey** a Briton or Englishman arose because sailors in the British Navy were formerly issued lime juice to prevent scurvy.

line [Old English *līne* and Old French *ligne*, both ultimately from Latin *linea (fibra)* 'flax (fibre)', from *linum* 'flax'] A rope, cord, or wire, hence **(a) hard lines** wet or icy ship's ropes, hard to manage, hence hard luck (19c) **(b) on line** directly connected (originally of a computer with a peripheral device, 1950s); (carried out while) connected to a computer network **(c)** a telephone connection (*a bad line*); **-line** a telephone service (*helpline*, 1960s). Hence **1** a row or series (originally of words, ME), hence **(a) line up** to form or be in one; **bring/come into line** to (cause to) agree or conform **2** a long, narrow mark (ME), hence **(a)** a trail; a track or route (*tramlines/mainline*, 18c); (a company running) a regular transport service; **liner** a ship belonging to one (19c), whence **airliner** (early 20c) **(b)** an imaginary line on the globe (ME); the equator (*crossing the line*, 16c) **(c)** (a real or imaginary line marking) a boundary (16c), hence **outline** (17c); a drawing showing only this (18c); (to give) a brief description of important features **(d) lines** the outline or plan of a building, ship, etc. (17c); *line(s)* overall shape (*fine lines, A-line skirt, c.*1910).

Old English *līne* appears as **Lin-** or **Lyn-** in place names (cf. LINEN). Latin *linea* produced **align**, **delineate**, **lineage**, **lineal**, and **linear**; *linum* is the ancestor of French **crinoline** [with Latin *crinis* 'hair'] a fabric made of horsehair and linen or cotton, used for linings and, formerly, to stiffen petticoats, hence a stiffened petticoat or skirt, of **linoleum** [with Latin *oleum* 'oil': shortened to **lino**], and probably of LINEN*.

linen [Old English *li(n)nen*, probably ultimately from Latin *linum*: see LINE*] Made of flax or flaxen cloth, hence such cloth (ME); articles (usually) made from it (*bed/table linen*); linen (under)clothing.

Related to **line** flax (fibre) [Old English *līn*], whence **Lin-** or **Lyn-** in place names (cf. LINE), **line** to cover or reinforce the inside (often with linen), **linseed**, French *lingerie* linen articles, later women's underwear and nightclothes, **linnet** (which eats flax seeds), and probably to **lint** the flax plant; a soft material originally made by scraping linen cloth, hence (a piece of) fluff.

lion [ME. Anglo-Norman French *liun* from Latin *leo, leonis,* from Greek *leōn*] The big cat (replacing *leo* below); a related or similar animal (*mountain lion*/**sea lion** from its lion-like profile). Hence **1** the lion as a symbol of **(a)** strength and courage; **lion heart** a brave person (17c, translating French *coeur de lion,* an epithet of Richard I of England) **(b)** ferocious cruelty **(c)** Great Britain (17c) **2** lions things worth seeing, curiosities (16c), hence *lion* a celebrity (17c); **lionize** to treat as one (19c).

An archaic form appears in **Lord Lyon** or **Lyon King of Arms,** the title of the chief herald in Scotland [from the lion on the royal shield], and in the surname **Lyon(s).** *Lion* produced the name **Lionel,** literally 'little lion'. Latin **Leo** was adopted for a constellation and its astrological sign, and as a name (traditionally given to lions): it produced **leonine,** and the names **Lennard, Leona, Leonard,** and **Leonie.** Greek *leōn* is the ancestor of **chameleon** [literally 'ground lion'] and **leopard,** once thought to be a cross between a lion and a **pard** a panther [Greek *pardos,* probably of Iranian origin], whence the name **Leppard, Lippard.** *Pard* is also found in **camelopard** [literally 'camel leopard', from its markings], an old name for the giraffe.

liquid [ME. Latin *liquidus,* from *liquere* 'to be fluid', also 'to be clear'] Of a substance: fluid at room temperature, hence **1** not fixed or stable; of assets: consisting of or easily converted into cash (19c) **2** clear and bright, like pure water (16c), hence **(a)** undisputed (surviving in Scots) **(b)** of sound: clear in tone, without harshness or discord (17c) **3** a liquid substance (18c); **liquids** liquid food.

Latin *liquidus* produced medieval Latin *liquidare* 'to make liquid or clear', whence **liquidate** to agree or clarify accounts (16–18c); to wind up a company and distribute its assets; to get rid of, to kill [translating Russian *likvidirovat',* from *liquidare*]. Latin *liquere* produced **deliquesce, liquefaction, liquefy,** and **prolix** [Latin *prolixus,* literally 'that has flowed out']. Related to Latin *liquor* a liquid; an (alcoholic) drink; a broth or sauce [adopted via Old French *licur* (the original English spelling), which evolved into *liqueur*].

list [16c. French *liste,* of Germanic origin] (A strip of paper etc. containing) a series of names, words, numbers, etc.; to make, or include in, a list (17c), earlier in **enlist** to enrol someone in the armed forces, which came to mean **1** to gain someone's help or support **2** to volunteer for the armed forces (18c).

Related to **list** [Old English *liste*] a border or hem (–17c), a limit or boundary (ME–17c); **lists** the barriers enclosing a place for tilting or tournaments, hence **enter the lists** to become involved in a contest or argument.

literal [ME. Via French or late Latin from Latin *lit(t)era* LETTER*] **1** sticking to the basic meaning of a word or text without interpretation or elaboration, hence **(a)** of a translation etc.: exact, accurate, word for word (16c) **(b)** actual, true, without metaphor or exaggeration (17c), hence **literally** actually, really, since the 18c often used simply for emphasis and sometimes introducing a wild exaggeration (*I literally died*) **(c)** of a person: apt to take a metaphor, joke, etc. at face value (18c) **2** to do with or expressed in letters of the alphabet; a typographical error (17c).

literate [ME. Latin *lit(t)eratus* 'lettered', from *lit(t)era* LETTER*] Able to read and write, hence knowledgeable or competent in a particular area (*computer/emotionally literate,* 1970s). The connection of literacy with knowledge is found in **illiterate**

unable to read and write (15c); ignorant, stupid, and in **numerate** [1950s, from Latin *numerus* 'number'] and **computerate** (1960s), both modelled on *literate*.

Latin *literatus* produced **literature** (knowledge of) books and good writing; written works on a particular subject; printed matter of any kind (*advertising literature*). **Literati** [plural of *literatus*] was adopted meaning intellectuals and those involved with literature or the arts, as a class, and inspired *glitterati* (at GLITTER).

lithe [Old English *līthe*] Gentle, meek (surviving, just, in Scots); soft, agreeable, mellow (surviving in dialect); flexible, supple, graceful (ME), whence **lithesome** (18c), soon altered to **lissom.**

litter [ME. Old French *litiere*, from medieval Latin *lectaria*, from Latin *lectus* 'bed' (whence *let* in **coverlet**)] A bed (–15c), hence **1** a curtained couch or a stretcher for carrying a person or a body **2** straw, rushes, etc. used as bedding, now only for animals (15c); mixed dung and straw, hence **(a)** things or rubbish strewn about (18c); to scatter such things; to lie about untidily (19c) **(b)** decomposing plant debris on the forest floor (*c.*1900) **(c)** material for a pet's toilet tray (1960s) **3** the young born to an animal at one time (15c); to produce a litter.

live [Old English *libban, lifian*] To be alive, to have life, hence **1** to stay alive, to continue to exist; to continue in the memory (16c) **2** (to supply yourself with) the means to live (*lives by farming/on fish*), hence **living** a means of maintenance or support (ME); **standard of living** (18c), **living standard** (1950s) the degree of material comfort in which you live; **living wage** on which you can live without hardship (19c) **3** to spend your life in a particular way or by certain principles; to express something in your life (*live a lie/your dream*, 16c); to enjoy life to the full (17c) **4** to reside (ME), hence *living* (landed) property (15c); (combining this and sense 2) a position as vicar or rector, with an income and/or property.

Related to **leave** to bequeath, also to go away (from), **life**, and **liver** once thought to produce blood and maintain life. *Life* produced **alive** (shortened to **live**), **enliven, livelihood** originally 'way of life' [with Old English *lād* meaning way, course: see LOAD*], and **lively**, originally 'having or giving life'.

livery [ME. Anglo-Norman French *liveré* or Old French *livrée* 'given out', ultimately from Latin *liberare* 'to set free' (in medieval Latin 'to hand out'): see LIBERAL] The provision of food and clothing to servants, hence **1 (a)** the food provided **(b)** the provision of food for horses, surviving in 15c **at livery** kept at a **livery stable** that boards people's horses (18c) **2** the clothing provided, hence the distinctive dress of a servant or a member of a **livery company**, one of the London City companies entitled to wear uniform; a design or colour scheme on a vehicle etc. that identifies its manufacturer or owner (1930s).

livid [ME. (Via French from) Latin *lividus*, from *livere* 'to be bluish'] Of a dull blue-grey colour, hence **1** discoloured (as if) by bruising, black and blue **2** tinged with grey (19c) **3** extremely angry, as if 'blue in the face' with rage (*c.*1910).

load [Old English *lād*] **1** carrying, conveyance (–16c); something carried (ME); the amount carried at one time; to put this in or on something (15c), hence **(a)** a burden (ME); to weigh down (15c); (to exert) a force (16c); to weight so as to affect performance (*loaded dice*, 18c); to weight an insurance premium for a specific risk or situation (19c) **(b)** to fill a machine etc. (*load a gun/camera*, 17c); what is loaded at one time **(c) download** to transfer data from a computer system to a

smaller one (1980s, whence the opposite **upload**); this action; the data transferred **2** surviving as **lode**: a way; a road or lane, hence **(a) lodestar** a star that
shows the way (ME) **(b)** a channel (15c); a vein of ore (17c) **(c) lodestone** (a piece
of) magnetite (16c); something that attracts.

Old English *lād* is one parent of *livelihood* (at LIVE): related to **lead** to go in front.

loafer [19c. Probably from German *Landlaufer* 'vagabond', from *land* 'land' +
laufen 'to run'] An idler, hence **loaf** to spend time idly, whence **Loafer** a proprietary name for a kind of casual shoe (1930s) or jacket (1950s).

  Landloper [*Landlaufer*'s early Dutch cousin] came to mean a poor or novice
sailor, *-loper* later replaced by **lubber** a clumsy oaf [perhaps related to LOB];
-loper is also found in **interloper**, originally an unauthorized trader who
encroached on a monopoly, and is related to LEAP*. German and Dutch *land* are
related to LAND.

loath [Old English *lāth*] **1** angry, hostile (–15c) **2** unpleasant, repulsive (–16c); a
repulsive or evil thing (–15c, surviving in **loathsome**) **3** reluctant, unwilling (ME).

  Related to **loathe** to be offensive or disgusting to someone (OE–16c), hence to
find disgusting; to dislike intensely.

lob [ME. Perhaps from Old English, or of Dutch origin and related to *lubber* (at
LOAFER): possibly more than one word] **1** a pollack (surviving in Scots) **2** a country bumpkin, a lout; to behave like one (16c); to move or throw clumsily (19c);
to strike a ball in a high arc; such a stroke **3** a lump (recorded in the 19c, but
producing or related to the place name **Lobb** (recorded in the Domesday Book),
whence the surname.

lobby [16c. Medieval Latin *lobia*: see LODGE*] A monastic cloister; a corridor, ante-
room, or entrance hall; an area in a legislative chamber where members may
meet non-members (17c), hence to seek to influence members (originally by
accosting them in the lobby, 19c, *US*); to frequent the lobby for this reason; a
group trying to get members or the public to support them.

local [ME. French, from late Latin *localis*, from Latin *locus* 'place'] **1** to do with,
acting on, or confined to, a particular part of the body (*local anaesthetic*); belonging to or to do with only part of something **2** to do with, existing in, or, later,
limited to, a particular place (*local time*, 15c); belonging to a region, town, etc.
rather than to the whole country (*local government/radio*); **the locals** the people
living in the immediate area (19c). Hence **local colour** the colour of one part of a
picture (18c); characteristic details of a time or place used to give verisimilitude
to a story, film, etc. (19c).

  Local produced **localize**; French *local* produced **locale** (respelt to indicate the
stress). Latin *locus* was adopted meaning a particular point, place, or position,
having produced ALLOW*, **locality**, **locomotive**, *locum tenens* (shortened to **locum**),
and French *lieu* (adopted in **in lieu** in place of, instead), whence *milieu* (at MEDIUM)
and **lieutenant** (literally 'one holding a place'; some early spellings omitted the *i*, and
the *u* was mistaken for a *v*, leading to the British pronunciation *leftenant*).

lock [Old English *loc*] A fastening mechanism, specifically one needing a key or,
later, knowledge of a code, to open it, hence **1 (a)** something that prevents movement, earliest in **oarlock** (ME), probably inspiring, and largely replaced by, **rowlock** (18c); a jam or blockage (*deadlock*, *gridlock*, 16c) **(b)** to fix or become fixed

(16c); **lock on(to)** to (cause to) find and track a target (1950s) **(c)** either of two fixed positions that a vehicle's front wheels can swivel between; the amount of such movement (*full lock*, 19c) **2** to fasten (with) a lock (ME) **3** a movable barrier (ME–18c); a section of a waterway enclosed by locks, allowing movement between different levels (18c), hence **(air)lock** allowing movement between areas of different pressure (19c) **4** to fix by fitting parts together (15c), hence **(a)** **interlock** to fit together (17c); to connect mechanisms so that they (must) work together (19c); tightly woven or knitted material (1920s) **(b)** **lock horns** of deer etc.: to entangle their horns when fighting (19c), hence to fight or argue with someone (*US*) **5** a gun's mechanism that explodes the charge (16c, probably because early ones resembled a lock), hence **flintlock**, **matchlock**, etc. (guns with) a certain kind of lock; **lock, stock, and barrel** the three main parts of a gun, hence everything, completely (19c).

Related to **locket** [Old French *locquet*, from *loc* 'latch, lock', of Germanic origin] originally a crossbar to secure a window (ME–16c), the current sense probably influenced by **lock** a tress, often worn in a locket [Old English *locc*, also perhaps related], the probable source of **fetlock** (the tuft of hair growing on) the lowest joint on a horse's leg.

lodge [ME. French *loge* 'arbour, summerhouse, hut', from medieval Latin *lobia*, of Germanic origin] A (small or temporary) house or dwelling; a tent (surviving in dialect, and revived for a wigwam or tepee, 19c), hence **1** to house temporarily, hence **(a)** to station an army, to take up a position (–16c, hence **dislodge**, originally to drive an enemy from one) **(b)** to provide with or stay in (temporary) accommodation; **lodging(s)** such accommodation; **lodger** who lives in someone else's house (16c) **2** a small house: **(a)** used by hunting parties **(b)** for a gatekeeper, hence a doorman's kiosk **(c)** an otter's or beaver's den (16c) **(d)** (the meeting place of) a branch of a Masonic or similar organization (17c) **3** to become caught or fixed (17c, 15c in *dislodge*) **4** to deposit (17c); to register a complaint etc. by depositing documents with the relevant authority (19c).

French *loge* produced **logistics** [via *logis* 'lodging, army encampment'] the organization of moving, lodging, and supplying troops, later of any complex task. Medieval Latin *lobia* fathered Italian **loggia** adopted for an open-sided gallery or arcade. Probably related to **louvre** [Old French *lov(i)er* 'skylight'] a turret with (slatted) openings for ventilation, hence (a slat in) such an opening.

loft [Old English, from Old Norse *lopt* 'air, sky, upper room'] **1** the air, the sky (–16c), surviving in **aloft** [ME, from Old Norse *á lopt* 'in the air']; to hit or kick a ball aloft (19c) **2 (a)** an attic (ME); an upper room or roof space used for storage; an upper storey, especially in a warehouse or factory (18c, *N American*), now one used as an apartment **(b)** a gallery in a church (*organ loft*, 15c) **(c)** a pigeon-house or dovecot (18c); its pigeons; to keep them (19c).

Loft produced **lofty** exalted, high-ranking; haughty, aloof; very high or tall; a nickname for someone tall. Old Norse *lopt* produced the surname **Lofthouse** or **Loftus** someone who lived in a house with a loft. Related to Old Norse *lypta*, whence **lift**.

log [ME. Origin unknown] A piece of a tree trunk or branch, hence **1** a lump of wood attached to a person or animal to impede movement (16c: cf. *waterlogged*), later also as **logger**, which was first recorded in **loggerhead: (a)** a fool, literally a blockhead **(b)** a large head, hence describing various large-headed creatures (*loggerhead turtle*, 17c) **(c)** a ball on a long handle, used for melting pitch etc., hence **go to loggerheads** to come to blows (perhaps using this as a weapon); **at loggerheads** squabbling (19c) **2** a wooden float trailed on a line to measure the speed of a ship (16c, cf. KNOT), hence **(a) logbook** a book containing a detailed record of the voyage (17c, shortened to *log*, 19c); a vehicle's registration document (1950s) **(b)** (to enter details in) a systematic record of events (19c), hence **log in/on** to 'sign in' to a computer application by entering your password etc. (1960s); **log out/off** to end access **(c)** *weblog* (at WEB) **3 backlog** a log at the back of a grate that smoulders on after the fire burns out (17c), hence something kept in reserve (19c); things waiting to be done (1930s, probably influenced by *log jam*) **4** to trim the branches off a tree (17c); to (fell trees and) cut the timber into logs (18c, *US*) **5 waterlogged** of a ship: difficult to handle because of water in the hold (lying or moving around like logs, 18c); water-damaged, saturated (19c).

long . [Old English *lang, long*] Extending a great, or greater than usual, distance in space or time: opposite of **short** [Old English *sceort*]. Hence **1 (a)** measuring a certain distance (*3 metres long*) **(b)** having the length greater than the breadth **2 (a)** lasting a certain length of time (*3 hours long*), or too much time (*seven long years*, ME); (during) such a period (*before long*, 16c) **(b)** a musical note (see LARGE sense 3b) **(c)** of a point in time: distant (ME) **3** describing a number, quantity, or measure greater than normal (e.g. **long hundred** 120, 16c); of a number, amount, price, etc.: large (18c, surviving mainly in *long odds*), **long suit** of which you hold several cards, hence your strong point; **long on** having plenty of (*c*.1910, *US slang*).

Short came to mean **1** not going far enough (*falling short/short circuit*); not meeting a standard **2** brittle, friable, crumbly (*short pastry*), perhaps from the idea of having short fibres, as in **short manure** well-rotted, with short, brittle straw fibres.

Old English *lang* produced ALONG*, the surname **Lang, Long** a tall person, and appears as **Lang-** or **Long-** in place names: other words that might seem to come from *lang* are actually from synonymous Latin *longus*: see LOUNGE*). Related to **length, lengthen,** LENTEN, **linger,** and **long** to grow or seem long, hence to yearn (from the idea of stretching out towards something). *Short* is related to SHEAR*.

loom [Old English *gelōma*] An implement or utensil (now Scots and N English dialect); a bucket or tub (ME, now Scots), hence **1** a tool or other chattel handed down from one generation to the next (surviving in **heirloom**) **2** a machine for weaving **3** flexible tubing protecting an insulated wire (*c*.1915); a group of insulated wires bound together (1940s).

lord [Old English *hlāford*, literally 'bread keeper', from *hlaf* 'bread, **loaf**' + *weard* WARD*], **lady** [Old English *hlǣfdige*, from *hlāf* + a Germanic word meaning 'to knead'] A man/woman due respect and (feudal) obedience: **1** The head of a household, especially in relation to servants; a ruler: replaced by *master* or *mistress* (see MASTER) except in *lady of the house* **2 The/Our Lord** God, or, later, Christ (hence **Lord's Day** the sabbath); **Our Lady** the Virgin Mary; **Lady Chapel** dedicated to her; **Lady Day** the feast of the Annunciation: also applied to various beautiful or beneficial creatures (**lady's mantle** a plant with medicinal uses, **ladybird/bug** that eats harmful aphids): her name is also found in **marigold**, a medicinal and pot herb (ME) and *rosemary* (at ROSE) **3** a landowner, hence **(a) landlord** (OE), **landlady** (16c), who lets land or property; the proprietor of a pub or boarding house (17c) **(b)** *lord* who held land directly from the king (ME: women at this time didn't), surviving in **lord of the manor** and in the Scots variant **Laird**, hence (a title or form of address for) a nobleman, *Lady* his wife or consort; now someone entitled to sit in the **House of Lords** the upper chamber of the British Parliament, and in the titles of some officials (*First Lord of the Admiralty/Lady Mayoress*, 16c). Hence *lady*: **4** a woman to whom a knight or lover is devoted (ME); **lady (love), old/good lady** your wife or sweetheart **5** a polite word or form of address for a woman (16c): the tendency of titles etc. to slide down the social scale is found also in *gentleman* (at GENTLE) and *mister* (at MASTER) **6** a courteous, refined, or dignified woman (19c: cf. *gentlewoman* at GENTLE).

In senses 1, 3, and 5 *lady* long co-existed with, and gradually replaced, **dame** [French, from Latin *domina*, feminine of *dominus* 'lord, master'], which survives as a title for a female member of a chivalric order, as a dialect and US slang word for a woman, as a ridiculous old woman in pantomime, in the shortened form **dam** a mother (now only an animal's: cf. SIRE), and in **madam** [French *ma dame* 'my lady'] a noblewoman, the mistress of a household or brothel, a precocious, petulant young girl, and as a respectful form of address (also shortened to **ma'am**). The Italian form *mia donna* produced **Madonna**, originally a polite way of addressing an Italian woman, later applied to the Virgin Mary. **Donna** was adopted as a given name and is also found in **prima donna** [literally 'first lady'] a principal female opera singer; a temperamental or demanding person.

The second element of Old English *hlǣfdige* is related to **dairy** and **dough**. Latin *domina* is the ancestor of **damsel** a young, unmarried lady, and DOMINATE*.

lose [Old English *losian* from *los* 'loss'] **1** to perish or be missing (–15c); to destroy (–17c): both surviving in **lost** destroyed, dead, damned (ME) **2** to mislay, to be unable to find, hence **(a) lose your way/yourself, be/get lost** to not know where you are or which way to go (ME); to fail to keep in sight (16c); to get away from or shake off **(c)** to become hidden (17c) **3** to cease to have (*lost his home/sight*, ME); to fail to keep or maintain (*lose your temper, a lost art*, 15c); to get rid of (17c) **4** to suffer loss (ME); to do so in war or in a game, hence to be defeated (16c); to fail **5** to cause loss (*the error lost him his job*, ME) **6** to fail to get something (ME); to waste money, an opportunity, etc.

Loss is partly from Old English *los*, partly a back-formation from *lost*. Related to FORLORN*, to **-less** devoid of (*worthless*), and to **loose** [Old Norse *lauss*].

lot [Old English *hlot*] Something used to reach an arbitrary decision, e.g. by being drawn at random; a share or portion decided in this way, hence **1** what fate allots, your destiny **2** a tax or due, chiefly in **scot and lot**, *scot* being a municipal tax [from Old Norse *skot* and Old French *escot*, both related to SHOOT*], hence **scot free** exempt from scot, later from injury or punishment) **3** (a number of people or things forming) a part (ME only); a group of people or things (16c); an item or a set of items sold at an auction (18c, hence a **bad lot** an undesirable item, a nasty person, 19c); **a lot, lots** a large number or amount (19c), to a great extent (*he's* *changed a lot*); much (*lots more/a lot better*); **the (whole) lot** everything; **your lot** all you're getting **4** a share of land (17c); a plot offered for sale or set aside for some purpose (*vacant/parking lot*); one where filming takes place (1920s).

Related to ALLOT, **lottery** [Dutch *loterij*], and **lotto** [(via French from) Italian, of Frankish origin].

lounge [16c. Probably from French *s'allonger* 'to stretch out', from *allonger* 'to lengthen', ultimately from Latin *longus* 'long', but sometimes said to be from obsolete *lungis* 'gangling, idle, stupid person', from Longinus, apocryphal name of the centurion who pierced Christ's side when he was on the cross] To move lazily, to slouch; to pass the time idly (17c); to recline comfortably (18c), hence a place for relaxing: **1** a sitting room in a house or hotel (19c); an airport waiting room; **lounge (bar)** a comfortably furnished bar in a pub etc.; **cocktail lounge** a smart bar serving cocktails (1920s), hence **lounge lizard** a man who frequents fashionable places, usually in search of wealthy women **2** a chair or couch for reclining on (19c, later **lounger**, 1960s) **3 loungewear** clothes suitable for relaxing in (19c), hence **lounge suit** a man's suit for ordinary day wear, less formal than a dress suit (*c*.1900).

French *allonger* produced LUNGE*. Descendants of Latin *longus* include **elongate**, *longitude* (at LATITUDE), **longevity**, **oblong** [via Latin *oblongus* 'rather long'], **prolong**, and **purloin** [Anglo-Norman French *purloigner*, from Old French *loing* 'far'] to put far away (–17c), hence to misappropriate or steal.

lour, **lower** [ME. Origin unknown] **1** to look sullen, angry, or (formerly) sad; of the sky etc.: to look dark and threatening (16c) **2** to lurk or skulk (mainly Scots).

Probably the source of **lurk**, whence, probably, **lurch** to lurk; to swindle or rob, whence **lurcher** a petty thief; a cross-bred dog with greyhound blood, popular with poachers. **Lurch** in **leave in the lurch** is apparently from French *demeurer lourche* [roughly 'to leave soundly beaten at *lourche*', a game resembling backgammon], hence to be discomfited. The origin of **lurch** (to make) a sudden unsteady sideways movement (*nautical*) is unknown.

loyal [15c. French, from Old French *loial, leial*, from Latin *legalis*, from *lex, legis* 'law'] Firm in your allegiance to your legitimate monarch or government, hence **1** faithful to a friend or ideal (16c) **2** expressing loyalty; **loyal toast** a toast to the British monarch (19c).

Latin *legalis* produced **legal**, originally referring to Mosaic law; *lex* is the ancestor of **legislation** (whence **legislate** and **legislature**), **legitimate**, and *privilege* (at PRIVATE).

lucid [16c. (Via French or Italian from) Latin *lucidus*, from *lucere* 'to shine', from *lux* 'light'] Bright, shining, luminous, hence **1** of a star: visible to the naked eye **2** translucent, clear (17c), hence **(a) lucid interval** [translating medieval Latin *lucida intervalla*] an interval between periods of dementia or insanity when the mind is clear, hence *lucid* rational, sane (19c) **(b)** clearly expressed, easily understood (19c).

Latin *lucere* produced **elucidate**, **lucerne** alfalfa [via French from Provençal *luzerno* 'glowworm', from Latin *lucerna* 'lamp': because of its shiny seeds], **pellucid**, and **translucent**. Latin **lux** was adopted as the SI unit of illumination, having produced Latin *Lucifer* [literally 'light-bringing'], applied to Venus as the morning star, and in the Bible to the King of Babylon, who boasted that he would ascend to the heavens and become God's equal but who was cast down to hell (Isaiah 14:12), hence, later, to the Devil, who also challenged God and was seen falling from the heavens 'as lightning' (Luke 10:18), and the name **Lucy** (variants **Lucille** and **Lucinda**, often shortened to **Cindy** or **Sindy**).

ludicrous [17c. Latin *ludicrus*, from *ludus* 'game, play'] Jocular, derisive, in fun (–18c), frivolous, witty, humorous (–19c); ridiculous, absurd (18c).

Latin *ludus* is the ancestor of **allude**, **collude**, ELUDE, ILLUSION*, **ludic** spontaneously playful, the game **ludo** [Latin, literally 'I play'], and **prelude**.

luff [ME. Old French *lof*, probably from Low German or Dutch] **1** a device for altering a ship's course (–15c) **2** the part of a ship facing the wind (–17c); to steer or sail closer to the wind (15c), hence **aloof** an order to steer to windward, away from a shore etc. onto which the ship might drift (16c), hence keeping your distance, reserved (17c).

lug [ME. Probably from or related to Swedish *lugga* 'to pull someone's hair', from *lugg* 'forelock'] To pull by the ear or hair (surviving in dialect), hence **1** to drag, tug, or carry with difficulty, hence **(a)** **luggage** (originally heavy or awkward) baggage (16c) **(b)** a box for shipping fruit (19c, US) **2** to move heavily or slowly, hence, perhaps, a clumsy or stupid man (1930s, *US*).

Probably related to **lug** an ear (*Scots*); a projection (originally one resembling an ear) by which something can be fixed or carried.

lumber [ME. Origin unknown] To move ponderously or clumsily; to rumble; to move with a rumbling noise (15c, surviving in the US). Probably the source of *lumber* **1** unwanted furniture or household items (16c, partly by association with *lumber* 'pawnshop' below); to fill up with lumber (17c); to encumber, now especially with an unpleasant task **2** timber sawn into rough planks (17c); to cut trees and produce lumber (18c), hence **lumberjack** someone who does so (19c); **lumberjacket** of a kind worn by lumberjacks (1930s).

In **lumber** in pawn, later in prison or trouble, comes from the **Langobards** or **Lombards**, a Germanic tribe (founders of the kingdom of **Lombardy** in N Italy), who took over the role of financiers and pawnbrokers when the Jews were expelled from England in 1290. **Lombard Street** often marks a financial district or the site of a pawnshop.

lunatic [ME. Via French from late Latin *lunaticus*, from Latin *luna* 'moon'] Suffering from intermittent insanity thought to be caused by changes of the moon; insane, crazy; a crazy person. Hence **loony** crazy, daft, foolish (19c); such a person: cf. *moonstruck* (at MOON).

Descendants of Latin *luna* include **lunar**, originally 'crescent shaped', largely replaced in this sense by **lunate**, **lunaria** the plant honesty, whose round shiny seed pods resemble the moon, and **lunette** applied to various crescent-shaped things.

lunch, luncheon [Two words intertwined, both of uncertain origin] **1** *lunch* [16c, perhaps from Spanish *lonja* 'slice', or from Middle English **lump**, of unknown origin] a piece or hunk of bread etc.: quickly lengthened to *luncheon*, both forms dying out in the 19c **2** *luncheon* [17c, perhaps from Middle English **nuncheon** [(from NOON) + *schench* 'drink' (Old English *scenc*)] a snack between meals, later a light midday meal: in this sense shortened to *lunch* (19c), now the usual term although originally widely deplored. *Luncheon* survives for a formal midday meal, and in **luncheon meat** processed meat (World War II: cf. SPAM). *Lunch* blended with *breakfast* (at FAST) to produce mid-morning **brunch** (19c).

lunge [18c. French *allonger* 'to lengthen': see LOUNGE*] A thrust with a weapon, especially in fencing; (to deliver a kick or blow with) a sudden forward movement; to thrust or move forward aggressively (19c).

French *allonger* produced **lune** a cord, a hawk's leash, and **lunge** a cord (17c only), later a long rein for training a horse, to train or exercise a horse using one.

lure [ME. Old French *luere*, of Germanic origin] A bunch of feathers on a long cord, used to call a hawk to its handler; to call a hawk with one, hence to entice; something that does so; a trap or snare; a decoy (17c).

Old French *luere* produced *aluere* 'to bring to the lure', whence **allure** to attract, tempt, or win over; enticement, charm.

lurid [17c. Latin *luridus*, from *luror* 'wan or yellow colour'] **1** pale, wan, sallow; of the sky: leaden, overcast **2** shining or glowing through darkness (18c, said of lightning, or of flames amid smoke); glaring, hence gaudy, showy; sensational, horrifying (19c).

lush [ME. Probably an alteration of **lash** 'loose, weak' (surviving in dialect), from Old French *lache* 'soft, succulent', ultimately from Latin *laxus* 'loose' (ancestor of RELEASE*)] Flaccid, soft, weak (now only dialect), hence **1** (probably influenced by *luscious* at DELICIOUS) **(a)** of vegetation: luxuriant (17c) **(b)** of a colour: deep and rich (18c) **(c)** luxurious, opulent (19c); voluptuous; fine, good, nice (1990s, *slang*) **2** (to ply with) alcoholic drink (18c); to drink it (19c); a (habitual) drunkard (*N American*).

lust [Old English] **1** (a source of) pleasure or delight (–17c); to give pleasure (ME–16c) **2** desire, appetite, inclination; strong sexual desire; to feel this (16c) **3** vigour, life, fertility (ME–17c, surviving in **lusty**).

Related to **list** to please; pleasure, joy; appetite, desire; to like or wish to do (obsolete by the late 17c, but revived by 19c Romantics), and surviving in **listless** without pleasure or desire, hence without interest or energy.

luxury [ME. Via Old French from Latin *luxuria*, from *luxus* 'abundance, (vicious) indulgence'] Lust, lechery (–19c); habitual self-indulgence (17c), especially in choice and expensive surroundings, food, etc.; (the comfort of) such surroundings; something enjoyable but not essential (18c).

The idea of abundance appears in **luxuriant** and in the original sense of **luxuriate** to grow profusely. Latin *luxus* fathered French *luxe*, adopted in **de luxe** [literally 'of luxury'].

lyric [16c. Via French or Latin from Greek *lurikos*, from *lura* '**lyre**'] To do with the lyre; meant to be sung (originally to the lyre), hence **1** of poetry: expressing

personal thoughts and emotions, often having a musical quality, hence **lyricism**
lyric style (18c), enthusiastic expression of emotions; **lyrical** to do with or
expressed in the language of lyric poetry (19c); effusive, gushing **2** a song or lyric
poem; **lyrics** lyric verses; the words of a song (19c), hence **lyricist** someone who
writes them (*c*.1910).

M

macabre [15c. Old French *macabré*] Earliest in **dance of macabre** in which Death leads a dance to the grave, hence grim, gruesome (19c) [translating French *danse macabre*, probably an alteration of *danse Macabé* 'dance of the Maccabees', a representation of the slaughter of the Maccabees in a miracle play]

macaroni [16c. Italian dialect *maccarone* 'dumpling, paste', probably from Greek *makaria* 'food made from barley'] **1** (a dish made with) small pasta tubes **2** a fop, a dandy (18c), originally a member of the Macaroni Club, whose members had travelled in Italy, affected foreign tastes, and are said to have introduced macaroni to England. Hence the **macaroni penguin**, whose crest was thought to resemble a foppish hairstyle (19c), and the line in *Yankee Doodle* (at YANKEE) 'stuck a feather in his cap and called it macaroni', Yankee Doodle thinking this enough to make him a dandy.

Italian *maccarone* produced **macaronic** describing a form of verse in which words from two languages, especially vernacular words and Latin, are mixed [perhaps from the idea of macaroni mixed with sauce] and **macaroon**.

machine [16c. Latin *machina*, ultimately from Greek *mēkhanē*: see MECHANIC] A structure or contrivance of any kind, hence **1** a scheme or plot, outlived by **machination** [15c, from Latin *machinari* 'to contrive, to plot', from *machina*] **2** a device for transmitting physical power; one for producing stage effects (cf. *deus ex machina* below), now usually a device consisting of a number of parts and for a stated purpose (*washing machine*); to produce or operate by means of one (19c). Hence something compared to a machine: **(a)** a person acting without thought or spontaneity (17c) **(b)** a complex system (19c).

Latin *machina* appears in ***deus ex machina*** [literally 'god from the machine' (the device that lowered actors onto the stage)] a god introduced to resolve the plot in ancient Greek or Roman drama, hence something/someone that turns up in the nick of time to solve a problem; an unconvincing plot device.

magazine [16c. Via French and Italian from Arabic *makhzanin*, 'storehouses', from *khazana* 'to store up'] A warehouse, hence **1** a storehouse for arms, ammunition, and explosives, hence **(a)** its contents (17c) **(b)** an ammunition chamber in a gun (18c); a device in a camera or projector holding film or slides (19c) **2** a book providing information on a particular subject (17–19c, from the idea of a storehouse of information); a periodical containing a number of articles, stories, pictures, etc. (18c), hence **(a)** **magazine (programme)** a regular radio or television programme containing a number of items (1940s) **(b)** **-zine** (*blogzine* at WEB, *fanzine* at FANATIC).

magnify [ME. (Via French from) Latin *magnificare* 'to make greater', from *magnus* 'great'] **1** to praise (especially God) highly **2** to make larger, greater, or more important, hence to make something appear larger (17c); to exaggerate its size or importance (18c).

Latin *magnificare* produced **magnificat** 'it magnifies', adopted as the name of the Virgin Mary's hymn, beginning *Magnificat anima mea Dominum* 'my soul doth magnify the Lord' (at the Bible, Luke 1:46–55). Latin **magnum** [neuter of *magnus*] was adopted for a large bottle of wine or spirits, as the proprietary name of (a gun using) a cartridge more powerful than normal for its calibre, and in *magnum opus* (at OPERATION). Latin *magnus* is the ancestor of *magnanimous* (at ANIMATE), **magnate** originally a great or noble person, **magnificence**, **magnitude**, MAJOR*, and MAXIMUM*.

magus [ME. Latin, from Greek *magos*, from Old Persian *maguš*] A member of the Zoroastrian priestly caste in ancient Persia, hence an astrologer or magician; one of the Three Wise Men (the **Magi**) who visited the infant Jesus (15c, see the Bible, Matthew 2).

Greek *magos* produced Latin *magica* 'the art of a magus', whence **magic** and **magician**.

maiden, maid [Old English *maegden*] **1** a female child, a young woman; a virgin (ME); unmarried, virgin (*maiden aunt*); an unmarried woman (surviving in dialect and as **old maid**) **2** now only *maid*: a female servant (ME); in Scotland, your daughter **3** only *maiden*: (describing) **(a)** something being done or used for the first time (*maiden speech*, 16c); an untried soldier or weapon **(b)** something without result: **maiden over** in cricket, in which no runs are scored (16c); **maiden assize** where there is no capital conviction (17c) or, later, no cases to try **(c)** a town or castle that has never been taken (16c) **(d)** a racehorse that has never won (18c); a race for such horses.

Sense 1 produced the surnames **Maiden, M(e)akin** an effeminate man, and **Maidman, Maidment** a young woman's servant.

mail [ME. Old French *male*, of Germanic origin] A travelling bag or pack; a bag of letters (17c), hence the letters themselves or the means of conveying them; to send letters (19c): cf. POST³. Hence (all *N American*) **1 junk mail** unsolicited (advertising) material (1950s) **2 electronic mail** sent from one computer to another (1970s), shortened to **e-mail** or **email** (1980s), hence (to send) such a message: this initially spawned terms such as *e-commerce*, now largely replaced by **on line** (*online banking*). Hence **snail mail** traditional mail, seen as unbearably slow (1980s).

main [Partly from Old English *maegen* 'physical force', partly from Old Norse *megenn, megn* 'strong, powerful'] **1** physical strength or force (–17c), surviving in *might and main*) **2** considerable, very great of its kind (ME); chief, principal, earliest in **mainland** the principal land mass, excluding outlying islands, shortened to *main* (16c), hence **Spanish Main** the mainland of Spanish America from the Isthmus of Panama to the mouth of the Orinoco, later applied to the adjacent sea or to the part of the Caribbean Sea crossed by Spanish ships (18c).

Related to **dismay** [via Old French *desmaier*, literally 'to deprive of power'], to **may** to be strong, powerful, or able (–15c), hence used to indicate that something could be, or have been, done, and to **might** power, ability, whence **mighty**.

major [ME. Latin, 'greater', from *magnus* 'great'] In senses 1, 3 and 4 the opposite of **minor** [ME. Latin, 'smaller', from *parvus* 'small']. Greater or more important, hence **1** legally adult (16c, hence **majority** legal adulthood); a legally adult person (17c) **2** a military officer [16c, via French, short for *sergent-major* (see *sergeant-major* at SERGEANT), once a higher rank], hence **drum major** the officer leading a drum corps or band (16c); **(drum) majorette** a girl who dances in front of a marching band (1930s, *US*) **3** *majority* the greater number (17c), hence the most powerful party or group; the difference in the number of votes by which one side beats the other (18c) **4** a student's main subject (19c, US); a student taking one (*a history major*); to do so (*majored in English*, 1920s): hence *minor* (to take) a secondary subject.

Latin *major* produced the surname **Mair**, **Mayer** a (self-)important person, **Majorca** (hence **majolica** a kind of pottery originally made there, from *Maiolica*, the island's old Italian name), **majuscule** originally (describing) a capital letter, and **mayor**, and is related to **majesty** and MASTER*. *Minor* first appeared in **friars minor** a Franciscan friar [medieval Latin *Fratres Minores*, literally 'lesser brethren', signifying their humility]; Latin *minor* produced MINISTER*, **Minorca**, Majorca's smaller neighbour, *minus* (at PLUS), and **minuscule** tiny, (describing) a lower case letter, and is related to MINUTE[2]*. Latin *magnus* appears as **Magna** in village names, usually contrasted with **Parva** [Latin *parvus*, whence *minim* (at LARGE sense 3b), and *minimum* (at MAXIMUM)], and produced MAGNIFY*.

malignant [16c. Late Latin *malignare* 'to plot or injure maliciously', from Latin *malignus* 'tending towards evil', from *malus* 'bad'] **1** likely to rebel against authority, especially God (applied during the English Civil War to Royalist sympathizers) **2** of a disease or infection: extremely virulent; likely to get worse; of cancer or a tumour: likely to spread, replacing **malign** [ME, via French from Latin *malignus*], the opposite of which is *benign* (at GENEROUS).

Late Latin *malignare* produced **malign** to plot, also to criticize angrily (ME–17c), later to slander. Latin *malus* is the ancestor of **mal-** 'ill, badly' (*maladjusted, malapropos* at PROPOSE), and **malice**, whence, probably, **malware** harmful software.

mallow [Old English *mealwe*, from Latin *malva*] Applied to a family of plants, typically with hairy leaves and stems, and pink, mauve, or white flowers, and to other plants thought to resemble them, e.g. the **marshmallow** [Old English], used in medicine and to make a soft sweet (19c), hence a soft-centred or sentimental person or thing.

Latin *malva* fathered French *mauve* 'mallow', adopted for a light purple dye or its colour. Related to **malachite** [Greek *malakhē* 'mallow'], thought to be the same colour as a mallow leaf.

man [Old English *man(n)*: related to MANIKIN*] A human being, regardless of sex or age; humans collectively, the human race (see also *mankind* at KIND); an adult male human (ME). Hence **1** a man with the virtues traditionally ascribed to men **2** a vassal; a male servant or worker (surviving as **-man** in many surnames); a (now low-ranking) soldier, sailor, etc.; to be or provide with troops or operators (*man the fort/pumps*), hence **(a)** a chess or draughts piece **(b)** a ship (*man of war, merchantman*, 15c) **3** a husband (surviving in *man and wife*); a male partner or lover.

The usual Old English word for an adult male person was *wer* [probably from Latin *vir*: see VIRAGO*] surviving in **werewolf**, and for an adult female *cwene* (see *quean* at KING) or *wif* **wife**, whose original meaning survives in archaic terms for some tradeswomen (*fishwife*), HOUSEWIFE, **midwife** [probably from Old English *mid* 'with', hence '(the person) with the woman'], **old wive's tale**, and **woman** [Old English *wifman*, literally 'woman person'].

manage [16c. Italian *maneggiare* (verb), *maneggio* (noun), ultimately from Latin *manus* 'hand'] to train a horse; this training; (the exercises done in) the riding school (17c, largely replaced by French *manège*, from Italian *maneggio*), hence to discipline and control animals or people; to organize or control a business, resources, etc.; to do so despite difficulties (18c); to find a way to get or do something; to cope or get by (19c).

Descendants of Latin *manus* include **maintain** [via French from Latin *manu tenere* 'to hold in the hand'], **manacle**, MANDATE*, MANIFEST, **manipulate**, **manner**, originally the way something is done [via Old French *maniere* 'way of handling'], MANUAL, **manufacture** [from Latin *manu factum* '(something) made by hand', the original English sense], MANURE*, MANUSCRIPT, and **mastiff** [French *mastin* (influenced by Old French *mestiff* 'mongrel'), from, ultimately, Latin *mansuetus*, literally 'used to the hand'].

mandarin [16c. Portuguese *mandarin* via Malay and Hindi from Sanskrit *mantrin* 'counsellor', from *mantra* 'thought', from *man* 'to think'] A high-ranking official of the Chinese Empire, hence **1 Mandarin** the form of Chinese spoken by officials and educated people (18c); a dialect of this, an official language of China (1930s) **2** something thought to resemble a mandarin: **(a)** a figure in Chinese robes with a nodding head (18c) **(b) mandarin (duck)** an Asian duck with bright, variegated plumage (18c) **(c) mandarin (orange)** a pale orange or yellowish citrus fruit [18c, from the officials' yellow robes] **(d) mandarin coat/collar/jacket/sleeve** resembling a Chinese robe (*c*.1910) **3** an important person, especially a high-ranking civil servant (*c*.1900).

Sanskrit *mantra* was adopted for a sacred word, text, etc., repeated during meditation, hence an oft-repeated thought or expression.

mandate [15c. Latin *mandatum*, from *mandare* 'to commit, entrust', later 'to order', from *manus* 'hand' + *dare* 'to give'] An order or injunction, hence **1** an official or legal instruction (16c); to order or require by one (17c, rare before the 1960s); **mandatory** compulsory (19c) **2** a contract by which someone agrees to perform a service free of charge (17c) **3** authority given to a delegate or representative (18c); to give this (1950s) **4** authority given by the League of Nations to control and develop a territory (1919); to give this; the territory concerned.

Latin *mandatum* produced **Maundy** a Christian ceremony in which an eminent person distributes alms and, originally, washed poor people's feet (see the Bible, John 13:5, 14, and 34); *mandare* produced COMMEND*, **countermand**, **demand**, and **remand** literally to order back; *manus* is the ancestor of MANAGE*, and *dare* of DATA*.

manifest [ME. (Via French from) Latin *manifestus* 'obvious', literally 'held in the hand', from *manus* 'hand' + *festus* 'gripped'] (To make something) obvious, hence **1** something that does so (16c, largely replaced by **manifestation**), hence

(a) a public declaration (17c, largely replaced by Italian *manifesto*) (b) a list of a ship's cargo (18c), later of the freight and/or passengers carried by a train or aircraft, hence **manifest (train)** a fast freight train (1920s, US) **2** of a ghost or spirit: to appear (19c).

Latin *manus* is the ancestor of MANAGE*; *festus* is related to DEFEND* and OFFEND.

manikin [16c. Dutch *manneken*, from *man* 'man'] A small man, a dwarf or pygmy, hence **1** a small model of a man used by artists or to teach anatomy **2 (a)** (usually as **manakin**) applied to various small birds of tropical America (18c) **(b)** (as **mannikin**) applied to similar but unrelated birds of Asia, Africa, and Australasia (1930s).

Dutch *manneken* produced French *mannequin* an artist's manikin; a dummy for displaying clothes, hence a fashion model. Related to MAN.

manor [ME. Old French *maneir* 'dwelling', from Latin *manere*: see MANSION*] The principal house of an estate; a lord's mansion and surrounding lands; a unit of English territorial organization based on this (16c); a police district (1920s), hence your own 'patch' (1950s).

mansion [ME. Old French, from Latin *mansio*, from *manere* 'to remain'] The action of living or staying in a place (–18c), hence to live: **1** part of a large building, surviving chiefly in the biblical phrase 'in my Father's house are many mansions' (John 14:2), and as **mansions** in the names of apartment blocks (19c) **2** a lord's main residence (16c), hence **(a) mansion house** an official residence, now that of the Lord Mayor of London **(b)** a manor house (17c); any large, imposing house.

Old French *mansion* evolved into *maison* 'house', whence *maisonette* a small house, later a two-storey apartment. Latin *mansio* produced MENIAL and the surname **Maynell, Meynell** someone who lived in an isolated house; *manere* is the ancestor of **manse** a manor house (15–18c), later a church minister's house, of French *ménage* 'household' (whence *ménage à trois*, literally 'household of three', *menagerie*, and, probably, **messuage** a dwelling house with its outbuildings and land), and of **permanent, remain**, and **remnant**.

mantle [Old English *mentel*, from Latin *mantellum* 'cloak'] Applied to various kinds of outer garment, now only to a woman's sleeveless cloak or a robe of State, hence **1** authority or responsibility handed down (from the passing of Elija's mantle to Elisha: see the Bible, 2 Kings 2:13) **2** something that surrounds or covers (ME); to do so; to cover, enfold, or conceal. The variant **mantel** appears in the surname **Mantel(l)** a mantle-maker, in **manteltree** a beam above a fireplace (15c), later in **mantel(piece)** the manteltree and its supports (16c), an ornamental framework around a fireplace, and in **mantel(shelf)** the projecting top of the mantelpiece (18c).

Latin *mantellum* is the ancestor of **dismantle** [via French *desmanteler* 'to tear down fortifications', from Old French *manteler* 'to enclose or fortify'], of French *manteau* a kind of robe or cloak (surviving in *portmanteau*: see PORT[1]), of Italian *mantelletta* a sleeveless vestment worn by bishops and cardinals, and of Spanish *mantilla*.

manual [ME. Via French from Latin *manualis*, from *manus* 'hand' (ancestor of MANAGE*)] To do with the hand or hands, hence **1** done by hand; (describing) a device worked by hand (16c) or one which is not automatic or electronic (1920s) **2** a small book; a (small) book of instructions (cf. *handbook*) **3** involving physical rather than mental effort (*manual labour*, 15c).

manure [ME. Old French *manouvrer* 'to work by hand', from medieval Latin *manu-operare*, from Latin *manus* 'hand' + *operari* 'to work': see OPERATION*] To occupy, manage, or cultivate land (–17c); to enrich land with dung or compost; the dung etc. used (16c).

Old French *manouvrer* evolved into **manoeuvre**; Latin *manus* is the ancestor of MANAGE*.

manuscript [16c. Medieval Latin *manuscriptus*, from *manu* 'by hand' (from *manus* 'hand') + *scribere*, *script-* 'to write'] (Something) written by hand, hence **1** a piece of writing not (yet) printed or published (17c); an author's original text, shortened in theatrical slang to **script**, which came to mean the text of a film, play, etc. (1930s, earlier in **scriptwriter**) **2** a person's (style of) handwriting (19c).

Latin *manus* is the ancestor of MANAGE*, and *scribere* of SCRIPT*.

marathon [1896. Marathon in Greece, scene of a Greek victory over the Persians in 490 BC: later traditions tell of a messenger running the 35 miles from the battlefield to Athens with the news] A long-distance running race, originally one of 35 miles held at the first modern Olympic Games in Athens, hence **1** any long race or endurance test (*c*.1900); a lengthy and difficult task (*c*.1910) **2** -(a)thon, used for an event or competition of long duration (*talkathon, telethon*, 1930s, *US*).

march [ME. Old French *marchier* 'to trample', later 'to walk', from late Latin *marcus* 'hammer'] To walk in a military manner, hence (all 16c) **1** this action, hence **(a)** the distance covered (*a day's march*) **(b)** a procession; **(protest) march** a procession as a protest or demonstration (early 20c); *march* to take part in one **(c)** a long difficult walk (17c) **2** to (make someone) walk or go **3** a drumbeat, later a piece of music to march to.

Old French *marchier* produced **mush** in dogsledding; late Latin *marcus* produced Spanish *machete*. Perhaps related to MARK*.

marine [ME. French, from Latin *marinus*, from *mare* 'sea'] **1** the coast or sea-shore, also a harbour (–18c, cf. *marina* below) **2** to do with, living in, or obtained from, the sea (15c); adapted for use at sea (18c) **3** to do with shipping or the navy (16c); a country's ships collectively (*merchant marine*, 17c) **4** a sailor (16–17c); a soldier trained to fight at sea (17c).

Latin *marinus* produced Spanish and Italian *marina* adopted for a seaside promenade, later for an artificial harbour for small boats, **marinade**, and **mariner**. Descendants of Latin *mare* include **maritime** [Latin *maritimus* 'belonging to the sea'] and **ultramarine** a blue pigment, originally one made from imported lapis lazuli [via obsolete Italian *oltramarino* 'beyond the sea'].

mark [Old English *me(a)rc* (noun), *mearcian* (verb)] A limit or boundary, surviving in **near/beyond the mark**); to trace out a boundary, hence something that indicates a boundary (–17c), position (*bookmark, landmark*), course, or progress (*waymark*); to show or record any of these. Hence **1** a visible sign; to designate (as if by putting a mark on (partly replaced by **earmark**, 19c) **2** (to produce or indicate by) a written symbol: **(a)** (one showing) a point awarded to a student for their work (19c) **(b) mark up** to note corrections and instructions on a text (19c); **mark-up** the process or result of doing so (1970s); in computing: the process or system of tagging elements to show their function (1980s) **3** to notice or pay attention to (ME, hence **marked** noticeable, 18c); to single out an opposing player (19c) **4** a label, inscription, stamp, etc. (*hallmark, trademark,* ME), hence **(a)** a particular make or design of an article (17c); one showing a stage of development (*Mark 1 Cortina*): cf. *marque* (at REMARK) **(b)** to label an item with its price (19c); **mark up/ down** to mark with a higher/lower price, to raise/lower the price; **mark-up** the amount added to the purchase price to provide a profit (1920s) **5** (to make) a visible patch, spot, etc. (ME).

Old English *me(a)rc* appears as **Mar-** in place- and surnames, and in **Mercia**, one of the Anglo-Saxon kingdoms which had borders with others as well as with Wales. Relatives include DEMARCATION, **march** [Old French *marche* from medieval Latin *marca*, of Frankish origin] a country's boundary or frontier (surviving mainly in **the Marches** the English/Welsh borderland), **margin**, REMARK*, and perhaps MARCH* and **mark** the currency, originally a unit of weight for gold and silver.

market   [Old English *markett*, ultimately from Latin *mercatus*, from *mercari* 'to trade', from *merx* 'goods'] A gathering for buying and selling, hence **1 (a) market(place)** its site (ME) **(b)** a collection of stalls or shops dealing in a particular commodity (*antiques market*) **(c) supermarket** a large self-service store (1930s); **hypermarket** a very large one [1970s, translating French *hypermarché*] **2** to buy or sell in a market (ME); to bring or send to market; **marketing** the promotion and selling of a product (19c); *market* to do so (1920s) **3** (also *marketplace*) (an opportunity for) buying and selling (16c); trade (17c), especially as controlled by **market forces** the effects of supply and demand, hence trade in a particular commodity (*housing/stock market*, 17c); **in/on the market** for sale (18c); **in the market for** wishing to buy (19c) **4** (a group or region providing) demand for a product or service (17c).

Latin *mercatus* produced **mart** [obsolete variant of Dutch *markt*] market, trade, now a large shop or auction room; *mercari* produced **mercantile** [via Italian *mercante*], *Mercator* (see CHEAP), and French *marchand*, whence **merchandise**, **merchant**, and the surnames **Marchant** and **Marquand**. Latin *merx* is the ancestor of **mercer** a dealer in fine fabrics, also as a surname, and of MERCURY.

marmalade   [ME. Via French from Portuguese *marmelada* 'quince jam', from *marmelo* 'quince', from Latin *melimelum*, a kind of sweet apple, ultimately from Greek *meli* 'honey' + *mēlon* 'apple'] A preserve originally made from quinces, later from citrus fruit and containing the peel, now applied to other sweetish preserves containing pieces (*ginger/onion marmalade*). Hence **1 marmalade tree** found in Mexico and the southern US, with brown edible fruit called **marmalade plums** or **natural marmalade** (18c) **2 marmalade cat** a ginger tabby (1920s, its stripes resembling orange peel).

Latin *meli* produced the name **Melissa**, and is related to Latin *mel* (see TREACLE). Greek *mēlon* produced **melocoton** a kind of peach [via French, Italian, and Latin from Greek *mēlon kudōnion* (literally 'apple of Cydonia', now Khaniá, in Crete, whence also **quince**)], and **melon** [Old French, ultimately via Latin from Greek *mēlopepōn*, with *pepōn* 'gourd'].

maroon [17c. French *marron* from Spanish *cimarrón* 'wild, a runaway slave', from *cima* 'a peak'] **1** (someone descended from) a runaway slave in the mountains and forests of Suriname and the West Indies **2 marooned** lost in the wilds, hence *maroon* to put someone ashore and abandon them in an inaccessible place (18c); *marooned* unable to escape from a place or position (*c*.1900).

Maroon meaning 'brownish purple' is from French *marron* 'chestnut' [via Italian from Greek *maraon*]: the sense 'warning device', originally a small box filled with explosive, may come from its supposed resemblance to a large chestnut.

marrow [Old English *mearg, maerg*] The pith of a plant or pulp of a fruit (–18c); the white fatty substance found in bones (also **bone marrow**), hence **1** the innermost or most essential part (15c); the essence or goodness; the source of vitality and strength, hence any rich or nutritious food **2 (vegetable) marrow (a)** the avocado (18–19c, rare, perhaps from its richness) **(b)** a squash with white flesh (19c) **3 marrowfat** a tallow-like substance made by boiling down bone marrow (*N American*), later a pea with a similar texture when cooked.

marshal [ME. Old French *mareschal* or late Latin *mariscalcus*, both of Germanic origin and related to **mare** (Old English *mearh*), originally simply 'horse'] A person who tends horses, especially a farrier (–18c, first recorded as a surname); to do so (–16c), hence (from the horse's importance in war, transport, etc.) a senior official in a royal household, hence **1** a senior (military) officer, hence **marshal of the field** responsible for lodgings and supplies, shortened to **field marshal** (17c), now the most senior rank in the British army (18c) **2** an official in a law court, responsible for keeping order and the custody of prisoners; an official with certain police duties (16c); in the US: a senior police or fire officer (*c*.1900) **3** a person in charge of a ceremonial occasion or sporting event, hence to place people correctly at a banquet etc.; to gather and organize troops, competitors, etc.; to organize resources to meet a need (18c).

A similar progression is found in **constable** [via Old French from Latin *comes stabuli*, literally 'count of the stable'] the senior official of the royal household; the governor of a royal fortress or castle; a military officer; an officer of the peace; a policeman; also in *equerry* (at SQUIRE), in GROOM, and in **Master of the Horse** originally in charge of the stables, now a high-ranking official who attends the monarch on State occasions, and is implied in HENCHMAN.

martial [ME. (Via French from) Latin *martialis* 'of Mars', the Roman god of war] **1** to do with or suitable for war, hence **(a)** warlike, brave; like a warrior (16c) **(b)** serving as training for combat (*martial arts*) **(c)** military (16c), surviving in **martial law** and **court martial** (17c) **2** to do with the planet Mars (17c), largely replaced by **Martian**, which originally meant to do with war (–16c), later with the month of March (17c, *March* being ultimately from Latin *Martius mensis* 'month of Mars').

Latin *Mars* produced the names **Marcus** (whence **Mark**, **Marcelle**, **Marcia**, and **Marsha**) and **Martin**, whence **martin** a bird whose markings resemble a short cloak [after St Martin of Tours, who gave half his cloak to a beggar: see also CHAPEL].

mash [Old English *masc-, max-*] Grain mixed with hot water for brewing, hence **1** to make this (ME); to brew beer (16c) or tea (18c) **2** grain or bran steeped in hot water and fed warm to animals (16c); any soft, pulpy mass or mixture, hence **(a) (mish)mash** a confused mixture **(b)** to make a mash (17c) **(c)** mashed potatoes (*c.*1900).

The variant **mush** originally meant maize porridge (N American), later any soft mixture, hence **1** sentimentality, romantic nonsense **2** (also **moosh**) the mouth or face, whence, perhaps, (a form of address to) a bloke **3** among surfers: the foam of a breaking wave. **Mosh** to dance violently, especially in the **mosh pit** in front of the stage at a rock concert, may be another variant.

mask [16c. French *masque* via Italian *maschera* from medieval Latin *masca* 'mask, spectre, nightmare', perhaps from Arabic *maskhara* 'ghost, mask, buffoon', from *sakhira* 'to ridicule'] A covering hiding (part of) the face, hence **1** to cover (as if) with a mask or screen, hence **(a)** a disguise or pretence **(b)** to cover meat with a glaze or sauce (19c) **2** a ball at which the guests wear masks and disguises (largely replaced by **masked ball** or *masquerade*); (the text for) a dramatic musical entertainment by masked performers (outlived by French *masque*) **3** a face: **(a)** in classical drama: a hollow head worn by actors to represent a character and amplify the voice (18c) **(b)** a likeness of someone's face in clay etc. (*death mask*) **(c)** an animal's face or head, especially as a trophy (19c) **(d)** a grotesque representation of a human or animal face worn at carnivals etc. **(e)** a face pack (1930s).

Italian *maschera* produced **mascara** and **masquerade** a masked ball, hence (to wear) a disguise; to pretend to be. Medieval Latin *masca* is the ancestor of **mascot** [via Provençal *mascotto* 'lucky charm, sorcery', from *masco* 'witch'].

mason [ME. Old French *masson*, ultimately of Germanic origin] Someone who works or builds with stone, hence **freemason** a skilled mason, especially one of those who moved from project to project, recognizing each other through secret signs and passwords, hence **(Free)mason** a member of an international society for mutual assistance, which has elaborate secret rituals (17c).

The source of the surnames **Freemason** and **Machin**, **Mason**, or **Meacham**, and of **Mason City**, Iowa, settled by Freemasons in 1853. Related to **make**, French *maquillage* cosmetic or stage make-up [from *maquiller* 'to apply make-up', ultimately from early Dutch *maken* 'to make'], and to MATCH[1].

master [Old English *maegester* (later reinforced by Old French *maistre*), from Latin *magister* 'chief', probably from *magis* 'more'] A man with power, authority, learning, or skill; a boss, teacher, or leader (*ship's master, master of the house/ceremonies*), hence **1** a victor (ME), hence **(a)** to overcome, to dominate **(b) (grand) master** a champion chess or bridge player (19c) **2** a title or form of address for: **(a)** a learned or upper-class man (ME): the pronunciation faded to *mister* and the title became attached to an ordinary man (usually written **Mr**, once the standard abbreviation for *master*) **(b)** an (originally upper-class) boy too young to be called *mister* (16c) **3** chief, principal, most powerful (ME); **master key** that opens all the locks (16c); *master* something from which a number of copies are made (*c.*1900) **4** to become skilled or proficient in a subject (17c).

The female equivalent, **mistress** [Old French *maistresse*, feminine of *maistre*] was a respectful title or form of address for a woman (surviving in the Caribbean), but also means a man's long-term lover (the mistress of his heart as his wife is of his household): shortened to **Miss** and, in writing, to **Mrs**, whence the spellings **missis** and **missus**. **Messrs**, the plural of *Mr*, is short for French *Messieurs*, plural of *Monsieur* [from *mon* 'my' + *sieur* 'lord', from Latin SENIOR*]; the plural of *Mrs*, **Mesdames**, is the plural of French *madame* (see LORD*).

Latin *magister* produced Italian **maestro**, **magisterial**, **magistrate**, and French **mistral** [via Provençal from Latin *magistralis ventus* 'dominant wind']. Related to MAJOR*.

match¹ [Old English *gemaecca*: related to MASON*. Cf. MATE] **1** a spouse, partner, or lover (–17c); to join a couple or their families by marriage (ME); a marriage or marriage contract (16c) **2** your fellow or companion, an equal in rank, age, etc. (–16c), hence **(a)** (to be) an equal or rival (ME); to bring opponents together; a sporting contest (16c) **(b)** someone/something corresponding exactly with another (ME); to resemble closely; to harmonize or go with (16c); **match (up)** to be, provide, or find a match or equal for.

match² [ME. Old French *mesche*, *meiche*, from Latin *myxa* 'spout of a lamp', in medieval Latin 'lamp-wick', from Greek *muxa*] A candle- or lampwick (–17c); a piece of this used as a slow fuse (16c, hence **matchlock** a gun fired with one); a piece of cord, paper, etc. dipped in sulphur, lit with a tinderbox and used to light a lamp etc.; a thin stick of wood with the end coated with a combustible material for the same purpose (19c).

mate [ME. Early Low German, from *gemate* 'messmate': related to MEAT. Cf. MATCH¹] An ordinary man (–17c); your equal, friend, or fellow-worker (ME: cf. *inmate* at INN), hence **1** to join in marriage; a spouse (16c), hence **(a)** either of a pair; to bring animals together for breeding (17c); of animals: to copulate (19c) **(b)** someone you share with (*playmate, flatmate*) **2** (an officer of) the ranks below captain of a merchant ship (*first/second mate*, 15c); an assistant to a naval officer or, later, a skilled worker (*plumber's mate*).

material [ME. Old French *materiel* from Latin *materialis*, from *materia*: see MATTER*] (To do with) matter, hence **1** what something is or may be made from; to do with the physical rather than the spiritual or intellectual (17c), hence **materialism**, **materialize** (both 18c) **2** important, relevant (15c).

Modern French **matériel** was adopted meaning 'available resources', especially the equipment and supplies (as opposed to the personnel) of the armed forces, a business, etc.

matrix [ME. Latin *matrix* 'breeding female, womb, register', from *mater, matris* 'mother'] The womb; the place, medium, or environment in which something develops (16c): **1** a mould or die (16c); an impression or image from which another is produced (*c*.1900) **2** rock in which gems, crystals, or fossils are embedded (17c); any fine material containing larger particles (19c); in biology: the space between cells or structures **3** in maths: values or symbols in rows and columns, treated as a single entity (19c); a grid-like arrangement of elements or data (1940s); in computing: a rectangular array of points, combinations of which are used to form images (1950s), chiefly in **(dot) matrix printer**.

Latin *matrix* produced **madrigal** originally a short lyric poem or simple song [via Italian from Latin *matricalis* 'from the womb, natural, simple'], and late Latin *matricula* [literally 'small list'] a register of members of an institution, whence **matriculate** to be enrolled as a member of a college or university; **matriculation** a qualifying exam; a set of exams for school leavers; *matriculate* to pass them. Latin *mater* is the ancestor of MATTER*.

matter [ME. Via Old French from Latin *materia* 'the wood at a tree's core' (as the source of growth), hence 'substance, subject', from *mater* 'mother'] What something is made of, hence **1** a physical substance; something having mass and occupying space **2** the 'stuff' of thought, speech, writing, dispute, or litigation; a business, affair, or case; a reason or cause (*what's the matter?*), hence to be important (16c) **3** corrupt matter, pus (15c).

Latin *materia* produced **Madeira** [Portuguese 'wood, timber'] a name given to a carpenter, a blockhead, and to the island (which produced timber, a sweet wine, and a kind of cake originally eaten with it), and MATERIAL*; *mater* is the ancestor of **maternal**, **maternity**, **matriarch**, **matrimony** [from *matrimonius* 'state of motherhood' (from the association of parenthood with marriage)], MATRIX*, and **matron** a married woman, regarded as mature, sensible, and dignified, hence a woman with authority.

mature [ME. Latin *maturus* 'timely, early', also 'ripe'] Fully grown or developed, hence **1** of wine, cheese etc.: having the flavour fully developed; of fruit: ripe; to ripen **2** involving serious thought **3** physically, mentally, or emotionally adult (16c); experienced; no longer young **4** to develop or perfect (17c); to develop into; to be perfected **5** of a bill etc.: (to become) due for payment (19c).

Latin *maturus* produced **immature** originally meaning 'too early', referring to death, and **premature**. Related to **Matuta**, the name of the Roman goddess of the dawn, whence French *matin* 'morning', whence **matinée** an early performance and **matins** morning service or prayer.

maudlin [16c. Old French *Madeleine* from ecclesiastical Latin *(Maria) Magdalena* 'Mary Magdalene' (literally 'Mary of Magdala', a town in Galilee), a follower of Christ (see the Bible, Luke 8:2), usually identified with the unnamed woman in Luke 7:37 and portrayed as a penitent sinner. *Maudlin*, the original pronunciation of *Magdalene*, survives also in Magdalen College, Oxford, and Magdalene College, Cambridge] **1** *Magdalen(e)* a reformed prostitute **2** **maudlin (drunk)** drunkenly tearful or sentimental (because Mary Magdalene was usually portrayed weeping); full of self-pity, mawkishly sentimental.

The name *Madel(e)ine* produced **Lena**, the German form **Marlene**, and the surname **Maudling**.

maul [ME. French *mail* from Latin *malleus* 'a hammer'] **1** a club; to strike or knock down with one (–17c), hence **(a)** to criticize someone severely (16c) **(b)** to beat (17c); to injure or damage; of an animal: to mangle its prey; to handle roughly and carelessly (18c) **2** a large hammer (15c), now specifically one for splitting logs or driving in stakes or wedges.

Latin *malleus* was adopted for one of the small bones in the ear (from its shape); it produced **malleable** and **mallet**, and is one parent of **pall-mall** a game in which the players tried to drive a ball through a ring with a mallet [via French from Italian *palla* 'ball' (see BALLOT*) + *maglio* 'mallet']. Charles I played it in an alley in London, now a street called *Pall Mall*; Charles II made a new alley in St James's Park, which eventually became **The Mall**, a fashionable, tree-lined walk, hence **mall** a pall-mall alley or a sheltered promenade, now a pedestrianized or indoor shopping centre (*N American*).

mawkish [17c. From **mawk** a maggot (ME, surviving in dialect), from Old Norse *mathkr*] Having a sickening or, later, insipid taste, hence feebly, falsely, or sickeningly sentimental (18c).

Related to **maddock** a worm or maggot (ME–17c), of which **maggot** is probably an alteration.

maxim [ME. Medieval Latin *maxima propositio*, literally 'greatest proposition'] A self-evident proposition (–17c); a pithy saying with some truth in it (16c); a (pithily expressed) general rule, principle, or truth.

maximum [17c. Neuter of Latin *maximus* 'greatest', from *magnus* 'great'] The opposite of **minimum** [neuter of Latin *minimus* 'smallest', from *parva* 'small']. The largest possible; (of) the greatest value; the highest amount or level; to the greatest extent. Sometimes shortened to **max** (19c, *US*), whence **to the max** to the limit, totally, and **maxed (out)** stretched to the limit (both 1980s).

Maximum produced **maximal** (**minimal** is earlier and more common), whence **maximalist** someone who rejects compromise, originally a member of an extremist faction of the Russian Socialist-Revolutionary party, later regarded as a translation of Russian *bol'shevik* [literally 'one of the majority', from *bol'she* 'more', from *bol'shoi* 'big'], whence **Bolshevik** a member of the largest faction of the Russian Social-Democratic party, also regarded as extreme, whence **bolshie** left-wing, argumentative, uncooperative. **Minimalist** was applied to more moderate reformers, specifically a **Menshevik** [Russian *men'shevik* 'member of the minority' (of the Social-Democratic party), from *men'she* 'less', from *malyi* 'little'], and went on to mean a lover or producer of **minimal art** (using simple, uncluttered forms and structures) or **music** (using repetition of musical patterns). Latin *maximus* produced MAXIM, **maximize**, and the name **Maximillian**, shortened to **Max**, whence the feminine **Maxina**. *Minimus* produced *minim* (see LARGE sense 3b) and **minimize**. *Magnus* is the ancestor of MAGNIFY*.

mayhem [15c. Old French *mahaing* 'mutilating injury', from *mahaignier*, of unknown origin] The crime of disabling someone; to maim (16c), hence malicious or violent destruction (19c); severe disruption, chaos.

Old French *mahaignier* is the ancestor of **maim** and probably of **mangle** to mutilate or destroy.

meagre [ME. Anglo-Norman French *megre*, Old French *maigre*, from Latin *macer*] **1** thin, lean, emaciated, surviving in the surnames **Meag(h)er**, **Meagers 2** poor in quality or quantity, inadequate, scanty (16c): cf. SLIM*.

Old French *maigre* was adopted in similar senses, and by the Roman Catholic church for (a dish suitable for) a day when meat was forbidden. Latin *macer* is the ancestor of **emaciate**.

meal¹ [Old English *mǣl*] **1** a measure (–15c, surviving in Middle English **piece-meal**) **2** a fixed time; one for eating food (ME); the food served.

meal² [Old English *melu*] The edible part of a grain or pulse ground to a powder, hence applied to powder from other ground substances (*bonemeal*, 16c), or to the powdery substance found on some plants.

Old English *melu* may be the ancestor of **mellow**, the underlying sense being 'soft and rich, like meal'. Related to Dutch **maelstrom** [from *maalen* 'to grind' + *stroom* 'stream'] originally the name of a huge whirlpool off the Norwegian coast, MILL*, **mould** loose soil, whence, perhaps, **moulder** to crumble or decay, and to **mull** (to grind to) a fine powder, hence **mull over** to 'grind' in your mind.

mean¹ [Old English *maenan*: related to MIND] To intend, to aim to do, hence **1** to (intend to) indicate, refer to, or signify; to be a sign or indication of (*a red sunrise means rain*); to be significant or important (*she means everything to me*, 19c) **2** to intend, design, or destine for a particular purpose or fate (ME); to cause or necessitate (*her new job will mean moving house*, 19c) **3** to have good/bad intentions (*he means well*, ME) **4** to be supposed or said to be (*it's meant to be good for you*, 19c).

mean² [ME. Old French *meien*, *moien*, from Latin *medianus*, from *medius* 'middle' (ancestor of MEDIUM*)] **1** coming between two points in **(a)** time, surviving in **meantime**, **meanwhile (b)** a sequence, hence a figure or value midway between the highest and lowest; this or some other point considered as a standard (*mean sea level*) **(c)** space (–17c), hence something in between; **means** a way of achieving something; the necessary (financial) resources (16c); money, wealth **2** of middling kind or quality; such a condition or course of action; **golden/happy mean** avoidance of excess (16c).

measles [ME. Strictly speaking the plural of *measle*, probably from early Low German *masele* or early Dutch *masel* 'a pustule or spot', but usually regarded as singular. Influenced by Middle English **mesel** leprous, a leper (from Latin *miser*: see MISERI-CORD*)] An infectious disease that produces catarrh, fever, and a rash, later applied to diseases of cattle, pigs, and trees. Hence **1 measly** infected with measles (16c); blotchy, spotty (18c); inferior, inadequate, disappointingly small (19c) **2 German** (formerly also **French**) **measles** a similar but usually less serious disease (19c: cf. *germane* at GERM).

measure [ME. Via French from Latin *mensura*, from *metiri*, *mens-* 'to measure'] **1** moderation, temperance, hence **(a)** proportion, symmetry; poetical or musical rhythm; a (stately) dance (*tread a measure*) **(b) measured** deliberate, restrained (19c) **2 measure (out)** to hand out in fixed amounts, hence **(a)** *measure* a unit or amount; **for good measure** as something extra **(b)** to give a punishment or reward (the only surviving sense of **mete** [Old English *metan*], which had most senses of *measure*) **3** (to determine) size or quantity (surviving in *made to measure*), hence **(a)** a device for doing so **(b)** a standard size or quantity **(c)** to be a certain size (*measures 24 x 12 cm*, 17c) **4** to assess character etc., especially by comparison with a standard, hence **measure up (to)** to be comparable, to be equal to (18c) **5 measures** rock strata, especially containing some mineral (*coal measures*, 17c) **6** [from French] a course of action (*take measures*, 17c); a bill to be enacted; a law.

Latin *metiri* produced **commensurate** [late Latin *commensuratus*, literally 'measured with or against'], **dimension** [Latin *dimetiri* 'to measure out'], and **immense**

[Latin *immensus* 'immeasurable']. *Mete* produced **meter** a person, later a device, that measures, hence to measure with a device; to measure out or regulate a flow (for -**meter** in *barometer* etc. see METRE), and is related to MEET[2].

meat [Old English *mete*] Food (as opposed to drink), hence **1** a meal **2** a kind of food (surviving in *sweetmeat* at SWEET): **(a)** animal flesh as food (ME); a person's flesh (19c); a person regarded solely as flesh; **meat market** a meeting place for those seeking sex **(b)** the edible part of a fruit, nut, egg, etc. (ME) **(c)** the most important or substantial part of something (19c) **(d) meaty** fleshy, muscular (18c); substantial (19c).

Related to MATE and probably to **mast** beech nuts, acorns, etc. as pig food.

mechanic/mechanical [ME. Greek *mēkhanikē*, from *mēkhanē*, from *mēkhos* 'contrivance'] To do with manual labour or machines, hence **1** (a person) having a manual occupation (16c), now (as *mechanic*) a skilled manual worker who works with or repairs machinery (17c) **2 mechanics (a)** the science of machines (17c); the study of energy and forces **(b)** the details of how something works **3** *mechanical* to do with or caused by physical forces or conditions (17c); explaining phenomena in terms of physical properties only **4** *mechanical* routine, without thought (17c).

Mechanic produced **mechanize**. Greek *mēkhanē* is the ancestor of MACHINE and **mechanism**.

meddle [ME. Old French *medler*, variant of *mesler*, ultimately from Latin *miscere*, *mixt-* 'to mix'] To mix, mingle, or combine (–17c), hence **1** to fight with (–17c) **2** to get mixed up or involved in; to interfere.

Old French *medler* produced **medley** conflict, (hand to hand) fighting, also a mixture. Old French *mesler* appears in *pesle mesle* 'in a confused mixture or disorderly rush', whence **pell-mell**, and produced modern French *mélange* and *mêlée*. Latin *miscere* is the ancestor of MIXED*.

mediate [ME. Latin *mediare*, from Latin *medius* 'middle'] **1** situated or coming between, intervening, hence **2 mediator** someone who acts as a go-between (originally Christ, as interceding between God and man); **mediation** intervention by a third party to bring about an agreement or reconciliation; *mediate* to do so (16c) **3** of a relationship (originally feudal): involving or depending on a third party.

In sense 1 *mediate* partly co-exists with **intermediate** [from medieval Latin *intermediatus*, ultimately from *inter* 'between' + *medius*], and *mediator* with **intermediary**. Latin *mediare* produced **immediate** [via *immediatus* 'direct, with nothing in between']; *medius* is the ancestor of MEDIUM*.

medium [16c. Latin, neuter of *medius* 'middle'] (Something in) a state or condition halfway between two extremes, hence **1** a substance through which something is conveyed or transmitted, hence **(a)** an intermediary (19c), now usually between the living and spirits of the dead **(b)** a means of communication, now especially in **the (mass) media** newspapers, radio, and television (1920s) **2** middling, midway between extremes (18c): cf. MEAN[2] **3 happy medium** a satisfactory compromise (18c) **4** a substance in which an organism lives (19c); your environment or social situation: cf. *milieu* below.

Descendants of Latin *medius* include MEAN², **medial, median**, MEDIATE*, **medi-eval** [Latin *medium aevum* 'Middle Age'], **mediocre** [(via French from) Latin *medi-ocris* 'of middle height', from *ocris* 'rugged mountain'], **Mediterranean** [Latin *mediterraneus (mare)* 'inland (sea)', from *terra* 'land' (whence TERRACE*)], MERIDIAN*, French **mezzanine** [from Italian *mezzanino*, literally 'small one in the middle'], Italian *mezzo* 'middle, half' (whence **intermezzo, mezzo-soprano**, etc.), French **milieu** (social) surroundings [literally 'middle place', from *lieu* 'place': see LOCAL*], **moiety** [via French *moité* 'half'], and probably **mitten** [French *mitaine*, probably from a word meaning 'glove cut off at the middle'], shortened to **mitt**.

meet¹ [Old English *mētan*: related to MOOT*] To come across, to find (now as **meet with**), hence to come together by accident or design (ME, but implied in **meeting** [Old English *gemēting*] a conference or gathering). Hence **1** to come to conform with someone's expectations or opinions (17c); to satisfy a demand or need (19c) **2 meet your eye/gaze/sight** or **ear** to come into sight or earshot (17c) **3** a gathering, originally of hunters and hounds (19c).

meet² [Old English *gemǣtan*: related to *mete* (at MEASURE)] Of the right size, made to fit (–19c); fitting, suitable (ME), hence **helpmeet** [17c, from *help meet* in the biblical phrase 'a help meet for him' (Genesis 2:18, 20), taken to be one word].

melody [ME. Via French and Latin from Greek *melōidia* 'singing, choral music', from *melos* 'song' + *(a)ōidē* 'song, singing': see ODE*] Sweet music, tunefulness; a tune (17c), hence the main tune in a harmony (19c).

Greek *melos* produced *melodrama* (at DRAMA) and **melodium** a small reed organ, altered to **melodeon**, which came to mean a kind of accordion and also a music hall (US, influenced by **odeon**, an alteration of **odeum** a building for musical performances, also from Greek *(a)ōidē*), hence **nickelodeon** a music hall or cinema charging a nickel (5 cents) to get in; an arcade of slot machines that take nickels; a juke box.

melt [Old English *m(i)eltan*] **1** to make or become liquid through heat, hence **(a)** to suffer from heat (17c); to (make someone) sweat excessively **(b) meltdown** the process of melting (1930s); the melting of part of a nuclear reactor (1960s), hence a disaster (1980s); **in meltdown** heading for one **(c)** a toasted open sandwich with melted cheese (1970s) **2** to digest or be digested (OE only); to dissolve. Hence **3** to be overcome by emotion (–17c); to soften or become softened by pity, love, etc. (ME) **4 melt (away)** to waste away, to dwindle; to vanish imperceptibly (17c) **5** to be absorbed into (ME); to blend into a mass (18c); to pass imperceptibly from one state to another.

Probably the source of **meld** to merge [*US*: with *weld* (see WELL²)], and related to **enamel, malt, mild, mulch**, Yiddish *schmaltz* melted chicken fat, later banal sentimentality, **smelt** a small fish, and **smelt** to melt ore to extract the metal [Low German or Dutch *smelten*].

member [ME. Via French from Latin *membrum* 'limb'] A part of the body, especially a limb or the penis, hence a part of a complex whole; any of the individuals, countries, etc. making up a community, club, or assembly.

Latin *membrum* produced **dismember** originally to remove a limb from, and **membrane** [via Latin *membrana* 'skin covering part of the body'].

memoir [16c. French *mémoire*: see MEMORY*] A note or (official) record; a biography or history written from personal knowledge (17c, hence **memoirs** an account of your experiences and events in which you took part); an essay on a scholarly subject (17c); **memoirs** the proceedings of a learned society.

memorandum [ME. Latin, literally 'thing to be remembered', from *memorare* 'to remember', from *memor*: see MEMORY*] To be remembered (placed at the beginning of a reminder or record), hence such a record etc. (15c); a document containing the terms of a contract etc. (16c); a record of a financial transaction (17c); an informal diplomatic message (cf. MEMORIAL); an informal business letter (19c, shortened to **memo**).

Latin *memorare* produced **commemorate** and **memorable** worth remembering, easy to remember, whence **memorables** souvenirs, replaced by Latin *memorabilia*.

memorial [ME. Latin *memorialis*, from *memoria*: see MEMORY*] Preserving the memory of someone/something; something that does so, hence a record or chronicle; a note or memorandum (16–19c); a diplomatic memorandum; a statement of facts accompanying a petition etc.

Latin *memorialis* produced **immemorial** [via medieval Latin *immemorialis*, literally 'not in the memory'], whence **time immemorial** the distant past.

memory [ME. Old French *memorie* (modern *mémoire*), from Latin *memoria*, from *memor* 'mindful, remembering'] **1** the capacity to retain knowledge or revive knowledge of the past, hence **(a)** someone's ability to remember (*a good/long/selective memory*) **(b)** the ability of some materials to return to their former state or shape after being altered (19c) **(c)** a computer's data storage capacity (1940s) **2** remembrance, commemoration (*in memory of*) **3** recollection: **(a)** what is remembered about someone after their death **(b)** someone's recollections of the past (*childhood memories*, 19c).

French *mémoire* produced MEMOIR. Latin *memor* is the ancestor of MEMORANDUM*, MEMORIAL*, and REMEMBER*.

menace [ME. Latin *minacia*, from *minax* 'threatening', from *minari* 'to jut out, to threaten', from *minae* 'projecting points, threats'] (To make) a threatening speech or action, hence a threat; (to be) a possible source of harm; a nuisance or pest (*Dennis the Menace*, 1930s).

Latin *minari* produced late Latin *minare* 'to drive on with threats', whence AMENABLE, DEMEANOUR*, and PROMENADE. Related to EMINENCE*.

menial [ME. Anglo-Norman French *meignial*, from *meignee* 'household', ultimately from Latin *mansio*: see MANSION*] To do with a household; of a servant: household, domestic, hence **1** a (man)servant kept mainly for show; a proud or arrogant one **2** a household drudge (17c); of work: suitable for one.

mercenary [ME. Latin *mercenarius*, from *merces* 'wages, reward'] Someone who works purely for money or material reward, hence **1** (describing) a professional soldier serving a foreign power (16c) **2** motivated solely by money (16c).

Latin *merces* developed the sense 'thanks, favour, grace', in Christian Latin 'pity', whence **mercy** [ME, via French *merci*].

mercury [ME. Latin *Mercurius*, the Roman god of commerce (associated with Hermes, the Greek god of commerce, science, and eloquence, and the gods' messenger), from *merx*, *merc-* 'goods, merchandise' (ancestor of MARKET*). Senses 1 and 2 follow Roman usage] **1** the planet nearest the sun **2** the metal, also known as quicksilver **3** a messenger or go-between (16c); a newspaper (17c, now only in titles) **4 mercurial** born under the influence of the planet (16c); eloquent, quick-witted and shrewd (from the influence of the god and planet); lively and volatile (from the metal).

mere¹ [Old English] The sea (–15, surviving in Middle English **mermaid**, whence 17c **merman**); later a lake. Appearing in names as **Mar-**, and in the names **Delamere, Mear(es)** or **Meers**, and **Merton**.

Related to **marram, marsh** a bog, also a surname of someone who lived by one, German *Meerschaum* [literally 'sea-foam' (from its foamy appearance), used to translate Persian *kef-i-daryā*], and **morass**.

mere² [ME. Via Anglo-Norman French from Latin *merus*] Pure, unmixed, diluted (–19c), hence **1** by itself, sole (*the mere thought infuriated her*, 15c) **2** just what is specified and no more (*a mere child*, 16c).

merge [17c. (Anglo-Norman French *merger* from) Latin *mergere*, *mers-* 'to dip or plunge'] To immerse, especially yourself (–19c); in Law: to incorporate a title, estate, company, etc. in a larger one (18c); to be incorporated, hence to be absorbed, to combine or blend.

Anglo-Norman French *merger* was adopted for such an incorporation. Latin *mergere* is the ancestor of **emerge** [via *emergere* 'to rise up or out', whence **emergency**, literally 'something that arises'], **immerse**, **merganser** a kind of diving duck [with Latin *anser* 'goose'], **submerge** and **submerse**.

meridian [ME. (Via French from) Latin *meridianus*, from *meridies* 'midday', from *medius* (see MEDIUM*) + *dies* 'day'] Midday, noon, hence **1** the point at which the sun or a star reaches its highest altitude, hence the peak of success, development etc. (16c) **2** the great circle of the celestial sphere than runs through both poles and the point above the observer; an imaginary line through the North and South poles on earth (which the sun crosses at noon).

Latin *meridiem* [neuter of *meridies*] appears in **a.m.**, **p.m.**, short for *ante/post meridiem*. *Dies* is the ancestor of JOURNEY*.

merit [ME. Via French from Latin *meritum* 'price, value', from *mereri* 'to deserve, to earn (money)'] Something deserved; the fact of deserving it, hence **1** what makes it deserved (15c); **merits** bad or, now usually, good qualities (16c); the rights and wrongs of a case etc. **2** to deserve (16c).

Latin *mereri* produced *emereri* 'to earn by service' (whence *emeritus* describing a soldier who has earned his discharge, **emeritus professor** who retains the title in retirement), **meretrix** a prostitute (rare), whence **meretricious** to do with or suitable for one, superficially attractive or plausible, and **turmeric** [from Old French *terre-mérite* 'saffron' (similar in colour), from Latin *terra merita*, literally 'worthy earth' (see TERRACE), both saffron and turmeric being used in cooking and formerly in medicine].

merry [Old English *myrige*] Pleasant, agreeable, delightful (*merry month of May*), hence **1** cheerful; jolly; full of fun, slightly drunk (16c) **2** funny, amusing (15c) **3** characterized by festivity, fun, or rejoicing (*merry Christmas*, 16c).

Related to **mirth** (a cause of) happiness or religious joy (–17c); rejoicing, merriment; hilarity.

mesh [ME. Early Dutch *maesche*] A space between the strands of a net, grid, etc., hence **1** a net, network, or grid (16c); a snare; to catch in one (largely replaced by 17c **enmesh**); to become entangled; of gears etc.: to (cause to) engage (19c), hence **(a) in/out of mesh** engaged/not engaged; **synchromesh** a mechanism that synchronizes gear wheels before they engage (1920s) **(b) mesh with/together** to fit in or combine (1940s) **2** a measure of the number of openings in a screen or grid (1930s). Cf. NET[1].

mess [ME. Old French *mes* from Late Latin *missus* 'course of a meal', from *mittere* 'to send': the underlying sense is something sent to the table] A portion of food; a course of a meal; a dish, hence **1** a portion or kind of (semi-)liquid food (cf. *slops* at SLIP[1]); an unappetizing one (19c); an unpleasant sloppy mixture, hence **(a)** confusion, a muddle; a dirty or untidy state, thing, or person (19c); **mess (up)** to make something dirty or untidy (19c); to ruin **(b) mess around/about** to busy yourself in a confused or desultory way; to treat someone inconsistently or unfairly; **mess with** to interfere or get involved with (*c*.1900, *US*); to trouble or annoy **(c) (to make a) mess** to defecate; *mess* excrement (*c*.1900) **2** a group of guests at a banquet served from the same dishes (15c); a group who regularly dine together; a division of a regiment, ship's company, etc. who share meals and sometimes accommodation (16c); the place where they eat and socialize; to share food, accommodation, and facilities (18c, cf. *muck in* below) **3** a quantity of food (16c); a (large) quantity or number (19c, N American).

Mess spawned the US variant **muss** an untidy state, **muss (up)** to make untidy, to crumple or ruffle. **Muck** mud, filth, dung [probably of Scandinavian origin and related to Old Norse *mjúkr* 'soft', whence **meek**] developed similar verbal senses, probably as a 'stronger' version of *mess*, as well as **muck in** to share food or accommodation (*army slang*), later also work, whence, probably, **mucker** a mate. Latin *mittere* is the ancestor of MISSION*.

message [ME. French, ultimately from Latin *mittere* 'to send' (ancestor of MISSION*)] A communication sent to or left for someone, hence **1** the carrying of one; a mission or errand, hence **messages** items bought on an errand, shopping (*c*.1900, Scots) **2** a communication from God via a prophet (16c); the import of this; a moral or meaning (19c) **3** to send a message (16c); **messaging** the sending and processing of electronic mail (1980s).

metal [ME. (Via French from) Latin *metallum*, from Greek *metallon* 'mine'] A kind of element that is typically hard and shiny, a good conductor of heat and electricity, and can be melted and formed into shapes; originally only gold, silver, copper, iron, lead or tin, later including alloys and other substances with similar properties. Hence **1** (something) made of metal, e.g. **(a)** a gun barrel (17c), a warship's guns (18c); **heavy metal** large guns or shot (19c); loud rock music with a powerful beat (1970s) **(b) metals** the rails of a rail- or tramway (19c) **2** material, matter, substance (16c), hence **(a)** what someone is made of, character, spirit (surviving as the variant **mettle**) **(b)** broken stone used in road-making (18c); to make or mend a road with it (19c).

Latin *metallum* produced **medal** [via French from Italian *medaglia*, whence also **medallion**].

meteor   [15c. Via modern Latin from Greek *meteōron*, literally 'something raised', from *meta* 'with, besides, beyond' + *aeirein* 'to raise'] Any atmospheric phenomenon (surviving in technical use and in 17c **meteorology** the study of the atmosphere, especially with regard to the weather); a mass of rock from space that burns up in the atmosphere (16c), hence **1 meteorite** a piece of a meteor that reaches a planet's surface (19c) **2 meteoric** to do with meteors (19c); shining brightly and briefly like one; sudden and rapid.

Greek *meta* is found in words such as *metabolism* (at BALLISTIC) and *metaphysics* (at PHYSIC). Greek *aeirein* is probably the source of ARTERY*.

meticulous   [16c. Latin *meticulosus* from *metus* 'fear'] Fearful, timid (–17c), re-appearing meaning over-anxious about details (19c); careful, precise.

metre   [Old English *meter* and, later, French *mètre*, both ultimately from Greek *metron* 'a measure'] (A kind of) rhythmic pattern in poetry; a pattern of beats in music (19c).

French *mètre* produced **metre** the basic SI unit of length. Greek *metron* produced **-meter** (*diameter, perimeter*), in the names of measuring instruments (*barometer, thermometer*) and poetic metres (*pentameter*), **metronome** [with Greek *nomos* 'law, rule'], and **-metry** (**geometry** (literally 'earth-measuring)', and SYMMETRY). Related to MEASURE*.

metropolis   [16c. Late Latin *metropolitanus*, ultimately from Greek *mētropolis* 'parent state', from *mētēr* 'mother' + *polis* 'city' (ancestor of POLICE*)] **1** the motherland of a colony (16c) **2** a capital city; any large city, hence **metropolitan** to do with one: **(a)** urbane, sophisticated; (to do with) such a person (18c), hence **metrosexual** (describing) a (heterosexual) man concerned with self-image, aesthetics, and good living (1994) **(b)** to do with an underground railway system in a city, originally in London (19c, hence **Metroland** the suburbs it serves), **metro** such a system (1920s, shortening of *metropolitan* or adopted from French *métro*, short for *Chemin de Fer Métropolitain* 'metropolitan railway') **3** the seat or see of a *metropolitan*, a high-ranking clergyman who oversees the bishops of a province, in the early church based in its chief city.

mew   [ME. French *mue*, from *muer* 'to moult', from Latin *mutare* 'to change'] A cage for a (moulting) hawk, hence **1 mew (up)** to confine, enclose, or conceal **2 Royal Mews** the royal stables, originally on the site of the royal hawk mews at Charing Cross, hence **mews** stabling facing a yard or alley; this converted into dwellings (19c); (one of) a row of town houses built in this style (now often in street names).

Descendants of Latin *mutare* include COMMUTE, **moult**, **mutation** (whence **mutate**), PERMUTE, and **transmute**. Related to **mutual** [Latin *mutuus* 'done in exchange'].

microcosm   [ME. Via French or Latin from Greek *mikros kosmos* 'little world'] Man as an epitome of the universe, later a structure or system regarded as a miniature representation of a larger one (16c). Hence **macrocosm** [Greek *makros kosmos* 'great world'] the universe, nature as a whole (17c); a complex structure or system, especially one epitomized by a microcosm (19c).

Greek *mikros* produced **micro-** (*microscope, microlight*); *makros* produced **macro-** (*macrobiotic, macro-economics*); *kosmos* is the ancestor of COSMOS*.

mill [Old English *mylen*, ultimately from late Latin *molinum*, from Latin *mola* 'grindstone, mill, meal' from *molere* 'to grind'] A building with machinery, originally for grinding corn (*windmill/sawmill/steel mill*), hence **1** (to make or process with) such a machine (16c), specifically to cut grooves in a coin edge (18c) **2** a grinder (*handmill/pepper mill*, 16c) **3** a rotary device (*treadmill*, 17c); a rotary motion (19c), hence **mill (about/around)** to move round aimlessly.

Mill appears in some instances of the surnames **Mellis** and **Mullen**, and as **Mil(l)-** in many place names. Latin *mola* produced **immolation** sacrifice [Latin *immolare* 'to sprinkle with meal', as was done to sacrificial victims] and **molar** a grinding tooth; *molere* is the ancestor of **emolument** [Latin *emolumentum*, probably a payment for grinding corn, from *emolere* 'to grind up'] and **ormulu** [via French *or moulu*, literally 'powdered gold']. Related to MEAL²*.

million [ME. French, from obsolete Italian *millione*, literally 'great thousand', from Latin *mille* 'thousand'] A thousand thousand; a million pounds or dollars (hence **millionaire**, 19c); **million(s)** a very large number or amount.

Million produced **zillion(s)** a huge, indefinite number (*US*). French *million* produced **billion** [substituting **bi-** 'twice, doubly, having two', from Latin] originally a million million, and **trillion** [substituting **tri-** 'thrice, trebly, having three', from Latin], originally a million million million. Large numbers were formerly written in groups of six figures, one billion being written 1 000000 000000, but in 17c France it became customary to use groups of three. The idea of a million squared was lost and a billion came to be written 1,000,000,000 (a thousand million); *trillion* then shrank to a million million. These became the standard values in the US, and were then adopted into British English to avoid confusion, although the original senses survive informally.

Latin *mille* is the ancestor of **mil** one thousandth of an inch, **mile** (at STADIUM), **millenary**, **millennium**, and **milli-** a thousandth (*millimetre*); a thousand, lots (*millipede*).

mime [17c. Latin *mimus* from Greek *mimos* 'imitator'] **1** a mimic or jester; to mimic (18c) **2** in ancient Greece and Rome: a farce with dialogue and music, and featuring ludicrous mimicry; a performer in one (18c) **3** to express action, character, or emotions without words; the art of doing so (1930s); a performance or artist using mime **4** to mouth words or pretend to play an instrument to pre-recorded music (1960s).

Latin *mimus* produced **mimosa**, the leaves of which fold when touched, appearing to flinch, and **mimulus** [literally 'little mime'], which has mask-like flowers (some mimes in classical farces wore masks). Greek *mimos* is the ancestor of **mimeograph**, **mimesis**, **mimic**, and PANTOMIME.

mince [ME. Old French *mincier*, ultimately from Latin *minutia*, literally 'smallness', from *minutus*: see MINUTE²*] **1** to chop or grind meat, hence **minced meat**, shortened to **mincemeat** (17c, first recorded in *make mincemeat of*). Both *minced meat* and *mincemeat* came to mean a mixture of dried fruit, suet, and, originally, chopped meat (earliest in **mince(d) pie**, 17c); *mincemeat* now refers only to this mixture, ground meat being called *mince* (19c) **2** to lessen or subtract from (15–19c); to minimize or disparage (16c); to make little or light of (*mince matters*); **mince your words** to speak euphemistically or tactfully **3** to walk or speak in an affectedly dainty way (16c).

Latin *minutiae*, plural of *minutia*, was adopted in the sense 'precise details'.

mind [Old English *gemynd*: related to MEAN[1]] Mental faculties: **1** memory (*bear in/ come to mind*; the ability to remember (–15c); to make someone remember (ME, largely replaced by 17c **remind**); to take care to remember; to make certain **2** intelligence, intellect (earliest in **mindless**); a person considered in terms of their intelligence or way of thinking (*a great mind, the criminal mind*, 16c) **3** a healthy condition of your mental faculties (*in his right mind*, ME). Hence **4** thoughts, intention, or desire (*have a good mind to, be in two minds*, ME); your thoughts (*keep your mind on your work, speak your mind*); your way of thinking or feeling; the state of your thoughts or feelings (*put his mind at ease*, 16c) **5** to pay attention to (*mind your manners*, 16c), hence **(a)** to heed and obey (*mind what I tell you*) **(b)** to look after temporarily (17c); to guard and protect, hence **minder** a (criminal's) body-guard (1920s); a public figure's assistant or adviser (1980s) **(c)** to watch out for (*mind the step!*, 17c); **mind (out)** look out, be careful **(d)** to object to, to be annoyed or troubled by (17c) **(e)** attention, heed (*pay no mind*, c.1910, US).

mine [ME. French *miner*, perhaps of Celtic origin] To dig or tunnel, hence **1** to tunnel under a wall to bring it down (largely replaced by **undermine**), hence **(a)** the tunnel made; an explosive charge laid in it; a hidden explosive device; to lay mines in (17c) **(b)** to destroy insidiously (–17c, replaced by *undermine*). Cf. *sap* below **2** an excavation from which a mineral is extracted, hence **(a)** to extract minerals from one **(b)** an abundant source (*a mine of information*, 16c).

Old French *miner* produced **mineral**, originally anything obtained by mining. **Sap** [via Italian or French from late Latin *sappa* 'a hoe or spade, spadework', perhaps ultimately from Arabic *sarab* 'tunnel'] originally meant a tunnel undermining a fortification, later (to dig) a covered trench leading to enemy territory, surviving in **sapper** a private in the Royal Engineers, formerly called the (Royal) Sappers and Miners. Hence to undermine; (to make) a stealthy attack; to destroy insidiously (*sap your strength*), probably influenced by SAP sense 4.

miniature [16c. Italian *miniatura*, from *miniare* 'to illuminate', from Latin *miniare* 'to colour with red' from *minium* 'red lead, vermilion'] Italian *miniatura* referred to (the small paintings in) manuscript illumination, hence *miniature* an image or representation on a small scale (16c, influenced by *minimum*); smaller than usual, tiny (18c); to reduce to such a size (19c, replaced by **miniaturize**, 1940s); something smaller than usual (c.1900 [originally translating German *minatur*, a chess problem involving few men or a game of few moves]). The Italian senses were adopted in the 17c.

Miniature produced **mini** the proprietary name of a very small car, and **mini-** 'small, miniature' (*minibar, mini-roundabout*).

minion [16c. French *mignon*, of uncertain origin] **1** dainty, neat, delicately pretty **2** a sweetheart, lover, or mistress (rare by the 18c); a ruler's favourite; a sycophant; a slave, servant, or attendant.

French *mignon* was adopted meaning 'delicately pretty', later a pretty child, and appears in *filet mignon* a small, tender piece of beef. It produced *mignonette* a delicate kind of lace, also a plant with small greenish white flowers, hence a similar colour or scent.

minister [ME. Via French from Latin *minister* 'servant' (the verb via *ministrare* 'to serve'), from *minus* 'less', from *minor*: see MAJOR*] An agent or representative; a servant or underling (–18c), hence **1** to attend to someone or their needs; to provide or give something beneficial (largely replaced by **administer** [ME, from Latin *administrare* 'to serve or to manage'] **2** a clergyman; one who conducts worship and administers sacraments; to do so, hence **ministry** a clergyman's duties or period of office [Latin *ministerium*, from *minister*] **3** a senior member of government (17c, originally regarded as the ruler's agent), hence **(a)** the head of a government department, hence *ministry* (the building housing) such a department (19c) **(b) Prime Minister** a ruler's chief agent; the leader of an elected government (also **Premier Minister**, shortened to **Premier**), hence *ministry* a Prime Minister's period of office (cf. **administration** an American President's government or period of office) **4** a diplomat ranking below an ambassador (18c).

Latin *minister* produced **minstrel** [via Old French from Provençal *menest(ai)ral* 'servant, entertainer, musician']. Latin *ministrare* fathered Italian *minestrare* 'to serve, to dish up', particularly to serve *minestra*, a dish of pasta, rice, beans, and vegetables, whence *minestrone*.

minster [Old English *mynster*, via ecclesiastical Latin from Greek *monastērion*, from *monazein* 'to live alone', from *monos* 'alone'] A monastery (–16c), hence a church belonging to one; any large or important church.

Greek *monastērion* produced **monastery**; *monos* is the ancestor of **monarch**, **monk**, **mono-** (*monochrome*, *monorail*), and *monotone* (at TONE).

mint [Old English *mynet*, ultimately from Latin *Moneta* (whence **money**), the name of a goddess identified with Juno, at whose temple coins were made] **1** a coin, money (dialect since the 16c) **2** a place where coins are made (ME), hence **(a)** to make them (16c) **(b)** a huge sum of money (17c) **(c)** pristine, as if straight from the mint (*mint condition*, c.1900).

minute¹ [ME. Latin *minuta* (feminine of *minutus*: see MINUTE²) in the medieval Latin phrase *pars minuta prima* 'first diminished part'] One-sixtieth: **1** of a degree of angular measurement **2** of an hour, hence **(a)** an instant, a particular moment **(b)** the distance you can travel in a minute (*5 minutes from the beach*, 19c).

The equivalent senses of **second** come from medieval Latin *secunda pars minuta* 'second diminished part', the result of dividing by sixty twice.

minute² [15c. Latin *minutus* from *minuere* 'to lessen or make small'] **1** of a tax or tithe: small, lesser (–17c), hence very small or insignificant (17c); attending to small details, precise **2** [via medieval Latin *minuta scriptura* 'draft in small writing'] a rough draft or memorandum (15c); a note of a meeting: cf. GROSS.

Latin *minutus* produced French *menu*, literally 'small', also 'a detailed list' (whence *menuet* 'small, delicate', whence *minuet*), MINCE*, and MINUTE¹. *Minuere* is the ancestor of **comminute**, **diminish**, **diminution**, and **diminutive**. Related to *minor** (at MAJOR).

mischief [ME. Old French *mesch(i)ef*, from *meschever* 'to end badly', from *chever* 'to end', literally 'to come to a head', from *ch(i)ef* 'head', ultimately from Latin *caput* 'head'] Misfortune, trouble, poverty, distress (–17c), hence **1** an injury (surviving in *do someone a mischief*); harm or misfortune attributable to some cause (15c); in law: a wrong or hardship for which there is a legal remedy (17c) **2** a cause of evil or injury (16c); the Devil, hence a 'little devil', a playful child, animal, etc. that is (deliberately) annoying; its behaviour (17c).

Old French *ch(i)ef* was adopted as **chef** (short for *chef de cuisine* 'head of the kitchen') and **chief**, and produced **coverchief**, literally 'cover head', which evolved into **kerchief** (whence **neckerchief** and **handkerchief**). Latin *caput* is the ancestor of CAPITAL*.

misericord [ME. Via French from Latin *misericors* 'merciful', from *misereri* 'to feel pity', from *miser* 'wretched' + *cor* 'heart'] Compassion, pity, mercy, hence **1** a small dagger for giving the *coup de grâce* to a wounded knight **2** a place in a monastery where certain rules were relaxed (15c) **3** a ledge on the underside of a tip-up seat in a choir stall, which a standing person could lean on (16c).

Latin *misereri* produced **miserere** Psalm 51, which begins *Miserere mei Deus* 'Have mercy on me, O God'. *Miser* was adopted for a person who lives miserably while hoarding wealth and produced French *misère* 'misery, poverty' a declaration that you do not expect to win any tricks in a card game, and **misery** originally physical hardship or poverty. *Cor* is the ancestor of CORDIAL*.

mission [16c. (Via French from) Latin *missio*, from *mittere, miss-* 'to send or let go'] Sending or being sent for a particular purpose, especially to promote a religion or establish trade, hence this purpose (17c); the people sent; their premises (18c). Hence **1 missionary** (characteristic of) a person sent out to promote their faith and do good works **2** a journey with a purpose (18c); a military or scientific expedition with a specific objective (1920s, *US*), hence **mission creep** a (gradual) change of objective changes without formal acknowledgement **3** a vocation (19c) **4** a special task or duty (done enthusiastically) (19c), hence **mission statement** a company's statement of its objectives and principles (1990s); **on a mission** travelling or working single-mindedly.

Descendants of Latin *mittere* include **emissary** and **emit** [via Latin *emittere* 'to send out'], **intermission**, **intermit**, and **intermittent** [via Latin *intermittere* 'to interrupt', literally 'to send between'], **Mass** [Old English *maesse*, from ecclesiastical Latin *missa* (whence **missal**), in *Ite, missa est* 'Go, it is the dismissal', which concludes the Mass], and **permit** [Latin *permittere* 'to let go through']. Other descendants include ADMIT, COMMIT, COMPROMISE*, DISMISS*, MESS*, MESSAGE, **missile**, **missive**, **omit**, PREMISE, REMIT, **submit**, SURMISE, and **transmit**.

mite [ME. Early Dutch or Low German: related to Old English **mite** a small insect or arachnid] **1** a Flemish coin of small value, hence any such coin; **widow's mite** a very small contribution, all you can afford (see the Bible, Mark 12:42–44, 17c) **2** a tiny amount, a little bit; somewhat, slightly **3** a very small thing, animal, or person, especially a small child (16c).

mixed [ME. French *mixte* from Latin *mixtus*, from *miscere* 'to mix or mingle'] Mingled or blended together, hence **1** consisting of different or conflicting elements or qualities **2** describing, to do with, containing, or intended for people of different backgrounds, races, etc., or of both sexes (17c) **3 mixed up** confused, originally through drink (19c). The verb **mix** (15c) is a back-formation, and produced the noun (16c).

French *mixte* was adopted for a bicycle frame suitable for both sexes. Latin *miscere*'s descendants include **admix**, MEDDLE*, *miscegenation* (at GENUS), **miscellaneous**, **miscible**, **mixture**, **mustang** [Mexican Spanish *mestengo* 'ownerless', literally 'mixed'(with ranchers' herds)'], and **promiscuous** consisting of indiscriminately mixed elements, hence indiscriminate, especially in your sex life.

mob [17c. Shortened from Latin *mobile vulgus* 'the excitable crowd', from *mobilis*: see MOBILE*: originally slang and widely deplored] The common people, the masses; a large, disorderly crowd, hence **1** to crowd round (18c); to gang up on (*c*.1910); **mob-handed** in a large, threatening group (1930s) **2** a gang of criminals (19c, hence **mobster** a gangster, *c*.1915, *US*); **the Mob** a society similar to the Mafia (1950s, US) **3** a herd of animals (19c, Australian).

mobile [ME. French, from Latin *mobilis*, from *movere* MOVE*] Capable of moving or being moved, hence **1** able to move or change quickly and easily (15c); of troops: able to be deployed rapidly (19c), hence **mobilize** [French *mobiliser*] to make troops ready for action; **demobilize** [French *démobiliser*] to disband troops, to release from military service, shortened to **demob** after World War I **2** operating from a vehicle (*mobile library*, 1930s); **mobile phone** a radio telephone used in vehicles (1960s); a cellphone (1970s) **3** a decorative structure that moves (1940s).

French *mobile* produced **automobile** [with Greek *autos* 'self': see AUTOMATON*] self-propelling, hence (describing) a motor vehicle, whence **auto-** in *autocross* etc. Latin *mobilis* produced MOB.

mode [ME. Latin *modus* '(proper) measure' (hence 'limit' and 'metre, rhythm, harmony, song'), also 'manner'] **1** the forms that show whether a verb expresses fact, a command, a question, or a condition (largely replaced by the 16c variant **mood**), hence **modal (verb)** an auxiliary verb (e.g. *should, may*) that shows the mood of another (18c) **2** [from the Latin sense 'song'] a tune; a musical scale, originally that of the ancient Greeks, later of medieval and modern music (18c) **3** a form, manner, or variety (*mode of travel*, 17c), hence **(a)** [via French] the current local style, practice, etc.; **modish** fashionable **(b)** a way in which something happens or is done; a way in which a machine can function or be used (*manual/automatic mode*, 19c).

Latin *modus* produced COMMODIOUS*, MODEL*, **modern** [(via French from) Latin *modo* 'in a certain manner', later 'just now'], Latin *modicum* 'a little way, a short time', adopted for a limited amount, and **modify**. Related to MODERATE and MODEST*.

model [16c. Via French from Italian *modello*, ultimately from Latin *modulus*, literally 'a small measure', from *modus*: see MODE*] A set of plans for a proposed building etc. (–18c), hence **1** a (smaller) copy of someone/something that exists or is planned; (to make) one that shows its parts and how it works (17c); a simplified version used to analyse problems or make predictions (*c*.1910); to devise one (1960s) **2** something to be copied or emulated: **(a)** a perfect example (17c); exemplary **(b)** a person who poses for an artist (17c) or who wears clothes to display them (*c*.1900); to do so (*c*.1910) **(c)** a person, place, or object on which a (fictional) one is based (17c); to base on a model **3** a particular version of a manufactured article (19c).

Latin *modulus* produced MODULATION, MODULE, and **mould** a frame or container for shaping; to shape with one.

moderate [ME. Latin *moderari* 'to regulate': related to MODE*] **1** to make, later to become, less extreme, violent, etc.; not excessive or extreme, hence middling, mediocre **2** to adjust (15–17c); to regulate, control, or supervise (16–19c), hence **moderator** someone who presides over a meeting, Presbyterian church, public examinations, etc. (16c); *moderate* to act as one.

modest [16c. Latin *modestus* 'keeping the proper measure': related to MODE*] **1** not conceited or boastful; not drawing attention to yourself; decorous and reserved, especially in sexual matters **2** of moderate size or quality (17c); simple, unpretentious.

modulation [ME. Latin *modulari, modulat-* 'to measure, regulate, adjust to rhythm, make melody', from *modulus*: see MODEL*] **1** the making of music, hence **modulate** to do so (16c): both now rare **2** the variation of something for artistic effect (16c); a change of musical key during a piece (17c) **3** tempering or toning down (16c) **4** *modulate* to vary the amplitude or frequency of a wave (*c.*1910, hence *modulation, c.*1920); to do so in order to transmit information (1950s), hence **modem** a device that converts computer information to a telephone signal and vice versa [1950s, short for *modulator/demodulator*] **5** a reversible variation in an organism in response to a changing environment (1930s); *modulate* to undergo one (1950s).

module [16c. (Via French from) Latin *modulus*: see MODEL] An allotted measure or span (–17c); a standard unit of measurement (17c); a standardized unit used to make up a larger structure (1950s); a self-contained part that can function independently (1960s); a unit that goes to make up a computer program or into which a complex process can be analysed; a discrete course of study which may form part of a training or academic course.

mole¹ [Old English *māl*] A mark, especially on cloth (–19c), hence **1** a blemish on the human skin (ME) **2 iron mole** a rust mark on cloth (17c), quickly altered to **iron mould**, probably by association with **mould** the fungus [ME, probably from the past tense of **moul** to go mouldy, of Scandinavian origin].

mole² [ME. (Via French from) Latin *moles* 'mass, a massive structure', hence 'a barrier, trouble'] Mass, bulk, a large mass or piece (–18c), hence a large (stone) structure forming a pier, breakwater, or causeway (16c); a harbour protected by one.

Latin *moles* is the ancestor of **demolish** [via French from Latin *demoliri*, literally 'to unbuild', from *moliri* 'to build'] and **molecule** [Latin *molecula* 'a small mass', whence [via German], **mole** the basic SI unit of amount of substance]. Related to **molest** [Latin *molestus* 'troublesome'] to trouble (ME–18c), to assault or interfere with, now especially sexually.

moment [ME. French, from Latin *momentum* 'movement', later 'an instant' (from the idea of a small movement), also 'importance', from *movere* MOVE*] **1** a short time (in medieval time-keeping, a fortieth or fiftieth of an hour), hence **(a)** a stage or turning point (17c); **moment of truth** the moment of the final sword-thrust in a bull fight (1930s), hence a crisis, a testing situation (1940s) **(b)** a brief but significant time (*the right/a sad moment*, 18c) **(c)** the present (*he's busy at the moment*, 18c) **(d) momentarily** briefly (17c); instantly (18c, N American); very soon (1920s) **2** significance, importance (16c), hence **momentous** extremely important (17c) **3** a turning motion (18c only, cf. *momentum* below); a tendency to cause rotation (19c).

Latin *momentum* was adopted for a turning motion (17–19c) and for a measure of motion, the product of an object's mass and velocity, hence the impetus gained by a moving object, later by an idea, course of events, etc.

monitor [16c. Latin, from *monere, monit-* 'to remind or warn'] **1** a student given special, including disciplinary, responsibilities **2** (something that gives) a reminder or warning (17c); a large tropical lizard, said to warn of the presence of crocodiles (19c) **3** a nozzle that regulates the flow of a water-jet (19c) **4** to check and regulate the quality of a transmission or signal (1920s), hence **(a)** someone who does so **(b)** a loudspeaker, originally in a recording studio **(c)** a screen in a television studio that shows the picture from a particular camera or the one being broadcast (1930s); a VDU connected to a computer (1970s) **5** to listen to and report on the content of broadcasts or telephone calls (1930s); to observe and check anything regularly or continuously (1940s); someone/something that does so.

Latin *monere* is the ancestor of **admonish**, MONSTER*, MONUMENT, **premonition**, and **summon** [via French from, ultimately, Latin *summonere*, literally 'to remind privately'].

monster [ME. Via French from Latin *monstrum* 'divine portent, warning', later 'a monster', from *monere*: see MONITOR*] An animal, plant etc. markedly different from normal; a deformed animal or fetus, hence **1** an imaginary hideous or evil creature; an inhumanly cruel or wicked person (15c); to treat someone as a monster, to criticize severely (1960s, Australian) **2** a huge thing or animal (16c); gigantic, huge (19c).

Latin *monstrum* produced DEMONSTRATION*, **monstrosity, monstrous**, and MUSTER, and probably **monstera** a kind of plant, some species of which have large perforated leaves.

monument [ME. French, from Latin *monumentum*, from *monēre*: see MONITOR*] **1** a tomb (–17c); a statue etc. commemorating a dead person; an old building etc. preserved because of its historical, cultural, or aesthetic significance (16c), hence **monumental** to do with or like a monument (17c); large, imposing, and permanent; historically important (19c) **2** a written document or record (15c). Hence **3** (combining 1 and 2) **(a)** anything that by its survival commemorates a person, period, event, etc. (16c); an enduring example or achievement (17c) **(b)** a permanent boundary marker recorded in a document (19c, US).

moon [Old English *mōna*] The earth's natural satellite (later any planet's, 17c); this as seen from the earth (*full/new moon*), hence **1** the period from one new moon to the next (ME); a month, hence **honeymoon** the first month after marriage (during which affection changes like the moon, 16c), hence **(a)** a period of harmony and goodwill at the beginning of a relationship (16c) **(b)** a newly married couple's holiday (19c) **2** a moon-shaped object (ME); the buttocks (18c); to expose them (1960s) **3** the light of the moon (15c): cf. *moonlight* below **4** **moonstruck** mad (17c), later dazed or dreamy, hence *moon* to act as if moonstruck (19c): the moon's supposedly harmful effects are also found in LUNATIC and in **mooncalf** a deformed fetus (16–19c); a simpleton (17c); an absent-minded or fickle person.

Hence **moonlight/moonshine** the light of the moon, hence **1** *moonlight* to carry on some illicit activity at night (19c): **(a) moonlight (flit)** a hurried removal to avoid paying rent **(b)** to work (illicitly) at an additional job (1950s) **2** *moonshine* **(a)** something insubstantial; foolish thoughts or speech **(b)** smuggled or illicitly distilled liquor (18c, N American); to make it (19c).

Old English *mōna* produced **Monday** [Old English *mōnandaeg* 'moon's day', translating late Latin *lunae dies*]. Related to **month**.

moot [Old English *mōt*] An assembly, a meeting or meeting place, hence **1** to argue or discuss; to discuss a hypothetical legal case; such a discussion or case (16c), hence in US law: hypothetical, theoretical, academic (19c) **2** debatable (*moot point*, 16c) **3** to put forward for discussion (17c).

Old English *mōt* produced the names **Mottram** and **Mustoe**, and perhaps EMPTY. Related to MEET[1].

moral [ME. Latin *moralis*, from *mos* 'custom'] To do with behaviour and the understanding of right and wrong, hence **1** of a story: dealing with such issues; a lesson contained in a story (15c); the part of the story that sums this up; **morality (play)** one with such a lesson (18c) **2** conforming to or supporting accepted standards of behaviour, hence **(a) morality** (16c), **morals** (17c) such standards; **demoralize** to undermine them (18c) **(b)** sexually virtuous (19c) **3** ethical (as opposed to legal, religious, intellectual, or practical) **4** affecting character or conduct (16c); producing confidence or discouragement, hence **morale** [18c, from French *moral*, respelt to indicate the stress] an individual's or group's degree of confidence and optimism; *demoralize* to undermine this (19c) **5** based on inner conviction or on knowledge of character (*moral certainty*, 17c).

Mores [plural of Latin *mos*] was adopted for the customs that embody a society's values (19c); *mos* produced **morose**, originally 'deliberate, painstaking'.

mordant [15c. French, literally 'biting', from *mordre* 'to bite', ultimately from Latin *mordere*] **1** sarcastic, caustically critical; pungent, biting (19c); of pain: acute **2** corrosive (17c); a corrosive used in etching (19c) **3** a fixative for a dye or stain (from the idea of biting into the fabric, 18c) or for gold leaf (19c); to treat with one.

Latin *mordere* is the ancestor of **morsel** [Old French, literally 'little bite'] and **remorse** [Latin *remordere* 'to torment'] originally in **remorse of conscience** the torment of a bad conscience, hence a strong feeling of guilt and regret, later of compassion, surviving in **remorseless** pitiless, relentless.

morn [Old English *morgen*] Dawn, sunrise; the early part of the day, between sunrise and noon; (this period of) the following day (surviving in Scots **the morn**).

Old English *morgen* produced **morning**, which has largely replaced *morn*, and which developed the sense 'before evening' (surviving in **morning dress/suit**), and **morrow**, surviving mainly in **tomorrow**. Related to **morganatic** [via French or German from medieval Latin *matrimonium ad morganaticam* 'marriage with a morning gift'] describing a marriage between a person of high rank and one of lower, the latter (and any children), having no right to the former's title or goods, only to a gift after consummation.

mortal [ME. (Old French from) Latin *mortalis*, from *mors, mort-* 'death'] Sure to die, hence **1** fatal (*a mortal wound*), hence **(a)** fighting or fought to the death; of an enemy or enmity: implacable, relentless **(b)** intense, extremely great (*mortal fear/a mortal fool*) **2** to do with humanity or earthly life as opposed to God, the gods, or an afterlife (15c) **3** of sin: deadly, causing damnation (15c): opposite of **venial** pardonable [ME, from Latin *venialis*, from *venia* 'forgiveness'] **4** a mortal being; a person (18c).

Descendants of Latin *mors* include **mortician** and MORTIFY, and probably the names **Mort**, **Mortimer**, **Mortlake**, and **Mortlock**. Latin *post mortem* 'after death' was adopted for an autopsy, hence an analysis or discussion following an event. Related to MORTUARY*.

mortar [Via Old French from Latin *mortarium* '(material prepared in) a bowl for mixing or pounding'] **1** a bowl for grinding spices etc. with a pestle, hence a short, wide cannon (likened to a bowl) or, later, a smooth-bore gun (16c); a device for firing a lifeline, firework, etc. (17c) **2** a mixture for holding bricks together; plaster etc. used as facing (15c), hence **mortarboard** a square board for carrying mortar (19c); a similarly shaped academic cap.

Pestle (ME) comes via Old French from Latin *pistillum*, from Latin *pinsere, pist-* 'to pound', whence also Italian *pesto*, French *piste* [via Italian *pistare* 'to trample'] originally the track made by a horse, **pistil** the female part of a flower (shaped like a pestle), the surname **Pestell**, **Pistol** an apothecary (the mortar and pestle being the trade's symbol: *pistol* the gun is unrelated, ultimately from Czech), and **piston**.

mortify [ME. Via French from ecclesiastical Latin *mortificare* 'to kill or subdue', from *mor*: see MORTAL*] To kill or destroy (–17c); to destroy vitality or vigour (–18c), hence **1** to subdue an appetite or passion by abstinence or self-inflicted discomfort (15c); to humble or shame (17c) **2** to become necrotic or gangrenous (15c).

mortuary [ME. Ultimately from Latin *mortuaries* 'to do with death', from *mortuus* 'dead', from *mori* 'to die'] **1** a gift formerly claimed by the incumbent of a parish from a deceased parishioner's estate **2** a funeral (15–17c); to do with burial, cremation, or death (16c), hence a place where corpses are kept (19c), partly replaced by **morgue** [19c, *US*, from *La Morgue* the name of a mortuary in Paris, possibly from French *morguer* 'to look at solemnly'], which now also means the department of a newspaper etc. where material is collected for future obituaries (*c*.1900).

Latin *mortuus* produced Old French *mortgage* [literally 'dead pledge', from *mort* 'dead' + *gage* 'pledge, security' (see WAGE*), because, if the borrower fails to pay, the property is 'dead' to them]; *mori* produced **moribund** (someone who is) dying, hence becoming obsolete, without vitality or purpose, and **murrain** a plague (ME–18c), a cattle disease, later the potato blight that caused the Irish famine. Related to MORTAL*.

moss [Old English *mos*] **1** a (peat) bog (Scots and N English dialect, surviving in place names) **2** a simple plant that grows in carpets in damp places, hence something resembling this, e.g. **moss agate/opal** with greenish markings, **moss campion/pink** with similar growing habits; **moss rose** with a moss-like coating on the calyx and stems.

Related to **mire** [Old Norse *mýrr*, whence the name **Myerscough**] and probably to French *mousse* 'moss, foam', adopted for a foamy mixture containing cream, eggs, and gelatine, later a hair-setting foam.

mote [Old English *mot*] A speck of dust, especially one seen in a sunbeam; an irritating particle in the eye or throat; a minor fault in one person spotted by another who has a greater one (see the Bible, Matthew 7:3); (a seed bearing) a tuft of fibre (16c).

Perhaps the source of **motley** multicoloured, hence **1** a jester's multicoloured costume **2** an (incongruous) mixture of colours or diverse elements; diverse, varied: **mottle** is probably a back-formation.

motion [ME. French, from Latin *movere, mot-* MOVE*] **1** moving, urging, hence **(a)** something that urges, an impulse, desire, or inclination (–18c); a reason for doing something (15–17c): replaced by **motive** [ME. French *motif* '(something) causing movement', from late Latin *motivus*, from *movere*] or **motivation (b)** a formal proposal (16c, replacing *motive*) **2** the action of moving or being moved (15c), hence **(a)** a commotion, agitation, shaking **(b)** (also **movement**) an emptying of the bowels (16c); **motion(s)** faeces (19c) **(c)** the way someone/something moves (16c) **(d)** (to make) a movement or gesture (*he motioned us to sit*, 17c) **(e) motions** the activities of an army in the field (17c, replaced by *movements*) **(f)** (also *movement*) a moving piece of mechanism (17c).

French *motif* was adopted meaning a distinctive or dominant idea, hence a recurrent feature or theme in art or literature; a repeated design, shape, or pattern; a decorative piece, originally one sewn onto a garment.

mount [ME. Old French *munter, monter*, ultimately from Latin *mons, mont-* 'mountain'] To rise or raise, hence **1** to rise to a higher level or rank; **mount (up)** to increase in amount or intensity (replacing **amount** [ME, from Old French *amounter* 'to go up' (the original English sense), from *amont* 'above', ultimately from Latin *mons*]) **2** to get or put onto (*mount a horse/stage, mounted the photo on a card*), hence **(a)** to get onto (a female) to mate (18c) **(b)** a support (*engine mount*, 18c) **(c)** an animal mounted and ridden (19c) **3** to add up to (–18c); a total (–17c), both outlived by *amount* **4** to put on, to launch (*mount an attack/play*, 19c).

Old French *monter* produced **surmount** [Old French *surmonter*, literally 'to climb over']; Old French *amont* produced **paramount**. Latin *mons* is the ancestor of the names **Montague** and **Montgomery** (**Monty** is short for both), Spanish *monte* 'mountain, heap of cards', adopted for a game in which the object is to win all the cards (one candidate for the disputed origin of **the full Monty**), **mount** a mountain, **mountain** [via Old French *montaigne*], MOUNTEBANK, and **tantamount** [from Italian *tanto montare* or Anglo-Norman French *tant amunter* 'to amount to as much'].

mountebank [16c. Italian *montambanco*, literally 'someone who climbs on a bench', from *montare* 'to climb up' (ultimately from Latin *mons* 'mountain': see

MOUNT*) + *banca* 'bench' (see BANK[2]*)] Someone selling (ineffective) medicines from a platform in the street, someone who pretends to have (medical) knowledge. Also called a **charlatan** [17c, via French from Italian *cialare* 'to babble'] or a **quacksalver** [16c, from Dutch *quacken, kwakken* 'to prattle' + *salf, zalf* 'medicine' (related to **salve**)], shortened to **quack** (17c), hence an army medical officer; any doctor (early 20c, *Australian*).

The mountebank's hapless assistant had to eat a toad (thought to be poisonous) to prove the medicine's efficacy, hence **toad-eater**, **toady** a sycophant, *toady* to fawn on.

mouse [Old English *mūs*] A small rodent, hence **1** something resembling one **(a)** a vole or shrew **(b)** something shaped like one: a muscle (–16c); a lump or bruise near the eye (19c); a device that moves a cursor on a VDU (1960s) **(c)** a small, insignificant person or thing (16c); a quiet, timid person **2** to hunt or catch mice (ME) **3** a greyish-brown colour, like a house mouse (17c); a light brown shade of hair.

Old English *mūs* appears as **Mus-** in the names of places infested with them. **Muscle** derives similarly from Latin *mus* 'mouse' (related to the similarly shaped **mussel**).

move [ME. Via Anglo-Norman and Old French from Latin *movere, mot-*] To (cause to) pass or be passed from one place or position to another; to put or keep in motion, hence **1** to be a motive or cause; to propose an action, now only formally in an assembly; such a proposal (15c, outlived by MOTION) **2** to take action; an action or manoeuvre (19c, influenced by sense 5) **3** to affect with emotion **4** to live or operate in particular (social) surroundings **5** (your turn) to change the position of a piece in a game (17c); such a change **6** to change your residence or business premises (18c); such a change (19c).

Latin *movere*'s offspring include EMOTION, MOBILE*, MOMENT*, MOTION*, **motor** [literally 'something that causes motion'], **mutiny** [obsolete *mutine* from French *mutin* 'rebellious', from *muete* 'movement, excitement'], PROMOTE, **remote**, and **remove**.

muddle [ME. Early Dutch *moddelen* 'to dabble in mud', from *modde* 'thick mud' (whence, probably, **mud**] To bathe or wallow in mud or muddy water; to make muddy or confused (16c), hence **1** to bewilder or fuddle (17c); (to bring about) confusion or disorder (19c); **muddle along/through** to get on in a confused, disorganized way **2** a mistake, misunderstanding, or mix-up (19c); **muddle (up)** to mistake one thing for another (19c).

mug [16c. Probably of Scandinavian origin] An earthenware pot or jug (Scots and N English); a large straight-sided drinking cup (17c), hence (probably, from the 18c practice of putting grotesque faces on mugs) the face, hence **1 mug (shot)** a photograph of the face, especially for police records (19c, *US*) **2** to hit in the face (19c); to attack and rob **3** a fool, a gullible person (19c); **mug's game** a thankless or pointless activity.

mule [Old English *mūl* and, later, Old French *mul*, both from Latin *mulus*] The offspring of a male ass and a mare, or of a female ass and a stallion (strictly speaking, a **hinny** [17c, via Latin from Greek *hinnos*]), used as a beast of burden despite its legendary obstinacy, hence **1** a stupid or obstinate person (ME) **2** a hybrid plant or animal (18c); a machine, vessel, etc. combining the characteristics of two distinct types (*spinning mule*) **3 (drug) mule** an (expendable) courier for illegal drugs (1930s) **4 (a) mule-deer** a long-eared N American deer (19c) **(b) mule** or **mule-ear(ed) rabbit** a jackrabbit (19c)

Latin *mulus* fathered Spanish and Portuguese *mulatto* [literally a young mule] someone with one White and one Black parent (now highly offensive).

multiple [17c. Via French from late Latin *multiplus*, alteration of Latin *multiplex*, literally 'many-fold', from *multus* 'much, many' + *plicare* 'to fold'] **1** (being) the product of multiplying one number by another **2** having several parts; of a disease: affecting several parts of the body (*multiple sclerosis*, 19c) **3** many and (often) various **4** of a system: having several access points (*c.*1900); **multiple (store)** a chain store.

In sense 1 and, largely, 2, *multiple* replaced Latin *multiplex* (which now means a system able to transmit more than one message simultaneously, and a building containing several cinemas, theatres, etc.) and **manifold** [Old English *maenigfeald*, probably a translation of Latin *multiplex*], which now means a pipe etc. with several branches, inlets, or outlets. Latin *multiplex* produced **multiply**. *Multus* produced **multi-** (*multicultural, multimedia*), **multifarious** varied, diverse [Latin *multifarius*, from *-farius* 'doing', from *facere* 'to do' (ancestor of FACT*)], and **multitude** literally the state of being numerous. *Plicare* is the ancestor of PLY*.

mumbo-jumbo The name of a W African idol (also *jumbo*, 18c), hence something worshipped without thought (19c), meaningless words or ritual.

Probably the source of **jumbo** a big (clumsy) person, later the name of an exceptionally large elephant in London Zoo. *Jumbo* became the traditional name for elephants, and was used to describe things larger than usual (*jumbo-size, jumbo jet*), hence **jumboize** to enlarge a ship by inserting a new middle section (largely replaced by STRETCH).

munition [ME. French, from Latin *munitio* 'fortification', from *munire* 'to fortify or secure', from *moenia* 'defensive walls'] **1** a right or privilege (–15c) **2** an apparatus (15c only) **3** anything serving as a defence or protection (16–19c); **munitions** weapons, ammunition, military equipment, and stores (the original sense of **ammunition** [French *la munition*, wrongly divided as *l'ammunition*: cf. EKE*]); the production of these; *munition* to supply with them.

Latin *munire* produced **muniments** documents supporting a claim [via *munimentum* 'defence, fortification', in medieval Latin 'title deed']. Related to MURAL*.

mural [ME. Via French from Latin *muralis* 'to do with a wall', from *murus* 'wall'] **1** describing an award to the first soldier to scale the enemy's wall **2** to do with or resembling a wall (16c), hence a painting done on one (1920s).

Latin *murus* produced **extramural** [Latin *extra muros* 'outside the walls'] and **immure** [Latin *immurare* 'to wall in']. Related to MUNITION*.

muse¹ [ME. (French, from) Latin *musa*, from Greek *mousa*] Each of the Greek goddesses believed to inspire learning and the arts, hence **1** (a goddess or person regarded as) a poet's, later any artist's, inspiration, hence an artist's individual style **2 the Muse** poetry (18c); **the Muses** the liberal arts.

Calliope, the Muse of epic verse [Greek *Kalliopē* 'beautiful voiced'] gave her name to a musical instrument consisting of a number of steam whistles played by a keyboard; **Terpsichore**, the Muse of dancing [from Greek *terpein* 'delight' + *khoros* 'dance, CHORUS*'] became a personification of the art of dance.

Greek *mousa* produced **mosaic** [via medieval Latin *musaicus, mosaicus*, from the mosaic work on shrines dedicated to the Muses], **museum** [Greek *mouseion* 'seat of the Muses'], **music** [Greek *mousika* '(art) of a Muse or the Muses'], and probably **musette** a small bagpipe, hence (a dance to) a pastoral tune with a similar sound; a small bag used by cyclists and soldiers.

muse² [ME. Old French *muser* 'to meditate', later 'to waste time', perhaps ultimately from medieval Latin *musum* **muzzle**, from the idea of a dog sniffing the air for a lost scent] To meditate or ponder; to gaze, contemplate, or speak thoughtfully; a contemplative or abstracted state (15c).

Old French *muser* produced *amuser*, whence **amuse** to distract someone in order to cheat them; to divert or entertain them, hence to make them laugh.

musk [ME. Late Latin *muscus* from Persian *mušk*, perhaps from Sanskrit *muṣka* 'scrotum' (from the shape of the musk deer's gland)] A strong-smelling secretion of the musk deer; a similar secretion in other animals, hence **1** in the names of **(a)** animals, birds, etc. with such secretions or a strong smell (*musk deer/beetle*, 15c); **musk duck** (originally from Central America, 17c) was altered (for no good reason) to **muscovy (duck)** '(duck) from Moscow': **muskrat** (17c) is an alteration of Algonquian *muscasus* 'it is red' (from its colour), although it does have musk glands **(b)** plants with a musky smell (*musk rose/melon*, 16c): cf. *muscari* below **2** synthetic musk (17c) **3** to perfume with (real or synthetic) musk (17c) **4** a musk-like smell (19c).

Late Latin *muscus* produced **moschatel** a plant with musk-scented flowers [via French from Italian *moscato*, later adopted for *muscatel* below], **muscadet** [via French *muscade* 'nutmeg'], **muscari** a grape hyacinth or related plant, Provençal *muscat* (wine from) a kind of grape with a musky smell, also called *muscatel* [literally 'little muscat'], which later came to refer to raisins from this grape, and **nutmeg** [via French from medieval Latin *nux muscata* 'musk-smelling nut': see also NUCLEUS*].

must [Old English, ultimately from Latin *mustus* 'new, fresh'] New wine; grape juice before or during fermentation, hence **mustard** [ME, via French from Latin *mustus*], originally made by crushing mustard seeds with new wine.

muster [ME. Old French *mo(u)stre* (noun), *mo(u)strer* (verb), ultimately from Latin *monstrare* 'to show': see MONSTER*] To show, report, or explain (–17c); to be shown, to appear (–16c); an exhibition or display (–17c), hence **1** an example or specimen **2** to bring or to come together (15c, originally soldiers for inspection or battle), hence **(a)** a gathering or roll-call; (16c); to call the roll (17c) **(b)** the (number of) those mustered; of an army: to comprise or number (19c) **(c) pass muster** to pass an inspection (16c); to be up to standard **(d)** to summon strength, courage, etc. (16c) **(e) muster in(to)** to enrol or be enrolled (now only US), hence **muster out** to discharge or be discharged (19c, US); a discharge **(f)** to round up cattle etc. (19c, Australia and New Zealand); a round-up.

mystery [ME. Via Old French or Latin from Greek *mustērion* 'secret rite', from *mustēs* 'an initiate', from *muein* 'to initiate'] A hidden divine presence or religious meaning (–17c), hence **1** religious belief based on divine revelation; (faith regarding) something beyond human knowledge or comprehension, hence (describing) someone/something puzzling or unknown; a puzzle or enigma **2** a religious rite: **(a)** a Christian sacrament (15c); **the mysteries** the consecrated bread and wine of the Eucharist **(b)** a rite reserved for the initiated; esoteric knowledge or practices (16c) **3** an incident in Christ's life with particular spiritual significance (17c); **mystery play** a medieval play based on a Bible story, performed by a craft guild (18c), hence erroneously connected with **mystery** an occupation, craft, or trade, later a guild [15c, ultimately from Latin *ministerium*: see *ministry* (at MINISTER)].

Old French *mystique* [Greek *mustikos*, from *mustēs*] was adopted for an aura of mystery designed to awe the uninitiated, and is the source of **mystic** to do with (religious) mystery; a believer in **mysticism**: **1** intuitive spiritual insight, later belief based on woolly, confused thinking **2** belief that union with God can be obtained by self-surrender and meditation.

mythology [15c. Via French or Latin from Greek *muthologia*, from *muthos* 'a myth'] The interpretation of a fable (–17c); (a story with) a symbolic meaning (16–18c); an ancient story purporting to explain the origins of natural or social phenomena (17c, replaced by 19c **myth**, also from Greek *muthos*); these collectively (18c, partly replaced by *myth*, which refers to such stories in general, *mythology* generally referring to those concerning a particular place or people); the study of these (19c).

Myth came to mean a widely held but false belief, hence **urban myth** a modern story of some bizarre event, told as if it were true.

N

name [Old English *nama, noma* (noun), *(ge)namian* (verb)] The word(s) by which someone/something is known and distinguished from others, hence **1** a name implying the person it belongs to; **in my name** with my authority **2** to give a name or specific epithet; to call, mention, or identify by it: **(a)** to declare someone to be, or to have done, something (*named as her successor/name and shame*) **(b)** to specify (*name your price/the day*, 16c) **(c)** an uncomplimentary epithet (*name-calling*, 17c) **3** reputation (*good/bad name*, ME); a famous or notorious person (17c, hence **name-dropping** speaking of famous people as though you know them personally, 1950s) **4 in name only** having no real validity, nominally (ME).

Similar senses are found in descendants of Latin *nomen* 'name', e.g. **ignominy** [(via French from) Latin *ignominia*, literally 'lacking a (good) name'], **nominal**, **nominate**, and **renown** [via Old French *renon, renom*, from *renomer* 'to make famous']. Latin *nomen* also produced **nomenclature** [French, from Latin *nomenclatura*, with *calare* 'to call'], and **noun** [Anglo-Norman French, whence also **surname**, literally 'name above'].

narcissus [16c. Latin, from Greek *narkissos*, from or influenced by *narkē* 'numbness', because of the plant's narcotic effects] A genus of flowering plants which includes the daffodil: in Greek mythology, the youth **Narcissus** was punished for rejecting the nymph Echo by being made to fall in love with his reflection; he pined away and was turned into the flower, giving his name to **narcissism** extreme vanity (19c). **Echo** faded away until only her voice remained, giving her name to reflected sound (ME).

Greek *narkē* is the ancestor of **narcolepsy** a condition causing an uncontrollable tendency to fall asleep, and **narcotic** a drug inducing numbness or sleep, now often applied to any illegally used drug (*US*).

native [ME. (Via French from) Latin *nativus*, from *nasci, nat-*: see NATURE*] **1** inborn, innate, natural; in a natural state, artless, unadorned, simple (16c, now rare, cf. *naïf* below **2** (someone/something) born in a particular place (15c), hence **(a)** to do with or belonging to someone because of their birthplace (*native land/language*, 16c) **(b)** an indigenous inhabitant of a colony (17c, now considered offensive); to do with or produced by indigenous inhabitants (*native art/village*, 18c).

Latin *nativus* is the ancestor of French *naïf* unaffected, artless, also innocent, simple, credulous (largely replaced by **naive**, from the feminine form of *naïf*), and of **nativity** (the circumstances surrounding) birth, especially Christ's.

nature [ME. French, from Latin *natura*, from *nasci*, *nat-* 'to be born'] An inherent or innate quality or disposition, hence **natural** based on instinct or an innate moral sense; simple, unaffected, spontaneous. Hence **1** innate and universal human impulses (*human nature*), hence **(a)** the unredeemed state of humankind, as distinct from a state of grace (17c) **(b)** heredity as it affects character (*nature versus nurture*, 19c) **2** (the forces that create and control) the world, often personified (*Mother Nature*), hence **(a)** living things and the countryside, as opposed to human creations; a state of existence uninfluenced by civilization (17c); **back to nature** to a simpler life (*c.*1900); **in a state of nature** naked (19c); **naturist** nudist (1920s) **(b)** physical needs (*call of nature*) **3** essential character (*the nature of the problem*).

Descendants of Latin *nasci* include **cognate**, **innate**, **nascent**, **nation** [French, from Latin *natio* 'birth race'] originally people of the same ethnic origin, later those forming a state, NATIVE*, NOEL*, **pregnant**, PUNY*, **Renaissance** [French, literally 'rebirth'], and the names **Renata** and **Renée**, both meaning 'reborn', referring to Christian baptism.

navigate [15c. Latin *navigare*, from *navis* 'ship' + *agere* 'to drive'] To sail on or across the sea or a waterway (implied in **navigable**); to travel by ship (16c), hence **1 navigation** travel by sea, sailing; **inland navigation** travel by inland waterways (18c), hence *navigation* such a waterway, now only a canal, whence **navigator** a labourer who digs a canal (18c), shortened to **navvy** and extended to other labourers (19c) **2** to plot or follow a course (18c); to make or find your way (19c).

Latin *navis* produced French *nacelle*, used briefly in its literal sense 'small boat', and re-adopted for various boat-shaped structures, the **nave** of a church (perhaps from its long narrow shape), French *navette* 'little boat, shuttle', adopted for a pointed oval jewel and later for a railway truck carrying cars through the Channel Tunnel, **navicular (bone)** a boat-shaped bone, and **navy** a fleet, later a country's fleet of ships, a seagoing military force, whence **navy (blue)** (of) the colour of the British naval uniform. Latin *navis* is related to NOISE*; *agere* is the ancestor of AGENT*.

neat [16c. French *net*: see NET[2]] **1** clean, pure, unadulterated (16c, now describing undiluted spirits) **2** smart, elegant, trim (16–17c, whence, probably, **natty**, 18c), hence tidy, well-organized, compact; attractive, desirable, excellent (19c).

nebula [15c, Latin 'mist'] A mist, cloud, or fog (in the Anglicized form *nebule*, reappearing as *nebula* in the 19c), hence **1** a film or cloudy patch on the cornea (17c) **2** cloudiness in the urine (17c) **3** a hazy appearance (18c); an indistinct or formless thing, hence **(a)** in astronomy: a hazy area representing a distant star cluster or, later, a cloud of gas or dust in deep space **(b) nebulous** hazy, vague, indistinct, formless (19c) **4 nebulizer** a device for turning a (medicinal) liquid into a spray (19c), whence *nebula* such a liquid.

nectar [16c. Latin, from Greek *nektar*] The drink of the Greek and Roman gods, hence **1** a delicious drink, now specifically a thick pulpy fruit juice; **amber nectar** beer (1980s, Australia) **2** the sweet liquid plants produce to attract pollinating insects etc. (17c) **3 nectarine (a)** like, or as sweet as, nectar (17c) **(b)** a smooth-skinned peach.

Ambrosia [Latin from Greek, from *ambrotos* 'immortal, divine' (whence the name **Ambrose** and its Welsh equivalent, **Emrys**), from *brotos* 'mortal'] referred to the gods' food, drink, or perfume, hence something that tastes or smells delicious.

negligence [ME. (Via French from) Latin *negligentia*, from *neglegere, neglect-* , literally 'to choose not to', from *legere* 'to choose', also 'to read'] Lack of attention to what needs to be done or taken care of, hence **1** failure to provide proper care; in law: a breach of a duty of care resulting in damage **2** carelessness in dress or artistic style (15c); freedom from artificiality or restraint.

Latin *neglegere* produced **neglect** and French *négligée* a woman's loose gown, later a flimsy dressing gown, hence informal or incomplete dress. Latin *legere* produced **diligence**, the opposite of *negligence* [Latin *diligere* 'to delight in doing, to love or esteem', literally 'to pick out', whence *prediligere* 'to choose before others', source of **predilection**], and LEGEND*.

negotiate [ME. Latin *negotiari* 'to do business', from *negotium* 'business', from *neg* 'not' + *otium* 'leisure'] **1** negotiation a private or business transaction (–18c) **2** to try to reach an agreement by discussion and/or compromise (16c); to achieve something by doing so (18c) **3** to deal with or manage something needing skill or care (17c), hence to get over, round, or through an obstacle or difficulty (19c) **4** to transfer ownership of a cheque etc. (17c); to give or receive money for one (more common in 18c **negotiable**).

Latin *otium* is the ancestor of **otiose 1** ineffective, futile; useless, worthless, superfluous **2** at leisure, idle, lazy.

Negro [16c. Spanish and Portuguese, from Latin *niger, nigr-* 'black'] (Someone descended from) a Black African: the standard term until the mid 20c, disparaging only in as far as Blacks were considered inferior to Whites: now considered offensive, and sometimes used by African-Americans for an Uncle Tom.

Spanish *negro* produced French *nègre*, whence **neger** a Negro: the variant **nigger** was also applied to other dark-skinned races and to dark colours (*nigger brown*), dark-coloured creatures, and to a screen used in film-making to cast shadows or avoid unwanted reflections. Among White Americans *nigger* has always been derogatory and appears in many phrases reflecting the Blacks' inferior social position, e.g. **nigger-driver**, **nigger minstrels** entertainers, usually blacked-up Whites, performing songs and dances based on a sanitized version of plantation life (now called **black-faced minstrels** where they exist at all), **White nigger** a White person doing menial work, later one who identified with Blacks or espoused Black causes. Among Blacks *nigger* and the variant **nigga** may express warmth, approval, or solidarity; used by a White person they are extremely offensive: the variants **nigra** (US) and **nig-nog** deliberately so.

Latin *niger* is the ancestor of DENIGRATE, of Italian *niello*, adopted for a black substance used to fill engraved designs, and of **nigella** a genus of plants with black seeds (**Nigel**, feminine **Nigella**, is not related, being a variant of **Neil**, from an Irish word meaning 'champion').

nephew [ME. French *neveu* from Latin *nepos* 'grandson, nephew, descendant'] **1** the son of your brother or sister, or of your brother- or sister-in-law **2** a descendant or successor (–17c); a euphemism for an illegitimate son, especially of an ecclesiastic who had taken a vow of celibacy (16c), hence **nepotism** [17c, via French from Italian *nipote* 'nephew', from Latin *nepos*], originally referring to the advantages enjoyed by 'nephews' of various popes.

Until the 17c *nephew* and **niece** [via French from Latin *neptis*, related to *nepos*] could be used for either sex, although the present division was always more common.

nerve [ME. Latin *nervus*] **1** a sinew or tendon (surviving in **strain every nerve** to make every effort); a rib or vein in a leaf or an insect's wing (15c), hence the main source of strength (17c); strength, vigour, energy; courage, coolness, boldness, impudence; to give someone courage (19c, 18c in **unnerve**) **2** the fibres or cells that carry impulses between the brain and the rest of the body, hence **nervous** to do with the nerves (15c), hence **(a)** well-supplied with nerves, sensitive; anxious, worried, hence *nerves* in phrases suggesting sensitivity or anxiety (*live/ get on your nerves*) **(b)** caused by a disorder of the nervous system (*nervous exhaustion*, 18c).

Latin *nervus* produced **enervate** [Latin *enervare*, literally 'to extract the sinews of']. Related to Greek *neuron* 'nerve', whence **neur(o)-** (*neuralgia, neurology*), **neuron** a cell that transmits nerve impulses, and **neurosis** a mild psychiatric illness causing anxiety and depression.

nest [Old English] A structure made, or a place chosen, by a bird to lay its eggs, hence **1** to have or build one **2** a cosy, private place (*love nest*); to settle in or create one (19c) **3** a place or structure where a creature rests or raises young (ME); the creatures living in one (15c) **4** a set of objects designed to fit into each other or into one container (*nest of tables*, 15c), hence **(a)** to put one thing inside another (19c); to group things together in a single unit **(b)** a group of machine guns (World War I).

Related to **nestle** to build or have a nest; to settle permanently or, later, comfortably; to snuggle up to or with someone; to be in a snug or sheltered position (*a village nestling in the foothills*).

net¹ [Old English *net(t)*] (A piece of) openwork fabric (*fishing/mosquito/football/ curtain net*); to make one (17c). Hence **1** to catch (as if) with a net (ME); to acquire (19c): cf. NET² **2** to cover or protect with a net (16c) **3 network** nets, netting (16c); a net-like structure; a system of interconnecting things or people (19c), hence **(a)** a system of linked radio or television transmitters (*c*.1915); a nation-wide broadcasting company (1940s) **(b)** to link computers (1960s); *net(work)* a set of interconnected computers (1970s); **internet** a set of linked computer networks operated by the US Defense Department, now a global computer network **(c)** to build up and maintain personal relationships, especially with those who can help you (1970s). Cf. MESH.

Related to **nettle** a plant with stinging hairs (whose fibres were used to make net cords), hence to sting, provoke, or annoy.

net², **nett** [ME. French *net* (whence NEAT), feminine *nette*, from Latin *nitidus* 'shining', from *nitere* 'to shine'] **1** trim, smart, elegant (–19c) **2** bright, clean, pure (–17c), not adulterated or diluted (–19c), hence with no deduction or discount (15c); left after deductions, hence to gain or bring in a net sum or profit (18c, cf. NET¹).

neuter [ME. (Via French from) Latin *neuter* 'neither', from *ne-* 'not' + *uter* 'either of two'] **1** to do with or belonging to the grammatical gender that is neither masculine nor feminine; a word belonging to this gender (16c), hence asexual (18c); a sexually undeveloped animal or insect; a castrated or spayed animal (*c.*1900); to castrate or spay; to make ineffective (cf. *neutralize* below) **2** (a person or state) not taking sides in a war or quarrel (15c) **3** not belonging to either of two categories (16c).

In senses 2 and 3 **neutral** [Latin *neutralis*, from *neuter*] is now more common: it went on to mean **1** made up of opposing elements that can cancel each other out, hence **neutralize** to cancel one thing out with another; to make harmless or ineffective (*US*) **2** neither acid nor alkaline; electrically neither positive nor negative, hence **neutrino**, **neutron** electrically neutral subatomic particles **3** without distinctive qualities; not brightly coloured **4** a gear in which no power is transmitted to the moving parts.

nib [16c. Probably from early Dutch or Low German] **1** a bird's beak, an animal's snout (surviving in dialect) **2** the tip of a (quill) pen (17c) **3** a projecting part, a point or spout (18c) **4** a small lump or knot in wool or raw silk (18c); a speck of matter in a coat of paint (1930s); **nibs** shelled and crushed coffee or cocoa beans (19c).

Nib shared senses 1, 2, and 4 with related **neb** [Old English *nebb*], the probable ancestor of *nipple* (at TIT)].

nice [ME. Old French, from Latin *nescius*, from *nescire* 'to be ignorant', from *scire* 'to know'] Ignorant, foolish, simple (–16c); modest, shy, coy (–17c); fastidious, discriminating, hence **1** precise, scrupulous, punctilious (15c); requiring great precision, discrimination, or tact; accurate, exact (16c); of differences: subtle. Hence **nicety** precision, accuracy **(a)** fine detail (18c) **2** delicate, sensitive (16c); refined, cultured, respectable (17c), hence pleasant, enjoyable (18c): ubiquitous and applied to a wide range of people and things, becoming almost meaningless through overuse.

Latin *nescire* produced **nescient** ignorant, later (an) agnostic; *scire* is the ancestor of *science* (at ART*).

niche [17c. French, from *nicher* 'to make a nest', ultimately from Latin *nidus* 'a nest'] A recess in a wall, especially for a statue, hence **1 (a)** a suitable or comfortable place or position in life (18c) **(b)** the role of an organism within its natural environment (1920s) **(c)** a specialized corner of the market (1960s) **2** a safe place, a retreat (18c) **3** a natural hollow in a rock or hill (19c) **4 (prayer) niche** (a motif on a prayer rug representing) the niche in a mosque that shows the direction of Mecca (*c.*1910).

Descendants, mainly technical, of Latin *nidus* include **nid(e)** a pheasant's brood or nest, and **nidify** to make a nest: *nidus* itself was adopted for a focus of infection in the body (a 'nest' of bacteria etc.), a spider or insect nest, a part of a plant where seeds or spores develop, or a place where something is formed or deposited.

nigh [Old English *ne(a)h*] **1** near in time or place; nearly, almost; of relatives or friends: close (ME) **2** of a road: short, direct (16c) **3** mean, stingy (16c, cf. CLOSE). The original comparative and superlative forms were **nar** [Old English *nearra*], which survives, just, in dialect, and **next** [Old English *nēhsta*]; the forms **nigher** and **nighest** arose in the 16c but are seldom used.

Replaced in ordinary use by **near** [related Old Norse *naer* 'nearer'], which developed the senses **1** to approach **2** left (referring to animals, traditionally handled or approached from the left side, which is thus nearer the handler): the **near side** of a vehicle is the one nearer the kerb.

nightmare [ME. From **night** (Old English *niht*) + *mare* 'goblin, incubus' (Old English *maere*)] A female spirit or monster that settled on sleeping people and animals, producing feelings of suffocation and distress; (a dream producing) such feelings (16c); a horrible or frightening dream or experience; (something) frightening or difficult to deal with (19c), sometimes shortened to **mare** (1990s).

A bad dream might also be caused by a **hag** [Old English *haegtesse*] a witch or evil spirit, later an ugly or spiteful (old) woman, or by an **incubus** [late Latin, from Latin *incubo* 'nightmare', from *incubare* 'to lie in or on', from *cubare* 'to lie'] a similar male spirit who also had sex with sleeping women: his female equivalent, the **succubus** [late Latin *succuba* 'prostitute', from *succubare* 'to lie under', from *cubare*] apparently did not give nightmares to the men she slept with.

Hag is related to **hex** [German *Hexe*] a witch; a spell or curse; to put one on someone; Latin *incubare* produced **incubate**; *cubare* is the ancestor of CUBICLE*.

nihilism [19c. (Via French, German, or Russian from) Latin *nihil* 'nothing'] **1** total rejection of religious and social mores; the beliefs of the Russian Nihilists that tradition and established authority must be destroyed before a just society can be built **2** in philosophy: an extreme form of scepticism involving the denial of all human values, of any objective basis for truth, and even of existence itself; in psychiatry: the belief that the world, or you yourself, no longer exist.

Latin *nihil* produced **annihilate** literally 'to make nothing', and was adopted meaning something of no value: the shortened form *nil* was adopted meaning 'nought, nothing'.

nimble [Old English *nǣmel*, from *niman* 'to take'] Quick to seize (OE only), hence **1** quick to take in or grasp (–15c: cf. CLEVER*); of the mind: quick, versatile, clever (16c) **2** quick, light, and agile.

Num, the past tense of Old English *niman*, evolved into **numb**, from the idea of having feeling taken away.

nip [ME. Probably from Low German or Dutch] (To give) a quick pinch, squeeze, cut, or bite, hence **1** nip **(off)** to cut or pinch off; to check or stop something growing or developing (16c) **2** to snatch or steal (15c, surviving in the US); to cadge, borrow, or extort money **3** to make narrower or tighter (*a nipped-in waist*, 16c) **4** of cold: to sting or bite (16c); a chilly feeling (*a nip in the air*); **nippy** chilly **5** pungency, a pungent flavour (19c, now mainly Scots) **6** to move nimbly, to go quickly (19c), hence **(a) nipper** a costermonger's boy (who nipped off to do errands); a child **(b) nippy** quick, sharp, nimble **7** nip **and tuck** neck and neck (19c: there are many theories for its origin, none very convincing); *nip* to beat narrowly (1940s, US).

Nip meaning a small quantity of spirits (originally a half-pint of ale) is probably an abbreviation of **nipperkin** a small measure or container [related to Dutch *nippen* 'to sip'].

Noel [ME. French *no(u)el*, variant of *nael*, from Latin *natalis* (*dies*) 'day of birth', from *nasci, nat-* 'to be born'. Spelt *nowel(l)* until the 19c] A cry of joy celebrating the birth of Christ, hence **1** a Christmas carol; Christmas (15c, now only in carols and on Christmas cards) **2** a name traditionally given to boys born on Christmas day, girls being called **Noelle, Noleen,** or **Natalie** [also from Latin *natalis*]: **Natasha** is the pet form of the Russian version, **Natalia.**

Latin *natalis* produced **natal** to do with (your) birth (hence *antenatal, neonatal,* etc.), and the name of the South African province of **Natal,** discovered on Christmas Day, 1497. *Nasci* is the ancestor of NATURE*.

noise [ME. French, from Latin *nausea* 'sea-sickness', perhaps later 'discomfort, annoyance, commotion', from Greek *nausia,* from *naus* 'ship'] Shouting, clamour, arguing, hence **1** a loud or unpleasant sound or sounds, hence **(a)** any sound **(b)** irregular fluctuations accompanying an electrical signal and interfering with it (1920s); useless data produced by a computer mixed up with the desired data (1970s) **2** talk, gossip, rumour, hence **(a)** to spread gossip or talk about (*noise abroad*) **(b) make a noise** to talk loudly or make a fuss about (17c); to be much talked about; *noise* someone who is; **big noise** someone important (1950s, *US*) **(c) make noises** to say or do something to express your (apparent) intentions (1950s).

Latin *nausea* was adopted for a general feeling of sickness, later of disgust or loathing; 'sea-sickness' appears later. Greek *naus* is the ancestor of **-naut** (*aeronaut* at AVIATOR) and **nautical.** Related to NAVIGATE*.

noon [Old English *nōn* from Latin *nona (hora)* 'ninth (hour)'] The ninth hour after sunrise, about 3 p.m.; prayers forming part of the Divine Office said at this time, later called **nones** [18c, also from Latin *nona*]. Benedictines held this service earlier, at about midday, and *noon* acquired its current meaning as the practice spread.

Noon produced *nuncheon* (at LUNCH); the surname **Noon** was given to a cheerful person, bright as the noonday sun.

normal [15c. (Via French from) Latin *normalis* 'made according to the square', from *norma* 'carpenter's square, pattern, standard'] **1** (describing) a regular verb (–16c) **2** right-angled, perpendicular (17c) **3** standard, regular, typical, ordinary (19c): the opposite in this sense is **abnormal** (19c), an alteration of **anormal** [16c. French, variant of *anomal,* via Latin from Greek *anomalos* 'uneven', from *homalos* 'even', from *homos* 'same'].

Latin *norma* produced ENORMITY* and **norm.** Greek *anomalos* produced **anomaly;** *homos* produced **homo-** (*homogeneous, homosexual*).

nose [Old English *nosu*] A mammal's organ of smell, hence **1** something resembling this: a nozzle (ME); the front of a ship, aircraft, etc. (16c) **2** the sense of smell (ME); to perceive by this (16c); **nose (out)** to sniff out, to discover (17c), hence *nose* the ability to do so (*a nose for scandal*); **nose about/into** to search furtively; **nosy** (objectionably) inquisitive (19c) **3** to push or rub the nose into or against (18c); to move forward cautiously (19c) **4** the aroma of a wine, tobacco, etc. (19c).

Nose produced **nozzle** and **nuzzle.** Related to **ness** a headland (mainly in place names, with the variant **Naze**).

note [ME. French, from Latin *notare* 'to mark', from *nota* 'a mark'] **1** to observe, to pay attention to; notice, regard, attention; importance, reputation; **notable**

remarkable, noticeable; **noted** distinguished, celebrated **2** to write down, hence **(a)** a brief written record (15c) **(b)** a brief comment or piece of information added to a text (16c) **(c)** a short informal written communication (16c), later briefly called a **notelet** (19c), which now means something resembling a greetings card for writing a note in (1950s) **(d)** a written promise to pay a certain sum (17c); **(bank) note** one issued by a bank and used as currency **(e)** a formal diplomatic communication (18c) **3** (a written sign for) a single musical tone, hence **(a)** a mark, sign, or token; a written or printed sign or character (16c) **(b)** any expressive sound or tone (*a note of caution*, 15c), hence a hint; a component of a flavour or smell (*c*.1900) **(c) notation** representation by signs or symbols (18c); a set of these, hence **notate** to write down using them (1920s).

Latin *notare* is the ancestor of **annotate**, **connote**, **denote**, and **notary** a clerk or secretary (ME–17c); someone authorized to draw up and certify legal documents, hence **notarize** to have a document certified by one (US).

notice [15c. French, from Latin *notitia* 'being known', from *notus* 'known', from *(g)noscere* 'to get to know'] Advance knowledge or information, a warning, hence **1** to inform of (–17c, outlived by **notify**, also from Latin *notus*); to mention, to draw attention to (16c); attention, heed; observation, perception (17c); **(to take) notice (of)** to pay attention to, to observe, perceive, or recognize (18c, replacing *notify*) **2** an announcement: **(a)** that a contract is to be terminated (18c), hence a period of warning **(b)** read out in church, school assembly, etc. (19c) **3** a sign, poster, etc. giving information (19c) **4** a brief mention in writing (19c), specifically a review of a book, play, etc.

Latin *(g)noscere* is the ancestor of **notion**, **notorious**, and QUAINT*. Related to IGNORE*, and distantly to GNOSTIC* and **noble** [Latin *nobilis* 'famous, celebrated, distinguished, well-born'].

nourish [ME. Old French *norir* from Latin *nutrire*] To rear a child or an animal (–16c); to suckle a baby or young animal (–17c, replaced by *nurse* below); to feed, to give people, animals, or plants what they need to grow or be healthy, hence to promote or foster; to help to grow or develop (partly replaced by *nurture* below).

Nourish produced the verb to **nurse**, which replaced it in some senses and overlaps with it in others, tending to mean 'to look after' rather than 'to feed': influenced by **nurse** [alteration of **nourice**, from Old French *nurice*, ultimately from Latin *nutrire*] a wet nurse; a nanny, hence **1** a carer; someone who looks after the sick; to do so **2** to hold or keep carefully.

Old French *norir* produced **nurture** originally meaning your upbringing or education; *nurice* produced the surnames **Norris** and **N(o)urse**, and **nursery** originally 'care, fostering'. Latin *nutrire* produced **nutrient**, **nutriment**, **nutrition**, and **nutritious**.

novel [Latin *novellus*, from *novus* 'new'] Strictly speaking, two words: **1** [15c, via Old French] young, fresh, newly made (–17c); original and interesting; something new (–18c, outlived by Middle English **novelty**) **2** [16c, via Italian *novella storia* 'new story'] a short story forming part of a longer work; a long fictional prose work (17c), hence **novelette** (18c) or Italian **novella** (*c*.1900) a short (romantic) novel.

Latin *novus* is the ancestor of **innovate**, French *nouveau* (feminine *nouvelle*), in phrases such as ***art nouveau, nouveau riche, nouvelle cuisine,*** **novice** [via Latin *novicius* 'newly enslaved or inexperienced person'] originally a person in a religious order who has not yet taken final vows, **nov(o)-** (**novocain** literally 'new cocaine', **Novocastrian** someone from Newcastle), and **renovate**. Latin *nova* [feminine of *novus*] was adopted for a 'new' star, later one which suddenly and briefly gets brighter. Related to Greek *neos* 'new', whence **neo-** (*neo-Nazi, neophyte* at PHYSIC) and **neon**, a gas not discovered until the 19c.

nucleus [18c. Latin, 'kernel', from *nuculus* 'little nut', from *nux, nucis* 'nut'] Adopted in various, mainly scientific, contexts meaning 'core, central part', hence something/someone around which others gather or may be collected, or from which something may grow. Hence **nuclear** being or forming a nucleus (*nuclear family,* 19c); to do with a nucleus or nuclei (19c), now atomic nuclei (1914); **nuclear energy/power** released by the fission or fusion of atomic nuclei (1930s); *nuclear* producing or using this power (1940s). Hence **nuke** a nuclear power station, weapon, etc. (1950s, US); to attack with nuclear weapons (1960s); to cook food in a microwave (1980s).

   Latin *nux* produced French ***nougat*** [via Provençal *noga* 'nut'] and *nutmeg* (at MUSK).

null [15c. (French, from) Latin *nullus* 'none', from *ullus* 'any', from *unus* 'one'] Amounting to nothing (*Scots legal term*), hence **1** not legally valid (16c, chiefly in *null and void*, hence **nullify** to make null, to invalidate: cf. *annul* below); insignificant, ineffective (18c) **2** a nought, a zero (17c); to do with, equal or amounting to, zero (19c); of a class or set: having no members (*c.*1900).

   Latin *nullus* produced **annul** to do away with, to abolish or cancel; to declare legally invalid. Latin *unus* is the ancestor of UNIT*.

nymph [ME. Via Old French from Latin *nympha*, from Greek *numphē* 'bride', later 'nymph'] A female nature spirit in classical mythology, hence **1** a beautiful young woman (16c) **2** the larva of some insects, resembling a small adult (16c); a fishing fly imitating a mayfly nymph (*c.*1900). Although nymphs inhabited woods and mountains as well as rivers, streams, and the sea, they became particularly associated with water, partly because of the Italian water spirits that were identified with them. Hence *nymph* a river or stream (16c, mainly in poetry); **nymphet** a white water lily (OE only, replaced by 16c **nymphaea** from the Latin name, *Nymphaea alba*): *nymphet* reappeared in 17c for a young or small nymph, later a desirable and sexually aware young girl (1955, in Vladimir Nabokov's novel *Lolita*).

   Latin *nympha* produced **nymphomania**. Greek *numphē* produced Latin *lympha* 'water nymph, water', whence **lymph** pure water, later a colourless bodily fluid.

O

object [ME. Partly from medieval Latin *objectum* 'something presented to the mind', partly from Latin *objectare* 'to keep throwing against', both from Latin *obicere* 'to put forward' (literally 'to throw against'), later 'to hinder or oppose', from *jacere* 'to throw' (ancestor of JET*)] To put something in the way (–19c); what is put, an obstacle or hindrance (*money no object*), hence **1** a statement opposing something (–19c, outlived by **objection**); to make one (15c); to oppose **2** something put before your eyes, hence **(a)** a visible or tangible thing; an entity; something that exists outside your mind (17c), hence **objective** not affected by emotions or personal bias (19c): cf. *subjective* (at SUBJECT) **(b)** (the image of) someone/something observed through a lens etc.; the focus of attention or emotion (16c) **(c)** someone/something to whom something is done; in grammar: a noun affected by the action of a verb (18c, cf. SUBJECT) **(d)** the aim or purpose of an action, hence **objective** (something) sought or aimed at.

obnoxious [16c. Latin *obnoxiosus* or *obnoxius*, from *noxa* 'harm'] **1** exposed to harm or injury, vulnerable (now rare) **2** subject to some authority, submissive, obsequious (–18c) **3** open to censure, reprehensible (17c) **4** (partly by association with 15c **noxious**, also from Latin *noxa*) harmful (17c only); offensive, odious.

observe [ME. Via French from Latin *observare* 'to attend to', from *servare* 'to watch or keep' (ancestor of CONSERVE*)] **1 (a)** to inspect or watch for omens **(b)** to watch or examine methodically (16c); in medical use, to do so without intervention **(c)** to perceive (16c); to note; to comment or mention that (cf. REMARK) **2** to comply with a law, custom, etc.; to mark a festival or other occasion in the proper way.

obsess [ME. Latin *obsidere*, *obsess-* 'to besiege', from *sedere* 'to sit' (ancestor of SESSION*)] Of an evil spirit: to haunt or possess, hence to beset or harass (16c); **obsession** something that occupies your mind to the exclusion of all else (17c), hence *obsess* to preoccupy (19c); to think or worry about something compulsively (1970s, *US*).

obtuse [ME. Latin *obtusus*, from *obtundere* 'to strike against, to blunt', from *tundere* 'to beat'] Not sharp or pointed, hence **1** slow to understand (16c) **2** of an angle: between 90° and 180° **3** of pain: dull (17c). Cf. ACUTE.

Latin *obtundere* produced **obtund** to blunt, dull, or deaden. Related to TOIL*.

obvious [16c. Latin *obvius*, from *ob viam* 'in the way', from *via* 'road, way']
1 frequently encountered, common (–18c) **2** in the way, in front of, facing (17c),
hence easy to see or understand.

Latin *obvius* produced **obviate**; *via* is the ancestor of TRIVIAL*.

occasion [ME. (Via French from) Latin *occasio* 'juncture, reason', from *occidere*,
occas- 'to go down', from *cadere* 'to fall'] **1** a set of circumstances: **(a)** a favourable
one, an opportunity **(b)** one requiring action (16c); necessary action or business;
something giving grounds for an action, a reason, motive, or cause **2** something
that happens, an incident or event (–17c); a time when something happens (16c);
a special event (19c).

Latin *occasio* produced **occasional** happening on or made for a particular occasion, hence irregular, infrequent; acting, employed, or designed to be used irregularly or on special occasions. *Occidere* produced **occident** [via *occidens* 'sunset,
west': cf. ORIENT]; *cadere* is the ancestor of CASE[1]*.

occult [15c. Latin *occulere*, from *celare* 'to hide' (ancestor of **conceal** and perhaps
CEILING)] Hidden, secret, hence **1** to hide, hence **(a)** **occultation** the hiding of a
celestial body by another one between it and the observer (16c); *occult* to hide or
be hidden in this way (18c) **(b)** of a lighthouse beam: to disappear as part of its
cycle (19c) **2** hidden from ordinary people (16c); to do with magic, alchemy, etc.
(17c); mysterious, magical, mystical; **the occult** the supernatural (*c*.1900).

occupy [ME. Via Old French from Latin *occupare* 'to seize', from *capere* 'to take'
(ancestor of CATCH*)] **1** to take possession of, to seize (–17c); to take over a country; to take over a building etc. as a protest (1960s) **2** to take up space or time,
hence **(a)** to live or stay in **(b)** to take up your time and attention, hence **occupation** being kept busy, employment; what you do for a living **3** to hold an office
or position **4** to cohabit or have a sexual relationship with (16–17c, leading to the
word almost falling out of polite use until the late 18c).

odd [ME. Old Norse *odda-* in *odda-mathr* 'third or odd man' (one holding a casting
vote), from *oddi* 'point, triangle, odd number'] Left over after division into pairs
or equal parts, hence **1** not divisible exactly by two; not even or equal (–16c);
odds inequalities (16c), hence **(a)** the ratio between the amounts staked by two
parties to a bet, based on the probabilities of the result, hence the chances of
something happening **(b)** a difference in advantage or significance (*it makes no
odds*, 17c) **2** slightly more or over (*fifty odd*) **3** single, solitary (surviving in dialect); separated from, or not part of, a pair or set (*an odd shoe*, 18c), hence
oddment(s), **odds and ends/bobs** miscellaneous articles, also **odds and sods**
(World War I, *Forces slang*, originally applied to men not attached to a particular
unit) **4** occasional, irregular, haphazard (*odd jobs, the odd day off*) **5** different,
strange, extraordinary (16c), hence **oddity** something/someone peculiar **6** in
conflict with (16–17c, surviving in *at odds with*).

ode [16c. French, from late Latin *oda*, from Greek *(a)ōidē* 'song, singing', from
aeidein 'to sing'] A poem intended or adapted for singing; a type of lyric poem,
usually with complex rhyme or metre (19c).

Greek *(a)ōidē*'s descendants include **hymnody**, MELODY*, **parody** [via Greek *parō-
idia* 'burlesque song'], **prosody** [via Latin from Greek *prosōdia* 'song sung to music,
(mark indicating) the tone of a syllable'], **psalmody**, **rhapsody**, and TRAGEDY*.

offend [ME. Via Old French from Latin *offendere* 'to strike against', from *fendere* 'to strike': see DEFEND*. **Offence** comes from *offendere* via Latin *offensus* 'annoyance' and *offensa* 'a knock against something, hurt, wrong'] To stub your toe, to trip or stumble (–15c); to trip up morally, to do wrong, hence **1** to attack, to act aggressively (–18c), hence **(a)** *offence* an aggressive act (15c); in sport: the attacking team or players (1920s, N American) **(b)** **offensive** to do with (an) attack (16c); an aggressive act or campaign (18c) **2** to hurt physically (–18c); to hurt someone's feelings; to cause annoyance, resentment, or disgust, hence *offence* such feelings; *offensive* causing offence (16c) **3** to break a law, hence *offence* a crime or misdemeanour; **offender** someone who commits one (15c).

offer [Old English *offrian* from Latin *offerre*, *oblat-* 'to bring to', from *ferre* 'to bring'] **1** to give as an act of worship **2** to tender (ME): **(a)** (to make) a suggestion; to volunteer to do or give something (*offered to help/offered us tea*); an expression of readiness to do so **(b)** to make available (*the trees offered welcome shade*, 16c) **(c)** to put up for sale (17c); an invitation to buy, especially at a reduced price (18c); (to make) a bid for something for sale **3** **offer (up)** to put something in place to see if it's right (19c).

Latin *offere* produced **offertory** the part of the Eucharist when the bread and wine are placed on the altar; the making of offerings at this time, hence a collection made at any religious service, and **proffer** [via Old French *proffrir* 'to hold out to someone']. *Oblat-* produced **oblate** someone devoted to a religious life, and **oblation** offering (specifically the bread and wine at the Eucharist) as a religious act; what is offered. Latin *ferre* is the ancestor of CONFER*.

office [ME. French, from Latin *officium* 'duty, performance of a task' (in medieval Latin also 'rite, divine service'), from *opus* 'work' + *facere* 'to do'] A duty, service, task, or function, hence **1** (tenure of) a position of trust or authority, hence **officer** someone holding a public or ecclesiastical one, as opposed to an **official** who originally had such a position in a private household **2** (the prescribed form of) a church service; a rite or ceremony (*last offices*); to preside at one (–16c, replaced by 17c **officiate**) **3** **offices** service or kindness done (*good offices*) **4** a place of business; one where clerical work or some specific function is carried out (*sales/lost property office*), hence **(a)** the part of a house or its outbuildings set aside for a specific purpose (*the usual offices*, 16c) **(b)** (the building housing) a government department (*Home Office*, 18c) **(c)** an official regulatory body (1980s), often abbreviated (*Ofcom*) **5** (to give) a hint or a (private) signal (19c) **6** *official* authorized, particularly by government (18c), hence formally accepted or agreed.

Latin *officium* produced OFFICIOUS; *opus* is the ancestor of OPERATION*, and *facere* of FACT*.

officious [15c. Latin *officiosus*, from *officium:* see OFFICE] **1** serving its purpose, functional, effective (–19c) **2** zealously doing your duty (16–18c), hence **(a)** attentive, obliging (–19c) **(b)** intrusive, interfering, domineering.

olive [ME. French, from Latin *oliva*, from Greek *elaia*, from *elaion* 'olive (oil)'] A Mediterranean tree; its fruit, yielding valuable oil. Hence **1** an olive leaf, branch, or wreath symbolizing peace and goodwill (because a dove released from Noah's ark brought back an olive branch, showing that the floods had subsided and God and mankind were reconciled, the dove also becoming a symbol of peace: see the Bible, Genesis 8) **2** something shaped like an olive (*beef olive*, 17c) **3 (a)** (of) the yellowish-green colour of an unripe olive (17c), hence **olivenite**, **olivine** olive-coloured minerals (both 19c) **(b)** (of) a yellowish-brown colour (*olive complexion*).

Greek *elaia* produced Latin *oleum* 'olive oil', whence *linoleum* (at LINE), **oil**, **oleaginous**, and *petroleum* (at PETRIFY). The names **Olive**, **Oliver**, and **Olivia** (introduced by Shakespeare in *Twelfth Night*) are not related, being forms of the Germanic name *Olaf*.

omnibus [19c. French from Latin, literally 'for all', from Latin *omnis* 'all' (whence **omni-** in *omnipotent* etc.)] **1** a large public passenger vehicle, quickly shortened to **bus**, which came to mean **(a)** to go or send by bus, hence **bussing** to transport schoolchildren to another area to help racial integration (1960s, *US*) **(b)** an aeroplane (*c*.1910), later a car **2 omnibus (bar)** a bar, wire, etc. that carries all the electrical power from a source (19c), hence **bus (bar)** a system of conductors that receives power from a number of generators (*c*.1900); *bus* a data channel in a computer system (1930s) **3** describing a book, broadcast, etc. containing several items or episodes (1920s) **4** a waiter's assistant who clears tables etc. (19c), later called a **bus boy** (*c*.1910, *US*), hence *bus* to clear tables.

one [Old English *ān*. In the 15c often spelt *won(e)*, whence the current pronunciation] The lowest cardinal number, 1, hence **1** the indefinite article (–16c, surviving as **an**, reduced to **a** before a consonant) **2** single, individual; something singular (ME) **3** (describing) a single entity; a single member of an (understood) set (*one of us*, *one of those things*), hence **(a)** referring to something previously mentioned (*a tabby cat and a black one*, ME) **(b)** (describing) an extreme example (*she's one sick girl/you are a one*, 19c) **(c) one of a kind** unique (1960s, *US*, based on *two of a kind*) **4** a typical person, often referring to the speaker (*one can't do any more*, ME, largely replaced by *you*), hence yourself, your own interest (16c, now usually **number one**, 19c).

One produced **once**. Old English *ān* produced *ānlīce* **only**, and *nān* 'not one', **none**, shortened to **no** (originally only before consonants): **no** expressing a negative is from Old English *na*, literally 'not ever'.

ooze [Old English *wōs*] Juice, sap (–15c), hence **1** to exude moisture, to seep (ME); a very slow flow or exudation (18c) **2** the liquid in a tanning vat (16c). Often associated with **ooze** wet mud or slime; a mud bank or marsh [Old English *wāse*].

opaque [ME. (French, from) Latin *opacus*: usually spelt *opake* until the 19c, when the French spelling was adopted] **1** lying in shadow, darkened, obscure (–18c); dark, dull (18c) **2** impervious to light (17c), hence **(a)** such a medium or space (18c); an opaque photographic pigment (*c*.1900) **(b)** hard to understand or make out (18c, 16c in **opacity** obscurity of meaning: cf. SEE*) **(c)** impervious to other forms of radiation (19c).

operation [ME. French, from Latin *operari*, *operat-* 'to work', from *opus*, *oper-* 'work'] **1** the exertion of force or influence to produce an effect; work, purposeful activity **2** an action or deed (–16c); an action or series of actions as part of a process, a procedure; a (military) action or campaign (18c); an (illegal) business or activity. **Operate** to work, to make a machine etc. work, to carry out or manage an operation, did not appear until the 17c.

Latin *opus* was adopted for an artistic or musical composition, originally in *magnum opus* [literally 'great work'] an artist's most important piece, and produced **cooperate**, **inure**, MANURE*, OFFICE*, and Italian *opera* (a) musical drama; an opera house: **opry**, representing a US dialect pronunciation, has been immortalized in **Grand Ole Opry** a radio show playing country music from Nashville, which helped establish the city as a musical centre.

opossum [17c. Virginian Algonquian *opassom*, literally 'white doglike creature'] A small American marsupial, quickly shortened to **possum** (some American dialects commonly drop unstressed syllables). Both forms were applied to similar animals found in Australia and New Zealand, *possum* being regarded as informal except in Australia, where it is standard and has become an affectionate or mildly derogatory term for a person (19c). Hence (because frightened possums play dead) **play possum** to feign sickness or ignorance (19c, *US*); **rouse/stir the possum** to add excitement or controversy (*c*.1900, Australia).

opportune [ME. Via French from Latin *opportunus*, describing wind blowing towards the harbour, hence favourable, from *portus* 'harbour'] Advantageous, useful (–17c); of a time or, formerly, a place: suitable, convenient (15c), hence fitting the time or circumstances; timely. Cf. IMPORTUNE.

Opportune produced **opportunism** originally political expediency (inspired by similar words in French and Italian), later simply making the most of opportunities. Latin *opportunus* produced **opportunity**; *portus* is the ancestor of PORT[1]*.

oppose [ME. French *opposer* from Latin *opponere*, *opposit-*, literally 'to set against', from *ponere* 'to put': see POSE*] **1** to face someone with objections or questions (–17c); to raise objections or ask difficult questions (16c), replacing **appose** [ME–17c, from French *aposer*, a variant of *opposer*], which was shortened to **pose** to ask a question; to perplex with a difficult one (16c), hence **poser** such a question **2** to be against someone/something, to contest, resist, or obstruct (15c) **3** to put something in front of or facing something else (16c, earlier and more common in **opposite**) **4** to set something up in contrast to something else (16c).

Latin *opponere* produced **opponent** originally someone who challenged a philosophical or theological thesis, and **opposite**.

optimism [18c. French *optimisme* from Latin *optimum* 'the best', from *optimus* 'best'] **1** the character or quality of being best or for the best (–19c) **2** the doctrine that this is the best of all possible worlds, hence the belief that, ultimately, good will prevail (19c); the tendency to expect or hope for the best; confidence in the future. The opposite is **pessimism** [18c, from Latin *pessimus* 'worst', modelled on *optimism*].

Latin *optimum* was adopted for the conditions most favourable for a plant; *optimus* produced **optimal**, **optimist**, and **optimize**. Except for **pessimist**, their opposites from *pessimus* are not in general use.

option [16c. (French, from) Latin *optare*, *opt-* 'to choose'] **1** (the making of) a choice; something that may be chosen, hence **(a) soft option** an easier course of action (1920s) **(b)** a piece of non-standard equipment available separately (1950s) **2** the right to choose, freedom of choice (17c), hence the right to buy or sell (originally shares) at an agreed price within a certain time (18c).

Latin *optare* is the ancestor of **adopt** [(via French from) Latin *adoptare* 'to choose as your own'] and **opt.**

oracle [ME. French, from Latin *oraculum*, from *orare* 'to speak or pray'] The place where, or the means by which, a god could speak to mortals; the priest(ess) who spoke on the god's behalf, hence **1** the Holy of Holies in the Jewish Temple **2** (a) divine inspiration or revelation; a wise or prophetic statement (15c); something believed to be an infallible sign (18c) **3** someone/something that teaches the word of God; a wise person, an infallible authority (16c) **4** the (cryptic) message delivered (16c); **oracular** cryptic, mysterious or ambiguous (18c).

Latin *orare* is the ancestor of ADORE, **inexorable**, ORATION, **orator**, ORATORY*, and **perorate.**

oration [ME. Latin *oratio* 'discourse, prayer', from *orare*: see ORACLE*] **1** a prayer **2** a formal public speech, especially one showing rhetorical skill (16c), hence **orate** to make one (19c, *US*); to speak pompously or at length. Hence **orator 1** an (eloquent or pompous) public speaker **2** a petitioner, originally to God, later in a law court (surviving in the US).

Latin *oratio* produced **orison** [via French *oraison*].

oratory [Two words, both from Latin *orare*: see ORACLE*] I [ME, via Anglo-Norman French from Latin *oratorium*] A place for prayer, a small chapel or a room for private worship. The **Oratory of St Philip Neri**, a society of priests whose aim was to bring people to God through plain preaching and attractive services, was founded in Rome in 1564 and named after the chapel where they met and their founder. They later moved to a larger church and held musical services, hence Italian **oratorio** (18c), and *oratory* a similar society (19c); a church belonging to either II [16c, via Latin *oratorius* 'to do with an orator'] (the art of) public speaking.

orb [ME. Latin *orbis* (ancestor of ORBIT*)] **1** a circle; something circular; to encircle (17c) **2** a sphere, originally the one thought to contain the earth (see SPHERE), hence **(a)** a celestial body **(b)** the eyeball or eye (17c): cf. ORBIT sense 1 **(c)** a sphere of action (cf. ORBIT sense 3) **(d)** a golden globe forming part of a monarch's regalia (18c) **3** to make circular or spherical (17c).

orbit [16c. Latin *orbita* 'course, track', in medieval Latin 'eye-socket', from *orbitus* 'circular' from *orbis* ORB] **1** the eye socket; the eye (18c, probably by confusion with ORB sense 2b); the area around a bird or insect's eye **2** the track a celestial body or a spacecraft follows around a planet or star (17c); one revolution of this, hence **(a)** a similar track of one thing around another (19c), hence **orbital** describing a road, railway, etc. that goes around a large town (1930s) **(b)** to travel in an orbit (1940s); to follow a regular (circular or elliptical) path (1950s) **3** a sphere of influence or activity (early 20c: cf. ORB sense 2c).

Latin *orbita* produced *exorbitare* 'to go off the track', whence **exorbitant.**

orchestra [17c. Latin, from Greek *orkhēstra*, from *orkheisthai* 'to dance'] The space in front of the stage in an ancient Greek theatre where the chorus performed; this space in a Roman theatre, where important people sat, hence **1 orchestra (stalls)** the front stalls (18c) **2 orchestra (pit)** the part of a theatre, usually in front of the stage, for the musicians (18c), hence *orchestra* the musicians; a large group of musicians playing classical music on a variety of instruments; the instruments (19c). Hence **orchestrate** to arrange music for an orchestra (19c); to direct or coordinate elements of a situation.

ordain [ME. (Old French *ordener* from) Latin *ordinare* 'to put in order, regulate, appoint', from *ordo, ordin-* 'row, array, degree, command'] **1 (a)** to appoint someone to a position or office, now only a religious one **(b)** to assign or appoint for a particular purpose (surviving in English dialect and in Canada) **2** to order or establish formally; to order something to be done, or someone to do it **3** to put in order: **(a)** to arrange in rows, especially in battle order (–16c) **(b)** to regulate **(c)** to plan or devise (–17c); to initiate or arrange **4** to prepare: **(a)** to prepare to do something (–15c) **(b)** to prepare something for a purpose (–16c); to fit out or equip.

Ordain's noun is **ordination**, which formerly shared the duty with **ordinance** [Old French *ordenance*, ultimately from Latin *ordinare*], now meaning an authoritative decree, regulation, law, or practice, also a sacrament. *Ordinance*'s earlier senses included 'something prepared or provided, specifically (military) equipment or supplies', surviving in **ordnance** [contraction of Old French *ordenance*], which came to mean an organization responsible for providing these, hence **Ordnance Survey** (the body set up to conduct) a survey of Great Britain and Ireland, originally for military purposes.

Latin *ordinare* is the ancestor of COORDINATE, *disordain* (ME–15c), survived by **disorder** (an alteration influenced by ORDER), **inordinate** literally 'not regulated', and SUBORDINATE*.

ordeal [Old English *ordāl, ordēl*: related to DEAL*] A form of trial in which the accused underwent painful or dangerous tests, the outcome being held to reflect divine judgement, hence any painful or harrowing experience (17c).

order [ME. Via French from Latin *ordo*: see ORDAIN*] **1** a rank: **(a)** of angels **(b)** of Christian clergy (surviving in **holy orders**) **(c)** in society (*lower orders*) **(d)** in maths: a degree of complexity (18c) **2** a group or class of people or things: **(a)** a monastic society; a fraternity of Christian knights; an institution partly imitating this founded by a monarch to confer honours (*Order of the Garter*) **(b) (natural) order** a grouping of related genera, now called a family (18c: see TAXONOMY) **3** (to bring about) a methodical or sequential arrangement **4** a (good, efficient, or peaceful) state or condition (*public order*, **out of order**: broken, not working; behaving unacceptably) **5** (to give) a command or (written) instruction (*postal/restraining order*, 16c), specifically one to supply something (18c); what is ordered (19c).

Descendants of Latin *ordo* include ORDER, **ordinal**, and ORDINARY*.

ordinary [ME. (Via Old French from) Latin *ordinarius* 'orderly, usual', from *ordo*: see ORDAIN*] A formula, rule, or custom (ME only), hence **1** a judge, archbishop, etc. having immediate rather than delegated authority **2** (something) customary, usual; commonplace, hence typical of common people, coarse, vulgar (17–19c), surviving in N America as **ornery** coarse, mean, cantankerous. Hence **3 extraordinary** [ME, Latin *extraordinarius*, from *extra* 'outside, beyond', from *exter* 'outward'] out of the ordinary, hence **(a)** in addition to the ordinary staff (*ambassador extraordinary*, 16c) **(b)** exceptional, remarkable, strange, extreme (16c).

English **extra** is probably from *extraordinary*. Latin *extra* produced **extra-** (*extrasensory*, EXTRAVAGANT) and *extraneus* (at STRANGE*); *exter* produced **exterior, external**, and **extreme**.

organ [Old English *organa* and Old French *organe*, both from Latin *organum* '(musical) instrument, engine, tool, pipe', from Greek *organon*] **1** a wind instrument (surviving in 17c **mouth organ**, originally meaning pan pipes); one using air passing through pipes (ME) **2** a part of a living being with a specific function (*vital organs*, ME) **3** a mechanical device (ME); a means of doing something, now a means of communication, specifically a newspaper or journal regarded as the mouthpiece of a group (18c).

Latin *organum* produced **organism** (a system similar to) a living being, and **organize** to provide with bodily organs, hence to form into an orderly whole. Greek *organon* produced ORGANIC, and was briefly adopted for a bodily organ, later for a set of principles for philosophical or scientific investigation. Latin *organum* was adopted, but rarely used, in the same senses; it is now applied to kinds of medieval polyphonic music.

organic [ME. Via French and Latin from Greek *organikos* 'to do with an organ, instrumental', from *organon* ORGAN*] **1** to do with or affecting a bodily organ or organs **2** to do with, derived from, or similar to, a living being (17c), hence **(a)** to do with or describing carbon compounds, originally those occurring naturally in living beings (19c) **(b)** from or produced using only natural substances (*organic fertilizer/chicken*) **(c)** appearing to develop naturally (1920s) **3** intrinsic, fundamental, structural (18c).

orgy [16c. Via French and Latin from Greek *orgia* 'rites'] **Orgies** secret rites, especially those in honour of Bacchus (the god of wine) marked by drinking, dancing, and song, hence *orgy* a celebration involving unrestrained eating, drinking, and sex (18c); a period of wild indulgence.

Bacchus gave his name to **bacchanalia** the Roman festivities in his honour, hence drunken revelry.

orient [ME. French, from Latin *oriens* 'rising, sunrise, east', from *oriri* 'to rise'. Cf. *occident* (at OCCASION)] The sky where the sun rises, hence **1** shining, radiant; (like) the sunrise **2** the east; now usually SE Asia; in, from, or belonging to this (largely replaced by **oriental**); of a pearl: high quality, lustrous, precious (15c, pearls from the Indian seas being finer than those from European mussels); (the lustre of) a top-quality pearl (18c) **3** to place facing the east (18c) or a particular direction (19c, also as **orientate**, a back-formation from *orientation*), hence **(a) orientation** the resulting position; the direction in which your thoughts or tendencies lie (*sexual orientation*) **(b)** to find the bearings of (19c), hence **orient yourself** to find out where you are; to find your way; to familiarize yourself with your surroundings: cf. **disorient** [17c, from French *désorienter*] and **disorientate** (18c), both meaning to make someone feel lost and confused.

Orient produced **orienteering** [via Swedish]. Latin *oriri* is the ancestor of ABORIGINES*.

ornament [ME. Via Old French from Latin *ornamentum*, from *ornare* 'to furnish, fit out, or adorn'] Equipment, furniture, trappings (–18c), hence **1 ornaments** church accessories, furnishings, vestments, etc. **2** a decoration or embellishment:

(a) a decorative object **(b)** a person or quality that is a source of pride (16c) **(c)** a grace note in music (17c) **3** adornment, embellishment, decoration (15c); to adorn or embellish (18c).

Latin *ornare* is the ancestor of **adorn**, **ornate**, and **suborn** to induce someone to do wrong by underhand means [via Latin *subornare*, literally 'to equip secretly'].

osculate   [17c. Latin *osculare* 'to kiss', from *osculum* 'a kiss', literally 'little mouth', from *os, or-* 'mouth, face'] To kiss, hence to come together (18c); of a curve: to touch another without crossing it.

Latin *osculum* was adopted for a pore or orifice, especially one through which a sponge expels water. Descendants of Latin *os* include **oral**, **orifice**, **orotund** (at ROTUND), **oscillate** [Latin *oscillare* 'to swing', from *oscillum* 'swing, mask', from the masks hung on trees during certain festivals], and **usher** [Anglo-Norman French *usser* from, ultimately, Latin *ostiarius* 'doorkeeper', from *ostium* 'door'].

ostentation   [15c. French, from Latin *ostentare, ostent-* 'to display or exhibit', from *ostendere* 'to show', literally 'to stretch out before', from *tendere* 'to stretch'] **1** a sign or portent of future events (–17c) **2** the act of showing, (an) exhibition, demonstration, or display; pretentious or vulgar display, hence **ostentatious** pretentious, showy, gaudy (17c); conspicuous (18–19c).

Latin *ostendere* produced **ostensible**, which once had both senses of *ostentatious*. Latin *tendere* is the ancestor of TEMPT*.

ostracism   [16c. Via French and Latin from Greek *ostrakismos*, from *ostrakon* 'shell, potsherd'] The ancient Greek custom of voting to banish a citizen, the votes being written on potsherds, hence **ostracize** to exclude someone from society or group (17c).

Greek *ostrakon* produced **ostracon**, an archaeologists' term for a potsherd used to write on. Related to **oyster** and to Greek *osteon* 'bone', whence **osteo-** (*osteoporosis*).

oust   [ME. Anglo-Norman French *ouster* 'to take away', from Latin *obstare* 'to oppose, hinder', literally 'to stand against', from *stare* 'to stand'] In law: to deprive someone of an estate, possession, or inheritance, hence **1** to take away a right or privilege (17c) **2** to force someone from a place or position (17c).

Latin *obstare* is the ancestor of **obstacle** and **obstetric** [Latin *obstetrix* 'midwife', who stands ready to receive the child], and *stare* of STATION*.

overture   [ME. Old French, from Latin *apertura*, from *aperire* 'to open or uncover'] A hole, an opening (–18c), hence **1 (a) overtures** an opening of negotiations or discussion (15c) **(b)** a proposal for consideration by a legislative body (16c), now only in the Presbyterian church **2** a beginning (16–18c), hence **(a)** an orchestral piece at the beginning of an opera etc. (17c) **(b)** an introductory passage of a poem or other written work (19c).

Latin *apertura* produced **aperture**. Latin *aperire* is the ancestor of **aperient**, and of French *apéritif* and *overt* [literally 'open'] not hidden or secret, which replaced **apert** [Old French, from Latin *apertus* 'open'] open(ly), public(ly); also straightforward, outspoken, insolent, surviving in the shortened form **pert**, which also meant beautiful, later lively, sprightly, cheerful (surviving in dialect and the US); jaunty and neat.

owe [Old English *āgan*] To have or possess, replaced except in dialect by **own** [Old English *agnian*, from the past participle of *āgan*, whence also **own** in *my own* etc.], hence **1** to have as a duty or obligation (–16c, hence **ought** [Old English *āhte*, past tense of *āgan*]); to have a moral or financial obligation (*owe you an explanation/£50*); to be indebted to, to have something because of (*owes her success to hard work*, 16c), hence **owing to** arising from, caused by (17c); because of (19c) **2** to have a certain feeling for someone (ME, surviving in *owe a grudge*).

P

pace [ME. Via French from Latin *passus*, literally 'a stretch (of the leg)', from *pandere* 'to stretch'] A step, hence **1** a gait: **(a)** one of a horse's gaits (trot, canter, etc.); **put through his/your** etc. **paces** to test a horse's action in all gaits; to make a person show their accomplishments (18c) **(b)** of an animal: to move both legs on the same side together (17c); this gait (cf. AMBLE) **2** the speed of your gait; speed in general, hence to set this (19c) **3** a narrow way between mountains, bogs, etc., a strait (–17c, surviving as the variant **pass**) **4** a section of a story or poem (–17c, replaced by Latin *passus*, 16c) **5** to step (16c); to walk to and fro or with regular strides; **pace (out)** to measure by counting steps.

Latin *passus* produced COMPASS*, PASS*, French *passage* in horse-riding: to (cause to) move sideways, and TRESPASS. Latin *pandere* is the ancestor of **expand**, **Spandex** a trade name for a stretchy fabric, and **spawn** [Old French *espandre* 'to spread or pour out', whence, probably, **spandrel** a space between beams, later between two arches].

pack [ME. Of early Dutch or Low German origin] **1** a collection of things tied or wrapped up together; to make up into a pack or put into a receptacle; to fill a receptacle or space (*pack a suitcase/the place was packed*), hence **(a)** to carry in a pack (15c); to carry or wear habitually (*pack a gun*); **pack a punch** to be able to hit hard (1920s), to be powerful (1930s) **(b) pack (up)** to pack your belongings and leave (15c), hence **send packing/pack off** to send away; **pack (it) up/in** to stop doing something (1940s) **(c)** to be able to be packed without harm (19c) **(d)** a receptacle: a rucksack (*c*.1915, *military*); a package or packet (1920s) **2** a group of animals living or hunting together; a group of people (often derogatory); a number of similar things (*pack of cards/lies*, 16c) **3** to press close together (16c) **4** to protect with material, padding, etc. (18c), hence **(a) packing** such material (19c); a charge made for doing so (*c*.1900) **(b)** a protective substance that hardens when dry, used in dentistry (1920s); **(face/mud) pack** a not dissimilar substance for cleaning the pores (1930s).

Ancestor of PACKAGE and PACKET.

package [16c. From PACK*] **1** the action of packing **2** a small bundle or parcel (18c); a number of things, services, etc. put or sold together (*package holiday/ salary package*, 1920s); to put things together in a package (cf. BUNDLE); to produce something complex for someone else to sell (1960s) **3** a box etc. in which goods are sold (19c); to present something attractively (1940s).

packet [16c. From PACK*] A small package, originally of letters or (State) dispatches, hence **1 packet (boat)** that travels regularly between two ports, originally carrying mail (17c) **2** a bullet or shell (World War I), surviving in *stop/cop a packet* **3** a large sum of money (*cost a packet*, 1920s: cf. BUNDLE).

pact [ME, from Latin *pacisci* 'to make an agreement'] An agreement or treaty; to enter into one (16c). Hence **pack** [the final *t* of *pact* being taken for *-ed*] to intrigue or conspire (16–17c); to select members of a jury etc. to get a favourable verdict.
Latin *pacisci* produced **compact** an agreement [via Latin *compacisci* 'to agree together']. Related to PAY*.

pagan [ME. Latin *paganus* 'villager', later 'civilian', also 'heathen' (partly because pre-Christian beliefs persisted longer in the countryside, partly because Christians were considered soldiers of Christ), from *pagus* 'country district'] A heathen, now specifically a follower of an ancient polytheistic or pantheistic religion.
Latin *paganus* is the ultimate ancestor of the surname **Payne** and some instances of **Pain**, of the place name **Painswick**, and of **peasant**.

page [ME. French, perhaps via Italian *paggio* from Greek *paidion* 'small child', from *pais, paid-* 'child, boy' (ancestor of PEDAGOGUE*)] A youth (–16c); a lower-class man or boy (–16c); a male servant, assistant, or apprentice (cf. BOY*), also as a surname, with the variants **Pa(d)get(t)** and **Paige**, hence **1** a youth attending a knight and training for knighthood (cf. SQUIRE); a personal servant in a royal or noble household **2 page (boy)** a uniformed errand boy in a hotel etc. (18c), hence *page* to send or search for someone by having their name called out by a page (*c.*1900, *US*) or over a loudspeaker etc. (1930s), or by using a **pager** a radio device with a bleeper (1960s) **3 page (boy)** a small boy attending a bride (19c).

pageant [ME. Medieval Latin *pagina*, perhaps from Latin *pagina* 'trellis, column of writing, page of a book', from *pangere* 'to fasten' (ancestor of IMPACT*)] A scene, especially from a mystery play; a tableau; the platform on which either is presented. Hence **pageantry** elaborate or ceremonial public display (17c); *pageant* such an event (19c), especially a parade, or scenes illustrating historical events; **(beauty) pageant** a beauty contest (1980s, US).

palace [ME. French *palais* from Latin *Palatium* the Palatine Hill in Rome where the Emperor Augustus built a house, and where the Caesars later lived] The official residence of a sovereign, later of an (arch)bishop, hence **1** a splendid, imposing, or luxurious house; a large, often ornate, building for public entertainments or refreshment (19c) **2** the monarch or the monarchy (1960s).
French *palais (de danse)* was adopted for a dance hall. Latin *Palatium* produced **paladin** one of Charlemagne's knights (see PEER), hence a legendary champion or knight errant, **palatial**, **palatine** originally describing a feudal lord having sovereign power within his territory (whence **palatinate** originally the territory ruled by the Count Palatine of the Rhine), and Italian *palazzo* a magnificent building.

palaver [18c. Portuguese *palavra* from Latin *parabola*: see PARABLE*] A discussion or conference, originally between local Africans and European traders, hence cajolery, flattery, time-consuming talk; fuss, bother, a to-do (19c).

pale [ME. Via French from Latin *palus*] A pointed fence stake; a vertical bar or slat in a fence; a fence made of pales, hence **1** an enclosing fence; a limit, boundary, or restriction (15c), **beyond the pale** beyond the limits of acceptable behaviour **2** an enclosed area (15c); a defined territory subject to a particular jurisdiction.

Pale produced **paling** (the building of) a fence with pales. Descendants of Latin *palus* include **impale** originally meaning to enclose with pales or a paling, **palisade**, the surnames **Palliser** someone who made pales and **Peel** a tall, thin person, **pole** a stake or rod, later a measure of length (see PERCH), and TRAVAIL*.

pall [Old English *paell*, from Latin *pallium* 'covering, cloak'] Fine (purple) cloth for robes, hence **1** a covering for an altar or chalice; a rich cloth spread over something, now usually a coffin, hearse, or tomb (15c, hence **pallbearer**, 18c); a dark or gloomy covering (*a pall of smoke*) **2** a (rich) robe: **(a)** one worn by a pope or a Roman Catholic archbishop (ME, outlived by the Latin form *pallium*) **(b)** one put on a monarch at their coronation (17c).

Pall is probably one parent of *tarpaulin* (at TAR). Latin *pallium* was adopted for a bird's or mollusc's mantle, later for the cerebral cortex, and produced *palliare* 'to cover or hide', whence **palliate** to relieve symptoms without curing the cause (*palliative care*).

pallet [ME. French *palette* 'small blade or spade', from *pale* 'shovel, spade, blade', from Latin *pala*] Applied in French and English to various tools, including: **1** a flat blade **2** a board: **(a)** an artist's palette (17c) **(b)** a board for carrying a newly moulded brick (19c) **(c)** a platform on which goods can be moved or stacked (1920s) **3** a valve in an organ (18c) **4** a projection on a machine that conveys motion by engaging with a toothed wheel (18c).

French *palette* was adopted for **1** an artist's paint-board, hence the range of colours, later other elements, used or available; **palette knife** with a flat blade used to mix or spread paint etc.; a similar kitchen knife **2** a kind of spatula a croupier uses to move money and cards.

palm [Old English *palm(a)*, from Latin *palma* **palm** (of the hand)] A tropical tree whose leaves spread out like a hand and fingers: the idea is also found in **date** the fruit, which grows on a palm tree [ME, via Old French and Latin from Greek *daktulos* 'finger']. Hence a palm leaf, especially as a symbol of triumph (hence **Palm Sunday** when palms are worn or carried to commemorate Christ's triumphal entry into Jerusalem: see the Bible, John 12:12–13) or of pilgrimage to the holy land (ME, hence **palmer** such a pilgrim (surviving as a surname).

Latin *palma* produced **palmette** an archaeologist's term for an ornament with radiating petals [French, 'small palm', later 'ornament on a window cornice', whence, probably, **pelmet**]. Greek *daktulos* produced **pterodactyl** [with *pteron* 'wing', whence also **helicopter**, literally 'spiral wing', with Greek *helix*].

pan [Old English *panne*, probably from Latin *patina* 'shallow dish', from Greek *patanē* 'plate'] A (metal) vessel for domestic use (*frying/bed pan*); a lavatory bowl (17c). Hence something resembling one: **1** in the body (ME), e.g. *brain pan*, **(knee) pan** the kneecap, replaced by *patella* [15c, Latin, literally 'small pan', from *patina*] **2** in the ground (ME), e.g. *saltpan*, **(hard)pan** a substratum of impermeable soil that causes water to gather on the surface (18c) **3** non-domestic vessels: **(a)** the hollow part of a flintlock that holds the gunpowder (16c), hence **flash in the pan** an ineffective explosion in it; short-lived brilliance **(b)** a dish for sorting gold etc. from gravel (19c); to seek gold in this way; **pan out** to yield gold, hence to turn out well **(c)** a metal drum in a steel band (1950s), hence (the lifestyle associated with) steel band music **4** to criticize a play etc. severely (*c*.1910, *US*), perhaps because it didn't 'pan out', or perhaps from the old custom of banging pans etc. to draw attention to a wrongdoer **5** the face (1920s, *US*), hence **deadpan** expressionless, impassive.

Latin *patella* produced Catalan *paella*. Latin *patina* was adopted for the greenish layer that forms on copper [via Italian, from the incrustation on ancient metal plates], hence a change in appearance caused by age and use, and produced **paten** the plate for the bread at the Eucharist, which is one parent of PLATEN.

pander [ME. Named after Pandarus in Chaucer's *Troilus and Criseyde*, who procured Criseyde for Troilus and acted as go-between for the lovers] A go-between in an illicit love affair; a male procurer or pimp, hence a person who encourages and caters for someone's weaknesses or vices (17c); to do so.

pane [ME. Via French from Latin *pannus*] A (piece of) cloth (–16c); a counterpane (–17c); a distinct part of a garment, hence a distinct section: **1** a facet **2** a piece of glass in a window (15c), hence a rectangular piece of ground or division of a surface (16c), a square in a chequered pattern **3** a section of a sheet of stamps (19c).

Latin *pannus* produced **panel** a piece of cloth, which developed similarly, and also came to mean a piece of parchment, especially one on which jury members were listed, hence a list, or later group, of members.

panoply [16c. Via French or modern Latin from Greek *panoplia* 'full armour', from Greek *pas, pan* 'all' + *hopla* 'arms'] A suit of armour, originally referring to 'the whole armour of God' (see the Bible, Ephesians 6:13–17). Hence a magnificent or impressive covering or array (19c); full ceremonial dress and accessories.

Greek *pan* appears in *pandemonium* (at DEMON), and produced *gene* (at GENESIS), **pan-** all, any, everyone (*pan-American*, PANORAMA), **panto-** 'all, complete' (PANTO-GRAPH, PANTOMIME), and *panegyric* (at PREDICAMENT).

panorama [18c. From *pan-* (see PANOPLY*) + Greek *horama* 'view', from *horan* 'to see'] A landscape or narrative scene which surrounds or is unrolled before the viewer (invented by a Scottish painter, Robert Barker, in 1788), hence **1** a continuous passing scene (19c) **2** a wide, unobstructed view, especially of a landscape (19c); a picture or photograph of such a view **3** a comprehensive survey of a topic (19c).

Panorama was shortened to **pan** to turn a camera to take a panoramic shot or to follow a moving object, and suggested **cyclorama** a panoramic picture viewed from the inside, and **diorama** a panorama with lighting effects simulating changes in the weather or time of day, or one with (moving) models in front of a painted backdrop.

pantaloon [16c. French *pantalon* from Italian *Pantalone*, probably from *Pantaleon*, the name of a popular saint] **Pantaloon** a foolish old man in Italian *commedia dell'arte* and comedies derived from it (see HARLEQUIN*), hence a feeble old man, described by Shakespeare as wearing 'youthful hose...too wide for his shrunk shank' (*As You Like It* II vii 158), influencing the modern meaning of **pantaloons**, originally tight-fitting breeches or hose, as worn by Pantaloon (17–18c); the tight trousers which replaced them (18c), later any trousers, now loose or baggy ones.

Pantaloons produced **pantalettes** long loose frilled knickers, and **pants** trousers (now US), hence **1 panties** boys' trousers or shorts, later women's knickers; **pantywaist** a child's garment of shorts attached to a bodice (US), hence a sissy or coward **2 (under)pants** men's or women's briefs, hence *pants* pathetically bad, rubbish **3 hot pants** women's brief shorts.

pantechnicon [19c. From *pan-* (see PANOPLY*) + Greek *tekhnikon*, the noun belonging to *tekhnikos* 'to do with (an) art': see TECHNICAL] The name of a London bazaar selling all kinds of artistic work: the building (and the word) came to be used for a furniture repository. The sense 'furniture van' arose in the 1890s, the building having burned down in the 1870s.

pantograph [18c. From *panto-* (see PANOPLY*) + *-graph* 'something that writes or records' (see GRAPHIC*] A copying device consisting of an adjustable parallelogram, hence something resembling it, especially the framework on an electric vehicle for picking up current from overhead wires (early 20c).

pantomime [16c. Via French or Latin from Greek *pantomimos* 'mime artist', from *panto-* (see PANOPLY*) + *mimos* 'imitator' (ancestor of MIME*)] **1** a mime artist in ancient Rome **2** a performance by a mime artist accompanied by music (17c); later a comedy featuring HARLEQUIN, now a comic tale with music and stock characters performed at Christmas, ostensibly for children (18c), hence an absurd event or action (1940s).

paper [ME. Via Old French from Latin *papyrus*, from Greek *papuros*] The material used for writing on, wrapping things, etc., hence **1** something resembling this, e.g. papyrus, the material of a wasps' nest **2** (a piece of) paper with writing on it (*exam paper/newspaper*, 15c), hence **(a) papers** identity documents, credentials (17c) **(b)** an essay or dissertation, especially one presented for publication or at a conference (17c) **(c)** bills of exchange; **paper (money)** banknotes (17c) **3** made of or resembling paper (16c); flimsy, insubstantial; **on paper** merely theoretical (17c); **paper tiger** someone/something apparently threatening but actually ineffectual (1950s, translating a Chinese expression) **4** a paper package (*a paper of pins*); a dose of an illicit drug, originally supplied in one (1930s) **5 (wall)paper** paper etc. pasted onto a wall for decoration (18c); to decorate with it; **paper over (the cracks)** to conceal or ignore a problem temporarily (*c*.1910, translating a phrase used by the 19c German statesman Bismarck). Hence *wallpaper* an unobtrusive background or background music (1920s).

Latin *papyrus* the plant was later used for (a document written on) the writing material made from it, and produced TAPER.

par [16c. Latin] Equality, an equal standing, level, or value (now chiefly in *on a par with*), hence **1 par (of exchange)** the accepted value of one currency in terms of another (17c) **2** equality between the face value (**par value**) and the market value of shares etc. (18c), hence **above/below par** at a premium/discount **3** an average or normal amount, quality, etc. (18c), hence **above/below par** above or below this; **below/under par** not very well **4** see BOGEY.

Latin *par* is the ancestor of **compare**, **disparage** to marry someone of lower rank or to be disgraced by doing so (–18c), hence to scorn, **pair**, **parity**, PEER*, *umpire* (at EKE*), and perhaps of APPAREL.

parable [ME. Via French from Latin *parabola* 'comparison' (in late Latin 'allegory, discourse'), from Greek *parabolē*, from *paraballein* 'to put alongside, to compare', from *ballein* 'to throw': cf. SYMBOL] A metaphorical or enigmatic saying; an allegory; a story used to convey a moral or spiritual lesson, especially one told by Christ.

Latin **parabola** was adopted for a symmetrical curve, and produced **palarie, polari**, or, later, **parlyaree** a variety of theatrical and gay slang [via Italian *parlare* 'to speak'], PALAVER, PARLIAMENT*, and PAROLE. Greek *ballein* is the ancestor of BALLISTIC*.

parade [17c. French, from Spanish *parada* or Italian *parata*, both ultimately from Latin *parare* 'to prepare or defend'] Ostentation, display, show, hence **1** (to assemble) a muster of troops for a display or inspection, hence a procession; a gathering or crowd of people marching or promenading, hence **(a)** to take part in one; to walk ostentatiously **(b)** to display in a parade for admiration or contempt (19c); to make a display of something (*parading their wealth*); to present or masquerade as (*old ideas parading as new*, 1940s) **2** a place for display: **(a)** a public square or promenade; a row of shops **(b) parade (ground)** a square for military parades (18c).

Italian *parata* produced **parry** to ward off a weapon or blow. Descendants of Latin *parare* include APPARATUS, **disparate**, IMPERIAL*, **para-** 'protector of, protection against' (*parachute* at CHUTE), **parapet**, *parasol* at SOLAR), **pare, prepare, rampart, repair** to mend, SEVERAL*, *vituperate* (at VICE), and perhaps APPAREL and SPAR.

paradise [ME. Via French and late Latin from Greek *paradeisos*, from Avestan *pairidaēza* 'enclosure', from *pairi* 'around' + *daeza* 'wall'] The Greek soldier and historian Xenophon (born *c*.430 BC), who served in Persia, used *paradeisos* to refer to the pleasure grounds of the Persian nobility, and its meaning was then extended to 'garden, orchard', and was used in Greek translations of the Bible for the Garden of Eden (see Genesis 2, 3) and for Heaven (the original English senses). Hence **1** in the names of plants, birds, etc. beautiful enough for Eden or Heaven **2** a (convent) garden or orchard; a park or pleasure ground (17c) **3** a wonderful place; a state of pure bliss **4** a place or state where the souls of the righteous await Judgement Day (17c).

In place names, *Paradise* was sometimes given to a street etc. built on the site of a park, orchard, or burial ground, or to a row of 'model' workmen's cottages.

paralysis [ME. Latin from Greek, from *paraluein* 'to disable', from *luein* 'to loosen'] Loss of the ability to move caused by disease or injury, hence a failure or inability to act (19c).

Latin *paralysis* fathered Old French *paralisie*, whence **palsy**, originally paralysis, later also an uncontrollable tremor. Greek *luein* produced **-lysis** (*analysis, dialysis*), **-lyst** (*analyst, catalyst*), and **-lyte** (*electrolyte*).

paraphernalia [17c. Medieval Latin, ultimately from Greek *parapherna*, from *para* 'beside, beyond' + *phernē* 'dowry'] Property that a woman kept after marriage, in English and Scots law restricted to her clothing, jewellery, and other trifles, hence anyone's personal belongings (18c); assorted items of equipment; bits and pieces.

Greek *para* is found in PARALYSIS*, **parasite** [Greek *parasitos* 'one who eats another's food', from *sitos* 'food'], and *parody* (at ODE), and produced **para-** (*paramedic, paranormal*).

parcel [ME. French *parcelle*, ultimately from Latin *particula* 'small part' (whence **particle** and PARTICULAR), from *pars*: see PART*] An item, a detail (–17c); a part or portion, hence **1 parcel (out)** to divide into portions, to share out **2** a piece, originally of land; a fragment; a (small) quantity or amount (15c); a (small) community; a group, a bunch (now US dialect, often as **passel**) **3** a wrapped item, a bundle or package (17c, hence **parcel (up)** to make up into a parcel); a number or quantity of things dealt with in one transaction (18c); a large amount of money gained or lost (*c*.1900): cf. BUNDLE.

pariah [17c. Tamil *paṟaiyar* 'hereditary drummers', from *paṟai* 'a drum'] A member of a low caste of agricultural and domestic workers in S India and Burma, later any low-caste or casteless Hindu, hence a social outcast (19c). Hence **pariah dog** a feral dog, originally in India: shortened to **pye dog**.

park [ME. Old French *parc* from medieval Latin *parricus*, of Germanic origin] An (enclosed) tract of land: **1** stocked and reserved for hunting (surviving in place names): many became ornamental grounds to which the public were sometimes admitted, hence such grounds in a town (17c) or, later, around a country house (18c); a piece of land for public recreation and conserving wildlife (*safari/theme park, National Park*, 19c); a sports ground **2** reserved for the artillery, vehicles, stores etc. in a military camp (17c); to arrange or leave such things there (19c); to leave a vehicle somewhere temporarily, hence **(a)** a place where vehicles can be left (*car/lorry park*, early 20c) **(b)** to leave someone/something temporarily in a convenient place (early 20c).

French **parquet** ['small space', literally 'small park', from *parc*] was adopted for flooring made of wooden blocks; and in the US for (part of) a theatre auditorium. Related to **parrock** [Old English *pearruc*] a fence or set of hurdles, hence the ground it enclosed, surviving mainly in the variant **paddock**.

parliament [ME. Old French *parlement* 'speaking', from *parler* 'to speak', from Latin *parabola*: see PARABLE*] Speaking, a speech, a conversation, conference, or debate (–16c), hence **1** a formal conference or council; one involving the king of England with his nobles and advisors to settle the affairs of the realm, gradually evolving into a more permanent assembly with some elected members, the legislative assembly of the United Kingdom, hence **(a)** its members; the period during which they meet, now the period between general elections **(b)** a similar assembly elsewhere **2** talks, under truce, with an enemy (–17c, replaced by 15c **parley**, also probably from Old French *parler*).

Old French *parler* is the ancestor of **parlance** speaking, speech, debate; a way of speaking (*legal parlance*), and of PARLOUR.

parlour [ME. Old French *parleor, parleur*, from *parler*: see PARLIAMENT*] A room for (private) conversation in a monastery or public building (*Mayor's parlour*); a sitting room in a private house, later often 'kept for best' and for entertaining visitors; a small quiet room in a hotel or public house (19c). Hence **1** to do with or suitable for the parlour (*parlour game/palm*, 18c); describing a comfortably-off person who professes support for radical causes (*parlour Bolshevik*, *c*.1910, largely replaced by **champagne socialist**, 1980s) **2** a room or building fitted up and used for a specified (commercial) purpose (*ice-cream/massage/milking parlour*, 19c).

parole [15c. French, ultimately from Latin *parabola*: see PARABLE*] (Originally and also as *parol*): something said, a word, hence **1 parole (of honour)** your word of honour; a prisoner of war's promise to abide by the terms of a conditional release, hence **(a) on parole** bound by such a promise **(b)** to release someone on parole (17c) **(c)** a prisoner's early and conditional release (*c*.1900) (17c) **2** describing a contract etc. made verbally or in an unsealed document (16c).

paroxysm [ME. Via French and medieval Latin from Greek *paroxusmos*, from *paroxunein* 'to goad, to exasperate', from *oxunein* 'to sharpen', from *oxus* 'sharp'] A sudden attack, recurrence, or worsening of a disease or symptom, hence a fit or convulsion (17c); a violent emotional outburst.

Greek *oxus* is the ancestor of **oxalis** a genus of plants including sorrel (from sorrel's sharp-tasting leaves), whence **oxalic acid** derived from them, of **oxygen** (because it was once thought to be an essential component of acids), and of **oxymoron** [Greek *oxumoros* 'pointedly stupid', from *moros* 'stupid' (whence **moron**, *US*)].

part [Old English, later also French, from Latin *pars*, *part-*; the verb via Latin *partire*] A portion or division (gradually replacing DEAL), later a component. Hence **1** an equal portion (ME), now usually understood, e.g. *a third (part)*, except in recipes etc. (*one part gin to two parts tonic*); a share, hence a share in an action, a duty, function, or role (*do my part, part song*); **take part** to share or play a part in, hence **partaking** doing so, whence **partake** (16c); cf. **participate** [15c, from Latin *participare*, from *pars* + *capere* 'to take'] **2** to divide or separate (ME), hence **(a)** to go away from or take leave of (each other) **(b)** to come apart, to break **3** a faction (ME–16c); one side in a contract, contest, etc. (largely replaced by PARTY), hence **partial** favouring one side; **partial to** liking, fond of (17c).

French *part* produced **apart** and probably **parse** to describe a word's function; to analyse a sentence grammatically; in computing: to analyse input etc. syntactically. Latin *participare* produced PARTICIPLE; *partire* produced DEPART*, **partite**, **partition**, **partner** originally a joint heir, owner, or participant, PARTY, and **repartee** [French *repartire* 'to retort', in Old French 'to set out again']; *pars* is the ancestor of IMPART, PARCEL*, and PARTISAN.

parterre [17c. French *par terre* 'on or along the ground', ultimately from Latin *terra* 'earth, land': see TERRACE*] A level space: **1** with flower beds arranged in a pattern **2** on which a house or village stands **3** the part of a theatre auditorium behind the orchestra (18c); (the occupants of) the part beneath the galleries.

participle [ME. Via French from Latin *participium*, from *particeps* 'partaker', from *participare* (see PART*)] Someone/something partly one thing and partly another (–17c), now only a word that is partly one part of speech and partly another, usually a verb form used as an adjective (*colouring book, coloured pictures*).

particular [ME. Via Old French from Latin *particularis*, from *particula* 'small part': see PARCEL] (Belonging to or affecting only) a part (–19c), hence **1** (to do with or describing) a detail, hence **(a) particulars** details, facts, especially used for identification (15c) **(b)** attentive to details, fastidious, scrupulous (17c) **2** to do with one individual or group among others; apart from the rest, individual, remarkable (15c).

partisan [16c. French, from Italian dialect *partigiano*, from *parte* 'part, side', from Latin *pars* PART*] A (zealous) supporter of a party, person, or cause, hence **1** a guerrilla, especially resisting occupying forces (17c); to do with guerrilla warfare (18c) **2** excessively devoted to a cause etc. (19c); prejudiced, one-sided.

party [ME. French *partie*, ultimately from Latin *partire*: see PART*] A part or portion, in various senses (–17c); one side in a battle, tournament, or legal case (cf. PART sense 3), hence **1** a group of people: **(a)** a detachment of troops (*raiding party*) **(b)** a national political group (18c) **(c)** a group acting or travelling together (*shooting/coach party*, 18c) **(d)** an informal social gathering (18c), hence to give, go to, or have fun at a party (1920s); to have (casual) sex (*c*.2000) **2** an individual: **(a)** who takes part in something (*I won't be party to it*) **(b)** the individual concerned or referred to (15c, largely replaced by PERSON).

Party in the sense 'shared' (*party line/wall*) [from related French *parti*] originally meant 'parted, divided, separate', also 'multicoloured, variegated' (replaced by **parti-coloured**).

pass [ME. French *passer*, ultimately from Latin *passus*: see PACE*] To (allow or cause to) go, hence to (allow or cause to) go across, by, over, through, or from one thing, person, or state to another; the action or an act of passing or being passed (16c): other senses stem from this.

The former past participle, **past**, survives mainly in **1** gone by in time; (to do with) an earlier time **2** beyond reach or limits (*past caring*).

Pass appears in words such as **passbook** and **password**, which give permission to pass, **passed master** someone who has passed the tests to be a master in his trade, an expert (later often altered to **past master**), PASSOVER*, and **pastime**. French *passer* produced **impasse** [with *im-* 'not'] a dead end; a deadlock, the name **Malpas** [literally 'bad (difficult) passage'], *pasque-flower* (at PASSOVER), PASSAGE*, *passport* (at PORT¹), **surpass**, and TRESPASS.

passage [ME. Old French, from *passer*: see PASS*] The action of going; movement, passing, hence **1** a route, road, or path; a corridor or alley (17c) **2** the possibility of going; leave or the right to go (*granted safe passage*); the right to be carried as a (ship's) passenger (17c) **3** travelling, a journey, hence **(a) bird of passage** one that migrates (17c); *passage* its migratory flight (18c); **passage migrant** one that interrupts its journey for a short period (1930s) **(b)** to make a voyage (19c) **4** transition, hence **(a)** the progress of a bill into law (16c) **(b) rite of passage** a ceremony or event that marks a significant transition, especially in human life (*c*.1910) **5** something that passes or takes place (16c): **(a)** a sequence of moves or occurrences **(b)** a short extract of a book, speech, musical work, etc.

Old French *passer* produced **passenger** a traveller, one carried in a train, car, ship, etc., other than a driver or crew member, hence someone who avoids their share of work.

passion [ME. French, ultimately from Latin *pati*, *pass-* 'to suffer'] **1 (a)** (an account of) Christ's suffering from the Last Supper until his death on the cross; a dramatic or musical work based on it, hence **passion flower** a plant with complex flowers whose parts are thought to resemble instruments of the crucifixion (17c); **passion fruit** the edible fruit of some varieties **(b)** a martyr's suffering; an account of it (*c*.1900) **2** the fact of being affected by an external force (largely replaced by *passivity*) **3** (a) powerful emotion, hence **(a)** (the object of) a strong sexual feeling, hence **pash** (the object of) an infatuation (*c*.1910) **(b)** a fit or outburst of emotion, especially rage (16c) **(c)** (the object of) a strong liking or enthusiasm (17c).

Latin *pati* produced *compati* 'to suffer with', whence **compassion** and **compatible** sympathetic (15–17c); mutually tolerant; able to co-exist or be used together, PASSIVE, and Latin *patientia* 'the ability to suffer pain or misfortune, endurance', whence **patience** and **patient**.

passive [15c. (Via French from) Latin *passivus*, from *pati*: see PASSION*] **1** (exposed to) suffering (–17c), hence **impassive** not subject to pain or suffering (17c); not feeling or showing emotion **2** influenced, affected, or produced by something external; acted on rather than acting or participating (*passive smoking*); inert; in grammar: expressing an action done to the subject of the verb **3** submissive, unresisting (17c); **passive resistance** non-violent resistance, non-cooperation (19c).

Passover The Jewish festival celebrating the angel of death passing over the Israelites without affecting them, but killing the Egyptian first-born (see the Bible, Exodus 12). *Passover* was used to translate Hebrew *pesaḥ*, whence [via Latin, Greek, and Aramaic] **Pasch** Easter [ME, Christ being identified with the lamb killed and eaten at Passover], surviving mainly in **paschal** and in **Pasch/pace egg** a decorated hard-boiled egg as an Easter gift (16c), and the names **Pascall**, **Pascoe**, **Pask** given to those born at Easter. **Pasque flower**, which flowers around Easter, is an alteration, by association with French *pasque* 'Pasch', of **passe-flower** [16c, from Old French *passe-fleur*, from *passer*: see PASS*].

paste [ME. Old French, from late Latin *pasta*, from Greek *pastē* 'barley porridge', from *pastos* 'sprinkled, salted', from *passein* 'to sprinkle'] The underlying sense is 'wet mixture'. **1** dough, pastry **2** a moist mixture: **(a)** used as an adhesive; to stick with it (16c), hence **pasteboard** made of paper or paper pulp stuck together **(b)** made with pounded or minced ingredients (*fish/tomato paste*, 15c) **(c)** of clay and water, used for making pottery (18c) **3** (imitation gems made from) clear flint glass (the ingredients being mixed wet, 17c) **4** to beat or thrash (19c), perhaps from the idea of pounding to a paste, but perhaps from *baste* (see *lambaste* at LAM).

Paste produced **pastry** and **pasty** to do with or like paste, unhealthily pale. Old French *paste* produced **pasty** a pie made from a folded round of pastry, and evolved into modern French *pâté*, adopted for a pie or pasty and again for meat paste, having produced **patty** originally a small pie. Late Latin *pasta* produced PASTEL* and PASTICHE*.

pastel [16c. (Via French from) Italian *pastello*, literally 'little paste', from *pasta* 'paste', from late Latin: see PASTE*] **1** [partly via Provençal] woad; the dye obtained from it, originally by pounding the twigs to a paste **2** (a crayon made of) a paste of ground pigment and gum; a drawing made with such crayons (19c); the art of pastel drawing; (describing) a pale shade of a colour (pastels being considered a pale imitation of oils).

Italian *pasta* came to mean (a dish based on) a type of food, e.g. spaghetti, made from flour, eggs, and water (19c).

pastiche [19c. French, from Italian *pasticcio* 'pie, pasty', especially one with mixed ingredients, ultimately from late Latin *pasta*: see PASTE*] A medley or hotchpotch, specifically a musical composition, literary work, etc. that is a mixture of elements from other works; one that imitates someone's work or style; to produce one (1950s).

Italian *pasticcio* was adopted earlier and was the more common until the early 20c. The sense 'mixture' is also found in French *pastis* a liqueur always mixed with water [medieval Latin *pasticium* (whence also French *pâtisserie*), from late Latin *pasta*].

pastor [ME. Via Old French from Latin, from *pascere, past-* 'to feed, to lead to pasture'] A herdsman or shepherd (now chiefly US), hence **1** someone having the spiritual care of a 'flock' of Christians; someone who gives care and guidance to a number of people (15c), hence **pastoral (a)** to do with a pastor or their work; **pastoral (letter)** from a bishop to their 'flock' (19c); **pastoral (staff)** a bishop's staff, resembling a shepherd's crook (19c) **(b)** describing a teacher's responsibility for a student's general well-being (1950s) **2** *pastoral* to do with shepherds, or with the care of sheep or cattle, hence **(a)** (describing) a work of art, literature, etc. depicting shepherds or (idealized) country life (16c), now often replaced by Italian *pastorale* (18c) **(b)** of land: used for pasture (18c).

Latin *pascere* is the ancestor of **antepast** (literally 'before the meal') an appetizer or first course, largely replaced by Italian *antipasto*, **pannage** the right to let pigs feed in a wood, or what they eat, **pastern** a shackle for a pastured animal (ME–17c), hence a horse's leg just above the hoof, where the shackle went, and of **pasture**, PESTER, and **repast**.

patent [ME. (French from) Latin *patere* 'to lie open'] **1 letters patent** an open document from a monarch or government recording a contract, authorizing an action, or conferring a privilege, hence *patent* (a document conferring) the right to make, use, or sell something; to obtain this (18c); protected by or manufactured under a patent (hence **patent leather** protected by varnish, 19c); the invention, process, etc. concerned (19c) **2** not enclosed or hidden; generally accessible or available for use (15c), hence (combining 1 and 2) **patent medicine** one patented and available without prescription (18c).

paternoster [ME. Latin, literally 'our father', the first two words of the Lord's Prayer (see the Bible, Matthew 6:9–13), from *pater* 'father' (ancestor of PATRON*)] The Lord's Prayer; a repetition of this as an act of worship, hence **1** any form of words repeated as a prayer or charm, whence **patter** to recite one rapidly or mechanically; to talk rapidly, to prattle, hence **(a)** the glib talk of a salesman, magician, etc. (18c), criminals' slang, or professional jargon; to use any of these (19c): cf. CANT **(b)** small talk, idle chat (19c) **2** a special bead on a rosary indicating that a paternoster should be said; the rosary itself, hence **(a)** in the names of streets where rosaries were made **(b) paternoster (line)** a fishing line with hooks or weights suspended on it at intervals (19c) **(c) paternoster (elevator/lift)** consisting of an endless moving chain of open compartments (*c*.1910).

pathos [16c. Greek, 'suffering, feeling, emotion'] **1** speech or writing that appeals to the emotions **2** a quality that arouses pity (17c); the power of doing so. Hence **pathetic**: **1** moving or stirring the emotions (–18c); arousing pity or sadness (18c); pitiable, miserably inadequate (1930s) **2** to do with the emotions (17c), surviving mainly in **pathetic fallacy** the attribution of human emotions to nature or inanimate objects (first used by John Ruskin, 19c writer and art critic).

Greek *pathos* is the ancestor of **apathy** [Greek *apathēs* 'without feeling'], **empathy** [Greek *empatheia* 'feeling within'], **homoeopathy** [with Greek *homoios* 'like'], whence -**pathy** a method of treating disease, -**path** a practitioner of one (*naturopath*), **patho-** 'disease' (*pathogen*, *pathology*), -**pathy** a particular kind or site of disease (*neuropathy*), whence -**path** a sufferer from one (*psychopath*), **sympathy** [Greek *sumpatheia* 'feeling together'], and **telepathy** [with *tele* 'far off': see TELEGRAPH*].

patriot [16c. Via French and late Latin from Greek *patriotēs*, from *patrios* 'of your fathers', from *pater* 'father'] **1** a fellow-countryman (–17c, outlived by **compatriot**, ultimately from Latin *com-* 'with, together' + Greek *patriotēs*) **2** a person devoted to their country (17c); a member of a resistance movement or militant nationalist organization (World War II).

Greek *pater* is the ancestor of **patriarch** and **patronymic**. Related to PATRON*.

patron [ME. French, from Latin *patronus* 'protector, defender', from *pater*, *patr-* 'father'] **1** a master, protector, or advocate, hence **(a)** someone who uses money or influence to support a person, charity, etc.; a (regular) customer of a business (17c); **patronize** to be one **(b)** *patronize* to treat or speak of someone condescendingly (18c) **(c)** *patron saint* (at SAINT) **2** someone with the right to appoint a clergyman to a benefice, hence **patronage** this power (15c); the control of appointments in public service (18c) **3** senses from French, spelt **pattern** since the 17c: a design, plan, model, etc. from which something is made; something to be copied, hence **(a)** a (repeated) decorative design (16c); to decorate with one (19c), hence a regular, repeated form, sequence, or way of doing something (*c*.1900) **(b)** a specimen or sample (*pattern book*, 17c) **(c) pattern after/on** to make from a pattern, to imitate (17c).

Latin *pater*'s descendants include Italian, Spanish, and Portuguese *padre*, used to address a priest, and adopted from Portuguese by British troops in India for a chaplain, **paternal**, **paternity**, PATERNOSTER*, **patr-** (*patrimony*), Latin *patria* 'native land, fatherland', whence **expatriate**, and Latin *repatriare* 'to return to your native land', whence **repair** to go somewhere and **repatriate**, *patrician* (at PLEBEIAN), and **perpetrate** [Latin *perpetrare*, from *patrare* 'to bring about, literally 'to father']. Related to PATRIOT*.

pay [ME. Via French from Latin *pacare*, from *pax*, *pac-* 'peace'] To appease, pacify, or satisfy (–16c), hence to give money in exchange for something or to discharge a debt (from the idea of appeasing a creditor); to give something due or deserved, hence **1** to make restitution or amends; to suffer for doing wrong **2** (to exact) retribution, to punish; to beat (16c, now only dialect) **3** wages, salary; **be in the pay of** to receive (regular) wages from (16c) **4** to give attention, a compliment etc.; to make a visit (15c) **5 pay out** to let out gradually (17c) **6** to give an adequate return (19c); to profit (*it would pay you to listen!*).

Pay produced **payola** payment, bribery, originally to a disc jockey for plugging a song [US: -*ola* is from *Victrola*, a make of gramophone]. Latin *pax* produced APPEASE*, **pacific** conciliatory, calming; peaceful, calm (the **Pacific Ocean** was named as being calmer than the Atlantic), and **pacify**. Related to PACT*.

peculiar [ME. Latin *peculiaris* 'not held jointly', from *peculium* 'private property', from *pecu* 'cattle, wealth': cf. CATTLE] **1 peculiar (to)** belonging exclusively to **2** particular, special, unique; strange, odd (17c) **3** separate, independent (16–18c); a church or parish exempt from the jurisdiction of the diocese in which it is situated (16c).

Latin *peculium* is the ancestor of **peculate** to embezzle, originally from the State. Latin *pecu* produced **pecorino** ewe's milk cheese [via Italian *pecoro* 'sheep'], and Latin *pecunia* 'money', whence **pecuniary** and **pecunious** wealthy, surviving mainly in **impecunious**.

pedagogue [ME. Latin *paedogogus* from Greek *paidogōgos*, from *pais, paid-* 'child, boy' + *agogos* 'leader', from *agein* 'to lead'] **1** a teacher, now especially a strict or pedantic one **2** a man, usually a slave, who supervised a child and accompanied it to school (the Greek meaning, 15c).

Latin *paedogogus* may be the ancestor, via French and Italian, of **pedant**, originally a teacher. Greek *pais* appears in **orthopaedic** to do with the treatment of bone disorders and deformities, originally in children, hence describing a firm, supportive mattress, **paediatric**, **paedophile**, and **pederast**, and produced PAGE; *agein* is the ancestor of AGONY*.

peel [OE. Latin *pilare* 'to strip hair from', also 'to pillage', from *pilus* 'hair'] To strip of possessions (–18c) or of a natural outer layer, hence **1** to pull, pare, or, formerly, pluck off (15c); to come off or away (16c) **2** the rind or skin of a fruit etc. (16c). In these senses replacing **pill** [OE, also from *pilare*] which survives mainly meaning to form balls of fluff on the surface of fabrics (1960s), probably influenced by *pill* a tablet (at PIPPIN) **3** to move away (World War II, originally of an aircraft leaving a formation) **4 peel off** to take off clothing (18c).

Latin *pilare* produced **pillage** and PLUCK; *pilus* produced **depilate**, the **pile** of a fabric, and **plush**. Probably related to **pilfer**.

peer [ME. Old French *pe(e)r*, from Latin PAR* 'equal'] Someone/something equal in any respect, hence **1 peerless** without equal, incomparable **2** someone equal in rank or status; a member of the same age group or social set (1940s) **3** a member of the paladins or *douzepers* [Old French, literally 'twelve peers'], an equal band of the bravest and noblest of Charlemagne's knights in medieval romances, later the twelve great spiritual and temporal lords of France (15c) **3** a member of the British nobility; **life peer** one whose title lapses when they die (19c).

peevish [ME. Origin unknown] Foolish, mad (–17c); contrary, self-willed, spiteful (15c); querulous, irritable (16c), whence **peeve** to annoy (*c*.1900, *US*); (to make) a peevish complaint.

pellet [ME. French *pelote*, ultimately from Latin *pilla* 'ball'] A small (rounded) mass, hence **1** a (stone) missile fired from a cannon, catapult, etc.; a bullet or piece of shot; an imitation bullet (16c) **2** a small ball of animal food, pesticide, etc. **3** a compacted mass of bones, fur, etc. regurgitated by a bird of prey (19c) **4** a small round piece of animal faeces (*c.*1920).

Pelt 'to throw things at', may be a contraction of *pellet*. French *pelote* produced *peleton* 'little ball, small troop' (whence **platoon**), adopted for the main field in a cycle race. Latin *pilla* is the ancestor of Spanish *pelota* a Basque and Spanish ball game, *pill* a tablet (at PIPPIN), and probably of **pile** a haemorrhoid (from the shape of an external one).

pen [Old English *penn*] An enclosure for animals, hence **1** to shut in or confine, hence **(a)** **pent** shut up, sealed (16c); **pent in/up** restricted, repressed, stifled (17c) **(b)** to put or keep in a pen (17c) **2** a weir or dam (16c) **3** a prison cell (17c, since the 19c also an abbreviation of PENITENTIARY) **4** a covered dock for a submarine etc. (World War I).

penance [ME. Old French, from Latin *paenitentia*, from *paenitere*, *paenitent-* 'to make sorry' (ancestor of PENITENTIARY and **repent**)] Repentance, contrition [–17c, outlived by **penitence**, also from *paenitere*]; in the Roman Catholic and Orthodox churches, a sacrament including confession, contrition, and absolution; (the performance of) a religious act, voluntarily or by order of a priest, to show contrition and atone for sin; an unpleasant task, especially one regarded as a punishment.

pencil [ME. Old French *pincel*, ultimately from Latin *penicillum*, from *peniculus* 'brush', literally 'small tail', from *penis* 'tail'] A fine paintbrush for delicate work; the art of painting with one; to do so (15c). Hence **1** a thin cylindrical writing or drawing implement (16c); to write or draw with one (17c); **pencil in** to arrange provisionally (because pencilled writing can easily be erased, 1940s) **2** something resembling a pencil: **(a)** in botany and zoology: a small tuft of hairs, feathers, etc. (16c) **(b)** something shaped like a pencil (*pencil beam/skirt*); the penis (16c), surviving mainly in **lead in your pencil** sexual potency (1940s).

Latin *penicillum* produced **penicillium** a kind of fungus with brushlike spore-bearing structures, whence **penicillin**, originally obtained from cultures of it. Latin *penis* was adopted for the male sex organ.

pendant [ME. French, 'hanging', from *pendre* 'to hang', from Latin *pendere*] **1** something hanging or suspended: **(a)** an architectural ornament hanging from a ceiling or roof **(b)** (a necklace or earring with) a hanging jewel, bead, etc. **(c)** a pennant (15c) **(d)** a short line hanging from a masthead etc., to which other tackle is attached (15c) **(e)** a hanging light fitting (19c) **(f)** an additional statement, a supplement (19c) **2** a companion piece (each 'hanging' from the other, 18c).

Pendant is one parent of **pennant**, the other being **pennon** [via Old French from Latin *penna*: see PIN*]. French *pendant* was Anglicized into **pending** during; awaiting action or decision, whence **pend** to leave pending. French *pendre* is the probable ancestor of **painter**, originally a rope that held a hanging anchor to the ship's side, now a mooring rope. Latin *pendere*'s descendants include APPEND*, DEPEND, **impend**, *penchant* and *propensity* (both at INCLINE), **pendulous**, **pendulum**, **perpendicular**, and **suspend** [Latin *suspendere* 'to hang up', later 'to stop temporarily, to delay']. Related to PENSION*.

penitentiary [15c. Medieval Latin *paenitentiarius* from Latin *paenitere*: see PEN-ANCE*] **1** a priest authorized to impose penance **2** a place of discipline or punishment for ecclesiastical offences; a refuge for prostitutes trying to reform (19c); a prison (N American).

pension [ME. French, from Latin *pendere, pens-* 'to weigh or pay'] A payment (–17c), hence **1** a contribution made by members towards the expenses of the Inns of Court and some other organizations (15c) **2** a regular payment: **(a)** a salary or stipend (15–19c) **(b)** to a noble, royal favourite, etc. to give them an appropriate standard of living (16c) **(c)** in recognition of past services or to avoid hardship (*retirement/widow's pension*, 16c), hence **pension off** to dismiss with a pension; to discard something no longer useful **3 (a)** payment for board and lodging (17–19c), reappearing in French *demi-pension* half-board (1950s) **(b)** a boarding house (17c), now only in the French form, referring to small hotels on the Continent.

Latin *pendere* is the ancestor of **compendium**, POISE*, SPEND*, and **stipend** [Latin *stipendium* 'soldier's pay', from *stips* '(small) payment']. Related to PENDANT* and PONDER*.

people [ME. Via Old French from Latin *populus*] **1** the folk making up a community, nation, or ethnic group, hence **(a) peoples** nations, races (regarded as incorrect until the 19c) **(b)** those belonging to a particular place, company, congregation, or class (*country/working people*) **(c)** human beings in general **2** persons in relation to others: **(a)** a ruler's subjects; the lower classes; the general public; the electorate (17c) **(b)** your servants or staff **(c)** the laity in relation to the clergy **(d)** your family **3** to populate (15c); to inhabit.

Descendants of Latin *populus* include **populace** [French, from Italian *populaccio*, a derogatory term for the common people], POPULAR, POPULATION, **populist** originally a member of an American political party that sought to represent all the people, and Spanish *pueblo* 'people, village', adopted for a village in Spanish or Latin America, specifically a settlement of certain Native American peoples in New Mexico and Arizona.

pepper [Old English *piper, pipor*, via a West Germanic word from Latin *piper*, via Greek from Sanskrit *pippalī* 'berry peppercorn'] An Indian and Sri Lankan shrub; a pungent condiment made from **peppercorns**, its dried berries, hence **1** a related plant **2** (a condiment made from) a sharp-tasting plant, e.g. *peppermint*, **chilli (pepper)** a species of capsicum [17c, via Spanish from Nahuatl], hence **sweet pepper** (the mildy pungent fruit of) another capsicum (19c), sometimes also called a **pim(i)ento** (also a former name of allspice or **Jamaica pepper**) [17c, Spanish, from Latin *pigmentum* 'pigment', later 'condiment', from *pingere*: see PICTURE*] **3** to sprinkle with pepper, hence to dot or stud a surface with small objects; to pelt with missiles; to fire bullets at (17c) **4** sharpness, pungency; indignation, anger; to liven up speech, writing, etc. (17c) **5 peppercorn (rent)** a rent of one peppercorn (17c); a notional or trifling amount **6** shortened to **pep** energy, spirit (*US*), hence **pep (up)** to invigorate or enliven (1920s); **pep pill, pep talk** intended to do so.

Latin *piper* produced Hungarian **paprika**, **pepperoni** [*US*, via Italian *peperone* 'chilli'], and **pimpernel** [Old French *pimpernelle*] originally a plant whose flowers have red sepals and whose seeds resemble peppercorns, later the **(scarlet) pimpernel** an unrelated plant with red flowers.

perambulate [ME. Latin *perambulare*, from *ambulare* 'to walk' (ancestor of AMBLE*)] To walk round or through a place; to stroll about (17c), hence **perambulator 1** a wheel for measuring distances (17c) **2** a baby carriage (19c, shortened to **pram**).

perch [ME. French *perche* from Latin *pertica* 'pole'] A pole or rod, hence **1** a measuring rod; a measure of length, standardized at 5½ yards (*c*.5.03 meters), also called a *pole* (at PALE) or **rod** [Old English *rodd* a thin straight stick] **2** a horizontal bar for a hawk to sit on; anything on which a bird may alight or rest (15c); to do so; (to stand or sit on) a small, raised, or precarious place (16c).

   Perk [from a variant of French *perche*] also meant a pole and (to sit on) a bird's perch, hence to sit on a high seat, to give yourself airs; to act in a conceited or jaunty way; **perk up** to make or become lively; **perky** cheerful.

percolate [17c. Latin *percolare* 'to strain through' from *colare* 'to strain', from *colum* 'sieve'] To strain, sift, or filter, hence **1** to go through a filter etc.; to (make something) ooze or trickle down or through; to (make something) pass, diffuse, or permeate gradually **2 percolator** an apparatus or substance for percolating (19c); one in which boiling water is passed through coffee grounds, hence *percolate*, **perk** to make coffee in one (1930s); of coffee: to bubble or boil.

   Latin *colare* fathered **colander**, Spanish *colar* 'to strain', whence *pina colada*, literally 'strained pineapple', and French *couler* 'to flow or slide', whence *coulee* a lava flow, also a deep gully, dry in summer, *coulis* a thin fruit or vegetable purée, *coulisse* a piece of sliding scenery or the space between two of them, hence a place 'behind the scenes', a groove in which something moves, a corridor [from *porte coulisse* 'sliding door', whence **portcullis**], and *couloir* a broad mountain gully.

percussion [15c. (French, from) Latin *percussio*, from *percutere*, *percuss-* 'to strike hard', from *quatere* 'to shake or strike'] The impact of one object striking another, hence **1** the playing of a musical instrument (a **percussion instrument**) by striking it (18c); this section of an orchestra **2** the striking of a **percussion cap** (containing explosive powder) to detonate the charge in some old firearms (19c) **3** in medicine: the gentle tapping of part of the body (19c); **percuss** to do so.

   Latin *percutere* produced *repercutere*, whence **repercuss** to beat or strike back; **repercussion** an echo, reverberation, or reflection; a blow given in return, hence an effect, an unintended or indirect consequence; *quatere* is the ancestor of QUASH*.

peremptory [ME. Via Anglo-Norman French from Latin *peremptorius* 'deadly, mortal, decisive', from *perimere* 'to take away entirely', from *emere* 'to buy, get, or take' (ancestor of EXAMPLE*)] Absolute, decisive (originally of a decree), hence of a person or their actions: dogmatic, imperious, dictatorial (16c).

perform [ME. Anglo-Norman French *parfourmer* from Old French *parfornir*, from *f(o)urnir* 'to accomplish, complete, or supply': see FURNISH*] To fulfil a promise, duty, undertaking, etc.; to carry out a public function or ceremony (17c), hence to present a play, ballet, etc.; to play a role in one; to act, sing, dance, etc. (19c).

period [ME. Via French and Latin from Greek *periodos* 'orbit, recurrence, course', from *peri* 'round, about' + *hodos* 'way' (ancestor of EPISODE*)] The time during which (an attack of) a disease runs its course, hence **1** the end of a course or process (16c); a punctuation mark at the end of a sentence, hence said after a statement for emphasis (1930s, *N American*) **2** a length of time marked by recurring (originally astronomical) events or phenomena (17c), hence **(a)** an identifiable length of time (*Roman/Cretaceous/free/menstrual period*, 18c); belonging to a historical time (*period furniture*) **(b)** the time taken by a complete cycle (18c). Hence **periodic** recurring at intervals (17c), hence **1 periodical** (describing) a weekly, monthly, etc. publication (18c) **2 periodic law** stating that the properties of the elements recur at regular intervals as their atomic numbers increase (19c); **periodic table** of elements arranged according to this.

peripatetic   [ME. Via French and Latin from Greek *peripatētikos*, from *peripatein* 'to walk about', from *patein* 'to tread'] **1** an Aristotelian philosopher (because Aristotle (see ARTERY) walked about while teaching); to do with or believed by Aristotelians (16c) **2** a walker or traveller (17c); an itinerant trader, hence travelling about (because of your work); working in more than one institution.

periphery   [ME. Via late Latin from Greek *periphereia* 'circumference', from *peri* 'round, about' + *pherein* 'to carry'] **1** used to translate medieval Latin *periferia*, each of the three atmospheric layers then thought to surround the earth **2** a boundary or circumference (17c), hence the area around the edge of a place (18c), hence **peripheral** to do with or situated at the periphery (19c); marginal, of minor importance (1950s); (describing) a device used with a computer but not part of it.

Descendants of Greek *pherein* include **amphora**, **euphoria** [via Latin from Greek *euphoros*, literally 'well borne', hence 'healthy'], **metaphor** [ultimately from Greek *metapherein* 'to transfer', literally 'to carry between'], **-phore** something that carries or causes, e.g. **semaphore** [originally a signalling apparatus [with Greek *sēma* 'a sign'].

perish   [ME. Via French from Latin *perire*, literally 'to go completely', from *ire* 'to go' (ancestor of EXIT*)] **1** to die or be killed; to be destroyed physically or spiritually, hence **(a)** to cause death or destruction, hence **perisher** an annoying person, especially a child (19c); **perishing** troublesome, confounded (19c) **(b)** in exclamations meaning 'may it perish' (*perish the thought!*, 16c) **2 perished/perishing** very hungry, thirsty, or (now usually) cold, hence **perishing (cold)** very cold **3** to rot (later to make something do so, 16c), hence **perishable** liable to rot (15c), **perishables** such goods (18c).

periwinkle   [16c. Probably ultimately from Old English *pīnewincel* (from Latin *pina* 'mussel' + Old English *wincel* 'snail shell'), influenced by **periwinkle** a small trailing plant (Old English, from Latin *pervinca*, from *pervincire* 'to wind about')] A small edible mollusc with a spiral shell, soon shortened to **winkle**. Hence **winkle out** to extract or elicit (as though pulling a winkle from its shell with a pin, World War II, *military slang*); **winklepickers** shoes with long pointed toes (1960s).

permute   [ME. Latin *permutare*, literally 'to change completely', from *mutare* 'to change' (ancestor of MEW*)] To change one thing for another (–19c); to change something's form, position, or state (largely replaced by *transform* or *transmute*), hence **1 permutation (a)** the transposition of two elements or terms (16c), hence

permutate to make this (19c) **(b)** a change in the order of a set of items; the resulting arrangement; *permute* to make such a change (19c) **(c)** a selection of a specified number of things from a larger group, especially matches in a football pool (1950s), hence **perm** (to make) such a selection **2** [via German] **permutite** a kind of ion exchanger used particularly in softening water (early 20c).

perquisite [ME. Medieval Latin *perquisitum* 'something sought', from Latin *perquirere* 'to search diligently for', from *quaerere* 'to seek' (ancestor of QUEST*)] **1** property acquired other than by inheritance (–18c) **2** casual income in addition to the regular revenues of a manor (16c); (now usually **perk**) any casual remuneration, benefit, or profit in addition to a regular salary; a customary tip (18c); something superfluous or no longer used which a subordinate or employee has a customary right to; something that someone has sole right to.

person [ME. Old French *persone* from Latin *persona* 'actor's mask, character in a play, human being'] **1** a character or role; a guise, an assumed identity (largely replaced by Latin *persona*, 1970s), hence **personate** to play the part of (16c); to assume someone's identity (17c), largely replaced by **impersonate 2** an individual human being: **(a)** one having a particular appearance, hence **personable** having a pleasant appearance or manner **(b)** an individual or group having legal rights and responsibilities **(c)** a distinguished individual (15c, earlier **personage** is more common) **(d)** one fulfilling a particular role (*chairperson/salesperson*, 1970s, often to avoid specifying the sex) **3** the self (*the king's person*); the body, sometimes including clothing etc. (*carried it on his person*); someone's presence (15c, surviving in *in person*) **4** one of God's three modes of existence (Father, Son, and Holy Spirit) **5** a grammatical category, according to whether someone is speaking (**first person**), spoken to (**second person**), or spoken about (**third person**) (16c), hence the **personal pronouns** (*I, you, he*, etc., 17c).

French *persone* produced **personify** to represent something abstract as a person (replacing *impersonate*), to embody or typify (replacing *personate* and the original sense of **personalize**). Latin *persona* is the ancestor of **parson**, **personal** to do with, affecting, later also intended for, a (particular) person, private, your own, **personality**, and French *personnel* (cf. *matériel* at MATERIAL).

perspective [ME. Via medieval Latin from late Latin *perspectivus* 'optical', from Latin *perspicere*, *perspect-* 'to look through, to look at closely' from *specere* 'to look'] **1** to do with sight, optical (–16c); an optical instrument (–18c) **2** a way of representing three-dimensional objects in two dimensions (16c), hence **(a)** a picture that does this (17c) **(b)** an understanding of the relative importance of things (17c); an individual's understanding, a point of view **(c)** the appearance of things according to distance, angle, etc. from the observer (19c) **(d)** (**sound/auditory**) **perspective** an apparent spatial distribution of perceived sound (1930s) **3** an (extensive) view (17c).

Latin *perspicere* produced **Perspex** a proprietary name for a transparent thermoplastic, **perspicacious** and **perspicacity**, both formerly referring to physical sight, and **perspicuity**, originally transparency, clarity, later clarity of sight or understanding (cf. SEE*). *Specere* is the ancestor of SPICE*.

pertinent [ME. (French, from) Latin *pertinere*, literally 'to hold to', from *tenere* 'to hold'] Belonging to (–17c, *impertinent* survived longer); appropriate, suitable;

relevant, to the point. Hence **impertinent** irrelevant (ME, now mainly in legal terms); out of place, absurd (16c); not keeping your place, interfering, presumptuous, insolent (17c).

Latin *pertinere* produced **pertain** to be attached to, to belong or relate to; *tenere* is the ancestor of TENOR*.

peruke [16c. French *perruque* from Italian *perrucca*, of unknown origin] A head of hair (–17c); an artificial one (17c, earlier as **periwig**, shortened to **wig**).

Bigwig (18c) comes from the large wigs then worn by important people (and still by judges), who probably administered a **wigging** a reprimand.

peruse [15c. From Latin *per-* 'through, thoroughly' + *usitari* 'to use frequently', from *uti*, *us-* 'to USE'*] **1** to use up or wear out (–16c) **2** to deal with or examine one by one (–18c); to consider in detail (16c); to go over and revise; to read through, strictly speaking to do so carefully, but now sometimes simply to look over or glance through.

pervert [ME. (Via Old French from) Latin *pervertere*, from *vertere* 'to turn' (ancestor of VERSE*)] **1** to overturn, overthrow, or ruin (–17c) **2** to turn away from the proper use, aim, etc., to misuse; to lead someone astray, hence **(a) perversion** this action, corruption, distortion; (preference for) an abnormal form of sexual activity (19c) **(b)** a misled or corrupted person; an apostate (17c); a sexual deviant (19c), shortened to **perv(e)** (1940s, *Australian*), which came to mean 'to act like a pervert', later to ogle (1980s) **(c) perverse** wicked; persisting in wrongdoing (16c); obstinate, contrary.

pest [15c. (Via French from) Latin *pestis* 'plague'] A (fatal) epidemic disease, specifically bubonic plague (outlived by **pestilence**, also from Latin *pestis*), hence an organism that harms livestock, crops, etc. (17c); an annoying person or thing.

pester [16c. French *empestrer*, ultimately via a Latin word meaning 'a hobble' from Latin PASTOR*] To encumber or impede; to clog up or overcrowd; to infest, hence (influenced by PEST) to plague with repeated requests.

petrify [ME. Medieval Latin *petrificare*, from Latin *petra* 'stone, rock', from Greek] To turn, later to be turned, to stone or a stony substance, hence to harden or deaden; to paralyse with fear (18c).

Descendants of Greek *petra* include **parsley** [with Greek *selinon* 'celery'], **petroglyph** a rock carving, **petrol** originally synonymous with its source, **petroleum** [literally 'rock oil'], now referring to refined petroleum (whence **petro-** in *petrochemical*, *petrodollar*, etc.), *saltpetre* (at SALT), and the name **Peter** originally given to Simon, one of the apostles, whom Christ regarded as the 'rock' on which his church would be built (see the Bible, Matthew 16:18), whose many descendants include the surnames **Parkins(on)**, **Pearce**, **Pearson**, **Perks**, **Perrin(s)**, and **Piers** (also as a given name), and perhaps **petrel** a small sea bird that flies low with dangling legs, appearing to walk on water as Peter tried to (Matthew 14:29–30): the French form *Pierre* produced *pierrot*, **samphire** [from *(herbe de) Saint Pierre* 'St Peter('s herb)'], and probably **parakeet** and **parrot**.

petty [ME. French *petit* 'small'] Small in size (surviving mainly in *petty cash*), hence minor, secondary, less important (*petty larceny/officer*, 15c); insignificant, trivial, small-minded.

Petty produced **petticoat** originally a padded coat worn under armour, and **pettifogger** a bad lawyer [with **fogger** a shyster, apparently from Fugger, the name of a 15c family of Bavarian merchants], whence **pettifogging** haggling about trivia; irritatingly trivial. French *petit* appears in combinations (*petit beurre/bourgeois/fours/point*), and produced the surname **Pettit**; the feminine form *petite* was adopted meaning small, trivial, now small and slender.

petulant [16c. Via French from Latin *petulans*, from *petere* 'to go towards, to aim at', also 'to seek, to demand or beg for'] Promiscuous, wanton, shameless; insolent, rude (17c), bad-tempered, peevish, sulky (18c).

Descendants of Latin *petere* include **appetite**, COMPETENT*, IMPETUS*, **petition**, **perpetual**, and **repeat**.

phantom [ME. Old French *fantosme*, ultimately from Greek *phantasma*, from *phantazein* 'to make visible, to cause to imagine', from *phanein* 'to show'. Originally as *fantom*, the Greek-style spelling emerged in the 17c] Unreality, (an) illusion, (a) delusion or deception (–17c), hence **1** an apparition, spectre, or ghost **2** a figment of the imagination; imaginary, false (*phantom pregnancy*, 15c); an image in a dream or in the mind (16c) **3** someone/something only apparently powerful (17c).

Greek *phantasma* produced **phantasm**, which shared most senses of *phantom*, and **phantasmagoria**, originally applied to an exhibition of optical illusions presented in London in 1802, hence a rapidly changing series of images; an ever-changing scene. Greek *phantazein* produced **pant** [via Old French *pantaisier* 'to be agitated']. Greek *phanein* is the ancestor of **diaphanous** [with Greek *dia* 'through'], **emphasis**, EPIPHANY*, FANTASY*, PHASE, **phenomenon** literally 'what appears', **phenyl** originally used for by-products of gas used for lighting (whence **pheno-** in *phenobarbitone* etc., and **phenol**), and SYCOPHANT.

phase [19c. French, from Greek *phasis* 'appearance', from *phanein*: see PHANTOM*] Any of the sequence of the moon's shapes as seen from the earth (replacing 17c *phasis*), hence **1** a stage in **(a)** a process, hence to organize or carry out in planned stages (1940s) **(b)** a recurrent sequence, hence **in phase** at the same stage at the same time; *phase* to bring into phase (1930s); to alter the phase of something, hence **phaser** a device that does so (1940s), a fictitious weapon using a laser beam whose phase can be altered to produce different effects (1960s, in the television series *Star Trek*) **2** a genetic or seasonal variety in an animal's appearance or behaviour **3** a state (e.g. solid, liquid) in which matter can exist.

philander [17c. Greek *philandros* 'fond of men', of a woman 'loving her husband', from *philos* 'loving' + *anêr, andr-* 'man'] Used in Greek and later literature as a name for a lover, perhaps from a misunderstanding of *philandros* as 'a loving man' (–19c), hence to flirt or have casual affairs with women (18c).

Greek *philos* produced **Philadelphia** [literally 'brotherly love', with Greek *adelphos* 'brother'], **-phile** 'loving, a lover of' (*bibliophile, paedophile*), **-philia** an affinity for or tendency towards (*Anglophilia, necrophilia*), **-philic** and **-philous** 'attracted by, liking', usually in scientific terms, **Philip** [Greek *Philippos* 'horse-lover', with *hippos* 'horse', whence HIPPODROME*], whose descendants include **Phelps, Philpott, Phipps,** and the **Philippines,** named after Philip II of Spain (the adjective **Filipino** is from the Spanish form), **phil(o)-** (*philharmonic, philosophy*), and **philtre** a love potion. *Anēr*'s descendants include **Andrea**, **Andrew**, **android**, **misandry** dislike of men, and **polyandry** the system of having more than one husband.

physic [ME. Old French *fisique* from Latin *physica*, from Greek *phusikē (epistēmē)* '(knowledge) of nature', from *phusis* 'nature', from *phuein* 'to plant, to make grow'] **1** the study of the body, especially of medicine and healing; medical treatment, (a) medicine, hence medical, medicinal (15c); **physic garden** for medicinal plants (16c) **2** physic(s) the study of natural phenomena (–19c), later as **physics** [15c, from Greek *ta phusika*, the collective title of treatises on the subject by Aristotle (see ARTERY)], now specifically the study of matter and energy (18c).

Old French *fisique* produced **physician**, and evolved into modern French *physique*, adopted for the shape and size of the body. Latin *physica* produced **physical** originally meaning medical, medicinal. Greek *phusis* fathered **physio-** to do with the body or matter (*physiotherapy*), and **physiognomy** [with *gnōmōn* 'judge, interpreter' (see GNOSTIC*)] the art of judging character from the face or body, hence the face, shortened to **phiz(og)**, and **physiology** originally natural science. Greek *phusika* produced **metaphysics** [ultimately from *ta meta ta phusika* 'the things after the physics', from the sequence of Aristotle's works]; *phuein* is the ancestor of EUPHUISM] and **neophyte** literally 'one newly planted'.

pick [ME. Origin uncertain] To dig into or pierce with something pointed (**picking**, a mark made by this, is recorded once in OE); to probe (*pick your nose*), hence to remove unwanted matter, to pluck a fowl, to hull fruit, hence **1** to detach or take with your fingers, hence **(a)** to pluck a flower, fruit, etc., later scraps from a carcass etc. (15c), guitar strings etc. (19c) **(b)** to steal or rob (surviving in **pickpocket**, *pick your brains*) **2** of a bird: to peck up corn etc., hence to eat fastidiously or without interest **3** to choose, hence **(a) pick a fight/quarrel** to seek one (15c) **(b)** the right to choose (18c); your choice; the best (*pick of the litter*).

Perhaps the source of **peck** and **pitchfork** (originally **pickfork**), and related to **picador**, **picaresque**, and **picaroon** [all from Spanish *picaro* 'rogue, roguish', perhaps from *picar* 'to prick'], PICKET*, and PIKE*.

picket [17c. French *piquet*, from *piquer* 'prick, pierce, sting', from *pic* 'pike'] **1 (a)** a pointed stake a soldier had to stand on as a punishment; to punish in this way (18c) **(b)** a stake as part of a fence, a tethering post, marker, etc.; to enclose with pickets **2** originally *piquet*: (to post) a sentry or group of sentries (18c), hence (to establish or take part in) a group stationed outside a workplace etc. to persuade people not to enter (19c).

Descendants of French *piquer* include *piquant*, **pique** (to cause) bad feeling or wounded pride, and *piqué* a fabric woven with a rib or raised pattern, originally imitating quilting. *Pic* is the ancestor of **Picardy**, whose inhabitants were notable pikemen (whence the surname **Pickard**), of **pick(axe)** [French *picois*, altered by association with *axe*], the surname **Piggot**, and **pike** the weapon, hence some instances of the name **Pike**, **Pyke** (cf. PIKE). Probably related to PICK*.

picture [ME. Latin *pictura*, from *pingere*, *pict-* 'to paint'] The art of making representational drawings and paintings (–19c); such a drawing, painting, or, now, photograph (15c), hence **1** to make one (15c) **2** a mental image (16c), hence **(a) clinical picture** the idea a physician forms of a case; the sum of its features, hence *picture* a situation (19c), hence **get/be in the picture** to understand one (*c*.1900) **(b)** to imagine (18c) **3** (to give) a vivid description (16c) **4** someone/something that embodies a quality or state (*a picture of health*, 16c); a person who strongly resembles another (18c); someone/something beautiful or striking (19c) **5** a visible image formed by optical or electronic equipment (17c); a film (19c), **pictures** films collectively; **picture show** (US), **the pictures** the cinema.

Picture was shortened to **pic(cy)**, *pictures* to **pix**, whence **pixel** [short for *picture element*]. Latin *pingere* produced **depict**, **paint** [via French *peindre*], **pictorial** and **picturesque** [both via Latin *pictor* 'painter'], **pigment** originally also a spice [Latin *pigmentum*, whence also *pim(i)ento* (at PEPPER), **pint** [French *pinte*, ultimately from Latin *pinctus* 'painted' (perhaps referring to a mark painted on a container)], and Spanish *pinto* 'painted, mottled', adopted for a piebald or skewbald horse (N American, sometimes also called a *paint*).

pie [ME. French, from Latin *pica*] A magpie, later a bird resembling one. Hence **1** (probably) a dish baked in, or topped with, pastry (the filling mixture resembling the objects collected in a magpie's nest) **2 (a) pied** black and white, later of any two colours **(b) piebald** (at BALD).

Magpie came from the addition of *Mag* (short for Margaret), a popular name for the bird, and was applied to someone who chatters (like a magpie's call), a curious person, a petty thief, or an avid or indiscriminate collector. Forms of Margaret became folk names for other creatures: **Madge** a barn owl; **Maggie** a guillemot (Scots), **Moggie** a cow or calf, later a cat. Latin *pica* was adopted for a size of type, and for an abnormal desire to eat clay, coal, etc. (the magpie being an indiscriminate feeder), and is the ancestor of the surname **Pye**.

piece [ME. Old French, probably of Gaulish origin] **1** a (detached) part (*piece of cake/land/string*); **piece (together)** to join pieces to form a whole (15c) **2** an item of a particular kind (*piece of furniture/news/music*), hence **(a) piece of money/gold**, etc.: a coin; *piece of eight* (at DOLLAR) **(b)** a gun (16c) **(c)** an object moved in a board game (*chess piece*, 16c) **3** a (specified) amount, hence **piecework** paid by the amount done (16c) **4 piece (of work): (a)** a work of art or skill (16c), hence **masterpiece** an outstanding work, the artist's finest (17c, shortened to *piece* an elaborate piece of graffiti, 1980s); a (short) musical or literary work (16c); an item for a newspaper, broadcast, etc.; a short recitation (19c), hence *say your piece, party piece* **(b)** a person, often contemptuous (1920s, perhaps influenced by Shakespeare's 'What a piece of work is a man' (*Hamlet* II ii 315) **5** a (financial) share in (*piece of the action*, 1920s, US).

Patch (with the general sense 'small piece') is believed to come from a variant of French *piece*. **Peat** is probably related.

piety [ME. Via Old French from Latin *pietas* 'dutifulness', from *pius* 'dutiful, devout, compassionate'] **1** mercy, clemency, mildness (–17c); compassion, sympathy; a reason or cause for this **2** devotion and reverence to God, later to parents, superiors, etc.

Pity [also from Latin *pietas*] originally shared both these senses, and went on to mean 'to feel sorry for'. *Pietas* also produced Italian *pietà* a depiction of the Virgin Mary with the dead Christ, and **pittance** a bequest to a religious house to provide food, wine, etc. on certain occasions, hence a small or meagre amount. Latin *pius* is the ancestor of **expiate** [Latin *expiare*, from *piare* 'to atone (by religious rite or sacrifice)] and **pious**, which has never meant 'compassionate'.

pike [Old English *pi(i)c*, of uncertain origin: probably related to PICK*] **1** a pickaxe (now dialect) **2** a sharp point, a spike (ME); a staff with an iron point, a pikestaff [**pikestaff** is from related Old Norse *pikstafr*, ME]. Hence **turnpike** a spiked, movable barrier across a road (15c); a tollgate (18c); **turnpike (road)** a toll road, later often shortened to *pike*, hence **piker**, **pikey** a tramp or gypsy (19c); **come down the pike** to appear, to turn up (US) **3** a narrow, tapering thing or part (ME, cf. *peak* below); a freshwater, predatory fish with a tapering jaw, whence **pickerel** a young pike; a smaller related species (18c, *N American*); the surname **Pickerell** an aggressive person **4** some instances of the name **Pike**, **Pyke**: cf. PICKET.

The variant **peak** came to mean something that sticks up or out (hence to do so), e.g. the front of a cap; part of the hairline on the forehead, especially a **widow's peak** in the middle, said to show that its owner would be widowed young; a narrow part of a ship's hull (*forepeak*); (a hill or mountain with) a pointed summit, hence highest part, specifically of a line on a graph, hence the point of maximum activity, demand, etc. (*peak-hour traffic*); to reach this.

pile [ME. French, from Latin *pila* 'pillar, pier, mole'] **1** a pillar, a bridge support (–18c) **2** a heap (15c), hence **(a)** any large group or collection of things (17c); **pile(s)** a large quantity, amount, or number **(b) pile (up)** to form a pile (17c); to amass or accumulate (19c); **pile-up** a multi-vehicle crash (1920s) **(c) galvanic/ voltaic pile** a stack of metal plates used to produce electric current (19c) **(d) atomic/nuclear pile** a nuclear reactor (consisting of uranium in a pile of graphite, 1950s) **3** a large, imposing building (17c).

Latin *pila* is the ancestor of **pillar** and possibly of **pillory**. Despite appearances **pile** 'a sunken support' is not related: it comes from Old English *pī* 'a dart or arrow, a pointed stake driven into the ground for a support', from Latin *pilum* 'spear'.

pilgrim [ME. Provençal *pelegrin* from Latin *peregrinus* 'stranger', from *peregre* 'abroad', literally 'through fields', from *ager* 'field'] A traveller; one who travels to a holy place for religious reasons; someone who embarks on a quest; someone on the journey through life. Hence **1 pilgrimage** a pilgrim's journey **2 Pilgrim Fathers** a later name for a group of Puritans who left England in search of religious freedom and 'fathered' the colony of Plymouth, Massachussets, in 1620.

Latin *peregrinus* produced **peregrination** a journey, originally through life towards heaven, and **peregrine** 'pilgrim', used to describe a falcon that was captured while on passage rather than taken from the nest; also as a name, with variants including **Peagrim** and **Pelerin**. Latin *ager* is one source of AIR*.

pillion [15c. Gaelic *pillean* or Irish *pillin*, literally 'little couch', from *pell* 'couch, cushion', from Latin *pellis* 'skin'] A light saddle; a pad fixed to the back of a saddle for goods or an additional rider, hence **pillion (seat)** a passenger seat behind the rider of a motorcycle etc. (1920s).

Descendants of Latin *pellis* include **pelisse** a long fur-lined cloak, **pellagra** a disease whose symptoms include skin inflammation, **pelt** an animal skin, **pilch** a fur-lined garment, later a leather or coarse woollen one, whence the surname **Pilcher**, **Pilger** someone who wore, made, or sold pilches, and **surplice** (which originally covered a pilch worn for warmth in church).

pin [Old English *pinn*, ultimately from Latin *pinna*, *penna* 'point, feather, wing'] A (pointed) device used as a fastener, marker, decoration, etc. (*hair/rolling/split pin*);

a small peg or projection (*three-pin plug*), hence **1** to fasten with one (ME); to attach firmly (16c), hence **pinafore** an apron with a bib, originally pinned 'afore' (to the front of) a dress (18c); a woman's sleeveless overall (both often shortened to **pinny**); **pinafore (dress)** resembling the overall (19c) **2** something resembling a pin: **(a)** pins legs (16c) **(b)** a skittle (16c), hence the games **ninepins** and **tenpin bowling 3 pin money** a wife's allowance, later a small amount she earns, for her personal expenses (17c).

Latin *pinna* produced **pinnate** like a feather, having parts arranged on each side of a common axis, and fathered late Latin *pinnaculum* [literally 'little *pinna*'], whence French *panache* originally a decorative plume of feathers, and **pinnacle** originally a turret (cf. PINION). *Penna* produced **pen** a writing implement, originally made from a quill, **pennate** winged, wing-shaped, the Italian pasta *penne*, literally 'quills', *pennon* (at PENDANT), and PINION.

pine¹ [Old English *pinian*, via Old French from Latin *poena* 'fine, penalty', from Greek *poinē*] To torment, torture, or distress (surviving in Scots), hence (all ME) **1** punishment, suffering, or loss inflicted as a penalty; physical or mental suffering: replaced in these senses by the variant **pain 2** to put to work; **pine yourself** to exert yourself, hence *pine* trouble taken in doing something (–17c), outlived by **pains 3** to wear someone out with starvation, disease, or grief (now dialect); **pine (away)** to waste away from grief or longing (15c), hence **(a)** to yearn for something unattainable (16c) **(b)** to lament, complain, or fret (17c, largely replaced by *pine*'s descendant, **repine**, 16c).

Latin *poena*'s descendants include **impunity**, **penal**, **penalty**, **punish**, **punitive**, and **subpoena** [Latin *sub poena* 'under pain of', the first words of the writ].

pine² [Old English *pīn* and Old French *pin*, both from Latin *pinus*] The coniferous tree; (made of) its wood (17c). Hence **pineapple** a pine cone (ME); a tropical fruit thought to resemble one (17c); a hand grenade (patterned like the fruit's skin, World War I).

Latin *pinus* produced **pineal (gland)** and **pinion** a cog wheel [both via Latin *pinea* 'pine cone', which they are thought to resemble], **pinnace** [via French and, probably, Spanish *pino* 'pine, boat'], and the French grape *pinot* [via French *pin* 'pine cone', from the shape of its cluster]: its earlier name, *pineau,* survives mainly for an aperitif made with grape juice and brandy.

pinion [ME. French *pignon*, ultimately from Latin *pinna*: see PIN*] **1** a turret or battlement (cf. *pinnacle* at PIN) **2** the end of a bird's wing, including the flight feathers; to cut this off to prevent flight (16c); to tie someone's arms.

pioneer [16c. French *pionnier* from Old French *paonier*, *peon(n)ier*, from *paon*, *peon*, from medieval Latin *pedon* 'foot soldier', from Latin *pes, ped-* 'foot'] A foot soldier who went ahead to prepare the way, hence an inventor, innovator, or forerunner (17c); an explorer or early settler; to be one (18c); **pioneer (species)** a plant or animal that establishes itself in new territory (*c.*1910).

Old French *paon* produced the **pawn** in chess. Descendants of Latin *pes* include EXPEDITION*, **-ped** (*biped, quadruped*), **pedal**, **-pede** (*centipede, velocipede*), **pedestal** (at STALL), **pedestrian**, **pedicure**, **pedigree** [Anglo-Norman French *pé de grue* 'crane's foot', used for a mark indicating succession in a family tree], French *pied-à-terre*, literally 'foot to earth'), TRIVET, VAMP, and perhaps *pedlar* (at HUCKSTER).

pipe [Old English, later also Old French, ultimately from Latin *pipare* 'to peep, chirp', imitating the sound] A simple wind instrument, later any woodwind instrument; an organ tube (ME); a boatswain's whistle (17c); **pipes** a wind instrument having more than one tube (*bagpipes, pan pipes*, 18c). Hence **1** to play a pipe or pipes, hence **(a)** to make a shrill, originally weak, sound (ME–15c, replaced by **peep**, also probably from Latin *pipare*); to hiss or whistle (hence **piping hot** sizzling); (to make) a high-pitched sound, song, or note (16c) **(b)** to call, lead, or signal to someone with a pipe (16c); **pipe down** to stand a crew down by blowing a boatswain's whistle (18c); to become quiet, to shut up (*c*.1900) **2** a tube for water, gas, etc., hence **(a)** a tube with a bowl for smoking tobacco etc. (16c, hence **pipe dream** an impractical notion, compared to those produced by smoking opium, 19c, *US*); a tubular part or structure **(b)** to convey by means of pipes; to transmit music, speech, etc. (1930s) **(c)** **pipeline** a continuous line of pipes (19c); a channel for supply or communication (1920s, hence **in the pipeline** being planned or prepared) **(d)** to decorate with **piping** a thin tube of cloth, or a line or twist of icing (19c).

Old French *pipe* produced *pipette*. Latin *pipare* produced **pipe** a cask or liquid measure [via Anglo-Latin *pipa*], and may be the ultimate ancestor of **fife**.

pippin [ME. French *pepin*, of unknown origin] The seed of some fruits (shortened to **pip**); a kind of apple grown from seed (also *pip* until the 17c); applied to people, originally meaning a fool (17c), later as a term of endearment (19c), hence an excellent person or thing (US), shortened to *pip* (1920s).

Possibly the same word as **pip** to blackball or reject; to defeat, especially narrowly or at the last minute; to fail an examination candidate: **pill** a medicinal tablet [via early Dutch or Low German from Latin *pilula* 'small ball', from *pilla* 'ball' (ancestor of PELLET*)] also had the senses 'to blackball' and 'to fail a candidate' at about the same time.

pirate [ME. Latin *priata* from Greek *peiratēs*, from *peiran* 'to attempt, to assault', from *peira* 'trial'] Someone who robs or plunders on, or from, the sea; their ship (16c); to rob or plunder; to be a pirate (17c). Hence **1 (a)** a person who uses or reproduces something in contravention of patent or copyright (17c); (describing) the thing used or reproduced; to do so (18c) **(b)** an unlicensed taxi or bus (19c) **(c)** (describing) an illegal broadcaster (*c*.1910) **2 (river) pirate** a river that captures the headwaters of another (19c).

Greek *peira* produced **empiric** a member of an ancient sect of physicians who based their treatments solely on experience, hence a physician with no scientific knowledge, a quack, and **empiricism** practice based on observation and experiment.

pit [Old English *pytt*] A large hole in the ground, later specifically one from which something is extracted (*chalk/gravel pit*), or where something is kept, hence **1 (a)** a waterhole or pond **(b)** a concealed pit as a trap (ME), hence **pitfall** an unexpected difficulty **(c)** the grave (ME), now only a mass grave (*plague pit*) **(d)** hell (ME) **(e)** (the shaft of) a coalmine (15c) **(f)** a sunken area for examining the undersides of vehicles (19c), hence **pits** a servicing area beside a motor-racing track (*c*.1910) **2** a hollow in the body (*armpit*, ME); one on a surface, hence **(a)** **pitted** having small hollows on the surface (15c) **(b)** a pockmark (17c) **(c)** **the pits** an unpleasant place or thing (1950s, *US*, short for *armpits*) **3** a pit where animals are kept or made to fight (16c, see also COCKPIT), hence **(a)** to make them do so (18c); to match your strength or skill against an opponent (19c) **(b) pit bull terrier** originally bred for fighting (1940s, *US*).

pitch [ME. Perhaps related to Old English *picung* 'stigmata'] **1** to drive something pointed into the ground etc. (–18c), hence to erect a tent; to put or fix something in a certain place, hence **(a)** to prepare a battlefield, troops, etc. for fighting, surviving in **pitched battle (b)** the place where something is put, someone stands, or something happens (17c, *US*); in cricket: the area between and around the wickets (19c), hence the playing area of a sports field (*c.*1900) **2** to fall heavily or head first; such a fall (16c), hence **(a)** to slope (*pitched roof*, 16c); the degree of slope **(b)** of a ship: to rise and fall alternately at bow and stern (17c) **3** to throw, hence **(a)** to send a ball to a batter (18c) or, in golf, towards the green (19c) **(b) pitch in** to throw yourself into something, to take part enthusiastically **4** the highest point (16–17c), hence **(a)** a degree of intensity, a level; the quality or frequency of a musical sound **(b)** the height of a roof or arch (17c) **5** persuasive speech or behaviour (19c, usually in *sales pitch*, perhaps from the idea of a pitch in a market); to go after business (1970s).

pith [Old English *pitha*: related to **pit** 'pip, seed'] The central spongy tissue in the stems of some plants; similar tissue lining the rind of citrus fruits, hence the central or essential part of something; its spirit or essence, hence **pithy** full of spirit, strength, or vigour (ME), full of significance (16c), of words etc.: forcible, concise, terse.

pixie [17c. Origin unknown] An (often mischievous) kind of elf (earliest in **pixie path**, which bewildered those following it), hence **pixilated** crazy, whimsical, bemused, drunk (19c, *US*, probably from *pixie-led*).

placard [15c. Obsolete French *placquart*, from *plaquier* 'to plaster, to piece together', from early Dutch *placken* 'to flatten or patch'] **1** a formal document, originally authenticated by a thin seal, hence an official announcement or decree (16c); a poster or notice, especially one carried by a demonstrator **2** an additional piece of armour worn under or over a cuirass (15c); a (decorated) garment worn under an open coat etc. (16c), hence the variant **placket** (a flap behind) an opening in a garment.

Dutch *placken* produced *plak* 'plate, patch', whence **plaque** an ornamental or commemorative (metal) plate; a flat raised patch, growth, etc.; a deposit on the teeth.

place [Old English from Old French, ultimately via Latin *platea* 'broad way, open space' from Greek *plateia*, feminine of *platus* 'broad, flat'] An open space in a town, hence **1** a location, a spot (ME), hence **(a)** an inhabited one; a town, city, etc.; your home; a small square or cul-de-sac (16c, now chiefly in their names) **(b)** the point reached in reading a book etc. **(c)** the point to which a falcon rises before swooping on its prey (17c, surviving mainly in **pride of place** the highest, now the most important, position) **2** position, standing: **(a)** in society (*know your place*, ME), hence a position or job (15c) **(b)** of a figure in a series (*two decimal places*) **(c)** of the (winner and) runners up in a race (19c), hence **be placed** to finish in such a position **3** to put someone/something in a particular place (15c);

to assign to a position, setting, date, etc. (16c); to recognize or remember correctly (19c, *US*).

The original sense survives in Italian *piazza* and Spanish *plaza* [both from Latin *platea*]. Greek *platus* produced PLATE*.

plague [ME. Latin *plaga*, probably from Greek] A blow, a wound (–16c); an affliction or calamity, hence **1** a large number of unpleasant things (*plague of frogs*); to afflict with one (15c), to torment or annoy (16c) **2** an illness (–17c); an infectious, often fatal, and rapidly spreading disease (16c).

plain [ME. Old French, from Latin *planum* 'something flat', from *planus* 'flat', of music: 'soft'] **1** **(a)** a level tract of country **(b)** see PLANE **2** level, flat, hence **(a)** unobstructed, clear; evident, easily understood; simple, uncomplicated (17c); (describing) the simplest knitting stitch (19c) **(b)** ordinary, undistinguished, unpretentious; not elaborate, embellished, or coloured; of food: not rich or highly seasoned (17c); of a woman: not pretty (18c) **(c)** of a person, their manner or speech: candid, straightforward.

Latin *planus* produced French **esplanade** originally a flat area on top of a rampart, **explain**, Italian *piano* and *pianissimo*, directions to play music (very) softly, and **plane** a tool for smoothing wood. Italian *piano et forte* (see FORCE*) 'soft and loud' produced **pianoforte** or **fortepiano** a keyboard instrument with soft and loud pedals, shortened to **piano**, whence **pianola** (a trade name for) a mechanical piano, hence a bridge hand that is easy to play, an easy task.

plait [ME. Old French *pleit*, ultimately from Latin *plicare* 'to fold'] **1** (to make) a fold, wrinkle, or crease, surviving mainly in the variant **pleat 2** to interweave or interlace; an interlaced length of three or more strands; a plaited tress of hair.

An Anglo-Norman variant of *pleit* produced **plight** a pleat, also a condition: the sense 'predicament' probably came about by association with *plight* '(to put in) danger' (see PLEDGE), but cf. PLY.

plan [17c. French *plant(e)*, ultimately from Latin *plantare* (see PLANT*): influenced by French *plan* 'flat' (see PLANE)] A diagram of the horizontal aspect of a (proposed) building; to make one (18c), hence **1** a detailed map of a small area **2** a table showing future events or tasks; (to prepare) a scheme for doing something.

plane [17c. A respelling of PLAIN, influenced by French *plan*, from Old French *plain*] (Describing) a flat surface, hence **1 plane sailing** a method of navigation that treats the earth's surface as flat (17c), originally as *plain sailing*: this spelling now usually means something very easy **2** a level or standard of existence etc. (19c) **3** a (flat) surface that generates an upward or downward force as it moves through air or water, hence **aeroplane** one that generates lift (19c–*c*.1900, replaced by **aerofoil** [FOIL²]): the sense 'aircraft' (19c), often shortened to **plane**, comes via French from Greek *planos* 'wandering'.

Aeroplane and *aerofoil* produced, by analogy, **hydroplane** and **hydrofoil** [Greek *hudōr* 'water', whence **dehydrate** and **hydro-** (*hydrogen*, *hydroelectric*)]. French *plan* produced **plane** to soar on outstretched wings (the wings being extended in a plane); to skim along the surface of water, and **planish** to smooth metal by rolling or hammering, and influenced PLAN. Greek *planos* produced **planet**, originally regarded as a wandering star, and **plankton** that 'wanders' the ocean.

plant [Old English, the noun from Latin *planta* 'sprout, slip, cutting', possibly from Latin *plantare*, literally 'to drive in with the sole of your foot' (whence the English verb), from *planta* 'sole of the foot'] To put a seed, bulb, sapling, etc. in the ground so that it may grow; a young tree, vegetable, etc. newly planted or to be planted. Hence **1** in various senses with the underlying meaning of **(a)** to fix firmly, hence something fixed, an industrial building (18c), hence heavy (movable) equipment **(b)** to introduce: to put an idea in someone's mind (15c); introduce covertly, especially to incriminate or mislead (17c); someone/something planted in this way (1920s) **2** a living thing other than an animal (16c).

Latin *planta* 'sprout etc.' is the ancestor of **clan** [via Gaelic *clann*, Old Irish *clan(d)* 'offspring, family, stock'] and **Plantagenet** [Latin *planta genista* 'sprig of broom', the family crest]. Descendants of Latin *plantare* include PLAN, **plantation**, and **transplant**; those of *planta* 'sole' include **plantain** a plant with broad prostrate leaves (the plantain of the banana family is an alteration of a Central or S American name), and SUPPLANT.

plaster [Old English, from medieval Latin *plastrum*, from Latin *emplastrum*, ultimately from Greek *emplassein* 'to daub on', from *plassein* 'to mould or form'] **1** a bandage spread with a salve, ointment, etc., now usually (a strip of) adhesive material for dressing a wound, hence a (temporary or inadequate) remedy (ME) **2 (a)** a soft, wet mixture that dries hard; to apply this to a wall etc.; to coat or daub unevenly or (too) thickly; to stick down as if with plaster (17c) **(b) plaster (of Paris)** a powder mixed with water to form a rapidly hardening paste, used to make casts and moulds; **plaster (cast)** a bandage stiffened with this (19c) **(c)** to mix or pound to a sticky mass (15c), hence to defeat heavily; **plastered** drunk (*c*.1900, cf. *shellacked* at SHELL).

Latin *emplastrum* produced **piastre** a Middle Eastern coin and currency [French, from Italian *piastra (d'argento)* 'plate (of silver)']. Greek *plassein* is the ultimate ancestor of **plasma** and PLASTIC.

plastic [17c. Via French or Latin from Greek *plastikos*, from *plassein*: see PLASTER*] To do with, or capable of, moulding or shaping clay, wax, etc.; able to be moulded or shaped. Hence **1 (a)** pliant, impressionable (17c); adaptable (*c*.1900) **(b)** (made of) a solid substance that is easily moulded or shaped (*plastic explosive*, 19c) **2** to do with or involving a permanent change of shape (19c), hence **(a)** to do with reconstruction of a body part (*plastic surgery*) **(b)** (made of) one of a number of synthetic materials that can be given a permanent shape while soft, often used in place of more traditional or expensive materials (early 20c), hence artificial, insincere (*plastic flowers, a plastic smile*, 1960s); **plastic (money)** (the use of) plastic credit or debit cards (1970s).

plate [ME. Old French, feminine of *plat* 'flat (surface)', ultimately from Greek *platus* 'broad, flat'] **1** a piece of metal used: **(a)** in armour **(b)** for writing, engraving, or printing (17c, hence a printed picture in a book), any surface used for printing (19c) **(c)** as an electrode (18c). Hence something resembling this: **(a)** a plaque or label (*book/name/number plate*, 17c) **(b)** a thin, flat structure in an animal or plant (17c), hence **platelet** a disc-shaped corpuscle in the blood (19c) **(c)** (to fit) a light horseshoe for racing (17c) **(d)** a sheet of glass etc. coated with light-sensitive material used in early cameras (19c), hence a standard size of photograph **(e)** a metal rail with a flange to hold a wheel (19c, surviving in **platelayer**) **(f)** a denture, originally the part shaped to fit the palate (19c) **(g) (tectonic) plate** one of the major sections of the earth's surface (early 20c) **2 (a)** (silver or gold) utensils for domestic use **(b)** metal items coated with another metal (16c); to coat an item (18c); the coating (early 20c) **(c)** a silver or gold cup given as a prize (17c); a race etc. with such a prize **3** a shallow (china) dish from which food is eaten; a similar item, e.g. one passed round a congregation to collect money (18c) **4** to cover, protect, or equip with a plate or plates (15c).

French *plat* produced *plateau*, **platform** [with *forme*: see FORM*] originally also meaning a plane surface, **platitude** flatness, dullness, insipidity (hence a banal statement), the surname **Platt** a thin person, and **platter**, and is one parent of PLATEN. Greek *platus* is the ancestor of PLACE*, **plaice**, **plane (tree)** (from its broad leaves), *platinum* (at GOLD), the name **Platt** (someone who lived on) a flat piece of land, and **platypus** [with Greek *pous* 'foot' (ancestor of PODIUM*)].

platen [ME. Partly an alteration of *paten* (at PAN), partly from French *plat* (see PLATE*)] **1** a paten (–17c) **2** a flat (metal) plate (16c): **(a)** in a printing press, which presses paper against inked type, hence in a typewriter or computer printer: the surface against which the paper is held (19c) **(b)** the movable table of a planing or milling machine (*c*.1900).

plausible [16c. Latin *plausibilis*, from *plaudere* 'to clap'] Commendable, deserving applause (–18c); pleasing, agreeable, popular (–19c); affable, ingratiating (–19c), hence (originally of a statement): convincing, persuasive, but probably deceptive.

Latin *plaudere* is the ancestor of **applaud**, EXPLODE*, and **plaudit** [Latin *plaudite* 'applaud!', called out by Roman audiences after a performance and adopted meaning (an appeal for) applause].

play [Old English *plega* (noun), *pleg(i)an* (verb)] (To take) physical exercise, to occupy yourself, hence **1** to do something for fun or recreation, hence **(a)** to take part in a game; to move or throw a counter, ball, etc. in one (16c); a move or manoeuvre **(b)** to toy with something/someone (ME) **2** action, movement (*swordplay/play of light on water*); free, unimpeded movement (17c) **3** a dramatic performance; to take part in one (ME); to represent a certain character in a drama or, later, in real life **4** to perform on a musical instrument.

The source of surnames such as **Player**, **Playfair**, and of place names such as **Plaistow**, **Playford**, where games were held or animals frolicked.

plea [ME. Anglo-Norman French *ple*, *plai*, Old French *plait*, *plaid* 'agreement, discussion, lawsuit', from Latin *placitum*, literally 'something that pleased', hence 'something agreed on, a decision or decree', from *placere*: see PLEASE*] **1** (the presentation of) a lawsuit; a statement made in court to support your case (both now Scots); a formal statement in answer to an allegation (*a guilty plea/plea of insanity*, 15c), hence **cop a plea** to plead guilty to avoid being tried for something more serious (1920s, US), **plea bargaining** this practice (1970s, US) **2** controversy, debate; argument; an apology or excuse (16c); a request or entreaty (cf. *plead* below).

Old French *plaid* produced *plaidier*, whence **plead** to discuss; to argue a case in court, hence **1** to entreat or implore **2** to enter a plea (of guilty etc.).

please [ME. Old French *plaisir* from Latin *placere*] To be agreeable, to give pleasure; to satisfy or gratify; to be pleased or satisfied; to be happy to do something,
hence as a polite request **(if you) please** if you wish to, if you would.

Old French *plaisir* produced **complaisant** [via *complair* 'to agree in order to
please'], **pleasa(u)nce** (something that gives) delight or pleasure, hence a quiet
(formal) garden, **pleasant**, **pleasantry**, and **pleasure**. Latin *placere* produced *com-
placere* 'to please very much', whence **complacent**, originally 'pleasant', later
'uncritically (self-)satisfied, smug', **placid**, and PLEA*.

The form *placebo*, literally 'I shall please', was adopted for a Roman Catholic
service for the dead (being the beginning of the first antiphon), and reborrowed
for a remedy given chiefly for its psychological benefit, also something with no
therapeutic value given as a control in trials.

plebeian [16c. Latin *plebeius*, from *plebs*] Belonging to, to do with, or typical of
the common people of Rome or, later, of any society; a commoner, hence commonplace, vulgar (17c). Hence **pleb** a commoner (17c); a coarse or uneducated
person; **pleb(e)** a freshman at a military or naval academy (19c, US); **plebiscite**
[Latin *plebiscitum*, with *scitum* 'a decree', ultimately from *scire* 'to know'] a law
enacted by the plebeians' assembly in ancient Rome (16c); a direct vote of a
state's whole electorate (19c).

Above the *plebs* in Roman society were the *patricii*, the Roman aristocracy [from
patricius 'of a noble father', from *pater* 'father'], hence **patrician** a member of the
patricii, aristocratic, an aristocrat. The lowest class were the *proletarii* [from *proles*
'child, offspring'], who owned no property, could not hold office, and were
regarded as contributing only their offspring to the State: hence **proletarian**
belonging to, to do with, typical of, or a member of, the *proletarii*, later of the
lowest class of any society; **proletariat** the lowest class, regarded as uncultured;
the working classes, sometimes including all wage earners; **prole** a derogatory
term for a lower-class person.

Latin *scire* is the ancestor of *science** (at ART*), *patricius* of the names **Patrick** and
Patricia, *pater* of PATRON*, and *proles* of **proliferate** and **prolific**.

pledge [ME. Via Old French from late Latin *plebium*, from *plebire* 'to assure', of
Germanic origin] **1** someone who acts as surety for another; to do so (–15c); to
deposit something as security for a loan or assurance that something will be done
(15c); what is pledged, hence a token of love and fidelity (16c) **2** a solemn commitment, promise, or vow, hence **(a)** to bind yourself or someone else with one
(16c) **(b)** a promise of support, love, or friendship sealed by drinking a toast
(16c); (to drink) such a toast **(c)** (a document containing) a promise, specifically
to abstain from alcohol (*sign the pledge*, 19c) **(d)** (the promise of) a donation to
charity in response to an appeal (1920s, *US*).

Probably related to Old English **plight** (to put in) danger, later of being forfeited, to give as a pledge, to pledge your faith, love, etc. (surviving mainly in *I
plight you my troth* in the Church of England marriage service: see also *troth* at
TRUCE).

plot [Old English, of unknown origin] A small piece of land kept or marked out
for a specific purpose, hence a ground plan (16c); (to make) a plan, graph, or
diagram; a plan or design of something to be made, hence **1** to make one; to plan

the sequence of events in a literary work; this sequence (17c) **2** [partly from French *complot* 'a crowd or conspiracy', of unknown origin] a secret plan or conspiracy (16c); to scheme (17c).

pluck [Old English *pluccian*, probably ultimately from Latin *pilare*: see PEEL*] To pick or pull off sharply, hence **1** to pull (at) abruptly, to tug, drag, or snatch (ME) **2** to pick at a string, harp, etc. (ME) **3** **pluck up** to raise or lift up, usually your courage (ME) **4** to pull out the hair, feathers, etc. (*pluck a chicken/your eyebrows*, 15c) **5** the heart, lungs, etc. of an animal pulled out of the carcass for food (17c), hence (the heart as the seat of) courage (18c); **plucky** brave and tenacious (19c).

plum [Old English *plūme*, ultimately via Latin *prunus* from Greek *prou(m)on*] The fruit, or the tree bearing it, later applied to various similar trees or fruits (17c), hence **1** (describing) something plum-shaped (*sugar plum/plum tomato*, 17c) **2** a raisin or other dried fruit used in a pudding or cake (probably originally replacing a prune, 17c), hence one of the best bits (19c); choice, coveted (*a plum job*, 1950s, 19c as **plummy**); *plummy* rich, good quality, desirable; of the voice: rich and resonant, also upper-class, posh.

Latin *prunus* fathered French *prune* a plum (ME–17c), hence **(dry) prune** a dried plum (the best ones coming from France); *prune* a type of plum suitable for drying. **Prunes and prisms**, referring to a mincing way of speaking, comes from Charles Dickens's *Little Dorrit* (1855–57), where the words are recommended as giving 'a pretty form to the lips': it may have contributed to *prune* a disagreeable person, later a useless one (World War II, *Air Force slang*: a training manual featured the incompetent Pilot Officer Prune).

plumb [ME. Old French *plomb* from Latin *plumbum* 'lead'] A ball of lead on a line for determining a vertical or depth, hence **1** **(a)** vertical(ly), straight down; completely, quite (16c); straight, direct; directly, precisely (17c) **(b)** to make something vertical (18c); to check that it is **(c)** to place or hang vertically (19c) **2** to measure the depth of water with a plumb line (16c); **plumb the depths** to reach the bottom.

French *plomb* produced **aplomb** [from *à plomb* 'straight down'] the state of being vertical or steady, hence poise, self-assurance. Descendants of Latin *plumbus* include **Pb** the chemical symbol for lead, PLUMBAGO, **plumber** someone who deals in or works with lead, hence, because water pipes were formerly made of lead, someone who installs and repairs pipes etc. for water and drainage (whence **plumb** to do so; **plumb in** to fit an appliance to a plumbing system), **plummet** a plumb; to (cause to) drop like one, and **plunge** to drop, fall, or throw yourself (originally into water).

plumbago [17c. Latin, from *plumbum*: see PLUMB*] **1** lead ore (17c only), also a red or yellow oxide of lead **2** graphite, black lead (18c) **3** a genus of plants, also called leadworts (18c), used by Pliny (see ANTHRAX) to translate Greek *molubdaina* 'piece of lead', used for the oxide and the plant, from *molubdos* 'lead', probably from the plant's bluish flowers but perhaps from the yellow pigment obtained from its roots).

Greek *molubdaina* produced **molybdenite** molybdenum sulphite, once thought to be a form of lead, and **molybdenum**.

plus [16c. Latin, 'more'] Opposite of **minus** [neuter of latin *minor*: see MAJOR*]
1 increased by (16c); with the addition of, hence **(a)** a quantity added (17c)
(b) (something) additional or extra (17c); an advantage **(c)** more or greater than
(*c*.1900, *US*) **(d)** as well, furthermore (1960s, *US*) **2** above zero by a specified
amount (16c) **3** positively electrically charged (18c).

Latin *plus* produced **pluperfect**, **plural**, and **surplus**; Latin *non plus* 'no more, no
further' produced **nonplus** a situation in which no progress can be made; a state
of confusion or perplexity, hence **nonplussed** confused, perplexed. Latin *minus*
produced **mis-** bad(ly), wrong(ly), in a few words borrowed from French (*misadventure, misnomer*): in most cases **mis-** is from Old English and related to **miss** to
fail to hit, catch, or do, also to feel the loss of.

ply [ME. French *pli*, from *plier* 'to bend or fold', from Latin *plicare*] **1** condition (*in
good/bad ply*, Scots): cf. *plight* (at PLAIT) **2** a fold or thickness (hence **plywood**, early
20c); a strand or twist of rope, yarn, or thread.

French *plier* produced **pliable**, **pliant**, and **ply** to bend or be bent, whence **pliers**.
Latin *plicare* is the ancestor of APPLY*, **accomplice** an associate or comrade, latterly
in crime (replacing *complice*) [Latin *complicare* 'to fold together', whence **complicate** and **complicity**], DISPLAY*, EXPLOIT*, IMPLY*, MULTIPLE*, PLAIT*, REPLICATE*, and
supple [Latin *supplex* 'submissive', literally 'bending under', whence **supplicate**].

poach [16c. French *pocher*, from Old French *pochier* 'to put in a bag', from *poche*:
see POCKET*] **1** to poke (now dialect) **2** to sink into mud (17c); to trample land
into mud; to become muddy **3** to encroach on someone's land or rights (17c); to
steal game by doing so (18c); to entice away employees, customers, etc.

Old French *pochier* produced **poach** to cook an egg by breaking it into swirling,
simmering water (when the white sets, enclosing the yolk), hence to simmer fish
etc.

pock [Old English *poc*] A small pustule, hence **1 pox** (formerly the plural) a disease causing pocks (*chickenpox, smallpox,* ME), hence **great/French/Spanish pox**
syphilis (16c); **the pox** any venereal disease; **poxed** (17c), **poxy** (1920s) infected
with the pox; ruined, worthless **2 pockmark** a scar left by a pustule (17c); any
disfiguring mark; to mark with one (18c, shortened to *pock*).

pocket [ME. Anglo-Norman French *poket(e)* 'small pouch', from Old Norman
French *poque, poke* 'pouch, bag, sack', a variant of Old French *poche*, of Germanic
origin] **1** a sack, now only a standard-sized one for hops or wool **2** a small bag or
pouch that you wear, now one sewn onto or into your clothing, hence **(a)** to put
something in it (16c); to hide or repress pride, resentment, etc.; to gain or appropriate money etc. (17c, cf. POACH) **(b) pocketbook** a small (note)book carried in
your pocket (17c); a wallet, handbag, or purse (now US) **(c)** money, means (*in/out of
pocket*, 18c) **3** a pouch or cavity (18c); the contents of one; something small and
isolated (*pocket of resistance*); a local atmospheric condition (*air pocket, c*.1910).

Old Norman French *poke* was adopted for a bag or sack, surviving in Scots and
in N American slang, where it means a purse or wallet, in **pig in a poke**, in **poke
bonnet** (from its deep brim), and as a surname for a bag-maker (also as **Pocket(t)**
and **Poucher**): it may be the source of **pucker**. Old French *poche* produced POACH,
French *pochette* [a small *poche*] adopted for a small, 'pocket' violin, later for a
small pouch or handbag, and **pouch**.

podium [18c. Latin, from Greek *podion* 'small foot', from *pous, pod-* 'foot'] **1** a raised platform: **(a)** surrounding the arena in an amphitheatre **(b)** for an orchestral conductor, speaker, prizewinner, etc. (1940s); a lectern **2** a low wall forming a foundation; a projecting structure around the base of a tower block (1960s).

Latin *podium* fathered French *puye* 'balcony', whence **pew**, originally a (raised) seating area in church for particular worshippers. Descendants of Greek *pous* include ANTIPODES, CHIROPODIST*, **-pod** (*arthropod, tripod* at TRIVET), and **-pus** (*octopus, platypus* at PLATE).

poesy [ME. French *poésie*, ultimately from Greek *poēsis* '(literary) creation', from *po(i)ein* 'to make'. The development was probably influenced by Greek *anthologia* 'a collection of flowers', later of epigrams or short poems, from *anthos* 'flower'] **1** (the art of) poetry; a poem (–19c) **2** an inscription of a motto or line of verse (15–17c) **3** a small bunch of flowers (15–17c). The shortened form **posy** preserves sense 2 (in **posy ring**, bearing such an inscription) and sense 3.

Descendants of Greek *po(i)ein* include **-poeia** 'the making of' (*pharmacopoeia*), **poem**, and **poet(ry)**; those of Greek *anthos* include the name **Anthea**, **anther** a medicine derived from flowers (16–17c), re-adopted for the pollen-containing part of the flower, **anthology**, **chrysanthemum** [with Greek *khrusos* 'gold'], and **dianthus** [with Greek *Dios* 'Zeus'].

poignant [ME. French, from *poindre* 'to prick', from Latin *pungere*: see POINT*] Sharp-pointed, piercing, hence **1** sharp-smelling or tasting **2** painful and distressing; deeply moving or touching **3** of remarks etc.: sharp, caustic, severe (15c).

Pungent [from Latin *pungere*] shared all these senses: it has largely replaced *poignant* in senses 1 and 3, and means 'sharp, pointed, prickly' in biology.

point [ME. French, from Latin *punctum* 'a prick or puncture', later a mark resembling one, and Latin *puncta* 'the action of piercing, something that pierces', both from *pungere, punct-* 'to prick'] **I** [from *punctum*] **1** a punctuation mark (*full/decimal point*) **2** a position in time or space **3** a measuring mark on a steelyard, hence a unit of measurement (*won on points*, 15c) **4** a distinguishing mark; a characteristic (*has his good points*) **5** a detail, an item (shown by a mark); in music: a short phrase, later an important one, hence **counterpoint** a melody accompanying the main one (16c) **6** a subject for discussion; the main subject, the aim or object; the sense or purpose (*what's the point?*, *c.*1900) **7** **point (to)** to indicate position or direction, hence **(a)** to hint at, to be evidence of **(b)** to aim, turn, or face in a particular direction (16c) **II** [from *puncta*] (something with) a sharp or pointed end, hence **1** to fill in the joints of brickwork (using the point of a trowel) **2 compass point** shown by a triangular mark (15c) **3** a headland or peak (16c) **4** an advance guard (16c); (the position) at the front of a herd (*to ride point*, early 20c, US) **5 points** extremities of a domestic animal (*brown with black points*, 19c), or a dancer's toes.

French *point* produced APPOINT*. Latin *pungere*'s descendants include **bung** a stopper, hence **bung up** to stop up, **compunction** [Latin *compunctio* 'sting (of conscience)', from *compungere* 'to sting strongly'], **counterpane** [alteration, influenced by PANE, of *counterpoint*, ultimately from Latin *culcit(r)a puncta* 'quilted mattress', from *culcit(r)a* 'cushion, mattress' (whence **quilt**)], **expunge** [Latin *expungere* 'mark for deletion by pricking'], **pincers** and **pinch** [both via Old French *pinchier*], POIGNANT*, PUNCH*, PUNCHEON, PUNCTUAL*, **punctuation** the marking (by pricking) of psalms to indicate pauses when chanting them (16–18c), hence the insertion of marks in a text to indicate pauses and clarify the meaning, and **puncture**.

poise [ME. Partly via Old French *pois*, *peis*, from Latin *pensum* 'something weighed', partly via Old French *peser*, from Latin *pensare* 'to weigh up or against', both from *pendere* 'to weigh or pay'] Heaviness, weight (–18c); to weigh a certain amount (–16c); (to measure or assess) the weight of something (–19c); to add weight to (16–18c), hence **(a)** originally **poise evenly/equally** to place or keep in equilibrium (16c); to hold or carry in balance or ready for use **(b)** originally **equal/even poise** equality of weight, balance, equilibrium (17c), hence **be poised** to be 'balanced' or undecided between alternatives (19c), later (influenced by *poise evenly* above) to be ready for, or to do, something (1930s) **(c)** bearing, posture (18c); a balanced, elegant way of standing or moving; aplomb, composure; **poised** composed, self-assured (1920s).

Old French *peis* is found in *aveir du peis* (at POUND[1]). Latin *pensare* produced *compensare* 'to weigh together, to balance out' (whence **compensate** and **recompense**), and French *penser* 'to think', whence **pansy** (appearing to nod thoughtfully) and **pensive**. Latin *pendere* is the ancestor of PENSION*.

poison [ME. Via Old French from Latin *potio*, from *potare* 'to drink'] A medicinal drink, especially one containing a potentially harmful ingredient; such an ingredient; any substance causing death or harm, hence **1** to give poison to, hence **(a)** to kill or injure in this way **(b)** to add poison to a substance **2** something morally harmful; to prove to be so; to corrupt or pervert **3** (also as **poisonous**) containing or acting like poison (16c); morally destructive; wicked, detestable, nasty (19c).

Latin *potio* produced **potion** a medicinal, poisonous, or magical drink; *potare* produced **potable**.

police [15c. French, from Latin *politia*: see POLICY*] Civil administration and public order (Scots); to maintain civil order and the rule of law (16–18c); the government department responsible for doing so (18c); a body or force that keeps order and enforces regulations (19c); to do so.

policy [ME. (Via French from) Latin *politia* from Greek *politeia* 'citizenship', from *politēs* 'citizen', from *polis* 'city'] **1** an established form of government or administration (largely replaced by **polity**, also from Greek *politeia*); (the art of) government, the conduct of public affairs (–18c, replaced by *politics* at POLITIC), hence **(a)** political sagacity (15c); prudent or expedient conduct; shrewdness, prudence: cf. *politic* **(b)** (the principles underlying) a government's or individual's (proposed) course of action (15c) **2** [by association with Latin *politus* 'polished, refined'] the improvement of an estate, building, etc. (–18c); such improvements (16–18c); **policies** the grounds of a country house (18c, Scot).

Policy referring to insurance comes via French and Italian from medieval Latin *apodixa* 'receipt', from Greek *apodeixis* 'evidence, proof', from *deiknunai* 'to show', whence also **paradigm** [via Latin from Greek *paradeigma* 'example', from *paradeiknunai* 'to show side by side']

Latin *politia* produced POLICE. Greek *politēs* produced POLITIC*: descendants of *polis* include **acropolis** the citadel in ancient Greece, usually on a hill [with *akron* 'summit'], *cosmopolitan* (at COSMOS), METROPOLIS*, and **necropolis**, literally 'corpse city' [Greek *nekros* 'corpse': related to INTERNECINE*].

polish [ME. Via French from Latin *polire, polit-*] To make, later to become, smooth and glossy by rubbing, hence **1** to free from roughness or coarseness; to refine or improve, hence **(a)** to embellish, to put the finishing touches to (15c); **polish off** to finish quickly, (19c) **(b)** refinement, elegance, culture (16c) **2** the glossy surface produced by polishing (18c); a substance used to produce it (*shoe/nail polish*, 19c).

Latin *polire* produced INTERPOLATE, **polite** polished, burnished (ME–18c); refined, cultured (*polite society*); well-mannered, courteous, and the surname **Poll(e)y** a polite person.

politic [ME. Via French and Latin from Greek *politikos* 'civic, civil', from *politēs*: see POLICY*] **1** to do with the administration and government of a state (surviving mainly in **body politic** and largely replaced by *political* below] **2** shrewd, prudent; cunning (16c).

Politic produced **political** to do with government or politics; shrewd, prudent, expedient; done for expediency rather than principle, **politician** originally a shrewd, cunning, or scheming person, and **politics** [translating Greek *ta politika* 'affairs of state'].

poll [ME. Perhaps of Low German or Dutch origin] A human head (now chiefly US and Scots), hence **1** the top of a human or animal head, hence **(a)** to cut someone's hair; to cut off the top of a tree or plant (15c), hence **pollard** (describing) a polled tree (17c); to poll a tree **(b)** to cut the edge of a sheet straight (16c); cut with a straight edge, hence **deed poll** a deed made and executed by one party only: cf. *indenture* (at INDENT), **(c)** to cut off cattle's horns (16c); to breed hornless cattle; *pollard* such an animal **2** a person as a unit (cf. HEAD sense 5), surviving in **(a) poll tax** levied at a fixed rate per person (17c) **(b)** a counting of heads (17c only), hence of voters or votes; to vote; voting (19c); the number of votes recorded; to receive a certain number **(c)** to seek someone's vote, to ask their opinion (17c); a survey of public opinion (*c*.1900); to sample opinion methodically, hence to check communication lines (systematically or repeatedly) in a computer network (1960s).

Poll is found in the surname **Pollard** someone with a large head, and **tadpole** [with Old English *tāde* **toad**], which looks like a large head with a tail. Probably related to **poleaxe** [early Dutch *pol(l)aex*, early Low German *pol(l)exe*] applied to various kinds of battle axe, later a butcher's tool for slaughtering animals, hence **poleaxed** felled with a poleaxe, stunned.

pollen [16c. Latin] Fine flour or powder (–18c), hence the fine powdery substance that contains the male reproductive cells of a plant (18c).

Possibly related to Latin *puls, pult-* 'porridge, pap', whence **poultice** and **pulse** a bean or pea, and to Latin *pulvis* 'dust', whence **powder** and **pulverize**.

polygraph [18c. *Poly-* (from Greek, from *polus* 'much' or *polloi* 'many') + *-graph*: see GRAPHIC*] **1** someone who copies another (18c only) **2** an apparatus for producing identical drawings etc. simultaneously (19c) **3** an apparatus producing a graph that records several physiological activities (e.g. pulse rate, perspiration) simultaneously (19c), now often specifically a lie detector.

Polygraph a prolific writer comes from Greek *polugraphos* 'writing much'. *Poly-* appears in many words, mostly from Greek, meaning 'much, many'. Greek *polloi* appears in *hoi polloi*, literally 'the many'.

pommel [ME. Old French *pomel*, ultimately from Latin *pomum* 'fruit, apple'] A spherical ornament on top of a tower, flag staff, etc., hence **1** any ornamental knob, boss, or button, specifically one at the end of a sword handle; to hit someone with this (16c); to hit repeatedly (surviving as the variant **pummel**) **2** a rounded projecting part (–17c), hence a saddle bow (15c); a projection for the rider's leg on a side saddle; a hand grip on a vaulting horse (19c).

Latin *pomum* produced Old French *pome* (see GRENADE), and is the ultimate ancestor of **pomace** crushed apples for making cider, hence any pulpy mass remaining after the extraction of juice, oil, etc., and of **pomade** (probably originally made with apples).

ponder [ME. Via French from Latin *ponderare*, from *pondus* 'weight'] To weigh (–17c), hence **1** to weigh mentally, to think over; to think long and carefully (17c) **2 ponderable** having appreciable weight or significance (17c), whence **imponderable** having little or no weight; (something) not measurable or quantifiable (19c).

Latin *ponderare* produced **preponderate** to be heavier or more significant, to predominate; *pondus* produced *pondorosus* 'heavy' (whence **ponderosa pine** and **ponderous** heavy, massive, clumsy, laborious, dull), and POUND[1]. Related to PENSION*.

pontiff [16c. French *pontife* from Latin *pontifex*, from *pons*, *pont-* 'bridge', earlier 'path, way', + *-fex* from *facere* 'to make'] A chief priest (perhaps a 'bridge' between God and humans), hence **1** a member of the principal college of priests in ancient Rome (17c, earlier and more commonly as *pontifex*) **2** (less commonly *pontifex*) a bishop of the early Christian church (17c), hence **(sovereign/supreme) pontiff** the Pope.

Latin *pontifex* produced **pontificate** to officiate as a bishop; to act like the Pope, to claim infallibility; to speak pompously, especially ignorantly. Latin *pons* was adopted for a piece of tissue joining two parts of an organ: its descendants include the name **Pontefract** [Latin *ponte fractus* 'broken bridge'], **pontoon** a flat-bottomed boat, (one used to support) a temporary bridge, a caisson, and **punt** a flat-bottomed boat. Welsh *pont* 'bridge', in names such as **Pontypool**, may well be related. Latin *facere* is the ancestor of FACT*.

pool [17c. French *poule* 'hen', later 'stake, kitty', ultimately from Latin *pullus* 'young animal'. Influenced by the **pool** of liquid [Old English *pōl*]] A card game in which all the stakes are put in a kitty (–19c), hence **1** the kitty or its container (18c); the total stakes bet on a race etc., shared among those who backed the winner (19c), hence **scoop the pool** to be the only winner **2** a form of billiards, originally played for a kitty (19c); a rifle shooting contest in which competitors pay for each shot, the winner taking the proceeds; **the (football) pools** an organized system of betting on the outcome of games, prizes coming from the total staked (early 20c) **3** a common fund (19c); to share money or resources; a shared resource (*car/typing pool*, early 20c); **gene pool** the stock of genes in a breeding population (1950s) **4** an agreement between suppliers to control the market (19c, US) **5** a competition in which each competitor plays all the others (early 20c).

French *poule* produced *poulet*, literally 'small hen', whence **poulter** a dealer in domestic fowl and game, which survives in the name of a London City company but is otherwise lengthened to **poulterer**, to **poultry** domestic fowl; a place where they are reared or sold (surviving in street names), and **pullet** a young hen, altered to **poult** which was extended to other young poultry and game birds. Latin *pullus* produced **catchpole** a tax collector, a bailiff entitled to seize poultry and domestic animals (surviving as a surname), the surname **Pullen** a horse-breeder or a frisky person [via French *poulain* 'foal', whence, probably, **pony** (via French *poulenet*, literally 'small foal')], *pusillanimous* (at ANIMATE), and probably PUNCH.

poor [ME. Old French *pov(e)re*, *poure* from Latin *pauper* 'poor, a poor man'] **1** needy, destitute; pitiable; thin and weak (15c), unwell (largely replaced by 18c **poorly**) **2** meagre, insufficient **3** poor quality, inferior; lacking in a particular substance or quality; of soil: unproductive (17c).

Old French *povere* produced **poverty** and **impoverish**. Latin *pauper* was adopted via the legal phrase *in forma pauperis*, literally 'in the form of a poor person', i.e. one judged too poor to pay legal costs.

poppet [ME. Ultimately from Latin *pupa* 'girl, doll', feminine of *pupus* 'boy'] **1** a small human figure used in witchcraft; a doll, hence **(a)** a small dainty person; a term of endearment for a child or young girl, shortened to **pop** (a term of endearment for) a girl or woman (18c), whence **popsy** a girl(friend) (19c) **(b)** now as the variant **puppet**: a marionette (16c); someone whose actions are controlled by another **2** one of the two upright pieces of a lathe (17c, perhaps likened to a small person), hence applied to various vertical supports; **poppet (valve)** one raised and lowered by a vertical guide.

Latin *pupa* was adopted for an insect's cocoon or the creature in it, and produced **pupil** of the eye (from the small images seen in it), and probably **puppy**, originally a tiny dog. *Pupus* produced *pupillus* 'small boy', whence **pupil** an orphan or ward; someone being taught.

popular [ME. (Via Old French from) Latin *popularis*, from *populus* PEOPLE*] Known or believed by the general public; intended for them (16c), hence **1** liked by many (17c) **2** **(a)** **pop(ular) song** one appealing to many, especially the young (1920s), hence **pop (music)** such songs as a genre (1950s), hence *pop concert/star* etc. **(b)** **pop art** using themes from popular culture (1950s).

population [16c. Late Latin *populatio*, from Latin *populare* 'to **populate**', from *populus* PEOPLE*] **1** an inhabited place (–17c) **2** its inhabitants (17c); the total number of them; all the people or, later, animals or plants, of a particular kind, living in a place (19c); a total number of people or things providing a sample for statistical analysis.

Latin *populare* produced *depopulari*, literally 'to swarm over', whence **depopulate** to lay waste (16–17c); to empty of inhabitants.

pork [ME. Via French from Latin *porcus* '(male) pig'] Pig flesh as food (see also BEEF*), hence **1 porker** a pig, especially one fattened for slaughter (17c); a fat person or animal (19c) **2 pork pie** a raised pie filled with chopped pork (18c), hence **(a) pork-pie hat** one with a flat crown (originally worn by women), thought to resemble a pork pie (19c) **(b) porky (pie)** rhyming slang for a lie (1970s) **3 porky** like pork or a pig (19c); fat **4 pork barrel** in which pork was preserved (19c), hence the State's financial resources (likened to a supply of food), their distribution, often for reasons of patronage (N American).

Latin *porcus* is the ancestor of **porcelain** [via French *porcelaine* from Italian *porcellana* '(polished surface of) a cowrie shell', thought to resemble a *porcella* 'a small sow'], **porcellanite** a kind of rock resembling unglazed porcelain, **porcine**, **porcupine** [Old French *porc d'espin* 'spiny pig'], **porpoise** [Old French *porpois*, literally 'pork fish'], **purslane** an edible succulent plant, and the surnames **Porcher** and **Purcell**, both swineherds.

port¹ [Old English, or, later, Old French, both from Latin *portus*] A harbour; a town with one, especially one with customs facilities, hence **1** in place names (*Bridport*, *Port Arthur*) **2** (probably) the left-hand side of a boat (looking forward), the side next to the wharf (16c), largely replacing **larboard** [alteration of Middle English *lad(d)borde*, probably from LADE* + BOARD*]; the opposite, **starboard**, is from Old English *steorboard*, from *steor* steering-paddle, placed on the right side (related to **steer** 'to guide' and **stern** 'the back')].

Latin *portus* is the ancestor of IMPORTUNE*, **Oporto** a port in Portugal, which gave its name to the country and to the wine, **port**, shipped from it, OPPORTUNE*, **passport** [French *passeport*, from *passer* PASS] originally meaning permission to pass through a port, and PORT³*. Related to PORT²*, Old English **port** a (walled) town, and perhaps to Cornish **porth** in place names.

port² [Old English, also later via Old French, from Latin *porta*] A gate or gateway (now chiefly Scots), hence **1** an opening, e.g. **(a)** in the side of a ship (*porthole, gun port*, ME) **(b)** to allow passage of steam, air, etc. (19c) **(c)** where a disk may be inserted or a peripheral device plugged in to a computer (1970s) **2** a curve or arch in a horse's mouthpiece (16c).

Latin *porta* produced **porch** [via French from Latin *porticus* 'porch, colonnade', whence also Italian *portico*], **portal**, **portcullis** (at PERCOLATE), and **porter** a doorman or caretaker. Related to PORT¹*.

port³ [16c. French *porter* from Latin *portare*, from *portus*: see PORT¹*] To carry, specifically **1** to carry a weapon across the chest with the barrel at the left shoulder (17c, probably influenced by PORT¹ meaning left-hand side) **2** to transfer computer software from one system to another (1970s).

French *porter* produced DISPORT* and **portmanteau** [with *manteau*: see MANTLE], applied by Lewis Carroll to a word where the sounds and senses of two words were 'packed up together'. Descendants of Latin *portare* include IMPORT*, **portable**, **portage** carrying or transporting, especially of a boat or cargo between two navigable waterways, hence a place where this is necessary, **porter** someone employed to carry luggage etc., whence **porter (beer)** originally drunk by market porters, hence **porterhouse** where this is sold, along with steak, chops, etc., whence **porterhouse steak**, *portfolio* (at FOLIO), PURPORT, REPORT*, **support** [via French from Latin *supportare*, literally 'to bear or hold up'], and TRANSPORT.

portion [ME. French, from Latin *portio*] One person's share, hence **1** a share of property inherited from your parents etc. or given as a dowry **2** your lot or destiny **3** a part; a limited quantity or amount; a serving of food (15c) **4** to divide into portions; to share out; to allot as someone's due (19c): **apportion** [16c: Latin *apportioner*, from *portio*] is more common.

The Latin phrase *pro portione* 'according to (each) share' is the ultimate ancestor of **proportion** a part in relation to its whole; a relationship between quantities; the relative size of things or parts of a thing, hence relative importance (*out of all proportion*).

portray [ME. Old French *portraire*, literally 'to draw out', from *traire* 'to draw', from Latin *trahere* (ancestor of TRACT*)] To depict a scene, object or, now usually, a person in a picture or sculpture; to describe them in words; to represent them dramatically (18c). Hence **1** this action (replaced by 19c **portrayal**) **2** the result, replaced by French *portrait* [16c, past participle of *portraire*], hence of a page, picture, etc.: vertical, taller than it is wide (1930s, cf. *landscape* at LAND).

pose [ME. French *poser* from late Latin *pausare* 'to stop or rest' (from Latin *pausa*, ultimately from Greek *pausein* 'to stop or cease'), which became confused with Latin *ponere*, *posit-* 'to put, place, or lay down'] **1** to make a statement or suggestion; to raise a question; to present a threat **2** to place someone in, later to assume, a particular attitude or position (19c); such an attitude or posture **3** to present yourself in a particular way for effect (19c); to pretend to be; a pretence, hence **poser** someone who does things for effect (partly translating French *poseur*).

Pose produced **repose** to place or put, now usually to put your trust in. Late Latin *pausare* is the ancestor of **pause** and of **repose** (to) rest. Descendants of Latin *ponere* include COMPOUND*, DEPOSE*, DISPOSE*, EXPONENT*, IMPOSE*, *juxtapose* (at JOUST), OPPOSE*, **posit**, POSITION*, POSITIVE, POST²*, **postpone** (at POSTERIOR), **posture**, **preposition**, PROPOSE*, **provost**, PUNT, **repository**, SUPPOSE*, and **transpose**. The expected spelling of many of these would end in *-pone* (as in *postpone*), and in some cases such a word existed but has not survived. The ending *-pound* evolved from Old French *pondre*, from *ponre*, a contraction of Latin *ponere* (the *d* was inserted to make it easier to say); the ending *-pose* also arose in Old French, by association with the verb *poser*.

position [ME. (French, from) Latin *positio*, from *ponere*, *posit*-: see POSE*] **1** the place where someone/something is or has been put, hence **(a)** the way in which something is placed, posture, disposition (18c) **(b)** a person's place in relation to others (19c); social standing; a job: cf. POST² **(c)** to put in the correct, or an advantageous, place or situation (19c) **2** the putting forward of an assertion or proposition; what is put forward (15c, largely replaced by *proposition* at PROPOSE).

positive [ME. (Via Old French from) Latin *positivus*, from *ponere*, *posit*-: see POSE*] **1** of law or justice: formally or explicitly laid down; precise, emphatic, irrefutable (16c), hence sure, having no doubts (17c); confident, optimistic (18c); affirmative, constructive **2** indicating the presence of a substance, amount, or quality, hence the opposite of **negative** [from Latin *negare* 'to deny': see RENEGADE*] in mathematical and scientific contexts **3** the basic form of an adjective or adverb, rather than the comparative or superlative; not relative, absolute, unconditional

(17c); downright (*a positive menace*, 19c) **4** practical, realistic, empirical (16c) **5** effective, mechanically efficient (*c.*1900).

posse [ME. Latin, literally 'to be able', from *potis, potent-* 'able, powerful' + *esse* 'to be'] Earliest in *posse comitatus* 'the force of the county', those able-bodied men that a sheriff could summon for help, or a band of these led by a sheriff, short-ened to **posse** (17c, surviving in the US), hence a powerful group of people; a group of friends; a Black, especially Jamaican, street gang (1980s, US and Carib-bean slang).

Latin *posse* produced **plenipotentiary** [literally 'having full power', with Latin *plenus* 'full', whence COMPLY*], **possible**, **potent**, **potentate**, **potential**, and **poten-tilla** [literally 'able little plant', from its use in medicine]. *Potis* is the ancestor of POSSESS* and **power**, and *esse* of ESSENCE*. Latin *comitatus* [literally 'a group of companions', from *comes* 'companion, attendant'] was used for the office, later the territory, of a *comes*, which had come to mean the governor of a territory, and produced **county** a shire meeting or court (retaining some idea of a group of people) or the shire itself. Latin *comes* produced **count** and **viscount** [both via Old French *conté*], and is one parent of *constable* (at MARSHAL).

possess [ME. Via Old French from Latin *possidere, possess-*, from *potis* (see POSSE*) + *sedere* 'to sit' (ancestor of SESSION*)] To own, hence **1** to hold or occupy a place **2** to take and keep (16c), hence **(a)** to have sex with **(b)** of a demon etc.: to take over and control a person or animal **(c)** of an idea etc.: to take over someone's mind; to influence someone strongly and persistently. Hence **self-possession** self-control, confidence, poise (17c); **prepossess** to influence someone beforehand, to prejudice (17c), hence **prepossessing** causing prejudice (17c); creating a favour-able first impression (19c).

post¹ [Old English, from Latin *postis*] A vertical piece of wood, metal, etc.: **1** one acting as a support (*fence/goalpost*, ME) **2** one for displaying notices (ME), hence to put up a notice (17c); to make something known by this means, hence **(a)** to publish the name of a ship, soldier, etc. as being missing (19c); to announce or publish (1960s, *N American*) **(b)** **poster** a notice (19c), now often a large printed (advertising) picture **3** one marking the start or finish of a race (17c).

post² [16c. Via French and Italian from Latin *positum* '(something) placed', from *ponere* 'to place': see POSE*] Someone's place or situation: **1** a job: cf. POSITION **2** a place where a soldier is stationed (17c); a strategic position occupied by troops, hence **(a)** your place of duty **(b)** (to station) troops, a sentry, etc. **(c)** a fort or gar-rison (18c); **outpost** (the place occupied by) troops away from the main body (18c) **(d)** a bugle call signalling the end of the day in the British army (19c); **last post** the final call of the day, also traditionally played at military funerals **3** **trad-ing post** a shop or centre for barter, especially in a remote area (18c).

post³ [16c. Latin *posita*, feminine of *positum*: see POST²] **1** one of a relay of riders posted at intervals to convey (originally the monarch's) mail, hence **(a)** (describ-ing) a person, vehicle, etc. that carries mail (hence used in the titles of newspa-pers) **(b)** the mail itself; that collected or delivered at one time **(c)** an organization for collecting and distributing mail (17c) **(d)** **post-haste** quickly, immediately (17c, from 'haste, post, haste' formerly written on letters) **(e)** to send mail (19c)

(f) to rise and fall in the saddle when trotting, as post riders did (19c) **2** to trans-fer an entry from a daybook etc. into a ledger (17c); to enter a transaction in a ledger; to update a ledger or, now, a database (18c), hence **keep me posted** keep me informed (19c).

Latin *posita* produced **postillion** [via Italian *postiglione*], originally a rider carry-ing mail or messages.

posterior [16c. Latin, literally 'coming further behind', from *posterus* 'following', from *post* 'after'] **1** coming after, later, subsequent, hence **posteriors** descendants (–19, outlived by Middle English **posterity**, also from *posterus*) **2** situated at the back, behind (16c, chiefly in anatomy), hence the buttocks (17c).

Latin *posterus* is the ancestor of **preposterous** [Latin *praeposterus* 'back to front'] and **postern** a back door, later a door or gate other than the main entrance. Latin *post* is found in words such as **posthumous** [Latin *posthumus*, an alteration, influ-enced by *humus* 'earth', of *postumus* 'last'], **postpone** [with *ponere* 'to place: see POSE*], **postscript** [Latin *postscriptum* 'written afterwards', from *scribere* 'to write' (ancestor of SCRIPT*)], and is the ancestor of **post-** (*postgraduate, postmodernism*) and PUNY*.

postulate [ME. Latin *postulare* 'to ask or request'] **1** to nominate or elect someone to an ecclesiastical office, subject to approval by a higher authority **2** to demand or claim (16c); to claim or assume the truth or existence of something (17c); the thing assumed; a precondition; a hypothesis.

Latin *postulare* is the ancestor of **expostulate** [Latin *expostulare*, literally 'to demand from'] originally to demand how or why, **postulant** a candidate, espe-cially one wishing to join a religious order, and of **postulator** someone who pleads for someone, especially for a candidate for beatification or canonization.

pot [Old English *pott*, ultimately of Latin origin] A deep rounded vessel (*cooking/chamber/tea/flowerpot*), hence **1** a pot and its contents (ME), a potful, hence a large sum of money, especially when bet (19c); the money bet on a card game; **jackpot** one that accumulates until a player can open with two jacks or better, hence any large prize **2** baked clay, earthenware (ME); to make articles from this (18c, ME in **potter**) **3** [possibly a different word] a pit (ME); a natural deep hole, especially in limestone (18c), hence **pothole** a bowl-shaped hole caused by an eddy in a river (19c); a deep hole or cavern (hence to explore underground cav-erns); a hole in the road (*c*.1900) **4** something made of earthenware or resem-bling a pot (*chimney/lobster pot*, 17c); a cup or other prize in a contest (19c) **5** to put in a pot: to plant in a flowerpot (17c); to preserve in a sealed pot, hence **potted** condensed, summarized (19c) **6 pot shot** one aiming to kill an animal for the cooking pot, not for sport (19c), hence *pot* to kill an animal with one; to win or bag something; in billiards: to get a ball in a pocket; in rugby: (to score) a dropped goal.

Probably related to POTAGE*, **potash** [Dutch *pot asschen* 'pot ash'] potassium carbonate (originally made by leaching vegetable ashes and evaporating the solu-tion in iron pots), whence **potassium**, and to **poteen** [Irish *(fuisce) poitin*, literally 'small pot (whisky)', from *pota* 'pot'].

potage [ME. French, from *pot*, probably from the same Latin word as POT*] Soup; Anglicized to **pottage**, which was altered to **porridge**, both forms meaning a thin stew or broth, sometimes thickened with cereal (16c), hence cereal, especially oats, cooked in water or milk (17c).

Potage produced **pottinger** a soup or porridge bowl (later altered to **porringer**). French *pot* is the ancestor of *pot pourri*, literally 'rotten pot', originally a stew made from scraps, **pottery** a place where earthenware goods are made, later (the making of) such goods, **putty** [French *potée*, originally 'potful'], and **hotchpot(ch)** [with *hocher* 'to shake'] a jumbled mixture; a stew with numerous ingredients; in law: the gathering of different people's property in order to divide it equally.

pound[1]   [Old English *pund* from Latin (*libra*) *pondo* 'a pound in weight', from *libra* 'balance, pound' + *pondus* 'weight' (see PONDER*)] A weight based on the Roman *libra*, varying in different times and places and for different commodities, and divided into anything from 12 to 27 ounces. Now **1** a British unit of currency, originally equal in value to a pound weight of silver, formerly divided into 20 shillings or 240 pence, since 1971 into 100 pence **2** a unit of weight: **(a)** in the **troy** system [ME, said to be based on a weight used at Troyes, France], divided into 12 ounces **(b)** in the **avoirdupois** system, divided into 16 ounces [ME, from Old French *aveir de peis* 'goods of (i.e. sold by) weight': see POISE*].

Before 1971 **£.s.d.** (sometimes still used to mean 'money') stood for pounds, shillings, and pence: the *s* stood, not for **shilling** (like **penny**, an Old English word), but for Latin *solidus* [in Latin *solidus nummus*, literally 'solid coin'] a Roman gold coin, later applied to a sloping line used to separate shillings from pence (*2/6d*); the *d* stood for Latin *denarius* (see DENIER*).

Punnet is probably from a dialect variant of *pound*. Latin *libra pondo* produced the abbreviation **lb** a pound, now only in weight, formerly also in money. *Libra* gave its name to the constellation and its sign of the zodiac (the scales), and produced LEVEL* and **lira** the currency. **Ounce** comes ultimately from Latin *uncia* 'a twelfth', whence also **inch**: the abbreviation **oz** came via Italian *onza*. Latin *solidus* is the ancestor of SOLID*.

pound[2]   [Old English *pund-*, of uncertain origin] An enclosure for stray animals; one where straying cattle or seized goods are kept pending payment of a debt or fine, hence **1** a prison (ME); a trap **2** an enclosed body of water (ME), largely replaced by the variant **pond** but surviving in dialect and for water behind a dam, e.g. the water above a canal lock. Hence **impound** to shut up in a pound (ME); to confiscate legally (17c); to store water in a reservoir (19c).

Old English *pund-* produced *pundfald* [with *fald* '**fold**, pen'], whence **penfold**, **pinfold** (to shut up in) a pound or pen, later a prison or trap: both forms survive as surnames, along with **Pender**, **Pinder**, **Pound**, **Pounder**, and **Poynder**, all originally people who lived by, or were keepers of, the village pound.

practise   [ME. Via French or medieval Latin from, ultimately, Greek *prattein* 'to make or do'] To do, to perform, hence to do habitually: **1** to follow a profession **2** to do something repeatedly to get or maintain a skill **3** to observe the demands of your religion.

In British English, *practise*'s noun is **practice**, which has largely replaced **practic** [ultimately from Greek *praktikos*, from *prattein*] except in **chiropractic** [with Greek *kheir* 'hand', whence SURGERY*]. In N America noun and verb are usually spelt *practice* (cf. ADVICE*).

precinct   [ME. Medieval Latin *praecinctum*, from *praecingere* 'to encircle', from *cingere* 'to gird'] **1** an enclosed or defined place: **(a)** an administrative district, now chiefly US **(b)** (usually **precincts**) the area surrounding and belonging to a cathedral, college, etc. (15c) **(c)** a designated area in a town (*pedestrian/shopping precinct*, 1940s) **2** (usually *precincts*) a boundary (16c).

Latin *cingere* is the ancestor of **cinch** [via Spanish *cincha*] a saddle-girth used in Mexico and the western US, hence a firm or secure hold; a certainty; something easily done, of Latin *cingulum* 'a girdle', (adopted as a technical term in biology for various girdle-like structures), whence **shingles** a disease producing a rash (sometimes encircling the body) and **surcingle** [via French *surcengle*, literally 'belt over'] a girth that goes over a horse's blanket, saddle, or pack, and of **succinct** surrounded; encircled or confined (as if) with a belt, hence **concise**.

precipitate   [15c. Latin *praecipitare*, from *praeceps* 'headlong', from *caput* 'head'] **1** to throw or fall down; (falling or descending) headlong (17c); steep, vertical (largely replaced by *precipitous* below) **2** to make something move suddenly or hastily (16c), or to happen suddenly or unexpectedly (17c), hence (replacing *precipitous*) **(a)** sudden, abrupt **(b)** hasty, impetuous, rash **3** **precipitation** the separation of a solid from a solution (15c), hence *precipitate* the solid (16c); to cause precipitation (17c) **4** to make moisture condense (19c); to make atmospheric moisture condense and fall as rain, snow, etc.; *precipitation* (the formation of) rain etc.

Latin *praeceps* produced **precipice** originally a sudden fall, and **precipitous**. Latin *caput* is the ancestor of CAPITAL*.

precocious   [17c. Latin *praecox* 'ripening early', from *praecoquere*, literally 'to precook', from *coquere* COOK*] Flowering or fruiting early, hence **1** bearing flowers before leaves **2** prematurely developed; of a child: (too) advanced for its age.

Latin *praecox* produced **apricot** [via Portuguese or Spanish from Arabic *al-barqūq*, ultimately from Latin *praecoquum*], which the Romans regarded as an early-ripening peach.

predicament   [ME. Late Latin *praedicamentum*, from Latin *praedicare* 'to state publicly', from *dicare* 'to state'] An assertion, what is asserted (used to translate Greek *katēgoria*, which Aristotle (see ARTERY) used for his classes of attributes, e.g. quality, quantity, that a thing may be said to have), hence a class or set (16c); a set of circumstances, a (difficult) situation.

Latin *praedicare* produced **preach** and **predicate** what is stated about the subject of a proposition or, later, of a sentence, hence to state that something exists or is true; *dicare* is the ancestor of ABDICATE*; Greek *katēgoria* produced **category**. *Katēgoria* comes from *katagorein* 'to assert' (whence **categoric(al)** explicit and absolute), from *agorein* 'to speak publicly' (whence **allegory**, via Greek *allēgorein* 'to speak otherwise'), from *agora* 'assembly, marketplace', whence **agoraphobia** and **panegyric** [via French from Latin *panegyricus* 'public eulogy', from Greek *panēguros* 'general assembly'].

premier   [ME. French, from Latin *primarius*: see PRIMARY*] First, most important, hence (the title of) the chief minister of a government (18c: see MINISTER).

French *première* (feminine of *premier*, in this case short for *première représentation*) was adopted for the first public presentation of a play etc., hence to show or be shown for the first time: now becoming naturalized and often written without the accent.

premise [ME. French *premisse* from medieval Latin *praemissa (propositio)* '(proposition) put in front', from Latin *praemittere* 'to send or put before', from *mittere* 'to send' (ancestor of MISSION*)] To say or write by way of an introduction, hence **1** a proposition that forms the basis of an argument or which leads to a conclusion; to put forward as a premise (17c) **2 premises** things already stated, the aforesaid (15c), hence the introductory part of a legal document, giving details of the parties etc. involved, hence the building(s) or land specified in a deed or conveyance; a house or building with its grounds (17c); a (part of) a building occupied by a business.

premium [17c. Latin *praemium* 'booty, reward', from *emere* 'to buy or take' (ancestor of EXAMPLE*)] A reward, a prize, hence **1** a sum payable: **(a)** for insurance **(b)** for changing one currency for another of greater value (18c) **(c)** for instruction in a profession etc. **2** an additional sum: **(a)** added to rent or interest (18c) **(b)** added to wages, a bonus **(c)** the value of one currency over another **(d)** the amount by which a prospective price exceeds the current one, or the actual exceeds the nominal price (19c), hence **at a premium** at more than the nominal or usual price; **put a premium on** to value highly (*c.*1900), hence *premium* superior and more expensive (1920s, *US*) **3 premium bond** that earns no interest but is eligible for lotteries (19c) **4** a free gift or loss-leader to attract customers (1920s, US).

present [ME. French, from Latin *praesens, praesent-*, from *praeesse* 'to be in front of', from *esse* 'to be': the verb via Latin *praesentare* 'to put in front of'] Being here, being with or in the same place as (the opposite of **absent** [ME, ultimately from Latin *ab-* 'away' + *esse*]), hence **1** existing or occurring now, hence **the present** this time, now; **presently** at this time, currently (now US and Scots); immediately; promptly; shortly, soon (15c) **2** being in the mind; to bring to mind, to describe or symbolize (15c), to act a character on stage (16c): largely replaced by **represent** [ME, from Latin *repraesentare* 'to show', from *praesentare*] **3** to bring or put forward; to introduce formally, now to introduce a show etc.; to exhibit or display, hence **(a) present yourself/itself** to appear or attend, cf. **absent yourself** to go or stay away **(b) present arms** to hold up a weapon as a salute (18c) **4** [from French *mettre une chose en present à quelqu'un* 'to put a thing into the presence of someone'] to offer or give (*present my compliments/a cheque*); a gift; a bribe (long obsolete, recently re-introduced as a euphemism). Hence **presentable** fit to be offered as a gift (17c) or introduced into society (19c); fit to be seen **5** alert, attentive, self-possessed (15–19c), cf. *absent* forgetful, preoccupied (18c), **absence of mind** (18c, suggested by 17c **presence of mind**); **absent-minded** (19c).

Absent produced **absentee**, whence **absenteeism** frequent absence from work or school, whence **presenteeism** the practice of working long hours to appear conscientious. Latin *esse* is the ancestor of ESSENCE*.

preserve [ME. Via French from Late Latin *praeservare*, literally 'to guard beforehand', from *servare* 'to watch or keep' (ancestor of CONSERVE*)] To keep safe, to take care of, to protect, hence **1** to maintain; to protect from decay (16c); to process food for this purpose, hence jam (cf. CONSERVE); **preserves** food preserved as jam, pickles, or by bottling **2** to protect game or its habitat for private use (17c); a place where this is done (19c, cf. RESERVE); a place or activity (regarded as) belonging to a particular person or group.

press [ME. Via French from Latin *pressare*, literally 'to keep pressing', from *premere*, press- 'to apply pressure to'] **1** to put pressure on something to change its shape, consistency, etc. (e.g. to iron clothes, to flatten and dry a flower etc. to preserve it, to make a record or CD); a device for doing so **2** to push, drive, or thrust, hence **(a)** to push your way, to make progress (now usually **press on**) **(b)** to compel or urge **3** (to form) a crowd or throng; to gather closely around; to harass or oppress (*hard pressed*); to put in difficulty, especially by the lack of something (*pressed for time*, 17c) **4** to print (16c, originally by pressing paper against inked type); a printing machine; a printing house or publishing business, hence **the press** newspapers (18c) and journalists (1920s) collectively; **good/bad press** good/bad publicity (*c.*1900).

Sense 2b influenced the alteration of obsolete **prest** (pay given on) enlistment [Old French, 'loan, advance pay', ultimately from Latin *praestare* 'to provide', from *stare* 'to stand' (ancestor of STATION*)], to **press** to force someone to enlist, surviving mainly in **press-gang** a gang of soldiers or sailors who forced others to join, hence to coerce. *Prest* survives in **imprest** an advance or loan, originally for military service or State business.

Latin *premere* is the ancestor of **compress**, **depress**, EXPRESS*, IMPRESS*, IMPRINT*, **oppress**, **pressure**, **print** [Old French *priente* from *preindre* 'to press'] an impression made by a stamp etc., hence to make one, **repress** [via Latin *reprimere*, whence also **reprimand**], and **suppress**.

prestige [17c. French, from late Latin *praestigium* 'illusion', probably ultimately from Latin *praestringere* 'to bind tightly' in *praestringere oculus* 'to bind the eyes, to blindfold', later 'to dazzle', from *stringere* 'to draw tight' (ancestor of STRICT*)] A conjuring trick, an illusion or deception (–18c); magic, glamour, dazzling influence (19c); influence or reputation gained by association or through achievements.

pretend [ME. Via French from Latin *praetendere* 'to stretch or put forward, to allege or claim', from *tendere* 'to stretch'] To put forward for consideration or acceptance (–17c); to make a claim for a right or title (–18c, surviving in **pretender**, 17c), hence to claim to be or to do something; to claim that something exists or is so; to make believe (16c).

Latin *tendere* is the ancestor of TEMPT*. **Pretext**, which would seem to belong here, is from Latin *praetextus* 'outward show', from *praetextere*, literally 'to weave in front', hence 'to disguise', from *texere* 'to weave' (ancestor of TEXT*).

pretty [Old English *praettig*, from *praett* 'a trick'] Cunning, crafty (OE only); clever, skilful; of a thing: cleverly made or done; of a person: admirable in appearance or behaviour, hence **1** attractive, nice to look at (15c) **2** considerable, great (15c, surviving mainly in *a pretty penny* a lot of money); rather, fairly (16c); **pretty much** more or less.

prevail [ME. Latin *praevalere* 'to be stronger', from *valere* 'to be strong' (ancestor of VALID*)] To gain vigour, power, or strength (–18c), hence **1 prevail against/over**

to be stronger or more influential (15c), hence to predominate (17c); to be or become more usual; to be in general use or effect (18c) **2** to be effectual, to succeed (15c); **prevail up(on)** to succeed in persuading someone.

prey [ME. Via Old French from Latin *praeda* 'booty'] **1** booty, spoil, plunder; to take this, to plunder or pillage (–17c) **2** a creature that is hunted and killed, now only by a carnivorous animal for food, hence **(a)** a vulnerable person or thing **(b) prey (up)on** to hunt as prey; *prey* the action of doing, or the instinct to do, so (16c, surviving in **bird of prey**).

Latin *praeda* produced *praedare* 'to hunt prey', whence **depredation**, **predator** (whence **predate**), and **predatory**, and may be the ultimate ancestor of SPREE.

price [ME. Old French *pris* from Latin *pretium*] **1** the cost of something in money, effort, suffering, etc., hence **(a)** to set a selling price (15c); to ask the price or compare prices (19c) **(b)** a sufficient bribe or inducement (*everyone has their price*, 18c); a reward (*a price on his head*) **(c)** the odds in betting (19c) **(d) pricey** expensive (1930s) **2** (high) value, (great) worth; appreciation of this; the expression of admiration or approval (–17c, replaced by *praise* below) **3** pre-eminence, superiority, victory, a symbol of this, a reward or trophy, surviving as the variant **prize**, which came to mean: **(a)** something won in a lottery etc. (16c) **(b)** a contest (16c), surviving in **prizefighter** (18c, from the phrase *to fight a prize*) **(c)** something worth working or competing for (17c) **(d)** having won a prize (*prize bull*, 18c); supreme, outstanding (*prize idiot*) **(e)** given as a prize (*prize money*, 19c) **4** the estimation of cost or worth (16c), hence **beyond price**, **priceless**.

The original sense of the verb **prize** [French *preisier* from, ultimately, Latin *pretium*] was to assess the price or value of (largely replacing **praise** [also from *preisier*] and replaced by **appraise** [alteration of **apprize**, from Old French *prisier*, from *pris*] and by *price*), hence to value highly (replacing *praise*). For *prize* meaning 'booty, something captured' see PRISE.

Old French *pris* evolved into *prix*, found in *grand prix*. Latin *pretium* produced APPRECIATE* and **precious** valuable, costly; valued and loved, later (over-)refined, fastidious, affected.

prig [16c. Origin unknown] **1** a tinker; a thief (17c), hence an unpleasant person (–18c) **2** [possibly a different word] an affectedly precise person, specifically **(a)** a dandy (17–19c) **(b)** someone with strict religious views, specifically a Nonconformist minister (–18c), hence (combining 1 and 2) a self-righteous moralist (17c).

primary [ME. Latin *primarius* 'chief', from *primus* 'first'] **1** original, fundamental, not caused by or based on anything else (*primary colour*) **2** to do with a first stage or period of time (*primary school*, 15c) **3** principal, chief (*primary feather*, 16c).

Latin *primarius* fathered PREMIER and **primer** [via Anglo-Norman French] a prayer-book for the laity, later a small prayer-book used in teaching children to read, hence any elementary text book or introductory work. Latin *primus* is the ancestor of PRIME*.

prime [Strictly speaking, four words, all ultimately from Latin *primus* 'first'] **I** [Old English *prīm* from Latin *prima (hora)* 'first (hour)'] the prayers appointed for the first hour of the monastic day (6 a.m. or sunrise); this hour, the early morning (ME) **II** [Old French *prime*, feminine of *prin* 'first, excellent'] **1** of the first quality, best, finest, choicest (ME), hence the best or most perfect state or stage (*in his prime*, 16c) **2** chief, most important (17c), hence *prime minister* (at MINISTER). **III** [partly from Old English *prīm*, partly from Old French *prime*] first, earliest, primitive; the beginning or first stage (ME), hence **1** spring as the first season of the year (16c), hence the 'springtime' of life, early adulthood **2** fundamental, basic (16c); **prime number** a number exactly divisible only by itself and one **IV** [evolution uncertain; the underlying sense is taking the first step] to fill, load, or charge (16c), hence to prepare something, e.g. a bomb with a fuse (16c), a surface with a preliminary coat of paint (17c), a pump with liquid.

Old French *prime* is the probable source of **prim**, which is one parent of *prissy* (at BROTHER): **primp** is almost certainly related. Descendants of Latin *primus* include **primal**, PRIMARY*, **primate** [via Latin *primas* 'of the first rank'], hence **1** a chief bishop **2** man, apes, and monkeys (regarded as the most advanced animals), **primeval** [with Latin *aevum* 'age'], **primitive** [via Latin *primitivus* 'first or earliest of its kind'], **primordial** [Latin *primordium* 'origin', from *ordiri* 'to begin (to weave)'], the early-flowering **primrose** and **primula**, and PRINCIPAL*.

principal [ME. French, from Latin *principalis* 'first, chief, original', from *princeps* 'chief man', from *primus* 'first' + *capere* 'to take'] Most important, greatest; leading, prominent, hence **1** a leader or ruler: **(a)** the person ultimately responsible for a crime or, later, an action or debt **(b)** the head of a school, college, etc. (15c) **(c)** either of the chief protagonists in a duel (18c) **(d)** a leading actor or performer (19c); **principal boy/girl** the leading male/female part in a pantomime **2** (being) the original sum invested or lent: cf. CAPITAL.

Latin *principalis* produced **principality** the rank or rule of a prince, later his territory. Latin *princeps* is the ancestor of **prince/princess** originally a monarch, later a ruler subject to another, or a member of the monarch's family, and PRINCIPLE. Latin *primus* is the ancestor of PRIME*, and *capere* of CATCH*.

principle [ME. Latin *principium* 'source', from *princeps*: see PRINCIPAL*] Beginning, the origin or source (–17c); a basis, hence a fundamental truth or proposition; a general law or rule as a guide to action (16c); an ethical standard; honour, integrity.

prior [ME. Latin, 'former, elder', from Old Latin *pri* 'before'] **1** a superior member of a religious community, specifically an abbot's deputy or the head of a house of friars, hence [both via Old French] **prioress** a female prior, **priory** a house ruled by a prior(ess) **2** earlier in time or order (18c, perhaps a new borrowing, or from Middle English **priority**), hence **(a)** having precedence, more important; *priority* something that takes precedence (early 20c); **prioritize** to treat as most important; to decide relative importance (1970s, US) **(b)** a previous criminal conviction (1970s, US).

Old Latin *pri* evolved into Latin *prae*, whence **pre-** (*pre-eminent*, *prenatal*), PRESENT, and PRETEND.

prise [ME. French, from *prendre* 'to take or seize', from Latin *prehendere* 'to grasp'] **1** the seizing of something by a feudal lord from his tenants; the requisitioning of something by or for the monarch; the thing requisitioned, hence the variant **prize** booty, a ship etc. captured in war **2** a lever (surviving in dialect); to raise, move, or open with one (17c), shortened to **pry** (19c).

French *prendre* produced ENTERPRISE*, **misprision** [from a variant of Old French *mesprison* 'error', from *mesprendre*, literally 'to mis-take'], **pregnable**, and REPRISE*. Descendants of Latin *prehendere* include APPREHEND*, COMPRISE*, **prehensile**, **prison**, and **surprise** [French, from *surprendre*, from medieval Latin *superprehendere*, literally 'to overtake'].

private [ME. Latin *privatus* 'withdrawn from public life', from *privare* 'to bereave or deprive' from *privus* 'single, alone'] **1** of a person: not holding office or taking part in community affairs; to do with someone's personal life rather than their public role, hence **private secretary** originally employed by an official to deal with personal correspondence related to his position (15c) **2** belonging to, or reserved for, one person or certain people (cf. PUBLIC), hence describing a business, services, etc. owned or provided by individuals rather than the State (18c, the idea appears earlier in 17c **privateer** a privately owned vessel authorized by the government to take part in war, hence its commander or a crew-member), hence **privatize** to transfer a state-owned utility or service to private ownership (1950s) **3** secret, concealed, confidential (15c), hence **(a)** secluded **(b)** reticent, secretive (16c); reserved, not gregarious **(c) private parts/privates** the genitals (17c, cf. PRIVY sense 2a).

Latin *privatus* produced PRIVY; *privare* produced **deprive** and **privation**, and *privus* produced **privilege** [via Old French from Latin *privilegium*, literally 'private law', with *lex, legis* 'law' (ancestor of LOYAL*)].

privy [ME. Via French from Latin *privatus*: see PRIVATE*] **1** belonging to your private circle, intimate (–17c), hence **(a)** an intimate friend or confidant **(b)** personal, private, surviving in **Privy Council** originally the British monarch's private advisors, and **Privy Purse** an allowance from public funds for the British monarch's private expenses (17c) **2** secret, concealed, surreptitious, hence **(a) privy parts** the genitals (cf. PRIVATE sense 3c) **(b)** an outside toilet or latrine **(c) privy to** sharing knowledge of something secret or private **3** in law: someone with an interest in the matter in hand (15c, cf. *stranger* at STRANGE).

probable [ME. (French, from) Latin *probabilis*, from *probare* 'to test, ascertain, or demonstrate', from *probus* 'good, honesty'] Able to be proved (–19c), believable, credible, (apparently) trustworthy (–19c), hence likely to exist, happen, or be so (15c); someone/something likely to succeed or be chosen (*c*.1900); an enemy aircraft or submarine probably destroyed (World War II).

Latin *probare* is the ancestor of APPROVE*, PROBATE, **probe**, PROVE, and REPROBATE*, and Latin *probus* of **probity**.

probate [15c. Latin *probatum* 'the thing proved', from *probare*: see PROBABLE*] To prove or demonstrate (–17c); proving or being proved, proof, evidence (–19c), hence the official proving of a will; the official verified copy of it given to the executors; to prove a will (18c, now N American).

Latin *probare* produced *probatio* 'testing, demonstration', whence **probation** the testing of character, conduct, or abilities (15c).

proceed [ME. French *proceder* from Latin *procedere, process-*, from *cedere* 'to go'] **1** to continue or resume an activity or journey; to go on to do something, specifically to institute a legal action, hence **proceedings** a legal action; the business transacted by a court, assembly, or society (16c); a published record of papers delivered at a conference etc. **2** to come from, hence **proceeds** money or profit resulting from an activity (17c).

Old French *proceder* produced **procedure** a way of proceeding, a course of action. Latin *procedere* is the ancestor of PROCESS*.

process [ME. Via French from Latin *procedere, process-*: see PROCEED*] **1** something that proceeds or continues; a continuous action or series of actions; to subject something to this (*processed peas*, 19c) **2** something that projects (16c), a protuberance, especially of a bone.

Latin *procedere* produced **procession** the action of going along together in a formal or ceremonial way; a number of people, vehicles, etc. doing so, hence **1** a series of things or people coming one after another **2** **process** to go in procession.

procurator [ME. Latin, from *procurare*: see PROCURE*] A Roman provincial officer whose duties included collecting fines, hence **1** someone who manages another's affairs and acts on their behalf **2** a legal representative (surviving in Scotland and in English ecclesiastical courts), in some cases shortened to **proctor 3** an elected officer with administrative and, formerly, legal duties in some universities (usually as *proctor* except in Scotland) **4 procurator fiscal** a local public prosecutor in Scotland, originally one who collected fines, fees, etc. (16c).

procure [ME. Via French from Latin *procurare* 'to attend to or manage', from *curare* 'to care for': see CURE*] To try to do something or to make something (bad) happen (–17c); to arrange or bring about, hence **1** to obtain, especially with an effort, hence **procurement** acquisition (17c), now of military equipment and supplies (1950s) **2** to prevail on someone to do something (now only in Scots and legal terminology) **3** to provide someone for prostitution (17c).

Latin *procurare* produced PROCURATOR and **proxy** [contraction of **procuracy** (a document giving authority to take) action on another's behalf] **1** a document authorizing someone to vote on another's behalf, the vote or the person who casts it **2** of a mineral: to occur in place of another; one that does so.

prodigal [ME. Medieval Latin *prodigalis* from Latin *prodigus* 'lavish', from *prodigere* 'to squander', literally 'to drive away', from *agere* 'to drive' (ancestor of AGENT*)] Recklessly extravagant or wasteful; a spendthrift (16c). Hence (see the Bible, Luke 15:11–32) someone who regrets such behaviour; **prodigal (son/daughter)** one who returns home after misbehaving; a returned wanderer.

prodigy [15c. Latin *prodigium* 'portent'] Something extraordinary taken as an omen; a marvellous or monstrous thing (16c, earlier in **prodigious**); a (young) person with an exceptional talent (17c).

Prodigious went on to mean abnormally big, hence **prodigiously** immensely, extremely.

produce [ME. Latin *producere, product-* 'to bring or lead forth', from *ducere* 'to lead'] **1** to bring out, to present or show **2** to extend, especially a line **3** to create, to make or cause (15c), hence **(a)** to yield offspring, crops, or a commodity; to manufacture (16c); what is produced (17c), now only by farms and gardens, otherwise replaced by **product**, which came to mean the value of what is produced (*gross national product*, 19c) **(b)** to supervise the making of a play, film, recording, etc. (19c), hence **production** (the making of) a film etc., hence an undertaking, a fuss or to-do.

Produce produced **reproduce** to re-create or regenerate; to create more of the same; to have offspring, whence **reproduction** the action or process of doing so; (describing) a copy, sometimes shortened to **repro**. *Ducere* is the ancestor of DEDUCE*.

profane [ME. (Via Old French from) Latin *profanus*, literally 'outside the temple', from *fanum* 'temple' (whence FANATIC)] Ritually unclean; to defile something sacred or deserving respect (15c); irreverent, blasphemous, hence **profanity** profane behaviour or language (17c, rare before the 19c).

profess [ME. Via French, from Latin *profiteri*, *profess-* 'to declare openly', from *fateri* 'to declare'] **1 be professed** to have taken religious vows **2** to declare openly (15c), hence to claim (falsely) to be, do, or have something (16c).

Latin *profiteri* produced PROFESSION and **professor**, originally someone qualified to teach, later the holder of a salaried or endowed teaching post, hence a senior university lecturer; (humorously) an expert. *Fateri* produced **confess**.

profession [ME. French, from Latin *profiteri*: see PROFESS*] The vow made on entering a religious order, hence **1** any solemn vow or declaration **2** a vocation; an occupation, especially one requiring advanced education or training; the people engaged in one (17c), hence **professional** to do with or engaged in a profession (18c), hence **(a)** (someone) doing something as a job or for money (18c) **(b)** a person engaged in a profession (19c); worthy of or suitable for one (1950s) **(c)** habitual, inveterate (*a professional busybody*, 19c) **(d)** (someone who is) competent and conscientious (1920s).

profile [17c. Italian *profilare* 'to draw in outline', from *filare* 'to draw a line', from late Latin *filare* 'to spin', from Latin *filum* 'a thread' (ancestor of FILE*)] (A drawing of) an outline, especially someone's head, seen from the side or in section, to draw in outline or cross-section (18c). Hence **1** a short biographical or character sketch (18c); an assessment of someone's attitudes and abilities (1930s); to prepare one (1940s, *US*) **2** to give something a specific outline or shape (19c) **3** (an outline on a chart representing) a set of data or characteristics (1930) **4** a degree of visibility, the extent to which something attracts attention (*keep a low profile*, 1970s).

profit [ME. French, from Latin *profectus* 'progress, profit', from *proficere*, *profect-* 'to advance', from *facere* 'to make or do'] Advantage, benefit, your good, hence **1** to benefit, to do someone good; to benefit from something **2 profits** income from an investment; *profit* a financial gain from a transaction or business activity (15c), especially the amount received for something above the cost of providing it.

French *profit* produced **profiterole**, literally 'little benefit'. Latin *proficere* is the ancestor of **proficiency** originally an improvement in skill or knowledge, and *facere* of FACT*.

profligate [16c. Latin *profligatus* 'dissolute, ruined', from *profligare* 'to overthrow', from *fligere* 'to strike down' (ancestor of **afflict**, **conflict**, and **inflict**)] Overthrown, overwhelmed, routed (–17c); overcome by vice, dissolute, licentious (17c); recklessly extravagant (18c).

programme [17c. French, via late Latin from Greek *programma*, from *prographein* 'to write publicly', from *graphein* 'to write' (ancestor of GRAPHIC*)] **1** a publicly displayed notice, especially one about a coming event (–19c, Scots, the English using *programma*) **2** a written preface (19c, replacing *programma*) **3** [from French] (a booklet etc. giving details of) an intended series of events or activities (19c); to create such a schedule. Hence (*US*, and therefore in the American spelling **program**) a sequence of operations that a machine can perform automatically (1940s); to set a machine to do so, hence **(a)** a list of instructions for a computer; to write one or load a computer with one **(b)** to train to behave in a predetermined way (1960s) **4** a radio or television broadcast (1920s); a radio station providing a series of programmes (largely replaced by CHANNEL), hence **(a)** to broadcast (1930s, US) **(b)** **programming** the selection and scheduling of radio or television programmes (1940s).

progress [ME. Latin *progredi*, *progress-*, 'to go forward', from *gradi* 'to walk', from *gradus* 'a step': the verb was obsolete in British English by the 18c: reintroduced from the US (*c*.1800), it was regarded as an Americanism until the mid 20c] The action of moving on, hence **1** a royal or official tour or visit; to make one (16c) **2** the course of a series of actions or events; advancement, development, improvement; to advance or develop (17c); to make or help something do so (19c) **3** forward movement (16c); to go forward.
Progress provided the model for *retrogress* (at RETROGRADE). Latin *gradus* is the ancestor of DEGREE*.

project [ME. Latin *projicere*, *project-* 'to throw forwards', from *jacere* 'to throw' (ancestor of JET*)] **1** to make something stand or jut out **2** to plan or propose (15c), hence a proposed scheme (17c); **projection** a forecast based on current trends (1950s); *project* to make one (1960s) **3** to throw something into a crucible, especially powdered philosopher's stone in the hope of transmuting metal (15c) **4** to throw forwards (16c), hence **projectile** a missile (17c).

promenade [16c. French, from *se promener*, literally 'to take yourself for a walk', from *promener* 'to take for a walk', from Latin *prominare* 'to drive forward', from *minare* 'to drive with threats': see MENACE*] (To take) a leisurely walk, especially to see and be seen, hence **1** a place for a promenade, especially at the seaside (17c, often shortened to **prom**, *c*.1900) **2** to lead a person or animal around to show them off (19c) **3** a school or college dance (19c, *US*, now usually **prom**) **4** applied to various dancing steps, especially a marching step in country or square dancing (19c) **5** **prom(enade) concert** in which (some of) the audience stands or walks about (19c), now often *prom*.

promote [ME. Latin *promovere*, *promot-* 'to move forward', from *movere* MOVE*] **1** to raise to a higher rank or position (hence **demote** to reduce to a lower rank, 19c) **2** to encourage or support; to support the passing of a bill into law (18c); to advertise a product etc. (thus promoting sales, 1930s). Hence **promotion** promoting or being promoted: **1** something designed to increase sales (1930s), hence **promo** a trailer for a film or broadcast (1960s, *US*); a promotional video **2** the organization of a (sporting) event (1950s, originally in boxing); the event.

prompt [ME. (French, from) Latin *promptus* 'ready', from *promere, prompt-* 'to produce', literally 'to take forward', from *emere* 'to take'] **1** to encourage someone to act; to inspire an action (17c); something that does so. Hence **(a)** to supply an actor with forgotten words (15c); this act (16c); the words said; the person who does so (1930s, partly replacing 16c **prompter**) **(b)** a signal a computer produces to tell the operator that some input is needed (1970s) **2** quick to act, ready and willing **3** (to be) done without delay (16c); immediate, punctual (19c); immediately, punctually (*c*.1900).

Latin *promptus* fathered **impromptu** [Latin *in promptu* 'in readiness'] (something done or composed) without preparation, on the spur of the moment, Italian **pronto** a direction to play music quickly, and Spanish **pronto** quickly, at once (*US*); *emere* is the ancestor of EXAMPLE*.

pronounce [ME. Via Old French from Latin *pronuntiare*, literally 'to declare before', from *nuntiare* 'to make known': see ANNOUNCE*] **1** to state firmly or officially, hence to announce, later to make, a judgement or decision (15c), hence **pronounced** firmly or clearly expressed (18c); decided, noticeable, obvious **2** to say a word etc. using certain sounds.

Latin *pronuntiare* produced **pronunciation** the way a word etc. is pronounced, often erroneously pronounced *pronounciation*.

propagate [ME. Latin *propagare* 'to multiply plants by layering', from *propago* 'slip of a plant, layer', ultimately from *pangere* 'to layer or fix'] **1** to cause to reproduce; to have offspring (17c); to pass a quality etc. to your descendants **2** to cause to grow (16c); to promote or spread an idea, practice, etc.; to increase or become widespread (17c) **3** to transmit a motion, sound, light, etc. in a particular direction or through a medium (17c); to be transmitted (1940s).

Latin *propagare* produced **propaganda**, originally in the **College** or **Congregation of the Propaganda** [Latin *congregatio de propaganda fide* 'congregation for propagating the faith'], a committee of cardinals founded in 1622 by Pope Gregory XV to oversee foreign missions, hence any organization for propagating a doctrine or practice; the systematic spreading of a doctrine, later (the spreading) of selected or distorted information. *Pangere* is the ancestor of IMPACT*.

proper [ME. Via French from Latin *proprius* 'your own, special'] **1** belonging to: **(a)** intrinsic, inherent **(b)** belonging exclusively or especially to, special, individual; **proper noun** belonging to a particular person, place, etc.; **proper** (**psalm**, **service**, etc.) appointed for a particular occasion or season (15c) **(c)** a possession (–16c, outlived by *property* at PROPRIETY) **2** appropriate, fit, suitable, hence **(a)** of good quality or character **(b)** strictly and accurately identified (*the suburbs outside the city proper, a proper meal*); genuine, accurate, correct (15c); correctly, complete(ly), veritable (*a proper little madam!*) **(c)** conforming to social standards, decorous, genteel, (over-)correct (18c, earlier in **improper**).

Latin *proprius* is the ancestor of APPROPRIATE and PROPRIETY*, which have had both strands of meaning, 'belonging to' and 'suitable, correct', and of **expropriate**, **proprietary**, and **proprietor**, concerned only with ownership.

propitious [15c. (Via Old French from) Latin *propitius*] Well-disposed, gracious, inclined to favour, hence favourable, auspicious, boding well (16c).

Latin *propitius* produced **propitiate** to make favourable, hence to appease or placate.

propose [ME. Old French *propos* (noun), *proposer* (verb), from Latin *proponere* 'to put forward', from *ponere, posit-* 'to put'] To suggest; to put forward for consideration, discussion, or acceptance (15c), hence **1** something proposed (–17c, replaced by **proposal**) **2** to consider doing or intend to do (15c); purpose, intention (15–16c); to state as an aim or intention (17c) **3** to nominate someone for office, membership, etc. **4 propose (marriage)** to offer to marry someone (17c); to ask them to marry you.

Propose has two nouns: **proposal** is the general term; the earlier **proposition** came to mean a question, a problem or riddle to be solved (surviving in maths and logic as an assertion to be proved), and now often refers to a suggestion likely to be advantageous to its maker: an offer of marriage is a *proposal* while a *proposition* is (merely) an offer of sex (hence to make one).

French *à propos* 'to the purpose' produced **apropos** appropriate, and **malapropos** inappropriate, whence **malapropism** a ludicrous choice or misuse of words [after Mrs Malaprop, a character given to this in Richard Sheridan's play *The Rivals* (1775)]. French *purposer*, a variant of *proposer*, produced **purpose**. Latin *proponere* produced **propone** to put forward for consideration, altered to **propound** except in Scots and in **proponent**; *ponere* is the ancestor of POSE*.

propriety [ME. Old French *proprieté* from Latin *proprietas*, from *proprius*: see PROPER*] **1** an essential quality or characteristic (–19c), outlived by **property** [from a variant of *proprieté*] **2** ownership; something owned (16c), replaced by *property* except in N America where it means someone's piece of land: cf. PROPER sense lc **3** suitability, (social) correctness (17c), replacing *property*.

prorogue [15c. Via French from Latin *prorogare* 'to prolong or extend', literally 'to ask the people' (to extend a term of office), from *rogare* 'to ask, to question'] To extend the time or duration of something (–19c); to postpone, hence to postpone the sittings of an assembly, especially Parliament, to suspend a session without dissolution; to be suspended (17c). Also as **prorogate**, which in Scotland came to mean to extend a judge's or court's jurisdiction by agreement with the parties involved (17c).

Latin *rogare* produced **abrogate**, **arrogant** [via *arrogare* 'to ask or claim for yourself'], DEROGATE, **interrogate**, **prerogative** [via French from Latin *prerogare* 'to ask first'], **rogation** (a day of) prayer and supplication, **subrogate** [via *subrogare* 'to ask for or choose as a substitute': the variant *surrogare* produced **surrogate**], and perhaps **rogue**, originally a beggar.

prosaic [16c. Via French from Latin *prosa* 'straightforward' (in *prosa oratorio* 'straightforward discourse, **prose**'), ultimately from *provertere* 'to turn forward', from *vertere* 'to turn (ancestor of VERSE*)] **1** a writer of prose (16c) **2** writing, or written in, prose (17c), hence unpoetic (18c); unromantic, dull (19c).

proscribe [15c. Latin *proscribere* 'to publish in writing', from *scribere* 'to write' (ancestor of SCRIPT*)] To publish or post up someone's name as being condemned to death or outlawed, hence to outlaw or banish; to reject or condemn (17c); to prohibit.

prospect [15c. Latin *prospicere* 'to look forward', from *specere* 'to look'] The action of looking outwards or towards a distant object, hence **1** to look at or towards a view, to command a view of (16–17c); a place that does so, a viewpoint; what can be seen from one (17c) **2** a mental survey, an inspection or investigation (16–18c); foresight, anticipation (17c, earlier in **prospective** having foresight); something anticipated; an expectation of wealth or success (*a career with prospects*); a potential customer (1920s) **3** to explore a region for gold etc. (19c); of a mine: to promise a good/poor yield.

Retrospect [with Latin *retro* 'backwards': see ARREAR] was modelled on *prospect*. Latin *prospicere* produced **prospectus** [literally 'a view or prospect'], adopted for a document for prospective investors, subscribers, or students. Latin *specere* is the ancestor of SPICE*.

protagonist [17c. Greek *protagŏnistēs*, from *protos* 'first, primary, elementary' + *agŏnistēs* 'contestant, actor', from *agŏn* 'contest': see AGONY*] The principal character in a drama, novel, etc.; the leading person in a contest, dispute, etc.; a prominent supporter of a cause (taken as the opposite of **antagonist** an opponent [16c, ultimately from Greek *antagŏnistēs*, from *antagŏnizesthai* 'to struggle against', from *agŏn*], partly because *pro-* was taken as meaning 'favouring', as in *pro-choice*); an advocate of a method, idea, etc. (1930s).

Greek *protos* appears in PROTOCOL and *prototype* (at TYPE), and is the ancestor of **protein** (from its importance to the body's functioning), **proto-** (*Proto-Germanic, protozoa*), and **proton** an elementary particle.

protest [ME. Via Old French from Latin *protestari* 'to declare publicly', from *testari* 'to assert or witness': see TESTAMENT*] To declare formally or solemnly; such a declaration (15–19c, outlived by **protestation**), hence **1 Protestant** (describing) one of those who protested against a decision ending toleration of Lutherans in Catholic districts (16c), hence (describing) any Christian denomination that rejected the authority and some doctrines of the Roman Catholic church **2** (to make) an expression of dissent (17c); to express disapproval or disagreement strongly (18c); such an expression; a public demonstration of disapproval or opposition (1950s).

protocol [ME. Via Old French and medieval Latin from Greek *protokollon* 'first page, table of contents, flyleaf', from *protos* (see PROTAGONIST*) + *kolla* 'glue'] **1** the original note or minute of a transaction, agreement, etc. which forms the legal authority for anything based on it, hence the original draft of a negotiation, treaty, etc. (17c); a formal statement of a proceeding (19c), specifically a detailed record of a scientific experiment, hence the procedure (to be) adopted for one **2** in some countries, (a department dealing with) the etiquette to be observed by the Head of State in official ceremonies and relations with other states (19c), hence diplomatic procedure and etiquette (1940s); any code of conventional or proper conduct (1950s); the rules for exchanging information between computers (1960s).

proud [Old English *prŭt, prŭd*, from Old French *prud, prod* 'valiant, worthy, wise', ultimately from Latin *prodesse* 'to be of value', from *esse* 'to be'] Having (exaggerated or unjustified) self-esteem, hence **1** conceited, haughty **2** self-respecting, dignified, independent **3** feeling honoured, pleased, or satisfied by something you do or have (*house-proud, proud of my daughter*, ME), hence producing this feeling (*a proud history*) **4** stately, magnificent, splendid (ME) **5** swollen, overgrown (*proud flesh*, 15c); projecting slightly from a surrounding surface (19c).

Proud became a surname for a haughty person, and appears in **Proudfoot** someone who struts. Old English *prūt* produced **pride** proudness (*pride of lions* comes from the animals' supposed dignity and courage), whence the name **Pryde**. Old French *prud* produced the name **Pridham** [from *prud homme* 'wise man'] and **prude** [via *prude femme* 'virtuous woman'], before evolving into *prou*, whence IMPROVEMENT and **prowess** exceptional courage or, later, ability. Latin *prodesse* produced the names **Prewett** and **Prowse**; *esse* is the ancestor of ESSENCE*.

prove [ME. Via Old French from Latin *probare*: see PROBABLE*] To test (*the exception proves the rule*); to find out by testing or experience; to ascertain or demonstrate the qualities, existence, or truth of something, hence **1** to establish the validity of a will etc. (cf. PROBATE) **2** to be established or demonstrated; to turn out to be **3 prove yourself** to show your worth (15c) **4** (less commonly *proof*) of bread: to rise before being baked (proving the efficacy of the yeast). See also *proof* below.

The original past participle is **proved**: **proven** is a Scottish variant, now common in the US but in British English used mainly as an adjective (*a proven remedy*). Prove's noun is **proof** something that proves; the action or fact of doing so (*burden of proof*). Hence **1** proven strength: **(a)** resistance, impenetrability; resistant or invulnerable to (*waterproof*); to make something so **(b)** of an alcoholic beverage: (having) a specified strength **2 (a)** a trial print of a text, engraving, etc., hence *prove*, *proof* to make one; **proof(read)** to check and correct one **(b)** a coin etc. struck to test the die or, later, as a specimen.

provide [ME. Latin *providere*, *provis-* 'to see or look ahead', from *videre* 'to see'] To foresee (–17c); to prepare for something foreseen (15c), hence **1** to stipulate in a will etc. that something be done (15c); to arrange something beforehand, hence **(a) provided**, **providing** on the condition or understanding that **(b) provision** a clause setting out a stipulation or condition (15c); **provisional** temporary and conditional (17c) **2** to supply (someone/something with) what is needed (15c); **provide for** to supply the means of support for. Hence *provision* this act (15c); **provisions** supplies of food, drink, etc.; *provision* to supply with provisions (19c).

Latin *providere* produced **improvise** [via French and Italian from Latin *improvisus* 'unforeseen'], PROVIDENCE*, **proviso** [medieval Latin *proviso quod* 'it being provided that'], and **purvey** [via Anglo-Norman French] also originally meaning 'to foresee or prepare for'. Latin *videre* is the ancestor of VISION*.

providence [ME. Latin *providentia*, from *providere*: see PROVIDE*] **1** the action of providing; foresight, care or preparation for the future, thrift (15c), hence **provident** farsighted (15c); frugal, thrifty (16c) **2** the wisdom, care, and guidance provided by a spiritual power, hence **Providence** that power, God; an instance or act of divine intervention (16c); **providential** ordained by Providence (18c), opportune, lucky.

In sense 1 *providence* and *provident* have largely been replaced by **prudence** and **prudent** [(via Old French) from Latin *prudentia*, alteration of *providentia*].

province [ME. French, from Latin *provincia* 'charge, (administration of) a conquered territory', from *vincere* 'to conquer' (ancestor of CONVICT*)] **1** a territory outside Italy under Roman rule (hence **Provence**, the first one), hence **(a)** an administrative division of a country etc.; a territory under the jurisdiction of an archbishop or metropolitan **(b) the provinces** the parts of a country outside the capital, traditionally regarded as culturally backward (17c); **provincial** unsophisticated, parochial **2** an area of knowledge, activity, or concern (17c) **3** an area containing a distinct group of animal or plant communities (19c), or with distinct features.

public [ME. (French, from) Latin *publicus*, from *pubes* '(an) adult'] To do with, affecting, or concerning the community or nation, hence **1 (a)** done by, or on behalf of, the community as a whole **(b)** available to everyone, not private, hence **public house** a public building (16c); (now usually **pub**) an inn or alehouse (17c) **(c)** to do with or provided by local or central government (*public library/sector*) **2 the public** the members of a community (15c) **3 (in) public** existing or done openly (15c).

Public produced **publicize**. French *public* produced **publicity**; Latin *publicus* produced **publican** a tax collector in ancient Rome, now the owner or manager of a pub, **publicist** originally an expert in public or international law, PUBLISH*, and *republic* (at REAL). Latin *pubes* is the ancestor of **puberty** and **pubescence**, referring to the coming of adulthood, and is related to Latin **pubis** either of the two frontal bones of the pelvis, whence *pubes* [plural of *pubis*] (the hair covering) this area.

publish [ME. Via Old French from Latin *publicare* 'to make public', from *publicus*: see PUBLIC*] To make something generally known, hence **1** to announce (now usually the banns) formally **2** to prepare and issue a book, newspaper, piece of music, etc. for sale to the public (16c).

Latin *publicare* produced **publication** publishing; the process of publishing a book etc.; the work published.

pudding [ME. French *boudin* 'black pudding', ultimately from Latin *botellus* 'pudding, small intestine, little sausage', from *botulus* 'sausage'] An animal's stomach or intestine stuffed with minced meat, suet, and cereal, and boiled, later a savoury or sweet mixture boiled, baked, or steamed in a cloth or basin, or in batter or a suet crust (16c), hence the sweet course of a meal.

Latin *botellus* fathered French *bouel*, whence **bowel**. Latin *botulus* is the ancestor of **botulin** the toxin causing **botulism** [German *Botulismus*, literally 'sausage poisoning'].

puddle [ME. Apparently from Old English *pudd* 'ditch'] A swamp; a water-filled pit, now a small muddy pool, hence **1** to splash about in shallow water; to potter or mess about **2** to wet with muddy water (16c); to make muddy; (to work wet clay and sand to make) a waterproof coating for embankments etc.; to cover or line with this **3** a small pool of any liquid (18c); one of molten metal (1930s), hence a piece of metal solidified from one **4** to heat molten iron in a furnace with an oxidizing agent to remove carbon (18c).

Puddle is probably one parent of **piddle** to urinate, the other being **piss** [from Old French, ultimately imitating the sound]: the earlier sense of *piddle* 'to potter or mess about' may be a different word. Related to **poodle** [German *Pudel(hund)*, from Low German *pudeln* 'to splash about'] and to the names of villages on the River **Piddle**, including **Piddletrenthide**, **Bryants Piddle**, and **Tolpuddle**.

pug [16c. Perhaps from Low German or Dutch] An ape, monkey, or, occasionally, a child, hence **pug (dog)** a small, thickset dog with a wrinkled 'monkey' face and a broad flat nose (18c), hence **1 pug nose** a short stubby nose (18c) **2** a short, thickset person, a dwarf (19c, Scots and N English) **3 pug (engine)** a small locomotive used for shunting (19c).

pulpit [ME. Latin *pulpitum* 'scaffold, platform'] A platform from which a clergyman preaches, hence **1 the pulpit** Christian ministers collectively (16c); **wayside pulpit** a board displaying a religious message (1920s) **2** a raised structure: **(a)** a platform or room from which machinery can be controlled (19c) **(b)** the harpooner's platform on the bowsprit of a whaler (19c); (an area enclosed by) a rail around a yacht's bow (1960s), hence **pushpit** a similar one at the stern.

pulse [ME. Via Old French from Latin *pulsus* 'beating', from *pellere, puls-* 'to drive or beat'] The rhythmical dilation of the arteries as blood is pumped through them, hence **1** the life force, vitality; a throb or thrill of emotion etc.; current attitudes, opinions, and feelings (*a finger on the pulse of society*) **2** to beat or throb, largely replaced by **pulsate** [19c, from Latin *pulsare*, from *pellere*]; beating, vibration, rhythmical strokes (17c); a beat, each stroke of a rhythmical series, hence **(a)** to send out in rhythmic beats **(b)** a short burst of (radiated) energy (*c.*1900) **(c)** a sudden, temporary change in a normally constant quality, e.g. a voltage (1930s, largely replacing *impulse* (at IMPEL).

Pulsate is one parent of **pulsar** a small dense star that emits intense bursts of radiation, the other being **quasar** [short for *quasi-stellar (object)*]. Latin *pellere* is the ancestor of APPEAL*, **compel** [Latin *compellere* 'to drive or force together', whence also **compulsion**], **dispel**, IMPEL*, **propel** originally 'to drive out', outlived by **expel** [also from *pellere*], **push** [via Old French *pou(l)ser*], and **repel** [Latin *repeller* 'to drive back', whence also **repulse**].

Punch [17c. Short for **Punchinello**, from *Pulchinello* a similar character in the Italian *commedia dell'arte* (see also HARLEQUIN), perhaps from *pollecena* 'young turkeycock', from *pulcino* 'chicken', ultimately from Latin *pullus* (ancestor of POOL*)] The hook-nosed, humpbacked, quarrelsome main character in a **Punch and Judy show** a comically violent puppet show. Hence **1** a short, fat person (17c); **Suffolk Punch** a short-legged draught horse (19c) **2** the title of a British satirical magazine, supposedly edited by Punch, which appeared in 1841 and finally ceased publication in 2002.

punch [ME. Partly a variant of **pounce**, from Old French *poinson, po(i)nchon* (see PUNCHEON); partly shortened from *puncheon*] To beat or emboss metal; to prick or puncture (as if) with a pointed instrument (–17c), hence **1** to poke or prod, hence **(a)** to drive cattle, originally by prodding (now N American); to press a key etc. (1950s) **(b)** (to give someone) a blow with the fist (16c), hence force, vigour (*c.*1910, *US*) **2** a tool or machine for making holes, driving in nails, or, later, stamping a design (16c, replacing *pounce*).

Pounce also meant a dagger, later a claw or talon, hence to seize with one; to attack by swooping down or jumping on; to seize on eagerly: the sense 'perforate' survives, just, in **pouncet** (pounced) **box**, a perfume box with a perforated lid (a Shakespearean term revived by Scott: see DOFF). *Pounce* may be the source of **ponce** a pimp; to act as one; to sponge on someone, hence a lazy or effeminate man.

puncheon [ME. Old French *poinson*, *po(i)nchon*, ultimately from Latin *pungere*, *punct-* 'to prick' (ancestor of POINT*)] **1** a prop, strut, or beam; a split trunk or piece of rough timber (18c, *US*) **2** a dagger (–17c); a tool for piercing, chiselling, or cutting (15c); a tool or machine for pricking, for stamping metal etc., or for making a die (cf. PUNCH) **3** (perhaps a different word) a cask, especially one used as a measure (15c).

punctual [15c. Medieval Latin *punctualis*, from Latin *punctum:* see POINT*] **1** sharp-pointed (–16c); to do with a point, prick, or dot (17c), later with punctuation; in maths: to do with a point in space (19c) **2** attentive to the smallest detail, especially correct behaviour (16c, replaced by **punctilious** [17c, via French from Spanish *puntillo* 'point of etiquette', ultimately from Latin *punctum*]); attentive to time (17c); on time, on the dot.

punt [18c. French *ponter*, from *pont* 'put, laid', from *pon(d)re* 'to put or lay': see POSE*] To lay a bet against the bank in some games, hence **punter** someone who does so; a gambler (19c); a swindler's accomplice or, later, victim (1930s); a prostitute's client (1960s); a (disparaging) term for any customer.

puny [16c. Variant of **puisne**, from Old French *puis* 'afterwards' (ultimately from Latin *post*) + *né* 'born' (ultimately from Latin *nasci*, *nat-* 'to be born'). Younger, junior; a junior or novice (–18c), hence **1** later, more recent (17c only, surviving as *puisne*) **2** (only as *puny*) small, weak, insignificant (17c).

French *née* (feminine of *né*) is put before a married woman's maiden name, later before any former name. Latin *post* is the ancestor of POSTERIOR*, *nasci* of NATURE*.

purchase [ME. Old French *pourchacier*, from *chasier* CHASE*] To (try to) bring about or get (–18c), hence to acquire, or the acquisition of, property by your own efforts (originally including pillaging) rather than by inheritance, hence **1** to buy; what is bought (16c); the act of buying (17c) **2** to pull in a rope hand over hand (16c, nautical); to raise an anchor using a capstan, pulley, etc.; such a device (18c); the mechanical advantage it gives, hence a grip or position that allows you to use or maximize power (*spikes give purchase on ice*); an advantage or influence.

pure [ME. Via French from Latin *purus*] Unmixed, unadulterated; uncontaminated, clean, hence **1** perfect(ly), absolute(ly) (*pure white*); in law: absolute, unconditional **2** morally undefiled, innocent; chaste (15c) **3** of unmixed ancestry (*pureblooded, purebred*, 15c) **4** to do with the essentials or theory of a subject (*pure maths*, 17c) **5** of a musical tone: free from discord, in tune (19c); of sound: consisting of a single frequency with no overtones.

Latin *purus* is the ancestor of *purée* [via French *purer* 'to squeeze out', literally 'to purify'], PURGE*, **Puritan** a member of a group in England and America who sought to purify the Protestant church of the remnants of Roman Catholic practices, hence someone with austere religious or moral beliefs, and perhaps of **pour** [Old Norman French *purer* 'to sift or pour out', from Latin *purare*].

purge [ME. Via Old French from Latin *purgare* 'to purify', from *purus* PURE*] To purify by removing dirt, sin, etc., to get rid of something impure or undesirable, hence **1** to clean out the bowels with a laxative (formerly also the stomach with an emetic); to evacuate the bowels or, formerly, to vomit (16c); a laxative or, formerly, an emetic (earlier as **purgative**); to act as one (17c) **2** in law: to atone for an offence, especially contempt of court (16c) **3** to rid an organization of undesirables (19c); to expel them; such expulsion.

Latin *purgare* produced **expurgate** [Latin *expurgare*, literally 'to clean out', whence also **spurge** a plant with purgative properties] and **purgatory** a place or period of spiritual purification, in Roman Catholicism, where souls remain after death until they have expiated their sins, hence a miserable but temporary condition or situation.

purport [ME. Via Anglo-Norman and Old French from medieval Latin *proportare*, literally 'to carry forward', from *portare* 'to carry': see PORT³*] To express, state, or imply; what is expressed or implied, hence **1** (a) meaning, (an) intention, (a) purpose (17c) **2** to profess or appear to be or to do (18c).

purse [Old English *purs* from medieval Latin *bursa*, *byrsa*, from Greek *bursa* 'hide, leather'] A small money pouch or (originally drawstring) bag, hence **1** its contents, money, funds (ME); money collected for a present or given as a prize (17c) **2** any bag, pouch, or sack (ME); a sac (16c); a bag-shaped part of a net (19c); a woman's handbag (1950s, N American) **3** to wrinkle the brow or pucker the lips (as if tightening the strings of a purse, 17c); to become wrinkled or puckered (18c).

Purse produced **purser 1** (the surname of) a purse-maker **2** a treasurer; one on a ship, who was also in charge of provisions; now the head steward on a passenger ship or aircraft. Latin ***bursa*** was adopted for a fluid-filled sac in the body, and is the ancestor [via French ***bourse*** 'purse', which was adopted in the sense 'money market, (Paris) stock exchange'] of **bursar** the treasurer of a college, in Scotland a student with a **bursary** an endowment, of **burse** a purse forming part of the Lord Chancellor's insignia, of **disburse**, of **imburse** originally to put in your purse, to stash away, later to pay or repay (largely replaced by **reimburse**), and of **sporran** [via Gaelic].

pursue [ME. Via Anglo-Norman French from, ultimately, Latin *prosequi* 'to follow after', from *sequi* 'to follow'] **1** to follow in order to harm; to harass or torment (largely replaced by *persecute* below); to hunt or chase, hence **(a)** to try to attain, to aim at **(b)** to prosecute or sue (chiefly Scots) **(c)** of troubles etc.: to dog (15c) **2** to follow a path or course of action; to follow up or go on with (15c); to carry on an occupation or profession, hence **pursuit** an occupation or recreation **3** to follow in time or order, hence **pursuant to** as a consequence of, in accordance with (17c).

Latin *prosequi* produced **prosecute**, which has largely replaced sense 1b and shares the sense 'to follow up'. **Persecute** [via Old French from, ultimately, Latin *persequi*, literally 'to keep following', from *sequi*] originally meant to hunt or chase, also to follow up. Latin *sequi* is the ancestor of SEQUEL*.

pygmy [ME. Latin *pygmaeus* from Greek *pugmaios* 'dwarf', from *pugmē* 'the length from elbow to knuckles'] A member of a mythical race of small people said to have lived in parts of Ethiopia and India, hence **1** a very small person, a dwarf or midget (16c) **2** a person of little significance or ability (*an intellectual pygmy*, 16c) **3** (describing) something smaller than average, especially an animal of a small breed (*pygmy hippopotamus*, 16c) **4** an elf or pixie (17c) **5** a member of any of several races of small people of Equatorial Africa (19c).

Paracelsus (16c German physician and alchemist) used Latin *gnomus* for the mythical pygmies, whence **gnome** a member of a race of small people said to live underground and guard the earth's treasures, hence **1** a small statue of a bearded man used as a garden ornament **2** an international financier or banker (*gnomes of Zurich*).

Q

quaint [ME. Old French *cointe, queinte*, from Latin *cognitus* 'known', from *cognoscere* 'to know or learn', from *(g)noscere* 'to know'] Wise, clever, cunning (–18c); ingeniously made (–17c), hence elaborate, beautiful (rare since the 17c); of speech or language: clever, affected, full of odd or witty turns of phrase (–18c), hence unfamiliar, odd (–19c); attractively odd or old-fashioned (18c).

Old French *queinte* fathered the surname **Quant, Quantrill**, or **Quintrell** a clever or elegant person. Latin *cognoscere* is the ancestor of **acquaint** [via Latin *accognoscere* 'to know well'], **cognition, cognizance**, French **connoisseur**, literally 'one who knows', Italian *incognito* [via Latin *incognitus* 'unknown'], and RECOGNIZE*. Latin *(g)noscere* is the ancestor of NOTICE*.

quake [Old English *cwacian*] To shake or tremble; a shaking or trembling (ME), hence **1 earthquake**, now sometimes shortened to *quake* **2** to shake with fear or cold; to be afraid, hence **Quaker** (originally a derogatory term for) a member of the Society of Friends, a Christian movement founded by George Fox (*c.*1650), who urged his followers to 'tremble at the name of the Lord'.

Quaker and **Shaker** were applied to various 17c sects said to shake or suffer fits during their devotions, *Shaker* specifically to an 18c sect noted for celibacy, ritual dances, and simple, well-made artefacts, hence describing furniture etc. supposedly in their style.

Probably related to **quag** a boggy spot that gives way underfoot (whence **quagmire**), and to **quaver** to tremble or quiver, hence (a symbol for) a musical note half as long as a crotchet (see also LARGE sense 3b); (to sing or speak with) a trill or tremble in the voice.

qualify [ME. French *qualifier*, ultimately from Latin *qualis* 'of what kind, of such a kind' (whence QUALITY)] To describe as a certain kind or as having a certain characteristic, hence **1** to have or get necessary qualities or accomplishments (16c); **2** to modify a statement etc. (16c); to moderate or mitigate; to make less good or complete (*a qualified success*).

quality [ME. Via French from Latin *qualitas*, from *qualis*: see QUALIFY] A person's nature or disposition; the nature of a thing, hence **1** the relative nature or standard of something (15c), hence **(a)** social standing; high rank (16c); **the quality** those of high rank **(b)** a degree of excellence; of a high standard (18c); excellence, superiority (19c) **2** a distinguishing characteristic of a person or thing (16c); an essential property.

quarantine [Strictly speaking, two words, both ultimately from Latin *quadraginta* 'forty': (related to QUARTER* and SQUARE*)] **I** [16c, via Italian *quarantina* 'forty days'] a period of forty days during which a widow had the right to remain in the marital home **II** [17c, via medieval Latin *quadrantena*] a period, originally of forty days, during which a traveller, ship, animal, etc. entering a country is isolated in case they are carrying an infectious disease; such isolation; to impose it (19c).

quarrel¹ [ME. Old French, ultimately from Latin *quadrum* SQUARE*] **1** a square-headed bolt shot from a crossbow **2** a square or diamond-shaped pane in a lattice window, largely replaced by **quarry**, an alteration of *quarrel* influenced by *quarry* below, hence **quarry tile** a square tile (16c).

Latin *quadrum* produced **quarry** a stone pit [via medieval Latin from Old French *quarriere*, ultimately from Latin *quadrare* 'to make square']. Related to QUARTER*.

quarrel² [ME. Via Old French from Latin *querel(la)* 'a complaint', from *queri* 'to complain' (ancestor of **querulous**)] (The cause of) a complaint against, or a disagreement with, someone; to complain about or object to, hence (to have) an angry dispute (16c); to fall out.

quarry [ME. Old French *cuiree*, *couree* (influenced by *cuir* 'leather' and *curer* 'to clean or disembowel'), ultimately from Latin *cor* 'heart' (ancestor of CORDIAL*)] The offal etc. of a deer placed on the hide for the hounds, also a heap of killed deer (–17c), hence any hunted animal (15c).

quarter [ME. Old French *quartier*, ultimately from Latin *quartus* 'fourth', from *quattuor* 'four'] A fourth, hence **1** each of four equal or corresponding parts; one of the four parts, each with a limb, of a body (*hindquarters*) **2** to divide into quarters **3** an area around one of the four main compass points, hence **(a)** a ship's side aft of the centre (16c) **(b)** an area, specifically one where certain people live (*Latin/artists' quarter*, 16c); a section of the community (*protests from some quarters*, 18c) **(c)** a suitable place or position (16c); **quarters** (temporary) lodgings, especially for soldiers, hence **quartermaster** an army officer whose responsibilities include finding quarters, a petty officer whose responsibilities included stowing stores (15c); *quarter* to lodge troops or stow things away (17c) **4 close quarters** barriers from which a ship's crew fought boarders (18c, replacing 17c *close fights*), hence close contact with the enemy (19c) **5** of a hunting animal or bird: to cross in a zigzag course, to range over (18c, cf. *cater* below).

Descendants of Latin *quartus* include **quart** a quarter of a gallon, **quartet**, and **quarto** a size of book or paper equal to a quarter of a printing sheet. Latin *quattuor* is the ancestor of **cater** the four on cards or dice (set in the four corners), hence (to move) from corner to corner, **cater-** or **catty-corner(ed)** diagonal(ly) (US), **quad bike**, **quadr(i)-** (*quadrangle*, *quadrilateral*), **quadruple**, **quaternary**, **quatrain**, and **quire** originally a pamphlet consisting of four folded sheets of parchment. Related to SQUARE*.

quash [ME. French *casser* 'to break', from Latin *quassare* 'to shake to pieces', from *quatere* 'to shake or strike'] To crush or overcome, hence **1** to suppress or stifle **2** to squeeze or press flat or to a pulp (15–18c), replaced by the alteration **squash** (16c), which came to mean: **(a)** a crowd (19c) **(b)** a small, soft rubber ball; **squash (rackets)** the game played with it (19c) **(c) lemon squash** a drink made from lemon juice, soda water, and ice (19c), hence *squash* (a drink made from) a concentrate made with crushed fruit.

Latin *quatere* is the ancestor of **cascara** a plant whose bark yields the laxative **cascara sagrada** [Spanish *cáscara (sagrada)* '(sacred) bark', from *cascar* 'to break off'], **concuss**, DISCUSS, PERCUSSION*, and **rescue** [via Old French from, ultimately, Latin *excutere* 'to shake out, to discard', from *quatere*].

Quash to annul comes via Old French from medieval Latin *quassare*, ultimately from Latin *cassus* 'null, void' (whence CASHIER). **Squash**, the vegetable, is ultimately from Narragansett *askútasquash* literally 'something you can eat raw'.

quay [ME. Old Norman French *cai*, of Celtic origin. Originally spelt *key* (hence the pronunciation): the current spelling was influenced by French *quai* (also from *cai*)] An artificial (stone) bank or landing stage.

The former spelling influenced **cay** a shoal, sandbank, or reef [from Spanish *cayo*, from *quai*], whence **key** a small island of sand or coral (*Florida Keys*).

queer [16c. Perhaps from German *quer* 'cross, oblique, perverse', from Old High German *twerh* 'oblique'] **1** strange, odd, eccentric; suspicious, dubious **2** bad, worthless, hence **(a)** to make worthless, to spoil someone's plans or chances (*queer his pitch*, 19c: cf. *thwart* below) **(b)** counterfeit (19c); a counterfeit coin or (US) banknote **(c) Queer Street** (the imaginary dwelling of those in) financial difficulties (19c) **3** nauseous or faint (18c) **4** homosexual; a (male) homosexual (1920s, derogatory and offensive, but adopted by some gay and bisexual people in the 1990s).

Perhaps related to **thwart** [Old Norse *thvert* 'transverse, cross'] **1** perverse, obstinate **2** to lie across, hence **(a)** to oppose (successfully), to foil **(b)** across, transverse (largely replaced by **athwart**): this influenced **thought** a rower's bench [Old English *thofte*], producing **thwart** a crosswise seat or structural member in a boat.

quell [Old English *cwellan*] To kill (surviving, just, in poetry until the 19c); to put an end to (ME), hence to overcome or subdue (16c).

Related to **kill**, and perhaps to **quail** to waste away; to come to nothing; to fail or give way, hence to do so through fear, to flinch, and to **qualm** a sudden feeling of faintness or sickness, later of fear, depression, or self-doubt, hence a misgiving or scruple.

quest [ME. Via Old French from, ultimately, Latin *quaerere*, *quaest-* 'to ask or seek'] **1** (the jury at) a judicial enquiry, especially into a cause of death (outlived by *inquest* at INQUIRE); (the object of) any inquiry or investigation (16c) **2** a search; a journey to find or achieve something, especially in medieval romances.

Latin *quaerere*'s descendants include **acquire**, **conquer** (at CONKER), **disquisition**, EXQUISITE, INQUIRE*, PERQUISITE*, **query**, **question**, and REQUIRE*.

queue [16c. French, ultimately from Latin *cauda* 'tail'] **1** in heraldry: an animal's tail **2** a plait or pigtail (18c, also as the variant **cue**) **3** *cue* the stick used in billiards etc. (18c) **4** a line of people, vehicles, etc. awaiting their turn (19c); to form or join one (1920s), hence in computing: a list of data items, commands, etc. accessible or done in order (1960s).

Latin *cauda* is the ancestor of Italian **coda** the final passage of a piece of music, **coward** (perhaps from the image of an animal with its tail between its legs: **cow** 'to intimidate' and **cower** are of Germanic origin and not related), and **curlicue** literally a curly tail.

quick [Old English *cwic(u)*] **1** living, alive, surviving in *the quick and the dead*, in **quickset** describing a hedge grown from live cuttings, and in **quick with child** (apparently an alteration of *with quick child*) at the stage of pregnancy when the fetus can be felt moving (15c), hence **quicken** of the mother or fetus: to get to this stage (16c) **2** resembling a living thing, moving, flowing, etc., hence **(a) quick-lime** that reacts vigorously with water, **quicksand** that moves under pressure, **quicksilver** the liquid metal mercury **(b)** mentally active, intelligent, alert; of the ear or eye: perceptive (ME); of the temper: easily roused (19c) **(c)** vigorous, energetic (ME); brisk, fast-moving; rapid, brief (16c); prompt, hasty **(d)** *quicken* to accelerate (17c).

Related to **quitch**, later altered to **couch (grass)**, so called from its vigorous growth.

quiet [ME. Old French, from Latin *quies, quiet-* 'rest, repose'] Freedom from war, strife, disturbance, or noise, hence **1** to free from an obligation (–15c): cf. QUIT **2** causing little noise or disturbance, hence **(a)** at rest, inactive **(b)** of an animal: gentle; of a person: reserved, discreet (16c), hence **on the quiet** discreetly, secretly (19c), informally shortened to **on the q.t. (c)** not obtrusive or showy (*a quiet wedding*) **3** undisturbed, peaceful: **(a)** not busy or crowded (16c) **(b)** relaxed, relaxing (*a quiet walk*) **4** to make or become quiet (16c, partly replaced by 19c **quieten**).

Latin *quies* produced **acquiesce** [Latin *acquiescere* 'to become quiet', hence 'to agree tacitly'], **quiescent**, and Latin *requies* 'rest', whence *requiem* the Mass for the dead, which begins *Requiem aeternam dona eis* 'give them eternal rest'. See also *acquit* (at QUIT).

quit [ME. (Via French from) Latin *quietus* 'still', from *quiescere* 'to be still', from *quies*: see QUIET*] (To) free (from), clear, or rid of, hence **1** to free yourself of a debt or obligation, to pay or pay up (cf. *acquit* below and QUIET), hence (now **quits**) out of debt, even; **call it quits** to agree that you are now even, to abandon a quarrel or venture; to cut your losses (19c) **2 quit yourself** to act or perform a task well/badly (cf. *acquit yourself* below) **3** to prove or declare innocent (–18c, outlived by *acquit* below) **4** to let go or renounce (15c); to cease to have, use, or be involved with; to leave, now especially your job or a rented property (*notice to quit*, 17c); to stop doing something (18c) **5** (as the variant **quite**) clear, clean; completely, fully, weakened to moderately, fairly, somewhat (19c).

Quit(e) produced **requite** to repay, reward, or retaliate. Latin *quietus* produced COY and appeared in *quietus (est)* (literally 'he is quit') an acknowledgement of payment of a debt, hence *quietus* a release from debt or obligation; death as a release from life; a final settlement or ending. Latin *quies* produced **acquit** [via Old French from medieval Latin *acquitare* 'to pay a debt', from *quitare* 'to set free'] to settle your own or, later, someone else's debt; to release someone from a liability or obligation, later to declare that someone is not responsible for a crime; **acquit yourself** to free yourself from an obligation by doing your part.

quiz [18c. Origin unknown: the story goes that a Dublin theatre proprietor had the word written on walls all over the city to win a bet that he could introduce a nonsense word into the language, the public supplying a meaning. There is no evidence to support this, and the first recorded usage of *quiz* predates it] An odd, eccentric, or strange-looking person, hence **1** to observe their peculiarities; to look at curiously; to ridicule, hence **quizzical** showing mild or amused puzzlement (19c) **2** a joker or hoaxer; a (practical) joke (19c); a witticism.

Quiz to question or interrogate (*US*), hence a set of questions; a (competitive) test of knowledge, is also of unknown origin, although it may be from the earlier *quiz*, influenced by *inquisitive*.

quorum [ME. Latin, 'of whom' (from *qui* 'who'), in *quorum vos...unum esse volumus* 'of whom we wish that you...be one', used in requests to certain people to serve on a committee etc.] Certain (eminent) justices of the peace whose presence was necessary to constitute a bench, hence the essential members of any body (16c); a fixed minimum number of members who must be present to make the business of a meeting valid (17c), hence **quorate** having this number present (1960s).

Latin *quibus* 'to or from whom' is the probable source of **quib** a trivial objection or distinction (16–17c, probably because *quibus* often appeared in legal documents and was associated with such niceties), replaced by its descendant **quibble** (literally a small quib), hence to make one.

quote [ME. Medieval Latin *quotare* 'to number', or medieval Latin *quota* 'how great', both from Latin *quot* 'how many'] To mark a book with chapter or page numbers, or with marginal references (–17c), hence **1** to give the page or chapter reference for a passage (16c); to cite a text or person; to repeat a passage, hence **(a) quotation** a quoted passage or remark (17c, now often *quote*) **(b) quotation mark** a punctuation mark indicating a quoted passage, direct speech, or a word regarded as inaccurate or slang (19c, now often *quote*) **(c) quote/unquote** used (originally in dictation) to indicate the beginning and end of a quotation (1930s) **2** to cite as an example (19c) **3** to state a price (19c), hence **(a)** *quotation* the price stated, especially for a job to be done, sometimes shortened to *quote* (1950s) **(b)** to state the odds in a race etc. (19c) **(c)** *quotation* a company's listing on the Stock Exchange that enables its shares to be traded officially (19c), hence **quoted** having a listing; **unquoted** not listed (1960s).

Medieval Latin *quota (pars)* 'how great (a part)' produced **quota** an amount or share which someone should contribute or receive, hence (a regulation imposing) a maximum number or quantity. Latin *quot* produced *quotidian* (at JOURNEY), and **quotient** the result of dividing one number by another.

R

rabbit [ME. Perhaps via Old French from early Dutch] The burrowing, short-tailed rodent: originally a youngster, the adult being a **cony** [ME, via Old French from Latin *cuniculus*: originally spelt *coney* and rhyming with *bunny*], hence **1** its flesh as food; **Welsh rabbit** (18c) probably came about because cheese was as commonly eaten in Wales as rabbit once was in England: **rarebit** is a gentrification **2** (also *cony*) a person, especially a novice or a dupe (16c) **3** to hunt or catch rabbits (19c) **4** a hare (19c, US), hence **jackrabbit** an American hare with very long ears (short for **jackass rabbit**) **5** rabbit fur (early 20c, largely replacing *cony*) **6** talk, to talk (1940s, from rhyming slang *rabbit and pork*).

Cony became a term of endearment for a woman, but was later considered indecent or abusive, probably by association with *cunt*, and was also used for the female genitals or for sexual activity: **puss(y)** [probably from Low German or Dutch], originally (a name for) a cat or a hare, then a pet name for a girl or woman, suffered the same fate. **Bunny** [origin unknown] a pet name for a rabbit or, occasionally, a person has escaped it, but the implication remains in **bunny girl**.

rabble [ME. Probably of early Dutch or Low German origin] To gabble, hence a lot of words with little meaning (–17c); a string, pack, or swarm of animals (15–16c); an untidy collection of things (16c); a disorderly crowd, the mob.

race¹ [ME. Old Norse *rás*] (Rapid) forward movement (–17c), hence **1** a course taken by something moving (–16c); that of the sun or moon through the sky or, later, of life (*my race is run*) **2** a strong current in the sea or a river; **mill race** (the channel for) a flow of water driving a mill wheel (15c), hence *race* any water channel (16c); a groove, channel, passage, etc. that directs movement (19c) **3** a contest of speed (15c) or towards an objective (*space/arms race*, 19c); to (make someone/something) take part in one **4** to move at full speed (18c); to go too fast or out of control (*his pulse is racing*).

race² [16c. French, from Italian *razza*, of unknown origin] A group with a common feature or features, hence **1** a group of beings with the same ancestry, hence **(a)** a breed, strain, or subspecies of an organism (16c) **(b)** humankind; any of its major divisions, a people (*the White/Japanese race*, 18c); the fact or condition of belonging to one of these **2** (the characteristic flavour of) a kind of wine, hence a characteristic, and especially lively, style of speech, writing, etc. (17c), hence **racy** vivid, uninhibited, risqué.

rack [ME. Early Dutch or early Low German *recken* 'to stretch'] **1** a bar or framework for carrying, holding, or storing things, hence **(a) rack up** to fill a rack (with fodder etc., 18c); to chalk up, to achieve or score (19c, *N American*) **(b)** a toothed bar that engages with a cogwheel etc. (18c) **2** a frame for stretching cloth; a device for torturing people by stretching, hence **(a)** to torture on the rack; to subject to severe pain or distress (16c); **on the rack** in great distress or suspense **(b)** to stretch something beyond its normal limits (*rack your brains*), hence to raise rent exorbitantly (16c); to extort money (especially excessive rent) **3** a joint of meat including the neck and ribs (16c, perhaps likened to sense 1, perhaps a different word).

racket [16c. Probably imitative] **1** a loud noise **(a)** disturbance or uproar; a large, noisy party (18c), hence **(a)** an exciting or trying situation (19c); **stand the racket** to cope with stress etc. **(b) racket about/around** to move around noisily, to make a racket (19c) **2** a prank, a trick (19c); a scheme involving fraud or intimidation, especially by organized criminals; a line of business or way of life.

radical [ME. Late Latin *radicalis* from Latin *radix, radic-* 'root'] To do with or forming a root or basis, hence **1** of action or change: going to the root of a matter, fundamental, far-reaching (17c); (someone) advocating such change (19c); progressive, unorthodox (1920s) **2** an element, atom, or group of atoms forming the basis of a compound (19c); a group of atoms etc. that behaves as a unit.

Latin *radix* was adopted for the root of a number (16–18c), later for the base of a numerical system, and produced **deracinate** and **eradicate**, both meaning literally 'to pull up by the roots', Italian *radicchio*, and **radish**.

radio [*c.*1900. Short for *radio-telephony* or *radio-telegram, radio-* being the form of Latin *radius* RAY used when combining it with another word] The transmission and reception of electromagnetic waves between the highest audio frequency and the shortest infra-red waves, especially as a means of telecommunication without a connecting wire (largely supplanting late 19c **wireless**); to send a message by this means (*c.*1910), hence **1** a device for sending or receiving radio messages or, later, broadcasts (*c.*1910) **2** sound broadcasting by this means (1920s) **3** these wavelengths (1960s).

Radio is one element of **radar** [*US*, from *radio detection and ranging*: in the UK originally called **radiolocation**], which provided the pattern for **sonar** [*US*, short for *sound navigation and ranging*], and produced **gaydar** the (supposed) ability to recognize that someone is gay.

raft [ME. Old Norse *raptr*: related to Old English *raefter* **rafter**] **1** a beam, spar, or rafter (now mainly dialect) **2** a collection of logs, barrels, etc. lashed together to be floated to another place (15c); one used as a boat or floating platform (16c), hence **(a)** to transport as, or on, a raft (17c); to use one (18c) **(b)** a large floating mass of vegetation, etc. (18c); a large flock of swimming birds; to form one **(c) raft up** to moor a boat to another (18c) **3 (life) raft** a small (inflatable) boat for use in emergencies (19c) **4** a concrete slab forming the foundations of a building (*c.*1900).

rag [ME. From **raggy** (from Òld English *raggig*) or **ragged**, both meaning 'rough, shaggy', and ultimately fom Old Norse *rögg* 'tuft, strip of fur'] A (frayed or worn) scrap of cloth, hence **1 ragged** worn, frayed; exhausted, hence **run ragged** (1920s, *US*) **2** a tattered garment, hence **(a) rags** tattered clothes; any clothes (19c, *US*), hence **rag trade** the clothing industry; **glad rags** fancy clothes, especially evening wear (*c.*1900) **(b)** *ragged* wearing tattered clothes; *rag* a poor person (16c), surviving in **rag, tag** (originally **tag, rag**) **and bobtail**, and **raggle-taggle** (*c.*1900) **3** an inferior newspaper (18c).

Ragged (from Old Norse) came to mean uneven, imperfect; of a sound: discordant, whence perhaps **rag** a dance or ball, especially to **ragtime** music (19c, *US*). Probably related to **rug** originally (a cloak made of) a coarse woollen cloth, and to **rugged**, originally 'hairy, rough-coated'.

rage [ME. French *rager*, ultimately from Latin *rabere*] To be or become mad (–16c); (a fit of) insanity, hence **1** (to indulge in) riotous behaviour or fun (–17c); (to have) a party or a good time (1980s, Australian) **2** (to have) a violent fit of temper, hence **(a)** of a fire, battle, etc.: to be violent, to go on unchecked (15c) **(b)** uncontrolled anger and violence in certain circumstances (*road rage*, 1990s) **3** intensity of feeling; an intense feeling or desire (16c); a widespread but short-lived fashion (*all the rage*, 18c).

Rave [Old French *raver*, possibly from *resver* 'to be delirious'] has a similar history (the noun is later): the verb developed the sense 'to praise enthusiastically', hence describing an enthusiastic review of a book, film etc. (*rave notices*, *US*).

Latin *rabere* produced **rabid** furious, raging; fanatical; to do with or suffering from rabies, and **rabies**. Old French *resver* produced **reverie** originally wild celebration, now a delusion or daydream.

rail [ME. Old French *reille* (modern *rail*) 'iron rod', from Latin *regula*: see RULE*] **1** a horizontal bar (*curtain/hand/fence rail*), hence **railing(s)** a fence made of uprights topped with one (15c) **2** **rail(s)** a metal bar or bars laid on the ground to support and guide a vehicle's wheels (17c), hence **railway**, **railroad** (18c), both shortened to *rail* (*rail travel*, *by rail*, 19c).

Modern French *rail* produced *dérailler*, whence **derail** to (cause a train to) come off the rails, and *derailleur* a device for changing gear on a bicycle that 'derails' the chain off one sprocket and onto another.

rake [Old English *raca*, *racu*: the verb partly from Old Norse *raka* 'to scrape, shave, or rake'] A toothed implement for gathering hay, leaves, etc. together, or for loosening the soil's surface, hence **1** to collect or gather together (as if) with a rake (ME); **rake in** to gather (large amounts of) money, profits, etc. (16c); **rake-off** a share of profits, winnings, etc. (19c, from the idea of raking gambling chips off the table) **2** to work over the soil with a rake (ME), hence **(a)** **rake up** to bring up a matter thought to be buried in the past (16c) **(b)** **rakehell** an immoral or dissolute man (16c), shortened to *rake* (17c), whence **rakish** dashing, jaunty, raffish (18c) **(c)** to sweep from end to end with gunfire (17c).

rally [17c. French *ral(l)ier*, literally 'to re-unite', from *allier* 'to unite or combine', from Old French *al(e)ier*, from Latin *alligare*, literally 'to bind to', from *ligare* 'to bind'] To bring together a scattered army or company, hence **1** to gather people for support or for a concentrated action; **rally to/round** to come together for such a purpose (19c) **2** a rapid reassembly of forces; a mass meeting of (political) supporters (19c, *US*), hence of any interest group (1920s); a social meeting of motorists including a run and, sometimes, driving competitions, hence a competition for cars over roads and tracks (1930s); to take part in one (1960s) **3** to concentrate or renew courage etc. by an effort of will (17c); to revive or rouse (18c), hence **(a)** to (temporarily) recover strength during illness (19c); a sudden or temporary recovery **(b)** to recover from a setback (19c) **(c)** in Boxing: to recover and renew an attack (19c); a prolonged exchange of blows or, in tennis, of strokes.

Old French *al(e)ier* produced ALLAY[2]* and **ally**. Latin *ligare* is the ancestor of LEAGUE*.

ram [Old English *ram(m)*] An uncastrated adult sheep, hence **1** a battering ram (originally having a ram's head); a device designed to beat, crush, press, or drive something, specifically **(a)** the hammer or weight of a pile driver (15c) **(b) (hydraulic) ram** a piston in a hydraulic press (19c) **(c)** (a warship with) a projecting underwater part designed to hole an enemy ship (19c), hence to collide with something deliberately and forcefully, hence **ramraid** to break into premises by ramming a vehicle through a window, wall, etc. (1990s); such an attack **2** to beat or flatten the earth with a heavy implement (ME); to drive piles into the soil (16c); to force anything into place; to force a charge into a firearm with a rod (a **ramrod**, 18c) **3** a sexually aggressive man (1930s).

Old English *ram(m)* appears as **Ram-** in place names (although this may also come from Old English *hramsa* '**ramsons**, wild garlic'). Related to RAMBLE.

ramble [ME. Early Dutch *rammelen* '(of an animal): to wander about in a state of sexual excitement', from *rammen* 'to copulate': related to RAM] Of the mind or thoughts: to wander, hence **1** to write or talk incoherently **2** to travel freely (17c); (to take) a walk for pleasure, especially in the country **3 rambler**, **rambling rose** a climbing rose (19c).

ramp [ME. Old French *ramper* 'to creep, crawl, or climb', of unknown origin] **1** of an animal: to stand on its hind legs, hence **2** in heraldry: to be **rampant**, i.e. portrayed in profile with the forepaws raised **3** to assume an aggressive posture or threatening manner, hence *rampant* fierce; out of control **4** to climb or scramble (16c); of a plant: to climb; to shoot up, to grow (too) luxuriantly, hence *rampant* growing vigorously and wildly (18c) **5** to gad about (16–17c); to play boisterously (17c, largely replaced by 18c **romp**, thought to be an alteration of *ramp* and to be one parent of 19c **rollick** (to have) boisterous fun, the other being **frolic** originally 'to be carefree and full of fun' [16c, from Dutch *vrolijk* from *vro* 'joyous']).

Ramp may be the source of **rampage** (*Scots*). Old French *ramper* produced **ramp** a difference in level between two supports of an arch etc.; a slope connecting different levels; an abrupt change in the level of a road.

random [ME. Old French *randon*, from *randir* 'to gallop', of Germanic origin and probably related to **rennet** and **run**] Great speed or impetuosity; a headless rush (–19c); a haphazard or aimless course (16c), hence **at random** haphazardly; *random* haphazard, without conscious choice or purpose (17c); **RAM** (random access memory) a computer memory or file with all parts directly accessible, not needing to be searched sequentially (1950s).

randy [17c. Perhaps via obsolete *rand* 'to rave', from obsolete Dutch *randen*, whence **rant**] Aggressive, rude, foul-mouthed (Scots); unruly, riotous (18c, Scots and N English); an unruly or foul-mouthed woman (19c); lustful, lewd, sexually eager (originally English dialect, repatriated from the US in the 1920s).

range [ME. Old French *rangier* 'to put in order', from *ranc* 'row, line', of Germanic origin] **1** to draw up in a row or rank (cf. *arrange* below), hence **(a)** to stretch out or stand in a row or straight line, to extend (15c) **(b)** a line or series, surviving mainly in *mountain range* (18c) **(c)** in maths: a set of points on a straight line (19c) **2** to roam over a large area, hence **(a)** a (large) area, e.g. one for jousting (cf. *rink* below), for target practice, or testing weapons (19c), or for hunting or grazing, hence **ranger (a)** a gamekeeper; the warden of a royal, now a national or state park; an officer who rounds up straying livestock (18c) **(b)** a wanderer (16c); a horse or dog used to travel or hunt over a wide area; **rangy** able to do so (19c), hence long and lean **(c)** a soldier from a troop that ranges over a tract of country (17c); a member of a regional police force **3** a set of hotplates and ovens around and heated by a fire (15c), now a large cooking stove **4** an area or category with defined limits (16c), hence **(a)** to be or move within one **(b)** the area or distance over which something is effective (*a range of two octaves/100 miles*) **(c)** the area or time period in which an animal or plant is found (19c) **(d)** the number and variety of things within a category (19c); to include or deal with a variety of things.

Old French *rangier* produced **arrange** originally meaning 'to draw up in rows' and **ranch** [Anglicized from Spanish *rancho* 'a group of people who eat together' (from Old Spanish *rancharse* 'to be billeted', from Old French *se rangier* 'to be arranged'), adopted in Latin America for a hut or small village]. Old French *ranc* is the ancestor of **derange** and RANK[1], and probably of **rink** originally a jousting ground or race-course. Related to **ring** a circular band [Old English *hring*].

rank¹ [ME. Old French *ranc*: see RANGE*] A row, line, or series, hence **1** (those people forming) a social stratum (15c); (high) social or military position, hence **(a)** (to put in or occupy) a position in a hierarchy (16c) **(b)** to have a higher rank or status (19c, N American: as **outrank** in British English) **2** a line of soldiers drawn up abreast (16c), hence **(a)** to (cause to) form a rank or ranks **(b)** **rank and file** the rows and columns of soldiers in military formation (16c); ordinary soldiers (18c); the ordinary members of any group **(c)** **the ranks** ordinary soldiers (19c); **other ranks** ordinary soldiers, seamen, etc. (1920s). Cf. *rating* (at RATE).

rank² [Old English *ranc*] Sturdy, strong (now dialect); growing (too) vigorously or luxuriantly (ME), hence **1** large and coarse or fat, gross (–17c) **2** overgrown with vegetation, choked (*rank with weeds*, 15c) **3** offensive or indecent; foul-smelling, rancid (16c) **4** utter, complete (*rank amateur*, 16c); blatant, flagrant (17c).

rankle [ME. Old French *rancler*, from *rancle*, a variant of *draoncle* 'festering sore' from medieval Latin *dranculus*, literally 'small dragon', from Latin *draco*: see DRAGON*] To fester; to cause festering (15–17c), hence to cause 'festering' bad feeling or resentment (16c).

ransack [ME. Old Norse *rannsaka*, from *rann* 'house' + *-saka* from *soekja* 'to seek': related to SAKE*] To search someone for stolen property (–15c); to search a place thoroughly, originally for stolen property; to do so causing damage or disorder, now especially in order to steal something.

In Scotland and N England *ransack* was altered to *ransackle*, hence *ransackled* 'ransacked', altered to **ramshackle**, originally meaning 'disorderly'.

rape [ME. Via Anglo-Norman French from Latin *rapere*, *rapt*- 'to seize', later 'to rush someone/something away'] To take by force; the taking (–18c), hence **1** abduction, especially of a woman; the forcing of a woman to have sex (15c); to do either (16c); (to carry out) the buggering of a man by force (1970s) **2** to carry someone away on a tide of emotion (17c, replaced by *enrapture* at RAPT) **3** to rob or plunder (18c).

Ravish [French *ravir*, *raviss*-, ultimately from Latin *rapere*] followed a similar path: it also meant to take up into heaven (cf. RAPT). Other descendants of Latin *rapere* include **rapacious**, **rapid**, RAPT*, **raptor** originally a plunderer or robber, later a bird of prey, RAVINE*, **ravish**, and **surreptitious** [Latin *surripere* 'to take away secretly', literally 'to seize from below'].

rapt [ME. Latin *raptus*, literally 'seized', from *rapere*: see RAPE*] Carried away by force (–17c) or religious ecstasy, hence **1** transported up to heaven (15c): cf. *ravish* (at RAPE) **2** moved by intense delight or joy (16c); enthralled, absorbed.

Rapture [via obsolete French, or medieval Latin *raptura*, from *rapere*] followed a similar path from 'capture, carrying off' via 'transportation to heaven' to 'great joy', hence to entrance or delight, largely replaced by **enrapture**.

rare [15c. Latin *rarus*] Widely spaced or scattered (–17c), hence **1** infrequent, uncommon, unusual, exceptional; exceptionally good **2** having widely spaced parts; of low density (–19c), surviving in **rarefied** [16c, from Middle English **rarefy** to make less dense, from Latin *rarus*].

Rare 'underdone' is from Old English *rear* [of unknown origin], and originally referred to an undercooked egg.

rate [15c. Old French, from medieval Latin *rata*, from Latin *pro rata parte* or *portione* 'according to the proportional share', from *ratus* 'firm, established', from *reri*, *rat*- 'to calculate, consider, or think'] (Estimated) value; to determine it, hence **1** a set price, fee, etc.; this as a basis for calculation (*an hourly rate*); **at any rate** at any cost (17c); under any circumstances, in any case (18c) **2** an amount in relation to another (*a rate of £1 per kilo/30 miles an hour*), hence **(a)** speed of movement (17c) **(b) rate (of exchange)** the value of one currency in terms of another (18c) **3 be rated** to be assessed or liable for (local) taxation (16c); **rate(s)** local tax (18c) **4** to consider, to regard as (16c); to regard highly (1970s) **5** a standard or rank (16c, now usually as *first/second* etc. *rate*), hence **(a) rating** a sailor's rank (17c); a non-commissioned sailor (19c, cf. RANK[1]) **(b)** to place someone/something in a particular class, grade, or rank (18c); to merit or be worthy of (1920s) **6** to specify the performance limits of a machine, material, etc. (18c) **7 rating(s)** an estimate of the size of a radio or television programme's audience (1930s); the programme's relative popularity based on this.

Latin *pro rata* was adopted meaning 'in proportion, proportional(ly)', and produced N American **pro-rate** to distribute or assess proportionately; to settle matters on the basis of proportional distribution. The strands of meaning of *rate* are found in other descendants of Latin *reri*: 'to determine or fix' in **ratify** and **ration**; 'proportion' in **ratio**; and 'to consider or think' in **ratiocination**, **rational**, **rationale**, and **reason**, and less obviously in **arraign** [Old Norman French *arainer* 'to call to account', ultimately from Latin *ad-* 'to' + *rationare* 'to reason, to talk reasonably'].

ravine [French, from Latin *rapina* 'plunder, pillaging' from *rapere* 'to seize']
Adopted on three separate occasions, the senses having developed in French:
1 violence, force (15c) **2** a violent rush of water (17c) **3** a deep, narrow gorge
(18c).

French *ravine* produced **ravage** and **ravenous** rapacious, later gluttonous, very
hungry, famished. Latin *rapina* produced **rapine** plundering, pillage; *rapere* is the
ancestor of RAPE*.

ray [ME. French *rai* from Latin *radius* 'staff, spoke, ray'] A narrow beam of light
(rare before the 17c), hence **1** a trace of something positive (*ray of hope*, 17c) **2** a
thin beam of energy or particles (17c); in science fiction: a destructive one (19c)
3 one of a system of lines, parts, or things arranged like the spokes of a wheel
(17c): **(a)** a straight line from the centre to the edge of a circle (outlived by *radius*
below); any one of a set of lines spreading out from a point (19c) **(b)** a starfish's
arm (18c).

Latin *radius* was adopted for a bar or staff, hence one of the two bones of the
forearm, also a straight line from the centre of a circle, whence a circular area
with a radius of a certain length (*within a radius of two miles from the factory*). Latin
radiare 'to emit rays' [from *radius*] produced **radiate**, with two main meanings, 'to
spread out from the centre' and 'to emit rays', also found to varying degrees in
other descendants of *radius*, including **radial**, **radiant**, **radiation** (now mostly
associated with the emission of energy from sub-atomic particles), RADIO, and
radium.

raze [ME. Old French *raser* 'to shave close', ultimately from Latin *radere*, *ras-* 'to
scrape'] (To make) a scratch, tear, cut, or mark (surviving in technical use in the
original spelling, **race**), hence to scrape, cut, or shave off; to scratch out writing
(15c, replaced by *erase* below); to level or obliterate (16c), now usually in *raze to
the ground*.

Old French *raser* produced **razor**. Latin *radere* appears in *tabula rasa* (at TABLE),
and produced **erase**, German *raster* 'screen, frame' [via Latin *rastrum* 'rake']
adopted for a pattern of parallel scanning lines on a cathode ray tube that creates
an image (whence **rasterize** to convert an image into points on a grid), and probably **rascal** (a member of) the rabble (whence, probably, *rascallion*, quickly altered
to **rapscallion**), and **rash** a skin disorder.

read [Old English *raedan*] **1** to control or guide (–ME); to advise **2** to solve a riddle
or interpret a dream; to peruse and interpret writing, a book, symbols, etc., later
musical notation (16c), hence **(a)** to occupy yourself by reading a book etc. **(b)** to
teach a subject, originally orally (ME–19c); to study one for a degree (19c) **(c)** to
present a bill to Parliament, originally by reading it aloud (16c) **(d)** to inspect a
measuring instrument (*read the meter*, 19c) **(e)** of a computer: to extract or transfer data (1940s), hence **ROM** (read-only memory), containing data that cannot be
altered (1960s) **3** to find something in a text, hence **(a)** to perceive a quality,
motive, etc. in someone's expression, words, or actions (16c); to believe that
something is implied (*don't read too much into it*, 19c) **(b)** to hear and understand
words by radio, telephone, etc. (1950s) **4** of a text: to contain certain words, to
say (19c); of an instrument: to show a measurement.

The sense 'to advise' survives, just, as **rede**, and in **Ethelred the Unready**, the
Saxon king who failed to repel the Danes, *unready* meaning 'lacking (good)

advice' rather than 'unprepared': *Ethelred* is made up of Old English *aethel* 'noble' + *raed* 'advice, counsel', so his nickname is both comment and a pun. Related to **dread** [Old English *ondraedan* 'to advise against, to fear'], **ready, -red** (*hatred, kindred* at KIN), and **riddle** a puzzle.

real [ME. Anglo-Norman French, from late Latin *realis*, from Latin *res* 'thing, matter'] **1** of a legal action: for the recovery of a specific thing **2** to do with, or consisting of, immovable property (*real estate*) **3** to do with things (16c), hence actually existing, happening, or true; not imaginary or artificial: earlier in **really** actually, truly (15c), hence very (17c), shortened to *real* (19c, Scots and N American). Hence **realize** to make real (17c), hence **1** to convert into cash (18c); to yield a specified return or fetch a specified price (19c) **2** to understand or become aware of something (18c).

Late Latin *realis* produced **surrealism** [via French], whence **surreal**. Latin *res* produced **re** [literally 'on the matter of'], hence with reference to, concerning, **rebus** [via French from Latin, literally 'by or about things', in the phrase *de rebus quae geruntur* 'about things that are happening', the title of 16c satirical pieces which included picture riddles], **reify** to regard an abstraction as if it were a thing, and **republic** [via French from Latin *res publica*, literally 'public matter'].

rear [Old English *raeran*: related to **rise**] **1** to set upright, to make stand up, hence to wake someone and make them get up; to stir up, incite, or stimulate: replaced by **raise** [ME, from *reisa*, the Old Norse equivalent of *raeran*], replaced in turn by ROUSE **2** to construct, build up, or establish, hence to produce (–18c), hence **(a)** to gather taxes, an army, etc. (ME–16c, replaced by *raise*) **(b)** (also as *raise*, US) to grow plants; to breed and keep animals; to bring up a child (16c) **3** to lift up or elevate (now usually *raise*) **4** to rise up (ME); of a horse etc.: to stand on its hind legs.

rebate [15c. French *rebattre* 'to beat back', from *abatre* 'to fell', from *batre* 'to beat': see BATTER*] To abate; to make or become less, hence to make a deduction from a sum (–17c); such a deduction (16c); a partial refund; to make one (1950s).

French *rebattre* produced *rab(b)at* 'recess', whence **rabbet**, later **rebate** a groove cut in a piece of wood etc. to allow the tongue of another piece to be slotted into it. *Abatre* produced ABATE*.

rebuff [16c. Via French from Italian *ribuffare* 'to scold', literally 'to blow back', from *buffo* 'puff', of imitative origin] To reject, repel, or snub; such a snub (17c), hence a sudden setback.

Italian **buffo** was adopted for a singer of comic roles in opera, having produced **buffoon**.

rebut [ME. Old French *rebo(u)ter*, literally 'to butt back', from *bo(u)ter* BUTT[1]*] To rebuke sternly (now Scots); to repel (–19c); in law: to bring forward a **rebutter** an answer to an accusation (16c), hence a refutation (18c), whence *rebut* to refute or disprove (19c).

recede [15c. Latin *recedere*, *recess-* 'to go back', from *cedere* 'to go'] To depart: **1** from your usual state or standard (–19c), hence to decline in value (19c) **2** from a place (15c), hence **(a)** of the hair: to stop growing at the front of the head (17c) **(b)** to become further away in space or time (17c) **(c)** to withdraw from an agreement (17c) **(d)** to slope backwards (18c).

Latin *recedere* produced RECESS; *cedere* is the ancestor of CEDE*.

receipt [ME. Anglo-Norman and Old Norman French *receite* from medieval Latin *recepta* 'received, taken', from Latin *recipere*: see RECEIVE*] **1** a formula for making or using a remedy, hence a list of ingredients and instructions, especially in cookery; the means of doing or achieving something (17c): largely replaced by **recipe** [15c, Latin, literally 'take!' (from *recipere*), originally used at the beginning of a medical prescription] **2** the act of receiving something, hence **(a)** an amount received, now usually **receipts** money received (15c) **(b)** a written acknowledgement of this (17c).

receive [ME. Old French *receivre, reçoivre* from Latin *recipere, recept-*, literally 'to take back', from *capere* 'to take'] **1** to accept something offered, given, or sent, hence **(a) receiver** someone who does so (replaced by 16c **recipient** except in **(official) receiver** an official appointed to administer property and receive moneys due; *receiver* someone who deals in stolen property) **(b)** to listen or pay attention to, hence **receptive** able and willing to accept impressions, information, etc. (15c) **(c)** to detect and interpret a signal (19c), hence *receiver* the part of the equipment that does this; **reception** the receiving, or the quality of, the signal **2** to be given or provided with; to have something conferred or inflicted **3** to (be able to) contain, hence **receptacle** a container **4** to greet a guest or visitor, hence *reception* **(a)** the action or manner of doing so (*a frosty reception*, 17c) **(b)** (describing) a place where this is done (19c) **(c)** a formal party (*wedding reception*, 19c) **5** to accept someone into a place or relationship, in a particular capacity (*receive in marriage*), or as a member (15c, hence *reception centre/class*, etc.) **6** to accept as authoritative or true (*received wisdom*, 15c).

Latin *recipere* produced RECEIPT*; *capere* is the ancestor of CATCH*.

recess [16c. Latin *recedere, recess-* 'to go back': see RECEDE*] Departure or withdrawal **1** from a place (–17c), hence a remote or secluded place (17c); a niche or alcove (18c); an indentation (19c) **2** from public life (17–18c), hence a time in which no work or business is done (17c); **recession** a temporary decline in economic activity (1920s). Hence **recessive** tending to recede (17c); of an inherited characteristic or gene: appearing only when inherited from both parents, 'giving way' to a dominant one (*c.*1900).

reclaim [ME. Via Old French from Latin *reclamare* 'to cry out against', from *clamare* 'to shout' (ancestor of CLAIM*)] **1** to call back a flying hawk (–18c), hence **(a)** to make one obedient; to tame an animal or subdue a person; to re-domesticate a feral animal; to bring wasteland into cultivation (18c); to recycle waste (19c) **(b)** to call or win a person away from immorality **2** to claim back property, a payment, etc. (16c).

recognize [ME. Old French *reconnaistre, reconniss-*, from Latin *recognoscere, recognit-*, 'to look over', literally 'to know again', from *cognoscere* 'to know': see QUAINT*] **1** to repossess land from a feudal tenant (–17c, Scots) **2** to acknowledge the existence or validity of (16c), hence **(a)** to appreciate or reward **(b)** to acknowledge or realize the nature of (19c) **(c)** to allow someone to speak in a meeting etc. (19c) **3** to identify someone/something that you have seen or been aware of, before (16c) **4** to enter into or bind over by a recognizance (17c, US).

Old French *reconnaistre* produced **recognizance** a bond by which someone promises to do something, later a sum pledged as surety for this. Latin *recognoscere* fathered French **reconnoître**: the later French form *reconnaître* produced **reconnaissance**: both shortened in military slang to **recce**.

recoil [ME. French *reculer*, ultimately from Latin *culus* 'buttocks'] **1** to drive or force back (–18c); to retreat or withdraw; retreat, withdrawal, hence a sudden backward movement from fear, horror, or disgust; to shrink from doing something (15–18c), or move quickly away (16c), in disgust; to feel disgust or repulsion **2** to fall or stagger back after a blow (16c); of a gun: to kick back from the force of a discharge; the extent to which it does so **3** to return to the original position or source (16c); to rebound; **recoil (up)on** of an action: to harm the perpetrator.

Latin *culus* fathered French *culotte* 'knee breeches', whence **culottes**, and is one parent of French ***bascule*** [the other being French *bas* 'low': see BASE²*].

record [ME. French, from Latin *recordari* 'to remember', from *cor* 'heart' (ancestor of CORDIAL*)] To repeat something (aloud or to yourself), especially in order to memorize it (–17c), hence **1** to tell, orally (–18c) or, later, in writing; an authentic or official written account; to make or include in one (16c), hence **(a)** the best achievement recorded (19c); **break/set a record** to do better **(b)** (an account of) the main facts of someone's life or career (19c); **(criminal) record** a list of their crimes and sentences (*c*.1900, *US*) **(c)** to convert a sound, performance, etc. into a permanent form (19c); a cylinder or, later, disc carrying recorded sound; to perform while being recorded (1920s) **(d)** a number of related items of information which a computer treats as a unit (1950s) **2** to sing (repeatedly), to practise a tune (15c), hence **recorder** a simple wind instrument.

recourse [ME. Latin *recurrere* 'to run back', from *currere* 'to run'] A return, a move backwards or in a particular direction (–18c); the act of turning to something/ someone for help, advice, etc., usually in *have recourse to*; the person or thing turned to.

Latin *recurrere* produced **recur**: *currere* is the ancestor of CURRENT*.

recruit [17c. Obsolete French dialect *recrute*, from Old French *recroître* 'to increase again', from Latin *recrescere*, from *crescere* 'to grow' (ancestor of CRESCENT*)] To reinforce, supplement, or replenish; a fresh or additional supply of goods, soldiers, etc., hence one of these soldiers (19c: **rookie** a novice soldier or policeman, is probably an alteration); a new employee or member of an organization; to enlist or obtain a recruit or recruits.

redeem [15c (earlier in **redemption**). (Via French from) Latin *redimere, redempt-*, from *emere* 'to buy'] To buy back; to get back something mortgaged or pledged by payment or by fulfilling an obligation, hence **1** to ransom someone; of Christ: to save someone from damnation by his own death **2** to make amends; to restore or put right; to make up for some inadequacy (*redeeming feature*, 16c) **3** to carry out a pledge or promise (19c) **4** to exchange a voucher etc. for cash or goods (*c*.1900, *US*).

Latin *redimere* fathered Old French *ransoun* 'redemption', whence **ransom**; *emere* is the ancestor of EXAMPLE*.

redolent [ME. Old French, from Latin *redolere* 'to smell strongly', from *olere* 'to smell'] Fragrant, aromatic; having a particular scent (16c), hence strongly suggestive or reminiscent of something (19c).

Latin *olere* produced **olfactory** and Spanish *oloroso* [literally 'fragrant'], a medium-sweet sherry. Related to **odour**.

reduce [ME. Latin *reducere*, literally 'to lead back', also 'to withdraw', from *ducere* 'to lead'] To bring back (–18c); to restore (–18c), hence **1** to put a fractured bone into alignment or dislocated part into its place (15c) **2** to turn someone from sin or error (–18c); to lead them towards faith, virtue, or to a certain state or opinion, hence to change something to a different state; to break up or pulverize, hence **(a)** to make (15c) or become (19c) smaller, less, or simpler; to boil down a sauce etc.; to slim (1920s) **(b)** to constrain or subdue (15c); to bring down (16c); to degrade or demote (*reduced to the ranks*, 17c); to be forced by poverty etc. to do something (*reduced to selling his medals*).

Latin *reducere* produced **redoubt** a fortification [via Italian and French from medieval Latin *reductus* 'refuge']; *ducere* is the ancestor of DEDUCE*.

redundant [16c. Latin *redundare* 'to overflow', from *undare* 'to surge', from *unda* 'a wave' (ancestor of SOUND³*)] Plentiful, abundant; excessive, superfluous (17c), hence **1** having an unnecessary part or feature (17c); of a part etc.: able to be removed without harm (19c); added as a back-up **2** of a person: no longer needed at work (1920s); unemployed for this reason.

reed [Old English *hrēod*] (The hollow stem of) a tall grass growing in water or marsh, hence **1** these stems used for thatching (ME), hence **(a)** wheat straw for thatching (15c) **(b)** some instances of the surnames **Read(er)**, **Re(e)dman** a thatcher **2** a hollow-stemmed plant made into a simple wind instrument (ME); part of the mouthpiece of some wind instruments, originally consisting of a thin piece of cane (18c); such an instrument (19c) **3** the wires (replacing reeds or canes) in a loom (16c).

reef [ME. Early Dutch *reef*, *rif*, from Old Norse *rif* 'ridge, rib'] A section of a sail that can be gathered or rolled up to reduce sail area; to do so (17c); to shorten a topmast or bowsprit (18c). Hence **1** **reefer (a)** someone who reefs a sail (19c); a midshipman **(b)** a sailor's thick warm jacket (19c), later an overcoat (N American) **(c)** a marijuana cigarette (1930s, *US*: probably from the idea of something rolled, but perhaps from or influenced by Mexican Spanish *grifo* 'marijuana') **2** **reef knot** used to tie a sail (19c).

Old Norse *rif* produced **reef** a ridge of rock etc. in the sea, and probably **reeve** to pass a rope through a hole.

reel [Old English *hrēol*, of unknown origin] A (rotating) cylinder on which thread etc. can be wound, hence **1** to wind something onto or off a reel (ME), hence **reel in** to pull in a hooked fish by winding in the line (16c); **reel off** to list things quickly and effortlessly (19c) **2** to whirl around (ME), hence **(a)** to be or become giddy or confused; to stagger back from a blow; to move unsteadily **(b)** (the music for) a lively folk-dance (16c).

refer [ME. Via French from Latin *referre*, *relat-* 'to carry or give back', from *ferre* 'to bring'] To bring back or restore (–17c); to trace something back to a source or cause, hence **1** to hark back or apply to **2** to pass a matter to some authority for consideration or action; to consult for advice or information (15c); to direct someone to a source of information or help (16c), hence to allude to (*refer you to* *my previous letter*, 17c) **3** to put back, to defer (–18c), hence **(a)** to put off discussion or treatment of a subject to another occasion (16c) **(b)** to postpone awarding a degree pending re-examination (*c*.1900).

Refer produced **referee**, **reference**, **referential**, and **referral**. Latin *referre* produced *referendum*, and **relate** with the main meanings 'to have a connection with' and 'to give an account of' (a later sense of *referre*, from the idea of bringing back news); *ferre* is the ancestor of CONFER*.

reflect [ME. Via Old French from Latin *reflectere*, *reflex-* from *flectere* 'to bend' (ancestor of FLEXIBLE*)] To turn back, redirect, or deflect, hence **1** to make light, sound, etc. rebound from a surface; to produce a reversed image in a mirror etc. by reflecting light (16c), hence **(a)** to correspond to in appearance or effect (17c); to show or express (*his manners reflect his upbringing*) **(b)** **reflect on** to show in a certain light (*his behaviour reflects well/badly on his parents*, 17c); to bring dishonour/credit to **2** to turn your thoughts back to, to ponder (17c, 15c in **reflection**); to say (to yourself) thoughtfully (18c) **3** to produce an impulse in response to a stimulus (19c), hence **reflex (action)** produced automatically by a stimulus, or unthinkingly in response to an event, hence **reflexology 1** the study of reflexes and their effect on behaviour (1920s) **2** the massaging of points on the feet and hands to treat a corresponding part of the body (1970s).

refraction [16c. Latin *refringere*, *refract-* 'to break up', from *frangere* 'to break'] **1** the action of breaking open or breaking up (–17c) **2** the deflection of light or other rays passing from one medium to another (17c); the degree to which this happens; the power of the medium to do it; (the measurement of) the eye's ability to deflect light so as to focus it on the retina (*c*.1900).

Latin *refringere* produced **refractory** [alteration of **refractary**, from *refractarius* 'stubborn'] originally (someone who is) obstinate or rebellious, later resistant to disease or heat, hence a heat-resistant material, and **refrain** a recurring phrase or verse (thought to 'break up' a song). *Frangere* is the ancestor of FRACTION*.

refund [ME. Via Old French from Latin *refundere*, from *fundere* 'to pour or melt' (ancestor of FUSE*)] To pour back; to give back, to restore, hence, by association with *fund* (at FOUND) to repay money (16c) or a person (18c).

regal [ME. (Old French, from) Latin *regalis*, from *rex*, *reg-* 'king'] **1** royal authority, sovereignty (–15c) **2** to do with or belonging to a monarch, hence **(a)** **regals** the emblems and insignia of royalty (15–17c, replaced by *regalia* below) **(b)** a royal right or privilege (16–18c), cf. *regalia* **(c)** fit for or resembling a monarch (18c); magnificent, stately.

Latin *regalis* produced medieval Latin *regalia* [literally 'royal things'] royal rights, privileges, or insignia, later the insignia of any organized group, and **royal** [via Old French *roial*]. Latin *rex* produced **interregnum** [via *regnum* 'royal authority', whence also **reign**], *Regis* added to the names of places with royal connections, **regius professor** whose chair was established by a monarch, and French *roy* 'king', whence the names **Elroy** and **Leroy**, and **viceroy** [with Latin *vice* 'in place of']. Latin *regina* 'queen' produced French *reine*, whence **vicereine**. *Rex* and *Regina* are used in British courts for the prosecution (representing the monarch), and were adopted as names (**Queenie** began as a pet form of *Regina*). Related to RULE*.

regiment [ME. French, from late Latin *regimentum*, from *regere*, *rect-* 'to guide, rule, or regulate'] Rule, government, especially royal authority (largely replaced by related RULE), hence **1** the office or function of a ruler (–17c); their period of rule (16–17c, replaced by *reign* at REGAL) **2** the place ruled (–17c), outlived by **realm** [ME, from Latin *regimen* below] **3** a method or system of government (15–17c), outlived by Latin *regimen* [15c, from *regere*] or its descendant, French *regime* **4** a prescribed diet or way of life (15–18c), outlived by *regimen* and *regime* **5** a permanent unit of troops under the control of a superior officer (16c), hence **(a)** to form into one; to organize people, society, etc. into a rigid system (17c) **(b)** a large or organized array (17c).

Descendants of Latin *regere* include CORRECT*, DIRECT*, **erect**, **rector** a ruler or governor, now only of a parish or educational establishment, **regent**, literally 'ruling', hence someone ruling, **region**, RESOURCE*, and SURGE*: see also REGISTER. Its past participle, *rectus*, literally 'guided, ruled', came to mean 'straight, right', whence **rectangle** [with *angulus* ANGLE¹] **rectify**, **rectitude** originally straightness, hence honesty, virtue (cf. RIGHT), **recto** [Latin *recto folio* 'on the right-hand leaf'], and **rectum** [Latin *rectum intestinum* 'straight intestine'].

register [ME. (Via French from) medieval Latin *registrum*, ultimately from Latin *regerere* 'to record or transcribe', from *gerere* 'to bring or carry'] (To enter in) a record book or list, hence **1 (a)** an entry in a register (17c); a specific memory location in a computer (1920s) **(b) register/registry office** where official records of births, marriages, and deaths are kept (18c) **(c)** to sign in or sign up (19c, *US*) **2** to make a mental note (16c); to be realized (*I heard a noise, but it didn't register*) **3** to record or indicate something automatically (18c), hence **(a)** a device for doing so (*cash register*, 19c); to be recorded by one (1930s) **(b)** of a person or their face: to show an emotion (*c*.1900) **4** (a device controlling) a set of organ pipes with similar tonal qualities (16c), hence the range of an instrument, voice, etc. (19c); a type of language used in a particular situation (1950s) **5** a device that controls a flow of air, smoke, etc. (17c); a grille through which warm or cool air is blown into a room (early 20c, *US*) **6** in printing: correct or precise alignment (17c); to be correctly aligned (19c).

Senses 5 and 6 arose by association with Latin *regere*: see REGIMENT*. Latin *registrum* produced **registrar** someone who keeps a register or records (a hospital registrar was originally a junior doctor whose duties included registering patients). *Gerere* is the ancestor of GESTURE*.

relay [15c. Old French *relayer*, from *laier* 'to leave' (whence **delay**), perhaps from Frankish or perhaps from Latin *laxare* 'to loosen': see RELEASE*] To set fresh hounds on a scent to replace tired ones (15c only); the fresh hounds, hence **1** to provide or use fresh horses etc. (16c), hence **(a)** a team of fresh horses, workers, etc. (17c) **(b) relay (race)** in which each team member covers part of the distance (19c) **(c)** a series of motor vehicles or drivers, each covering part of a route (World War II) **2** a device enabling a weak signal to initiate a stronger one for onward transmission (19c), hence **(a)** to receive and pass on a message, information, broadcast, etc. **(b)** a device that receives, amplifies, and retransmits a signal (1920s) **(c)** a device that enables one electrical circuit to open or close another (1930s).

release [ME. Old French *relaiss(i)er* 'to let go', later 'to leave behind', from Latin *relaxare*, from *laxare* 'to loosen', from *laxus* 'loose'] **1** to cancel or lessen a sentence or punishment (–17c), to free from confinement, distress, an obligation, or debt; liberation from these; a written discharge **2** to give up a right or claim, hence **(a)** to make over money or property to another; (a deed affecting) such transference **(b)** to return requisitioned property (World War I) **3** to set free, hence **(a)** to free a moving part in a machine etc.; a device that does so (19c) **(b)** to let out an emotion (early 20c); to ease, or an easing of, tension **4** to make available (*c*.1900); to issue, or the issuing of, a book, film, etc. (*US*); the item issued (*c*.1910); written permission to publish (1960s).

Old French *relaiss(i)er* produced RELISH. Latin *relaxare* produced **relax**; *laxare* produced **laxative**, **lease** [via French *laisser* 'to let', whence also, from a later sense 'to let run on a loose lead', **leash**], and perhaps RELAY*; *laxus* is the ancestor of **lax** and probably LUSH. Related to Latin *languere* 'to be faint or weary', whence **languid**, **languish**, and **languor**.

relegate [ME. Latin *relegare* 'to send away', from *legare* 'to depute' (ancestor of LEGATE*)] **1** to exile or banish, hence to send to an inferior or less important place (18c); to demote a football team etc. to a lower league (*c*.1910) **2** to refer something for action or judgement (19c), perhaps influenced by *delegate* (at LEGATE).

relieve [ME. French *relever* from Latin *relevare*, literally 'to raise again', from *levis* 'light'] To 'lift up' out of trouble or danger, hence **1** to bring help, originally to a besieged town, later to the needy **2 (a)** to free (mainly Scots); to free from a task, duty, or obligation, especially by being or providing a replacement (16c) **(b)** to deprive of a possession, especially by theft **3** to free from, or lessen, pain or distress; **relieve yourself** to urinate or defecate (1930s) **4** to make less onerous (15c) or tedious (18c).

Relieve's noun is **relief** [French, from *relever*]. Latin *relevare* produced **relevant** [from a medieval Latin sense 'to take up'], and is the ultimate ancestor of Italian *rilievo*, whence **relievo** and **relief** moulding, carving, etc. in which the design stands out from a surface, hence **1** *relieve* to make something stand out from a surface **2** *relief* the (amount of) variation in height in a geographical area; **relief map** showing this. Latin *levis* is the ancestor of LEVER*.

relish [ME. Old French *relais* 'remainder', from *relaiss(i)er*: see RELEASE*] A taste, after-taste, odour, or flavour, hence **1** (to give something) an appetizing flavour (16c); to make something enjoyable or satisfying; to enjoy or look forward to very much **2** a sauce or chutney (17c).

rely [ME. Via Old French from Latin *religare* 'to bind closely', from *ligare* 'to bind' (ancestor of LEAGUE*)] To come or bring together (–17c), to associate with or turn to (15–17c), hence to depend on (17c); to have faith and confidence in.

remark [16c. French *remarquer*, from *marquer* 'to mark', ultimately from Old Norse *merki* 'a mark'] To take notice of; to perceive, hence **1** (to make) an observation or comment (17c) **2 remarkable** noteworthy, unusual, striking (17c). Cf. OBSERVE sense 1c.

French *remarquer* produced *remarque* a mark made in the border of an engraved plate to show its state of production; *marquer* produced *marque* (adopted meaning a make or brand: cf. MARK sense 4a), whence *marqueter* 'to variegate', ancestor of **marquetry**. Related to MARK*.

remember [ME. Old French *remembrer* from late Latin *rememorari*, from Latin *memor* 'mindful'] To recall; to bring to, or keep in, mind, hence **1** to bring to someone else's mind (*remember me to your mother*) **2** to keep in mind as being entitled to a gift, etc. (*remember him in your will*, 15c).

Old French *remembrer* produced **remembrance**. Latin *memor* is the ancestor of MEMORY*.

remit [ME. Latin *remittere, remiss-*, literally 'to send or let go back', also 'to relax or release', from *mittere* 'to send'] **1** to send back: **(a)** to refer to another person or authority; to send a person or case to another tribunal (16c), especially back to a lower court (17c), hence (a brief statement of) the area of responsibility of a tribunal, person, etc. (1960s) **(b)** to refer someone to a source of information (15c) **(c)** to restore to a previous condition or position (16c) **(d)** to send money or valuables to (16c), hence **remittance** what is sent (18c) **(a)** payment **(e)** to postpone **2** to pardon or forgive; to cancel or not enforce a debt or punishment (15c, earlier in **remission**, now usually meaning early release from prison for good behaviour) **3** to relax or relieve tension, standards, or diligence (15c) **4** to abate or diminish (16c), now mainly in *remission* (temporary) abatement of a disease (17c), and in **unremitting** (18c).

Latin *remittere* produced **remiss** careless, negligent; *mittere* is the ancestor of MISSION*.

rend [Old English *rendan*: related to **rind**] To tear or wrench off, away, etc.; to tear apart; to split or divide. Hence **1** to tear, to burst or split open (ME); a split or tear (16c) **2** to tear your clothes or hair in grief (ME) **3** to tear someone's heart, to cause emotional pain (16c).

The past tense, **rent**, became a verb in its own right with a similar range of senses; as a noun it took over the general sense 'a split or tear' from *rend*, and also came to mean a rift in a relationship, and a fissure or gorge.

render [ME. French *rendre*, ultimately from Latin *reddere* 'to give back', from *dare* 'to give'] **1** to repeat something learned (–16c); to reproduce in another language, to translate; to reproduce or depict artistically (16c) **2** to bring into a specific state, hence **(a)** to purify or extract fat by melting **(b)** to cover with a preliminary coat of plaster (18c, 17c in **rendering** this coat, later also called *render*, 19c) **3** to hand over, to give up or relinquish, hence **(a)** to surrender a place to an enemy (16c); **render yourself** to give yourself up, to surrender, later to present yourself, to be at a certain place (17c, cf. *rendezvouz* below) **(b)** **(extraordinary) rendition** the transferring of prisoners for interrogation probably involving torture from a country that does not officially sanction it (1990s, *US*) **4** to give out or give back (15c), hence **(a)** to present something for consideration, approval, or, later, payment **(b)** to give what is due (16c); to show respect or obedience; to do a service; to pay as rent, tax, or tribute; such a payment in money, goods, or services (17c: cf. *rent* below).

Old French *rendre* produced *rendez-vous* 'present yourselves!' (whence **rendezvous** originally a mustering-place for troops), and **surrender**. Latin *reddere* produced French *rente*, whence **rent** (a source of) revenue or income, specifically a tax or charge (ME–18c), hence an amount paid by the tenant to the landlord, later (the amount paid) to hire something. Latin *dare* is the ancestor of DATA*.

renegade [ME. Medieval Latin *renegare*, literally 'to deny again', from Latin *negare* 'to deny'. Originally spelt *renegate*, the current spelling is from Spanish *renegado* (also used in English, 16–19c)] A convert to another religion, especially a Christian who becomes a Muslim, hence someone who abandons their party or principles (17c); to do so (18c); (describing) a rebel or outlaw. The alteration **runagate** [16c, influenced by *run* + obsolete *agate* 'on the way, in motion', from GATE²*] came to mean a deserter, fugitive, or tramp.

Medieval Latin *renegare* produced RENEGE; Latin *negare* produced **abnegate**, **deny**, **negate**, and *negative* (at POSITIVE). Related to Latin *neg-* in *neglect* (at LEGEND) and NEGOTIATE.

renege [16c. Medieval Latin *renegare*: see RENEGADE*] **1** to renounce a person or your faith (16c); to go back on your word (18c, *US*) **2** to refuse or decline (16c); in card games: to not follow suit (17c).

repertory [16c. Late Latin *repertorium* 'inventory', from Latin *reperire* 'to find out', from *parere* 'to get, beget, or give birth'] An index, calendar, or catalogue (–18c); a store or stock, originally of information, hence a stock of material that a person or company can perform (19c, more common in the French form *repertoire*); the system by which a theatre company performs a number of works during a season (shortened to **rep**, 1920s); (describing) one that performs in this way (early 20c).

Latin *parere*'s descendants include **parent** and VIPER*.

replicate [ME. Latin *replicare*, literally 'to fold back', later 'to turn back, to go over, to repeat', from *plicare* 'to fold'] **1** to do or say again, hence **(a) replication** an echo or reverberation (17c) **(b)** to repeat an experiment to check a result (1920s) **2** *replication* a reply; the plaintiff's response to the defendant's plea; *replicate* to reply (16c) **3** to fold or bend back (17c) **4** *replication* (the making of) a copy (17c); *replicate* to make (19c) or be (1950s) a reproduction or replica of (1950s); of genetic material: to reproduce itself exactly (1970s).

Latin *replicare* fathered Italian *replica* originally a repeated sequence of musical notes, and **reply**; *plicare* is the ancestor of PLY*.

report [ME. Via Old French from Latin *reportare* 'to bring back', from *portare* 'to bring': see PORT³*] To bring (back) information (–16c), hence **1 (a)** (to give or produce) an account of an event, proceedings, etc., now especially of the result of an investigation (17c), of a student's progress and conduct (19c), or of a serviceman's misbehaviour (chiefly in **on report**) **(b)** to be accountable to a superior (19c); to present yourself to a person or at a place **2** gossip, rumour; how someone/something is spoken of, reputation **3** a musical note played in response to another (16–17c), hence a sudden loud noise.

French *rapport* [from *rapporter* 'to bring back', from *apporter* 'to bring', ultimately from Latin *portare*] was briefly borrowed meaning 'report, talk', and again meaning 'communication, relationship', now especially a relationship of mutual understanding.

reprise [ME. French, feminine of *repris*, past participle of *reprendre* 'to take back or again', from *prendre* 'to take', from Latin *prehendere*] **1** to reprove (–15c), outlived by **reprehend** [Latin *reprehendere*, also meaning 'to take back or again', from *prehendere*], surviving mainly in **reprehensible 2** to begin again (–17c); in music: the repetition of, or return to, the original theme (18c); to repeat, or the repetition of, a passage, performance, etc. (1950s) **3** to take or get back; the action or fact of doing so, later as an act of retaliation (17–18c, outlived by *reprisal* below).

French *repris* produced **reprieve**, originally to send back to prison, later to 'take back' a punishment, specifically to stop or delay an execution; this act; (to give someone) a temporary respite. Latin *reprehendere* produced **reprisal** the seizing of another state's property or people in retaliation or compensation for your losses, hence an act of retaliation, especially in wartime. Latin *prehendere* is the ancestor of PRISE*.

reprobate [ME. Latin *reprobare*, from *probare* 'to test, ascertain, or demonstrate': see PROBABLE*] To disapprove of, to censure or condemn; of God: to reject or condemn someone (15c), hence **1** rejected, damned, beyond salvation; such a person, a hardened sinner (16c); (someone) without religious or moral principles **2** rejected as worthless or inferior (16c); to do so (17c). Hence, probably, **rep** an immoral person, especially a man (18c, now usually as the variant **rip**); a worthless article.

Latin *reprobare* produced French *reprover*, whence **reproof** and **reprove**.

require [ME. Via Old French from, ultimately, Latin *requirere*, literally 'to ask in return', from *quaerere* 'to ask or seek'] To ask a question (–17c); to ask for something, hence **1** to demand (15c) **2** to need (15c).

Latin *requirere* produced **request**, **requisite**, and **requisition**; *quaerere* is the ancestor of QUEST*.

reserve [ME. French *reserver* from Latin *reservare*, from *servare* 'to watch or keep'] To keep back, to set aside for future use, hence **1** to postpone (*reserve judgement*) **2** to keep for a particular person or use, e.g. a place kept for game or wildlife (17c, cf. PRESERVE); **reservation** an area set aside for a particular race (originally for Native Americans in the US, 18c), hence to secure for yourself (19c) **3** something kept back (17c), hence **(a) reserve(s)** troops kept back to be deployed as and when needed; (a member of) armed forces not on active service who can be called up if necessary (19c); in sport: a substitute (*c.*1900); **reserves** the second team (1960s) **(b)** *reserves* funds kept to meet future needs and contingencies (19c); oil, gas, etc. known to exist but not yet exploited (*c.*1910); extra energy, stamina, etc. that a person can use in an emergency (1920s) **(c) reserve (champion)** a runner-up who would get a prize if a prizewinner were disqualified (19c) **(d) reserve (price)** the minimum acceptable price for something at an auction, below which it will be withdrawn (19c) **4** restraint, self-control (17c), hence **(a)** *reserved* reticent, cool, distant, formal; *reserve* reticence, a lack of frankness or friendliness (18c) **(b)** *reservation* (the making of) a tacit limitation to an agreement (17c); *reservations* limitations, scruples, doubts.

French *reserver* produced **reservoir**; Latin *servare* is the ancestor of CONSERVE*.

residence [ME. French, or medieval Latin *residentia*, from Latin *residere* 'to stay behind', from *sedere* 'to sit'] The fact of living in a particular place, hence **1** the fact, or a period, of living or staying in a particular place to carry out (official) duties (15c), now often in **in residence**, also applied to a creative artist employed by an institution (*writer-in-residence*, 1950s). Hence **(a) resident** in residence, living on the premises (19c); a medical graduate undergoing a period of specialized training in a hospital (19c, *N America*), hence **residency** this period (1920s) **(b)** *residency* a band's or a musician's regular gig at a club etc. (1960s) **(c)** an intelligence agent living in a foreign country (1960s, translating Russian *rezident*), hence *residence/residency* a group of them, a cell **2** your dwelling (16c), hence **(a)** the time you live there (17c) **(b)** an (imposing) house (17c); (also as *residency*) an official dwelling, specifically a colonial governor's (19c).

Reside, originally to settle or take up residence, is probably a back-formation. Latin *residere* produced **residue**; *sedere* is the ancestor of SESSION*.

resolve [ME. Latin *resolvere, resolut-*, literally 'to loosen up', from *solvere* 'to loosen, to dissolve'] To melt or dissolve; to disintegrate or decompose, hence **1** to separate something into its constituent parts (hence **resolution** the act or process of doing so); to distinguish constituent parts (18c), hence *resolution* the power of an optical instrument to do so (19c) **2** to reduce a statement etc. to a simpler form or a set of principles; to answer a question or solve a problem, hence to clarify or settle a matter (16c); to determine or decide on, hence **(a)** what is decided, an intention (16c); *resolution* a formal decision **(b)** firmness, determination (16c, 15c in *resolution*).

Latin *resolvere* produced **resolute** dissolved, friable, also morally lax (outlived by *dissolute* (at SOLVE*), also from Latin *solvere*), later determined, purposeful: the sense 'to make or pass a resolution' (US) is a back-formation from *resolution*.

resort [ME. Old French *resortir*, literally 'to come or go back', from *sortir* 'to come or go out'] **1** to come out again (–15c) **2** to return to a place, subject, habit, condition, etc. (15–18c); to visit regularly, frequently, or in large numbers, hence the place visited (15–18c), now usually a holiday destination **3** to go to for help, information, etc. (15–18c), hence this act; a source of help; a possible course of action (*prison should be the last resort*); **resort to** to adopt an (unpleasant or extreme) expedient (17c).

French *sortir* produced **sortie**, literally 'come or gone out', adopted for an attack by troops from a defensive position, hence **1** to make one **2** an operational flight by a single military aircraft; a series of photographs taken during a single flight.

resource [French *ressource, ressourse*, from Old French dialect *resourdre* 'to rise again, to recover', from Latin *resurgere*, from *surgere* 'to rise': see SURGE*] A store of something you can draw on (17c, now often plural), hence **1** a possible source of help (17c); a possible strategy or expedient **2 resources** a country's natural, economic or military assets (18c); an individual's or company's available funds or assets; to provide with resources (1970s). Hence **3 your own resources** your own talents and ingenuity (18c); *resource* such capabilities (19c), **resourceful** having them.

Latin *resurgere* produced **resurgam** 'I shall rise again', adopted by Christians to proclaim their faith in the resurrection of the dead, **resurge, resurrection** the raising of Christ from the dead, or of the dead at the Last Judgement (whence **resurrect** and **resurrectionist** a body-snatcher), and Italian **Risorgimento** the movement that led to the unification of Italy in 1870, a revival in any sphere.

respect [ME. (French, from) Latin *respectus*, from *respicere* 'to regard', literally 'to look back on', from *specere* 'to look at' (ancestor of SPICE*)] **1 in/with respect to**, later **respecting** in relation to, with regard to **2** a facet (largely replaced by ASPECT); a point or detail (*in some respects*) **3** to postpone (15–17c); a delay requested or granted, a (temporary) reprieve or rest (15–16c), outlived by **respite** [ME, via French from Latin *respectus*] **4** attention, heed, consideration (15c); **respects** polite attention (*pay my respects*, 17c) **5** (to treat with) admiration and deference (16c), hence **(a) respectable** deserving this (16c); of good social standing (18c); honest, decent; presentable; satisfactory, considerable (*a respectable amount*) **(b)** to refrain from harming, insulting, or interfering with (17c), hence **disrespect**, informally shortened to **diss** (1980s, *US*) **6 (a)** discrimination, partiality (16c, usually in **without respect to**) **(b) respective** belonging or relating separately to different people or things (17c).

response [ME. Via Old French from Latin *respondere, respons-*, literally 'to promise in return', from *spondere* 'to pledge or betroth'] A reply (**respond** 'to reply' does not appear until the 16c), hence **1** an anthem sung alternately by a soloist and choir (also as **responsory**); a part of the liturgy said or sung by the congregation in reply to the priest **2 respondent** someone who answers, particularly someone who responds to questioning (16c); also a defendant in a lawsuit, especially a divorce, hence **co-respondent** the alleged lover (19c) **3 responsible** answerable, accountable, hence **(a)** reliable, trustworthy (17c) **(b)** at fault, to blame **(c) responsibility** accountability; something you are accountable for (18c) **4** a reaction to a stimulus (18c in *respond* and in **responsive** responding readily).

Latin *respondere* produced **correspond** [Latin *correspondere*, literally 'to answer to each other'], and [via Italian *rispondere*] French **riposte** (to make) a quick thrust in fencing after parrying a lunge, hence (to make) a quick retort. Latin *spondere* is the ancestor of SPONSOR*.

rest [Old English *r(a)est* (noun), *r(a)estan* (verb)] Repose, hence **1** refreshment through sleep; to lie down (as if) asleep, hence **(a) restless** unable to rest, uneasy, fidgety: cf. *restive* below **(b)** a place to rest; a bed or couch (–ME); a shelter or lodging (*seamen's rest*) **2** to lie dead or in the grave **3** peace, tranquillity; the peace of death (ME) **4** (to take or allow) a break from work or activity; in music: (a sign indicating) a period of silence (16c) **5** to stop: **(a)** to settle or alight **(b)** to finish presenting evidence in a law suit (*I rest my case*, 19c, *US*) **6** to lie or lay on; to lean on for support (ME); to depend on; a prop or support (*footrest*, 16c).

Sense 5 probably influenced **rest** to remain (surviving mainly in *rest assured*), what remains, those remaining [via Old French from Latin *restare* 'to stay behind', from *stare* 'to stand' (ancestor of STATION*)], whence **restive** still, inactive; of a horse: refusing to go forward, especially by moving backwards or sideways, hence restless, fidgety.

restore [ME. Old French *restorer* from Latin *restaurare*] To give back, to make restitution or amends, to make good loss or damage, hence to renew, re-erect or reconstruct; to bring something back to its original state or condition, hence **1** to bring someone back, originally to a state of grace, later to their former or rightful position, hence **Restoration** (the period following) the re-establishment of the English monarchy in 1660 (18c) **2** to give someone renewed health and vigour (ME).

Old French *restorer* evolved into *restaurer*, whence **restaurant** and **restaurateur**. Related to **store** [Latin *instaurare*] to supply or stock; to keep for future use, hence what is kept; a place where things are kept, now specifically for sale.

resume [15c. French *résumer* or Latin *resumere*, from *sumere* 'to take up'] To take something up again after losing or relinquishing it; to return to an activity after a pause; to repeat a word or phrase; to recapitulate or summarize.

French **résumé** [past participle of *résumer*] was adopted for a summary or curriculum vitae (US). Latin *sumere* is the ancestor of SUMPTUOUS*.

retain [ME. Anglo-Norman French *retei(g)n-*, from Old French *retenir*, ultimately from Latin *retinere*, *retent-* 'to hold back', from *tenere* 'to hold'] To restrain or hold back (–18c), hence **1** to keep possession of (hence **retainer** a payment made to reserve rented accommodation while you are away, 19c); to keep or have in mind, to remember (15c) **2** to keep with you or in your service (15c): **(a)** to engage or hire (16c), to secure someone's professional services by a preliminary payment (a *retainer*) (18c) **(b)** *retainer* a dependant or servant (16c): cf. *retinue* below **3** to keep in custody (16c); to keep under control or in place.

Old French *retenir* produced **retinue** someone's attendants. Latin *retinere* produced **retention** and **retentive**, and is the ultimate source of **rein**. Latin *tenere* is the ancestor of TENOR*.

retort [Via French from medieval Latin *retorta*, literally 'twisted back', from Latin *retorquere*, *retort-* 'to twist again, to twist back', from *torquere* 'to twist'] A (glass) vessel with a long bent neck, used for heating and distilling liquids (17c), hence a large container or furnace used to heat minerals to extract metals, oil, etc.; a machine that sterilizes packaged food by heating (19c).

Latin *retorquere* also produced **retort** to turn back an insult, accusation, etc., hence (to give) a witty or angry reply. *Torquere* is the ancestor of TORTURE*.

retrieve [15c. Old French *retrover*, from *trover* 'to compose in verse, to invent', later 'to find', perhaps ultimately from Greek *tropos* 'turn'] **1** of a dog: to re-find game temporarily lost, to flush a bird for the second time (hence **retriever** any dog used to do so, –17c); to find and bring back a shot bird (19c), hence *retriever* a dog bred to do so **2** to recover or regain, specifically information, originally by investigation (16c), later from your own or a computer's memory **3** to save from being lost or destroyed (16c); to remedy a loss, error, etc. (17c).

Old French *trover* produced **trove** in **treasure trove** literally 'treasure found', and is related to **troubadour**. Greek *tropos* is the ancestor of **contrive**, **heliotrope** [with Greek *helios* 'sun'] a plant that turns to follow the sun's path, and **trope** [via Latin *tropus* 'figure of speech']. Related to **atropine** [named after Atropos, the Fate who cut the thread of life (whose name means 'inflexible'), from *trepein* 'to turn'] and to TROPHY*.

retrograde [ME. Latin *retrogradus*, from *retro* 'backwards' + *gradus* 'a step'] **1** originally of a planet: (apparently) going against the prevailing direction; to do so (16c) **2** to turn back or reverse (16c), hence inverse; reversed; pointing or moving backwards; to do so (17c) **3** tending to go back to an earlier time or condition (16c); to do so, to revert or decline (17c), hence **retro** (something) imitating or reviving a style etc. from the past (1970s).

Some senses of *retrograde* are shared by **regress** [ME, from Latin *regredi, regress-*, literally 'to walk back', from *gradi*: see DEGREE] originally meaning a return or re-entry, and **retrogress** [formed on the pattern of PROGRESS]: cf. *retrospect* (at PROS-PECT). Latin *retro* produced ARREAR*; *gradus* is the ancestor of DEGREE*.

review [15c. Obsolete French *reveue* 'inspection', from *revoir* 'to inspect', literally 'to see again', from Latin *revidere*, from *videre* 'to see'] **1** (to hold) an inspection of military or naval forces **2** to view, inspect, or examine again (16c), hence **(a)** to refer a case, sentence, etc. to a higher court or authority; its deliberations (17c) **(b)** the examination and correction of a book (largely replaced by **revision**); to carry this out (17–18c, outlived by **revise**, also ultimately from Latin *videre*) **(c)** a general survey, inspection, or examination (*in/under review*, 17c) **(d)** a criticism of a book, performance, film, etc. (17c); to write one; a periodical containing such pieces (18c).

French *reveue* evolved into *revue*, adopted for a theatrical entertainment consisting of a (satirical) review of current events, later of a series of skits and musical numbers (also Anglicized as *review*). French *revoir* appears in *au revoir* [literally 'to the seeing again']. Latin *videre* is the ancestor of VISION*.

revolve [15c. Latin *revolvere*, literally 'to turn or roll back', later 'to overturn', from *volvere* 'to roll'] The basic sense 'to (make something) turn in a circle or rotate on an axis' does not appear until the 16c, but is implied in senses such as 'to roll or move something by rolling', 'to wrap up a limb' (both 15–17c), 'to turn over in your mind' (15c), and in **revolution** a complete orbit (ME).

The later sense of Latin *revolvere* produced **revolt** (to rise in) a rebellion; to turn against, hence to turn away from in disgust, surviving mainly in **revolting** disgusting, and *revolution* originally 'alteration, change', now a period or instance of significant change, especially the overthrow of (an) authority by those it rules. Latin *volvere* is the ancestor of VAULT*.

reward [ME. From *rewarder*, the Anglo-Norman and Old Norman French form of Old French *regarder*, literally 'to consider fully', from *garder* 'to guard or judge': see WARD*, and cf. WALLOP*] **1** (to give) a payment or recompense; remuneration, wages, also a bonus (15–18c); a part of the kill given to a hound or hawk (15–17c), hence something given for effort or success (16c); money for catching a criminal or recovering something lost; to give these. Hence **rewarding** intended as a reward (17c); gratifying, satisfying, worthwhile **2** to heed, consider, or observe; consideration, attention, heed **3** estimation, worth. Replaced in senses 2 and 3 by **regard** [from Old French *regarder*], which came to mean **4** something heeded or taken into account (16c) **5** (to feel) respect or affection (16c), **regards** an expression of these (18c).

rheum [ME. Via Old French and late Latin from Greek *rheuma* 'bodily humour, flow', from *rhein* 'to flow'] A watery substance secreted by the mucous membranes, hence **1** (a mucous discharge caused by) a cold **2** (a flow of) any abnormal or harmful bodily humour (15c), hence **rheumatism** applied to various pains in the joints and muscles, once thought to be caused by such humours (17c).

Greek *rhein* is the ancestor of **catarrh** [via French and late Latin from Greek *katarrhein* 'to run down'], **haemorrhoid** [via Old French and Latin from Greek *haimorroides* 'bleeding piles', from *haima* 'blood' + *-roos* 'flowing'], **rheo-** to do with flow or (electric) current (*rheostat*), **rhyolite** [via Greek *rhuax* '(lava) stream'], and -**rrhoea** flow, (abnormal) discharge (*diarrhoea, logorrhoea*). Related to RHYTHM*.

rhythm [16c. French *rhythme* or medieval Latin *rithmus* from Latin *rhythmus*, from Greek *rhuthmos*. Related to RHEUM*] The pattern of stress in verse or, later, prose, hence a particular form of this (17c); a pattern of beats in music (18c); any regularly recurring pattern of events etc.

Medieval Latin *rithmici versus* 'rhythmic verse' was used for poetry based on the number of stresses, rather than the number of syllables, in a line, and, as this usually rhymed, *rhythm* briefly became synonymous with the noun **rhyme** [via French *rime* from medieval Latin *rithmus*: originally, and occasionally still, spelt **rime**: the spelling was changed to conform with Latin *rhythmus*] a verse with corresponding sounds at the end of lines, hence **1** (to have) such correspondence **2** to compose (scurrilous) rhymes.

rich [Old English *rīce*, later also from related Old French *riche*, ultimately of Celtic origin] **1** noble, powerful, strong (–16c); of a colour: strong and deep (ME); of a voice: strong and mellow (16c) **2** (the) wealthy, hence fit for them: **(a)** costly, splendid (ME) **(b)** containing plenty of a quality or of 'good' things (*rich food/soil rich in minerals*) **(c)** full, ample (16c); highly developed; highly amusing (18c); absurd, preposterous.

Rich produced **enrich** to make rich, especially to fertilize soil or improve food by adding vitamins etc., the place name **Richmond**, and the name **Richard**, whence **Pritchard**, **Rickert(s)**, **Rickwood**, and **Ritson**; descendants of the short form **Dick** include **Dicken(s)**, **Dixon**, **Digance**, and (via the variant **Hick**) **Eakin**, **Ickes**, and names beginning **Hig-**, **His-**, and **Hitch-**. Related to German **Reich**, to -**ric** in *bishopric*, and to the names **Eric** and **Frederick**.

rickets [17c. Origin uncertain, but associated by medical writers with Greek *rhakhitis*, literally 'inflammation of the spine', from *rhakhis* 'spine, ridge'] A disease that causes softening and deformation of the bones (17c). Hence **rickety** suffering from rickets, hence badly constructed, likely to collapse (18c).

Greek *rhakhitis* produced **rachitis** formerly the medical name of rickets (surviving mainly in **rachitic** to do with rickets); *rhakhis* fathered modern Latin *rachis*, adopted in botany and zoology for various spine- or ridge-like structures, including the main axis of a compound leaf and the shaft of a feather.

ride [Old English *ridan*] To sit on and control an animal, cycle, etc.; to travel like this or in a vehicle, hence **1** to move or be carried with a smooth, easy motion, hence **(a)** of a ship: to float buoyantly; to withstand a storm (16c), hence to survive trouble or pressure; to reduce the impact of a blow by yielding to it **(b)** an animal's or vehicle's motion (*a lively/smooth ride*, 1930s) **2** to go through on horseback (*ride the range*, ME), hence **(a)** **riding** a path, originally for riders, especially through woodland (partly replaced by 19c *ride*: cf. related ROAD) **(b)** of land: to be suitable for riding (*the course rides well*, 19c) **3** to have sex with a woman (ME, now coarse but once standard); this act (1950s) **4** to rest on a pivot (16c), hence to depend on **5** of a nightmare or witch: to sit on and use like a horse (16c), hence to oppress or harass **6** a journey or (pleasure) trip on an animal or in a vehicle you are not driving (18c), hence a lift in a vehicle; **for the ride** for fun, just as an observer (1960s, *US*) **7** something to ride: a horse (18c); a roundabout or roller-coaster (1930s, *US*); a motor vehicle (1930s, *N American slang*). Hence **rider (a)** someone who rides, originally a mounted warrior (ME, also as a surname, with the variant **Ryder**) **(b)** something added afterwards, specifically a clause or condition (17c).

rifle [ME. French *rifler* 'to plunder', also 'to graze or scratch', probably of Germanic origin] **1** to search someone's pockets or goods to rob them; to ransack or pillage; to search through vigorously and thoroughly (1960s) **2** to cut spiral grooves in a gun barrel (17c); these grooves; a gun having them (18c); a soldier or hunter armed with a rifle (19c).

French *rifler* may be one ancestor of *riffle* (at RUFFLE), and fathered French *rif* in *rif et raf* 'small bits of plunder', whence **riff and raff** everything, everybody, shortened to **riffraff** the poor, the rabble, also worthless items (in Scotland also as **scaff and raff**, **scaffraff**). *Scaff* [of unknown origin] originally meant food, later to eat voraciously, altered to **scoff**, partly by association with **scoff** food, a meal [Afrikaans *skof* from Dutch *schoft* 'a quarter of a day', hence one of the four daily meals]. **Raff** came to mean 'a large number of' (altered to **raft** under the influence of RAFT sense 2), and produced **raffish** (attractively) disreputable.

right [Old English *riht*] **1** the opposite of **left** [Old English *lyft*, originally 'weak']: (describing or towards) the side on the east when you face north, for most people the stronger and easier side to use, hence **(a)** (describing) political conservatives or their opinions (19c: from the arrangement in the French National Assembly of 1789, where the nobles sat on the President's right, the Commons sitting on the left) **(b)** (the position of) a sportsman who plays on the right side of the pitch (19c) **(c)** a blow with the right hand (19c) **2** the opposite of **wrong** [ME, originally 'bent, crooked, awry' (cf. sense 3): of Scandinavian origin]: perhaps from the idea of the right side as the 'correct' one to use: legally, morally, socially, or factually correct, hence **(a)** moral or legal grounds for having or doing something **(b)** to make correct, just, or fair (*right a wrong*); to restore or return to a proper state or position (17c) **(c)** true, genuine, utter (*Right Honourable/a right idiot*); quite, really; precisely (*right now*) **3** straight, direct, hence **(a)** a **right** (literally 'straight') **angle** (ME: cf. *rectangle* at REGIMENT) **(b)** **-right** in *forthright*, *upright*, etc. **4** in good health or spirits (*all right, not in his right mind*, 17c).

The idea of *right* 'good', *left* 'bad' is found in **adroit** [French *à droit* 'at or to the right'], AWKWARD, **cack-handed** left-handed, clumsy [from dialect **cack** 'excrement', from Old English *cac*], **dexterity** [Latin *dexter* 'right, right-hand', whence **ambidextrous**, literally 'right-handed on both sides'], French *gauche* [literally 'left, left-handed'], adopted meaning socially awkward, **gawky** [from **gawk(-handed)** 'left(-handed)', of unknown origin], **left-handed** ambiguous, doubtful (*left-handed compliment*), and in SINISTER. Straight 'good', curved 'bad' is also found in *bent* (at BEND), CROOK, PERVERT, and *rectitude* (at REGIMENT).

riot [ME. Old French *riote* (noun), *ri(h)oter* (verb), perhaps ultimately from Latin *rugire* 'to roar', whence also **rut** (to be in) an annual period of sexual excitement] (To have) a dissolute, debauched, or wildly extravagant lifestyle, hence **1** a noisy or unrestrained celebration; a disturbance arising from it; (an instance of) serious public disorder; to take part in this (18c), hence **Riot Act** (1715) read by a magistrate to order an unruly crowd to disperse, hence **read the riot act** to reprimand sternly (19c) **2** a hound's indiscriminate following of any scent, hence **run riot** to follow any scent (16c), to act without restraint **3** **riotous** extravagant, lavish, vivid (15c); *riot* a lavish or spectacular display (19c) **4** (to take part in) wild revelry (18c); an uproariously successful performance or show (*c.*1900); someone/something very entertaining or exciting.

rip [15c. Perhaps from Flemish *rippen*] To cut, pull, or tear away or out, apart, or open; to tear up (19c); to become torn; a split or tear. Hence **1** to swear or curse (18c); **rip (into)** to attack verbally (1940s) **2** to rush along (19c, *US*); a rapid rush, hence **(a)** to let something go without restraint (*let her rip*); **let rip** to let yourself go **(b)** **ripping** very fast (19c only), hence very good or exciting (slang, now dated) **3** to pull the **rip(ping) cord/line** a cord that lets gas out of a gas balloon (early 20c); **rip cord** that activates a parachute **4** to steal or rob (*c.*1900); **rip off** to embezzle, swindle, or overcharge (1970s); to copy or plagiarize; **rip-off** a swindle, an act of plagiarism.

   Possibly the same word as **rip** an area of rough water caused by conflicting tides or currents, whence **rip (current/tide)** a strong intermittent current flowing out from the shore. Flemish *rippen* is related to ROBE*.

riviera [18c. Italian, literally 'seashore', from Latin *ripa* 'bank'] The coast around Genoa, later applied to that between Marseilles and La Spezia, and then to any coastal region with a warm climate, good beaches, and fashionable resorts.

   Latin *ripa* produced **riparian**, **river**, and obsolete French *riveret* small stream, possibly the source of **rivulet**, although this may be from Italian *rivoletto*, ultimately from Latin *rivus* 'stream' (whence DERIVE*).

road [Old English *rād*: related to RIDE] **1** (a journey) riding on horseback (–17c, replaced by RIDE); a mounted expedition or attack (–17c), surviving in **inroad** a sudden attack (16c), later a forceful or gradual encroachment, and in the Scottish variant **raid** (15–16c, revived by Scott: see DOFF) **2** a sheltered stretch of water providing safe anchorage (ME) **3** a path or track (16c, but implied in Old English *streamrād* 'the course of a stream', *hwēolrād* 'wheeltrack', and poetic terms for the sea such as *seglrād* 'sail road' and *swanrād* 'swanroad'); one wide enough for vehicles and with a made-up surface, hence **(a)** a way, route, or course (16c) **(b) on the road** on the way, on tour, travelling (17c) **(c) (rail)road** a railway (18c, *US*) **(d)** an underground passage in a mine (19c) **(e) road(way)** the carriageway.

robe [ME. French, literally 'spoils', hence 'clothes taken as spoils', of Germanic origin] A long outer garment worn by both sexes in the Middle Ages, hence **1** a ceremonial robe, or one showing a person's rank, office, or profession **2** to dress (someone) in a robe: partly replaced by **enrobe** (16c), whence **enrober** a machine that covers centres with chocolate (early 20c) **3 (bath)robe** a dressing gown (19c, US) **4** a dressed skin used as a garment or blanket (19c, N American).

   Related to BEREAVE*, **rob**, and probably to RIP and RUBBISH*.

robot [1920s. Czech, from *robota* 'forced labour', used in Karel Čapek's play *R.U.R.* (Rossum's Universal Robots) for a mechanical person] A machine that performs tasks usually done by a person; one that does, or can be programmed to do, such work automatically; a person who works or obeys orders without thinking. Hence **robotics** the technology of making and using robots (1941, originally a science-fiction term, coined by the writer and biochemist Isaac Asimov).

Robo- and, increasingly, **-bot** have been used in names of automatic devices (*Robocop, dogbot*). The earliest, but short-lived, example was **robomb**, short for the equally short-lived **robot bomb** a pilotless aircraft with an explosive warhead used by the Germans in World War II, also called a **buzz bomb, doodlebug, flying bomb**, or a **V-I** (short for German *Vergeltungswaffe* 'reprisal weapon').

robust [16c. Via French from Latin *robustus* 'made of oak, firm, hard, solid', from *robur* 'oak, strength'] Sturdy; stout, thickset; vigorous, healthy, tough (17c), hence **1** needing physical strength **2** uncompromising, blunt, direct (18c) **3** able to cope with setbacks or unforeseen circumstances (18c) **4** of food, wine, etc.: full-flavoured, full-bodied (1960s).

The source of **robustious** big and strong; boisterous, noisy, whence, probably, **rumbustious** [perhaps by association with **rumble** in sense 'commotion, uproar', or with **rum(bullion)** '(a drink of) rum'], altered to **rumbunctious** and further to **rambunctious** (N American). Latin *robustus* produced **robusta** (beans or coffee from) a disease-resistant African plant; *robur* is the ancestor of **corroborate** [Latin *corroborare*, from *roborare* 'to strengthen', from *robur*], originally to make physically stronger.

roil [16c. Perhaps via Old French *ruiler* 'to mix mortar', from late Latin *regulare* 'to regulate': see RULE*] To make a liquid cloudy by stirring up sediment, hence to disorder, disturb, or excite; to annoy (18c, largely replaced by the variant **rile**).

roll [ME. Via Old French *ro(u)lle* (noun), *rol(l)er, rouler* (verb), from Latin *rotula* 'small wheel', from *rota* 'wheel'] **1** a scroll; an (official) document in this form; an (official) list, register, or catalogue, hence **(a)** to enter information or a name on one (–17c), outlived by **enrol** [ME, from Old French *enroller*, from *ro(u)lle*] **(b) rigmarole** [18c, alteration of obsolete *ragman roll* a list or catalogue (ME–17c), of unknown origin] **2** to form, or to be formed, into a cylinder or rounded shape; the thing formed (*roll of carpet*), hence **(a)** round a food item formed by wrapping pastry etc. round a filling (*sausage/Swiss roll*, 15c); cf. 19c **roly-poly (pudding)** and French *roulade* [from *ro(u)lle*] **(b)** a small loaf, shaped by rolling the dough (16c) **(c) (bank)roll** a roll of bank notes (19c); *bankroll* to finance a project (1920s, *US*) **3** to (make something) turn over and over, to revolve, hence **(a) roller** a revolving cylinder **(b)** to (make something) go forward by rolling or on wheels or rollers (16c) **(c)** of a wave: to flow with an undulating motion (hence *roller* a long swelling wave of land: to undulate) (*rolling hills*, 19c) **4** to turn over or writhe (15c), hence **(a)** to wallow or luxuriate, to have plenty of (*rolling in money*) **(b)** (to perform) a somersault (19c) **(c)** of an aircraft: (to perform) a sideways rotation (early 20c); to make an aircraft do so **5** to sail, later to walk, unsteadily (15c); such a motion (19c); of a car: to lean when cornering (early 20c) **6** to press or stretch with a roller or rollers (15c), hence **rolling mill/pin**, etc. **7** of a sound: to reverberate (16c), hence to pronounce with a reverberation or trill; an almost continuous reverberating sound (*drum roll*, 17c).

Old French *ro(u)lle* produced **rouleau** adopted for a cylindrical packet of gold coins, before evolving into *rôle* 'a roll of paper containing an actor's part', adopted for the part itself, hence a part someone/something plays, their function. Old French *roller* produced German *rollen* 'to roll, trill, or burble', whence **roller** applied to various birds that roll and twist in flight, also to a canary that trills, and **rollmop(s)** a rolled pickled herring fillet [with German *Mops* 'blockhead']. Latin *rotula* produced CONTROL; *rota* is the ancestor of ROTATE*.

romance [ME. Old French *roma(u)nz*, *roma(u)nt*, ultimately from Latin *Romanicus* 'in the Roman style', from *Romanus*, from *Roma* 'Rome'] The vernacular language of France, hence **1** (describing) those European languages descended from Latin **2** a vernacular tale of derring-do, chivalry, and courtly love; this genre; to recite one (15c), hence **(a)** a wildly exaggerated account or explanation (15c); wild exaggeration; to exaggerate or distort the truth (17c) **(b)** an imaginative tale of adventure and love, especially depicting love in an idealized or sentimental way (17c); such a book, play, film, etc.; this genre, hence a love affair; to woo (1940s), hence to court a potential client etc. (1960s, *US*) **(c)** a mysterious, exciting, sentimental, or nostalgic feeling or quality (17c).

Old French *roma(u)nt* produced **romantic** characteristic of or involving romance, specifically *Romantic* describing an artistic movement of the 18–19c that emphasized nature and the expression of feelings over classical form, hence **romanticism** (the style and theories of) this movement; **romanticize** to make or describe as romantic; to indulge in romantic thoughts. Latin *Roma*'s descendants include **Romanesque** a style of architecture combining Roman and Byzantine elements, **Romania**, once an outpost of the Roman Empire, and **Romeo**, an Italian name given to someone who had made a pilgrimage to Rome, adopted by Shakespeare for the hero of his play *Romeo and Juliet*, hence a romantic lover or (serial) seducer.

root [ME. Old Norse *rót*] The underground base of a plant or body part, hence **1** an origin or basis, hence **(a)** a number multiplied by itself (*square/cube root*, 15c) **(b)** **roots** social, ethnic, or cultural origins, especially producing an attachment to a place (1920s); of music: expressing a distinctive West Indian culture (1970s) **2** to implant deeply, to establish; to grow roots **3** **root out/up** to pull or dig up root and all (cf. *deracinate* and *eradicate* at RADICAL).

Relatives include **mangel-wurzel** [German *Mangoldwurzel*, from *Mangold* 'beet' + *Wurzel* 'root'], **rutabaga** [Swedish dialect *rotabagge*, literally 'baggy root'], and **wort** a (medicinal or edible) plant, surviving in plant names (*lungwort*, *St John's wort* at SAINT: see also *collard* at COLE), and the **wort** used in brewing [both Old English].

rose [Old English *rōse*, later also Old French *rose*, both from Latin *rosa*, from or related to Greek *rhōdon*] The plant or flower, originally referring to the wild rose but now usually to the cultivated double flower; a related or similar plant or flower; any plant with beautiful flowers (15c). Hence **1** (someone/something regarded as) a symbol of beauty or perfection, in early use often the Virgin Mary **2** a pinkish colour (ME); of this colour (16c), earlier as **roseate** [from Latin *roseus*, from *rosa*] or **rosy 3** the flower as a symbol of England (15c) or of the House, later the county, of York (a white rose) or of Lancaster (a red rose), hence **Wars of the Roses** between these houses for the English throne (the name may have been invented by, or derived from, Scott: see DOFF) **4** something resembling the flower, e.g. **(a)** the shape of one in plaster (15c); a circular mounting for a ceiling light (19c, also called **rosette** [French, literally 'little rose']) **(b)** now usually *rosette* an ornamental bunch of ribbons (17c) **(c) compass rose** a circular pattern showing the points of the compass (16c) **(d)** a perforated cap on a hose etc. (18c) **(e) rose window** a round window with tracery radiating out like flower petals (19c) **5** in phrases for favourable circumstances (*bed of roses, rose garden, coming up roses*, 16c) **6 under the rose** privately, in strict confidence [16c, probably a translation of German *unter der Rose*: legend says that Cupid bribed Harpocrates with a rose not to reveal Venus amours], now more familiar in the Latin form *sub rosa* (17c).

French *rose* produced *rosé* 'pink', adopted for a light red wine. Latin *rosa* produced **rosacea** a condition that reddens the face, **rosary** [via Latin *rosarium* 'rose garden'] (a string of beads used to count) a series of Roman Catholic prayers, and **roseola** a red rash. Descendants of Greek *rhôdon* include **rhododendron** [with *dendron* 'tree'], and the minerals **rhodium** (from its pinkish compounds) and **rhodonite** (from its pink crystals).

The name **Rose** is probably from the same Germanic element, meaning 'horse', that produced **Rosalind** and **Rosamund**. **Rosemary** the herb, later adopted as a name, is an alteration of *rosmarine* [ultimately from Latin *ros* 'dew' + *marinus* 'of the sea', from its mist of blue flowers].

rotate [15c. Latin *rotare* 'to go round', from *rota* 'wheel'] **1 (a) rotation** an alchemists' term for the transmutation of the four elements into each other (15c only) **(b)** to change or be changed in a recurring cycle (17c) **2** to (make something) turn around a centre or axis (19c, 16c in *rotation*).

Latin *rotare* produced Spanish *rodeo* a cattle round-up, later a competition of cowboy skills, *rotator* adopted for a muscle that turns a part of the body, later any device causing rotation, shortened to **rotor**, ROTUND*, and French *rouer* 'to break on the wheel', whence *roué* someone deserving this, hence a debauched man. Latin *rota* was adopted for a rotation of duties, a roster (cf. TURN*), and produced **barouche** [German *Barutsche* from Italian *biroccio*, ultimately from late Latin *birotus* 'two wheeled', although a barouche has four], ROLL*, **rotary**, and **rowel** [via Old French *roel(le)*, literally 'little wheel', whence *roulette*].

rotund [15c. Latin *rotundus*, from *rotare*: see ROTATE*] Circular, spherical, hence **1** plump, podgy (19c) **2** sonorous, rich (19c), also of style: inflated, grandiloquent: cf. **orotund** [alteration of Latin *ore rotundo* 'with a round mouth', from *os* 'mouth' (see OSCULATE*)] of speech: clear, resonant, imposing (18c); of style: grandiloquent, pretentious (19c).

Latin *rotundus* produced **prune** to trim a plant [via Old French *pro(o)ignier*, literally 'to cut in a rounded shape in front'], whence **preen** (influenced by obsolete *preen* 'a pin' [Old English *prēon*], from the idea of a bird 'stabbing' and tidying its plumage), **rotunda** [via Italian *rotonda (camera)* 'round (chamber)'], surnames including **Rounce** and **Rundle**, and Old French *ro(u)nd*, whence **round** and Old French *rondel* [literally 'small round'] adopted for a circle or circular object, later a kind of poem with a refrain, whence **roundel**, and **roundelay** a song with a refrain. *Rondeau* [a later form of *rondel*] was adopted for a similar poem, and produced Italian *rondo* a piece of music with a recurring theme.

rough [Old English *rūh*] Uneven, irregular; coarse in texture, hence **1** shaggy, unclipped; unfinished, unrefined, crude (ME), hence **(a)** uncouth (16c)

(b) approximate, preliminary (16c); **rough (out)** to produce a preliminary plan etc. (18c) **2** of land: uncultivated, hence wasteland, scrub (17c); in golf: the unmowed land off the fairway (early 20c) **3** harsh, severe, forceful, violent (ME), hence **(a)** loutish, rowdy; such a person (19c); of an area: inhabited by roughs **(b) rough up** to beat up (15c) **(c)** of the sea or weather: stormy, wild (15c) **(d)** the harsh or unpleasant part (*take the rough with the smooth*, 15c); **rough it, live rough** to live in harsh conditions (18c); harsh, unpleasant, unfair (19c) **(e)** of work: needing strength, manual (18c); heavy or dirty housework (1940s) **4** unwell, miserable, dejected (19c).

Old English *rūh* appears in place- and surnames as **Ro-**, **Rough-**, **Row-**, and **Ru-**, and probably produced **ruff** a decorative frill, later a ring of feathers, hair, etc. resembling one. Related to **gruff** [Dutch or Low German *grof*], originally meaning coarse-grained (*Scots*).

rouse [15c. Origin unknown: its early use in hunting and falconry suggests Anglo-Norman French ancestry] **1** of game: to rise from cover; to make it do so (16c) **2** of a hawk: to raise and shake its feathers (16c). Hence to (cause to) wake and get up (cf. REAR), hence **(a)** to stir or be stirred into action; to stir up emotions (*a rousing chorus*); to agitate or anger (19c) **(b)** in military use: the reveille (19c).

Roust to rouse or stir up, later to harass (N American) is probably an alteration of *rouse*. **Rouseabout** began as a dialect word for an energetic or wandering person: both it and **roustabout** are used for a (casual) labourer in various contexts.

route [ME. French, 'road', from Latin *rupta (via)*, literally 'broken (road)', from *ruptus* 'broken', from *rumpere*, *rupt-* 'to break'] A path or road, the course of (regular) travel from one place to another, hence **1** a regular course or way of doing something (18c, partly replaced by *routine* below) **2** a regular round to collect, deliver, or sell goods (19c, *N American*) **3** to mark a ticket for use on a particular route (19c); to send or direct by a certain route; to direct an electrical signal or transmission via a particular circuit etc. or to a particular location (1940s) **4 route march** a long training march for troops over a designated route (19c); any long tiring march **5** a numbered highway (*Route 66,* early 20c), hence **Route One** the most direct route (1960s); in football: a long high kick upfield (1980s).

French *route* appears in **en route** on the way, and produced **routine** and probably **rut** a wheel track. Descendants of Latin *ruptus* include **abrupt**, *bankrupt* (at BANK[2]), **corrupt**, **disrupt**, **erupt**, **interrupt**, **rupture**, and **rout** a (disorderly) band of people; a herd of animals [via Anglo-Norman French *rute* 'dispersed troop'], probably the same word as **rout** (to bring about) a disorderly retreat.

rove [15c. Probably of Scandinavian origin] To shoot arrows at random targets (–17c); to shoot at random or wide (16–17c), hence to diverge or digress; to wander aimlessly, hence **1 roving eye** a tendency to ogling or infidelity (17c) **2 roving** of an ambassador, reporter, etc.: travelling to different places to deal with events as they arise (1930s).

rub [ME. Perhaps from Low German *rubben*, of unknown origin] To press and move one thing against another vigorously; to clean, polish, or smooth by doing so. Hence **1 rub along** to get by with some difficulty (15c) **2 rubber** a hard brush, a cloth, stone, etc. (16c), later a soft pad (19c) for rubbing, polishing, etc. **3** to annoy (16c), now only in *rub (up) the wrong way* **4 rub off/out/away** to erase by rubbing (16c), hence *rubber* a substance made from latex, used to erase pencil marks (18c), later applied to similar substances or things made from it, including an eraser (*c*.1900) **5** of a bowl: to be diverted by a rough patch on the green (16c), hence such an impediment; a hindrance (*there's the rub*) **6 rub up** to brush up or refresh your knowledge of something (16c) **7** to chafe or abrade (19c).

Rubber a set of games, originally in bowls, may be the same word, although the derivation is not clear.

rubbish [ME. Anglo-French *rubbous*, probably from or related to Old French *robe* 'spoils': see ROBE*: probably related to **rubble**] Waste material, litter, refuse; worthless, contemptible (16c, obsolete by the mid 18c and replaced by **rubbishy**: revived *c*.1980); worthless material or articles (17c); absurd ideas, nonsense; to reject as worthless or nonsense, to criticize severely (1950s, *Australia and New Zealand*).

rubric [ME. (Via Old French from) Latin *rubrica terra* 'red earth or ochre', from *rubeus, ruber* 'red'] **1** text in distinct (originally red) lettering, hence **(a)** a printed explanation or instruction, originally for conducting a Christian service, now introducing an examination paper or question, hence a general rule or custom (19c) **(b)** a saint's name, written in red, in a church calendar (15c), hence a calendar of saints' days; **rubricate** to enter a saint in it (16c). Hence **red-letter day** a church festival or saint's day (18c); a happy or special day **(c)** a title or heading (15c); things gathered under a heading, a category (19c) **2** to write in red (15c, largely replaced by *rubricate*); written or printed in red **3** red ochre (15c) **4** containing or contained in a rubric (15c).

Descendants of Latin *rubeus* include **rubella** (from its red rash), the river **Rubicon** (from the surrounding red soil), **ruby**, and French *rouge* 'red', adopted for the cosmetic, and later for various polishing powders, originally ferric oxide (from its red colour).

rude [ME. French, from Latin *rudis* 'unworked, uncultivated'] **1** uneducated, ignorant, hence **(a)** not cultured, refined, or sophisticated **(b)** rough, harsh, unkind, hence **rude awakening** (17c) **(c)** ill-mannered (cf. *uncouth* at CAN[1], *ignorant* at IGNORE); indecent, lewd (1960s) **2** unworked, untreated; roughly made or done, hence **(a)** coarse or misshapen but big and strong (15c); of health: vigorous, robust (18c) **(b)** in an early or primitive state. Cf. CRUDE.

Latin *rudis* is the ancestor of **erudite** [via *erudire* 'to instruct', from *ex-* 'out of' + *rudis*] and of **rudiment** [Latin *rudimentum* 'a first attempt, a beginning'].

rue [Old English *hrēow* (noun), *hrēowan* (verb)] **1** sorrow, repentance, regret, hence to make someone feel remorse for a sin or regret an action (–15c); to repent (ME); to regret an action because of its consequences **2** pity, compassion (ME). Hence **rueful** sorrowful, remorseful, pitiable.

Old English *hrēowan* produced **ruth** sorrow, compassion, pity, surviving mainly in **ruthless**.

ruffle [ME. Origin unknown] To crease or wrinkle, to disturb a smooth surface or neat arrangement, hence **1** to make hair or feathers stick up irregularly (15c); of a bird: to raise its feathers to display or in anger (17c), hence **ruffle someone's**

feathers to vex or annoy them **2** to search or rummage through (15–16c, cf. *rifle*); to flick through the pages of a book (17c); to shuffle cards by flicking two piles together so that they overlap (the 17c senses largely replaced by *riffle* below) **3** to rise and fall irregularly or in folds (16c); to gather into folds or pleats (17c); a decorative frill.

Riffle may be a variant of *ruffle*, or may be partly from Old French *rifler* (see RIFLE*), influenced by **ripple** [of unknown origin]: it originally meant a slight scratch, or to caress one another, later **1** to ripple (*N American*); a patch of ripples, hence, perhaps, **riff** a repeated musical phrase **2** *ruffle* sense 2.

rule [ME. Old French *reule* (noun), *reuler* (verb), from late Latin *regulare*, from Latin *regula* 'straight stick, measuring rod, standard'] **1** a governing principle, regulation, or maxim, hence **(a) Rule** the code of a religious order; **rule(s)** a code of practice or set of regulations **(b)** a dominant custom, habit, or fact; the normal state of things (*as a rule*) **2** to guide or control; to exercise authority; to make a formal or judicial decision (15c); (also **ruling**) a judicial decision to deal with a particular case or circumstance **3** control, government, hence **misrule** bad government, disorder, chaos, anarchy; **unruly** disorderly, disobedient **4** a rod: **(a)** (more commonly **ruler**) a piece of wood etc. marked with units of length and used to measure or draw straight lines; *rule* to mark paper etc. with parallel straight lines; to make a straight line (as if) with a ruler (16c) **(b)** a metal strip for separating columns of type, headings, etc., or to keep type level and in place (17c) **(c)** a printer's term for a short or long dash used in punctuation (17c).

Latin *regula* produced RAIL*, **regular** conforming to a rule, pattern, or standard, **regulate** to control or govern by rules, whence **regulation** and **regulo** (a proprietary name for) a thermostatic control for a gas oven, hence its temperature setting. Related to REGAL* and REGIMENT*.

rummage [15c. Old French *arrumage*, from *arrumer* 'to stow', from *run* 'ship's hold', of Germanic origin and related to **room**] The stowing of goods in a ship's hold (–17c); to stow them (–18c), hence **1** to rearrange them (16c); to disarrange, especially by searching, hence **(a)** to ransack (17c); such a search (18c) **(b)** (to make) a thorough search (17c), now one by customs officials (19c) **2** miscellaneous articles, lumber, rubbish (16c), hence **rummage goods** out-of-date goods (19c); **rummage sale** a sale of these, later a jumble sale.

ruse [15c. Old French, from *ruser* 'to drive back', from Latin *recusare* 'to reject or refuse', from *causari* 'to dispute', from *causa* CAUSE*] The doubling back of a hunted animal to evade capture (15c only), hence a trick or plot (16c).

Old French *ruser* produced **rush** to dash, hurry. Latin *recusare* is the ancestor of **recuse** to reject (hence **recusant** a religious dissenter), and probably of **refuse** [influenced by Latin *refutare* 'to repel' (from *futare* 'to beat') whence **refute**].

russet [ME. Old French *ro(u)sset* 'reddish', from *rous* 'red', ultimately from Latin *russus*] A kind of (reddish-brown) woollen cloth worn by country people, hence **1** made of or clad in this (15c); rustic, homely (16c) **2** reddish brown (15c) **3** a variety of apple or potato, formerly also pear, with a reddish-brown skin (18c).

Old French *rous* produced some instances of the name **Rouse** someone with red hair, whence **Russel**, before evolving into French *roux*, adopted for a mixture of flour and fat browned and used to thicken sauces. Latin *russus* is the ancestor of French *rissole* [Old French *ruissole*, ultimately from late Latin *russeolus* 'reddish'].

rustic [ME. Latin *rusticus*, from *rus, ruris* 'the country'] From, found in, or to do with, the country, hence **1** a country-dweller, a peasant (15c), hence **(a)** rough, uneducated, unsophisticated (16c): cf. CHURL* **(b)** living or working in the country (17c) **2** plain, simple (16c); made in a rough or simple style, specifically **(a)** made of untrimmed branches **(b)** (made of) rough or pitted masonry.

Latin *rusticus* produced **roister** [via French *rustre* 'ruffian'] and **rusticate 1** to imbue with or adopt country ways or a rustic style; to settle in the country **2** to suspend temporarily from university as a punishment (from the idea of sending back to the country). Latin *rus* is the ancestor of **rural**.

rustle [ME. Probably an imitation of the sound] To make or, later, cause something to make a series of soft crackling sounds; to (make something) move with such a sound (16c). Hence **1** this sound (18c) **2** to move something quickly (19c); **rustle up** to produce or acquire something quickly when needed; to round up cattle; *rustle* to round up cattle and steal them (19c, *US*).

S

sack [Old English *sacc* via Latin *saccus* from Greek *sakkos*, of Semitic origin] A large strong bag, hence **1** later **sackcloth**: coarse fabric used to make sacks, hence **sackcloth and ashes** a show of mourning or repentance: in biblical times mourners and penitents wore sackcloth garments and sprinkled ash on their heads, hence **Ash Wednesday** the first day of the penitential period of Lent **2** a sack and its contents (ME) **3** a woman's loose dress (16c) **4** a hammock (19c), later a bed, now mainly in *hit/in the sack* (*US*) **5 the sack** dismissal from your job (19c); *sack* to dismiss someone: a phrase similar to *get the sack* existed in 17c France, and perhaps referred to a workman's toolbag; when dismissed he would get it and go **6** a paper bag (*c.*1900, *US*).

Latin *saccus* fathered French *sac*, adopted for a baglike cavity (whence *sachet*, literally a small sack), and **sack** to plunder [French *mettre à sac* 'to put in a sack', from Italian *far il sacco*]. Latin *saccus* produced **satchel** [via *saccellus* 'little sack'].

sacrifice [ME. French, from Latin *sacrificium*, ultimately from *sacer* 'holy'] To make an offering to a god by killing a person or animal, or by giving up something valuable; this act; what is offered, hence **1** Christ's giving up his life at his crucifixion; the Eucharist symbolizing this (16c) **2** to devote your life, time, etc. to a deity, person, or cause; this action; **self-sacrifice** the surrender of your own desires and needs for someone else's benefit (19c); **the supreme sacrifice** dying for your country (World War I) **3** to give up, or the surrender of, something desirable for something more worthy or important (16c); what is sacrificed **4** to allow someone/something to be killed, hurt, or damaged for a cause or your own advantage (18c); to kill an experimental animal for the sake of scientific knowledge (*c.*1900) **5** to sell, or the sale of, something at a loss to get rid of it or attract trade (19c).

Descendants of Latin *sacer* include EXECRABLE*, **sacrilege** [via French from Latin *sacrilegium* 'the stealing of sacred objects'], **sacristy** a room where sacred objects are kept [Latin *sacrista*, whence also **sacristan** the person responsible for it, and **sexton** the person who looks after a church, often acting as bell-ringer and gravedigger, hence **sexton beetle** that buries carrion], **sacrosanct** [Latin *sacrosanctus* 'consecrated with sacred rites', from *sacrum* 'sacred (rite)' + *sancire* 'to sanctify: see SANCTION], and **sacrum** the bone forming the back of the pelvis [Latin *os sacrum* 'sacred bone', because the soul was thought to reside there]. Related to SANCTION*.

sad [Old English *sǣd*: related to *sate* (at SATISFY)] **1** satisfied, sated, weary of (–15c) **2** firm, strong, steadfast, constant (ME–17c); trustworthy; dignified, grave, serious, hence (combining 1 and 2) sorrowful, mournful, miserable (ME); causing sorrow, regrettable, shameful; pitiable, pathetic, hence **(a) sad sack** a pathetically inept person [1940s, *US*, the name of an inept G.I. in cartoons: said to be short for *sad sack of shit*] **(b) saddo** a pathetic or boring person, especially a nerd (1990s).

safe [ME. Old French *sauf*, from Latin *salvus*] **1** uninjured, unharmed (*safe and sound*); healthy (–16c) **2** delivered from sin (–17c) **3** secure, not likely to be harmed or lost; offering security or protection (*safe conduct/house*); unable to escape or do harm (16c) **4** not risky or dangerous (15c) **5** trustworthy, dependable (17c); convincing, hence **unsafe** of a verdict or conviction: based on unreliable evidence **6** to make safe or secure (17c, rare thereafter until revived in the 1940s).

Latin *salvus* produced SAGE*, **saviour** originally referring to saving from sin and to Christ as the one who does so, SALVAGE*, **salvation**, and **salver** [from French *salve* 'tray for presenting something to the king', from Spanish *salva* 'testing food, tray on which tested food was presented', from *salvar* 'to make safe'], **salvo** a simultaneous discharge of weapons in battle or as a salute [via Italian and French from Latin greeting *salve!*, literally 'be well!'], **save** and **saving** meaning 'except', and **save** to make or keep safe, to keep for future use, a container for doing so (now spelt *safe*). Related to SALUTE*.

saga [18c. Old Norse and Icelandic] An epic narrative in Old Norse, especially one based on Icelandic and Norwegian history and the lives of kings, hence an epic legend handed down orally (19c); a novel or series of novels following the lives of a family or community over several generations; (an account of) a long or convoluted series of events.

Related to **saw** [Old English *sagu*] a saying or speech (–17c), hence a pithy saying, a maxim, and to **say**.

sage [ME. French *sauge* from Latin *salvia* 'healing plant', from *salvus* 'uninjured, healthy, healed'] Any plant of the genus *Salvia*, specifically a greyish-green herb formerly much used in medicine, now mainly in cookery, hence applied to various similar or related plants (15c); **sage (brush/bush)** (an area covered by) a kind of artemisia with greyish downy leaves (19c, *US*).

Latin *salvia* is now usually applied to an ornamental member of the genus. Latin *salvus* is the ancestor of SAFE*.

saint [Old English *sanct* and Old French *seint, saint*, both from Latin *sanctus* 'holy', from *sancire* 'to consecrate': see SANCTION*] (The title of) an exceptionally holy person considered to be worthy of veneration by the Christian church, also added to things connected with God or Christ (*St Cross, St Sophia* at SOPHIST). Hence **1 patron saint** one regarded as the special guardian of a country, trade, etc. (ME) **2** one of God's chosen people (ME), adopted by various more or less Christian sects for their members (16c); **Latter-Day Saints** the Mormons (19c) **3** a good person; one with exemplary compassion and patience (ME) **4 saint's day** on which a particular saint is celebrated by the Church (15c); the festival of the saint you were named after (18c).

Saints are important in Roman Catholic worship, and before the Reformation their names were part of everyday language and often given to children (Protestants preferred biblical names: see also FAITH). Many churches were dedicated to saints and gave their names to their surroundings, and such names could be transferred, e.g. *St Kilda wren*, the surname **Sinclair** from either of two places in France named after St Clare. Plants were named after saints because they were beneficial or because they bloomed around the saint's day: (**St John's wort**, long used as an antidepressant, flowers around 24 June, the feast of John the Baptist). Diseases were named after saints believed to cure them (*St Vitus' dance*). Other things were named after a patron saint: French *gâteau St Honoré* after the patron saint of pastry-cooks; **St Elmo's fire** a ball of light sometimes seen on a ship, after the patron saint of sailors (also called **corposant** [via Spanish or Portuguese from Latin *corpos sanctum* 'holy body', or *corpus sancti* 'saint's body']), or from the saint's martyrdom, e.g. **Catherine wheel** because St Catherine was broken on the wheel.

sake [Old English *sacu*: related to FORSAKE, RANSACK*, and SEEK*] **1** strife, contention; a legal case or action (–ME); (grounds for) an accusation (ME–15c) **2** guilt, sin, (a) crime (–15c) **3 for the sake of, for someone's/something's sake** out of consideration for, because of your regard for or interest in (ME); for the purpose of; in order to obtain or preserve (this sense may be from a related Old Norse word); also in oaths (*for God's/pity's sake*). Hence **keepsake** something given or kept in remembrance (19c); **namesake** a person with the same name as another (17c, perhaps from the idea of being connected 'for the name's sake').

salad [15c. Via French from Provençal *salada*, ultimately from Latin *sal* 'salt'] A mixture of raw vegetables and leaves, often with other (cold) ingredients, hence **1** (describing) a vegetable or herb that can be eaten raw **2 salad days** a time of youthful inexperience [1606, from Shakespeare's *Antony and Cleopatra* I v 73 'My salad days, when I was green in judgement, cold in blood'] **3** a mixture (*fruit salad*, 17c).

Latin *sal* appears in the names of some medicinal salts (*sal volatile* at VOLATILE), and is the ancestor of *cellar* in **salt cellar** [obsolete *saler* from Old French *salier* 'salt box'], Italian **salami**, **salary** [via Latin *salarium* a soldier's salt money], **saline, saltpetre** [via Old French from medieval Latin *salpetrae* 'salt of rock' (i.e. found as an incrustation), from *petra* 'rock': see PETRIFY*], SAUCE*, and **taramasalata** [from Greek *taramas* 'preserved roe' (from Turkish) + *salata* 'salad'].

salient [16c. Latin *salire* 'to leap'] **1** of an animal in heraldry: having the forelegs raised as if leaping **2** leaping, jumping (17c); in zoology: adapted for leaping; of water: rushing upwards **3** of an angle: pointing outwards (17c), hence **(a)** of a fortification: having such angles; such an angle or part (19c) **(b)** sticking up or out (18c); prominent, noticeable; **salient point** an important factor **(c)** a spur of land, especially one that juts out into enemy territory (19c).

Latin *salire* is the ancestor of **assail** and **assault** [both via medieval Latin *assalire* 'to jump on'], DESULTORY, **exult** originally to jump for joy [via French from Latin *exsalire* 'to leap up'], INSULT, **resilient** [Latin *resilire*, literally 'to spring back'], **result** [Latin *resultare* 'to spring back, to reverberate'], **salacious, sally** originally (to make) a sudden attack from a besieged place, French *sauté* [from French *sauter* 'to jump', from the idea of food jumping about in the hot fat], and **somersault** [via French from Old Provençal *sobresaut*, from *sobre* (from Latin *supra* 'above') + *saut* 'a leap']. Latin *supra* is a form of *super* (see SUPERANNUATED*), and produced Italian **soprano**.

salon [17c. French, from Italian *salone* 'large room, hall', from *sala* 'hall'] A reception room in a large house, hence **1** (a gathering in) one belonging to a (Parisian) lady of fashion (19c) **2** a commercial establishment where hairdressers, beauticians, etc. work (*c*.1910).

The Anglicized form **saloon** was later used for various public rooms, sometimes with a suggestion of gentility: in the US it meant a public house, in the UK the **saloon (bar)** was more comfortable and expensive than the public bar. A **saloon (car)** is one with an enclosed body and no partition between the driver and passengers (hence more 'public'): its N American name, **sedan**, presumably comes from **sedan chair** an enclosed chair carried by porters in the 17–18c [perhaps ultimately from Latin *sedes* 'seat'].

salt [Old English *s(e)alt* (noun), *s(e)altan* (verb)] Sodium chloride, hence **1** to do with or containing it (*salt marsh/pan*) **2** to preserve with it (cf. CORN), hence **salt away** to put away, to save (19c) **3** to season with it, hence **(a)** to make piquant, poignant, or more interesting (16c); the quality that does so, hence **salty** of conversation etc.: spicy, racy (19c) **(b)** to put ore, gold dust, etc. into a mine to make it seem more promising (19c); to add to an invoice etc. fraudulently **4** to sprinkle or strew with salt (ME) **5** a salt cellar (ME), hence **below the salt** seated further from the head of the table than the salt cellar, of low social standing. Hence something resembling salt, especially a solid obtained by evaporation (like salt from sea water), and, later, having a distinct taste (ME), hence **(a)** **salts** a crystalline compound used as a medicine, cosmetic, etc. (*Epsom/smelling salts*, 18c) **(b)** a crystalline compound formed by the neutralization of an acid with a (metallic) base (18c): cf. *sal* (at SALAD).

Because of its preservative qualities salt was highly valued in the ancient world: it was used in religious rites (see the Bible, Leviticus 2:13), Roman soldiers were paid in it (hence **worth your salt** efficient, capable) or given money to buy it (see *salary* at SALAD), and Christ described his disciples as **the salt of the earth** to emphasize their important role (Matthew 5:13): the phrase was taken to mean 'the best', hence the aristocracy or the wealthy, now a decent, honest person.

Old English *s(e)alt* appears in names as **Sal-** or **Salt-**, usually referring to a place where salt was made or to a salt maker, and is related to **silt** and **souse**.

salute [ME. Latin *salutare*, from *salus* 'health, welfare', later 'a spoken or written wish for your good health, a greeting': cf. *salvo* (at SAFE)] To greet (respectfully), hence **1** such a greeting; a formal or ceremonial sign of respect, such as the raising of flags, firing of guns, etc. (17c) **2** to express respect for formally, to honour or praise (*we salute your courage*, 16c).

Latin *salus* is the ancestor of **salubrious** good for the health, hence of a place: pleasant, decent, of **salutary** beneficial, useful (*salutary experience*), and of **salutatory** (describing or to do with) a welcoming address. Related to SAFE*.

salvage [17c. French, via medieval Latin *salvagium* from Latin *salvare*: see SAFE*] Compensation paid to those who have saved a ship or its cargo from destruction; the action of saving a ship etc. (18c), hence **1** property salvaged (18c) **2** to save a ship etc. (19c, replacing the back-formation **salve**); this action; the saving and collection of waste material for recycling (World War I); to do so (World War II); recyclable waste.

sanction [15c. French, from Latin *sancire, sanct-* 'to make sacred or inviolable'] **1** a law, an (ecclesiastical) decree **2** a solemn oath (17c); (what gives) its binding force. Hence **3** the enforcement of a law (17c); a penalty for breaking it, later also a reward for obeying it, hence **(a)** the considerations that encourage you to comply with a law or custom **(b)** to support a law by rewards and penalties (18c) **(c) sanctions** military or economic actions aimed at making a state etc. comply with an international agreement (*c*.1920) **4** the act of making something legally binding (17c); confirmation or ratification of a law; to do so (18c) **5** authorization for an action (18c), hence **(a)** approval; to allow, tolerate, or accept **(b)** in military intelligence: permission to kill someone (1980s).

Descendants of Latin *sancire* include *sacrosanct* (at SACRIFICE), SAINT, **sanctify**, **sanctimonious** holy, now only pretending holiness or piety, and SANCTUARY*.

sanctuary [ME. Via Anglo-Norman and Old French from Latin *sanctuarium*, from *sanctus* 'holy', from *sancire*: see SANCTION*] A holy place; (the most holy part of) a place of worship, hence a church etc. in which, formerly, a fugitive or debtor could not be arrested; immunity from arrest or punishment by taking refuge in one; (a place of) refuge or shelter, hence a place where animals and plants are protected (19c).

Sanctum [neuter of Latin *sanctus*] and **sanctum sanctorum** [Latin, 'holy of holies'] trod a somewhat similar path from 'holy place or shrine in a church' to 'refuge from disturbance or intrusion, a private room or study'.

sanguine [ME. Via Old French from Latin *sanguineus* 'bloody', from *sanguis* 'blood'] **1** blood-red (surviving in heraldry and in the names of animals and plants) **2** to do with, consisting of, or containing blood (15c); causing or delighting in bloodshed (18c, outlived by **sanguinary**) **3** having blood as the predominant humour (15c, see HUMOUR), hence confident, optimistic (16c).

Latin *sanguis* fathered French *sang*, appearing in *sang-froid*, literally 'cold blood', hence coolness, self-possession, and Spanish *sangre* 'blood', whence *sangria*, literally 'bleeding', hence the red-wine mixture (the altered form **sangaree** had been used earlier for similar spiced drinks). **Blue blood** 'aristocratic descent' is a translation of Spanish *sangre azul*, said of aristocratic Castilian families claiming to have no Moorish or Jewish blood (probably from the blue veins easily seen in fair-skinned people).

sanity [15c. Latin *sanitas*, from *sanus* 'healthy'] Good physical health (15c, now rare); mental health (17c).

Latin *sanitas* produced **sanitary**, whence **sanitation** and **sanitize** to make sanitary or hygienic, later to make or present as less unpleasant (*US*). Latin *sanus* produced **sainfoin** [obsolete French *saintfoin* from Latin *sanum foenum* 'healthy hay', from its medicinal properties] and **sanatorium** [via Latin *sanare* 'to heal']: the US form, **sanitarium**, is from *sanitas*. Latin *insanus*, literally 'unhealthy', always referred to mental health, as have its offspring, **insane** and **insanity**: this influenced **sane**, where the sense 'physically healthy' has always been rare.

sap [Old English *saep*] The juice in plant stems, hence **1** the younger, softer wood between the heartwood and the bark (ME, now usually **sapwood**), hence **saphead, sapskull** (both 18c) a simpleton, shortened to *sap* (19c) **2 sapling** a young tree (ME), whence *sap* a club or cosh, originally one made from a sapling (19c, US); to beat with one (1920s) **3** vigour, vitality (16c) **4** to drain of sap (18c).

satellite [16c. (French, from) Latin *satelles*] An (obsequious) underling, hence **1** a celestial object that orbits a larger one (17c); an artificial object placed in orbit round the earth etc. (1930s), hence **satellite (broadcasting/navigation/television)** using signals transmitted via such a satellite (1960s) **2** something linked with or close to something larger (18c); a country, State, town, or community dependent on another (19c) **3** a computer (terminal) away from but linked with another (1960s).

satire [15c. Latin *satira* 'a verse dealing with a variety of subjects', from *satura* 'mixture, medley', from *satur* 'full' (ancestor of **saturate**). Related to SATISFY*] A composition, originally in verse, ridiculing an individual's or society's vices (15c); this genre; the use of sarcasm, irony, etc. in this way (17c). Associated with, and originally spelt, **satyr** a lustful woodland god in Greek or Roman mythology [ME, ultimately from Greek *saturos*], partly because of the ancient Greek **satyr play** ridiculing a mythological subject, with a chorus dressed as satyrs.

satisfy [15c. Via Old French from Latin *satisfacere*, from *satis* 'enough'] **1** to fulfil an obligation or pay a debt; to make reparation or atone for (–18c), earlier and surviving in **satisfaction** penance, atonement, and in **demand satisfaction** to challenge someone who has offended you to a duel (17c) **2** to fulfil or comply with a request or demand; to meet someone's expectations, needs, or desires; **be satisfied** to be content with what is supplied; **satisfactory** acceptable, (just) enough or good enough (17c) **3** to resolve a doubt or difficulty; to provide someone with enough proof to convince them.

Descendants of Latin *satis* include ASSET, **insatiable**, and **satiate** to satisfy hunger or some other desire completely, later to excess, which encouraged *sade* [Old English *sadian*: related to SAD] to change to **sate** (17c). Related to SATIRE*.

saturnine [ME. Via French or medieval Latin from Latin *saturnus* 'Saturn', the Roman god of agriculture or the planet named after him] Born under the influence of the planet, associated by astrologers with the metal lead and with slowness and gloom, hence **1** being or looking gloomy **2** to do with lead (17c); caused by or suffering from lead poisoning (19c).

Latin *Saturnus* produced *Saturday* (at THUNDER) and **Saturnalia** the Roman festival of Saturn and the winter solstice, celebrated with feasting and unrestrained revelry (the precursor of Christmas), hence a wild celebration.

sauce [ME. Old French, ultimately from Latin *salsus* 'salted', from *sal*: see SALT*] Any condiment eaten with meat or fish; a thick liquid that adds moisture and flavour to food; to season or serve with sauce. Hence **1** to add flavour, piquancy, or excitement (15c); something that does so, hence **saucy** flavoured with sauce, savoury, piquant (16c), hence mildly titillating; impertinent, (endearingly) cheeky, hence *sauce* an impertinent person; impertinence (19c); to speak insolently to someone, to answer them back (19c). **Sassy** and **sass** (verb) are N American variants (19c) **2** **saucepan**, originally a small skillet for making sauces (17c) **3** **the sauce** alcoholic liquor (1940s, *US*); **sauced** drunk.

Old French *sauce* produced **saucer** originally a small dish for condiments or sauces, and **sausage**. Latin *salsus* is the ancestor of Spanish *salsa* a spicy sauce, extended in Latin American Spanish to a kind of dance or its music.

saunter [ME. Origin unknown] To muse or talk idly (–16c); to wander aimlessly (17c), hence (to take) a leisurely walk; (to go for) a stroll.

savage [ME. French *sauvage* from late Latin *salvaticus*, from Latin *silvaticus* 'of woodland, wild' from *silva* 'a wood'] **1** undomesticated, uncultivated, wild; (someone considered to be) primitive or barely civilized (15c, now offensive) **2** bold, courageous, later reckless, ungovernable (–15c). Hence (to some extent combining 1 and 2) ferocious, cruel, hence **(a)** to act cruelly (16–17c); to treat or criticize cruelly (18c); of an animal: to attack ferociously (19c) **(b)** a violent or cruel person (17c); a fierce animal (–19c); a bad-tempered horse (19c).

Descendants of Latin *silva* include **sylvan** (a person, animal, etc.) living in or belonging to woodland, **sylviculture** the cultivation of woods, and the names **Silas** [a shortening of **Silvanus**, the Roman god of the woods], **Sylvester**, **Sylvia**, and **Transylvania** literally 'beyond the woods'.

savour [ME. Old French, from Latin *sapor*, from *sapere* 'to have or perceive a taste, to be wise'] **1** relish, delight, satisfaction; to enjoy or appreciate **2** a (distinctive) taste or, later, smell: cf. FLAVOUR), hence **(a)** to have (an agreeable) one; (to have) a pleasant or attractive quality; an essential virtue or quality (see the Bible, Matthew 5:13). Hence **savoury** tasty, appetizing; pleasant, acceptable; **unsavoury** unpleasant, (morally) objectionable **(b)** to show traces of; a slight trace (18c) **(c)** to flavour with salt or spice (–17c), hence *savoury* salty, spicy, piquant (17c); a light, savoury dish.

Latin *sapere* is the ancestor of **sage** wise, a wise person, **sapid** tasty, palatable [Latin *sapidus*, whence also **insipid**], **sapient** wise; in anthropology: to do with modern man, *homo sapiens*, French *savant* (literally 'knowing') a learned person, now often in *idiot savant* someone with psychiatric or learning difficulties but with an exceptional talent, French *savoir faire* literally 'to know how to do', and **savvy** [Black or pidgin English, based on Spanish *sabe (usted)* '(you) know', from *saber* 'to know'] to know or understand; common sense, shrewdness; shrewd, knowledgeable.

saw [Old English *saga*] The cutting tool; to use or cut something with one (ME); to (make something) move to and fro like a saw (18c).

Saw produced the surname **Sawyer**, and **see-saw** originally a sawyers' chant representing the saw's motion (whence the nursery rhyme *See saw, Margery Daw*), hence (moving with) a to-and-fro or up-and-down motion; the child's toy, a teeter-totter. Related to SAXON*, **scythe**, and **sedge** [Old English *secg*] a plant with tapering leaves like a handsaw.

Saxon [ME. Via French from late Latin *Saxones* (plural), from Greek, ultimately of Germanic origin] A member of a N German people who began to spread west in the fifth century AD; one who settled in England; their language. These settlers became described as **Anglo-Saxons** (to distinguish them from the continental Saxons, later called **Old Saxons**); this term was stretched to include all the Germanic settlers (Angles, Saxons, Frisians, and Jutes) and also used for Old English (18c).

Hence **1 (Anglo-)Saxon** (describing) a person of English or British descent (19c); an English person as distinct from a Scots, Irish, or Welsh one; a Lowland as opposed to a Highland Scot (cf. *Sassenach* below) **2** the English language (19c); plain, robust, or coarse English (1920s, *US*) **3** in place names such as **Saxby, Saxton, Pensax**, and the less obvious **Sixpenny Handley**, pinpointing Saxons in areas mainly populated by other folk.

Said to be related to Old English *seax*, whence **sax** a (Saxon) knife, sword, or dagger, now a tool for trimming slates: an imaginative reconstruction of a Saxon sword appears on the coats of arms of **Essex, Middlesex, Sussex**, and **Wessex**, the homes of the East, Middle, South and West Saxons respectively. The continental Saxons gave their name to **Saxony**, whence (the dye producing) **saxe blue** [from the French form of Saxony]; the German form *Sachsen* produced the surname **Sachs**, whose variant, **Sax**, appears in **saxophone** [invented by the Belgian instrument maker Adolphe Sax]. Latin *Saxones* produced Gaelic *Sasunnoch* and Irish *Sasanach*, whence **Sassenach** an English person, not 'one of us'.

scab [ME. Old Norse *skabb*] A skin disease causing pustules or scales (–18c), hence **1** a disease of sheep or cattle, now one resembling mange (partly by association with **scabies** [Latin, from *scabere* 'to scratch']); a fungal disease of plants (18c) **2** the crust that forms on a wound or pustule when healing; to encrust with scabs (17c); to form a scab (18c) **3** mean, nasty, contemptible (replaced by 18c **scabby** except in Scots: cf. *scurvy* at SCURF and *shabby* below); a mean, nasty person (16c); a strike-breaker (18c); to be one (19c).

Perhaps influencing, or influenced by, **blackleg 1** a disease of cattle and sheep that makes the flesh of their legs go black and die **2** a swindler, especially a dishonest bookmaker (said to be from the long black boots bookmakers used to wear), hence to work during a strike, cheating workers of their traditional weapon; someone who does so, hence **black** of work or goods: handled by blackleg labour and hence boycotted by trade union members; to declare something black.

Scab largely replaced related **shab** [Old English *sceabb*], which survives mainly in **shabby** covered in scabs; worn out, threadbare, scruffy, also mean, inconsiderate, unfair. Latin *scabere* produced **scabious** [medieval Latin *scabiosa (herba)*] a plant once used to treat skin disease. Related to **scabrous** [via French or late Latin from Latin *scaber* 'scurfy, scaly'] harsh, unmusical (16–17c); rough to the touch, later risky, risqué; scandalous, obscene.

scaffold [ME. Old French *(e)schaffaut*, earlier *escadafaut*, ultimately from the same unrecorded Latin word as **catafalque**] A platform: **1** a temporary one used by builders, decorators, etc., hence **scaffolding** a system of such platforms and poles; *scaffold* to put scaffolding round a building **2** a raised platform on which a (mystery) play is performed or on which someone is exposed to view (15–17c); one on which a criminal is executed (16c); **the scaffold** execution **3** any supporting platform or framework (16c).

scale [ME. Latin *scala*: the verb via French *escaler* or medieval Latin *scalare*] A ladder (–19c); a rung (–17c), hence **1** to climb up or over, originally using ladders **2** a series of marks representing units of measurement; one that shows the relationship between distances on a map and those on the ground; this relationship (17c); the relative size of a model, diagram, etc. to the thing it represents, hence relative magnitude, length etc. (*large/small scale*) **3** a series of musical notes ascending or descending at fixed intervals (16c); any graduated series (17c), hence **(a) scale up/down** to increase/decrease according to a scale (18c, *US*) **(b)** a graduated table of prices, charges (18c), or wages (1920s).

Latin *scalare* produced **echelon** and **escalade** the climbing of a wall with ladders; to do so, whence **escalator** (originally a US trade name, modelled on *elevator*), hence **escalate** to travel on an escalator; to make or become greater or more serious in stages, originally applied to a conflict developing into nuclear war. Related to SCAN*.

scallop, scollop [ME. French *escalope* 'shell', of Germanic origin] (The shell of) a large marine mollusc, hence **1** the shell as a symbol of St James (reflected in French *coquille St Jacques* 'St James's shell'), hence (a representation of) the shell worn as a souvenir of a pilgrimage to his shrine (ME, 17c as **escallop**) **2** something shaped like the shell (15c), especially **(a)** a small pan or dish for baking or serving food; to cook food in one, or in a scallop shell, especially in cream or a sauce and topped with breadcrumbs (18c) **(b)** an ornamental wavy edging (17c, 15c as *escallop*); to make, or trim with, one **3** to gather scallops (19c).

French *escalope* was adopted for a thin slice of meat, especially veal, and is related to **scaloppine** or **scallopini** a dish of small escalopes in a sauce [US, from Italian *scaloppina* 'little escalope', from *scaloppa* 'escalope'], and probably to SHELL*. French *coquille* comes ultimately from Greek *kogkhē* 'cockle, mussel': see CONKER*.

scamp [18c. Probably from early Dutch *schampen* 'to slip away, to decamp', from Old French *esc(h)amper*, ultimately from Latin *campus* 'field'] (To be) a highway robber (–19c), hence **1** a rogue (19c); a mischievous person or child **2** to wander about, especially intending mischief (19c, *Scots*) **3** to do a job etc. badly or carelessly (19c).

Sense 3 may be a different word and related to **scrimp** (*Scots*) and **skimp** originally meagre, scanty, and possibly to **scrump** a small, withered apple (whence **scrumpy** rough cider), to steal fruit from orchards, and to **shrimp** [of uncertain, probably Germanic, ancestry].

Dutch *schampen* probably produced **scamper** to run away (17–19c); to run quickly, nimbly, or playfully. Latin *campus* is the ancestor of CAMP*.

scan [ME. Latin *scandere* 'to climb', in late Latin 'to scan a verse' (from raising and lowering your foot to mark the rhythm): cf. THESIS] To analyse the metre of verse, hence **1** to investigate, examine, or consider closely (16c); to look over something intently or quickly (18c); to search for, hence **(a)** to pass a beam of light or electrons over a surface to produce (and transmit) an image (1920s); this act; the image produced (1950s) **(b)** to move a radar beam in a systematic pattern in search of a target (World War II); in computing: to search stored data automatically for specific information (1960s) **2** of verse: to be metrically correct (19c).

Latin *scandere* is the ancestor of **ascend**, **condescend** [Latin *condescendere* 'to lower yourself', from *descendere* 'to go down', whence **descend**] and **transcend** [via Old French from Latin *transcendere* 'to climb over, to surmount']. Related to SCALE*.

scandal [ME. French *scandale*, a later form of *escandle*, via ecclesiastical Latin from Greek *skandalon* 'snare, stumbling block'] (Discredit to religion from) the bad behaviour of a religious person, hence **1** an obstacle to faith in, or obedience to, God (16c) **2** defamatory talk, malicious gossip (16c); such a statement (17–19c), outlived by **slander** [ME, from Old French *esclandre*, an alteration of *escandle*] originally and chiefly as a legal term for making such a statement in speech: cf. LIBEL **3** something/someone that causes public outrage or criticism (16c) or brings something into disrepute (17c); such outrage or offence.

scavenger [16c. Alteration of 15c **scavager**, from Anglo-Norman French *scawager*, from *scawage*, from Old Norman French *escauwer* 'to inspect', from Flemish *scauwen*: related to SHOW*] A scavager was an official who collected **scavage**, a tax levied in London on foreign merchants, and who also kept the streets clean. Hence *scavenger* a street cleaner, hence **1** a refuse or carrion eater; **scavenger (cell)** one that ingests waste or foreign matter in the blood stream (19c) **2 scavenge** to clean (17c, long rare); to clean the streets or a river (19c) **3 scavenger** a person who collects discarded items for reuse (19c), hence *scavenge* to do so.

scene [16c. Latin *scena* from Greek *skēnē* 'tent' (in which the actors dressed), 'stage, scene'] A subdivision of (an act of) a play, often marked by a change of setting (16c), hence **1** the backcloth, later all, or any piece of, the **scenery**, i.e. the backcloths, props, etc., that show the setting **2** the setting of (part of) a play, later of a novel etc.; the place where something happens or has happened, now a 'place' where people with common interests meet (*the music scene*, 1930s); a situation (*a bad scene*, 1950s, *US*) **3** a play in performance (surviving in *the scene opens/unfolds* etc.); an episode in a play, film, etc., or in real life (*a love scene*, 17c); a (public) display of emotion (*make a scene*, 18c) **4** a view or picture of a place or activity (17c); *scenery* the (picturesque) natural features of landscape (18c).

Scenery comes from Italian **scenario** [from Latin *scena*], adopted for the outline of a play's plot, hence a film script with all the details needed for shooting, later a description of a possible situation or course of action. Greek *skēnē* produced **proscenium** [Greek *proskēnion*, literally 'front scene'] the stage (in front of the background) in classical theatre, now the stage area in front of the curtain, and **scenic** to do with the theatre or with stage or natural scenery.

schedule [ME. Via French from late Latin *schedula* 'slip of paper', ultimately from Greek *skhedē* 'page, papyrus leaf'] A slip or scroll of parchment or paper with writing on it (–17c); a sheet accompanying a document containing additional information (15c); an appendix to a legal document containing an inventory or (a table of) details, hence any list, table, or classification; a price list; a timetable or programme (19c, *N American*); to put something on a list or in a timetable etc., hence **scheduled** included in a schedule; of a flight etc.: part of a regular service.

scheme [16c. Latin *schema* from Greek *skhēma* 'form, figure'] **1** a figure of speech (–17c) **2** a diagram, originally one showing the positions of celestial objects, especially at the time of someone's birth; an illustrative drawing or map (17c), hence an outline or design; a plan; a policy, programme, or project, hence **(a)** (to devise) an underhand plot (18c) **(b)** an arrangement of elements according to a plan (*housing/colour scheme*, 18c).

Latin **schema** was adopted by the German philosopher Immanuel Kant (b.1774) for a general or essential type or form; it now usually means an outline, plan, or synopsis.

school [Old English *scōl, scolu,* and, later, Old French *escole,* ultimately via Latin *schola* from Greek *skholē* 'leisure', hence, from the idea of using your leisure, 'disputation, philosophy, (place for) study'] A place where a Greek or Roman philosopher taught, later where children or students are educated or a skill is taught. Hence **1** something regarded as instructive (*the school of hard knocks*) **2** a school's pupils; someone's students or disciples (17c); (the people following) a particular practice or doctrine **3** to teach or train (ME), hence **(a)** to discipline (*schooled himself to keep silent,* 16c) **(b)** to train or put a horse through its paces (19c); a place for this [modelled on French *école,* a later form of *escole,* adopted in *haute école* [literally 'high school'] advanced dressage.

Latin *schola* produced **scholar** a student, later a learned person, hence a student given financial support (a **scholarship**) because of their aptitude. Greek *skholē* produced **scholastic** to do with the teachings of the **Schoolmen** the teachers of philosophy and theology at the medieval 'schools' (universities), hence **scholasticism** their teachings.

scion [ME. Old French *ciun, cion, sion,* of unknown origin] A shoot or twig, especially one used for grafting, hence an heir or descendant, especially of a noble family (rare before the 19c). Cf. IMP, *offshoot* (at SHOOT), and SLIP[3].

scold [ME. Old Norse *skáld* 'poet', probably also 'satirist'] A person, especially a woman, using ribald or abusive language; one who persistently nags or grumbles (15c); to do so; to rebuke someone angrily or at length (18c).

Old Norse *skáld,* Anglicized to **skald,** was adopted meaning a medieval Scandinavian poet.

scoop [ME. Early Dutch or Low German *schōpe* 'bailer': related to **shape** and to **-ship** (*ladyship, craftsmanship*)] Something for moving liquids, e.g. a bucket, bailer or ladle; a small, deep, short-handled shovel for moving grain, coins, etc. (15c); a device for moving soft material (*ice-cream scoop,* 18c). Hence **1** to move something (as if) with a scoop; what is scooped (18c), hence **(a)** to take all or a large quantity of (19c) **(b)** to outdo a rival reporter, newspaper, etc. by reporting a story first or exclusively (*US*); the story **2** to hollow out with a scoop (18c); a hollowed-out place; **scoop neck(line)** a wide, low-cut, round neckline (1950s).

scope [16c. Italian *scopo* 'aim', from Greek *skopos* 'watcher, thing watched, target'] A target (–17c), hence **1** an aim or purpose (now rare); the main purpose or intent of a writer or work **2** a projectile's range, hence **(a)** the length of a mooring cable, hence space or opportunity for movement; (limited) freedom to act **(b)** the range of an activity or subject **(c)** the range of someone's/something's capabilities or potential **(d)** to assess scope or range (19c only); **scope out** to investigate or examine, to check out (1970s, US).

Greek *skopos* produced *bishop* and *episcopal* (both at SUPERINTENDENT), and *horoscope* (at TIDE). Related to **sceptic** [Greek *skeptesthei* 'to observe or consider'] originally applied to a follower of the Greek philosopher Pyrrho of Ellis (*c.*300 BC), who held that real knowledge is impossible, and to Greek *skopein* 'to watch or examine', whence **-scope** in the names of instruments for observing or examining (*telescope, stethoscope*), and **-scopy** in words for scientific examination, especially using such an instrument.

score [ME. Old Norse *skor* 'notch, tally', later 'twenty' (presumably shown by a notch on a tally stick): related to SHEAR*] **1** a group or set of twenty; **scores** lots, a great many **2** a line; a crack or crevice; a cut, notch, or scratch, hence **(a)** to cut (cf. SCOTCH); to make, or mark with, one or more lines, cuts, or scratches; **score out/through** to cross out (17c) **(b)** a notch on a stick or tally (–16c); an account kept by such marks; to keep count (originally in this way), hence the points achieved in a game (18c); to gain a point or points, hence to achieve a success (19c); to make a (dishonest) gain, an illegal drug deal (1930s), or a sexual conquest (1960s) **(c)** a written or printed copy of a piece of music, showing all the parts (18c, from the lines originally connecting the staves); to orchestrate or arrange a piece of music (19c); (to compose) the music for a film etc. (1920s).

scotch [ME. Origin unknown] (To make) a cut, score, or gash, hence **1** a line marked on the ground (17c), hence **hopscotch** a game in which players hop over a pattern of such lines (19c) **2** to (temporarily) disable (18c): based on a later reading of Shakespeare's 'we have scorched the snake, not killed it' (*Macbeth* III ii 13), **scorch** in this case being a 15c alteration of SCORE in the sense 'to cut', hence to stamp out or put a stop to (19c).

Scottish [Old English *Scyttisch*, from *Scottas* 'Scotsmen, Irishmen', from late Latin *Scotti* 'Irishmen'] To do with the ancient Scots, a Gaelic-speaking people who migrated from Ireland to northern Britain in the 6c, and gave their name to Scotland (–15c), hence to do with Scotland or its inhabitants (ME); originating in or belonging to Scotland.

Scottish has long existed alongside its contracted form **Scotch** and **Scots** [a contraction of *Scottis*, the northern variant of *Scottish*]. Until the 19c *Scotch* was the more common form in England, *Scottish* being regarded as more formal. *Scots* was the usual form in Scotland until the 18c, when *Scotch* was adopted and used by Scottish writers; it later appeared in official language. However, in the 19c *Scots* reasserted itself, and *Scotch* fell into disuse, firstly in Scotland and later in England; it survives in certain fixed terms, notably **Scotch (whisky)**. Nowadays *Scots* is the more common adjective (always used for people), and also means the form of English spoken in (Lowland) Scotland. *Scottish* usually refers to the whole country with its culture and institutions, and also describes animals originating there (*Scottish terrier*).

The surname **Scott** was given to someone from Scotland, or by Scots to a Gaelic speaker. Related to **schottische** [German *Schottischetanz* 'Scottish dance'].

scour [ME. Via early Dutch and French from Latin *excurare* 'to clean off', from *curare* 'to take care of': see CURE*] To clean, especially by hard rubbing or an abrasive; to clear out a ditch or channel (15c), hence to give or be given a purgative; of livestock: to have diarrhoea (16c).

scout [ME. Old French *escouter* 'to listen', ultimately from Latin *auscultare*] (Someone sent) to travel about in search of (military) information. Hence **1** a spy (16c); someone employed by an oil-drilling company, or, later, a sports team, to monitor another (19c), hence to do so (early 20c, *US*); someone who seeks out and recruits those with talent or ability (now usually **talent scout**) **2** a reconnaissance ship (18c), later an aircraft or other vehicle **3 (boy) scout** a member of an international organization for boys founded in 1908 by Lord Baden-Powell (who had trained military scouts); **girl scout** a girl guide (US: cf. GUIDE sense 3).

Latin *auscultare* produced **auscultation** listening, now only to the heart, lungs, etc. to assist diagnosis.

scramble [16c. Perhaps a blend of dialect *cramble* 'to crawl' and *scamble* 'to struggle for', both of unknown origin] **1** to climb using hands and feet, to clamber; a walk or climb involving scrambling (18c), hence **(a)** a motorcycle race over rough ground (1920s) **(b) scramble/scrambling net** by which you can climb (1940s, *nautical*, now also one on a child's climbing frame) **2** to struggle or compete frantically for; such a struggle (17c) **3** to move, cause to move, or gather up hastily or clumsily (perhaps the source of **scram** to go away quickly, 1920s, *US*), hence (to make) a jumbled mess, hence **(a) scrambled egg** egg beaten with milk and cooked (19c); the gold braid on an officer's cap (World War II) **(b)** to make a transmitted signal unintelligible to those without a decoding device (1920s) **(c)** to launch a number of fighter planes quickly (World War II); such a launch.

scrape [Old English *scrapian*, later also from related Old Norse *skrapa* or early Dutch *schrapen*] To scratch with fingernails or claws (–17c), hence **1** to abrade or scuff (ME), hence **(a)** to move something with a scratching sound (16c), hence to play the violin badly **(b)** a slight scratch or graze (16c) **(c)** a layer of thinly spread butter or margarine (19c); cheap margarine **2** to scratch at the earth (15c), hence **(a)** to make a hollow by doing so (15c); such a hollow (18c) **(b) scrape (together/ up)** to get or gather with difficulty, as though scratching it up (16c) **(c)** to bow while drawing back one leg as if scraping the ground with it (17c), surviving in **bow and scrape** to act obsequiously **3** to just get through or by (*scrape along the bottom/through an exam*), hence an awkward situation, especially resulting from an escapade (18c); a skirmish or brawl (19c, US, cf. *scrap* below).

Scrap, (to take part in) an argument or brawl, may be a variant of *scrape*, although an earlier sense 'a plot' casts doubt. Related to **scrap** a fragment or remnant [Old Norse *skrap*], and probably to **scrabble**, **scratch**, and SCRUB.

screen [ME. Old Norman French *escren*, *escran*, from early Dutch *scherm* 'shield': related to SKIRMISH*] **1** a light, upright structure giving protection from heat, light, sight, etc., hence to shield, shelter, or conceal (as if) with one (15c); something that does so (16c); protection, concealment **2** a partition (15c); to shut off or in with one (18c) **3** a large sieve (16c), hence **(a)** to sift with one (17c); to 'sift out' those having a particular disease, quality, etc., or who are suitable/unsuitable (1940s) **(b)** a (frame covered with) fine mesh to keep out insects (19c) **4** a vertical surface onto which an image may be projected (19c), hence **(a)** to project an image or a film onto a screen (*c.*1910), hence films collectively, cinema **(b)** the part of a television on which the image appears (1920s), hence **small-screen** television, as opposed to **big-screen** cinema (1940s) **(c)** a computer's monitor (1970s); the data currently displayed on it.

screw [ME. Old French *escroue* 'female screw', ultimately from Latin *scrofa* 'sow', later 'screw' (presumably because of the pig's curly tail)] A pin with a spiral thread around it (a male screw) that you wind into a socket with a corresponding thread (a female screw); a spiral pin (*corkscrew*, 16c), hence **1** to twist; a twist (18c); something twisted (*a screw of paper*, 19c) **2** to fix with a screw or screws (17c) **3** to tighten a screw (17c); **the screws, thumbscrew** an instrument of torture that applies pressure by doing so, hence **turn the screw, put the screws on** to put pressure on, to extort money; *screw* to exploit or cheat **4** a (skeleton) key (17c criminals' slang), hence a prison warder (19c) **5** to propel with a spiral motion (17c); to give spin or a curved trajectory to a ball (19c), hence **screwball** in baseball: one pitched with spin against the natural curve, hence eccentric, zany (*screwball comedy*, 1930s, *US*); an eccentric person **6** to have sex with (18c); the sex act; a person considered in sexual terms; **screw up** to blunder or make a mess of (1930s, *US*); **screwed up** mismanaged, ruined; mentally or emotionally disturbed.

Latin *scrofa* produced *scrofula* (to which pigs were thought particularly susceptible), whence **scrofulous** like or having scrofula; scabby, (morally) shabby.

script [ME. Via Old French from Latin *scriptum*, from *scribere* 'to write'] Something written, hence **1** handwriting as opposed to print (19c), hence **(a)** a typeface that imitates this **(b)** an original or principal legal document **(c)** an examinee's written answer paper (1920s) **2** a system of writing, an alphabet (19c) **3** see MANUSCRIPT.

Descendants of Latin *scribere* include **ascribe, circumscribe** [Latin *circumscribere* 'to draw a line round', hence 'to limit'], CONSCRIPTION, DESCRIBE*, **inscribe**, MANUSCRIPT, **prescribe** [Latin *praescribere* 'to write beforehand', hence 'to direct in writing'], PROSCRIBE, *postscript* (at POSTERIOR), **scribble, scribe** (also as a surname), **scripture, scrivener** a copyist or clerk (also as a surname with the variants **Scribner** and **Scriven(s)**), SHRIVE*, SUBSCRIBE*, and TRANSCRIBE*.

scroll [ME. Alteration, influenced by *roll*, of *scrowe*, from Old French *escroue* 'strip or scrap of parchment', from medieval Latin *scroda*, ultimately from a Germanic word meaning 'to cut'] A roll of paper or parchment with writing on it, hence **1** something shaped like a partly unrolled one: a convoluted spiral ornament (15c); the curved head of a violin etc. (19c) **2** a piece of writing, a letter, list, or roster (16c) **3** a long strip of paper or, in heraldry, a ribbon, bearing a motto (16c) **4** in computing: to move displayed text etc. up and down as if winding or unwinding a scroll (1970s).

Old French *escroue* produced **escrow** a bond, deed, etc. held in trust until a certain condition is met; a deposit or fund held in trust or as a security (N American), hence **in escrow** in trust; *escrow* to place in trust. Related to SHRED* and SHROUD.

scrub [ME. Probably from early Dutch or Low German *schrobben*] To groom a horse (ME only). Re-borrowed meaning to rub or clean (as if) with a hard brush (16c), hence **1** a menial servant, a drudge (18c, cf. SHRUB) **2** to remove impurities from a gas (19c) **3** to erase (19c); to eliminate or cancel.

scruple [ME. Via French from Latin *scrupulus*, from *scrupus* 'small sharp stone', hence 'anxiety' (first used by the Roman orator and statesman Cicero, probably from the idea of a stone in your shoe)] **1** an apothecaries' weight equal to 20 grains, hence a very small quantity, amount, or portion (16c) **2** a source of unease (15c); a moral or ethical doubt, hence **(a) scrupulous** troubled by scruples; (too) concerned to do the right thing (16c) **(b)** to have such doubts (17–19c); to hesitate because of them.

scrutiny [15c. Latin *scrutinium* 'a search', from *scrutari* 'to search', originally 'to sort rags', from *scruta* 'rubbish'] **1** the taking of a vote to choose someone or decide a question **2** investigation, (a) critical inquiry or examination (16c, hence **scrutineer** someone who carries one out; **scrutinize** to do so, 17c); a searching gaze (18c).

Latin *scrutari* produced **inscrutable** [via medieval Latin *inscrutabilis* 'that cannot be found by searching']; **scrutable** is a back-formation.

scum [ME. Early Dutch or Low German *schüm*] Foam, froth (–17c); a layer of froth, dirt, algae, etc. on the surface of a liquid; an unwanted surface layer or deposit, hence **1** the dregs of society (16c); a despicable person **2** semen (1960s, US), hence **scumbag** a condom; a despicable person (1970s).

Probably the source of **scumble**, originally to apply a thin coat of paint to soften the underlying colours, and related to German *Meerschaum* (at MERE[1]), and to **skim** [French *escumer* 'to remove scum', from *escume* 'scum'].

scurf [Old English *sceorf*, perhaps of Scandinavian origin] **1** any disease that makes the skin flake off (–17c) **2** the flakes of skin which come off as new skin forms underneath; dandruff **3** any incrustation or scaly deposit on a surface (ME).

The variant **scruff** produced **scruffy** scaly, scurfy, later dirty, shabby, unkempt, whence *scruff* a scruffy person, and **scurvy** scurfy (15–19c), hence **1** rough, despicable (*scurvy knave*) **2** **scurvy (disease)** causing debility, loosening of the teeth and bleeding under the skin, hence **scurvy grass** eaten to ward it off.

scuttle[1] [Old English *scutel* from Old Norse *skutill*, from Latin *scutella* 'dish, tray', from *scutra* 'wooden platter'] **1** a dish or platter (–18c) **2** a basket for winnowing corn (ME); a wide-mouthed basket for corn, vegetables, earth, etc. (15c); a similarly shaped metal container for coal (18c); the part of a car between the bonnet and windscreen, containing the instrument panel (early 20c).

Latin *scutella* fathered French *escuele* 'dish', whence **scullery** the household department concerned with the care of crockery and kitchen utensils; a back kitchen where the washing up is done, and **skillet** a small metal cooking pot with a long handle and three or four feet, now usually a frying pan (*US*).

scuttle[2] [15c. Perhaps via French from Spanish *escotilla* 'hatchway', from *escotar* 'to cut out', of Germanic origin and related to SHOOT*] (The covering of) a small opening in a ship's side, hence **1** to make an opening (17c); to sink a ship by letting water in **2** (the covering of) an opening in the wall, floor, or roof of a building (18c, now only US).

Scupper [Old French *escopir*, from a Romanic word meaning 'to spit'] would appear to have a similar development, from 'ship's drainage hole' to 'sink a ship'. However, the verb originally meant to (ambush and) kill, hence to defeat, ruin, or put an end to, whence, probably, to sink a ship (by association with *scuttle*). ·

seal [ME. Old French *seel*, from Latin *sigillum* 'small picture, engraved figure', from *signum*: see SIGN] A piece of wax or similar material, often stamped with a design, fixed to a document to show its authenticity, or used to fasten a letter. Hence **1** a stamp engraved with such a design; an (impressed) mark of authenticity or ownership (16c) **2** to put a seal on a document, hence to conclude an agreement etc. (15c); to decide irrevocably (*sealed their fate*, 19c) **3** to fasten with a seal or, later, with an adhesive (17c), hence **(a)** (what is used) to close something so that it cannot be opened secretly or to make it water- or airtight **(b) seal (up)** to confine in a sealed receptacle (15c); **seal (off)** to close off an area to prevent people entering or leaving (1930s) **(c)** to apply **sealant** an impervious coating (1940s) **4** an obligation, especially to keep silent (*seal of the confessional*).

Latin *signum* produced **signet** a small seal (especially one engraved on a finger-ring, hence **signet ring** with a monogram or design); one used by English and Scottish sovereigns and later by the Scottish Court of Sessions, hence **writer to the signet** a clerk in the Secretary of State's office who prepared writs for the royal seal, later a solicitor authorized to prepare crown writs.

season [ME. Old French *seson, saison*, from Latin *satio* 'act or time of sowing', from *serere, sat-* 'to sow' (ancestor of SEMINARY*)] A traditional division of the year; a particular time or period. Hence **1** the (right) time (of year) for a particular activity (*hunting/holiday season*), of the greatest or least activity (*high/low season*), when a plant blooms or produces fruit (hence to flavour food with salt, spices, etc., from the idea of fruit tasting better as it ripens); when an animal is ready to breed, or marked by a particular festivity (*Christmas season*, 18c); a period during which a connected series of events or performances takes place (*film noir season*, 19c); such a series **2** to prepare something for use by exposing it to the weather or other conditions it will later encounter (16c), hence **seasoned** acclimatized, experienced (*seasoned traveller*, 17c).

secret [ME. French, from Latin *secretus* (adjective), *secretum* (noun) '(something) set apart', from *secernere, secret-* 'to sift out', from *cernere* 'to sift'] (Something) kept hidden or private, hence **1** (describing) something that is not obvious (*the secret of success*) **2** remote, secluded (16c) **3** unacknowledged (*secret admirer*, 16c); undercover (*secret agent*, 17c); acting or meeting surreptitiously **4** to keep secret, to conceal (16–18c), altered to **secrete** (18c).

Latin *secretum* produced late Latin *secretarius* (whence French *secretaire* a writing desk and *secretariat*) and **secretary** originally someone entrusted with private matters. Latin *secernere* produced *secretio* 'separation', whence **secretion** the production and release of a substance from a gland etc., whence **secrete** to do so. Latin *cernere* is the ancestor of CRIME*.

section [ME. (French, from) Latin *secare, sect-* 'to cut'] **1** a division or subdivision, hence **(a)** to divide into sections (19c) **(b)** to admit someone to a psychiatric hospital compulsorily under the appropriate section of the Mental Health Act (1980s) **2** the action of cutting (16c); a cut or incision, now usually in surgery (*Caesarian section*) **3** a view of something cut through to show its internal features or structure (17c), hence **(a)** to cut something to show this (19c) **(b) cross section** a cut through at right angles to the (longest) axis (19c); (a representation of) the surface this reveals, hence a representative sample, group, etc. (*c*.1900).

Latin *secare*'s progeny include **bisect**, **dissect**, INSECT, **intersect**, French *secateurs*, **sector**, **segment**, **sickle** [Old English *sicol*], and **vivisection** (at VICTUAL).

sedate [15c. Latin *sedatus* 'settled', from *sedare* 'to settle', literally 'to make sit', from *sedere* 'to sit'] Calm, quiet, composed; sober, dignified, decorous, staid.

Latin *sedare* produced **sedative** calming or inducing sleep; a sedative medicine, and **sedation**, whence **sedate** to do so. Latin *sedere* is the ancestor of SESSION*.

seduce [15c. Latin *seducere* 'to lead away', from *ducere* 'to lead'] To persuade someone to abandon their allegiance or duty or to do something foolish or wrong, especially to have (illicit) sex (16c).

Latin *seducere* produced **seduction**, originally an attempt to overturn a government (ME–15c), replaced by **sedition** [Latin, literally 'a separation, a going apart', from *ire* 'to go' (ancestor of EXIT*)]. Latin *ducere* is the ancestor of DEDUCE*.

see [Old English *sēon*] To perceive with the eye, hence (all ME) **1** to experience; to witness; to be the time or scene of **2** to perceive mentally, hence **(a)** to predict (*I saw that coming*) **(b)** to recognize **(c)** to understand **(d)** to consider or regard as **(e)** to find out **3** to watch over (–17c), hence **(a)** to ensure that something is done or is as it should be **(b)** to escort (*I'll see you out*, 17c) **4** to meet (socially); to receive as a visitor (*Doctor will see you now*, 15c) **5** to look (at), especially as an order to do so (*see here!*, *see paragraph 4*).

The connection between seeing and thinking or understanding is found in many English words, e.g. CLEAR, **consider**, **contemplate**, *enlighten* (at LIGHT[2]), **foresee**, ILLUMINATE, ILLUSTRATE, **insight**, LUCID*, **obscure**, OBVIOUS, OPAQUE, PERSPECTIVE, *regard* (at REWARD), and VIEW: also in **blind** meaning 'wilfully ignorant', **bright** meaning 'clever', **dim** meaning 'stupid', and MUDDLE: cf. CLEVER*. Related to **sight** originally 'something seen'.

seek [Old English *sēcan*] To try to find or find out, hence **1** to look for or pursue with hostile intent, to attack (–17c): the dialect variant **sick** (19c) came to mean to incite (especially a dog) to attack **2** to try or want to get something or to make something happen; to ask for or demand, hence **sought after** desirable, in demand (17c).

Old English *sēcan* produced **beseech**. Related to SAKE*.

seem [ME. Old Norse *soema* 'to conform to', from *soemr* 'fitting'] **1** to be suitable or fitting (–17c, surviving in **seemly**) **2** to appear to be, to do, or to be true.

seethe [Old English *sēothan*] **1** to cook food by boiling or stewing; to boil, be boiled, or bubble up (ME); to be or become boiling hot, hence to be full of (unexpressed) anger or resentment (16c), or of hectic activity **2** to soften by boiling or soaking; to steep or soak.

The original past participle was **sodden**, which now only means 'soaked, saturated' and is no longer associated with *seethe*. Probably related to **suds**.

seize [ME. Old French *seizir*, *saisir*, from Frankish Latin *sacire* 'to claim', of Germanic origin and probably related to SET*] **1** in law (often spelt **seise**): to put someone in legal possession of land, property, etc., hence **seisin** [ME, from Old French *seisine*, from *seizir*] (the action of taking) legal possession; the property concerned **2** to take forcibly or by warrant; to confiscate or impound (15c); to arrest or imprison **3** to grab, hence **(a)** to affect someone suddenly and forcefully (*seized by panic*, 15c), hence **seizure** a sudden attack of illness, a fit or stroke (18c) **(b)** **seize (up)on** to exploit or point out an error etc. (15c); to use or take advantage of quickly and eagerly (*seize an opportunity/the day*, 17c) **(c)** to grasp mentally

(19c): cf. CLEVER* **4** to fasten with several turns of thin rope (17c, nautical); **seize up** to tie someone up for a flogging; to become stiff or unable to move (19c).

sell [Old English *sellan*] To grant, give, or hand over voluntarily (–ME); to give up or betray someone, especially for a reward, hence to hand over in exchange for money.

Related to, and probably influenced by, **sale** [Old Norse *sala*], which has always meant a financial transaction.

seminary [ME. Latin *seminarium*, from *semen* 'seed', from *serere* 'to sow'] A seed plot (–19c), hence a place where something originates or is developed (16c); a place of education, now specifically a training college for priests or rabbis.

Latin *seminarium* produced German **seminar** a meeting of (originally, advanced) students under a tutor or professor; a conference of specialists (*US*); a short intensive course of study. Latin **semen** was adopted for sperm-bearing fluid, and produced **disseminate** to spread ideas, information, etc. like seed, **inseminate**, and **seminal** to do with semen or seed, hence capable of development, original and influential. *Serere* is the ancestor of SEASON.

senior [15c. Latin, 'older, older man', comparative of *senex*, *senis* 'old (man)'] Opposite of **junior** [15c, comparative of Latin *juvenis* 'young (person)']. Elder, older, hence **1 (a)** an older person **(b)** used after a father's (15c) or older brother's (19c) name to distinguish them from a younger family member with the same name: *junior*, used in the same way, is now sometimes a nickname or given name for a boy, especially your son (1940s, *US*) **(c)** a specified amount older than you (*12 years my senior*, 15c) **(d) senior citizen** someone past retirement age (1930s, *US*) **(e) senior moment** an elderly person's moment of forgetfulness (1990s) **2** of earlier origin, longer service, or higher rank (16c); of a student: more advanced (17c); suitable or reserved for senior staff or students (*senior common room*, 18c).

Latin *senex* is the ancestor of French *sieur* 'lord' (at MASTER) and **seigneur** a feudal lord, whence **Monseigneur** a title or form of address for an eminent person, whence Italian **Monsignor** applied to senior Roman Catholic clergy, **senate** the highest council of the ancient Roman Republic and Empire, hence applied to various governing bodies or the place where they meet, **senescent** growing old, ageing, **senile**, and SIRE*. Latin *juvenis* produced **juvenescent** 'ageing' from infancy to youth, **juvenile**, and **rejuvenate**.

sense [ME. Latin *sensus* 'the faculty of feeling, thought, meaning', from *sentire*, *sens-* 'to feel or perceive, to be of the opinion'] **1** the meaning of a word, text, etc. (15c); satisfactory or intelligible meaning (16c); wisdom, hence **(a)** (a) reason (*no sense waiting here*, 17c) **(b)** the ability to understand (*road sense, sense of humour*, 17c); **common/horse sense** natural or practical wisdom **2** one of the five physical faculties (sight, hearing, etc.), or a mental faculty, through which you perceive the world (16c), hence **(a)** to get information through (one of) these; to be or become vaguely or intuitively aware of (19c); of a machine etc.: to detect, observe, or measure (1940s) **(b) senses** your mental faculties when sane (*brought to his senses*, 16c).

Descendants of Latin *sentire* include **assent**, **consent**, **dissent**, **resent**, **scent** originally a hunting term meaning to find and track by smell [via French *sentire* 'to feel or perceive', later also 'to smell': the *c* is unexplained], **sensible**, **sensitive**,

sensuous, SENTENCE*, **sentient**, SENTIMENT*, and probably **sentinel** [via Italian *sentire*], whence, probably, **sentry** [from the variant *centrinel*].

sentence   [ME. French, from Latin *sententia*, from *sentire*: see SENSE*] An opinion or decision (–17c), hence **1** a court's decision about a guilty person's punishment; the punishment; to condemn them to it (16c) **2** someone's expressed opinion, hence **(a)** the meaning or gist of a passage (–16c) **(b)** a pithy or memorable saying (Latin *sententia* was adopted in this sense *c*.1915); a group of words containing a finite verb that expresses a statement, question, exclamation, or command (15c).

    Latin *sententia* produced **sententious** full of meaning or wisdom (ME–17c); full of, or tending to use, maxims or aphorisms, later full of, or given to, pompous moralizing.

sentiment   [ME. Old French *sentement* and medieval Latin *sentimentum*, both from Latin *sentire*: see SENSE*] **1** your own experience or feeling **2** a physical sensation. These senses, spelt *sentement*, died out: the following senses are from modern French *sentiment* **3** a feeling or emotion (17c), hence **(a)** **sentiment(s)** the general feeling or opinion of a group **(b)** the feeling expressed by a work of art or literature, or behind an action (18c) **(c)** an opinion based on emotion (18c); the tendency to be swayed by emotion; mawkishness, hence **sentimental** showing exaggerated or superficial tenderness, nostalgia, etc.

    French *sentiment* produced **presentiment**, literally 'a feeling beforehand'.

sequel   [15c. (Via French from) Latin *sequel(l)a*, from *sequi* 'to follow'] **1** a band of followers (–17c); your descendants or successors **2** what follows: **(a)** a result or consequence (16c); an ensuing train of events; a book, film, etc. that takes up the story of a previous one, hence **prequel** [with **pre-** 'before', from Latin *prae*] a film, book, etc. about events before those in a previous one (1970s) **(b)** an age or period following and influenced by another (19c).

    Latin *sequela* was adopted for a condition resulting from a previous disease or accident. Descendants of Latin *sequi* include **consecutive**, **consequence**, **ensue**, EXECUTE, Latin *non sequitur* [literally 'it does not follow'], **obsequious** originally 'dutiful, obedient', PURSUE*, **second** [via Old French from Latin *secundus* 'following, second', from *sequi*: see also MINUTE[1], **sect** [Latin *secta* 'course or belief followed': see also SET], **segue** [Italian, literally 'it follows'] a direction in music to move on to the next section without interruption, hence (to make) an uninterrupted transition from one melody, state, subject, etc. to another, **sequence**, **subsequent**, **sue** to follow or pursue (ME–19c), hence to pursue a legal action, **suitor**, originally an attendant, and SUIT*. SEQUESTER is related.

sequester, **sequestrate**   [ME. (Via French from) late Latin *sequestrare* 'to place in safe keeping', from Latin *sequester*, literally 'follower', later 'agent, trustee': related to SEQUEL*] To remove or set aside, hence **1** now *sequester*: to isolate, to make secluded (15c) **2** in law: **(a)** to seize property until a debt is paid or a condition fulfilled (15c); to take the income of a benefice to pay the incumbent's debts or for the next incumbent (17c) **(b)** *sequestrate*: in Scots law: to give a bankrupt's property to a trustee to pay creditors (18c); to declare someone bankrupt **3** to seize or demand an enemy's property (16c).

serene [15c. Latin *serenus*] **1** of the weather, air, or sky: clear, fine, and calm, hence of a place, time or person: tranquil, untroubled (17c) **2** (also as **Serenity**) a title given to dignitaries, especially princes (*His Serenity, Her Serene Highness*, 15c).

Latin *serenus* fathered **serenade** [French, from Italian *serenata*] (to entertain someone with) music performed in the open air, especially a lover's song sung under his beloved's window, later an instrumental composition for a small ensemble (also as *serenata*, which was adopted earlier for an elaborate cantata).

sergeant [ME. Old French *sergent* from Latin *serviens* 'servant', later 'public official', from *servire*: see SERVE*] **1** a servant (–16c) **2** a soldier (–15c); an army officer (16c), now a non-commissioned officer in the army, air force, or marines, ranking next above a corporal, hence **(a)** **sergeant-major** an officer ranking below a lieutenant-colonel (16–18c: cf. MAJOR sense 2); a non-commissioned officer of the highest rank (19c); **(b)** a police officer ranking next above a constable (19c) **3** an official who implements the decisions of a court or some other authority, surviving in **sergeant/serjeant-at-arms** a nobleman's or monarch's armed attendant, now an officer of each of the two British Houses of Parliament (later of other legislative assemblies) who maintains order and security (18c).

serve [ME. Via French from Latin *servire*, from *servus* 'slave'] **1** to be, or to work for someone as, a servant or slave, later as a soldier etc. (16c) or employee (19c), hence **(a)** to work for and worship God (earlier in *service* below) **(b)** to wait on; to give or offer food, goods, etc. **(c)** to fulfil a need or do a job (*a box served as a table*) **(d)** to be an assistant, specifically one in real tennis, one of whose duties was to put the ball in play (16c), hence in lawn tennis, badminton, etc.: to start play; the act or way of doing so (17c) **2** to treat someone in a particular way (*serve you right*, 16c) **3** to hold, or do the duties of, an official position **4** of a male animal: to mate with a female, later also as *service* (1960s) **5** to deliver a legal document (15c).

The earliest sense of **service** [OE, via French from Latin *servitium*, from *servus*] was (liturgy prescribed for) an act of public worship; the other main senses are **1** the status, occupation, or duties of one who serves, hence **active service** actual warfare **2** work done for someone else, hence **services** things other than goods provided or sold, hence *service* to (regularly) provide services; (to do) routine maintenance **3** an organization of public servants (*Civil/diplomatic service*); **the services** the army, navy, and airforce.

Descendants of Latin *servus* include **serf** originally a slave, later someone in a state of semi-slavery, specifically a farm labourer tied to the land, SERGEANT, **servant**, **serviette**, **servile** to do with or suitable for a slave, hence slave-like, submissive, fawning, **servitude**, and **servo**, originally short for **servomotor** an auxiliary motor.

session [ME. (French, from) Latin *sedere, sess-* 'to sit'] **1** a place for sitting (–15c) **2** a sitting of an official body (15c); (the period of) a series of them (16c), hence **(a)** **sessions** periodical court sittings (*quarter sessions*, 15c) **(b)** the part of the academic year in which teaching takes place (18c, *Scots*); a period of time set aside for a particular activity (1920s); one in which musicians perform (*jam/recording session*), hence **session man/musician** hired for a recording session, not a regular member of the band (1950s).

Latin *sedere* is the ancestor of **dissident** [Latin *dissidere* 'to sit apart'], **insidious** [Latin *insidere* 'to lie in wait for', literally 'to sit on'], **preside** [via French from

Latin *praesidere*, literally 'to sit in front of': earlier in **president** (the person) presiding], French *séance* a session or meeting, later specifically a spiritualist one, **sedentary** originally meaning staying in one place, not migratory, **sediment**, *see* (at CHAIR), **siege** a seat, also the act of 'sitting' round a town etc. (earlier in **besiege**), and **supersede** [via Old French from Latin *supersedere* 'to set above']. *Sedere* is also the ancestor of ASSIZE*, OBSESS, POSSESS*, RESIDENCE*, SEDATE, **sediment**, **sessile**, and SUBSIDY*, and probably *sedan* (at SALON).

set [Old English *settan*] The main strands of meaning, from which all senses evolved, were established in Old English: they are: **1** to sit someone down, to seat or (now dialect) be seated **2** to subside or go down (now mainly of a celestial body) **3** to establish or be established in a more or less permanent place, position, condition, or relationship **4** to appoint or prescribe **5** to arrange, fix, or adjust **6** to (make something) go in a particular direction. The variant **sett** survives in a few technical uses, and for a badger's burrow (19c).

Set 'a group of people' is from, and originally meant, *sect* (at SEQUEL); this merged with *set* above to mean a group or series of things, hence a collection of tools etc. for a specific purpose; a piece of (now electronic) apparatus (*TV set*).

Old English *settan* produced **beset** to set near, to surround, now only with hostile intent. Related to Old English *cotsaeta* (see COTTAGE), German *ersatz* 'replacement' [from Old High German *irsezzan* 'to set in place of'], adopted describing a poor substitute, to **saddle**, **seat**, SETTLE, **sit**, and **soot**.

settle [Old English *setl*: related to, and probably influenced by, SET*] A place to sit, a chair, bench, or stool, hence **1** to (make someone) sit down (–17c); to make or become still or calm (ME), hence **(a)** to make something stable or permanent (15c); to establish in a place or situation (*settled on the couch/in London*, 16c); to establish as colonists; to colonize an area **(b)** to resolve a matter or argument (16c); to put affairs in order (17c); to pay a bill or debt **2** a bench with a high back and arms (16c): **settee** is probably a fanciful alteration (18c).

several [ME. Anglo-Norman French, from Anglo-Latin *separalis*, from Latin *separare*, literally 'to arrange apart', from *parare* 'to make ready'] Having a distinct, individual identity, position, or status (–18c); distinctive, individual, separate (15c), hence **1 (a)** different, various, diverse (15c), hence (since variety implies number) more than two but not very many **(b)** in law: more than one (15c, earlier in **severally** individually, not jointly); applied or regarded separately (16c); regarding each of a number of people individually **2** private, privately owned (15c); a piece of privately owned land (surviving in field names and in **several fishery** fishing rights derived through ownership of land).

Latin *separare* produced **separate** and **sever**; *parare* is the ancestor of PARADE*.

shade, **shadow** [Both from Old English *sceadu*] Originally sharing most senses. **I** as *shade* or *shadow*: **1** partial darkness; shelter from light or the sun; a sheltered area **2** something insubstantial or unreal (ME), an illusory image, hence **(a)** *shade* a spirit, a ghost **(b)** *shadow* a weak remnant (*shadow of his former self*, 16c) **(c)** a tinge, touch, or hint **3** comparative obscurity or inferiority (16c) **4** to conceal or disguise (16c), hence **shadowy** indistinct, mysterious (18c), **shady** dubious, disreputable (19c). **II** now mainly or always *shade*: **1** to screen from the light or sun; something that does so (*lampshade/eyeshade*, 18c); **shades** sunglasses (1950s, *US*)

2 (to produce) an area of darkness in a painting etc. (15c) **3** a colour's degree of darkness (17c); a lighter or darker variant of a colour, hence **(a)** a slight variation (*shades of opinion*, 18c) **(b)** to merge shades (19c); to change imperceptibly from one shade to another. **III** now mainly or always *shadow*: **1** the (growing) darkness of evening or night; darkness, gloom; a foreboding, a threat (ME) **2** the darkened shape on a surface when something blocks the light, hence **(a)** hanger-on or inseparable companion (following like a shadow, 16c); to follow and imitate or watch closely (17c) **(b)** an imitation, copy, or counterpart (17c), hence the Opposition counterpart of a government minister or cabinet; to act as shadow to a minister (1960s).

Shed 'an outbuilding or lean-to' is thought to be a variant of *shade*.

shag [Old English *sceacga*] (A mass of) rough matted hair, wool, etc., hence **shagged**, *shag*, **shaggy** having such hair; of hair: long and/or matted (16c in all three forms). Hence **1** to be or make rough or shaggy (16c) **2** (cloth with) a long or coarse nap (16c), hence **(a)** a rug of such material (17c) **(b)** *shaggy* (17c), *shag* (1940s) of pile: long and rough **3** (describing) strong tobacco cut into shreds (18c) **4** *shagged* covered with scrub or rough undergrowth (18c); *shag* a mass of shrubs, trees, etc. (19c).

Perhaps the same word as **shag** a small cormorant with a shaggy crest. Related to **shaw** [Old English *sc(e)aga*] a thicket, coppice, or grove; a field border of trees or bushes: surviving mainly in place- and surnames.

shamble [Old English *sc(e)amul*, ultimately from Latin *scamellum, scamnum* 'stool, bench'] **1** a low stool, a footstool (–15c) **2** a table displaying goods, especially meat, for sale, hence **shambles** a meat market (15c, surviving in a few street names); a slaughterhouse (16c); a scene of carnage, later of devastation or disorder (1920s, *US*); a muddle or mess, hence **shambolic** chaotic (1950s).

Shamble 'to walk clumsily' probably comes from dialect *shamble legs* 'ungainly legs', perhaps from the rickety legs of a market stall.

shame [Old English *sc(e)amu* (noun), *sc(e)amian* (verb)] A feeling of humiliation or distress because of some wrongdoing; to (make someone) feel this, hence **1** disgrace, dishonour; to bring this on someone (ME); what does so, specifically the loss or violation of a woman's chastity; a cause of reproach or disappointment (*it's a shame the way she treats him, shame they can't come*) **2** shameless without shame or modesty; impudent, brazen, hence *shame* the capacity to feel shame (ME); regard for propriety; modesty, shyness **3** put to shame (ME), *shame* (16c) to outdo, to make someone/something look or feel inferior **4** to make someone retreat or do something for fear of disgrace (16c).

Shame produced **ashame** to feel shame (surviving mainly in **ashamed**), the northern variant **sham** a trick or hoax, to trick or deceive (17–19c); to pretend or feign; imitation, counterfeit **(a)** fake, and **shamefast** [Old English *sc(e)amfaest*, literally 'held fast by shame'] modest, shy, later embarrassed, ashamed, altered in both senses to **shamefaced**. **Scam** (to perpetrate) a trick, swindle, or fraud (1960s, *US*) may be related, but evidence is lacking.

shampoo [18c. Hindi *chāmpo* 'press!', from *chāmpnā* 'to press or knead'] To massage, especially as part of a Turkish bath, hence a preparation for massaging and cleansing the scalp; to wash the hair and scalp with it (19c); (to wash something with) a similar preparation for cleaning carpets, upholstery, etc.

shard [Old English *sceard*: related to SHEAR*] **1** a broken place in a hedge etc. **2** a piece of broken pottery (the variant **sherd** survives in ME **potsherd**, now used chiefly by archaeologists), hence a fragment or sliver of something brittle (*shards of bone*, 16c).

The sense 'beetle's wing-case', hence 'shell, hard covering', arose from a misunderstanding of Shakespeare's *shard-born* 'born in dung' (*Macbeth* III ii 42) to mean 'born on fragments', which Johnson (see ACHE) surmised to mean the sheaths of insects' wings. **Shard** 'cow dung' is a variant of *sharn*, from Old English *scearn*: cf. *scearnbudda* (at BUG).

shatter [ME. Of Old English origin] **1** to disperse, to throw, later to be thrown, about in all directions (outlived by the variant **scatter** except in dialect) **2** to smash or be smashed, hence **(a)** to destroy (16c); to ruin someone's health (17c); to tire out (18c); to shock and distress **(b)** **shatterbrain(ed)** absent-minded, disorganized (18c), outlived by **scatterbrain(ed)**, whence **scatty** (*c*.1910) **3** (only as *scatter*) to squander money or goods, hence the surname **Scattergood** a spendthrift or, perhaps, a philanthropist.

shear [Old English *scēar* (noun), *sceran* (verb)] **1** **shears** scissors (now Scots and dialect), later applied to various large two-bladed cutting instruments, and more recently to mechanical cutters (19c). Hence (also **sheers**, later **shear/sheerlegs**) a lifting apparatus consisting of a pulley supported on poles joined at the top like the blades of shears (17c) **2** to cut with a sword, later with shears; to cut or shave your hair or beard; to cut off a sheep's wool, hence (all ME) **(a)** **shearling** a sheep after its first shearing **(b)** to cut off a part; to lose something (as if) by cutting (*shorn of his dignity*, 18c) **(c)** to cut through, hence **shearwater** a low-flying seabird whose wings seem to cut the surface (17c) **3** strain produced when parallel planes in a structure move in relation to each other (19c), hence **(a)** to subject to this; to fracture or be distorted by it **(b)** **wind shear** a difference in wind direction and speed at slightly different altitudes (1950s).

Related to SCORE, SHARD, **share** a portion, to divide and distribute, *share* in **ploughshare** [Old English *scaer*], **short** (at LONG), SKIRT*, and probably to **sheer (off/away)** to change direction, and **shore** land by the sea [early Low Dutch or Low German *schōre*, perhaps from the idea of the dividing line between sea and land].

shed [Old English *scead* (noun), *sc(e)adan* (verb)] To divide or separate (surviving mainly in farming contexts, e.g. to separate sheep from a flock), hence **1** to disperse, scatter, or rout (ME–17c); to throw off or repel (15c) **2** to spill or pour out liquid (*shed tears*, ME); to cause blood to flow (hence **bloodshed** slaughter, 15c) **3** to throw light on (ME) **4** to lose hair, slough skin, etc., naturally (ME), hence to get rid of something unwanted or unnecessary (19c) **5** to part the hair (ME); a parting; a ridge of high ground separating two valleys (19c), first recorded in **watershed** separating waters flowing to different rivers, hence an event or period that marks a turning point; in the UK, the time after which television programmes unsuitable for children may be shown.

Related to **sheath**, **sheathe**, **shiver** a fragment or splinter, hence to SHATTER, and to SKID*.

sheen [Old English *scēne*: related to **shine**, which has influenced the sense, and to SHOW*] Beautiful; bright (surviving mainly in names such as **Shenfield**), shining, resplendent, hence radiance, brightness (17c); a gloss or lustre on a surface, hence a film of oil (1970s).

sheer [ME. From obsolete *shire* (Old English *scir*) 'bright, shining, translucent', later 'pure, unmitigated'] **1** free, clear, acquitted (–15c) **2** of the hair: thin, sparse (15c only); of fabric: fine, diaphanous (16c) **3 (a)** unmixed, unadulterated, undiluted (16c) **(b)** absolute, unmitigated (16c); of a cliff etc.: perpendicular (19c).

Old English *scir* appears in **Sheerness** and in other names as **Sher-** or **Shir-**. Related to SHOW*.

sheet [Old English *scēat(a)*] The lower corner of a sail; a rope etc. attached to it (ME), hence **sternsheets** (15c), **foresheets** (18c) the (boarded) stern or bow part of an open boat, from which the rope was handled.

Old English *scēat(a)* appears in names as **-shot(t)**, probably meaning 'corner of land'. Related to **sheet** a large piece of fabric [OE *scēte, sciete*], hence a flat piece of paper, ice, metal, etc., and more distantly to SHOOT*.

shell [Old English *sc(i)ell*] A hard protective covering, originally of an egg or mollusc, hence **1** one of the small plates covering a fish, reptile, etc. (–17c), replaced by related **scale** [ME, from Old French *escale*, of Germanic origin, which went on to mean the deposits formed on kettles, teeth, etc.]; a thin flat plate or fragment (ME) **2** a husk or pod (ME) **3** to remove from a shell or pod (16c) **4** a hollow (hemi)spherical object or container (16c): **(a)** a scale pan (*Scots*): cf. *scale* below **(b)** a case for explosives, fireworks, cartridges, etc. (17c), hence an explosive projectile; a cartridge (18c, *US*) **(c)** the external structure of a building, ship, car, etc. (17c) **(d)** a hollow or empty form (18c); **shell (company)** one left dormant or used only to channel funds (1950s).

Shell produced **shellac** [translating French *lacque en écailles*] lac in thin plates used to make varnish etc., hence to coat with shellac; to beat or defeat soundly (cf. PASTE); **shellacked** drunk (US slang, cf. *plastered* at PLASTER). Related to Old Norse *skál* 'bowl', in the plural 'weighing scales' (whence **scale** a drinking-bowl or cup (surviving in Scots and also in S Africa, where it means a measuring pot); a scale pan, hence **(pair of) scales** a weighing device), and probably to SCALLOP* and to **shale** the sedimentary rock.

sherbet [17c. Turkish *şerbet*, Persian *šerbet*, from Arabic *šarba(t)* 'drink', from *šariba* 'to drink'] **1** a drink made of sweetened, diluted fruit juice **2** a flavoured sweet powder eaten or made into a fizzy drink (19c); this drink **3** a water-ice (19c, N *American*).

Turkish *şerbet* produced French *sorbet* sherbet (sense 1 and sense 3). Arabic *šariba* is the ancestor of **shrub** a drink of sweetened fruit juice and rum, later a cordial made of raspberry juice, vinegar, and sugar (*US*), and of **syrup**.

shibboleth [17c. Hebrew *šibbōlet* 'ear of corn'] A word used as a test of a speaker's origin because of a distinctive local pronunciation (see the Bible, Judges 12:6), hence **1** a way of speaking, later a custom, style of dress, etc., that indicates a person's nationality, class, etc., or identifies an outsider **2** a custom, belief, or saying of long standing, held or used without much thought; a taboo (1930s).

shield [Old English *sc(i)eld*] A piece of armour carried in the hand or on the arm, hence **1** to protect; to cover or hide (as if) with a shield; someone/something that does so (ME); a protective screen or cover (18c) **2** a representation of a shield: **(a)** bearing the owner's coat of arms (ME), also called an **escutcheon** [ME, via Old Norman French from Latin *scutum* 'shield'] **(b)** given as a trophy (19c) **(c)** as a police officer's badge (*c*.1900, *US*).

Old English *sc(i)eld* produced **sheltron** a testudo or phalanx [–15c, from Old English *scieldtruma* 'shield troop'], whence, probably, **shelter**. Latin *scutum* is the ancestor of SQUIRE*.

shift [Old English *sciftan*] To divide or distribute (OE only); to arrange or put in order (–15c), hence **1** to deal with (ME–16c); to manage or get by (16c, surviving mainly in **shift for yourself** to manage by your own efforts); a means of getting by, hence **(a) make shift with** to get by with inferior resources, hence **makeshift** (19c) **(b)** an expedient, an underhand scheme, hence to be evasive or deceitful, hence **shifting** evasive, cunning, replaced by **shifty** (19c) **(c)** ingenuity, initiative, surviving mainly in **shiftless** (17c) **2** to change, transform, or swap (ME), hence **(a)** to put on fresh clothes (15c), especially underwear, hence a long, loose undergarment, originally worn by both sexes, later by women (16c, replacing *smock* and largely replaced by *chemise*: see below), hence a loose dress (1950) **(b)** a relay, originally of horses (18c), later of workers; their period of work (*the night shift*) **3** to change the position of (ME), hence **(a)** to dispose of (17c); to consume (a lot of) food or money quickly (19c); to sell (a lot of) goods quickly or dishonestly (1970s) **(b)** a mechanism for doing so, hence the **shift key** on a typewriter etc. (19c); the gear lever in a car, hence **down/upshift** a change, or to change, to a lower/higher gear: **downshifter** someone who changes to a less stressful career or simpler lifestyle (1980s).

Smock [Old English *smoc*] came to mean a farm labourer's tunic (also as *frock* or **smock-frock**), hence **1 smocking** traditional decoration on one, formed by pleating and ornamental sewing; *smock* a dress or blouse decorated with smocking **2** a loose (smocked) overall as worn by artists; **(camouflage) smock** a loose camouflage tunic. French *chemise* comes from late Latin *camisia* 'shirt, surplice', whence also French *camisole* and Arabic *qāmis*, whence **kameez** a tunic worn on the Indian subcontinent and by some Muslims elsewhere.

ship [Old English *scip*] A large seagoing vessel, hence **1** to fit out or launch one (ME–16c: cf. *equip* below) **2** to board one (ME); to take passengers or cargo onto one, hence to go or send by ship; to transport goods by any means (19c, *US*) **3** a ship's crew (ME); to employ (17c) or to be employed (19c) as crew **4** something resembling a ship (*ship of the desert/spaceship*, ME) **5** to put something into the ship it belongs to (earlier in **unship**) or in its proper place (17c), hence **(a)** to bring an oar into a boat, or fit it into the rowlock **(b) shipshape** orderly, tidy **(c)** *unship* to unbalance or upset (19c); of a horse: to unseat its rider **6** of a vessel: to take in water over the side (17c).

Related to Low German or Dutch *schip*, whence Dutch **schipperke** [literally 'little boatman'] a breed of barge dog, **skipper** [Low German or Dutch *schipper* 'boatman'] the captain of a ship, later a sports team, and **yacht** [Dutch *jaghte*, from *jaghtschip* 'fast pirate ship', from *jagen* 'to hunt']. Probably related to **equip**

[French *équiper*, probably from Old Norse *skipa* 'to man or fit out a ship', from *skip* 'ship'] and **skiff** [via French from Italian *schifo*, probably from High German *schif*].

shire [Old English *scīr*] Administrative office, the position of a governor, bishop, etc. (OE only), hence an area ruled by one; in Anglo-Saxon England, an administrative district governed by an alderman and a sheriff; under the Normans, an administrative division equivalent to a county, hence in the names of counties in the S England and the Midlands (*Hampshire, Leicestershire*). Hence **the Shires** these counties, specifically those in the Midlands (18c); **shire (horse)** a heavy horse bred there.

In Anglo-Saxon England, a **reeve** [Old English *(ge)rēfa*] was the chief official or magistrate of a town or district: the equivalent in a shire was the *scirgerēfa* or **sheriff**, who in England now has ceremonial and some judicial duties, in Scotland presides over the lower courts, and in the US is elected to keep the peace.

shirk [17c. Perhaps from German *Schurke* 'scoundrel'] To prey and sponge on others; someone who does so (cf. *shark* below), hence to be evasive; to evade or dodge a person (18c), later, work or a duty.

German *Schurke* is probably the ancestor of **shark** in *loan shark*, influenced by the predatory fish [origin unknown].

shoal [Old English *sceald*] Of water: not deep (first recorded as **Shal-** in place names); largely replaced by related **shallow** (ME), hence **1** an area of shallow water (15c, also as *shallows*); a sandbank visible at high water **2** to become shallower (16c, also as *shallow*); to move into shallower water (17c).

shoddy [19c. Origin unknown] Old unravelled woollen cloth; cloth made from a mixture of this and new wool, hence (describing) something inferior, especially if it looks better than it is, hence **1** poorly made **2** shabby, disreputable; dishonest.

shoot [Old English *scēotan*] To (make something) go quickly and suddenly; to throw something suddenly or violently, to stick or, later, to push out suddenly. So **1 (a)** to fire a missile or weapon; to kill or wound by doing so **(b)** to dart a glance, remark, question, etc. (17c), hence *shoot!* 'come on, tell/ask me!' (*c.*1910, US: cf. *fire away!* at FIRE) **(c)** to send a ball towards a goal (19c) **(d)** to photograph or film something (19c); a session of doing so (*photoshoot*, early 20c) **(e)** **shoot up** to inject an illicit drug (*c.*1910, *US*: cf. *shooting gallery* at GALLERY) **2** to push home a bolt (the original sense of related **shut**) **3** to tip or empty out grain, rubbish, etc. (ME), hence (to pour it down) a slope or channel (18c); a narrow passageway for cattle etc. (also as the variant **shute**: see also CHUTE) **4** a young branch or sucker (ME): **(a)** to produce one (16c); of a bud etc.: to appear and grow **(b)** **offshoot** a branch, originally of a family tree (18c); a spin-off or by-product (19c) **5** to pass (rapidly) across or through (*shooting star, shoot the rapids*, ME); in weaving: to pass the weft thread through the warp (16c); to weave with the warp of one colour and the weft of another, so that the different colours show at different angles (*shot silk*).

Skeet a form of clay pigeon shooting (1920s, *US*) may be an alteration of *shoot*. Old English *scēotan* produced the names **Shooter**, **Shutte** given to archers, and some place names beginning **Shot-** or **Shut-** (referring to a steep slope). Related to *scot* (at LOT), SCUTTLE[2], SHEET*, **shot** an act of shooting (most of whose senses parallel or derive from *shoot*), SHUTTLE, and perhaps **shout** and SKITTISH*.

show [Old English *scēawian*] To look at, inspect, or consider (–15c); to cause or allow to be seen (ME); to appear or be visible, hence **1** a demonstration or exhibition (*show of strength/dog show*, 15c); a public entertainment (16c); a light entertainment programme on radio or television (1930s); any broadcast (*US*) **2** external appearance (16c); an appearance or display of a quality, feeling, etc.; ostentatious display, hence **showy** striking, ostentatious, gaudy (18c) **3** a sign or trace (16c).

Show produced **showdown**, when card players lay their cards down face up, hence a declaration or trial of strength; a confrontation. Related to SCAVENGER, **scone** [Scots, from early Low German or Dutch *scho(o)nbrot* 'fine bread'], SHEEN, SHEER, and **shimmer**.

shred [Old English *scrēad* (noun), *scrēadian* (verb): related to SCROLL*] To prune, cut off, or cut to pieces; a piece broken or cut off, hence **1** a thinly cut or torn strip (ME); to cut or tear into shreds **2** the smallest fragment or remnant (*not a shred of evidence*, ME).

The variant **screed** came to mean **1** a long roll or list, hence a long, often tedious, piece of writing or, later, speech **2** a strip of plaster, wood, etc. used as a guide to the correct thickness of plaster; a board or tool to level fresh plaster etc.; a smooth layer forming part of a floor etc.

shrew [Old English *scrēawa*] A small mouselike creature once believed to be harmful to humans, hence a villain (ME); a scold or a bad-tempered person, now only a woman, hence to curse someone (largely replaced by its offspring, 15c **beshrew**).

Shrew produced **shrewd** evil, malignant, depraved; dangerous, harmful, hence **1** cunning, artful, later astute, perceptive **2** sharp to the senses; of wind etc.: keen.

shrine [Old English *scrīn*, ultimately from Latin *scrinium* 'case for books or papers'] A box, chest, or cabinet (–17c), hence **1** a reliquary, hence **(a)** to put relics in one (ME); to enclose and protect as a shrine does (16c), outlived by **enshrine** (15c) **(b)** a container for a sacred or precious object (16c); a niche for a religious icon **2** a coffin (ME), later an elaborate tomb, especially of a saint, pope, or other revered figure. Hence **3** a place regarded as holy because of its association with a person or event (17c); a place kept to preserve someone's memory (19c).

shrive [Old English *scrifan*, ultimately from Latin *scribere* 'to write', also 'to describe, to draft': in English and the Scandinavian languages the underlying sense is 'to prescribe a penalty'] To hear someone's confession, prescribe a penance, and absolve them; to make your confession and be absolved.

The past tense, **shrove**, produced **Shrove Tuesday**, the day before the penitential period of Lent, when it was customary to go to confession, to eat pancakes (made of eggs symbolizing creation, flour as the staff of life, and milk symbolizing purity), and take part in general merrymaking. Feasting and merrymaking before Lent are also referred to in **carnival** [via Italian from medieval Latin *carnelevanum*, *carnelevarium*, literally 'the removal of meat', from Latin *caro*, *carn-* 'flesh' (ancestor of CARRION*) + *levare* 'to remove', more commonly 'to raise': see LEVER*], and in French *Mardi gras* [literally 'fat Tuesday'].

Old English *scrifan* produced **shrift** penance (–15c); absolution **(a)** confession; **short shrift** a short time allowed for confession before being executed, surviving in **give short shrift to** to treat curtly or unsympathetically.

shroud [Old English *scrūd:* related to SCROLL*] A garment (–17c); to clothe or adorn (ME–16c), hence **1** to protect or shelter, hence **(a)** to hide or disguise (15c, later also as **enshroud**); a covering, veil, or disguise (18c) **(b)** a (protective) covering on machinery (15c) **2 shrouds** a set of ropes supporting the mast of a ship (15c, from the idea of 'clothing' the mast with them: a mast without shrouds is said to be naked), hence *shroud* a similar rope etc. on land (18c); **shroud (line)** a strap joining the canopy of a parachute to the harness (1920s) **3** to wrap a corpse in a sheet or sheetlike garment for burial (16c, also as *enshroud*); such a garment (18c).

shrub [Old English *scrubb, scrybb*] A woody plant smaller than a tree; an area planted with these (replaced by 18c **shrubbery**). The variant **scrub** came to mean a stunted tree (ME, surviving in Australia, New Zealand, and English dialect), hence **1** one of a breed of small cattle (16c); a stunted or poorly bred animal; a worthless, contemptible person: also as *shrub* (16–17c), and later as **scrubber** (19c, probably by association with SCRUB a menial servant), hence a prostitute or tart (1950s) **2** (an area overgrown with) stunted trees and brushwood (19c, 17c in **scrubby**).

shun [Old English *scunian*, of unknown origin: probably the source of SHUNT] To loathe (OE only); to hide or run away from (–17c); to shrink (back) with fear; to avoid out of fear or, now usually, disgust (ME).

shunt [ME. Probably from SHUN] To move aside suddenly, to shy away (–18c); to push aside (18c), hence **1** (to use) a device that diverts a flow (19c) **2** to move railway rolling stock from one set of rails to another (19c), hence a motor accident, especially a nose-to-tail collision (1920s, likened to shunted trucks).

shuttle [Old English *scytel*] An arrow (OE only), hence **1** in weaving: a bobbin with pointed ends that carries the weft thread back and forth through the warp (ME), hence to move something quickly back and forth like a shuttle (16c, earlier in the game of *battledore and shuttlecock* below); to move or travel in this way (19c), hence a train, bus, aircraft, etc. that goes back and forth at frequent intervals, hence **(a) (space) shuttle** a reusable space craft (1960s) **(b) shuttle diplomacy** involving a mediator travelling to and fro between the parties (1970s) **2** a device that carries the thread in tatting, embroidery, a sewing machine, etc. (18c) **3** a shuttle-shaped mollusc (18c).

Battledore and shuttlecock was an early form of badminton, the **shuttlecock** [from *shuttle* + COCK a male bird, because of its feathers] being hit back and forth with a **battledore**, originally a kind of paddle used in washing, later applied to various similarly shaped things including the racket used in the game [perhaps a mixture of **beetle** a mallet (Old English *bytl*) and Old Provençal *batedor* 'a bat', ultimately from Latin *battuere* (whence BATTER*)]. The modern game of **badminton** evolved at Badminton House in W England in the 1870s.

shy [Old English *sceoh*] Easily frightened (–17c), hence **1** to take fright suddenly (17c); of a horse: to jump back or sideways in fright (18c) **2** reluctant to approach, or to do, something (17c), hence **(a)** bashful, diffident (17c); showing such feelings (*a shy smile*) **(b)** **shy away from**, **fight shy of** to avoid (both 18c) **(c)** of a plant or bird: not prolific, reluctant to breed (19c), hence short of, lacking (19c, *US*) **3** to throw (18c, supposedly from throwing things at a reluctant cockerel to make it fight) **4** dubious, suspect (19c), perhaps influenced by **shyster** an unscrupulous person, especially a lawyer [perhaps from the name *Scheuster*, an unscrupulous New York lawyer in the 1940s, or from German *Scheisser* 'bastard, villain', from *Scheisse* 'shit'].

Related to **eschew** [from Old French *eschiver* 'to avoid' (of Germanic origin), whence also **skew**, which has also meant 'to swerve or jump sideways', and 'to throw'], and perhaps to **skive** (*military slang*).

sign [ME. Via French from Latin *signum*] A gesture, mark, or symbol that conveys a meaning, hence **1** an indication or evidence (*signs of life*), hence **(a)** an omen **(b)** a miracle as evidence of a supernatural power **(c)** in medicine: an objective indication of disease, e.g. a rash or swelling (19c), as opposed to a subjective **symptom** [15c, via Latin from Greek *sumptôma* 'chance, accident', from *sumpiptein* 'to happen to', from *piptein* 'to fall'] **2** a board etc. carrying an identifying symbol, later one giving information or directions **3** to mark with a sign; to add your signature to something, especially to show consent, hence **(a)** to write your name as a signature (17c) **(b)** **sign (on/up)** to employ or be employed by signing a contract (19c) **(c)** **sign in/out** to sign your name when you arrive/leave (19c) **4** to give an indication or sign; to make a significant gesture (18c); to communicate using signs **5** (the symbol belonging to) each of the divisions of the zodiac.

Latin *signum* is the ancestor of **assign**, CONSIGN, DESIGN*, ENSIGN*, **resign** [via Old French from Latin *resignare* 'to unseal, cancel, or give up'], SEAL*, SIGNAL, SIGNATURE*, **signify** [Latin *significare* 'to be a sign or symbol of'], **tocsin** an alarm sounded by ringing a bell, later the bell [French, from Provençal *tocasenh*, from *tocar* 'to strike' + *senh* 'bell', from a late Latin sense, 'signal bell', of Latin *signum*], and probably of **scarlet**.

signal [ME. French, ultimately via late Latin *signalis* from Latin *signum* SIGN*] A visible sign: **1** a badge or symbol (–17c) **2** an indication of a fact, quality, or (future) occurrence (15c), hence **(a)** a sound or gesture conveying information or a warning (16c); a device used to make one (*traffic signal*, 17c) **(b)** a series of electrical impulses or radio waves transmitted or received (19c) **(c)** to be, make, indicate, or communicate by, a signal (19c).

Signal meaning 'remarkable, notable' comes via French from Italian *segnalato* 'distinguished', from *segnalare* 'to make famous', from *segnale* 'a signal, a distinguishing mark', from Latin *signum*.

signature [(French, from) medieval Latin *signatura*, from Latin *signare* 'to mark', from *signum* SIGN*] A person's name, initials, etc. written by them and used to sign a document. Hence a distinguishing mark (17c): **1** a character at the foot of a page or pages of a printed sheet to show the order for binding; a folded sheet distinguished by one (18c) **2** a sign at the beginning of a piece of music showing its key or time (19c) **3** a distinctive feature, way of behaving, etc. by which someone/something can be identified (1930s, earliest in **signature tune** a tune associated with, and used to introduce, a performer) **4** **sig** text, a logo, etc. at the end of an on-line communication that identifies or gives information about the sender (1990s).

Latin *signare* produced **signatory**, originally describing a ring etc. used in sealing documents (17c only, outlived by *signet* at SEAL), later (describing) a person or state that has signed a document or treaty.

silly [Old English *sǣlig*] Happy, fortunate, blessed, hence pious; innocent, harmless, defenceless (ME, probably the meaning in *silly sheep*); unworldly, naive; foolish; absurd, ridiculous (16c); in cricket: describing positions (dangerously) close to the batsman (19c). Cf. DAFT, *naive* (at NATIVE), and **ninny** [from **innocent**, ultimately from Latin *nocere* 'to harm', whence **innocuous** and **nuisance**].

A Middle English spelling, *seely*, survives as a surname for a happy or innocent person (variants include **Sealey** and **Sellick**), whence **Se(a)lman** their servant.

simple [ME. French, from Latin *simplus*: related to *single* (at DOUBLE)] **1** free from duplicity, open, honest **2** poor, humble (*a simple shepherd*), hence uneducated, inexperienced; foolish (15c), hence *simpleton* (at TOWN) **3** unpretentious, unadorned, plain **4** unadulterated, mere, pure; not composite or complex, hence **(a)** of a wound or disease: without complications **(b)** of a remedy: made from one plant (16c), hence a medicinal plant.

simulate [ME. Latin *simulare* from *similis* 'like'] **Simulation** feigning, deceitful pretence; *simulate* to feign or imitate (17c), hence to reproduce the features of a situation or process, especially for training purposes (1940s).

Latin *simulare* produced *dissimulare* 'to disguise completely', whence **dissimulate** and **dissimule**, the latter altered to **dissemble** by association with **semblance** [Old French, from *sembler* 'to seem' (whence **resemble**), from Latin *simulare*]. Descendants of Latin *similis* include **assimilate**, FACSIMILE*, **similar**, and **verisimilitude** [Latin *verisimilis* 'like the truth', from *verus* 'truth' (ancestor of VERY*)].

sinister [ME. Latin, literally 'left, left-hand'] **1** adverse, unfavourable, also malicious (–18c), underhand, shady, corrupt (15c); inauspicious, threatening (16c) **2** in heraldry: **bend** or, later, **bar sinister** a stripe running from the top right to the bottom left of a shield, a mark of illegitimacy (15c). See also RIGHT*.

sink [Old English *sincan*] To fall or go slowly downwards; to go below the surface, especially of a liquid; to cause to do so (ME). Hence **1** a container for liquid: **(a)** in a kitchen (ME) **(b)** a cesspool (15c), hence a wicked or corrupt place (16c), now describing a socially deprived one (*sink school*, 1970s) **(c)** a place where water collects or sinks into the ground (16c); **sink (hole)** a swallow hole (18c) **(d)** a device for absorbing energy (*heat sink*, 19c) **2** to (make something) penetrate (ME), hence **(a)** to drill a well, shaft, etc. (ME); to force something into the ground etc. (*sink piles/a putt*, 19c) **(b)** **sink in** to penetrate your mind or heart **3** to slump or collapse (ME); to subside; to deteriorate; to cause to do so; to ruin; **sunk** ruined, doomed **4** to invest money, especially unsuccessfully (18c).

sire [ME. French, ultimately from Latin *senex* 'old': see SENIOR*] **1** a polite form of address for a man, especially your superior, or for a certain kind of man (*Sire Knight/Priest* etc.), or used before the first name of a knight or baronet: quickly shortened to **sir** except when speaking to a king. **Sirrah** is an archaic form, usually contemptuous (16c) **2** the father or forefather of a person or quadruped (16c, cf. *dam* at LORD), hence to father (17c).

Sir produced **sirly** lordly, haughty, imperious (ME–17c), whence **surly** bad tempered, morose.

siren [ME. Via Old French from Latin *Sirena*, feminine of *Siren*, from Greek *Seirēn*] **1** a monster in Greek mythology, half woman and half bird, whose singing lured sailors to destruction on the rocks, hence **(a)** someone who sings sweetly (16c) **(b)** a temptress (16c) **(c)** a warning device that makes a loud wailing sound (19c) **2** an imaginary serpent (based on glosses of Latin *sirenes* in the Vulgate version of the Bible, Isaiah 13:22: later translated as 'flying serpents' or 'dragons'), hence a kind of eel-like N American amphibian (18c).

site [ME. (Anglo-Norman French, from) Latin *situs* 'position'] Someone/something's place or position (–18c), now **1** the location of a town, building, etc., especially with reference to its surroundings (15c); the ground on which it stands or is to be built, hence **sited** situated, located, whence *site* to locate (16c) **2** a place where something happened or is happening (17c); in archaeology: a place containing traces of former human habitation (*c.*1910).

Latin *situs* also produced **situate** to put in a particular place or, later, in particular circumstances, and **situation** the place or position of something in relation to its surroundings, hence **1** someone's place in life; a position, a job **2** a set of circumstances, whence **situation comedy** based on characters in unusual circumstances, shortened to **sitcom** (*US*), which has encouraged formations such as **romcom** romantic comedy.

skep [Old English *sceppe* from Old Norse *skeppa* 'basket, bushel'] A tub or basket, hence **1** a straw or wicker beehive (15c); to make bees go into one (19c) **2** as the variant **skip** a bucket, cage, etc. for raising and lowering miners and mining materials (19c); a large metal container for (builders') rubbish.

skid [17c. Possibly from or related to Old Norse *skith* 'piece of split wood, snowshoe'] **1** a supporting beam or plank, especially in boat-building **2** (to apply) a shoe that grips a wheel, hence of a wheel: to slide (19c); of a vehicle etc.: to slide out of control after braking (19c); (to cause) such a movement (early 20c), hence of an aircraft: to slip sideways, especially while turning **3** a plank or roller on which something heavy may be moved (18c), hence **(a)** **skid road** one made of half-sunken logs along which logs are hauled (19c, N American), hence an area of town frequented by lumberjacks (*c.*1900), later by down-and-outs, usually altered to **skid row (b)** in phrases describing impending failure or defeat (*put the skids under/on the skids*, *c.*1910) **(c)** a runner under an aircraft (*c.*1910).

Old Norse *skith* produced Norwegian **skí**. Related to SHED*.

skirmish [ME. Old French *eskirmir* and/or Old Italian *scaramuccia* 'to fight with swords, to fence', of Germanic origin] **1** (to take part in) a brief fight involving a small number of troops; a brief struggle, argument, or battle of wits (16c) **2** to search or rummage around for something (19c, *US*, cf. *scrimmage* below).

Skirmish changed to **scrimmage** a fencing bout; a fight (now only US), hence **1** a rough or confused struggle, particularly for possession of the ball in some games, in rugby football as the variant **scrummage**, shortened to **scrum** a set-piece formation to decide possession, hence **scrum (down)** to form or take part in one; *scrum* to crowd or jostle; a confused or disorderly crowd **2** to search roughly and thoroughly (chiefly Scots); such a search.

Old Italian *scaramuccia* was adopted as the name of a cowardly braggart in the *commedia dell'arte* (see also HARLEQUIN): the French form **Scaramouche** is more familiar. Related to SCREEN.

skirt [ME. Old Norse *skyrta* 'shirt'] The lower part of a woman's dress; a separate garment corresponding to this (16c); the lower part of a coat or robe. Hence **1** something resembling this: **(a)** a saddle flap (15c) **(b)** a border, edge, or verge (surrounding as a skirt does the legs, 15c); an edging (16c); a **skirting (board)** around a room (18c). Hence to border (17c); to go around (18c); to avoid **(c)** an animal's diaphragm and other membranes, especially as food (18c); the trimmings of a carcass or fleece (19c); a cut of meat from the lower flank; **2** a (sexually attractive) woman (16c); women regarded in this way (*a bit of skirt*).

The Old English equivalent, *scyrte*, produced **shirt**: both probably meant some kind of tunic before separating into the top and bottom half of one. Related to SHEAR*.

skittish [15c. The eldest of a family thought to be from or related to Old Norse *skjota* 'to shoot' (related to SHOOT*) and sharing ideas of quick movement, unreliability, and vanity] Light, frivolous, playful; changeable, fickle (16c); restive, fidgety, nervous.

Other family members are **skit** originally a vain, flighty woman, **skitter**, and probably **scoot**.

slack [Old English *slaec*] **1** lazy, lackadaisical, lax, negligent, hence to be idle (16c); to make little effort; **slack off** to become less energetic or diligent: replacing **slake** [Old English *slaecian*, from *slaec*] **2** slow, unhurried, sluggish, hence **(a)** of the tide: neither ebbing or flowing (15c); (describing) an area of comparatively still water (19c) **(b)** of trade: not busy or brisk (15c) **3** not tight or firm (ME), hence **(a)** to loosen (16c), replacing *slake*, largely replaced by **slacken** (17c) **(b)** the loose part of a rope (18c) or garment (19c); **slacks** loose casual trousers **4** to make less intense (16c), partly replacing *slake*, later also as *slacken*; *slake* remains predominant meaning 'to quench your thirst', and came to mean 'to moisten' (15c), hence to treat lime with water to produce calcium hydroxide (**slaked lime**, 17c).

slag [16c. Early Low German *slagge*, perhaps from *slagen* 'to strike'] (A piece of) waste material from smelting metallic ore, hence **1** a similar lump of lava (18c) **2** a despicable person (18c); a promiscuous woman, hence, probably, **slag (off)** to insult or criticize (1970s).

Related to **onslaught**, **slaughter** [Old Norse *slátr* 'butcher's meat'], **slay**, and *sledge* in **sledgehammer**.

slap [ME. Probably an imitation of the sound] To hit smartly, especially with the open hand; (the sound of) such a blow. Hence **1** a reprimand or rebuff (18c) **2** to put on or put down sharply, forcefully, or carelessly (17c), hence **(a) slap-bang shop**, an 18c fast-food shop demanding payment in advance, hence **slap (bang)** immediately, directly, precisely (cf. *slap/smack dab* at DAB) **(b) slapdash** hastily, careless(ly) (17c) **(c)** (theatrical) make-up, especially applied thickly or carelessly (19c) **3 slapper** a large thing or person (17c); a big fat woman; a tart **4 slapstick** a device used to simulate the sound of a slap in pantomime etc. (19c), hence knockabout comedy (*c*.1900) **5 slaphappy** punch-drunk, dazed (1930s); cheerfully irresponsible **6 happy slapping** attacking someone, the attack being recorded and transmitted on a mobile phone (*c*.2005).

Smack [imitative Dutch or Low German *smacken*] now also means 'to hit with an open hand': the original sense was as in *smack your lips*, hence to kiss noisily (surviving in Scots and in **smacking kiss** or **smacker**).

slate [ME. Old French *esclate*, feminine of *esclat* 'splinter, piece broken off', from *esclater* 'to split', probably of Germanic origin] A sedimentary rock that splits easily into flat plates, hence **1** a roofing tile made of it (15c) **2** a piece of it for writing on (15c), hence (to add something to) a list, record, or schedule, originally one written on a slate (19c) **3** (of) the colour of slate (19c) **4** to beat or thrash (19c: this development is not clear, but some early examples refer to knocking someone's hat over their eyes, so there may be a connection with roof slates: *tile* was used to mean 'hat', though there are no records of *slate* in this sense); to scold or criticize harshly.

Old French *esclat* produced **slat** originally a roof or writing slate. Probably related to **slice** and **slit**.

slave [ME. Old French *esclave*, from medieval Latin *sclavus* 'Slavonic (captive)', from *Sclavus* 'Slav', from late Greek *Sklabos*, an alteration of Old Slavic *Slovenine* (whence also **Slovak** and **Slovene**), probably from *slovo* ' word, language', applied to those speaking mutually intelligible languages] A human chattel, hence **1 (a)** someone completely dominated by someone/something (16c) **(b)** someone who works hard without reward or thanks (18c); to do so; **slavey** a servant, especially a female drudge (19c); **slave (jib)** a working jib which is almost permanently set (1940s) **(c) white slave** an enslaved White person (18c); a woman forced into prostitution (early 20c) **(d)** an ant captured by and made to work for another species (19c) **(e)** (describing) a device controlled by another (*c*.1900) **2** to make someone a slave (16c, replaced by **enslave**, 17c) **3 slavish** servile, submissive (16c); strictly imitative, showing no originality (18c).

sleazy [17c. Origin unknown] Of fabric: thin, flimsy, hence of poor quality; cheap and tawdry; squalid, disreputable, sordid (1940s), hence **sleaze** squalor, sordidness (1960s); (someone with) low moral standards (1970s).

sleuth [ME. Old Norse *slóth*, whence, probably, **slot** an animal's track or trail, a deer's footprint (16c, via Old French)] The track or trail of a person or animal (–15c), hence **sleuth-hound** a hound used for tracking criminals; *sleuth* a detective (19c); to act as one (*c*.1900).

slick [ME. Probably from Old English and related to SLIGHT*] (To make) smooth, glossy, elegant, or fine, hence **1** of an animal: healthy-looking with a shiny coat (15c, now only as the variant **sleek**) **2** smooth, plausible (16c); superficially attractive (19c), hence **(a) (city) slicker** a sophisticated and perhaps dishonest city dweller (1920s, *US*) **(b)** to cheat or swindle (1930s); a swindler (1950s) **3** polished, efficient, running smoothly (19c) **4** something smooth or glossy: **(a)** a smooth patch on water, especially one caused by oil (19c) **(b)** **slicker** a raincoat (19c, N American) **(c)** a glossy magazine (1930s, *US*) **(d)** a smooth tyre (1950s).

slide [Old English *slīdan*] Shares some senses with SLIP². To glide or slip on a smooth surface; this action (16c); to make something do so (17c). Hence **1** to slip away, to be forgotten or neglected (ME); **let slide** to let something take its course; **on the slide** declining or degenerating rapidly (19c) **2** to move quietly or stealthily; to change imperceptibly (ME) **3** a landslip (17c), largely replaced by **landslide** (19c), which came to mean an overwhelming victory in an election **4** a surface, slope, or chute to slide on or down (17c) **5** something that slides, hence **(a)** a fastener that slides on a cord (17c); an ornamental hair clasp **(b)** something designed to slide into place (19c), hence a photograph in a holder to slide into a projector; a specimen prepared to slide under a microscope.

Old English *slīdan* produced *sliderian*, literally 'to keep sliding', whence **slidder**, largely replaced by the alteration **slither**. Related to **sled**, **sledge**, and **sleigh**.

slight [ME. Old Norse *slēttr* 'level'] **1** (to make) smooth, level, or sleek (now dialect); to raze to the ground (17c); to demolish **2** small; slender, frail, insubstantial; barely perceptible; unimportant, trifling, hence **(a)** of a person: humble, lowly, worthless (15–17c); to treat as such, to snub (16c); a snub (18c) **(b)** half-hearted (17c); to do half-heartedly (19c).

Related to **slime**, SLIP²*, and probably to SLICK*.

slim [16c. Low German or Dutch] **1** a (lanky and) idle person (–19c, from a sense 'bad' found in German and Dutch, which also produced the S African sense 'sly, spiteful', 17c); to idle or skive (19c) **2** slender, slight (17c), hence **(a)** meagre, insufficient (cf. LEAN², MEAGRE) **(b)** not overweight (19c), hence **slim (down)** to make slim; to (try to) lose weight (1930s); a spell of doing so (*sponsored slim*, 1970s) **(c)** unhealthily thin, delicate, poorly (19c, US) **(d)** to reduce in size (19c), hence stripped of unnecessary elements, efficient, economical (1970, cf. LEAN²) **(e)** Slim (disease) the Central African name for AIDS (1980s, from the severe weight loss it causes).

slip¹ [Old English *slyppe*] Slime, mud (–15c), hence **1** dung, surviving in **cowslip**, **oxslip**, literally 'cow/ox dung', applied to the yellow flowers that appear to spring from it **2** curdled milk (ME), hence a mixture of clay and water used in pottery-making (17c).

Probably the source of **slop** a muddy place, later to spill or splash liquid, hence **slops** semi-liquid, unappetizing food, dregs, and of **sloppy** wet, muddy; of work etc.: careless, messy; of a garment: loose, ill-fitting [perhaps influenced by **slop** a loose garment, **slops** loose trousers, of unknown origin].

slip² [ME. Probably from early Dutch or Low German *slippen*] Shares some senses with SLIDE. To move easily, smoothly, or imperceptibly; to make or allow to do so, hence **1** **slip (away)** to leave or escape; **(let) slip** to allow to do so; **give someone the slip** to elude them (16c) **2** to slide (inadvertently) on a smooth surface, hence **(a)** to make a mistake; a (slight) error or oversight (16c); to lapse, deteriorate, or fall behind schedule (*c*.1900) **(b)** a man-made slope for launching boats (15c) **(c)** an act of slipping or sliding down (16c); a place where land has subsided (16c, now usually **landslip**); (the amount of) such a movement or (of) deviation from what is expected (later also **slippage**, *c.*1900) **3** to put on or off quickly and easily (implied in 15c **slipper** a loose indoor shoe), hence **(a)** a loose garment (18c), now an underskirt **(b) slipshod** wearing slippers or loose shoes (16c), hence shabby, unkempt (17c); slovenly, careless (19c) **(c) slips** the sides of the stage, from whence the scenery is 'slipped' on (18c).

Slippery comes from related dialect **slipper**, which also meant 'morally repugnant', whence *slippery*'s sense 'deceitful, untrustworthy, unreliable'.

slip³ [ME. Probably from early Dutch or Low German *slippe*] A cut or slit (–17c), hence **1** a cutting from a plant for grafting or planting (15c); a descendant or offshoot (16c): cf. SCION* **2** a strip of material (16c); a small piece of paper (17c) **3** a young person of either sex, especially a small or slender one (16c, now usually in *a slip of a girl*) **4** something elongated or narrow (18c); a long narrow window, passage, etc. (18c); **slips** the sides of the gallery of a theatre (19c).

Related to dialect **slive** to split, divide, or cut off, whence **sliver** a piece cut off; to cut one; to cut or tear to slivers.

slob [18c. Irish *slab* 'mud' from English *slab* 'ooze, sludge', probably of Scandinavian origin: perhaps influenced by Middle English **slobber**, from Dutch *slobbern*, imitating the sound] **1** (soft) mud, muddy land (18c) **2** a large soft worm used as bait (18c); a coarse, fat, or slovenly person (19c).

slog [19c. Origin unknown] (To give) a hard blow (also, and now more commonly, as **slug**), hence in cricket: (to make) a vigorous attacking stroke; to score runs by sustained and aggressive hitting, hence to work long and hard; a long spell of hard work; a long hard walk; to walk doggedly.

slogan [16c. Gaelic *sluagh-ghairm*, from *sluagh* 'multitude, army' + *gairm* 'shout'] A war cry, hence the distinctive cry or watchword of a person or group (18c); a short, memorable phrase used to promote something (1920s).

The variant **slughorn** came to mean a kind of trumpet, perhaps from a misunderstanding of *horn*. Gaelic *sluagh* is the ancestor of **slew** a crowd, a large number (US). The origin of **slew** 'to turn or twist round' is unknown.

slot [ME. Old French *esclot*, of unknown origin] The hollow of the breastbone (now rare), hence a slit, channel, or groove (15c); to put something into one (19c), hence **1 slot machine** activated by putting a coin into its slot (19c), now often shortened to *slot* for gambling machines, however operated **2** (to fit something into) a position in a hierarchy, scheme, or schedule (1940s) **3** in football: to kick a ball through a narrow gap (1970s); to score by doing so **4** a rectangular socket on a computer (*expansion slot*, 1970s).

slow [Old English *slāw*] **1** not readily understanding, thinking, etc., dull **2** inactive, sluggish, lazy; not willing or quick to do something (ME) **3** needing, taking, or lasting a long time (ME), hence **(a)** moving at a low speed (15c) **(b)** of fire: smouldering (15c); of an oven: merely warm (18c) **(c)** of business: not brisk (19c) **(d)** tedious, lifeless (19c).

Slow produced **sloth** laziness, reluctance to act or work; slowness, hence applied to various slow-moving mammals of Central and S America, and creatures resembling them.

slug [15c. Probably of Scandinavian origin] A lazy, inactive person (outlived by related Middle English **sluggard** and by 16c **slugabed** someone reluctant to get up); to be lazy and slow (15c). Hence **1 sluggish** not active or vigorous (15c) **2** a slow sailing boat (16–17c); a sluggish animal, vehicle, etc. (17c); a slow-moving creature like a snail with no shell, hence, perhaps (from its shape), a bullet, hence **(a)** a drink of spirits (having a similar effect, 18c) **(b)** a thick piece of metal or other material (19c); in printing: a line of type cast in a single strip; a (temporary) line of type carrying identifying marks; **slug (line)** a temporary title identifying a news story in draft (1920s).

slur [ME. Origin unknown] Thin semi-liquid mud, largely replaced by related **slurry** (15c), which now means any mixture of water and an insoluble solid. Hence to smear (17c): **1** to smear someone's reputation; such a smear **2** in music: a line over notes to be played in a smooth, uninterrupted way; to play in this way (18c); to speak or write so that sounds or letters run together (19c) **3** to gloss over or minimize.

slush [17c. Origin unknown] Partly melted snow or ice; watery mud (18c), hence **1** grease obtained by boiling meat (18c, sailors' slang), hence **slush fund** money from selling this, used to buy luxuries for the sailors (19c); a fund used to supplement the salaries of government employees or for illicit political or business activities **2** sentimental drivel (19c) **3** sloppy food, mush (1940s 19c as the variant **slosh**).

Slosh also means **1** to splash through slush or water; to splash or soak; (the sound of) a splash; **sloshed** drunk **2** to hit; a blow.

sly [ME. Old Norse *sloegr* 'able to strike', later 'adept', from *slá-* 'to strike'] Capable, skilful, dexterous, clever; cunning, evasive; stealthy, hence **1** mischievous, roguish (18c) **2 on the sly** in secret, stealthily (19c).

Old Norse *sloegr* produced **sleight** skill, dexterity, cunning, surviving in **sleight of hand**.

smack [Old English *smaec*] A (characteristic) taste, originally also a smell, hence to have a characteristic taste or smell; to taste or smell of something; (to have) a trace or suggestion of something (16c).

Smack a hard drug, usually heroin (*US*), is probably an alteration of related Yiddish *schmeck* 'a sniff or smell', also used for heroin.

smart [Old English *smeart* (adjective), *smeortan* (verb)] (To be) acutely painful; (to cause or feel) a sharp physical or mental pain (ME); of pain: sharp (–17c), hence forceful, vigorous; of a person: quick, active, hence **1** impudent, forward (ME, now mainly US and Scots) **2** alert (17c); quick-witted, clever, astute, hence **(a) smart alec** a know-all [19c, *US*, said to be from Alex Hoag, a clever and remarkably elusive thief], but perhaps a euphemism for **smart-arse** (not recorded in polite society until the 1960s): **smarty pants** (1940s, *US*) may be another euphemism, and **smarty boots** (1960s, US) perhaps a euphemism of a euphemism **(b)** of a device: apparently able to make judgements and act by itself (*smart card/bomb*, 1970s) **(c) smarts** intelligence, acumen (1970s, US) **3** brisk, spruce; neat and stylish (17c), hence **(a)** fashionable and sophisticated (*the smart set*, 18c) **(b) smarten (up)** to make smart, to improve the appearance of (19c).

smear [A falling together of Old English *smeoru* (noun) and *smeirwan* (verb)] Fat, grease, ointment (–17c); to coat or mark with this or with something sticky. Hence **1** to put oil on as a sign of consecration (gradually becoming contemptuous and replaced by *anoint* at UNGUENT) **2** (a mark caused by) a thin layer of grease etc. smeared on (17c); a sample of cells etc. smeared onto a microscope slide (*cervical smear*, *c*.1900) **3** to blot, smudge, or obscure (19c); to (try to) discredit someone or their reputation by slander; a slanderous story (1940s, *US*).

Old English *smeoru* appears as **Smar-** in place names, perhaps meaning rich pasture. Related to Swedish *smör* 'butter', whence *smorgasbord*.

smoulder [ME. Probably an alteration of *smorther*, from Old English *smorian* 'to suffocate' (whence **smother**)] **1** to suffocate (surviving in dialect) **2** smoke from a slow fire; to burn slowly with no flame (15c: rare from the 17c, revived by 19c Romantics), hence **(a)** a slow-burning fire (16c) **(b)** to exist in a suppressed state (19c); to feel a suppressed emotion.

smug [16c. Low German *smuk* 'pretty'] Trim, neat; smooth, sleek; well-groomed, presentable; conscious of being so; complacent, conceited.

snag [16c. Probably of Scandinavian origin] A sharp point or projection, especially a broken stump; a trunk or branch in a waterway causing danger to shipping (19c), hence **1** to catch or tear on a snag; such a tear **2** a hidden difficulty or drawback.

Snag is the source of **snaggly** and **snaggled** tangled, knotty, whence **snaggle** a tangle, and of *snaggle* in **snaggle-tooth** (someone with) a broken or projecting tooth.

snap [15c. Probably from early Dutch or Low German *snappen* 'to seize'] Of an animal: to give a sudden (audible) bite; such a bite, hence **1 snap (up)** to catch, seize, or snatch suddenly (15c); **snap (at)** to snatch at, to try to catch or bite (17c), hence *snap* something worth having (19c) **2** to speak sharply or irritably (16c) **3** to bite, cut, or break off sharply, cleanly and/or with a sharp sound, hence **(a)** such a sound; to (cause to) make one (*snap your fingers*) **(b)** a scrap or morsel (17c); a mouthful, a bite (cf. *schnapps* and *snack* below) **(c)** a break or fracture (18c) **4** quick, sudden (*snap decision*, 18c, *Scots*); a sudden, short spell (*cold snap*) **5** (to make) a short, quick movement (19c), hence **(a)** applied to various games involving one **(b) snap(shot)** a hurried shot without time to aim (19c); a casual photograph; *snap* to take one **(c)** to change your behaviour, mood, etc. with a sudden effort (*snap to attention*, *snap out of it*, early 20c).

Low German and Dutch *snappen* produced *snaps* 'a mouthful', whence German *schnaps* 'a dram of liquor', adopted for various strong dry liquors: Dutch *snappen*'s variant, *snacken*, produced **snack** (to give) a bite or snap, later a mouthful, a light meal, something (designed to be) eaten between meals, to eat a snack or snacks. Related to the name **Snape** [from Old English and Old Norse words for poor grazing], probably to **snatch** to grab (the noun had the senses 'a small amount, a fragment' and 'a light, hurried meal'), and **snoop** [Dutch *snoepen* 'to eat on the sly'] to steal and eat; to act secretively; to pry, and perhaps to **snip** [Low German or Dutch *snippen*] to cut with scissors, whose senses include 'a small piece', 'something worth having, a bargain', and 'to snatch' (now only Canadian dialect).

snare [Old English *sneare* from Old Norse *snara*] A trap or noose for catching small creatures; to trap with one, to entangle (ME, later also as **ensnare**). Hence a trial or temptation; to catch by tempting, to seduce (15c).

Snare produced **snarl** (to catch in) a snare; to tangle or become tangled; a knot or tangle; **snarl (up)** (to produce) a muddle, now especially a traffic jam. Related to Dutch *snaar* 'a string', whence, probably, **snares** strings or wires across a drum.

snipe [ME. Probably of Scandinavian origin] A marsh bird, hence **1** a worthless or contemptible person (17c); **guttersnipe** someone who lives by collecting rubbish from gutters (19c); a child brought up 'in the gutter' **2** to shoot at people one at a time from cover, as in snipe shooting (18c); to make snide remarks, to carp (19c).

snivel [Old English, probably imitative] To have a runny nose; to sniff audibly, hence **1** mucus in or running from the nose (ME) **2** to make sniffling and whining sounds (17c); to complain tearfully; (to pretend) to be tearful; the act or the sound of this (19c).

Related to Early Dutch *snuffen*, whence **snuff** and **snuffle**, and to modern Dutch *snuf tabak* 'sniffing tobacco', whence **snuff** (*Scots*, apparently brought from the Low Countries by Scottish soldiers stationed there).

snob [18c. Origin unknown: often said to be short for Latin *sine nobilitate* 'without nobility', added to someone's name on a list to mark them as a commoner, but evidence is lacking] A shoemaker, later a cobbler or his apprentice, hence **1** in Cambridge university slang: someone not a member, a townsman (cf. *cad* at CADET) **2** a lower-class person (19c), later, after a series of articles by Thackeray (see BOHEMIAN) in *Punch*, one who tries to imitate or associate with their social superiors (see below) or who despises those they consider socially inferior, or lacking in education or good taste (*wine snob*) **3** in Australia, the last sheep to be shorn [19c, altered from *cobbler*, a pun on *cobbler's last*].

Shoemaking was known as 'the gentle craft' (its patron saints, Crispin and Crispinian, were said to be brothers of noble birth who supported themselves by shoemaking while spreading the Gospel), and shoemakers considered themselves a cut above cobblers, so *snob* may come from the idea of a cobbler claiming the status of shoemaker. The status of cobblers is also found in **cobble** [a backformation from **cobbler**, of unknown origin] to mend shoes; to patch up or make roughly or clumsily.

snout [ME. Early Dutch and Low German *snūt*] The nose: an elephant's trunk; an animal's muzzle; a (large or misshapen) human nose. Hence **1** something resembling this, e.g. a ship's prow, a projecting piece of land (both 15c) **2** to nose or root about (19c); (to act as) a police informer (early 20c).

Snooty 'haughty, snobbish' may be from the variant **snoot**, or may be an alteration of **snotty** [from related **snot** nasal mucus] (having a nose) full of snot; unpleasant, contemptible; short tempered, supercilious. Also related are German *Schnauzer* a breed of dog with a bearded muzzle [1920s, from German *Schnauze* 'snout', whence, via Yiddish, **schnozz** and **schnozzle** (Anglicized as **snozzle**) 'nose' (*US*)], and **snorkel** [originally *schnorkel*, a tube enabling a submarine's engine to 'breathe' underwater, from German *Schnorchel*].

snub [ME. Old Norse *snubba*] The underlying sense is 'to check': **1** to rebuke or rebuff; to treat coldly or with disdain; an action or remark that does so (16c) **2** to restrain, also a restraint or hindrance (–17c); to stop a line from running out, especially by hitching it round something (19c) **3** to stop something growing (17c); to shorten or cut off the end of, hence **snub nose** a short, blunt one; **snub-nosed** having a snub nose; short and broad at the front (1920s, *US*); of a handgun: small with a short barrel (1950s, *US*).

snuff [ME. Origin unknown] The charred part of a candle or lamp wick; to cut it off (15c); to extinguish a candle etc. (17c), hence to put an end to (19c), hence **snuff it** to die; **snuff out** to murder (1930s); **snuff movie** a film depicting actual torture or murder (1970s).

sober [ME. Via Old French from Latin *sobrius*, from *se* 'without, not' and *ebrius* 'drunk' (whence **inebriate**)] **1** moderate, especially in eating or drinking; temperate, abstemious; not drunk; **sober (up)** to make or become sober (18c) **2** grave, serious, staid, hence **(a)** calm, dispassionate (16c) **(b)** subdued, not showy or extravagant (16c).

social [ME. (French, from) Latin *socialis* 'allied', from *socius* 'companion, friend'] **1** describing a war between traditional allies or confederates **2** living or preferring to live in communities; gregarious; in zoology: living or breeding in colonies (18c) **3** characterized by, or giving an opportunity for, friendly interaction or companionship (17c); such a gathering or party (19c) **4** to do with (the organization of) society (17c), hence **(a)** to do with fashionable or wealthy society (*social calendar*, 19c) **(b)** to do with the problems of (the members of) society (19c); of an activity etc.: for the benefit or improvement of society (1960s); provided by government for the poorer members of society (*social security/housing*).

Social produced **socialize**. Descendants of Latin *socius* include ASSOCIATE, **sociable**, which overlaps in meaning with senses 2 and 3 of *social*, **socialism**, SOCIETY, and **socio-** society, social (*sociology, socio-economic*).

society [16c. Via French from Latin *societas*, from *socius*: see SOCIAL*] (Friendly) association with others (16c), hence an organized body of people united by a common aim, interest, profession, etc.; an ordered community united by traditions, institutions, or nationality, hence **1** the members collectively (17c); the wealthy, fashionable, or prominent ones (19c) **2** a community's mores (17c).

socket [ME. Anglo-Norman French, literally 'small ploughshare', from Old French *soc* 'ploughshare', probably of Celtic origin] The head of a lance or spear (likened to a ploughshare), hence a hollow part or piece that something fits in (like the shaft of a spear, 15c).

sofa [17c. French, ultimately from Arabic *ṣuffa* 'long bench'] A raised part of a floor, especially in Arab countries, covered in carpets and cushions, hence a long upholstered seat (18c).

soil [ME. Old French *soiller*, *suiller* 'to wallow, to make dirty', from *souil* 'pigsty, wallow', ultimately from Latin *sucula* 'small pig', from *sus* 'pig'] **1** to make or become dirty, stained, or polluted, originally with sin, hence **(a)** a physical or moral stain (16c) **(b)** dirt, (liquid) waste (17c); excrement, manure, hence **night**

soil human excrement collected at night, often used as fertilizer (18c) **(c)** to feed livestock on green fodder, originally as a laxative (17c); such fodder (19c) **2** a wild boars' wallow (15c); a piece of water where a hunted animal takes refuge; to do so.

Old French *suiller* probably produced **sully**. **Soil** meaning 'earth, mould' is Anglo-Norman French, from Latin *solium* 'seat': the original sense '(a piece of) land' survives in phrases such as *my native soil*.

solar [ME. Latin *solaris*, from *sol* 'sun'] To do with or coming from the sun, hence **1** determined by (observing) the sun's course (*solar time*, 16c) **2** in astrology: influenced by the sun (17c) **3** sacred to the sun (18c) **4** like the sun (18c), hence **solar plexus** a bundle of nerves in the upper abdomen, spreading out like the rays of the sun; this area [18c, with Latin *plexus*, from *plectere* 'to plait': ancestor of COMPLEX*] **5** using the sun as a source of energy (*solar panel*, 18c).

Latin *sol* produced **parasol** [French, from Italian *parasole*, literally 'against the sun'], **solar** an upper room open to the sun [via Old French from Latin *solarium*, which was adopted for a sundial, later a sun room, now a place equipped with sun lamps], and **solstice** [with Latin *sistere*, *stit-* 'to stand still'].

sole [ME. Old French, from Latin *solea* 'sandal', also 'sill', from *solum* 'bottom'] **1** the underside, later the ball, of the foot; the part of a shoe, sock, etc. covering this, hence **(a)** a piece of material forming the sole; one worn inside the shoe (now usually as **insole**, 19c) **(b)** to put a (new) sole on a shoe (16c) **2** the foundation or site of a building etc. (15–17c), hence applied to the base or floor of various objects (17c).

Latin *solea* produced **sole** a flatfish [Old French, from Provençal *sola*, because of its shape].

solicit [15c. Via French from Latin *sollicitare* 'to agitate', from *sollicitus* 'anxious, concerned', literally 'completely moved' from *sollus* 'entire' + *citus* 'moved' from *ciere* 'to set in motion'] **1** to make anxious (–18c); to pester, hence **(a)** to ask for something (16c) **(b)** to incite or tempt someone to do something wrong (16c); to accost someone and offer yourself or someone else as a prostitute (17c) **2** to be concerned, especially to attend to business (–18c), hence **solicitor** an agent or representative; someone who conducts legal business, a lawyer (16c).

Latin *sollicitare* fathered French *soucier* 'to care', whence **insouciant** unconcerned; *sollicitus* produced **solicitous** and **solicitude**; *sollus* produced **solemn** [via Latin *sollemnis* 'celebrated ceremonially on a fixed date']; *ciere* is the ancestor of CITE*].

solid [ME. (Via French from) Latin *solidus*] **1** three-dimensional; such a body or figure; to do with one (16c) **2** not hollow, hence **(a)** dense, firm and compact (16c); substantial, strong; dependable, sound (17c) **(b)** uninterrupted (17c); of the same colour or substance throughout (18c) **(c)** unanimous, united (19c, *US*) **3** having a definite shape and volume, not liquid or gaseous (16c); such a substance (17c).

Latin *solidus* produced **consolidate** [via French *consolider*, whence, probably, **console**), **solder** [via French from Latin *solidare* 'to fasten'], and **soldier** [via French from Latin *soulde* 'soldiers' pay', from *solidus* (*nummus*) 'a gold coin', whence also French *sou* a small coin, surviving in **not a sou** no money at all]. For the English use of *solidus*, see POUND¹.

solve   [15c. Latin *solvere*, *solut-* 'to loosen, unfasten, or free'] **1** to loosen or break up (–17c), outlived by **dissolve** [Latin *dissolvere*, from *solvere*], now usually referring to breaking up an assembly or a marriage **2** to melt in a liquid, largely replaced by *dissolve*, but surviving in **soluble**, **solute**, **solution**, and **solvent 3** to find an answer to a problem, riddle, equation, etc., or a means of dealing with a difficulty (16c, earlier in *solution* this action, the answer or means found): cf. ABSOLVE, RESOLVE **4** to pay money, a debt, etc. (16c), hence *solvent* able to do so (17c).

Dissolve also meant 'to melt away, to be melted', also 'to fade away', hence in cinematography, to make an image fade into another. Latin *solvere* is the ancestor of ABSOLVE* and RESOLVE, which shares some senses with *dissolve* and *solve*: *dissolvere* produced **dissolute** disconnected, disunited (–17c), later lax, unrestrained (–18c), hence lacking moral restraint (cf. *resolute* at RESOLVE).

sonic   [Latin *sonus* SOUND²*] To do with or operated by (especially reflected) sound waves (1920s). Slightly earlier in **supersonic** to do with or describing frequencies higher than humans can hear (*c*.1919, now largely replaced by **ultrasonic**, 1920s); faster than the speed of sound (1930s), hence **sonic boom** the sound caused by the shock wave of a supersonic aircraft (1950s).

soothe   [Old English *sōthian*, from *sōth* 'true, truth'] To prove that something is true (–16c); to declare that something is true, whether it is or not (16–18c), hence **1** to support someone's statement, or, later, actions (16–18c) **2** to flatter, cajole, or humour (16–19c). Hence (combining 1 and 2) to appease, pacify, or comfort (17c); to lessen pain or discomfort (18c).

Old English *sōth* survives, just, in **forsooth** and **soothsayer** someone who tells the truth or claims to foretell the future.

sop   [Old English *sopp*] A piece of bread dipped or soaked in wine, gravy, etc., hence **1** milksop a weak-willed or ineffectual man (ME, as a surname); shortened to *sop* (17c), hence **soppy** silly, foolishly sentimental or affectionate (early 20c) **2** to soak (17c) or soak up (19c); to be or become soaking wet (19c), hence **sopping** soaking, drenched **3** something given to appease (17c, originally alluding to the sop given to Cerberus, the monstrous dog that guarded the entrance to Hades, who would then let you pass); a minor concession, a (small) bribe.

Related to SOUP* and **sip** [Old English *supan*, whence also **sup** to sip; to eat by the spoonful].

sophist   [ME. Latin *sophistes* from Greek *sophistēs*, from *sophizesthai* 'to devise', also 'to become wise', from *sophos* 'wise, clever'] A member of a school of professional philosophers in ancient Greece who taught rhetoric and debating skills, but who gained a reputation for specious reasoning, hence someone using clever but fallacious arguments.

Latin *sophistes* produced SOPHISTICATE. Greek *sophos* produced **Sofia** the Bulgarian capital (named by the Turks when they converted its church of St Sophia into a mosque, *Sophia* here being God's wisdom: see SAINT), **Sonia** Slavic pet form of **Sophia** or **Sophie**, **sophism** a plausible but fallacious argument, **sophister** and **sophomore**, applied to second- or third-year students at various universities, **sophistry** specious or over-subtle reasoning, especially intending to deceive, and the name of **Sophocles**, the 5c BC Greek dramatist [literally 'famous for wisdom', with Greek *kleos* 'fame, glory'].

sophisticate [ME. Medieval Latin *sophisticare* 'to quibble', also 'to tamper with', ultimately from Latin *sophistes*: see SOPHIST*] To adulterate; to corrupt (16c); to mislead someone or distort an argument, especially by over-complication; to deprive someone/something of natural simplicity or innocence (17c), hence **sophisticated** experienced, worldly (19c); of a technique, equipment, etc.: highly developed and complex (1940s).

sore [Old English *sār*] (Causing or suffering) physical or mental pain (–16c), hence **1** painful, inflamed, raw; a raw or tender place; a source of pain, distress, or annoyance (ME) **2** pitiful, wretched (ME, outlived by *sorry* below) **3** involving great hardship or difficulty (surviving in Scots); grievous, serious (ME); **sorely** greatly, extremely **4** suffering pain or distress (ME); sorrowful; irritated, angry, resentful (17c, *US*).

Related to **sorry** [Old English *sārig*] distressed, sorrowful (now particularly from pity, sympathy, or regret); causing distress, sorrow, or pity; pitiful, deplorable.

sot [Old English *sott*, later Old French *sot* 'foolish', both from medieval Latin *sottus*, of unknown origin] A fool (now dialect), hence **1** to confuse or stupefy (ME), replaced by **besot** (16c), now usually as **besotted** foolishly infatuated **2** a habitual drunkard (16c); to drink to excess (17c).

sound¹ [Old English *sund*: related to **swim**] The action of swimming (–15c), hence **1** the swim bladder of some fish (ME) **2** a narrow channel between the mainland and an island, or between two bodies of water; an inlet of the sea (ME, probably influenced by related Old Norse *sund* 'swimming', also 'strait').

sound² [ME. Via Old French from Latin *sonare* 'to sound', from *sonus* '(a) sound'] What is or may be heard, hence **1** to make a sound (*the trumpet sounded*), hence **(a)** to make something do so; to give a signal in this way (*sound the all-clear*, 16c) **(b) sound off** of a band: to strike up (*c.*1910, *US* military), hence of a person: to speak or complain loudly or at length (*c.*1915) **2** music, melody (–16c), re-invented as **sounds** popular music (1950s, *US*); *sound* a particular kind of this (*the Mersey sound*, 1960s) **3** to give an impression (as if) by sounds (*the menu sounds nice*); the impression given (*I don't like the sound of it*, 17c) **4** the dialogue, music, and other noises of a film (1920s).

Sound produced *sonar* (at RADIO) and **resound**. Latin *sonare* produced **assonance**, **consonance** agreement or harmony [Latin *consonare* 'to sound together', whence **consonant** a speech sound pronounced with a vowel], **dissonance**, **resonance** and **resonate** [both from *resonare* 'to sound again'], Italian **sonata**, and **sonorous**. *Sonus* produced SONIC*, **sonnet** [(French, from) Italian *sonetto* 'little sound', from *suono* 'sound'], and **unison** [ME, from Latin *unisonus* 'of the same pitch', from *unus* 'one'].

sound³ [ME. French *sonder*, ultimately from Latin *sub-* 'under' + *unda* 'a wave'] To use a line and lead (or, now, an electronic device) to find the depth of water, hence **1 sound (out)** find out someone's opinions or feelings by discreet questioning (16c) **2** in medical use: to probe a wound or, later, a body cavity using a long rodlike implement (16c); this implement (18c) **3** of a sounding lead: to touch bottom (17c); of a whale etc.: to dive to a great depth (19c).

Latin *unda* is the ancestor of ABOUND*, **inundate**, REDUNDANT, **surround** originally to flood or submerge [via Old French from late Latin *superundare* 'to overflow', from Latin *undare* to flow], and **undulate**.

soup [ME. Old French *soupe* 'sop, broth poured on bread', from late Latin *suppa*, ultimately of Germanic origin] A liquid food made by boiling meat, fish, vegetables, etc. in stock or water, later applied to various (thickish) liquids including nitroglycerine and a stimulant given to horses (both early 20c), hence, probably, **soup up** to make more powerful (1930s).

Old French *soupe* produced **supper** a (light) meal in the evening, and **sup** to eat it. Related to SOP*.

spade [16c. Italian, plural of *spada* 'sword', from Latin *spatha* 'sword, spatula' from Greek *spathē* 'blade, paddle, shoulder blade'] (A card bearing) a black shape like a spearhead, hence **1 in spades** very much, abundantly, extremely (spades being the highest ranking suit in bridge, 1920s, *US*) **2** a Black person (1920s, *US*): now considered offensive, but formerly used among African-Americans, for one with very dark skin.

Latin **spatha** was adopted in botany for a large sheathing bract (now usually **spathe**), and a kind of broadsword. It produced French **épée** a fencing sword [via Old French *espee* 'sword', whence **spay** to cut out an animal's ovaries], and Latin **spatula** [literally 'small *spatha*'], which was adopted for various broad-bladed implements, and produced **epaulette** [via French *épaule* 'shoulder'] and French **espalier** [from Italian *spalliera* 'shoulder support', from *spalla* 'shoulder'] adopted for a fruit tree or shrub trained on a support.

Spam [1930s. Apparently short for *spiced ham*] A trade name for a kind of tinned meat (*US*), sometimes loosely applied to similar products. During World War II Spam was often available when fresh meat was not, and came to be regarded as commonplace, hence **Spam medal** a campaign medal awarded to all troops. In the 1970s the Monty Python team produced a sketch in which Spam was served with everything whether you wanted it or not, hence *spam* junk emails, sent to everyone and impossible to avoid (1990s, *US*); to send them (*c*.2003).

span[1] [Old English *span(n)*, later also related to Old French *espan*: related to SPIN*] The distance between the tips of the thumb and little finger when fully extended; this as a measure of length; to measure or encircle something with your hand. Hence **1** (something taking up) a short space or time (ME) **2** to reach or extend from one place to another (16c); the full extent (*life/attention/wing span*, 17c); the space between a bridge's pillars, hence **(a)** the sections between the pillars (19c) **(b)** to bridge.

span[2] [Old English *spannan*, later mainly from related Dutch and Low German *spannen* 'to unite'] **1** to harness or yoke draught animals together (now mainly S African, from Dutch) **2** to extend, stretch, or make tight (16c) **3** to fasten (18c, *nautical*); a rope or chain for doing so; to tether or hobble an animal (19c).

Low German *spannen* produced **spancel** a hobble or fetter, and **spanner** originally a device for winding up a spring. Related to SPIN* and probably to **spangle** [from obsolete *spang* a glittering ornament', from early Dutch *spange* 'brooch, clasp'].

spar [Old English *sperran, spyrran*, perhaps ultimately from Latin *parare* 'to prepare or defend' (ancestor of PARADE*)] To spring, to strike or thrust rapidly (–15c); of a cock: to fight with its feet or spurs (16c), hence **1** to engage in an argument (17c) **2** to box for practice (18c).

Spartan [ME. Latin *Spartanus*, from *Sparta*, capital of the ancient Greek region of Laconia] A native or inhabitant of Sparta (renowned for courage, endurance, discipline, and frugality); to do with Sparta or the Spartans (16c); like a Spartan, hence **1** simple, austere (17c) **2** a kind of apple bred in Canada to withstand the cold winters (1960s).

The Laconians were known for their terse speech, hence **laconic** terse.

spatter [16c. Perhaps of Low German origin] To spit or splutter, hence **1** to (make something) come out in small drops or particles **2** to splash with drops of liquid (17c), hence **(a)** to fall on or strike with (the sound of) drops; (the sound of) a splash or sprinkle (18c) **(b) spatterdash** a gaiter or legging to protect trousers while riding, shortened to **spat** a short gaiter just covering the ankle (19c); a cover for the upper part of an aircraft wheel (1930s) **3** to splash through mud etc. (19c).

speak [Old English *sprecan*, later *specan*] To say, to express by saying, hence **1** to talk with; to be on good terms with (*we're not speaking*); talk, conversation (ME), outlived by **speech** [related to Old English *spēc*] **2** to deliver an address or lecture; such an address (16c, outlived by *speech*) **3** to express in words (ME, outlived by **say** [Old English *secgan*]); to be expressive or significant (16c) **4** (to be able) to use a language (*she speaks French*, ME); a language or dialect (outlived by *speech*) **5** a way of speaking (ME–15c); the ability to speak (outlived by *speech*) **6** to approach someone about something (ME); to ask for or order (16c); to propose marriage (17c), the last two surviving in *spoken for* **7 speak for** to speak on others' behalf, to express their views, hence the surname **Spackman**, **Speakman** for a **spokesman** someone who does so **8** -**speak** a particular kind of language or jargon (*computerspeak*) [1960s, based on **Newspeak** and **Oldspeak** in George Orwell's novel *1984*, the former being the artificial language used for official propaganda, the latter being standard English.

spectacle [ME. French, from Latin *spectaculum* 'public show', from *spectare* 'to watch', from *specere* 'to look'] **1** a (large or lavish) public performance or display; a regrettable one (*made a spectacle of herself*); a (remarkable or impressive) sight (15c) **2** a means of seeing: **(a)** a window or mirror (–17c) **(b) spectacles** eyeglasses.

Spectacle produced **spectacular**; Latin *spectare* produced **spectator**, whence **spectate**; *specere* is the ancestor of SPICE*.

spectrum [17c. Latin *spectrum* 'image, apparition', from *specere* 'to look'] **1** an apparition (largely replaced by *spectre* below); an image; one left on the retina after looking at a bright light (18c) **2** the coloured bands into which white light can be split, hence **(a)** (any part of) the entire range of wavelengths of electromagnetic radiation (19c) **(b)** any range (*the whole spectrum of opinions*, 1930s).

Spectrum produced **spectro-** as in **spectroscopy** the study of spectra; Latin *spectrum* fathered French *spectre* an apparition, a ghost, an unpleasant prospect (*the spectre of poverty*). Latin *specere* is the ancestor of SPICE*.

speculation [ME. (French, from) Latin *speculari*, *speculat-* 'to spy out, to observe', from *specula* 'watchtower', from *specere* 'to look'] Contemplation, consideration, study; (a conclusion reached by) hypothetical reasoning or conjecture rather than knowledge (15c), hence (the action of making) a risky investment (18c).

Latin *speculari* produced **speculate**; *specere* is the ancestor of SPICE*.

speed [Old English *spēd* (noun), *spēdan* (verb)] Prosperity, success; to prosper or get on well, hence **1** rapid progress; swift movement, hence **(a)** quickness, rapidity; a rate of movement (*high/low speed*), hence a gear ratio (*three-speed gears*, 19c); a degree of sensitivity of a photographic film **(b)** to (cause to) go, move, or pass quickly (ME); to drive (too) fast (1930s) **(c) speed up** to (make something) go more quickly (ME) **(d)** amphetamine (1960s) **2** to help someone/something get on or succeed (ME, surviving mainly in **God speed**) **3** as a surname for a fortunate person or a fast runner.

spell¹ [Old English *spel(l)*: related to SPELL²] Talk, speech; (the telling of) a tale or news (cf. GOSPEL); words believed to have magical powers (ME), hence **1** an attraction or fascination, a mysterious power or influence (16c) **2 spellbound** held (as if) by a spell (18c), whence **spellbind** to fascinate (19c).

spell² [ME. Old French *espeller*, from Frankish: related to SPELL¹] To read letter by letter; to write or say (correctly) the letters of a word in sequence, hence **1** to signify, to amount or lead to (*drought spells disaster for farmers*, 17c) **2** to form a word letter by letter (*C A T spells 'cat'*, 19c); **spell out** to explain in detail (1940s, *US*).

spell³ [16c. Later form of dialect *spele* 'to take someone's place', from Old English *spelian*, of unknown origin] To take a worker's place to let them rest; a shift or relay of workers; a turn of work to relieve someone else (17c). Hence a period of activity (18c, also of rest: now dialect and Australian); a short period of time, specifically **1** of a certain kind of weather (18c) **2** of being unwell (*a dizzy spell*, 19c).

spend [Old English *spendan*, from Latin *expendere*, later also from obsolete *dispend*, from Latin *dispendere*: both meaning 'to weigh or pay out', and both from *pendere* 'to weigh or pay'] To pay out money; to use money, effort, etc. in a particular way, hence **1** to pass time, or your life, in a particular place, state, or activity **2** to use up completely, hence **spent** consumed, used up, done for, no longer effective (ME); worn out, exhausted (16c) **3** to waste or squander, hence the surname **Spendlove**, **Spen(d)low** someone free with his affections **4** the action of spending money (17c); the amount spent.

Latin *expendere* produced **expend** to spend or use up, whence **expendable** able to be expended, readily sacrificed, and **expense** what is spent (–18c, replaced by **expenditure**); the cost of doing or getting something (hence **expensive** costly); the cause of spending (*the car is a big expense*). Latin *dispendere* produced DISPENSE*; *pendere* is the ancestor of PENSION*.

sphere [ME. Via Old French and Latin from Greek *sphaira* 'ball'] (The shape of) a globe or ball; a hollow globe once thought to enclose the earth; each of a series of concentric transparent globes once thought to revolve round the Earth carrying the celestial bodies, hence **1 the music/harmony of the spheres** a harmonious sound believed to be caused by their movement **2** the sphere carrying a particular planet etc.; a place believed to be occupied by a god, person, or thing, hence your place in society (16c); your field of knowledge, activity, or influence (17c).

sphinx [15c. Latin, from Greek *Sphigx*, apparently from *sphiggein* 'to draw tight'] A winged creature in Greek mythology with a lion's body and a woman's head, who strangled anyone who could not solve its riddle, hence **1** an ancient Greek or Egyptian stone figure with a lion's body and a human or animal head (16c), specifically the one at Giza **2** an inscrutable or enigmatic person or thing (17c).

Spinnaker comes from a mispronunciation of *Sphinx*, the name of the first yacht to have one. Greek *sphiggein* is the ancestor of **sphincter**.

spice [ME. Via Old French *espice* from Latin *species* 'seeing, something seen, a kind', in late Latin 'merchandise', from *specere* 'to look or look at'] **1** a sort, a kind (–17c, outlived by *species*: see also TAXONOMY) **2** a strongly flavoured or aromatic substance used in cookery and, formerly, in medicine (surviving in the surname **Spicer** a spice merchant or apothecary).

Latin *species* produced **special** [Latin *specialis* 'of a particular type', whence Old French *especial*], **specific**, and **specify** [late Latin *specificus*, literally 'making a kind']. *Specere*'s descendants include ASPECT, AUSPICE, **conspicuous**, DESPITE*, **expect**, *frontispiece* (at FRONT), **inspect**, **introspect**, PERSPECTIVE*, PROSPECT*, RESPECT, Latin *specimen* literally 'something looked at', **specious** beautiful, later deceptively attractive or plausible, SPECTACLE*, SPECTRUM*, SPECULATION, **speculum**, and SUSPECT.

spike [ME. Early Low German and Dutch *spiker*, or Old Norse *spik* 'nail'] A sharp-pointed piece of metal or wood, hence **1** to fasten with one (17c); to make into one; to provide with one or more (18c); to stick up in a spike or spikes (1950s) **2** a pointed steel plug used to sabotage a cannon if it had to be abandoned (17c), hence **spike your guns** to thwart you **3** a sharp, brief increase (as) shown on a graph (18c) **4** the workhouse (19c slang, said to be from the hard narrow bed and sharp 'welcome'); a hostel for the homeless **5** to lace a drink with alcohol or a drug (19c, perhaps from the idea of making it sharper); (to add) a small quantity of a radioisotope etc. as a tracer (1950s) **6** to decide not to publish a newspaper story (*c*.1900, from the spike on which it was impaled) **7** a hypodermic needle (1930s); to inject someone with a narcotic drug.

Related to SPIT[2]* and to the **spoke** of a wheel [Old English *spaca*]: **put a spoke in someone's wheel** comes from a later sense 'a bar, stake, or pole'.

spill [Old English *spillan*, of unknown origin] To kill (–17c); to destroy or ruin (obsolete by the 17c, replaced by SPOIL: revived as an archaism in the 19c), hence to shed blood; (to allow something to) flow accidentally from a container (ME); to come out of a confined space (*fans spilled onto the pitch*), hence **1** to waste or squander, hence the surnames **Spiller** and **Spillman** a waster or spendthrift **2** to cause or allow wind to be lost from a sail (17c) **3** to (make someone) fall from a horse or vehicle (19c); such a fall **4** a quantity spilled (*oil spill*, 19c) **5** **spill (the beans/your guts)** to confess, to divulge information (*c*.1915).

spin [Old English *spinnan*] **1** to draw out and twist wool etc. to form a thread, hence **(a)** to make a thread by drawing out and/or spinning (*spun sugar*, ME) **(b)** of the Fates: to 'spin out' the thread of your life (ME), hence to tell a tale, especially at length, especially in *spin a yarn* (at YARN) **(c)** of a spider etc.: to produce silken thread from its body (16c); to make a web from it **(d)** **spin (out)** to prolong or extend; to eke out (17c) **2** of blood etc.: to gush or spurt out (ME–19c), hence to move or travel quickly (15c); a rapid run or ride; a short pleasure drive or flight (19c). Hence **3** to (make something) turn or revolve rapidly (17c); to rotate freely

(19c); a rapid or free rotation (*wheelspin*), hence **(a)** of a ball: to travel with such a motion (19c); to make a ball spin so that it changes direction (*c.*1900), hence (to produce) an interpretation intended to present something in a favourable light (1970s); **spin doctor** a (political) spokesperson who does so (1980s, *US*) **(b)** to (make an aircraft) go into a deep spiral dive (*c.*1915); such a dive **(c)** a state of confusion or agitation (1920s, cf. WHIRL).

Old English *spinnan* produced **spider** [Old English *spīthra*, literally 'spinner'] and **spinster** a female spinner, later a woman who had never married (spinning, originally done in the home, was a respectable occupation for women: cf. BACHELOR): spinning as 'women's work' is also found in **distaff side**, the wife's side of the family. Related to SPAN[1,2] and SPINDLE.

spindle   [Old English *spinel*: related to SPIN*] A rod used in hand-spinning, later a rod or pin on which something revolved (ME), and applied to various things resembling this in shape or use. Hence **1** the surname **Spindler** a spindle-maker or seller **2** of a plant: to grow (too) long and thin (16c); **spindly** long, tall, thin, and weak-looking (17c).

spine   [ME. (Old French *espine* from) Latin *spina* 'thorn, backbone, quill'] **1** a thorn or prickle, hence **(a)** a spike or quill on an animal or fish (17c) **(b)** a spine-shaped natural formation (18c); a tall mass of lava sticking up from a volcano's cone (*c.*1900) **2** the backbone (15c); something resembling this: **(a)** a support or source of strength (17c) **(b)** a sharp ridge (18c) **(c) spineless** without a backbone (19c); weak and cowardly **(d)** the back of a book (1920s) **(e) (pay) spine** a pay scale that can take individual circumstances into account (1980s, from the backbone's flexibility).

Latin *spina* fathered **spinet** [via French from Italian *spinetta*, because the strings are plucked with quills], **spinifex** [literally 'thorn-maker', with *facere*: see FACT*], **spinney** [Old French *espinei,* from Latin *spinetum* 'thicket'], and probably influenced **spinach** [Old French *espinache*, ultimately from Persian *aspanākh*], which has prickly seeds. Related to Latin *spica* 'spike', whence **spigot** [Provençal *espigou(n)* from Latin *spiculum* 'small *spica*'] and **spike** an ear of corn; a cluster of flowers up a stem.

spirit   [ME. Anglo-Norman French, or Old French *esprit*, from Latin *spiritus* 'breath, spirit', from *spirare* 'to breathe'] **1** the essence of a living being, hence **(a) Holy Spirit** the essence of God (cf. *Holy Ghost* at GHOST) **(b)** the mind, soul, and/or emotions, hence **spirits** a mood (*in good/low spirits*); *spirit* anger, arrogance, later assertiveness, courage, hence **spirited** assertive, lively, energetic (16c); **high-spirited** lively, full of fun (17c) **(c)** an essential character, attitude, or feeling (16c); that belonging to a particular time, place, group, etc. (19c) **(d)** real intent or meaning, as opposed to a literal interpretation (19c) **2** one of the highly refined substances once thought to permeate the body, hence a liquid essence (17c), hence **(a)** a solution of a substance in alcohol **(b)** a distilled (alcoholic) liquid; *spirits* strong alcoholic liquor **3** a supernatural being, e.g. an angel, demon, or fairy; a ghost **4** a breath of air, a breeze, hence **spirit away** to remove suddenly and secretly (17c, originally to kidnap someone to work on the West Indian or American plantations).

Sense 3 survives as the variant **sprite**, altered to **spright**, which survives in **sprightly**. French *esprit* appears in ***esprit de corps*** and ***esprit d'escalier*** [literally 'spirit of the staircase'] a witty remark you think of too late (when descending the stairs, away from the gathering). Latin *spiritus* produced **spiritual** to do with or affecting the spirit or soul, whence **spiritualism** the belief that the spirit exists independently of matter, or that the spirits of the dead can communicate with the living. Latin *spirare* is the ancestor of **aspire**, CESSPOOL, **conspire**, INSPIRE*, **perspire**, **respiration**, and TRANSPIRE.

spit¹ [Old English *spittan*: related to **spew**, **spittle**, and **spout**] **1** to eject saliva from your mouth; to do so as a sign of contempt or anger, hence **(a)** (a glob of) saliva (ME); **spit and polish** thorough or exaggerated cleaning (19c, *military*, soldiers using spit to clean their boots) **(b)** an act of spitting (17c) **2** to eject something else from your mouth (ME), hence **(a)** **spit out** to say vehemently; **spit it out!** go on, say it! **(b)** **the (very/dead) spit of** just like (19c, from a 17c idea of being so like someone that they might have spat you out), lengthened to **spit and image**, which was then corrupted to **spitten**, later **spitting**, **image** (*c.*1900) **3** to emit or throw out in a similar way (ME); **spit (with rain)** to rain in scattered spots (16c).

spit² [Old English *spitu*] A rod on which meat is cooked, hence **1** to skewer or impale (ME) **2** any pointed rod or stick (ME); an instrument used by customs officers to search cargo (1920s) **3** a horizontal stroke used in ancient manuscripts to mark a word or passage (ME); a dagger-shaped mark with a similar function (–17c), outlived by the Latin word for a spit, *obelus* [ME, from Greek *obelos*], and by **obelisk** [16c, from Greek *obeliskos* 'small obelus'], which also means a tapering stone pillar (cf. *spire* below) **4** a tongue of land, a narrow reef or sandbank (17c).

Related to SPIKE*, **spire** [Old English *spīr*] the stem of a long, slender plant (the variant **spear** survives for an asparagus or broccoli shoot), hence a tall, tapering structure, and to German *Spitz(hund)* a breed of dog with a pointed muzzle.

spoil [ME. Via Old French from Latin *spoliare* 'to strip', from *spolium* 'animal's hide', hence 'clothes, armour, etc. stripped from an enemy': partly also from Middle English **despoil**, from Latin *despoliare* 'to strip completely', from *spoliare*] **1** to strip, pillage, or plunder; to take by force or stealth; **spoils** booty, plunder; something gained by effort (18c); profit or advantage connected with public office or a high position **2** (partly from sense 1, partly replacing SPILL) to destroy or damage (16c), hence **(a)** to mar a child's character by leniency (17c); to indulge or pamper **(b)** of food: to go bad (17c), hence **spoiling for** eager for (going bad for want of), especially a fight (19c) **(c)** to prevent or obstruct (*spoiling tactics*, 19c) **3** *spoil(s)* a sloughed or stripped-off skin (17c); *spoils* the remains of a carcass; *spoil* waste material from mining, dredging, etc. (19c).

sponsor [17c. Latin, from *spondere* 'to promise solemnly', also 'to betroth'] A godparent; someone who presents or supports a person at their baptism or confirmation, hence one who stands surety for or supports another; to do so (19c); a person or organization that promotes or gives financial support to a broadcast, sporting event, competitor, etc. (1930s); to do so.

Latin *spondere* is the ancestor of **despond** to give up hope [Latin *despondere* 'to give up, to abandon'], RESPONSE*, and [via Old French] **spouse** a husband or wife, also to marry, replaced by **espouse**, which came to mean to 'marry yourself' to a cause, way of life, etc.

spook [19c. Dutch, of unknown origin] A ghost (*US*), hence **1** an African-American term for a White person (as being pale and ghostlike); a White American term for a Black person (1940s) **2** to go around like a ghost; to haunt a person or place; to make or become fearful (1920s) **3** a spy (1940s).

spoon [Old English *spōn*: related to **spade** a digging tool] **1** a chip or splinter (–16c) **2** the utensil, originally wooden (ME), hence **(a)** something resembling it: a surgical instrument (15c); a golf club with a concave head (18c); a shiny oval fishing lure (18c) **(b) spoon-feed** to feed with a spoon (17c); to give someone so much help or information that they need not think or work (19c) **(c)** (also **spoony**) a simple or stupid person (18c), perhaps from the idea of a spoon-fed child, but perhaps connected with the wooden spoon awarded to the lowest student in mathematics at Cambridge University, although this is recorded later (19c), and subsequently to the losing team in a tournament **(d)** to eat, scoop, or carry with a spoon (18c) **(e)** to kiss and cuddle (19c, said to be because Welsh boys traditionally carved an ornate wooden spoon for their sweethearts, but perhaps from (c) above); (also **spooner**, *spoony*) a foolish and sentimental lover; *spoony* foolishly sentimental and amorous **(f)** to lie together like spoons in a drawer (19c) **(g)** to make hollow or concave (19c) **(h)** a spoonful (1920s); a small quantity of heroin etc. (1960s, *US*) **3** the surname **Spooner**, originally someone who covered a roof with shingles, later one who made spoons.

spot [ME. Of Germanic origin: perhaps more than one word] **1** a small speck or discoloration, hence **(a)** a pimple: a (moral) blemish (15c) **(b) spotless** perfectly clean, without stain or blemish (cf. IMMACULATE) **(c)** to mark or decorate with a spot or spots (15c) **2** a small area or definite point, hence **(a) on the spot** at the very place or time (17c), hence **spot cash/check** etc. paid/done on the spot **(b) spotlight** with a narrow beam (*c*.1900); to light with one (1920s); (to bring to) public attention: cf. *limelight* (at LIME) **(c)** an awkward position or situation (*in a spot*, 1920s) **3** a small piece, amount, or quantity (*a spot of rain/lunch*, 15c) **4** to mark or note as being suspicious (18c); to notice or catch sight of (19c); to identify beforehand (*spot a winner*); to watch for and note (*trainspotter, c*.1920).

spray [ME. Probably of Old English origin and related to **sprig**] Small twigs (growing or as firewood); a slender twig or shoot, hence **1** one with flowers, berries, etc., hence a flower arrangement, especially one that fans out (19c, perhaps influenced by a **spray** of water [17c, from Dutch *sprayen* 'to sprinkle']); a brooch resembling a bouquet or flowering twig **2** the surname **Spray** a thin person.

spree [19c. Perhaps via Scots *spreath* '(cattle taken as) spoils, booty', also 'a cattle raid', from Scottish and Irish Gaelic *spréidh* 'cattle', ultimately from Latin *praeda* 'booty' (ancestor of PREY*)] **1** a lively outing (*Scots*) **2** a drinking bout; a binge (*spending spree*) **3** a fight (Scots and Irish dialect).

spring [Old English *springan*] To move quickly and suddenly, to rush or flow out, hence **1** a place where water flows from the earth; the source of a stream (also as **wellspring**) **2** to arise or be descended from (implied in OE **offspring** progeny)

3 to begin to grow, hence **(a)** a beginning (in **dayspring** sunrise, dawn); the first season of the year (ME) **(b)** to grow, to increase (15c); **spring tide** a very high tide after the new and full moon (16c) **4** to jump or leap (up) (ME); of a game bird etc.: to break cover; to make one do so (hence **springer spaniel**, 19c); to (cause to) escape or be released from prison (*c*.1900, *US*) **5** to break or split under pressure (*spring a leak*, ME) **6** to make something move or open with a sudden movement (*sprung the lock*, ME) **7** something that can go back quickly to a previous shape or position (15c), hence **(a)** (to be able) to do so (17c) **(b)** elasticity, bounce, liveliness (*a spring in his step*, 17c); to give elasticity or bounce to (*sprung floor*, 19c) **8** a mooring rope that enables the bow or stern of a ship to swing clear when leaving (18c) **9** the surname **Springer** someone who lived by a spring, or a lively person.

spruce [ME. An alteration of early forms of *Prussia*] Prussia (–17c); Prussian (15c), hence **1** [probably from *spruce (leather) jerkin*] (to make) neat, dapper, or smart (16c) **2** **spruce (fir)** a kind of conifer found in Prussia and elsewhere (17c), later applied to similar or related species.

Prussia gave its name to **Prussian blue** (the colour of) a deep blue pigment discovered in Berlin in 1704, and to **prussic acid** obtained from it.

spur [Old English *spura*: related to **spurn**] A spike on a boot for urging a horse on, hence **1** something resembling one: **(a)** a claw or spike (ME) **(b)** something sticking out like a spur, e.g. a short diagonal strut (15c); a ridge extending from a mountain range (17c); a side shoot; a branch of a road or railway (19c) **2** to prick with spurs (ME); to urge on, incite, or encourage; a stimulus or incentive (16c).

square [ME. Old French *esquarre*, ultimately from Latin *quadrum*] (A figure) having four straight equal sides and four right angles, hence **1** an implement for producing or measuring right angles (*set square*); (to set) at right angles (16c), hence, probably, **square away** to set a ship's yards at right angles to the keel (as when docked, 17c), hence to tidy up **2** to make or reduce to a square; to regulate (16c); to make consistent with, hence **(a)** (to make) even or equal (*all square*, 19c); to balance an account **(b)** to ensure acquiescence, especially by bribery (19c) **3** a square space (*town square, back to square one*, 15c); to mark off in squares (*squared paper*) **4** describing a square with sides of a certain length (*3 metres square*, 15c), hence to multiply a number by itself (16c); (equal to) the product of this **5** a square piece (*headsquare*, 16c) **6** honest, fair (16c), hence **(a)** **square meal** (19c) **(b)** straight, direct, uncompromising (19c); **square up to** to take up an assertive position **7** conventional, old-fashioned (early 20c, *US*, originating among jazz musicians, sometimes said to be from the square traced by a conductor's arms for music in 4/4 time), hence a cigarette containing tobacco rather than marijuana (1970s, *US*).

Latin *quadrum* is the ancestor of CADRE*, QUARREL[1]*, and of **squad** and **squadron** [both via Italian *squadra*]. Related to QUARANTINE and QUARTER*.

squat [ME. Old French *esquatir* 'to flatten', from *quatir* 'to press down, to crouch', ultimately from Latin *coactus* 'forced together', from *cogere* 'to drive together, to compel', from *agere* 'to drive'] **1** to push down violently or forcefully; to crush or flatten (now dialect); to fall or hit hard (–16c): the idea of crushing or hitting survives in the variant **swat** (18c) **2** to crouch with your heels under your thighs

(15c), hence **(a)** in such a posture (15c), hence thickset, dumpy (17c) **(b)** such a posture (18c), now mainly in weightlifting **(c)** to settle on unoccupied land (18c, implied in **squatter**); to take over empty premises (19c).

Latin *cogere* produced CACHET* and **cogent**; *agere* is the ancestor of AGENT*.

squeal [ME. Imitative] To give a loud, high-pitched cry; to make a similar sound (16c); such a sound (18c), hence **1** to become an informer (19c, *US*) **2** (to make) a call for police assistance (1940s, *US*).

Squall to howl or cry is probably a mixture of *squeal* and **bawl** [probably of Scandinavian origin]. **Squall** 'a sudden strong wind' may be the same word.

squire [ME. Old French *esquier*, from Latin *scutarius* 'shield-bearer', from *scutum* 'shield'] A young nobleman training for knighthood, who acted as an attendant to a knight (cf. PAGE); (a title for) a man ranking next below a knight (also as a surname, with variants including **Swyer**), hence **1** to escort a lady, as a chivalrous knight should; a woman's escort or lover (16c) **2** (a title for) a country gentleman, especially the chief landowner in a district (17c), hence a polite form of address to a gentleman (19c), now informal or humorous.

Old French *esquier* produced **equerry** [via Old French *esquierie* 'company of squires', also (probably by association with Latin *equus* 'horse') 'prince's stables'] (an officer or officers in charge of) the royal stables, now an officer acting as attendant to a member of the Royal family (cf. MARSHAL*), and **esquire**, which shared most of *squire*'s senses and survives as an old-fashioned equivalent of *Mr*, placed after the man's name, often abbreviated (*John Smith, Esq.*). Latin *scutum* is the ancestor of *escutcheon* (at SHIELD) and perhaps of *skewbald* (at BALD).

stadium [ME. Latin, from Greek *stadion*] An ancient Greek and Roman measure of length, varying from time to time, but usually equal to one-eighth of a Roman mile [Old English *mil*, ultimately from Latin *mil(l)e* 'thousand' (ancestor of MIL-LION*), a Roman mile being one thousand paces], hence (as in Latin) a race course, originally of this length (17c); an arena or sports ground (19c).

In the Bible, Latin *stadium* was translated by **furlong** [Old English *furlang*, literally 'furrow long', the length of a furrow in the common field], standardized at an eighth of an English mile.

staff [Old English *staef*: the plural *staves* produced the variant **stave**] A stout stick, hence **1** one used as a walking stick; a prop or support (*flagstaff/bread is the staff of life*); the military officers supporting a commanding officer; the workers in an organization, especially permanent employees with some authority (19c); to be or provide staff **2** one used as a weapon, hence **stave off** to ward off (as if) with one (17c) **3** a rod carried in your work or as a sign of office, e.g. a shepherd's crook, a surveyor's measuring rod, hence **tipstaff** (a court official who formerly carried) one with a metal tip (16c) **4** one of the pieces making up a barrel or the bottom of a boat (ME, also *stave*), hence *stave* to break up a barrel etc. (16c); **stave in** to crush inwards (18c), later also as **stove in**, from the past tense of *stave* **5** now usually *stave*: the lines on which music is written (17c).

stage [ME. Old French *estage* 'dwelling', also 'stay', from Latin STATUS*] The underlying sense is a place to stand or stop. **1 (a)** a workmen's scaffold **(b)** a shelf or shelving, now only in a greenhouse, hence to put plants on it (19c); to exhibit them at a show **(c)** the platform in a theatre where actors perform (16c); the setting for (an) action (*the world stage*); the theatre as a profession; to put on a play (19c); to organize an event (*staged a coup/comeback*, *c*.1920, *US*) **2** a (regular) stopping-place (hence **landing stage**, **fare stage**), hence **(a)** the distance between stages (16c); a point or phase in a journey, life, or a process; **old stager** someone who has seen many stages, an old hand **(b)** to travel, now also to make something happen, in stages (17c, hence **stagecoach**); to make a brief stop on a journey (1970s) **(c)** a section of a rocket which is jettisoned when its fuel is exhausted (1930s).

stake [Old English *staca*] A post stuck in the ground, hence **1** one to which someone was tied for execution, especially by burning (ME); **the stake** death by burning **2** to mark out an area with stakes (ME); to claim land by doing so **3** to fasten to or with a stake (ME), hence **stake out** to place under surveillance (1940s, probably from the practice of keeping watch on a tethered decoy); **stake-out** a surveillance operation **4** money etc. wagered (15c, perhaps because the item wagered was put on a post while the outcome was decided, although evidence is scant), hence **(a)** the total amount bet on a race etc. (16c); **stakes** the total bet, or entrance fees, offered as a prize (17c); a race etc. offering such a prize (18c: see also *sweepstake* at SWEEP) **(b)** to wager (16c); to risk losing (17c); **at stake** at risk **(c)** a personal or financial interest (18c) **5** money, provisions, etc. necessary to survive an initial period (18c), specifically **grubstake** those advanced to a prospector (19c, *N American*); to give (financial) support.

Related to ATTACH*, ATTACK, **stack**, **stagger**, STICK*, **stockade** [via French from Spanish *estacada*, from *estaca* 'stake', of Germanic origin], and possibly to STOCK and TACK.

stalk [ME. Probably related to STEAL*] To walk quietly (–16c), hence **1** to approach or pursue stealthily, hence **(a)** **stalking horse** a horse, or horse-shaped screen, behind which a hunter hides (16c); a decoy; a pretext concealing your real actions or intentions **(b)** to follow or harass someone obsessively (1980s) **2** to walk with a stiff-legged, hence haughty, gait (16c).

stall [Old English *steall*, partly also from related Old French *estal*] A place, a position (–17c), hence **1** a cowshed or stable; a compartment for a single animal, hence **(a)** a small enclosed area: a pool (surviving in place names); a container or shelter (*finger stall*, 15c); a cubicle (1960s) **(b)** to keep or fatten an animal in a stall (ME) **2** **bring to stall** to bring to a standstill (ME–15c), hence *stall* to (suddenly) stop or be stopped (15c); of an aircraft: to suddenly lose lift (early 20c); the resulting dive **3** a throne (ME), hence **(a)** to induct or appoint officially (–17c), outlived by **instal** [related medieval Latin *installare*, from *stallum* 'a stall'] **(b)** a fixed seat or bench in a church etc. (*choir stalls*, 15c); **stalls** the seats on the ground floor of a theatre etc. (19c) **4** a bench in front of a shop (ME); a trader's stand in a market etc.

Old English *steall* appears as **Stal-** or **-stall** in place names, and produced *foresteall* **forestall** an ambush (–17c), hence to lie in wait for, to intercept (ME–18c); to prevent by acting beforehand. Old French *estal* produced INSTALMENT*. Related to German *Gestalt*, literally 'form, shape', **pedestal**, **stallion** [Old French *estalon*: stallions were often kept stalled], **still** motionless, and probably to STAND*.

stalwart [ME. Scots variant of **stalworth**, from Old English *staelwierthe*, from *stael* 'place'+ *w(e)orth* WORTH] Serviceable; sturdy, robust; resolute, determined; courageous, loyal; such a person, an uncompromising supporter or partisan.

Stalwart and *stalworth* died out during the 16c (surviving in the surnames **Stallard**, **Stollard**, and **Stal-** or **Stolworthy**), being revived by Scott (see DOFF). Old English *stael* is probably related to **staddle** [Old English *stathol*] a foundation (–ME); a support, surviving mainly in **staddle (stone)** that keeps stored hay etc. off the ground.

stamen [17c. Latin, literally 'warp, warp thread', adopted by Pliny (see ANTHRAX) for a lily's stamen] **1** the male organ of a flower **2** the thread of life spun by the Fates; the amount of vitality given at birth that determined your life span (18c only, surviving into the 19c as the plural **stamina**, which also meant endurance or staying power).

Related to **penstemon** [Greek *penta-* 'five' + *stēmōn* 'thread, stamen'], whose flowers have five stamens.

stamp [ME. Probably from Old English, influenced by related Old French *estamper*: related to **stampede** (Spanish *estampida* 'crash, uproar')] **1** to crush; to slam your foot down to do so, later to express anger, hence to trample (16c); **stamp out** to extinguish a fire by stamping on it (19c), to eradicate **2** (to impress or print with) a die or block (15c); the impression made (16c), hence **(a)** a characteristic mark, quality, or type (16c) **(b)** an embossed mark made on a document to show that tax (**stamp duty**) has been paid (17c); a small gummed label serving a similar function (*postage/insurance stamp*, 19c); to stick one on a letter etc. **(c)** to give approval to (as if by putting a stamp on it, 17c): cf. **rubber stamp** a person or institution that automatically approves others' decisions (early 20c); to do so (1930s) **(d) stamp (out)** to cut out with a die etc. (18c).

stance [ME. French, from Italian *stanza* 'standing, stopping-place', ultimately from Latin *stare* 'to stand'] A place to stand, a position, hence **1** a site (Scots): **(a)** one to be built on (17c) **(b)** one where a fair or market is held; a street-trader's pitch **(c)** a bus stop or taxi rank (1920s) **2** the position of a golfer's feet when hitting the ball (18c), hence **(a)** a posture (19c) **(b)** a standpoint, a point of view (1950s) **3** a workman's platform (19c); a place where a mountaineer can pitch and belay (1920s).

Italian *stanza* was adopted for a verse of a poem (from the idea of stopping at the end of it), hence a session of a game etc. Latin *stare* is the ancestor of STATION*.

stand [Old English *standan*] To be, or get into, an upright position; to be, stay, or put in a particular place, position, or condition, hence **1** of liquid: to collect and remain; of food etc.: to rest undisturbed **2** (also as **withstand**, literally 'to stand against') to resist or bear the brunt of, hence **(a) (to make a) stand** (to take up) a determined position (16c) **(b)** (to be exposed) to risk (*stand to win/lose*, 16c) **(c)** to endure or tolerate (17c) **3** a place where someone/something stands or is placed (*grand/hallstand, witness stand*, ME) **4** to act in a particular capacity (*stand surety*, ME), hence **(a)** to be a candidate (16c) **(b)** of a male animal: to be available for breeding (18c) **(c)** to treat to food, drink, etc. (19c) **5** a set of objects (15c), now often a group of growing plants, especially trees (19c, *US*) **6** a stop (16c); one on a theatrical tour (19c), hence **one-night stand**, now often a casual sexual encounter.

Related to STEAD*, STEM, STOOL, STOW*, and STUD*, and probably to INSTALMENT*, STALL*, and STANDARD.

standard [ME. Anglo-Norman French *estaundart*, Old French *estendart*, from *estendre*, perhaps from Latin *extendere* 'to stretch out', from *tendere* 'to stretch' (ancestor of TEND*), or of Frankish origin and related to STAND*] **1** a flag etc. as a rallying-point for troops; the distinctive flag of a monarch, regiment, etc. **2 king's standard** the official measuring rods, vessels, etc. that ensured uniform weights and measures throughout the realm, perhaps regarded as a symbol of his authority like his flag, hence *standard* an official or recognized measure; an example, norm, or criterion against which things are judged (15c); serving as, or conforming to, a standard (17c); regarded as a norm, ordinary (19c) **3** an upright timber, pole, etc.; (describing) a tree or shrub growing on an upright stem and needing no support (17c).

staple [ME. Old French *estaple* 'market', from early Low German and Dutch *stapel* 'pillar, platform, heap'] A town whose merchants had the exclusive right to deal in certain export commodities; to receive or deal with goods there (15c), hence **1 (a)** (describing) merchandise handled at the staple (15c); (describing) a country's most important commodity (17c), hence of diet etc.: usual, predominant **(b)** (probably) fibre considered with regard to its strength and fineness, assessed at the staple (15c); the fibre of which a thread or textile is made (16c) **2** a commercial centre (15c).

Related to **staple** [Old English *stapol*] a pillar or post (hence the names **Staple(ton)** and **Stapley**), later a U-shaped fastener with pointed ends.

star [Old English *steorra*] A celestial object shining in the night sky, now a gaseous body, but formerly also a planet, comet, or meteor (surviving in *falling/shooting star*), hence **1** something resembling or representing one: **(a)** a starfish **(b)** a white spot on a horse's forehead (ME) **(c)** a star-shaped mark, an asterisk (ME); a (star-shaped) badge of rank or merit (*five-star general/hotel*, 19c); to mark with or award a star (19c) **(d)** a 'brilliant' person (19c); (to be) a leading performer; of a film etc.: to feature someone as the star **2** the planet or constellation believed to influence your destiny (ME); **your stars** your horoscope.

Old English *steorra* probably produced **sterling** an English penny (some of which bore a star), hence **1** a **pound of sterlings** a pound weight of pennies, the English pound in money; *sterling* British money **2** (describing) money or silver of the same quality as a sterling, or meeting a standard quality (hence **sterling silver**, 92% pure), hence admirable, valuable, excellent (*sterling qualities/work*).

stark [Old English *stearc*] Hard, unyielding, severe, hence (all ME) **1** strong, powerful; of liquor: potent (16c, surviving in Scots) **2** rigid, stiff **3** sheer, absolute, absolutely, utterly (*stark raving mad*), hence **stark (naked)** (18c), **starkers** (19c) completely naked (influenced by *start naked*, from Old English *steort* 'tail', which also survives in **redstart** a bird with red tail-feathers); of landscape etc.: bare, barren (19c), hence unadorned, brutally simple, plain, or obvious.

Related to **starch**, **stare**, **starve** [Old English *steorfan* 'to die' (of cold, lack of food etc., from the idea of going stiff)], **stern** strict, severe, and STRUT, and probably to **stork**, from its rigid upright posture.

start [Old English] To jump or caper, to leap on or into (–16c); to move or jump up or out suddenly (ME), hence (all ME) **1** to force an animal from cover, hence to 'put up' an idea etc. for discussion (16c) **2** to (cause to) move to avoid danger;

(to make) a sudden involuntary movement **3** to awake suddenly **4** a sudden, brief movement or effort (surviving mainly in *fits and starts* at FIT²) **5** to go or come quickly, suddenly, or hastily (–17c), hence to begin to move or to do something, originally to begin running in a race (16c), hence **(a)** a beginning (16c); **start (out)** to begin a journey, career, etc. (18c); an opportunity to do so (*fresh start/ start in life*, 19c) **(b)** an advantage or lead (*five minutes start*, 16c) **(c) start (up)** to initiate or set going (17c) **(d)** a race or contest (*won his last three starts*, 1940s, US).

Related to **startle** to kick or struggle (OE only); to caper or rush about (surviving in dialect), later to start in fear or surprise; to frighten or surprise.

state [ME. (Old French *estat* from) Latin STATUS*] Status or condition, hence **1** someone's status, profession, or rank, hence **(a)** high rank, greatness, power (–17c); the trappings of this: pomp, ceremony (hence **stately** dignified, imposing); property and possessions (–19c): cf. *estate* below **(b)** a class of people or the members of a profession (–17c); one traditionally having political power (–18c): cf. *estate* **(c)** to assign a certain rank to (16–18c); to instal in an office or position (17c, largely replaced by its descendant, **instate**) **2** the condition of a country etc., especially as regards its prosperity and government (–17c), hence **(a) the State** a country's government; *State* to do with, owned, or run by it (16c) **(b) state** a community, nation, etc. under one government (16c); a largely autonomous region of a federal country (17c) **3** a particular condition (cf. *estate*): **(a)** an agitated mental or emotional one (15c) **(b)** a dirty or untidy one (19c) **(c)** the current one (*state of play/the art*, 19c) **4** to express something fully, formally, or authoritatively (17c); to lay down or specify (18c), hence **statement** this action; what is stated; an account.

Old French *estat* produced **estate**, which shared some senses: its main strands of meaning are: **1** property, possessions: **(a)** a (large) landed property (hence **estate agent**, originally the manager of one); a planned district (*housing/industrial estate*) **(b)** a (deceased) person's assets and liabilities **(c) estate (car)** designed to carry possessions as well as passengers **2** an influential class: **Estates of the Realm**, now the Lords Spiritual, the Lords Temporal, and the Commons, hence **the fourth estate**, originally the mob, now usually the Press **3** a particular condition: surviving, just, in *man's/woman's estate* and *the estate of matrimony*.

static [16c. Via modern Latin from Greek *statikos* 'causing to stand', from *statos* 'standing', from *histainai* 'to cause to stand, to weigh'] The study of weight and equilibrium (replaced by 17c **statics**); to do with things in equilibrium or at rest (19c), hence fixed, stationary, not moving or changing; **static (electricity)** 'stationary' electricity (as opposed to current), often caused by friction and producing sparks or crackling, hence **1 (electro)static** to do with or producing stationary electricity or a steady electrical field **2** (the sound of) electrical disturbances that interfere with broadcasts and telecommunications (*c.*1910), hence interference, aggravation (1920s, *US slang*).

Static was the first form of electricity known, produced by rubbing amber, hence **electric** [Latin *electricus*, from *electrum* 'amber', from Greek *elektron*].

station [ME. French, from Latin *statio* 'standing', from *stare*, *stat-* 'to stand'] **1** your role in society; your job; your social standing (17c) **2** one of a series of holy places which pilgrims visit in sequence, hence **(a) Stations of the Cross** a series of images of Christ's passion (16c) **(b)** a stopping-place on a journey (16c); one where passengers may join or leave trains (18c), hence **bus/coach station** (1940s) **3** a port or harbour; one to which naval ships are posted, hence **(a)** a place where something/someone is, or should be, found (15c) **(b)** to assign, originally a ship, to a place to carry out duties (16c); the place; **station yourself** to place yourself (18c) **4** a place designated and equipped for a particular purpose (*police/pumping station*, 19c); one from which radio or television broadcasts can be made (*c.*1910); a broadcasting channel **5** a large sheep or cattle farm (19c, Australia and New Zealand): cf. American Spanish *estancia* cattle ranch [ultimately from Latin *stare*].

Latin *statio* produced **stationary** and **stationer** a bookseller [via medieval Latin *stationarius* 'shopkeeper, bookseller' (a 'stationary' one, not a pedlar)], later a seller of writing materials etc., hence **stationery** such goods. Latin *stare*'s descendants include **circumstance** [Latin *circumstare* 'to stand around'], REST 'to remain, the remainder', **stable** steady [from Latin *stabilis*, whence also **establish**], *stable* for horses (at MARSHAL), and **stanchion** [Old French *estance* 'prop, support']. Other descendants include **arrest**, CONSIST*, **constant**, **cost**, DESTINE*, **distance**, INSTANCE*, **obstinate**, OUST*, STANCE*, STATUS*, STAY*, SUBSTANCE, **superstition**, and probably STAUNCH*.

status [17c. Latin, 'standing, state', from *stare*: see STATION] **1** the crisis of a disease (late 17c only) **2** someone's legal position (*refugee status*, 18c); their social standing (19c); someone/something's (relative) importance **3** a state or condition (19c), often in Latin phrases such as *status quo* [literally 'the state in which'].

Latin *status* produced STAGE, STATE*, **stature** natural height, hence an achieved 'height' or eminence, and Latin *statuere* 'to set up or establish', whose descendants include **constitute** [Latin *constituere* 'to establish, to make up', whence also **constituency** and **constituent**], **destitute** [Latin *destituere* 'to set down, to abandon'], INSTITUTE, **prostitute** [Latin *prostituere* 'to offer for sale'], **restitution** [ultimately from Latin *restituere* 'to restore', literally 'to re-establish'], **statistic** [German *Statistik* 'political science', from Italian *stato* 'state'] originally the collection of figures as a political activity, **statue**, **statute** [via French from late Latin *statutum*, literally 'something established'], and **substitute** originally (to appoint) a deputy or delegate.

staunch [15c. Old French *estanche*, probably ultimately from Latin *stare*: see STATION*] Watertight; firm, strong, substantial; reliable, dependable (16c, originally of a sporting dog); resolute, unwavering, dependable, loyal (17c).

Related to **stanch** [Old French *estanchier*] to stop, quell, or allay, now usually to stop a flow, also to make watertight. Both words can be spelt *staunch* or *stanch*: these are the more common usages.

stay [15c. Old French *este(i)r*, from Latin *stare*: see STATION*] To stop, hence **1** to linger **2** a stop or pause (16c), hence in law: a suspension of proceedings, sentence, etc. (*stay of execution*) **3** to dwell (16c), usually temporarily (*stayed in a hotel/with my parents*), but permanently in Scotland, S Africa, and the US; (the duration of) a period of temporary residence **4** to remain in a place or condition (*stayed in her memory/warm all week*); to remain for some reason (*stay and meet them/stay for dinner*) **5** to show stamina (19c); **stay with** keep up with (*US*).

The original past tense and participle, **staid**, came to mean fixed, settled, hence set in your ways, steady, sedate.

stead [Old English *stede*] A particular place (–16c), hence **1 (home)stead** a settlement; a village (surviving in place names, e.g. *Ham(p)stead*, *Binstead*), hence **(a)** *homestead* a house with its outbuildings (17c, hence, probably, **farmstead**, 19c); a piece of land that will support one family (17c, *US*), specifically one granted to a settler under the Homestead Act of Congress (1862) **(b) steading** a farmstead (15c), later the outbuildings only (Scots and N English dialect) **2** the place where something is or should be found, hence **bedstead** originally the place for a bed **3** a person's official position (–17c), hence **in his stead** in his place, as his successor (ME); **instead (of)** in place of, as a substitute for.

Stead produced **steadfast** and **steady**, with the underlying sense 'not giving ground': related to STAND*.

steal [Old English *stelan*] To take furtively, dishonestly, or by deceit, hence **1** to sneak away, to move secretly or quietly (ME); **steal up on** to sneak up on; to come insidiously (15c); to move or happen imperceptibly (17c); **steal a march** to gain an advantage (originally that of a day's march) by moving troops secretly (18c) **2** a theft (ME); something stolen or purloined, hence **(a)** (an act of) large-scale fraud or dishonesty (19c, US) **(b)** a bargain (1940s, US) **3** to gain or accomplish something surreptitiously (*steal a kiss*, ME): **(a)** to entice away (*stole my boyfriend*, 16c) **(b)** to pass someone's ideas, words, etc. off as your own (16c); **steal your thunder** to stop you getting credit for something by doing it, using it, etc. first (*c*.1900, said to refer to pirating a method of producing stage thunder) **(c) steal the scene/show**, etc. to make such an impression that no one else gets a look-in (1920s, *US*).

Related to STALK and to **stealth** stealing, (a) theft (ME–18c); covert or furtive activity; the ability to move secretly, hence **Stealth** (describing the products of) a branch of US military technology developing weapons that are hard to detect.

steel [Old English *stȳle*, *stēli*] A hard, malleable alloy of iron, hence **1** something made of this, e.g. a weapon or weapons (*cold steel*); a rod to sharpen knives on (16c) **2** hardness, toughness (ME); to make hard, strong, or determined (16c); **steely** hard, cold, relentless; **steel yourself** to prepare yourself for a difficulty **3** a cold grey, the colour of steel (19c).

Related to **stay** a rope supporting a mast [Old English *staeg* 'to be firm'], whence **mainstay** that supports the mainmast, your chief support, and to **stay** [French *estay*] a support, to give support, whence **stays** corsets.

steep [Old English *stēap*] **1** tall, high, lofty, hence excessive, unreasonable (19c); of a story etc.: incredible, 'tall' **2** sloping sharply, almost perpendicular (ME); of a rise or fall: sharp (19c).

Related to **steeple** a tall tower or building (–19c), now only one forming part of a church, and to **stoop** to bend down.

stem [Old English *stemn*, *stefn*] A main part or line: **1** of a plant, hence a stalk, especially bearing leaves, flowers, or fruit (16c); something resembling this (*pipe stem*, 17c); a support (stem of a wine glass, *brainstem*, etc.) **2** the main timber at either end of a ship, now only at the bow, hence to head in a certain direction

(15c); to make headway against the wind etc. (16c), hence **stem the tide**, which may also mean 'to stop a flow' [**stem** to stop or staunch (ME), from Old Norse *stemma*: related to **stammer**] **3** the main line of a family's descent (16c), hence **(a)** ancestry, pedigree, partly by association with Latin *stemma* a family tree [17c, from Greek, 'crown, garland', from *stephein* 'to crown or encircle'] **(b)** to spring from (1930s, US) **4** the part of a word to which endings etc. are attached (17c) **5** the main line of a railway (19c); a (main) street; one frequented by tramps and beggars (early 20c, US), hence to beg on the street.

Greek *stephein* produced *stephanos* 'crown, wreath', whence **stephanotis** [literally 'fit for a garland'], a plant with fragrant flowers, and the name **Stephen**, given to the first Christian martyr (from the idea of martyrs wearing crowns in heaven). Related to STAND*.

step [Old English *st(a)epe* (noun), *st(a)eppan* (verb)] To lift your foot and put it down elsewhere; this movement; to walk, hence **1** a pace; a very short distance; to measure a distance by pacing it out (19c) **2** a structure to step on when going up or down, a stair, hence **(a)** something resembling this, e.g. a block in which the heel of a mast is fixed, hence to fix the mast in it (18c); to fix securely in a groove etc. **(b)** a degree in an ascending or descending scale, or later, in a process; one of a series of actions towards a goal **3 (foot)steps** a course (of action) (*retrace your steps, follow in someone's footsteps*) **4** a foot movement in a dance (17c); in the names of dances (*quickstep, two-step*, 19c).

Step produced **instep**, and is related to Afrikaans *stoep* a raised verandah [from Dutch, whence also N American **stoop** (the steps up to) a small porch or verandah]. **Step-** in *stepmother* etc. is from Old English *stēop* 'orphan'.

stereotype [18c. French *stéréotype* (noun), *stéréotyper* (verb), ultimately from Greek *stereos* 'solid' + *tupos* 'blow, impression': see TYPE*] A method of replicating a printing plate by taking a cast of it; a plate produced from the cast (19c), hence to reproduce, or the thing reproduced, many times without change or thought, hence **1** a standardized, oversimplified idea that one group has of another (1920s); someone apparently conforming to it (1960s) **2** in zoology: an action or series of actions an animal repeats for no apparent reason (1960s).

A French alternative for *stéréotyper* is *clicher* (apparently imitating the sound made when the matrix is dropped into molten metal), whence *cliché* a stereotype plate; a hackneyed saying or idea.

Greek *stereos* produced **stereo-** in **stereophonic** and **stereoscope**, both of which use multiple inputs to produce a 'solid' or three-dimensional effect (both often shortened to **stereo**), and is one parent of *cholesterol* (at HUMOUR).

stew [ME. Old French *estuve* (noun), *estuver* (verb), perhaps ultimately from Greek *tuphos* 'smoke, vapour, stupor'] **1** a cauldron (–17c); to cook (slowly) in one (15c); to simmer, hence **(a)** a dish of meat and vegetables simmered in a pot (18c) **(b)** to be overheated (19c); (to be in) an agitated or angry state (19c); to fret (*c*.1915) **2** a heated room; one used for hot or steam baths, hence a brothel (the baths often being used for this purpose).

Greek *tuphos* produced **typhus**, whence **typhoid**. Possibly related to STOVE.

stick [Old English *stician*] To stab or pierce, hence **1** of a spear, knife, etc.: to have its point embedded, hence **(a)** to (cause to) be or become fastened, jammed, or set; to fix or be fixed with adhesive (ME) **(b)** to stay in the same place (*sticks in the mind*); to stop or hesitate (16c), especially from confusion or scruples **2** to (make something) protrude (as if thrust through, 16c).

Related to STAKE*, **steak** [Old Norse *steik* 'meat roasted on a spit'], **stick** a thin piece of wood, **stickleback** [Old English *sticel* 'thorn'], STITCH, and **stoke**.

stilt [ME. Of Germanic origin: related to STOUT] A plough handle; a crutch (both surviving in dialect), hence **1 stilts** a pair of poles with footrests for 'walking tall'; long slender legs (16c); *stilt* a long-legged wading bird (18c) **2** one of a series of poles on which a building is raised above ground or water (17c), hence **stilted** built on stilts, raised; of language etc.: lofty, affected, stiff and pompous (19c).

stint [Old English *styntan*, influenced by Old Norse *stytta* 'to shorten'] **1** to make blunt or dull (OE only) **2** to (cause to) stop or shorten (ME); to stop something growing (18c, influenced by sense 3 and by *stunt* below) **3** a portion or ration (15c), hence **(a)** (to impose) a limitation; to be mean or grudging with food, money, etc. (16c) **(b)** a quota of work, especially to be done in a shift (16c); a shift or spell of work; to impose one (18c).

Stunt [Old English: perhaps related to *stump* (at STUB)] originally meant stupid (–ME), later stubborn; blunt, curt, hence to bring to a sudden stop (16–17c); to stop or check growth. **Stunt** a daring trick (*US college slang*) also meant a task or exercise, so may be related to *stint*, though evidence is lacking.

stipulate [Latin *stipulari*, probably from *stipula* 'straw', from the Roman custom of breaking a straw to confirm a promise] To make a (verbal) agreement or contract (16c), hence to specify or demand as part of this.

Latin *stipula* is the ultimate ancestor of **etiolated** pale and drawn, originally of a plant deprived of light [French *étioler*, from Norman French *etieuler* 'to grow into stalks', from *éteule* 'stalk', from Old French *estuble*, whence also **stubble**].

stitch [Old English *stice*: related to STICK*] A prick, puncture, or stab (OE only), hence **1** a stabbing pain, now only cramp in the side **2** (the thread left by) a single pass of a needle, hence **(a)** to sew (ME) **(b)** (the loop produced by) a single movement of a knitting or crochet needle (16c) **(c)** a particular way of sewing, knitting, etc. (*cable/feather stitch*, 17c).

stock [Old English *stoc(c)*] A tree trunk or stump (surviving in names, e.g. *Stockleigh*, *Stockbridge*, and in **stock dove** that nests in hollow trees); a log or block of wood (now Scots), hence **1** a post or stake (–17c); the main (upright) part or support (ME), hence **(a) stocks** a frame (with two upright supports) which confined the ankles, later one for immobilizing a large animal (19c) **(b)** *stocks* the framework supporting a ship under construction (15c), hence **on the stocks** planned or in progress (17c) **(c)** the body to which a (moving) part is attached, a rifle butt, whip handle, etc. (15c) **2** a plant stem (ME); one that takes a graft, hence a progenitor; a line of descent (16c); a race or type **3** a supply (ME); to supply or keep supplied, hence **(a)** money, capital (15c); *stocks* shares in capital or in a commodity, industry, etc. (17c), hence *stock* your apparent worth or reputation (*her stock rose after her success*, 1930s) **(b)** a store of goods for sale or use (15c); to (habitually) have something in it; kept in stock (17c, hence ordinary, unoriginal); **take stock** to count your stock (18c); to assess your situation **(c)** a farm's machinery (**dead**

stock) and animals (**livestock**) (16c) **(d) laughing stock** a source of amusement (16c) **(e)** a liquid from which soup, gravy, etc. is made (18c) **(f)** raw material (*film stock*, 19c) **4** *stocks* (perhaps from sense 1a: tight boots were once called *shoemaker's stocks*): **(a)** close-fitting hose (15c), replaced by **stocking** (16c), whence, probably, **stockinet(te)** a fine knitted fabric (18c) **(b)** a close-fitting neckcloth (17c).

Stock produced **stocky** strong, sturdy (originally of a plant); now often short and thickset. Perhaps related to STAKE*.

stoic [15c. Via Latin from Greek *stōikos*, from *stoa* 'porch'] A follower of the Syrian philosopher Zeno, who lectured in the *Stoa Poikilē* (Painted Porch) at Athens around the turn of the 3c BC, teaching that passions and appetites should be subdued, hence **stoical** unemotional, patient in adversity, unmoved by pleasure or pain (16c); *stoic* such a person.

stooge [Early 20c. Origin unknown] **1** a stagehand (*c*.1910); a conjuror's assistant (1920s); a comedian's straight man, hence a loyal and unthinking subordinate; someone's puppet (1930s) **2** a novice (1930s), specifically **(a)** a first offender **(b)** a trainee (World War II, *RAF slang*), hence, probably, **stooge (about/around)** (to go on) a routine flight not expecting to meet the enemy, hence to wander about aimlessly (1950s).

stool [Old English *stōl*: related to STAND*] A chair or throne (–19c), hence **1** a footstool (ME) **2** a seat for offenders (*ducking stool*, ME) **3** a seat without arms or back (ME), hence **(a)** **toadstool** which resembles one, and is found in similar places to toads **(b)** a bird, originally a pigeon tied to a stool, used as a decoy in wildfowling (19c, *US*), hence **stool (pigeon)** someone acting as a decoy; (also **stoolie**) a police informer (*c*.1900) **4 (close) stool** a seat with a chamber pot (15c), hence the place for, later the act of, defecating (16c); **stools** faeces **5** a tree stump (16c); the part from which new shoots spring (18c); (to produce) new growth from a stool or root; to cut back a plant to make it do so (*c*.1900).

stout [ME. Old French dialect, of Germanic origin and related to STILT] **1** brave, dauntless, steadfast **2** strong, vigorous, robust (surviving in US dialect), hence **(a)** of a beer: strong, with body (17–19c: see *stout* at BEER) **(b)** strongly built, thickset (18c); fat (19c).

stove [15c. Early Dutch and Low German: possibly related to STEW*] A steam room or heated room (–18c), hence a heating apparatus, a furnace, kiln, or cooker (16c), hence to heat in one (17c); to stew meat etc. (Scots and N English), surviving mainly in **stoved tatties** or **stovies** potatoes stewed with onions and perhaps a little meat (19c).

stow [Old English *stōw*] A place (surviving in place names, e.g. *Chepstow* at CHEAP), hence to place or lodge (ME), hence **1 stow (away)** to put away tidily so as to be easily accessible (16c, originally on a ship); to put cargo in the hold (17c), hence **stow away** to hide on a ship (19c); **stowaway** someone who does so **2** to invest or spend time, effort or, later, money in a particular activity (ME–18c).

Stow produced **bestow**, which also meant to place or spend, and came to mean to settle or give in marriage (ME–18c), hence, probably, to give as a gift. Related to STAND* and to Old English *stoc* 'place, outlying farm', later 'monastery, cell', which survives in place names (*Halstock*, *Stoke-on-Trent*).

straight [ME. Former past tense of STRETCH. Formerly also spelt, and confused with, STRAIT] Not curved, bent, or angular, without deviation, hence **1** direct, directly, hence candid(ly), frank(ly) **2** immediately, replaced by **straightaway** (17c) **3** **(a)** not crooked, honest, trustworthy **(b) the straight and narrow** a conventional, law-abiding way of life (19c, from a misunderstanding of the Bible, Matthew 7:14: 'strait is the gate, and narrow is the way, which leadeth unto life') **(c)** orthodox, conventional (19c); heterosexual (1930s) **(d)** of drama etc.: not comic or experimental (19c) **4** of an account: settled (16c), hence even, without debt or obligation (17c) **5** not disturbed or disarranged (19c): **(a)** tidy **(b) straight face** without expression, not laughing; **straight man** who 'feeds' a comedian with lines **6** not mixed, modified, or adulterated, neat (19c, *US*) **7** consecutive(ly) (19c) **8** a straight part, especially of a race course (19c).

strain¹ [Old English *strēon*] Something gained (–ME), hence offspring, progeny (ME); a line of descent, hence **1** a hereditary quality (16c) **2** a variety developed by breeding (17c); a natural or cultured variety of a micro-organism (19c).

strain² [ME. Old French *estreindre, estreign-*, from Latin *stringere*: see STRICT*] To pull tight, hence **1** to bind tightly, to confine, control, or restrain (–16c); to clasp or squeeze tightly, hence, perhaps, to push through a sieve; to separate liquid from solids **2** to (over-)stretch, hence **(a)** to tighten the string of a musical instrument, hence, perhaps, to play an instrument (16–17c); a melody or tune; a passage of a song or poem **(b)** to (over-)exert yourself or part of your body; (to make) an extreme effort (16c); to cause injury by doing so (17c); such an injury (*eyestrain*) **(c)** to distort (15c); (the cause of) such distortion (17c); force, load, stress **(d)** to pull strongly (*straining at the leash*, 18c) **(e)** (to make) extreme demands (*a strain on resources*, 19c).

strait [ME. French *estreit* from Latin *stringere*: see STRICT*. Formerly also spelt, and confused with, STRAIGHT] **1** cramped, confined, narrow, tight (see also *straight and narrow* at STRAIGHT), hence **(a)** a narrow passage; **strait(s)** a narrow piece of water connecting two seas **(b)** of means: limited, inadequate (–18c), hence *strait(s)* a time of great need or hardship (ME) **2** rigorous, severe (–17c), hence **(a)** of a rule etc.: strictly worded or enforced (cf. STRICT) **(b)** of a person: exacting, strict, scrupulous, hence **strait-laced** prudish (16c): the sense 'wearing a tightly laced garment' is later (17–18c) **(c)** of confinement: strict, close, hence **strait-waistcoat** (18c), **strait-**, now usually **straightjacket** (19c).

strand [Old English] A shore, specifically between the low and high water marks, or just above the latter, hence **1** a (foreign) land (ME) **2** a landing place, a quay (ME–19c): senses so far shared by **shore** [ME, early Dutch or Low German *schore*: sense 2 survives in Scots] **3** in the names of roads, promenades, etc. following the line of the shore **4** to drive or wash ashore (17c, cf. BEACH), hence **stranded** abandoned with no means of leaving (19c).

strange [ME. Old French *estrange* from Latin *extraneus*, from *extra* 'outside': see *extraordinary* (at ORDINARY)] From another country, foreign, alien (–18c); new to or unknown in a place, hence **stranger** a foreigner; someone you don't know. Hence **1** not belonging to your family, hence *stranger* **(a)** a guest or (infrequent) visitor (now usually in **don't be a stranger** make yourself at home, come again soon) **(b)** a non-member; in law: someone who is not party to an action etc. (16c, cf. PRIVY) **2** new, unfamiliar; remarkable, odd **3** (also, and now usually, **a stranger to**) unacquainted with, unaccustomed to (16c).

Latin *extraneus* produced **extraneous** introduced from outside, foreign, irrelevant, and **estrange** [Old French *estranger* from Latin *extraneare* 'to treat as a stranger'].

streak [Old English *strica*: related to STRIKE*] A line, a mark, a pen stroke (–18c); (to mark with) a line or strip of contrasting colour (16c), hence **1** a strain of an unexpected quality (*a streak of meanness*, 17c) **2** a line of light in darkness (16c); a flash of lightning (18c), hence to move rapidly (properly a variant of obsolete *streek* 'to stretch', but long regarded as moving like lightning), hence **streaking** running naked in public (1970s) **3** a run or spell (*a lucky streak*, 19c).

street [Old English *straet* from late Latin *strata (via)* 'paved (way)', from *sternere*, *strat-* 'to lay down'] A paved road, a highway, surviving in the names of some ancient, mostly Roman, roads and of places on them (*Stratford, Streatley, Stretton*); an urban public road, usually lined with buildings, hence **1** the public space outside the buildings (ME), hence **(a)** describing things and people found there (*street furniture/trader*, 18c) **(b)** **in/on the street(s)** outdoors, homeless (19c); out of prison, at liberty (*US*) **(c)** the realm of ordinary people (*the man in the street*, 19c); (to do with) modern urban culture, especially of youth or the underworld (*streetwise*, 1930s) **2** the buildings or people of a street (*the whole street can hear you*, ME).

Latin *sternere* is the ancestor of **consternation**, **prostrate**, **stratum** literally 'something laid down' (whence **stratify**), **stratus** a flat cloud formation (whence **strato-** in *stratocumulus* etc.), and possibly *stray* (at EXTRAVAGANT).

stretch [Old English *streccan*] **Stretch (out)** to lie down with arms and legs straight out, hence *stretch* to extend or be extended, especially beyond normal limits; this action (16c), hence an extended or continuous length (17c); a continuous period of time, work, imprisonment, etc.

Stretch produced STRAIGHT and influenced *distraught* (at DISTRACT). Related to **straggle**.

strict [ME. Latin *stringere*, *strict-* 'to pull tight'] Restricted in space or extent, later in amount, meaning, or scope (16–18c), hence **1** of a law etc.: rigorously framed or enforced (16c); of a person: severe, not lenient **2** of confinement or imprisonment: close (16c) **3** precise, exact (17c) **4** conforming rigidly to rules or principles (17c).

Latin *stringere* is the ancestor of **astringent**, PRESTIGE, STRAIT, **stricture**, **stringent**, and of pairs of words, most with overlapping meanings, ending in -*strict* and [via an intermediate language, usually French] -*strain*: **constrict/constrain**, DISTRESS*, **restrict/restrain**, and *strict*/STRAIN².

stride [Old English *stride* (noun), *strīdan* (verb)] To stand or walk with the legs wide apart; (the distance covered by) a single long step. Hence **1** to walk vigorously, purposefully, or with long steps (ME); to take a long step; to step over or across with one (16c) **2** your gait determined by the length of your stride (17c); the cut or fit of trousers etc. to accommodate this (19c); **strides** trousers **3** (the length of) a coordinated forward movement by an animal (17c); a horse's regular pace or speed (19c); **get into your stride** to reach a steady rate of progress **4** *strides* progress (*make strides*, 17c) **5** the surname **Stride**, someone with long legs or a purposeful gait.

Stride produced **astride**, **bestride**, and **straddle** [alteration of **striddle**, back-formation from **striddling(s)** 'astride']. Possibly related to STRIVE*.

strike [Old English *strīcan*] **1** of water: to flow, hence to go, to proceed (ME); **strike out** to set out **2** to pass your hand over lightly: largely replaced by **stroke** [related to Old English *stracian*: not the same word as *stroke* below] **3** to hit (ME), hence **(a)** of light: to fall on (15c), hence to reach the eye, mind, or ear (16c); to catch your attention (18c, in **striking**); to make an impression on (19c) **(b)** to happen (to) suddenly or violently (ME); (to launch) a sudden attack; to punish or afflict; to seize with terror etc. **(c)** to slap or shake hands to seal an agreement (15c), hence **strike a bargain** (16c: the idea is found earlier in **swap** to slap palms to seal a bargain, hence to barter or exchange) **(d)** of a clock: to sound the hour (15c) **(e)** to produce by percussion or friction (*strike a coin/light*, 15c) **(f)** the act of striking (15c: cf. *stroke* below); in baseball: the act of hitting the ball (19c), hence a **(foul) strike** an illegal stroke or a miss, three of which disqualify the hitter, hence **three strikes you're out** referring to a mandatory jail sentence for a third offence **(g)** to touch a drum, key, string, etc. to produce a sound (16c) **(h)** to hit upon, to find (18c); a sudden (lucky) find or success (*oil strike*, 19c) **4** to take down a flag, mast, tent, etc. (ME), hence to **strike (work)** to down tools; a refusal to work etc. as a protest (*hunger/rent strike*, 19c) **5** to mark with a line (15c: cf. related STREAK); to cross out, hence **struck off** removed from a professional register and no longer allowed to practise (19c) **6** of a plant: to put down roots (17c); to root a cutting etc.

Closely related to **stroke** an act of striking: **1** a blow, a sudden destructive act or occurrence (now especially a cerebral vascular accident) **2** a single completed movement (*brush/keystroke*, **stroke of work** the minimum amount), hence **(a)** a single pull of an oar, hence the rower whose rate sets the time for the others (19c) **(b)** a style of movement (*back stroke*) **(c)** a single instance (*a stroke of wit/luck*). Also related are the surname **Straker**, **Striker** someone who levelled measures of grain etc. by removing the excess with a stick, and French *tricot* a knitted fabric [from *tricoter* 'to knit', from Old French *tricote* 'small stick', from *(es)trique* 'a straker's stick', from *estriquer* 'to strike off'].

strive [ME. Old French *estriver*, from or related to *estrif* strife, of Germanic origin. Possibly related to STRIDE*] To be mutually hostile, to quarrel; to fight or compete for something, hence to try hard to do, later to get, something.

strop [ME. Early Dutch and Low German, probably ultimately from Greek *strophos*, from *strephein* 'to turn'] A (leather) thong or loop (–18c, partly replaced by the variant **strap**, 16c), hence **1** a (leather or rope) band used as a fastening (15c, chiefly nautical), later also *strap*, which came to mean **(a)** a loop for pulling your boots on (17c) or to hang onto in a moving vehicle **(b)** a strip of leather, cloth, etc.; to bind, fasten, or beat with one (18c) **2** a strip of leather, or leather-covered wood, for sharpening a razor (18c, also *strap*), hence to do so, whence, probably, *strap* to work energetically, later specifically to groom a horse (19c), but cf. **strapping** vigorous, robust, sturdy (17c).

Strapped for cash is probably from a variant of **strip** to remove the last drops of milk from a cow [perhaps from or related to **strip** to undress, probably of Old English origin]. *Strop* is probably related to **strip** a narrow band, piece of land, etc., and **stripe** [both from Dutch or Low German]. Greek *strephein* is the ancestor of CATASTROPHE*.

strut [Old English *strūtian*: related to STARK*] **1** to stick up or out stiffly (–19c); a rigid plank etc. used as a support (16c) **2** to quarrel or bluster (ME–15c); **strut (it)** to behave arrogantly, to swagger or show off (15c, surviving in N American **strut your stuff**, 1920s, which is probably partly from the following sense); to walk stiffly with exaggerated dignity (16c); such a walk (17c).

stub [Old English *stub(b)*, *styb*] A tree stump; the remaining piece of a broken-off branch (ME), hence **1 stub (up)** to dig up, or clear land of, stumps (ME) **2** something short and thick, e.g. a nail or stud (ME) **3** something (appearing to be) cut, worn down, or stunted (*cigarette/ticket stub*, 15c); to reduce in length; **stubby** short and thick (16c) **4** to stumble over a stump etc., hence to strike your toe on one (19c, *US*); to put out a cigarette by crushing it against something hard (1920s).

Senses 1, 3, and 4 were shared by unrelated **stump** [early Dutch *stomp*, Low German *stump(e)*], originally the remains of an amputated limb, which came to mean **1** a stake or post **2** a rudimentary or deformed limb; a wooden leg; to walk heavily as if with one **3 stump up** to 'fork out' money (as if digging out stumps); *stump* to bring to a halt, to baffle (perhaps from ploughing poorly cleared land) **4** a tree stump used as a speaker's platform (*US*), hence **(to go on the) stump** to travel around making (election) speeches.

stud [Old English *stōd*] A place where horses are bred; the horses kept there, hence **1 (a) stud(-horse)** a stallion, hence a man considered good at sex **(b) at stud** (also of other animals) available for breeding **2** horses collectively (–15c, surviving as **Stad-**, **Stod-**, and **Stud-** in place names, and in surnames such as **Stoddart** someone who kept horses); the horses bred and/or kept by one person (17c); one person's collection of (breeding) animals (18c), later also of cars.

Related to STAND* and **steed** a stallion (surviving in the surname **Ste(a)dman** a lusty man, or one who looked after a stallion); a powerful, spirited mount.

studio [19c. Italian, from Latin *studium*: see STUDY*] An artist's workplace, hence **1 studio (apartment/flat)** consisting of one large room, originally with large windows like an artist's studio (early 20c, *US*) **2** *studio(s)* a place where films (*c*.1910), or broadcasts and recordings (1920s) are produced.

study [ME. Via Old French from, ultimately, Latin *studium* 'zeal, mental effort', from *studere* 'to study'] (To apply your mind to) the pursuit of knowledge, hence **1** a room set aside for studying **2** to try to do or achieve something; (the object of) the effort or thought applied, hence **studied** deliberate, not spontaneous (*studied indifference*, 15c) **3** to examine in detail; a book, report, etc. describing the thing studied (19c) **4** interest in something/someone, hence affection, friendliness (–17c); to heed and consider someone's feelings or needs (18c) **5** an artistic work, especially a preparatory sketch etc. (18c); a piece of music that develops a point of technique or shows off the performer's skill (19c, more common in the modern French form *étude*).

Latin *studium* produced **student** and STUDIO, and is the ultimate ancestor of **stew** a pond for keeping edible fish [French *estui* 'place of confinement', whence modern French *etui* a small ornamental case for small items, quickly but briefly Anglicized to *tweeze*, whence **tweezers**].

stuff [ME. Old French *estoffe* (noun), *estoffer* (verb), probably of Germanic origin] **1** quilted material worn under, or instead of, chain mail (–16c), hence **(a)** (woollen) cloth **(b)** to pad a garment **(c)** an army's materials, stores, or supplies (–15c); provisions (15c, now only Scots); (household) goods, (raw) materials; miscellaneous things; your belongings; rubbish, nonsense **2** to place knights in tight formation; to cram people together or into a confined space; to pack a receptacle tightly (15c) **3 (a)** to gorge yourself with food (15c) **(b)** to fill with forcemeat etc. (15c, hence **stuffing**, 16c); to fill a dead animal's skin to make it look lifelike (16c) **(c)** to clog or choke (15c); to block an opening (16c); to push something into a cavity **(d)** *stuffy* badly ventilated, full of stale air (19c), hence conventional, formal, pompous.

Probably related to **stifle** [Old French *estoufer* 'to smother', of Germanic origin], and perhaps to **stop** [Old English *(for)stoppian* 'to block an opening', ultimately from late Latin *stuppare* 'to stuff'].

stultify [17c. Late Latin *stultificare*, from Latin *stultus* 'foolish'] In law: to allege, prove, or claim to be, insane; to make someone/something seem foolish or ridiculous (19c), hence to make useless or ineffective; to make someone bored and enervated.

sturdy [ME. Old French *estourdi* 'dazed, reckless', from *etourdir* 'to stun', ultimately from Latin *turdus* 'thrush' (from the behaviour of a thrush 'drunk' on rotting fruit)] Brave, foolhardy, violent, ferocious, cruel (all –17c); rebellious, intractable, obstinate (–18c), hence tough, strong, robust, well built.

style [ME. French, from Latin *stilus*: the spelling influenced by Greek *stulos* 'column'] An ancient writing implement (replaced by **stylus**, a misspelling of Latin *stilus*, 19c), hence **1** a literary work (–16c); a way of writing, later of producing other works of art, and of living and behaving, hence **(a)** elegance and refinement in doing so (16c); **stylish** elegant, fashionable (18c); *style* fashionable status (*out of style*, 19c) **(b)** a distinctive type or fashion (*the Egyptian style*, 18c) **(c)** to design or arrange in a (fashionable) style (1920s) **2** a correct or official title; to give someone a name or title (16c); to describe as being (*self-styled genius*) **3** something shaped like a stylus: a pointer or probe (16c); a stalk-like extension of a flower's ovary (17c); a small slender pointed part of an animal, insect, etc. (19c). Cf. *stylet* below.

Stylus came to mean a machine's tracing pen and a record-player's needle. Latin *stilus* produced Italian **stiletto**, whence French **stylet**, adopted for a probe or an animal's style. Probably related to Latin **stimulus**, literally 'a goad'.

suave [ME. (French, from) Latin *suavis* 'pleasant, sweet'] Pleasing, agreeable; (superficially) polite and charming (19c); sophisticated; of wine: smooth, bland.

Latin *suavis* produced **assuage** [via Old French *assuagier*, literally 'to sweeten'].

subject [ME. Via French from Latin *subjicere* 'to put or throw under', from *jacere* 'to throw' (ancestor of JET*)] **1** ruled, controlled, or protected by a person or government; someone who is (*British subject*); to make someone so. Hence **(a)** bound by a rule or law; conditional (*subject to status*, 19c) **(b)** liable, vulnerable, or susceptible to; to expose or make liable to (16c) **2** [via Latin *subjectum*, literally 'that which underlies', a translation of Greek *to hupokeimon* as used by Aristotle (see ARTERY)] what something is made of (–18c), hence **(a)** what a book etc. is about or what a picture etc. represents (15c) **(b)** what is being studied, discussed, treated, or judged (16c) **(c)** **(thinking) subject** the conscious mind (17c), hence **subjective** to do with this (18c); originating in the mind; coming from or expressing someone's thoughts or feelings (cf. *objective* at OBJECT) **(d)** in grammar: the performer of a verb's action (17c, cf. *object*).

sublime [16c. Latin *sublimis* 'high, elevated' (the underlying meaning is perhaps 'up to the lintel'), from *sub* 'under, up to' + a second element probably related to *limen*: see THRESHOLD*] Dignified, aloof, proud; of language or style: elevated, grand, hence exalted, outstandingly beautiful, awe-inspiring (17c).

Latin *sublimis* produced *sublimare* 'to elevate', whence **sublime** to change a solid to a gas without an intermediate liquid phase; to extract something by doing so, hence to purify (now especially morally or spiritually); to transform to something purer or more elevated. **Sublimate** [from *sublimare*] shared these meanings: it now usually means to divert a (sexual) instinct into a creative or more socially acceptable activity. *Sub* was added to many Latin words (sometimes as **sup-** or **sus-**); **sub-** is also used in English (*submarine*, *substandard*).

subordinate [15c. Medieval Latin *subordinare* 'to place below', from Latin *ordinare* 'to put in order': see ORDAIN*] Lower in rank, hence **1** dependent or subservient; to make so (16c); such a person (17c) **2** (to make something) secondary or minor (17c). Hence **subordination 1** arrangement by rank or degree (15–19c) **2** subservience, submission, deference to authority (16c), hence **insubordination** (18c), whence **insubordinate** disobedient, rebellious (19c).

subscribe [ME. Latin *subscribere* 'to write underneath', from *scribere* 'to write'] Write on or sign a document, especially at the bottom, hence **1** to do so to show support for its contents, hence **subscribe to** to agree with, to have a certain opinion (16c) **2** to put your name on a list of contributors to a charity etc. (17c); to (promise to) contribute, later to buy goods or services, regularly, hence **subscriber** someone who does so (17c); **subscription** a regular contribution or payment; **subscription price** a reduced price for subscribers or advance payment **3** to promise to pay for an issue of shares (17c), hence **scrip** a receipt for shares (18c, short for *subscription receipt*); a provisional certificate entitling the holder to dividends; these certificates collectively; **scrip issue** an issue of extra shares to existing shareholders (1950s).

Latin *subscribere* produced **subscript** something written at the bottom of a document, later (a number or symbol) written below the line (the opposite of **superscript**). Latin *scribere* is the ancestor of SCRIPT*.

subsidy [ME. Via Anglo-Norman French from Latin *subsidium* 'reserve troops', ultimately from *sedere* 'to sit'] Help, assistance, hence a (government) grant (15c), now one to a business, charity, etc. (19c). Hence **subsidize** to give a grant, originally to pay for mercenary or foreign troops (18c).

Latin *subsidium* produced **subsidiary** auxiliary, supplementary, secondary, hence **1** such a person or thing; (describing) a company owned by another **2 subsidiarity** the theory that an authority should have a less important role, most tasks and power being devolved. Latin *sedere* is the ancestor of SESSION*.

substance [ME. French, from Latin *substantia*, from *substare* 'to stand under, to underlie', from *stare* 'to stand' (ancestor of STATION*)] An essential part, the essential nature; what something is made of, hence **1** a thing or being; something tangible and real (16c); reality, truth, hence **substantial** real (16c), (mostly) true (18c), **substantiate** to prove or support with evidence (19c) **2** a particular kind of material or matter; a chemical compound, hence **substance abuse** misuse of drugs, alcohol, etc. (1970s) **3** possessions, wealth (*a man of substance*) **4** the subject of an artistic work; the meaning or gist of something (15c) **5** solidity, seriousness, hence *substantial* stout, solid, fairly large; weighty, important, worthwhile (15c).

suffrage [ME. (French, from) Latin *suffragium* 'support, (right to) vote', from *suffragari* 'to express support, to vote for', from *fragor* 'din, shouts (of approval)'] **1** prayers on someone else's behalf; intercessory prayers or petitions **2** (someone who gives) assistance (–17c) **3** a vote in favour (16c), hence **(a)** the collective vote of a body of people (16c); a consensus **(b)** the casting of a vote or votes (17c); the right to do so (18c, US).

Suffrage produced **suffragist** someone who advocated widening the franchise, specifically to women, and **suffragette** a female suffragist, especially one taking part in militant protests. Latin *suffragium* produced **suffragan** an assistant bishop. Related to FRACTION*.

sugar [ME. Old French *suk(e)re*, via Italian from Latin *succarum*, *saccarum*, from Arabic *sukkar*, ultimately via Persian and Prakrit from Sanskrit *śarkarā*] A sweet substance obtained from plants, hence **1** to 'sweeten', to make less unpleasant **2** to coat or sprinkle with sugar (16c) **3** applied to similar inorganic substances (17c), or to simple, usually sweet-tasting, carbohydrates, e.g. glucose, fructose.

Descendants of Latin *saccarum* include **saccharin** an intensely sweet substance used instead of sugar, and **saccharine** to do with or like sugar; sickeningly sweet. See also CANDY.

suit [ME. Old French *si(e)ute*, ultimately from Latin *sequi* 'to follow'] **1** attendance at your lord's court as a feudal obligation, later attendance at a sheriff's court etc.; a process or an action in a law court; a petition or entreaty, especially to someone in authority (15c), hence a man's attempts to persuade a woman to marry him (16c) **2** a group of witnesses, or of followers or attendants, hence a uniform; a set of outer clothes (15c); a set of clothes for a particular occasion or activity (*swimsuit*): **(a) birthday suit** worn on the monarch's birthday (18c), now your bare skin, worn at birth (19c) **(b)** a matching jacket and trousers or skirt for office or formal use (early 20c), hence **the (men in) suits** bosses, faceless bureaucrats (1980s) **3** a set of things (15c), largely replaced by *suite* below, except in **(a)** one of the four sets of cards in a pack (16c) **(b)** a set of sails for a boat (17c) **(c)** a complete set of armour (19c). Hence **suitable** matching, corresponding (16–18c); fitting, appropriate (17c).

Old French *si(e)ute* evolved into modern **suite** a retinue; a set of things belonging together (*hotel/three-piece suite*), also in **en suite 1** in harmony (18–19c) **2** as
part of a set of rooms. Latin *sequi* is the ancestor of SEQUEL*.

sullen   [ME. Anglo-Norman French *solain, sulein*, from Old French *sol* 'alone',
from Latin *solus*] Single, sole, solitary (–16c), hence unsociable, bad-tempered
and sulky; gloomy, dismal (16c); of water: flowing sluggishly (17c).

French *sol* produced **sole** single, alone. Latin *solus* is the ancestor of **desolate**
[Latin *desolare* 'to leave alone, to abandon'], **soliloquy** [with Latin *loqui* 'to speak',
whence ELOCUTION*], French *solitaire* a recluse, (a ring set with) a single stone, a
game for one person, **solitary**, **solitude**, and Italian *solo*.

sum   [ME. Via Old French from Latin *summa* 'highest or most important thing',
feminine of *summus* 'highest'] A quantity of goods; a stated amount of money;
(to find) a total, hence **1** to gather everything into a small space (17c); **sum up** to
summarize; to form a quick opinion of (19c) **2** a series of numbers to be added up
(16c); a numerical calculation (19c); **sums** simple arithmetic.

Latin *summus* is the ancestor of **consummate**, **summary**, and **summit**. Related
to Latin *super* 'above' (see SUPERANNUATED*).

sump   [ME. Early Dutch and Low German] A marsh or swamp (surviving in dialect); a dirty puddle, hence a pit at the bottom of a mine shaft to collect water
(17c); any pit or hollow where liquid collects, hence the bottom of an engine's
crankcase which acts as a reservoir for lubricating oil (*c.*1900).

Probably related to **swamp** a piece of waterlogged land, hence to submerge or
inundate, to overwhelm.

sumptuous   [ME. Via French from Latin *sumptuosus*, from *sumptus* 'cost', from
sumere 'to take up'] Costly (–17c); lavish, extravagant (15c); splendid, magnificent (16c).

Scrumptious (shortened to **scrummy**) may be an alteration. Latin *sumptus* produced **sumptuary** to do with expenditure; *sumere* is the ancestor of ASSUME*, **consume** [Latin *consumere*, literally 'to take up completely'], and RESUME.

sunder   [Old English *sundor*] Separate, apart, private (–15c). Hence **1 (a)** to separate or part, later to become separated or estranged **(b)** to break in pieces (ME)
2 asunder in or to a separate place (–16c); apart or separate (ME); in two, into
pieces (15c).

Sunder appears in **Sunderland**, meaning either 'detached land' or 'private land'.
Related to **sundry** separate, distinct (surviving in dialect); miscellaneous; **sundries**
miscellaneous articles.

superannuated   [17c. Medieval Latin *superannuatus*, from Latin *super* 'above' +
annus 'year'] Antiquated, obsolete; worn out; old and infirm, hence **superannuate** to discard or dismiss because of age; to pension off, whence **superannuation**
a pension (18c); *superannuate* to make a post pensionable (19c); to reach retirement age.

Latin *super* produced **insuperable** [via *superare* 'to overcome'], Italian *soprano*,
French *soubrette* [from Provençal *soubret* 'conceited, coy'], **sovereign**, **superb**,
superior, **superlative** [with Latin *ferre, lat-* 'to bear': see CONFER*], **superscript** (at
SUBSCRIBE), **supreme**, and **suzerain**. *Super* was added to many Latin words, and is

also used in English (e.g. *supermarket* (at MARKET), **superfine**, shortened to **super** 'excellent'): its French descendant, **sur-**, appears in words borrowed from French (*surrealism*, *surtax*). Related to SUM*. Descendants of Latin *annus* include **annals**, *anniversary* (at VERSE), *anno Domini* (at DOMINATE), **annual, annuity, biennial, millennium**, and **perennial**.

superintendent [16c. Ecclesiastical Latin *superintendere* 'to oversee, to **superintend**' (used to translate Greek *episkopein* below), from *intendere* 'to turn your mind to': see INTEND*] **1** a bishop; a presiding minister of a non-episcopal church **2** an overseer: **(a)** the director of a business or institution; the governor of a district (18c) **(b)** a police officer next above an inspector (19c); the head of a police department (US).

Greek *episkopein* is from *episkopos* 'overseer' [from *skopos* 'watcher, thing watched': see SCOPE*], whence, ultimately, **bishop** [Old English *bisceop*] and **episcopal** (ME).

supplant [ME. (Via French from) Latin *supplantare*, from *sub* '(from) underneath' + *planta* 'sole of the foot' (ancestor of PLANT*)] To trip up (–17c); to overthrow (–18c), hence to replace one person or thing with another, especially by underhand means.

supply [ME. Via Old French from Latin *supplere*, literally 'to fill up', from *plere* 'to fill': see COMPLY*] To help, support, or maintain, specifically to provide with troops or reinforcements (–19c); to compensate for a loss or satisfy a need (15c); something that does so (16–18c, outlived by *supplement* below), hence **1** to fill a vacancy (15c); (describing) the person who does (*supply teacher*) **2** to provide something needed (15c), hence **(a)** to do so regularly or commercially (16c) **(b)** a stock or store of goods (to be) provided (16c); the amount of goods or services available (*supply and demand*, 18c), hence **supply-side economics** favouring the producers of goods and services (1970s, *US*) **(c) supplies** provisions and equipment (17c).

Latin *supplere* produced **supplement** something added, especially to remedy a deficiency; to provide or add a supplement.

suppose [ME. French *supposer*, based on Latin *subponere*, literally 'to place under', from *ponere* 'to place': see POSE*. Influenced by Greek *hupothesis* (see *supposition* below)] **1** to assume for the sake of argument or as a precondition, hence to infer (16c); to think something is probably true **2** to expect, hence **(a) be supposed to** to be expected or obliged to **(b) I suppose (so)** expressing hesitant or reluctant agreement.

French *supposer* produced **presuppose**; Latin *subponere* produced **supposition** [translating Greek *hupothesis* 'foundation, basis', whence **hypothesis**, from *hupo* 'under' + *thesis* 'placing' (see THESIS*)], and **suppository** [medieval Latin *suppositorium* 'something placed underneath'].

sure [ME. Via Old French from Latin *securus* 'untroubled', from *cura* 'care'] **1** safe, protected or giving protection from danger (–18c), largely replaced by *secure* below **2** trustworthy, steadfast, dependable **3** certain: **(a)** in your mind **(b)** to be, have, happen, etc., or to be true.

Latin *securus* produced ENSURE*, **secure**, which shared sense 3 of *sure* (–18c) and produced the verb meaning 'to ensure', specifically that a sum of money will be paid, and **security** safety [via Latin *securitas*], later property pledged, or someone who promises, to guarantee payment of a debt: a sense shared by **surety** [also from *securitas*].

surf [17c. Apparently from *suff* (16–17c), of unknown origin] The swell of the sea that breaks on the shore, hence **1** the line of foam formed (18c) **2** to lie or stand on a board and ride a wave into shore (*c.*1915), hence **(a)** to ride on the outside of a moving train for kicks (1980s, a practice originating in Rio de Janeiro which spread to the US and later to the UK) **(b)** to keep changing television channels (1990s, hopping from one to another as if from wave to wave), hence to browse the internet, also in various phrases meaning to move or change continually.

surge [15c. French *sourdre*, *sourge-* 'to rise', and Old French *sorgir* 'to anchor', both ultimately from Latin *surgere* 'to rise', from *regere* 'to rule'] **1** a fountain or spring, the place where a stream rises (–16c, outlived by *source* below); of a stream etc.: to rise from its source (16–17c) **2** to anchor (16c); to ride at anchor; to rise and fall on the waves. Hence **3** to rise and fall in great waves (16c), hence **(a)** a sudden rush, onset, or rapid (often temporary) increase or upward movement **(b)** to increase suddenly and rapidly (19c); to move suddenly, forcefully, or in great numbers.

French *sourdre* produced **source** the fountainhead of a stream, hence the place, person, or thing from which something comes or can be obtained. Latin *surgere* produced *insurgere* 'to rise up', whence **insurgent** and **insurrection**, and *resurgere*, whence RESOURCE*. Latin *regere* is the ancestor of REGIMENT*.

surgery [ME. Old French *surgerie*, *cirurgerie*, via Latin *chirurgia* from Greek *kheirourgia*, from *kheirourgos* 'working by hand', from *kheir* 'hand' + *ergon* 'work'. The spelling *chirurgery*, adopted during the Renaissance, survived into the 20c] **1** medical treatment involving cutting into, or manipulation of, the body **2** the place where, or the regular time when, a medical practitioner sees and treats patients (19c), hence the time when a Member of Parliament, councillor, etc. may be consulted by members of the public (1950s).

Greek *kheir* appears in CHIROPODIST and *chiropractic* (at PRACTISE); *ergon* is the ancestor of **argon** an inert gas [Greek *argos* 'idle', from *a* 'without' + *ergon*], **energy**, **erg** the SI unit of energy, **ergonomics**, **georgic** a literary work dealing with rural life [Greek *georgos* 'farmer', literally 'earth-worker', with *ge-* 'earth' (whence geo- in *geography* etc.)], **liturgy** [Greek *leitourgia* 'public service', from *lēos*, *leit-* 'people'], **metallurgy**, and **synergy**.

surmise [15c. Anglo-Norman French and Old French *surmis*, from *surmettre*, from late Latin *supermittere*, literally 'to put on or over', from *mittere* 'to send' (ancestor of MISSION*)] To lay a charge on someone, (to make) an accusation; (to form) a conjecture or suspicion (16c); an unfounded or unproven one.

suspect [ME. Latin *suspicere*, *suspect-*, literally 'to look up at', later 'to look at secretly', from *specere* 'to look' (ancestor of SPICE*)] **1** regarded with or deserving suspicion or distrust (–18c); someone who is (16–18c): both revived in the 19c after French *suspect* was used for someone believed not to support the Revolution **2** to imagine something bad about someone without proof (15c, earlier in

suspicion and **suspicious**); to think that something (especially bad) may exist or happen (16c). Both *suspect* and *suspicion* were shortened to **suss** in slang (1930s), hence **suss (out)** to find or to work out the truth (1960s), **sussed** aware, in the know (1980s).

suture [ME. (French, from) Latin *sutura*, from *suere* 'to sew'] **1** the closing of a wound or incision by stitching; the material used; a single stitch made with it; to stitch (18c) **2** a groove, ridge, or seam in an organ or tissue (–18c); an immovable joint between two bones, especially those in the skull (16c); the (visible line of) a junction between parts of an organism (17c) or between tectonic plates (1970s).

Latin *suere* is the ancestor of French **couture** literally 'sewing' [Old French *cousture*, from Latin *consuere* 'to sew together'], adopted meaning the design and making of fashionable clothes, whence **couturier** fashion designer, *haute couture* high fashion.

swag [ME. Probably of Scandinavian origin: possibly more than one word] **1** a bulging bag (ME only), perhaps surviving unrecorded and producing **(a)** a large, blustering man (16–18c) **(b)** a bundle of personal belongings (18c, now Australia and New Zealand); to carry your belongings in one (19c) **(c)** stolen goods, illicit gains; to pilfer **2** to sway, lurch, or stagger (16c, cf. *swagger* below); (to cause) such a movement (now Scots and dialect) **3** to hang down loosely (17c); (a carving of) a festoon of flowers supported at both ends and hanging down in the middle (18c); a curtain etc. that hangs in this way.

Probably the source of **swagger** to sway or stagger; to bluster; to brag; to behave or walk arrogantly; such a manner or walk.

swain [OE. Old Norse *sveinn* 'lad'] **1** a (young) male servant or attendant, originally to a knight (–17c), hence **(a)** boatswain, often pronounced and written as **bosun** (19c) an officer responsible for a ship's rigging and sails **(b)** coxswain (ME, usually pronounced *coksun*), shortened to **cox** (19c) a helmsman, originally of a **cock(boat)** a ship's small rowing boat used as a tender [via Old French *coque* and Old Italian *cocca* from medieval Latin *caudica*, from Latin *codex* 'lump of wood' (whence CODE*)] **2** a lad (ME–17c); a country lad (16c), hence a girl's sweetheart **3** appearing in names as **Swan-**.

swan [Old English] A large graceful waterbird, hence **1** an excellent or faultless person or thing (ME), from the swan's grace and pure white plumage: often contrasted with *goose*: also as a surname **2** a singer or poet (17c, because the swan was sacred to Apollo, the Greek god of, among other things, music and poetry), hence **swansong** your last work, performance, or action (19c: the mute swan was believed to sing only when dying) **3** to swim like a swan (19c); to move about freely (World War II, originally of armoured cars reconnoitring); to wander about in a relaxed or ostentatious way.

swear [Old English *swerian*] To appeal to, or invoke the name of, someone/something sacred to confirm the truth of a statement, hence **1** to make a solemn statement or promise with or without such an invocation; to make someone else do so (*swore him to silence*) **2** to take an oath; **swear (in)** to make someone do so before performing a duty (*the jury/witness was sworn in*) **3** (because the names of sacred beings or objects were often invoked in anger) to use bad language (ME):

oath [Old English *āth*] originally (the words of) a solemn declaration or vow, usually invoking the name of a sacred person, developed the sense 'swear word' at about the same time. Hence of an animal: to make angry sounds (17c); of a colour: to clash (18c).

Related to **answer** [Old English *andswaru*, literally 'a swearing against', with the underlying sense 'to respond, or a response, to an accusation'].

sweat [Old English *swāt* (noun), *swaetan* (verb)] (To exude) perspiration, hence **1** to exude moisture like sweat; this moisture; to make something do so (*sweat the onions*, 17c) **2** to work hard; hard work, hence (a) to work someone (too) hard (*sweated labour*, *sweat shop*, 19c) (b) as the variant **swot**: to study hard (19c); someone who does so **3** a fit of sweating (ME); to cause one (16c), hence **sweater** a woollen vest or jersey worn during exercise to induce sweating and cause weight loss (19c); one worn for warmth after exercise, later any jersey; **sweatshirt** a thick cotton jersey worn after exercise or as leisure wear (1920s).

sweep [Old English *swāpan*: related to German *schweifen* 'to move in an arc', probably the underlying meaning] **1** to clean with a broom; to remove or collect up dirt etc. with one (ME); this action (16c, now only in *clean sweep* below); someone who does (*chimney sweep*, 18c) **2** to take or cut off with a swinging stroke (ME), hence (a) to remove or abolish swiftly and decisively (16c) (b) (to make) such a stroke (17c) **3** to move or be moved swiftly, confidently, or forcibly (*Labour swept to power/were swept out of office*, 15c); to move swiftly or extend over an area (16c), hence (a) to move over and search an area; such a survey (18c) (b) to affect widely and radically (*sweeping changes*, 18c) (c) a wide (curving) stretch of land etc. (18c) **4 sweepstake** someone who wins all the stakes in a game (15–17c), hence a race where the prize is the total entrance fees (18c, cf. STAKE; **sweep(stake)** in which the winner wins all the participants' stakes. Hence *sweep* to clear or gather everything in one action; **sweep the board** to win all the cards or prizes on the table (17c); **make a clean sweep** to win every game or place in a contest (19c, N American).

Old English *swāpan* probably produced **swipe** and **swoop**. Related to **swift** and **swivel**.

sweet [Old English *swēte*] Smelling, sounding, looking or tasting pleasant; to make sweet; replaced by **sweeten** (15c). Hence **1** having the taste of sugar, honey, or ripe fruit, hence (a) **sweetmeat** (a small piece of) sweet food (b) **sweetie** a piece of confectionery (17c, Scots), in England shortened to *sweet* (19c) (c) a dessert (19c) **2** of food or water: fresh and wholesome **3** affectionate, amiable, kind **4** beloved, precious, hence **sweetheart** a lovable or beloved person (ME) **5** pretty, charming, attractive (18c), now often bordering on **twee** [*c*.1900, from a childish pronunciation of *sweet*] **6** the surnames **Sweatman**, **Sweet(ing)**, **Swett**, a pleasant or popular person.

Sweetheart is probably the source of **tart** (a term of endearment for) a girl or woman [probably influenced by **tart** a (usually sweet) open pie (Old French *tarte*, of uncertain origin)], later a bawdy woman or a prostitute, hence **tart up** to titivate, especially in a cheap and showy way.

swell [Old English *swellan*] To expand or be distended; to rise or raise above the surrounding level, hence **1** to 'puff up' with pride or vanity (ME); to behave proudly or arrogantly, hence, perhaps, someone with wealth or high social status (18c); a dandy; fashionable, stylish (19c); fine, excellent **2** of the sea: to rise and fall in long waves (ME); this motion (16c), hence **groundswell** deep waves caused by an earthquake or distant storm (19c); a strong growth of feeling or opinion **3** to increase (15c); to cause to do so (17c); a gradual increase (18c).

swelter   [From **swelt** to die (Old English *sweltan*); to faint (ME), specifically from heat, which survives in dialect] To be uncomfortably hot (15c); to cause to be so (16c), hence **sweltering** uncomfortably or oppressively hot (16c).
   Possibly related to **sultry** hot and humid, later sensual, lascivious.

switch   [16c. Probably from Low German or Dutch] **1** a thin riding whip; to strike, beat, or drive with one (17c); a blow with one (19c) **2** a thin flexible twig (17c), hence a movable rail or pair of rails that makes a train branch off onto another line (18c), hence **(a)** to divert a train with one (19c); to change a course or position (hence such a change, 1920s); to change one thing for another, especially to deceive; such an exchange (1930s) **(b)** a device for making and breaking an electrical circuit (19c); to turn an electrical device on or off **(c)** in computing: a program instruction that selects one of a number of possible paths (1950s); an electronic connection that transfers funds from the purchaser's bank account to the retailer's, using a debit or Switch card (1980s) **3** a long tress of (false) hair (19c).

sycophant   [16c. Via French or Latin from Greek *sukophantēs*, from *sukon* 'fig' + *phanein* 'to show' (ancestor of PHANTOM*)] An informer or slanderer in ancient Greece (once said to be one who informed against illegal exporters of figs, but more likely because *sukon* was also a slang term for the vulva, as though the tell-tale was making an obscene gesture to the victim); an obsequious flatterer (probably ingratiating himself by maligning others).

symbol   [15c. Via Latin from Greek *sumbolon* 'outward sign, distinguishing mark', from *sumballein* 'to compare', literally 'to throw together', from *ballein* 'to throw' (ancestor of BALLISTIC*). Cf. PARABLE] **1** a formal statement of Christian doctrine, specifically the Apostle's Creed (regarded as the distinguishing mark of a Christian) **2** something that stands for or represents something else (16c); a written mark that does so (17c).

symmetry   [16c. Via French or Latin from Greek *summetria*, literally 'similar measure', from *metron* 'measure' (see METRE*)] Proportion, the relative measurement of parts, hence **1** (beauty or harmony resulting from) correct or pleasing proportions **2** exact correspondence in size, shape, or position of parts relative to a central point or line.

symphony   [ME. Via Old French and Latin from Greek *sumphōnia*, literally 'sounding together', from *phonē* 'sound'] (Musical) harmony, hence **1** agreement, accord (16c); a harmonious combination of sounds or colours **2** (a performance of) music for an ensemble of instruments and/or voices (16c); a large-scale composition for full orchestra (18c).
   Greek *sumphōnia* produced Italian *sinfonia* and *sinfonietta*.

symposium   [16c. Latin, from Greek *sumposion*, from *sumpotēs* 'fellow drinker', from *potēs* 'drinker'] A drinking party, especially one held in ancient Greece for drinking, music, and philosophical discussions, hence a meeting for the discussion of a particular subject (18c); a series of papers delivered at one; a collection of essays by a number of authors (19c).

synthesis [Latin from Greek, from *suntithenai*, from *sun* 'together' + *tithenai* 'to put'] **1 (a)** the process of reasoning from first principles to a conclusion (17c) **(b)** see THESIS **2** the forming of a compound, specifically the artificial production of an organic compound (18c), hence **synthesize** to do so (19c), **synthetic** man-made (19c); artificial, imitation, phoney (1930s) **3** the action of putting elements together to produce something complex (19c); the result of this, hence **(a)** the production of white light by combining its constituent colours **(b)** the production of complex musical sounds by combining simple elements; **synthesizer** an instrument for producing and combining signals of different frequencies (*c*.1900), especially a computerized (keyboard) instrument that creates a variety of musical sounds electronically (1950s) **(c)** the combining of information from different senses into an intelligible whole.

Greek *sun* was added to many Greek verbs, appearing in English as **syn-**, **syl-**, and **sym-**; *tithenai* is the ancestor of THESIS*.

syrinx [17c. Latin, from Greek *surigx* 'pipe, channel'] **1** a set of pan pipes **2** a narrow gallery or corridor in an ancient Egyptian tomb (17c) **3** a bird's vocal organ (19c).

Latin *syrinx* produced **syringe**; Greek *surigx* produced **syringa** a shrub formerly used to make pipe stems.

T

tabby [16c. French *tabis*, from Arabic *al-ʿAttābiyya*, the quarter of Baghdad where tabby was manufactured] A kind of silk taffeta, originally striped, later with a watered finish, hence (describing) a brown or grey cat with darker stripes (17c); any (female) domestic cat; a derogatory term for an old maid or a spiteful gossip.

Tabby produced **tabaret** a striped fabric, and **tabinet** one of watered silk and wool. **Tibby** [a pet form of Isabel(la)], is said to have become a popular name for a (tabby) cat after a besieged Queen Isabella (possibly of Castile) vowed not to change her underwear until the siege was lifted, by which time it might well have been tabby-coloured: this may also account for the greyish-yellow colour known as **Isabella**.

tabernacle [ME. (French, from)] Latin *tabernaculum* 'tent, booth, small hut', from *taberna* 'hut', whence also **tavern**] A structure used as a portable sanctuary for the Ark of the Covenant while the Israelites were in exile (see the Bible, Exodus 25–26), hence **1** an ornate canopied structure (–15c); a canopied recess for an image; an ornate receptacle for consecrated bread and wine for the Eucharist **2 Feast of Tabernacles** a Jewish festival commemorating their exile, when the people lived in tents; now called **succoth** [19c, plural of **succah**, one of the booths used in the festival, from Hebrew *sukkāh* 'hut'] **3** a (temporary) dwelling place, e.g. the body as the soul's dwelling on earth; a socket for a mast which can be lowered or removed (19c) **4** a place of worship: **(a)** the Jewish temple in Jerusalem, where the Ark was eventually housed **(b)** a temporary one used after the Great Fire of London in 1666 **(c)** a Nonconformist one (18c).

table [Old English (later also French), from Latin *tabula* 'plant, tablet, list'] A flat slab, hence **1** one bearing or intended for an inscription (replaced by *plaque* at PLACARD, or TABLET); a board on which a picture is painted, or the picture (ME–18c, cf. *tableau*) **2 table(s)** the old name of backgammon, from the hinged board on which it is played (ME); (a section of) a backgammon board (15c); a board for chess or similar games, hence **turn the tables** to reverse the contestants' positions (17c) **3** a raised board on which things can be placed or work done (*billiard/dining/operating table*, ME), hence a systematic display of numbers, words, etc. (as though laid out on a table), usually in columns and lines; the information contained (*multiplication/league/time table*): see also *tab* (at TAG sense 5) **4** a high plateau (16c); a horizontal structure or surface (17c).

French *table* appears in **table d'hôte** [literally 'host's table'] where all the guests ate together, hence a set meal at a fixed price, and produced **tableau** originally a picture. Latin *tabula* appears in **tabula rasa** [literally 'scraped tablet'] a blank slate, a mind with no innate ideas. Descendants of *tabula* include **entablature** the upper part of a classical building, supported on columns [Italian *intavolatura*, from *tavola* 'table'], TABLET, TABULATE, and **taffrail** the rail round a ship's stern [alteration of **tafferel** a (carved) panel, later the flat part of a ship's stern above the transom, from Dutch *taffereel* 'panel', from *tafel* 'table'].

tablet [ME. Old French *tablete*, literally 'small table', ultimately from Latin *tabula* TABLE*] **1** a small slab or flat surface with, or intended for, an inscription; a thin sheet of wood, ivory, etc. on which to write; a writing pad, a notebook (19c, *N American*: see also *tab* at TAG sense 5) **2** a small flat piece or cake of something (*a tablet of soap*), specifically a dose of a drug, a pill (16c). Hence **1 tabloid**, originally the proprietary name of a medicine sold in tablets (19c), hence any small medicinal tablet; something in a compressed or concentrated form, hence a popular newspaper, originally one with pages half the size of a broadsheet (early 20c) **2 tab** a pill, especially of an illegal drug (1960s).

taboo [18c. Tongan *tabu*: introduced into English by Captain Cook] Consecrated, sacred, hence forbidden to all or some sections of society; (the imposing of) such a prohibition. Hence (something) socially unacceptable (*taboo words*, 19c); to prohibit or discourage certain language, subjects, etc.

tabulate [16c. Latin *tabulare*, from *tabula* TABLE*] **1** broad and flat like a table; to give something a flat top (17c) **2** to enter on a roll (17–18c, Scots); arrange or show figures etc. in a table (18c), hence the **tab(ulator) key** on a typewriter or computer keyboard (19c).

tacit [17c. Latin *tacitus*, from *tacere* 'to be silent'] Wordless, noiseless, silent, hence implied but not stated.

Latin *tacitus* produced **taciturn**; *tacere* is the ancestor of **reticence** [via Latin *reticere* 'to keep silent'].

tack [ME. Probably related to Old French *tache* 'fibula, clasp, large nail', and possibly to STAKE*] (To fasten or attach with) a clasp, buckle, etc.; to attach temporarily, hence **1 (a)** a small broad-headed nail or pin (15c) **(b)** a rope, wire, etc. for securing a sail (15c), hence to alter course (using the tacks to move the sail) to make the most of the wind (16c); to zigzag by doing so repeatedly (17c); one leg of the zigzag, hence **(change) tack** (to make) a change in a policy or course of action **(c)** a strip or band used for fastening (16c) **(d)** (to sew with) a long temporary stitch (18c) **2** the ability to hold or hold on (15c, now Scots and dialect), hence **tacky** slightly sticky (18c) **3** to bring or fasten disparate elements together (17c); (to add on as) an appendix or supplement.

tackle [ME. Probably from Low German *takel*, from *taken* 'to take hold of'] **1** apparatus, equipment, later specifically a horse's harness (now as **tack**); to equip with this (15c) **2** to grasp, take hold of, or grapple with (19c), hence to take on a task or difficulty; to approach someone with a question or problem; in sport: to intercept another player to get the ball; the interception.

tacky [19c. Origin unknown] A worthless horse (US), later a poor White in some southern states, hence cheap, shabby, trashy, in bad taste, whence **1 ticky-tacky** (made of) cheap and inferior (building) material (1960s) **2 tack** trashy stuff, tat, kitsch (1980s).

tact [17c. (French, from) Latin *tactus* 'touch', from *tangere, tact-* 'to touch'] **1** a principal accent or rhythmic unit in music (replaced by *tactus*, 18c) **2** (the sense of) touch, hence an ability to make fine distinctions, likened to the sense of touch (18c); sensitivity and discretion in dealing with people or situations (19c).

Latin *tangere* is the ancestor of **contact**, **contagious**, **contaminate**, CONTINGENT*, ENTIRE*, **tactile**, **tangent** (a line) touching, but not intersecting, another line or a surface, **tangible**, perhaps of TASTE* and TAX*, and is one parent of TAINT*.

tag [ME. Origin unknown: probably related to **dag** 'ornamental point' below, and **tab** a small flap, loop, etc. attached to an object, which share some senses] **1** an ornamental hanging point on a garment, formerly also *dag* (ME–17), cf. also JAG, TATTER, later any ragged or torn piece (see also *tagrag* etc. at RAG), or a hanging bit of cloth, ribbon, etc., hence any small hanging piece: **(a)** a matted lock of hair or of sheep's wool (17c, also *dag*) **(b)** something added to a text or speech, especially a stock phrase (18c); the refrain of a song **2** a metal or plastic end on a shoelace etc. (16c): earlier as *dag* (ME–17c) and as *tab* in dialect **3** to add or provide with a tag (17c) **4** to trail behind, to follow closely (*tag along*, 17c); to follow and spy on (19c); someone who does so (1960s); **(electronic) tag** an electronic device attached to a person, animal, or thing for monitoring purposes (1970s) **5** a label, badge, etc. specifying ownership or giving other information (19c, *US*, less commonly as *tab*), hence **(a) price tag** a price label (19c), the price itself (1940s); *tag* an account or bill: more commonly as *tab* (perhaps in this sense from TABLE or from TABLET meaning 'notebook'), hence **keep tabs on** to keep a check on; *tab* to watch (1920s) **(b)** in computing: a set of characters added to a piece of data to identify it (1960s) **(c)** an epithet (1960s): cf. *tab* to name or dub (1940s) **(d)** a graffiti artist's signature design (1980s).

Dag came to mean 'to clog with or trail in dirt', and then produced **daggle** and **draggle** (whence **bedraggled**): the sense 'matted lock of wool' survives in Australia and has influenced **dag** and **daggy** (someone who is) scruffy or unfashionably dressed, which stem from **dag** a (likeable) eccentric [origin unknown].

tail [ME. Old French *taillier* 'to cut (off)', ultimately from Latin *talea* 'twig, cutting'] To cut up, trim, or cut to shape (–16c), hence to decide in a particular way, specifically to limit the inheritance of property to a designated heir or heirs (see also *fee tail* at FEE), hence **entail** to settle, or the settlement of, inheritance inalienably to designated heirs (ME); to attach something inseparably (16–18c); to necessitate, lead to, or involve (19c).

Old French *taillier* produced DETAIL, **retail** [Old French *retaille* 'piece cut off'], **tailor** [literally 'a cutter'], whence the surname **Taylor**, the surnames **Tallis** someone who lived in a clearing, and **Telfer**, **Telford** [with *fer* 'iron'] a strong man or ferocious warrior (the Shropshire town of *Telford* was named after the engineer Thomas Telford, b.1757). Latin *talea* produced Italian *intaglio* [via *intagliare* 'to engrave'] and *tagliatelle* [from *tagliare* 'to cut into strips'], and TALLY.

taint [ME. Partly from Latin *tingere* 'to colour or dye', partly from **attaint** (via Old French from Latin *attingere* 'to touch on, to reach' from Latin *tangere* 'to touch'), which shared some senses of *taint*] **1** to convict or condemn (–18c), to accuse of a crime or wrongdoing (16c); a conviction or accusation **2** (to make) a touch or hit in jousting (–18c) **3** a stain, blemish, or impurity (15c), hence **(a)** to corrupt, contaminate, or sully (16c) **(b)** an unpleasant smell (1920s).

Latin *attingere* produced **attain** to accomplish or achieve, to succeed in (outliving *attaint*); to arrive at or live to. Latin *tangere* is the ancestor of TACT*, and *tingere* of TINCTURE*.

talent [Old English *talente*, *talentan*, via Old High German and Latin from Greek *talenton* 'weight, sum of money'] An ancient unit of weight; a sum of money based on this weight in silver or gold. The sense 'natural aptitude or ability' (15c), comes from a Bible story (Matthew 25:14–30) in which three men are entrusted with small sums and judged by the use they make of them, abilities or aptitudes being regarded as entrusted by God to be used and improved. Hence **(the) talent** talented people collectively (19c); women, less often men, considered as possible sexual partners (1940s).

tall [ME. Ultimately from Old English *getael* 'swift, prompt'] **1** ready, active (–17c) **2** fine, handsome (15–17c) **3** bold, strong, good at fighting (15–17c, revived briefly in the 19c). Hence (apparently from the association of height with good looks and strength), of greater than average height (16c), hence **(a)** lofty, grand, pretentious (17–19c); of a story etc.: exaggerated, unlikely (19c) **(b) stand/walk tall** stand/walk erect, proudly, and courageously (19c) **(c)** of a game bird: high-flying (early 20c).

tally [15c. Via Anglo-Norman French or Anglo-Latin from Latin *talea*: see TAIL*] A wooden stick with notches cut in it representing the amount of a debt or payment, which was split lengthways, one half being kept by each party, hence **1** to mark on a tally, hence **(a)** (to record) an amount or score (16c); to count or reckon up **(b)** (to mark with) a distinguishing mark, tag, etc. **2** a set of marks representing a number (usually 5), used in counting (17c) **3** either of the halves of a tally (17c); a duplicate or counterpart; to agree or correspond (18c).

tan [Old English, probably from medieval Latin *tannare*, from *tannum* 'crushed bark used in tanning', perhaps of Celtic origin: later also from related Old French *tanner*] To make skin or hide into leather, hence **1 tan (bark)** crushed bark used in tanning (ME); (of) its yellowish brown colour (16c) **2 (sun)tan** to brown your skin by sunbathing (16c); of the skin: to become brown; browned skin (18c) **3** to thrash, originally and often as **tan your hide** (17c, probably from the idea of hardening the skin: cf. HIDE) **4** to harden chemically (19c).

Latin *tannum* produced **tannin**, used in tanning, dyeing, and as an astringent, and **tawny**.

tang [ME. Old Norse *tange* 'point'] **1** a snake's tongue (once believed to have a sting), hence an insect's sting; a sharp taste or smell (15c, later also as **twang**); an aftertaste, hence **(a)** a trace or touch of some quality (16c) **(b) tangy** pleasantly sharp or spicy (19c) **2** the (tapered) part of a blade that fits into a handle (15c).

tanga [*c*.1910. Portuguese, ultimately of Bantu origin] A small covering for the pubic area worn by indigenous peoples in tropical America; (the lower half of) a minimal bikini (1970s).

tank [17c. Gujurati *ṭānku* or Marathi *ṭānkẽ* 'underground cistern', from Sanskrit *taḍāga* 'pond', probably influenced by Portuguese *tangue* 'pond', from Latin *stagnum* (ancestor of **stagnant** and **stagnate**)] In the Indian subcontinent, a (manmade) pool or lake used as a reservoir, hence **1** a natural pond (dialect and US) **2** a (large) receptacle for liquid or gas (*fuel/fish tank*), hence **(a)** to put or store in a tank (19c) **(b) tanked up** full of alcohol, drunk (19c) **(c)** a holding cell for several prisoners, especially drunks (*c*.1910, US) **3** an armoured combat vehicle moving on tracks (World War I, originally the code name for the new weapon).

tap [Old English *taeppa* (noun), *taeppian* (verb)] A bung for the vent-hole of a cask; a valve and spout for regulating the flow of liquid from a container or pipe: **faucet** [ME, from Old French *fausset*, from *fausser* 'to break in', ultimately from Latin *fallere* 'to deceive or disappoint' (ancestor of FAIL*)] followed the same path without developing further senses. Hence **1** to draw off and sell (alcoholic) liquid (ME); this liquid (17c) **2 tap (into)** to pierce or open up a cask etc. to get at the contents (16c), hence **(a)** to obtain by doing so **(b)** to use a resource or supply **(c)** *tap* to connect a listening device to a telephone line (19c); such a device (1920s); the use of one (1950s) **3** an object shaped like a tapering cylinder (*tap root*, 17c) **4** a tool for cutting an internal screw thread (17c); to cut one (19c).

Related to **tampion** a plug or stopper [French *tampon* (itself adopted for a plug used in the body), a variant of *tapon* 'rag for plugging a hole', of Frankish origin], whence, probably, **tamp**, and to TATTOO.

taper [Old English, from Latin *papyrus* (see PAPER) because papyrus pith was used for candle wicks] A wax candle, later a long, slender one, hence something of a similar shape (16c, rare before the 20c); to make or become progressively narrower (17c); such a narrowing (18c).

tar [Old English *te(o)ru*: related to TREE*] A thick black liquid used as a protective coating; a similar substance produced by burning tobacco. Hence **1 tarmacadam** broken stone mixed with tar [19c, from **macadam** broken stone used in layers to make roads, named after John McAdam, Scottish surveyor, who advocated its use], whence **Tarmac** a proprietary name for (a surface made of) iron slag bound with tar (*c*.1900) **2** (probably) **tarpaulin** [17c, with PALL] a waterproof covering or cloth made of tarred canvas, hence a nickname for a sailor (who wore a tarpaulin jacket), probably the source of **tar** in this sense.

tarantism [17c. Italian *tarantismo*, named after the Italian town of Taranto] A nervous condition characterized by an urge to dance, common in the 15–17c in S Italy, and thought to be caused, or sometimes cured, by the bite of the **tarantula** (16c): another 'cure' was to dance the **tarantella** (18c) until you dropped.

tardy [16c. French *tardif, -ive,* ultimately from Latin *tardus* 'slow'] **1** slow, sluggish, reluctant, replacing **tardive** (15–17c), which reappeared as a medical term meaning 'appearing or developing late' (*c*.1900) **2** later than the expected or usual time (17c); late for an appointment etc. (*N American*).

Latin *tardus* produced **bustard** [via Old French from Latin *avis tarda* 'slow bird' (it can actually run quite fast)], **retard**, and **tardigrade** walking or moving slowly; (to do with) a kind of slow-moving microscopic water creature.

targe [Old English *targa*, *targe*: later also from related Old French *targe*] A (light) shield or buckler. Hence **target** a small targe (ME), later applied to a variety of round objects and eventually to the concentric circles that an archer etc. aims at (18c), hence anything aimed at, or made the focus or object of an action, policy, etc. (19c); to make someone/something a target; to plan or schedule something to achieve a desired aim (1940s).

Related to **targa** (a car having) a kind of detachable roof, especially one that leaves a roll bar [the name of a Porsche having one, from Italian *targa* 'plate, shield', referring to the *Targa Florio* (Florio Shield), a Sicilian time-trial].

tariff [16c. Via French and Italian from Turkish *tarife*, from Arabic *taʿrif(a)*, from *ʿarrafa* 'to notify'] An arithmetical table (–18c); an official list or system of Customs duties for various goods; a table of fixed charges (18c); a scale of standard sentences for different crimes (1950s); a sentence in accordance with this (1980s).

taste [Old French *tast* (noun), *taster* (verb), ultimately perhaps from a blend of Latin *tangere* 'to touch' and *gustare* 'to taste', from *gustus* 'taste'] The sense of touch, a touch (–15c); to touch, feel, or handle; to examine by doing so (–17c), hence **1** (to have) a first or slight experience of **2** to eat or drink a small quantity to test the flavour or, later, whether it was poisoned, hence **(a)** such a quantity **(b)** to discern, or the discernment of, flavour; a characteristic flavour; to have one (16c); **tasty** having a nice one (17c) **3** a mental perception of quality; a sense of what is aesthetically pleasing or socially acceptable (15c) **4** a liking or predilection for (15c), hence **distaste** dislike, (a) mild aversion (16c), influenced by **disgust** (to cause) strong aversion or repugnance [16c, Old French *desgouster* or Italian *disgustare* 'to lose your appetite', both from Latin *gustare*].

Disgust is probably the source of slang **scuzz**, **scuzzbag**, etc. a despicable person (US slang), whence **scuzzy** disgusting. Latin *gustare* produced **gustation**; *gustus* fathered Italian **gusto** and French **ragoût** [from *ragoûter* 'to revive the taste of']. Latin *tangere* is the ancestor of TACT*.

tatter [15c. Old Norse *tötrar* 'rags'] A hanging or torn piece of cloth, slightly earlier in **tattered**, which also referred to ornamental hanging points: cf. TAG. Hence **tatters** ragged clothing, later also a coat made of cloth strips worn by mummers or Morris dancers.

Related to **tatty** tangled, matted, shaggy (*Scots*), whence, probably **tat** a rag; a shabby person; cheap or poor quality clothing or goods, whence **tatty** scruffy, shabby, tawdry.

tattle [15c. Flemish *tatelen*, *tateren*, imitating the sound] To falter or stammer (–18c, surviving in the surname **Tatler**); of a small child: to make meaningless sounds, hence to chatter or gossip (16c); to tell tales or reveal secrets. Hence **1** **tittle-tattle** (to indulge in) idle gossip (16c) **2** **twaddle** [alteration of obsolete *twattle*, itself an alteration of *tattle*] senseless talk, nonsense (18c).

tattoo [17c. Originally *tap-too*, from Dutch *taptoe*, literally 'to close the tap (of a cask)': related to TAP*] An evening drum, later bugle, signal to recall troops to their quarters, hence **1** a drum beat; a continuous beating or tapping (18c); to produce this **2** a military entertainment, originating in an elaboration of the evening signal (18c).

tawdry [17c. From *tawdry lace*, a shortening of *St Audrey's lace*] **Audrey** is a later form of Etheldreda, the name of a 7c Saxon princess who founded a religious house at Ely (in E England) and became the city's patron saint. A fair was held there on her feast day, where you could buy a **tawdry lace,** a fine silk cord or ribbon worn as a necklace, or, if money was short, an imitation or some other piece of cheap finery. Hence *tawdry* such goods (17c); cheap and gaudy; unpleasant and slightly sordid.

tax [ME. French *taxe* (noun), *taxer* (verb), from Latin *taxare* 'to censure, charge, or reckon', perhaps from Greek *tassein* 'to arrange', or from Latin *tangere* 'to touch'] **1** to assess the amount of a penalty, damages, etc., now only legal costs **2** (to impose) a compulsory contribution to the State's finances, hence to impose a task or duty (–19c); to make heavy demands on (17c); a demand or strain **3** to censure or accuse (16c).

French *taxe* 'tariff' produced *taximètre* **taximeter**, whence **taxi(meter) cab**, shortened to **taxi** or *cab* (at CABRIOLET); the sense of an aircraft moving slowly along a runway may come from a taxi moving up the rank. Latin *taxare* produced medieval Latin *tasca* 'tax, duty', whence **task**. Greek *tassein* produced TAXONOMY*; Latin *tangere* is the ancestor of TACT*.

taxonomy [19c. Greek *taxis* 'arrangement' (from *tassein* 'to arrange') + **-nomy** from Greek *nomos* 'law'] (The study or principles of) classification, especially of living organisms, hence the back-formation **taxon** a taxonomic group (1920s): in biology the main ones are (from the top) *kingdom* (see KING), **phylum** [Greek *phulon* 'tribe, race'], CLASS, ORDER, FAMILY, GENUS, and *species* (at SPICE).

Greek *taxis* produced **taxidermy** [with Greek *derma* 'skin': see HYPE]; *tassein* produced **tactic** and, perhaps, TAX; *nomos* produced *metronome* (at METRE), and **numismatic** [via French and Latin from Greek *nomisma* 'custom, current coin'].

tea [17c, probably via Dutch from Chinese *te* (Amoy dialect), *chá* (Mandarin)] (A drink made from) the dried leaves of an evergreen shrub, originally from China, hence **1** an infusion made in a similar way from other plants; such a plant; marijuana, especially when taken in this way (1930s, *US*) **2** a meal at which tea is served (18c): **(a)** in the UK, Australia, and New Zealand: an evening meal, sometimes the main meal of the day (cf. *dinner* at JEJUNE) **(b)** in Guyana and Jamaica: breakfast **(c)** **(afternoon) tea** the drink with sandwiches and cake; **high tea** with a light cooked dish.

Chinese *chá* was adopted as **cha**, an alternative word for the drink (17c), rare in the 18–19c, re-emerging in the early 20c as **chai**, now usually a spiced tea, or **char** (*military slang*).

tease [Old English *taesan*] To pick wool, flax, etc. into separate fibres, hence **1 tease out** to gradually separate entangled things; to obtain or extract gradually (1950s, *US*) **2** to torment with persistent annoying behaviour (17c); to make fun of playfully or spitefully, hence **(a)** someone who does so (17c) **(b)** to arouse hope, curiosity, or sexual desire while refusing to satisfy it (19c), hence **teaser** an inferior ram or stallion used to excite the females before the stud animal mates with them (19c); **(cock-)teaser** (1950s), *tease* (1970s), a woman who teases sexually; **striptease** an entertainment in which a woman gradually takes her clothes off (1920s, *US*) **3** to comb cloth to raise a nap (18c), originally using the prickly dried seed heads of the **teasel** [related to Old English *taesel*]; to back-comb the hair (1950s, US).

technical [17c. Greek *tekhnikos* 'of art', from *tekhnē*: see TECHNOLOGY*] To do with or involving an art, science, or occupation, now the applied arts and sciences; of a person: having specialist knowledge (of one) of these; of a writer, book, etc.: treating a subject in a specialist way or using specialist terminology (18c), hence according to such terminology or to a strict interpretation of words or rules (*technical knockout*, 19c); **technicality** a minor point arising from a strict application of a rule etc.

technology [17c. Greek *tekhnologia* 'systematic treatment', from *tekhnē* 'art, craft'] A treatise on an art or arts (17c); (the study or use of) the applied arts or sciences (19c); a particular one of them (1950s).

Greek *tekhnē* produced **architect** [Greek *arkhitekton*, literally 'chief builder'], PANTECHNICON, TECHNICAL, and words referring to method rather than creativity, notably **technician** and French *technique*.

teem [Old English *tēman*: related to TUCK*] To bear offspring (–17c); to be or become pregnant; to be full of (as if about to give birth, 16c); to swarm with.

Teem meaning 'to pour' (*teeming with rain*) is from Old Norse *toema* 'to empty' (the original sense in English).

telegraph [18c. French *télégraphe*, ultimately from Greek *tēle* 'far off' + *graphein* 'to write or draw': see GRAPHIC*] A kind of semaphore device for relaying messages, later applied to various devices or systems for sending messages a long way, specifically a transmitter connected to a receiver by a wire, along which messages were sent by making and breaking an electric circuit. Hence **1 telegraph (board)** a large information board, visible from a distance (19c) **2** to send a message by telegraph (19c), hence to act in a way that signals your intentions (1920s, originally in sport) **3 bush telegraph** the people who kept bushrangers informed of police actions (19c, Australian), hence the means of a rapid spread of information or rumour (the similar **grapevine telegraph** in the American Civil War was quickly shortened to **grapevine**) **4 telegram** a written message sent by telegraph (19c, originally used for urgent messages but later for greetings, hence the *Gorillagram*, *strippergram*, etc. delivered by an appropriately (un)dressed messenger (1970s)).

By the 1930s the telegraph, the **telephone** (originally applied to various signalling systems using musical notes or other sounds), and other methods of communicating over a distance were covered by the term **telecommunications**, which produced words such as *teleconference*, *telemarketing*, etc. (from the 1950s, proliferating in the 1970–80s). As technology progresses these are being replaced (*videoconference* has largely replaced *teleconference*), and written messages that were sent by **teleprinter** (1920s) or **telex** [1930s, from *teleprinter* + *exchange*] now go by *email* (at MAIL) or by TEXT.

Greek *tēle* was added to many Greek words, and produced **tele-** in words such as *telephone*, **telescope** [Italian *telescopio*], and **television** [originally referring to various theoretical methods of transmitting moving images], whence **tele-** in *telethon, televangelist,* etc.

temper [Old English *temprian* from Latin *temperare* 'to mix in proper proportions, to moderate, to restrain yourself', probably ultimately from *tempus* '(right) time, season'] **1** to prepare by mixing, hence to mix or blend in the right proportions (ME); (the character or quality brought about by) a (correct) mixture of elements or qualities (–19c, the original sense of **temperament** and **temperature**, both also from Latin *temperare,* ME), hence **(a)** your physical or mental constitution, thought to result from a combination of humours (16c, formerly also as *temperament* and *temperature*): see HUMOUR, and cf. COMPLEXION; your disposition or frame of mind (17c), largely replaced by *temperament* except in *good/bad/even tempered,* hence composure, restraint (*keep/lose your temper*); a tendency to anger (18c); an angry state (19c) **(b)** to bring clay to the required consistency by mixing it with water (ME), whence **tamper** in the same sense (16–18c), which also means to meddle with **(c)** to prepare pigments by mixing them with oil etc. (ME: cf. DISTEMPER) **2** to modify, moderate, or mitigate; to keep within limits (hence **temperate** mild, moderate); to restrain or control yourself, hence **temperance** moderation, self-restraint, especially in eating and drinking, now usually abstinence from alcohol **3** to adapt or make suitable (ME–17c); to harden steel, especially by heating and cooling, hence to make stronger by hardship **4** how hot or cold something is (16–19c), formerly also as *temperament,* replaced by *temperature* (17c).

Latin *tempus* is the ancestor of CONTEMPORARY, CONTRETEMPS, **tempest** [via Latin *tempestas* 'season, weather, storm'], **temple** the flat side of the forehead [*tempus* here meaning 'right place' (for a fatal blow) rather than 'right time'], whence perhaps **template**, Italian *tempo*, **temporal** to do with secular rather than sacred (and therefore eternal) matters, **temporary, temporize,** and the **tense** of verbs.

temple [Old English *temp(e)l,* later also Old French *temple,* both from Latin *templum* 'consecrated space', also 'place for observing omens'] A building regarded as the dwelling place, and/or devoted to the worship of, a god, gods, or a sacred object, hence **1 (a)** each of the two successive Jewish religious buildings in Jerusalem, hence **(Knights) Templars** a military and religious order whose headquarters were on the site of these, founded in the 12c, mainly for the protection of Christian pilgrims to the Holy Land. *Temple* in place names indicates ownership by the Templars, specifically **The Temple** the site of their establishment in London, which now contains the **Temple Church** (the surname *Temple* was given to foundlings baptized there) and the **Inner** and **Middle Temple** two of the four Inns of Court (hence *Templars* those with chambers there, 16c) **(b)** a synagogue (16c, now mainly N American) **2** any place where something precious is kept or maintained (*the body is the temple of the soul*) **3** a large Christian church (ME); the central place of Mormon worship (19c).

The name *(Knights) Templars* was adopted for an American Masonic order, and **(Good) Templars** for an American temperance society organized on Masonic lines. Latin *templum* is the ancestor of **contemplate** [Latin *contemplari* 'to observe carefully'].

tempt [ME. Via Old French from Latin *temptare* 'to handle, test, or try', from *tendere* 'to strive or stretch'] To put to the test, hence **1** to try in a way that involves risk; to provoke or defy, now chiefly in *tempt fate/providence* **2** to encourage to do something (wrong or unwise) by promising something attractive; to incite desire; to attract or allure **3** to try, specifically to try to kill, overthrow, or take by force (–16c), outlived by **attempt** [ME, from Latin *attemptare* 'to try for', from *temptare*], which came to mean a try (16c); an attack or assault; (something produced by) an endeavour, especially when not (wholly) successful (19c).

Latin *temptare* produced **tentacle** and **tentative**. Latin *tendere* is the ancestor of French *détente* literally 'relaxation' (1908), **portend** and **portent** [via Latin *portendere* 'to stretch forward' (into the future)], **tender** (to make) an offer, hence what may be offered in payment (*legal tender*), **tendon** [via medieval Latin *tendo*, used to translate Greek *tenōn* 'sinew', from *tenein* 'to stretch'], **tent** [canvas etc. stretched over a framework], and **tenter** a framework that holds cloth taut during manufacture, hence **tenterhook** one of the hooks that holds the cloth; **on tenterhooks** anxiously expectant, in suspense. *Tendere*'s other descendants include ATTEND*, **contend**, **distend**, **extend**, INTEND*, OSTENTATION*, PRETEND*, TEND*, and TENSION.

tend [ME. Via French from Latin *tendere* 'to stretch' (ancestor of TEMPT*)] To move towards or away from, hence to be inclined to do or be something, or towards some state, opinion, etc. (16c); to lead, or be conducive, to an action or result. Hence **tendency** such an inclination (17c); a drift in a certain direction; a political group within a larger party (*Militant Tendency*, 1970s), and **tendentious** having an underlying drift or purpose (*c.*1900).

tenor [ME. Via Old French from Latin *tenor* 'uninterrupted course', i.e. something held to, from *tenere* 'to hold'] **1** the thinking or argument running through a document, speech, etc. (cf. VEHICLE sense 2); the general sense, substance, or content; an exact copy of a document or its actual wording (15c) **2** a continuous or prevailing course or direction, especially of someone's life or habits; a prevailing state, especially of the mind (16c) **3** a male voice that usually sings the main melody rather than a descant or counterpoint; someone having this voice (15c); an instrument, bell, etc. with a similar range (16c).

Latin *tenere* is the ancestor of ABSTAIN, CONTAIN*, **detain**, **detention**, ENTERTAIN, *maintain* (at MANAGE), PERTINENT*, RETAIN*, **sustain** [via Old French from Latin *sustinere*, literally 'to hold up'], **tenacity** [Latin *tenax* 'holding fast', whence also **pertinacity**], **tenement**, **tenet** [Latin, literally 'he holds', hence something held], and TENURE*.

tension [16c. (French, from) Latin *tendere*, *tens-* 'to stretch' (ancestor of TEMPT*): the equivalent senses of **tense** are generally later] The condition or feeling of being stretched or strained, originally of part of the body, hence **1** (the stress produced by) a stretching force (17c) **2** (a state or source of) mental or emotional strain (18c); a state of anxiety or suppressed hostility (19c); (the effect produced by) the interaction of characters or elements in a work of art (1940s) **3** the degree of tightness or looseness of knitting or sewing stitches (19c) **4** to tighten or make taut (19c, 17c as *tense*).

tenure [15c. Old French, from *tenir* 'to hold', from Latin *tenere*] **1** the right by which, or the conditions under which, land or property is held **2** the possession of property, a position, etc. (16c), hence **(a)** the duration of tenure **(b) (security of) tenure** the right to continue a tenancy; the right to remain in an (academic) post until retirement (1950s); **tenured** of a post: giving this right; of the holder: having it, hence *tenure* to give it (1970s).

Old French *tenir* produced **tenable**, **tenant** (whence the surname **Tennant**, **Tennent** a tenant farmer), **tenon**, and **tennis** [apparently from *tenez!* 'take!', called by the server to the opponent] originally the indoor game now known as **real tennis** to distinguish it from the newfangled outdoor game, **lawn tennis**, which, however, is now sometimes played indoors. Latin *tenere* is the ancestor of TENOR*.

term [ME. Via French from Latin *terminus* 'end, boundary, limit'] A limit in space or time, hence **1** a definite time; the beginning or end of a period, hence a period or duration: **(a)** the period during which a court sits or a school etc. teaches **(b)** a tenancy limited to a certain period (15c) **(c) (full) term** the normal length of pregnancy (19c) **(d) long/short term** (lasting) from now for a long/short time (*c*.1900) **2 terms** conditions or stipulations, hence **come to terms (with)** to agree such conditions; to reach agreement; to come to accept **3** a word or expression used in a precise or special way (*technical term, in no uncertain terms*) **4** a mathematical quantity in a ratio, series, or sum **5** the condition of your relationship with someone (*bad/friendly/speaking terms*, 16c) **6** a pillar or pedestal bearing a statue or bust (17c, also as *terminus*: statues or busts of the Roman god Terminus being used for boundary markers).

Latin *terminus* was adopted for the goal of an action or the end of a journey, now of a rail, bus, etc. route, and is the ancestor of DETERMINE, **exterminate** to banish (ME–17c), later to wipe out, **interminable**, **terminal**, and **terminology**.

termagant [ME. Old French *Tervagant* from Italian *Trivigante*, of uncertain origin] A god that medieval Christians thought was worshipped by Muslims, and who appeared in mystery plays as a violent and overbearing character, hence a violent or quarrelsome person (16c), later especially a woman (17c).

terrace [16c. Old French, 'rubble, platform', ultimately from Latin *terra* 'land, earth'] **1** an open gallery or colonnade; a balcony **2** a raised level place for walking or sitting; the levelled top of a natural slope etc., hence **(a)** a natural formation with a flat top (17c) **(b)** a levelled strip on a hillside for cultivation (18c) **(c)** a row of houses built along the top or face of a slope (18c); any row of adjoining houses; **terrace (house)** one such house (19c) **(d) the terraces** (the people standing on) wide, shallow steps for spectators at a sports ground (1950s) **3** to make, or provide with, one or more terraces (17c).

Latin *terra* appears in the names of various kinds of earth and pigments (*terra rosa/sigillata* etc.), in **terra firma** dry land and in **terra incognita** unknown land, hence an unexplored area of study, experience etc. Its descendants include *fumitory* (at FUME), **inter** to bury in the earth, *Mediterranean* (at MEDIUM), PARTERRE, *pied-à-terre* (at PIONEER), **subterranean**, *terracotta* (at COOK), **terrain**, **terrarium** originally for small land animals, **terrestrial**, **terrier** a kind of dog that pursues a hunted animal into its burrow, TERRINE*, **territory** originally the area surrounding and ruled by a (Roman) town or city, and *turmeric* (at MERIT).

terrine [18c. French, feminine of *terrin* 'earthen', from Latin *terra*: see TERRACE*] **1** an (earthenware) lidded bowl from which soup, stew, etc. is served, now called a **tureen** [an alteration of *terrine*, perhaps by association with the Italian city of

Turin] **2** a dish for cooking (and serving) stew, pâté, etc.; the food cooked in or served from it, now usually a coarse pâté.

terror [ME. (Via Old French from) Latin, from *terrere* 'to frighten'] (A state of) intense fear, hence **1** something that causes this; a formidable person (19c); **(holy) terror** a troublesome person or child **2** the use of fear to repress opposition, specifically in **the (Reign of) Terror** a period of the French Revolution (1793–94) when thousands were executed as potential enemies of the regime. Hence **terrorism** and **terrorist** [both 18c, from French], originally referring to (the violence and intimidation used by) the Jacobins and their supporters; **terrorize** to fill with or coerce by terror (19c).

Latin *terrere* produced **deter**, **terrible** causing terror, dreadful, appalling, **terrific** causing terror, very great (cf. *awful* at AWE), hence extremely good, and **terrify**.

terse [17c. Latin *tergere*, *ters-* 'to wipe or polish' (ancestor of **detergent**)] Polished, trim, spruce (–19c); of language: polished, polite (–18c), hence of writing or speech: concise and to the point (18c); brusque, curt.

test [ME. Via Old French *teste* from Latin *testu(m)* '(earthenware) pot', variant of *testa* 'tile, jug, shell, pot'] A porous pot used in assaying precious metals, hence a trial or examination to determine the presence, identity, or nature of something (16c); to subject to one (17c). Hence **1** to try someone's patience or endurance (17c); (to subject someone/something to) a procedure that determines performance or competence (*c.*1900) **2** to undergo a test (1930s); to come out with a certain result (*tested positive*).

Latin *testa* produced **testaceous** describing certain invertebrates with shells (whence **test** the shell), **tester** the canopy over a bed, **testudo** a tortoise (surviving chiefly as the genus name), also a shelter against missiles from above, either a portable 'roof', or one formed by soldiers covering themselves with their shields, and **testy** [Anglo-Norman French *testif* from Old French *teste* 'head'] headstrong; argumentative; irritable, peevish. Old French *teste* evolved into modern *tête*, adopted in several English phrases, *tête-à-tête* being the most common.

testament [ME. Latin *testamentum* 'a will', from *testari* 'to make one', also 'to testify', from *testis* 'a witness'] **1** a will, formerly concerning personal rather than real property, now only in *last will and testament* **2** the covenant between God and mankind [from the use in Bible translations of Latin *testamentum* for Greek *diathēkē* 'distribution, arrangement', which usually meant a will, but sometimes an agreement], hence the **Old Testament** telling of God's covenant with the Israelites, and the **New Testament** telling of the new covenant established through Christ **3** a witness or their evidence (15c, originally in error for **testimony** [ME, from Latin *testimonium*, from *testis*]).

Latin *testari* produced **attest**, CONTEST, **detest**, PROTEST, **testate** (someone) having made a will (the opposite, **intestate**, is more common); *testis* produced **testicle** [via Latin *testiculus*, literally 'small witness', the testicles perhaps being seen as evidence of their owner's virility], **testify**, and **testosterone**, and the plural, *testes*, was adopted as the medical term for the testicles; Latin *testimonium* produced **testimonial** (something) serving as evidence; a formal recommendation; a gift presented (publicly) as a mark of respect or gratitude, hence **testimonial (match)** played in honour of someone who receives the proceeds.

text [ME. Via Old Norman French from Latin *textus* 'woven material', hence 'literary composition' (in medieval Latin 'Gospel'), from *texere* 'to weave'] A piece of writing; the main body of a book as distinct from illustrations, notes, appendices, etc., hence **1** the wording of a piece of writing; the author's actual words (not a translation, summary, etc.); the actual words of the Scriptures; a Scriptural passage as a basis of a sermon etc. **2** (a book containing) a version of a written work (*good/corrupted text*, 18c), hence **(a) textbook** a student's edition of a classical work; a version accepted or set for study (often shortened to *text*); the standard work for the study of any subject, hence as in a textbook, perfect (*textbook example*) **(b)** the written version or transcript of a speech **3 subtext** an underlying meaning or theme (1950s) **4** data stored in a computer that appears as words on the screen (1960s); **text (message)** sent from a mobile phone that appears as words on the phone receiving it (*c*.2000); *text* to send one.

Latin *texere* produced CONTEXT, *pretext* (at PRETEND), TEXTURE*, and TISSUE. Related to TOILET*.

texture [ME. Latin *textura* 'weaving, web', from *texere*: see TEXT*] The art or process of weaving (–18c); a woven fabric (replaced by **textile**, also from *texere*), hence the look and feel of a fabric's surface, determined by its weave (17c), hence **1** the look, feel, or consistency of any surface or substance **2** the character or quality of a work of art, music, etc. produced by the combination of its elements **3** to give something a rough or raised surface.

Textile came to mean (fibres for making) any kind of cloth, and is used by naturists for someone who is not one, or a place from which naturists are banned. Latin *textura* produced Italian **tessitura** the range within which most notes of a melody or vocal part lie.

thank [Old English *thanc* (noun), *thancian* (verb): related to **think**] A thought (–ME); a favourable or kindly thought or feeling (–17c), hence a feeling or expression of gratitude (long only as **thanks**); to give thanks; (to give) credit to someone, to hold them responsible (*thanks to you/you've only yourself to thank*).

thatch [Old English *thaec* (noun), *theccan* (pronounced *thetchan*, verb). The earlier form of the noun was **thack** (surviving in dialect), which changed its ending by association with the verb. In turn the verb changed its vowel by association with *thack*. The spelling and sense of the two words came together in Middle English] To cover (OE only); a roof (–16c). Hence roofing material, now only reeds or straw, hence **1** to make, or to provide with, such a roof **2** something resembling thatch: your hair (17c); (a matted layer of) plant debris, moss, etc. in a lawn (1950s, *US*).

Old English *thaec* is found in the place names **Thakeham**, **Thatcham**, and **Thaxted**, and surnames such as **Thacker**, **Thake**, **Thatcher**, and **Theaker**. Related to DECK and to the name **Thackeray** [Old Norse *thak* 'reeds' + *vrá* 'corner'].

theme [ME. Via Old French and Latin from Greek *thema* 'proposition': related to THESIS*] The subject of, or the idea running through, a talk, piece of writing, exhibition, etc., hence **1** to provide with a theme (16c, usually as **themed**), hence **theme park** an amusement park designed around a unifying idea (1960s, *US*), hence **theme pub/restaurant** (1980s) **2** a written exercise on a given subject, a school essay (16c, now US) **3** a prominent or recurring melody in a composition

(17c), hence **theme music/song/tune** that recurs in a film, musical, etc. (1940s); a signature tune.

theory [16c. Via Latin from Greek *theōria* 'contemplation, speculation', from *theōros* 'spectator', ultimately from *thea* 'viewing'] An idea, also a statement of the rules or principle, for doing something, hence (all 17c) **1** the general principles, as opposed to the practice, of an art or science **2** abstract thought or speculation (often opposed to *practice*); an idea formed by speculation, a hypothesis (18c) **3** a set of principles and propositions that seem to explain or account for known facts; a hypothesis confirmed by observation.

Greek *theōros* produced **theorem**: *thea* is the ultimate ancestor of **theatre** a place where plays are performed, hence the scene of an action (*theatre of war*), especially one that can be watched, hence **operating theatre** where observers were formerly allowed.

thermal [18c. French, from Greek *thermē* 'heat', from *thermos* 'warm, hot'] **1** to do with, or having, hot springs; of a spring: naturally warm **2** to do with or caused by heat (19c), hence **(a)** a rising current of warm air (1930s) **(b)** of clothing: retaining body heat (1970s); **thermals** such clothing, especially underwear.

Greek *thermē* produced **therm** a proposed unit of heat (19c only), later the official British unit for the supply of gas, and **thermo-** (*thermometer*, *thermostat*). Greek *thermos* was adopted as the trade name for a vacuum flask.

thesis [ME. Latin from Greek, literally 'putting, placing', from *tithenai* 'to place'] **1** Greek *thesis* was used by ancient writers for the tapping of the foot in keeping time, hence the stressed syllable in verse or beat in music (cf. SCAN). Latin writers used it for the lowering of the voice on an unstressed syllable, thus reversing the meaning. Hence in English, a stressed beat or an unstressed syllable. The opposite, also originally ambiguous, is **arsis** [ME, late Latin from Greek, from *airein* 'to raise'] **2** a proposition put forward as the premise in an argument (16c), hence **(a)** the first stage in dialectical reasoning, opposed by the **antithesis** [16c, late Latin from Greek *antitithenai* 'to set against']: the final stage, SYNTHESIS, produces a new idea that resolves the differences **(b)** a dissertation in support of a proposition, especially one counting towards an academic degree.

Descendants of Greek *tithenai* include ANATHEMA, APOTHECARY*, *bibliotheca* (at BIBLE), *discotheque* (at DISC), **epithet** [Greek *epitithenai* 'to put or add on'], *hypothesis* (at SUPPOSE), **prosthesis** originally the addition of a letter or syllable at the beginning of a word [Greek *prostithenai* 'to add to'], and SYNTHESIS: THEME is related.

thick [Old English *thicce* (adjective), *thiccian* (verb)] **1** broad, wide; large in diameter; of clothes: made of heavy material, hence too 'heavy', too much to take (*that's a bit thick*, 19c) **2** dense, hence **(a)** densely packed or crowded; densely, closely; in quick succession (*thick and fast*); the most dense or active part (*in the thick of it*, ME) **(b)** a dense group of bushes or trees, largely replaced by **thicket** [Old English *thiccet*, from *thicce*] **(c)** of a liquid: viscous **(d)** stupid (16c); a stupid person (19c school slang), largely replaced by **thickhead** (19c) and **thicko** (1970s): cf. *crass* at GREASE **(e)** intimate, chummy (*thick as thieves*, 18c) **3** to make or become thick (largely replaced by **thicken**) **4** not clear (ME), hence **(a)** of the voice: husky, indistinct; of an accent: strong and hard to understand **(b)** of the air or atmosphere: stuffy (17c).

thing [Old English] A meeting, also a court or council (OE only); a matter brought before a court (–16c), hence **1** an affair, a matter, often plural (*how's things?*); your particular interest (*do your own thing*, 19c); an obsession or preoccupation (*make/have a thing about*, 1930s) **2** something that happens or is done, said or thought **3** an (unspecified) object or entity; *things* possessions (ME); clothes (17c); equipment or utensils (*breakfast things*).

The original sense is found in place names (e.g. *Fingest*, *Tingley*, **Thinghill**): related Old Norse *thing* produced similar names in N England and Scotland, and survives denoting a (legislative) assembly in Scandinavian countries and in **Tynwald** the Manx parliament.

thorough [Old English *thuruh*, an alteration of *thurh* THROUGH*] **1** through, surviving in **thoroughfare**, literally a way through (15c) **2** throughout, affecting every part or detail, hence **(a)** comprehensive, meticulous, painstaking (15c) **(b)** complete, utter, absolute (17c), hence **thoroughbred** pure bred (18c); an (originally English) breed of horse, carefully bred for racing.

thrall [Old English *thrael* from Old Norse *thraell*] A slave or villein; a servant or subject, later a captive or prisoner, hence **1** enslaved, captive (ME); **enthral** to enslave; to captivate or fascinate (16c) **2** servitude, captivity (15c, usually as *in thrall*).

Old Norse *thraell* appears in names as **Threl-**, and also in **Thirlby**.

thrash [OE. Variant of **thresh**, from Old English *therscan*, *threscan*: related to THRESHOLD] (Usually *thresh*) to separate grain from its husk, originally using a flail. Hence (now *thrash*) **1** to hit or beat (as if) with a flail or whip; (now as **thrashing**) such a beating (19c) **2** to defeat decisively (ME): cf. BEAT **3** to sail or make way against the wind and tide (19c): cf. BEAT **4** to make wild flailing movements (19c) **5 thrash out** to reach a decision by discussion (19c). Only as *thrash* **6** a lavish or wild party (1950s) **7** a short, energetic, and usually loud piece of jazz or rock music (1950s), hence **thrash (metal)** a kind of heavy metal music influenced by punk (1980s) **8** an exciting car ride or race (1970s).

threshold [Old English *threscold*] A door sill; a doorway or entrance, hence **1** the edge of an area, now specifically of the take-off or landing area of an airfield **2** a starting point (*on the threshold of his career*, 16c) **3** the level at which something begins to be felt or to have an effect (*pain threshold*, 19c): psychologists use Latin *limen* 'threshold' in this sense, whence **subliminal** below the level of conscious awareness.

Threshold is related to THRASH. Latin *limen* is the ancestor of **eliminate** [Latin *eliminare* 'to turn out of doors'] originally to drive or throw out, and **preliminary**: perhaps related to SUBLIME.

thrift [ME. Old Norse, from *thrifask* 'to grab for yourself', later 'to flourish or prosper' (whence **thrive**) from *thrifa* 'to grasp'] Prosperity, success, luck; acquired wealth; profit or savings, hence **1** economical management, frugality (16c), hence **thrift club/society** a savings and loan association (19c, US); **thrift shop/store** selling second-hand goods, usually in aid of a charity (1940s, US) **2** the sea pink (which thrives in poor conditions, 16c) **3 spendthrift** someone who wastes money, originally by squandering an inheritance (17c).

thrill [ME. Variant of **thirl** (to pierce) a hole, hence to pass through, to penetrate, from Old English *thyr(e)l*, from *thurh* THROUGH*] A sound, emotion, etc. that goes right through you; the feelings, now of joy or excitement, it produces (16c); to produce such a feeling.

Old English *thyr(e)l* produced **nostril** [OE *nosthyrl* 'nose hole'], and the name **Thirlwell** literally a gap in a wall.

throttle [15c. Probably from **throat** (Old English *throte*)] To strangle or choke (15c), hence to control an engine's flow of fuel (19c); (the mechanism controlling) a valve for doing so; **throttle back/down** to close the throttle (1930s).

through [Old English *thurh* (whence also THRILL*). Spellings beginning *thr-* appeared in Middle English and became standard in the 16c: the original form survives in THOROUGH. The original abbreviation was **thro**: **thru** is N American] From one end or side to the other, or into one and out at the other, hence **1** from beginning to end in time or space, hence **(a)** (going) all the way (*through road/train*, 16c); at or to the (far) end of (18c) **(b)** having finished with (*we're through*, 18c) **(c)** up to and including (*Monday through Friday*, 18c, N American) **2** also **throughout**: extending to all parts, everywhere in **3** between, among (*tiptoe through the tulips*) **4** by means of; on account of, owing to.

throw [Old English *thrāwan*: related to **thread**] **1** to twist or turn, hence to form by doing so (ME), surviving in pottery (*throw pots on a wheel*) and in the surname **T(h)rower**, originally a maker of silk thread, later a potter **2** to hurl or toss (ME); this act; **throw (away/out)** to discard or get rid of. Cf. WARP*.

thug [19c. Hindi *ṭhag* 'swindler, thief', ultimately from Sanskrit *sthagati* 'he conceals'] A member of a secret organization in India who robbed and murdered in the name of the goddess Kali, hence a brutal, vicious criminal.

thunder [Old English *thunor* (noun), *thunrian* (verb)] (To produce) the noise that accompanies or follows lightning, hence **1** to speak loudly and angrily (ME); vehement speech or criticism **2 thunderbolt** a flash of lightning accompanied by thunder (ME); a missile hurled to Earth by a god, accompanied by lightning, hence **thunderstricken** (16c), **thunderstruck** (17c) struck by lightning or a thunderbolt; extremely surprised or shocked **3** great force or energy (16c: see the Bible, Job 39:19) **4** any deep, loud or rumbling noise (16c).

Old English *thunor* produced *thunresdaeg* 'day of thunder', later *thuresdaeg* 'Thor's day', now **Thursday** [a translation of Latin *Jovis dies* 'Jove's day', Thor (Old English *Thunor*) being the Norse god of thunder as Jove was the Roman]. All the days of the week are based on the Latin names: **Sunday** 'day of the sun', **Monday** 'day of the moon' and **Saturday** 'Saturn's day' are direct translations, the others having Norse gods substituted for Roman ones: **Tuesday** [Tiw, the Norse god of war, replacing Mars], **Wednesday** [Woden replacing Mercury], and **Friday** [the goddess Frigg replacing Venus]. Thor also appears in the place names **Thundersley** and **Thursley**, Tiw in **Tuesley** and **Tysoe**, and Woden in **Wednesbury**, **Wednesfield**, and **Wensley** (see also GRIM).

Related to Dutch *donder*, whence **blunderbuss** [alteration of Dutch *donderbus*, literally 'thunder gun'], and perhaps **dunderhead**.

tiara [16c. (Via Italian from) Latin, from Greek] A tall turban worn by Persian kings, hence a similarly shaped ceremonial headdress with three jewelled bands worn by the Pope (17c); a woman's jewelled headband (18c).

tick [ME. Probably of Germanic origin] To touch or tap lightly; a light touch, tap or stroke (15c). Hence **1** (to make) such a sound, or a clicking sound like a clock (16c), hence **(a) tick-tack** a regular tick (16c, largely replaced by 19c **tick-tock**); bookmakers' sign language (19c, perhaps from the clicking of mechanical semaphore devices) **(b)** a moment (between two ticks of a clock, 19c) **(c)** to function (1930s, chiefly in *what makes someone tick*) **2** a children's game in which one chases the others, the one they touch becoming the pursuer (17c), the variant **tig** probably produced **tag** in the same sense, whence **tag wrestling** in which pairs of wrestlers take turns, changing places when one touches the other (1950s) **3** a small mark put beside an item as a record, or to show it is correct (19c); to mark with one, hence **(a) tick off** to reprimand (World War I, *military slang*: cf. *tell off* at COUNT) **(b)** an item on a list of things you have seen or hope to see (1970s) **(c) tick the box** to record that something has been done, whether or not it was any use (*c.*2000); **tick (all) the boxes** to satisfy all requirements.

Perhaps the source of **tickle** originally (to be or make) delighted or thrilled, which may, however, be an alteration of Scots and N English dialect **kittle** to tickle physically.

ticket [16c. Obsolete French *étiquet*, from Old French *estiquet(te)* 'notice, label', from *estiquier*, *estechier* 'to stick or fix', from early Dutch *steken* 'to stick or stab'] A short document, a note, hence **1** a promise to pay: **(a)** an IOU (–18c), hence *on the ticket* on credit, shortened to **on tick** (17c) **(b)** a (discharge) warrant stating the pay due to a serviceman, hence **work your ticket** to wangle your discharge **2** a notice; a label (*price ticket*) **3** a certificate or licence; a sailor's or airman's qualification (19c) **4** a slip of paper etc. that entitles you to something (*theatre/ train/lottery ticket*, 17c) **5** a list of candidates for an election (18c, US); their policies, hence, perhaps, **that's the ticket** that's what's wanted (19c) **6** an official notification of a traffic offence (1930s, *US*).

Old French *estiquette* evolved into **étiquette** 'ceremonial' (court ceremonies being noted in a book known as *l'étiquette*), adopted meaning correct behaviour at court, in diplomatic circles, polite society, or a profession. Early Dutch *steken* is the ancestor of *snick* in **snick or snee** the cut and thrust of knife fighting [17–18c, with *snee* from *snijen* 'to cut'], altered to **snickersnee** (a knife for) such combat: **snick** to snip, later to strike sharply, is probably the same word.

tide [Old English *tīd*] A period or point in time: largely replaced by related **time** [Old English *tīma*] or **hour** [ME, via Old French and Latin from Greek *hōra* 'season, time'], but surviving in **1** *eventide* (at EVENING), *noontide*, *Eastertide*, etc. **2** the time between low and high water, or between two points of high water (ME); the regular rise and fall of the sea, hence **(a)** a (recurrent) flowing of water, emotion, etc.; a marked turn or trend **(b)** to flow and surge like the tide (16c) **(c)** to carry along (as if) on the tide (17c), hence **tide over** to help someone over a difficult time (19c).

Tide produced TIDY*. Related to **tide** to happen [Old English *tīdan*], whence **betide** to happen to, to **tidings** [Old English *tīdung*, probably from Old Norse], and to German *Zeit* 'time' (whence *Zeitgeist* at GHOST). Greek *hōra* is the ancestor of **horology** and **horoscope** [via Latin from Greek *hōroskopos*, literally 'observer of the hour (of birth)'].

tidy [ME. From TIDE] **1** timely, opportune (–18c) **2** good: **(a)** in good condition, healthy; attractive, bonny; of good character; able, skilful, hence as a surname for someone with any of these attributes **(b)** fairly good, satisfactory, pleasing (18c); considerable (*a tidy sum*, 19c) **(c)** methodical, systematic (18c); orderly, neat (19c), hence **tidy (up)** to make neat and tidy; to clear up or put things away, hence, perhaps, **titivate** (originally **tidivate**, 19c), modelled on *cultivate*.

till¹ [Old English *tilian*] To strive for, to get by working (–15c); to exert yourself, to work hard (–ME), hence to prepare land for planting, especially by ploughing (ME).

Old English *tilian* produced **tilth** agricultural work; (a piece of) tilled land; its surface soil. Related to **till** a goal, a fixed point, hence to a point in time, up to the point when something happens or is done (*shop till you drop*). Hence **until** [from Old Norse *und* 'as far as, till' + *till*], which produced, and outlived, **unto** [Old English **to** replacing *till*].

till² [15c. Origin unknown] A drawer or compartment for valuables, hence a cash drawer in a shop or bank, particularly the drawer of a cash register (17c); the register itself.

tilt [ME. Perhaps of Scandinavian origin] To fall, topple, or upset (–16c), hence **1** (to take part in) a joust (16c), hence **(a)** (to take part in) a dispute or debate **(b)** to rush at, to charge, hence **at full tilt** at full speed **(c)** (to poise a lance for) a thrust (18c); (to make) a verbal thrust **2** to (cause to) lean or slant (16c); a slanted surface or position; a preference, a bias (1970s, US).

timber [Old English] A building (–ME), hence **1** to build a house or other structure, later specifically of wood, hence **half-timbered** built with a brick or stone ground floor and a wooden upper part (19c) **2** building material, now only wood; (the wood from) suitable trees; growing trees, whether or not for building (18c); woodland **3** a beam (ME); **timbers** the wooden ribs of a ship (18c) **4** names such as **Timbersbrook** and **Timperley** where timber is obtained, and **Timsbury** a timber fort.

tincture [ME. Latin *tinctura* 'dyeing', from *tingere, tinct-* 'to dye or colour'] **1** a pigment or (cosmetic) dye (–19c), hence **(a)** a tinge or tint (15c); to add one (17c) **(b)** a quality imparted to something as a colour is imparted by a dye (16–19c); to impart one (17c); a trace or hint of one **2** the spirit, quintessence, or soul of something (15–17c); a solution of the active principle of a substance in alcohol (17c); an alcoholic drink, a nip (*c*.1910).

Latin *tingere* is the ancestor of **stain** and **tint**, and is one parent of TAINT.

tinker [ME. Origin unknown: first recorded as a surname, with the Scots and northern variant **Tinkler**] An (itinerant) seller or mender of pots and pans, hence **1** a gypsy or similar traveller (16c, usually derogatory, often shortened to **tink**); a disreputable person; a mischievous person or animal (1920s) **2** to mend pots and pans (16c); to bodge (17c); to fiddle about trying to repair or improve something.

Tink to clink (ME–17c) may be from *tinker*, or may be an imitation of the sound: it produced **tinkle** to ring (originally of the ears); **tingle** is probably a variant.

tinsel [ME. Old French *estinceler*, *estanceler* 'to sparkle', from *estencele* 'a spark', ultimately from Latin *scintilla*] Fabric woven with metallic thread or decorated with spangles (–18c), hence **1** decorated with tinsel (15c); sparkling, glittering, flashy, gaudy; (something) superficially glamorous, hence **Tinseltown** Hollywood or its film industry (1970s) **2** spangles, metallic threads, etc. used as decoration (16c), now especially strips of metal foil used in Christmas decorations.

Old French *estanceler* produced **stencil**, originally to decorate with bright colours or precious metal. Latin *scintilla* was adopted for a tiny piece or amount, having produced **scintillate**.

tip¹ [ME. Old Norse *typpi* (noun), *typpa* (verb)] The (pointed or rounded) end of something; a small piece attached to form one; to attach it. Hence, probably, (to give) a light touch, stroke, or tap (15c, from the idea of touching with the tip), whence, probably, to give, to hand (17c), hence **1** (to give) a gratuity (18c) **2** (to give) a hint or piece of advice (19c); **tip off** to advise or warn; **tip the wink** to do so (originally) by winking.

Tit for tat, an alteration of *tip for tap*, became rhyming slang for a hat, shortened to **titfer**. Related to **toupee** [alteration of French *toupet* 'tuft of hair', ultimately from Frankish] and probably to **top** [Old English *topp*] the highest point, the upper surface, originally also a tuft of hair or feathers, whence **topple** and, probably, **topsy-turvy** [with *terve* 'to overturn', probably from Old English *tearflian* 'to roll over and over'].

tip² [ME. Perhaps of Scandinavian origin] To (make something) fall, overbalance, or overturn, hence **1** the surname **Tiplady** (with the variants **Toplady** and **Topley**), given to a lecherous man or one said to have seduced a woman of higher rank **2** to make unsteady or drunk (17–18c, but implied in **tipsy**, 16c) **3** to empty out a container (or its contents), by tilting or overturning it (19c), hence a place for doing so, a dump; a very untidy place.

tissue [ME. Old French *tissu* 'woven', from *tistre* 'to weave', from Latin *texere* (ancestor of TEXT*)] **1** a rich material, often interwoven with gold or silver threads **2** any woven fabric (16c), hence **(a)** a delicate, gauzy one (18c) **(b)** a network or series (*a tissue of lies*, 18c) **(c)** the 'fabric' of an animal's or plant's body, consisting of interconnected cells (19c) **3** **tissue (paper)** perhaps named from its resemblance to thin gauze, or because it was put between folds of rich or delicate fabric (18c), hence *tissue* a piece of soft paper used as a handkerchief (1920s).

tit [Old English] A nipple, especially when feeding young, largely replaced by **teat** [ME, from Old French *tete*, of Germanic origin: probably related] and **nipple** [16c: see NIB]. Hence **1** **titty** (18c), **tit** (1920s, US) a woman's breast: often plural, whence rhyming slang *Bristol Cities*, shortened to **bristols** (1960s) **2** something resembling a nipple, specifically a push-button (World War II, forces' slang).

Teat came to mean the mouthpiece of a baby's bottle. *Nipple* also means the analogous structure to a teat in a male, and came to mean something resembling a nipple, specifically a device for dispensing measured amounts of a fluid, or a small lump on a surface.

title [Old English *titul*, from Old French *title* (modern *titre*) 'name, qualification, quality (of gold or silver alloy)', from Latin *titulus* 'placard, inscription'] **1** a label (–17c), originally the one on Christ's cross (see the Bible: Matthew 27:37), for which Latin **titulus** was adopted (*c.*1915). Hence **(a)** the descriptive heading of each section of a book or legal document (ME) **(b)** the name of a book etc. (ME); a publication (*Penguin publishes thousands of titles*, 19c) **(c)** a word added to someone's name to show their status, profession, etc. (*Lady Muck/President Obama*, ME); the status of champion in a sport (1920s) **(d) titles** writing on a film screen giving the credits (early 20c); **subtitles** at the bottom of the screen, usually representing dialogue, hence **supertitles**, **surtitles** above the stage, translating the lyrics of an opera (1980s) **2** grounds for a claim (ME); a right, especially (the evidence for) a right of ownership (15c) **3** to give a name or right to (ME, largely replaced by **entitle**, 15c) **4** the expression in carats of the purity of gold (19c).

French *titre* was adopted for the concentration of a chemical as determined by **titration**, the process of adding a reagent of known concentration to a known quantity of a test solution until the reaction it causes is complete. Latin *titulus* produced **tittle** a small mark or stroke, an accent [a medieval Latin sense], hence a very small amount, usually in *not one jot or tittle* 'nothing at all' (based on the Bible, Matthew 5:18: *jot* is at IOTA).

toast [ME. Old French *toster* 'to roast', ultimately from Latin *torrere, tost-* 'to burn, parch, or scorch'] To heat with dry or radiant heat, hence **1** to brown bread over a fire or under a grill (15c); toasted bread (18c); a small piece of sweetened or spiced toast used to be put into wine or other drinks, hence a person, originally a woman, whose health is drunk (17c, her name flavouring the drink as the toast does), hence someone who is honoured or celebrated; (a call to the company) to drink to someone/something (18c); the drink **2** to warm yourself, or part of your body, especially by the fire (17c), hence **toasty** warm and snug (19c).

Latin *torrere* is the ancestor of **torrefy** to subject to intense heat, **torrent** [French, from Italian *torrente*, from Latin *torrens* 'burning, boiling'], and **torrid** scorched, burned, intensely hot, hence ardent, passionate.

tog [18c. Apparently an abbreviation of *togemans* a light cloak (16–18c underworld slang), from French *toge* a Roman toga (15–17c), from Latin *toga* 'a covering or garment', adopted for the cloth draped around the body by Roman citizens (17c): related to DETECT*] An outer garment, a coat, hence **togs** clothes, a costume, hence **1 togged (up)** dressed (up) **2** a measure of the insulation properties of clothes, duvets, etc. (1940s: modelled on an American unit, the **clo** [short for *clothing*]).

toil [ME. Anglo-Norman French, from Old French *tooilier, tooil*, from Latin *tudiculare* 'to stir up', from *tudicula* 'machine for bruising olives', from *tudes* 'hammer'] (To take part in) a fight, struggle, or dispute, hence to struggle towards some objective or for a living; to work long and hard; such labour (16c).

Old French *tooilier* produced French dialect ***ratatouille*** a ragout (19c only), re-adopted as ***ratatouille (Niçoise)*** the vegetable dish.

toilet [16c. French *toilette* 'cloth, wrapper', from Old French *toile, teile* 'cloth, web', from Latin *tela* 'web, woven material'] A cloth used as a wrapper for clothes (–17c); one put round your shoulders while doing your hair (17c only), hence (the paraphernalia involved in) washing, dressing, doing your hair, and applying make-up, hence **1** a dressing room (19c); one with bathing facilities (*US*); a bathroom; a lavatory (early 20c), hence to help a child or invalid use the lavatory (1950s) **2 toilet water** (19c); **toiletries** (1920s) used for grooming yourself.

Old French *toile* was adopted briefly for a painting canvas (15–16c, re-adopted for a painting on canvas, *c.*1920), later for various sheer fabrics, hence a muslin prototype of a fashion garment: it is the source of **toil** a net, trap, or snare, now usually as **toils**. Latin *tela* produced **subtle** [Latin *subtilis* 'fine, thin, delicate', from *sub tela*, literally 'beneath the weaving', probably meaning 'finely woven'] and **tiller** [via medieval Latin *telarium* 'weaver's beam']. Related to TEXT*.

token [Old English *tāc(e)n* (noun), *tacnian* (verb)] (To be) something that acts as a sign or symbol, hence **1** an omen or portent, hence **betoken** to be a sign or omen of (ME) **2** serving as a sign of, now usually existing or done as a gesture towards something expected, nominal (*a token woman director*); **tokenism** the making of gestures to avoid real change (1960s, *US*) **3** a characteristic mark; a spot or blemish indicating disease, especially the plague (ME, cf. *tetchy* below); **4** a mark, object, or password that proves authenticity, identity (ME), or entitlement (16c), hence a stamped metal disc showing that the bearer may take Holy Communion, or issued by traders or employers to make up for a lack of small coins, hence a voucher (*c.*1900); a disc used to operate a machine (1960s).

Related to **teach** [Old English *taecan* 'to show, point out, or teach'] and probably to **tetchy** [probably from **tache** a spot or blemish, later a stain on your character; a (bad) characteristic, from Old French *teche* 'blemish', ultimately from Gothic *taikins* 'sign'].

toll [Old English, ultimately via Latin from Greek *telōnion* 'toll-house', from *telos* 'tax'] A tax, fee, or other charge, now mainly one for using a road or bridge (15c) or for making a (long-distance) telephone call (19c, N American), hence a cost, loss, or damage caused by disaster etc. (*death toll*, ME, rare before the 19c); **take its toll** to affect badly.

Greek *telos* is the ancestor of **philately** stamp collecting [French *philatélie*, from Greek *philein* 'to love' + *atelēs* 'toll free' (used for a franking mark or postage stamp exempting the recipient from payment), from *a-* 'not' + *telos*].

tome [16c. French, from Latin *tomus*, from Greek *tomos* 'section, cutting', from *temnein* 'to cut'] **1** a single volume of a multi-volume work; a (large, weighty) book **2** (translating Latin *tomus*) a papal letter (18c).

Descendants of Greek *temnein* include **anatomy** [ultimately from Greek *anatomē* 'dissection'], ATOM, **dichotomy** [via Latin from Greek *dikhotomia* 'division in two'], *entomology* (at INSECT), EPITOME, and **-tomy** in words for surgical operations (*vasectomy*, *lobotomy*).

tone [ME. Via French from Latin *tonus*, from Greek *tonos* 'tension, stretching', from *teinein* 'to stretch'] **1** [mainly from Latin] a characteristic quality: **(a)** of a voice or musical instrument, hence to sound with the proper tone (–16c); to say with a musical lilt (17c), outlived by **intone** [15c, from Latin *intonare*] **(b)** of a colour (15c); the general effect of light and shade in a picture etc. (19c); to alter this, hence **tone (in)** to blend in, to go with (19c); **toner** something used to modify colour (19c); a pigment used in xerography to make an image visible

(1950s) **(c)** in speaking or writing, expressing a mood, attitude, etc. (*tone of voice*, 17c) **(d)** of a place, society, etc. (*lower the tone*) **2** [mainly from Greek] (correct) musical pitch (–18c, cf. *tune* below), hence **(a)** a sound (originally a musical note) produced by a regular vibration (15c), now one automatically generated in a telephone system etc. (*dialling tone*, early 20c) **(b) (whole) tone** the interval between successive notes on the **diatonic scale** [Greek *dia* 'through'] (17c) **(c)** (an accent on) a stressed syllable of a word (19c) **3** the normal firmness of a healthy body (17c), hence to bring the body to this state (19c); to strengthen or improve something.

The variant **tune** originally meant **1** a musical sound, hence a string of them, a melody **2** correct musical pitch (mainly in **in/out of tune**), hence to put an instrument in tune; to adjust a radio to receive a certain frequency or an engine for efficient working.

Greek *tonos* produced **baritone** [with Greek *barus* 'deep'], **monotone** (the continuance or repetition of) a single tone, hence **monotonous** lacking variety, boring, and TONIC. Greek *dia-* appears in many English words, e.g. *diaphanous* (at PHANTOM), *diabetes* (at BASE[1]).

tongue [Old English *tunge*] The fleshy organ in the mouth, one of the speech organs, hence **1** something resembling this (*tongue of flame, of a shoe*, etc.); a narrow strip of land or water (ME) **2** the speech of a people or community; a way of speaking or, later, writing (ME): partly replaced by **language** [ME, from French *langage*, from *langue* 'tongue, speech', from Latin *lingua*], which came to mean a non-verbal system of communication (*body language*, 17c); a common way of thinking (*talk the same language*, 19c) **3** to touch or move with the tongue (17c).

Latin *lingua* is the ancestor of **lingo** [probably via Portuguese], Italian **lingua franca** [literally 'Frankish tongue'] originally a mixture of Italian with other languages used in the eastern Mediterranean, Italian **linguine** [literally 'little tongues'], and **linguist**.

tonic [17c. Via French from Greek *tonikos* 'of or for stretching', from *tonos*: see TONE*] **1** to do with or producing physical tension, especially muscle contraction **2** to do with or producing the normal tone or condition of the body; tending to restore or increase tone (18c); a substance that does so, hence (something) bracing or invigorating; **tonic (water)** originally drunk to stimulate the appetite (1920s) **3** (to do with or based on) the keynote of a musical scale (18c); the principal key of a piece (19c).

topic [15c. Latin *topica*, from Greek *Ta Topika*, literally 'Matters concerning Commonplaces' (from *topos* 'a place, commonplace'), the title of a treatise by Aristotle (see ARTERY) largely concerned with searching for an argument to support or refute a thesis. Greek *koinoi topoi* 'common places' meant (a collection of) general arguments that might be applied to particular cases, regarded as a 'place' where rhetoricians could seek suggestions on how to treat a subject] **1** a set or book of general rules, maxims, or ideas on various subjects **2** a (stock) argument (17–19c); a heading under which arguments or subjects could be arranged, hence the subject of an argument, conversation, book, etc. (18c); **topical** to do with this (19c), now especially to do with whatever is currently in the news.

Commonplace originally meant a general rule, or a text cited in argument (16c only), hence **1** a notable passage, quotation, etc. collected and kept for future use **2** an ordinary topic or saying, a platitude; (something) trivial, trite, or hackneyed. Greek *topos* produced UTOPIA*.

torture [ME. (French, from) Latin *tortura* 'twisting, torment', from Latin *torquere*, *tort-* 'to twist', hence 'to twist the limbs'] **1** (a disorder characterized by) twisting or distortion; to distort or twist violently (17c) **2** (the infliction of) severe physical or mental pain (15c); this as a means of punishment, interrogation, or coercion (16c); to subject someone to it; the means of doing so.

Descendants of Latin *torquere* include **contort**, **distort**, **extort**, **nasturtium** [Latin *nasturcium* 'nose-twister' (because of its pungency), from *naris* 'nose'], RETORT, **torch** originally a twist of tow dipped in wax, **torment** [via Latin *tormentum* 'the rack'], **torque** a twisting or rotating force, also [via French] a (twisted) metal collar worn by Celts, **tort** injury, wrong (ME–18c), now a wrongful act for which damages can be sought, **tortuous**, and probably **truss** (to tie in) a bundle [via Old French *trusser*, whence also *trousseau* (literally 'a small bundle'), adopted for a bride's clothes etc., and French *retroussé* (from *retrousser* 'to turn up')].

Tory [17c. Probably from Irish *toraidhe* 'outlaw, highwayman', from *tóir* 'to pursue'] One of the Irish peasants who became outlaws when dispossessed by English settlers, hence a derogatory term for an Irish Catholic or Royalist, or for anyone who supported James II's claim to the English throne despite his Catholic faith. They formed a parliamentary grouping opposed by the **Whigs** [probably an abbreviation of **whiggamore**, literally 'horse driver', applied to Scottish Presbyterian rebels against Charles I], forerunners of the British Liberal Party, from which the Labour Party sprang. After James II was ousted the Tories gradually became associated with the Established Church of England, landed gentry, and businessmen, and the Whigs with constitutional reform, Nonconformism, and the rising manufacturing classes. *Tory* has remained an epithet of the British Conservative Party: *Whig* was adopted by those who sought to rid America of British rule (18c), and later by those who sought to limit the president's power and the role of government, the forerunners of the Republican party.

tour [ME. French, from Latin *tornus* 'a turn', from Greek *tornos* 'lathe'] **1** your turn to do something; a spell of work etc. (*tour of duty*, 19c) **2** a circular movement (–18c, French *tour* survives in ballet), hence a period of travel taking in several places before returning to your starting place (17c); one taken as a holiday; a series of performances, matches, etc. at different places on a route, hence to make a tour (18c); to take a play etc. on tour (19c). Hence **tourer** a car, bicycle, etc. suitable for touring (1920s); **tourist** someone making a tour (18c); **tourism** travelling for pleasure (19c); the business of attracting and catering for tourists.

French *tour* is found in **tour de force**, and produced **contour**, **detour**, and French **entourage** [via *entourer* 'to surround'] and **tournedos**. Latin *tornus* is the ancestor of TURN*.

touse [ME. Of Germanic origin] To knock about, to handle roughly, hence **1** to disorder, to dishevel or rumple (outlived by its descendant **tousle**, 15c, now usually as **tousled**) **2** of a dog: to tear at (now dialect and Scots), hence **towser** a large powerful dog used in bear-baiting etc. (17c, also as a dog's name); a violent or uncouth person **3** horseplay (18c, also as *tousle*).

Probably the source of **tussle** to pull or push roughly (*Scots and N English*), later (to take part in) a vigorous struggle or scuffle.

tout [Old English *tȳtan*] To peep or look out, to keep watch (–18c), hence **1** to watch or spy on (17c), specifically **(a)** to spy on a racehorse in training (19c); someone who does so and sells the information gained **(b)** an informer (19c, mainly Scots and N Ireland) **2** to be on the lookout for business or customers (18c), hence **(a)** to try to attract customers, sometimes by pestering; someone who does so **(b)** to try to sell something (1920s); to advocate or recommend; someone who does so, specifically **(ticket) tout** someone who buys up tickets for a popular event to resell them at a profit (1950s).

Related to **toot** to stick out, later to look out; a look-out place, surviving in place names such as **To(o)thill**, **Totternhoe**, etc., and subsequent surnames, e.g. **Tootal**, **Tottle**.

town [Old English *tūn*] An enclosed piece of land (–15c); one surrounding a building (surviving in Scots); the building(s) inside, a homestead or farmstead; a village; an urban area smaller than or lacking the status of a city, hence **1** the chief town or city of an area, specifically London (*going to town*) **2** the centre of a village, now of a town or city, hence **downtown** (in or to) the centre, business district, or poorer part, **uptown** (in or to) the residential or more prosperous area (both 19c, *US*) **3** an urban area or lifestyle; town as the scene of social life, entertainment, or vice (*man about town*, 17c); **townie** one used to and preferring urban life (19c) **4** (also as **townsfolk**, **townspeople**) the people of a town or city; the civic community as opposed to that of the local university (*town and gown*, 17c).

Old English *tūn* appears as **Ton-**, **Tun-**, and **-ton** in place and subsequent surnames, whence **simpleton** a fool (as if a surname derived from SIMPLE), and produced the surname **Toner** someone who lived in an enclosure or village. Related to DOWN*.

toxic [17c. Latin *toxicum* 'poison', from Greek *toxikon (pharmakon)* '(poison for) arrows', from *toxon* 'bow'] Poisonous (hence **toxic assets/debt** bad debts likely to 'kill off' a creditor, 2008, *US*); a poisonous substance (replaced by its descendant, **toxin**, 19c); caused by poison (*toxic shock*, 19c). Hence **detoxify** to remove the poison from (*c.*1900, largely replacing 19c **detoxicate**, based on *intoxicate* below); to treat an alcoholic or drug addict by controlled withdrawal of the addictive substance, shortened to **detox** (1970s, *US*).

Latin *toxicum* produced **intoxicate** to poison (15–19c); to stupefy or madden with strong drink or a drug; to excite or exhilarate. **Toxophilite** a lover of archery is from Roger Ascham's book *Toxophilus* [1545, coined from Greek *toxon + -philos* 'lover'], hence **toxophily** archery.

toy [ME. Origin unknown] (A) flirtation, amorous play (–18c), to indulge in this (16c); to amuse yourself with, hence **1** a trifle or piece of nonsense; **toy with** to play with, to treat as unimportant **2** a plaything (16c), hence **(a)** a person considered as one (16c), hence **toyboy** (1970s) **(b)** describing a model etc. used as a plaything (*a toy train*, 19c) **(c)** an animal of a small breed or variety (*toy poodle*, 19c) **3** the surname **Toye**, a frivolous person.

trace [ME. Via Old French from Latin *tractus*: see TRACT*] The path taken by an animal, person, or thing (–18c); a mark or sign showing that someone/something has passed or existed, hence **1** to follow such signs; to find the origin or whereabouts of; (also as **tracer**) something used to do so (19c) **2** to make marks on, to ornament with marks or lines, hence **tracery** such ornamentation, specifically the intersecting patterns in Gothic windows etc. (17c) **3** a hint or suggestion (*a trace of a smile*); (an indication of) a minute amount of something in a mixture (19c); **trace element** found or needed only in minute quantities (1930s) **4** to mark out or chart the course of something (15c), hence **(a) tracing** the copying, or a copy, of a drawing etc. using a transparent sheet laid over it; *trace* to make one (18c) **(b)** to follow the course or shape of something with your finger, eye, mind, etc. (18c) **(c)** the line made by a recording instrument (19c).

track [15c. Old French *trac*, perhaps from early Dutch or Low German *tre(c)k* 'draught, drawing', from *trecken* 'to pull' (ancestor of TREK*)] The sign(s) left by someone/something in passing, hence **1** to (find and) follow a course or movement (16c), hence **(a) track down** to find (as if) by doing so (19c) **(b)** of a vehicle's back wheels: to follow the front ones exactly (19c) **2** a course or route (to be) followed (16c), hence **(a)** a rough path (17c) **(b)** a course for running or racing (19c), hence **track (events)** races for athletes (*c.*1900, *US*); **fast track** a horse-racing track whose surface encourages high speeds (1930s); a road to rapid promotion or success (1960s); to promote someone or progress something rapidly (1980s) **(c)** a groove in a gramophone record (*c.*1900), hence (the grooves containing) a single item on an album (1940s) **(d)** a strip of magnetic tape containing a sequence of signals (*soundtrack*, 1920s) **(e)** a moving assembly line (1980s) **3** what something moves on (*curtain/railway track*, 19c), hence **(a)** a continuous articulated band that a tank etc. moves on (19c) **(b)** of a film camera (originally running on rails): to move in relation to an object (1950s).

tract [ME. Latin *tractus*, literally 'a drawing out', from *trahere, tract-* 'to pull'] **1** course or duration **2** a stretch of land, territory, water, etc. (16c) **3** an elongated natural structure, especially in the body (*digestive tract*, 17c).

Latin *trahere* is the ancestor of ABSTRACT, ATTRACT, CONTRACT, **detract**, DISTRACT, **extract**, PORTRAY, **protract** [Latin *protrahere* 'to draw out'] to draw (surviving mainly in **protractor** the drawing instrument), also to prolong, **retract** to pull something back [Latin *retrahere*, whence also **retreat** (via French *retraire* 'to draw back, to retire')], **subtract**, TRACE, TRACTION*, TRAIL*, TRAIN, TRAIT*, and TREAT*.

traction [15c. (French, from) medieval Latin *tractio*, from Latin *trahere*: see TRACT*] The action of pulling (originally by the contraction of a muscle etc.), hence **1** the action of drawing a vehicle or load (19c), hence **(a) traction engine** a (steam) engine used to pull heavy loads **(b)** the (amount of) force that enables a load to be moved **(c)** a wheel's grip on a surface that allows movement **2** the sustained pulling of a part of the body for surgical purposes (19c).

Tractor 'something that pulls' came to mean a traction engine, now a sturdy motor vehicle used particularly on farms, or the powered section of an articulated lorry.

trade [ME. Early Low German, 'track': related to TREAD*] A way or path (–17c), hence **1** a (habitual) course of action, hence **blow trade** to blow constantly in the same direction (16–18c), hence **trade winds/trades** that do so (17c) **2** buying and selling, originally by travelling merchants; (a branch of) commerce; to buy, sell, barter, or exchange (17c); the goods etc. traded **3** a way of life; (the habitual practice of) an occupation (16c), often a skilled one requiring an apprenticeship, hence **the trade** those following one (17c).

tradition   [ME. (French, from) Latin *tradere*, *tradi-* 'to deliver or betray', from *trans* 'across, over' + *dare* 'to give'] **1** the (oral) delivery of information or instruction; a statement, belief, or custom handed down (orally) from one generation to another, hence a long-established custom (16c); those of a society, profession, etc. **2** betrayal or handing over (15–17c), hence **(a)** a legal transfer of property (16c) **(b)** the surrender of sacred books in a time of persecution (19c).

Latin *tradere* is the ancestor of **betray**, **extradite**, **traitor**, and **treason**; *dare* of DATA*.

traffic   [16c. French *traf(f)ique*, Spanish *tráfico*, or Italian *traffico*, possibly from Catalan *trafegar* 'to decant', ultimately from Latin *trans* 'across, over' + *faex, faec-* 'dregs' (whence **faeces**)] The business of transporting goods or passengers, hence **1** what is transported; the flow of people, vehicles, ships, etc., later of messages through a communications system (19c); the amount of this **2** commerce, trade, hence **(a)** to trade, now especially illegally **(b)** social intercourse; to have dealings, later secret or illicit ones, with someone **3** (combining 1 and 2) the illegal transporting of people from one country to another, often in conditions tantamount to slavery (1990s).

tragedy   [ME. Via French and Latin from Greek *tragōidia*, apparently and inexplicably from *tragos* 'goat' + *(a)ōidē* 'song', from *aeidein* 'to sing' (ancestor of ODE*)] A medieval story or poem typically dealing with the downfall of an important person (–16c); a drama in which a great man's downfall is caused by his own error or a flaw in his character (15c); this genre; any literary work with a sad ending; a fatal, terrible, or very unhappy event.

Comedy [via French and Latin from Greek *kōmōidia*, from *kōmōidos* 'comic actor', from *kōmos* 'revel' + *aiodos* 'singer', from *aeidein*] followed a similar path, originally being a narrative poem with a happy ending (surviving in Dante's *Divine Comedy*). Both **tragedian** and **comedian** originally meant a writer of such works.

trail   [ME. Old French *traillier* 'to tow', or early Low German *treilen* 'to haul', both ultimately from Latin *tragula* 'dragnet', from *trahere* 'to pull'] To pull or be pulled, especially along the ground, hence **1** something that trails, originally the train of a dress **2** to drag yourself along wearily; to follow slowly (15c); to straggle (17c) **3** to hang down loosely (*trailing plants*, 15c) **4** (to follow) a track, scent, or trace (16c); a beaten path (19c); a marked route with things to see along the way (*nature trail*) **5** to 'drag into' a course of action (17c); to persuade or entice, hence, perhaps, **trailer** an excerpt used to publicize a film etc. (1920s, shortened to *trail*, 1970s), hence *trail* (1940s), *trailer* (1960s) to advertise with one **6** *trailer* a vehicle pulled by another (19c); a caravan (1950s, US), hence *trail* (19c), *trailer* (1970s) to transport on a trailer.

Latin *tragula* is probably the source of **trawl** (to fish with) a large net towed through the water, hence (to make) a thorough search. Latin *trahere* is the ancestor of TRACT*.

train [ME. French *train* (noun), *tra(h)iner* (verb), ultimately from Latin *trahere* 'to pull' (ancestor of TRACT*] **1** time 'dragged out', delay (–16c); to spin out tediously (15–17c) **2** to entice, to lead on; to control and direct (15c), hence **(a)** to make a plant grow into the desired shape; to discipline and teach a skill (16c); to prepare for a task or competition (17c) **(b)** to aim a gun etc. at a target (19c) **3** to pull along (15c); what is pulled (–18c), surviving in **(a)** the train of a dress (replacing TRAIL) **(b)** a connected series (*train of events/thought*), hence (originally *train of carriages*) a string of railway carriages, trucks, etc., now including the locomotive that pulls them (19c, perhaps influenced by sense 4) **4** (the vehicles carrying) a retinue (15c); a number of people, animals, and vehicles travelling together; an army's equipment and supplies in transit.

trait [15c. French, from Latin *tractus* 'a drawing out' see TRACT*] **1** arrows or other missiles (15c only, rare) **2** a pen or pencil stroke (16c) **3** a line or feature of the face (18c); a distinctive feature or characteristic; in genetics: an inherited one.

French *trais* (plural of *trait*) produced **trace** originally a pair of chains, straps, etc. connecting a draught animal with its load, now one of them; also a thread that attaches a fly to a fishing line.

tram [16c. Early Low German and Dutch *trame* 'balk, beam'] A shaft of a cart, wheelbarrow, etc. (Scots), hence a barrow, later a four-wheeled cart, used in a coalmine (16c); **tram(road)** the track on which it runs (19c); **tram(car)** a passenger vehicle running on rails (19c).

tramp [ME. Of Germanic origin] To walk with heavy steps, hence **1** to trample (15c); to tread or stamp on (16c) **2** to walk steadily, to trudge (17c); (to take) a long walk over rough ground, hence **(a)** a vagrant (17c) **(b)** **(ocean) tramp**, **tramp steamer** a boat having no regular route but taking available cargoes to any destination (19c); *tramp* a similar aircraft (early 20c); to transport goods by road as and when required (1950s) **(c)** a promiscuous woman (1920s, US).

Tramp produced **trample**. Probably related to **trampoline** [Italian *trampolino*, from *trampoli* 'stilts', of Germanic origin].

trance [ME. Old French *transir* 'to be numb with fear', originally 'to depart, to die', from Latin *transire* 'to pass away', literally 'to go across', from + *ire* 'to go'] To die; (to be or put into) a state of doubt or fear, or of abstraction, hence **1** a semiconscious state, hence **(a)** **entrance** to put someone into one (16c) **(b)** **trance (music)** electronic dance music with hypnotic rhythms (1990s) **2** exaltation, rapture (15c), hence *entrance* to produce this, to delight (16c).

Latin *transire* produced **transient**, **transit**, **transition**, and **transitive**; *ire* is the ancestor of EXIT*.

transact [ME. Latin *transigere*, *transact*- 'to settle (a matter)', literally 'to drive through', from *agere* 'to drive'] **1** **transaction** in Roman and Civil law: the settling of a dispute, an agreement **2** to negotiate or do business with (16c); to conduct business (17c); *transaction* the business; (the making of) a deal **3** to deal with, treat, or discuss (17c); **transactions** the published proceedings of a learned society.

Intransigent 'obdurate, uncompromising' comes via French from Spanish *los intransigentes*, a name adopted by the extreme republicans in the Cortes, ultimately from Latin *transigere*. Latin *agere* is the ancestor of AGENT*.

transcribe [ME. Latin *transcribere, transcript-*, literally 'to write across', from *scribere* 'to write' (ancestor of SCRIPT*)] **1 transcript** a written copy, e.g. of something dictated, hence *transcribe* to make one (16c); to write out in full from notes or shorthand, to transliterate or translate, hence to adapt a piece of music for a different voice or instrument (19c) **2** to record something for later broadcasting (1940s) **3** to synthesize a nucleic acid using an existing one as a template (1960s).

translate [ME. Latin *transferre, translat-*, literally 'to carry across', from *ferre-* 'to bear'] **1** to move or take from one place, person, time, circumstance, etc. to another, largely replaced by **transfer** [ME, also from Latin *transferre*] except in certain ecclesiastical uses: e.g. to move a bishop from one see to another, or to take someone (alive) up into heaven **2** to express the sense of writing or speech in another language, in different words, or in a different medium, hence to (make something) change from one form to another; to be converted into, to result in (*lower taxes translate into spending cuts*, 1970s).

    Transfer is one parent of **transistor** [with *resistor*]. Latin *ferre* is the ancestor of CONFER*.

transpire [ME. French *transpirer* or medieval Latin *transpirare*, literally 'to breathe through', from Latin *spirare* 'to breathe' (ancestor of SPIRIT*)] To make a gas or liquid pass through a body as a vapour, hence to give off moisture through the skin or leaves (17c); of moisture: pass through the pores, hence to leak out, to become known, to be disclosed (18c), hence to turn out to be, to happen.

transport [15c. (Via French from) Latin *transportare*, literally 'to carry through', from *portare* 'to carry': see PORT³*] To move or carry from one place or person to another, hence **1** to move people or goods in a vehicle; the act or business of doing so; (describing) a means or system of doing so (*transport plane/have you got transport?*, 17c) **2** to make someone imagine themselves in another place or time (15c); to affect strongly (and now pleasurably) with emotion (16c); such an emotional state, rapture (17c) **3** to move away or emigrate (16–17c); to make someone do so, especially to send a convict to a penal colony (17c).

trap [Old English *traeppe*] A device for catching vermin or game, hence **1** betrap to catch (as if) in a trap (replaced by *trap*, from the noun, then by *entrap* below); *trap* to set traps, especially for a living (19c) **2** a way of catching out the guilty or unwary (ME); to catch someone out with one (17c) **3** a pivoted device used in the game of trap-ball (16c, the ball placed on one end and the other hit with a bat), hence any device that suddenly releases something, e.g. a clay pigeon (19c); a greyhound (1920s) **4** a light carriage [18c, said to be from **rattletrap** a rickety vehicle, although this is recorded later] **5** a device that prevents the escape of steam, water, etc. (19c); the U-bend in a waste pipe **6** some instances of the name **Trafford** (someone who lived by) a ford with a fishtrap.

    Entrap comes from related French *entrapper*, from Old French *trappe*, the ultimate source of the **Trappist** monastic order, which originated at Soligny-la-Trappe in N France, the name indicating a place where animals and birds were caught.

travail [ME. French *travailler*, ultimately from medieval Latin *trepalium* 'instrument of torture', probably from Latin *tres* 'three' + *palus* 'stake' (ancestor of PALE*)]

(To subject to) suffering or hardship, hence **1** to weary; to exert yourself; (to undertake) a painful or exhausting task; (to undergo) the pains of childbirth **2** to go from place to place; (to undertake) a journey: outlived by the variant **travel**.

treacle [ME. Old French *triacle*, via Latin from Greek *thēriakē (antidotos)* '(antidote to) venom', ultimately from *thērion* 'wild or venomous animal', from *thēr* 'beast'] An antidote to poison or snake bite, also applied to other medicines, hence (from disguising a medicine's taste with something sweet) golden syrup or molasses (17c). The original sense survives in the popular names of plants believed to have medicinal properties (*treacle mustard, poor man's treacle*).

Technically, *treacle* is the syrup from partly refined sugar, that from raw sugar being **molasses** [via Portuguese from late Latin *mellaceum* 'must', from Latin *mel* 'honey']. Latin *mel* also appears in **mellifluent** and **mellifluous** [both with Latin *fluere* 'to flow' (ancestor of FLUENT*)], and is related to MARMALADE* and more distantly to **mildew** [Old English *meledēaw*] originally meaning honeydew.

tread [Old English *tredan*] To walk; to walk on, along, etc., hence **1** to step on or trample, hence **(a)** to press grapes, thresh corn, full cloth, etc. by doing so (hence the surname **Tre(a)dwell** a fuller: cf. *walker* at WALK) **(b)** to suppress or subdue, surviving mainly in 16c **downtrodden (c)** of a male bird: to mate with a hen (ME) **2** a footprint (ME), hence **(a)** a line of them; a track or path (–19c); a habit, custom, or occupation (16c, surviving in Scots: cf. TRADE) **(b)** the horizontal surface of a step (18c) **(c)** the part of your sole that you tread on (18c); the part of a wheel that touches the ground; the patterned part of a tyre that grips the ground (19c) **3** a way or the sound of walking, a footstep (ME).

Old English *tredan* produced **treadle** originally a step or stair. Related to TRADE.

treasure [ME. Old French *tresor*, ultimately from Greek *thēsauros* 'treasure, store(house)'] Wealth, riches, especially precious stones or metals, accumulated or hoarded, hence **1** something precious; a loved or valued person (16c) **2** to hoard as treasure; to cherish or prize (*c.*1900).

Old French *tresor* produced **treasury** a place where treasure or money is stored, hence **the Treasury** the government department responsible for raising and managing funds; **treasurer** [Old French *tresorier*] the person responsible for managing them. Greek *thēsauros* fathered Latin **thesaurus**, adopted for a dictionary (a 'treasure house' of words), later a book of words arranged by their meanings, hence a classified list of keywords used for indexing and information retrieval.

treat [ME. Anglo-Norman French *treter*, Old French *traitier*, from Latin *tractare* 'handle, deal with' (the underlying sense here), from *trahere, tract-* 'to pull'] **1** to discuss terms, to negotiate **2** to ask earnestly, to beg (largely replaced by **entreat** [ME, from French *entraitier*], which has shared most senses of *treat*) **3** to deal with or act towards in a particular way: **(a)** to represent a subject in art or literature **(b)** to regard as and deal with accordingly (*don't treat me like an idiot!*) **(c)** to try to heal or cure (15c) **(d)** to show respect and kindness to (15–16c); to provide someone with food etc. at your own expense (16c); what is provided (17c); something out of the ordinary that gives real pleasure (18c) **(e)** to apply a substance or process to something (*treated against rust*, 19c).

Old French *traitier* produced **treatise** a formal written treatment of a subject, and **treaty** originally a literary or artistic treatment. Latin *tractare* produced **retract** to take back an offer, accusation, etc., **tract** a book on a particular subject, now a (religious or political) pamphlet, **tractable** easy to deal with or manage (**intractable** is earlier and more common), and Italian *trattoria* [from *trattore* 'host', from *tratari* 'to treat']. Latin *trahere* is the ancestor of TRACT*.

tree [Old English *trēow*] A large upright plant with a woody stem, hence **1** wood, timber; an (originally) wooden structure, especially one that forms or supports (*roof/saddle/shoe tree*) **2** something shaped and branched like a tree (*family tree*, ME) **3** to (make a hunted animal) take refuge in a tree (16c).

Old English *trēow* appears as **-tree**, **-trey**, **-trow**, and **-try** in place names, and fathered **treen** wooden, now applied to small wooden domestic articles regarded as collectable. Related to TAR*, **tray**, TRIM, **trough** (**trug**, originally a shallow basin, is probably a variant), the name **Trowbridge** probably originally from a tree-trunk used as a bridge, and probably to TRUE*.

trek [19c. Dutch and Afrikaans *trekken* 'to draw, pull, or travel', from Dutch *trecken* 'to pull'] (To undertake) a journey or migration by ox-wagon (19c, *S African*), hence **1** (to make) a long and difficult journey, especially on foot **2 pony trekking** riding across country as a holiday activity (1970s) **3 trekker**, **trekkie** a fan of the television series *Startrek* (1970s).

Dutch *trekken* produced **trigger** something pulled to set off a mechanism, hence applied to various things that initiate a process or chain reaction; to do so. Dutch *trecken* is the ancestor of TRACK.

tremendous [17c. Latin *tremendus*, from *tremere* 'to tremble'] Fearsome, frightening (17c); awe-inspiring; large and impressive, hence remarkable, excellent (19c). Cf. AWE*.

Latin *tremere* is the ancestor of **tremble**, **tremella** a kind of fungus that forms jelly-like masses, **tremor** terror (ME–15c), a shaking or vibration, Italian *tremolo* a vibrating effect produced in singing or on a musical instrument, and **tremulous**.

trench [ME. Old French *trenche* 'a cut, a cut piece', *trenchier* 'to cut', ultimately from Latin *truncare*, from *truncus*: see TRUNK*] A path cut through a wood (–16c); a ditch (15c), hence **1** a deep ditch and parapet to shelter troops; **trenches** a system of these; the front line (World War I) **2** to dig a trench or channel (16c); to drain land with ditches (19c).

Old French *trenche* evolved into *tranche* a slice, now an instalment of money, shares, etc. Old French *trenchier* produced **entrench** literally to surround or defend with trenches, **retrench**, **trenchant**, and **trencher** a cutting instrument, later a board for cutting and serving meat, hence a plate, surviving mainly in (good) **trencherman/woman** someone with a hearty appetite. Latin *truncare* produced the surname **Tranchant** a butcher, and **truncate**.

trend [Old English *trendan*] To turn round, to rotate or revolve (–17c); to make something do so (ME); to bend or go in a particular direction (16c), hence the direction taken (18c); the general direction or course of thought, events, fashion, etc. (19c); a fashion, hence **trendy** fashionable, up to the minute (1960s); a trendy person.

Old English *trendan* produced the surname **Trinder** someone who made braid. Related to **trundle**.

trespass [ME. Old French *trespasser* from medieval Latin *transpassare*, literally 'to step over', ultimately from Latin *passus* 'a step': see PACE*]. The underlying sense is of stepping over a limit: cf. *transgress* (at DEGREE)] (To commit) a sin, offence, or unlawful act, to injure someone or damage their property; to enter land or property without permission (15c); wrongful entry (with subsequent damage), hence to encroach or intrude (17c); (to make) an unfair claim on someone, their time, hospitality, etc.

tribe [ME. (Via Old French from) Latin *tribus* (possibly from *tres, tria* 'three'), originally applied to the three divisions of early Roman society, later used to translate Greek *phulē*, a division of society originally based on family, which the Greeks also applied to the Israelites] **1** each of the twelve divisions of the Israelites, descended from Jacob (see the Bible, Genesis 27–49), hence any group of families with a common ancestry, culture, religion, etc. (15c), hence **(a)** a set of people with something, e.g. an occupation or viewpoint, in common (16c) **(b)** a large or extended family **2** a Roman *tribus* (16c); a Greek *phulē* (17c) **3** a taxonomic grouping between a subfamily and a genus (17c); a class or sort.

Latin *tribus* produced TRIBUNAL* and TRIBUTE*; Latin *tria* (or related Greek *treis*) produced **tri-** (*triangle*, TRIVET*); Greek *phulē* is related to *phylum* (at TAXONOMY).

tribunal [ME. (French, from) Latin, from *tribunus*, literally 'tribal leader', applied to various Roman officials, specifically to an elected representative of the common people, from *tribus*: see TRIBE*] A raised platform where magistrates sat, hence a judge's seat; a court of justice (16c); a body appointed to adjudicate or to investigate something of public concern (early 20c).

Latin *tribuna*, an alteration of *tribunal*, produced **tribune** a platform, hence **1** (the apse of a basilica containing) the bishop's raised throne **2** a platform or gallery with seats. Latin *tribunus* produced **tribune**, applied to similar officials in other societies, hence a popular leader.

tribute [ME. Latin *tribuere, tribut-* 'to assign', originally 'to divide between tribes', from *tribus*: see TRIBE*] (The obligation to make) a periodical payment from one state to another, from a subject to a ruler, etc., as a sign of dependence, hence something done, said, or given as a mark of respect or gratitude (16c); something that shows a good effect (*her success is a tribute to the school*, 1920s). Hence **tributary** [Latin *tributarius*] **1** (a person) required to pay tribute (ME), hence subsidiary (17c); a subsidiary thing (19c), specifically a river that flows into a larger one **2** offered as a tribute or mark of respect (16c).

Latin *tribuere* is the ancestor of **attribute, contribute, distribute**, and **retribution**.

trice [ME. Early Dutch *trīsen* or Low German *trīssen*] To pull sharply (–17c), hence **1** to pull up and fasten a sail etc. (15c) **2** a sharp pull (15c); the time this takes, an instant, **in a trice** instantly (16c).

trick [ME. French *trichier* 'to deceive', probably from Latin *tricare* 'to play tricks': see INTRIGUE*] A ruse; to deceive or cheat with one (16c), hence **1 (a)** an (optical) illusion (16c); intended to create one (*trick photography*, 19c) **(b)** a prank or practical joke (16c) **(c)** a clever way of doing something, a knack (16c), a skilful act; one designed to amuse (17c), hence **tricksy**, **tricky** difficult, needing skill (18c) **2 trick out/up (as)** to dress up (as); to adorn (15c), hence *trick* a particular style of dress (16c); a particular habit, mannerism, or practice, hence a spell of duty (originally a sailor's, 17c); a prostitute's (time with her) client (1920s, *US*) **3** the cards in one round of play (16c); the points gained **4** as a surname (also **Tricker** and **Trickett**) a devious person.

French *trichier* produced the surname **Treacher**, and **treachery**.

trim [Old English *trymman*, *trymian*: related to TREE*] To make firm, to strengthen, to arrange (OE only). The word then disappeared, re-emerging meaning 'to prepare for a particular purpose', which underlies the modern senses (16c, but implied in the surname **Trimmer** and the adjective *trim* neat, smart, neatly prepared or arranged, 15c).

trip [ME. Old French *trippen* 'to stamp or kick', from early Dutch *trippen* 'to hop or skip'] **1** to skip, to dance lightly and nimbly (whence some instances of the surname **Tripp**); (to move with) a light, nimble gait, hence (to make) a journey or excursion, originally for pleasure (17c), hence (to have) a drug-induced hallucination (1950s) **2** to (cause to) catch your foot and stumble, hence **(a) trip (up)** (to make) a mistake (16c); to make someone do so or catch them doing so **(b)** to activate a mechanism by means of a switch (19c); **trip (out)** of an electrical circuit: to disconnect automatically as a safety measure (1940s); **trip (switch)** that makes it do so.

triumph [ME. Via Old French from Latin *triump(h)us*, probably from Greek *thriambos* 'hymn to Bacchus' (see ORGY)] A victory parade in ancient Rome, hence **1** (the glory of) victory, conquest, or a great achievement (15c) **2** to hold a triumph (16c); to celebrate a victory or achievement; (to feel) joy and pride from conquering or succeeding **3** to be victorious (16c) **4** (the playing of) a card of a suit that outranks the other three (16c), quickly shortened to **trump** (perhaps by association with **trump** to deceive or cheat [ME–17c, from Old French *tromper*, whence also **trumpery**]), which went on to mean **(a)** to play a trump; to take a trick by doing so; (to gain) an advantage; **turn up trumps** to turn out to be an asset (18c) **(b) trump up** to fabricate evidence or make a false accusation (*trumped-up charge*, 17c).

A lesser Roman victory was celebrated by a more low-key event, an *ovatio* [from *ovare* 'to rejoice or celebrate'], whence **ovation** an ovatio; an enthusiastic reception; sustained applause.

trivet [15c. Latin *tripes*, literally 'three-footed', from *pes* 'foot'] A three-legged stand, hence **1** a stand over a fire, later a bracket on the bar of the grate, for a cooking pot; a stand for a hot pan etc. **2** a three-legged seat, table, or support (16–17c), replaced by **tripod** [17c, from Latin *tripus*, *tripod-*, from Greek *tripous* 'three-footed', from *pous*, *pod-* 'foot'].

Tripos [an alteration of Latin *tripus*] had the same meaning (16–19c), and was then applied to a graduate at Cambridge University who sat on a three-legged stool and debated humorously with degree candidates (17c), hence **tripos (verses)** originally composed by him; **tripos (list)** the list of candidates for a degree in mathematics, originally printed on the back of the verses; **Tripos** the final honours examination for a Cambridge BA, originally in mathematics, now in any subject.

Latin *pes* is the ancestor of PIONEER*, Greek *pous* of PODIUM*.

trivial [ME. Latin *trivialis* 'belonging to the street' (literally 'to the crossroads'), from *trivium*, literally 'where three ways meet', from *via* 'road, way'] **1** to do with the trivium, regarded as the lower division of the liberal arts (see ART) **2** commonplace, ordinary (16c); unimportant, trifling; **trivia** insignificant things or facts (*c.*1900).

Latin *via* appears in the names of some (Roman) roads or routes (*Via Dolorosa*), and was adopted meaning 'by way of, through', hence 'by means of'. Its descendants include CONVEY*, **deviate**, **devious**, ENVOY*, OBVIOUS*, **pervious**, **previous**, **viaduct**, and **voyage** originally a long journey by land or sea [via Old French from Latin *viaticum* 'something for the road', which was later adopted meaning money or provisions for a journey, or Holy Communion administered to someone near death].

troop [16c. French *troupe*, back-formation from *troupeau* 'flock', from medieval Latin *troppus*, probably of Germanic origin] A large group of people, animals, or things, hence **1** to gather or go in one **2 (a) troops** armed forces, soldiers **(b)** applied to various military units, later to units in the Boy Scouts etc. (1908) **3 troop the colours** to parade the regimental colours ceremonially before the troops (17c).

Troop produced **trooper** a private soldier in a cavalry or, later, an armoured unit, hence **1** (also as **troop horse**) a cavalry horse, hence a mounted policeman (Australian); **(State) trooper** a mobile State policeman (US) **2 paratrooper** a soldier who drops into action by parachute, shortened to **para** (originally referring to the French *parachutistes*). French *troupe* was adopted for a theatrical troop, and produced **trouper** a member of one; a veteran performer; a reliable and selfless colleague.

trophy [16c. Via French and Latin from Greek *tropaion*, from *tropē* 'a rout, a turning'] In ancient Rome or Greece: a display of the enemy's weapons set up on the battlefield to mark the victory (15c), hence **1** a prize, a souvenir of hunting or war; a token of victory or success (now especially one awarded for victory in a sporting contest), hence **trophy wife** one chosen to demonstrate and enhance the husband's status (1980s) **2** a painting, carving, etc. of the Greek or Roman battle trophy (17c); an ornamental group of symbolic objects.

Greek *tropē* produced **entropy** and **tropic** originally either of the furthest points the sun reaches north and south of the equator before it 'turns'. Related to RETRIEVE*.

trouble [ME. Old French *turbler*, *trubler* (verb), *truble* (noun), ultimately from Latin *turbidus* 'confused, muddy', from *turba* 'crowd, agitation', probably from Greek *turbē* 'turmoil'] To disturb physically, mentally, or emotionally, hence **1** to worry, grieve, or distress **2** to harm or injure; to be painful or cause pain (*my leg's troubling me*, 15c) **3** public disturbance, civil unrest (15c) **4** (to cause) effort or inconvenience (*you've gone to a lot of trouble*, 15c); to ask or pester someone for something (16c) **5** a disturbing or distressing experience (16c); unpleasant, difficult, or embarrassing circumstances, specifically those of an unmarried pregnant woman (*get into trouble*, 19c) **6** (a problem caused by) a malfunction (*heart/engine trouble*, *c.*1900), hence **(a) troubleshooter** someone who traces and corrects such faults, later one who solves difficulties, e.g. a mediator **(b)** (a source of) difficulty (*money trouble*, 1980s).

Latin *turba* produced **disturb**, **perturb**, **turbid,** and **turbulent**. Greek *turbē* probably produced Latin *turbo*, *turbin-* 'spinning top, whirlwind', whence French **turbine**, originally a high-speed waterwheel, sometimes altered to **turbo**, whence **turbo-** in *turbo(super)charger* etc. Latin **turbo** was adopted for a mollusc with a spiral shell.

trounce [16c. Origin unknown] Afflict, distress (–17c); to beat, especially as a punishment), hence **1** to censure, scold or punish severely **2** to defeat decisively (19c): cf. BEAT*.

truce [Old English *trēowa*, plural of *trēow*] Good faith, trust (OE only, replaced by **trow** [from *trēow*]); a pledge or agreement, hence (an agreement that brings about) a suspension of hostilities (ME, as *trewe* or the plural *trewes*), probably because each party gave a pledge.

Old English *trēow* produced *trēowian* 'to trust or believe in', whence the verb **trow**. Related to TRUE*.

truck [ME. Probably from **truckle** 'a pulley wheel, a small wheel or roller', via Anglo-Norman French from Latin *trochlea* 'pulley', from Greek *trokhielia*] A small solid wooden wheel or roller, specifically on a ship's gun carriage, hence a flat trolley, originally for moving stone blocks (18c); an open railway wagon (19c); a motor vehicle for heavy goods (*c*.1915, *US*): **lorry** [19c, of unknown origin] followed a similar path from 'flat trolley'.

Truckle produced **truckle bed** a bed on castors that can be stored under another bed, hence (because servants often had truckle beds) *truckle* to act obsequiously. Latin *trochlea* was adopted for an anatomical structure with a smooth surface over which a tendon, bone, etc. slides.

true [Old English *(ge)trīewe*] **True (to)** loyal, faithful, steadfast, constant, hence **1** honest, straightforward, sincere **2** faithful to the facts or reality (ME), hence **(a)** telling the facts; speaking sincerely or honestly **(b)** genuine, authentic, not false or imaginary (*true love*) **(c)** certainly, admittedly **(d)** accurate, precise; accurately positioned; exact alignment (*out of true*, 19c) **3** conforming to a pattern, standard, or ancestral type (16c).

True produced the surname **Trueman**, and **truth** originally (a promise of) loyalty, a solemn pledge, outlived by the variant **troth**, whence **betroth** to promise formally to marry. Related to the surname **Trigg** [Old Norse *triggr* 'trustworthy'], TRUCE*, and **trust** [from Old Norse], and probably to TREE* and **tryst** [Old French *triste*, of Germanic origin].

truffle [16c. Probably via Dutch from French, ultimately from Latin *tubera*, plural of *tuber* 'lump, swelling'] An underground edible fungus, hence **(chocolate) truffle** a chocolate with a filling of chocolate and cream, thought to resemble the fungus in shape, colour, and as a delicacy (1920s).

Latin *tuber* was adopted for the thickened underground stem of a potato etc., and in medicine for a small raised area on the body. It is the ancestor of **protuberance**, **tubercle** [from Latin *tuberculum* 'small lump'] a small protuberance or swelling (whence **tuberculosis**), and **tuberose** a flowering plant with a tuberous root. Related to Latin *tumere* 'to swell' (whence **tumescent**, **tumid**, and **tumour**), and to Latin *tumulus* 'heap of earth', adopted by archaeologists for a burial mound.

trump [ME. Old French *tromp* 'horn', of Germanic origin] A trumpet, hence **1** a trumpeter (–15c); someone/something that proclaims loudly, summons, or warns (16c), hence the **last trump** that will wake the dead on Judgement Day **2** a sound like a trumpet (19c); (to let out) an audible fart.

Old French *tromp* fathered modern **trompe,** adopted for a device that produces blast in a furnace, and *trompette*, literally 'small horn', whence **trumpet.** Related to Italian *tromba*, literally 'large horn', whence **trombone.**

trunk [15c. French *tronc* from Latin *truncus* 'maimed, mutilated'] The torso without the head and limbs; the main stem of a tree, without roots or branches, hence **1** a (large) box or chest (originally one made from a tree trunk), hence **(a)** a large travelling chest (17c); the luggage compartment of a car (1920s, *US*) **(b)** a casing (17c); an enclosed shaft or duct for pipes, cables, etc. **2** to cut short, hence **trunks** (16–17c); **trunk hose** (17c) men's short baggy breeches; *trunks* men's shorts for swimming, boxing etc. (19c, *US*); men's underpants with short legs (1920s) **3** the main part of a branching structure (16c), e.g. **trunk road** a main road (19c); **trunk (line)** a telephone line linking two exchanges, hence **trunk call** a long-distance call **4** [partly by association with TRUMP] a cylinder or pipe (16–18c); an elephant's nose.

French *tronc* developed the sense 'collecting box', and was adopted for the tips collected and distributed to hotel or restaurant staff. Latin *truncus* produced TRENCH*, **truncheon**, the surname **Trunchion** a short, fat person, and probably **trunnion** a supporting pin or pivot.

try [ME. Old French *trier* 'to sift', of unknown origin] To pick out, to distinguish (rare since the 16c), hence to 'sift out' the truth (–18c): **1** to examine the facts of a law suit; to put someone on trial (16c) **2** to test strength, effectiveness, etc., hence **(a)** to test your own ability; to attempt to do or achieve something; such an attempt (17c) **(b)** to test someone's patience, endurance, etc. (16c), hence **trying** hard to endure (18c).

Old French *trier* produced **triage** the sorting of goods by their quality, later of casualties by the urgency of their needs, and **trial.**

tuck . [Old English *tucian*, later influenced by early Dutch and Low German *tucken* 'to pull sharply' and High German *zucchen* 'to twitch or snatch'] To punish, torment, or ill-treat (–ME); to pluck or tug at (ME), hence **1** to finish or stretch woven cloth (whence the surnames **Tucker, Tuckwell,** and **Tugwell**) **2** to pull or gather cloth into folds; (to make) a fold in a garment to shorten, tighten, or decorate it, hence **(a)** to put away (as if) in such a fold (16c), hence **tuck away/in** to eat heartily or greedily (18c), *tuck* food, especially schoolchildren's sweets etc. (19c); **tucker** a station-hand or gold-miner's daily ration (19c, Australia and New Zealand), hence food in general **(b)** to push in the end of something to secure it (17c), hence *tucker* a piece of lace, linen, etc. tucked into the top of a bodice, surviving in *best bib and tucker*.

Related to **team,** originally a set of draught animals, TEEM, **tow** 'to pull', **tug,** and **wanton** [Old English *wan* 'un' + *togen* 'disciplined, trained', from *tēon* 'to train'].

tuft [ME. Old French *toffe*, of unknown origin] A small bunch of fibres, hairs, feathers, etc.; something resembling this: **1** an ornamental tassel on a cap (15c), specifically one formerly worn by titled Oxbridge undergraduates, whence, probably, **toff** a smart, rich, or upper-class person (19c) **2** a cluster of short-stemmed flowers, shoots, or stems with a common root (16c), hence **candytuft** a plant with flowers in dense clusters [17c, with *Candia*, a former name of Crete, whence it came] **3** a small grassy mound (17c): the variant **tuffet** came to mean a hassock or footstool (19c), perhaps by association with Miss Muffet's seat.

tun [Old English *tunne* from medieval Latin *tunna*, probably of Gaulish origin] A large (wine or beer) cask, hence **1** one of a specific capacity used as a measure (ME); such a measure. The variant **ton** came to be used for various measures of volume or weight, specifically a weight of 2,240 lb (approx 1,016 kg), now largely replaced in the UK by the 1000 kg **metric ton** or *tonne* [19c, French, originally 'cask', also from medieval Latin *tunna*]. Hence **(a) ton(s)** a large amount, lots (18c) **(b)** one hundred, originally as a score in darts (1930s) **2** a brewer's vat (18c), hence **tundish** a shallow funnel, originally one used in brewing (16c), later a trough for molten metal.

French *tonne* had earlier produced *tonel* 'a small cask', whence **tunnel** a long tapering net for catching game birds, later applied to various funnels or tubes, and hence to an underground passage. *Tonel* evolved into *tonneau,* adopted for a measure for French wine, and later for the barrel-like rear body of some early cars, or the rear compartment of an (open) car, hence **tonneau (cover)** a removable cover for an open car, later for the cockpit of a small aircraft or boat.

turban [16c. Via French, Italian, Spanish or Portuguese from Turkish *tülbent*, from Persian *dulband*] A length of cloth wound round the head, worn especially by Muslims and Sikhs, hence a woman's hat of a similar shape (17c); a scarf, towel, etc. wound round the head.

Persian *dulband* also produced **tulip** [via obsolete French *tulipan*, from its turban-shaped flowers].

turn [Old English *tyrnan, turnian* from Latin *tornare*, from *tornus* 'lathe' from Greek *tornos* 'lathe, circular movement', probably influenced later by related French *t(o)urner*] To (cause to) rotate or revolve, hence (all ME) **1** to (cause to) change position or direction by doing so **2** to shape something on a lathe; to shape elegantly (17c), hence a character or style (*turn of phrase*) **3** the action of turning, a full or partial rotation (15c) **4** a time for doing something that comes round to each person in succession; a spell of work or activity (cf. BOUT, CHAR, *rota* at ROTATE, and TOUR), hence **(a)** a deed (*good/bad turn*) **(b)** an attack of illness, dizziness, or fear (*gave me a turn/a funny turn,* 18c) **(c)** a short performance as part of a show (18c).

Turn may be the first element of TURNIP. Latin *tornus* is the ancestor of **attorney** [via Old French *atorn* 'to assign or appoint', literally 'to turn over to'], **return**, *tornado* (at ASTONISH), TOUR*, and **tournament** and **tourney** [both from Old French *torneier* 'to take part in a tournament', perhaps from the idea of turning to face your opponent].

turnip [16c. From **neep** (Old English *naep* from Latin *napus*): the first element may be TURN, from its round root] (The plant producing) an edible white root, earlier called a *neep* or **rape** [ME, from Latin *rapa*: transferred to oilseed rape from the the 16c: see also *Kohlrabi* (at COLE)]. A vegetable with a larger, purple root was introduced to Scotland from Sweden, and was called the **Swedish turnip** (18c). In S England this was shortened to **swede turnip** and later to **swede**, while the Scots and N English used *neep* and *turnip* for both. Eventually the Scots adopted **(new) turnip** for the small white vegetable (often called a *swede* in N England), using the older word *neep* for the newcomer.

Neep influenced the spelling of **parsnip** [Old French *pasnaie,* from Latin *pastinaca*].

tutor [ME. (Via Old French from) Latin, from *tueri, tut-* 'to watch, to guard or look after'] A custodian or protector (–17c); the guardian of a ward; a (private) teacher; one in a university etc. who oversees a student's work and conduct (17c), hence **tutorial** a lesson with a tutor for an individual or small group (1920s). Hence to teach or instruct (16c); a book of instruction (17c); *tutorial* a printed explanation or computer program providing individual instruction (1970s).

Latin *tueri* produced **tuition**, originally meaning 'caring, guardianship', and **tutelage**, and Latin *intueri* 'to look at, to consider', whence **intuition 1** an inspection (15–17c) **2** (spiritual) insight; the ability to understand immediately without thinking, whence **intuit** to know intuitively.

twill [ME. Scots and N English variant of obsolete *twilly,* from Old English *twili* (from *twi-* 'double, two': see TWIST*), translating Latin *bilix,* from *licium* '(warp) thread'] A fabric with a ridged surface made by passing the weft thread under two warp threads; to weave fabric in this way; this method (18c).

Tweed comes from a misreading of *twill*'s variant, **tweel**, influenced by the Scottish river Tweed, near which it was made. Latin *licium* produced *trilicium* 'three ply', whence [via German *drillich*] **drilling** a twilled fabric (shortened to **drill**), and **trellis**.

twine [Old English *twīn, twigin,* ultimately from *twi-* 'two': see TWIST*] Linen; (strong) thread made by twisting two or more strands of hemp etc. together; to make thread in this way (ME), hence to (cause to) wind round something; of a plant: to grow around a support. Hence **entwine** to wind or twist together (16c).

twist [Old English, ultimately from or related to *twi* 'two, double'] A divided object (only in OE compounds such as *candeltwist* 'candle snuffers', shaped like tongs); to divide (ME), hence **1** the point at which something divides, hence **(a)** a twig or branch (–17c: **twig** itself is from related Old English *twigge*) **(b)** a turning or bend (*twists and turns,* 18c); a deviation; an unexpected development in a story (1930s) **2** to take away (ME–15c); to wrench off, later to distort or shape, with a rotating motion: other modern senses stem from this.

Old English *twi* appears as **Twy-** in names, and produced **twilight** (*twi-* here perhaps meaning 'half'), TWILL*, and TWINE*. Relatives include **between, (be)twixt, twain, twelve, twenty, twice, twin,** and **two**.

tyke [ME. Old Norse *tík* 'bitch'] A (mongrel) dog, hence **1** an unpleasant or rude man (cf. DOG*), also said playfully to a child, hence a small child, usually a boy (19c) **2** a Yorkshireman (17c, perhaps from their legendary plain-speaking, or because *tyke* is a common word in Yorkshire); originally meant as an insult but adopted by Yorkshiremen themselves.

A similar development is found in **mongrel** [probably ultimately from Old English *gemang* 'mixture': related to **among** and **mingle**] a cross-bred dog; a contemptible person (now Australian). **Mutt** [short for *mutton head*] a stupid person (US), later a scruffy or mongrel dog, seems to have reversed it.

Tyke used contemptuously for a Roman Catholic (Australia and New Zealand) is a variant of the Irish surname **Teague**, used as a nickname for an Irishman (the majority of Irish emigrants being Catholic); another variant, **Taig**, is used by N Irish Protestants as a derogatory term for their Catholic neighbours.

type [15c. (French, or) Latin *typus* from Greek *tupos* 'impression' (the underlying sense here), 'figure, type', from *tuptein* 'to strike'] **1** a sign, a foreshadowing, especially one in the Old Testament of something/someone in the New **2** a characteristic or distinguishing form (17c, originally of a fever), hence (something distinguishing or exemplifying) a class of people or things (19c), hence **(a)** resembling, having similar characteristics (*Cheddar-type cheese*) **(b)** a person of a particular kind (*the sporty type/not my type*) **(c)** to assign to a class (*tissue typing*, *c.*1900) **3** a small block with a raised symbol to be printed (18c); such blocks or printed characters collectively, hence **(a)** -type in words for methods of printing (*collotype*, STEREOTYPE) **(b)** typewriter a machine that produces characters resembling printed ones, using small types activated by a keyboard (19c).

Greek *tuptein* produced *tupon* 'mould, model', whence **archetype** and **prototype** (both meaning 'first or chief model'), and *tumpanon* 'drum', whence Italian *timpani* kettle drums [via Latin *tympanum*, which was adopted for the eardrum, a recess over a door or window, and a (drum-shaped) wheel for raising water].

U

ullage [15c. Anglo-Norman French *ulliage*, ultimately from Latin *oculus* 'eye', here meaning 'bunghole' (ancestor of INOCULATE*)] The amount by which a container is short of being full, or the amount of liquid lost, after leakage, evaporation, or use, hence **1** the amount of liquid left (19c); the dregs, hence a useless member of a ship's crew **2** (the volume of) the empty part of a rocket's fuel tank (1950s).

ulterior [17c. Latin, 'further away', from *ultra* 'beyond'] Beyond the present, further on; beyond or outside a point or boundary (18c); beyond the obvious, underlying, concealed.
Latin *ultra* was adopted as a prefix meaning 'beyond' (*ultraviolet*), hence 'extreme(ly)' (*ultralight*), and produced **outrage**, originally 'extravagance, exaggeration' [via Old French *outre* 'to exceed, to exaggerate', literally 'to go too far', whence modern French *outré* 'eccentric, unusual'], **ultramarine** originally a pigment made from imported lapis lazuli [via Italian *azzurro oltramarino* 'azure from beyond the seas']. Related to Latin *ultimus* 'last, final', whence **penultimate** [with Latin *paene* 'almost'], **ultimate**, and **ultimatum** a final statement of terms.

umbrage [ME. Old French, ultimately from Latin *umbra* 'shade, shadow'] Shade, shadow (–18c), hence **1** something giving shade (16c) **2** a shadowy outline, a vague shape (17c) **3** (grounds for) suspicion (17c); annoyance, offence (*take umbrage*, 18c).
Latin *umbra* was adopted meaning a ghost, and again for the deepest part of a shadow, especially that cast in an eclipse, as opposed to the lighter **penumbra** [with Latin *paene* 'almost']. It produced **adumbrate**, **sombre** [French, ultimately from Latin *sub* 'under' + *umbra*, whence also Spanish *sombrero*], and **umbel** a cluster of small flowers coming from one stalk [via French from Latin *umbella* 'parasol', whence also **umbrella**].

unction [ME. Latin *unctio*, from *ung(u)ere* 'to smear'] The action of anointing with oil for medicinal or religious purposes, specifically **(extreme) unction** the Roman Catholic rite of anointing the sick or dying, hence **1** a spiritual influence (regarded as balm for the soul); (a manner suggesting) real or, later, pretended spiritual earnestness (17c); one expressing appreciation or enjoyment (19c) **2** an ointment, salve, or lubricant (15c); a soothing influence (17c).
Latin *ung(u)ere* is the ancestor of **anoint** (replacing SMEAR), **ointment**, **unctuous** greasy, fatty, or oily, hence, of a person: oily, obsequiously flattering, and **unguent**.

unit [16c. Latin *unus* 'one', probably suggested by DIGIT] One as a whole number and the basis of all numbers, hence **1** **units** the right-hand column in a sum, containing numbers under ten (17c) **2** an individual thing, person, or group that is complete in itself, but forms part of a whole (17c) **3** a quantity adopted as a standard of measurement (18c), hence **(a) (course) unit** a measure of educational achievement representing so many hours of study (19c, *US*) **(b) unit of account** a monetary unit in which accounts are kept, which does not have to correspond to any actual currency (19c).

Descendants of Latin *unus* include NULL*, **uni-** 'one, single, having or consisting of one' (*unicorn*, *unilateral*), **unify**, **union** [(French, from) Latin *unio* 'unity', later 'a large pearl', whence also **onion**, either from a supposed resemblance to a pearl or from the 'unity' formed by the layers], **unique**, *unison* (at SOUND²), **unite** [Latin *unire* 'to join together'], **unity**, and UNIVERSE*.

universe [ME. Via French from Latin *universum* 'the whole world', neuter of *universus* 'turned into one, whole', from *vertere* 'to turn'] **1 in universe** applying to everything and everybody (–15c), outlived by **universal 2 the universe** the cosmos, all existing matter and energy considered as a (systematic) whole (16c), hence **(a)** the world and its inhabitants (17c); the human race; human history **(b)** the sphere in which something exists or happens (17c).

Universe produced **multiverse** an infinite realm of which our universe is only a part. Latin *universum* produced Latin *universitas* 'the whole, the whole number', in late Latin 'guild, college', whence **university**, abbreviated to **versity**, later **varsity**, and now **uni** (*Australia and New Zealand*): cf. COLLEGE. Hence **multiversity** a university with numerous departments, colleges, etc., more than one campus, and affiliated institutions (US). Latin *vertere* is the ancestor of VERSE*.

uphold [ME] To hold up, support, or sustain, hence **1** to keep in good condition, hence **upholder**, **upholdster** someone who mends and/or sells second-hand clothing, furniture, etc., later specifically beds and bedding, evolving into **upholster** (15c), expanded to **upholsterer**, someone who makes, repairs, or sells furniture with a fabric covering, padding, and/or springs (17c), hence **upholstery** these features, whence *upholster* to fit a piece of furniture with them (19c, *US*) **2** to maintain or defend against opposition (15c) **3** to lift up (15c).

urbane [16c. Latin *urbanus*, from *urbs* 'city'] To do with or characteristic of a city or town (replaced by **urban**, 17c), hence sophisticated, courteous, suave (17c, sophistication and refined manners being associated with urban life).

Latin *urbanus* produced **suburb** [via French from Latin *suburbium*] a district immediately outside a city, now a residential area on the outskirts, hence **1 suburban** a resident of a suburb; typical of suburbs or their residents, provincial, conventional, boring: the abbreviation **burb** (*US*) is similarly dismissive. Cf. *subtopia* at UTOPIA **2 exurb** a district beyond the suburbs (1940s, *US*).

use [ME. Via French from, ultimately, Latin *uti*, *us*-] **1** to perform a rite; to follow a custom, hence habitual or common practice; to do something customarily, hence **used to** formerly did or was (*used to smoke/be a teacher*); **be/get used to** be/become accustomed or inured to **2** to employ; the fact of being employed (*in/out of use*) or the way in which something is employed; the power or opportunity to employ (*have the use of a car*); a purpose or function, hence **(a) use (up)** to consume; *use* to take a drug etc. habitually (*c*.1900) **(b)** to deal with or treat in a particular way (15c); to exploit or manipulate **(c)** the effectiveness of what is used or the advantage of using it (*it's no use*, 16c), hence **useful**, **useless (d)** a need (*have no use for*, 17c).

Descendants of Latin *uti* include ABUSE, **disuse** originally to make someone lose a habit, PERUSE, **usual**, **usurp** [via Latin *usurpare* 'to seize for use'], **usury** [Latin *usura* 'use of money lent, interest'], **utensil** [Latin *utensilis* 'fit for use'], UTILITY*, and **utilize**.

utility [ME. Via French from Latin *utilitas* 'useful', from *uti*: see USE*] Usefulness, serviceability, practicality, hence **1** (describing) someone/something (merely) useful (15c): **(a)** e.g. **utility (actor)** who plays the minor roles (19c); **(public) utilities** gas, water, electricity, etc. (1930s); **(utility) truck/vehicle** for passengers and goods (*Australia and New Zealand*, often shortened to **ute**), **sport utility vehicle** or **SUV** one that can be driven on- or off-road (1980s, US); **utility program/routine** a computer program that performs a routine task (1960s) **(b)** (describing) clothing and household goods made to an official standard using only the materials allowed (World War II) **2** the ability to satisfy the needs and desires of the majority (18c), hence **utilitarianism** the greatest good of the greatest number as a guiding principle (19c).

Utopia [16c. Ultimately from Greek *ou* 'not, no' and *topos* 'place'] The title of a treatise by the scholar and statesman Thomas More (b.1478) which contrasted England with the perfect society of the imaginary land of Utopia, hence an ideal state or place: *utopia* and its opposite, **dystopia** (19c), come together in **suptopia** suburbia regarded either as an ideal place or a soulless urban sprawl (1950s).

Greek *topos* was adopted for a traditional theme in literature or rhetoric, and is the ancestor of **ectopic** [Greek *ektopos* 'out of place'], **isotope** [with Greek *isos* 'equal, same'] one of two or more atoms with the same atomic number (hence the same place in the periodic table), but different numbers of neutrons, **topiary** [via French from Latin *topia* 'ornamental gardening', from Greek *topion* 'field', literally 'small place'], TOPIC, **topical** meaning 'local', and **topography**.

utter [Old English *ūtera*, from *ūt* 'out'] Further out; (towards) the outside; further from the centre (replaced by **outer**), hence at the furthest or most extreme point (ME); complete, absolute.

Old English *ūt* is also found in BUT*. Related to **utter** to say [early Dutch *ūteren* 'to drive or send out'].

V

vagary [16c. Latin *vagari* 'to wander', from *vagus* 'wandering, uncertain'] To ramble or wander, a ramble (–19c), hence a wandering from the subject or from accepted norms (–18c); a prank; a whim (17c); an unpredictable change.

Latin *vagari* produced EXTRAVAGANT* and **vagabond** originally a criminal, and probably influenced **vagrant** [believed to be an alteration of Old French *wacrant*, from *wacrer* 'to wander', of Germanic origin]. Latin *vagus* produced French *vague*, and was adopted describing nerves serving the heart, lungs, stomach, and various other organs.

vain [ME. Via French from Latin *vanus* 'empty, without substance'] Without real worth or significance, hence **1** ineffectual, futile, hence **vanity** futility, something worthless or futile **2** foolish, thoughtless; conceited, especially about your appearance. Hence *vanity* such conceit, hence **vanity case** for cosmetics, a mirror, etc. (*c*.1900), **vanity publishing** at the author's expense (1960s), **vanity unit** a washbasin set into a dressing table (1970s), earlier in the trade name **Vanitory** [1950s, US, on the pattern of *lavatory*] **3** something (worthless) that you are proud of or attached to (17c), hence **Vanity Fair** a place of frivolous entertainment and worthless show (coined by John Bunyan in *Pilgrim's Progress*, 1678).

Latin *vanus* produced **evanescent** [via *evanescere* 'to pass or die away', whence **vanish**] and **vaunt** to brag [via late Latin *vanitare* 'to talk frivolously'].

valet [15c. Old French *vaslet*, from a medieval Latin word, probably of Celtic origin] A horseman's servant, hence **1** a gentleman's servant responsible for his master's clothes and appearance (16c); a man in a hotel etc. who cares for guests' clothes (19c); to be a valet; to look after clothes etc. (1930s) **2** **valet parking** a service provided by a restaurant etc. where attendants park and retrieve customers' cars (1960s). Hence **3** (a person employed) to clean and/or park cars (1970s).

Old French **varlet** [a variant of *vaslet*] was adopted for a male servant or groom, later a rascal, or as a (mock) contemptuous form of address for either. Probably related to **vassal**.

valid [16c. (Via French from) Latin *validus* 'strong, well', from *valere* 'to be strong'] **1** legally acceptable or binding, hence **validate** to make valid, to ratify (18c) **2** of an argument etc.: well-founded and relevant (17c); effective, having some force, hence *validate* to confirm truth or effectiveness (18c); to examine data for accuracy (1950s) **3** of a person: healthy, robust (17c), surviving mainly in **invalid** infirm or disabled; such a person (18c); to treat someone as infirm; **invalid out** to release from active service because of injury or sickness.

Latin *vale* [literally 'be well', from *valere*], was used as a way of saying goodbye, and appears in *valedicere* 'to say vale', whence **valediction** a farewell, a farewell speech. Other descendants of *valere* include AVAIL, **ambivalent**, **convalesce**, **equivalent**, **valency**, **Valentine** ('sweetheart' and related senses came about because two Italian saints of that name had their feast day on 14 February, when, traditionally, birds choose their mates), **Valerie**, **valetudinary** in poor health, delicate [Latin *valetudo* 'state of health'], **valiant** originally also 'strong, robust, well-built', and VALUE*.

value [ME. Old French, from *valoir* 'to be worth', from Latin *valere*: see VALID*] **1** material or monetary worth; to judge or estimate this (15c), a sense shared by **evaluate** [18c, French *evaluer*, from Old French *value*]. Hence **valuable** able to be evaluated (17c only, 16c and surviving in **invaluable**) **2** status, especially that earned in battle (–17c), hence courage, fortitude (outlived by **valour**, also from Latin *valere*) **3** what something is worth to you, hence **(a)** to regard as important or precious (16c) **(b) values** the principles or standards important to a person or society (early 20c) **4** a (relative) size, quantity, number (16c), or quality (18c).

valve [ME. Latin *valva*] One leaf of a double or folding door, hence **1** one half of the hinged shell of a mussel or similar creature (17c): also applied in botany and zoology to other halves or paired organs **2** a device, originally opening like a door, that allows a flow in one direction (17c).

vamp [ME. Old French *avantpié*, from *avant* 'in front' (from late Latin *abante*: see ADVANCE) + *pied* 'foot' (from Latin *pes*, *ped-*, ancestor of PIONEER*)] The foot of a stocking; the front of a shoe (17c). Hence to provide with a new vamp (16c); to refurbish or renovate (partly replaced by 19c **revamp**); to put together from old materials (17c); to present as new; to improvise an accompaniment etc. (18c).

vandal [Old English *Wendlas* (plural), later also from Latin *Vandalus*, of Germanic origin] A member of a Germanic people that sacked Rome in AD 455, hence someone who attacks or destroys something beautiful, valuable, or useful (17c), hence **vandalism** (18c), **vandalize** (19c).

vanilla [17c. Spanish *vainilla* 'small pod', from *vaina* 'sheath, pod', from Latin *vagina* 'sheath, scabbard'] A kind of tropical climbing orchid; a fragrant substance originally derived from a vanilla pod and used in perfumery and to flavour food, especially ice cream, where it was the basic flavour, hence vanilla-flavoured or coloured (19c); ordinary, plain, unexciting (1970s); basic, without extras.

Latin *vagina* produced **evaginate** to turn a tubular organ inside out, and was adopted for the tube between the vulva and cervix.

vaudeville [18c. French, from *vau de ville*, alteration of *(chanson du) Vau de Vire* '(song of) the valley of Vire' (in Normandy), a kind of convivial song originally composed by Olivier Basselin, a 15c fuller and poet born in Vire] A satirical or topical song, especially one sung on the stage, hence a stage play or comedy with songs (19c); variety, music hall (US).

vault [ME. Old French *voute*, *vaute*, ultimately from Latin *volvere* 'to roll'] An arch or series of arches forming a roof over a space in a building, hence **1** an enclosed space with an arched roof; one (partly) underground, used as a storeroom (15c);

a burial chamber (16c) **2** something resembling an arched ceiling, e.g. the sky (*vault of heaven*, 15c); a structure in the body (16c).

Latin *volvere*'s descendants include **convolute** and **convolvulus** [both via Latin *convolvere* 'to coil round'], **devolve** [Latin *devolvere* 'to roll down'], **evolve** [Latin *evolvere* 'to unfold, to roll out'], **involve**, REVOLVE*, **vault** to leap [via French *vo(u)lter* 'to turn a horse', also 'to gambol or leap'], French *volte* [from Italian *volta* 'a turn'] originally a lively dance in which each partner lifts the other off the ground (16–17c), later a sudden movement to avoid a thrust in fencing, now a circular movement made by a horse in dressage (also found in *volte-face* [literally 'turn face'] a sudden complete change in attitude or opinion), VOLUBLE, VOLUME*, **volute** a spiral shape or object, a spiral-shelled mollusc, and **Volvo** [Latin *volvo* 'I roll', the name of a subsidiary of a ball-bearing company where designers of the original car worked].

veer [16c. French *virer* 'to turn', perhaps ultimately from Latin *gyrare* 'to turn round', from *gyrus* 'ring, circle', from Greek *guros*] Of the wind: to change direction; of a ship: to turn away from the wind (17c), hence, generally, to change direction, especially suddenly or uncontrollably, to swerve.

French *virer* produced **environ** to surround, whence **environment** and **environs**. Latin *gyrus* was adopted for a convolution in the brain. Descendants of Greek *guros* include **autogiro**, Italian *girasole* (SEE ARTICHOKE), Italian *giro* a circuit, also the circulation of money, whence [via German] a system of transferring money between banks etc., later adopted by the British Post Office, hence a social security or similar cheque cashable at the Post Office (1970s), **gyre**, largely replaced by related **gyrate**, and **gyro-** in *gyroscope* etc.

vegetable [15c. (Old French, from) Latin *vegetabilis* 'animate, able to grow', from Latin *vegetare* 'to animate', from *vegere* 'to be active'] Living and growing as a plant (–17c), hence **1** a plant (16c); an edible one (18c) **2** to do with, consisting of, or derived from, a plant or plants (16c).

Vegetable produced **vegan** and **vegetarian**. Latin *vegetare* produced **vegetate**, which has the paradoxical meanings **1** to grow or sprout **2** to have a boring or empty life, to stagnate, whence *vegetable* someone leading such a life or being in a **vegetative state** with little physical and mental function; **veg out** to kill time in meaningless inactivity.

vehement [ME. (Via French from) Latin *vehemens* 'impetuous, carried away', perhaps ultimately from *vehere* 'to carry' + *mens* 'mind'] Of pain, heat, wind, etc.: strong, intense, severe, hence done or said forcefully (15c); of thoughts or feelings: strong, fervent (16c).

Latin *vehere* is the ancestor of VEHICLE*, *mens* produced **demented** and **mental**, and is related to **comment**, **mention**, and **reminisce**.

vehicle [17c. (Via French from) Latin *vehiculum*, from *vehere*, *vect-* 'to carry'] **1** a liquid etc. with which a substance is mixed to make it easier to use or apply **2** a means or medium for conveying ideas; the literal meaning of words used metaphorically (1930s: the opposite of TENOR sense 1) **3** a conveyance **4** a film, song, etc. intended to display a particular performer's talents (19c).

Latin *vehere* produced **convection**, **invective** abusive [the noun is later, from Latin *invectiva (oratio)* 'abusive or censorious (language)'], **inveigh**, **vector**, and perhaps VEHEMENT.

velvet [ME. Via Old French from, ultimately, Latin *villus* 'hair, tuft, down'] (Made of) a soft fabric with a short dense pile, hence **1** the soft downy skin covering a deer's growing antler (15c) **2** soft and smooth like velvet, hence **velvet revolution** [translating Czech *sametová revoluce*, referring to the events leading to the end of communist rule in 1989] a non-violent political revolution **3** gain, profit, especially winnings (*c.*1900); **to the velvet** to the good.

Velvet produced **velveteen**, a similar cotton fabric. Latin *villus* was adopted for a long hair or hairlike growth (usually as the plural *villae*), and produced **velour** a similar fabric to velvet [via French *velours*, whence the tradename **Velcro**, from *velours croché* 'hooked velvet'], French *velouté* [literally 'velvety'] adopted for a rich white sauce, and **velutinous** describing a plant etc. covered in short, soft hairs [via Italian *vellutino* 'velvety'].

venal [17c. Latin *venalis*, from *venum* 'thing for sale'] For sale, able to be bought, hence of support, a post, privilege, etc.: obtainable for a payment or bribe; of a person: able to be bribed; of a person, system, or conduct: corrupt (18c).

Latin *venum* is one parent of **vend**, the other being Latin *dare* 'to give': see DATA*.

venerable [ME. (French, from) Latin *venerabilis*, from *venerari* 'to revere'] Worthy of reverence because of religious or historical associations or, later, age, hence **1** as a title: in the Roman Catholic church, for someone who has reached the first stage of canonization; in the Anglican church: for an archdeacon **2** ancient, old (18c).

Latin *venerari* produced **venerate**. Related to Latin *venus*, *vener-* 'love, desire', whence **venereal** and **Venus** (the planet named after) the Roman goddess of love. Despite similarities in form, meaning, and use, **reverence**, **reverend**, and **revere** are not related, being from Latin *vereri* 'to be in awe of'.

vent [ME. (Via French from) Latin *ventus* 'wind'] (To provide with) an opening through which a gas or liquid can escape (ME), or air or light get in (16c), hence **1** the anus, now only of an animal or bird (15c) **2** an outlet for an emotion etc. (16c); to release or express emotion; such release (17c) **3** a hole or crack (16c); the touch hole of a cannon etc. (17c); **ventage** a finger hole in a wind instrument.

Latin *ventus* produced **ventail** the part of a knight's helmet that can be raised to let air in, and **ventilate** [via *ventilare* 'to fan or winnow' (the original sense in English)]. **Vent** 'slit in the back of a garment' is a variant of **fent** [via French from, ultimately, Latin *findere* 'to split', whence **fission** and **fissure**].

venue [ME. French, from *venir* 'to come', from Latin *venire*] **1** a hostile approach, an attack (ME only), re-emerging in fencing as a hit, thrust, or wound (16c), also a bout (replaced by the variant **veny**) **2** a former legal term for the locality in which a case must be tried, originally near the scene of the crime (16c), hence the scene of, or a place for, an action or event (19c).

Latin *venire* is the ancestor of ADVENTURE*, AVENUE*, **circumvent**, CONVENE, CONVENT, **event** [Latin *envenire* 'to happen', literally 'to come out'], **intervene**, INVENT*, **prevent** [via Latin *praevenire* 'to anticipate, to hinder', literally 'to come before'], French *revenue* [from *revenir* 'to return', from Latin *revenire*], and French *souvenir* [from *souvenir* 'to remember', from Latin *subvenire* 'to come to mind'].

vermin [ME. Old French, ultimately from Latin *vermis* 'worm'] Snakes and other reptiles considered harmful; animals, birds, insects, etc. harmful to game, domestic animals, or crops, hence **1** such a creature (15c) **2** despicable people, a despicable person (16c). Hence the variant **varmint** such a creature or person (16c).

Descendants of Latin *vermis* include Italian **vermicelli**, literally 'little worms', **vermiculated** covered or ornamented with fine wavy lines, like worms, **vermiculite** a hydrous silicate aluminium, magnesium, or iron [because flakes of it expand into long, writhing shapes when heated], **vermiculture** the cultivation of earthworms to produce compost, **vermiform** wormlike (*vermiform appendix*), and **vermillion** [via Old French: the underlying sense is 'worm-coloured'].

verse [Old English *fers*, later also French *vers*, from Latin *versus* 'a turn of the plough, a furrow, a line of writing', from *vertere* 'to turn'] A line of poetry, hence **1** to compose such lines (largely replaced by **versify** [ME, from Latin *versificare*]); a group of them (ME), hence **(a)** poetry **(b)** a stanza; part of a song between choruses (1920s) **2** a clause or sentence, especially an article of the Creed (–16c); a short (biblical) sentence as part of the liturgy (largely replaced by **versicle** [ME, from Latin *versiculus* 'short verse']); a short division of a Bible chapter (16c).

Latin *vertere*'s offspring include **anniversary** [Latin *anniversarius* 'returning yearly', from *annus* 'year'], **retrovert** (at RETROGRADE), **revers** [Latin *revertere* 'to turn back', whence **reverse** and **revert**], **transverse** [late Latin *tra(n)sversare*, literally 'to turn across', whence **traverse**, and the names **Maltravers** a bad crossing, **Travers**, and **Travis**], **versed** knowledgeable about [via Latin *versari* 'to occupy yourself with', from *versare* 'to keep turning' (whence **versatile**)], **version**, Latin *verso* [literally 'being turned'], adopted for the left-hand page of a book or the back of a leaf, coin, etc., Latin *versus* [literally 'turned towards', in medieval Latin '(turned) against'], **vertigo** [Latin, literally 'spinning'], and *vice versa* (at VICAR). Other descendants include ADVERTISE*, **avert**, **controversy**, CONVERSE*, CONVERT, DIVERS*, **evert**, INTROVERT*, **inverse**, **invert**, **obverse**, PERVERT, PROSAIC, **subvert**, UNIVERSE*, **version**, **vertebra**, and VERTEX*.

vertex [ME. Latin, 'whirlpool' (surviving in the variant **vortex**), later 'crown of the head, highest point', from *vertere*: see VERSE*] **1** the crown or top of the head; the highest point (17c), specifically that of a celestial body's apparent motion **2** the point of a triangle or pyramid opposite and furthest from the base (16c), hence **vertical** situated at or passing through this; at right angles to the horizontal (18c); upright, hence consisting of, or to do with, different levels or stages (19c). Hence **vert** in skateboarding, snowboarding, etc.: (a manoeuvre performed on) a more or less vertical surface (1990s).

very [ME. Via Old French from, ultimately, Latin *verus* 'true'] Rightly named, true, genuine, hence **1** truly, really, extremely **2** complete, absolute, in the fullest sense **3** exact, right (*the very man!*).

Descendants of Latin *verus* include **veracious**, **veracity**, **verdict** [with Latin *dicere* 'to say' (ancestor of DICTATE*)], **verify**, **verily**, *verisimilitude* (at SIMULATE), **veritable**, **verity**, and the name **Veronica** [Latin *vera icon* 'true image'], from the legend of a woman who wiped Christ's face with her veil on the way to his crucifixion, the veil being left with an image of his face. The woman became known as St Veronica and a cloth or other object bearing Christ's face as a *veronica* or **vernicle**: *veronica* in bullfighting is said to come from the matador holding out the cape to the bull, like St Veronica offering her veil. Despite its appearance the name **Vera** is actually from a Russian word meaning 'faith'.

vessel [ME. Via Anglo-Norman and Old French from late Latin *vascellum*, 'small dish, vase', also 'ship', from *vas* 'dish, utensil' (whence **vase**)] **1** a ship or boat; an airship (*c.*1915); a hovercraft (1950s) **2** (gold or silver) dishes and utensils collectively; any receptacle, hence **(a)** a person who embodies a particular quality **(b)** a tube or duct in the body containing liquid: also as Latin *vas*, whence **vascular** to do with such a structure or structures, especially the blood vessels (17c); *vas deferens* a sperm duct (16c, *deferens* from Latin *deferre* 'to carry away': see DEFER*], whence **vasectomy** surgical cutting and tying off of the sperm ducts (19c), and **vaso-** (*vasodilator, vasomotor*).

vest [15c. Ultimately from Latin *vestis* 'garment, clothing', the verb via Latin *vestire* 'to clothe'] **1** to establish someone in a position of authority (from the idea of dressing them in the appropriate robes: largely replaced by **invest**); to give someone power, authority, or property, hence **vested interest** (a person or group having) a (future) interest in property etc. recognized as belonging to them (18c); an interest in protecting or promoting something for your own advantage, hence **vested interests** those who try to maintain or control a system etc. for their own benefit **2** to (formally or ceremonially) dress someone in a robe etc. (16c) **3** a robe or gown (17c); a man's long sleeveless garment worn under a coat, hence **(a)** a (sleeveless or short-sleeved) undergarment for the upper body (19c); a similar garment worn as a casual top; an athlete's singlet in the team's colours (1970s) **(b)** a short sleeveless jacket (*c.*1900, N American); (also **vestee**) a waistcoat.

Descendants of Latin *vestis* include **divest**, **transvestism** [via German], **travesty** [from French *travestir* 'to change clothes, to disguise', from Italian *travestire*], **vestment** a (ceremonial) garment, especially a clergyman's, and **vestry** the part of a church etc. where vestments are kept.

veteran [16c. Via French from Latin *veteranus*, from *vetus* 'old'] Someone with long experience, originally a soldier, hence **1** long-serving, experienced (17c) **2** old, long-lasting (17c); **veteran car** made before 1919 or, strictly speaking, before 1905 (cf. VINTAGE) **3** anyone who has served in the armed forces (18c, sometimes shortened to **vet**, 19c).

Latin *vetus* produced INVETERATE and perhaps **veterinary** [Latin *veterinus* 'to do with (mature) cattle or beasts of burden'].

vicar [ME. Via Old French from Latin *vicarius* 'substitute, deputy', from *vix, vic-* 'turn, position, change'] Christ or the Holy Ghost as representing God; a person representing God on earth, originally St Peter or the Pope, also a parish priest, later specifically an Anglican priest in charge of a parish who receives a salary but not the tithes (16c); a priest in the Roman Catholic church or a lay person in the Anglican church who stands in for a bishop or rector.

Latin *vicarius* produced **vicarious** being, or done by, a substitute, later experienced through another by imagination. Latin *vix* is the ancestor of **vice-** 'deputy' (*vice-president*), *vice* in **vice versa** literally 'the position being reversed' [with *vertere* 'to turn' (ancestor of VERSE*)], VICISSITUDE, the surnames **Vickar(y)**, **Vicker(y)** (a layman who substituted for) an absentee clergyman, and **Vickers** a clergyman's son or servant, and *viscount* (at POSSE).

vice¹ [ME. French, from Latin *vitium* 'fault, flaw'] Moral depravity, hence **1** immoral or criminal activity, especially involving prostitution, pornography, or drugs; a bad habit or addiction **2** a flaw in someone's character; an animal's bad temperament (18c). Hence **vicious** depraved, immoral (ME); bad-tempered (18c); spiteful, violent, savage (19c).

Latin *vitium* is the ancestor of **vitiate** and **vituperate** [Latin *vituperare* 'to accuse of a fault', with *parare* 'to prepare' (ancestor of PARADE*)].

vice² [ME. French *vis* from Latin *vitis* 'tendril, vine' (whence **viticulture**)] **1** a spiral staircase **2** a screw; a device (now for gripping) operated by one.

vicissitude [16c. (French, from) Latin *vicissitudo*, from *vicissim* 'by turns', from *vix, vic-*: see VICAR*] Change, variability **(a)** regular change, especially from one extreme to another, hence **vicissitudes** the ups and downs of life (17c).

victual [ME. Old French *vitaille* from late Latin *victualia*, from Latin *victus* 'food, nourishment', from *vivare* 'to live'. Originally spelt *vitail*, the *c* was added in the 17c following a similar change in French to conform to the Latin. The original spelling survives in the pronunciation and in the variant **vittles**] Food, hence **victuals** provisions, supplies; *victual* **1** to supply (especially an army or ship) with provisions; **licensed victualler** a publican (19c) **2** to lay in stores (17c).

Descendants of Latin *vivare* include CONVIVIAL, **revive**, **survive**, **viand** [French, from Latin *vivenda* 'things for living'], VIPER*, **vivacious**, **vivarium** originally a warren or fish pond, medieval Latin *viva voce* [literally 'with the living voice'] orally, now an oral examination following a written one, usually shortened to **viva**, which also means to give or undergo one, the names **Vivian** and **Vivienne**, **vivid** originally 'full of life', **vivify**, and **vivisection**, whence **vivisect**.

vie [16c. Shortening of *envy* (ME–17c), via French *envier* from Latin *invitare* 'to invite, summon, or challenge' (whence **invite**)] **1** in card playing: to bet a certain amount on the strength of your hand (–17c); to declare that you can win **2** to set one thing against another (–19c); to compete with, to rival (17c).

view [ME. Anglo-Norman French *vewe*, Old French *vëue*, from *vëoir* 'to see', from Latin *videre*] The act of seeing or observing, hence **1** a formal inspection, now mainly of objects for sale, hence to inspect something (now especially a property) you may wish to buy (16c) **2** mental perception or contemplation; to contemplate or consider something (16c); your way of doing so, your attitude or opinion **3** what you can see, especially a landscape seen from a particular place (16c); a painting etc. of this (17c).

Old French *vëue* evolved into *vu*, which appears in *déjà vu* [literally 'already seen'], and Old French *vëoir* into *voir*, whence *clairvoyant* literally 'clear-seeing', **interview**, and *voyeur*. Latin *videre* is the ancestor of VISION*.

vigil [ME. Via French from Latin *vigilia*, from *vigil* 'awake, watchful'] The day or night before a holy day as a time of prayer, hence (usually **vigils**) prayer or a religious service at this time (15c); nocturnal prayers; *vigil* a period of staying awake or keeping watch through the night (17c); a stationary, peaceful, and often silent demonstration in support of a cause (1950s).

Latin *vigil* produced *invigilare* 'to keep watch', whence **invigilate** originally simply 'to watch over', **vigilant**, Spanish *vigilante* (US), and French *veiller*, whence *reveille* [French *reveiller* 'to wake up'] and *surveillance* [from French *surveiller* 'to watch over']. Related to Latin *vigere* 'to be lively', whence **invigorate** and **vigour**.

vignette [ME. Old French, literally 'small vine', from *vigne* 'vine', from Latin *vinum* (ancestor of VINTAGE*)] A carved decoration of leaves and tendrils; a small decorative design (originally of a vine) printed in the margin of a book, later in any blank space (18c); one that shades away at the edges, hence (to produce) a photograph of someone's head and shoulders with the edges shading into the background (19c); a short description of a person, later an anecdote, a short essay, or an evocative episode in a play etc.

vilify [15c. Late Latin *vilificare* from Latin *vilis* 'cheap, worth little' (ancestor of **revile** and **vile**)] To reduce the value of (–19c); to regard as worthless (16–17c), hence to disparage, to defame or revile.

village [ME. Old French, from Latin *villa* 'country house, farm'] A rural community larger than a hamlet; its inhabitants (16c), hence **1** a small self-contained district or community within a town (*Greenwich village*); a temporary one (*Olympic village*, 1970s) **2** a group of bird or animal dwellings (19c) **3** an out-of-town shopping centre (1980s, *Australian*).

VILLAIN, **-ville** in place names, and the surname **Villiers** all come via French from Latin *villa*, which now usually means a (semi-)detached house in a residential district or a holiday home abroad.

villain [ME. Old French *vilain, vilein* from medieval Latin *villanus* 'villager', from Latin *villa*: see VILLAGE*] A peasant (surviving in **villein** a serf), a churlish rustic (cf. CHURL*), later a scoundrel, hence an evil character, the hero's main enemy in a play etc. (19c); a culprit, hence **1** a troublesome person or animal (19c) **2** a professional criminal (1960s).

Old French *vilein* may be the ancestor of **nasty** originally 'disgustingly dirty' [perhaps from Old French *nastre*, short for *villenastre*, from *vilein* + the derogatory suffix *-astre* (from Latin *-aster*, also found in **poetaster**)]. Medieval Latin *villanus* produced Italian **villanella** a rustic Italian part-song, whence French **villanelle** in the same sense (16–17c), re-adopted for a kind of pastoral or lyric poem (19c).

vindicate [16c. Latin *vindicare* 'to claim' also 'to liberate or avenge', from *vindex* 'a claimant', later 'a protector, liberator, or avenger' (from the idea of claiming on someone else's behalf)] **1** to vent your anger by taking revenge (16c only); to avenge or revenge (17–18c) **2** to claim something for yourself; to defend a cause or right (17c) **3** to set free (–18c); to free from suspicion or blame (17c); to justify or prove right.

Latin *vindicare* produced **avenge** [via French *vengier*, whence **revenge**, **vengeance**, and **vengeful**] and **vindictive** [via Latin *vindicta* 'vengeance', whence also Italian **vendetta**].

vintage [ME. Via French from Latin *vindemia*, from *vinum* 'wine' + *demere* 'to remove', from *emere* 'to buy, get, or take'] (The time of) grape harvesting; the grapes or the wine produced from them, hence **1** the yield in a season, especially that of a particular district or vineyard; the wine made from it, hence (describing) wine produced from a named district in a good year (18c), hence classic, the best or most typical of its time or kind (*vintage Hitchcock*, 19c) **2** the time when someone was born or something was produced (19c); describing something made in a certain period; **vintage car** made between 1919 and 1930 (cf. VETERAN).

Descendants of Latin *vinum* include VIGNETTE, **vindaloo** [Portuguese *vin d'alho* 'wine and garlic sauce'], **vine**, **vinegar** [via French *vinaigre* (whence *vinaigrette*), from Old French *vyn egre* 'sour wine', with Latin *acer* 'sour' (ancestor of ACID*)], **vintner**, **vinyl**, **wine** [via Old English *wīn*], and surnames such as **Vine(s)**, **Vyner**, and **Winyard**. Latin *emere* is the ancestor of EXAMPLE*.

violate [ME. Latin *violare* 'to treat with violence', from *vis* 'force, power'] **1** to break or disregard a law, promise, etc., hence to accuse a convict of, or find them guilty of, violating the terms of their parole (1970s, *US*) **2** to assault sexually, to rape (15c) **3** to treat with disrespect: **(a)** to desecrate or defile (15c), hence desecrated, profaned; impure, corrupt (more common in **inviolate**) **(b)** to interrupt or disturb rudely (17c).

Latin *violare* produced **inviolable**; *vis* produced **vim** and **violent**, and is found in sundry Latin phrases (none of them common): its plural, *vires*, appears in the legal phrases **intra** and **ultra vires** within/beyond someone's authority or powers.

viper [16c. (Via French from) Latin *vipera* 'snake', from *vivus* 'living' (from *vivare* 'to live') + *parere* 'to get, beget, or give birth'] Applied to various poisonous snakes, especially the adder, hence a spiteful, treacherous, or ungrateful person (from Aesop's fable, in which a farmer finds a frozen viper and warms it under his clothes, whereupon it bites him); cf. *snake* (at WORM).

Latin *vipera* produced **wyvern** originally a viper (ME–15c), now a winged dragon with two legs and a barbed tail. Latin *vivare* produced VICTUAL*; *parere* produced REPERTORY*, the two together producing **viviparous** 'bearing live young'.

virago [OE. Latin, from *vir* 'man'] **1** woman (–16c, with reference to the Vulgate translation of the Bible, Genesis 2:23, where Adam names Eve *Virago* because she comes from man: the King James Version says *woman*) **2** a vigorous woman, an Amazon (the Latin sense, ME), hence a domineering or abusive one.

Latin *vir* is the ancestor of **virile**, VIRTUE*, and perhaps *were* in *werewolf* (at MAN).

virtue [ME. Via French from Latin *virtus* 'manliness', hence 'courage, strength, skill', etc., from *vir*: see VIRAGO*] **1** power, efficacy, or influence: **(a)** that of a supernatural being (–19c); such a being, especially one of the fifth order of the celestial hierarchy (see ANGEL) **(b)** the magical (healing) power of a stone etc. (–16c); the efficacy of a herb, drug, etc. **(c) by virtue of** by the power, or later, authority of, through, because of **(d)** a particular power or beneficial quality **2** behaviour showing high moral standards; a morally good quality; chastity (16c).

Christian virtues (e.g. *faith, charity, grace, mercy, prudence*) were popular with Puritans as girls' names: other Puritan names, such as *Fly-fornication* and *Repentance*, were mercifully short-lived. Latin *virtus* produced Italian **virtu** (love of or expertise in) the fine arts, and *virtuoso* 'learned, skilled', adopted for a learned person (17–18c), now an extremely skilful one, and **virtual** having certain virtues or strengths, hence in effect, more or less (*traffic at a virtual standstill*); appearing to exist, now owing to computer software (*virtual reality*).

virus [ME. Latin, 'slimy liquid, poison'] **1** venom **2** a substance produced in the body by a disease which can pass the disease on to others (18c), hence **(a)** a morally corrupting influence (18c); an infectious fear **(b)** a minute parasitic particle that can only replicate within living cells, often causing disease (19c); such a disease (1950s) **(c) (computer)** virus a self-replicating program that can destroy or interfere with other programs (1970s).

Latin *virus* produced *virulentus* 'poisonous', whence **virulent** of a wound etc.: containing poison, purulent (15–18c); (extremely) poisonous, noxious, or harmful; bitter, spiteful.

visage   [ME. French, from Old French *vis* 'face', from Latin *visus* 'sight, appearance', from *videre*, *vis-* 'to see'] **1** someone's face or expression, hence the face or visible side of the sun or moon **2** the appearance or look of something (15c).

French *visage* produced **envisage** to look at, to regard in a particular way, to imagine as a future possibility. Old French *vis* produced VISOR and appears in **vis-à-vis** [literally 'face to face'], now usually meaning 'regarding, to do with'. Latin *visus* produced **visual**, whence **visualize** 'to form a mental image of'; *videre* is the ancestor of VISION*.

vision   [ME. French, from Latin *videre*, *vis-* 'to see'] **1** something seen in a dream, trance, etc. and regarded as significant or prophetic, hence **(a)** imaginative insight or foresight, far-sightedness (15c); **visionary** far-sighted, percipient (17c) **(b)** to see (as if) in a vision, to imagine (18c), largely replaced by **envision**, or by *envisage* or *visualize* at VISAGE), hence *visionary* imaginative, fanciful; impractical, unlikely to be realized **2** the ability to see, sight (15c); the visual component of a television broadcast (*c.*1910).

Descendants of Latin *videre* include ADVICE, Italian **belvedere** [literally 'beautiful sight'] a summerhouse etc. with a view, **evident** and **evidence** (that makes something evident), INVIDIOUS*, PROVIDE*, PROVIDENCE*, REVIEW*, **supervise** and **survey** [both via Latin *supervidere* 'to oversee'], **video(-)**, VIEW*, **visa** [French from Latin, literally 'things seen'] originally an endorsement in a passport showing that it has been examined, VISAGE*, **visible**, **visit** [via French from Latin *visitare* 'to go to see'], and Italian *vista* a view.

visor   [ME. Old French *visiere*, from *vis* 'face': see VISAGE*] **1** the movable front part of a helmet, hence the peak of a cap (like a raised visor, 19c, *US*); an eyeshade resembling it; a small screen to shield your eyes from glare (1920s) **2** a mask, later altered to **vizard** (16c).

vital   [ME. (Via French from) Latin *vitalis*, from *vita* 'life'] To do with life, the life force, or, later, living things, hence **1** essential to life or continuing effectiveness (*vital organs*, 15c); extremely important, paramount (17c) **2** full of life or energy (15c); invigorating (17c) **3** capable of living (17c), replaced by **viable** [19c, French, from *vie* 'life', from Latin *vita*].

Latin *vitalis* produced **vitality** the life force, later energy, liveliness. *Vita* produced **vitamin** [with **amine**, a derivative of ammonia, which vitamins were mistakenly thought to contain], and appears in *aqua vitae* [literally 'water of life'], adopted for a strong spirit, especially brandy, whence Norwegian, Swedish, and Danish *aquavit* and French *eau de vie*. The same idea appears in **whisky** [from **usquebaugh**, from Gaelic *uisge* 'water' + *beatha* 'life'].

vitriol   [ME. (French, or) medieval Latin *vitriolum*, from Latin *vitrum* 'glass'] Applied to sulphates of various substances with a glassy appearance, hence

(oil of) vitriol sulphuric acid; *vitriol* (an expression of) extreme bitterness and hatred (18c).

Latin *vitrum* is the ancestor of **vitreous**, **vitrify**, and French *vitrine* a glass display case.

vogue [16c. French, literally 'rowing', hence 'smooth course, trend, fashion', probably of Germanic origin and related to WAG*] **1** natural bent (16c only); general tendency or character (17–18c) **2** the greatest popularity (–18c); (short-lived) popularity (*in vogue*, 17c); the prevailing fashion; fashionable. Hence **vogueing** a form of dance that imitates the postures of fashion models (1980s, US, named after the fashion magazine *Vogue*).

voice [ME. Via Old French from Latin *vox, voc-*] The sound made by the vocal organs, hence **1** someone's style of speaking, singing, etc. **2** the right or opportunity to express an opinion; (the expression of) people's opinion or will; to express an opinion, emotion, etc. in speech (17c) **3** a singer (16c); a vocal part in music (17c) **4** to utter a sound with the vocal cords loosely together, giving vibration or resonance (19c); **voiced/voiceless** having/not having this quality **5** to be the unseen narrator of a film etc., or the 'voice' of a cartoon character (1940s); **voice-over** narration by an unseen voice.

Latin *vox* produced *aequivocus*, literally 'equal-voiced', whence **equivocal** uncertain, ambiguous, questionable, and **equivocate** to use a word in more than one sense or apply it to more than one thing (–17c), hence to speak ambiguously or evasively, *viva voce* (at VICTUAL), **vocal**, **vociferate**, **vowel**, and *vox populi* [literally 'voice of the people'], whence **vox pop** impromptu comments from members of the public, gathered by an interviewer, especially for a broadcast. Related to VOUCH*.

void [ME. Old French *voider* 'to empty', *voide* 'empty, vacant', from an alteration of Latin *vocivus, vacivus*, a variant of *vacuus*, from *vacare* 'to be empty'] **1** originally of a benefice: vacant, hence unoccupied, empty; emptiness; a vast empty space (*the void*, 17c) **2** to empty; to excrete (15c); this act (1980s) **3** free from or lacking, outlived by **devoid** [ME, from Old French *devoidier*, literally 'to empty out'] **4** of speech or an action: useless, ineffective, hence (to make something) legally invalid **5** to leave a place, to withdraw (–17c); to shun, to keep away or escape from; to ward off (17c).

Old French *voide* produced **avoid**, which shared *void*'s verbal senses and replaced it in sense 5. Latin *vacuus* produced **evacuate**, **vacuous**, and Latin *vacuum*; *vacare* is the ancestor of **vacant**, **vacate** originally 'to make null and void', and **vacation**.

volatile [ME. (Via Old French from) Latin, from *volatilis* 'flying', from *volare* 'to fly'] **1** birds collectively, especially wildfowl (–17c); any winged creature **2** of meal: fine, light, apt to fly about (16c only); (capable of) flying (17c), hence **(a)** moving or flitting (rapidly) from place to place **(b)** of a substance: tending to evaporate at relatively low temperatures; transient, changeable, unstable, hence of markets, shares, etc.: subject to sudden fluctuations (1930s); of a computer: losing data when the power is switched off (1950s) **(c)** of a person: changeable, moody, unpredictable, fickle (17c).

Latin *volatile* appears in ***sal volatile*** [literally 'volatile salt'], adopted for ammonium carbonate used as smelling salts. Latin *volare* is the ultimate ancestor of French ***vol-au-vent*** [literally 'a flight in the wind'] and VOLLEY.

volley [16c. French *volée*, ultimately from Latin *volare*: see VOLATILE*] **1** the discharging of a number of weapons simultaneously, hence a shower of arrows, stones, words, etc. **2** the flight of a ball, hence a stroke that hits a ball in flight; to make one (19c).

voluble [ME. (French, from) Latin *volubilis*, from *volvere* 'to roll' (ancestor of VAULT*] **1** readily turning around a point or axis; of a plant: twining (18c) **2** changeable, inconstant; moving rapidly or easily (16c), hence speaking or spoken easily or at length.

volume [ME. Via Old French from Latin *volumen* 'a roll', from *volvere* 'to roll'] A roll of parchment with writing; a written work, originally in this form, hence **1** one of the separately bound parts of a written work (16c) **2** size or extent, originally of a book (16–18c), hence **(a)** size or mass (17c); the size of a three-dimensional space within, or occupied by, an object (18c) **(b)** the amount or quantity of something, e.g. traffic or trade (19c) **(c)** in music: richness of tone (19c); loudness (now of any sound).

Latin *volumen* produced **voluminous**, which also meant 'convoluted' and 'producing many books'; *volvere* is the ancestor of VAULT*.

voluntary [ME. (Via French from) Latin *voluntarius*, from *voluntas* 'will, choice', from *velle*, *vol-* 'to wish'] **1** of a feeling: spontaneous, hence improvised music added to a piece (16c only); an improvised (solo) performance; a solo played before, during, or after a church service or other ceremony (18c) **2** arising, acting, or resulting from your own free will, hence of work: unpaid (15c); (a person) serving of their own free will and usually without payment (16–17c, outlived by **volunteer**); (an organization) maintained (largely) by donations and staffed by volunteers (18c).

Latin *velle* produced **volition**. Related to **voluptuous** [Latin *voluptas* 'pleasure'].

voodoo [19c. Louisiana French, from Fon *vodū* 'protective deity', also 'fetish'] A Black religious cult of W Africa, subsequently of the Caribbean and southern US, involving sorcery and communication with the spirits of the dead; a voodoo deity, spell, practitioner, or priest.

The alteration **hoodoo** originally meant a person who practised voodoo, hence **1** a hidden cause of bad luck; to bring bad luck to **2** a tall rock column, often with an overhanging cap of harder material, probably thought to resemble a strange or sinister human figure (US).

vouch [ME. Old French *vo(u)cher* 'to summon', ultimately from Latin *vocare* 'to call'] To summon someone to court to prove ownership of property, hence to assert; to confirm or substantiate, especially by producing evidence (16c); **vouch for** to give your personal assurance for, to guarantee (17c). Hence **1 voucher** such a summons (16c); a corroborative document (17c); a document showing that payment has been made or promised, which can be exchanged for goods or services (1940s) **2 vouchsafe** (ME, originally in *to vouch something safe on* 'to guarantee something granted to').

Descendants of Latin *vocare* include ADVOCATE*, **convocation**, INVOKE*, **irrevocable**, **provoke**, **revoke**, and **vocation**. Related to VOICE*.

vow   Strictly speaking, two words: I [ME. Old French *vo(u)*, from Latin *vovere*, *vot-* 'to vow', also 'to wish for'] **1** a solemn promise, hence **(a)** to make one, to swear **(b)** to dedicate something to a god, person, or cause (15c) **2** an earnest wish or desire (15c) II [ME. Shortened from **avow**, from Old French *avouer*, from Latin *advocare* (see ADVOCATE), confused with Old French *avo(u)er* 'to vow', from Latin *vovere*, and further confused with **avow** to bind with, or to make, a vow (ME–19c, from *vow*)] to acknowledge; to state solemnly, to declare.

Latin *vovere* is the ancestor of **devote**, **devout**, **votary**, **votive**, and **vote** a vow; (the formal expression of) a wish or choice; to express a choice.

vulgar   [ME. Latin *vulgaris*, from *vulgar* 'to make common', from *vulgus* 'the common people'] **1** in ordinary use: **(a)** measured or calculated according to common or standard practice, surviving in **vulgar** (as opposed to decimal) **fraction** **(b)** of language: commonly used by the people, vernacular (as opposed to Latin, 15c) **(c)** commonplace, ordinary (16c) **2** to do with, or characteristic of, the common people (16c), hence unrefined; coarse, crude, indecent (17c).

Latin *vulgus* produced *vulgare* 'to spread among the masses, to publish', whence **divulge** to announce publicly (15–18c), later to disclose something private, and **Vulgate** the name given to the 4c Latin translation of the Bible [late Latin *vulgata editio* 'edition for ordinary people', as all educated people then read Latin].

W

wad [16c. Origin unknown] A kind of material used for padding (replaced by **wadding** except in Scots), hence **1** a small piece of it used as a pad or plug, hence **(a)** to insert such a plug **(b)** a disc or plug keeping powder and shot in position in a gun or cartridge (17c) **(c)** a tight roll (especially of banknotes, 18c), hence an amount, a large sum of money, etc. (19c, Scots and N England) **(d)** a bun, cake, or sandwich (World War I, *forces slang*) **2** to line, pad, or protect (as if) with wadding (18c).

wade [Old English *wadan*] To go on, through, or into (–17c); to walk through water, mud, etc. (ME); to plod through something tedious; to progress with difficulty.

Probably the source of **waddle**. Related to Old English *gewaed* 'ford', which appears as **Wade-** or **-wade** in place names, and to synonymous Old Norse *vath*, which appears as **-wath**, **-with**, or **-worth** (*-worth* is more commonly from Old English *worth*, *wyrth* 'enclosure, homestead').

wafer [ME. From *wafre*, the Anglo-Norman French form of Old French *gaufre* (cf. WALLOP*), from early Low German *wāfel*] A thin crisp biscuit, hence **1** a disc of unleavened bread used in the Eucharist **2** a disc of paste used to seal a document (18c) or to hold a medicinal powder (19c) **3** an ice cream between wafers (1930s) **4** a very thin slice of a semiconductor crystal (1950s) **5** a very small gold ingot (1970s).

Old French *gaufre* also meant 'honeycomb', and produced **goffer** to crimp with a hot iron, and probably GOPHER. Low German *wāfel* is the ancestor, via Dutch, of **waffle** a pancake cooked on an iron (*US*), and is related to WEB*. **Waffle** meaning 'to go on and on without saying much' originally meant 'to yap', and comes from dialect **waff** an imitation of a dog's bark.

waft [16c. Back-formation from obsolete *wafter* 'armed convoy escort ship', from Dutch or Low German *wachter*, from *wachten* 'to watch over, to guard': related to WAKE*] To escort ships in a convoy (–17c); to sail (–19c); to blow (originally a sailing ship) along, hence **1** a signalling flag; a signal using flags **2** to move or carry (as if) on the breeze (17c); a scent, sound, etc. carried in this way.

wag [ME. From or related to Old English *wagian* 'to sway'] To move; to (make something) wave or sway, hence **1** to do so quickly and repeatedly (15c); to brandish **2** **waghalter** someone likely to be hanged (16c), hence **wag** **(a)** a mischievous boy (16–17c); a joker, a wit **(b)** **wag (off)** to play truant (19c).

Wag produced **waggle** and the surnames **Waghorn(e)** a trumpeter, and **Wagstaff** an official with a staff of office: both may also refer to a medieval flasher. Related to *wig* in **earwig** [Old English *earwicga*, from *wicga* 'earwig', *ear* added as the creature was believed to crawl into people's ears], to **wiggle**, and probably to VOGUE.

wage [ME. The Norman form of Old French *gage* (cf. WALLOP*), of Germanic origin] **1** someone/something given as security (–16c); to give one (–18c), hence **(a)** (to give) a pledge of willingness to fight, (to make) a challenge (–16c), hence **wage war** (15c) **(b)** to risk (15c); to stake or bet (replaced by *wager* below): these senses shared by *gage* (ME) **2** a payment for work etc., originally a fee or salary to a professional, now a fixed regular payment to any worker, hence **(a)** a reward or result (sometimes plural but treated as singular: *the wages of sin is death*) **(b)** to pay someone a wage, hence **waged** receiving a wage, in paid work, more common in **unwaged**).

Norman French *wage* produced **wager** a pledge (ME only), later (to make) a bet; Old French *gage* produced ENGAGE. Related to **wed** [Old English *wedd*] (to give) a pledge or promise, hence to marry, to link or unite.

wagon [15c. Dutch *wag(h)en*] A large, sturdy four-wheeled cart, hence **1** a chariot, a carriage (both 16–17c); (now usually **wagonette**) a light four-wheeled carriage (19c) **2** a truck used in a mine (17c); a railway truck or open coach (18c); any railway vehicle **3** a gypsy's or showman's caravan (19c) **4** applied to various vehicles with a specified use (*chuck/patrol wagon*): **(a) station wagon** a covered carriage for taking passengers and luggage from a railway station to a hotel (19c, US); an estate car (1920s) **(b) water wagon** for carrying water to workers or animals, or for laying dust (19c), hence **on the (water) wagon** abstaining from alcohol.

Wagon replaced **wain** [related to Old English *waeg(e)n*] except in poetry, in names such as **Wainfleet**, **Wainwright**, and **Wayne**, and in **Charles's Wain** [literally 'Charlemagne's chariot'] the Plough, apparently from a confusion of *Arcturus*, the brightest star in this constellation, with Latin *Arthurus* 'Arthur', plus a popular association of King Arthur with Charlemagne. Related to **wainscot** [Low German *wagenschot*, from *wagen* 'wagon' + *scote* 'boarding, panelling'] good-quality oak used for coachwork and panelling, hence a panelled area, especially the lower part of a wall, to WAY*, and more distantly to WEIGH*.

waif [ME. Anglo-Norman French *weyf*, ultimately of Scandinavian origin] A piece of ownerless property, hence an abandoned or neglected child (17c); a fashionable young person who cultivates a fragile appearance (1990s).

Anglo-Norman French *weyf* produced *weyver* 'to abandon, to allow to become a waif', whence **waive** to deprive of legal protection, later to give up a right, whence **waiver** the act of doing so or a document showing that you have.

wait [ME. Old Norman French *waitier*, of Germanic origin: related to WAKE*] **1** to watch for in order to harm (–16c); an ambush (*lie in wait*) **2** to keep watch (–17c); a watchman (hence the surname **Wait(e)**, **Waites**); one with a trumpet etc. to sound the alarm, hence a member of a town band; **waits** a group of musicians and singers that performs Christmas carols in the street (18c) **3** to watch for someone/something to appear or happen (usually **wait for** or **await**); to stay put or do nothing until it does, hence **(a)** to be ready or available (15c); to be ready to receive orders; to be an attendant or servant, hence **waiter** a household servant; one who serves at table in a restaurant etc. (16c, hence **waitress**, 19c); *wait* to do so (19c); **wait on** to serve **(b)** to be put off for a while (16c) **(c) waiting** (a period of) attendance at court (*lady-in-waiting*, 17c) **(d)** a period of waiting (19c).

wake [Old English *wacan, wacian*] **1** to be or stay awake; to do so in order to look after someone or as a (religious) duty; a period of doing so, especially the night before a festival, hence **(a)** an annual parish festival, originally on the feast day of the church's patron saint (ME); an annual holiday period, originally at this time, especially in N English industrial towns (*wakes week*, 18c: cf. FAIR²) **(b)** to keep watch beside a body before burial (ME, now mainly Irish); a convivial gathering before or after a funeral (15c) **2 wake (up)** to end your own or someone else's sleep (ME, earlier as **awake** [Old English *awacian*] or **awaken**); to make or become lively, alert, or aware; to stir up feeling, strife, etc. Hence **awake** not asleep, alert, vigilant.

Related to WAFT, WAIT, **Wake-** in place names [Old English *wacu* 'vigil' or *waca* 'watchful person'], WATCH, and WITCH*, and probably to BIVOUAC.

wale [Old English *walu*: related to WALK*] A ridge of earth or stone (OE only), hence **1** a ridge on the skin caused by a blow, replaced by the variant **weal**, which came to mean an itchy swelling, and by **welt** [origin uncertain], originally a strip attaching a shoe's upper to its sole (ME). Hence to mark with wales (15c, later as *weal* or *whale*) **2** one of a ship's horizontal timbers (ME), hence **(a)** the top of a ship's side: largely replaced by **gunwale**, as the ship's guns were mounted on it (15c, now pronounced, and often spelt, **gunnel**) **(b) wale (piece)** a horizontal timber between the piles of a dam (17c) **3** a raised line of threads in a woven fabric (16c); the texture produced **4** a ridge on a horse's collar (18c).

walk [Old English *wealcan*] Of waves: to roll or toss (–15c); to roll around, to wander (–16c), hence **1** to go about in public, to appear (*the ghost walks*, ME) **2** to go on foot (ME), hence a short journey on foot; a place for walking (15c); a route or path (16c), hence **walk of life** your path in life, your social position, trade or occupation (18c) **3** (to move at) the slowest pace (15c).

Related to GALLANT*, SWELL, WALE*, **walk** to full cloth [Low German or Dutch *walken*], whence the surname **Walker** (cf. *fuller* at FOIL¹, *Treadwell* at TREAD), WALLOP*, WALLOW, **waltz**, **whelk**, **willow**, and probably to GABERDINE, **wallet** originally a bag for carrying food, clothing, etc. on a journey, and WELL¹.

wall [Old English, from Latin *vallum* 'rampart', from *vallus* 'stake'] A rampart or embankment; a structure that encloses, protects, or divides a space, or that supports a roof. Hence **1** to surround with a wall or walls; w**all (up) (a)** to block up with masonry (16c) **(b)** to brick in, to immure (16c) **2** something resembling a wall in function or appearance: **(a)** a barrier (ME) **(b)** the sides of a ship, tent, horse's hoof, etc. (16c).

Wall appears as **Wal-** in place names (but see WELL² and WELSH), and produced the surnames *Thirlwell* (at THRILL) and **Wall(er)** someone who lived by a wall, or a stonemason (but see WELL²). Latin *vallum* is the ancestor of **interval** [via Old French from Latin *intervallum* 'space between ramparts'].

wallop [ME. *Waloper*, the Norman form of Old French *galoper*, perhaps from Frankish *wala* 'well' + *hlaupan* 'to run'] **1** of a horse: (to run at) its fastest pace (replaced by **gallop** [from *galoper*]) **2** (to boil with) a noisy bubbling sound (16c, surviving in dialect) **3** (the sound made by) a violent or clumsy movement (16c); to make one (18c) **4** a heavy blow (19c); to hit or beat; the ability to do so, hence, probably, alcoholic drink, especially beer. Sometimes said to be the source of **codswallop**, one Hiram Codd having invented a bottle for fizzy drinks, *Codd's wallop*, the theory goes, became a derogatory term for gassy beer: there is no evidence for this.

Wallop and *gallop* are one of a number of pairs, one from Old Norman French and spelt with *w*, the other coming from Old French and spelt with *g*: see REWARD*, WAFER*, WAGE*, WAR*, WARD*, WARDROBE*, WARRANT*, and WICKET.

Frankish *wala* is related to WALK*, and *hlaupan* to LEAP*.

wallow [Old English *walwian*: related to WALK*] To roll about, hence **1** to roll or lie relaxed in mud etc., hence **(a)** to indulge in a vice, emotion, etc. (*wallowing in self-pity*, ME) **(b)** a place where animals wallow (16c); this action **2** of a ship: to roll or be tossed about (ME) **3** to move clumsily or with a rolling gait (16c).

wan [Old English *wann*, of unknown origin] Especially of the sea: dark, gloomy, hence **1** of an unhealthy greyish colour (–17c); sickly, pallid (ME) **2** sad, dismal (ME) **3** of the moon, stars, etc.: faint, partly obscured (17c).

want [ME. Old Norse *vanr* 'lacking', *vanta* 'to lack': related to Old English *wanian* **wane**] **1** to be missing or unavailable; a lack of, a deficiency, now usually in *for (the) want of* **2** to be without; to have too little of, hence **(a)** need, poverty; something needed (16c) **(b)** to desire or wish for (18c); to wish to do or be (hence **wannabe** (describing) someone who wishes to be something/someone they are not, 1980s); to wish someone/something to do or be; to wish to see or speak to (*wanted by the police*).

war [ME. *Werre*, the Norman form of Old French *guerre*, of Germanic origin. Cf. WALLOP*] The state or a time of (declared) armed conflict between nations or states; any conflict or contest between opposing people, forces, or principles; **civil war** armed conflict between sections of the same nation or state. Hence **1** to make war; to be at war **2** the methods of armed conflict (*guerrilla/nuclear war*) **3** a serious and sustained attempt to defeat or eradicate something (1930s).

Werre produced **warrior** and the surnames **Warr(e)** and **W(h)arrier** a belligerent person. Related to Spanish *guerrilla* [literally 'little war', from *guerra* 'war': introduced during the Peninsular War, 1808–14], **worse**, and German *Wurst* sausage [Old High German *wurst* 'mixture'].

ward [Old English *weard* (noun), *weardian* (verb): later reinforced by related *warde*, *warder*, the Norman forms of Old French *garde*, *garder* (cf. WALLOP*)] To keep safe, take care of, guard, or protect; this duty or action, hence **warden** someone who does so [ME, from *wardein*, the Norman form of Old French *garden*, whence **guardian**, which replaced it in some senses], hence **1 (a)** to take legal responsibility for the affairs of a minor etc. (–15c); the person cared for (ME) **(b)** the care or charge of a prisoner (ME); custody, imprisonment, surviving mainly in *warden* a prison governor; **warder** a prison officer (19c) **2** a company of watchmen or sentries: replaced by **guard** [Old French *guarde*], hence a division of an army (*advance/rearguard*, ME) **3** to provide a guard (–17c); to protect or rule an area, hence such an area: **(a)** between the inner and outer walls of a castle etc. (ME) **(b)** a guarded entrance (ME) **(c)** an administrative district of a borough etc. (ME), or of the Mormon church (19c) **(d)** (a part of) a prison (ME) **(e)** a room for patients in a hospital (17c) **4** (to adopt) a defensive posture or position (ME); to parry a blow, hence **ward off** to repel an attack (16c); to avert danger, to guard against.

Old English *weard* produced the names **Ward(law)** and some instances of **Wardle**, and is one parent of **steward** [with Old English *stig* 'house, hall', whence also (pig) **sty**] originally someone who managed a large household, also as a surname (also as **Stewart**, **Stuart**), and of LORD, and is related to WARE[1]*. Old Norman French *warder* produced AWARD, REWARD*, and WARDROBE*.

wardrobe [ME. *Warderobe*, the Norman form of Old French *garderobe*, from *garder* (see WARD*) + ROBE] A room for storing clothes (or sometimes armour or other expensive goods), especially one adjoining a bedroom; a bedroom, dressing room, or other private room (–19c); a privy (–15c): these senses shared by *garderobe* (15c). Hence **1** (a building housing) the department in charge of clothing in a royal or noble household (15c, hence the surname **Wardrop** the person in charge of it); (a room housing) the costumes or costume department of a theatre etc. (18c) **2** all someone's clothes (15c); their clothes for a particular season or activity **3** a clothes cupboard (16c).

ware[1] [Old English *waer*] **1** conscious of (largely replaced by **aware**, from Old English *gewaer*, from *waer*) **2** on your guard, cautious (largely replaced by its descendant, **wary**, 15c).

Old English *waer* produced **beware**, which has replaced related **ware** [Old English *warian*] except as a huntsman's warning cry (*ware wire!*). Related to WARD*, WARE[2], and **warn**.

ware[2] [Old English *waru*: related to WARE[1]*] Goods; those of a certain kind or origin (*glassware, Manchester ware*), hence **1 hardware** ironmongery (16c), hence **(a)** weapons (19c) **(b)** the physical components of a computer system (1940s), as opposed to **software** the operating system (1960s), hence different kinds of software (*shareware*, 1980s); **warez** pirated software (1990s) **2 warehouse** a storehouse for goods (ME), hence **(a)** to store goods in one (18c), hence **warehousing** the (covert) buying up of shares in the hope of a rise in price or a takeover (1970s) **(b)** a large wholesale or retail store (18c) **(c) warehouse party** a large illicit party held in a warehouse or other large building (1980s), hence *Warehouse* a Chicago nightclub which gave its name to **house (music)**, first played there.

warlock [Old English *waer-loga*, from *waer* 'oath, pledge' + *-loga* 'liar', from *lēogan* 'to **lie**'] A traitor (–15c); a scoundrel (now mainly Scots); the Devil (–16c), hence a man in league with the Devil, a male witch (ME, *Scots and N English*, brought into wider use by Scott: see DOFF).

Old English *lēogan* produced **belie** to deceive by lying (OE only); to tell lies about (–19c), hence **1** to give a false impression of **2** to show to be false.

warp [Old English *weorpan*] **1** to throw (surviving in dialect) **2** the lengthwise threads in weaving or woven fabric (perhaps from the idea of 'throwing' the shuttle across them, or because they are twisted tighter than the weft threads)

3 a rope around a piling, capstan, etc., used to move a ship (ME); to move a ship using one (16c) **4** to make or become bent or distorted (15c), hence **(a)** to bias or pervert (16c) **(b)** a distortion (17c); **space** or **time warp** a hypothetical distortion of the space-time continuum that enables travel outside the laws of physics (1930s).

The senses 'throw' and 'turn or twist' are also found together in CAST, HURL, THROW, and WHIRL.

warrant [ME. *Warant*, the Norman form of Old French *guarant* (cf. WALLOP*), from Frankish *werēnd* 'to be surety for'] **1** to keep safe or protect (−16c); to ensure security of possession or title (15c), hence **warranty** a guarantee of title **2** to answer for the truth of a statement etc.; someone who does so; to give an assurance (a *warranty*) that goods etc. are as represented (15c) **3** a command or document sanctioning or authorizing something (*death/search warrant*), hence **(a)** to give one, to authorize or sanction (16c) **(b)** a writ of authority given to a non-commissioned officer (17c), hence **warrant officer (c)** (sufficient grounds) to justify an action, belief, etc. (16c).

Warrant and *warranty* have been partly replaced by **guarantee** [from *guarant*] or related **guaranty**. Related to French **garage** [from *garer* 'to shelter'], GARNISH*, GARRET*, and WARREN.

warren [ME. *Warenne*, the Norman form of Old French *garenne* 'game-park' (cf. WALLOP*), of Germanic origin and related to WARRANT*] A reserve for small game (surviving in field and farm names), hence **1** one for breeding rabbits and, formerly, hares; a wild rabbit colony or its network of burrows, hence an area which is crowded or has a complicated layout (17c) **2 (free) warren** the right to keep and hunt **beasts** or **fowls of warren**, e.g. rabbits, hares, and some birds (15c) **3** the surnames **Warrener**, **Warriner**, and some instances of **Warren** and **Warner** a warren-keeper.

wash [Old English *waescan*] To clean (originally clothes) with water or, later, other liquid; this action, hence **1** (the sound of) breaking waves on the shore (perhaps resembling the sound of washing clothes); erosion caused by this; a wave caused by a passing boat (19c); a current of air caused by a passing aircraft (*c*.1910) **2** to wet thoroughly (ME); of water: to flow over the land, hence **(a)** a piece of land that floods periodically (15c); the dry bed of an intermittent stream (19c, US) **(b) awash** covered in water (19c); of a ship: having water coming over the sides, hence full of, having too much of (*c*.1910) **3** of water: to carry something away (ME); **wash down** to follow food etc. with a drink **4** waste liquid (15c), hence **(hog)wash** (semi-)liquid food, originally kitchen waste, for pigs, hence rubbish, nonsense (18c): **swill** [Old English *swilian*] made a similar journey from 'to wash or rinse out' to 'pig food' (16c) **5 (a)** (an application of) a medicinal or cosmetic liquid, or one for cleaning, colouring, etc. (16c) **(b)** (to apply) a thin coat of paint, distemper, or watercolour (16c); paint etc. for this (*whitewash*, 17c) **6** insipid liquid (16c); watery beer, hence **washy** weak, sloppy (17c), later as **wishy-washy**.

Wash is related to **water**, **wet**, and probably to **Wash-, -was(h)** in place names, and **winter**. *Swill* is probably related to **swallow** to gulp down, whence **groundsel** [Old English *grundeswylige*, literally 'pus-swallower', from the plant's use in poultices].

waste [ME. Old Norman French, ultimately from Latin *vastus* 'void, empty, unoccupied, deserted', also 'immense' (ancestor of **devastate** and **vast**)] Of land: unoccupied or not worth cultivating; such land (partly replaced by 19c **wasteland**); to bring to this state (now usually as **lay waste**), hence to destroy or consume, hence **1** of disease etc.: to make someone thin or weak; to lose health or strength; to lose weight by dieting and training (18c) **2** useless consumption or expenditure; to consume or spend uselessly or extravagantly, hence **(a)** superfluous, needless, useless (–16c); (something) discarded as being so (17c) **(b)** to give or do something with no result or reward (18c) **(c)** to fail to use or take advantage of (19c) **3** damage caused by neglect (15c); gradual loss by wear, pilfering, etc. (largely replaced by 18c **wastage**, whence **(natural) wastage** reduction in staff from resignations, retirement, etc. rather than dismissal, early 20c) **4** to murder (1960s, *US*); **wasted** drunk or stoned.

watch [Old English *waecce* (noun), *waecan* (verb): related to WAKE*] To be or stay awake, to keep a vigil (–17c), later to be alert (ME); to keep guard, hence **1** night watch a lookout or guard kept during the night (ME), hence **(a)** the period of it; *watch* a period of duty (16c); those on duty during it (17c) **(b)** *(night) watch*, **watch(man)** a person or people who keep watch (15c), especially in a town before there were police (16c); **neighbourhood watch** a system of vigilance by residents to prevent crime (1970s, *US*) **(c) watchdog** a guard dog (17c); a person or body of people appointed to guard against undesirable practices (19c) **(d)** *watch* a company of irregular Highland troops (18c), surviving in **Black Watch** the 42nd Highland Regiment (19c) **2** to observe closely for a period (ME) **3** to wait or look out for (16c); to beware of **4** an alarm clock (16–17c), later a small portable clock, hence **deathwatch (beetle)** applied to various insects which make a noise like a watch's tick, and were thought to foretell a death (17c).

wave [Old English *wafian*: later also from related Old Norse *veifa* 'to wave or brandish'] To move (originally your hands) up and down or from side to side, hence **1** of something with a fixed end: to move (ME) or be moved (17c) from side to side; this action **2** to vacillate (ME–18c), outlived by **waver** [from related Old Norse *vafra* 'to move unsteadily'] **3** an undulation in water (15c), hence **(a)** (to form or to ornament with) an undulating shape or line (16c); a loose curl in the hair; an oscillation, especially of energy (18c) **(b)** to move like a wave (18c); to undulate; to surge, hence (the movement of) a large number of advancing people etc. (19c); a swelling (and subsidence) of an emotion or activity (19c); the ripple effect of groups in a crowd alternately standing and sitting (1984, US, called a **Mexican wave** after the crowd at the football World Cup in Mexico City performed it, 1986).

Old Norse *veifa* produced **weave**. Related to WEB*.

way [Old English *weg*] A (main) road, a path or track: surviving in **highway**, **byway**, and in the names of Roman roads or ancient tracks: in modern street names it is virtually meaningless. Hence **1** a route (*the way to London/on the way*) **2** your path through life; a course of action; a method of doing something; a characteristic manner of behaving (*I did it my way*, 17c); **ways** customs (18c) **3** the distance (to be) travelled (*a long way*) **4** a place you can go through (*way in/out, doorway*, ME); the opportunity of going through, forward, etc. (15c), unimpeded passage, hence **(a)** freedom of movement or action (*get his own way*, 15c) **(b) right of way** the right to cross someone's property (18c); a path by which you may do so (19c); the right of a vehicle to move before another (early 20c) **5** the movement of a boat through water (17c), hence **under way** having begun to move (18c) **6** baulks of timber laid so that something can be moved over them (17c); **(rail)way** parallel rails to carry wagons, trains, etc. (18c).

Way produced **always** [Old English *ealne weg* 'all the way', hence covering the whole distance, perpetually, on all occasions], **anyway**, AWAY, **waybill** originally a list of stagecoach passengers, **wayfarer**, **waylay**, and -**ways** (*lengthways*, *sideways*). Related to WAGON*.

wealth [ME. Either from **weal** (Old English *wela*), which it has largely replaced, or from related WELL[1]*] Happiness and prosperity, (the possession of) riches, hence **1** an abundance (*a wealth of detail*, 16c) **2** (the value of) a person or country's assets (17c).

Weal produced **commonweal** literally 'the common good', hence a nation or state as a political entity in which everyone has a stake, replaced by **commonwealth**, which came to mean **1** a federation of states (16c) **2** a republic or democracy (17c).

weather [Old English *weder*] The state of the atmosphere with regard to temperature, rainfall, sunshine, wind, etc.; (a spell of) a certain kind of weather (surviving mainly in *in all weathers*). Hence **1** to expose or be exposed to the weather (ME); to change or be changed by this; to withstand bad weather or troubles (*weather the storm*, 17c) **2** in nautical use: **(a)** towards the wind (ME); to sail to windward (16c) **(b) make good/bad weather of it** to sail well/badly in a storm (17c), hence **make heavy weather of it** to make a task more difficult than it is.

Wither 'to dry up and shrivel' is apparently a variant. Probably related to **wind** moving air, **window** [Old Norse *vindauga*, literally 'wind's eye'], and **wing** [of Scandinavian origin].

web [Old English] (A piece of) woven fabric, hence **1** to weave, whence the surnames **Webb** and **Webster** [Old English *webba*, feminine *webbestre* 'weaver': cf. *brewster* (at BREW)] **2** the net a spider makes (ME), also as **cobweb** [ultimately from Old English *coppa* 'spider'] **3** a membrane or similar structure in the body (ME); the membrane between the toes of a duck etc. (16c) **4** any intricate construction or network (16c), now especially the **(World Wide) Web** the system of linked items accessible via the internet (1991), whence **website** a 'place' on the Web where a person, organization, etc. gives information about themselves, **web**-referring to items disseminated via the Web (*webisode*, *webliography*); **weblog** someone's on-line diary, observations, or opinions, which others may interact with (*c.*2005), quickly shortened to **blog**; to produce or keep one, hence **blogosphere** blogs and bloggers collectively; **blogzine** an on-line magazine (2007); by analogy **blook** an on-line 'book'.

Relatives include WAFER*, **wasp** [from its intricate nest], WAVE*, **weave** (fabric) [Old English *wefan*, whence **weft** and **woof**, both meaning the crosswise threads], **weevil**, and **wobble**.

wee [ME. Ultimately from Old English *wēge*, *waege* 'weight': originally and mainly Scots: related to WEIGH*] **1** a small thing (ME only); a child (replaced in Scots by

wean, and in N English by **wain**, both short for *wee ane* 'wee one', 17c) **2** a small quantity; a short time (*bide a wee*). Hence small, tiny (15c), whence **weeny** (18c).

weigh [Old English *wegan*] **1** to lift up or carry, surviving mainly in **weigh anchor** (16c) **2** to determine the weight of, hence to measure or consider the value, importance, or desirability of, hence **(a)** to be important to, or to influence, someone (ME) **(b) weigh up** to appraise (19c) **3** to be a certain weight; to equal in weight, value, etc. (16c) **4** to be affected by weight (ME); **weigh down** to force or bend down by weight; to oppress or burden.
Related to WEE and **weight**, and more distantly to WAGON*.

weird [Old English *wyrd*] Fate, destiny; **Weirds** the Fates, hence **1** (thought to be) able to foresee or control someone's fate or future events (ME, originally in **weird sisters** the Fates, later the witches in Shakespeare's *Macbeth*); someone claiming or believed to have this ability, a witch or wizard (17c) **2** to do with fate or the supernatural (19c); uncanny, eerie, odd, bizarre, hence **weirdie** (19c), **weirdo** (1950s) an odd or eccentric person.

well¹ [Old English] In a good way, satisfactorily, hence **1** ethically, properly; kindly, considerately; good-naturedly or with equanimity (*took it well*) **2** fully, certainly (*well able/aware*); very, more than a little (*well worn/well after midnight*, ME); very, extremely (*well busy*, 1980s slang, apparently originating in N England and possibly reflecting dialect use) **3** happily, fortunately; happy, fortunate, hence **(a)** prosperous(ly) (ME, surviving in *well-to-do, well off*); profitably, advantageously (*married well*) **(b)** of a ship etc.: sound, undamaged (ME); of a person: in good health (16c).
Well produced *welfare* (at FARE) and perhaps WEALTH*. Related to WALK*.

well² [Old English *wellan* (verb), *wella* (noun)] **1** to boil (–17c); to melt or soften metal (ME–16c); to join pieces of metal by heating (15c, altered to **weld** except in dialect) **2** a (bubbling) spring of water (surviving in place names), hence **(a)** one regarded as sacred or having magical or healing properties (hence *Wells* in the names of spa towns); a shaft sunk to reach underground water, later oil, gas, etc., hence any shaft, pit, or deep receptacle (*stairwell, inkwell*, 17c) **(b)** to produce or pour out water etc. (ME); **well (up)** to come or bring to the surface and pour out; **well over** to overflow (19c).
Well appears in many place names, usually as **Wal(l)-**, **-wall**, **Wel-**, **-well**, or **Wil-**. Hence the surname **Well(er)** someone who lived by a spring (see also *Halliwell* etc. at HOLY): the variant **Waller** sometimes meant someone who boiled down sea water for salt. Cf. WALL, WELSH).

Welsh [Old English *Welisc*, *Waelisc*, etc., from *w(e)alh* 'foreigner, Briton, Celt', later 'serf', ultimately from Latin *Volcae*, the name of a Celtic people of southern Gaul] **1** (to do with) the native Celts of England as opposed to the Anglo-Saxons **2** a native or inhabitant of Wales; from or to do with Wales.
Welsh produced the surnames **Walsh(e)** and **Welch** (a 17c spelling which also survives in the *Royal Welch Fusiliers*). Old English *w(e)alh* produced the place names **Cornwall** [with *Cornovii*, the Latin name of the British tribe that lived there] and many beginning **Wal-**, **Wales**, **walnut** [literally 'foreign nut'], which was introduced from southern Europe, the surname **Wellesley**, and probably the

Scots surname **Waugh**. Related to **Wallace** and **Walloon** but, despite various theories, not to **welsh** to avoid paying a debt.

wend [Old English *wendan*] To turn something round or over (–15c), hence **1** to turn your steps, to go; to make your way: largely replaced by **go** [Old English *gan*: related to GANG] **2** of a ship: to turn in the opposite direction (ME–18c); to turn a ship's bow to the opposite tack (16c).

The original past participle was **went**, now the past tense of *go* and replaced by **wended**. Related to WIND*.

whelm [Old English *hwylfan*] To overturn or capsize (–16c); to overturn something hollow, especially to put it upside down over something else (ME), hence to cover (–17c); now **overwhelm** (probably originally used for emphasis): to drown or bury something like a flood or avalanche, to overcome someone emotionally. **Underwhelm** 'to fail to impress' was made up as a joke in the 1950s.

while [Old English *hwīl*] A period of time, hence **1** during the time that something (else) exists, is happening, etc. (ME), hence **(a)** so long as, provided that (*not while I can stop him*) **(b) (all) the while** during the whole time (15c): cf. *meanwhile* (at MEAN²) **(c)** although (*while she's silly, she's good fun*, 16c) **2** the time and effort spent in doing something (ME, surviving in *worth your while*) **3 while (away)** to pass a period of time pleasantly (17c: cf. *wile* at GUILE).

whimper [16c. Dialect *whimp*, an imitation of the sound] To make a weak, intermittent crying sound; to complain feebly or peevishly; such a sound or complaint (17c); a disappointing ending, an anticlimax, alluding to T. S. Eliot's 'This is the way the world ends: Not with a bang but a whimper', 1925.

The source of **whimbrel** a small curlew with a tremulous call, and probably of **wimp** a weak, timid, or ineffectual person, hence **wimp out** to fail to do or finish something through fear.

whip [ME. From or related to early Dutch and Low German *wippen* 'to swing or leap'] **1** of a bird: to flap its wings vigorously (ME only) **2 whip (it)** (to make, or to move something with) a sudden movement (cf. *whippet* below), hence **(a)** to snatch or steal (19c) **(b) whip (round)** an impromptu collection of money (19c) **(c)** a fairground ride where the cars make a quick sweeping movement (1920s) **3** a switch, or a rod with a lash, for inflicting pain, hence **(a)** to hit with one **(b) whip (up)** to urge a horse on with one (16c, hence *whip* (the skill of) a coachman, 18c); to arouse strong feelings (19c) **(c)** to defeat or outdo (16c) **(d)** to beat eggs, cream, etc. (17c); a dessert made by doing so (18c) **(e) whip in** to chase a straying hound back into the pack with a whip (18c), hence **whipper-in** the huntsman who does so; someone who makes members of a political party conform to its aims (19c), shortened to *whip*, hence a whip's written instruction to members (underlined according to its importance, a **three-line whip** being the most serious); **the whip** party discipline (1950s) **4** to bind a rope etc. with cord wound tightly round it (15c); **whip(stitch)** (to sew with) an overlapping stitch (16c).

Descendants of *whip* include **whipcord** thin cord used to make whiplashes, later a kind of ribbed worsted, **whiplash** the lash of a whip, hence (describing) an injury caused when the head is thrown forward and suddenly back, **whippersnapper** (implying noise and unimportance) an impudent (young) person, and

whippet to move briskly [from *whip it* above], hence a kind of small greyhound. Related to **wipe**.

whirl [ME. Old Norse *hvirfla* (verb), the noun partly from Old Norse *hvirfill* 'circle', partly from related early Dutch and Low German *wervel* 'spindle'] To (make something) move in a curve or circle, hence **1** to spin, hence **(a)** a rapid rotation (15c); an eddy or vortex (16c) **(b)** a convolution or coil (16c, mainly as the variant **whorl**) **(c)** to spin round and face the other way (19c) **2** to rush around, hence **(a)** to move something swiftly **(b)** hurried and confused activity (16c); of the brain: to become confused, cf. SPIN **3** to throw, especially with a rotating movement (15c, cf. WARP*) **4 give it a whirl** give it a try (19c, *US*): the equivalent in Australia and New Zealand is **give it a burl** (early 20c), from Scots and N English dialect **burl** to rotate (18c), also to toss a coin.

Whirl produced **whirligig** [with **gig** a flighty girl, later a spinning top] and **whirlpool**. Old Norse *hvirfill* produced **whirlwind** [with *vindr* 'wind']. **Whirr**, originally 'to throw violently or with a noise', is probably related.

whisk [ME. Probably of Scandinavian origin] A quick, light, sweeping movement, hence **1** to (make something) move in this way, or quickly and suddenly (15c) **2** to brush or beat with a bundle of twigs, grass, etc. (16c), hence **(a)** to brush away lightly (17c) **(b)** to beat eggs, cream, etc. (17c) **(c)** a broom or utensil for whisking (17c).

Whisk produced **whisker** something that whisks or sweeps, e.g. a switch or a bunch of grass etc., hence **whiskers** facial hair; *whisker* a single hair or bristle, and probably **whist** the card game (the cards being 'whisked up' after each play). Probably related to **wisp** [from or related to Frisian *wisp* 'handful of straw'].

whittle [ME. Variant of *thwittle*, from Old English *thwītan* 'to cut off'] **1** a knife **2** to cut shavings from a wooden stick (16c), hence **(a)** to reduce or deplete something a little at a time (18c) **(b)** to make something by whittling (19c).

Related to **thwaite** [Old Norse *thveit(i)*] a piece of land, especially reclaimed scrub, surviving in place names.

whole [Old English *hāl*] Without disease, injury, or damage, hence **1** well, healthy (surviving in the Northern form **hale**: cf. *wassail* below), hence **wholesome** conducive to health and well-being (ME) **2** intact, undivided, hence **(a)** of a number: not containing a fraction or decimal (15c) **(b) wholesale** the selling of goods in large quantities, to be divided up by the retailer (15c), hence (done) on a large scale (19c) **3** entire, complete, hence **(a) the whole** all, the total; the full duration or extent (*cried the whole night*, ME) **(b)** containing all and only its proper constituents, unmixed, pure (*wholemeal, whole food*, 17c) **4** something made up of parts, a complex entity (16c), hence **on the whole** taking everything together, in general (17c).

Related to **heal, health**, HOLY*, and to **wassail** [Old Norse *ves hail* 'be healthy!'] a toast to someone's health, to which the answer was **drink hail** '(I) drink (your) health', whence **hail** (used) to greet someone, now implying respect, hence **1** to call or wave to (*hailed a taxi*) **2 hail from** to come from.

wicket [ME. *Wiket*, the Norman form of Old French *guichet* (cf. WALLOP*), of Scandinavian origin: related to **wicker** and **wych elm**] A small door or gate in or beside a larger one, hence **1** a small opening, often protected by a grille; one in the window of a ticket office or cashier's desk (19c, *US*): *guichet* was adopted in a similar sense in British English **2 wicket (gate)** a small gate for pedestrians **3** in cricket: the stumps and bails (thought to resemble a gate) at which the bowler aims (17c); a batsman's turn to bat (18c); the ground between the wickets (19c) **4** a croquet hoop (19c, US).

wield [Old English *wieldan*] To rule, guide, or control; to have and be able to use, hence to handle a tool, weapon, etc. (skilfully), hence **wieldy** easy to use, manageable, handy (16c), surviving mainly in **unwieldy**.

wight [Old English *wiht*] **1** a living being (–16c), hence **(a)** a supernatural being (now Scots) **(b)** a person (ME, surviving in poetry) **2** a thing, a (small) amount (–15c: the variant **whit** survives in **not a whit** not/nothing at all) **3** worth something, worthy (ME only: cf. *naught* below).

Old English *wiht* produced *awiht*, whence **aught** or **ought** anything, to any extent, at all, with the opposites **naught** or **nought** nothing, later zero, the figure 0 (now only as *nought*); good for nothing; worthless (now old-fashioned, although the forms **owt** and **nowt** are current in N England). *Naught* came to mean 'worthlessness, wickedness', whence **naughty** wicked, evil, immoral; indecent, titillating; disobedient, mischievous. *Nought* produced **not**. Related to EVER* and to German *Nichts* 'nothing', whence **nix**.

wild [Old English *wilde*] In a natural state, not domesticated or cultivated; not controlled or restrained, hence **1** uninhabited, uninhabitable; such a place (largely replaced by *wilderness* below except in *the wilds of* **2** turbulent, disorderly (ME); outside the rules, hence **wild card (a)** one worth whatever its holder decides (1920s); a symbol that can represent any character (1980s) **(b)** a competitor entered after the regular places are taken (1970s, *US*) **3** uncivilized, savage (ME); fierce; angry (17c); passionate (18c), enthusiastic, elated (19c) **4** beyond reasonable limits, fantastic (*wildest dreams*, 16c).

Old English *wilde* produced **wilderness** land inhabited only by wild animals [with Old English *deor*: see BEAST], and probably **wilder** to lead astray (into the wilderness), to (make someone) lose the way, surviving mainly as **bewilder**, which now usually means 'to confuse'.

will [Old English *willa* (noun), *wyllan* (verb)] (To have) a desire, wish, or liking, hence **1** to be inclined to do something (also as **be willing**), hence **willy-nilly** [17c spelling of *will I, nill I* 'whether I want to or not']; to do persistently **2** used with verbs to form their future tense (probably originally expressing an intention to do something, strictly speaking only in the second and third persons (*you, he, they*), the first person (*I, we*) using **shall** [Old English *sceal* 'ought to, must', the sense surviving in the past tense **should**]; however, *will* is now commonly used for all **3** what you want (*have your will*) **4 (free) will** the exercise of choice, volition, hence **(a) wilful** strong-willed, stubborn (ME); (done) on purpose (*wilful murder*) **(b) will(power)** control over your desires (ME); *will* to control or influence by willpower (19c) **(c) at will** as and when you like (ME) **5** (to leave) instructions about the disposal of your property when you die; a document containing them; to bequeath something (ME) **6** feeling towards someone, earliest in **goodwill**.

Would, past tense of *will*, is used for something that may not happen (*you would know him if you saw him*), and in polite requests or offers (*would you help me/like some tea?*): *should* in such offers is now old-fashioned.

Old English *willa* produced the name **Wilfred**, and is related to WALK*, **welcome** [Old English *wilcuma* 'someone/something welcome', from *wil-* 'pleasing' + *cuma* 'comer': the spelling changed by association with WELL[1], influenced by French *bien venu* or Old Norse *velkominn*], and **William**. *Shall* produced **shilly-shally** [based on *shall I*, with the idea 'shall I, shall I not?'].

win [Old English *winnan*] To work, strive, contend, or fight (–ME); to overcome, to capture and subdue, hence **1** to gain with an effort (ME); to gain a woman's love or hand in marriage; **win over** to gain someone's support or sympathy **2** to be victorious in a race, contest, etc. (ME); to gain something by doing so; **win (through** or, US, **out)** to overcome opposition or difficulties (19c) **3** the surname **Win-, Wimpenny** an acquisitive person.

Related to **ween** to think or believe (surviving in **overweening**), **winsome**, **wish**, and to **wont** a habit or custom, and **wonted** customary [both ultimately from Old English *(ge)wunian* 'to remain or reside'].

wind [Old English *windan*] To move quickly and forcefully (–15c); to turn or writhe (surviving in dialect); to curve, bend, or twist (–17c), hence **1** to plait or intertwine (now Scots); to twine or wrap one thing round another (ME), hence **(a)** to haul or lift with a winch or windlass **(b)** to turn thread etc. round a reel or roll it into a ball, hence **wind up** to bring to an end (18c, from the idea of using all the thread); to dissolve a company, to cease trading; to end up (*wound up in jail*, early 20c) **(c)** to wrap a corpse, hence **winding sheet** a shroud (15c) **2** to meander (ME) **3 wind (up)** to tighten by turning a screw, key, etc. (17c), hence **(a)** *wind up* to intensify, to bring to a pitch; to tease or hoax (1970s); **wind-up** a hoax or prank (1980s) **(b) wind down** to come to an end gradually (1950s); to relax (earlier in **unwind**) **4** of a ship: to turn round; to turn a ship round (17c, perhaps really a form of WEND).

Related to **wander**, WEND, **windlass** [ultimately from Old Norse *vinda* 'to wind' + *áss* 'pole'], to the names **Windlesham** and **Windsor**, both referring to places with a windlass, and probably to **wand** [Old Norse *vondr* 'flexible stick'].

wink [Old English *wincian*] To close your eyes, hence **1 (a)** a closing of the eyes in sleep (*forty winks*, ME); to doze (–17c) **(b) wink at** to 'close your eyes to' wrongdoing (15c) **(c) hoodwink** to cover the eyes (as if) with a hood (16c); to deceive (17c) **2** to blink, hence **(a)** of a light: to flash or twinkle (16c); to send a signal with a flashing light (*c.*1910) **(b)** a brief moment (16c); in time and motion study: 1/2000 of a second (1930s) **3** to close one eye, originally when taking aim (ME–17c); the quick closing and opening of one eye (16c); to do so (19c).

wise [Old English *wīs*] Sagacious, sensible, prudent, hence **1** a wise person; wise people collectively **2** clever, skilled, later especially in magic, hence **(a)** well-informed, aware (*worldly wise/streetwise*) **(b) wise man/woman** one skilled in magic, astrology, or healing (ME: the Three Wise Men who visited the infant Jesus were probably astrologers: cf. MAGUS): *wise man* meaning 'magician' has been largely replaced by **wizard** [ME, from *wise* + *-ard* (see HARD)] originally a philosopher or sage, later (someone who is) extremely good at something; now also a computer program that simplifies a process for the user.

Old English *wīs* produced **wisdom** (your **wisdom teeth** emerge when you have achieved adulthood and, hopefully, some wisdom). Related to **wiseacre** [early Dutch *wijseggher* 'soothsayer'] and WIT*.

wistful [17c. Apparently an alteration of *wistly* (15–18c), ultimately from Middle English **whis(h)t** 'hush!'] Attentive, intent (–19c); eagerly expectant, later (by association with *wishful*) yearning; pensive and sad.

Whisht survives mainly in Scotland, Ireland, and N England: in Scotland it came to mean 'silence', chiefly in **hold/keep your whisht!** 'be quiet!'.

wit [Old English] The mind (–17c), hence **1** wit(s) your right mind, sanity (*scared witless/out of his wits*); your mental faculties or resources (*at your wits' end, keep your wits about you*, ME) **2** wisdom, common sense (ME, earlier in **witty** [Old English *wittig*] 'wise, sensible'), surviving mainly in *have the wit to* and **mother wit** innate good sense (15c) **3** intelligence, intellect (ME); ingenuity, inventiveness, also cunning (*lives on her wits*); (someone with) the ability to use words and ideas inventively and amusingly (16c), hence *witty* having or showing this; **witticism** a witty remark [1677, coined by John Dryden from *witty* and *criticism*].

Wit produced WITNESS. Related to GUIDE*, GUISE*, **twit** to tease or taunt [Old English, from *wītan* 'to blame'], WISE*, **wit** to know, surviving mainly in **unwitting** [Old English *witan*, whence also **wot**], and to **witan** [plural of Old English *wita* 'counsellor, wise man'] the counsellors of an Anglo-Saxon king.

witch [Old English *wicca* (masculine), *wicce* (feminine): related to WAKE*] A magician or sorcerer, hence **1 (a)** a woman thought to act malevolently with the help of evil spirits; to do so (surviving mainly in **witching hour** midnight, when witches were believed to be active). Hence **witch hunt** persecution of (those believed to be) witches (17c) or those with unpopular views (1930s) **(b) white witch** who uses supernatural powers benevolently (17c), now sometimes used by Wiccans (see below) **2** a hag (ME) **3** a seductive young woman (18c).

Witch produced **bewitch** to put a spell on, to charm or enchant. Old English *wicca* was revived, as **Wicca**, for the modern religious cult of witchcraft, and may be the source of **wicked** evil, cruel; formidable (*US*); excellent, wonderful (youth slang, *US*).

withdraw [ME. From *with* meaning 'against, from', and DRAW*] **1** to take back or away, hence to take money from a bank etc. (18c) **2** to retire or retreat, hence **withdrawing chamber/room** a private room adjoining a more public one, shortened to **drawing room**, later a room to which the ladies withdrew after dinner (18c).

witness [Old English *witnes*, from WIT*] Knowledge, understanding (–15c), hence **1** evidence, proof: **(a)** evidence of religious faith through actions; someone who gives this, originally a Christian martyr (ME) **(b)** (to serve as) a sign or token (ME) **2** a person who gives evidence: **(a)** one who is present at an event (originally the signing of a document) and can say what took place **(b)** someone invoked to confirm your actions (*as God is my witness*, ME) **(c)** to be a witness to (ME); to 'see', to be the scene or time of (*the 1930s witnessed mass unemployment*, 18c).

work [Old English *weorc*] All the main senses existed in Old English: later senses include 'to function' (ME) and **works** (the parts of) a mechanism (17c), hence **the works** the whole lot, everything (19c, *US*). The original past tense, **wrought**, survives describing something that has been worked on (ME), especially metal shaped by hammering (*wrought iron*, 16c), in **overwrought** over-elaborate, over-excited, distraught (17c), and in the altered form **wrot** dressed timber (1930s).

Related to *wark* (in BULWARK), and to **wright** a craftsman (*playwright/wheelwright*), whence the surnames *Arkwright* (at ARK), *Cartwright* (at CART), *Wainwright* (at WAGON), and **Wright**.

world [Old English *w(e)orold*: related to *old* (at ELDER), so the underlying sense is probably 'the age of mankind'] Man's life on earth, also an afterlife (*this world and the next*), hence **1** human society; (secular) concerns and activities, hence **(a) worldly** secular; materialistic (ME) **(b)** someone's sphere (16c); a particular part of society (*the world of fashion*, 17c); **underworld** the lowest stratum of society (19c, largely replaced by **underclass**); criminals **2** the earth, hence **(a)** a particular part of it (*the western world*) **(b) the (whole) world** all the earth contains (ME); to do with or affecting all countries (*World Bank/world record*, 17c) **(c)** a vast amount (16c) **(d)** another place regarded as (possibly) inhabited (17c), hence *underworld* the home of the dead, thought to lie beneath the earth.

worm [Old English *wyrm*] A snake or dragon (replaced by *serpent* below), also applied to other reptiles and to insects (*slow-worm, glow-worm*), to maggots and caterpillars, especially destructive ones (*woodworm*), and to various long invertebrates (*earthworm, tapeworm*). Hence **1** a parasitic tick or mite infesting the skin (surviving in **ringworm**); a (self-replicating) program designed to sabotage a computer (1975, in John Brunner's science fiction novel *The Shockwave Rider*: it became a reality in the 1980s) **2** a despicable person (cf. *serpent*) **3** applied to various spiral objects (16c) **4** to proceed or gain something deviously (16c); to insinuate yourself (17c) **5** to treat plants for insect infestation (17c), or an animal for parasitic worms (1930s).

Serpent [Old French, from Latin *serpens* 'creeping', from *serpere* 'to creep'] often referred to the Devil (from the snake's role as tempter in the Garden of Eden, see the Bible, Genesis 3:1–5), hence **1 serpentine** to do with or resembling a snake **2** a treacherous or spiteful person (largely replaced by *snake*): **snake** [Old English *snaca*] has never meant a dragon or the Devil, the sense 'treacherous person' coming partly from Aesop (see VIPER) and partly from **snake in the grass**, from Virgil.

Wormwood, a bitter-tasting plant, is from unrelated Old English *wermōd*: the spelling changed by association with *worm* and *wood*: related to **vermouth** [ultimately from German *Wermut* 'wormwood', which was originally used to flavour it].

worry [Old English *wyrgan*] To strangle (surviving in Scots); to choke (ME); to seize by the throat and pull about, hence **1** to kill by biting and tearing; to bite or tear repeatedly (19c) **2** to harass, to attack repeatedly; to annoy by persistent demands (17c); to make anxious or uneasy (19c); something that does so; to fret about it.

worship [Old English *weorscipe*, from *w(e)orth* WORTH] Worth, dignity, merit, hence **1** possession of high rank, prominence, importance; in a title for a magistrate, mayor, or other important person (*Your Worship*, 16c) **2** respect and honour shown to someone; religious reverence and devotion (ME); to honour or revere, hence to adore or idolize (*worships his daughter/money*, 18c).

worth [Old English *w(e)orth*: ancestor of STALWART and WORSHIP] **1** (having) monetary value, being equal in value to a certain sum; having a certain amount of wealth (ME) **2** moral or social value (ME); moral character (16c); merit, excellence (17c) **3** value or importance (ME); sufficiently valuable or important to justify or repay (*not worth the trouble*). Hence **worthy** having value (ME), hence **1** (someone) deserving respect **2** deserving of or meriting (also in *trustworthy* etc.) **3** sufficiently good, suitable (also in *roadworthy* etc.).

wrangle [ME. Probably from Low German or Dutch: related to **wring** and **wrong**] To argue angrily, noisily, or vehemently; such an argument (15c), hence **1** to debate (publicly), to dispute or defend a thesis (16c), hence **wrangler** someone who does so; a student receiving first class honours in the Mathematical Tripos at Cambridge University (see *Tripos* at TRIVET) **2** to get something, or to drive someone out of a place, by persistent argument (17c), hence [partly by association with Spanish *caverango* 'stable hand'] to herd horses (19c, western US); to train and manage animals on a film set (*swan wrangler*, 1990s).

wreak [Old English *wrecan*] To drive or drive out, to banish (–15c); to punish (–17c); to take revenge or exact retribution; to cause harm or damage (*wreak havoc*).

Related to WRECK and **wretch** originally a banished person, hence one to be pitied or despised.

wreck [ME. Anglo-Norman French *wrec*, of Scandinavian origin: related to WREAK*] (**Ship**)**wreck 1** debris washed ashore from a ship that has foundered (replaced by 19c **wreckage**), hence (kinds of) seaweed floating in the sea or growing on the shore (15c), replaced by related **wrack** [Dutch *wrak*, also originally meaning 'shipwreck'] **2** the destruction of a ship at sea (15c); to cause or suffer it (*shipwrecked sailors*, 17c). Hence *wreck* **(a)** the remains of a wrecked ship (15c); something damaged or dilapidated (18c); a sick or exhausted person **(b)** ruin, downfall (16c), chiefly in **wreck and ruin**, replaced by **rack and ruin** [16c, ultimately from related Old English *wraec* 'vengeance']; to cause this (19c). Hence **wrecker**: a ship or person that salvages wrecked ships or their cargo (18c), hence **(a)** someone who lures vessels onto the rocks to plunder them (19c) **(b)** a railway vehicle for removing wrecked trains (*c*.1900); a breakdown truck **(c)** a demolition worker (1930s).

write [Old English *wrītan*] To score or draw the outline of something (–16c); to carve or engrave letters, symbols, etc., hence to form letters etc. on paper with a pen, pencil, later a typewriter etc., hence **1** to produce something by doing so (*write a letter/cheque/novel/song*); to state, describe, or record in writing **2** to be an author or clerk **3 underwrite** to sign a document at the bottom; to confirm or agree to its contents, especially to accept liability for specific losses, by doing so (17c), hence to issue insurance (later also as *write*, 19c), or to give financial support **4 write off** to note a deduction, a reduction in value, or the cancellation of a bad debt, in accounts (17c); to regard something as worthless, hence to damage beyond repair (World War I, *Air Force slang*); **write-off** something worthless or beyond repair; a complete failure (1960s) **5** to transfer data to a storage medium (*write to disk*, 1940s).

Related to **writ** written matter, especially the Scriptures; a formal document, especially a court order, hence authority or influence.

writhe [Old English *wrīthan*] To wrap or bind (–15c); to coil or twist something, hence **1** to twist together, to plait or intertwine, to form a wreath by doing so (ME–16c): largely replaced by *wreathe* below **2** to squirm (ME); to twist or contort (part of) your body; to do so expressing pain, grief, embarrassment, etc.

Related to **wreathe** [partly from *wreathen*, a variant of *writhen*, the original past participle of *writhe*; partly from related **wreath** (Old English *writha*)], and to **wrath** and **wroth** [both from Old English *wrāth* 'angry'].

wry [Old English *wrīgian*: related to **wriggle**] To tend or incline (–16c), hence to (cause to) turn away or back (ME–17c), hence **1** a twisting movement (ME) **2 on wry** twisted, askew, amiss (ME–16c, Scots), outlived by **awry 3** to twist or turn your body, neck, etc. (ME); to contort your face or mouth to express dislike, disgust, or, later, quiet amusement (16c), hence drily amusing, sardonic (1920s).

XYZ

X The 24th letter of the English alphabet, long used **1** to express something unknown, e.g. the first unknown quantity in an algebraic equation, hence **X-ray** [1890s, translating German *x-Strahl*], because when the rays were discovered their nature was not known **2** to represent the Greek letter *khi*, the first letter of Greek *khristos* 'Christ' (*Xmas, Xtianity*).

Xanadu [1960s. Alternation of Shang-tu, an ancient city in SE Monogolia: the residence of Kublai Khan, 13c ruler of an empire stretching from the Blank Sea to China] An imaginary place of almost unbelievable magnificence and luxury (after S. T. Coleridge's poem *Kublai Khan*, which describes the ruler's 'pleasure dome' in Xandadu).

Yankee [18c. Probably from Dutch *Janke* 'Johnny', from *Jan* 'John'] A derisive nickname, probably originally used for the Dutch inhabitants of New England by their English neighbours (hence for any New Englander), later for American soldiers by the British in the American War of Independence, and then by people in the southern states for northerners, especially Unionist soldiers in the American Civil War. It has come to mean any American (also as **Yank**).

    Yankee Doodle, adopted as a patriotic song in the US, appears to have been introduced by British troops in the Anglo-French War, deriding those provincial soldiers who wore elaborate uniforms (see also MACARONI).

yard¹ [Old English *gerd*] **1** a long spar supporting a sail **2** a rod or staff; one used as a measure, hence **(a)** applied to various units of length, now standardized at 3 feet (0.9144 metres); a cubic yard of something, especially sand (19c) **(b) yardstick** a 3-foot measuring stick (19c); a standard used for comparison.

yard² [Old English *geard*] **1** a building, a house, a home (OE only, but perhaps surviving unrecorded): reappearing or re-created in the West Indies (19c), where it means a house with its land, or a collection of dwellings sharing facilities, hence **(a)** used by expatriate Jamaicans for 'home, Jamaica' (1970s) **(b) yardie** a member of a West Indian, especially Jamaican, criminal gang (1980s: in Jamaica, one who has been a gang-member abroad **2** a small uncultivated or paved area next to a building or surrounded by buildings, hence **(a)** a garden (ME, earlier in *orchard* (at COURT), now mainly N American) **(b)** land and buildings for a particular purpose (*dockyard, farmyard*, ME), hence to pen cattle or store corn etc. in a yard (18c); **yardage** a charge for doing so (19c).

    Related to **garden** [Old Norman French *gardin* (whence the surname **Gardener**, **Gard(i)ner**), variant of Old French *jardin* (whence the surname **Jardine**), of Germanic origin], **garth** a yard [Old Norse *garthr*], whence the surnames **Garth** and **Garton**, and to *kindergarten* (at KIN).

yarn [Old English *gearn*] Spun flax, cotton, wool, etc. fibre (now that prepared for weaving, knitting, etc.); (one of) the threads making up a rope (17c), hence **spin a yarn** to tell a long, rambling, and unlikely story (as sailors did to while away time spent mending ropes, 19c); *yarn* (to tell) such a story; (to have) a chat (Australia and New Zealand).

yelp [Old English *gielp(an)*] Pride, arrogance (OE only); to speak arrogantly, to boast (–15c); to cry or sing loudly (ME–16c), hence (to utter) a short, shrill cry or bark (16c).
  Related to *gale* in **nightingale** [Old English, from *night* + *galan* 'to sing'] and **yell**.

yen [19c. Chinese (Cantonese) *yan*] An addict's craving for a drug, originally opium (*US slang*), hence (to have) a desire or longing (*c*.1900).

yield [Old English *gield* (noun), *g(i)eldan* (verb)] To give in payment, compensation, or restitution (17c); such a payment (–16c: cf. *geld* below), hence **1** to reward or repay (ME); to produce (a certain amount of) a commodity, later revenue or profit; the amount produced **2** to hand over (ME); to give up a position; to admit defeat; to give way or collapse **3** to give out (*yield a sigh*, 15c).
  Related to *geld* in **Danegeld** [from Old Norse *gjald* 'payment, tribute'], probably originally a tax to finance fighting the Danes, later identified with protection money paid to them, and probably to **guild** [probably from Low German or Dutch] an association of people for mutual benefit or the pursuit of common aims, especially a medieval association of craftsmen etc., hence a group of species with similar needs and functions.

yoke [Old English *geoc*] A frame that joins two draught animals at the neck, hence **1** something resembling this: **(a)** a framework put on a conquered enemy; something symbolizing this that the person had to walk under, hence subjection, servitude, oppression; to subjugate or oppress (ME) **(b)** a crossbar or crosspiece (ME) **(c)** a shaped piece of wood worn across the shoulders to carry things hung from each end (17c), hence a fitted part of a garment, usually covering the shoulders, from which the rest of it hangs (19c) **(d)** the control column of an aircraft (1930s, from its yoke-shaped handle, *US*) **2** to put a yoke on a pair of animals, hence **(a)** a pair of (yoked) animals **(b)** to join, link, or couple (ME); (to become linked by) a bond, especially marriage.

young [Old English *g(e)ong*] Not very old, hence **1 (a)** a young person (–15c, partly replaced by **youngster**); **the young** young people collectively **(b)** a young animal (ME–18c); offspring (15c) **2** characteristic of youth or the young (*my young days*) **3 (a)** newly initiated, inexperienced **(b)** newly begun, in an early stage (15c) **4** referring to the younger of two people with the same name (ME), replaced by **(the) younger** or by *junior* (at SENIOR): the source of the surname **Young**.
  Probably the source of *yeo* in **yeoman** originally a servant in a royal or noble household (ME: *young man* was also used in this sense). Related to, and sharing some senses with, **youth** [Old English *geoguth*].

zap [1920s] Used in comic strips to represent the sound of a lightning strike, bullet, ray gun, etc., hence **1** to kill or destroy, originally with a (ray) gun (1940s) **2** to move briskly (1960s), hence **(a)** liveliness, energy, drive **(b)** to fast-forward through advertisements etc. on a video tape (1980s); to change or flick through television channels with a remote control unit (hence **zapper** such a unit, 1990s) **(c)** to cook something quickly in a microwave (1990s).

zeal [ME. Ecclesiastical Latin *zelus* from Greek *zēlos*] Strong emotion (originally in biblical translations); fervent love; strong desire; great energy and enthusiasm for a task or a cause.

Latin *zelus* produced **jealous** [via Old French *gelos*]; Greek *zēlos* produced **zealot** originally a member of a Jewish sect passionately opposed to Roman rule.

zenith [ME. (Via Old French from) medieval Latin *cenit*, ultimately from Arabic *samt (ar-ra's)* 'path (over the head)'] The point of the heavens directly overhead, hence the highest point reached by a celestial object (17c); a high point or climax.

Arabic *samt* produced **azimuth** [via French from Arabic *as-samt* 'the way or direction'] and **nadir** [via French, Italian, or Spanish from Arabic *naẓīr (as-samt)* 'opposite (the zenith)'].

zodiac [ME. Via French and Latin from Greek *zōidiakos (kuklos)* '(circle) of carved figures', from *zōidion* 'carved animal, sign of the zodiac', from *zōion* 'animal'] A band in the sky in which the sun, moon, and major planets appear to move, hence **1 (a) signs of the zodiac** the twelve equal parts of this, each named after the constellation (and represented by its symbol, some being animals) through which the sun progressed **(b)** a diagram or chart of this or a similar system **2** a recurring cycle (16c).

Greek *zōion* produced **zoology** the study of animals: the first **zoological gardens**, where live animals were exhibited, opened in Regent's Park, London, in 1829: its name was soon shortened to **zoo**, which was applied to other such places, hence to a chaotic place or situation, hence **zoo format** describing a radio or television show with multiple presenters who chat to each other.

zombie [19c. From a W African language] The name of a voodoo snake-god, later applied to a spirit that could revive a corpse, hence such a re-animated corpse; a slow-witted, unresponsive, or apathetic person (1930s).

zoom [19c. Imitating the sound] To make a continuous humming or buzzing sound, hence to move (as if) with such a sound; to move at speed, hence **1** of an aircraft: to climb steeply and rapidly (World War I); of prices etc.: to rise sharply (1970s) **2 zoom (lens)** a camera lens that can change the apparent distance of the subject (quickly) without losing focus (1930s); **zoom (shot)** made with a zoom lens; **zoom (in/out)** to use a zoom lens (1940s) **3** zest, energy (1960s).

Zing (*c*.1910, *US*) and **zip** (19c) followed a similar path, from '(to make) such a sound' to '(to move with) energy or vigour'; *zip* produced the **zip (fastener)** or **zipper** (1920s).

PENGUIN POCKET REFERENCE

THE PENGUIN POCKET BOOK OF FACTS
EDITED BY DAVID CRYSTAL

The Penguin Pocket Book of Facts is a goldmine of information, figures and statistics on every conceivable subject – from the world's highest mountains and longest rivers to the gods of mythology, and from time zones to Nobel Prize winners. The ultimate one-stop factfinder, this is the essential book for browsers, crossword and trivia addicts, and for anyone who needs to check facts at home or at work.

– Up-to-date information about everything from astronomy to zoology

– Easy to use

– Illustrated throughout with maps and diagrams

PENGUIN POCKET REFERENCE

THE PENGUIN POCKET DICTIONARY OF QUOTATIONS
EDITED BY DAVID CRYSTAL

The Penguin Pocket Dictionary of Quotations is essential reading for anyone searching for the perfect quotation – whether you need a snappy one-liner for a speech or a remark of brilliant insight for your written work. With this pithy and provocative selection of wit and wisdom, you will never be lost for words again.

– Includes quotations from a vast range of people, from film stars to politicians

– Arranged alphabetically by name of person quoted, with the original source for each quotation given

– Provides a full index of key words to help you find each quotation quickly and easily

www.penguin.com

Penguin Pocket Reference

THE PENGUIN POCKET SPELLING DICTIONARY
EDITED BY DAVID CRYSTAL

The Penguin Pocket Spelling Dictionary is indispensable for anyone who wishes to check a spelling quickly and easily. It shows how to spell virtually all the words you are likely to encounter on a daily basis and highlights areas where mistakes are commonly made.

- Includes over 70,000 entries

- Gives capsule definitions for unusual and frequently confused words, and panels discussing points of interest

- Provides British and American spellings

PENGUIN POCKET REFERENCE

THE PENGUIN POCKET ENGLISH DICTIONARY

This pocket edition of the bestselling *Penguin English Dictionary* is the
perfect reference book for everyday use. Compiled by Britain's
foremost lexicographers, up to date and easy to use, it is the ideal
portable companion for quick reference.

- Includes a wealth of words, phrases and clear definitions, with more
  information than other comparable dictionaries
- Covers standard and formal English, as well as specialist terms,
  slang and jargon
- Provides invaluable guidance on correct usage, commonly confused
  words and grammar and spelling

www.penguin.com

PENGUIN REFERENCE LIBRARY

THE PENGUIN DICTIONARY OF FIRST NAMES

EDITED BY DAVID PICKERING

What's in a name? Rather more than you might at first suspect, for names are steeped in history and myth and have much to tell us about our past, our beliefs – even our personality traits. Now fully updated for its second edition, with 150 new entries, *The Penguin Dictionary of First Names* is much more than just an inspiration for expectant parents. Each entry is a carefully researched mini-masterpiece in cultural and linguistic history, as David Pickering offers a wealth of information fitted for the twenty-first century reader. He takes a close look at over 5000 examples – ranging from the familiar to the comparatively obscure – drawn from all parts of the English-speaking world. No other book provides the same authoritative detail and quality of definition.

- Gives the meaning or origin of each name, its variants and diminutives

- Highlights names that have become popular from literature, films, culture and celebrities

- Shows how names have changed in use and popularity over time

- Lists the most popular girls' and boys' names from 1700 to the present, from *Siobhan* and *Iolanthe* to *Hayden* and *Sherlock*

- Examines trends and changing tastes in the twenty-first century

ONLY PENGUIN GIVES YOU MORE

Penguin Language

THE STORIES OF ENGLISH
DAVID CRYSTAL

How did a language originally spoken by a few thousand Anglo-Saxons become one used by more than 1,500 million people? How have all the different versions of English evolved and changed? In this compelling global tour, David Crystal turns the traditional view of the history of the language on its head and tells the *real* stories of English that have never before been fully told.

'A spirited celebration . . . Crystal gives the story of English a new plot' *Guardian*

'Rejoices in dialects, argots and cants . . . enlightening – in a word, excellent' *Sunday Times*

'An exhilarating read . . . Crystal is a sort of latter-day Johnson' *The Times Higher Education Supplement*

'*The Stories of English* reads like an adventure story. Which, of course, it is' Roger McGough

'A marvellous book . . . for anyone who loves the English language(s) it will be a treasure-house' Philip Pullman

PENGUIN LANGUAGE

SHAKESPEARE'S WORDS
DAVID CRYSTAL AND BEN CRYSTAL

A vital resource for scholars, students and actors, this book contains glosses and quotes for over 14,000 words that could be misunderstood by or are unknown to a modern audience. Displayed panels look at such areas of Shakespeare's language as greetings, swear-words and terms of address. Plot summaries are included for all Shakespeare's plays and on the facing page is a unique diagrammatic representation of the relationships within each play.

'This is a fascinating guide to Shakespeare's language, a more or less indispensable treasure-chest for anyone who loves watching or reading the plays and is curious about the meaning, use and derivation of the language' Sir Richard Eyre

'Detailed, comprehensive – fascinating' Kenneth Branagh

'*Shakespeare's Words* is one of the very few works of reference that deserves a place on the shelves of all Shakespeare lovers and for that matter all lovers of the English language' Professor Jonathan Bate, author of *The Genius of Shakespeare*

PENGUIN REFERENCE LIBRARY

THE PENGUIN BOOK OF FACTS

EDITED BY DAVID CRYSTAL

'One of the greatest reference books ever published' *Independent on Sunday*

Funafuti is the capital of which south Pacific island? Which dog-toting film star's real name is Frances Gumm? How far is Brussels from Paris? *The Penguin Book of Facts* is the most comprehensive and authoritative general factbook available. Calling upon his famously encyclopaedic knowledge, David Crystal has compiled this international information bible with meticulous precision, layering fact upon fact in a logical order, from the beginnings of the universe to the World Water Skiing Union. It is not only the authoritative and infinite breadth of knowledge that sets this dictionary apart; Crystal has added an invaluable and comprehensive index that makes finding that elusive fact all the easier.

- Contains more facts than any other book of its kind and is illustrated throughout

- Includes contributions from over 250 experts

- This is the updated edition of *The New Penguin Factfinder*

ONLY PENGUIN GIVES YOU MORE

PENGUIN WRITERS' GUIDES

HOW TO WRITE BETTER ENGLISH
ROBERT ALLEN

The Penguin Writers' Guides series provides authoritative, succinct and easy-to-follow guidance on specific aspects of written English. Whether you need to brush up your skills or get to grips with something for the first time, these invaluable guides will help you find the best way to communicate clearly and effectively.

In this age of rapid communication, we all need to write fluent and accurate English, but getting it right can seem daunting. This reassuring guide explains how you can increase your word power and make language work for you. It tells you how to choose the right style for your audience, avoid hackneyed expressions and find ways of brightening up your writing. The glossaries, tables and 'hitlist' of awkward words and phrases will help you find solutions to problems quickly and easily.

Get your message across

PENGUIN POCKET REFERENCE

PORTABLE   **DESIRABLE**   **INDISPENSABLE**

Penguin Pocket Babies' Names

Penguin Pocket Book of Facts

Penguin Pocket Crossword Finisher

Penguin Pocket Dictionary of Quotations

Penguin Pocket English Dictionary

Penguin Pocket Famous People

Penguin Pocket French Dictionary

Penguin Pocket German Dictionary

Penguin Pocket Italian Dictionary

Penguin Pocket Jokes

Penguin Pocket Kings and Queens

Penguin Pocket On This Day

Penguin Pocket Rhyming Dictionary

Penguin Pocket Roget's Thesaurus

Penguin Pocket School Dictionary

Penguin Pocket Spanish Dictionary

Penguin Pocket Spelling Dictionary

Penguin Pocket Thesaurus

Penguin Pocket Writer's Handbook

Our Penguin Pockets are part of the extensive Penguin Reference
Library – a resource that draws on over 70 years of experience bringing
reliable, useful and clear information to millions of readers around the
world. We want to make knowledge everybody's property.

PENGUIN SUBJECT DICTIONARIES

Penguin's Subject Dictionaries aim to provide two things: authoritative complimentary reference texts for the academic market (primarily A level and undergraduate studies) *and* clear, exciting and approachable reference books for general readers on subjects outside the core curriculum.

Academic & Professional

ACCOUNTING
ARCHEOLOGY
ARCHITECTURE
BUILDING
BUSINESS
CLASSICAL MYTHOLOGY
CRITICAL THEORY
ECONOMICS
INTERNATIONAL RELATIONS
LATIN
LITERARY TERMS & THEORY
MARKETING (forthcoming)
MEDIA STUDIES
MODERN HISTORY
PENGUIN HUMAN BIOLOGY (forthcoming)
PHILOSOPHY
PSYCHOLOGY
SOCIOLOGY

Scientific, Technical and Medical

BIOLOGY
CHEMISTRY
CIVIL ENGINEERING
COMPUTING
ELECTRONICS
GEOGRAPHY
GEOLOGY
MATHEMATICS
PHYSICAL GEOGRAPHY
PHYSICS
PSYCHOANALYSIS
SCIENCE
STATISTICS

English Words & Language

CLICHÉS
ENGLISH IDIOMS
PENGUIN ENGLISH GRAMMAR
PENGUIN RHYMING DICTIONARY
PROVERBS
SYNONYMS & ANTONYMS
SYNONYMS & RELATED WORDS
ROGET'S THESAURUS
THE COMPLETE PLAIN WORDS
THE PENGUIN A–Z THESAURUS
THE PENGUIN GUIDE TO PLAIN ENGLISH
THE PENGUIN GUIDE TO PUNCTUATION
THE PENGUIN WRITER'S MANUAL
USAGE AND ABUSAGE

Religion

BIBLE
ISLAM (forthcoming)
JUDAISM (forthcoming)
LIVING RELIGIONS
RELIGIONS
SAINTS
WHO'S WHO IN THE AGE OF JESUS

General Interest

BOOK OF FACTS
FIRST NAMES
MUSIC
OPERA
SURNAMES (forthcoming)
SYMBOLS
THEATRE

Penguin Reference – making knowledge everybody's property